Government Giveaways for Entrepreneurs IV

First Edition

by

Matthew Lesko

Best Selling Author of *Information USA* and *Getting Yours*

Editor: Andrew Naprawa

Contributing Editor: Toni Murray

Researchers:
Jennifer Jones
Pam Schultz
Mary Ann Martello
Sarah Churner
Sharon McGinnis
Audry Elias
Charles Lorenz
Elaine Sikorski
Denise Burek
Caroline Pharmer
Bradley Sowash
Cindy Owens

Production Coordinator: Beth Meserve

GOVERNMENT GIVEAWAYS FOR ENTREPRENEURS IV, First Edition, Copyright 2000 by Matthew Lesko. All rights reserved. Printed in the United States of America. Published by Information USA, Inc., P.O. Box E, Kensington, MD 20895.

Cover Design: Lester Zaiontz

Cover Cartoon: Galen D. Bailey

Photo: Kevin Gilbert

Library of Congress Cataloging-in-Publication Date

Lesko, Matthew

Government Giveaways for Entrepreneurs IV Sixth Edition.

ISBN 1-878346-59-8

Most books by Matthew Lesko are available at special quantity discounts for bulk purchases for sales promotions, premiums, fund-raising or educational use. Special books or book excerpts also can be created to fit specific needs.

For details, write Information USA, Special Markets, Attention: Kim McCoy, P.O. Box E, Kensington, MD 20895; or 1-800-797-7811, Marketing; {www.lesko.com}.

Acknowledgements

We would like to thank the thousands of bureaucrats who contributed their time and expertise in explaining what opportunities are available to entrepreneurs.

A Word Of Caution To The Reader

We have to warn you that **this book is out of date**. You have to realize that the moment any book is printed, it is out of date. Especially this one with its over 9,000 sources. A book of this size is sure to have some telephone numbers that have changed. But don't be discouraged. You can live with these small inconveniences. If you are calling a government office listed in the book and the telephone number gets you a local diner, or some other wrong number, here's what you can do.

* Call the operator for the area and ask for the number of the office you're after. The directory assistance operator can be located by dialing the area code followed by 555-1212. To inquire about a toll-free number, call directory assistance at 1-800-555-1212.

* Or, call the Federal Information Center at 1-800-688-9889.

* If you have questions, write to us at Information USA, Inc., P.O. Box E, Kensington, MD 20895, or contact us at our web site: {www.lesko.com}. We will be happy to help you any way we can.

You can keep up to date with the information in this book by ordering our new editions when they become available. Each new edition will not only verify all the sources identified in the book but include updated information as well as new chapters and much more. We hope to be publishing updates every year.

Happy Hunting,

Matthew Lesko

Other books available from Matthew Lesko:

Free Stuff for Seniors

Free Health Care

Free Legal Help

Free Stuff For Busy Moms

Free Stuff For Women's Health, Fitness and Nutrition

Free College Money And Training For Women

Free Money And Help For Women Entrepreneurs

Free Money to Change Your Life

Free Money to Change Your Life CD-ROM

Free Money to Change Your Life 6-hour audio

Free Stuff for Pet Lovers

For ordering information on any of Matthew Lesko's publications, call 1-800-UNCLE-SAM, or contact his web site at {www.lesko.com}.

Table Of Contents

Uncle Sam Wants To Make You A Millionaire 1

The Good And Bad Of Entrepreneuring
    a. Six Reasons Why Now Is The Best Time To Start A Business 3
    b. What Entrepreneurs Don't Need 5
    c. Choosing The Business That Is Right For You:
       Trust Your Heart As Well As Your Head 8
    d. Don't Believe In Instant Success 10
    e. Key Pointers When Applying For Money 13
    f. Jumping Over Bureaucratic Hurdles 15

Tips On Finding Information
    a. The Art Of Getting A Bureaucrat To Help You 16
    b. Case Study: Jelly Beans 19
    c. Coping With MisInformation 22
    d. Using Industry Sources And Overcoming The "Negative Researching Syndrome" ... 24
    e. What's Good And Bad About Using Computers In The Information Age ... 28
    f. The Freedom Of Information Act 32

Federal Money Programs For Your Business 46

State Money And Help For Your Business
    a. Who Can Use State Money 53
    b. Types Of State Money And Help Available 53
       - Information 53
       - Funding Programs 53
       - Assistance Programs 54
    c. State-by-State Listing 55

Small Business Development Centers 132

Loans for Entrepreneurs With No Money 160

Technical Assistance Programs for Entrepreneurs With No Money 177

Real Estate Ventures
    a. Federal Money For Housing And Real Estate 186
    b. State Money For Housing And Real Estate 194

Venture Capital: Finding A Rich Angel 206

Uncle Sam's Venture Capital 210

**Get Free Help With The Americans With Disabilities Act (ADA)
Which Requires Businesses To Accommodate The Disabled** 223

Franchising: How To Select The Best Opportunity 227

**Government Contracts: How To Sell Your Goods And Services
To The World's Largest Buyer** 233
    a. Free Local Help: The Best Place To Start To Sell To The Government ... 236
    b. Government Buys Bright Ideas From Inventors:
       Small Business Innovative Research Programs (SBIR) 241
    c. State Procurement Assistance 242

Government Giveaways for Entrepreneurs

Help For Inventors
- a. Patents, Trademarks, and Copyrights ... 245
- b. Invention Scams: How They Work ... 250
- c. Free Help For Inventors ... 251
- d. State Sources for Inventors ... 253

Home-Based Business Resources ... 260

Women Entrepreneurs: Special Money, Help And Programs
- a. For Women Only ... 270
- b. For Starters: Call Your Local Women's Business Ownership Representative ... 273
- c. State Women Business Assistance Programs ... 277
- d. Commissions, Committees, and Councils on the Status of Women ... 281

Green Entrepreneuring: Making Money While Protecting The Environment ... 285

Videos From Uncle Sam To Help Your Business ... 299

Money And Help To Companies Which Want To Use Or Sell Technology ... 302

Free Technology Help: Futuristic Solutions To Today's Business Problems ... 306

2,000 Productivity Specialists Offer *Free* Analysis ... 312

Company Intelligence
- a. How To Find Information On Any Company ... 316
- b. Every Company Has To File With The State ... 324
- c. Who Owes Money To Whom ... 330
- d. Companies That Only Sell Stock In One State ... 335
- e. State Licensing Offices ... 338
- f. State Company Directories ... 344
- g. Company Background Reports Free From Better Business Bureaus ... 348

Market Studies, Demographics And Statistics
- a. Existing Market Studies ... 352
  - Traditional Published Sources
  - Market Studies From Associations
  - A $1500 Market Study For Free
  - Free Government Market Studies
- b. Nine Federal Statistical Agencies ... 359
- c. Hotlines For Monitoring The Economy and Your Markets: Listen To Tomorrow's News Today ... 361
- d. State Data Centers ... 363
- e. State Labor Information Centers ... 371
- f. State Statistical Abstracts ... 377
- g. State Forecasting Agencies ... 381
- h. State Division of Motor Vehicles ... 387

Selling Overseas: Foreign Markets ... 392
- Country Experts
- Money For Selling Overseas
- Marketing Data, Custom Studies, and Company Information
- Trade Fairs And Missions
- Special Programs For Agricultural Products
- Export Regulations, Licensing, and Product Standards
- Cheap Office and Conference Space Overseas
- Other Services, Resources, and Databases
- Read All About It: Helpful Publications
- U.S. Department of Commerce/US & FCS Field Offices
- State Government Assistance To Exporters
- State International Trade Offices
- Overseas Travel: Business Or Pleasure

Table Of Contents

Legislation
- a. How To Monitor Federal Legislation 410
- b. Tracking State Legislation 413

Government Auctions And Surplus Property
- a. Federal Auctions 418
- b. Donations To Non-Profit Organizations 427
- c. State Government Auctions 429

Unclaimed Property: Does The Government Owe You Money? 435

Free Tax Help
- a. Federal Tax Help 439
- b. Tax Hotlines 464
- c. Recorded Messages 466
- d. IRS Tax Forms and Publications 468
- e. State Tax Assistance 493

Free Experts
- a. Free Help In Finding A Free Expert 496
- b. State Starting Places For Finding Experts 499

Free Research on Any Topic 504
- a. Animals and Agriculture 507
    - Agriculture Exports Clearinghouse
    - Economic Research Service (Agriculture)
    - National Agricultural Statistics Service
    - Alternative Farming Systems Information Center
    - Animal Welfare Information Center
    - Aquaculture Information Center
    - Food and Nutrition Information Center
    - Alternative Farming Systems Information Center (Horticulture)
    - Meat and Poultry Hotline
    - Organic Gardening
    - Plant Information Service
    - Rural Information Center
    - Seafood Hotline
- b. Business and Industry 509
    - Advertising Practices
    - Federal Aviation Administration
    - Board of Governors of the Federal Reserve System (Banking)
    - Business Assistance Service
    - Central and Eastern Europe Business Information Center
    - Commodity Futures Trading Commission
    - Federal Communications Commission
    - Export Country Experts
    - Economic Research Service
    - Economics: National, Regional, and International
    - Exporter's Hotline
    - Fishery Statistics and Economics Division
    - Office of Industries
    - Technical Data Center (Job Safety)
    - Federal Mediation and Conciliation Service (Labor-Management)
    - Federal Labor Relations Authority
    - Labor Statistics Clearinghouse
    - Mine Safety Clearinghouse
    - Mineral Commodity Statistics Information
    - Minority Energy Information Clearinghouse
    - Overseas Private Investment Corporation
    - Pension Benefit Guaranty Corporation
    - Pension and Welfare Benefits Administration

Government Giveaways for Entrepreneurs

Free Research on Any Topic (continued)
- Federal <u>Procurement</u> Data Division
- <u>Science, Technology and Business</u> Division
- U.S. <u>Securities and Exchange Commission</u>
- U.S. <u>Small Business</u> Administration
- National Center for <u>Standards and Certification</u>
- <u>Transportation</u> Research Information Services
- <u>Women's Bureau</u> Clearinghouse
- Office of American <u>Workplace</u>

c. Consumer and Housing 514
- <u>Animal Welfare</u> Information Center
- <u>Auto Safety</u> Hotline
- Federal <u>Communications Commission</u>
- <u>Consumer Product Safety</u> Commission
- <u>Credit</u> Information
- National <u>Credit Union</u> Administration
- <u>Food and Nutrition</u> Information Center
- Federal Trade Commission (<u>Fraud</u>)
- <u>Horticulture</u> Clearinghouse
- HUD USER (<u>Housing</u>)
- <u>Housing Discrimination</u>
- Public <u>Housing Drug Strategy</u> Clearinghouse
- National <u>Injury</u> Information Clearinghouse
- U.S. Postal Service (<u>Mailing</u>)
- <u>Meat and Poultry</u> Hotline
- <u>Mortgage</u> Information Center
- <u>Organic Gardening</u>
- <u>Pension</u> Benefit Guaranty Corporation
- <u>Pension and Welfare</u> Benefits Administration
- <u>Plant</u> Information Service
- <u>Seafood</u> Hotline
- <u>Social Security</u> Administration
- Internal Revenue Service (<u>Taxes</u>)
- <u>Women's Bureau</u> Clearinghouse

d. Criminal Justice 518
- Bureau of <u>Alcohol, Tobacco, and Firearms</u>
- National <u>Criminal Justice</u> Reference Service
- <u>Drug and Crime Data</u> Center and Clearinghouse
- National Clearinghouse on <u>Election</u> Administration
- <u>Equal Employment Opportunity</u> Commission (EEOC)
- Bureau of <u>Justice Assistance</u> Clearinghouse
- <u>Justice Statistics</u> Clearinghouse
- <u>Juvenile Justice</u> Clearinghouse
- National Clearinghouse for Poverty Law (<u>Legal Services</u>)
- National Center for <u>Missing and Exploited Children</u>
- Office for <u>Victims</u> of Crime Resource Center

e. Education and the Arts 520
- ERIC Clearinghouse on <u>Adult, Career, and Vocational</u> Learning
- ERIC Clearinghouse on Educational <u>Assessment and Evaluation</u>
- <u>Bilingual Education</u> Clearinghouse
- ERIC Clearinghouse on <u>Counseling and Student Services</u>
- ERIC Clearinghouse on <u>Disabilities and Gifted Education</u>
- ERIC Clearinghouse on <u>Educational Management</u>
- <u>Educational Research</u>
- <u>Educational Resources</u> Information Center
- ERIC Clearinghouse on <u>Elementary and Early Childhood Education</u>
- ERIC Clearinghouse on <u>Higher Education</u>
- ERIC Clearinghouse on <u>Information and Technology</u>
- ERIC Clearinghouse on <u>Community Colleges</u>
- ERIC Clearinghouse on <u>Languages and Linguistics</u>
- National Clearinghouse on <u>Literacy Education</u>

Table Of Contents

- Museum Reference Center
- Performing Arts Library
- ERIC Clearinghouse on Reading, English and Communication Skills
- ERIC Clearinghouse for Science, Mathematics, and Environmental Education
- ERIC Clearinghouse for Social Studies/Social Science Education
- ERIC Clearinghouse on Teaching and Teacher Education
- ERIC Clearinghouse on Urban Education

f. Energy and Environment 524
- EPA Control Technology Center Hotline (Air Pollution)
- BACT/LAER Clearinghouse (MD-13) (Air Pollution)
- Asbestos and Small Business Ombudsman Clearinghouse
- Boating Safety Hotline
- National Climatic Data Center
- Energy Efficiency and Renewable Energy Clearinghouse
- Safe Drinking Water Hotline
- EROS Data Center (Earth Resources)
- Earth Science Information Centers
- National Earthquake Information Center
- Emergency Planning and Community-Right-To-Know Information Hotline
- Emissions Clearinghouse
- National Energy Information Center
- National Environmental Data Referral Service
- Environmental Financing Information Network
- U.S. Environmental Protection Agency (EPA)
- Center for Environmental Research Information
- National Marine Fisheries Service
- Forest Service
- Geologic Inquiries Group
- National Geophysical Data Center
- National Response Center (Hazardous Chemicals)
- RCRA Hotline (Hazardous Waste)
- National Water Information Center
- Indoor Air Quality Information Clearinghouse
- Bureau of Land Management
- U.S. Nuclear Regulatory Commission
- National Oceanic and Atmospheric Administration
- Oceanographic Information
- National Park Service
- National Pesticide Telecommunication Network
- Pollution Prevention Information Clearinghouse
- EPA Radon Information Hotline
- National Sea Grant Depository
- Small Business Ombudsman Clearinghouse
- National Snow and Ice Data Center
- Solid Waste Information Clearinghouse
- National Space Science Data Center
- Technology Transfer Competitiveness
- Technology Transfer Program
- Toxic Substance Control Act
- Undersea Research
- EPA National Small Flows Clearinghouse (Wastewater)
- Watershed Resource Information System
- National Weather Service
- Wetlands Protection Hotline

g. Health 531
- National Institute on Aging
- National AIDS Information Clearinghouse
- National Clearinghouse for Alcohol and Drug Information
- National Institute of Allergy and Infectious Diseases
- Alzheimer's Disease Education And Referral Center
- National Arthritis and Musculoskeletal and Skin Diseases Information Clearinghouse

v

Government Giveaways for Entrepreneurs

Free Research on Any Topic (continued)
- Asthma Clearinghouse
- Blood Resources
- The Cancer Information Service
- National Clearinghouse on Child Abuse and Neglect Information
- National Institute of Child Health and Human Development
- National Information Center for Children and Youth with Disabilities
- Cholesterol Information
- National Institute on Deafness and Other Communication Disorders Clearinghouse
- National Institute of Dental and Craniofacial Research
- National Diabetes Information Clearinghouse
- National Digestive Diseases Information Clearinghouse
- Disabilities Information Clearinghouse
- Disease Information
- Drug Evaluation Clearinghouse
- National Eye Institute
- Food and Drug Information
- National Health Information Center
- Health Care Delivery
- Health Care Policy Clearinghouse
- Clearinghouse on Health Indexes
- National Heart, Lung, and Blood Institute Information Center
- High Blood Pressure Information
- Homelessness
- Public Housing Drug Strategy Clearinghouse
- Indian Health Clearinghouse
- National Kidney and Urologic Diseases Information Clearinghouse
- National Maternal and Child Health Clearinghouse
- Medical Devices Clearinghouse
- National Library of Medicine
- Mental Health Clearinghouse
- Minority Health Clearinghouse
- National Institute of Neurological Disorders and Stroke
- Center for Nutrition Policy and Promotion
- National Institute for Occupational Safety and Health
- National Clearinghouse For Primary Care Information
- National Rehabilitation Information Center
- Office on Smoking and Health
- National Clearinghouse for Professions In Special Education
- Sudden Infant Death Hotline
- Family Violence and Sexual Assault Institute

h. National and World Affairs 538
- Agriculture Exports Clearinghouse
- Arms Control and Disarmament Agency
- Central Intelligence Agency
- Export Country Experts
- Country Officers
- U.S. Customs Service
- Defense Technical Information Center
- Defense Clearinghouse704
- Federal Emergency Management Agency704
- American Foreign Policy Information Clearinghouse704
- Immigration and Naturalization Service704
- Agency for International Development (AID)704
- National Clearinghouse for U.S.-Japan Studies704

i. Other 540
- Boating Safety Hotline
- Children's Literature Center
- Congressional Research Service
- Federal Assistance Programs Retrieval System
- American Folklife Center

vi

Table Of Contents

- Forest Service
- Genealogy Research
- Geographic Names Information
- Geography and Map Division
- Bureau of Indian Affairs
- Library of Congress
- Manuscript Division
- Motion Picture Broadcasting and Recorded Sound Division
- National Park Service
- Performing Arts Division
- Prints and Photographs Division
- Rare Books and Special Collections
- Rural Information Center
- Science and Technology Division
- Women's Bureau Clearinghouse

j. Statistics 544
- National Agricultural Statistics Service
- Federal Aviation Administration
- National Clearinghouse for Census Data Services
- Census Information on Business
- Crime Statistics
- Economics: National and Regional
- Educational Research
- Fishery Statistics Division
- Clearinghouse on Health Indexes
- United States International Trade Commission
- Justice Statistics Clearinghouse
- Labor Statistics Clearinghouse

Index 546

vii

Your Uncle Sam Wants To Make You A Millionaire

Each year the government makes more millionaires than all the state lotteries and Regis Philbin combined. Even famous ones like H. Ross Perot and Donald Trump have been large recipients of government giveaways.

This book identifies programs that give out money to over one million entrepreneurs each and every year. Not one in one million like the lotteries, but 1,000,000 each and every year.

Why aren't you one of them? It's probably because you don't know about the programs. You see, the government doesn't advertise that these programs are available. Unlike the state lotteries that have large advertising budgets, these programs don't spend a nickel telling taxpayers that they exist. Also, turning to the government is not the first place that pops into an entrepreneur's head. With all the bad press the government gets, it's the last place people think of for anything but getting a driver's license or paying taxes. And these two experiences certainly do not leave people wanting to come back for more.

But if the fat cats are using it, you should too. The government is the world's largest source of money, help and information that no entrepreneur can live without. There are programs that give out:

- $100,000 to open up a coffee shop,

- $3,000 to buy a computer for a home-based business,

- $25,000 to train your employees,

- $3,000 to travel overseas looking for customers,

- $500,000 to buy out your employer,

- $2 million to start a hot new Internet company,

- a mailing list of all men over 6 feet tall in your zip code,

- free help to write a business plan,

- $15,000 to start a craft business in your home,

- $50,000 for your foreign clients to buy your products,

- $250,000 to work on your invention,

- financial information on your competitors,

- free legal help if you get audited,

- free help in collecting bad debts,

Your Uncle Sam Wants To Make You A Millionaire

- over 300,000 experts who will do free research on any topic,

- $50,000 a year in freelance writing contracts,

- free consulting help to make your business more profitable,

- free market studies, free management help and free tax help,

- $125,000 in web design contracts, and

- free legal help in dealing with consumer complaints, disgruntled employees, false advertising, harassment charges or EEOC or disability laws.

Why be turned down at the bank for money when the government is set up to give money to people who can't get it elsewhere? And if the bank will give you money, why ask them for it when the government will give it to you cheaper or even for free? Why hire a lawyer to solve a legal problem when you can get free legal help from the people who wrote the laws? Why hire an engineer to solve a technology problem when the government will send out an engineer to solve your problem for free? Why hire a marketing consultant to identify new opportunities for your business to grow when can tap into $3 billion dollars worth of free market studies?

Successful entrepreneurs are those who know how to get the most out of all the resources that are available to them. Here's a book that gives you access to the world's largest pot of money, help, and information. And now it's up to you to use it. Remember your tax dollars pay for all these programs, whether you use them or not.

The Good And Bad Of Entrepreneuring:
Six Reasons Why
Now Is The Best Time To Start A Business

I believe the current conditions in our country make it an excellent environment for entrepreneuring. Here's why.

1) Big Business Is Forcing Entrepreneurism

Most creative people who work in large companies feel frustrated and believe their real talents go unused. They see that the company they work for is not much different than a government agency. They see that 20% of the people are doing 80% of the work. They are also fed up with having 10 months of meetings before any little decision is made.

Few people working in big business feel that their efforts go towards making a difference. Office politics seem to be just as important as actual work. People feel unfulfilled and search for ways to feel needed.

As an entrepreneur you know you are needed from the first day you open up for business. You immediately see the direct correlation between your efforts and the success of your business. It's not office politics or 10 months of meetings that will determine your success; it's going to be hard work, fast decision making, mixed with a dose of good luck.

The more big business makes people feel unimportant and just a cog in the wheel, the more they will force entrepreneurs to go out and do it themselves.

2) The Best Tax Shelter

As long as our society is based on capitalism, having your own business offers the best of all tax advantages, no matter how Congress tinkers with the tax code. This is because under the tax laws, money spent in an attempt to generate a sale for your business is tax deductible. This is how people who own their own business write off their house, their car, their country club, their travel, their entertainment, and even their boats.

When I was a young, single entrepreneur, I paid almost no taxes. Almost everything I did was a business expense. But now that I am married with two children, things are a little different. I haven't figured a way to deduct such expenses as computer games and toys.

3) A Bad Economy Helps

Bad economic times show employees that the security of having a job is not secure at all. No matter how good you are at your work, or no matter how high you are up the ladder, you can still lose your job. It is that fear of losing that security that keeps so many people from starting their own business. Life is just as unpredictable whether you are working for yourself or working for someone else. You might as well have fun and be your own boss. This way you'll never be fired again!

The Good And Bad Of Entrepreneuring

The success of your business also will improve if you start it during hard times. If you start a business during a boom, customers can come easily and you'll get fat and happy. Then, when the first economic downturn hits, you may not be able to handle it. You won't know how to operate in a mean and lean mode. This is why a lot of businesses go belly up in bad economic times.

However, if you start your business when times are tough, it will make your business stronger. You will figure out ways to make it work when times are bad and you'll make a bundle when the economy makes a comeback and business get easier. You will also learn how to handle things when the economy turns sour again. You'll be ready to operate a lean and mean company and you won't become a business failure statistic.

4) Opportunities in a Post-Industrial Society

When our country was a growing industrialized society, it took a lot of money to get into business. You needed to invest in a factory, equipment, and high priced unionized employees. Now we live in an information and service-based economy, and most of these types of businesses take very little money to start. For many service businesses, all you need is a phone, a desk and business card, and you are in business. The factory for my information business is between my ears. I don't have to invest in a plant, equipment or anything, except computers and paper.

Employees in the post-industrial society are a lot cheaper. People working in the industrialized society made $20 to $30 per hour. You can now get people to work in information and service-based businesses at $5 to $10 per hour. That's a real bargain.

5) Big Business Creates Opportunities For You

As big business gets bigger and bigger, it creates more and more opportunities for the small entrepreneur. When my Fortune 500 clients look for new businesses opportunities, the first thing they ask is: "How big will this business eventually be?" And if the answer wasn't at least $100 million, they were not interested. It takes them just as much effort to get into a $100 million business as it does for them to get into a $1 million business. So they concentrate only on the big ones, and leave the $1 million crumbs for the small entrepreneurs. Well, I don't know about you, but a $1 million business is not a bad living. I see myself as an entrepreneur cockroach, living off $1 million crumbs that fall through the cracks from the big guys. And if my history serves me well, the cockroach outlived the dinosaur by a long shot.

6) An Information Explosion Equals An Open Society

The information explosion has greatly expanded what once was just a little club of entrepreneurs. Before the information explosion, you had to know someone to get the legal, marketing, technical or competitive information needed to launch a venture. Now you don't have to know someone to get this kind of help, you just have to understand the process of accessing information. Why can anyone tap into this information gold mine? Because this information is in our government, and by living in an open democracy we all have the same right to this information whether you're Donald Trump or a street cleaner.

What Entrepreneurs Don't Need

Everybody is always telling entrepreneurs about all the essentials they need. I think it's just as important to tell entrepreneurs what they don't need. After starting four businesses of my own and even after having two failures, here is what I believe you should be extra careful to avoid.

1) Too Much Professional Advice

If you're starting a business with a limited supply of capital, too much professional advice is going to kill you. If you try to surround yourself with all the trappings of business success, you're soon going to go out of business.

Remember, you and your time are the most important resources in your business. Succeeding in business is a "beat the clock" game. If you're spending a lot of your time meeting with lawyers and accountants or choosing fancy "power" furniture, you'll have little time to concentrate on the <u>one</u> thing that is important to your success...getting a client. This is the most critical success factor of any new business. Without a client, everything else is meaningless.

When I started my first business, I got the high priced accountants, the high priced lawyers, the power business cards and power furniture, but I went out of business. And who won? It was the accountants, lawyers, and furniture salesmen. They were all smart enough to get paid in the good times and I was out on the street.

Your clients don't care what kind of accounting system you use or what legal structure you have formed. And having the right look, whether it be impressive business cards or furniture, may only affect your business 5% or 10%. This is a very insignificant percentage if you have no business. Furthermore, it's a waste of time if you're spending a half a day choosing furniture when you could be spending a half a day getting a client. And 99% of the clients don't care what kind of furniture you have. The only person who cares about what kind of furniture you have is the furniture salesman.

2) Too Much Money

Anyone can start a business if given a million bucks. It doesn't take a lot of creativity to spend money to buy advertising in your local newspaper. But what are you going to do next year when your business doesn't have an extra $1 million lying around? Instead of learning how to buy space, you should first learn how to get your local paper to write a FREE story about your business! The price is right and it's more effective than advertising because you're also getting a big, respected institution, the newspaper, to endorse you (or so it seems to most readers).

Too much money for a novice entrepreneur can make you fat, lazy, and uncreative. The key to developing a strong business is learning how to get sales using the least amount of money, not the most amount of money.

The Good And Bad Of Entrepreneuring

3) Too Perfect A Product

A beginner entrepreneur can easily get hung up trying to develop the perfect product. Most of us can never be perfect, but we can still be successful. Entrepreneurs can get easily trapped into believing that their product or service has to be perfect before they offer it to the public.

Trying to be flawless can lead to failure. Being a perfectionist can cause you to go broke before you get to market. Be careful that your perfectionist attitude isn't really a mask for your own insecurities. What your family and friends will think about your product doesn't matter. The object of a product is to sell it to a customer. Your relatives and pals don't have to be your customers. Customers come with all different kinds of needs, and very few are willing to pay for perfection. Go open up your own closets and look at all the mediocre stuff you have purchased.

Until you start asking people for money you really don't know what they will buy. Your product is probably going to change dozens of times before it reaches its final form. And this metamorphosis is due to customer feedback, your most important information source. The most important thing is to introduce your product as soon as possible so that you can stay in business long enough to find out how to improve it.

Few of us are smart enough to read minds but we're all smart enough to listen. If you offer a product to ten people and five of them say they would buy it if it were green, go right out and paint the damn thing green, so you can make a few sales.

If you spend too much time designing the ultimate product you'll probably be wrong anyway and have few resources left to learn from your mistakes. Overdesigning isn't just a disease of the small entrepreneur. Do your remember Ford's Edsel or Coca-Cola's New Coke?

4) A Board of Directors

Anytime you get three people in a room to talk about an idea there will always be one naysayer. Finding potential problems is always easy to do. If an idea was perfect, it wouldn't be an idea anymore; it would already be a product or service fulfilled by someone else.

For ideas to work, it usually takes the passion and commitment of one person. This kind of spirit doesn't come from a board of directors which engages in group decision making. Although democratic, this process usually results in ideas where everyone owns a small piece of the end product and no one person is committed to the complete picture.

Also, board meetings can be a waste of time for struggling entrepreneurs. Entrepreneurs have to live from moment to moment, often making quick, reflexive decisions so they can immediately move to the next decision. The temperament required for entrepreneuring is different than the temperament needed to placate a diverse group such as a board of directors.

5) An MBA

I have a BS in Business and an MBA. I believe it took me two failing businesses to unlearn all that I was taught in my six years of business school. I was brainwashed into believing such things as: "if you need money, you go to the bank." When I was starting my businesses I quickly learned that a bank is the last place an entrepreneur with no money should go. Business schools spend a lion's share of the time teaching you how to run big businesses like General Motors. And from the shape that General Motors is in, you can see that they don't do such a good job at that.

The jargon you learn in business school certainly is helpful if you want to get a job in big business. But if you are a small entrepreneur, much of what they teach you will just interfere with your instincts. There is no magic to most operations of running a business. Accounting is keeping a checkbook. Production is making sure that your product costs less than what you sell it for. But, in the beginning marketing can seem magical. Finding a customer is what any new business is all about, and that doesn't take an MBA. It takes a lot of door pounding.

6) Government Forms

Don't tell the government this because I may get in trouble. I believe that entrepreneurs should even forget about government licenses and forms for starting a business.

After I had two businesses that failed, I got rid of the accountants, the lawyers, the power furniture and power business cards, and I also didn't file any local, county, state or federal forms. Don't get me wrong; I did file my tax return. Never mess around with the IRS. The government forms I'm talking about are the permits, licenses and applications to do business. My theory is that filing all these forms takes time and energy. Your time is very important. You'd be better off to concentrate that time on what is the critical success factor of your business...getting customers.

If you don't file the necessary forms there isn't much that can happen to you. The way the government works, it will take them three years to find you. And by then, you'll either be out of business, or you'll be successful enough to pay the $25 fine and file whatever is necessary.

Choosing The Business That Is Right For You: Trust Your Heart As Well As Your Head

Choosing the business that is right for you can be a daunting prospect. Take heart, however, there are as many different businesses as there are ideas. One of them is right for you.

To begin with, choose an area that excites you. To succeed, you must love what you do. I know that this sounds deceptively simple, but everything else depends upon this one principle.

Find out if there's a market for your products or services. Study your competition, suppliers, and new customers. Once this is done, trust your instincts. Choosing a business is a very personal decision. After all, you may end up spending the rest of your life with this business.

Following your heart, as well as your head, will greatly increase your chances of financial and personal success. I'm not advocating that you rely upon instinct alone, but the elements that lead to success often have little to do with advanced business degrees or perfectly balanced ledgers.

When you love what you do -- magic happens. Your business is no longer work. You may find yourself thinking about your business all the time, not because you have to, but because it is fun, fulfilling, and exciting.

Your chances of success skyrocket because you won't be easily discouraged. If you look around at the people who run businesses, you'll see that it doesn't take a rocket scientist to run a successful company. Most of us are bright enough to run a business if we decide to try.

Perseverance, not intelligence, is the key. If you love what you're doing, you won't give up at the first economic downturn and try to find something more profitable. You'll stay and learn how to make money even when the economy sours. Eventually, you'll become better at what you do than anyone else.

We pride ourselves in making all our decisions "by the numbers." Numbers are safe. Yet, those who meet the needs of our fast changing society look past the numbers. They see beyond the present and anticipate the future.

Choosing The Business That Is Right For You

Steps for Choosing a Business

(1) **Use Your Imagination.** Clear your mind and let your imagination go. Explore new ideas and opportunities. Ask yourself questions such as:

a) What is my fantasy business?
b) What would I do even if I didn't get paid for doing it?
c) What people do I really admire in the world and why do I admire them?

(2) **Research Your Idea NOW.** Reach for that calculator and explore as many ideas as you can. Your job is to take the best ideas that you have at the moment and see how they grow. You can expect a lot of duds. Don't worry if all of your ideas aren't winners. With work and the help of a calculator, your ideas will lead to interesting opportunities. Do the research, study the options. Remember, all the information you need to find out about any business is out there. Start by looking through this book. It will give you plenty of ideas of where to start.

(3) **Trust Your Instincts.** The final decision can be difficult. If you did enough research you probably came up with more than one potentially good idea. But, be sure to make the final decision with your heart as well as your head. You are the one who has to be happy. And when you are, you will work like hell to make that business a success.

The Good And Bad Of Entrepreneuring

Don't Believe In Instant Success

The Glorification of Failure Will Bring More Success

Everybody fails, but no one ever tells you about it. I had two failing businesses before I got lucky with what I am doing now. In 1975, I even had a computer software company that failed. Looking back at the growth of the computer business since then, I feel that I must have been the only person in the country with a computer company that didn't make it.

It's not only me. Everybody who does anything in the world has to experience failure. We all know that Henry Ford was responsible for manufacturing the first mass produced automobile called the Model T. But very few people are aware that the Model T was not his first automobile. He went through models from A to S that all were failures before he got it right. Coca-Cola was only selling a dozen cases a week for a long time before they got it right. Even Thomas Edison failed over 1,000 different times while working on the filament for the light bulb before he was successful.

Our society should glorify failure the same way it glorifies success. The stories we read about in the general press and in special interest magazines like *Success*, all make success sound easy. They tell you stories of some housewife who was selling her "Can't Beat Em" cookies at school bake sales when her son's teacher suggested she should sell them in stores. Within no time at all, she's a millionaire. Face it: that's probably not going to happen to you.

A millionaire friend of mine, Dr. Fad, didn't make his money instantly either. Maybe you've heard about him. He's responsible for the Wacky Wall Walker fad a number of years ago and he made a bundle from it. He was successful with the Wall Walker only after dozens of other products failed. His business sounds glamorous now. He's got his own television show and 60 Minutes did a story on him. But when he started, his little import/export business struggled for years as he lived in an efficiency apartment with his wife and his business shared a one room office. Some of his early failures included importing Japanese fish parts and face masks for industrial use. He struggled with this unglamorous business for years before he hit the jackpot.

Success Merchants Lie To You

Go out and fail...that is the only way you are going to get anywhere. The odds of being an instant success are about the same as you being hit by lightning. If you live in Florida, where lightning has a habit of striking often, your odds may not be so bad. If you're waiting for the right idea that is sure to be an instant success like you see in the magazines, you'll never do anything. Magazines lie by making you believe that you, too, can be an instant success, just like the people they profile. This is how they sell magazines.

The magazines are not the only liars. I do it too, when I tell success stories on TV Talk shows. And the people on TV infomercials are among the worst offenders. They make you believe that instant success will happen to you just like the people they have on their success panel.

Don't Believe In Instant Success

Success Stories Can Stop YOUR Success

The problem with these instant success stories is instead of encouraging you, they are more likely to stop you from fulfilling your dream. When the announcer introduces one of the panel members, it's usually something like this..."Do you see Joe and his wife here? Yesterday Joe was a garbage collector in Chattanooga, Tennessee. Last night he listened to my 15-hour "How To Make A Million" success tapes and today Joe owns 15 beautiful properties in Southern California."

Any rational person knows that kind of instant success probably won't happen to him. But now you feel jealous. You're thinking..."If that garbage collector can do it, why can't I?" And then you think about buying the 15-hour cassette program but you don't, because your rational side knows that you can't listen to hours of tapes at night, and own 15 properties by the next morning. If that garbage collector really did it and you can't, you're going to feel dumb. How can a garbage collector be smarter than you? No one wants to know that a garbage collector is smarter than you are so you don't do anything about it.

Or, if you buy the tapes and listen to them, you get angry because your life didn't change overnight. You get discouraged, throw the tapes in the closet, and hang up your success dreams, leaving it for the folks on TV.

Failure Helps You Unlearn What You Learned in School

It took me two failing businesses to unlearn all I was taught in my six years of business school. I marched out into the world with an MBA in Computer Science and that was why my first two businesses failed. I was trying to put into practice what I learned in school. They were telling me things like..."If you need money go to the bank." No matter how good the economy is, a bank is the last place an entrepreneur with no assets is likely to find money for his or her business.

In my consulting business, I was trying to do things just like the big consultants, such as preparing mahogany-bound reports and renting fancy offices. I couldn't perform the services of a big consulting firm as well as a big consulting firm could. The clients who expected that from me were not satisfied in the end. What I learned was that I was a small consulting firm, but there were a lot of companies who didn't want a big consulting firm. They wanted someone who was operating out of their bedroom. I discovered my niche and that uniqueness gave me a real edge.

Friends, Loved Ones, and Teachers Are Bad For Entrepreneurs

We all have misconceptions about the way things work and what will be successful. We are inundated from all sides with opinions. Our associates, friends, families, and teachers all continually tell us why they believe someone is a success. They don't really know. If they did, they would be doing it too. The truth is, what makes one person a success is not likely to make you a success. The reason for your success will be because you are different than anyone else and your product will be different than anyone else's.

The Good And Bad Of Entrepreneuring

Another way all sorts of well-meaning folks hinder your success is by protecting you. All these people who care for you will not want to see you hurt. They will show you 15 ways your idea is likely to fail. Teachers are the worst. It seems that the more schooling you receive in this country, the more reasons you can think of as to why the idea won't work. Remember, the founder of Federal Express first presented his idea as a paper in business school and the professor barely gave him a passing grade because he thought the idea wouldn't work. And that was at Harvard! So trust your instincts and set your idea in motion, regardless of what some people might say.

If you want to succeed, most likely you are going to experience failure. And you shouldn't let anyone protect you from it. It's the best springboard to your future success.

Key Pointers When Applying For Money

The following are tips meant to offer advice and encouragement to both the novice and the "old pro" government money seeker.

1) Don't Always Believe A Negative Answer

If you call a government office and ask about a particular money program and they tell you that no such program exists, don't believe them. No one person in the government can know everything. Senator Kerry of Massachusetts recently surveyed all the local Small Business Administration offices to see how they were administering a program which provides money to Vietnam era veterans starting their own businesses. <u>Only half the offices knew that such a program existed.</u> These are the same offices which are in charge of giving out the money. Other times, programs are consolidated under new names. For example, there used to be a program at the U.S. Department of Agriculture which gave money to farmers to build golf courses and tennis courts in their fields so that they could get into the resort business. The program was called the Recreation Facility Loan Program. I think the name made politicians uneasy, so they folded the money into the Farm Operating Loan Program. The lesson here is not to throw up your hands when told that a program does not exist. Keep asking questions like:

- "Did such a program ever exist?"
- "What happened to the program?"
- "Are there any similar programs?"
- "Can I get a descriptive listing of all your current programs?"
- "What other programs or agencies might offer money in similar areas?"
- "Is there anyone who may know more about this program?"

2) Apply To More Than One Program

There is no rule which says that you can apply only to one program for your businesses. For example, if you want to build condominiums in a town of less than 50,000, investigate programs at the Small Business Administration, the Department of Housing and Urban Development, the Department of Agriculture, as well as programs at the state and city level. The worst that can happen to you is that all of your applications are approved. This is a nice predicament to be in. You may not be able to accept the money from everyone. Many of the applications do not even ask if you are applying for money elsewhere.

3) Don't Be Discouraged If You Think You Are Not Eligible

If you happen to contact a program office and they tell you that the program was changed so that only non-profit organizations can now receive the money, don't let this discourage you. What you can do is find a non-profit or existing organization to work with you. This is done every day in Washington, DC. Entrepreneurs locate federal money programs and find passive partners who will get a percentage of the money.

The Good And Bad Of Entrepreneuring

4) Talk To Those Who Give The Money

Before you actually fill out any application, it is well worth your time to review the forms with the program officials, either in person if at all possible, or over the telephone. Many of the funding agencies have offices throughout the country to assist you. Such contact should help you tailor your answers to meet the government's expectations. It will give them what they want to see.

5) Give Them What They Want

When you prepare your application, give the government exactly what it asks for, even though it may not make much sense to you. Don't fight it. You will need all your energy to get your money. It is unlikely that you will have any chance in changing the government's ways even if you are right.

6) Starting Small Or Big?

You have to be careful about when to ask for a lot of money and when to ask for just a little. This depends upon the program. So before you say how much money you need, be sure you have some understanding of the maximum amount as well as the average amount of monies given to applicants. Each program office listed can give you this information.

7) Try Again

If your proposal is rejected, learn what you did wrong and try again next year, or try with a different program. Many proposals are rejected because of bad timing or a relatively minor hitch. Don't worry. Being turned down will not be held against you. Some programs deny first time applications just for drill. They want to make sure that you are serious about your project.

8) When the Bureaucracy Is Stuck, Use Your Representative

Contact the office of your U.S. Senator or Congressperson only when the bureaucracy comes to a halt on your paperwork. Sometimes this is the only way to get action. Playing constituent is a very effective resource and should be used only when all else fails.

9) Don't Overlook State Programs

Investigate opportunities from the state agencies at the same time you are exploring federal financial assistance. State real estate programs are listed under "Real Estate Ventures" and state business money programs are listed under "State Money and Help for Your Business."

Jumping Over Bureaucratic Hurdles

Remember you are not going to make one telephone call and as a result, some bureaucrat will send you a check. If it were that easy, our mammoth deficit would be 10 times as big as it is now. What normally happens is that bureaucratic hurdles will be put in your way, and how you handle them will determine the success or failure of your getting the money. An example of the ultimate success in overcoming such bureaucratic roadblocks is depicted by a Boston entrepreneur named Steven Stern. His story follows:

A few years ago, Steven Stern saw me on the David Letterman Show one night when I talked about a government program which gave money to teenage entrepreneurs. The next day Steven called my office and asked for more details about the program. He explained that he was 16 years old and wanted to start a lawn mowing business in Boston. I told him that I really didn't know much about the details of the program, but I did give him the name and address of the office which runs the program.

Steven called me back about two days later and said that the Washington DC office told him to contact the regional office located in Boston. When he called the regional office, he was told that he could not apply for that program because the money was set aside for teenagers in rural areas. He asked me what he could do now, and I suggested he call Washington back and get a copy of the law which authorizes the program. I told him that the law would give him all the facts.

When Steven got a copy of the law, he was surprised to find that it stated that the money was indeed intended for teenagers in rural areas, but it also said that it could be used to start lawn mower businesses anywhere. What a match. So he took a copy of the law to the government office in Boston and rubbed their noses in the facts. The local office then conceded that he should apply for the money, and gave him an application.

But, at this point Steven was stopped again. Just as they handed him an application, they asked if he belonged to a 4-H club. This was another eligibility requirement for the financial assistance. Well, Steven attended a city high school where students didn't know one end of a cow from another, let alone belong to a 4-H club. But this did not stop Steven. He went to school the next day and rounded up four of his buddies and started what may have been one of the first and only inner city 4-H clubs.

Now completely eligible to apply for the money, Steven sent in his application and three months later received $3,000 to start his business. Within two years, Steven was making $10,000 a year and able to support himself through Babson College.

Not all cases are going to be as difficult as Steven's, but they can be, and you have to have the stamina to overcome any hurdle the government puts in your path. Remember that someone is going to get the money every year, and it might as well be you.

Tips On Finding Information: The Art Of Getting A Bureaucrat To Help You

Our greatest asset as information seekers is that we live in a society inhabited by people who are dying to talk about what they do for a living. However, in this world of big bureaucracies and impersonal organizations, it is rare that any of us get a chance to share what we know with someone who is truly interested. Perhaps that explains why psychiatrists are in such great demand. They are great listeners, and not many average Americans are these days.

This phenomenon can actually work to your advantage — almost anyone can find an expert on any topic if you are willing to make an average of seven telephone calls to eventually locate that expert.

The Value Of Experts In Today's Information Age

Using experts can be your answer to coping with the information explosion. Computers handle some problems of the information explosion because they are able to categorize and index vast amounts of data. However, many computerized databases fail to contain information that is generated by non-traditional sources, like documents that are buried in state and federal agencies.

Another problem is that many databases suffer from lack of timeliness because they offer indexes to articles and most publishers have long lead times for getting the material into print. And in our fast changing society, having the most current information is crucial, and these articles are often not as current or up to date as they should be.

Computers also contribute to a more serious problem. Because of their ability to store such large quantities of data, computers aggravate the information explosion by fueling the information overload. If you access one of the major databases on a subject such as Maine potatoes, most likely you will be confronted with a printout of 500 or more citations. Do you have the time to find and read all of them? How can you as a non-expert tell a good article from one that will just waste your valuable time retrieving and reading it?

The first step to cut through this volume of information is to find an expert specializing in Maine potatoes. Yes, such an individual exists! This person already will have read those 500 articles and will be able to identify the relevant ones that meet your information needs. This expert will also be able to tell you what will be in the literature next year on the subject of Maine potatoes, because he is probably in the midst of writing or reviewing forthcoming articles right now. And if you are in search of a fact or figure, this government bureaucrat might know the answer right off the top of his head. The best part of this research strategy is that all this valuable information can be accumulated for just the price of a telephone call.

Case Study: How To Find Mr. Potato

The techniques for locating an expert can best be illustrated by a classic story from the days when I was struggling to start my first information brokerage company in 1975.

At the time the business amounted to just a desk and telephone crowded into the bedroom of my apartment. As so often happens in a fledgling enterprise, my first client was a friend. His problem was this: "I've got to have the latest information on the basic supply and demand of Maine potatoes within 24 hours."

My client represented a syndicate of commodity investors which invests millions of dollars in Maine potatoes. When he called, these potatoes were selling at double their normal price and he wanted to know why. I knew absolutely nothing about potatoes, but thought I knew where to find out. The agreement with my client was that I would be paid only if I succeeded in getting the information (no doubt you've guessed I no longer work that way).

Luck With The First Telephone Call

The first call I made was to the general information office of the U.S. Department of Agriculture. I asked to speak to an expert on potatoes. The operator referred me to Mr. Charlie Porter. I wondered if this Mr. Porter was a department functionary with responsibility for handling crank calls, but the operator assured me that he was an agriculture economist specializing in potatoes. I called Mr. Porter and explained how I was a struggling entrepreneur who knew nothing about potatoes and needed his help to answer a client's urgent request. Charlie graciously gave me much of the information I needed, adding that he would be happy to talk at greater length either over the phone or in person at his office. I decided to go see him and meet a real expert face to face.

Only Problem Was Getting Out Of Charlie Porter's Office

For 2 1/2 hours the next morning, the Federal government's potato expert explained in minute detail the supply and demand of Maine potatoes. Charlie Porter showed me computer printouts that reflected how the price had doubled in recent weeks. For any subject that arose during our conversation, Charlie had immediate access to a reference source. Rows of books in his office covered every conceivable aspect of the potato market. A strip of ticker tape that tracked the daily price of potatoes from all over the country lay across his desk.

Here in Charlie's office was everything anyone might ever want to know about potatoes. The problem, it turned out, was not in getting enough information, but how to gracefully leave his office. Once Charlie started talking, it was hard for him to stop. It

The Art Of Getting A Bureaucrat To Help You

seemed that Charlie Porter had spent his lifetime studying the supply and demand of potatoes and finally someone with a genuine need sought his expertise on the subject closest to his heart.

One Potato....Two Potato....

When I finally had to tell Charlie that I really had to leave, he pointed across the hall in the direction of a potato statistician whose primary responsibility was to produce a monthly report showing potato production and consumption in the United States. From this statistician I was to learn about all the categories of potatoes that are tallied. It turns out the U.S. Department of Agriculture counts all the potato chips sold every month, even how many Pringle potato chips are consumed in comparison to say, Lay's Potato Chips. The statistician offered to place me on the mailing list to receive all this free monthly data.

The Art Of Getting An Expert To Talk

The information explosion requires greater reliance on experts in order to sift through this proliferation of enormous data. Cultivating an expert, however, demands an entirely different set of skills from using a library or a publication. You must know how to treat people so that they are ready, willing, and able to give you the information that you need. It is human nature for almost anyone to want to share their knowledge, but your approach will determine whether you ultimately get the expert to open up to your questions. So it is your job to create an environment that makes an individual want to share his expertise. Remember when dealing with both public and private sector experts, they will get the same paycheck whether they give you two weeks worth of free help or if they cut the conversation short after a minute or two. They will decide whether you'll get all of the information that you're asking for.

Expectations:
The 7-Phone Call Rule

There is no magic to finding an expert. It is simply a numbers game which seems to take an average of seven telephone calls to find the answer you're looking for. Telephone enough people and keep asking each for a lead. The magic lies in how much information the expert will share once you find the right individual. This is why it is essential to remember "the 7-phone call rule", and never stop at the second or third lead that seems to be going nowhere.

If you make several calls and begin to get upset because you are being transferred from one person to another, you will be setting yourself up to fail once you locate the right expert. What is likely to happen is that when your "Charlie Porter" picks up his telephone he is going to hear you complaining about how sick and tired you are of getting the runaround from his organization and colleagues. If you don't sound like you are going to be the highlight of Charlie's day, he will instantly figure out how to get rid of you fast.

This explains why some people are able to get information and others fail. Seasoned researchers know it is going to take a number of telephone calls and they will not allow themselves to get impatient. After all, the runaround is an unavoidable part of the information gathering process. Consequently, the first words that come out of your mouth are extremely important because they set the stage for letting the expert want to help you.

Ten Basic Telephone Tips

Here are a few pointers to keep in mind when you are casting about for an expert. These guidelines amount to basic common sense but are very easy to forget by the time you get to that sixth or seventh phone call.

1) Introduce Yourself Cheerfully
The way you open the conversation will set the tone for the entire interview. Your greeting and initial comment should be cordial and cheerful. They should give the feeling that this is not going to be just another telephone call, but a pleasant interlude in his or her day.

2) Be Open And Candid
You should be as candid as possible with your source since you are asking the same of him. If you are evasive or deceitful in explaining your needs or motives, your source will be reluctant to provide you with information. If there are certain facts you cannot reveal such as client confidentiality, explain just that. Most people will understand.

3) Be Optimistic
Throughout the entire conversation you should exude a sense of confidence. If you call and say "You probably aren't the right person" or "You don't have any information, do you?" it makes it easy for the person to say "You're right, I can't help you." A positive attitude will encourage your source to stretch his mind to see what information he might have that could possibly help you.

4) Be Humble And Courteous
You can be optimistic and still be humble. Remember the old adage that you can catch more flies with honey than you can with vinegar. People in general, and experts in particular, love to tell others what they know, as long as their position of authority is not questioned or threatened. In fact, if they are made to feel like an expert by the way you treat them, chances are that they will give you more information than they originally intended.

5) Be Concise
State your problem simply. A long-winded explanation may bore your contact and reduce your chances for getting a thorough response.

6) Don't Be A "Gimme"
A "gimme" is someone who says "give me this" or "give me that", and has little consideration for the other person's time or feelings. Remember to "ask" for information or a particular document that you're interested in.

7) Be Complimentary
This goes hand in hand with being humble. A well placed compliment about your source's expertise or insight about a particular topic will serve you well. In searching for information in large organizations, you are apt to talk to many colleagues of your source, so it wouldn't hurt to convey the respect that your

Tips On Finding Information

"Charlie Porter" commands, for example, "Everyone I spoke to said you are the person I must talk with." It is reassuring for anyone to know that they have the respect of their peers.

8) Be Conversational
Avoid spending the entire time talking about the information you need. Briefly mention a few irrelevant topics such as the weather, the Washington Redskins, or the latest political campaign. The more social you are without being too chatty, the more likely that your source will open up to you.

9) Return The Favor
You might share with your source information or even gossip you have picked up elsewhere. However, be certain not to betray the trust of either your client or another source. If you do not have any relevant information to share at the moment, it would still be a good idea to call back when you are further along in your research when you might have information of value to offer.

10) Send Thank You Notes
A short note, typed or handwritten, will help ensure that your source will be just as cooperative in the future.

Case Study: Jelly Beans

In our information society, which produces thousands of databases and other resources every day, it seems that most decision makers rely primarily on traditional information sources. More often than not executives will spend lots of time and money trying to determine the size of a market or information about a competitor, and if the answer cannot be found through conventional sources, the corporate decision is made without the information. This does not have to be the case.

We believe that you can find solid information for almost any problem, no matter how sensitive the issue may be, if you use some unorthodox research techniques. To illustrate this point, here is a step-by-step account of how one of our researchers succeeded in gathering figures on the U.S. market for jelly beans when a Fortune 500 firm came up emptyhanded after exhausting all traditional sources. The prevailing view both inside and outside the industry was that this piece of the information puzzle could not be obtained.

It should be said at the outset that the estimates Information USA, Inc. finally obtained must not be regarded as 100% accurate, but they do represent the best available figures and, most likely, come within 10% to 15% of the actual number.

Opening Round

Faced with the problem of finding the U.S. market for jelly beans, we already knew that our client had contacted the major market research firms, did some literature searches, and came up with practically no useful information. As is evident from this case study, this information hunt occurred when Ronald Reagan was President and jelly beans happened to be the candy of choice of several very high government officials.

1) The first call was to the U.S. Department of Commerce to locate the government's jelly bean expert. We were referred to Cornelius Kenny, the confectionery industry expert. Mr. Kenny was out that day and would call us back when he returned to the office.

2) A search of Gale's *Encyclopedia of Associations* identified four relevant trade associations. However, upon contacting them we were told that they provide information only to their members.

3) The White House seemed like a good bet because of Ronald Reagan's fondness for jelly beans and the resulting publicity. The Public Affairs office at 1600 Pennsylvania Avenue said that it never obtained statistical information on the industry but could tell us tales about a lifesize water buffalo and portraits of the President constructed of jelly beans. However, they suggested that we contact several lobbying organizations. Calls to these groups proved fruitless.

4) A call to the U.S. Bureau of the Census uncovered John Streeter, an analyst who monitors the panned candy industry. He told us:

* jelly beans have never been counted and there would be no way to get the answer;

* the non-chocolate panned candy category within the Bureau's Annual Confectionery Survey contains jelly beans;

* the seasonal category of the non-chocolate panned candies, according to his estimates, contains 90% jelly beans because most jelly beans are sold during Easter and that jelly beans are about the only non-chocolate panned manufactured candy sold on a seasonal basis;

* $37,804,000 worth of non-chocolate panned candy was shipped by U.S. manufacturers in 1984, which represents about 48,354,000 pounds; the figures for total non-chocolate panned candy for 1984 totaled $251,525,000 and 237,308,000 pounds; and

* government regulations prohibited him from revealing the names of jelly bean manufacturers, but he did refer us to two trade associations he thought might help.

So this analyst at the Census Bureau, who tried to discourage us with warnings that no such figure for the jelly bean market exists, actually gave us quite a lot of concrete information as well as some valuable leads to pursue.

Armed and Dangerous With a Little Information

At this point, we had a market estimate from one government expert based on a figure generated by the U.S. Bureau of the Census. It may have sounded like the answer we were after, but taking that figure to our client at this juncture would have been premature and possibly irresponsible. The main drawback was that the estimate reflected only one person's opinion, and although he was an expert, he was not a true industry observer as one would be if they were actually in the business of selling jelly beans. Our strategy now was to find people in the industry who could give us their interpretation of these figures.

The Census expert referred us to one of the trade associations we had already contacted. However, when we called back saying that Mr. Streeter at the Census Bureau suggested we call them, the association promptly responded with a list of the 25 major jelly bean manufacturers. This is an example of how using the name of a government expert can get you in the door and get you the information you're looking for. When we phoned several manufacturers, they laughed when we told them of our effort to ascertain the market for jelly beans. Jelly beans had never been counted, they told us, and their advice was to give up.

At this point Mr. Kenny, the confectionery expert at the U.S. Department of Commerce called us back and he, too, said that the market had never been measured. However, he did hazard a guess that the jelly bean market could be roughly 50% of the total Census figure for Non-Chocolate Panned Candy.

Tips On Finding Information

A separate call to a private research group which does trend analysis by surveying grocery stores shared its estimate that 90% of all jelly beans are sold at Easter.

Easier to Be a Critic Than a Source

Our lack of success in dealing with a few manufacturers caused us to change tactics. Instead of asking them to estimate the size of the jelly bean market, we began asking them what they thought of the figures we received from the industry analysts at the Commerce Department, as well as the Census Bureau. We decided to try to find someone who actually filled out the Census survey and get a reaction to the Census figures. We spoke with the owner of Herbert Candies, a small candy company. He gave us his 1984 jelly bean production and cost statistics, told us he filled out the Census report, and readily explained what he thought the Census statistics meant in terms of jelly bean production and cost. Furthermore, using his calculator, he helped us arrive at national figures for 1984. He also told us which companies manufacture 80% of the jelly beans produced in the country.

Now, armed with actual figures for 1984 jelly bean production, average cost per pound, average number of jelly beans in a pound, and the percentage of jelly beans produced during Easter, we resumed calling manufacturers — this time to get their opinion of our figures. This was the real turning point in dealing with the manufacturers. Because everyone in the industry knew that there were no exact numbers on the size of the jelly bean market, as professionals they were afraid to give a figure because anyone could say it was wrong. However, because they were experts in the business, they were not afraid to criticize someone else's information. Reactions from insiders were just what we needed to help hone a good working number. The manufacturers were able to tell us why our figures were good or not and they gave us sound reasons why the numbers should be adjusted, such as "Based on our sales figures your numbers sound a little low," or "Not all manufacturers report to the Bureau of the Census, so that figure may be low."

To show how this tactic prompted many manufacturers to be candid about both the industry and their sales in particular, here are highlights of our conversations with nine companies. What is presented below may seem to be too detailed, but after reviewing them we hope that it proves our point about how open business executives can be about their company.

1) Owner, Herbert Candies (small manufacturer and retailer)

* 90% of jelly beans are sold at Easter
* 60% of Census seasonal category are jelly beans
* average cost of jelly beans is $1 per pound
* when President Reagan first got into office the jelly bean market shot up 150% but now it is back to normal
* four companies have 80% of the market, with E.J. Brach the largest at 40%, Brock the second largest, followed by Herman Goelitz and Maillard
* Herbert Candies sold 30,000 pounds of jelly beans this past year and 90% at Easter; 10,000 were gourmet beans at $3.20 per pound and 20,000 were regular jelly beans at $2.80 per pound

2) Marketing Department, Nabisco Confectionery

* suggested we call SAMI, a private market research firm
* estimated 90% of jelly beans are sold at Easter
* confirmed that E.J. Brach has 40% of the market

3) Vice President of Marketing and Sales, Herman Goelitz (producer of "Bellies," Ronald Reagan's favorite)

* between 35% and 50% of his jelly beans are sold at Easter
* $1.00 per pound could be the average retail price
* a retailer can purchase jelly beans at $.60 per pound
* the retail price ranges between $1.25 and $5 per pound

4) General Manager, Burnell's Fine Candy (manufacturer of hanging bag jelly beans)

* 75% of jelly beans are sold at Easter
* $.60 to $.75 per pound is average manufacturer's price
* $1.59 is the average retail price
* 75% of Census seasonal category is probably jelly beans

5) Senior VP of Marketing and Sales, E.J. Brach (largest manufacturer)

* produces 24 million jelly beans annually at an average price of $.86 per pound
* there are approximately 100 beans per pound
* Brach's selling price is about industry average
* they have about 50% of the market
* 90% of the jelly beans sold at Easter sounds too high

6) Product Manager of Marketing Department, Brock Candy (second largest manufacturer)

* 85% to 95% of all jelly beans are sold at Easter
* average price paid by retailers is $.59 to $.99 per pound
* there are 130 to 140 jelly beans in a pound
* E.J. Brach has 40% to 50% of the jelly bean business — 32 to 45 million jelly beans sold in a year sounds correct given Brock's production figures; but probably it is closer to the high side
* Brock Candy is number 2 in the industry
* there are not many jelly bean manufacturers and basing total production on E.J. Brach's sales figures is a good way to arrive at an industry estimate

7) Traffic Manager, Powell Confectionery (medium size producer)

* 75% of jelly beans are sold at Easter judging from Powell's sales
* average retail price $.75 to $.80 per pound and the average manufacturer's price is $.65 to $.70 per pound
* 35 to 45 million jelly beans per year sounds reasonable
* it seems fair to double E.J. Brach production figures to get the total market because it has about 50% share of the market

8) President, Ferrara Panned Candy (largest panned candy producer)

* familiar with Census data and believes that jelly beans represent about 75% to 80% of the seasonal sales; 80% to 90% of all jelly beans are sold at Easter
* 32 to 45 million pounds per year seems a bit low
* E.J. Brach has 50% of the packaged jelly bean market but has less than half of the bulk jelly bean market

9) New Product Development Manager, Farley Candy

* familiar with Census data and believes that the numbers are understated because not all companies report their figures
* an industry estimate of 32 to 50 million pounds per year seems low

So much for all those who discouraged us from even tackling this issue of the market for jelly beans. All the data poured forth during these telephone conversations provided more information than our Fortune 500 client ever expected.

Deciding on an Estimate

As you can see from the interviews outlined above, traffic managers all the way up to company presidents were willing to give us their best estimate of the size of the market and even divulge their own company's sales figures.

After government experts, the figure seemed to cluster around the 45 to 50 million pound range. It may not be that obvious from just reading the highlights of our interviews, but that consensus became apparent after talking with about a dozen people associated with the industry.

Information Exchange Is a People Business

It is just surprising what company executives and government experts are willing to tell you if they are approached in the right way. You can find the answer to any question (or at least a good estimate) as long as you expect to make many phone calls and you treat each person on the other end of the telephone in a friendly, appreciative way.

The biggest difference between those who succeed in their information quest and those who fail boils down to whether or not they believe the information exists. If you persist in thinking the information can be found, nine times out of ten you will get what you need.

Tips On Finding Information

Coping With Misinformation

One of the major problems encountered by researchers is determining the accuracy of the information that they have collected. If you are doing traditional market research and using primary sources, accuracy is not that complicated. Traditional market researchers are well aware of survey methods, sampling techniques, and computing errors using statistical standard deviation analysis. However, if you are a desk researcher, like Information USA, Inc. which relies on secondary sources and expert opinion, how do you compute the standard deviation for error? The answer is that you cannot use hard statistical techniques, but you can employ other soft forms of error checking.

Major Causes for Error and Prevention Tactics

Problem #1: Lost in the Jargon

It is not uncommon for researchers to be dealing frequently in areas of expertise where they do not have complete command of the industry jargon. In such situations it is easy to believe that you have found the exact information needed only to find out later that you missed the mark considerably. This is a common trap to fall into when fishing in unfamiliar waters. And if you have to do the job quickly, it is easy to believe that you know more than you really do or to avoid getting the complete explanation of specific jargon because you do not want to waste the time of the expert who is giving you the information. Here is an experience of a U.S. Department of Agriculture expert which illustrates this point.

This government expert received a call one day from an assistant at the White House. This hot shot, who acted pretty impressed with himself, said he was in a meeting with both the President and the head of the Meat Packers Association and needed to know right then the official number of cows in the United States. The livestock expert asked the presidential aide if that was exactly what he meant and then when he impatiently responded "Yes," the bureaucrat told him the figure. Within minutes the White House staffer called back and said the president of the Meat Packers Association laughed at him and claimed that there were twice as many cows. The assistant then realized he needed the number of all cows — including "male cows" — as well as all female ones.

The White House aide had a problem with semantics, probably a city slicker who never knew the difference between cows and cattle. This can happen to anyone, not only a cocky Presidential aide. For example, if you want to know the market for computers, a more specific question to ask is are you talking about free standing units or central processing units?

Solution #1: Act a Little Dumb

In order to prevent this type of embarrassment, you have to find an expert with whom you are comfortable. When I say comfortable, I mean someone you can go to and ask dumb questions. You will get the most help if you act very humble in your approach. If you request information with the arrogance of the White House staffer, you may be given only the facts you ask for and nothing more. However, if you call up an expert and say something like "Oh God, can you please help me? I don't really know much about this, but my boss needs to know how many cows there are in the country." With more than a hint of indecision in your voice and honestly admitting you don't know much about the field, the expert is more likely to ask you some key questions that will ensure that you get the right figures. He may even enjoy giving you the information that you need, and not just resent your phone call.

Problem #2: Believing the Written Word or a Computer

This is a more serious problem than the difficulties and confusion surrounding industry jargon. Mastering the terminology just requires a little homework. However, overcoming a deep seated belief that information either from a computer, in published sources, or from the government is always accurate can be like changing your religion. It took me years, as well as dozens of professional embarrassments, to overcome this problem.

Just because a figure appears in print does not make it gospel. Remember the saying, "Figures don't lie, but liars can figure." Keep this in mind before betting the farm on anything you read in print, even if it comes out of a computer. A good illustration which follows pertains to Census Bureau information.

A few years ago we were doing a market study on stereo speakers and discovered that the figures the U.S. Bureau of the Census had for this market were off by over 50 percent. No one in the industry complained to the government because the industry was small and couldn't be bothered. But most of the companies involved knew that the figure was misleading and so had no use for the Census report. Another case is a Fortune 500 company which told us that for over five years it filled out the U.S. Census form under the wrong Standard Industrial Code (SIC). An important caveat—this firm ranks as the number two manufacturer in the industry.

You have to remember that number crunchers at the Census Bureau and other such organizations are not always interested in the meaning behind the numbers. Much of their work is simply taking a number from block A, adding it to the number in block B, and placing the result in block C. Verifying where the numbers come from is not their job.

Published sources are an even bigger problem than government data. Many believe that what you read in a magazine or a newspaper or hear on television or radio must be true. Nonsense! Anyone and their brother can be interviewed by a magazine or newspaper, and usually what they say will get printed in a magazine or quoted on the air as long as it is not too outrageous. Sometimes you are more likely to get it into print if what you're saying **is** outrageous. After all, most news stories are just accounts of what someone said as interpreted by a journalist.

The more general the media, the less accurate its reporting may be about an industry. In other words, an article in the ice cream industry trade magazine is more likely to be accurate than a similar story in the *New York Times*. The trade journal will have reporters who cover that particular industry and they will more than likely be able to flush out bad data. The newspaper, on the other hand, will do only one ice cream story a year, and will print almost anything it hears. So just because someone is quoted in an article does not mean that the information is correct.

I have seen much of this firsthand when on nationwide book promotion tours. In newspaper interviews or on radio and television talk shows, I can say almost anything and they will print or broadcast it, as is. I will give countless facts and figures based on my own biased research (remember that I am trying to sell books), and hardly ever will I be questioned or seriously challenged about the authenticity of my research. I don't know if it is laziness, apathy, or just plain lack of time that allows so much unchallenged information to be presented in the media. I have even blatantly lied to a reporter who thought of himself as a clone of CBS' Mike Wallace of *60 Minutes*. Before I started doing media interviews, I assumed that any good reporter worth his or her salt could find holes in what I presented and would expose me as some kind of fraud. I didn't know how they would do it, but I guess my own insecurity prompted me to prepare for the worst. The reality is that most reporters spend little or no time studying the topic before they interview you, and if you become annoyed or angry, especially with this Mike Wallace type described above, you can blow them away with an exaggerated fact or half-truth that he will never be able to verify.

Solution #2: Find Another Industry Expert

Whether a figure comes from the Census Bureau, a trade magazine or off a television program, your best bet for determining whether the number is accurate is to track down an industry expert and ask him to comment on the figure. What you are seeking is their biased opinion about the accuracy of the stated figure. If the expert believes the figure is correct but doesn't know why, find another expert.

Problem #3: Trusting an Expert

This may seem to contradict what I just said in the solution to problem #2, but stick with me and you'll see the difference.

There are many times when you cannot start with published or printed data and all you can do is pick the brains of experts within the industry. This means that you will be getting facts and figures based on the best available guess from experts. Many times this is the only way to get the information you need.

Getting this type of soft data can be full of danger. After having worked for hours trying to find a friendly soul to share with you his inner-most thoughts about the facts and figures of an industry or company, you do not want to turn him off with an antagonistic remark about the accuracy of his data.

Solution #3: Ask Why?

The best way to judge whether a source is knowledgeable about the fact or figure they have given you is to ask them how they arrived at that number. Such a question will likely initiate one of the following responses:

"I don't know. It's the best I can think of."
- A response like this will be a clue that the expert may not know what he is talking about and you should continue your search for a more knowledgeable and willing expert.

"This is the figure I read from an industry association study."
- This should lead you to verify that such a study was conducted and to attempt to interview people involved with the report and its findings.

"The industry figure is XX because our sales are half that and we are number 2 in the industry."
- This is probably one of the best types of answers you can get. Any time an industry expert gives you a figure based on something he is positive about, you can almost take it to the bank. The best you can do after this is to find other industry analysts and ask them to comment on the figure you were given.

Misinformation can lead to a decision making disaster. Following the simple techniques described above can take you a long way down the road to making good decisions based on near perfect information.

Tips On Finding Information

Using Industry Sources And Overcoming The "Negative Researching Syndrome"

When you cannot find company information from traditional sources or government documents, it may be necessary to dig around the industry in order to uncover it. This is likely to be the only place you can turn to when you really want:

1) the scoop on a company's pricing policy;
2) facts on distribution channels for a given product;
3) details about a company's potential future strategy; or
4) estimates on the profitability of a privately held company.

The researchers at Information USA, Inc. are seeing many more research projects which fall into this category, and would like to share with you some of our recent experiences in solving this type of problem.

Two Pronged Approach

Unlike traditional research work, hunting for specific information within an industry involves two separate approaches. The first is identifying potential sources. The second and equally difficult job is developing a strategy for interviewing these sources.

Although most researchers probably would think that the biggest problem is figuring out what organizations and companies to contact, we find this not to be the case when dealing with industry sources. We believe that the toughest challenges our researchers face are improving their techniques and attitudes for obtaining information. Other types of research are not as "technique sensitive," because relying on industry sources means getting in close range to the target company. Although technique can be the major trouble spot, let's tackle the problem of sources first.

Identifying Industry Sources

When I refer to industry sources, I am talking about those organizations and individuals whose business it is to know what is going on in the overall industry as well as activities among individual companies. These are the sources which can provide sensitive information that you cannot find elsewhere. Those who know their business and industry have to know about pricing, profitability, and even the strategy of those companies which comprise a particular industry. Most likely these individuals have never seen a given company's in-house strategic plan or a private company's profit and loss statement, but they are usually knowledgeable enough to give you estimates which can be as close as plus or minus 15% of the actual figures. They also will be familiar with an industry's "rule of thumb" in terms of operation, and can offer educated guesses on important figures, like sales based on the number of employees, or production based on the size of equipment, or strategy based on purchasing plans and sales literature. A researcher's job is to find industry people in a position to know and then to get them to share this knowledge.

Starting Points For Sources

Here are six major checkpoints for identifying industry sources:

I. Government Experts:

These sources can be the easiest to talk with and also can usually suggest leads to sources who in turn will identify others within the industry. Normally these are analysts within the Federal government and sometimes within state government. Their job it is to monitor a specific industry either for the purpose of formulating government policy or preparing market analysis which is used by both the public and private sectors. These people are the most plugged into a given industry.

Examples of U.S. government industry experts whose focus is primarily on policy are Energy Department specialists who study potential applications for wind energy, or biotechnology experts at the Department of Agriculture who stay current on this research field as it pertains to the food industry. In contrast, those federal experts whose orientation is geared toward market analysis are found at the Department of Commerce who produce the annual *U.S. Industrial Outlook*, and the analysts at the U.S. International Trade Commission who investigate the impact of imports on American industry.

Finding policy oriented experts can be difficult because they are scattered throughout the vast federal bureaucracy. Try to determine which agency in the government probably follows a particular industry under which a given company falls. For food products, try the U.S. Department of Agriculture and the U.S. Food and Drug Administration; for products involving pesticides, check with the U.S. Environmental Protection Agency; for companies in new technologies, contact the Office of Technology Assessment on Capitol Hill. Other resources which will help you identify where these policy experts are hiding include:

1) *U.S. Government Manual* (Government Printing Office);

2) *Lesko's Info-Power III* by Matthew Lesko, (published by Information USA, Inc.);

3) Local Federal Information Center (look in the U.S. government section of your local telephone book under General Services Administration); or

4) The Washington or district office of your U.S. Representative or Senator.

Below are the main telephone numbers for finding the two major offices which have 100 or more experts with market analysis orientation who cover most every industry. Simply call and ask to speak to the expert who studies golf balls or music instruments or whatever industry you are investigating:

- International Trade Administration (ITA), U.S. Department of Commerce, Washington, DC 20230, 202-482-1461: over 100 analysts who monitor all the major industries in the U.S. and the companies within these industries ranging from athletic products to truck trailers; and

- U.S. International Trade Commission (ITC), Office of Industries, 500 E St., SW, Room 504, Washington, DC 20436, 202-205-3296: experts who analyze the impact of world trade on U.S. industries ranging from audio components to x-ray apparatus.

There are no concrete rules for locating state industry experts. Every state government works differently, and the level of expertise varies tremendously. However, there is a trend at the state level to accumulate more data especially within those industries, for instance, high-tech companies, which the state sees as having potential for contributing to their economic development. The starting place for finding a specialist is the state's Department of Commerce and Economic Development. These offices are located in the state capital and are easy to track down by telephoning the state government operator.

II. Industry Observers:

Industry observers may be affiliated either with trade magazines or trade associations. They are in a position to oversee what is going on in the industry and they collect details about specific companies within that industry. Associations can identify the magazines and other publications that report on their industry and vice versa. If you have trouble getting started, contact either the federal analysts at the ITA and ITC described above or consult the *Encyclopedia of Associations* (Gale Research Company) at a local library.

You have to be careful who you talk to when contacting these various organizations. Usually when you call a trade association looking for information about the industry, they will connect you with the library; and when you contact a magazine, you are likely to be switched to the research department. These offices are good to touch base with, but they normally know about only the more obvious published material and are not very helpful in getting answers to more difficult questions.

After you have contacted the libraries or research departments of these organizations, be sure to call back with a different tactic in order to get through to the association executives and editors of trade magazines. These are the people who are immersed in the industry and pick up bits and pieces of information about companies which rarely show up in the published literature.

III. The Distribution Chain:

People within the chain of distribution can be wholesalers, jobbers, distributors or anyone who acts as an intermediary between the manufacturer and the end user. Although not all products are sold through middlemen, many are, and if the company under investigation uses middlemen they can be an information bonanza. Most people in these kinds of businesses are down to earth types who generally like people and are approachable. What is also advantageous about dealing with distributors is that they normally handle the products of the company you are interested in as well as those of its competitors. As a result they can be very helpful in comparing strategies and assessing market share.

Who do you talk to in these organizations? You try to talk to the buyers or sales reps. This normally does not leave many people in between. How do you find these organizations? Usually it is quite easy — most trade associations or magazines can provide you with lists. Or, it is also easy to call up your target company and pretend you want to purchase one of their products, at which point they will be more than happy to inundate you with the names and telephone numbers of suppliers.

IV. Customers:

This may sound foolish to some, but for most industries customers are approachable and often prove to be valuable sources of company information. By talking to the buyers of a half dozen major retail chains, you can determine the market for goods ranging from tablecloths to toys. And the buyers at a dozen or so major food chain stores can give you a clear picture of almost any consumer food product. What is selling like hotcakes and what is gathering dust on the shelves can be invaluable marketing information.

How do you find a company's customers? If they fall into groups like supermarkets or department stores, their industry will be organized enough so you can contact the relevant trade association or trade magazines for a listing of members. Many times the target company's literature will proudly display major clients or customers. Most industries also produce a buyer's guide which will identify these sources. Again, the association or trade magazines should be aware of such publications.

V. Competitors:

Contacting the competitors of a target company may be difficult if they are also your competitor. If the company is not in the same industry as your firm, or someone else is doing the research, competitors can often provide all the information sought. Obviously these are the people who really have to know about the target company. They are in the best position to know how well the company is doing compared to them and what their competitor is likely to do in the future.

VI. Suppliers And Complimentary Product Manufacturers:

Don't overlook suppliers to the target company. These companies can be very helpful because the target company is just a customer to them and what they know about a company they are likely to assume that everyone knows. Many suppliers are directly dependent upon the success of their customer and make it their business to know how well they are doing and can offer predictions about future plans. Their livelihood depends upon knowing this information. Tire manufacturers have to know all about automobile companies and the manufacturers of equipment which make shoes have to know all about shoe companies. The same holds true for complimentary products like BBQ utensils and charcoal briquettes, or electric popcorn poppers and popcorn kernels.

The same technique described earlier for finding customers can also be used for locating suppliers and complimentary product manufacturers.

Tips On Finding Information

Preventing Early Pitfalls and Other Techniques

Developing a good technique is crucial when digging for information within an industry. Finding a source is simply a numbers game, and by following the outline presented above anyone doing the research will eventually run into a couple of people who will have most of the answers you need. However, creating the proper atmosphere for that source to want to share information with you is contingent on both attitude and technique. Here are some of the major problems you are likely to encounter.

A bad start leads to depression. I've seen this happen to even the best of researchers. They will start out confident about a project investigating a company's pricing policy or profitability. After spending a half a day on the project and talking to a half dozen industry experts, they are ready to throw in the towel and give up. What normally happens is that the researcher has run into trouble getting through to anyone who knows much about the company or anyone they did talk to has been full of negative comments such as "There's no way to get that kind of information."

After initial feedback like this, it's natural for researchers to begin to believe what they are hearing and to forget about their past research triumphs. This faulty start can be even more devastating to a novice who has yet to complete a number of research projects. This problem intensifies as the researcher continues because all the negative feedback poisons their relaxed, friendly interviewing style and upbeat attitude. This pessimism creeps into their voice when talking to people within the industry. Soon they will start a conversation by saying things like "You don't have any information on company X, do you?"

Once this begins to happen the researcher should stop immediately and get some help. This "Negative Researching Syndrome" will begin to feed on itself and will only get worse and worse unless something drastic happens to change this course.

How do you cure "Negative Researching Syndrome"? Well it isn't easy, and unless the researcher is very experienced, it usually requires the help of a senior researcher. What we usually do when we sense a researcher falling into this trap is to tell him that it is a bad time of day to be making these kinds of calls, or to quit for the day. Another approach is to suggest the researcher pick up the next day but only after we have had a chance to get together to talk about the project. Before our session I try to make sure the researcher is given an easy short term project just to build up their confidence. Then we brainstorm about one or all of the following strategies:

1) Try a different segment of the industry. Instead of talking with distributors, switch to retailers; move from customers to government experts and so on. Try anything to find someone in the industry who may be more willing to talk.

2) Describe past success stories. We will remind the researcher of projects in the past where we started out thinking that we were never going to get anything and how it all eventually came together. I'll even describe some of my own personal experiences doing research where experts said it couldn't be done. And, of course, we'll remind them that this is really the reason we are getting paid. If it was easy, no one would need us.

3) Try a different "story line." This is explained next.

A Bad "Story Line" Can Kill A Project

A bad story line can also be the chief cause of "Negative Researching Syndrome." What do we mean by a story line? It is the explanation or reason the researcher gives for needing the information. If the researcher is uncomfortable with the story, a potential source will sense this unease and be reluctant to talk. In most research this is not a problem. In traditional projects, conventional reference sources are used for gathering information, and all you have to do is identify yourself and ask whether certain information is available. However, in dealing with industry sources the situation changes markedly; they are not comfortable just knowing the researcher's name and affiliation. Industry sources want to know what you are after and why. And this is when the story line can make or break your chances for success.

Being comfortable with a "story line" can be a complicated process. The bottom line is that you are not after information that is proprietary. Consequently, it is essential for **you** to feel comfortable with what you are saying, because if you don't no one will open up to you and give you the real facts that you need to write a credible research report for your client.

If you are uneasy that your story line is too far fetched or something you don't know enough details about, you will fail to convince yourself or the people that you're speaking to, and as a result your efforts will backfire. Saying that you work for the FBI or write for the *Nuts and Bolts* Magazine are the kinds of stories that spell trouble. Furthermore, most researchers are basically too honest to stretch the truth that far and it begins to eat into their conscience. As they do get deeper into the research, the guilt that they feel will aggravate the troubling "Negative Researching Syndrome," and the researcher is bound to wind up empty handed, with little or no relevant information.

Here are a few sample explanations that may not be too improbable:

- Your company is doing a market study on all the companies within the industry. [Not just the target company.]

- You are trying to write an article about the industry and plan to submit it to a trade magazine.

- You are a student working on a paper. [Not a highly useful story but usually one that is easy to live with.]

- You have a client or your boss wants you to investigate the possibility of developing a competing brand and you are trying to get industry comments about such an idea. [People will more likely give opinions than information on a company, but their opinions will often include company information.]

- You are working on a speech about the industry and trying to get some background material.

Also, if your story is too negative or "predatory," no one will **want** to give you the information. This, too, will show up when you are talking with industry experts and cause a researcher to come up empty handed. In other words, don't call up an industry source and say, "I am with company X, which is a major

Using Industry Sources

competitor of company Y. Can you tell me about the pricing strategy of company Y so that we can try to put them out of business?" Many researchers worry that this is really what they are doing through their research efforts, and this anxiety and belief will lead to "Negative Researching Syndrome", along with failure to gather any valuable information.

Choosing the right story line can determine the success or failure of your project. Be sure you can live with it and feel comfortable and honest, and that this explanation will make those in the industry comfortable enough to share information with you. If a researcher's story line does not meet these two criteria, be prepared for a long, hard, and more than likely, frustrating and unsuccessful hunting expedition.

Tips On Finding Information

What's Good and Bad About Using Computers In The Information Age

Food Processors, PCs, and Other Miracle Products

Before you purchase a database, first think about what you are actually buying. Is it the steak or the sizzle? Many of today's commercial database vendors are selling their services the way food processor sales reps sold their wares a few years back. Remember the sales pitch that this kitchen appliance could make the entire meal every day of the week? However, after buying this expensive gadget we found that puree of steak did not taste as good as a charcoaled piece of meat and that carrot mousse didn't suit our children's taste buds. Now we all have this expensive equipment cluttering up the kitchen counter that we use a few times a month to make coleslaw or milk shakes because the blender we bought 10 years ago is stashed away in the attic. Remember when simple was better?

This phenomenon has struck personal computers. A few years ago, buyers were sold on the belief that the world would pass them by if they did not have a PC. Furthermore, this sophisticated machine would solve all their problems and organize their lives like never before. We were told that daily tasks such as balancing the checkbook or keeping track of recipes would virtually disappear. However, PC owners discovered that because they never balanced their checkbook by hand, they were never going to do it by computer. It actually was more complicated and took longer to use the computer than the old fashioned way. And, keeping 50 or so recipes in a $1,000 machine that is located at the other end of the house proved to be inconvenient. Soon people realized that the "practical applications," like word processing and spread sheets, were not typical household functions. As a result of this revelation, computer sales began to plummet.

Waiting For The Technology To Mature

One can safely predict that computers will eventually be easier, cheaper, and more practical to use as the sophistication of the technology improves. The same pattern occurred with the introduction of the automobile. It took decades to get it right, and even now, cars are being improved in subtle ways all the time.

When cars first rolled off the assembly line, the primary advantages they offered over the horse as a traditional means of transportation were technology and novelty. An automobile cost at least ten times more than a horse. These complex machines were difficult to start and required special fuel that was hard to come by. Special clothing, goggles, and other paraphernalia were necessary for protection against dust and the elements. And cars were very limited in where they could go due to the lack of good roadways. All of these problems could not compare with the simple act of jumping on a horse and going anywhere. It was obvious that the horse still was the fastest, most convenient, and most inexpensive mode of transportation. But even then people were willing to be oversold on the use of a new technology. In other words, they bought the sizzle instead of the steak. And those who waited until the cost was worth the benefit of the application found that as the technology improved, the new product was faster, cheaper, and easier to use than the original. With the increase in available software, or highways in the case of automobiles, there were many more uses and applications for the new product than the old one.

By waiting for the technology to evolve into a cost effective alternative for a specific application, consumers who held on to their horses before buying the first automobiles found that they got to their destinations a lot sooner for a lot less money than the new car buyer. And when these patient consumers purchased the later model of automobile, they found that their later model machine could do a great deal more than the ones that rolled off the first production line, with a lot less kinks to be worked out.

Pros And Cons Of Databases

Overselling Computerized Databases

A similar story continues to unfold with online databases. Slick sales reps tell us that we can solve all of our information problems with their databases. Again buyers, because of their infatuation with the technology, are dazzled with the notion of getting the answer to a million dollar question by simply dialing up an all knowing computer. In order to avoid spending money on novelty items, one has to see if the price of obtaining information via high tech means is worth the money compared to relying on traditional alternatives.

Helpful With Large Amounts of Info

Databases are especially good at handling large amounts of information, and there are literally hundreds of computerized systems that perform this function. These services index and abstract everything from all business-oriented periodicals to those that can provide such bibliographic help only in a certain subject area such as energy. If this is your field of interest, you should think about what you will be paying for. Most of these types of databases are aimed at the professional user and can be expensive. Studies show that the average professional user of databases spends about $100 per hour. What kind of information will you be able to access at that price?

A $100 Seminar On How To Shop At Macy's

Many of the professional databases are also very complicated to use. It is the only industry where commercial vendors charge their customers for taking a course on how to spend money on their products. Wouldn't it be something if Macy's Department Store charged you to take a class on how to shop at their store? This should be a clue that databases and their applications are not for everyone. Especially if you know that you'll be using a database very infrequently.

Using Computers In The Information Age

Much of the material that is online is also available in print form. So you may be paying $100 per hour for the convenience of not dropping by your local library to look up the indexes manually. At $100 an hour, you could buy an awful lot of library help.

Non Discriminating Computers

Also remember that these bibliographic databases sometime create more problems than they solve. Searching a large database on a subject can easily churn out 500 articles for you to review. The problem now comes in trying to identify the worthwhile articles, not to mention actually obtaining those which you select. The computer is attempting to cope with the information explosion by providing the capability to index any and all data that are generated. However, the computer does a very poor job at being selective. It cannot tell you whether an article is good or bad. This problem is only getting worse because anyone with a word processor can be a publisher within days and the commercial vendors are always eager to acquire new databases.

After you get bombarded with some 500 citations racing across the screen, you still may have to make a half dozen telephone calls to locate a real expert in the field who can suggest which are the best and most current articles to read. Or this expert may be able to give you the answer right over the telephone. Even better, he may be able to tell you what will be online next year because he is in the midst of writing or reviewing articles and manuscripts on that subject. **Remember, even though a report or survey is contained in a database, that does not guarantee it is the latest available information.** Many databases still rely on printed documentation, so many times there may be less expensive and easier ways to get your hands on more current information. In the chapter "Using Industry Sources And Overcoming The Negative Researching Syndrome", use the resources listed in the section "Government Experts".

Is Speed Worth The Price?

Getting information to you quickly is another function that databases and telecommunications do exceedingly well. Here again, you must decide whether the convenience is worthy of the expense. Having the Associated Press wire service available during the day at $10 to $20 per hour may not be cost effective for you and your business unless you are a million dollar business. Most of us barely get through the morning newspaper which costs a mere 50 cents and usually contains the highlights of what is reported on the wire service. And it's not yet feasible to scan your newspapers via computer either in bed or while commuting to work. No doubt getting the price of stocks as they are traded on the floor of the stock exchange at $75.00 per hour may be worth it if you are a big time investor and have to know what the stock market is doing minute-by-minute. But for most of our investment decisions, reading the stock quotes in our local morning paper is usually good enough. There are many professional applications in addition to big time investing in which speed would be worth a significant premium. It is wise to make sure that paying for this convenience is honestly necessary to you and your organization.

Help If You Are Reinventing The Wheel

Another aspect of telecommunications which appears to have much more usable potential is the ability of like minded people to communicate instantly. The pace at which civilization develops seems dependent upon the speed at which ideas are refined and shared with others. Thus, it seems reasonable to assume that some day soon one person on one side of the street will not waste his or her time wrestling with a problem which has already been solved by someone else on the opposite side of the street. Telecommunications can aid in the process of making information more available.

We once spoke to a veterinarian in Iowa who was faced with treating a three-legged dog and was uncertain how to proceed. As a member of a veterinarian bulletin board, he posed his question to this professional forum via computer. By the next morning, there were answers from doctors in Florida and Massachusetts who had treated similar cases. He did not have to wait for the next annual meeting of veterinarians or for a relevant article to be published in the Journal of Veterinarian Medicine. Overnight, he had his question answered and was free to tackle other unsolved problems because his time was now free to go on to other things.

Databases Are Here To Stay

By presenting all these negative aspects, we hope it is now more obvious that databases contribute only a few pieces to solving a big information puzzle. Many times the cost far exceeds the benefit. However, like the automobile, online databases are here to stay, and in time, they will become more reasonably priced and offer applications users never dreamed could exist.

The online database business, like other segments of the information industry, is a buyer's beware market. **Access to a $1,000 computerized information system that one firm is selling may be available for free or a modest charge from some public or non-profit organization.**

Some suggestions about purchasing databases are described next which are intended to help you save some money while utilizing this current technology.

Money Saving Online Tips

Use The Free Database First

This may sound obvious, but the real problem is that you may not be aware of **free online databases**. The free ones cannot afford to hire an expensive sales team to promote their systems. Here are some examples of how prices may vary widely for the same product:

- You can tap into weather information on over seven systems at prices ranging from $3 to $90 an hour, or you can access the National Weather Service's free database provided by the Federal government, which happens to be the basis for all the other sources of weather information.

- Online encyclopedias can cost up to $75 per hour if you are accessing systems like Dow Jones or BRS, or you can pay as little as $6 per hour on CompuServe or Delphi. Oftentimes, it is the exact same file.

- City or state demographics can cost over $100 an hour from such vendors as DIALOG, BRS or Chase Econometrics, or

Tips On Finding Information

you can use the free database offered by Conway Data, Inc. in Atlanta, Georgia (404-446-6996).

- The latest economic statistics that are sold on such systems as DRI and Chase for as much as $160 an hour can also be accessed for free from an electronic bulletin board maintained by the U.S. Department of Commerce. Chances are the data are probably available sooner from this free source.

Consider Off-Line Alternatives

Typically what many commercial database vendors do is find data that are available in other formats, such as hard copy, off-line printout and computer tape. You can often save a lot of money by not accessing online systems but rather getting the information in less high tech ways. Here are some examples:

- Legi-Slate, Commerce Clearing House, and Congressional Quarterly will charge you up to $190 an hour to find out the current status of legislation, or you can telephone for free searches and even obtain computer printouts on all the bills you are monitoring by using a free database maintained by the U.S. Congress.

- Services such as Data Resources, I.P. Sharp, and Chase Econometrics will charge you $100 per hour to obtain demographic information on any country in the world, or you can call the International Demographic Center at the U.S. Bureau of the Census and request a free printout of the same information which may even be more current.

- Dialog charges $45 an hour for information on U.S. exports, and the Trade Information Branch at the U.S. Department of Commerce will give you much of the same information for free. Also, the data will be more current because this government office is where Dialog gets the information it sells.

- Control Data Corp. allows you to access a file called FARPS that will tell you where to get money in the government for your project, or you can contact the U.S. General Services Administration which maintains the file and this government agency will do free searches for you.

- An energy bibliographic database maintained by the U.S. Department of Energy in Tennessee is sold by DIALOG or it can be accessed directly from the government for free.

Use Database Wholesalers and Intermediaries

Many commercial vendors have initiation fees and monthly minimums which can increase your hourly cost considerably if you are not going to be a large user. One way to cut out these extra fees, at least until you see what your volume will be, is to use a database wholesaler or intermediary. For example, if you are a subscriber to MCI, you receive access to the Dow Jones service without paying an additional initiation charge. You may begin to see more of these opportunities as the telecommunications industry develops further.

If you are a first time database user and are interested in the non-consumer oriented electronic systems, it may be wise to have someone else do your searching. Even some so-called "user friendly" databases are not as easy to use as their vendors claim. Online charges at $100 an hour can translate into a hefty bill if you are just learning the system. Companies called information brokers will usually handle this for you. The best way to find available brokers is to contact your local reference librarian. They are in a good position to tell you what is available locally. If you have trouble with this approach, you may find help by calling: DIALOG Information Services, Customer Service, 1-800-334-2564.

This major commercial database vendor maintains a list, by city, of those organizations which will provide this service tailored to your needs. Be sure to ask if a nearby public, academic, or specialized library might perform online retrieval services because chances are, this would be a cheaper alternative. For example, the Brooklyn Business Library will do database searches and charge only for direct out-of-pocket costs. An information broker is likely to cost you three to four times as much. The following reference book identifies over 8,400 databases available in a variety of electronic formats:

Gale's *Directory of Databases*
    1994, 2 volume set ($300)
    Gale Research Co.
    P.O. Box 33477
    Detroit, MI 48232-5477
    313-961-2242
    1-800-877-4253
    Contact: Sandy Gore, extension 1394

If you have a PC with a modem but have been reluctant to access the more complicated business databases, you can call Easynet. This firm will search some seven major vendors for you and send the results to you via your computer. Easynet covers most of the major business databases and claims that their average search cost is $17.00.

    EASYNET Telebase Systems, Inc.
    435 Devon Park Dr., Suite 600
    Wayne, PA 19087
    1-800-220-9553
    610-293-4700

Save With Evening Discounts

Most of the commercial database vendors offer discounts if you access their systems during the evening hours and other non-prime times. According to a survey of vendors, the average savings amounted to 50%, which means that if you encounter any volume at all, it would pay for you to hire someone to come into your office in the evening just to access certain databases. Here is a sample of such discounts offered by some of the major vendors:

ADP Network Services	50%
BRS	62% to 80.9%
CompuServe	52%
DataNet	84.4%
Dialog	53.3%
Dow Jones	22% to 78%
Delphi	45%
Mead Data Central	50%
NewsNet	25%
Source	62.7%

Save On Telecommunications Software

In this case, the cheapest may be the best. A paper presented at the 1985 National Online Conference concluded that there was little difference between using a free telecommunications product for the IBM-PC called PC-TALK and a $120 product called Instantcom. To obtain a copy of PC-TALK, contact your local IBM users group.

Tips On Finding Information

The Freedom of Information Act

A Citizen's Guide on Using the Freedom of Information Act and
the Privacy Act of 1974 to Request Government Records

Introduction

A popular Government without popular information or the means of acquiring it, is but a Prologue to a Farce or a Tragedy or perhaps both. Knowledge will forever govern ignorance, and a people who mean to be their Governors, must arm themselves with the power knowledge gives. — James Madison

The Freedom of Information Act (FOIA) established a presumption that records in the possession of agencies and departments of the Executive Branch of the United States government are accessible to the people. This was not always the approach to federal information disclosure policy. Before enactment of the Freedom of Information Act in 1966, the burden was on the individual to establish a right to examine these government records. There were no statutory guidelines or procedures to help a person seeking information. There were no judicial remedies for those denied access.

With the passage of the FOIA, the burden of proof shifted from the individual to the government. Those seeking information are no longer required to show a need for information. Instead, the "need to know" standard has been replaced by a "right to know" doctrine. The government now has to justify the need for secrecy.

The FOIA sets standards for determining which records must be made available for public inspection and which records can be withheld from disclosure. The law also provides administrative and judicial remedies for those denied access to records. Above all, the statute requires federal agencies to provide the fullest possible disclosure of information to the public.

The Privacy Act of 1974 is a companion to the FOIA, and serves to regulate federal government agency recordkeeping and disclosure practices. The Act allows most individuals to seek access to federal agency records about themselves. The Act requires that personal information in agency files be accurate, complete, relevant, and timely. The Act allows the subject of a record to challenge the accuracy of the information. The Act requires that agencies obtain information directly from the subject of the record and that information gathered for one purpose not be used for another purpose. As with the FOIA, the Privacy Act provides civil remedies for individuals whose rights have been violated.

Another important feature of the Privacy Act is the requirement that each federal agency publish a description of each system of records maintained by the agency that contains personal information. This prevents agencies from keeping secret records.

The Privacy Act also restricts the disclosure of personally identifiable information by federal agencies. Together with the FOIA, the Privacy Act permits disclosure of most personal files to the individual who is the subject of the files. The two laws restrict disclosure of personal information to others when disclosure would violate privacy interests.

While both the FOIA and the Privacy Act encourage the disclosure of agency records, both laws also recognize the legitimate need to restrict disclosure of some information. For example, agencies may withhold information classified in the interest of national defense or foreign policy, trade secrets, and criminal investigatory files. Other specifically defined categories of confidential information may also be withheld.

The essential feature of both laws is that they make federal agencies accountable for information disclosure policies and practices. While neither law grants an absolute right to examine government documents, both laws provide a right to request records and to receive a response to the request. If a requested record cannot be released, the requester is entitled to a reason for the denial. The requester has a right to appeal the denial and, if necessary, to challenge it in court.

These procedural rights granted by the FOIA and the Privacy Act make the laws valuable and workable. The disclosure of government information cannot be controlled by arbitrary or unreviewable actions.

Which Act to Use

The access provisions of the FOIA and the Privacy Act overlap in part. The two laws have different procedures and different exemptions. As a result, sometimes information exempt under one law will be disclosable under the other.

In order to take maximum advantage of the laws, an individual seeking information about himself or herself should normally cite both laws. Requests by an individual for information that does not relate solely to himself or herself should be made under the FOIA.

Congress intended that the two laws be considered together in the processing of requests for information. Many government agencies will automatically handle requests from individuals in a way that will maximize the amount of information that is disclosable. However, a requester should still make a request in a manner that is most advantageous and that fully protects all available legal rights. A requester who has any doubts about which law to use should always cite both the FOIA and the Privacy Act when seeking documents from the federal government.

The Scope of the Freedom of Information Act

The federal Freedom of Information Act applies to documents held by agencies in the executive branch of the federal

The Freedom Of Information Act

government. The executive branch includes cabinet departments, military departments, government corporations, government controlled corporations, independent regulatory agencies, and other establishments of the executive branch.

The Freedom of Information Act (FOIA) does not apply to elected officials of the federal government, including the President, Vice President, Senators, and Congressmen, or the federal judiciary. The FOIA also does not apply to private companies; persons who received federal contracts or grants; tax-exempt organizations; or state or local governments.

All states and some localities have passed laws like the FOIA that allow people to request access to records. In addition, there are other federal and state laws that may permit access to documents held by organizations not covered by the FOIA.

What Records Can Be Requested Under FOIA?

The Freedom of Information Act (FOIA) requires agencies to publish or make available some types of information. This includes: (1) Description of agency organization and office addresses; (2) statements of the general course and method of agency operation; (3) rules of procedure and descriptions of forms; (4) substantive rules of general applicability and general policy statements; (5) final opinions made in the adjudication of cases; and (6) administrative staff manuals that affect the public. This information must either be published or made available for inspection and copying without the formality of an FOIA request.

All other "agency records" may be requested under the FOIA. However, the FOIA does not define "agency record." Material that is in the possession, custody, or control of an agency is usually considered to be an agency record under the FOIA. Personal notes of agency employees may not be agency records. A record that is not an "agency record" will not be available under the FOIA.

The form in which a record is maintained by an agency does not affect its availability. A request may seek a printed or typed document, tape recording, map, computer printout, computer tape, or a similar item.

Of course, not all records that can be requested must be disclosed. Information that is exempt from disclosure is described below in the section entitled "Reasons Access May Be Denied Under the FOIA."

The Freedom of Information Act (FOIA) carefully provides that a requester may ask for records rather than information. This means that an agency is only required to look for an existing record or document in response to an FOIA request. An agency is not obliged to create a new record to comply with a request. An agency is not required to collect information it does not have. Nor must an agency do research or analyze data for a requester.

Requesters may ask for existing records. Requests may have to be carefully written in order to obtain the information that is desired. Sometimes, agencies will help a requester identify the specific document that contains the information being sought. Other times, a requester may need to be creative when writing an Freedom of Information Act request in order to identify an existing document or set of documents containing the desired information.

There is a second general limitation on FOIA request. The law requires that each request must reasonably describe the records being sought. This means that a request must be specific enough to permit a professional employee of the agency who is familiar with the subject matter to locate the record in a reasonable period of time.

Because different agencies organize and index records in different ways, one agency may consider a request to be reasonably descriptive while another agency may reject a similar request as too vague. For example, the Federal Bureau of Investigation has a central index for its primary record system. As a result, the FBI is able to search for records about a specific person. However, agencies that do not maintain a central name index may be unable to conduct the same type of search. These agencies may reject a similar request because the request does not describe records that can be identified.

Requesters should make their requests as specific as possible. If a particular document is required, it should be identified as precisely as possible, preferably by date and title. However, a request does not have to be that specific. A requester who cannot identify a specific record should clearly explain his or her needs. A requester should make sure, however, that the request is broad enough to cover the information that is needed.

For example, assume that a requester wants to obtain a list of toxic sites near his home. A request to the Environmental Protection Agency for all records on toxic waste would cover many more records than are needed. The fees for such a request might be very high, and it is possible that the request might be rejected as too vague.

A request for all toxic waste sites within three miles of a particular address is very specific. But is unlikely that EPA would have an existing record containing data organized in that fashion. As a result, the request might be denied because there is no existing record containing the information.

The requester might do better to ask for a list of toxic waste sites in his city, county, or state. It is more likely that existing records might contain this information. The requester might also want to tell the agency in the request letter exactly what information is desired. The additional explanation will help the agency to find a record that meets the request.

Many people include their telephone number in their requests. Sometimes questions about the scope of a request can be resolved quickly when the agency employee and the requester talk. This is an efficient way to resolve questions that arise during the processing of FOIA requests.

It is to everyone's advantage if requests are as precise and as narrow as possible. The requester benefits because the request can be processed faster and cheaper. The agency benefits because it can do a better job of responding to the request. The agency will also be able to use its scarce resources to respond to more requests. The FOIA works best when both the requester and the agency act cooperatively.

Tips On Finding Information

Making an FOIA Request

The first step in making a request under the Freedom of Information Act (FOIA) is to identify the agency that has the records. An FOIA request must be addressed to a specific agency. There is no central government records office that services FOIA requests.

Often, a requester knows beforehand which agency has the desired records. If not, a requester can consult a government directory such as the *United States Government Manual*. This manual has a complete list of all the federal agencies, a description of agency functions, and the address of each agency. A requester who is uncertain about which agency has the records that are needed can make FOIA requests at more than one agency.

All agencies normally require that Freedom of Information Act (FOIA) requests be in writing. Letters requesting records under the FOIA can be short and simple. No one needs a lawyer to make an FOIA request. The Appendix to this section contains a sample request letter.

The request letter should be addressed to an agency's FOIA officer or to the head of the agency. The envelope containing the written request should be marked "Freedom of Information Act Request" in the bottom left-hand corner.

There are three basic elements to an FOIA request letter. First, the letter should state that the request is being made under the Freedom of Information Act. Second, the request should identify the records that are being sought as specifically as possible. Third, the name and address of the requester must be included.

In addition, under the 1986 amendments to the FOIA, the fees chargeable vary with the status or purpose of the requester. As a result, requesters may have to provide additional information to permit the agency to determine the appropriate fees. Different fees can be charged to commercial users, representatives of the news media, educational and non-commercial scientific institutions, and individuals. The next section explains the new fee structure in more detail.

There are several optional items that are often included in an FOIA request. The first is the telephone number of the requester. This permits an agency employee processing a request to talk to the requester if necessary.

A second optional item is a limitation on the fees that the requester is willing to pay. It is common for requesters to ask to be contacted if the charges will exceed a fixed amount. This allows a requester to modify or withdraw a request if the cost is too high.

A third optional item sometimes included in an FOIA request is a request for waiver or reduction of fees. The 1986 amendments waived or reduced the rules for fee waivers. Fees must be waived or reduced if disclosure of the information is in the public interest because it is likely to contribute significantly to public understanding of the operations or activities of the government and is not primarily in the commercial interest of the request. Decisions about granting fee waivers are separate from and different from decisions about the amount of fees that can be charged to requesters.

Requesters should keep a copy of their request letter and related correspondence until the request has been fully resolved.

Fees and Fee Waivers

FOIA requesters may have to pay fees covering some or all of the costs of processing their request. As amended in 1986, the law establishes three types of charges that may be imposed on requesters. The 1986 law makes the process of determining the applicable fees more complicated. However, the new rules reduce or eliminate entirely the cost for small, non-commercial requests.

First, fees can be imposed to recover the costs of copying documents. All agencies have a fixed price for making copies using copying machines. Requesters are usually charged the actual cost of copying computer tapes, photographs, or other nonstandard documents.

Second, fees can also be imposed to recover the costs of searching for documents. This includes the time spent looking for material responsive to a request. Requesters can minimize search charges by making clear, narrow requests for identifiable documents whenever possible.

Third, fees can be charged to recover review costs. Review is the process of examining documents to determine whether any portion is exempt from disclosure. Before the effective date of the 1986 amendments, no review charges were imposed on any requester. Effective April 25, 1987, review charges may be imposed on commercial requesters only. Review charges only include costs incurred during the initial examination of a document. An agency may not charge for any costs incurred in resolving issues of law or policy that may arise while processing a request.

Different fees apply to different categories of requesters. There are three basic groups of FOIA requesters. The first includes representatives of the news media, and educational or noncommercial scientific institutions whose purpose is scholarly or scientific research. Requesters in this category who are not seeking records for commercial use can only be billed for reasonable standard document duplication charges. A request for information from a representative of the news media is not considered to be for commercial use if the request is in support of a news gathering or dissemination function.

The second group includes FOIA requesters seeking records for commercial use. Commercial use is not defined in the law, but generally includes profit making activities. Commercial users pay reasonable standard charges for document duplication, search, and review.

The third group of FOIA requesters includes everyone not included in either of the first two groups. People seeking information for their own use, public interest groups, and non-profit organizations are examples of requesters who fall into the third group. Charges for these requests are limited to reasonable standard charges for document duplication and search. No review charges may be imposed. The 1986 amendments did not change the fees charged to these requesters.

Small requests are free to requesters in the first and third groups. This includes all requesters except commercial users. There is no

The Freedom Of Information Act

charge for the first two hours of search time and the first 100 pages of documents. Noncommercial requesters who limit their requests to a small number of easily found records will not pay any fees.

In addition, the law also prevents agencies from charging fees if the cost of collecting the fee would exceed the amount collected. This limitation applies to all requests, including those seeking documents for commercial use. Thus, if the allowable charges for any FOIA request are small, no fees are imposed.

Each agency sets charges for duplication, search, and review based on its own costs. The amount of these charges is included in the agency FOIA regulations. Each agency also sets its own threshold for minimum charges.

The 1986 FOIA amendments changed the law on fee waivers. The new rules require that fees must be waived or reduced if disclosure of the information is in the public interest because it is likely to contribute significantly to public understanding of the operations or activities of the government and is not primarily in the commercial interest of the requester.

The new rules for fees and fee waivers have created some confusion. Determinations about fees are separate and apart from determinations about eligibility for fee waivers. For example, a news reporter may only be charged duplication fees and may ask that the duplication fees be waived. There is no need for a reporter to ask for a waiver of search and review costs because search and review costs are not charged to reporters.

Only after a requester has been categorized to determine applicable fees does the issue of a fee waiver arise. A requester who seeks a fee waiver should include a separate request in the original request letter. The requester should describe how disclosure will contribute to the public understanding of the operations or activities of the government. The sample request letter in the Appendix includes optional language asking for a fee waiver.

Any requester may ask for a fee waiver. Some will find it easier to qualify than others. A news reporter who is charged only duplication costs may still ask that the charges be waived because of the public benefits that will result from disclosure. Representatives of the news media and public interest groups are very likely to qualify for a waiver of fees. Commercial users will find it more difficult to qualify.

The eligibility of other requesters will vary. A key element in qualifying for a fee waiver is the relationship of the information to public understanding of the operations or activities of government. Another important factor is the ability of the requester to convey that information to other interested members of the public. A requester is not eligible for a fee waiver solely because of indigence.

Requirements for Agency Responses

Each agency is required to determine within ten days (excluding Saturdays, Sundays, and legal holidays) after the receipt of a request whether to comply with the request. The actual disclosure of documents is required to follow promptly thereafter. If a request for records is denied in whole or in part, the agency must tell the requester the reasons for the denial. The agency must also tell the requester that there is a right to appeal any adverse determination to the head of the agency.

The FOIA permits agencies to extend the time limits up to ten days in unusual circumstances. These circumstances include the need to collect records from remote locations, review large numbers of records, and consult with other agencies. Agencies are supposed to notify the requester whenever an extension is invoked.

The statutory time limits for responses are not always met. Agencies sometimes receive an unexpectedly large number of FOIA requests at one time and are unable to meet the deadlines. Some agencies assign inadequate resources to FOIA offices. The Congress does not condone the failure of any agency to meet the law's limits. However, as a practical matter, there is little that a requester can do about it. The courts have been reluctant to provide relief solely because the FOIA's time limits have not been met.

The best advice to requesters is to be patient. The law allows a requester to consider a request to be denied if it has not been decided within the time limits. This permits the requester to file an administrative appeal. However, this is not always the best course of action. The filing of an administrative or judicial appeal does not normally result in any faster processing of the request.

Agencies generally process requests in the order in which they were received. Some agencies will expedite the processing of urgent requests. Anyone with a pressing need for records should consult with the agency FOIA officer about how to ask for expedited treatment of requests.

Reasons Access May Be Denied Under the FOIA

An agency may refuse to disclose an agency record that falls within any of the FOIA's nine statutory exemptions. The exemptions protect against the disclosure of information that would harm national defense or foreign policy, privacy of individuals, proprietary interests of business, functioning of government, and other important interests.

A record that does not qualify as an "agency record" may be denied because only agency records are available under the FOIA. Personal notes of agency employees may be denied on this basis.

An agency may withhold exempt information, but it is not always required to do so. For example, an agency may disclose an exempt internal memorandum because no harm would result from its disclosure. However, an agency is not likely to agree to disclose an exempt document that is classified or that contains a trade secret.

When a record contains some information that qualifies as exempt, the entire record is not necessarily exempt. Instead, the FOIA specifically provides that any reasonably segregable portions of a record must be provided to a requester after the deletion of the portions that are exempt. This is a very important requirement because it prevents an agency from withholding an entire document simply because one line or one page is exempt.

Tips On Finding Information

Exemption 1: Classified Documents

The first FOIA exemption permits the withholding of properly classified documents. Information may be classified to protect it in the interest of national defense or foreign policy. Information that has been classified as "Confidential," "Secret," or "Top Secret" under the procedures of the Executive Order on Security Classification can qualify under the first exemption.

The rules for classification are established by the President and not the FOIA or other law. The FOIA provides that, if a document has been properly classified under the President's rules, the document can be withheld from disclosure.

Classified documents may be requested under the FOIA. An agency can review the document to determine if it still requires protection. In addition, the Executive Order on Security Classification establishes a special procedure for requesting the declassification of documents. If a requested document is declassified, it can be released in response to an FOIA request. However, a document that was formerly classified may still be exempt under other FOIA exemptions.

Exemption 2: Internal Personnel Rules and Practices

The second FOIA exemption covers matters that are related solely to an agency's internal personnel rules and practices. As interpreted by the courts, there are two separate classes of documents that are generally held to fall within exemption two.

First, information relating to personnel rules or internal agency practices is exempt if it is a trivial administrative matter of no genuine public interest. A rule governing lunch hours for agency employees is an example.

Second, internal administrative manuals can be exempt if disclosure would risk circumvention of law or agency regulations. In order to fall into this category, the material will normally have to regulate internal agency conduct rather than public behavior.

Exemption 3: Information Exempt Under Other Laws

The third exemption incorporates into the FOIA other laws that restrict the availability of information. To qualify under exemption three, a statute must require that matters be withheld from the public in such a manner as to leave no discretion to the agency. Alternatively, the statute must establish particular criteria for withholding or refer to particular types of matters to be withheld.

One example of a qualifying statute is the provision of the Tax Code prohibiting the public disclosure of tax returns and tax law designating identifiable census data as confidential. Whether a particular statute qualifies under Exemption 3 can be a difficult legal determination.

Exemption 4: Confidential Business Information

The fourth exemption protects from public disclosure two types of information: trade secrets and confidential business information. A trade secret is a commercially valuable plan, formula, process, or device. This is a narrow category of information. An example of a trade secret is the recipe for a commercial food product.

The second type of protected data is commercial or financial information obtained from a person and privileged or confidential. The courts have held that data qualifies for withholding if disclosure by the government would be likely to harm the competitive position of the person who submitted the information. Detailed information on a company's marketing plans, profits, or costs can qualify as confidential business information. Information may also be withheld if disclosure would be likely to impair the government's ability to obtain similar information in the future.

Only information obtained from a person other than a government agency qualifies under the fourth exemption. A person is an individual, a partnership, or a corporation. Information that an agency created on its own cannot normally be withheld under Exemption 4.

Although there is no formal requirement under the FOIA, many agencies will notify a submitter of business information that disclosure of the information is being considered. The submitter can file suit to block disclosure under the FOIA. Such lawsuits are generally referred to as "reverse" FOIA lawsuits because the FOIA is being used in an attempt to prevent rather than to require disclosure of information. A reverse FOIA lawsuit may be filed when a submitter of documents and the government disagree whether the information is confidential.

Exemption 5: Internal Government Communications

The FOIA's Exemption 5 applies to internal government documents. One example is a letter from one government department to another about a joint decision that has not yet been made. Another example is a memorandum from an agency employee to his supervisor describing options for conducting the agency's business.

The purpose of the exemption is to safeguard the deliberative policymaking processes of government. The exemption encourages frank discussions of policy matters between agency officials by allowing supporting documents to be withheld from public disclosure. The exemption also protects against premature disclosure of policies before final adoption.

While the policy behind the fifth exemption is well accepted, the application of the exemption is complicated. Exemption 5 may be the most difficult FOIA exemption to understand and apply. For example, the exemption protects the policymaking process, but it does not protect purely factual information related to the policy process. Factual information must be disclosed unless it is inextricably intertwined with protected information about an agency decision.

Protection for the decision making process is appropriate only for the period while decisions are being made. Thus, the Exemption 5 has been held to distinguish between documents that are pre-decisional and therefore may be protected, and those which are post-decisional and therefore not subject to protection. Once a policy is adopted, the public has a greater interest in knowing the basis for the decision.

The exemption also incorporates some of the privileges that apply in litigation involving the government. For example, papers prepared by the government's lawyers are exempt in the same way that papers prepared by private lawyers for clients are not available through discovery in civil litigation.

The Freedom Of Information Act

Exemption 6: Personal Privacy

Exemption 6 covers personnel, medical, and similar files the disclosure of which would constitute a clearly unwarranted invasion of personal privacy. This exemption protects the privacy interests of individuals by allowing an agency to withhold from disclosure intimate personal data kept in government files. Only individuals have privacy interests. Corporations and other legal persons have no privacy rights under the sixth exemption.

The exemption requires agencies to strike a balance between an individual's privacy interests and the public's right to know. However, since only a clearly unwarranted invasion of privacy is a basis for withholding, there is a perceptible tilt in favor of disclosure in the exemption. Nevertheless, the sixth exemption makes it hard to obtain information about another individual without the consent of the individual.

The Privacy Act of 1974 also regulates the disclosure of personal information about individuals. The FOIA and the Privacy Act overlap in part, but there is no inconsistency. Individuals seeking records about themselves should cite both laws when making a request. This ensures that the maximum amount of disclosable information will be released. Records that can be denied to an individual under the Privacy Act are not necessarily exempt under the FOIA.

Exemption 7: Law Enforcement

Exemption 7 allows agencies to withhold law enforcement records in order to protect the law enforcement process from interference. The exemption was amended slightly in 1986, but it still retains six specific subexemptions.

Exemption (7)(A) allows the withholding of law enforcement records that could reasonably be expected to interfere with enforcement proceedings. This exemption protects active law enforcement investigations from interference through premature disclosure.

Exemption (7)(B) allows the withholding of information that would deprive a person of the right to a fair trial or an impartial adjudication. This exemption is rarely used.

Exemption (7)(C) recognizes that individuals have a privacy interest in information maintained in law enforcement files. If the disclosure of information could reasonably be expected to constitute an unwarranted invasion of personal privacy, the information is exempt from disclosure. The standards for privacy protection in Exemption 6 and Exemption (7)(C) differ slightly. Exemption (7)(C) refers only to unwarranted invasions of personal privacy rather than to clearly unwarranted invasions.

Exemption (7)(D) protects the identity of confidential sources. Information that could reasonably be expected to reveal the identity of a confidential source is exempt. A confidential source can include a state, local, or foreign agency or authority, or a private institution that furnished information on a confidential basis. In addition, the exemption protects information furnished by a confidential source if the data was compiled by a criminal law enforcement authority during a criminal investigation or by an agency conducting a lawful national security intelligence investigation.

Exemption (7)(E) protects from disclosure information that would reveal techniques and procedures for law enforcement investigations or prosecutions or that would disclose guidelines for law enforcement investigations or prosecutions if disclosure of the information could reasonably be expected to risk circumvention of the law.

Exemption (7)(F) protects law enforcement information that could reasonably be expected to endanger the life or physical safety of any individual.

Exemption 8: Financial Institutions

Exemption 8 protects information that is contained in or related to examination, operating, or condition reports prepared by or for a bank supervisory agency such as the Federal Deposit Insurance Corporation, or the Federal Reserve, or similar agencies.

Exemption 9: Geological Information

Exemption 9 covers geological and geophysical information, data, and maps about wells. This exemption is rarely used.

FOIA Exclusions

The 1986 amendments to the FOIA gave limited authority to agencies to respond to a request without confirming the existence of the requested records. Ordinarily, any proper request must receive an answer stating whether there is any responsive information, even if the requested information is exempt from disclosure.

In some narrow circumstances, acknowledgement of the existence of a record can produce consequences similar to those resulting from disclosure of the record itself. In order to avoid this type of problem, the 1986 amendments established three "record exclusions." However, these exclusions do not broaden the ability of agencies to withhold documents.

The exclusions allow agencies to treat certain exempt records as if the records were not subject to the FOIA. Agencies are not required to confirm the existence of three specific categories of records. If those records are requested, agencies may state that there are no disclosable records responsive to the request. However, these exclusions give agencies no authority to withhold additional categories of information from the public.

The first exclusion is triggered when a request seeks information that is exempt because disclosure could reasonably be expected to interfere with a current law enforcement investigation. There are specific prerequisites for the application of this exclusion. First, the investigation in question must involve a possible violation of criminal law. Second, there must be a reason to believe that the subject of the investigation is not already aware that the investigation is underway. Third, disclosure of the existence of the records — as distinguished from contents of the records — could reasonably be expected to interfere with enforcement proceedings.

When all three of these conditions are present, an agency may respond to an FOIA request for investigatory records as if the records are not subject to the requirements of the FOIA. In other words, the agency's response does not have to reveal that it is conducting an investigation.

Tips On Finding Information

The second exclusion applies to informant records maintained by a criminal law enforcement agency under the informant's name or personal identifier. The agency is not required to confirm the existence of these records unless the informant's status has been officially confirmed. This exclusion helps agencies to protect the identity of confidential informants. Information that might identify informants has always been exempt under the FOIA.

The third exclusion applies only to records maintained by the Federal Bureau of Investigation which pertain to foreign intelligence, counterintelligence, or international terrorism. When the existence of those type of records is classified, the FBI may treat the records as not subject to the requirements of FOIA.

This exclusion does not apply to all classified records on the specific subjects. It only applies when the records are classified and when the existence of the records is also classified. Since the underlying records must be classified before the exclusion is relevant, agencies have no new substantive withholding authority.

In enacting these exclusions, congressional sponsors stated that it was their intent that agencies must inform FOIA requesters that these exclusions are available for agency use. Requesters who believe that records were improperly withheld because of the exclusions can seek judicial review.

Administrative Appeal Procedures

Whenever a Freedom of Information Act (FOIA) request is denied, the agency must inform the requester of the reasons for the denial and the requester's right to appeal the denial to the head of the agency. A requester may appeal the denial of a request for a document or for fee waiver. A requester may contest the type or amount of fees that were charged. A requester may appeal any other adverse determination including a rejection of a request for failure to describe adequately the documents being requested. A requester can also appeal because the agency failed to conduct an adequate search for the documents that were requested.

A person whose request was granted in part and denied in part may appeal the partial denial. If an agency has agreed to disclose some but not all of the requested documents, the filing of an appeal does not affect the release of the documents that are disclosable. There is no risk to the requester in filing an appeal.

The appeal to the head of an agency is a simple administrative appeal. A lawyer can be helpful, but no one must have a lawyer to file an appeal. Anyone who can write a letter can file an appeal. Appeals to the head of the agency often result in the disclosure of some records that have been withheld. A requester who is not convinced that the agency's initial decision is correct should appeal. There is no charge for filing an appeal.

An appeal is filed by sending a letter to the head of the agency. The letter must identify the FOIA request that is being appealed. The envelope containing the letter of appeal should be marked in the lower left hand corner with the words "Freedom of Information Act Appeal."

Many agencies assign a number to all FOIA requests that are received. The number should be included in the appeal letter, along with the name and address of the requester. It is a common practice to include a copy of the agency's initial decision letter as part of the appeal, but this it not required. It can also be helpful for the requester to include a telephone number in the appeal letter to insure a faster response.

An appeal will normally include the requester's arguments supporting disclosure of the documents. A requester may include any facts or any arguments supporting the case for reversing the initial decision. However, an appeal letter does not have to contain any arguments at all. It is sufficient to state that the agency's initial decision is being appealed. The Appendix to this section includes a sample appeal letter.

The FOIA does not set a time limit for filing an administrative appeal of an FOIA denial. However, it is good practice to file an appeal promptly. Some agency regulations establish a time limit for filing an administrative appeal. A requester whose appeal is rejected by an agency because it is too late may refile the original FOIA request and start the process again.

A requester who delays filing an appeal runs the risk that the documents could be destroyed. However, as long as an agency is considering a request or an appeal, the agency must preserve the documents.

An agency is required to make a decision on an appeal within twenty days (excluding Saturdays, Sundays, and federal holidays). It is possible for an agency to extend the time limits by an additional ten days. Once the time period has elapsed, a requester may consider a that the appeal has been denied and may proceed with a judicial appeal. However, unless there is an urgent need for records, this is not always the best course of action. The courts are not sympathetic to appeals based solely on an agency's failure to comply with the FOIA's time limits.

Filing a Judicial Appeal

When an administrative appeal is denied, a requester has the right to appeal the denial in court. An FOIA appeal can be filed in the United States District Court in the district where the requester lives. The requester can also file suit in the district where the documents are located or in the District of Columbia. When a requester goes to court, the burden of justifying the withholding of documents is on the government. This is a distinct advantage for the requester.

Requesters are sometimes successful when they go to court, but the results vary considerably. Some requesters who file judicial appeals find that an agency will disclose some documents previously withheld rather than fight about disclosure in court. This does not always happen, and there is no guarantee that the filing of a judicial appeal will result in any additional disclosure.

Most requesters require the assistance of an attorney to file a judicial appeal. A person who files a lawsuit and substantially prevails may be awarded reasonable attorney fees and litigation costs reasonably incurred. Some requesters may be able to handle their own appeal without an attorney. Since this is not a litigation guide, details of the judicial appeal process have not been included. Anyone considering filing an appeal can begin by reviewing the provisions of the FOIA on judicial review.

The Freedom Of Information Act

The Privacy Act of 1974

The Privacy Act of 1974 provides safeguards against an invasion of privacy through the misuse of records by federal agencies. In general, the Act allows citizens to learn how records are collected, maintained, used, and disseminated by the federal government. The Act also permits individuals to gain access to most personal information maintained by federal agencies and to seek amendment of any incorrect or incomplete information.

The Privacy Act applies to personal information maintained by agencies in the executive branch of the federal government. The executive branch includes cabinet departments, military departments, government corporations, government controlled corporations, independent regulatory agencies, and other establishments in the executive branch. Agencies subject to the Freedom of Information Act (FOIA) are also subject to the Privacy Act. The Privacy Act does not generally apply to records maintained by state and local governments or private companies or organizations.

The Privacy Act grants rights only to United States citizens and to aliens lawfully admitted for permanent residence. As a result, foreign nationals cannot use the Act's provisions. However, foreigners may use the Freedom of Information Act to request records about themselves.

The only records subject to the Privacy Act are records about individuals that are maintained in a system of records. The idea of a "system of records" is unique to the Privacy Act and requires explanation.

The Act defines a "record" to include most personal information maintained by an agency about an individual. A record contains information about education, financial transactions, medical history, criminal history, or employment history. A system of records is a group of records from which information is actually retrieved by name, social security number, or other identifying symbol assigned to an individual.

Some personal information is not kept in a system of records. This information is not subject to the provisions of the Privacy Act, although access may be requested under the FOIA. Most personal information in government files is subject to the Privacy Act.

The Privacy Act also establishes general records management requirements for federal agencies. In summary, there are five basic requirements that are more relevant to individuals.

First, agencies must establish procedures allowing individuals to see and copy records about themselves. An individual may also seek to amend any information that is not accurate, relevant, timely, or complete. The rights to inspect and to correct records are the most important provisions of the Privacy Act. This section explains in more detail how an individual can exercise these rights.

Second, agencies must publish notices describing all systems of records. The notices include a complete description of personal data recordkeeping policies, practices, and systems. This requirement prevents the maintenance of secret record systems.

Third, agencies must make reasonable efforts to maintain accurate, relevant, timely, and complete records about individuals. Agencies are prohibited from maintaining information about how individuals exercise rights guaranteed by the First Amendment to the U.S. Constitution unless maintenance of the information is specifically authorized by statute or relates to authorized law enforcement activity.

Fourth, the Act establishes rules governing the use and disclosure of personal information. The Act specifies that information collected for one purpose may not be used for another purpose without notice to or the consent of the subject of the record. The Act also requires that agencies keep a record of some disclosures of personal information.

Fifth, the Act provides legal remedies that permit individuals to seek enforcement of rights under the Act. In addition, there are criminal penalties that apply to federal employees who fail to comply with the Act's provisions.

Locating Records

There is no central index of federal government records. An individual who wants to inspect records about himself or herself must first identify which agency has the records. Often, this will not be difficult. For example, an individual who was employed by the federal government knows that the employing agency or the Office of Personnel Management maintains personnel files.

Similarly, an individual who receives veterans' benefits will normally find the related records at the Veterans Administration or at the Defense Department. Tax records are maintained by the Internal Revenue Service, social security records by the Social Security Administration, passport records by the State Department, etc.

For those who are uncertain about which agency has the records that are needed, there are several sources of information. First, an individual can ask an agency that might maintain the records. If that agency does not have the records, it may be able to identify the proper agency.

Second, a government directory such as the *United States Government Manual* contains a complete list of all federal agencies, a description of agency functions, and the address of the agency and its field offices. An agency responsible for operating a program normally maintains the records related to that program.

Third, a Federal Information Center can help to identify government agencies, their functions, and their records. These centers, which are operated by the General Services Administration, serve as clearinghouses for information about the federal government. There are several dozen Federal Information Centers throughout the country.

Fourth, the Office of Federal Register publishes an annual compilation of system of records notices for all agencies. These notices contain a complete description of each record system maintained by each agency. The compilation — which is published in five large volumes — is the most complete reference for information about federal agency personal information practices. The information that appears in the compilation is also published occasionally in the *Federal Register*.

Tips On Finding Information

The compilation — formally called Privacy Act Issuance — may be difficult to find. Copies will be available in some federal depository libraries and possibly in other libraries as well. Although the compilation is the best single source of detailed information about personal records maintained by the federal agencies, it is not necessary to consult the compilation before making a Privacy Act request.

A requester is not required to identify the specific system of records that contains the information being sought. It is sufficient to identify the agency that has the records. Using information provided by the requester, the agency will determine which system of records has the files that have been requested.

Those who request records under the Privacy Act can help the agency by identifying the type of records being sought. Large agencies maintain dozens or even hundreds of different record systems. A request is processed faster if the requester tells the agency that he or she was employed by the agency, was the recipient of benefits under an agency program, or had other specific contacts with the agency.

Making a Privacy Act Request for Access

The fastest way to make a Privacy Act request is to identify the specific system of records. The request can be addressed to the system manager. Few people do this. Instead, most people address their requests to the head of the agency that has the records or the agency's Privacy Act Officer. The envelope containing the written request should be marked "Privacy Act Request" in the bottom left-hand corner.

There are three basic elements to a request for records under the Privacy Act. First, the letter should state that the request is being made under the Privacy Act. Second, the letter should include the name, address, and signature of the requester. Third, the request should describe as specifically as possible the records that are wanted. The Appendix to this section includes a sample Privacy Act request letter. It is a common practice for an individual seeking records about himself or herself to make the request both under the Privacy Act of 1974 and the Freedom of Information Act. See the discussion in the front of this section concerning which act to use.

A requester can describe the records by identifying a specific system of records, by describing his or her contacts with an agency, or by simply asking for all records about himself or herself. The broader and less specific a request is, the longer it may take for an agency to respond.

It is a good practice for a requester to describe the type of records that he or she expects to find. For example, an individual seeking a copy of his service record in the Army should state he was in the Army and include the approximate dates of service. This will help the Defense Department narrow its search to record systems that are likely to contain the information being sought. An individual seeking records from the Federal Bureau of Investigation (FBI) may ask that files in specific field offices be searched in addition to the FBI's central office files. The FBI dose not routinely search field office records without a specific request.

Agencies generally require requesters to provide some proof of identity before records will be disclosed. Agencies may have different requirements. Some agencies will accept a signature; others may require a notarized signature. If an individual goes to the agency to inspect records, standard personal identification may be acceptable. More stringent requirements may apply if the records being sought are especially sensitive.

Agencies will inform requesters of special identification requirements. Requesters who need records quickly should first consult regulations or talk to the agency's Privacy Act Officer to find out how to provide adequate identification.

An individual who visits an agency office to inspect a Privacy Act record may wish to bring along a friend or relative to review the record. When a requester brings another person, the agency may ask the requester to sign a written statement authorizing discussion of the record in the presence of that person.

It is a crime to knowingly and willfully request or obtain records under the Privacy Act under false pretenses. A request for access under the Privacy Act can be made only by the subject of the record. An individual cannot make a request under the Privacy Act for a record about another person. The only exception is for a parent or legal guardian who can request records for a minor or a person who has been declared incompetent.

Fees

Under the Privacy Act, fees can be charged only for the cost of conveying records. No fees may be charged for the time it takes to search for the records or the time it takes to review the records to determine if any exemptions apply. This is a major difference from the FOIA. Under the FOIA, fees can sometimes be charged to recover search costs and review costs. The different fee structure in the two laws is one reason many requesters seeking records about themselves cite both laws. This minimizes allowable fees.

Many agencies will not charge fees for making copies of files under the Privacy Act, especially when the files are small. If paying the copying charges is a problem, the requester should explain in the request letter. An agency can waive fees under the Privacy Act.

Requirements for Agency Responses

Unlike the Freedom of Information Act (FOIA), there is no fixed time when an agency must respond to a request for access to records under the Privacy Act. It is good practice for an agency to acknowledge receipt of a Privacy Act request within ten days and to provide the requested records within thirty days.

At many agencies, FOIA and Privacy Act requests are processed by the same personnel. When then is a backlog of requests, it takes longer to receive a response. As a practical matter, there is little that a requester can do when an agency response is delayed.

Agencies generally process requests in the order in which they were received. Some agencies will expedite the processing of

The Freedom Of Information Act

urgent requests. Anyone with a pressing need for records should consult the agency Privacy Act Officer about how to ask for expedited treatment of requests.

Reasons Access May Be Denied Under the Privacy Act

Not all records about an individual must be disclosed under the Privacy Act. Some records may be withheld to protect important government interests such as national security or law enforcement.

The Privacy Act exemptions are different from the exemptions of the Freedom of Information Act (FOIA). Under the FOIA, any record may be withheld from disclosure if it contains exempt information when a request is received. The decision to apply an FOIA exemption is made only after a request has been made. In contrast, Privacy Act exemptions apply not only to records but to systems of records. Before an agency can apply a Privacy Act exemption, the agency must first issue a regulation stating that there may be exempt records in that system of records. Thus, there is a procedural prerequisite for the application of the Privacy Act exemptions.

Without reviewing agency regulations, it is hard to tell whether particular Privacy Act records are exempt from disclosure. However, it is a safe assumption that any system of records that qualifies for an exemption has been exempted by the agency.

Since most record systems are not exempt, the exemptions are not relevant to most requests. Also, agencies do not automatically rely upon the Privacy Act exemptions unless there is a specific reason to do so. Thus, some records that are exempt may be disclosed upon request.

Because Privacy Act exemptions are complex and used infrequently, most requesters need not worry about them. The exemptions are discussed here for those interested in the law's details and for reference when an agency withholds records. Anyone interested in more information about the Privacy Act's exemptions can begin by reading the relevant sections of the Act.

The Privacy Act's exemptions differ from those of the FOIA in another important way. The FOIA is essentially a disclosure law. Information exempt under the FOIA is exempt from disclosure only. That is not true under the Privacy Act. It imposes many separate requirements on personal records. No system of records is exempt from all Privacy Act requirements.

For example, no system of records is ever exempt from the requirement that a description of the system be published. No system of records can be exempted from the limitations on disclosure of the records outside the agency. No system is exempt from the requirement to maintain an accounting for disclosures. No system is exempt from the restriction against the maintenance of unauthorized information on the exercise of First Amendment rights. All systems are subject to the requirement that reasonable efforts be taken to assure that records disclosed outside the agency be accurate, complete, timely, and relevant. Agencies must maintain proper administrative controls and security for all systems. Finally, The Privacy Act's criminal penalties remain fully applicable to each system of records.

1. General Exemptions

There are two general exemptions under the Privacy Act. The first applies to all records maintained by the Central Intelligence Agency. The second general exemption applies to selected records maintained by an agency or component whose principal function is any activity pertaining to criminal law enforcement. Records of these criminal law enforcement agencies can be exempt under the Privacy Act if the records consists of (A) information compiled to identify individual criminal offenders and which consist only of identifying that and notations of arrests, the nature and disposition of criminal charges, sentencing, confinement, release, and parole or probation status: (B) criminal investigatory records associated with an identifiable individual; or (C) reports identifiable to a particular individual compiled at any stage from arrest through release from supervision.

Systems of records subject to these general exemptions may be exempted from many of the Privacy Act's requirements. Exemption from the Act's access and correction provisions is the most important. Individuals have no right under the Privacy Act to ask for a copy of records that are generally exempt or to seek correction of erroneous records.

In practice, these exemptions are not as expansive as they sound. Most agencies that have exempt records will accept and process Privacy Act requests. The records will be reviewed on a case-by-case basis. Agencies will often disclose any information that does not require protection. Agencies also tend to follow a similar policy for requests for correction.

Individuals interested in obtaining records from the Central Intelligence Agency or from law enforcement agencies should not be discouraged from making requests for access. Even if the Privacy Act access exemption is applied, portions of the records may still be disclosable under the FOIA. This is a primary reason individuals should cite both the Privacy Act and the FOIA when requesting records.

The general exemption from access does not prevent requesters from filing a lawsuit under the Privacy Act when access is denied. The right to sue under the FOIA is not changed because of a Privacy Act exemption.

2. Specific Exemptions

There are seven specific Privacy Act exemptions that can be applied to many systems of records. Records subject to these exemptions are not exempt from as many of the Act's requirements as are the records subject to the general exemptions. However, records exempt under the specific exemptions are exempt from the Privacy Act's access and correction provisions. Nevertheless, since the access and correction exemptions are not always applied when available, those seeking records should not be discouraged from making a request. Also, the FOIA can be used to seek access to records exempt under the Privacy Act.

The first specific exemption covers record systems containing information that is properly classified. Classified information is also exempt from disclosure under the FOIA. Information that has been classified in the interest of national defense or foreign policy will normally be unavailable under either the FOIA or the Privacy Act.

Tips On Finding Information

The second specific exemption applies to systems of records containing investigatory material compiled for law enforcement purposes other than material covered by the general law enforcement exemption. The specific law enforcement exemption is limited when — as a result of the maintenance of the records — an individual is denied any right, privilege, or benefit to which he or she would be entitled by federal law or for which he or she would otherwise be entitled. In such a case, disclosure is required except where disclosure would reveal the identity of a confidential source who furnished information to the government under an express promise that the identity of the source would be held in confidence. If the information was collected from a confidential source before the effective date of the Privacy Act (September 27, 1975), an implied promise of confidentiality is sufficient to permit withholding of the identity of the source.

The third specific exemption applies to systems of records maintained in connection with providing protective services to the President of the United States or other individuals who receive protection from the Secret Service.

The fourth specific exemption applies to systems of records required by statute to be maintained and used solely as statistical records.

The fifth specific exemption covers investigatory material compiled solely to determine suitability, eligibility, or qualifications for federal civilian employment, military service, federal contracts, or access to classified information. However, this exemption applies only to the extent that disclosure of information would reveal the identity of a confidential source who provided the information under a promise of confidentiality.

The sixth specific exemption applies to systems of records that contain testing or examination of material used solely to determine individual qualifications for appointment or promotion in federal service, but only when disclosure would compromise the objectivity or fairness of the testing or examination process. Effectively, this exemption permits withholding of questions used in employment tests.

The seven specific exemption covers evaluation material used to determine potential for promotion in the armed services. The material is only exempt to the extent that disclosure would reveal the identity of a confidential source who provided the information under a promise of confidentiality.

3. Medical Records

Medical records maintained by federal agencies — for example, records at Veterans Administration hospitals — are not formally exempt from the Privacy Act's access provisions. However, the Privacy Act authorizes a special procedure for medical records that operates, at least in part, like an exemption.

Agencies may deny individuals direct access to medical records, including psychological records, if the agency deems it necessary. An agency normally reviews medical records requested by an individual. If the agency determines that direct disclosure is unwise, it can arrange for disclosure to a physician selected by the individual or possibly to another person chosen by the individual.

4. Litigation Records

The Privacy Act's access provisions include a general limitation on access to litigation records. The Act does not require an agency to disclose to an individual any information compiled in reasonable anticipation of a civil action or proceeding. This limitation operates like an exemption, although there is no requirement that the exemption be applied to a system of records before it can be used.

Administrative Appeal Procedures for Denial of Access

Unlike the FOIA, the Privacy Act does not provide for an administrative appeal of the denial of access. However, many agencies have established procedures that will allow Privacy Act requesters to appeal a denial of access without going to court. An administrative appeal is often allowed under the Privacy Act, even though it is not required, because many individuals cite both the FOIA and Privacy Act when making a request. The FOIA provides specifically for an administrative appeal, and agencies are required to consider an appeal under the FOIA.

When a Privacy Act request for access is denied, agencies usually inform the requester of any appeal rights that are available. If no information on appeal rights is included in the denial letter, the requester should ask the Privacy Act Officer. Unless an agency has established an alternative procedure, it is possible that an appeal filed directly with the head of the agency will be considered by the agency.

When a request for access is denied under the Privacy Act, the agency explains the reason for the denial. The explanation must name the system of records and explain which exemption is applicable to the system. An appeal may be made on the basis that the record is not exempt, that the system of records has not been properly exempted, or that the record is exempt but no harm to an important interest will result if the record is disclosed.

There are three basic elements to a Privacy Act appeal letter. First, the letter should state that the appeal is being made under the Privacy Act of 1974. If the FOIA was cited when the request for access was made, the letter should state that the appeal is also being made under the FOIA. This is important because the FOIA grants requesters statutory appeal rights.

Second, a Privacy Act appeal letter should identify the denial that is being appealed and the records that were withheld. The appeal letter should also explain why the denial of access is improper or unnecessary.

Third, the appeal should include the requester's name and address. It is good practice for a requester to also include a telephone number when making an appeal. The Appendix at the end of this section includes a sample letter of appeal.

Amending Records Under the Privacy Act

The Privacy Act grants an important right in addition to the ability to inspect records. The Act permits an individual to request a correction of a record that is not accurate, relevant, timely, or complete. This remedy allows an individual to correct errors and to prevent those errors from being disseminated by the agency or used unfairly against the individual.

The right to seek a correction extends only to records subject to the Privacy Act. Also, an individual can only correct errors contained in a record that pertains to himself or herself. Records disclosed under the FOIA cannot be amended through the Privacy Act unless the records are also subject to the Privacy Act. Records about unrelated events or about other people cannot be amended unless the records are in a Privacy Act file maintained under the name of the individual who is seeking to make the correction.

A request to amend a record should be in writing. Agency regulations explain the procedures in greater detail, but the process is not complicated. A letter requesting an amendment of a record will normally be addressed to the Privacy Act Officer of the agency or to the agency official responsible for the maintenance of the record system containing the erroneous information. The envelope containing the request should be marked "Privacy Act Amendment Request" on the lower left corner.

There are five basic elements to a request for amending a Privacy Act record.

First, the letter should state that it is a request to amend a record under the Privacy Act of 1974.

Second, the request should identify the specific record and the specific information in the record for which an amendment is being sought.

Third, the request should state why the information is not accurate, relevant, timely, or complete. Supporting evidence may be included with the request.

Fourth, the request should state what new or additional information, if any, should be included in place of the erroneous information. Evidence of the validity of the new or additional information should be included. If the information in the file is wrong and needs to be removed rather than supplemented or corrected, the request should make this clear.

Fifth, the request should include the name and address of the requester. It is a good idea for the requester to include a telephone number. The Appendix includes a sample letter requesting amendment of a Privacy Act record.

Appeals and Requirements for Agency Responses

An agency that receives a request for amendment under the Privacy Act must acknowledge receipt of the request within ten days (not including Saturdays, Sundays, and legal holidays). The agency must promptly rule on the request. The agency may make the amendment requested. If so, the agency must notify any person or agency to which the record had previously been disclosed of the correction.

If the agency refuses to make the change requested, the agency must inform the requester of: (1) the agency's refusal to amend the record; (2) the reason for refusing to amend the request; and (3) the procedures for requesting a review of the denial. The agency must provide the name and business address of the official responsible for conducting the review.

An agency must decide an appeal of a denial of a request for amendment within thirty days (excluding Saturdays, Sundays, and legal holidays), unless the time period is extended by the agency for good cause. If the appeal is granted, the record will be corrected.

If the appeal is denied, the agency must inform the requester of the right to judicial review. In addition, a requester whose appeal has been denied also has the right to place in the agency file a concise statement of disagreement with the information that was the subject of the request for amendment.

When a statement of disagreement has been filed and an agency is disclosing the disputed information, the agency must mark the information and provide copies of the statement of disagreement. The agency may also include a concise statement of its reasons for not making the requested amendments. The agency must also give a copy of the statement of disagreement to any person or agency to whom the record had previously been disclosed.

Finding a Judicial Appeal

The Privacy Act provides a civil remedy whenever an agency denies access to a record or refuses to amend a record. An individual may sue an agency if the agency fails to maintain records with accuracy, relevance, timeliness, and completeness as is necessary to assure fairness in any agency determination and the agency makes a determination that is adverse to the individual. An individual may also sue an agency if the agency fails to comply with any other Privacy Act provision in a manner that has an adverse effect on the individual.

The Privacy Act protects a wide range of rights about personal records maintained by federal agencies. The most important are the right to inspect records and the right to seek correction of records. Other rights have also been mentioned here, and still others can be found in the text of the Act. Most of these rights can become the subject of litigation.

An individual may file a lawsuit against an agency in the federal district court in which the individual lives, in which the records are situated, or in the District of Columbia. A lawsuit must be filed within two years from which the basis for the lawsuit arose.

Most individuals require the assistance of an attorney to file a judicial appeal. An individual who files a lawsuit and substantially prevails may be awarded reasonable attorney fees and litigation costs reasonably incurred. Some requesters may be able to handle their own appeal without an attorney. Since this is not a litigation guide, details about the judicial appeal process have not been included. Anyone considering filing an appeal can begin by reviewing the provisions of the Privacy Act on civil remedies.

Appendix: Sample Request and Appeal Letters

A. Freedom of Information Act Request Letter

Agency Head [or Freedom of Information Act Officer]
Name of Agency
Address of Agency
City, State, Zip Code
Re: Freedom of Information Act Request.

Tips On Finding Information

Dear ____:

This is a request under the Freedom of Information Act.

I request that a copy of the following documents [or documents containing the following information] be provided to me: [identify the documents or information as specifically as possible].

In order to help determine my status to assess fees, you should know that I am (insert a suitable description of the requester and the purpose of the request).

[Sample requester descriptions:
    a representative of the news media affiliated with the newspaper (magazine, television station, etc.) and this request is made as part of news gathering and not for a commercial use.
    affiliated with an educational or noncommercial scientific institution and this request is made for a scholarly or scientific purpose.
    an individual seeking information for personal use and not for a commercial use.
    affiliated with a private corporation and am seeking information for use in the company business.]

[Optional] I am willing to pay fees for this request up to a maximum of $XXX. If you estimate that the fees will exceed this limit, please inform me first.

[Optional] I request a waiver of all fees of this request. Disclosure of the requested information to me is in the public interest because it is likely to contribute significantly to public understanding of the operations or activities of the government and is not primarily in my commercial interest. [Include a specific explanation.]

Thank you for your consideration of this request.

Sincerely,
Name
Address
City, State, Zip Code
Telephone number [Optional]

B. Freedom of Information Act Appeal Letter

Agency Head or Appeal Officer
Name of Agency
Address of Agency
City, State, Zip Code
Re: Freedom of Information Act Appeal

Dear ____:

This is an appeal under the Freedom of Information Act.

On (date), I requested documents under the Freedom of Information Act. My request was assigned the following identification number: XXXXX. On (date), I received a response to my request in a letter signed by (name of official). I appeal the denial of my request.

[Optional] The documents that were withheld must be disclosed under the FOIA because * * *.

[Optional] I appeal the decision to deny my request for a waiver of fees. I believe that I am entitled to a waiver of fees. Disclosure of the documents I requested is in the public interest because the information is likely to contribute significantly to public understanding of the operations or activities of government and is not primarily in my commercial interests. (Provide details)

[Optional] I appeal the decision to require me to pay review costs for this request. I am not seeking the documents for a commercial use. (Provide details)

[Optional] I appeal the decision to require me to pay search charges for this request. I am a reporter seeking information as part of news gathering and not for commercial use.

Thank you for your consideration of this appeal.

Sincerely,

Name
Address
City, State, Zip Code
Telephone number [Optional]

C. Privacy Act Request for Access Letter

Privacy at Officer [or System of Records Manager]
Name of Agency
City, State, Zip Code
Re: Privacy Act Request for Access.

Dear ____:

This is a request under the Privacy Act of 1974.

I request a copy of any records [or specifically named records] about me maintained at your agency.

[Optional] To help you to locate my records, I have had the following contacts with your agency: [mention job applications, periods of employment, loans or agency programs applied for, etc.).

[Optional] Please consider that this request is also made under the Freedom of Information Act. Please provide any additional information that may be available under the FOIA.

[Optional] I am wiling to pay fees for this request up to a maximum of $ XXX. If you estimate that the fees will exceed this limit, please inform me first.

[Optional] Enclosed is [a notarized signature or other identifying document] that will verify my identity.

Thank you for your consideration of this request.

Sincerely,

Name
Address
City, State, Zip Code
Telephone number [Optional]

D. Privacy Act Denial of Access Letter

Agency Head or Appeal Officer
Name of Agency
City, State, Zip Code
Re: Appeal of Denial of Privacy Act Access Request.

Dear ____:

This is an appeal under the Privacy Act of the denial of my request for access to records.

On (date), I requested access to records under the Privacy Act of 1974. My request was assigned the following identification number: XXXXX. On (date), I received a response to my request in a letter signed by (name of official). I appeal the denial of my request.

[Optional] The records that were withheld should be disclosed to me because * * *.

[Optional] Please consider that this appeal is also made under the Freedom of Information Act. Please provide any additional information that may be available under the FOIA.

Thank you for your consideration of this appeal.

Sincerely,

Name
Address
City, State, Zip Code
Telephone number [Optional]

The Freedom Of Information Act

E. Privacy Act Request to Amend Records

Privacy Act Officer [or System of Records Manager]
Name of Agency
City, State, Zip Code
Re: Privacy Act Request to Amend Records

Dear ____:

This is a request under the Privacy Act to amend records about myself maintained by your agency.

I believe that the following information is not correct: [Describe the incorrect information as specifically as possible].

The information is not (accurate) (relevant) (timely) (complete) because * * *.

[Optional] Enclosed are copies of documents that show that the information is incorrect.

I request that the information be [deleted] [changed to read:]

Thank you for your consideration of this request.

Sincerely,

Name
Address
City, State, Zip Code
Telephone number [Optional]

F. Privacy Act Appeal of Refusal to Amend Records

Agency Head or Appeal Officer
Name of Agency
City, State, Zip Code
Re: Privacy Act Request to Amend Records

Dear ____:

This is an appeal made under the Privacy Act of the refusal of your agency to amend records as I requested.

On (date), I was informed by (name of official) that my request was rejected. I appeal the rejection of my request.

The rejection of my request for amendment was wrong because * * *.

[Optional] I enclose additional evidence that shows that the records are incorrect and that the amendment I requested is appropriate.

Thank you for your consideration of this appeal.

Sincerely,

Name
Address
City, State, Zip Code
Telephone number [Optional]

Federal Money Programs For Your Business

Federal Money Programs for Your Business

The following is a description of the federal funds available to small businesses, entrepreneurs, inventors, and researchers. This information is derived from the *Catalog of Federal Domestic Assistance* which is published by the U.S. Government Printing Office in Washington, DC. The number next to the title description is the official reference for this federal program. Contact the office listed below the caption for further details. The following is a description of the terms used for the types of assistance available:

Loans: money lent by a federal agency for a specific period of time and with a reasonable expectation of repayment. Loans may or may not require payment of interest.

Loan Guarantees: programs in which federal agencies agree to pay back part or all of a loan to a private lender if the borrower defaults.

Grants: money given by federal agencies for a fixed period of time and which does not have to be repaid.

Direct Payments: funds provided by federal agencies to individuals, private firms, and institutions. The use of direct payments may be "specified" to perform a particular service or for "unrestricted" use.

Insurance: coverage under specific programs to assure reimbursement for losses sustained. Insurance may be provided by federal agencies or through insurance companies and may or may not require the payment of premiums.

* Grants to Producers of Honey, Cotton, Rice, Soybeans, Canole, Flaxseed, Mustard Seed, Rapeseed, Safflower, Sunflower Seed, Feed Grains, Wheat, Rye, Peanuts, Tobacco, and Dairy Products.
(10.051 Commodity Loans and Purchases)
U.S. Department of Agriculture
Farm Service Agency
Price Support Division
Stop 0512, 1400 Independence Ave., SW
Washington, DC 20250-0512   202-720-7641

Objectives: To improve and stabilize farm income, to assist in bringing about a better balance between supply and demand of the commodities, and to assist farmers in the orderly marketing of their crops. Types of assistance: direct payments with unrestricted use; direct loans. Estimate of annual funds available: Commodity purchases: $61,700,000 in 1998; Loans: $7,451,289,000.

* Grants to Dairy Farmers Whose Milk Is Contaminated Because of Pesticides
(10.053 Dairy Indemnity Program)
U.S. Department of Agriculture
Farm Service Agency
1400 Independence Ave., SW
Washington, DC 20250-0512   202-720-7641

Objectives: To protect dairy farmers and manufacturers of dairy products who through no fault of their own, are directed to remove their milk or dairy products from commercial markets because of contamination from pesticides which have been approved for use by the federal government. Dairy farmers can also be indemnified because of contamination with chemicals or toxic substances, nuclear radiation or fallout. Types of assistance: direct payments with unrestricted use. Estimate of annual funds available: Direct payments: $450,000.

* Grants to Producers of Corn, Sorghum, Barley, Oats, and Rye
(10.055 Production Flexibility Payments for Contract Commodities)
Philip W. Sronce
U.S. Department of Agriculture
Farm Service Agency
Economic and Policy Analysis Staff
Stop 0532, 1400 Independence Avenue SW
Washington, DC 20250-0532   202-720-4418

Objectives: To support farming certainty and flexibility while ensuring continued compliance with farm conservation and wetland protection requirements. Estimate of annual funds available: Contract Payments: $700,921,515.

* Money to Run an Agriculture Related Business, Recreation Related Business or Teenage Business
(10.406 Farm Operating Loans)
Director
Loan Making Division
U.S. Department of Agriculture
Farm Service Agency
Ag Box 0522
Washington, DC 20250   202-720-1632

Objectives: To enable operators of not larger than family farms through the extension of credit and supervisory assistance, to make efficient use of their land, labor, and other resources, and to establish and maintain financially viable farming and ranching operations. Types of assistance: direct loans; guaranteed/insured loans. Estimate of annual funds available: Direct Loans: $500,000,000; Guaranteed Loans: $1,700,000,000.

* Money to Farmers, Ranchers, and Aquaculture Businesses
(10.407 Farm Ownership Loans)
Director, Loan Making Division
U.S. Department of Agriculture
Farm Service Agency
Ag Box 0522
Washington, DC 20250   202-720-1632

Objectives: To assist eligible farmers, ranchers, and aquaculture operators, including farming cooperatives, corporations, partnerships, and joint operations, through the extension of credit and supervisory assistance to: Become owner-operators of not larger than family farms; make efficient use of the land, labor, and other resources; carry on sound and successful farming operations; and enable farm families to have a reasonable standard of living. Types of assistance: direct loans; guaranteed/ insured loans. Estimate of annual funds available: Direct Loans: $85,000,000; Guaranteed Loans: $425,031,000.

* Loans to Family Farms That Can't Get Credit
(10.437 Interest Assistance Program)
FmHA County Supervisor in the county where the proposed farming operation will be located

or

Director, Loan Making Division
U.S. Department of Agriculture
Farm Service Agency
Ag Box 0522
Washington, DC 20250   202-720-1632

Federal Money Programs For Your Business

Objectives: To aid not larger than family sized farms in obtaining credit when they are temporarily unable to project a positive cash flow without a reduction in the interest rate. Types of assistance: guaranteed/insured loans. Estimate of annual funds available: Subsidized Guaranteed Loans: $200,000,000. (There have been no funds authorized for Subsidized Farm Ownership Loans.)

* Grants to Market Food Related Products Overseas
(10.600 Foreign Market Development Cooperation Program)
Deputy Administrator
Commodity and Marketing Programs
Foreign Agricultural Service
U.S. Department of Agriculture
Washington, DC 20250   202-720-4761

Objectives: To develop, maintain and expand long-term export markets for U.S. agricultural products through cost-share assistance and the opportunity to work closely with FAS and its overseas offices. Types of assistance: direct payments for specified use (cooperative agreements). Estimate of annual funds available: Direct payments: $27,500,000.

* Grants to Sell Food Related Products Overseas
(10.601 Market Access Program)
Deputy Administrator
Commodity and Marketing Programs
Foreign Agricultural Service
U.S. Department of Agriculture
Washington DC 20250   202-720-4761

Objectives: To encourage the development, maintenance, and expansion of commercial export markets for U.S. agricultural commodities through cost-share assistance to eligible trade organizations that implement a foreign market development program. Priority for assistance is provided for agricultural commodities or products in the case of an unfair trade practice. Funding of the program is accomplished through the issuance by the Commodity Credit Corporation (CCC) of a dollar check to reimburse participants for activities authorized by a specific project agreement. Types of assistance: direct payments for specified use (cooperative agreements). Estimate of annual funds available: Direct payments: $90,000,000.

* Money to Local Communities Near National Forests to Help Businesses Grow or Expand
(10.670 National Forest-Dependent Rural Communities)
Deputy Chief
State and Private Forestry
Forest Service
U.S. Department of Agriculture
P.O. Box 96090
Washington, DC 20090-6090   202-205-1657

Objectives: Provide accelerated assistance to communities faced with acute economic problems associated with federal or private sector land management decisions and policies or that are located in or near a national forest and are economically dependent upon forest resources. Aid is extended to these communities to help them to diversify their economic base and to improve the economic, social, and environmental well-being of rural areas. Types of assistance: project grants; direct loans; use of property, facilities, and equipment; training. Estimate of annual funds available: $3,500,000.

* Loans to Nonprofits to Lend Money to New Businesses
(10.767 Intermediary Relending Program)
Rural Business and Cooperative Development Service
Room 6321, South Agriculture Building
Washington, DC 20250-0700   202-690-4100

Objectives: To finance business facilities and community development. Types of assistance: direct loans. Estimate of annual funds available: Loans: $35,000,000.

* Loans to Businesses in Small Towns
(10.768 Business and Industry Loans)
Administrator
Rural Business and Cooperative Development Service
U.S. Department of Agriculture   202-690-4730
Washington, DC 20250-3201   Fax: 202-690-4737

Objectives: To assist public, private, or cooperative organizations (profit or non-profit), Indian tribes or individuals in rural areas to obtain quality loans for the purpose of improving, developing or financing business, industry, and employment and improving the economic and environmental climate in rural communities including pollution abatement and control. Types of assistance: Direct loans; guaranteed/insured loans. Estimate of annual funds available: Direct Loans: $50,000,000; Guaranteed Loans: $1,000,000,000.

* Grants to Nonprofits to Lend Money to New Businesses
(10.769 Rural Development Grants)
Director
Specialty Lenders Division
Rural Business-Cooperative Service
U.S. Department of Agriculture
Washington, DC 20250-3222   202-720-1400

Objectives: To facilitate the development of small and emerging private business, industry, and related employment for improving the economy in rural communities. Types of assistance: project grants. Estimate of annual funds available: Grants: $40,300,000.

* Loans to Companies That Provide Electricity to Small Towns
(10.850 Rural Electrification Loans and Loan Guarantees)
Administrator
Rural Utilities Service
U.S. Department of Agriculture
Washington, DC 20250-1500   202-720-9540

Objectives: To assure that people in eligible rural areas have access to electric services comparable in reliability and quality to the rest of the Nation. Types of assistance: direct loans. Estimate of annual funds available: Direct Loans: $366,000,000; Guaranteed FFB: $700,000,000.

* Loans to Companies That Provide Telephone Service to Small Towns
(10.851 Rural Telephone Loans and Loan Guarantees)
Assistant Administrator
Rural Utilities Services
U.S. Department of Agriculture
Washington, DC 20250   202-720-9554

Objectives: To assure that people in eligible rural areas have access to telecommunications services comparable in reliability and quality to the rest of the Nation. Types of assistance: Direct loans; guaranteed/insured loans. Estimate of annual funds available: Hardship Loans: $50,000,000; Cost of Money Loans: $300,000,000; FBB Treasury Loans: $120,000,000.

* Extra Loans to Companies That Provide Telephone Service to Small Towns
(10.852 Rural Telephone Bank Loans)
Assistant Governor
Rural Telephone Bank
U.S. Department of Agriculture
Washington, DC 20250   202-720-9554

Objectives: To provide supplemental financing to extend and improve telecommunications services in rural areas. Types of assistance: direct loans. Estimate of annual funds available: Direct Loans: $175,000,000.

* Grants and Loans to Telephone Companies That Then Provide Financing to Small Businesses
(10.854 Rural Economic Development Loans and Grants)
Director
Specialty Lenders Division
Rural Business-Cooperative Service
U.S. Department of Agriculture
Washington, DC 20250   202-720-1400

Objectives: To promote rural economic development and job creation projects, including funding for project feasibility studies, start-up costs, incubator projects, and other reasonable expenses for the purpose of fostering rural development. Types of assistance: direct loans; project grants. Estimate of annual funds available: Loans: $15,000,000; Grants: $11,000,000. (Note: Grants to establish Revolving Loan Fund Programs.)

Federal Money Programs For Your Business

* Free Plants to Nurseries
(10.905 Plant Materials for Conservation)
Deputy Chief For Science and Technology
Natural Resources Conservation Service
U.S. Department of Agriculture
P.O. Box 2890
Washington, DC 20013 202-720-4630

Objectives: To assemble, evaluate, select, release, and introduce into commerce, and promote the use of new and improved plant materials for soil, water, and related resource conservation and environmental improvement programs. To develop technology for land management and restoration with plant materials. To transfer technology on plant materials. Types of assistance: provision of specialized services. Estimate of annual funds available: Salaries and expenses: $8,745,000.

* Grants to Communities That Provide Money And Help to Small Business Incubators
(11.300 Economic Development Grants for Public Works and Infrastructure Development)
David L. McIlwain, Director
Public Works Division
Economic Development Administration
Room H7326, Herbert C. Hoover Building
U.S. Department of Commerce
Washington, DC 20230 202-482-5265

Objectives: To promote long-term economic development and assist in the construction of public works and development facilities needed to initiate and encourage the creation or retention of permanent jobs in the private sector in areas experiencing substantial economic distress. Types of assistance: project grants. Estimate of annual funds available: Grants: $160,200,000.

* Grants to Communities to Help Small Businesses Start or Expand
(11.302 Economic Development Support for Planning Organizations)
Luis F. Bueso
Director Planning Division
Economic Development Administration
Room H7319, Herbert C. Hoover Bldg. 202-482-3027
Washington, DC 20230 Fax: 202-482-0466

Objectives: To assist in providing administrative aid to multi-county Economic Development Districts, Redevelopment Areas and Indian Tribes to establish and maintain economic development planning and implementation capability and thereby promote effective utilization of resources in the creation of full-time permanent jobs for the unemployed and the underemployed in areas of high distress. Types of assistance: project grants. Estimate of annual funds available: Grants: $20,000,000.

* Grants to Communities That Help Finance New or Old Businesses Due to New Military Base Closings
(11.307 Special Economic Development and Adjustment Assistance Program-Sudden and Severe Economic Dislocation (SSED) and Long-Term Economic Deterioration (LTED))
David F. Witschi, Director
Economic Adjustment Division
Economic Development Administration
Room H7327, Herbert C. Hoover Building
U.S. Department of Commerce
Washington DC 20230 202-482-2659

Objectives: To assist state and local areas develop and/or implement strategies designed to address structural economic adjustment problems resulting from sudden and severe economic dislocation such as plant closings, military base closures and defense contract cutbacks, and natural disasters (SSED), or from long-term economic deterioration in the area's economy (LTED). Types of assistance: project grants. Estimate of annual funds available: Grants: $175,393,116 (includes funds for economic adjustment, defense adjustment, disaster recovery and trade impacted areas).

* Grants to Fishermen Hurt by Oil and Gas Drilling on the Outer Continental Shelf
(11.408 Fishermen's Contingency Fund)
Chief
Financial Services Division
National Marine Fisheries Service
1315 East West Highway
Silver Spring, MD 20910 301-713-2396

Objectives: To compensate U.S. commercial fishermen for damage/loss of fishing gear and 50 percent of resulting economic loss due to oil and gas related activities in any area of the Outer Continental Shelf. Types of assistance: direct payments with unrestricted use. Estimate of annual funds available: Direct payments: $500,000.

* Grants to Develop New Technologies for Your Business
(11.612 Advanced Technology Program)
Dr. Lura Powell, Director
Advanced Technology Program
National Institute of Standards and Technology
Gaithersburg, MD 20899 301-975-5187
E-mail: {lura.powell@nist.gov}
To receive application kits:
ATP customer service staff 1-800-ATP-FUND

Objectives: To work in partnership with industry to foster the development and broad dissemination of challenging, high-risk technologies that offer the potential for significant, broad-based economic benefits for the nation. Types of assistance: project grants (cooperative agreements). Estimate of annual funds available: Cooperative Agreements: $209,931,000.

* Grants to Organizations That Help Minorities Start Their Own Businesses
(11.800 Minority Business Development Centers)
Mr. Paul R. Webber
Acting Deputy Director
Room 5087, Minority Business Development Agency
U.S. Department of Commerce
14th and Constitution Avenue, NW
Washington, DC 20230 202-482-3237

Objectives: To provide business development services for a minimal fee to minority firms and individuals interested in entering, expanding, or improving their efforts in the marketplace. Minority business development center operators provide a wide range of services to clients, from initial consultations to the identification and resolution of specific business problems. Types of assistance: project grants. Estimate of annual funds available: Grants: $6,900,000.

* Grants to Organizations That Help American Indians Start Their Own Businesses
(11.801 Native American Program)
Mr. Joseph Hardy
Business Development
Specialist for the Office of Operations
Room 5079, Minority Business Development Agency
U.S. Department of Commerce
14th and Constitution Avenue, NW
Washington, DC 20230 202-482-6022

Objectives: To provide business development service to American Indians interested in entering, expanding, or improving their efforts in the marketplace. To help American Indian business development centers and American Indian business consultants to provide a wide range of services to American Indian clients, from initial consultation to the identification and resolution of specific business problems. Types of assistance: project grants. Estimate of annual funds available: Grants: $1,000,000.

* Grants to Help Minority Businesses Enter New Markets
(11.802 Minority Business Development)
Mr. Paul R. Webber, Acting Deputy Director
Room 5055, Minority Business Development Agency
U.S. Department of Commerce
14th and Constitution Avenue, NW
Washington, DC 20230 202-482-3237

Objectives: The resource development activity provides for the indirect business assistance programs conducted by MBDA. These programs encourage minority business development by identifying and developing private markets and capital sources; expanding business information and business services through trade associations; promoting and supporting the mobilization of resources of federal agencies and state and local governments at the local level; and assisting minorities in entering new and growing markets. Types of assistance: project grants (cooperative

Federal Money Programs For Your Business

agreements). Estimate of annual funds available: Cooperative Agreements/Contracts: $1,448,000.

* Grants to Organizations That Will Help You Sell to the Department of Defense
(12.002 Procurement Technical Assistance For Business Firms)
Defense Logistics Agency
Office of Small and Disadvantaged Business
 Utilization (DDAS)
8725 John J. Kingman Rd., Suite 2533
Ft. Belvoir, VA 22060-6221   703-767-1650

Objectives: To increase assistance by the DoD for eligible entities furnishing PTA to business entities, and to assist eligible entities in the payment of the costs of establishing and carrying out new Procurement Technical Assistance (PTA) Programs and maintaining existing PTA Programs. Types of assistance: Cooperative agreements. Estimate of annual funds available: Cooperative Agreements: $12,000,000.

* Loans to Start a Business on an Indian Reservation
(15.124 Indian Loans - Economic Development)
Office of Economic Development
Bureau of Indian Affairs
1849 C Street, NW, MS-2061
Washington, DC 20240   202-208-5324
Contact: Orville Hood

Objectives: To provide assistance to Federally Recognized Indian Tribal Governments, Native American Organizations, and individual American Indians in obtaining financing from private sources to promote business development initiatives on or near Federally Recognized Indian Reservations. Types of assistance: Guaranteed/ insured loans. Estimate of annual funds available: Guaranteed Loans: $5,005,000.

* Grants to Small Coal Mine Operators to Clean Up Their Mess
(15.250 Regulation of Surface Coal Mining and Surface Effects of Underground Coal Mining)
Chief
Division of Regulatory Support
Office of Surface Mining Reclamation and Enforcement
U.S. Department of the Interior
1951 Constitution Ave., NW
Washington, DC 20240   202-208-2651

Objectives: To protect society and the environment from the adverse effects of surface coal mining operations consistent with assuring the coal supply essential to the Nation's energy requirements. Types of assistance: project grants; direct payments for specified use. Estimate of annual funds available: $50,656,000. (Includes all cooperative agreements and State Grants except SOAP grants.) Small Operator Assistance: $3,800,000.

* Money to Fishermen Who Have Their Boats Seized by a Foreign Government
(19.204 Fishermen's Guaranty Fund)
Mr. Stetson Tinkham
Office of Marine Conservation
Bureau of Oceans and International
 Environmental and Scientific Affairs
Room 5806, U.S. Department of State   202-647-3941
Washington, DC 20520-7818   Fax: 202-736-7350

Objectives: To provide for reimbursement of losses incurred as a result of the seizure of a U.S. commercial fishing vessel by a foreign country on the basis of rights or claims in territorial waters or on the high seas which are not recognized by the United States. Effective November 28, 1990, the United States acknowledges the authority of coastal states to manage highly migratory species, thus reducing the basis for valid claims under the Fishermen's Protective Act. Types of assistance: insurance. Estimate of annual funds available: Reimbursement of Losses: $500,000.

* Grants to Build an Airport
(20.106 Airport Improvement Program)
Federal Aviation Administration
Office of Airport Planning and Programming
Airports Financial Assistance Division, APP-500
800 Independence Avenue, SW
Washington, DC 20591   202-267-3831

Objectives: To assist sponsors, owners, or operators of public-use airports in the development of a nationwide system of airports adequate to meet the needs of civil aeronautics. Types of assistance: project grants; advisory services and counseling. Estimate of annual funds available: Grants: $1,700,000,000.

* Grants to Bus Companies
(20.509 Public Transportation for Nonurbanized Areas)
Federal Transit Administration
Office of Grants Management
Office of Capital and Formula Assistance
400 Seventh Street, SW
Washington, DC 20590   202-366-2053

Objectives: To improve, initiate, or continue public transportation service in nonurbanized areas by providing financial assistance for the operating and administrative expenses and for the acquisition, construction, and improvement of facilities and equipment. Also to provide technical assistance for rural transportation providers. Types of assistance: formula grants. Estimate of annual funds available: Grants: $203,164,311.

* Grants to Become a Women-Owned Transportation Related Company
(20.511 Human Resource Programs)
Director
Office of Civil Rights
Federal Transit Administration
U.S. Department of Transportation
400 Seventh Street, SW
Room 7412
Washington, DC 20590   202-366-4018

Objectives: To provide financial assistance for national, regional and local initiatives that address human resource needs as they apply to public transportation activities. Such programs may include but are not limited to employment training programs; outreach programs to increase minority and female employment in public transportation activities; research on public transportation manpower and training needs; and training and assistance for minority business opportunities. This description is applicable only to projects awarded directly by the Federal Transit Administration (FTA) under the authority of Section 5314(a), the National component of the Transit Planning and Research Program. Types of assistance: project grants (cooperative agreements); dissemination of technical information. Estimate of annual funds available: Grants, Cooperative Agreements: $1,189,000.

* Grants to U.S. Shipping Companies That Have to Pay Their Employees Higher Salaries Than Foreign Shipping Companies
(20.804 Operating Differential Subsidies)
Edmond J. Fitzgerald, Director
Office of Subsidy and Insurance
Maritime Administration
U.S. Department of Transportation
400 Seventh Street, SW
Washington, DC 20590   202-366-2400

Objectives: To promote development and maintenance of the U.S. Merchant Marine by granting financial aid to equalize cost of operating a U.S. flag ship with cost of operating a competitive foreign flag ship. Types of assistance: direct payments for specified use. Estimate of annual funds available: $51,030,000 in 1998.

* Money for Airlines to Fly to Small Towns and Make a Profit
(20.901 Payments for Essential Air Services)
Director
Office of Aviation Analysis, X-50
U.S. Department of Transportation
400 Seventh Street, SW
Washington, DC 20590   202-366-1030

Objectives: To assure that air transportation is provided to eligible communities by subsidizing air carriers when necessary to provide service. Types of assistance: direct payments for specified use. Estimate of annual funds available: Direct payments to air carriers: $50,000,000.

Federal Money Programs For Your Business

* Grants to Women-Owned Businesses to Help Get Contracts from the Department of Transportation

(20.903 Support Mechanisms for Disadvantaged Businesses)
Office of Small and Disadvantaged Business
  Utilization, S-40
Office of the Secretary
400 Seventh Street, SW
Washington, DC 20590   800-532-1169

Objectives: To develop support mechanisms, including liaison and assistance programs, that will provide outreach and technical assistance to small disadvantaged business enterprises (DBEs) to successfully compete on transportation-related contracts. Recipients will provide a communications link between the Department of Transportation; its grantees, recipients, contractors, subcontractors; and minority, women-owned and disadvantaged business enterprises (DBEs) in order to increase their participation in existing DOT programs and DOT funded projects. Types of assistance: project grants (cooperative agreements). Estimate of annual funds available: Cooperative Agreements: $1,100,000.

* Loans to Start a Credit Union

(44.002 Community Development Revolving Loan Program for Credit Unions)
Ms. Joyce Jackson
Community Development Revolving Loan Program
  for Credit Unions
National Credit Union Administration
1775 Duke St.
Alexandria, VA 22314-3428   703-518-6610

Objectives: To support low-income credit unions in their efforts to: (1) stimulate economic development activities which result in increased income, ownership, and employment opportunities for low-income residents; and (2) provide basic financial and related services to residents of their communities. Types of assistance: direct loans. Estimate of annual funds available: Direct Loans: $2,400,000.

* Money if Your Business Was Hurt by a Natural Disaster or Drought

(59.002 Economic Injury Disaster Loans)
Herbert Mitchell
Office of Disaster Assistance
Small Business Administration
409 3rd Street, SW
Washington, DC 20416   202-205-6734
E-mail: {disaster.assistance@sba.gov}

Objectives: To assist business concerns suffering economic injury as a result of Presidential, Small Business Administration (SBA), and/or Secretary of Agriculture declared disasters. Types of assistance: direct loans; guaranteed/insured loans (including immediate participation loans). Estimate of annual funds available: $901,000,000 (Includes funds for 59.002 and 59.008).

* Money for Businesses Hurt by Physical Disaster or Drought

(59.008 Physical Disaster Loans)
Herbert Mitchell
Office of Disaster Assistance
Small Business Administration
409 3rd Street, SW
Washington, DC 20416   202-205-6734

Objectives: To provide loans to the victims of declared physical-type disasters for uninsured losses. Types of assistance: direct loans; guaranteed/insured loans (including immediate participation loans). Estimate of annual funds available: Loans: $901,000,000 (Includes funds for 59.002 and 59.008).

* Money to Start a Venture Capital Company

(59.011 Small Business Investment Companies)
Associate Administrator for Investment
Investment Division
Small Business Administration
409 Third Street, SW
Washington, DC 20416   202-205-6510

Objectives: To establish privately owned and managed investment companies, which are licensed and regulated by the U.S. Small Business Administration; to provide equity capital and long term loan funds to small businesses; and to provide advisory services to small businesses. Types of assistance: direct loans; guaranteed/ insured loans; advisory services and counseling. Estimate of annual funds available: Loans: $1,526,119,000.

* Up to $750,000 to Start Your Own Business

(59.012 Small Business Loans)
Director, Loan Policy and Procedures Branch
Small Business Administration
409 Third Street, SW
Washington, DC 20416   202-205-6570

Objectives: To provide guaranteed loans to small businesses which are unable to obtain financing in the private credit marketplace, but can demonstrate an ability to repay loans granted. Guaranteed loans are made available to low-income business owners or businesses located in areas of high unemployment, non-profit sheltered workshops and other similar organizations which produce goods or services; to small businesses being established, acquired or owned by handicapped individuals; and to enable small businesses to manufacture, design, market, install, or service specific energy measures. The SBA's 7(a) lending authority includes: 1) the Low Documentation Loan Program (Low Doc); 2) the Cap Line Program; 3) FA$ TRAK Program, formerly the Small Loan Express; 4) the Women's Prequalification Program; and 5) Minority Prequalification Program. Types of assistance: guaranteed/insured loans (including immediate participation loans). Estimate of annual funds available: Loans: $10,000,000,000.

* Help for Contractors and Others to Get Bonded to Obtain Contracts

(59.016 Bond Guarantees for Surety Companies)
Assistant Administrator Robert J. Moffitt
Office of Surety Guarantees
Small Business Administration
409 3rd Street, SW
Washington, DC 20416   202-205-6540

Objectives: To guarantee surety bonds issued by commercial surety companies for small contractors unable to obtain a bond without a guarantee. Guarantees are for up to 90 percent of the total amount of bond. Types of assistance: insurance (guaranteed surety bonds). Estimate of annual funds available: Guaranteed Surety Bonds: $1,672,000,000.

* Money to Local Organizations to Finance Small Businesses

(59.041 Certified Development Company Loans [504 Loans])
Office of Loan Programs
Small Business Administration
409 3rd Street SW
Washington, DC 20416   202-205-6485

Objectives: To assist small business concerns by providing long-term fixed rate financing for fixed assets through the sale of debentures to private investors. Types of assistance: guaranteed/insured loans. Estimate of annual funds available: Guaranteed Loans: $3,000,000,000.

* Grants to Local Organizations That Help Women Start Their Own Businesses

(59.043 Women's Business Ownership Assistance)
Harriet Fredman
Office of Women's Business Ownership
Small Business Administration
409 3rd Street, SW
Washington, DC 20416   202-205-6673

Objectives: To fund non-profit economic development organizations to assist, through training and counseling, small business concerns owned and controlled by women, and to remove, in so far as possible, the discriminatory barriers that are encountered by women in accessing capital and promoting their businesses. Types of assistance: project grants (cooperative agreements or contracts). Estimate of annual funds available: Cooperative Agreements: $9,000,000.

* Grants to Local Organizations That Help Veterans Start Their Own Businesses

(59.044 Veterans Entrepreneurial Training and Counseling)
William Truitt
Office of Veteran Affairs
Small Business Administration

Federal Money Programs For Your Business

6th Floor, 409 3rd Street, SW
Washington, DC 20416   202-205-6773

Objectives: To design, develop, administer, and evaluate an entrepreneurial and procurement training and counseling program for U.S. veterans. Types of assistance: project grants (cooperative agreements). Estimate of annual funds available: Grants: $40,000.

* Money to Local Organizations to Provide Micro-Loans

(59.046 Microloan Demonstration Program)
Small Business Administration
Office of Financial Assistance
Microenterprise Development Branch
409 Third Street SW, Eighth Floor
Washington, DC 20416
Mail Code 7881   202-205-6490

Objectives: To assist women, low-income, and minority entrepreneurs, business owners, and other individuals possessing the capability to operate successful business concerns and to assist small business concerns in areas suffering from lack of credit due to economic downturns. Under the program, the Small Business Administration (SBA) will make loans to private, non-profit and quasi-governmental organizations (intermediary lenders) who will use the loan funds to make short-term, fixed interest rate microloans in amounts up to $25,000 to start-up, newly established, and growing small business concerns. These microloans are to be used exclusively for working capital, inventory, supplies, furniture, fixtures, machinery, and/or equipment. In addition, the SBA will make grants to participating intermediary lenders to provide marketing, management, and technical assistance to borrowers receiving microloans. In addition, the SBA will make grants to non-profit organizations, which are not intermediary lenders, to provide marketing, management, and technical assistance to low-income individuals seeking private sector financing for their businesses. Under the program, SBA will also provide training for intermediary lenders and non-lenders participating in the program. Types of assistance: formula grants; project grants; direct loans. Estimate of annual funds available: Direct Loans: $60,000,000; Loan Guarantees: $11,995,000; Formula Grants: $12,000,000.

* Money for Disabled Veterans to Start New Businesses

(64.116 Vocational Rehabilitation for Disabled Veterans)
Veterans Benefits Administration
Vocational Rehabilitation and Counseling Service (28)
U.S. Department of Veterans Affairs
Washington, DC 20420   202-273-7413

Objectives: To provide all services and assistance necessary to enable service-disabled veterans and service persons hospitalized or receiving outpatient medical care services or treatment for a service-connected disability pending discharge to get and keep a suitable job. When employment is not reasonably feasible, the program can provide the needed services and assistance to help the individual learn skills to achieve maximum independence in daily living. Types of assistance: direct payments with unrestricted use; direct payments for specified use; direct loans; advisory services and counseling. Estimate of annual funds available: Direct payments: $402,907,000; Loan advances: $2,401,000.

* Help for Retired Military to Start a Business

(64.123 Vocational Training for Certain Veterans Receiving VA Pension)
Veterans Benefits Administration
Vocational Rehabilitation and Counseling Service (28)
U.S. Department of Veterans Affairs
Washington, DC 20420   202-273-7413

Objectives: To assist new pension recipients to resume and maintain gainful employment by providing vocational training and other services. Types of assistance: direct payments for specified use; advisory services and counseling. Estimate of annual funds available: Direct Payments: $234,000 in 1998.

* Money to Invest in Companies Overseas

(70.002 Foreign Investment Guaranties)
Information Officer
Overseas Private Investment Corporation
1100 New York Ave., NW
Washington, DC 20527   202-336-8799
    Fax: 202-336-8700
E-mail: {OPIC@opic.gov}
www.opic.gov

Objectives: To provide financing for projects sponsored by eligible U.S. investors in friendly developing countries and emerging economies throughout the world, thereby assisting development goals and improving U.S. competitiveness, creating American jobs and increasing U.S. exports. Types of assistance: guaranteed/insured loans; direct loans. Estimate of annual funds available: $50,000,000 in subsidy obligations is expected to support $2,000,000,000 in loans and direct loans.

* Insurance Against Your Business in Another Country Being Hurt by Foreign Politics

(70.003 Foreign Investment Insurance)
Information Officer
Overseas Private Investment Corporation
1100 New York Ave., NW
Washington, DC 20527   202-336-8799
    Fax: 202-336-8700
E-mail: {OPIC@opic.gov}
www.opic.gov

Objectives: To insure investments of eligible U.S. investors in developing countries and emerging markets, against the political risks of inconvertibility, expropriation, and political violence. Special programs include insuring contractors and exporters against arbitrary drawings of letters of credit posted as bid, performance or advance payment guaranties, energy exploration and development, and leasing operations. Types of assistance: insurance. Estimate of annual funds available: Insurance Issued: $9,000,000,000.

* Free Patent Rights to Government Discoverers of Energy Saving Ideas

(81.003 Granting of Patent Licenses)
Robert J. Marchick
Office of the Assistant General Counsel for Patents
U.S. Department of Energy
Washington, DC 20585   202-586-2802

Objectives: To encourage widespread utilization of inventions covered by Department of Energy (DOE) owned patents. Types of assistance: dissemination of technical information. Estimate of annual funds available: (Salaries) Not identifiable.

* Money to Work on an Energy-Related Invention

(81.036 Energy-Related Inventions)
Sandra Glatt
Office of Industrial Technologies (EE-23)
U.S. Department of Energy
1000 Independence Avenue, SW
Washington, DC 20585   202-586-3987

Objectives: To encourage innovation in developing non-nuclear energy technology by providing assistance to individual and small business companies in the development of promising energy-related inventions. Types of assistance: project grants; use of property, facilities, and equipment; advisory services and counseling; dissemination of technical information. Estimate of annual funds available: Grants: $2,900,000.

* Grants to Local Organizations That Help Women and Minorities Get Department of Energy Contracts

(81.082 Management and Technical Assistance for Minority Business Enterprises)
Sterling Nichols
Office of Economic Impact and Diversity
U.S. Department of Energy
ED-1, Forrestal Building, Room 5B-110
Washington, DC 20585   202-586-8698

Objectives: (1) To support increased participation of minority, and women-owned and operated business enterprises (MBE's); (2) to develop energy-related minority business assistance programs and public/private partnerships to provide technical assistance to MBE's; (3) to transfer applicable technology from national federal laboratories to MBE's; and (4) to increase the Department of Energy's (DOE) high technology research and development contracting activities. Types of assistance: advisory services and counseling. Estimate of annual funds available: Contracts and Grants: $480,000.

* Grants to Develop Energy Saving Products

(81.086 Conservation Research and Development)
Energy Efficiency and Renewable Energy Programmatic Offices:

Federal Money Programs For Your Business

Office of Building Technology
State and Community Programs
Contact: Lynda Dancy — 202-586-2300

Office of Transportation Technologies
Contact: Nancy Blackwell — 202-586-6715

Office of Industrial Technologies
Contact: Beatrice Cunningham — 202-586-0098

Office of Utility Technologies
Contact: Gloria Elliott — 202-586-4142

Objectives: To conduct a balanced long-term research effort in the areas of buildings, industry, transportation. Grants will be offered to develop and transfer to the nonfederal sector various energy conservation technologies. Types of assistance: project grants. Estimate of annual funds available: Grants: not separately identified. (Note: Discretionary funds for grants are not specifically contained in the President's request for Energy Conservation Programs. However, the Department does issue grants if found to be appropriate as a result of unsolicited proposals that clearly are consistent with program objectives and are appropriate as grants in lieu of other contractual methods. Unsolicited proposals have received grants totalling approximately $2,000,000 to $2,500,000 over the past 5 years.)

* Grants to Work on Solar Energy Products

(81.087 Renewable Energy Research and Development)
Energy Efficiency and Renewable Energy Programmatic Offices:
Office of Building Technology
State and Community Programs
Contact: Lynda Dancy — 202-586-2300

Residential, Commercial and Institutional Buildings
Contact: Regina Washington — 202-586-1660

Office of Industrial Technologies
Contact: Beatrice Cunningham — 202-586-0098

Office of Transportation Technologies
Contact: Nancy Blackwell — 202-586-6715

Office of Utility Technologies
Contact: Gloria Elliott — 202-586-4142

Objectives: To conduct balanced research and development efforts in the following energy technologies; solar buildings, photovoltaics, solar thermal, biomass, alcohol fuels, urban waste, wind, and geothermal. Grants will be offered to develop and transfer to the nonfederal sector various renewable energy technologies. Types of assistance: project grants. Estimate of annual funds available: Grants: not separately identified. (Note: Discretionary funds for grants are not specifically contained in the President's request for Renewable Energy Research and Development Programs. However, the Department does issue grants if found to be appropriate as a result of unsolicited proposals that clearly are consistent with program objectives and are appropriate as grants in lieu of other contractual methods. Unsolicited proposals have received grants totalling approximately $1,500,000 to $2,000,000 over the past 5 years.)

* Grants to Develop Uses of Fossil Fuels

(81.089 Fossil Energy Research and Development)
Mary J. Roland
Fossil Energy Program, FE-122
U.S. Department of Energy
Germantown, MD 20545 — 301-903-3514

Objectives: The mission of the Fossil Energy (FE) Research and Development program is to promote the development and use of environmentally and economically superior technologies for supply, conversion, delivery and utilization of fossil fuels. These activities will involve cooperation with industry, DOE Laboratories, universities, and states. Success in this mission will benefit the Nation through lower energy costs, reduced environmental impact, increased technology exports, and reduced dependence on insecure energy sources. Types of assistance: project grants; project grants (cooperative agreements). Estimate of annual funds available: Grants and cooperative agreements: $7,000,000.

* Grants to Businesses That Employ People with Disabilities

(84.234 Projects with Industry)
Ms. Martha Muskie
Rehabilitation Services Administration
U.S. Department of Education
600 Independence Ave.
Washington, DC 20202 — 202-205-7320

Objectives: To create and expand job and career opportunities for individuals with disabilities in the competitive labor market, to provide appropriate placement resources by engaging private industry in training and placement. Types of assistance: project grants; project grants (cooperative agreements). Estimate of annual funds available: Grants: $22,071,000. (Note: This amount may change upon enactment of the Rehabilitation Act.)

State Money and Help For Your Business

Who Can Use State Money?

All states require that funds be used solely by state residents. But that shouldn't limit you to exploring possibilities only in the state in which you currently reside. If you reside in Maine, but Massachusetts agrees to give you $100,000 to start your own business, it would be worth your while to consider moving to Massachusetts. Shop around for the best deal.

Types Of State Money And Help Available

Each state has different kinds and amounts of money and assistance programs available, but these sources of financial and counseling help are constantly being changed. What may not be available this year may very well be available next. Therefore, in the course of your exploration, you might want to check in with the people who operate the business "hotlines" to discover if anything new has been added to the states' offerings.

Described below are the major kinds of programs which are offered by most of the states.

Information

Hotlines or One-Stop Shops are available in many states through a toll-free number that hooks you up with someone who will either tell you what you need to know or refer you to someone who can. These hotlines are invaluable -- offering information on everything from business permit regulations to obscure financing programs. Most states also offer some kind of booklet that tells you to how to start-up a business in that state. Ask for it. It will probably be free.

Small Business Advocates operate in all fifty states and are part of a national organization (the National Association of State Small Business Advocates) devoted to helping small business people function efficiently with their state governments. They are a good source for help in cutting through bureaucratic red tape.

Funding Programs

Free Money can come in the form of grants, and works the same as free money from the federal government. You do not have to pay it back.

Loans from state governments work in the same way as those from the federal government -- they are given directly to entrepreneurs. Loans are usually at interest rates below the rates charged at commercial institutions and are also set aside for those companies which have trouble getting a loan elsewhere. This makes them an ideal source for riskier kinds of ventures.

Loan Guarantees are similar to those offered by the federal government. For this program, the state government will go to the bank with you and co-sign your loan. This, too, is ideal for high risk ventures which normally would not get a loan.

Interest Subsidies On Loans is a unique concept not used by the federal government. In this case, the state will subsidize the interest rate you are charged by a bank. For example, if the bank gives you a loan for $50,000 at 10 percent per year interest, your interest payments will be $5,000 per year. With an interest subsidy you might have to pay only $2,500 since the state will pay the other half. This is like getting the loan at 5 percent instead of 10 percent.

Industrial Revenue Bonds Or General Obligation Bonds are a type of financing that can be used to purchase only fixed assets, such as a factory or equipment. In the case of Industrial Revenue Bonds the state will raise money from the general public to buy your equipment. Because the state acts as the middleman, the people who lend you the money do not have to pay federal taxes on the interest they charge you. As a result, you get the money cheaper because they get a tax break. If the state issues General Obligation Bonds to buy your equipment, the arrangement will be similar to that for an Industrial Revenue Bond except that the state promises to repay the loan if you cannot.

Matching Grants supplement and abet federal grant programs. These kinds of grants could make an under-capitalized project go forward. Awards usually hinge on the usefulness of the project to its surrounding locality.

Loans To Agricultural Businesses are offered in states with large rural, farming populations. They are available solely to farmers and/or agribusiness entrepreneurs.

Loans To Exporters are available in some states as a kind of gap financing to cover the expenses involved in fulfilling a contract.

Energy Conservation Loans are made to small businesses to finance the installation of energy-saving equipment or devices.

Special Regional Loans are ear-marked for specific areas in a state that may have been hard hit economically or suffer from under-development. If you live in one of these regions, you may be eligible for special funds.

High Tech Loans help fledgling companies develop or introduce new products into the marketplace.

Loans To Inventors help the entrepreneur develop or market new products.

Local Government Loans are used for start-up and expansion of businesses within the designated locality.

Childcare Facilities Loans help businesses establish on-site daycare facilities.

Loans To Women And/Or Minorities are available in almost every state from funds specifically reserved for economically disadvantaged groups.

State Money and Help For Your Business

Many federally funded programs are administered by state governments. Among them are the following programs:

The SBA 7(A) Guaranteed and *Direct Loan* program can guarantee up to 90 percent of a loan made through a private lender (up to $750,000), or make direct loans of up to $150,000.

The SBA 504 establishes Certified Development Companies whose debentures are guaranteed by the SBA. Equity participation of the borrower must be at least 10 percent, private financing 60 percent and CDC participation at a maximum of 40 percent, up to $750,000.

Small Business Innovative Research Grants (SBIR) award between $20,000 to $50,000 to entrepreneurs to support six months of research on a technical innovation. They are then eligible for up to $500,000 to develop the innovation.

Small Business Investment Companies (SBIC) license, regulate and provide financial assistance in the form of equity financing, long-term loans, and management services.

Community Development Block Grants are available to cities and counties for the commercial rehabilitation of existing buildings or structures used for business, commercial, or industrial purposes. Grants of up to $500,000 can be made. Every $15,000 of grant funds invested must create at least one full-time job, and at least 51 percent of the jobs created must be for low and moderate income families.

Farmers Home Administration (FmHA) Emergency Disaster Loans are available in counties where natural disaster has substantially affected farming, ranching or aquaculture production.

FmHA Farm Loan Guarantees are made to family farmers and ranchers to enable them to obtain funds from private lenders. Funds must be used for farm ownership, improvements, and operating purposes.

FmHA Farm Operating Loans to meet operating expenses, finance recreational and nonagricultural enterprises, to add to family income, and to pay for mandated safety and pollution control changes are available at variable interest rates. Limits are $200,000 for an insured farm operating loan and $400,000 for a guaranteed loan.

FmHA Farm Ownership Loans can be used for a wide range of farm improvement projects. Limits are $200,000 for an insured loan and $300,000 for a guaranteed loan.

FmHA Soil And Water Loans must be used by individual farmers and ranchers to develop, conserve, and properly use their land and water resources and to help abate pollution. Interest rates are variable; each loan must be secured by real estate.

FmHA Youth Project Loans enable young people to borrow for income-producing projects sponsored by a school or 4H club.

Assistance Programs

Management Training is offered by many states in subjects ranging from bookkeeping to energy conservation.

Business Consulting is offered on almost any subject. Small Business Development Centers are the best source for this kind of assistance.

Market Studies to help you sell your goods or services within or outside the state are offered by many states. They all also have State Data Centers which not only collect demographic and other information about markets within the state, but also have access to federal data which can pinpoint national markets. Many states also provide the services of graduate business students at local universities to do the legwork and analysis for you.

Business Site Selection is done by specialists in every state who will identify the best place to locate a business.

Licensing, Regulation, And Permits information is available from most states through "one-stop shop" centers by calling a toll-free number. There you'll get help in finding your way through the confusion of registering a new business.

Employee Training Programs offer on-site training and continuing education opportunities.

Research And Development assistance for entrepreneurs is a form of assistance that is rapidly increasing as more and more states try to attract high technology-related companies. Many states are even setting up clearing houses so that small businesses can have one place to turn to find expertise throughout a statewide university system.

Procurement Programs have been established in some states to help you sell products to state, federal, and local governments.

Export Assistance is offered to identify overseas markets. Some states even have overseas offices to drum up business prospects for you.

Assistance In Finding Funding is offered in every state, particularly through regional Small Business Development Centers. They will not only identify funding sources in the state and federal governments but will also lead you through the complicated application process.

Special Help For Minorities And Women is available in almost every state to help boost the participation of women and minorities in small business ventures. They offer special funding programs and, often, one-on-one counseling to assure a start-up success.

Venture Capital Networking is achieved through computer databases that hook up entrepreneurs and venture capitalists. This service is usually free of charge. In fact, the demand for small business investment opportunities is so great that some states require the investor to pay to be listed.

Inventors Associations have been established to encourage and assist inventors in developing and patenting their products.

Annual Governors' Conferences give small business people the chance to air their problems with representatives from state agencies and the legislature.

Small Business Development Centers (SBDCs), funded jointly by the federal and state governments, are usually associated with the state university system. SBDCs are a god-send to small business people. They will not only help you figure out if your business project is feasible, but also help you draw up a sensible business plan, apply for funding, and check in with you frequency once your business is up and running to make sure it stays that way.

Tourism programs are prominent in states whose revenues are heavily dependent on the tourist trade. They are specifically aimed at businesses in the tourist industries.

Small Business Institutes at local colleges use senior level business students as consultants to help develop business plans or plan expansions.

Technology Assistance Centers help high tech companies and entrepreneurs establish new businesses and plan business expansions.

On-Site Energy Audits are offered free of charge by many states to help control energy costs and improve energy efficiency for small businesses. Some states also conduct workshops to encourage energy conservation measures.

Minority Business Development Centers offer a wide range of services from initial counseling on how to start a business to more complex issues of planning and growth.

Business Information Centers (BICs) provide the latest in high-tech hardware, software, and telecommunications to help small businesses get started. BIC is a place where business owners and aspiring business owners can go to use hardware/software, hard copy books, and publications to plan their business, expand an existing business, or venture into new business areas. Also, on-site counseling is available.

Alabama

Alabama Development Office
401 Adams Avenue
Montgomery, AL 36104-4340
800-248-0033
334-242-0400
Fax: 334-242-0415
www.ado.state.al.us

Alabama Department of Revenue
P.O. Box 327001
Montgomery, AL 36132-7001
334-242-1170
alaweb.asc.edu

* Business Assistance

For all items without a separate address, contact the Alabama Development Office at the address listed above.

Alabama Development Office: A one-stop source for business support and incentives that will tailor programs to meet individual companies' needs.
Economic Development Association: Members exchange information and ideas and participate in courses and other professional development seminars.
Technology Assistance Program: Assists with technology-oriented problems, maintains a database containing information about technical assistance available from federal sources and from other sources throughout the State of Alabama. Contact: Alabama Technology Assistance Program, University of Alabama at Birmingham, 1717 11th Ave. South, Suite 419, Birmingham, AL 35294; 205-934-7260.

Department of Agriculture and Industry: Supplies both information and technical support to farmers, businesses and consumers. Contact: Department of Agriculture and Industry, P.O. Box 3336, Montgomery, AL 36109; 334-240-7171.
Alabama Industrial Development Training: Offers recruiting, assessing and training potential employees; developing and producing training materials, and locating facilities; and, delivering customized services. Contact: Alabama Industrial Development and Training, One Technology Court, Montgomery, AL 36116; 334-242-4158.
Alabama Answers: Comprehensive handbook on doing business in Alabama.

* Business Financing

For all items without a separate address, contact the Alabama Development Office at the address listed above.

Industrial Revenue Bonds: Financing available for land, buildings and equipment.
Economic Development Loan Program: Loans for the purchase of land, buildings, machinery and equipment for new and expanding businesses.
Revolving Loan Funds: Gap financing for land, buildings, equipment, renovation and working capital for companies creating jobs.
Business Loan Guarantee Program: Provides funding for the acquisitions of fixed assets or working capital for companies creating or retaining jobs in economically distressed areas.
Guaranteed Business and Industrial Loan Program: Companies located in communities under 50,000 can receive guaranteed long-term loans for real estate improvements.
Rural Economic Development Loan and Grant Program: Offered through the Rural Electrification Administration for project feasibility studies, start-up costs and incubator projects.
Venture Capital Funds: Small companies may receive equity capital and long-term loans.
Local and Regional Development Organizations: More than 100 throughout the state assist in securing loan assistance.
Section 108 Loan Guarantee: Provides communities with an efficient source of financing for economic development and large-scale physical development projects.
Tennessee Valley Authority's Economic Development Loan Fund: Multi-million dollar revolving loan program that provides financing for new industrial plants, plant expansions, plant retention, and infrastructure development such as speculative industrial buildings and industrial parks.

* Tax Incentives

For all items without a separate address, contact the Alabama Development Office at the address listed above.

No inventory tax for businesses.
Corporate income tax limited to five percent.
Income Tax Capital Credit: If a business entity invests in a qualifying project that meets certain requirements and is approved by the Alabama Department of Revenue, the company may receive an annual credit against its income tax liability generated from the qualifying project. The capital credit is equivalent to 5% of the capital costs of the qualifying project, and can be utilized for a period of 20 years beginning during the year the project is placed in service.
Net Operating Loss Carryforward: Corporate income tax law provides for a 15-year carryforward of net operating losses. In computing net income, a corporation is allowed a deduction for the sum of the net operating losses which are carried forward. Each net operating loss may be carried forward and deducted only during the 15 consecutive year period immediately following the year in which it arose.
Pollution Control Equipment Deduction: All amounts invested in pollution control equipment/materials acquired or constructed in Alabama primarily for the control, reduction, or elimination of air or water pollution are deducted directly from the income apportioned to Alabama.
Enterprise Zone Credit: The corporate income tax enterprise zone credit is offered to help encourage economic growth to areas in Alabama that are considered economically depressed. To qualify for this credit, a business must meet detailed requirements concerning site location and employee qualifications.
Educational Tax Credit: An employer could qualify to receive a credit of 20% of the actual cost of an employer sponsored educational program that enhances basic skills of employees up to and including the twelfth grade functional level.
Foreign Corporation Deduction for Manufacturing Facilities: Alabama law contains several provisions to allow foreign corporations to significantly reduce or almost eliminate their corporate franchise tax liability.

State Money - Alaska

Assessed Value fixed by Alabama Constitution: Amendment 373 of the Constitution provides that business property will be assessed at 20% of its fair market value. That is, for property with a fair market value of $1,000,000, the assessed value would be $200,000 ($1,000,000 x 20%). The combined state and local millage rate would then be applied to the assessed value.

Low Millage Rates: Section 214 of the Constitution limits the state millage rate on both real and personal property to 6.5 mills. This rate is equivalent to a tax of $6.50 for every $1000 of assessed value. However, both cities and counties may levy millage rates in addition to the state's 6.5 mills. These local rates vary but the average rate for any one locality is 43 mills, including the state's 6.5 mills. For business property with a fair market value of $1,000,000 the average property tax would be only $8,600 ($1,000,000 x 20% x .043).

Tax Incentive Reform Act: Allows qualified industries to receive abatements of non-educational ad valorem taxes for new businesses locating to Alabama, and for expansions of existing facilities in Alabama.

Inventory and Raw Materials Exemption: All stocks of goods, wares, and merchandise held for resale, as well as raw materials, are statutorily exempt from ad valorem taxes.

Corporate Shares Tax Deductions: Domestic corporations (incorporated in Alabama) are responsible for the payment of corporate shares tax. This tax is actually an ad valorem tax on the assessed value of capital stock of the corporation. The shares tax is calculated like any other ad valorem tax. There are several deductions from the value of shares that can be considered as tax incentives for Alabama domestic corporations.

* Exports

For all items without a separate address, contact the Alabama Development Office at the address listed above.

International Trade Center: Services offered include foreign market research, strategic planning and consulting, implementation recommendations, training seminars and general information. Contact: Alabama International Trade Center, University of Alabama, Box 870396, Tuscaloosa, AL 35287; 205-348-7621.

Alabama Development Office: Offers trade promotion services to Alabama manufacturers, including:
- Participation in overseas catalog shows, trade shows, and trade missions
- Opportunities to meet one-on-one with foreign buyers visiting Alabama
- Listing in the *Alabama International Trade Directory*, a publication that is disseminated worldwide
- *Public/Private Grant Program*: Designed to assist Alabama companies in expanding export activities through participation in foreign trade shows and missions
- *Representative Offices*: Germany, Japan, and South Korea

* Women and Minorities

For all items without a separate address, contact the Alabama Development Office at the address listed above.

Office of Minority Business Enterprise: Assists minorities in achieving effective and equitable participation in the American free enterprise system and in overcoming social and economic disadvantages that have limited their participation in the past. Management and technical assistance is provided to minority firms on request. Contact: Office of Minority Business Enterprise, 401 Adams Ave., Montgomery, AL 36130; 334-242-2224; 800-447-4191.

* Small Business Administration Offices

James Barksdale
2121 8th Avenue North., Suite 200
Birmingham, AL 35203
205-731-1344
Fax: 205-731-1404

Alaska

Alaska Department of Commerce and Economic Development
P.O. Box 110800
Juneau, AK 98111
907-465-2017
800-478-LOAN
Fax: 907-465-3767
www.commerce.state.ak.us

* Business Assistance

For all items without a separate address, contact the Alaska Department of Commerce and Economic Development at the address listed above.

Division of Trade and Development: Has information on assistance programs, licensing requirements, taxation, labor laws, financial assistance programs and state sources of information. They have a Small Business Advocate that provides assistance in cutting red tape and has information and expertise in dealing with state, federal and local agencies

Alaska Product Preference, Forest Product Preference, and The Alaska Recycled Product Preference Programs: These programs provide incentives for Alaska businesses responding to bids or proposals for state contracts by giving preferential consideration. The Alaska Product Preference Program and the Alaska Forest Product Preference Program can provide a cost preference of up to 7%, while the Recycled Product Preference Program offers a 5% preference. For these programs, contact Division of Trade & Development, 3601 C Street, Suite 700, Anchorage, AK 99503; 907-269-8121; {www.commerce.state.ak.us/trade/econ/prodpref.htm}.

Buy Alaska: The Buy Alaska Program's mission is to assist businesses, consumers, and government entities in finding competitive Alaskan sources for goods and services with the goal of keeping more dollars in Alaska. The Buy Alaska Program offers the free service of researching buying needs and "matching" buyers with sellers. Businesses and consumers seeking to buy competitively-priced goods and services can get help from Buy Alaska in identifying local Alaskan vendors and providers from which to make their purchases. For these programs, contact Buy Alaska, University of Alaska, Small Business Development Center, 430 W. 7th Avenue, Suite 110, Anchorage, AK 99501; 907-274-7232; 800-478-7232; {www.alaskanet.com/buyalaska}.

* Business Financing

For all items without a separate address, contact the Alaska Department of Commerce and Economic Development at the address listed above.

Sustainable Development Program: The program's primary function is to provide (grant) seed money to entities that propose viable sustainable development projects that are community based and supported. The program is not intended to fund pure research. The maximum funding available for any one project is $50,000. But, it's anticipated that most applicants will receive less, thereby allowing the program to fund between six to twelve sustainable development projects. This program is not intended to provide the sole or majority funding of a project. The program will continue funding projects for as long as money is available.

Alaska Science and Technology Foundation Grants (ASTF): Major individual grants of over $2,000 and group grants are both available under this program. Projects that provide economic development, direct benefits and utilize end user participation are considered ideal. ASTF typically requires a financial match equal to the amount they contribute and technology projects that develop a product or process are required to repay ASTF funds through revenue, license fees or profit from sales of the product. For this program, contact Alaska Science and Technology Foundation, 4500 Diplomacy Drive, Suite 515, Anchorage, AK 99506; 907-272-4333; {pprc.pnl.gov/pprc/rfp/astf.html}.

Alaska Growth Capital: This is a commercial financial institution, licensed and regulated by the State of Alaska. It is not regulated as a bank, but rather as a Business and Industrial Development Corporation (BIDCO). BIDCOs do not accept deposits and do not provide consumer lending. BIDCOs focus exclusively on financing businesses. For more information, contact Alaska Growth Capital, 201 Arctic Slope Avenue, Suite 100, Anchorage, AK 99518; 907-349-4904; 888-315-4904; {www.akgrowth.com}.

Power Project Fund: Provides loans to local utilities, local governments or independent power producers for the development or upgrade of electric power facilities, including conservation, bulk fuel storage and waste energy conservation, or potable water supply projects. Loan term is related to the life of the project. For more information, contact Department of Community and Regional Affairs, Division of Energy, 333 West 4th Avenue, Suite 220, Anchorage, AK 99501-2341; 907-269-4625; {www.comregaf.state.ak.us/doehome.htm}.

The Polaris Fund: The purpose of the Polaris Fund is to finance young companies with potential to achieve profitable sales by providing equity capital. Ideal companies should have an experienced management team, an innovative, distinctive product with a $100-$500 million growing market and a well-defined channel for sales. Polaris investments are usually in the $100,000 to $500,000 range, and favor companies that align Polaris closely with management. For more information, contact Jim Yarmon, c/o Yarmon Investments, 840 K Street, #201, Anchorage, AK 99501; 907-276-4466.

Business Incentive Program: Under this program companies will be reimbursed

State Money - Arizona

(rather than be paid up front) for designated portions of relocation costs, site development costs, special employee training not covered by other programs, and special analysis of sites in Alaska. The program was passed into law in April 1998 and is limited to $3 million annually. Contact: Bill Paulick, Division of Trade & Development, P.O. Box 110804, Juneau, AK 99811-0804; 907-465-3961; {E-mail: Bill_Paulick@commerce.state.ak.us}.

Small Business Economic Development Revolving Loan Fund: This program was established in 1987 in conjunction with the U.S. Department of Commerce, Economic Development Administration (EDA). The purpose of the program is to provide private sector employment in the areas designated by EDA. The maximum loan amount is $300,000. Applicants are required to obtain additional private, non-public financing of approximately twice the amount requested. The interest rate of prime minus 4 points is set by the Loan Administration Board consisting of three members from the existing divisional loan committee and two members from the private sector. The board is responsible for setting loan policy and for making all major loan decisions. For more information, contact Alaska Department of Commerce and Economic Development, Division of Investments, P.O. Box 34159, Juneau, AK 99803; 907-465-2510; {www.commerce.state.ak.us/investments/}.

Commercial Fishing Revolving Loan Fund: Commercial fishing loans are available for various purposes at prime plus two percent (up to a maximum of 10.5%) for a 15-year term. All loans must be secured by adequate collateral. Contact: Alaska Department of Commerce and Economic Development, Division of Investments, P.O. Box 34159, Juneau, AK 99803; 907-465-2510; {www.commerce.state.ak.us/investments/}.

Development Finance: Alaska Industrial Development and Export Authority (AIDEA) may own and operate projects that provide infrastructure support for resource development and bring economic benefits to Alaska. To qualify a project must be endorsed by the local government where the project will be sited and be economically feasible. Contact: Alaska Industrial Development and Export Authority, 480 West Tudor, Anchorage, AK 99503; 907-269-3000; Fax: 907-269-3044; {www.alaska.net/~aidea}.

* Tax Incentives

For all items without a separate address, contact the Alaska Department of Commerce and Economic Development at the address listed above.

Work Opportunity Tax Credit (WOTC): Offers employers tax credits as an incentive to hire people from seven target groups including Alaska Temporary Assistance Program (ATAP) and Aid for Families with Dependent Children (AFDC) recipients, food stamp recipients, veterans, vocational rehabilitation recipients, ex-felons, and high risk youth. The credit amount is 40% of up to $6,000 in qualified first year wages with a maximum credit of $2,400.

Welfare-to-Work Tax Credit (W2W): The W2W tax credit is available for hiring long-term ATAP and AFDC clients. The W2W tax credit is 35% of the first $10,000 in wages paid the first year, and 50% of the first $10,000 paid for the second year. The maximum tax credit is $3,500 the first year and $5,000 the second year for a total of $8,500.

For information on these programs, contact Alaska Employment Service, WOTC Coordinator, P.O. Box 25509, Juneau, AK 99802; 907-465-5925; {www.state.ak.us/local/akpages/LABOR/offices/win_of.htm}.

Exploration Incentive: Up to $20 million in qualifying costs can be credited against future state corporate income tax, mining license tax and production royalties. Geophysical and geochemical surveys, trenching, bulk sampling, drilling, metallurgical testing and underground exploration are included as qualifying costs. Unused credit can be retained for 15 years and may be assigned to successors in interest. For more information, contact Department of Natural Resources, Division of Mining, 3601 C Street, Suite 884, Anchorage, AK 99503; 907-269-8600; {www.dnr.state.ak.us}.

Depreciable Property: 18% of the federal income tax credit for investment in specified depreciable property can be applied to Alaska state corporate income tax. Each tax year, as the property is put into use in the state, up to $20 million of qualified investments may be claimed with the exception of the unlimited credit allowed on pollution control facilities. Contact: Alaska Department of Revenue, Income & Excise Audit Division, P.O. Box 110420, Juneau, AK 99811-0420; 907-465-2320; {www.revenue.state.ak.us/index.htm}.

* Exports

For all items without a separate address, contact the Alaska Department of Commerce and Economic Development at the address listed above.

Division of Trade and Development: Trade representatives help to promote Alaska products and services by providing information and access to markets, acting as liaisons between domestic and foreign markets, and promoting investment in Alaska's natural resources. Contact: Division of Trade & Development, 3601 C Street, Suite 700, Anchorage AK 99503; 907-269-8121; {www.commerce.state.ak.us/trade/econ/prodpref.htm}.

Alaska Industrial Development Export Authority (AIDEA): AIDEA assists businesses through two programs:

1. *Loan Participation*: New or existing projects can receive long term financing or the refinancing of existing loans. Eligible projects include commercial facilities such as office buildings, warehouses, retail establishments, hotels, and manufacturing facilities. AIDEA participation may total up to 80% of a commercial lending institution loan with a maximum of $10 million.

2. *Business and Export Assistance*: This loan guarantee program provides financial institutions with up to an 80% guarantee on the principal of a loan. AIDEA's added support can make project financing, refinancing, and working capital guarantees up to $1 million available to borrowers who might not otherwise find commercial financing.

Accelerated Amortization Program: Under this program, AIDEA may allow the financial institution to amortize its portion of the loan using an accelerated amortization schedule if the project can support the increased debt service, and if the shortened schedule is necessary for the bank's participation. Borrowers may obtain such financing for manufacturing facilities, real estate and equipment under the Loan Participation Program.

Contact: Alaska Industrial Development and Export Authority, 480 West Tudor, Anchorage, AK 99503; 907-269-3000; Fax: 907-269-3044; {www.alaska.net/~aidea}.

* Small Business Administration Offices

Frank Cox
222 W. 8th Avenue
Box 67 Room A36
Anchorage, AK 99513
907-271-4022
Fax: 907-271-4545

Arizona

Department of Commerce
3800 N. Central, Suite 1650
Phoenix, AZ 85012
602-280-1480
800-542-5684
Fax: 620-280-1339
www.commerce.state.az.us/fr_abc.shtml

* Business Assistance

For all items without a separate address, contact the Arizona Department of Commerce at the address listed above.

Arizona Business Connection: A resource center for information, referrals and advice for every stage of small business development. Representatives are available to answer questions and provide a free custom packet.

Small Business Advocate: Works with chambers of commerce and other groups to develop policies and programs that will address fundamental statewide issues of concern to all small businesses.
- Develops customized packets of information and licenses required for small business start-up, expansion, and relocation.
- Provides the booklet *Guide To Establishing and Operating a Business In Arizona* which includes an extensive directory and resources for referrals and networking opportunities.
- Provides coordination and publicity for programs and services that assist minority and women business owners, and assists state agencies in certification of minority and women owned businesses.
- Conducts seminars to help local companies procure goods and services from qualified firms.
- Assists entrepreneurs in resolving matters involving state government offices.
- The High Technology Division aids and assists the growth of high technology companies in Arizona.

The Community Planning Staff: Provides technical assistance on development-related issues, such as community-strategic planning, land-use planning, design review, zoning and infrastructure development, and financing. Provides direct assistance to rural communities in organizing an economic development program or effort, and evaluating community resources. Provides assistance with downtown revitalization projects. Provides support for rural community tourism development efforts. This program helps organizations responsible for retention and expansion develop a program to retain and encourage expansion

State Money - Arkansas

of existing businesses. The program places significant emphasis on creating a business environment for stable, successful companies. It also provides resources to aid in the design and implementation of a locally defined and community-based Business Retention and Expansion program. It provides assistance with designing, implementing and monitoring cost-effective energy conservation projects in residential, commercial and industrial buildings throughout the state.

Arizona's Work Force Recruitment and Job Training Program: Provides job training assistance to businesses creating net new jobs in Arizona. The program is designed to provide companies with a well equipped work force while ensuring maximum leverage of state and federal training funds.

* Business Financing

For all items without a separate address, contact the Arizona Department of Commerce at the address listed above.

Strategic Finance Division: Offers a wide range of loan and grant programs which provide economic development resources for companies relocating to or expanding in Arizona including the following:

Commerce & Economic Development Commission (CEDC): A low-interest rate loan program funded by proceeds from the Arizona Lottery. The CEDC's activities include:
- *Direct Assistance To Arizona Business*: to provide expansion capital to existing companies.
- *Technology Sector Capital*: financing that supports the development and growth of high-tech industries.
- *Intermediary Participation Program*: partnerships with other groups that provide economic development loans.
- A *CEDC loan* can be used to purchase fixed assets. A grant component tied to specific wage levels may also be available. In general, projects are weighted based on job creation, the presence of other investors and projected tax revenues. Final loan approval is determined by a six-member commission appointed by the Governor of Arizona. Attractive terms and a fixed interest rate are available.

Revolving Energy Loans for Arizona (RELA): A loan fund to promote and assist energy-related projects and companies. Arizona non-profit entities, political subdivisions or companies that purchase energy-conserving products for use in their own facilities are eligible. In addition, manufacturers of energy-conserving products may apply. Loan requests may range from $10,000 to $500,000 up to a maximum of 60% of total project costs. The RELA program offers a 5% interest rate and variable terms depending on energy payback. Projects have varied in size from window tinting and light fixture replacement to major equipment retrofits of air conditioning systems and solar heaters.

Economic Strength Projects (ESP) offers grants for road construction. This is a very competitive program based on the economic impact of applicant projects in the community in which it will be located. Applications are submitted by a town, city or county.

Loan fund to promote and assist energy-related projects and companies.

50/50 matching grants to schools and hospitals to improve the energy efficiency of their buildings.

Grants for road construction.

Technical and financial assistance to local and tribal governments with the development of public infrastructure projects.

* Tax Incentives

For all items without a separate address, contact the Arizona Department of Commerce at the address listed above.

Tax credits and technical assistance for low-income housing development.

The Enterprise Zones Program: Offers income tax credits and property tax reclassification for eligible companies meeting employment and industry requirements. Benefits are based on net new job creation, employment of economically disadvantaged or dislocated workers and location in an enterprise zone.

* Exports

For all items without a separate address, contact the Arizona Department of Commerce at the address listed above.

The Arizona Department of Commerce provides export counseling, access to federal documents assisting with market research, contact facilitation, access to Arizona State offices in several foreign cities, publications including *Arizona International Business Resource Guide*.

* Women and Minorities

For all items without a separate address, contact the Arizona Department of Commerce at the address listed above.

Minority/Women-Owned Business Enterprises Office: Acts as a resource and advocate for women and minority small businesses. Services include: a statewide directory of women/minority-owned businesses, Professional Women's conference sponsorship, newsletter containing calendar of events and relevant articles, marketing to state agencies and businesses, and certification seminars.

* Small Business Administration Offices

Bob Blaney
2828 N. Central Avenue, Suite 800
Phoenix, AZ 85004
602-745-7200
Fax: 602-745-7210

Arkansas

Arkansas Economic Development Commission
1 State Capitol Mall
Little Rock, AR 72201
501-682-1121
Fax: 501-682-7341
www.aedc.state.ar.us

* Business Assistance

For all items without a separate address, contact the Arkansas Economic Development Commission at the address listed above.

Existing Workforce Training Program (EWTP): Provides financial assistance to Arkansas manufacturing industries for upgrading the skills of their existing workforce. Secondary objectives are to build the capacity within their state-supported institutions to supply the ongoing training needs of Arkansas industries and to increase industry participation in the state's School-to-Work initiative.

ScrapMatch: A program designed to help Arkansas manufacturers find markets for their industrial scrap materials, thereby lowering the cost of doing business. ScrapMatch uses an electronic data management system to match industrial waste generators with secondary material markets.

Industrial Waste Minimization Program and Resource Recovery: Reduction, reuse, and recycling of industrial waste is the Industrial Waste Minimization Program's focus. By-product and surplus asset marketing assistance are also provided. The program provides on-site waste reduction audits and technical assistance to industry.

Environmental Permitting Services: The Arkansas Department of Environmental Quality works in a pro-business manner with companies looking to locate or expand operations in Arkansas. The agency recognizes the need for business growth in Arkansas while maintaining their state's positive environmental quality. Contact: Arkansas Department of Environmental Quality, 8001 National Dr., Little Rock, AR 72219; 501-682-0821.

Customized Training Incentive Program: Provides intensive pre-employment training for Arkansas workers to meet the increasing technical employment needs of the state's new and expanding businesses. Additionally, financial assistance to manufacturing industries for upgrading the skills of their existing workforce is also available.

* Business Financing

For all items without a separate address, contact the Arkansas Economic Development Commission at the address listed above.

Bond Guaranty Programs: For companies that have a financial history but are unable to sell industrial revenue bonds to the public, the Arkansas Economic Development Commission (AEDC) can assure bond holders of repayment by guaranteeing up to $4 million of a bond issue. The state's guaranty allows the bonds to be sold at a higher credit rating, therefore lowering the effective interest rate for the company. The AEDC charges a 5% fee for guaranteeing issues of this type.

Arkansas Capital Corporation: A privately-owned, nonprofit organization established in 1957 to serve as an alternative source of financing for companies in

Arkansas. Its main goal is to improve the economic climate in the state by providing long-term, fixed-rate loans to Arkansas companies. As a preferred lender for the Small Business Administration, ACC makes loans to existing operations and business start-ups for everything from new construction and equipment to working capital. ACC loans may be used in combination with bank loans, municipal bond issues, or other sources of financing. Contact: Arkansas Capital Corporation, 225 S. Pulaski St., Little Rock, AR 72201; 501-374-9247; {www.arcap.com}.

ASTA Investment Fund: The Arkansas Science and Technology Authority (ASTA) administers a special Investment Fund of $2.8 million which can provide seed capital for new and developing technology-based companies through loans, royalty agreements, and limited stock purchases. Contact: Arkansas Science and Technology Authority, 100 Main St., Suite 450, Little Rock, AR 72201; 501-324-9006.

Economic Development District Revolving Funds: Several planning and development districts in Arkansas have revolving loan funds for economic development purposes. The loans are limited to $100,000 per business, must involve specific levels of job creation, and must be matched by a bank loan.

Create Rebate Program: Companies hiring specified net new full-time permanent employees within 24 months after completion of an approved expansion and/or new location project can be eligible to receive a financial incentive to be used for a specific purpose. This incentive ranges from 3.9% to 5% in areas with an unemployment rate in excess of 10%, or more than 3% above the state's average unemployment rate for the preceding calendar year.

Industrial Revenue Bonds: Provide manufacturers with below-market financing. Interest on tax exempt issues is normally 80% of prime, but this may vary depending on terms of the issue. For real estate loans, 15 years is the most common term. The primary goal of this financing program is to enable manufacturers to purchase land, buildings, and equipment to expand their operations

* Tax Incentives

For all items without a separate address, contact the Arkansas Economic Development Commission at the address listed above.

Arkansas Economic Development Act (AEDA): To utilize the AEDA program, companies must sign a financial agreement prior to construction outlining the terms of the incentives and stipulations. There are two basic incentives provided: A state corporate income tax credit up to 100% of the total amount of annual debt service paid to the lender financing a project; Refund of sales and use taxes on construction materials, machinery, and equipment associated with a project during the period specified by the financial agreement.

Advantage Arkansas Program: A job tax credit program for qualifying new and expanding companies which provides corporate income tax credits and sales and use tax refunds to companies locating or expanding in Arkansas.

Corporate Income Tax Credit: Provides a credit on corporate income tax equal to the average hourly wage of each new worker times a multiplier of 100, with a $2,000 cap per employee. The multiplier increases to 200 when a company locates in a county where the unemployment rate is at least 10% or 3% above the state average for the preceding calendar year.

InvestArk Tax Credit: Available to industries established in Arkansas for 2 years or longer investing $5 million or more in plant or equipment. A credit against the manufacturer's state sales and use tax liability of 7% of the total project cost, not to exceed 50% of the total sales and use tax liability in a single year, is allowed.

Free Port Law: No tax on goods in transit or raw materials and finished goods destined for out-of-state sales; no sales tax on manufacturing equipment, pollution control facilities, or raw materials; no property tax on textile mills.

Day Care Facility Incentive Program: Companies can receive a sales and use tax refund on the initial cost of construction materials and furnishings purchased to build and equip an approved child care facility. Additionally, a corporate income tax credit of 3.9% of the total annual payroll of the workers employed exclusively to provide childcare service, or a $5,000 income tax credit for the first year the business provides its employees with a day care facility is also available.

Tourism Development: Provides state sales tax credits up to 10% of approved project costs for the creation or expansion of eligible tourist attractions exceeding $500,000, and 25% of project costs exceeding $1,000,000.

Recycling Equipment Tax Credit: Allows taxpayers to receive a tax credit for the purchase of equipment used exclusively for reduction, reuse, or recycling of solid waste material for commercial purposes, whether or not for profit, and the cost of installation of such equipment by outside contractors. The amount of the credit shall equal 30% of the cost of eligible equipment and installation costs.

Motion Picture Incentive Act: Qualifying motion picture production companies spending in excess of $500,000 within six months, or $1 million within 12 months may receive a refund of state sales and use taxes paid on qualified expenditures incurred in conjunction with a film, telefilm, music video, documentary, episodic television show, or commercial advertisement.

Biotechnology Development and Training Act: Offers three different income tax credits to taxpayers furthering biotechnical business development. The first credit is a 5% income tax credit applied to costs to build and equip eligible biotechnical facilities. The second credit allows a 30% income tax credit both for eligible employee training costs and for contract with state-supported institutions for higher education to conduct qualified cooperative research projects. The third credit allows an income tax credit for qualified research in biotechnology, including but not limited to the cost of purchasing, licensing, developing, or protecting intellectual property. This credit is equal to 20% of the amount the cost of qualified research exceeds the cost of such resource in the base year.

Enterprise Zone Program: Corporate income tax credits and sales tax refund.

Sales and Use Tax Exemptions: For many manufacturing materials, equipment, and machinery; and, air and water pollution control equipment.

* Exports

For all items without a separate address, contact the Arkansas Economic Development Commission at the address listed above.

The *Arkansas Economic Development Commission's (AEDC)* international offices assist Arkansas companies in exporting their products and services by arranging personalized meetings with potential distributors, sales representatives or end users in the countries targeted for AEDC's export promotion efforts. In addition to this service, they also offer the following:
- Market research
- Assisting companies exhibiting in international trade fairs
- Planning and coordinating trade missions
- Obtaining trade leads
- Representing and/or advising companies on export transactions
- Accompanying company representatives on export sales trips
- Promoting companies in meetings with prospective buyers

* Small Business Administration Offices

Joe Foglia
2120 Riverfront Drive, Suite 100
Little Rock, AR 72202
501-324-5871
Fax: 501-324-5199

California

California Trade and Commerce Agency
801 K St., Suite 1700
Sacramento, CA 95814
916-322-1394
www.state.ca.us/s/business

California's business resources are many and varied with many local and regional programs. The following is not all-inclusive:

* Business Assistance

For all items without a separate address, contact the California Trade and Commerce Agency at the address listed above.

Office of Small Business: Offers workshops, seminars, individual counseling, and publications for those interested in small businesses. They have information and expertise in dealing with state, federal, and local agencies.

* Business Financing

For all items without a separate address, contact the California Trade and Commerce Agency at the address listed above.

The Loan Guarantee Program: Assists small businesses that cannot qualify for bank loans. Normally, 80% of the loan amount, with the guaranteed portion of the loan not exceeding $350,000 is offered. Microloans, up to $25,000, are fully guaranteed.

Energy Technology Export Program: The California Energy Commission assists California companies through several energy export programs. For more

State Money - California

information, contact California Energy Commission, Energy Technology Export Program, 1516 Ninth St., MS-45, Sacramento, CA 95814; 916-654-4528; {www.energy.ca.gov}.

Fishing Vessel: Direct loans to finance commercial fishing vessel equipment and modifications that result in fuel savings. Loans are from $10,000 to $25,000.

Hazardous Waste: Direct loans to finance equipment or a production practice that reduces waste or lessens hazardous properties. The minimum loan is $20,000. The maximum loan is $150,000.

Bond Guarantees: Access to surety bonds that allow greater participation by small and emerging contractors in state public works contracts. Maximum is $350,000 liability per contract.

Small Corporate Offering Registration Network: Raise up to $1 million by issuing shares directly to investors through a state-registered public offering.

Sudden and Severe Economic Dislocation (SSED): The California Trade and Commerce Agency provides gap financing to businesses in areas of the state affected by plant and military base closures, defense downsizing, industry layoffs, presidentially declared disasters and other economic problems which have contributed to job loss in California.

Old Growth Diversification Revolving Loan Fund: The California Trade and Commerce Agency provides low cost capital to businesses that create jobs in targeted timber-dependent areas. Businesses may borrow from $25,000 to $100,000 at a reduced interest rate to purchase machinery and equipment or for working capital.

The California Capital Access Program: The California Pollution Control Financing Authority (CPCFA) provides a form of loan portfolio insurance which provides up to 100% coverage on certain loan defaults, encouraging banks and other financial institutions to make loans to small businesses that fall just outside of most banks' conventional underwriting standards. The maximum loan amount is $2.5 million. The maximum premium CPCFA will pay is $100,000 (per loan). Contact: California Pollution Control Financing Authority, Attention: SBAF Program Manager, 915 Capitol Mall, Room 466, Sacramento, CA 95814; 916-654-5610.

California Industrial Development Financing Advisory Commission (CEDFAC): The Treasurer's office assists California manufacturing businesses in funding capital expenditures for acquisitions or expansions. Allows a business to borrow funds at competitive rates through the issuance of tax-exempt bonds enhanced by a letter of credit. The maximum face amount of an IDB bond issue is $10 million per applicant per public jurisdiction. Contact: California Industrial Development Financing Advisory Commission, 915 Capitol Mall, Sacramento, CA 95814; 916-653-3843.

* Tax Incentives

For all items without a separate address, contact the California Trade and Commerce Agency at the address listed above.

Manufacturers operating in California are eligible for a 6% manufacturers' investment credit (MIC). This credit is generally unlimited.

Provides "new" or start up companies the option of a 5% partial sales or use tax exemption on all qualifying manufacturing property purchased or leased generally during the company's first three years of operation.

Research tax credits allow companies to receive a credit of 11% for qualifying research expenses (research done in-house) and 24% for basic research payments (payments to an outside company), making it the highest in the nation.

Net Operating Loss Carryover: Allows businesses that experience a loss for the year to carry this loss forward to the next year in order to offset income in the following year.

Enterprise Zone Program: Encourages business development in 39 designated areas through numerous special zone incentives.

Local Agency Military Base Recovery Area: Designations which are similar to enterprise zones allowing communities to extend the aforementioned California tax credits to companies locating in a LAMBRA zone.

Child Care Tax Credit: For employers who pay or incur costs for the start up of a child care program or construction of an on-site child care facility are eligible for a credit against state income taxes equal to 30% of its costs, up to a maximum of $50,000 in one year. Excess credits may be carried over to succeeding years.

* Exports

For all items without a separate address, contact the California Trade and Commerce Agency at the address listed above.

International Trade and Investment: Acts as a catalyst to create jobs in California through vigorous and sustained promotion of exports to global markets and foreign investment into the Golden State. They have offices in California and ten foreign locations. They offer promotion of California products and companies abroad through the Office of Export Development, current information on foreign market opportunities, the Special American Business Internship Training Program, and assistance with attracting foreign investment through the California Office of Foreign Investment. They also provide exporting financial assistance for going global through several economic development programs provided by the California Export Finance Office, a division of California's Trade and Commerce Agency. The maximum guarantee amount is $750,000. That is 90% of an $833,000 loan.

* Women and Minorities

For all items without a separate address, contact the California Trade and Commerce Agency at the address listed above.

Child Care and Development Facilities Loan Guarantee Fund and Child Care and Development Facilities Direct Loan Fund: Together, these funds support the California Child Care Facilities Finance Program. The Department of Housing and Community Development will deposit $3.1 million from the Child Care and Development Facilities Loan Guarantee Fund into the Small Business Expansion Fund. Corporations can issue guarantees against this fund as long as the transaction adheres to the following HCD rules: The loan must be used for creating new child care spaces or preserving spaces that would otherwise be lost; the projects must fit into the HCD priority categories. A direct loan may not exceed 20% of the total project cost if the same facility is also utilizing a guaranteed loan. In no case can a direct loan exceed 50% of the project cost. Home-based child care will be financed by non-profit microlenders. Both small businesses and non-profit organizations will be eligible for either guarantees and/or direct loans.

* Small Business Administration Offices

Viola Canales
455 Market Street, S-2200
San Francisco, CA 94105
415-744-2118
Fax: 415-744-2119

Antonio Valdez
2719 N. Air Fresno Drive
Suite 200
Fresno, CA 93727
559-487-5791
Fax: 559-487-5636

Alberto Alvarado
330 N. Brand Boulevard
Suite 1200
Glendale, CA 91203
818-552-3210
Fax: 818-552-3286

Jim O'Neal
660 J Street, Room 215
Sacramento, CA 95814
916-498-6410
Fax: 916-498-6422

George Chandler
550 W. C Street, Suite 550
San Diego, CA 92101
619-557-7252
Fax: 619-557-5894

Mark Quinn
455 Market Street, 6th Floor
San Francisco, CA 94105
415-744-8474
Fax: 415-744-6812

Sandy Sutton
200 W. Santa Ana Boulevard, Suite 700
Santa Ana, CA 92701
714-550-7420
Fax: 714-550-0191

Colorado

Office of Economic Development
1625 Broadway, Suite 1710
Denver, CO 80202
303-892-3840
Fax: 303-892-3848
TDD: 800-659-2656
www.state.co.us

* Business Assistance

For all items without a separate address, contact the Colorado Office of Economic Development at the address listed above.

Office of Economic Development: The Office of Economic Development (OED) works with companies starting, expanding or relocating in Colorado. OED offers a wide range of services to assist new and existing businesses of every size.

Marketing Colorado: Marketing activities are conducted nationwide to promote sectors of the Colorado economy which are growing and provide high quality jobs. Marketing activities include attendance at selected trade shows, company visits, cooperative marketing with local enterprise zones and community economic development councils and industry research. *Colorado Facts* is published annually by OBD and includes statistics and comparisons of key indicators to evaluate Colorado's economic climate and to provide information of special interest to the business community.

Job Training: Colorado First and Existing Industries Job Training Programs assists employers with customized job training. Assistance is provided to new and existing businesses to retrain workers and improve their workplace skills. The goal of the Colorado First program is to assist companies in training employees to fill newly created full-time permanent quality jobs.

* Business Financing

For all items without a separate address, contact the Colorado Office of Economic Development at the address listed above.

Revolving Loan Fund Programs (RLFs): Administered locally in 15 geographic regions covering the rural areas of the state. RLFs have considerable flexibility to make small loans of two or three thousand dollars up to $100,000. Applicants can be existing or startup businesses.

Larger Business Loans: Between $100,000 and $250,000 are provided by OBD through the Community Development Block Grant Business Loans Program when the local government is willing to assume the risk on the loan in order to create or retain jobs. Larger loans may be considered on a case by case basis.

Economic Development Commission: Will provide interest rate write-downs, low interest rate loans or subsidies to companies interested in relocating to or expanding in Colorado.

Private Activity Bonds (PABs): Provide a tax-exempt financing vehicle for facilities and equipment used in the manufacture or production of tangible personal property.

* Tax Incentives

For all items without a separate address, contact the Colorado Office of Economic Development at the address listed above.

Investment Tax Credits: The Colorado Tax Equity Act, signed into law during the 1987 legislative session, reinstates the Colorado Investment Tax Credit, up to $1,000 per year, for tax years beginning on or after January 1, 1998, based on 10% of what the Federal Investment Tax Credit would have been had such credit not been restricted by the Tax Reform Act of 1986. Excess credits may be carried forward up to three years.

Enterprise Zone Tax Credits: Enterprise Zones are geographic areas designated to promote economic development. Sixteen such zones have been designated in Colorado. They cover most rural areas of the state with the exception of the ski area/resort counties. There are also urban zones designated to attract investment and jobs to selected areas. Enterprise Zones offer the following advantages to businesses locating or expanding within their boundaries:
- A $500 credit for each new full-time employee working within the Zone.
- Double job tax credit for agricultural processing.
- $200 job tax credit for employer health insurance.
- Local government incentives.
- 3% investment tax credit for businesses making investments in equipment used exclusively in an Enterprise Zone.
- Exemption from state sales and use taxes for manufacturing equipment.
- Income tax credit of up to 3% for expenditures on research and development activities (as defined in federal tax laws) in an Enterprise Zone.
- A credit of 25% of qualified expenditures up to $50,000 to rehabilitate buildings which are at least 20 years old which have been vacant at least two years.
- A 25% tax credit for private contributions to local zone administrators for qualifying projects or programs within zones.
- A 10% tax credit for employer expenditures for qualified job training and school-to-work programs.

Sales Tax Exemptions: For purchases over $500 on machinery and machine tools purchased for use in manufacturing; Purchases of electricity, coal, gas, or fuel oil for use in processing, manufacturing, and all industrial uses; Sale of tangible personal property for testing, modification, inspection, or similar types of activities in Colorado; Interstate long distance telephone charges.

Local Governments: May provide incentive payments or property tax credits based on the amount of increased property taxes for qualifying new business activity in their jurisdictions.

* Exports

For all items without a separate address, contact the Colorado Office of Economic Development at the address listed above.

Colorado International Trade Office (ITO): Responsible for assisting Colorado companies with all aspects of exporting, including counseling, protocol, leading trade missions, and conducting trade shows abroad. By promoting Colorado exports and attracting foreign investment, the ITO helps to build Colorado's identity as an international business center, encouraging foreign buyers to look to Colorado for products and services. The ITO is open to the public and most services are rendered at no cost.

* Women and Minorities

For all items without a separate address, contact the Colorado Office of Economic Development at the address listed above.

Women's Business Office: Strives to keep the women entrepreneurs of Colorado informed about pertinent issues through all modes of communication.

Office of Economic Development Minority Business Office: Acts as a clearinghouse to disseminate information to the minority business community. Promotes economic development for minority businesses in cooperation with the state economic development activities. Establishes networks between majority and minority business sectors. Promotes minority participation in state procurement. Assists Colorado in achieving its Minority Procurement Goals of 17%. Works with the Minority Business Advisory Council and the minority community in promoting minority business development.

* Small Business Administration Offices

Kathleen Piper
721 19th Street, Suite 400
Denver, CO 80202
303-844-0500
Fax: 303-844-0506

Patricia Barela Rivera
721 19th Street, Suite 426
Denver, CO 80202
303-844-4028
Fax: 303-844-6468

Connecticut

Economic Resource Center
Connecticut Department of Economic and Community Development
805 Brooks St., Bldg. 4
Rocky Hill, CT 06067-3405
860-571-7136
800-392-2122
Fax: 860-571-7150
www.cerc.com

State Money - Connecticut

* Business Assistance

For all items without a separate address, contact the Connecticut Economic Resource Center at the address listed above.

One Stop Centers: Authorized to enable businesses to obtain many necessary permits and licenses in one location.

Connecticut Economic Resource Center (CERC): A non-profit private-sector organization formed and managed through a unique partnership of utility/telecommunication companies and state government. The CERC coordinates Connecticut's business-to-business marketing and recruitment efforts on behalf of the state. As a one-stop gateway to the state's programs and services for business, the CERC helps businesses obtain quick and accurate information in the areas of financing, export assistance, licensing, manufacturing programs, job training, utility, telecommunications and real estate help, all at no cost.

Business Resource Index: The Connecticut Economic Resource Center's website {www.cerc.com} offers a large and comprehensive database of programs and services for businesses. The database contains information from the public and private sectors on federal, state and local levels including license and permit information. The *Business Resource Index* is divided into three major sections, each of which can be searched individually or collectively. The sections include *Resources By Agency, Licensing,* and *Helpful Fact Sheets*. Available business resources are often divided by city or region. Listings are extensive. To illustrate, a search with the keyword "Small Business" yielded 119 documents including loans, technical assistance, consulting services, grants, and economic development assistance among others. As an example, the Entrepreneurial Loan Program offers loans up to $100,000 insured by the Connecticut Development Authority, for the benefit of start-up and early stage business anywhere in Connecticut. The website also features a real estate search engine enabling the user to input parameters such as size of building and desired location to aid with business site selection.

Technology Extension Program: Provides direct technical assistance to small and mid-sized manufacturing firms.

Institute for Industrial and Engineering Technology: Offers assistance with process improvement, technical training, procurement, human resources, business incubators, and others.

SiteFinder: A comprehensive computer database of available commercial and industrial properties.

Demographic and Economic Analysis: Services include industry profiles, competitive intelligence, regional analysis, survey research, bench marking and evaluation.

* Business Financing

For all items without a separate address, contact the Connecticut Economic Resource Center at the address listed above.

Entrepreneurial Loan Program: Provides up to $1000,000 in start-up and expansion financing. 75% of past loans were made to women and minority owners.

URBANK: Loans up to $500,000 for any small business enterprise in targeted communities that are unable to obtain conventional financing.

Business Loans: Up to $10 million for medium size enterprises.

Junior Participation Loans: Up to $5 million to assist the lender in meeting the company's total borrowing requirements.

Inducement Loans: Up to $10 million at below market interest rates restricted to significant competitive business retention or recruitment.

Industrial Revenue Bonds: Low rate, tax exempt financing for manufacturers, utilities, certain non-profits and others.

Environmental Assistance Revolving Loan Fund: Provides loans, lines of credit or loan guarantees for Clean Air Act compliance and pollution prevention.

Job Training Finance Program: Pays up to 25% of the cost of improving skills of manufacturing workers.

Custom Job Training Program: Department of Labor will pay up to 50% for eligible training expenses.

For all the above loan programs, contact Connecticut Development Authority, 999 West St., Rocky Hill, CT 06067; 860-258-7800.

Manufacturing Assistance Fund: Program includes loans, defense diversification project funding, tax credits and funding for new machinery and equipment.

Naugatuck Valley Loan Fund: Fund can be used to purchase land or buildings, construction, renovation, rehabilitation, and/or the purchase and installation of machinery and equipment. Maximum loan is $200,000.

Connecticut Programs Fund: Program provides venture capital, including minority-focused venture capital, mezzanine financing and funds for restructuring.

For the above loan programs, contact Department of Economic and Community Development, 249 Thomaston Ave., Waterbury, CT 06702; 203-596-8862.

Community Economic Development Fund: Provides financing for a wide range of projects in certain targeted investment and public investment communities throughout the state.

Regional Revolving Loan Funds: Provide supplemental financing to stimulate job growth and business activity.

Community-Based Development Organizations: Local economic development organizations offering financing on varying conditions and terms.

For the above loan programs, contact Community Economic Development Fund, 50-G Weston St., Hartford, CT 06120; 800-656-4613; 860-249-3800.

Connecticut Venture Group: A non-profit membership organization that brings entrepreneurs and investors together.

Innovations Technology Financing: Offers a wide range of support from research assistance to financing for product development and marketing.

For the above loan programs, contact Connecticut Venture Group, 891 Post Rd., Suite F, Fairfield, CT 06430; 203-333-3284.

Product Development and Product Marketing Financing: Recipients of funding frequently gain the credibility that they need to leverage investment capital from more traditional, private sources. Typical investments range from $50,000 to $1,000,000.

Yankee Ingenuity Initiative Funding: Provides funding for collaborative research between businesses and colleges.

Technology Partnership: Invests $50,000 to $500,000 in businesses pursuing funding through federal research and development programs.

For more information regarding the loan programs listed above, contact Connecticut Innovations Technology Fiancing, 999 West St., Rocky Hill, CT 06067; 860-563-5851; {www.ctinnovations.com}.

* Tax Incentives

For all items without a separate address, contact the Connecticut Economic Resource Center at the address listed above.

Corporate Income Tax Credits:
- 50% for financial institutions constructing new facilities and adding new employees.
- 5% annual credit for fixed capital investment in tangible personal property.
- 4% annual credit for investments in human capital, employee training, childcare, and donations to higher education for technology training.
- 10% credit for increased investment in machinery and equipment for companies with 250 or fewer full-time permanent employees.
- Research and development credits.
- 100% credit for property taxes paid on data processing hardware, peripheral equipment and software.
- 25% credit for an increase in grant to institutions of higher learning for R&D related to technology advancement.
- 100% credit for investment over 10 years in an investment fund creating insurance related facilities and jobs.
- Other credits for low-income housing, contributions to neighborhood assistance programs, and alternative employee transportation.

Corporate Income Tax Exemptions:
All insurance companies, passive investment companies, and financial services companies.
- Property Taxes: 100% exemption for newly installed machinery and equipment, inventories, unbundled software, new commercial motor vehicles.
- Sales Tax: 100% exemption on newly acquired and installed machinery and equipment, inventories, unbundled software and commercial motor vehicles.
- Enterprise Zones and Targeted Investment Communities: 40 - 80% real and personal property tax exemptions, 25% corporate business tax credits for firms conducting research & development, 15 - 100% corporate business tax credits depending on industry and jobs created, $750 - $2,250 grants for each new job created for eligible companies.
- Department of Labor: Tax credits up to $4,800 are available for qualified apprenticeships in the manufacturing and construction trades.

* Exports

For all items without a separate address, contact the Connecticut Economic Resource Center at the address listed above.

Access International: Program designed to put businesses in touch with resources to support exporting efforts including consultants, suppliers, services and support.

* Women and Minorities

For all items without a separate address, contact the Connecticut Economic Resource Center at the address listed above.

State Money - Delaware

Procurement Program: Set-Aside Program requires state agencies and political subdivisions to set aside 25% of their budget for construction, housing rehabilitation and the purchasing of supplies. These services are awarded to certified small business contractors, minority businesses, enterprises, non-profit corporations and individuals with a disability. 25% of this amount is to be awarded to certified minority owned firms.

Minority Supplier Development Council: A non-profit organization whose mission is to foster business relationships between corporations and certified minority businesses. Services include training seminars, matchmaking activities, bid notifications, networking functions and a large trade expo.

For these programs, contact Minority and Small Business Contractors Set-Aside Program, Department of Economic and Community Development, 505 Hudson St., Hartford, CT 06106, Attn: Set Aside Unit; 860-270-8025; {www.state.ct.us/ecd/setaside}.

* Small Business Administration Offices

Marie Record
330 Main Street, 2nd Floor
Hartford, CT 06106
860-240-4700
Fax: 860-240-4659

Delaware

Delaware Economic Development Office
John S. Riley
99 Kings Highway
P.O. Box 1401
Dover, DE 19903
302-739-4271
Fax: 302-739-5749
www.state.de.us/dedo/index.htm

* Business Assistance

For all items without a separate address, contact the Delaware Economic Development Office at the address listed above.

Delaware Economic Development Office: Offers referrals to appropriate state agencies and other organizations. Free tabloid, *Small Business Start-Up Guide* is available. Provides support for new businesses and coordinates the efforts of organizations statewide that assist small businesses.

Workforce Development Section: Works to ensure the availability of a skilled, multilevel workforce for new and existing Delaware businesses. Helps employers obtain, upgrade and retain suitable workers, by helping Delawareans gain the education and training to get and keep quality jobs and steady employment.

Business Research Section: Collects, analyzes and distributes statistical data on the state's economy and business climate and develops research regarding the economic vitality of the State of Delaware

Delaware Tourism Office: Assists the tourism industry.

The State Data Center: Provides economic and demographic data for Delaware.

Business Calendar: Maintained by the Delaware State Chamber of Commerce (DSCC), it is the state's central location for listing business-related events.

Advanced Technology Centers (ATCs): Public/private partnerships designed to bolster Delaware's technology base and to create and retain quality high-tech jobs. The State of Delaware has committed $11 million to date in grants to establish five Centers. Funding for the program comes from the state's 21st Century Fund. Amounts are not available without a specific inquiry. For more information, contact Delaware Economic Development Office, 820 French St., Wilmington, DE 19801; 302-577-8477.

Green Industries Initiative: Targets specific businesses for receipt of financial and technical assistance to further the goals of Governor Castle's Executive Order #82 and Delaware's Pollution Prevention Program. The State of Delaware provides corporate income tax credits and/or gross receipts tax reductions for existing Delaware firms and those choosing Delaware as a location for new operations. The type of financial assistance is dependent upon the category under which assistance is requested.

* Business Financing

For all items without a separate address, contact the Delaware Economic Development Office at the address listed above.

Industrial Revenue Bonds: Statewide financial assistance to new or expanding businesses through the issuance of bonds (IRBs). The maximum for IRBs issued annually in Delaware is $150 million.

Economic Development Loan Program: Assists Delaware businesses to finance projects when 100% financing cannot be obtained through a bank. The program does require 70% bank financing. The remaining 30% is financed through the program up to a maximum of $450,000. In most cases the interest rate for monies loaned through the Economic Development Loan Program is 60% of the prime lending interest rate.

The Delaware Access Program: Designed to give banks a flexible and extremely non-bureaucratic tool to make business loans that are somewhat riskier than a conventional bank loan, in a manner consistent with safety and soundness. It is designed to use a small amount of public resources to generate a large amount of private bank financing, thus providing access to bank financing for many Delaware businesses that might otherwise not be able to obtain such access. The program sets minimum and maximum limits for the borrower's payment. At a minimum, it must be at least 1-1/2% of the loan amount. The maximum is 3-1/2% . (The premium payment, and other up-front expenses, may be financed as part of the loan.)

Small Business Innovation Research (SBIR): Bridge grant assistance to encourage Delaware businesses to participate in the federal Small Business Innovation Research (SBIR) grant program. The SBIR program requires that 1.25% of all federal research dollars be made available to small businesses. Phase I awardees are granted up to $100,000 by the federal government.

The Delaware Innovation Fund: Assists in the initial capitalization of pre-seed and seed stage enterprises within the State of Delaware. The Fund provides financial and technical assistance to Delaware based businesses which have the potential to launch innovative products and processes into national markets, to create new jobs, and to make a significant contribution to the economic diversity and the technology base of Delaware's communities.

Demonstration Funding: Limited one-time availability, provides $10,000 to $25,000 to aid in establishing patents, business plans and proof of concept issues.

Commercialization Funding: Ranging from $25,000 to $250,000, this funding is used to begin the commercialization process of early-stage businesses and may be available in multiple years.

Venture Capital Funds: Three funds — Anthem Capital, L.P., Triad Investors Corporation, and Blue Rock Capital — have the ability to fund a variety of seed stage, early stage, and later stage companies in both technology-related and non-technology fields. The investment focus of each fund varies. Investments can range from $150,000 for seed stage companies up to $2,000,000 or more for later stage companies.

City of Wilmington: Projects located within the city limits of Wilmington may also apply for financing through the Wilmington Economic Development Corporation (WEDCO). Financing programs offered include SBA Section 504 Loans, Revolving Loan Funds, and other special purpose financing. Contact: Wilmington Economic Development Corporation, 605A Market St., Wilmington, DE 19801; 302-571-9088.

Sussex County: Operates an Industrial Revenue Bond program with a cap of $15 million each year for industrial projects in the County. Project review requires a letter of commitment for placement of the bond before a project recommendation is made by the Industrial Revenue Bond Review Committee to Sussex County Council (political jurisdiction). The Industrial Revenue Bond process may require as little as five weeks from inception to bond closing. Contact: Sussex County Office of Economic Development, P.O. Box 589, 9 S. Dupont Hwy., Georgetown, DE 19947; 302-855-7770.

* Tax Incentives

For all items without a separate address, contact the Delaware Economic Development Office at the address listed above.

Bank Franchise Tax Credits: For taxable years beginning after December 31, 1996, credits against bank franchise taxes are available to qualifying firms. Credits are $400 per year for each new qualifying employee in excess of 50 new employees and are for a period of ten years.

Export Trading Company Exemption: Delaware exporters who qualify as an Export Trading Company can receive exemption from Delaware income and mercantile taxes.

Targeted Area Tax Incentives: Firms which qualify for targeted industry credits and are located in one of the targeted areas, qualify for corporate income tax credits of $650 for each new employee and $650 for each new $100,000 investment.

Retention and Expansion Tax Credits: Corporate income tax credits and gross receipts tax reductions are available to qualifying manufacturers and wholesalers planning new facilities or large expansions. The maximum annual credit cannot exceed $500,000. Gross receipts tax reductions are limited to a maximum total credit of $500,000 over the ten-year life.

State Money - District of Columbia

Green Industries Tax Credits: Manufacturers that reduce their chemical waste, as reported under the Toxics Release Inventory, by 20% or their other wastes by 50%, are granted a $400 corporate income tax credit for each 10% reduction.

Public Utility Tax Rebates for Industrial Users: Industrial firms meeting the criteria for targeted industries tax credits are eligible for a rebate of 50% of the Public Utilities Tax imposed on new or increased consumption of gas and electricity for five years.

Property Tax Incentives: The cities of Wilmington, Newark, Dover and the counties of New Castle and Kent offer a variety of property tax incentives for new construction, renovation, and property improvements. Amounts vary.

* Exports

For all items without a separate address, contact the Delaware Economic Development Office at the address listed above.

The International Trade Section: A one-stop resource for exporter assistance and international trade information in Delaware. Contact the International Trade Section, Delaware Economic Development Office, 820 French St., Carvel State Office Bldg., 10th Floor, Wilmington, DE 19801; 302-577-8477.

* Small Business Administration Offices

Jayne Armstrong
1318 North Market Street
Wilmington, DE 19801
302-571-5225
Fax: 302-573-6060

District of Columbia

Office of Economic Development
441 4th St., NW, Suite 1140
Washington, DC 20001
202-727-6365
www.dchomepage.net

* Business Assistance

For all items without a separate address, contact the District of Columbia Office of Economic Development at the address listed above.

Welcome To Washington D.C. Online: A useful website with links to business & finance opportunities in the district.

Certifies business as *local business development* for purposes of procurement from the District of Columbia government.

Transferable Development Rights: Permits businesses to purchase the right to develop at higher densities in designated TDR "receiving zones."
Contact Local Business Development, 441 4th St., NW, Suite 970N, Washington, DC 20001; 202-724-1385.

Business Location Assistance:
D.C. Chamber of Commerce, 1301 Pennsylvania Ave., NW, Suite 309, Washington, DC 20004; 202-347-7201; {www.dcchamber.org};
D.C. Building Industry Association, 5100 Wisconsin Ave., NW, Suite 301, Washington, DC 20016; 202-966-8665; {www.reji.com/associations/dcbia}.

* Business Financing

For all items without a separate address, contact the District of Columbia Office of Economic Development at the address listed above.

Enterprise Zone: Eligible for up to $15 million per business in tax exempt bonds for businesses within an Enterprise Zone; $20,000 of additional expensing of business equipment.

Bond Financing and General Information: Contact D.C. Revenue Bond Program, 441 4th St., NW, Suite 360, Washington, DC 20001; 202-727-6055; 202-727-2778; {www.dccfo.com/dcbons.htm}.

* Tax Incentives

For all items without a separate address, contact the District of Columbia Office of Economic Development at the address listed above.

Enterprise Zones: Consists of 65 census tracts with 20% and higher poverty rate. Benefits include:
- *Tax-Exempt Bond Financing*: Up to 15 million.
- *Federal Capital Gains Exemption*: Requires 80% of the business' total gross income be derived from a business or trade conducted within the enterprise zone.
- *Employment Tax Credit*: Up to $3,000 for each employee at the EZ facility who is also a D.C. resident.
- *Special Expensing Allowance*: $20,000 available for business equipment and depreciable property purchase by EZ businesses.

Public Schools Tax Credit: Available for contributions to school rehabilitation and repair, the provision of school equipment, materials and teacher training and the advancement of innovative K-12 programs.

Work Opportunity Tax Credits: $2,400 first time work opportunity tax credit for each worker in the first year of employment.

Welfare-To-Work Tax Credit: $8,500 welfare to work one-time tax credit for employees certified by D.C. DOES.

* Exports

For all items without a separate address, contact the District of Columbia Office of Economic Development at the address listed above.

The DC Office of International Business: OIB was created to support the District of Columbia's development and expansion of local business through international trade and joint-venture partnerships, and to attract outside investment to the District of Columbia. Programs offered include:
- *International Trade Counseling and Technical Program*: OIB offers counseling and assistance on all aspects of international business to firms, organizations and residents of the District of Columbia.
- *Resource Center for International Trade Information*: Offers country market profiles, current export licensing regulations, information on trade and financing, a comprehensive database of trade resources and a directory of Washington-based international firms.
- *Trade and Investment Program*: Offers a database of local, small, and medium sized businesses, using criteria and categories useful for the analysis of the local market; match making potential for local small business, and investment needs; facilitates trade and investment leads; identifies overseas markets for local goods and services; supports trade and investment missions; hosts foreign buying delegations; works in tandem with its sister agencies in devising strategies and marketing activities to attract foreign investment and business entities to the District of Columbia; establishes regular and close relationships with the diplomatic community, chambers of commerce and other regional and state agencies to identify export and investment opportunities for local and area businesses.
- *OIB Seminar Series*: Provides hands-on training through an eight week course designed to provide concise, nuts-and-bolts instructions on how to conduct import, export, and joint venture transactions. Topics cover every aspect of international trade with emphasis on small business involvement. Upon successful completion of the course, participants receive a "Certificate of Achievement."
- *OIB Internship Program*: OIB offers a high school and college internship program that provides local youth with on-the-job training, skill development and an orientation to international trade.

* Women and Minorities

For all items without a separate address, contact the District of Columbia Office of Economic Development at the address listed above.

Minority Business Opportunity Commission: Promotes equal opportunity in all aspects of District life and fosters minority business development through:
- *Business Marketing Directory*: listing of Local, Small, Disadvantaged and Minority Business Enterprises.
- *Minority Business Certification Program*
- *Technical Assistance Program*: Aids minority business enterprises through workshops, contracting conferences, referrals and the MBOC Directory to bid and compete on District Government contracts.
- *Bonding Assistance Program*: Establishes a financial assurance pool to serve as limited collateral for surety bonds on public construction projects awarded by the DC government.

For these programs, contact D.C. Department of Human Rights and Local Business Development, DC Department of Human Rights and Minority Business Development, 441 4th Street, NW, Suite 970, Washington, DC 20001; 202-724-1385; Fax: 202-724-3786.

State Money - Florida

* Small Business Administration Offices

Darryl Hairston
1110 Vermont Avenue, NW, Suite 900
Washington, DC 20005
202-606-4000
Fax: 202-606-4225

Florida

Florida Economic Development Council
502 East Jefferson Street
Tallahassee, FL 32301
805-222-3000
Fax: 850-222-3019

Enterprise Florida
390 North Orange Avenue, Suite 1300
Orlando, FL 32801
407-316-4600
Fax: 407-316-4599
www.floridabusiness.com

* Business Assistance

For all items without a separate address, contact the Florida Economic Development Council at the address listed above.

Enterprise Florida: Offers information and referral services for current and potential small business owners. Also serves as ombudsman to small businesses to help resolve problems being experienced with state agencies. They sponsor workshops and business forums and an annual Small Business Development Workshop that brings together local, state, and federal agency representatives. Distributes and publishes the *Florida New Business Guide Checklist* for small businesses.

Innovation and Commercialization Centers: Sponsored by Enterprise Florida, Technology Development Corporation provides services and assistance designed to help entrepreneurs and emerging technology-based companies grow, launch new products and succeed in the marketplace. Services include business planning, market development, technology access, commercialization assistance, financial expertise and additional services.
- *Vendor Bid System*: An online computer service allowing searches for state bids that fit a particular business.
- *Quick Response Training*: Up to 18 months of employee training for businesses that produce exportable goods or services, create new jobs and employ Florida workers who require customized entry-level skills training.
- *Info-bid*: Helps businesses locate bid opportunities to sell to federal, state and local government agencies, as well as some commercial firms.

* Business Financing

For all items without a separate address, contact the Florida Economic Development Council at the address listed above.

Enterprise Bonds: Tax-exempt Industrial Development Bonds (IDBs). These bonds provide a cost-effective means for qualified manufacturers, processors and nonprofit organizations to access public and private bond markets, particularly for small fixed asset investment projects with limited access to those markets. Minimum loan size is $500,000. Maximum loan size is $2,000,000 unless a larger amount is strongly supported by local economic development officials.

The Economic Development Transportation Fund: Commonly referred to as the "Road Fund," provides funding to units of local government for the elimination of transportation problems that adversely impact a specific company's location or expansion decision. Up to $2,000,000 may be provided to a local government to implement the improvements.

Florida Energy Loan Program: Provides low interest loans for energy conservation measures (ECM) to encourage eligible Florida businesses to reduce energy consumption while increasing energy efficiency. Maximum to $75,000; Minimum of $1,500.

The Florida Recycling Loan Program: Provides funding for machinery and equipment for manufacturing, processing, or conversion systems utilizing materials which have been or will be recycled; collection systems are not eligible. Direct Loans — Maximum to $200,000; minimum of $20,000. Maximum amount for leveraged loans will be $200,000, or 40% of total eligible costs, whichever is less.

Florida Export Finance Corporation: Makes available pre- and post-shipment working capital to small and medium size Florida exporters. Programs include state-supported direct loans and guarantees as well as packaging services that provide access to EXIM Bank and SBA export finance and working capital guaranty programs. Direct loans for the lesser of 90% of the product cost or $50,000. Loan guarantees for the lesser of 90% of a loan provided by a lender or $500,000. No minimum size.

Community Development Corporation Support and Assistance Program: Provides funds to local community development corporations, which in turn make loans to private businesses for the establishment of new businesses; provide financial assistance to existing businesses; or purchase equity interest in businesses located within a service area.

Rural Revolving Loan Program: Designed to provide gap funding for economic development projects in rural counties. Loan size to $200,000 or 10% of the project being assisted, whichever is less.

Florida Venture Finance Directory: Acts as a "wholesaler" in providing information to assist in the guidance of financing searches, Capital Development developed and published *The Florida Venture Finance Directory*. The *Directory* serves as an effective tool for economic development organizations (primary distributors) to assist local businesses in their fund raising efforts.

Venture Capital Network Development: Financial support, within budget limitations, is provided to a limited number of venture capital conferences at which Florida entrepreneurs have opportunity to present their ventures to members of the venture capital community. Enterprise Florida also is specifically interested in supporting initiatives leading to increased participation of private individual investors in Florida business ventures.

The Technology Investment Fund: Makes co-investments with Florida companies in promising technology-related projects with near-term commercial potential. Investments fall within a range of $25,000 to $250,000, depending upon the project's scope, commercial potential, matching funds, leveraged funds, the number and quality of other proposals received and the amount of funding requested in the highest ranked proposals.

Cypress Equity Fund: A $35.5 million venture capital "fund of funds" organized to facilitate investment in the venture capital asset class by Florida financial institutions, and to provide a platform to showcase Florida to the national venture capital community.

* Tax Incentives

For all items without a separate address, contact the Florida Economic Development Council at the address listed above.

No corporate income tax on limited partnerships, individuals, estates, and private trusts.
No state personal income tax.
No inventory tax.
No collected or assessed property tax at the state level.
No sales tax on groceries, prescription medicines, household fuels, and most services.
No sales tax on "Boiler Fuels" used at a fixed Florida location in an industrial manufacturing, processing, production or compounding process.
No sales and use tax on goods manufactured or produced in the state for resale for export outside the state.

The Qualified Target Industry Tax Refund Program: A tool available to Florida communities to encourage quality job growth in targeted high value-added businesses. The program provides tax refunds to pre-approved applicants of up to $5,000 per new job created ($7,500 in an enterprise zone).

Enterprise Zone Program: Offers financial incentives to businesses to encourage private investment as well as employment opportunities for residents of 30 designated Enterprise Zones. Tax incentives are available to all types of businesses located within a designated zone which employ zone residents, rehabilitate real property or purchase business equipment to be used in the zone. Tax credits, sales tax exemptions and refunds are also available.

* Exports

For all items without a separate address, contact the Florida Economic Development Council at the address listed above.

Enterprise Florida offers on-staff multi-language capabilities and are prepared to help businesses open and operate companies in Florida or to engage in trade. A sophisticated and experienced network of financial, trade, transportation, and commercial services, including freight forwarders and the largest number of customs brokers and insurers in the United States, supports the global marketing efforts of the state's business community. A statewide network of world trade centers, bi-national chambers of commerce, and international

State Money - Georgia

business associations also can assist companies wishing to explore international business opportunities.

* Women and Minorities

For all items without a separate address, contact the Florida Economic Development Council at the address listed above.

Minority Business Development Centers: Offers existing and potential minority entrepreneurs a wide range of free services, from initial counseling on how to start a business to the more complex issues of planning and growth.

Minority Business Advocacy and Assistance Office: Responsible for certifying minority business enterprises to do business with state agencies.

Office of Minority Business Development: Develops statewide initiative to help minority and women-owned businesses prosper in Florida and the global marketplace. Advocates for minority economic development and provides assistance to minority businesses and organizations. Contact: Office of Minority Business Development, 2801 Ponce de Leon Blvd., Suite 700, Coral Gables, FL 33134; 305-569-2654.

Black Business Investment Board: Oversees the state's investment in black business investment corporations, which provide technical assistance and loans to black-owned businesses. For more information, contact Florida Black Business Investment Board, 1711 S. Gadsen St., Tallahassee, Fl 32301; 850-487-4850.

Black Business Investment Corporations: Provides loans, loan guarantees, joint ventures, limited partnerships or any combination thereof. For more information, contact Florida Black Business Investment Board, 1711 S. Gadsen St., Tallahassee, Fl 32301; 850-487-4850.

Black Business Venture Corporation: A vehicle for initiating business acquisitions and engaging in real estate development. Serves a twofold purpose: to provide real and/or commercial office space for Black businesses; and to address the larger community needs such as local employment and retail centers.

Florida Contractors' Cooperative Surety Bond Support and Management Development Program: Assists the African American contractor in developing a relationship with a surety company that is equipped to meet long-term bonding needs of the business.

* Small Business Administration Offices

Wilfredo Gonzalez
7825 Baymeadows Way, Suite 100-B
Jacksonville, FL 32256
904-443-1970
Fax: 904-443-1912

Gary Cook
100 South Biscayne Boulevard, 7th Floor
Miami, FL 33131
305-536-5533
Fax: 305-536-7566

Georgia

Office of Economic Development
60 Executive Park South, NE, Suite 250
Atlanta, GA 30329-2231
404-679-4940
Fax: 800-736-1155
www.dca.state.ga.us

* Business Assistance

For all items without a separate address, contact the Georgia Office of Economic Development at the address listed above.

Georgia Department of Community Affairs (DCA): Responsible for state administration of many incentive programs as well as providing technical assistance in the area of economic development to local governments, development authorities, and private for-profit entities. Provides information on financing programs and other services offered by the state government.

DCA maintains a highly skilled and extremely dedicated graphics and editorial staff to ensure that the information it gathers is effectively digested and promptly disseminated. Some of the department's many publications include:
- *Small Business Resource Guide*: Manual for small business owners with useful instruction, organization addresses and telephone numbers and resources.
- *Georgia's Communities-Planning, Growing, Achieving*: Publication contains information about various federal, state, and local financing programs that benefit businesses located in Georgia.
- *Economic Development Financing Packet*
- *Regional Development Center Listing*: List of Georgia's 16 RDCs with addresses and telephone numbers.

One-Stop Environmental Permitting: Georgia offers one-stop environmental permitting through its Department of Natural Resources, Environmental Protection Division. The state has the full authority of the U.S. Environmental Protection Agency (EPA) to issue permits that meet Federal standards, thus allowing a single permit to meet all requirements.

Emissions Credit Banking and Trading System: Companies can buy, sell or trade credits received for reducing the amount of pollutants it emits beyond those required by Federal regulations. These credits can be used at a later time to offset requirements on pollution created by the company's new growth, or could be sold or traded to another company.

Industrial Revenue Bonds: Taxable and tax-exempt industrial revenue bond financing is available through the state or local development authorities at competitive, below-prime rates.

Supplier Choice Power: Georgia companies with electricity demands of 900 kilowatts or higher may choose among competing suppliers, taking advantage of a competitive market. This cost-saving option has been available to Georgia consumers long before deregulation of the industry was even contemplated.

Georgia Secretary of State: First Stop Business Information Center provides the small business owner and the prospective entrepreneur with a central point of information and contacts for state regulatory requirements for opening a business. Contact: Georgia Secretary of State, 214 State Capitol, Atlanta, GA 30334; 404-656-2881; Fax: 404-656-0513; {www.sos.state.ga.us}.

* Business Financing

For all items without a separate address, contact the Georgia Office of Economic Development at the address listed above.

The Employee Incentive Program: A financing program that may be used in conjunction with traditional private financing to carry out economic development projects which will result in employment of moderate and low income persons. Amounts not available.

The Entrepreneurial Development Loan Fund (EDLF): A loan program to facilitate economic development, particularly in targeted Atlanta Project cluster areas by making credit available to small businesses located within those areas, particularly businesses owned by minorities and women. Typically, loans range from a low of $25,000 to a maximum of $100,000; however, smaller amounts and larger amounts may be considered.

Community Home Investment Program (CHIP): Created by the National Affordable Housing Act of 1990, the Home Investment Partnerships (HOME) Program is the first federally funded block grant designed to address state and local affordable housing concerns with a maximum amount awarded per local government applicant of $200,000.

Lead Safe Homes Demonstration Program: Exists for the purpose of reducing lead-based paint hazards in approximately 475 homes occupied by low and moderate income persons. There is no set amount that each applicant can receive.

Immediate Threat and Danger Program: Funds community development, having a particular urgency because existing conditions pose a serious and immediate threat to the health or welfare of the community. The maximum amount an applicant may receive is $20,000, which shall not exceed half of total project cost.

Local Development Fund: A state funded grant program that provides local governments with matching funds for community improvement projects. The maximum grant amount is $10,000 for single community projects and $20,000 for multi-community projects.

Appalachian Regional Commission (ARC): An economic development program providing matching grant funds to eligible applicants for projects that will benefit the entire 35-county area of Appalachian Georgia.

Appalachian Region Business Development Revolving Loan Fund: A $2.2 million pool that can be used in the Appalachian Region for loans to projects that create or save jobs. The maximum loan amount is $200,000 per qualifying business, or 50% of total project cost, whichever is less. There is no maximum project cost and no minimum loan amount.

Regional Assistance Program (RAP): Grants are available on a competitive basis to local governments, development authorities, and regional development centers for regional industrial parks and similar facilities, regional water and sewer treatment facilities, regional transportation and communication facilities, regional marketing and recruitment programs, and other projects important to regional economic development. Grants will be available up to $250,000 per multi-county or regional economic development implementation project with no minimum match required.

Research and Development Tax Credit: Companies are eligible for a tax credit on research expenses for research conducted within Georgia for any business or headquarters of any such business engaged in manufacturing, warehousing and distribution, processing, telecommunications, tourism, and research and development industries. The credit is 10% of the additional research expense over the base amount and may be carried forward ten years, but may not exceed 50% of the business' net tax liability in any one year.

Small Business Growth Companies Tax Credit: Tax credit is granted for any business or headquarters of any such business engaged in manufacturing, warehousing and distribution, processing, telecommunications, tourism, and research and development industries having a state net taxable income which is 20% or more above that of the preceding year if its net taxable income in each of the two preceding years was also 20% or more. The credit applies to companies whose total tax liability does not exceed $1.5 million.

The Business Improvement Loan Fund (BILF) Program: Designed to encourage the revitalization of targeted business districts in Atlanta, and to support commercial/ industrial development in other eligible areas. Direct loans and loan participation up to $50,000 are available to businesses that are not able to obtain a market rate loan.

The Phoenix Fund: A program created to assist small and medium-sized businesses providing loan amounts from $10,000-$100,000 for construction or renovation of privately-owned commercial buildings, equipment purchases needed to operate a business, and, in some cases, working capital. Contact: Atlanta Development Authority, 230 Peachtree St., Suite 100, Atlanta, GA 30303; 404-568-7000.

Atlanta Export Assistance Center: Provides marketing assistance, a resource center and financial assistance. The professional counseling services provided by EAC counselors are free of charge. Most market research and trade information is furnished at no cost to the client. Contact: Export Assistance Center, 285 Peachtree Center Ave., Suite 200, Atlanta, GA 30303; 404-657-1964.

The Georgia Procurement Assistance Center: Assists firms in their efforts to do business with the federal government. The Center helps firms solicit bids and locate procurement opportunities with the Department of Defense and area military facilities seeking certain goods and services. Although assistance is given upon request to any firm, the majority of clients are small and disadvantaged businesses. Contact Georgia Tech Economic Development Institute, 208 O'Keefe Bldg., Atlanta, GA 30332; 404-894-6121.

Business Retention and Expansion Process: Provides a process for local governments, chambers and/or development authorities to survey existing industries and identify the perceptions and potential problems of private sector firms concerning issues like future plans, international trade, labor and manpower, local government services, energy requirements, and community linkages.

Surety Bond Guarantee Program: Enables small contractors to obtain the surety bonds necessary to compete for government and non-government contracts.

* Tax Incentives

For all items without a separate address, contact the Georgia Office of Economic Development at the address listed above.

Georgia Employment Tax Credit Program: A tax credit on Georgia income taxes for eligible businesses that create new jobs in counties or "less-developed" census tract areas.

Job Tax Credit: Companies engaged in manufacturing, warehousing and distribution, processing, telecommunications, tourism or research and development that create 25 or more jobs may receive between a $500 and $2,500-per-job tax credit. Companies that locate in industrial enterprise zones are required to create 10 new jobs to be eligible for this tax credit.

Investment Tax Credit: Taxpayers operating an existing manufacturing or telecommunications facility or telecommunications support facility in Georgia for three years may obtain a 1% credit against their income tax liability when they invest $50,000. That credit increases to 3% for recycling, pollution control and defense conversion activities.

Industrial Enterprise Zones: The City of Atlanta, as authorized under a special provision of Georgia law, has designated two industrial parks as industrial enterprise zones. Companies in both the Atlanta and Southside industrial parks receive 100% freeport on all three classes of inventory and may receive real property tax reduction for up to 25 years. All buildings constructed in these enterprise zones are exempted from local property taxes at levels that begin at 100%. These exemptions decrease in increments of 20% every five years. New businesses in both parks are eligible for a $2,500-per job tax credit for a payroll of ten or more persons.

The Atlanta Empowerment Zone: Businesses which locate in the federally designated City of Atlanta Empowerment Zone and employ residents from this zone are eligible for various federal and state tax incentives, job training benefits and other assistance. A local executive board decides and manages the allocation of federal funds that are channeled through the State of Georgia.

Commercial Enterprise Zone: City of Atlanta offers a commercial enterprise zone designation for office employers applying in portions of the city including the central business district. Substantial property tax relief is possible.

Tax Exemptions

Computer Software: Taxable software includes canned prewritten software and canned software modified for specific applications. All other software is exempt.

Electricity Exemption: Electricity purchased that interacts directly with a product being manufactured is exempt from sales taxes when the total cost of the electricity makes up 50% or more of all the materials used in making the product.

Goods Delivered Out of State: Exemptions are provided for the sale of tangible personal property manufactured or assembled in Georgia for export when delivery is taken outside Georgia; aircraft, watercraft, motor vehicles and other transportation equipment mailed, manufactured or assembled in Georgia, when sold by the manufacturer or assembler by the purchaser within Georgia for the sole purpose of removing the property from this state under its own power when the equipment does not lend itself more reasonably to removal by other means.

Manufacturing Machinery: Tax exemptions are provided for machinery used directly in the manufacture of tangible personal property under two conditions: (1) the machinery is bought to replace or upgrade machinery in an existing manufacturing plant, and (2) the machinery is incorporated as additional machinery for the first time into an existing manufacturing plant. Machinery used directly in the remanufacture of aircraft engines, parts and components on a factory basis may also be exempt from sales and use tax.

Primary Material Handling: Primary material handling equipment purchased for direct use in storage, handling and movement of tangible personal property in a new or expanding warehouse or distribution facility is exempted from sales and use tax when such new facility or expansion is valued at $5 million or more and does not engage in direct retail sales.

Transportation: Exemptions are provided on and for charges made for the transportation of tangible personal property including, but not limited to, charges for accessorial services such as refrigeration, switching, storage and demurrage made in connection with interstate and intrastate transportation of the property.

* Exports

For all items without a separate address, contact the Georgia Office of Economic Development at the address listed above.

The *Atlanta Export Assistance Center* offers the following resources: Marketing Assistance, Resource Center, Financial Assistance, The Atlanta Export Assistance Center combines the export promotion and finance resources of the following eight agencies: U.S. Department of Commerce, U.S. Small Business Administration, The Georgia Department of Agriculture, The Georgia Department of Industry, Trade & Tourism, The Georgia Housing and Finance Authority, Georgia's Institute of Technology's Center for International Standards and Quality, and the Service Corps of Retired Executives.

The *Atlanta Region* houses consulates, trade offices, and Chambers of Commerce for 44 countries. These organizations provide assistance with foreign exporting, importing and investing.

International Trade Data Network (ITDN): A not-for-profit data multiplier, GDITT provides the business community with the timely, detailed market intelligence needed to be competitive in the global arena.

For these programs, contact Atlanta Regional Export Assistance Center, 285 Peachtree Center Avenue,, Suite 200, Atlanta, GA 30303; 404-657-1900; Fax: 404-657-1970.

* Women and Minorities

For all items without a separate address, contact the Georgia Office of Economic Development at the address listed above.

Georgia Minority Subcontractors Tax Credit: Provides for an income tax adjustment on the State Tax Return, to any company which subcontracts with a minority-owned firm to furnish goods, property or services to the State of Georgia. The law allows a corporation, partnership, or individual, in computing Georgia taxable income, to subtract from federal taxable income or federal adjusted gross income, 10% of the amount of qualified payments to minority subcontractors. For more information, contact Small and Minority Business

State Money - Hawaii

Program, 200 Piedmont Ave., Suite 1304, West Floyd Bldg., Atlanta, GA 30334; 404-656-6315; 800-495-0053.

Atlanta Economic Development Corporation (AEDC): Provides financial and technical assistance to small minority and female owned businesses to expand and/or relocate in the city. In cooperation with local financial institutions and government agencies, it provides a variety of financial aids for business development projects that have corresponding public benefits.

Minority Small Business Resource Organizations: These organizations provide a variety of technical counseling and financial assistance to minority small businesses:
- *Atlanta Business League*, PO Box 92363, Atlanta, GA 30314; 404-584-8126
- *Atlanta Public Schools,* Contract Compliance Office, 1631 LaFrance Street, NE, Atlanta, GA 30307; 404-371-7129
- *Business Development Center – NAACP*, 2034 Metropolitan Parkway, SW, Atlanta, GA 30315; 404-768-5755
- *Department of Commerce*, Minority Business Development Agency (MBDA), Summit Building, Room 1715, 401 West Peachtree Street, NW, Atlanta, GA 30308; 404-730-3300
- *Small Business Administration*, Minority Small Business Division, 1720 Peachtree Road, NW, Suite 606, Atlanta, GA 30309; 404-347-7416.

* Small Business Administration Offices

Billy Max Paul
233 Peachtree Street, NE, Suite 1800
Atlanta, GA 30303
404-331-4999
Fax: 404-331-2354

Charles Anderson
1720 Peachtree Road, NW, 6th Floor
Atlanta, GA 30309
404-331-0100
Fax: 404-331-0101

Hawaii

Department of Business, Economic Development and Tourism
P.O. Box 2359
Honolulu, HI 96804
No. 1 Capitol District Bldg.
250 S. Hotel Street
Honolulu, HI 96813
808-586-2593
Fax: 808-586-2589
www.hawaii.gov/dbedt/index.html

* Business Assistance

For all items without a separate address, contact the Hawaii Department of Business, Economic Development and Tourism at the address listed above.

Business Resource Center: Assists both new and existing businesses with information on government permit and license requirements, government procurement, sources of alternative financing, marketing, preparing a business plan, and available entrepreneurship training programs. Access to statistical, economic and marketing information, as well as information and services available from other government sources. Contact Business Resource Center, Department of Business, Economic Development and Tourism, No. 1 Capitol District Bldg., 250 S. Hotel St., 4th Floor, EWA Wing, Honolulu, HI 96813; 808-586-2423.

Small Business Information Service: Responsible for providing referrals and information on government licenses, permits and procurement, funding source, and entrepreneurship training.

Business Services Division: Helps new and existing businesses with direct business loans, community development projects, information programs, licensing and permit information and referral, and business advocacy.

Business Action Center: Provides Hawaii's entrepreneurs with the information, business forms, licenses and permits they need to make their small business dreams a reality. Contact: Business Action Center, State Department of Business, Economic Development and Tourism, 1130 N. Nimitz Hwy., Suite A-254, Honolulu, HI 96817; 808-586-2545.

Financial Assistance Branch: Administers loan programs.

Business Resource Center: Accurate timely statistical and economic information for Hawaii. Access to information and services available from other government sources in the State of Hawaii, nationally and internationally. 15,000 titles relating to business, government and economic development in the State of Hawaii with an emphasis on statistical information.

Pacific Business Center Program University of Hawaii at Manoa: The Pacific Business Center matches faculty, students, and facilities at the University of Hawaii at Manoa with requests for assistance from businesses and community development organizations in Hawaii and the U.S. territories in the Pacific Islands. Consultation with program staff is free of charge, and after that clients may be assessed a modest consulting fee to pay faculty and students working on individual projects. Contact: Pacific Business Center, College of Business Administration, University of Hawaii at Manoa, 2404 Maile Way, 4th Floor, Honolulu, HI 96822; 808-956-6286.

Alu Like, Inc. offers a wide range of office support services and technical assistance to all individuals regardless of race. The organization charges a nominal fee, and has several sites. Contact: Alu Like, Business Development Center, 1120 Maunakea St., Suite 271, Honolulu, HI 96817; 808-542-1225.

University of Hawaii Office of Technology Transfer & Economic Development (OTTED) works to involve the University of Hawaii system in economic development support activities for the state. OTTED is responsible for patenting and licensing technologies developed at the University, for funding University-based R&D projects and the development of unique computer applications, and for matching University-based technical, educational and business development resources with the needs of the community.

Hawaii Island Economic Development Board: HIEDB's mission is to facilitate federal resource programs and implement appropriate economic development projects. HIEDB provides valuable information and contacts for area businesses and industries, as well as key liaison to federal, state, county and private sector resources in financing, business planning, permitting, legal advice and other business services. Contact Hawaii Island Economic Development Board, Box 103-281, Hilo, HI 96720; 808-966-5416; Fax: 808-966-6792.

Opportunity Hawaii: Offers information of strategic business advantages to locating Hi-Tech industries in Hawaii. Contact High Technology Development Corporation, 2800 Woodlawn Dr., Suite 10, Honolulu, HI 96822; 888-677-4292; {www.hawaii.htdc.org}.

Employment and Training Fund Program: Business-specific training, upgrade training, new occupational skills training, management skills training, and other similar activities are available to both employers and individuals.

High Technology Development Corporation: Promotes the growth of commercial high-technology industry and assists in promoting hi-tech products and software. Contact High Technology Development Corporation, 2800 Woodlawn Dr., Suite 10, Honolulu, HI 96822; 888-677-4292; {www.hawaii.htdc.org}.

* Business Financing

For all items without a separate address, contact the Hawaii Department of Business, Economic Development and Tourism at the address listed above.

Innovation Loan Program: Controls loans up to $100,000 to start-up companies with innovative projects.

Hawaii Department Of Agriculture Loan Programs:
1. The Agricultural Loan Program is intended to provide financing to "Qualified Farmers" and "New Farmers" engaged in agricultural production of food, feed and fiber. Loans can be made to qualifying sole proprietorships, corporations, partnerships and cooperatives. In addition, qualifying corporations and cooperatives can obtain funding for enterprises engaged in marketing, purchasing, processing and for those who provide certain farm business services.
2. Aquaculture Loan Program: Aquaculture means the production of aquatic plant and animal life in a controlled salt, brackish, or freshwater environment situated on real property. Loans can be made to "Qualified Aquaculturists" organized as sole proprietorships, corporations, cooperatives and partnerships.

For these, contact Department of Agriculture, Agricultural Loan Division, P.O. Box 22159, Honolulu, HI 96823; 808-973-9460; 808-468-4644, ext. 39460.

Hawaii Small Business Innovation Research Grant Program: Its purpose is to expand science and technology-based economic development in Hawaii, increase revenues and quality job opportunities in the State.
1. Federal SBIR Program: Phase I awards determine the feasibility of a new technology and are valued up to $100,000. Phase II awards are a continuation of successful Phase I efforts. Phase II awards typically involve developing a prototype and are valued up to $750,000
2. Hawaii SBIR Matching Grant Program: To encourage Hawaii companies to participate in the program, the High Technology Development Corporation provides a matching grant of up to $25,000 to Hawaii companies that receive Phase I awards

State Money - Idaho

The Rural Economic Transition Assistance: Hawaii (RETA-H) Program provides a limited "window of opportunity" to existing and potential entrepreneurs who would like to take part in the transition of Hawaii's agricultural economy from sugar caned-based monoculture to diversified agriculture and are willing to support the Program's goals. Any individuals, especially displaced sugar workers, and community and agricultural associations with an entrepreneurial spirit, are invited to determine if their ideas are eligible for RETA-H funds. These funds are only available for establishing or expanding businesses which produce, process and/or service agricultural products where funds will ultimately go to establishing former sugar workers as business owners and which will speed the transition toward a diversified agriculture in Hawaii. Most grants are in the range of $50,000 - $200,000.

State of Hawaii Government: May finance exports through its Department of Business, Economic Development & Tourism's Hawaii Capital Loan Program (HCLP). The loan program's objective is to provide standard commercial loans to small businesses unable to get financing from private lenders. With an average loan award amount of $250,000 (maximum $1 million) for terms of up to 20 years, HCLP is available to all SBA- defined small businesses with two bank turndowns. The interest rate is set at a very attractive prime rate minus 1%, which is not to exceed 7.5%.

Hawaii Strategic Development Corporation (HSDC) is a state agency created in 1990 to promote economic development and diversification in conjunction with private enterprise. HSDC has established four venture funds, some of which have new funds in formation. Keo Kea Hawaii is typical of the four funds, which are:
- Keo Kea Hawaii LP (KKH) is a Hawaii Based venture capital limited partnership that invests in start-up, emerging and established companies located in the state of Hawaii with an emphasis on high technology. KKH will purchase up to a maximum of 50% of the limited partnership units offered by each Venture Company, while the other units are purchased by third parties who are not directly involved with the Venture Partnership or the project, nor otherwise directly affiliated with the Venture Partnership or its general partner(s). KKH's maximum commitment is $50,000 per investment and may assist in identifying other investment partners when requested.
- HMS Investments, L. P.
- Hawaii Venture Fund, L. P.
- Tangent Growth Hawaii, L. P.: Mezzanine and Later Stage Fund

Contact: Hawaii Strategic Development Corporation, No. 1 Capitol District Building, 250 South Hotel Street, Suite 503, P.O. Box 2359, Honolulu, HI 96804; 808-587-3829; Fax: 808-587-3832.

* Tax Incentives

For all items without a separate address, contact the Hawaii Department of Business, Economic Development and Tourism at the address listed above.

Hawaii has only two levels of government taxation: state and local.
No personal property tax.
No tax on inventories, furniture, equipment or machinery.
Credit against taxes paid on the purchase of capital goods, machinery, and equipment.
No state tax on goods manufactured for export.
No stock transfer tax: All security exchange transactions are exempt from general excise tax, as an incentive to financial institutions.
No unincorporated business tax.
Banks and financial institutions pay only one business tax.
Manufactured products or those produced for export are exempt from the general excise tax, including custom computer software.
Manufacturers, wholesalers, processors, millers, refiners, packer and canners are taxed on 0.5% of gross proceeds.
Insurance solicitors and agents are taxed at .15 percent.
Contractors are taxed 4% of gross proceeds. All sales of retails goods and services are taxed at 4% of gross income.
Purchase of depreciable and tangible property is allowed with a refundable tax credit against excise and use taxes.
General excise tax exemptions are in effect for air pollution control facilities, certain scientific contracts with the United State, ships used in international trade and commerce, sugar and pineapple manufacturers, and sales of tangible personal property to the federal government.
Enterprise Zones (EZ) Program: A joint state-county effort intended to stimulate--via tax and other incentives--certain types of business activity, job preservation, and job creation in areas where they are most appropriate or most needed. Incentives include 100% exemption from the General Excise Tax (GET) and Use Tax every year. Contractors are also exempt from GET on construction done within an EZ for an EZ-qualified business. An 80% reduction of state income tax the first year. (This reduction goes down 10% each year for 6 more years.) An additional income tax reduction equal to 80% of annual Unemployment Insurance premiums the first year. (This reduction goes down 10% each year for 6 more years.)

* Exports

For all items without a separate address, contact the Hawaii Department of Business, Economic Development and Tourism at the address listed above.

U.S. Department of Commerce-Commercial Service (Honolulu District office): The trade specialist at the Honolulu District office assists U.S. companies seeking to expand into export markets. The Honolulu District office provides companies with trade leads, foreign market research, and information on trade events, seminars, and conferences.

Foreign Trade Zones: Ports designated for duty-free entry of goods. Merchandise may be stored, displayed, or used for manufacturing within the zone and re-exported without duties being paid. Contact: Foreign Trade Zone #9, 521 Ala Moana, Pier 2, Honolulu, HI 96813; 808-586-2507.

Local Chambers of Commerce: Provide exporters with copies of and instructions for completing a general Certificate of Origin. This certificate is a notarized statement authenticating the country of origin of an export good.

Consulate Generals in Hawaii: Various consulate generals in Hawaii offer limited trade counseling and a few have trade libraries.

Thai Trade Representative Office: Focuses primarily on the promotion of Thailand products in Hawaii.

* Women and Minorities

For all items without a separate address, contact the Hawaii Department of Business, Economic Development and Tourism at the address listed above.

The Honolulu Minority Business Development Center: The objectives of the Honolulu Minority Business Development Center are to 1) promote the creation and/or expansion of viable and competitive minority-owned businesses, 2) increase contracting opportunities from public and private sources for minority-owned businesses, and 3) provide management and technical assistance to qualified minority individuals and firms in the areas of planning, finance, construction assistance, and general management to improve the overall performance, profit, and net worth of minority firms.

* Small Business Administration Offices

Andrew Poepoe
300 Ala Moana Blvd.
Box 50207, Room 2-235
Honolulu, HI 96850
808-541-2990
Fax: 808-541-2976

Idaho

Idaho Department of Commerce
700 West State Street
P.O. Box 83720
Boise, ID 83720-0093
208-334-2470
Fax: 208-334-2631
www.idoc.state.id.us/pages/businesspage.html

* Business Assistance

For all items without a separate address, contact the Idaho Department of Commerce at the address listed above.

Economic Development Division: This office can provide information and expertise in dealing with state, federal, and local agencies. They also have information on financing programs and other services offered by the state government.

Idaho Business Network (IBN): Operated by the Idaho Department of Commerce to help Idaho companies bid on federal, state and large corporation contracts.
- *Opportunity Notices*: Every day bid notices on federal, state and private contracts are entered into the Idaho Business Network computer. These bidding opportunities are matched with the capabilities of Idaho businesses participating in the IBN. When a match occurs the client company is notified with a printed or e-mail version "opportunity notice" alerting them to the opportunity and providing information

State Money - Illinois

- needed to obtain the bid package.
- *Military and Federal Standards*: Federal bid packages often reference military and federal specifications by name or number without providing the actual documents. The Idaho Business Network maintains a CD-ROM library of all military and federal standards and specifications. Printed copies of required specifications and standards are provided at no charge to businesses participating in the IBN.
- *Federal Acquisition Regulations (F.A.R.)*: Contains the rules and regulations used by federal agencies to purchase products and services. Bid packages often refer to F.A.R. clauses by name or number without providing the text of the document. The IBN maintains the F.A.R. on CD-ROM, and provides printed copies of needed clauses to participating companies at no charge.
- *Trade Missions*: All IBN clients are welcome to attend periodic trade missions to visit large corporations, military sites, and other government agencies. Businesses attending the trade missions have the opportunity to meet with buyers to market their products and services.
- *Workshops and Seminars*: The IBN holds workshops statewide on topics such as selling to Mountain Home Air Force Base, selling to the INEEL, how to package for the military, quality assurance, etc.
- *The Governor's Business Opportunity Conference*: Annually, the IBN hosts the Governor's Business Opportunity Conference with over 60 large private corporations and government agencies sending buyers to meet with representatives of Idaho businesses. Concurrent training workshops are also held during the conference on a wide range of topics, such as introduction to procurement and marketing strategies for small businesses.
- *Electronic Bulletin Board*: Provides computer and modem access to all bid notices obtained by the IBN for the most current ten days.
- *CAGE Code*: All companies wishing to do business with the U.S. Department of Defense must have an identification number known as a Commercial and Government Entity Code, or CAGE Code. Companies applying for a CAGE Code must be sponsored by a government agency. The Idaho Business Network provides CAGE Code application forms and sponsors participating Idaho business applications
- *New Industry Training Program*: Provides customized job training for new and expanding industries.
- *Work Force Training*: Funds are available to provide skilled workers for specific economic opportunities and industrial expansion initiatives.

* Business Financing

For all items without a separate address, contact the Idaho Department of Commerce at the address listed above.

Revenue Allocation Finance Areas: Any city in Idaho can have established urban renewal areas. New facilities located within designated revenue allocation area boundaries may qualify for tax exempt bonds. Tax revenues from increases in property value within the urban renewal area are dedicated to servicing the bonds. Also known as Tax Increment Financing, these funds can be used to pay for infrastructure development costs of a project.

Industrial Revenue Bonds: Idaho cities and counties are able to form public corporations for the purpose of issuing industrial revenue bonds (IRBs). The IRB program provides for loans of up to $10 million, at tax-exempt interest rates, to finance the improvement or purchase of land, buildings, and machinery or equipment used in manufacturing, production, processing, or assembly.

Rural Economic and Community Development Administration: Offers guarantees up to 90% of loans between $500,000 and $10 million made to small businesses located in areas not within the boundaries of a city of 50,000 or more. Loan proceeds can be used for the purchase, development or improvement of land, buildings and equipment, or a start-up and working capital.

* Tax Incentives

For all items without a separate address, contact the Idaho Department of Commerce at the address listed above.

Idaho's Investment Tax Credit: Equal to 3% of qualified investment (not to exceed more than 45% of a given year's tax liability) and may be carried forward for seven years.

Nonbusiness-Related Contributions: Corporations are allowed credit for certain nonbusiness-related contributions, e.g., education and rehabilitation. Net operating loss carrybacks are limited to $100,000 per tax year. The $100,000 loss limit may be carried back three years and if it is not absorbed by the income in those three years, the rest of the loss may be carried forward 15 years. Instead of carrying a loss back, a taxpayer may choose to carry the loss forward for up to 15 years or until it has been completely absorbed.

Property Tax Exemptions: Include inventories, livestock, stored property in transit, pollution control facilities, household belongings, clothing, and properly licensed motor or recreational vehicles. Statewide, tax rates vary generally from 0.8 to 2.8 percent, with an average of 1.7 percent.

Excluded from a 5% sales tax: Utilities, motor fuels (which are taxed separately), and tangible personal property used for production activities involved in manufacturing, farming, processing, mining, and fabricating.

Mining Claims: Non-patented mining claims are exempt from property taxation.

* Exports

For all items without a separate address, contact the Idaho Department of Commerce at the address listed above.

The Idaho Department of Commerce's Division of International Business: Provides a variety of services and assistance to all Idaho firms interested in doing business overseas, with special programs for small- and medium-sized firms.

Idaho International Business Development Center (IIBDC): Seeks to coordinate efforts statewide to promote Idaho in the global marketplace. The division, in partnership with the Boise Branch Office of the U.S. Department of Commerce, maintains regular contact with importers, distributors, wholesalers, and retailers in foreign countries and can supply market data and information on foreign packaging, labeling requirements, language barriers, consumer preferences, and other trade factors.

Idaho Department of Agriculture: Offers a broad range of assistance to Idaho companies which export Idaho agricultural commodities and processed and specialty food products. The Department of Agriculture sponsors many special agricultural trade events and participates with the Department of Commerce in joint seminars, workshops, and trade shows.

* Small Business Administration Offices

Tom Bergdoll
1020 Main Street, Suite 290
Boise, ID 83702
208-334-1696
Fax: 208-334-9353

Illinois

Department of Commerce and Community Affairs
620 E. Adams
Springfield, IL 62602
217-782-7500
Fax: 217-524-3701
www.commerce.state.il.us

100 West Randolph St.
Suite 3-400
Chicago, IL 60601
312-814-7179
Fax: 312-814-2370

* Business Assistance

For all items without a separate address, contact the Illinois Department of Commerce and Community Affairs at the address listed above.

Department of Commerce and Community Affairs: Provides information, assistance and advocacy to facilitate and advance the economic development process in partnership with Illinois' communities, businesses, and their network of public and private sector providers.

Small Business Division: Responsible for an environment that supports small business success resulting in increased employment opportunities and prosperous communities throughout Illinois. Provides advocacy, business assistance, training and information resources to help entrepreneurs, small companies and their partners enhance their competitiveness in a global economy. Serves customers through a dynamic, integrated small business assistance delivery system that matches the diversity of their customers' current and future needs.

Business Association Directory: Includes organization mission, location and member information.

State Money - Illinois

Workforce Development & Manufacturing Technology Assistance: Provides programs to assist manufacturers to improve employee job skills and manufacturing efficiency. Labor-Management programs are also available.

First Stop Business Information Center: Provides individuals with comprehensive information on state business permits and licenses, business startup assistance, regulatory guidance, demographic and census data. Guides them through permitting, licensing and regulatory processes. Phone: 800-252-2923.

Procurement Technical Assistance Centers (PTAC): Provide one-on-one counseling, technical information, marketing assistance and training to existing Illinois businesses that are interested in selling their products and/or services to local, state or federal government agencies. The services are offered through PTACs located at community colleges, universities, chambers of commerce and business development organizations.

Small Business Innovation Research Centers (SBIRC): Provide counseling, technical information and training to Illinois entrepreneurs and small businesses interested in pursuing research and development opportunities available to them through various federal and state programs. These programs provide small businesses with a means of developing new and marketable technologies and innovations and also for enhancing existing products and services.

* Business Financing

For all items without a separate address, contact the Illinois Department of Commerce and Community Affairs at the address listed above.

Participation Loan Program, Development Corporation Participation Loan Program, Minority, Women and Disabled Participation Loan Program: Through these loan participation programs, the Illinois Department of Commerce and Community Affairs (DCCA) helps small businesses obtain financing through Illinois banks, development corporations, and lending institutions for business start-up, expansion, modernization and competitiveness improvement. Generally, the Department may provide subordinated small business loans up to 25% of the total amount of a project, but not less than $10,000 or more than $750,000.

Title IX Revolving Loan Fund: Provides low-cost supplemental financing to small and medium-sized manufacturers located in areas declared eligible for assistance. Proceeds may be used for the acquisition of land, buildings, machinery and equipment, building construction or renovations, and leasehold improvements.

Rural Development Loan Program: Assists businesses in communities with populations less than 25,000. Proceeds may be used to purchase land, construct or renovate buildings and purchase machinery and equipment.

Farm Development Authority Programs: 85% guarantee for loans by local lenders; up to $300,000 for farm owners. Proceeds may be used for land acquisition, building construction and improvements and the purchase of machinery and equipment.

State Treasurer's Economic Program: Provides companies with access to affordable capital to expand their operations and retain or create jobs in the state. For each permanent full-time job that is created or retained, the Treasurer can deposit $25,000 at well below market rates into the borrower's financial institution. That institution will then lend the money at below prevailing interest rates to the borrower.

Enterprise Zone Financing Program: Designed to encourage businesses to locate within an Illinois Enterprise Zone. DCCA may participate in an eligible loan for no less than $10,000, nor more than $750,000. In no case shall the amount of DCCA's subordinated participation exceed 25% of the total project. Ineligible uses of funds are debt refinancing and contingency funding.

Development Corporation Participation Loan Program: Provides financial assistance through a Development Corporation to small businesses that provide jobs to workers in the region served by the Development Corporation. The state will participate in loans up to 2% of the total amount of a project but not less than $10,000 nor more than $750,000.

Capital Access Program (CAP): Designed to encourage lending institutions to make loans to businesses that do not qualify for conventional financing. CAP is based on a portfolio insurance concept where the borrower and DCCA each contribute a percentage of the loan amount into a reserve fund located at the lender's bank. This reserve fund enables the financial institution to make loans beyond its conventional risk threshold and is available to draw upon to recover losses on loans made under the program.

Technology Venture Investment Program (TVIP): Provides investment capital for young or growing Illinois businesses in cooperation with private investment companies or investors. Program investments will be used for businesses seeking funding for any new process, technique, product or technical device commercially exploitable by Illinois businesses in fields such as health care and biomedical products, information and telecommunications, computing and electronic equipment, manufacturing technology, materials, transportation and aerospace, geoscience, financial and service industries, and agriculture and biotechnology. Program funds shall be used for such costs including, but not limited to, research and development costs, acquisition of assets, working capital, purchase or lease of machinery and/or equipment, and the acquisition and/or improvement or rehabilitation of land and buildings.

Affordable Financing of Public Infrastructure Program: Provides financial assistance to or on behalf of local governments, public entities, medical facilities and public health clinics.

Community Services Block Grant Loan Program: Provides long-term, fixed-rate financing to new or expanding businesses that create jobs and employment opportunities for low-income individuals.

Industrial Training Program: Assists companies in training new workers or upgrading the skills of their existing workers. Grants may be awarded to individual companies, multi-company efforts and intermediary organizations offering multi-company training.

Prairie State 2000 Programs: Businesses that need to retrain employees may utilize these funds. Loans are available to cover 100% of direct training costs. Grants covering 50% of those costs are also available.

Industrial Revenue Bonds: IDFA issues tax-exempt bonds on behalf of manufacturing companies to finance the acquisition of fixed assets such as land, buildings and equipment. Proceeds may also be used for new construction or renovation.

* Tax Incentives

For all items without a separate address, contact the Illinois Department of Commerce and Community Affairs at the address listed above.

No personal income taxes.
Retirement income is not taxed.

Enterprise Zones: Incentives for businesses within a designated Enterprise Zone include:
- Sales tax exemption on building materials to be used in an Enterprise Zone.
- Sales tax exemption on purchases of tangible personal property to be used in the manufacturing or
- Assembly process or in the operation of a pollution control facility within an Enterprise Zone.
- Tax exemption on gas, electricity and the Illinois Commerce Commission's administrative charge is available to business located in Enterprise Zones.
- Tax credit of 0.5% is allowed a taxpayer who invest in qualified property in a Zone.
- Dividend Income Deduction for individual, corporations, trust, and estates are not taxed on dividend income from corporation doing substantially all their business in a Zone.
- Jobs tax credit allows a business a $500 credit on Illinois income tax for each job created in the Zone for which a certified eligible worker is hired.
- Financial institutions are not taxed on the interest received on loans for development within a Zone.
- Businesses may deduct double the value of a cash or in-kind contribution to an approved project of a designated Zone organization form taxable income.

Corporate Income Tax: Corporate income is taxed at 7.3% which includes a 4.8% state income tax and a 2.5% personal property replacement tax.

Incentives include:
- The 2.5% replacement tax may be deducted from the 4.8% state income tax.
- After 2000, apportionment will be based on sales alone.

Tax Credits include:
- 0.5% credit for investment in mining, manufacturing or retailing, plus an additional 0.5% if employment increases over 1%; a 1/6% training expense tax credit; and a 6.5% Research and Development credit.
- There are no local corporate income taxes in Illinois.

Sales Tax Exemptions: Purchases of manufacturing machinery as well as replacement parts and computers used to control manufacturing machinery; purchases of farm machinery; pollution controls, building materials to be used in an Enterprise Zone; and materials consumed in the manufacturing process in Enterprise Zones. Purchases or manufacturing machinery receive a credit equal to 50% of what the taxes would have been if the manufacturing machinery was taxable, making it possible for the manufacturers to use this credit to offset any other sales tax liability they incur. Food and drugs are taxed at the reduced rate of 1%.

Property Tax Exemptions: All property other than real estate is exempt from the property tax. Taxing bodies within Enterprise Zones may abate property taxes without a dollar limit for the life of the zone.

State Money - Indiana

* Exports

For all items without a separate address, contact the Illinois Department of Commerce and Community Affairs at the address listed above.

International Trade Centers/NAFTA Opportunity Centers (ITC/NOC): Provide information, counseling and training to existing, new-to-export Illinois companies interested in pursuing international trade opportunities. The NOCs provide specialized assistance to those firms seeking to take advantage of the trade opportunities in Mexico and Canada made possible by the North American Free Trade Agreement.

Foreign Trade Zones: Offering low-cost production and warehousing facilities for imported and export-bound products.

* Women and Minorities

For all items without a separate address, contact the Illinois Department of Commerce and Community Affairs at the address listed above.

Business Enterprise Program for Minorities, Females, and Persons with Disabilities (BEP): Promotes the economic development of businesses owned by minorities, females, and persons with disabilities. The Business Enterprise for Minorities, Females, and Persons with Disabilities Act is designed to encourage state agencies to purchase needed goods and services from businesses owned and controlled by members of minority groups, women, and/or persons with disabilities.

Surety Bond Guaranty Program: Designed to provide Illinois' small, minority and women contractors technical assistance, help them receive experience in the industry and assist in obtaining bid, performance and payment bonds for government, public utility and private contracts.

Minority, Women and Disabled Participation Loan Program: (See Business Financing above) Additional information: The Minority, Women and Disabled Participation Loan Program guidelines differ, in that the program funding may not exceed 50% of the project, subject to a maximum of $50,000.

* Small Business Administration Offices

Barbara Notestein
500 West Madison Street
Suite 1240
Chicago, IL 60661
312-353-0357
Fax: 312-353-3426

Judith Roussel
500 West Madison Street
Chicago, IL 60661
312-353-5031
Fax: 312-886-5688

Curt Charter
511 W Capitol Street, Suite 302
Springfield, IL 62704
217-492-4416
Fax: 217-492-4867

Indiana

Indiana Department of Commerce
One North Capitol, Suite 700
Indianapolis, IN 46204
317-232-8888
800-463-8081
317-233-5123 Fax
www.ai.org/bdev/index.html

* Business Assistance

For all items without a separate address, contact the Indiana Department of Commerce at the address listed above.

Indiana Department of Commerce: This office can provide information and expertise in dealing with state, federal, and local agencies. They also have information on financing programs and other services offered by the state government.

Technical & Marketing Assistance

Quality Initiative: Provides quality-awareness education, assessments and information to companies attempting to implement or improve quality-management programs.

Energy Policy Division Services: A wide range of assistance in energy efficiency, alternative energy and recycling market development programs.

Enterprise Advisory Group: Counsels emerging and mature businesses.

Government Marketing Assistance Group: Helps companies that wish to sell to federal, state or local governments.

Indiana Micro-Electronics Center (IMC): Assists businesses in using Application Specific Integrated Circuits (ASICs). Contact: Indiana Business Modernization and Technology corporation, One N. Capitol Ave., Suite 925, Indianapolis, IN 46204; 317-635-3058.

The Indiana Quality Initiative: Quality-awareness education, assessments and information. Contact: Indiana Business Modernization and Technology corporation, One N. Capitol Ave., Suite 925, Indianapolis, IN 46204; 317-635-3058.

International Trade Services: Assistance to Indiana companies in export development in order to increase the sale of Indiana products worldwide.

Office of Regulatory Ombudsman: Acts as a mediator, expediter and problem-solver in areas affecting business.

Government Marketing Assistance Group: Provides counseling to businesses interested in obtaining federal or state government contracts.

Regional Manufacturing Extension Centers (RMEC): Helps small and medium-sized businesses assess and solve problems related to technology, training, marketing and financing. Contact: Indiana Business Modernization and Technology corporation, One N. Capitol Ave., Suite 925, Indianapolis, IN 46204; 317-635-3058.

Trade Show Assistance Program (TSAP): Provides reimbursement for a portion of the costs incurred while companies exhibit their products at overseas trade shows.

* Resources

For all items without a separate address, contact the Indiana Department of Commerce at the address listed above.

Indiana Development Finance Authority (IDFA): Helps Indiana businesses obtain financial assistance through loan guaranty programs, tax-exempt private activity bonds for industrial development, Ex-Im Bank loan guarantees, insurance and direct loans for export products and flexible lending through case reserve accounts. Contact: Indiana Development Finance Authority, One N. Capitol, Suite 320, Indianapolis, IN 46204; 317-233-4332.

Indiana Small Business Development (ISBD) Corporation: Offers conferences and workshops, one-on-one counseling and up-to-date information on new market opportunities. The ISBD Corp. also identifies contracting opportunities with the government, assists growth-oriented companies in approaching new market opportunities and serves as a statewide advocate for contracting and marketing with Indiana's women- and minority-owned businesses. Contact: Indiana Small Business Development Corp., One N. Capitol, Suite 1275, Indianapolis, IN 46204; 317-264-2820.

Indiana Economic Development Association (IEDA): Provides continuity to a statewide community development effort. The organization has two objectives: (1) to utilize the knowledge and resources of the association to make economic development activities in the state more effective, and (2) to cooperate and interact with all state and local organizations engaged in promoting the economic welfare of Indiana. Contact: Indiana Economic Development Association, One N. Capitol, Indianapolis, IN 46204; 317-573-2900.

Indiana Economic Development Council (IEDC): Helps to shape long-term state goals, strategies and policies on economic development matters through non-partisan planning, evaluation, policy development and coordination. The role of the IEDC includes providing independent performance reviews and recommendations relating to governmental budgets and the economic development support systems of public and private entities, both state and local. Contact: Indiana Economic Development Council, One N. Capitol, Suite 425, Indianapolis, IN 46204; 317-631-0871.

* Business Financing

For all items without a separate address, contact the Indiana Department of Commerce at the address listed above.

Loans

Product Development/Commercialization Funding: Provides loans for businesses in need of financing to support research and development projects, or to support commercialization of new technology. Loan amounts vary.

State Money - Indiana

Capital Access Program (CAP): Helps financial institutions lend money to Indiana businesses that don't qualify for loans under conventional lending policies. CAP loans may be of any amount

Certified Development Companies (CDC): Long-term, fixed-rate financing for a business's fixed-asset needs. CDC provides up to 40% of the cost with a commercial bank financing 50% of the total cost. The CDC portion is limited to $750,000. Minimum project cost is $125,000. Contact: Indiana Statewide Certified Development Corp., 8440 Woodfield Crossing, Suite 315, Indianapolis, IN 46240; 317-469-6166.

Hoosier Development Fund: Loans for small to medium-sized businesses. Loans range from $250,000 to several million dollars.

Indiana Community Business Credit Corporation (ICBCC): Loans for small to medium-sized businesses that exceed banks' customary limits. Loan amounts range from $100,000 to $750,000, and must be at least matched by a participating lender. Minimum project is $200,000. Contact Indiana Community Business Credit Corp., 8440 Woodfield Crossing, Suite 315, Indianapolis, IN 46240; 317-469-9704.

Industrial Development Infrastructure Program (IDIP): Supplemental financing for infrastructure projects in support of job creation/retention for low- to moderate-income persons. Amounts determined based on project needs. The program is designed to supplement local funding sources.

Industrial Development Loan Fund: Revolving loans for industrial growth. Loans up to $1 million are available.

Industrial Energy Efficiency Fund: The Energy Policy Division provides loans for improving energy efficiency in industrial processes. The maximum amount available per applicant is $250,000 or 50% of the total eligible project costs, whichever is less.

Loan Guaranty Programs: Financing for land or building acquisition or improvements, structures, machinery, equipment, facilities and working capital. Loan guaranties are available up to $2 million.

Product Development/Commercialization Funding: Loans for research and development or to support commercialization of new technology. Loan amounts are determined by the Business Modernization and Technology Corporation (BMT) and the business. Leveraging of outside funds is encouraged in the loan consideration.

Recycling Promotion and Assistance Fund: Loans to enhance the development of markets for recyclable materials.

Small Business Investment Company Program: Long-term and/or venture capital for small firms.

Strategic Development Fund (SDF): Loans or grants for not-for-profits and cities, towns and counties whose purpose is to promote industrial/business development. Generally $100,000 to $500,000, but can vary depending on the particular SBIC.

Trade Finance Program Financing: Assistance for companies exporting internationally. Amounts: Varies with programs.

Grants

Industrial Energy Efficiency Audits: The Energy Policy Division provides grant to manufacturers to study energy use in their facilities and recommend ways to reduce energy use and energy costs. Maximum amount available per applicant is $5,000.

Alternative Energy Systems Program: The Energy Policy Division offers grants to businesses to fund eligible alternative-fuel technologies and infrastructure development. The maximum amount available per project is $10,000.

Community Development Action Grant (CDAG): Grants to help organizations whose missions include economic development to expand administrative capacity and program development by offsetting miscellaneous expenses. In the case of organizations serving at least two counties, the amount of the grant may not exceed one dollar for every one dollar raised by the organization. The maximum grant award for organizations serving two or more counties may not exceed $75,000. Contact: Community Development Division, Indiana Department of Commerce, One N. Capitol, Suite 600, Indianapolis, IN 46204; 317-232-8911; 800-824-2476.

Industrial Development Grant Fund: Grants for non-profits and local units of government for off-site infrastructure projects in support of new business development. The grant amount is determined based on project needs. However, the program is designed to supplement local funding sources

National Industrial Competitiveness Through Energy, Environment and Economics Grant: The Energy Policy Division has information about Federal grants, with possible state matching funds, to improve energy efficiency, promote a cleaner production process and improve the competitiveness of industry. The maximum amount of federal grant available per applicant is $400,000.

Strategic Development Fund (SDF): Grants or loans for not-for-profits and cities, towns and counties whose purpose is to promote industrial/business development. Grant or loan funds may not exceed 50% of the cost of the project. The maximum grant amount is $250,000. The maximum grant and loan combination may not exceed $500,000.

Tire Recycling Market Development Program: The Energy Policy Division has grants to businesses involved in the production of a product that uses scrap tires as a feedstock. Recycled Tire Product Marketing grants up to $20,000. Recycled Tire Product Procurement grants up to $40,000.

Scrap Tire Market Development Research and Prototype Grant Program: Provides grant to support research on new products or machinery for handling scrap tire recycling. Grant range from $5,000 to $50,000.

Tire-Derived Fuel Testing Grant Program: Provides grants to develop fuel uses for scrap tires. Amount based on project needs.

Trade Show Assistance Program (TSAP): Provides reimbursement for a portion of the costs incurred while companies exhibit their products at overseas trade shows. Reimbursement includes 100% of exhibit space rental or $5,000, whichever is less.

Training 2000: Grants for reimbursement of eligible training costs. Up to 50% of eligible training costs. Awards for retraining have a maximum ceiling of $200,000. For companies seeking to become QS-9000 certified, up to 75% of QS-9000 related costs may be reimbursed.

Bonds

Tax-Exempt Bonds: Provide fixed-asset financing at competitive rates. Limits vary according to the type of project. Most manufacturing facilities are limited to $10 million. Contact: Indiana Development Finance Authority, One N. Capitol, Suite 320, Indianapolis, IN 46204; 317-233-4332.

Tax Increment Financing (TIF): Allows use of TIF revenues for purpose of developing an area. Amounts: Depends on the new property taxes generated as a result of development in the TIF allocation area.

* Tax Incentives

For all items without a separate address, contact the Indiana Department of Commerce at the address listed above.

Indiana Corporate Income Tax: Taxpayers eligible for state corporate income tax credits apply the value first against gross tax liability, then against corporate adjusted gross tax liability and finally against supplemental net liability. Some credits may be applied against future tax liabilities if the amount of current credit exceeds taxes due.

College and University Contribution Credit: A credit for contributions to Indiana colleges and universities. Limited to the lesser of: (a) $1,000; (b) 50% of the contribution; or (c) 10% of the adjusted gross income tax.

Neighborhood Assistance Credit: Credit to corporate or individual taxpayers contributing to neighborhood organizations or who engage in activities to upgrade disadvantaged areas. Up to 50% of the amount invested, not to exceed $25,000 in any taxable year.

Drug and Alcohol Abuse Credit: Maximum credit is $6,250 for corporations with more than 1,000 employees, and $3,750 for corporations with fewer than 1,000 employees.

Research Expense Credit: Credit to any corporate taxpayer entitled to the Federal Research Expense Credit who incurs qualified Indiana research expenses.

Teacher Summer Employment Credit: Credit to persons who hire a public school teacher during the summer in a position that is relevant to a teaching-shortage area in which the teacher is certified. Limited to the lesser of: (a) $2,500; or (b) 50% of the compensation paid.

Enterprise Zone Employment Expense Credit: A taxpayer who conducts business in an enterprise zone is entitled to a maximum credit of $1,500 for each employee who is an enterprise zone resident and who is employed primarily by the taxpayer.

Enterprise Zone Loan Interest Credit: A credit equal to 5% of the lender interest income from qualified loans made in an enterprise zone.

Enterprise Zone Investment Cost Credit: Credit to individual taxpayers against state tax liability equal to a percentage times the price of qualified investment in an enterprise zone business.

Industrial Recovery Tax Credit: Credit for qualifying investments to rehabilitate vacant industrial facilities ("dinosaurs") that are at least 20 years old and at least 300,000 square feet in size.

Personal Computer Tax Credit: Credit for donations of computer units to the "Buddy-Up with Education Program." A credit of $125 per computer unit is allowed.

Twenty-First Century Scholars Program Support Fund Credit: Credit for contributions to the fund. A maximum credit of the lesser of (a) $1,000; (b) 50% of the contribution made; or (c) 10% of the adjusted gross income tax is available.

Maternity Home Credit: Credit for maternity-home owners who provide a temporary residence for a pregnant woman (women).

Prison Credit: Credit for investments in Indiana prisons to create jobs for prisoners. The amount is limited to 50% of the inventory in a qualified project plus 25% of the wages paid to the inmates. The maximum credit a taxpayer may claim is $100,000 per year.

State Money - Indiana

Property Tax Abatement: Property tax abatement in Indiana is authorized under Indiana Code 6-1.1-12.1 in the form of deductions from assessed valuation. Any property owner in a locally designated Economic Revitalization Area (ERA) who makes improvements to the real property or installs new manufacturing equipment is eligible for property tax abatement. Land does not qualify for abatement. Used manufacturing equipment can also qualify as long as such equipment is new to the state of Indiana. Equipment not used in direct production, such as office equipment, does not qualify for abatement.

Real-Property Abatement Calculation: Real-property abatement is a declining percentage of the increase in assessed value of the improvement based on one of the three following time periods and percentages as determined by the local governing body.

Enterprise Zones: The purpose of the enterprise zone program in the state of Indiana is to stimulate local community and business redevelopment in distressed areas. An enterprise zone may consist of up to three contiguous square miles. There are 18 enterprise zones in Indiana. In order to stimulate reinvestment and create jobs within the zones, businesses located within an enterprise zone are eligible for certain tax benefits. These tax benefits include:
- A credit equal to 100% of property-tax liability on inventory.
- Exemption from Indiana Gross Income Tax on the increase in receipts from the base year.
- State Investment Cost Credit (up to 30% of purchase price) for individuals purchasing an ownership interest in an enterprise zone business.
- State Loan Interest Credit on lender interest income (5%) from qualified loans made in an enterprise zone.
- State Employment Expense Credit based on wages paid to qualified zone-resident employees. The credit is the lesser of 10% of the increase in wages paid over the base year, or $1,500 per qualified employee.
- Tax deduction to qualified zone-resident employees equal to the lesser of 50% of their adjusted gross income or $7,500.

Interstate Inventory Tax Exemption: Indiana has a modest inventory tax with a number of deductions available, including the Interstate Inventory Tax Exemption. Finished goods awaiting shipment to out-of-state destinations are usually exempt from the inventory tax. In most instances, a taxpayer may determine the exemption by applying the percentage of that location's total shipments, which went out of state during the previous year.

Industrial Recovery Site (Dinosaur Building): Much like the dinosaurs, many large buildings that were once used for mills, foundries and large manufacturers are obsolete for today's new production methods and technologies. Because of this, these buildings now stand vacant. This program offers special tax benefits to offset the cost of adaptive reuse. Tax benefits are available for 10 years from date of project approval and include the following:

Investment Tax Credit: A credit against the cost of remodeling, repair or betterment of the building or complex of buildings.

Local Option Inventory Tax Credit: A municipality or county has the option of awarding an Inventory Tax Credit to tenants of "dinosaur" buildings.

Maritime Opportunity District: A geographical territory designated at Indiana ports by the Indiana Port Commission. Companies located in a designated district are eligible for tax benefits through the authority of the commission.

Tax Increment Financing (TIF): provides for the temporary allocation to redevelopment or economic districts of increased tax proceeds in an allocation area generated by increases in assessed value. Thus, TIF permits cities, towns or counties to use increased tax revenues stimulated by redevelopment or economic development to pay for the capital improvements needed to induce the redevelopment or economic development. Bond amounts are determined by the size of the project and the amount of the increment available.

Economic Development for a Growing Economy (EDGE): Provides tax credits based on payroll. Individual income tax withholdings for the company's employees can be credited against the company's corporate income tax. Excess withholdings shall be refunded to the company.

* Exports

For all items without a separate address, contact the Indiana Department of Commerce at the address listed above.

International Trade Services Program: The driving force behind the International Trade Services Program is a group of individuals whose job title is international trade specialist. Many of these people have lived and worked overseas and are proficient with foreign languages. They understand the cultural differences that must be overcome for successful exporting. And they are dedicated to helping Indiana companies -- at no cost -- in the following areas: export assistance, export documentation, foreign buyer visits to Indiana, overseas trade show identification, financial assistance, attendance at overseas trade shows, enrollment of employees in export-related classes/seminars, developing international markets, identification and selection of foreign agents, representatives and distributors, representation of companies at foreign trade shows, provision of economic and political information on other nations.

The Trade Finance Program (TFP): Provides Indiana manufacturers with the tools for export finance. On behalf of Indiana manufacturers and lending institutions, trained representatives at the Indiana Department of Commerce process applications Ex-Im Bank guarantees, loans and export credit insurance. The TFP helps exporters face the challenges of expanding their existing market by becoming more competitive in terms of price, performance, service and delivery by enabling Indiana's exporters to: get paid upon shipment, offer extended credit terms to minimize risk, offer foreign buyers better payment terms.

Available programs
- 90% working-capital loan guarantees, and may be used to purchase finished products, materials, services and labor to produce goods for export.
- Medium- & long-term export guarantees and loans.
- Guarantees provide repayment protection. Loans provide competitive, fixed-rate financing for U.S. export sales.
- Export credit insurance: Protects exporters against political and commercial risk.

Trade Show Assistance Program: Helps small and medium-sized companies realize their full export potential by participating in international trade shows and exhibitions. Financial assistance is available for qualified Indiana exporters who need a little help getting to their trade show of choice. The program also reimburses firms up to $5,000 for booth rental costs at overseas trade shows.

Foreign Trade Zones: Offer great financial incentives for conducting import/export business in the state.

Foreign Trade Zone or Free Trade Zone: An enclosed, secure area that is located outside U.S. Customs territory. A company located within a Foreign Trade Zone does not pay duties or personal property taxes on goods stored within the zone. Foreign and domestic goods may enter a zone to be stored, processed, distributed, manufactured, assembled or exhibited. Benefits to companies located in a Foreign Trade Zone include the following:
- Duty is deferred on imported goods admitted to the zone, thus improving cash flow for the company.
- No U.S. duty is assessed when exporting goods from the zone.
- Processing goods within the zone can eliminate or lower tariffs.
- Duties can be avoided on defective or damaged goods by inspecting and testing imported goods within a zone.
- Savings may be realized in transport insurance.
- Inventory stored in a Foreign Trade Zone is exempt from local property tax.

Contact International Trade Division, Indiana Department of Commerce, One North Capitol, Suite 700, Indianapolis, IN 46204; 317-233-3762.

* Women and Minorities

For all items without a separate address, contact the Indiana Department of Commerce at the address listed above.

LYNX: A privately owned company established to link capital to minority business opportunities. The fund provides subordinated debt to minority-owned businesses in Marion and surrounding counties. Capital can be provided in the form of equity or debt. Minimum project amount is $75,000. Contact Cambridge Capital Management Corporation, 8440 Woodfield Crossing, Suite 315, Indianapolis, IN 46240; 317-469-3925.

Women and Minorities in Business Group (WMBG): Eligibility: Indiana businesses owned by women and/or minorities. Services/Uses: Counsels emerging and mature businesses. Client needs are determined, evaluated and advised at no cost. Services include: workshops and seminars, direct counseling, information clearinghouse and referral source, general information, including statistics regarding women- and minority-owned businesses, administers Minority Outreach Resource Executive (MORE) Program in six regions. Contact Indiana Small Business Development Corporation (ISBD Corp.), One N. Capital Ave., Suite 1275, Indianapolis, IN 46204; 317-264-2820; 888-ISDB-244; {www.isbdcorp.org/index.htm}.

Minority Outreach Resource Executives (MORE): Extension of WMBG services in Gary, South Bend, Fort Wayne, Indianapolis, Evansville and Jeffersonville. Contact: Indiana Small Business Development Corporation (ISBD Corp.), One N. Capital Ave., Suite 1275, Indianapolis, IN 46204; 317-264-2820; 888-ISDB-244; {www.isbdcorp.org/index.htm}.

* Small Business Administration Offices

Janice Wolfe
429 N. Penn. Avenue, Suite 100
Indianapolis, IN 46204
317-226-7272
Fax: 317-226-7259

Iowa

Department of Economic Development
200 East Grand Ave.
Des Moines, IA 50309-1827
515-242-4700
800-245-IOWA
Fax: 515-242-4809
TTY: 800-735-2942
www.state.ia.us/ided

* Business Assistance

For all items without a separate address, contact the Iowa Department of Economic Development at the address listed above.

Workforce Development Fund: Programs under this fund provide training for new and existing employees and include: Jobs Training, Business Network Training, Targeted Industries Training, Innovative Skills Development.

Professional Site Location/Expansion Services, Resources, and Confidential Consultation for Growing Companies: Provides expanding companies with many valuable and unique services, with the end goal of streamlining the site location process. Iowa Department of Economic Development (IDED) confidential services include:
- Working on a confidential basis with companies to determine expansion project needs
- Providing data and information on available buildings, sites and communities
- Coordinating community/site visits
- Packaging appropriate financial assistance and job training programs
- Serving as a liaison with state environmental permitting officials
- IDED Incorporates Information and Technology Into Team Approach

Multimedia Economic Development Information Access system (I-MEDIA): Working in partnership with local economic development groups and utilities, IDED maintains a comprehensive statewide database of community data, available buildings and industrial sites.

Center for Industrial Research and Service: Assists companies with management, production, marketing, engineering, finance, and technology problems and/or contact with resource people, organizations, and agencies that can help provide solutions, and operates as an industrial arm of University Extension, Iowa State University. Contact: Center for Industrial Research and Service, ISU Research Park, 2501 N. Loop Park, Suite 500, Ames, IA 50010; 515-294-3420; {www.ciras.iast.edu}.

Cooperative Services: Provides free technical assistance to help rural residents form new cooperative ventures and improve operations of existing cooperatives. Contact: USDA-Rural Development, 873 Federal Bldg., 210 Walnut St., Des Moines, IA 50309; 515-284-4714.

Manufacturing Technology Center: A resource for small and mid-sized manufacturers. Helps identify problems and resources, conducts formal needs assessments, and develops strategic plans. Also assists with modernizing facilities, upgrading processes, and improving work force capabilities through the use of effective training and skill development. Contact: Iowa Manufacturing Technology Center, Advanced Technology Center, Building 3E, 2006 S. Ankeny Blvd., Ankeny, IA 50021; 515-965-7125; {www.tecnet.org/iowamtc}.

Procurement Outreach Center: Helps businesses successfully compete for federal government contracts.

Regulatory Assistance Programs: Provide assistance with environmental permitting, regulations, and compliance with the EPA Clean Air Act.

University of Northern Iowa/Market Development Program: Provides customized market research, analysis, and strategic planning services to existing businesses, primarily manufacturers. Contact: University of Northern Iowa, College of Business Administration, The Business Building, Suite 5, Cedar Falls, IA 50614; 319-273-2886.

Virtual Management Assistance Program: Maintains and monitors a comprehensive, confidential, database system designed to act as a clearinghouse to foster business-to-business connections by connecting entrepreneurs with prospective management consultants and/or strategic alliance partners.

* Business Financing

For all items without a separate address, contact the Iowa Department of Economic Development at the address listed above.

New Jobs Training Program: Provides training funds for companies creating new jobs, including assistance with screening, skills assessment, testing and custom-designed training and other training programs. Companies can be reimbursed up to 50% of new employees' salaries and fringe benefits during the training period.

Community Economic Betterment Account (CEBA): Provides financial assistance to companies that create new employment opportunities and/or retain existing jobs, and make new capital investment in Iowa. The amount of funding is based, in part, on the number of jobs to be created/retained. Funds are provided in the form of loans and forgivable loans. The CEBA program can provide assistance up to $1 million. As an alternative, non-traditional, short-term float loans or interim loans greater than $1 million may be available. The funding level for start-up companies varied depending upon employee wage rates. Assistance through CEBA's "Venture Project" component is provided as an "equity-like" investment, with a maximum award of $100,000.

Economic Development Set-Aside Program (EDSA): Provides financial assistance to companies that create new employment opportunities and/or retain existing jobs, and make new capital investment in Iowa. The amount of funding is based, in part, on the number of jobs to be created/retained. Funds are provided in the form of loans and forgivable loans. The EDSA program can provide assistance up to $500,000.

Entrepreneurs with Disabilities Program: Provides technical and financial assistance to individuals with disabilities who are seeking self-sufficiency by establishing, maintaining, expanding, or acquiring a small business.

Self Employment Loan Program: Offers low-interest loans to low-income entrepreneurs of new or expanding small businesses. Maximum amount is $10,000 with a 5% simple interest rate.

Value-Added Products and Processes Financial Assistance Program (VAAPFAP): Seeks to increase the innovative utilization of Iowa's agricultural commodities. It accomplishes this by investing in the development of new agri-products and new processing technologies. The program includes two components:
- Innovative Products and Processes encourages the processing of agricultural commodities into higher-value products not commonly produced in Iowa, or utilizing a process not commonly used in Iowa to produce new and innovative products from agricultural commodities.
- Renewable Fuels and Co-Products encourages the production of renewable fuels, such as soy diesel and ethanol, and co-products for livestock feed.

Any single project may apply for up to $900,000 in assistance. Financial assistance is provided in the form of loans and forgivable loans. Generally, assistance of $100,000 or less is provided as a forgivable loan, while larger awards are usually a combination of loans and forgivable loans, with the forgivable portion decreasing as the award size increases.

Small Business Loan Program and Economic Development Loan Program: Provides financing to new and expanding businesses through the sale of tax-exempt bonds. The maximum loan is $10 million.

Link Investments for Tomorrow (LIFT): Assists with rural small business transfer, and horticulture and alternative agricultural crops. Contact: Treasurer of State's Office, Capitol Bldg., 1st Floor, Des Moines, IA 50309; 515-281-3287.

USDA Business and Industrial Loan Guarantee Program: Provides guarantees on loans up to $10 million or more made by private lenders for start-up or expansion purposes to for-profit or non-profit businesses or investors of any size.

Iowa Capital Corporation (ICC): A for-profit venture capital corporation established with funds provided by the state of Iowa and equity investments by Iowa financial institutions, insurance companies and electric utilities. The corporation's primary purpose is to provide an attractive risk-adjusted rate of return on investment to the corporation's shareholders and advance economic development in Iowa. The corporation provides financing for a broad range of business capital needs. Financing may be in the form of equity participation, loans with stock purchase warrants, royalties, etc. and is tailored to the particular business situation. Investments generally range from $50,000 to $1 million, with the average expected to be approximately $250,000.

Rail Economic Development Program: The Iowa Department of Transportation provides funds for construction or rehabilitation of rail spurs to serve new or existing industries. The rail project must be a key to the creation or retention of jobs.

Revitalize Iowa's Sound Economy (RISE): Administered by the Iowa Department of Transportation for expenditures on city, county and state highways to help attract new development or to support growth with existing developments. Projects are evaluated on economic potential and impact. Funding may be used in conjunction with other sources of federal, state, local and private financing for the purpose of improving area highways and specific access to roads.

Public Facilities Set-Aside Program: Administered by the Iowa Department of Economic Development, provides financial assistance to cities and counties to provide infrastructure improvements for businesses which require such improvements in order to create new job opportunities. The form of assistance is limited to grants to cities under 50,000 population and counties for the

State Money - Iowa

provision of or improvements to sanitary sewer systems, water systems, streets and roads, storm sewers, rail lines and airports. Assistance is limited to two-thirds of the total cost of the improvements needed. The emphasis of this program is to increase the productive capacity of the state. Priority will be given to projects that will create manufacturing jobs, add value to Iowa resources and/or export out-of-state.

Tax Increment Financing (TIF): City councils or county boards of supervisors may use the property taxes resulting from the increase in taxable valuation due to construction of new industrial or commercial facilities to provide economic development incentives to a business or industry. Tax increment financing may be used to pay the cost of public improvements and utilities which will serve the new private development, to finance direct grants or loans to a company, or to provide a local match for federal or state economic development assistance programs. TIF does not increase a company's property taxes, but it allocates virtually all of the taxes, which are paid back to the city or county, where they may be spent to benefit the company.

Seed Capital Corporation: Invests in start-up companies that are bringing new products or processes to the marketplace. Generally takes the form of royalty agreements or equity participation.

Venture Capital Resource Fund: A for-profit corporation whose mission is to stimulate economic development and provide an attractive rate of return to shareholders by investing in businesses with significant growth potential.

* Tax Incentives

For all items without a separate address, contact the Iowa Department of Economic Development at the address listed above.

New Jobs and Income Program (NJIP): Provides a package of tax credits and exemptions to businesses making a capital investment of at least $10.38 million and creating 50 or more jobs meeting wage and benefit targets. Qualifying businesses participating in NJIP receive substantial benefits, including:
- A 3% withholding tax credit applied to the company's job training fund, essentially doubling the training funds otherwise available.
- An investment tax credit of up to 10% for use against Iowa's corporate income tax. The credit, based on machinery, equipment, buildings, and improvements, can be carried forward for seven years.
- A 13% research and development activity corporate tax credit may be carried forward or refunded.
- A refund will be paid for Iowa sales, service or use taxes paid to contractors or subcontractors during the construction phase of the project.
- Foreign-owned companies may receive exemptions from land ownership restrictions.
- The local government involved may elect to exempt property tax the improvements to land and buildings for a period not to exceed 20 years. These exemptions can cover all or a portion of the value added by the improvements.

Enterprise Zones: Manufacturers and other businesses expanding or locating in new or existing facilities and creating new jobs in economically distressed areas of Iowa have a new incentive to do so. Businesses expanding or locating in an Enterprise Zone can receive the following benefits:
- Property tax exemptions on all or part of the costs of improvements to land and buildings for up to 10 years.
- An investment tax credit of up to 10% on corporate income taxes for investments on machinery and equipment, new buildings, and improvements to existing buildings.
- Refunds of sales, services, or use taxes paid to contractors or subcontractors during construction.
- A 13% research and development activities credit (refundable) on corporate income taxes.
- Supplemental new jobs training withholding credit of 1 1/2% of the gross wages. This credit is in addition to, and not in lieu of, the withholding credit of 1 1/2% authorized for the Iowa New Jobs Training Program.

Supplemental New Jobs Credit From Withholding: This program is designed to create high-quality jobs by doubling the withholding credit for companies participating in the Iowa New Jobs Training Program. Starting wages must be at least the county average or regional average wage, whichever is lower. Eligibility for the credit is based on a one-time determination by the community college of the starting wage.

New Jobs Tax Credit: Businesses entering into an agreement under the state's training program, and which increase workforce by at least 10 percent, may qualify for this credit to their Iowa corporate income tax. This credit is equal to 6% of the state unemployment insurance taxable wage base. The tax credit can be carried forward up to 10 years.

Exempt Sales and Services: 911 surcharge, advertising, aircraft sales, rental and services, agriculture, containers, coupon books and gift certificates, educational, religious or charitable activities, finance charges, food, freight charges, fuel, government entities, green houses, hospitals, industrial machinery and equipment design and installation, industrial machinery, equipment computers, replace parts, insulin, interstate commerce, lease and rental, medical, mobile homes, newspapers, nonprofit organizations, prescription drugs, printers and publishers, prizes, processing, railroads, repair, resale, resales of property connected with a service, transportation, vehicles, vehicle manufacturing.

* Exports

For all items without a separate address, contact the Iowa Department of Economic Development at the address listed above.

Export Trade Assistance Program: Promotes international trade though financial assistance for increased participation in overseas trade shows and trade missions.

* Women and Minorities

For all items without a separate address, contact the Iowa Department of Economic Development at the address listed above.

Targeted Small Business Financial Assistance Program (TSBFAP): Designed to assist in the creation and expansion of Iowa small businesses that have an annual gross sales of $3 million and are at least 51% owned, operated and managed by women, minorities or persons with a disability. The business must be certified as a "Targeted Small Business" by the Iowa Department of Inspections and Appeals before applying for or receiving TSB funds. Awards may be obtained in one of the following forms of assistance:
- Low-interest loans - Loans of up to $25,000 may be provided at interest rates of 0-5 percent, to be repaid in monthly installments over a five- to seven-year period. The first installment can be deferred for three months for a start-up business and one month for an existing business.
- Loan guarantees are available up to $40,000. Loan guarantees can cover up to 75% of a loan obtained from a bank or other conventional lender. The interest rate is at the discretion of the lender.
- In limited cases, equity grants - to be used to leverage other financing (SBA or conventional) - are available in amounts of up to $25,000.
- TSB funds may be used to purchase equipment, acquire inventory, provide operating capital or to leverage additional funding.

Self-Employment Loan Program (SELP): This program is designed to assist in the creation and expansion of businesses owned, operated and managed by women, minorities, or persons with a disability. To qualify for a SELP loan, applicants must have an annualized family income that does not exceed current income guidelines for the program. An applicant is automatically eligible for SELP if he or she is receiving Family Investment Plan (FIP) assistance or other general assistance such as disability benefits. The applicant can also qualify for SELP funds if determined eligible under the Job Training Partnership Act, or is certified as having a disability under standards established by the Iowa Department of Education, Division of Vocational Rehabilitation Services. SELP loans of up to $10,000 are available. The interest rate is 5 percent, and the loan is to be repaid in monthly installments over a five-year period. The first installment can be deferred for three months for a start-up business and one month for an existing business.

Entrepreneurs With Disabilities (EWD): Helps qualified individuals with disabilities establish, acquire, maintain or expand a small business by providing technical and financial assistance. To be eligible for the program, applicants must be active clients of the Iowa Department of Education Division of Vocational Rehabilitation Services or the Iowa Department for the Blind. Technical Assistance grants of up to $10,000 may be used to pay for any specific business-related consulting service such as developing a feasibility study or business plan, or accounting and legal services. Financial Assistance grants of up to $10,000 may be used to purchase equipment, supplies, rent or other start-up, expansion or acquisition costs identified in an approved business plan. Total financial assistance provided to an individual may not exceed 50% (maximum of $10,000) of the financial package. EWD financial assistance must be fully matched by funding from other sources.

Institute of Social and Economic Development: Focuses on minorities, women, persons with disabilities and low-income individuals. Encourages self-sufficiency through the growth of small business and self-employment opportunities, and provides services for any person who wants to start or expand a business employing up to five employees, including the owner(s). Contact Institute of Social and Economic Development, 1901 Broadway, Suite 313, Iowa City, IA 52240; 319-338-2331; Fax: 319-338-5824.

State Money - Kansas

* Small Business Administration Offices

James Thomson
215 4th Avenue Road, SE Suite 200
Cedar Rapids, IA 52401
319-362-6405
Fax: 319-362-7861

Cheryl Eftink
210 Walnut Street, Room 749
Des Moines, IA 50309
515-284-4026
Fax: 515-284-4572

Kansas

Department of Commerce and Housing
700 SW Harrison Street, Suite 1300
Topeka, KS 66603-3712
785-296-5298
Fax: 785-296-3490
TTY: 785-296-3487
www.kansascommerce.com

* Business Assistance

For all items without a separate address, contact the Kansas Department of Commerce and Housing at the address listed above.

First-Stop Clearinghouse: A one-stop Clearinghouse for general information. It also provides the necessary state applications required by agencies which license, regulate and tax business, and furnishes information about starting or expanding a business.

From the Land of Kansas Trademark Program: Offers marketing opportunities for Kansas produced food, arts, crafts, and plants.

Agricultural Value Added Center: Identifies new technologies and assists companies in commercialization efforts. Both food/feed and industrial related projects are potential candidates for assistance.

Kansas Match: Promotes economic growth in the state by matching Kansas manufacturers who are currently buying products from outside Kansas with Kansas suppliers of those same products. The benefit to the buyer includes reductions in freight, warehousing, and communication costs.

Business First: Drawing from the existing KDOC&H business retention and expansion instrument, this new survey software program assists communities of any size in establishing a customized local retention and expansion program.

Business Retention & Expansion Program: Offered to Kansas communities and counties who wish to sustain existing industry, support its modernization and competitiveness, foster its expansion and provide an environment that encourages new industry creation and recruitment. The Department works with community leaders and volunteers to conduct on-site surveys of local businesses. The information gathered is then analyzed and the results are used to solve immediate short-term problems, as well as to develop long-term local retention and expansion strategies.

Partnership Fund: Provides financial assistance to Kansas cities and counties by making low-interest loans for infrastructure projects needed to encourage and assist in the creation of new jobs either through the relocation of new businesses or the expansion of existing businesses.

Industrial Training Program (KIT): Provides training assistance primarily to manufacturing, distribution and regional or national service firms in the process of adding five or more new jobs to a new or existing Kansas facility. KIT will pay the negotiated cost of pre-employment, on-the-job and classroom training expenses that include instructor salaries, travel expenses, minor equipment, training aids, supplies and materials, and curriculum planning and development.

Industrial Retraining Program (KIR): Provides retraining assistance to employees of restructuring industries who are likely to be displaced because of obsolete or inadequate job skills and knowledge.

* Publications

For all items without a separate address, contact the Kansas Department of Commerce and Housing at the address listed above.

The Kansas Department of Commerce & Housing (KDOC&H) distributes a variety of publications to help Kansas residents, businesses and visitors find the information needed about their state. Here are a few:

Data Book: The information found in the *Data Book* gives a good idea of what Kansas has to offer new and expanding businesses. The book is filled with information about the Kansas economy, labor and workforce training. It briefly describes taxes and incentives for new and expanding businesses. It also includes sections on finance, technology and education, markets and transportation, and the environment.

The Kansas Aerospace Directory: A complete resource for aircraft production, parts, equipment, research and development, etc. *Directory* includes a wide range of aviation products and companies.

Kansas Agribusiness Directory: A complete resource for agriculture-related business, the *Kansas Agribusiness Directory* offers assistance in contacting any firm or business as well as finding specialized products or services.

Steps to Success: A Guide to Starting a Business in Kansas: Created to give entrepreneurs and small business owners all the information needed on licenses, forms, rules and regulations required by State agencies. It discusses the aspects of business development including finance, incentives and taxation. Plus, it has referrals to programs such as Small Business Development Centers, development companies, the Kansas Technology Enterprise Corporation, Inc. and the Small Business Administration.

* Business Financing

For all items without a separate address, contact the Kansas Department of Commerce and Housing at the address listed above.

Venture Capital & Seed Capital Programs: Instituted to increase the availability of risk capital in Kansas. These programs make use of income tax credits to encourage investment in venture and seed capital pools as a source of early stage financing for small businesses. Businesses demonstrating strong growth potential but lacking the financial strength to obtain conventional financing are the most likely candidates for risk capital funding. The Business Development Division has in operation and continues to develop a network of venture capital resources to assist qualified small businesses in locating potential sources of venture capital financing.

Economic Opportunity Initiatives Fund (KEOIF): A funding mechanism to address the creation/retention of jobs presented by unique opportunities or emergencies. The fund has a higher level of flexibility than do many of the other state financing programs and allows the State to participate as a funding source when other options have been exhausted.

Existing Industry Expansion Program (KEIEP): Performance based, with a focus on the expansion/retention of jobs that are associated with the activities of existing firms.

Investments In Major Projects And Comprehensive Training (IMPACT): A funding mechanism designed to respond to the training and capital requirements of major business expansions and locations in the state. SKILL (State of Kansas Investments in Lifelong Learning) funds may be used to pay for expenses related to training a new work force. MPI (Major Project Investment) funds may be used for other expenses related to the project such as the purchase or relocation of equipment, labor recruitment, or building costs. Individual bond size may not exceed 90% of the withholding taxes received from the new jobs over a 10-year period.

Network of Certified Development Companies: Provides financial packaging services to businesses, utilizing state, Small Business Administration, and private financial sources. The state provides supplemental funding to these organizations in recognition of the service they provide.

Private Activity Bonds (PABs): Tax-exempt bonds (IRBs) for facility and equipment financing for qualifying manufacturers and processors. The reduced financing costs generated through these bonds are passed through to the company.

Training Equipment Grants: Provide area technical schools and community colleges an opportunity to acquire instructional equipment to train or retrain Kansas workers.

Kansas Job Training Partnership Act (JTPA): Primarily targeted toward economically disadvantaged workers, dislocated workers, and workers facing severe barriers to employment. JTPA can reimburse a company for up to 50% of the employee's wages during training. JTPA may be used together with the KIT or IMPACT programs.

* Tax Incentives

For all items without a separate address, contact the Kansas Department of Commerce and Housing at the address listed above.

Enterprise Zone Act: Establishes a non-metropolitan regional business incentive program and provides for business expansion and development incentives on a statewide basis. Businesses throughout the state may be eligible for 1) a Sales Tax Exemption on the personal property, materials, and services

State Money - Kentucky

associated with the project; 2) a Job Creation Tax Credit; and 3) an Investment Tax Credit. Tax credits may be used to offset up to 100% of the business' annual Kansas income tax liability. Unused credits may be carried forward indefinitely.

High Performance Incentive Program (HPIP): Provides incentives to qualified companies which make significant investment in employee training and pay higher than average wages. Incentives include 1) a Sales Tax Exemption; 2) a potentially substantial Training Tax Credit; 3) a generous Investment Tax Credit; and 4) priority consideration for other business assistance programs. Tax credits may be used to offset 100% of the business' annual Kansas income tax liability. Unused credits may be carried forward and must be used within a 10-year time frame.

Tax Exemptions In Connection With The Usage Of Industrial Revenue Bonds: Property financed with the proceeds of an IRB issue can be exempt from property taxation for a period of 10 years. In addition, the cost of building materials and permanently installed equipment are exempt from state and local taxes.

Property Tax Exemptions: Can be made available by the governing body of a city or county for up to ten years. The exemptions apply to land, building, machinery and equipment for new or expanding businesses.

Sales Tax Exemption On Manufacturing Machinery & Equipment: Manufacturing machinery and equipment used directly and primarily for the purposes of manufacturing, assembling, processing, finishing, storing, warehousing, or distributing articles of tangible personal property intended for resale are exempt from sales tax.

Research & Development Tax Credits: May be claimed at 6.5% of the amount which exceeds the business' average R&D expenditures during the preceding three years. A maximum of 25% of the total credits may be used in any given year and unused credits may be carried forward indefinitely.

Child Day Care Tax Credits: Available to businesses that pay for, or provide, child day care services to their employees. The credit is 30% of the annual cost of providing the service, not to exceed $30,000 total credit. A credit of up to 50%, not to exceed $45,000, may be earned during the first year on the costs of establishing a child day care facility. Multiple taxpayers may work together to establish such a facility.

Venture Capital Tax Credit: Designed to encourage cash investments in certified Kansas venture capital companies. Tax credit is equal to 25% of the taxpayer's cash investment in a venture capital firm in the year in which the investment is made.

Local Seed Capital Pool Tax: Designed to encourage cash investments in certified local seed capital pools. Credit is equal to 25% of the taxpayer's cash investment.

Job Expansion And Investment Tax Credit Act Of 1976: Allows an income tax credit for a period of 10 years, up to 50% of a business' Kansas income tax liability. The Job Expansion Tax Credit is $100 for each qualified business facility employee. The Investment Tax Credit is $100 for each $100,000 in qualified investment.

Economic Development Tax Abatement Assistance Program: Provides technical application assistance as well as consulting services to companies and communities applying for economic development and/or industrial revenue bond (IRB) tax exemptions. The Assistance Program serves as liaison between the applicant and the Board of Tax Appeals to ensure quality service and enhance approval success.

* Exports

For all items without a separate address, contact the Kansas Department of Commerce and Housing at the address listed above.

Export Loan Guarantee Program: Allows financial institutions to provide working capital loans to help Kansas companies pay for costs associated with an export transaction. The guarantee protects the financial institution against exporter non-performance risk. In addition to significantly reducing a lender's risk on an export loan, expertise available through the Kansas Export Finance Program can assist a lender in the area of international trade.

Kansas Export Financing Program: Allows the state to enter into agreements with Kansas exporters and financial institutions, and other public and private agencies to provide guarantees, insurance, reinsurance, and coinsurance for commercial pre-export and post-export credit risks.

Kansas Trade Show Assistance Program: Allows a Kansas company to receive a reimbursement of up to 50% of their international trade show expenses to a maximum of $3,500 per show and $7,000 per state fiscal year.

Foreign Trade Zones: Provide a duty-free and quota-free entry point for foreign goods into specific areas under customs' supervision for an unlimited period of time.

Kansas International Trade Resource Directory: A complete resource for anyone needing assistance in exporting goods to foreign countries and to other states. The guide offers a comprehensive listing of government agencies. It lists the state's six regent universities and the international trade services and information provided by each. It also lists international law firms, bankers, consultants and freight forwarders/ customhouse brokers. Also, it lists foreign consulates, U.S. Embassies, international telephone country and city codes, metric conversion tables and a complete glossary of terms used in international trade.

* Women and Minorities

For all items without a separate address, contact the Kansas Department of Commerce and Housing at the address listed above.

Office of Minority & Women Business Development: Promotes and assists in the development of minority-owned and women-owned businesses in Kansas. The program provides assistance in procurement and contracting, financing resources, business planning, and identification of business opportunities. A directory of minority-owned and women-owned businesses in Kansas is published annually.

Single Source Certification Program: Responsible for certifying minority-and-women-owned businesses as small disadvantaged businesses for non-highway related firms.

* Small Business Administration Offices

Liz Auer
271 West Third Street North, Suite 2500
Wichita, KS 67202-1212
316-269-6566
Fax: 316-269-6499

Kentucky

Kentucky Cabinet for Economic Development
2300 Capital Plaza Tower
500 Mero Street
Frankfort, KY 40601
502-564-7670
800-626-2930
www.thinkkentucky.com

* Business Assistance

For all items without a separate address, contact the Kentucky Cabinet for Economic Development at the address listed above.

Kentucky Cabinet for Economic Development: The Cabinet is the primary state agency responsible for creating new jobs and new investment in the state.
- Job Recruitment, Placement And Training: Provides a package of time- and cost-saving employee recruiting and placement services to Kentucky employers, at no cost to either employers or employees.
- Industrial Location Assistance: Provides a comprehensive package of assistance to large manufacturing, services, and administrative facilities, both before and after their location in Kentucky.

Business Information Clearinghouse: Provides new and existing businesses a centralized information source on business regulations, licenses, permits, and other business assistance programs. Call 800-626-2250.

* Business Financing

For all items without a separate address, contact the Kentucky Cabinet for Economic Development at the address listed above.

Kentucky Economic Development Finance Authority (KEDFA): Provides business loans to supplement other financing. KEDFA provides loan funds at below market interest rates. The loans are available for fixed asset financing (land, buildings, and equipment) for business startup, locations, and expansions that create new jobs in Kentucky or have a significant impact on the economic growth of a community. The loans must be used to finance projects in agribusiness, tourism, industrial ventures, or the service industry. KEDFA may participate in the financing of qualified projects with a secured loan for up to $10,000 per new job created, not to exceed 25% of a project's fixed asset cost. The maximum loan amount is $500,000 and the minimum is $25,000. Small businesses with projects of less than $100,000 may receive loans on fixed assets for up to 45% of the project costs if enough jobs are created. Interest rates are fixed for the life of the loan, and are determined by the length of the loan term.

KEDFA Direct Loan Program: Offers a loan program to work in conjunction with private financing. The program is designed to allow businesses to obtain the long term financing needed to encourage growth. Maximum loan amount is $500,000. Minimum amount is $25,000.

Commonwealth Small Business Development Corporation (CSBDC): Works with state and local economic development organizations, banks, and the SBA to achieve community economic development through job creation and retention by providing long-term fixed asset financing to small business concerns. The CSBDC can lend a maximum of 40% of project cost or $750,000 per project (in certain circumstances $1,000,000).

Linked Deposit Program: Provides loans up to $50,000 for small business and agribusiness. Credit decisions are the responsibility of the lender making the loan. The state will purchase certificates of deposit from participating lenders through the State Investment Commission, at the New York Prime interest rate less four percent, but never less than 2%.

Local Financial Assistance: Several local governments and area development districts offer loans and other financial incentives for economic development projects. The levels and terms of financial assistance provided generally are negotiable, and are based upon the availability of funds, jobs created, economic viability of the project, and other locally determined criteria.

Bluegrass State Skills Corporation (BSSC): An independent dejure corporation within the Cabinet for Economic Development, provides grants for customized skills training of workers for new, expanding and existing industries in Kentucky.

Industrial Revenue Bonds (IRB): Can be used to finance manufacturing projects and their warehousing areas, major transportation and communication facilities, most health care facilities, and mineral extraction and processing projects.

Utility Incentive Rates: Electric and gas utility companies regulated by the Kentucky Public Service Commission (excluding municipal systems) can offer economic incentive rates for certain large industrial and commercial customers.

Kentucky Investment Fund (Venture Capital): Encourages venture capital investment by certifying privately operated venture funds, thereby entitling their investors to tax credits equal to 0% of their capital contributions to the fund.

Kentucky Tourism Development Act: Provides financial incentives to qualifying tourism projects. Tourism projects are defined as a cultural or historical site, recreation or entertainment facility, or area of natural phenomenon or scenic beauty.

Local Government Economic Development Fund: Grants are made to eligible counties for specific project that enable the counties to provide infrastructure to incoming and expanding business and industry.

Job Development Incentive Grant Program: Grants are made to eligible counties from their coal severance accounts for the purpose of encouraging job development. The grant amount cannot exceed $5,000 per job created.

* Tax Incentives

For all items without a separate address, contact the Kentucky Cabinet for Economic Development at the address listed above.

Kentucky Industrial Development Act (KIDA): Investments in new and expanding manufacturing projects may qualify for tax credits. Companies that create at least 15 new full-time jobs and invest at least $500,000 in projects approved under KIDA may receive state income tax credits for up to 100% of annual debt service costs (principal and interest) for up to 10 years on land, buildings, site development, building fixtures and equipment used in a project, or the company may collect a job assessment fee of 2% of the gross wages of each employee whose job is created by the approved project and who is subject to Kentucky income taxes.

Kentucky Rural Economic Development Act (KREDA): Larger tax credits are available for new and expanding manufacturing projects that create at least 15 new full time jobs in counties with unemployment rates higher than the state average in each of the five preceding calendar years and invest at least $500,000.

Kentucky Jobs Development Act (KJDA): Service and technology related companies that invest in new and expanded non-manufacturing, non-retail projects that provide at least 75% of their services to users located outside of Kentucky, and that create new jobs for at least 25 full-time Kentucky residents may qualify for tax credits.

Kentucky Industrial Revitalization Act (KIRA): Investments in the rehabilitation of manufacturing operations that are in imminent danger of permanently closing or that have closed temporarily may qualify for tax credits. Companies that save or create 25 jobs in projects approved under KIRA may receive state income tax credits and job assessment fees for up to 10 years limited to 50% of the costs of the rehabilitation or construction of buildings and the reoutfitting or purchasing of machinery and equipment.

<u>Other Income Tax Credit:</u>
- A credit of $100 is allowed for each unemployed person hired for at least 180 consecutive days.
- Credits are allowed for up to 50% of the installed costs of equipment used exclusively to recycle or compost business or consumer wastes (excluding secondary and demolition wastes) and machinery used exclusively to manufacture products substantially from recycled waste materials.
- A credit is allowed for up to 4.5% of the value of Kentucky coal (excluding transportation costs) used for industrial heating or processing.

Kentucky Enterprise Zone Program: State and local tax incentives are offered to businesses located or locating in zones, and some regulations are eased to make development in the area more attractive. A zone remains in effect for 20 years after the date of designation.

Tourism Sales Tax Credit: Approved new or expanding tourism attractions will be eligible for a sales tax credit against sales tax generated by visitors to the attraction.

Property Tax Exemptions: Manufacturing machinery, pollution control facilities, raw materials and work in process, tangible personal property in foreign trade zones.

Favorable Tax Treatments: Available for finished goods in a transit status, private leasehold interest in property owned and financed by a governmental unit through industrial revenue bonds.

Sales Tax Exemptions: Machinery for new and expanded industry, raw materials, supplies used directly in manufacturing, industrial tools, energy and energy-producing fuels used in manufacturing, industrial processing, mining or refining, pollution control equipment and facilities, fee processor or contract manufacturers that do not take title to the tangible personal property that is incorporated into a manufactured product for raw materials, supplies and industrial tools directly used in the manufacturing process, containers, packaging and wrapping materials, equipment used to collect, separate, compress, bale, shred or handle waste materials for recycling, customized computer programs, gross receipts from the sales of newspaper inserts or catalogs purchased for storage, use, or other consumption outside this state, motor fuels for highway use, motor vehicles, trailers, and semi-trailers registered for highway use, locomotives, rolling stock, supplies, and fuels used by railroad in interstate commerce, air carriers, parts and supplies used for interstate passenger or freight services, marine vessels, and supplies, farm machinery, livestock, feed, seed, fertilizer, motion picture production companies.

* Exports

For all items without a separate address, contact the Kentucky Cabinet for Economic Development at the address listed above.

Kentucky International Trade Office: The Office offers the following services:
- Export Consulting
- Export Marketing
- Education and Training
- Overseas Offices
- International Trade Directory
- Kentucky Export Guide

* Small Business Administration Offices

William Federhofer
600 Dr. MLK, Jr. Place
Downtown Stat., Room 188
Louisville, KY 40202
502-582-5978
Fax: 502-582-5009

Louisiana

Department of Economic Development
P.O. Box 94185
Baton Rouge, LA 70804
225-342-6000
225-342-5388
www.lded.state.la.us

* Business Assistance

For all items without a separate address, contact the Louisiana Department of Economic Development at the address listed above.

Economically Disadvantaged Business Development Division: Division was created to assist businesses owned by economically disadvantaged individuals. It offers Development Assistance Program where a preliminary assessment analysis of

State Money - Maine

a business is conducted; Mentor-Protégé Program; Recognition Program; Small Business Bonding Program; and more. Contact: Division for Economically Disadvantaged Business Development, 339 Florida Blvd., Suite 212, P.O. Box 44153, Baton Rouge, LA 70804; 225-342-5373.

Quality jobs: Provides an annual refundable credit of up to 5% of payroll for a period of up to 10 years for qualifying companies.

Cost-free training: Louisiana's QuickStart Training Program utilizes the state's vocational-technical institutes to provide cost-free pre-employment training customized to a company's requirements. The Jobs Training Partnership Act Program can help a company find trainees and will also pay a portion of their wages while they are in training.

Workforce development and training: Develops and provides customized pre-employment and workforce upgrade training to existing and prospective Louisiana businesses.

Business Matchmakers: Seeks to pair small and medium-sized suppliers in the state with larger companies which are currently making purchases out of state.

* Business Financing

For all items without a separate address, contact the Louisiana Department of Economic Development at the address listed above.

Small Business Loan Program: Provides loan guarantees and participations to banks in order to facilitate capital accessibility for businesses. Guarantees may range up to 75% of the loan amount, not to exceed a maximum of $1.5 million. Loan participations of up to 40% are also available. Applicants must have a business plan and a bank that is willing to fund the loan.

Business Linked Deposit Program: Provides for a 1% to 4% interest rate reduction on a maximum of $200,000 for a maximum of 2 to 5 years on term loans that are funded by banks to Louisiana businesses. Job creation, statistical area employment, and cash flow requirements for underwriting are all criteria, which will effect the percentage and term of the linked deposit.

Micro Loan Program: Provides loan guarantees and participations to banks that fund loans ranging from $5,000 to $50,000 to Louisiana small businesses.

Contract Loan Program: Intended to provide a loan participation and guarantee to a bank for government contract loans. These loans are intended to help businesses finance working capital for contracts with local, state, or federal government agencies. Loans may range from $5000 to $1,000,000 and must be for terms of one year or less.

Exim Bank City/State Program: LEDC has a relationship with the U.S. Export-Import Bank in Washington, DC Under this program, LEDC facilitates export working capital loans for small Louisiana businesses.

Venture Capital Match Program: Provides for a match investment for Louisiana venture capital funds. The fund must have at least $5 million of private investment for which LEDC may provide $5 million.

Venture Capital Co-Investment Program: Provides for a co-investment in a Louisiana business of up to 1/4 of the round of investment, but not more than $500,000, with any qualified venture capital fund with at least $7.5 million in private capital. The venture capital fund may be from outside of Louisiana.

BIDCO Investment Program: Provides for a match or co-investment in certified BIDCOs. BIDCOs are state-chartered, non-depository alternative financing sources for small businesses. BIDCOs frequently provide equity and subordinated debt financing to new and growing companies, as well as to companies requiring turnaround assistance. A BIDCO must have at least $2 million in private capital. LEDC may match the investment $1.00 for $2.00 of private capital up to $2.5 million. Co-investments are considered on a project by project basis and cannot exceed 33% of the total investment.

Specialty BIDCO Investment Program: Provides for a match or co-investment in certified Specialty BIDCOs. Specialty BIDCOs are BIDCOs established with a particular focus on assisting disadvantaged businesses and businesses located in impoverished and economically disadvantaged areas. The BIDCO must have at least $250,000 in private capital. LEDC may match the investment $1.00 for every $1.00 of private capital up to $2.5 million. Co-investments are considered on a project by project basis and cannot exceed 50% of the total investment.

Small Business Bonding Assistance Program: The primary goal of this program is to aid certified Economically Disadvantaged Businesses (EDBs) in acquiring quality bid, performance, and payment bonds at reasonable rates from surety companies. EDBs receive help reaching required bonding capacity for specific projects. Contractors often do not reach these levels on their own due to balance sheet deficiencies and a lack of adequate managerial and technical skills. After certification by the Division and accreditation by LCAI, contractors are eligible to receive bond guarantee assistance to be used as collateral when seeking bonds. The Division will issue a letter of credit to the surety for an amount up to 25% of the base contract amount or $200,000.

Economic Development Award: Provides financial incentives in the form of linked deposit loans, loan guarantees and grants to industrial or business development projects that promote economic development and that require state assistance for basic infrastructure development.

All of the above financing programs are available through Louisiana Economic Development Corporation, P.O. Box 44153, Baton Rouge, LA 70804; 225-342-5675.

* Tax Incentives

For all items without a separate address, contact the Louisiana Department of Economic Development at the address listed above.

Industrial property tax exemption: Exempts any manufacturing establishment entering Louisiana or any manufacturing establishment expanding its existing Louisiana facility from state, parish, and local property taxes for a period of up to ten years.

Enterprise zone: Provides a tax credit of $2,500 for each net new job created in specially designated areas. Also provides for a rebate of state sales/use taxes on building materials and operating equipment. Local sales/use taxes may also be rebated. Credits can be used to satisfy state corporate income and franchise tax obligations.

Restoration tax abatement: Encourages restoration of buildings in special districts by abating Ad Valorem taxes on improvements to the structure for up to ten years

Inventory tax credit: Provides tax credits against state corporate income and franchise tax obligations for the full amount of inventory taxes paid. When credits are in excess of tax obligations, a cash refund is made.

* Exports

For all items without a separate address, contact the Louisiana Department of Economic Development at the address listed above.

Freeport law: Cargoes in transit are exempt from taxation as long as they are kept intact within their smallest original shipping container. Most manufacturers can bring raw materials into the state without paying taxes on them until they are placed in the manufacturing process.

Foreign trade zones: Louisiana's six Foreign Trade Zones (FTZ) make it possible to import materials and components into the U.S. without paying duties until they enter the U.S. market. Goods shipped out of the country from FTZs are duty-free. Contact: International Trade Division, 101 France St., Baton Rouge, LA 70802; 225-342-4320.

* Women and Minorities

For all items without a separate address, contact the Louisiana Department of Economic Development at the address listed above.

Minority Venture Capital Match Program: Provides for a match investment for qualified minority venture capital funds. The fund must have at least $250,000 of private investment for which LEDC may invest $1.00 for every $2.00 of private capital up to $5 million.

* Small Business Administration Offices

Randy Randolph
365 Canal Place, Suite 2250
New Orleans, LA 70130
504-589-2744
Fax: 504-589-2339

Maine

Office of Business Development
Department of Economic and Community Development
59 State House Station
Augusta, ME 04333
207-287-3153
Fax: 207-287-5701
TTY: 207-287-2656
www.econdevmaine.com

* Business Assistance

For all items without a separate address, contact the Maine Office of Business Development at the address listed above.

State Money - Maine

Small Business Energy Conservation Program: This program provides small businesses with free energy audits, conservation recommendations and low-interest loans for the purpose of energy conservation.

Business Answers: Maine's toll-free business information hotline provides rapid responses to questions about doing business in Maine. Call 800-872-3838.

One-Stop Business License Center: This central clearinghouse for state regulatory information helps simplify the process of complying with state business regulations. Callers may request business license and permit applications, as well as information on state regulations.

Business Answers/Small Business Advocate: Serves as a central clearinghouse of information regarding business assistance programs and services available to state businesses. Also helps small businesses resolve problems they may be experiencing with state regulatory agencies.

Plus 1 Campaign: This program represents Maine's long-term strategy to foster small business growth and remove barriers to business development. Among the program's initiatives are the $5-million Small Enterprise Growth Fund and the $6-million Agricultural Marketing Loan Fund administered by FAME. In addition, financing packages for hardware and software acquisitions which help businesses go online are available under the Plus 1 Computer Loan Program. For more information, visit the Plus 1 Web site at {www.mainebusiness.com/plus1}.

Maine Products Marketing Program: Provides marketing assistance to producers of Maine-made consumer goods. Members of the program promote their message of Maine quality through the use of product tags and labels, literature and package design, which carry the unified theme, "Maine Made America's Best." The program also publishes the "Maine Made" Buyer's Guide, which is sent to more than 25,000 wholesale buyers.

Apprenticeship Program: Maine's Apprenticeship Program provides customized training and instruction so workers can obtain professional credentials. Many of Maine's larger firms have taken advantage of this innovative workforce development program, which will underwrite 50% of apprenticeship-related tuition for new and existing employees. For more information contact Kenneth L. Hardt, Maine Apprenticeship Program, Maine Department of Labor, 55 State House Station, Augusta, ME 04333-0055; 207-624-6390; Fax: 207-624-6499; E-mail: {k.skip.hardt@state.me.us}.

School-to-Work Initiatives: This public-private partnership is designed to provide Maine industry with a competitive workforce. The program employs three strategies to train Maine youth. These include:
- Maine Career Advantage: a nationally recognized two-year combination of business internship and integrated academics, including one free year at the technical college level.
- Registered Pre-Apprenticeship: four years of employer-driven high school academics, coupled with two summers of on-the-job training. This culminates in permanent employment and a Registered Apprenticeship upon high school graduation.
- Tech Prep: sequential, industry-driven academic and technical training beginning in eleventh grade and progressing through completion of Certificate, Associate and/or Bachelor Degrees.

For more information contact Susan Brown, Center for Career Development, Maine Technical College System, SMVTC, Fort Road, South Portland, ME 04106; 207-767-5210 ext. 111; Fax: 207-767-5210; E-mail: {susan@ccd.mtcs.tec.me.us}; {www.mtcs.tec.me.us}.

Maine Quality Centers Program. This is an economic development initiative of the Maine Technical College System, which provides new and expanding businesses with a trained and ready workforce. New or expanding firms creating at least eight new full-time jobs with benefits may be eligible to receive state financing for 100% of pre-hire classroom training. For a packet of information and application contact Michael M. Aube, Director, Maine Quality Centers, Maine Technical College System, 323 State Street, Augusta, ME 04330; 207-287-1070; Fax: 207-287-1037; E-mail: {MMAube@syst.mtcs.tec.me.us}; {www.mtcs.tec.me.us}.

Governor's Training Initiative: This program reimburses training costs when they are required for business expansion, retention or unique upgrading issues. Businesses that meet eligibility requirements may receive reimbursements for on-the-job training, competitive retooling, specialized recruitment, workplace literacy, high-performance skills or customized technical training. For an application contact Bureau of Employment Services, Maine Department of Labor, 16 State House Station, Augusta, ME 04333-0016; 207-624-6490; Fax: 207-624-6499; E-mail: {caroline.p.morgan@state.me.us}; {www.state.me.us/dolbes/labor.htm}.

Safety Education and Training: At no cost to a company, Maine's Bureau of Labor Standards provides customized health and safety training, site evaluation and technical support. Priority is given to small and mid-sized employers and large employers with documented health and safety problems. For more information contact Alan Hinsey, Director, Bureau of Labor Standards, Maine Department of Labor, 45 State House Station, Augusta, ME 04333-0045; 207-624-6400; Fax: 207-624-6449; E-mail: {alan.c.hinsey@state.me.us}.

* Business Financing

For all items without a separate address, contact the Maine Office of Business Development at the address listed above.

The Finance Authority of Maine (FAME) is Maine's business finance agency. FAME supports start-up and expanding businesses by working closely with Maine banks to improve access to capital. FAME offers a wide array of programs, ranging from traditional loan guarantees for small and large businesses to tax credits for investments in dynamic manufacturing or export-related firms. FAME has also established taxable and tax-exempt bond financing programs that provide loans to creditworthy firms at very favorable rates and terms.

- *The Commercial Loan Insurance Program*: This program provides large business borrowers, who would otherwise have problems securing conventional loans, with access to capital. FAME can insure up to 90% of a commercial loan, not to exceed $7 million, for most types of business projects. There is a $2.5-million limitation on recreational projects; additional limitations and restrictions apply.
- *Major Business Expansion Program*: Any business proposing to expand or locate in Maine and whose borrowing needs fall in the $5,000,000 to $25,000,000 range is eligible for tax-exempt or taxable bond financing for up to 100% of project's cost.
- *Economic Recovery Loan Program*: Designed as a supplemental financial resource to help small businesses access the capital required to become more productive and more competitive. Maximum request is $200,000 for businesses seeking last-resort financial assistance.
- *Agricultural Marketing Loan Fund Program*: Helps natural resource based industries by providing a source of subordinated debt for eligible projects and borrowers. Maximum loan size is $25,000 for any person or organization in the business of growing or harvesting plants, raising animals, growing or obtaining plant or animal byproducts, aquaculture or engaged in the producing, processing, storing, packaging or marketing of a product from such business.
- *Small Enterprise Growth Program*: Provides financing for small companies that demonstrate a potential for high growth and public benefit. Financing is limited to a maximum of $150,000 per loan and borrower must be engaged in at least one of the following: Marine Science, Biotechnology, Manufacturing, Exporting, Software Development, Environmental Sciences, Value Added Natural Resource and/or other enterprises that the Board determines will further the purposes and intent of the program.
- *Marine Technology Investment Fund*: Provides investment in businesses with technology that can lead to product or process innovation. Targets funding for the next step required to bring a promising idea from the bench to commercialization.
- *Tax Increment Financing (TIF) Districts*: Municipalities can use Tax Increment Financing as an economic development incentive within their community. The program enables a municipality to designate a TIF District in which new or expanding businesses can receive financial support based on the new property tax revenues generated by their project. The municipality may choose to fund a portion of the project improvements or to return a percentage of the tax revenues to the company to offset the costs of development.
- *Business Assistance Program*: Provides a grant to a local government to either loan or grant up to $400,000 to businesses to finance fixed assets including capital equipment, commercial or industrial buildings, fixtures or property improvements.
- *Development Fund Loan Program*: Can provide up to $200,000 or gap financing for up to 40% of a business' development activities.
- *Investment Banking Service*: FAME helps borrowers seeking large amounts of capital for major commercial projects find and secure financing alternatives.
- *Occupational Safety Loan Program*: In cooperation with the Maine Department of Labor, FAME administers a program to provide direct loans to businesses making workplace safety improvements.
- *Plus 1 Computer Loan Program*: This program provides lenders with loan insurance on an expedited basis for small businesses that need to borrow money to acquire and install computer equipment and software. For more information on this program, visit the Plus 1 Web site at {www.mainebusiness.com/plus1}.
- *Rapid Response Guarantee*: FAME's Rapid Response Guarantee provides lenders with loan insurance on an expedited basis for small business loans that meet certain minimum credit standards.
- *Regional Economic Development Revolving Loan Program*: This program distributes $10 million to community, regional or statewide public-sector or non-profit entities that, in turn, loan the funds to eligible small business borrowers.
- *Small Business and Veterans' Small Business Loan Insurance Program*: This program is designed to help small businesses that cannot obtain conventional commercial financing. FAME can insure up to 90% of a small

State Money - Maryland

business loan, to a maximum insurance exposure of $1 million. If the borrower is an eligible wartime veteran, the authority may insure up to 100% of a loan of $75,000 or less, and up to 90% of a loan up to a maximum exposure of $1.1 million.

- **Small Enterprise Growth Fund**: This program was created to provide Maine entrepreneurs with access to "patient" sources of venture capital. The Fund targets the needs of entrepreneurs with financial requirements of between $10,000 and $300,000.
- **Bond Financing Programs**: FAME, using its authority to issue taxable and tax-exempt bonds, provides reduced-rate financing to large projects. Under the SMART-E Bond Programs, FAME issues tax-exempt bonds for manufacturing projects, which must meet eligibility requirements established under the Internal Revenue Code. The SMART Bond Program and Major Business Expansion Program offer reduced interest rates by using FAME's guarantee authority to put the strength of the State of Maine's credit rating behind financing for larger projects.

For information on the above programs, contact Finance Authority of Maine, 83 Western Ave., P.O. Box 949, Augusta, ME 04332; 207-623-3263.

* Tax Incentives

For all items without a separate address, contact the Maine Office of Business Development at the address listed above.

Business Equipment Property Tax Reimbursement Program: Program reimbursed, for up to 12 years, all local property taxes paid on eligible business property.

Employee-Assisted Day Care Credit: Provides an income tax credit of up to $5,000. The credit is limited to the lesser of $5,000, 20% of the cost incurred or $100 for each child of an employee enrolled on a full-time basis or for each full-time equivalent throughout the tax year.

Employer Provided Long-term Care Benefits Credit: Provides an income tax credit equal to the lesser of $5,000, 20% of the cost incurred or $100 per employee covered by a long-term care policy as part of a benefits package.

Employment Tax Increment Financing (ETIF): This program returns between 30 and 50% of new employees' income withholding tax to companies who add new workers. To qualify, employees must be paid a wage equal to or above the per capita wage in their labor market area, and be provided group health insurance and access to an ERISA qualified retirement program. The company must also demonstrate that ETIF funding is an essential component of the expansion project's financing.

High-Technology Investment Tax Credit: Offers businesses engaged in high-tech activities that purchase and use eligible equipment a credit amount equal to the adjusted basis of equipment place in service less any lease payments received during the taxable year.

Jobs and Investment Tax Credit: This program helps businesses with an income tax credit on equipment and facilities that generate new jobs. The program provides a 10% credit against Maine income taxes for investment in most types of personal property that generates at least 100 new jobs within two years, as long as the investment is at least $5 million for the taxable year. The credit amount is tied to the federal investment tax credit and is limited to $500,000 per year with carry-forwards available for seven years.

Research and Development Tax Credit: Maine's R&D tax credit provides an income tax credit for qualifying research and development activities. The program is based on definitions within the Internal Revenue Code; therefore, Maine's Bureau of Taxation recommends a careful study of Section 41 of the Code. In general, qualified research expenses include in-house and contract research related to discovering information that is technological in nature and is intended for use in developing a new or improved business.

Custom Computer Programming Sales Tax Credit Program: Exempts from sales tax the purchase of custom computer programming.

Biotechnology Sales Tax Exemption: Exempts sales tax of purchase of machinery, equipment, instruments and supplies used by any biotechnology company directly and primarily in a biotechnology application.

Manufacturing Sales Tax Exemptions: Sales of machinery and equipment used by any manufacturing company directly and primarily in the production of tangible personal property is eligible for a sales tax exemption.

Partial Clean Fuel Vehicle Sales Tax Exemption: Businesses that sell clean fuel vehicles to the general public are eligible for an exemption amount based on a portion of the sales or lease price of a clean fuel vehicle.

Research and Development Sales Tax Exemption: Sales of machinery and equipment used by the purchaser directly and exclusively in research and development by any business is eligible for a sales tax exemption.

Fuel and Electricity Sales Tax Exemption: Program exempts any business from sales tax 95% of the sales price of all fuel and electricity purchased for use at the manufacturing facility.

Business Property Tax Reimbursement Program: Maine reimburses what companies pay in local property taxes on facilities built after April 1, 1995. Taxes on this property may be reimbursed by the state for a maximum of 12 years. The definition of qualified business property for this program is broad and specified by law.

Maine Seed Capital Tax Credit Program: FAME authorizes state income tax credits to investors in an amount equal to 30% of the cash equity they provide to eligible Maine businesses.

For more information, contact Maine Revenue Services, 24 State House Station, Augusta, ME 04333; 207-287-2336.

* Exports

For all items without a separate address, contact the Maine Office of Business Development at the address listed above.

Maine offers businesses and organizations international assistance through the Maine International Trade Center. The Trade Center's mission is to expand Maine's economy through increased international trade in goods and services and related activities such as:

- Trade missions
- Training programs in international trade
- Conferences, such as a major Trade Day event
- Publications, including the Trade Center newsletter
- Special member-only programs and one-on-one counseling and technical service assistance
- Comprehensive international library resources

For more information on the Maine International Trade Center, including membership information, contact Perry Newman, Trade Director, Maine International Trade Center, 511 Congress Street, Portland, ME 04101; 207-541-7400; Fax: 207-541-7420; E-mail: {newman@ mitc.com}; {www.mitc.com}.

Export Financing Services: Working Capital Insurance from FAME provides additional security to lenders and encourages greater lending activity for international business ventures. Export Credit Umbrella Insurance, provided by the Export-Import Bank of the United States (Eximbank) and administered by FAME, reduces international credit risk and allows an exporter to offer credit terms to foreign buyers in a competitive market.

* Small Business Administration Offices

Mary McAleney
40 Western Ave., Room 512
Augusta, ME 04330
207-622-8378
Fax: 207-622-8277

Maryland

Department of Business and Economic Development
217 East Redwood St.
Baltimore, MD 21202
410-767-6300
800-811-0051
Fax: 410-333-6792
TDD/TTY: 410-333-6926
www.mdbusiness.state.md.us

* Business Assistance

For all items without a separate address, contact the Maryland Department of Business and Economic Development at the address listed above.

Department of Business and Economic Development (DBED): This office can provide information and expertise in dealing with state, federal, and local agencies. They also have information on financing programs and other services offered by the state government.

Workforce Resources: Maryland offers several training and grants for training programs to meet a variety of workforce needs. The following are two of their many programs:

1. Maryland Job Service: Provides recruitment and screening services based on the specifications of a company at no costs. It maintains a state/ nationwide data bank of job seekers and acts as the state's labor exchange agent to match qualified workers with available employment opportunities.

Industrial Training Program: Provides incentive grants for the development and training of new employees in firms locating or expanding their workforce in Maryland. MITP reimburses companies for up to 100% of the direct costs associated with training programs customized to the work process.

State Money - Maryland

2. Partnership for Workforce Quality: Targets training grants to manufacturing firms with 500 or fewer employees to upgrade skills for new technologies.

Regional Response Resources: Coordinates services designed to improve the quality, productivity and competitiveness of a business and help develop new and innovative products and processes.

Engineering Assistance: Provides a gateway for companies to access the expertise of the University of Maryland faculty, staff and resource of the University's Engineering Resource center.

Technology Support: Helps companies diversify into new markets. In addition, the office: provides technical assistance to firms seeking to commercialize new technologies; facilitates collaboration between businesses and universities and federal laboratories; and oversees the Strategic Assistance Fund, which provides matching funds to support the cost of private sector consultants to aid in both strategic plan development and new market strategies.

Regulatory and Permitting Assistance: The Office of Business Advocacy assists businesses in navigating through the processes and regulations of local, state and federal government. The Office provides ombudsman service to businesses and acts an information source and liaison on behalf of the business community.

* Business Financing

For all items without a separate address, contact the Maryland Department of Business and Economic Development at the address listed above.

Investment Financing Programs: Provide for direct investment in technology-driven Maryland-based companies through three programs. All three provide a novel alternative to grants, direct loans or credit enhancements available through other State financing programs. All three involve the use of private sector capital, including venture capital, on a co-investment basis, and while having an underlying economic development agenda, are capital gains and return-on-investment driven.

Challenge Investment Program: Provides emerging or early "seed" stage, technology-driven companies with a capital formation capability of $100,000 through a direct investment of $50,000 from the Challenge Program, which facilitates a required 1:1, $50,000 co-investor match. A return on investment is potentially achieved through a repayment of up to $100,000 over a ten year period for DBED's original $50,000 investment, based on a contingent stream of royalty payments. The contingency is based in turn on the achievement of certain revenue and capital structure thresholds by the company during that time period. The Challenge Program invests $500,000 annually, in two "rounds" of five $50,000 investments, about six months apart.

Enterprise Investment Fund: An investment financing tool that enables DBED to make direct equity investments in "second-stage" technology driven companies located in the state. Investments range from $150,000 to $250,000 per entity. Investment decisions are based on the potential for return on investment, as well as the promotion of broad-based economic development and job creation initiatives.

Maryland Venture Capital Trust: Administered by DBED through the Division of Financing Programs and the Investment Financing Group. As a "Fund of Funds", the trust has invested a total of $19,100,000 directly in eight separate, private sector venture capital funds. The source of this funding from the State, from the Maryland Retirement System, and from the Baltimore Retirement System. In the aggregate, these eight venture capital funds seek to make direct investments of at least $19,100,000 on a pro-rata basis, in Maryland-based, technology-driven companies. The Enterprise Investment Fund will work closely with these eight venture capital funds in attempting to facilitate its co-investment requirements.

Community Financing Group (CFG): Consists of programs that support the effort of local jurisdictions to create jobs and enhance their communities. These innovative programs have been very successful in revitalizing downtown areas, creating attractive business areas, developing industrial sites, creating attractive business locations, and in general, improving the State's industrial and commercial base.

The Four CFG programs include the Maryland Industrial Land ACT (MILA), the Maryland Industrial and Commercial Redevelopment Fund (MICRF), the Community Development Block Grant for Economic Development (CDBG-ED), and the Economic Development Opportunities Program Fund (Sunny Day). Each has unique attributes that allow effective and timely support of the needs and priorities of Maryland's local jurisdictions.

- *Maryland Industrial Land ACT (MILA)*: MILA loans provide a financial resource in cases where the need to develop industrial sites is not fully met by the private sector. Loans are made to counties or municipalities at below market interest rates and are secured by the full faith and credit of the borrowing government. The Act authorizes loans for acquisition of industrial land, development of industrial parks, improvement to infrastructure of potential industrial sites, construction of shell buildings for industrial use, installation of utilities, and rehabilitation of existing buildings for business incubators.

- *Maryland Industrial & Commercial Redevelopment Fund (MICRF)*: MICRF financing is intended to encourage private investment to facilitate industrial and commercial development or redevelopment. Loans are made to counties or municipalities who can then re-loan the proceeds to an eligible end user.

- *Sunny Day Fund*: Created to allow the State to take advantage of extraordinary economic development opportunities where assistance from other sources are constrained by program design, timing or available resources. The fund has been an extremely valuable tool in both business retention and recruiting. Maryland has taken advantage of opportunities with rapid and creative proposals that have assisted in the establishment of several high-profile private sector enterprises, including prized technology and research companies.

Maryland Industrial Development Financing Authority (MIDFA): Available to industrial/commercial businesses except certain retail establishments. Normal project range is $35,000 to $5 million. Insured up to lower of 80% of loan or $1 million. The amount of insurance varies with each loan and is determined after discussing the lender's needs. Typically, MIDFA insures from 20% to 50% of the loan.

Tax Exempt Program: Available to manufacturers or 501(c)(3) non-profit organizations. Normal project range is $1 million to $10 million. May insure up to 100% of bond. Normal policy: financing not to exceed 90% or real estate value or 75% of equipment cost. The actual amount of insurance generally varies with each project.

Taxable Bond Program: Available to industrial/commercial businesses with certain exceptions. Normal project range is $1 million or more. Insurance level varies with each project but is limited to $5 million. May be insured up to 100% of bond amount. Approved Uses of Funds: To finance fixed assets.

Seafood & Aquaculture Loan Fund: Available to individuals or businesses involved in seafood processing or aquaculture. Normal Project Range: $20,000 to $800,000. Maximum Program Participation: The lesser of $250,000 or 80% of the total investment needed.

Energy Financing: Eligible applicants are businesses seeking to conserve energy, to co-generate energy, to produce fuels and other energy sources, and to recycle material. Normal Project Range: $800,000 to $160 million. Maximum Program Participation: 80% to 90% of value not exceeding 100% of cost.

Contract Financing Program: Eligible applicants are businesses owned 70% or more by socially and economically disadvantaged persons. Normal Project Range: Up to $500,000. Maximum Program Participation: Direct up to $500,000. Loan guarantee up to 90% not to exceed a maximum participation of $500,000. Approved Uses of Funds: Working capital required to begin, continue and complete government or public utility contracts. Acquisition of machinery or equipment to perform contracts. Interest Rates: For guaranteed loans, maximum rate is prime plus 2%. For direct loans, maximum is 15%

Long Term Guaranty Program: Eligible applicants are businesses owned 70% or more by socially and economically disadvantaged persons. Must have 18 successive months of experience in the trade or business for which financing is sought. Normal Project Range: $50,000 to $1 million. Maximum Program Participation: Loan guarantees may not exceed the lesser of 80% of the loan or $600,000.

Surety Bond Program: Eligible applicants are independently owned small businesses generally employing fewer than 500 full-time employees or those with gross annual sales of less than $50 million. Normal Project Range: Guaranty Program - None. Direct Bonding Program - Up to $750,000. Maximum Program Participation: Guaranty Program - Guarantees up to 90% of face value of the bond not to exceed a total exposure of $900,000. Direct Bonding Program - Can directly issue bonds not to exceed $750,000. Approved Uses of Funds: Guaranty Program - Guarantees reimbursement of losses on a bid, payment or performance bond required in connection with projects where the majority of funds are from government or a regulated public utility. Direct Bonding Program - Issues bid, payment or performance bonds on projects where the majority of funds are from government or a regulated public utility.

Equity Participation Investment Program - Technology Component & Business Acquisition Component: Eligible applicants are technology based businesses and business acquisitions which will be owned 70% or more by disabled, socially or economically disadvantaged persons. Normal Project Range: $100,000 to $3 million. Maximum Program Participation: The lesser of $250,000 or 80% of the total investment needed.

Equity Participation Investment Program - Franchise Component: Eligible applicants are franchises that are or will be owned 70% or more by disabled, socially or economically disadvantaged persons. Must have at least 10% of total project cost in owner's equity. Normal Project Range: $50,000 to $1.5 million. Maximum Program Participation: Equity investments or loans up to 45% of initial investment or $100,000, whichever is less.

State Money - Maryland

Challenge Investment Program: Eligible applicants are technology-driven companies, with principal activity located in Maryland; applicants must have complete business plan as a minimum requirement. Size of Investment: $50,000.

Enterprise Investment Program: Eligible applicants are technology-driven companies, with principal activity located in Maryland; applicants must have complete business plan as a minimum requirement. Size of Investment: $150,000 to $250,000.

Defense Adjustment Loan Fund (DALF): The primary purposes of this program are: (1) to stimulate and support the development of defense and non-defense enterprises in Maryland that have the potential to create employment in areas hurt by defense downsizing; and (2) to support the diversification of Maryland defense companies. On average, DALF intends to create or retain one job for every $35,000 loaned. The fund will lend capital to companies with growth potential for working capital, product development, technology commercialization, or manufacturing modernization. Preference will be given to loans that will catalyze investment or loans from other sources. Loans as small as $25,000 are permitted, but it is expected that loans will average $100,000 to $250,000. Committed funds may be released by DALF against the achievement of specified milestones.

Neighborhood Business Development Program (NBDP): Initiative to help stimulate Maryland's established, older communities, NBDP provides flexible, gap financing (up to 50% of total project cost) for many small businesses starting up or expanding in targeted urban, suburban or rural revitalization areas throughout the State. Terms and conditions are established on an individual basis. Financing ranging from $25,000 to $500,000, up to 50% of total project cost, where other funds clearly are unavailable. Contact Maryland Department of Housing and Community Development, Neighborhood Business Development Program, Revitalization Center, 1201 W. Pratt Street, Suite D, Baltimore, MD 21223; 410-514-7288; Fax: 410-685-8270; {www.dhcd.state.md.us}.

* Tax Incentives

For all items without a separate address, contact the Maryland Department of Business and Economic Development at the address listed above.

No unitary tax on profits.
No income tax on foreign dividends.
No gross receipts tax on manufacturers.
No corporate franchise tax.
No separate school taxes.

Job Creation Tax Credits: income tax credits granted to businesses for the creation of jobs. Credit granted will be the lesser of $1,000 or 2 1/2% of a year's wages for each qualifying permanent job.

Employment of Individual with Disabilities Tax Credit: Includes tax credits for wages paid and for child care or transportation expenses for qualifying individuals with disabilities.

Employment Opportunity Tax Credit: Includes credits for wages and child care or transportation expenses for qualifying employees who were recipients of state benefits from the "Aid to Families with Dependent Children" program immediately prior to employment.

Neighborhood and Community Assistance Program Tax Credit: Provides tax credits for business contributions to approved, non-profit Neighborhood and Community Assistance Programs.

Property Tax Exemptions and Credits: Maryland does not impose a personal property tax on business. For those jurisdictions that do tax personal property, exemptions and credits available include the following: machinery, equipment, materials and supplies use in manufacturing or research; manufacturing inventory; commercial inventory for warehousing and distribution; custom computer software.

Enterprise Zones Tax Credits:
1. Property Tax Credits: Ten year credit against local property taxes on a portion of real property improvements. Credit is 80% the first five years, and decreases 10% annually thereafter to 30% in the tenth and last year.
2. Income Tax Credits: One to three year credits for wages paid to new employees in the zone. The general credit is a one-time $500 credit per new workers. For economically disadvantaged employees, the credit increases to a total of $3,000 per worker distributed over three years.
3. Priority access to Maryland's financing programs.

Empowerment Zone Incentives: Firms locating in the federally designated Empowerment Zone in Baltimore, one of six in the nation, may be eligible for state enterprise zone incentives including: income tax credits for job creation; property tax credits for real property improvements. Businesses in the Zone may also qualify for potential federal incentives such as: wage tax credits; increased depreciation on equipment; tax exempt bond financing; employment development incentives.

Brownfields Tax Incentives: The counties, Baltimore City or incorporated municipalities may elect to grant a five-year credit equal to 50% of real property taxes attributable to the increase in the assessment resulting from cleanup and improvement of a qualified Brownfields site. The Brownfields real property credit may be expanded as follows: localities may grant an additional credit of up to 20%; localities may extend the credit by an additional five years if the site is in a state-designated enterprise zone; a credit will also apply against state real property taxes for the same percentage and duration.

Sales Tax Exemptions: The following are major business-oriented exemptions from the Maryland Sales and Use tax. Local jurisdictions do not impose a sales tax:
1. Sales of capital manufacturing machinery and equipment, including equipment used for testing finished products; assembling, processing or refining; in the generation of electricity; or used to produce or repair production equipment.
2. Sales of noncapitalized manufacturing machinery and equipment; safety and quality control equipment use on a production activity site; and equipment used to move a finished product on the production site.
3. Sales of tangible personal property consumed directly in manufacturing, testing of finished products, assembling, processing or refining, or in the generation of electricity.
4. Sales of fuels used in manufacturing, except those used to cool, heat and light the manufacturing facility.
5. Sales for resale and sales of tangible personal property to be incorporated in other tangible personal property manufactured for resale. In addition, there is an exemption for sales of computer programs reproduced for sale or incorporated in whole or in part into another computer program intended for sale.
6. Sales of customized computer software.
7. Sales of equipment and equipment used or consumed in research and development, to include testing of finished products.
8. Sales of aircraft, vessels, railroad rolling stock, and motor vehicles used principally in the movement of passengers or freight in interstate and foreign commerce.
9. Sales of certain end-item testing equipment used to perform a contract for the U.S. Department of Defense and transferred to the federal government.

* Exports

For all items without a separate address, contact the Maryland Department of Business and Economic Development at the address listed above.

Trade Financing Program: Eligible applicants are industrial/commercial businesses which are engaged in the export and import of goods through Maryland ports and airport as well as service providers to the overseas market. Normal Project Range: $10,000 to $5 million. Maximum Program Participation: Insured up to lower of 90% of obligation or $1 million for export financing and 80% for all others. The actual amount of insurance generally varies with each transaction.

The State of Maryland's Office of International Business (OIB): Offers export assistance to small and medium-sized Maryland firms with internationally competitive products and services. OIB's international trade professionals provide Maryland companies with access to international market intelligence, targeted trade activities, financial assistance and high-level introductions to potential customers.

- *Exporter's Hotline & Referral Service*: OIB marketing specialists deliver basic trade information to companies in all stages of the export process. The Exporter's Hotline handles inquiries concerning the exporting process, assistance offered to Maryland firms by international trade service providers, and data on Maryland's international business activity. The hotline's number is 410-767-6564.

Export Assistance Network: An alliance of international business assistance centers, was developed by the State of Maryland to facilitate the transition of small and medium-sized companies to the global marketplace. The Network gives Maryland businesses convenient access to foreign market reports, profiles of the top industries for export, trade leads and contacts, travel information, trade statistics, and other information needed for entering the global market. The five centers are:
- World Trade Resource Center, Baltimore; 410-576-0022
- Eastern Shore Export Assistance Center, Salisbury; 410-548-5353
- Southern Maryland Export Assistance Center, La Plata; 301-934-2251
- Suburban Maryland Export Assistance Center, Rockville; 301-217-2345
- Western Maryland Export Assistance Center, Cumberland; 301-777-5867

Maryland's Trade Finance Program: Offers up to $1 million in loan insurance per borrower for export and import financing. The trade finance office also provides access to the export financing and foreign credit insurance programs of the United States Export-Import Bank and the Overseas Private Investment Corporation.

Sister State Relationships: Promotes business, educational and cultural exchanges between Maryland and regions in Asia, Europe and Latin America. This program, which is managed through alliances with the World Trade Center Institute and the Maryland Business Center China, facilitates high-level international contacts, meetings with visiting delegations and networking with Maryland's international executives. Maryland has active sister state relationships in Belgium, China, Japan, Korea, Poland and Russia.

Foreign Offices & Representatives: Network of foreign offices and representatives provide exporters with in-country resources and expertise around the globe. These foreign offices in China, Japan, the Netherlands and Taiwan -- and representatives in Argentina, Brazil, Chile, Israel and Mexico -- deliver support in the following areas: agent/distributor searches and business appointments; credit reports, competitor analysis and regulatory information; marketing and logistical support at trade shows; market research and analysis.

Export Credit Program: Businesses conducting substantial economic activity in Maryland may submit proposals to receive export offset credits accrued from state purchases.

Publications

- *Trade Secrets: The Export Answer Book*: This guide contains over 100 answers to the most commonly asked questions concerning international trade; provides contact information for export experts; and describes more than 300 current publications, software programs and other international trade resources. The book, produced by the Maryland Small Business Development Center, is distributed for free to Maryland businesses through the State's Export Assistance Network.
  - *World View*: A collaborative effort of the State's international office and other international service providers, the World View newsletter covers exporting issues, events and other topics of interest to Maryland's international executives. *World View* is published bimonthly by the Office of International Business and distributed for free.

* Women and Minorities

For all items without a separate address, contact the Maryland Department of Business and Economic Development at the address listed above.

Day Care Facilities Guarantee Fund: Eligible applicants are individuals or business entities involved in the development or expansion of day care facilities for infants and children, the elderly, and disabled persons of all ages. Normal Project Range: Up to $1 million. Maximum Program Participation: Loan guarantee up to 80%.

Child Care Facilities Direct Loan Fund: Eligible applicants are individuals, business entities involved in the development of day care facilities for children, either center-based or home-based. Normal Project Range: Minimum $15,000. Maximum Program Participation: Maximum of 50% of fixed assets.

Child Care Special Loan Fund: Eligible applicants are individuals, business entities for expanding or improving child care facilities, meeting state and local licensing requirements and improving the quality of care. Normal Project Range: $1,000 to $10,000. Maximum Program Participation: Direct loans up to $10,000.

* Small Business Administration Offices

Allan Stephenson
10 S. Howard St., Suite 6220
Baltimore, MD 21201
410-962-4392
Fax: 410-962-1805

Massachusetts

Massachusetts Office of Business Development
10 Park Plaza, 3rd Floor
Boston, MA 02116
617-973-8600
800-5-CAPITAL
Fax: 617-973-8797
www.state.ma.us/mobd

* Business Assistance

For all items without a separate address, contact the Massachusetts Office of Business Development at the address listed above.

Massachusetts Office of Business Development (MOBD): Through five regional offices, they will advise and counsel businesses and individuals in utilizing federal, state, and local finance programs established to help businesses with their capital formation needs.

Entrepreneurial Group: Provides funding, oversight, and, in some cases, the operation of a number of entrepreneurial training programs designed to help dislocated workers start their own businesses or consulting practices.

Achieving the Competitive Advantage Program: An intensive 10-week course designed to introduce entrepreneurs to strategic skills, methods, and models that are critical in planning and implementing a successful business plan. The classes provide training in the areas of business management, technology and financing, as well as such concepts as strategic partnerships, quality assurance and motivational vision.

One-Stop Business Centers: Offers a streamlined approach to economic development assistance. Offices located throughout the state are staffed with professionals who know about Massachusetts' programs and opportunities for businesses throughout the state's diverse regions.

Massachusetts Site Finder Service: Offers confidential, statewide searches for industrial land or buildings to fit defined specifications for expanding businesses. MOBD can also provide up-to-date Community Profiles of communities being considered as a business location. Information provided includes the local tax structure, local permitting requirements, and a demographic profile of area residents. For more information, contact Massachusetts Alliance for Economic Development, 800 Boylston St., Suite 1700, Boston, MA 02199; 617-247-7800; 800-872-8773; {www.massecon.com}.

Economic Development Incentive Program (EDIP): To stimulate economic development in distressed areas, attract new businesses, and encourage existing businesses to expand in Massachusetts.

Business Finance Specialists: Assists companies with financing targeted to urban and economically disadvantaged areas through the Community Development Finance Corporation and other public funds.

One-Stop Permitting Program: For all construction-related, state-issued permits. Project Managers act as advocates, assisting with identifying all required permits and moving the application through the entire process.

Massachusetts Energy Advisor Service: Helps companies identify energy efficiency opportunities in facilities and manufacturing processes. The University of Massachusetts and the Corporation for Business, Work, and Learning provide a similar service focusing on smaller and medium-sized manufacturing plants.

Economic Development Programs: Designed to encourage businesses to expand their operations, to move into the state, or to address specific utility needs. Within a year, businesses will be able to shop around for electricity, thereby creating competition among electric providers. This new opportunity will position Massachusetts in a more competitive environment regarding utility costs and will bring about lower commercial and industrial rates.

Business Consulting and Municipal Loan Pools: Professional staff are available at the municipal level who can offer business and technical assistance, as well as valuable insights on the local business climate and available local resources. Some municipalities also administer loan pools that can provide businesses with low-interest financing.

Massachusetts Manufacturing Partnership (MMP): Helps plan and implement a strategy for increased competitiveness, whether by adopting new production technologies and management techniques, finding new markets, or training a work force. Industry led regional offices are staffed by Field Agents who will work with a company to create the best combination of assistance.

The Commonwealth has resources to assist smaller and medium-sized manufacturers to stay competitive and to ensure that their work force has the skills necessary to be re-employed. Through the Corporation for Business, Work, and Learning, the Commonwealth provides training and job search services to unemployed workers, and offers consulting services and a loan fund/loan guarantee program for turnarounds.

The New England Suppliers Institute (NESI): Helps manufacturing companies become better suppliers to their larger customers by assisting them to develop quality business relationships, implement continuous improvement strategies, achieve supplier certification, and enhance company-wide work force and management skills.

Massachusetts Manufacturing Network Program: Provides technical assistance and funding to help them leverage resources, share information, and accomplish tasks that they could not do on their own.

Office of Defense Adjustment Strategy: Provides information about federal and state defense conversion programs. MOBD experts can discuss how defense companies wishing to diversify into new commercial markets may be eligible for federal grants.

Environmental Agency has an Office of Technical Assistance that has helped many firms replace or reduce the use of toxic substances in production, increasing productivity while lowering treatment and disposal costs. Massachusetts' Energy Advisor Service helps companies reduce pollution related to energy use while cutting their consumption and cost of energy. The Industrial Extension Service has expertise in helping firms make greater use of recycled materials.

State Money - Michigan

Starting a Business in Massachusetts: A comprehensive guide for business owners available from MOBD.

* Business Financing

For all items without a separate address, contact the Massachusetts Office of Business Development at the address listed above.

The Capital Access Program (CAP): Designed to assist small businesses throughout the Commonwealth in obtaining loans to start, expand or continue operating profitably. The program is designed to gain access to capital where none currently exists. The state provides "cash collateral" guarantees for banks willing to make loans to smaller, "less bankable" businesses. Any person or business authorized to do business in Massachusetts may borrow through CAP. There are no minimum loan amounts.

The Emerging Technology Fund (ETF): A useful tool for economic growth for technology based companies. Targeting the fields of biotechnology, advanced materials, electronics, medical, telecommunications and environmental technologies, the fund provides companies in these industries with a greater opportunity to obtain debt financing. Loans can be guaranteed for tenant build-out, construction or expansion of facilities and equipment purchased for up to $1.5 million or 50% of the aggregate debt, whichever is less. Loans are also provided for hard asset-owned facilities and equipment, with a maximum amount of $2.5 million or 33 1/3% of the aggregate debt, whichever is less.

Equipment Lease/Purchase Program: The tax-exempt lease/purchase program provides manufacturers, non-profit institutions and environmental enterprises with a low-cost alternative for financing $300,000 or more in new equipment needs. By enabling leasing companies to furnish below-market, tax-exempt interest rates, the program offers companies sizable cost savings. Offers fixed interest rates approximately 70% of traditional leasing rates. 100% financing is available. Institutions must qualify as a 501(c)(3), not-for-profit entity and be located in Massachusetts. Potential borrowers include educational institutions, cultural institutions, long term care facilities, and other non-profits.

Tax-Exempt Industrial Development Bonds: Companies can borrow money via a tax-exempt Industrial Development Bond (IDB) to provide the lowest possible borrowing rates. Funds for an IDB can be used to purchase land, buildings and new equipment as well as to construct or renovate buildings. Based on the proposed project, the purchase of a new site, any new equipment needs and renovation or construction of facilities could be financed through an IDB. Should the project require a more flexible financing structure, the Massachusetts Development Finance Agency can work with the particular company to structure a taxable bond. Project size ranges from approximately $1.5 million to a federally imposed maximum of $10 million.

* Tax Incentives

For all items without a separate address, contact the Massachusetts Office of Business Development at the address listed above.

Investment Tax Credit: Massachusetts gives businesses a 3% Investment Tax Credit against the corporate excise tax for the construction of manufacturing facilities. The credit also applies to the purchase or lease of equipment. It is available to companies involved in manufacturing, research and development, agriculture or commercial fishing.

R&D Tax Credit: Massachusetts has permanent 10% and 15% R&D tax credits with a fifteen-year or indefinite carry-forward provision for companies investing in research and development. Companies are allowed to compute defense and non-defense R&D separately. This constitutes one of the highest R&D tax credits in the nation.

Economic Opportunity Areas: Qualified businesses operating within one of 36 Economic Target Areas are eligible for tax and financing incentives: A 5% Investment Tax Credit for all businesses, not just manufacturing; A 10% Abandoned Building Tax Deduction (at least 75% vacant for at least 24 months); Local Property Tax Benefits (Special Tax Assessment or Tax Increment Financing); Priority status for state capital funding.

Economic Target Areas (ETA) are designated throughout Massachusetts. Within ETAs, Economic Opportunity Areas of particular economic need and priority are further defined. Businesses that undertake certified projects within Economic Opportunity Areas can qualify for additional investment incentives: 5% Investment Tax Credit for Certified Projects, 10% Abandoned Building Tax Deduction within designated areas, Municipal Tax Benefits (Tax Increment Financing or Special Assessments on Property Values), Priority for state capital funding.

Tax Increment Financing: Businesses may also benefit from the substantial property tax savings offered through Tax Increment Financing (TIF). TIF enables municipalities to enter into agreements with private companies to determine a baseline property value level at which taxes will be levied for a specified number of years.

* Exports

For all items without a separate address, contact the Massachusetts Office of Business Development at the address listed above.

Massachusetts Export Center: One-stop resource for international business. The Export Center is a cooperative effort of the Massachusetts Office of International Trade and Investment, the Massachusetts Port Authority, the Massachusetts Small Business Development Center, Mass Development and the Massachusetts Office of Business Development. Offers:
- One-on-one Export Counseling
- Export Workshops, Training Programs and Conferences
- Overseas Market Research, Statistics and Trade Leads
- International Marketing Activities, including Trade Missions and Exhibitions
- Network of International Offices
- Meetings with International Business Delegations
- Export Financing
- International Business Resource Library
- Bimonthly Newsletter on International Trade Opportunities

Contact the Massachusetts Export Center, Fish Pier West, Bldg., II, Boston, MA 02210; 617-478-4133; {www.state.ma.us/export}.

Assistance is also provided through the *Massachusetts Trade Office*. This office's home page provides information on upcoming trade missions and lists events and seminars about doing business in the global market. Contact Massachusetts Trade Office, State Transportation Bldg., 10 Park Plaza, Boston, MA 02116; 617-367-1830; {www.state.ma.us/moiti}.

* Women and Minorities

For all items without a separate address, contact the Massachusetts Office of Business Development at the address listed above.

State Office of Minority and Women Business Assistance (SOMWBA): Certifies companies as minority or women-owned or controlled, and publishes a directory listing of verified firms. SOMWBA provides management and technical assistance seminars and workshops for minority and women entrepreneurs on a wide variety of business topics.

Minority Business Financing: A MOBD Business Finance Specialist can guide a company to several targeted financing programs including the Community Development Finance Corporation's Urban Initiative Fund, the Economic Development Fund and others.

* Small Business Administration Offices

Patrick McGowan
10 Causeway Street, Suite 812
Boston, MA 02222
617-565-8415
Fax: 617-565-8420

Elaine Guiney
10 Causeway Street, Suite 265
Boston, MA 02222
617-565-5561
Fax: 617-565-5598

Harold Webb
1441 Main Street, Suite 410
Springfield, MA 01103
413-785-0484
Fax: 413-785-0267

Michigan

Michigan Jobs Commission
201 North Washington Square
Victor Office Center, 4th Floor
Lansing, MI 48913
517-373-9808
Fax: 517-335-0198
www.mjc.state.mi.us

State Money - Michigan

* Business Assistance

For all items without a separate address, contact the Michigan Jobs Commission at the address listed above.

Michigan Business Ombudsman: Serves as a "one-stop" center for business permits. Acts as a mediator in resolving regulatory disputes between business and the various state departments and also provides consultation and referral services.

Michigan Works! is the state's workforce development resource agency. Offers workforce development services at 25 locations.

MiProSite: Lists more than 2,600 sites that can be searched based on client criteria for industrial site locations.

Economic Development Jobs Training: Provides financial assistance to companies that need to train or retrain workers to meet marketplace needs. Grant average: $2,000 per employee.

Business and Economic Services Team: Provides a broad variety of business and economic services to employers, entrepreneurs, and to those seeking to do business with the State of Michigan, which enable businesses to keep pace with civil rights and equal employment opportunity legal standards.

Customer Assistance: Provides a centralized intake unit in which economic development and workforce customers obtain services quickly and efficiently, and where individuals can receive information about starting a business in Michigan.

Economic Development Corporations: Provides a flexible tool to assist in job creation at the local level by acquiring, developing, and maintaining land, buildings, machinery, furnishings, and equipment necessary to complete a project plan.

Michigan Business Development: Assists existing companies with a wide array of business services which are customized to meet the specific needs of the business.

Michigan Business Strategies 2000: Provides affordable high quality management consulting services for small businesses seeking to position themselves for long-term growth. Businesses can receive expert consulting services in areas such as accounting, marketing, information systems, financial management, and internal operations.

Certified Industrial Park Program: Industrial park developers and communities have used this identification as a marketing tool to show prospective clients that they are prepared to accept the new client without delay. For more information, contact Michigan Economic Developers Association, P.O. Box 15096, Lansing, MI 48901; 517-241-0011.

Child Care Clearinghouse: Employers and organizations needing general information on employer-sponsored child care can obtain a resource kit which includes a series of fact sheets on topics related to workplace child care and information about a variety of tax issues. For more information, contact Michigan Child Care Clearinghouse, 201 N. Washington Square, Lansing, MI 48913; 517-373-9808; 800-377-2097.

Michigan Technical Assistance Center Network: Assists companies with government contracting and exporting.

Research Services: Detailed information concerning Michigan's economy and business climate. Information is also available regarding various industrial sectors critical to Michigan.

Employee Ownership Program: Provides information, technical assistance, and financing to enhance the establishment of employee-owned companies and Employee Stock Ownership Plans.

* Business Financing

For all items without a separate address, contact the Michigan Jobs Commission at the address listed above.

Alternative Investments Division: Invests in businesses with strong management that show a substantially above-average potential for growth, profitability, and equity appreciation. A typical initial investment is $5,000,000 and up. Contact: Michigan Department of Treasury, Alternative Investments Division, P.O. Box 15128, Lansing, MI 48901; 517-373-4330.

Capital Access Program: An extremely flexible and non-bureaucratic program designed to assist banks in making business loans that are somewhat riskier than conventional bank loans. The program utilizes a special loss reserve to assist banks in covering losses from a portfolio of loans that a bank makes under the program. The program is very broad based and can be used to finance most types of Michigan businesses. Due to premium payments that range from 3% to 7% of the amount borrowed [which are made to help fund the special loss reserve], loans under the program are generally more expensive than conventional bank loans. The key point is that, through the program, banks can provide access to bank financing for many businesses that otherwise might not qualify. Although there are no loan size limits, the average loan is approximately $53,000.

Business and Industrial Development Corporations (BIDCOs): Many sound businesses are unable to obtain growth capital because their finances are considered too risky for conventional bank lending, yet they cannot provide the high rates of return required by venture capitalists. BIDCOs are a new type of private institution designed to fill this growth capital gap. BIDCOs offer an array of financing options that can be structured flexibly to suit the needs of individual companies. In addition, they can provide management assistance to help businesses grow. As a privately owned and operated corporation, each BIDCO establishes its own criteria for the kinds of businesses it will finance and for the types of loans and investments it will make. BIDCOs do not normally finance start ups.

Industrial Development Revenue Bond Program (IDRB): Tax-exempt bonds issued on behalf of the borrower by the Michigan Strategic Fund and purchased by private investors. These loans can be made for manufacturing and not-for-profit corporation projects and solid waste facilities. Bond proceeds can only be used to acquire land, building and equipment. Working capital and inventory are not eligible for this type of financing. These bonds are generally used when financing of $1 million and higher is required.

Pollution Control Loans: Intended to provide loan guarantees to eligible small businesses for the financing of the planning, design, or installation of a pollution control facility. This facility must prevent, reduce, abate, or control any form of pollution, including recycling. SBA can guarantee up to $1,000,000 for Pollution Control Loans to eligible businesses. The 7(a) Program interest rates and maturities apply and are negotiated with the lender.

Equipment and Real Property Purchases: Municipal Bonds provide streamlined tax-exempt, fixed interest rate financing well suited to equipment purchases. For more information, contact Michigan Municipal Bond Authority, Treasury Bldg., 3rd Floor, 430 West Allegan, Lansing, MI 48922; 517-373-1728.

Freight Economic Development Project Loans/Grants: Provides financial assistance to non-transportation companies which promote the development or expansion of new business and industries, by financing freight transportation infrastructure improvements needed to operate a new venture. For more information, contact Michigan Department of Transportation, Bureau of Urban and Public Transportation, Freight Services and Safety Division, 425 W. Ottawa, P.O. Box 30050, Lansing, MI 48909; 517-373-6494.

Industrial Development Revenue Bonds (IRBs): Provides healthy, profitable firms locating or expanding in Michigan with capital cost savings stemming from the difference between taxable and tax exempt interest rates. Maximum size of bonds is limited to: $1,000,000 free of any restriction on capital expenditures, or $10,000,000 subject to certain conditions.

Private Rail Loans: Privately owned railroad companies may receive capital loans up to 30% of the total project cost to improve or expand the privately owned infrastructure. For more information, contact Michigan Department of Transportation, Bureau of Urban and Public Transportation, Freight Services and Safety Division, P.O. Box 30050, Lansing, MI 48909; 517-373-6494.

Taxable Bond Program: Provides small and medium sized companies access to public capital markets normally available to larger companies.

Venture Capital Fund: Provides venture capital to growth-oriented firms ranging from $3 - $10 million.

* Tax Incentives

For all items without a separate address, contact the Michigan Jobs Commission at the address listed above.

Enterprise Zones: The program allows a designated community to provide a business and property tax abatement reducing property taxes approximately 50% on all new investment.

Tax-Free Renaissance Zones: 11 regions of the state designated as virtually tax free for any business or resident presently in or moving to a zone. The zones are designed to spur new jobs and investment. Each Renaissance Zone can be comprised of up to six smaller zones (sub zones) which are located throughout the community to give businesses more options on where to locate.

MEGA Jobs Tax Credit: Companies engaged in manufacturing, research and development, wholesale and trade, or office operations that are financially sound and that have financially sound proposed plans, are eligible to receive a tax credit against the Michigan Single Business Tax for a new location or expansion project and/or the amount of personal income tax attributable to new jobs being created.

Property Tax Abatements: Can be granted by the state and by local units of government. They reduce property tax on buildings, machinery and equipment by 50% for new facilities, 100% for existing.

Air Pollution Control Systems Tax Exemptions for Installation: Relieves a company of sales tax, property tax, and use taxes for air pollution control equipment.

Economic Growth Authority: Awards credits against the Single Business Tax to eligible companies for up to 20 years to promote high quality economic growth and job creation that otherwise would not occur without this program.

State Money - Minnesota

Registered Apprenticeship Tax Credit: Makes available a tax credit of up to $2,000 annually per apprentice to employers who, through registered apprenticeships, train young people while they are still in high school.

Work Opportunity Tax Credit: The tax credit is 35% of the first $6,000 in wages paid during the first year of employment for each eligible employee.

* Exports

For all items without a separate address, contact the Michigan Jobs Commission at the address listed above.

Export Working Capital Program (EWCP): The EWCP was designed to provide short-term working capital to exporters. It is a combined effort of the SBA and the Export-Import Bank. The two agencies have joined their working capital programs to offer a unified approach to the government's support of export financing.

International Trade Loan (ITL): This program provides short- and long-term financing to small businesses involved in exporting, as well as businesses adversely affected by import competition. The SBA can guarantee up to $1.25 million for a combination of fixed-asset financing and working capital. Loans for facilities or equipment can have maturities of up to 25 years. The working capital portion of a loan has a maximum maturity of three years. Interest rates are negotiated with the lender and can be up to 2.25% over the prime rate.

Export/Foreign Direct Investment Program: Promotes the export of Michigan-produced goods and services and attract investment in Michigan by foreign-based companies.

* Women and Minorities

For all items without a separate address, contact the Michigan Jobs Commission at the address listed above.

Minority And Women's Prequalification Loan and the Women's Pre-Qualification Loan Program: Use intermediaries to assist prospective minority and women borrowers in developing viable loan application packages and securing loans. The women's program uses only nonprofit organizations as intermediaries; the minority program uses for-profit intermediaries as well.

The Women Business Owner Advocacy Unit: Provides information to women business owners regarding government contracting, financing, legislation, and other business issues. It is establishing a statewide network to facilitate the sharing of information, resources, and business expertise, and more. Contact Women's Business Owner Advocate, Michigan Jobs Commission, 201 N. Washington Square, 1st Floor, Lansing, MI 48913; 517-335-1835; Fax: 517-373-9143.

Disadvantaged Business Enterprise Certification: Insures that firms owned and controlled by disadvantaged individuals, minorities, and women participate in federal-aid contracts and grant entered into and administered by MDOT.

Small Business Group: Promotes job creation and retention in small firms by fostering communication, coordination partnerships between the Michigan Jobs Commission and those public and private sector groups and organizations which advocate for and/or provide services to small companies and minority, women, and handicapped-owned businesses.

* Small Business Administration Offices

Eugene Cornelius
477 Michigan Avenue, Suite 515
Detroit, MI 48226
313-226-6075
Fax: 313-226-4769

Minnesota

Department of Trade and Economic Development (MTED)
500 Metro Square Blvd.
121 7th Place East
St. Paul, MN 55101-2146
612-297-1291
800-657-3858
www.dted.state.mn.us

* Business Assistance

For all items without a separate address, contact the Minnesota Department of Trade and Economic Development (MTED) at the address listed above.

Minnesota Small Business Assistance Office: Provides accurate, timely, and comprehensive information and assistance to businesses in all areas of start-up, operation, and expansion. They can also provide referrals to other state agencies.

Business Development and Site Location Services: For businesses interested in expanding or relocating to a Minnesota site, it serves as a bridge between government and the resources that businesses are seeking. Business Development Specialists act as liaisons between businesses and state and local government to access financial and technical resources. The program also serves as an important information source, providing businesses with data on topics ranging from the availability of buildings and property or the labor supply in a particular location, to transportation or tax comparisons. The one-on-one nature of this program provides businesses with assistance throughout every phase of their expansion or location projects.

Computer and Electrical Components Industry Services: Exists to foster the growth of jobs, revenues, and investment in Minnesota's computer and electrical components industries. A specialist provides technical review of projects, coordination of statistical analysis, overview of prospect proposals, participation in development efforts with industry associations and other agencies.

Healthcare and Medical Products Industry Services: Exists to seek business investment and job growth in the healthcare industry while promoting Minnesota companies' capabilities in this industry. A specialist provides information to businesses on financial programs, suppliers, business planning, trade opportunities, venture partners and other needed resources. The specialist also works to attract direct investment in existing Minnesota businesses with problems and opportunities involving sources, product development, marketing, financing, site selection, and by marketing Minnesota actively at industry gatherings.

Printing and Publishing Industry Services: Exists to foster the growth of jobs, revenues, and investment in Minnesota's printing and publishing industry. A specialist provides information on resources, markets, technologies, buildings and sites, transportation, and other issues, both in response to inquiries and by marketing Minnesota actively at industry gatherings.

Wood Products, Plastics, and Composites Industry Services: Exists to foster the growth of jobs and added value in Minnesota's wood processing and related businesses and to attract new industry consistent with environmental protection. A specialist represents the industry and the Department of Trade and Economic Development by reviewing projects, organizing statistical data, participating in development efforts with Department of Natural Resources, University of Minnesota, Minnesota Technology, Inc., National Resources Research Institute and other agencies, and by helping to coordinate demonstration projects like model homes. This position has evolved from a primary focus on wood products, to a wider interest in plastics and composite materials that are more frequently used in conjunction with wood.

A Guide to Starting a Business in Minnesota: Provides a current discussion of many of the major issues faced by persons planning to start a new business in Minnesota, including forms or organizations, business name filing, business licenses and permits, business plans, financing, employers' issues, business taxes and small business resources.

* Business Financing

For all items without a separate address, contact the Minnesota Department of Trade and Economic Development (MTED) at the address listed above.

Minnesota Investment Fund: To create new and retain the highest quality jobs possible on a state wide basis with a focus on industrial manufacturing and technology related industries; to increase the local and state tax base and improve the economic vitality for all Minnesota citizens. Grants are awarded to local units of government who make loans to assist new expanding businesses. Maximum available: $500,000. Only one grant per state fiscal year can be awarded to a government unit.

Minnesota Job Skills Partnership Board: Awards grants for cooperative education and training projects between businesses and educational institutions.

Small Business Development Loan Program: Provides loans to industrial, manufacturing or agricultural processing businesses for land acquisition, building construction or renovation, machinery and equipment. Maximum available: $500,000 minimum up to a maximum of $6 million.

Rural Challenge Grant Program: Provides job opportunities for low-income individuals, encourage private investment, and promote economic development in rural areas of the state. The Business and Community Development Division has a partnership with each of six regional organizations to provide low-interest loans to new or expanding businesses in rural Minnesota. Eligible projects: Up to 50% of start-up or expansion costs, including property acquisition, site improvements, new construction, building renovation, purchase of machinery and equipment, and working capital. Maximum available:

$100,000. Most loans will be smaller due to the high demand for funds compared with the funds available.

Tourism Loan Program: Exists to provide low-interest financing to existing tourism-related businesses providing overnight lodging. Additionally, the program assists with the development of business plans. Businesses with feasible business plans qualify to receive financing for up to half of all eligible costs. Business owners meet with DTED staff to determine project eligibility and receive counseling. Direct loans, or participation loans in cooperation with financial institutions, can be made for up to 50% of total project cost. The maximum state loan may not exceed 50% of the total project cost, or $65,000, whichever is less. Maximum available Septic System Loans: Participation Loans - State funds are used in conjunction with loaned funds from financial institutions. Loans for septic system replacement or upgrade are eligible for an additional $65,000. Direct Loans - Only septic system projects of under $10,000 may receive a direct loan. The borrower must fund 50% of the project with private financing. The maximum direct loan is $5,000.

Certified Community Development Corporation: Certified CDCs may apply for grant funds for several purposes: 1. specific economic development projects within a designated area, 2 dissemination of information about, or taking application for, programs operated by DTED, or 3 developing the internal organizational capacity to engage in economic development activities.

Capital Access Program: To encourage loans from private lending institutions to businesses, particularly small-and medium sized-businesses, to foster economic development. When loans are enrolled in the program by participating lending institutions, the lender obtains additional financial protection through a special fund created by the lender, borrower and the State. The lender and borrower contribute between 3% and 7% of the loan to the fund. The amount of funds contributed by the borrower/lender must be equal; however, the funds contributed by the bank may be recovered from the borrower as additional fees or through interest rates. If the amount of all enrolled loans is less than $2,000,000, the State contribution will be 150% of the borrower/lender contribution. The borrower/lender contribution can be financed as part of the loan.

Contamination Cleanup/Investigation Grant Program: The Department of Trade and Economic Development can award grants towards contamination investigations and the development of a Response Action Plan (RAP) or for the cleanup of contamination on sites which will be redeveloped. The contamination investigation grants will allow smaller, outstate communities to access sites believed to be contaminated which are typically not addressed due to limited financial resources. The Contamination Cleanup grants address the growing need for uncontaminated, developable land. In both cases, grants are awarded to those sites where there is serious, imminent private or public development potential.

Minnesota Pathways Program: Act as a catalyst between business and education in developing cooperative training projects that provide training, new jobs and career paths for individuals making the transition from public assistance to the workforce. Grants are awarded to educational institutions with businesses as partners. Maximum available: $200,000 of Pathway funds per grant can be awarded for a project.

Underground Petroleum Tank Replacement Program: Exists to provide low interest financing to small gasoline retailers for the replacement of an underground petroleum tank. Business owners submit an application on the approved form along with supporting documentation including third party cost estimates from a certified installer, prior year federal tax return, schedule of existing debt and proof of gasoline volume sold in the last calendar year. Loans can only be made to businesses that demonstrate an ability to pay the loan from business cash flow. The maximum loan in $10,000.

* Exports

For all items without a separate address, contact the Minnesota Department of Trade and Economic Development (MTED) at the address listed above.

Minnesota Trade Office: Acts as an advocate for Minnesota businesses pursuing international markets and to promote, assist and enhance foreign direct investments that contribute to the growth of Minnesota's economy. Services provided for Minnesota companies include information on trade shows and trade missions; education and training; and financial assistance programs for Minnesota companies.

Services for International Companies: Resources, services and direct counseling for all companies interested in international trade.

Minnesota World Trade Center Corporation: An international business resource for Minnesota and the upper Midwest.

Minnesota Export Finance Authority: Assists with the financing of exports through four focus areas: working capital guarantees for purchase orders, receivable insurance for foreign buyers, ExIm bank, and agency liaison.

* Women and Minorities

For all items without a separate address, contact the Minnesota Department of Trade and Economic Development (MTED) at the address listed above.

Microenterprise Assistance Grants: To assist Minnesota's small entrepreneurs successfully startup or expand their businesses and to support job creation in the state. Any type of business is eligible to receive assistance, especially nontraditional entrepreneurs such as women, members of minority, low-income individuals or persons currently on or recently removed from welfare assistance who are seeking work. Startup entrepreneurs and expanding businesses receive technical assistance and, in some cases, financial support through selected nonprofit business development organizations. Businesses are eligible for up to $4,000 of technical assistance through this program. Participating organizations are reimbursed by DTED for up to half of this amount for approved expenses they incur on behalf of the grant recipient. The participating organization provides the other matching amount.

Minnesota Job Skills Partnership Program: Acts as a catalyst between business and education in developing cooperative training projects that provide training for new jobs or retraining of existing employees. Grants are awarded to educational institutions with businesses as partners. Preference will be given to non-profit institutions, which serve economically disadvantaged people, minorities, or those who are victims of economic dislocation and to businesses located in rural areas. Maximum available: $400,000 of Partnership funds per grant can be awarded for a project.

Urban Initiative Loan Program: Exists to assist minority owned and operated businesses and others that will create jobs in low-income areas of the Twin Cities. Urban Initiative Board enters into partnerships with local nonprofit organizations, which provide loans and technical assistance to start-up and expanding businesses. Project must demonstrate potential to create jobs for low-income people, must be unable to obtain sufficient capital from traditional private lenders, and must be able to demonstrate the potential to succeed. Eligible projects: Start-up and expansion costs, including normal business expenses such as machinery and equipment, inventory and receivables, working capital, new construction, renovation, and site acquisition. Financing of existing debt is not permitted. Micro enterprises, including retail businesses, may apply for up to $10,000 in state funds. Maximum available: The maximum total loan available through the Urban Initiative Program is $300,000. The state may contribute 50% of the loan up to $150,000.

* Small Business Administration Offices

Nancy Gilbertson
100 N 6th Street, Suite 610
Minneapolis, MN 55403
612-370-2306
Fax: 612-370-2303

Mississippi

Department of Economic and Community Development
P.O. Box 849
Jackson, MS 39205-0849
601-359-3040
800-340-3323
Fax: 601-359-4339
www.decd.state.ms.us

* Business Assistance

For all items without a separate address, contact the Mississippi Department of Economic and Community Development at the address listed above.

Department of Economic and Community Development: This office can provide information and expertise in dealing with state, federal, and local agencies. They also have information on financing programs and other services offered by the state government.
- *Training*: Customized industrial training programs provided through the State Department of Education. Job Training Partnership Act assistance provided through the Mississippi Department of Economic and Community Development.
- *Site Finding*: The Mississippi Resource Center in Jackson offers an

State Money - Mississippi

- interactive video for site viewing and detailed data on video, computer disk, or hard copy for later study.
- *One-stop environmental permitting*.

* Business Financing

For all items without a separate address, contact the Mississippi Department of Economic and Community Development at the address listed above.

Loan Guarantee Program: Provides guarantees to private lenders on loans made to small businesses allowing a small business to obtain a loan that may not otherwise be possible without the guarantee protection. The maximum guarantee is 75% of the total loan or $375,000, whichever is less.

Industrial Development Revenue Bond Program: Reduces the interest costs of financing projects for companies through the issuance of both taxable and tax-exempt bonds. Additionally, ad valorem and sales tax exemptions are granted in conjunction with this type of public financing. There is a $10 million cap.

Small Enterprise Development Program: Provides funds for manufacturing and processing companies to finance fixed assets. Although a company may qualify for more than one loan under this program, the aggregate amount loaned to any company cannot exceed $2 million.

Department of Economic and Community Development Finance Programs: Through the issuance of State General Obligation Bonds, low-interest loans are provided to counties or cities to finance improvements that complement investments by private companies.

Airport Revitalization Revolving Loan Program: Funds from the issuance of state bonds provide loans to airport authorities for the construction and/or improvement of airport facilities. Maximum loan amount is $500,000.

Port Revitalization Revolving Loan Program: Designed to make loans to port authorities for improvement of port facilities. Maximum is $500,000.

Agribusiness Enterprise Loan Program: Designed to encourage the extension of conventional financing by lending institutions by providing interest-free loans to agribusinesses. Maximum loan is 20% of the total project cost or $200,000, whichever is less. Proceeds may be used to finance buildings and equipment and for costs associated with the purchase of land.

Small Business Assistance Program: Established for the purpose of providing funds to establish revolving loan funds to assist in financing small businesses. Maximum is $100,000.

Energy Investment Program: Provides financial assistance to individuals, partnerships or corporations making energy conserving capital improvements or designing and developing energy conservation processes. This program offers low-interest loans of up to $300,000.

Local Industrial Development Revenue Bonds: Local political entities have the authority to issue tax-exempt and taxable industrial development revenue bonds to finance new or expanding industrial enterprises up to 100% of total project costs.

General Obligation Bonds: Local political entities have the authority to issue general obligation bonds for the purpose of acquiring sites and constructing facilities for lease to new or expanding industries.

* Tax Incentives

For all items without a separate address, contact the Mississippi Department of Economic and Community Development at the address listed above.

Jobs Tax Credit: Provides a five-year tax credit to the company's state income tax bill for each new job created by a new or expanding business. Amounts: $2,000 per new job for less developed counties, $1,000 per new job for moderately developed counties, and $500 per new job for developed counties.

R&D Jobs Tax Credit: Provides a five-year credit of $500 per year for each net new R&D job created by new or expanding businesses.

Headquarter Jobs Tax Credit: Provides a five-year tax credit of $500 per year for each net new job created by the transfer of a national or regional headquarters to Mississippi.

Child/Dependent Care Income Tax Credit: An income tax credit of 50% of qualified expenses is offered to any employer providing child/dependent care for employees during working hours.

Basic Skills Training Tax Credit: Provides a tax credit to new or existing businesses that pay for certain basic skills training or retaining for their employees. Credit is equal to 25% of qualified expenses of the training.

Rural Economic Development Credits: Companies financing projects through the Small Enterprise Development or Industrial Revenue Bond Program may be eligible to receive credits on corporate income taxes.

Mississippi State Port Income Tax Credit: Provides an income tax credit to taxpayers who utilize the port facilities at state, county, and municipal ports in Mississippi. The taxpayer receives a credit in an amount equal to certain charges paid by the taxpayer of export cargo.

County Property Tax Exemptions: For new or expanding manufacturers, certain properties may be exempted from county property taxes, except school taxes, for up to ten years at the local option.

Local authorities may grant a fee in lieu of taxes, including school taxes, on projects over $100 million.

Free Port Warehouse Law: Exempts finished goods from property taxes, including school taxes.

No state property tax except school taxes.

Sales Tax Exemptions: No sales tax on purchases of raw materials, processing chemicals, or packaging materials. No sales tax on direct purchases of construction materials, machinery, and equipment for businesses that are financed through certain bonds or located in less developed counties.

Partial Sales Tax: 50% sales tax exemptions for purchases of construction materials, machinery and equipment in moderately developed and developed counties. A 1 1/2% sales tax on machinery and parts used directly in manufacturing and on industrial electricity, natural gas, and fuels.

* Exports

For all items without a separate address, contact the Mississippi Department of Economic and Community Development at the address listed above.

Foreign Trade Zones (FTZ): A safe area where goods can be landed, stored, processed, and transhipped--all without incurring custom duties (import tax). Foreign trade zones can provide customers with manufacturing, assembling, packaging, and display facilities, all free of duties. They are considered outside the customs territory of the United States in reference to many factors relating to international trade.

* Women and Minorities

For all items without a separate address, contact the Mississippi Department of Economic and Community Development at the address listed above.

Minority Business Enterprise Division (MBED): Provides assistance to businesses in those categories. The division acts as principal advocate on behalf of minority- and women-owned business enterprises and promotes legislation that will help them operate more effectively. Developing funding sources, including state funding, bonding resources, federal and local funds, and others is among the major aims of MBED. But identifying funding sources represents only one aspect of MBED's service to Mississippi's women- and minority-owned firms. The division also attempts to put those businesses in touch with potential customers; MBED maintains an outreach program designed to include them in contracting of goods and services and procurement of contracts. A regional and statewide network of workshops, seminars, and trade shows continually provide training to stimulate the role of entrepreneurship in Mississippi's economic development.

Minority Surety Bond Guaranty Program: Program enables minority contractors, not meeting the surety industry's standard underwriting criteria, to obtain bid and performance bonds on contracts with state agencies and political subdivisions. Maximum bond guarantee is 75% of contract bond amount, or $112,500, whichever is less.

Minority Business Enterprise Loan Program: Designed to provide loans to socially and economically disadvantaged minority-or women-owned small businesses. Loan proceeds may be used for all project costs associated with the establishment or expansion of a minority business, including the purchase of fixed assets or inventory or to provide working capital. The minimum loan is $2,000 and the maximum loan is $25,000. MBFC may fund up to 100% of a total project.

* Small Business Administration Offices

Janita Stewart
101 West Capitol Street, Suite 400
Jackson, MS 39201
601-965-5371
Fax: 601-965-5335

Charles Gillis
2909 13th St , Suite 203
Gulfport, MS 39501
228-863-4449
Fax: 228-864-0197

Missouri

Department of Economic Development (DED)
Truman Building, Room 720
P.O. Box 118
Jefferson City, MO 65102-0118
573-751-4962
800-523-1434
Fax: 573-526-2416
www.ecodev.state.mo.us

* Business Assistance

For all items without a separate address, contact the Missouri Department of Economic Development (DED) at the address listed above.

First Stop Shop: Serves to link business owners and state government and provides information on state rules, regulations, licenses, and permits.

Business Assistance Center: Provides information and technical assistance to start-up and existing businesses on available state and federal programs. Offers several useful publications. Contact: 888-751-2863.

University Outreach and Extension: Programs to help citizens apply university research knowledge to solve individual and community problems. Working with business owners and managers on a one-to-one basis, B&I specialists help entrepreneurs identify problem areas and find solutions.

Workforce Development System: Integrates previously fragmented employment and training programs into a comprehensive workforce development system. Services benefit both job seekers and employers through One-Stop Career Centers. Contact Workforce Development Transition Team, P.O. Box 1928, Jefferson City, MO 65102-1928; 573-751-7039; Fax: 573-751-0147.

Small Business Incubators: Buildings that have been divided into units of space, which are then leased to new small businesses. In addition to low-cost physical space, incubators can help clients with access to necessary office machines, reception and secretarial services, furniture, conference rooms and technical expertise in business management.

Innovation Centers: Provide a wide range of management and technical assistance to businesses. These centers are familiar with up-to-date business management and technology innovations and help businesses apply these innovations to help increase profits.

Mid-America Trade Adjustment Assistance Center: Available to small and medium-sized manufacturers who have been hurt by foreign competition. Helps firms analyze their strengths and weaknesses, develop a strategy to offset foreign competition, pay for implementing this strategy with federal cost-share fund.

Regional Planning Commissions: Services provided include business assistance, development, education, job training programs, loan preparation request, community assistance, airport planning, environmental assessments, grant administration and writing, hazardous waste planning, housing programs, legislative activities, local emergency planning, research, rural assistance, solid waste management, transportation planning, water and sewer planning, workshop development.

* Business Financing

For all items without a separate address, contact the Missouri Department of Economic Development (DED) at the address listed above.

Action Fund Program: The program provides a subordinate loan to certain types of for-profit companies that need funds for start-up or expansion and have exhausted other sources. The projected growth of the company, economic impact, the risk of failure, and the quality of management are critical factors for approval. DED must determine that the borrower has exhausted other funding sources and only the least amount needed to complete the project may be provided. In any event, an Action Fund Loan would be limited to the lower of: $750,000 per project; 30% of the total project cost; or $20,000 per new full-time year-round job.

Brownfield Redevelopment Program: The purpose of this program is to provide financial incentives for the redevelopment of commercial/industrial sites owned by a governmental agency that have been abandoned for at least three years due to contamination caused by hazardous substances. The program provides state tax credits for eligible remediation costs. DED may provide a loan or guarantee for other project costs, or a grant for public infrastructure. Also, tax credits may be provided to businesses that create jobs at the facility. The program provides Missouri state income tax credits for up to 100% of remediation costs. Guaranteed loans or direct loans to an owner or operator of the property are limited to $1 million. Grants to public entities are also available up to $100,000 or 50% for feasibility studies or other due diligence costs. Grants can also be issued up to $1 million for the improvement of public infrastructure for the project. The total of grants, loans or guarantees cannot exceed $1 million per project.

CDBG Loan Guarantee Program: The purpose of this program is to provide "gap" financing for new or expanding businesses that cannot access complete funding for a project. "Gap" financing means other sources of financing (including bank loans and owner equity) have been maximized, and a gap exists in the total project cost. The Department of Economic Development (DED) will guarantee 50% to 80% of the principal balance (after liquidation of assets) of a loan made by a financial institution. DED must determine that the borrower has exhausted other funding sources and only the least amount needed to complete the project may be provided. The maximum funding available is based on the lower of: $400,000 per project or $20,000 per new full-time permanent job created or retained. Approval is based on the good character of the owners, sufficient cash flow, adequate management and reasonable collateral.

Certified Capital Companies (CAPCO): Purpose is to induce private investment into new or growing Missouri small businesses, which will result in the creation of new jobs and investment. DED has initiated the formation of private venture capital firms (CAPCOs). These firms have certain requirements to make equity investments in eligible businesses in Missouri. The amount a CAPCO may invest in one Missouri business depends on various factors, however the maximum amount is 15% of the CAPCO's certified capital. Funding decisions are made by each CAPCO based on their evaluation of the return on investment relative to the risk. CAPCO funds may be used for equity investments, unsecured loans or hybrid investments in eligible businesses. Typically, venture capitalists require a projected 25-40% annual ROI, depending on the risk.

Economic Development Administration Revolving Loan Funds: Designed to provide gap financing for start-up as well as existing business and industry in rural areas. The Revolving Loan Funds are administered by various agencies throughout the state and are available in cooperation with area financial institutions.

Industrial Development Bonds (IDBs): Developed by the US Congress and the Missouri General Assembly to facilitate the financing of business projects. The interest received by the bondholders may be exempt from federal and state income taxes, if the project is eligible.

Missouri Market Development Program: Financial assistance is targeted toward developing and expanding manufacturing capacity in the state by assisting businesses with the development, purchase and installation of specialized equipment needed to convert manufacturing facilities to utilize recovered materials. The maximum amount of financial assistance for any one project is $75,000.

Linked Deposit Program: The State Treasurer will provide a deposit of state funds to a lender selected by an approved company. The rate of deposit is lower than market rates, and the difference is passed on to the borrower as a lower interest rate on the loan.

Neighborhood Improvement Districts Program: General obligation bonds are issued to finance public improvements requested by benefiting property owners. The bonds are paid by special assessments to the property owners. The project should realistically be in excess of $150,000 due to the financing costs. The outstanding bonds cannot exceed 10% of the city or county's assessed valuation.

Urban Enterprise Loan Fund (UEL): A micro lending instrument established by the State of Missouri, Department of Economic Development and administered in Kansas City by the downtown Minority Development Corporation and in St. Louis by the St. Louis Development Corporation. The program is designed to assist Missouri residents with the creation, expansion, and retention of micro-enterprises. Eligible enterprises must be located - or aspire to locate - within the Federally designated Enhanced Enterprise Community and the State Enterprise Zone. One job must be created for every $20,000 in Urban Enterprise Loan proceeds invested. Loans from the State fund range from a minimum of $10,000 up to a maximum of $100,000. The Urban Enterprise Loan Fund also has a matching funds requirement and new job creation criteria.

Missouri First: The State Treasurer has reserved a portion of available linked deposit funds for small businesses. State funds are deposited with participating lending institutions at up to 3% below the one-year Treasury Bill rate, with the lender passing on this interest savings to the small business borrower. A company must have less than 25 employees, be headquartered in Missouri, and be operating for profit. Small Business MISSOURI FIRST Linked Deposit loans are available for working capital. The maximum loan amount is $100,000. Contact State Treasurer's Office, P.O. Box 210, Jefferson City, MO 65102-0210; 800-662-8257.

Market Development Loans for Recovered Materials: The Environmental Improvement and Energy Resources Authority funds activities that promote the development of markets for recovered materials. Loans of up to $75,000 are available to companies for equipment used in the production or manufacture of products made from recovered materials. After three years, if all contract

State Money - Missouri

obligations are met, the loan is forgiven and repayment is not required. Contact: Environmental Improvement and Energy Resources Authority, P.O. Box 744, Jefferson City, MO 65102; 573-526-5555.

Financial Aid for Beginning Farmers: Beginning farmers can receive federally tax-exempt loans from commercial lenders at rates 20 to 30% below conventional rates through this program. A qualified borrower can borrow up to $250,000 to buy agricultural land, farm buildings, farm equipment and breeding livestock in Missouri. The borrower must be a Missouri resident, at least 18 years old and whose chief occupation must be farming or ranching after the loan is closed. The borrower's net worth must not exceed $150,000, and he or she must have adequate working capital and experience in the type of farming operation for which the loan is sought. A beginning farmer is one who has not previously owned more than 15% of the medium-sized farm in their county. Land cannot be purchased from a relative. For more information, contact Missouri Agricultural and Small Business Development Authority, Beginning Farmer Program, P.O. Box 630, Jefferson City, MO 65102; 573-751-2129.

Small Corporation Offering Registration (SCOR): Missouri's Small Corporate Offering Registration (SCOR) provides a process for entrepreneurs to register their securities. The SCOR process has been designed by state securities regulators to make it easier and less expensive for small companies to raise needed capital from Missouri residents. All securities registered through this process need to complete form U-7 available from the Secretary of State's Office. For more information, contact Securities Division, Secretary of State's Office, P.O. Box 1276, Jefferson City, MO 65102; 573-751-4136.

Working Capital, St. Louis: Working Capital is a micro-lending program which identifies small business people in the St. Louis area and makes available to them the commercial credit and business support which enables them to expand their business. Working Capital utilizes a peer-lending technique. At required monthly meetings borrowers receive continuing assistance in the marketing of their goods or services. The maximum first-time loan is $500 payable in four to six months; subsequent loans can have increased amounts (up to $5,000) and longer duration. Working Capital gives priority to individuals already in business to minimize loan risk; will consider applications from start-ups. Contact Working Capital, 3830 Washington, St. Louis, MO 63108; 314-531-4546.

Economic Council of St. Louis County: Services include Business Development Fund (BDF), Metropolitan St. Louis Loan Program, Minority/ Disadvantaged Contractor Loan Guarantee, Recycling Market Development Loan Program, SBA 504 Loan Program and Minority & Women's Prequalified Loan Program. Economic Council of St. Louis County, 121 South Meramec St., St. Louis, MO 63105; 314-889-7663.

St. Charles County Economic Development Council: Program assists eligible companies with fixed asset and working capital needs; acts as the certified development company which packages SBA 504 loans. Contact St. Charles County Economic Development Council, 5988 Midrivers Mall Dr., St. Charles, MO 63304; 314-441-6880.

St. Louis Development Corporation:
1. St. Louis City Revolving Loan Fund: Provides direct, low interest, subordinated loans for working capital, machinery and equipment, purchasing land and buildings, renovation and constructing facilities and leasehold improvements. Business must be located in the City of St. Louis and be licensed to do business in the City. Must create one full-time job for every $10,000 of funds. Loans can provide up to 1/3 of the project cost to a maximum loan amount of $150,000.
2. St. Louis Urban Enterprise Loan, St. Louis Development Corporation: Provides loans to businesses located within the Enterprise Community area or the Enterprise Zone within the City of St. Louis. Eligible borrowers must be for profit businesses with current employment of less than 100. Eligible program activities will include fixed asset or working capital needs. Eligible projects must retain existing or create new jobs (one job created for every $20,000 of funding). The UEL can lend up to 50% of the project costs to a maximum loan amount of $100,000.
3. LDC Micro Loan Program, St. Louis Development Corporation: Microloans are available to start-up companies or businesses less than one year old located within the City of St. Louis; one job, other than the owner's, must be created. Successful applicants must demonstrate a viable business plans and the inability to secure bank financing. Companies must show the ability to start or grow the business with a maximum loan amount of $25,000. Loans may be used to cover start-up costs, working capital and purchase of machinery and equipment.

Contact St. Louis Development Corporation, 1015 Locust St., #1200, St. Louis, MO 63101; 314-622-3400.

First Step Program, Kansas City: The First Step Fund (FSF) offers training in business basics such as record keeping, budgeting and marketing; assistance in completing a feasibility study for a business; opportunity to apply for loans of up to $2,500; and ongoing support group. FSF participants must be residents of Jackson, Clay or Platte counties in Missouri and must meet federal guidelines for low to moderate income. During a 10-week business training program, students work on a feasibility study for the proposed business. Potential borrowers receive continuing education at monthly meetings. Participants review each others' feasibility studies and approve loans. The maximum loan amount for first-time borrowers is $2,500 and $5,000 for second-time borrowers. Contact First Step Fund, 1080 Washington St., Kansas City, MO 64105; 816-474-5111, ext. 247; Fax: 816-472-4207.

Kansas City's Urban Enterprise Loan Fund, Kansas City: Fund is designed to assist with the creation, expansion and retention of small businesses located, or aspiring to locate, within the federally designated Enhanced Enterprise Community and the State Enterprise Zone. Eligible applicants include any Missouri resident with a for-profit business with gross annual revenues of less than $250,000 and less than 100 employees. Loan amounts can range from $10,000 to $100,000; matching funds are required as well as new job creation (minimum of one job per $20,000 borrowed). Contact First Business Bank, 800 West 47th St., Kansas City, MO 64112; 816-561-1000.

Community Development Corporation of Kansas City: Provides microloan business assistance to small businesses located in a five-county area; assists entrepreneurs whose credit needs are $25,000 and under. Contact Community Development Corporation of Kansas City, 2420 E. Linwood Blvd., Kansas City, MO 64109; 816-924-5800; Fax: 816-921-3350.

Thomas Hill Enterprise Center, Macon: The Thomas Hill Enterprise Center established a Revolving Loan Fund (RLF) to fill financing gaps not covered by conventional lenders. While certain restrictions exist, the RLF is designed to provide financing for businesses which cannot obtain adequate funds from conventional sources. Contact: Thomas Hill Enterprise Center, 1709 Prospect Dr., Suite B, Macon, MO 63552; 660-385-6550; 800-470-8625.

In$Dent Small Business Support: Peer lending program designed to assist low income residents of Dent County attain economic self-sufficiency by helping them start and/or maintain profitable businesses. All borrowers complete an approved business management training program and must be a member of a peer lending group. Loans will not be for more than $1,000 for any one group member. After the initial loan is repaid, members can apply for larger loans up to $2,000; each loan thereafter will have a ceiling of twice the previous loan, up to a maximum of $10,000. Contact: Bryan Adcock, Child and Family Development Specialist, 112 E. 5th St., Jucicial Building, Suite 4, Salem, MO 65560; 573-729-3196.

CDBG Industrial Infrastructure Grant: This program assists local governments in the development of public infrastructure that allows industries to locate new facilities, expand existing facilities or prevent the relocation or closing of a facility. The use of this program is based on the local government exhausting their available resources. DED has targeted a 20% match by the community base upon the availability of unencumbered city or county funds.

* Tax Incentives

For all items without a separate address, contact the Missouri Department of Economic Development (DED) at the address listed above.

Small Business Investment "Capital" Tax Credit: The state of Missouri, through the Small Business Investment Capital Tax Credit Program offers a 40% tax credit to eligible investors in qualified businesses. Eligible investors may not be principle owners in the business. Only unsecured investments are considered eligible. All businesses wishing to participate in the program must make application to the Department of Economic Development prior to accepting investments for which tax credits are to be issued.

Business Facility Tax Credit Program: State income tax credits are provided to the business based on the number of new jobs and amount of new investment created at the qualifying facility. The credits are provided each tax year for up to ten years after the project commences operations. The tax credits are earned each tax period for up to 10 years. The formula to earn the tax credits is based on:
- $100 (or $75 for a new MO company) for each new job created at the project.
- $100 (or $75 for a new MO company) per $100,000 of the new capital investment at the project.

Capital Tax Credit Program: The investors of an approved business will receive a 40% state income tax credit on the amount of their equity investment or, in the case of a qualified investment in a Missouri small business in a distressed community, may receive a 60% state income tax credit. The percentage of stock purchased by the investors is negotiated with the business. The minimum amount of tax credits allowed per investor is $1,500 ($3,750 investment). The maximum amount of tax credits allowed per investor is $100,000 ($250,000 investment).

Community Bank 50% Tax Credit: The purpose of this program is to induce investment into Community Banks, which then invest in new or growing businesses or real estate development, resulting in an expansion of the tax base, elimination of blight, reduction of reliance on public assistance and the creation of jobs. A contributor may obtain state tax credits based on 50% of

State Money - Missouri

investments or contributions in a Community Bank. The Community Bank then makes equity investments or loans to a business, or investment in real estate development within a target area. No more than $750,000 can be invested or loaned by the Community Bank for any one business (including any affiliated or subsidiary of the business) or real estate development.

Enterprise Zone Tax Benefits: State income tax credits are provided to the business based on the number of new jobs and amount of new investment created at the qualifying facility. The business may earn credits based on the facility's new jobs and investment, the number of zone residents and "special" employees hired and trained for the facility.

Historic Credit Tax Credit: The program provides state tax credits for 25% of eligible costs and expenses of the rehabilitation of an approved historic structure.

Infrastructure Tax Credit Program
- *Missouri Development Finance Board (MDFB):* Provides state tax credits to a contributor based on 50% of the contribution. The contributed funds are granted to a public entity to finance infrastructure needed to facilitate an approved project. Eligible contributors receive a tax credit of 50% of the contribution against Chapter 143 (excluding certain withholding taxes), 147, and 148 taxes. Contributions may be eligible for federal tax deductions also.
- *Distressed Communities Tax Credit Program*: Based on demographic requirements. Some entire cities qualify, and some areas qualify based on census block group demographics. The total maximum credit for all businesses already located within distressed communities shall be $750,000 for each calendar year.
- *Research Expense Tax Credit Program*: Purpose of the Research Expense Tax Credit Program is to induce existing businesses to increase their research efforts in Missouri by offering a tax credit. The amount of qualified research expenses for which tax credits shall apply, may not exceed 200% of the taxpayer's average qualified research expenses incurred during the three-year period immediately prior to the tax period the credits are being claimed. The aggregate of all tax credits authorized shall not exceed $10 million in any taxable year.
- *Seed Capital Tax Credit Program*: Purpose is to stimulate investment in new or young Missouri companies to fund the research, development and subsequent precommercialization phases of new, innovative products or services. Any person who makes a qualified contribution to a qualified fund shall be entitled to receive a tax credit equal to 50% of the amount of their contribution. This credit may be used to satisfy the state tax liability due within the year of the qualified investment, or in any of the ten tax years thereafter.
- *Small Business Incubator*: The purpose of the Small Business Incubator Tax Credit Program is to generate private funds to be used to establish a "protective business environment" (incubator) in which a number of small businesses can collectively operate to foster growth and development during their start-up period. The minimum tax credit is $1,500 per contributor. The maximum tax credit is $50,000 per contributor if made to a single incubator and $100,000 per contributor if made to multiple incubators. There is no maximum if the contribution is made to the Incubator Fund. The overall maximum amount of tax credits that can be issued under this program in any one calendar year is $500,000.
- *Tax Increment Financing Program*: A method to invent redevelopment of a project that otherwise would not occur. TIF redirects an approved portion of certain local taxes caused by the project to reduce project costs. The amount and length of the increment is negotiated by the TIF Commission based on the least amount to cause the project to occur. The "increment" may be up to 100% of the increased amount of real property taxes and 50% of local sales, utility and (in St. Louis and Kansas City) earnings taxed for a period of up to 23 years, as approved by the municipality.
- *Transportation Development Tax Credit Program*: A company (or individual) may be provided a state income tax credit for up to 50% of a contribution to a public entity for eligible activities. The project is needed to facilitate a business project or is a community development/public infrastructure improvement.
- *Wine and Grape Production*: To assist vineyards and wine producers with the purchase of needed equipment and materials by granting tax credits. A grape grower or wine producer is allowed a 25% state income tax credit on the amount of the purchase price of all new equipment and materials used directly in the growing of grapes or the production of wine in the state.

* Exports

For all items without a separate address, contact the Missouri Department of Economic Development (DED) at the address listed above.

Missouri Office Of International Marketing: Services include: International Consulting Service, Competitive Analysis Reports, Trade Show Reports, Trade Exhibitions, Catalog Shows, Missouri International Office Assistance, Foreign Company Background Checks, Rep-Find Service, International Travel Program, Marketing Program, Trade Opportunity Program, Foreign Trade Missions, Strategic Alliance Program, Export Finance Assistance, Made In Missouri Catalogs, Missouri Export Directory, Recognition Program.

Missouri's Export Finance Program: Missouri companies that need financial assistance exporting to foreign markets can use programs of the Export and Import Bank of the United States(Ex-Im Bank) and the Small Business Administration (SBA) through a joint project that provides local access for Missouri businesses. There are primarily two programs available, Working Capital Loan Guarantees and Export Credit Insurance. These programs are designed to help small and medium-sized businesses that have exporting potential but need funds or risk insurance to produce and market goods or services for export.

Export Credit Insurance: The state of Missouri offers assistance in obtaining export credit insurance through the Export/Import Bank of the US to take the risk out of selling to customers overseas. The Missouri program, which insures both commercial and political risks, guarantees an exporter that once his goods are shipped, he will be paid. Insured receivables can enhance an exporter's ability to obtain export financing and allow an exporter to offer more attractive credit terms to foreign buyers. For more information contact Missouri Export Finance Program, P.O. Box 118, Jefferson City, MO 65102-0118; 573-751-4855.

* Women and Minorities

For all items without a separate address, contact the Missouri Department of Economic Development (DED) at the address listed above.

Missouri Women's Council: To help Missouri women achieve economic self-sufficiency by supporting education, training, and leadership opportunities. Each year the Missouri Women's Council reviews pilot program proposals across the state and selects projects to fund which promote training, employment, and support Missouri women in the work place.

Workplace Readiness for Women: This particular program provides skills for employment in manufacturing industries for women living in Camden, Laclede, and Pulaski Counties. Training includes classroom instruction, one-on-one instruction and tutoring, computer training and work experience assignments with private employers who agree to provide the necessary supervision and work experience to assist participants with skills development and transition into employment in the manufacturing industry. For more information on this program, please contact Trish Rogers, Central Ozarks Private Industry Council, 1202 Forum Drive, Rolla, MO 65401; 800-638-1401 ext. 153; Fax: 573-634-1865.

Workforce Preparation for Women: This program is currently served in two Missouri locations; Mineral Area College in Park Hills and Jefferson College in Hillsboro. These programs focus on self-esteem, foundation skills and competencies as identified by an assessment process, and a workforce preparation plan developed by each student. Experts from education, business, and industry serve as speakers and consultants for the training sessions. Furthermore, the program matches each student with a mentor. For more information on this program, please contact Dr. Nancy Wegge, Consortium Director, Jefferson College, Hillsboro, MO 63050; 573-431-1951; Fax: 573-431-9397.

Capital for Entrepreneurs, Kansas City: Seed capital fund divided into three separate funds of $1 million each: Fund for Women, Fund for Hispanics, and Fund for African-Americans. Contact: Capital for Entrepreneurs, 4747 Troost Ave., Kansas City, MO 64110; 816-561-4646; Fax: 816-756-1530.

Office of Minority Business (OMB): Charged with the responsibility of identifying and developing support systems that assist the minority business community in gaining a foothold in the mainstream of Missouri's economy. This responsibility entails counseling minority small businesses on business start-up, retention, expansion, financing, and procurement; also including but not limited to providing ready access to information regarding current legislation and regulations that affects minority business. The staff of the Office of Minority Business can provide assistance with; administering technical and financial assistance programs; providing new and small businesses with management expertise; business development information; tying minority firms to national and global markets; connecting minority firms to the labor market; accessing research and technology; and other customized assistance.

* Small Business Administration Offices

Brad Douglas
323 W. 8th Street, Suite 307
Kansas City, MO 64105
816-374-6380
Fax: 816-374-6339

State Money - Montana

Dorothy Kleeschulte
323 W. 8th Avenue, Suite 501
Kansas City, MO 64105
816-374-6708
Fax: 816-374-6759

Robert Andrews
815 Olive Street, Room 242
St. Louis, MO 63101
314-539-6600
Fax: 314-539-3785

James Combs
620 S. Glenstone Street
Suite 101
Springfield, MO 65802
417-864-7670
Fax: 417-864-4108

Montana

Department of Commerce
1424 Ninth Ave.
P.O. Box 200505
Helena, MT 59620-0505
406-444-3814
800-221-8015 (in MT)
Fax: 406-444-1872
http://commerce.state.mt.us

* Business Assistance

For all items without a separate address, contact the Montana Department of Commerce at the address listed above.

- *Economic Development Division*: Offers a variety of programs aimed at assisting start-up and existing businesses with the technical and financial assistance necessary for their success. Works closely with other department divisions, state agencies, and federal and private programs, as well as local development groups, chambers and similar organizations.
- *Business Location Assistance*: Provides prompt referrals of prospective expanding or relocating firms to Montana communities meeting the company's physical, economic and/or demographic requirements; provides assistance to communities in working with recruitment prospects; works with individual communities or groups of communities and/or other organizations to design and implement proactive recruitment efforts to attract specific types of firms in industries targeted by the community; works with companies new to Montana to identify and utilize available technical assistance and resident suppliers of materials and services. If in-state demand for particular goods or services exists, the program will attempt to recruit one or more firms to fill that demand. Special services, including visa consulting and assistance, is available to investors from Canada or subsidiaries of international corporations. The program distributes prospects lists to Certified Community Lead organizations and appropriate Department of Commerce staff, unless otherwise requested and authorized by the prospective company.
- *The Census and Economic Information Center (CEIC)*: The official source of census data for Montana, the Center maintains a collection of documents and computer-retrievable files that address the economy and population of the state (historical as well as current), including special papers and annual, quarterly and monthly statistical reports from federal agencies and other Montana state agencies
- *Montana Health Facility Authority*: Issues revenue bonds or notes to finance or refinance projects involving construction, renovation, or equipment purchases for public or private non-profit health care programs. The MHFA lends its bond proceeds to participating health care facilities at costs below those offered by commercial lending institutions, thereby substantially lowering the facilities' borrowing expenses. In some instances, however, the MHFA includes commercial lending institutions in the financing to provide credit enhancement or private placement for the bonds. The MHFA may issue its notes and bonds, which are not general obligations of the state, for a single entity or a pool of health care facilities. Eligible health facilities may include hospitals, clinics, nursing homes, centers for the developmentally disabled or a variety of other health facilities.
- *Montana Manufacturing Extension Center (MMEC):* Improves the competitiveness of Montana manufacturers through direct, unbiased engineering and managerial assistance in partnership with public and private resources. MMEC field engineers help companies obtain the highest output from their people, equipment, and capital. They make "house calls" and provide free initial consultation. Their assistance includes, but is not limited to: productivity and quality audits, facility layouts, materials handling, ISO 9000 and quality assurance, benchmarking, managing growth, capacity planning, feasibility assessment, equipment justification, process design and improvement, cycle time reduction, production management, cost/benefit analysis, cost reduction, product costing, make/buy analysis, inventory analysis, supplier identification and relations, payroll incentive systems, materials requirements planning (MRP), and more. Contact: MMEC/ UTAP, 315 Roberts Hall, Montana State University-Bozeman, Bozeman, MT 59717; 406-994-3812.
- *University Technical Assistance Program*: For more than 10 years, the University Technical Assistance Program (UTAP) has provided technical assistance to Montana manufacturers through engineering graduate students who work half-time during the academic year and full-time in the summers. It continues as an integral part of MMEC with the MMEC Bozeman field engineer serving as the UTAP supervisor. Undergraduates who have completed certain engineering course work may be hired as summer interns under the supervision of other field engineers. The UTAP staff engineers complete some projects and provide valuable support to the MMEC field engineers on other projects. Contact: MMEC/ UTAP, 315 Roberts Hall, Montana State University-Bozeman, Bozeman, MT 59717; 406-994-3812.

* Business Financing

For all items without a separate address, contact the Montana Department of Commerce at the address listed above.

- *Microbusiness Finance*: Montana "micro" business companies with fewer than 10 full-time equivalent employees and annual gross revenues under $500,000 can receive loans of up to $35,000 from the program's network of regional revolving loan funds lending directly to businesses. The loan program is designed to fund economically sound business projects that are unable to obtain commercial financing. Companies must provide a detailed written business plan and may be required to participate in business training classes. In addition to financing, borrowers receive technical assistance and consulting to help assure their success.
- *Job Investment Loans (JIL):* This program is intended to provide funding for loans to Montana businesses as part of a financing package to permit business expansion, job creation and job retention. The program will provide a portion of the financing necessary to permit business expansion, job retention, and job creation. JIL monies will be used only in conjunction with equity and other debt financing in cases where other funding would not satisfy the total need and would not be available without this piece of additional financing.
- *Research and Development Financing*: Montana Science and Technology Alliance provides $13.1 million in matching capital, from the Permanent Coal Tax Trust Fund, for research and development projects at Montana public universities.
- *Risk Capital Financing*: The Montana Science and Technology Risk Capital Financing program may provide additional funding for current Montana companies. To receive MSTA financing, these businesses must meet the MSTA Board's investment criteria and have potential for achieving significant growth, benefiting the state's economy, and providing a substantial return on the board's investment. The MSTA structures all risk capital financing as loans. These loans may be convertible to company stock or would otherwise be structured to provide a risk-adjusted return on investment.
- *Growth Through Agriculture*: Projects must embody innovative agricultural products or processes. Amounts: $50,000 in any one round, $150,000 to any one firm.
- *REA Loan and Grant Program*: Provides zero-interest loans and grant to RE Act borrowers for relending to projects promoting rural economic development and job creation.
- *Seed Capital Program*: provides funding for early-state entrepreneurial companies. The emphasis for funding is on technological companies but other companies can receive financing as well. The program may loan up to $350,000 in a single financing round, and up to a maximum of $750,000 to any one company over time.

* Tax Incentives

For all items without a separate address, contact the Montana Department of Commerce at the address listed above.

- *New and Expanding Industry Tax Credit*: Credit is equal to 1% of new wages paid by any corporation that is either brand new or has expanded its number of jobs by 30% or more.

State Money - Nebraska

Reclamation and Recycling Equipment Credit: Investment tax credit for businesses equal to 25% of the cost of property purchased to collect or process reclaimable material or to manufacture a product from reclaimed material.

Recycling Tax Credit: Income tax deduction for purchase of recycled material.

Wind Energy Generation Tax Credit: Income tax or license severance tax credit equal to 35% of the eligible costs for an investment of $5,000 or more in a commercial wind-powered energy generation system.

Small Business Investment Tax Credit: Corporation income, licenses, or coal severance tax credit for investment in a small business investment company. Credit is limited to 50% of the investment to a maximum credit of $250,000 for each taxpayer.

Research and Development Exemption: Exemption from the corporation income of license tax on the net income of a newly organized research and development firm during its first 5 years of operation.

Dependent Care Assistance Credit: A company can claim a credit for the amount paid or incurred during the taxable year for dependent care assistance actually provided to or on behalf of an employee.

Infrastructure Fees Credit: A nonrefundable tax credit is available against the corporation license tax or income tax for the portion of the fees that are charged to a specified new business for the use of the infrastructure that is built with loans.

Inventory Tax Exemption: Business inventories are exempt from property tax.

Property Tax Incentives for Selected Businesses: Reduction in property tax rates are available to: real and personal property used in the production of gasohol, machinery and equipment used in electrolytic reduction facilities (production of aluminum), market value on machinery and equipment used in a maltiny barley facility, market value on machinery and equipment used in a canola seed oil processing facility.

Property Tax Incentives for Specific Industries: Reduction in property tax rates are available to: industries that manufacture, mill, mine, produce, process, or fabricate materials; that convert materials unserviceable in their natural state into commercial products or materials, engage in the mechanical or chemical transformation of materials of substance into new products, engage in the transportation, warehousing or distribution of commercial products or materials, or if 50% or more of their annual gross income comes from out of state sales. Additional property tax reductions are available to: research and development firms, agricultural or timber product processing plants, and property used in the production of motion pictures or television commercials.

Local Option Property Tax Incentives: Property tax reduction is available to: new and expanding industries, businesses making improvements, machinery and equipment, business incubators, industrial parks, buildings or land sold or donated to a local economic development organization, and air and water pollution-control equipment.

* Exports

For all items without a separate address, contact the Montana Department of Commerce at the address listed above.

Trade Program: Mission is to identify opportunities for worldwide and domestic trade and to provide representation, information and technical assistance. More specifically, the Trade Program provides: trade consultation, Marketing/Country reports, trade leads, trade show assistance, special promotions for Montana made products and services, tourism promotion services in the Far East.

Made in Montana program: Works to elevate the status of Montana-made products in the marketplace and to educate Montanans about the diversity of products manufactured in their state.

* Small Business Administration Offices

JoAlice Mospan
301 S. Park, Room 334
Helena, MT 59626
406-441-1081
Fax: 406-441-1090

Nebraska

Department of Economic Development
P.O. Box 94666
301 Centennial Mall South
Lincoln, NE 68509
402-471-3111
800-426-6505 (in NE)
Fax: 402-471-3365
TDD: 402-471-3441
www.ded.state.ne.us

* Business Assistance

For all items without a separate address, contact the Nebraska Department of Economic Development at the address listed above.

One-Stop Business Assistance Program: Provides assistance on identifying, marketing and finance information; business information and research, regulations, licenses, fees, and other state requirements for business operation.

Skilled Training Employment Program (STEP): Offers a comprehensive, on-the-job training program for new and expanding businesses.

Government Procurement Assistance: Helps create additional markets.

Match Marketing: Assists with matching Nebraska buyers and suppliers.

Technical Assistance: Increases productivity and competitiveness.

Site Location Assistance: Includes facilitating access to programs.

* Business Financing

For all items without a separate address, contact the Nebraska Department of Economic Development at the address listed above.

Industrial Revenue Bonds (IRB): All Nebraska counties and municipalities, as well as the Nebraska Investment Finance Authority, are authorized to issue IRBs to finance land, buildings and equipment for industrial projects. The rate of interest is normally lower than on most loans.

Nebraska Investment Finance Authority: Issues IRBs for land, building and equipment for industrial enterprises, as well as provides financing for housing.

Dollar and Energy Saving Loans: Energy saving loans are offered statewide by the Nebraska Energy Office and the state's lending institutions. The interest rate is 6% or less, but may be adjusted semi-annually. Adjustments do not affect existing loans. Check with a lender or the Nebraska Energy Office for the current rate. Contact: Nebraska Energy Office, Box 95085, Lincoln, NE 68509; 402-471-2867.

Community Improvement Financing: This is Nebraska's version of Tax Increment Financing, a method of financing public improvements associated with a private development project in a blighted and substandard area by using the projected increase in the property tax revenue which will result from the private development.

Local Option Municipal Economic Development Act: Provides the ability for communities to add a sales or property tax for economic development projects.

Nebraska Energy Fund: Provides low-interest loans for energy efficiency improvements.

Nebraska Redevelopment Act: Authorizes Community Improvement Financing for real estate and equipment in a project that adds at least 500 new jobs and $50 million of new investment.

Adams County Central Community College: Total Loan Funds: $30,000 as of April 24, 1996. Sources: Private money. Loan Terms: Low interest rates, 3 year term, collateral required, payments put on amortization schedule, $10,000 maximum. Loan Eligibility: Serves the 25-county Central Community College area. Services: Counseling, CCC business courses, SCORE available. Contact Person: Jim Svoboda, Coordinator, P.O. Box 1054, Hastings, NE 68902-1024; 402-461-2461; 402-461-2506; Email: {svohbus@cccadm.gi.cccneb.edu}.

Mid-Nebraska Community Services: A caring, non-profit community action agency that provides resources to help people and communities in 27 counties grow within themselves for a better future. Total Loan Fund: $130,000. Contact Person: Robert E. Hobbs, Loan Coordinator, 16 West 11th Street, P.O. Box 2288, Kearney, NE 68848-2288; 308-865-5675; 308-865-5681.

Rural Business Development Fund, Small Enterprises Economic Development Project, Rural Economic and Community Development, State of Nebraska. LB144, private grants. Provides microenterprise loans, loan counseling, credit analysis, developing business plan and entrepreneurial training. Contact Person: Robert E. Hobbs, Loan Coordinator, 16 West 11th Street, P.O. Box 2288, Kearney, NE 68848-2288; 308-865-5675; 308-865-5681.

Northeast Nebraska Development District Business Loan Programs: Exists to promote and assist the growth and development of business and industrial concerns within Northeast Nebraska. Priority will be given to fixed asset financing (land, building, equipment); however, working capital can also be financed. Generally, loans will range from $10,000 to $100,000 (maximum). Contact: Northeast Nebraska Economic Development District, 111 S. 1st St., Norfolk, NE 68701; 402-379-1150; {www.nenedd.org}.

State Money - Nevada

* Tax Incentives

For all items without a separate address, contact the Nebraska Department of Economic Development at the address listed above.

Employment and Investment Growth Act: With a $3 million investment in qualified property and addition of 30 full-time employees, a business qualifies for: direct refund of all sales and use taxes paid on purchases of qualified property; 5% tax credit on the amount of the total compensation paid to employees; 10% tax credit on total investment in qualified property, 5 and 10% tax credits applied to income tax liability or used to obtain refund of sales and use taxes paid on other purchases. With a $10 million investment in qualified property and addition of 100 full-time employees, a business qualifies for: all of the above plus up to a 15 year personal property tax exemption on newly acquired: turbine-powered aircraft, mainframe computers and peripheral components, equipment used directly in processing agricultural products. Investment in qualified property resulting in a net gain of $20 million with no increased employment qualifies a business for direct refund of all sales and use taxes paid on purchases of qualified property.

Employment Expansions and Investment Incentive Act: Provides tax credits for any business which increase investment by at least $75,000 and increase net employment by an average of two full-time positions during a taxable year. Credits of $1,500 per net new employee and $1,000 per $75,000 net new investment may be used to reduce a portion of the taxpayer's income tax liability or to obtain a refund of sales and use taxes paid.

Quality Jobs Act: Authorizes a wage benefit credit to new employees of approved companies that add at least 500 new jobs and $50 million in new investment or 250 new jobs and $100 million in new investment.

Enterprise Zones: Within these areas, tax credits are given for qualifying businesses which increase employment and make investments in the area.

For more information, contact Nebraska Department of Revenue, 301 Centennial Mall South, P.O. Box 94818, Lincoln, NE 68509; 402-471-2971; 800-742-7474.

* Exports

For all items without a separate address, contact the Nebraska Department of Economic Development at the address listed above.

Office of International Trade and Investment (OITI): Works with existing businesses to expand their international marketing efforts, as well as foster international manufacturing investments in the state.

* Small Business Administration Offices

Glenn Davis
11145 Mill Valley Road
Omaha, NE 68154
402-221-4691
Fax: 402-221-3680

Nevada

State of Nevada Commission on Economic Development
5151 South Carson St.
Carson City, NV 89710
775-687-4325
800-336-1600
Fax: 775-687-4450
www.state.nv.us/businessop

555 E. Washington Avenue
Suite 5400
Las Vegas, NV 89101
702-486-2700
Fax: 702-486-2701

* Business Assistance

For all items without a separate address, contact the State of Nevada Commission on Economic Development at the address listed above.

Commission on Economic Development: Publishes a pamphlet, *Business Assistance*. Acts as a clearinghouse for information and technical assistance. Operates several business assistance programs and performs advertising and public relations activities on behalf of Nevada business. Maintains a computerized inventory of available manufacturing and warehousing buildings, land and corporate office space, and customized site selection.

Procurement Outreach Program: Assists businesses in successfully tapping into this lucrative market by: introducing firms to federal agencies that purchase the products and services they sell; providing assistance to ensure that companies are prepared with all of the tools, knowledge and skills necessary to meet the federal government's specifications and standards, and properly complete bids; offering seminars, marketing fairs, mailing lists and direct assistance as well as the Automated Bidline which is a fax-on demand system allowing instant access to the latest bid and requests for proposal information.

Community Business Resource Center: A one-stop center for business information designed to enhance the economic self-sufficiency of low-and moderate-income individuals by developing their entrepreneurial skills. Services available include training, technical assistance and access to credit. Contact Community Business Resource Center, 116 E. 7th St., Suite 3, Carson City, NV 89701; 800-337-4590.

* Business Financing

For all items without a separate address, contact the State of Nevada Commission on Economic Development at the address listed above.

Nevada Development Capital Corporation: A private development fund designed to finance growth opportunities for small, sound Nevada businesses which do not qualify for conventional financing. The financing provided by NDCC includes but is not limited to the following: working capital loans secured by primary or subordinated assets; loans secured by fixed assets with longer terms than could be provided by conventional lending sources; loans for the acquisition of a business or interest in a business; subordinated loans in cases where available bank financing is sufficient; loans to refinance existing debt in cases where existing terms present a hardship for the business. Most loans will probably be in the $50,000 to $150,000 range. Contact: Nevada State Development Corporation, 350 S. Center St., Suite 310, Reno, NV 89501; 775-323-3625; 800-726-2494.

Nevada Self-Employment Trust: A start-up business may be eligible to borrow from $100 to $7,500 while existing companies may borrow a maximum of $25,000. Contact: Community Business Resource Center, 116 E. 7th St., Suite 3, Carson City, NV 89701; 800-337-4590.

Venture Capital: A potential source of venture capital is the State Public Employees Retirement System that disperses funds through several venture capital pools.

Industrial Revenue Bonds: A special type of loan to qualified manufacturers who are buying land, building new facilities, refurbishing existing buildings and purchasing new equipment.

Rural Business Loans: Companies in rural Nevada have additional avenues for financial assistance designed to: lend money to small businesses in need of expansion or start-up financing; assist small businesses in obtaining gap financing to complete their business expansion projects; provide financing to small businesses which meet job creation requirements. Assistance is available through the Nevada Revolving Loan Fund, Rural Economic and Community Development Services, and Rural Nevada Development Corporation.

Train Employees Now: Grants to training providers up to 75% of the total eligible costs with a cap of $1,000 per trainee.

Business Assistance Program: Helps businesses understand environmental rules and explain the permitting process as well as identify sources of financing for pollution control equipment and provide access to the latest information regarding environmental issues.

* Tax Incentives

For all items without a separate address, contact the State of Nevada Commission on Economic Development at the address listed above.

No Personal Income Tax
No Corporate Income Tax
No Franchise Tax on Income
No Unitary Tax
No Inventory Tax
No Inheritance, Estate, or Gift Tax
No Admissions or Chain Store Tax

Freeport: Protects shipments in transit from taxation and cuts the cost of doing business both domestically and internationally.

Sales and Use Tax Abatement: Partial sales/use tax exemption on machinery and equipment purchases.

State Money - New Hampshire

Sales and Use Tax Deferral: Tax deferral on machinery and equipment purchases in excess of $100,000.
Business Tax Abatement: A 50% tax exemption determined on a case by case basis.
Personal Property Tax Abatement: 50% tax exemption for businesses operating in Nevada for 10 or more years.
Property Tax Abatement: 75% tax exemption on real and personal property for qualified recycling businesses.

* Exports

For all items without a separate address, contact the State of Nevada Commission on Economic Development at the address listed above.

Nevada's International Trade Program: Goal is to assist Nevada businesses to begin, or expand, exporting to international markets. Services include: Trade Missions, Export Seminars, Export Counseling, International Trade Database, Foreign Buyers Delegations, International Trade Directories.
Foreign Trade Zones: Two zones allow international importers duty-free storage and assembly of foreign products.
Export Financing: Assistance is available through private sector financial institution, the International Trade Program and the federal Export/Import Bank.

* Small Business Administration Offices

John Scott
300 Las Vegas Boulevard, South, Suite 100
Las Vegas, NV 89101
702-388-6611
Fax: 702-388-6469

New Hampshire

State of New Hampshire
Department of Resources and Economic Development
172 Pembroke Road
P.O. Box 1856
Concord, NH 03302-1856
603-271-2341
800-204-5000 (in NH)
Fax: 603-271-6784
www.ded.state.nh.us/obid

* Business Assistance

For all items without a separate address, contact the State of New Hampshire Department of Resources and Economic Development at the address listed above.

Office of Business and Industrial Development: Provides assistance and publications designed to support and promote business and industry in the state. Information in areas such as licensing and permits, financial counseling, marketing, and exporting, labor markets, and more.
Economic Development Data System: A comprehensive database of all the communities and available industrial properties within the state.
Business Visitation Program: Local volunteers visit businesses to gather information about firms' development issues, economic concerns and opinions about their community as a place to do business. Once aware of these issues, local, state and federal programs can be accessed to assist the firms. A referral network coordinates questions, issues and concerns.
Vendor Matching Program: A database that can be used to match a prospective client's product needs with the appropriate New Hampshire vendor of those products.
Procurement Technical Assistance Program: Provides the necessary tools to be competitive in the federal marketplace through procurement counseling; contract announcements; specifications and standards; and support databases.
Industrial Research Center: Assistance in basic and applied research, development and marketing through a matching grants program; hands-on training in Design of Experiment methods; and helping inventors develop patent and commercialize their ideas. Contact: New Hampshire Industrial Research Center, University of New Hampshire, 222 Kingsbury Hall, Durham, NH 03824; 603-862-0123.
Job Training Council: Provides job training for citizens while helping businesses gain capable workers. Contact: New Hampshire Job Training, 64 Old Suncook Rd., Concord, NH 03301; 603-228-9500.

Manchester Manufacturing Management Center: Serves as a crucial link between the university and the manufacturing community through sponsorship of industry-specific programs, including seminars, symposia, expos, and internships. Contact: Manchester Manufacturing Management Center, 150 Dow St., Manchester, NH 03101; 603-625-0106.

* Business Financing

For all items without a separate address, contact the State of New Hampshire Department of Resources and Economic Development at the address listed above.

Regional and Local Revolving Loan Funds: Many local and regional revolving loan funds exist throughout New Hampshire. These funds have been capitalized from a variety of services, many with federal monies. The administration of these funds is generally handled by a non-profit corporation, while the local funds most often are overseen by governing bodies with the help of a loan committee. The loans may be used in conjunction with other sources to leverage additional monies or independently finance the project.
Finance Clearinghouse: Offers companies assistance in obtaining financing. A complete listing of programs can be obtained through the clearinghouse.
Business Finance Authority: Has several loan programs designed to foster economic development and create employment with an emphasis on small business assistance.
1. Capital Access Program: Start-up businesses or business expansion are eligible for loans from $5,000 to $250,000 for business purposes.
2. Working Capital Line of Credit Guarantee: Up to $2,000,000 for business needing working capital line of credit.
3. Guarantee Asset Program: Provides assistance to capital intensive businesses.
4. Industrial Development Revenue Bond: Up to $10 million for any trade or business that is eligible for tax-exempt financing for acquisition of land, buildings and improvements, machinery and equipment.
5. Assistance to Local Development Organizations: Provides funding to municipalities and development organizations to assist in the promotion and development of New Hampshire businesses.

Contact: New Hampshire Business Finance Authority, Suite 101, 14 Dixon Ave., Concord, NH 03301; 603-271-2391.
Business Development Corporation: A non-profit company in the business of funding loans to small businesses that qualify. For more information, contact Business Development Corporation, 1001 Elm Street, Manchester, NH 03101; 603-623-5500; Fax: 603-623-3972.
Capital Consortium: A venture capital partnership that makes investments between $250,000 and $12,000,000 in high-potential companies. For more information, contact Business Development Corporation, 1001 Elm Street, Manchester, NH 03101; 603-623-5500; Fax: 603-623-3972.

* Tax Incentives

For all items without a separate address, contact the State of New Hampshire Department of Resources and Economic Development at the address listed above.

No general sales or personal income tax
No tax on personal property or inventories
No property tax on machinery or equipment
No higher assessments or higher property tax rates for commercial or industrial real estate

* Exports

For all items without a separate address, contact the State of New Hampshire Department of Resources and Economic Development at the address listed above.

International Trade Resource Center: A one-stop location when businesses, both current and potential exporters, can access the assistance and information necessary to effectively explore, develop and penetrate the foreign marketplace. Offers counseling, education and training seminars, automated trade leads, market research, marketing promotion, library and finance assistance.
New Hampshire Export Finance Program: To support export sales in providing working capital for the exporter to produce or buy a product for resale; provide political and/or commercial risk insurance in order to provide open account terms to foreign buyers; provide access to funding to qualified foreign buyers who need medium-term financing in order to purchase capital goods and services from New Hampshire Exporters. Rates and premiums arranged per sale or as needed. No dollar limit. Contact: New Hampshire Office of International Commerce, 17 New Hampshire Ave., Portsmouth, NH 03801; 603-334-6074.

State Money - New Jersey

Foreign Trade Zones: Provides economic incentives to companies doing business in foreign countries.

* Small Business Administration Offices

Bill Phillips
143 North Main Street, Suite 202
Concord, NH 03301
603-225-1400
Fax: 603-225-1409

New Jersey

New Jersey Economic Development Authority
P.O. Box 990
Trenton, NJ 08625-0990
609-292-1800
www.njeda.com

* Business Assistance

For all items without a separate address, contact the New Jersey Economic Development Authority at the address listed above.

Division of Economic Development: Develops and administers comprehensive marketing and support programs. Helps access public and private services which address a broad array of issues, ranging from financial, technical and regulatory concerns to employee training and site location.

Office of Account Management: Offers assistance to existing companies to maintain or expand operations.

Office of the Business Advocate and Business Information: Assists businesses that are having difficulty navigating through State regulations.

Entrepreneurial Training Institute: An eight week program is offered to help new and aspiring entrepreneurs learn the basics of operating a business.

Small Business Contracts: State law requires that at least 15% of the contracts awarded by the State be given to small businesses. In the first half of 1998, these "set-aside contracts" amounted to more than $425 million.

Doing Business in New Jersey Guidebook: Provides information on starting and operating a business in the state. Topics include requirements and advice for starting a new business, information on tax and employee regulations, state and federal financial information, franchising, procurement opportunities, and exporting.

Selective Assistance Vendor Information Database: A computer database designed especially to assist business owners that wish to do business with the State of New Jersey and the private sector. SAVI-II matches buyers and vendors for public and private contracting opportunities.

Department of Labor's Division of Field Support: New Jersey provides the Business Resource Network, a coordinated interdepartmental resource to identify and market programs available to employers through various New Jersey agencies.

Department of Labor's Division of Workforce Development: The State provides matching customized training grants and technical assistance to upgrade the technical skills of incumbent workers.

Maritime Services: New Jersey offers several services to support businesses engaged in this enterprise. These include advice and assistance with permits and economic development issues, facilitation of dredging-related activities, and assistance in reducing or minimizing the creation of sediment.

Manufacturing Extension Partnership: Provides assistance to manufacturers in securing a wide variety of technical resources.

New Jersey Economic Development Authority's Trade Adjustment Assistance Center: Can provide technical assistance to manufacturers or certify manufacturers for eligibility for federal government assistance.

Real Estate Development Division: Businesses may be able to lease state-of-the-art, affordable laboratory, production, and research facilities in the Technology Centre of New Jersey. New high-technology businesses may be able to utilize inexpensive lab and office space at one of several technology business incubators throughout the state. These incubators typically offer administrative and consulting services to their tenants.

Technology Transfer Program: Businesses may be able to partner with an academic institution, facilitating the transfer of new technology from research to commercial application.

Technology Help Desk Hotline: Businesses may take advantage of a one-stop Technology Help Desk Hotline, 1-800-4321-TEC. The hotline offers answers to business and technology questions as well as financial advice, referrals to sources of commercialization assistance, help with research and development grant proposals, and advice on using a statewide and national network of business development resource organizations.

The New Jersey Economic Development Authority's Finance Finder: Helps match companies with appropriate finance programs administered by the NJEDA.

Technology Centre of New Jersey: State-of-the-art, affordable laboratory production and research facilities are available for emerging and advanced technology driven companies.

Consulting Assistance for Manufacturers Impacted By Imports: Manufacturers who can demonstrate that their employment and either sales or production have declined due to foreign competition of a like or similar product may be eligible for consulting assistance.

* Business Financing

For all items without a separate address, contact the New Jersey Economic Development Authority at the address listed above.

Bond Financing: Bonds are issued to provide long-term loans at attractive, below-market interest rates for real estate acquisitions, equipment, machinery, building construction, and renovations. Minimum loan size is approximately $1 million. Maximum tax-exempt bond amount for manufacturers is $10 million.

Statewide Loan Pool For Business: Loans from $50,000 up to $1 million for fixed assets and up to $500,000 for working capital are available to businesses that create or maintain jobs in a financially targeted municipality or represent a targeted industry such as manufacturing, industrial, or agricultural. Assistance usually will not exceed $35,000 per job created or maintained.

Business Employment Incentive Program (BEIP) Grant: Businesses creating at least 25 new jobs in designated urban areas, or 75 jobs elsewhere, may be eligible to receive a BEIP grant. These grants, which may last for up to 10 years, may be for up to 80% of the value of the income taxes withheld annually from the paychecks of new employees.

Loan Guarantees: Guarantees of conventional loans of up to $1 million for working capital and guarantees of conventional loans or bond issues for fixed assets of up to $1.5 million are available to credit worthy businesses that need additional security to obtain financing. Preference is given to businesses that are either job intensive, will create or maintain tax ratables, are located in an economically distressed area, or represent an important economic sector of the state and will contribute to New Jersey's growth and diversity.

Direct Loans: Loans are made for up to $500,000 for fixed assets and up to $250,000 for working capital for up to 10 years to businesses that are unable to get sufficient bank credit on their own or through the Statewide Loan Pool or with and EDA guarantee. Preference is given to job-intensive enterprises located in economically targeted areas or representing a targeted business sector.

New Jersey Seed Capital Program: Loans are made from $25,000 to $200,000 at a market rate of interest for working capital and fixed assets to technology businesses that have risked their own capital to develop new technologies and need additional funds to bring their products to market.

New Jersey Technology Funding Program: EDA participates with commercial banks to make term loans from $100,000 to $3 million for second stage technology enterprises.

Fund For Community Economic Development: Loans and loan guarantees are made to urban-based community organizations that in turn make loans to micro-enterprises and small businesses which may not qualify for traditional bank financing.

Urban Centers Small Loans: Loans ranging from $5,000 - $50,000 are available to existing retail and commercial businesses located in the commercial district of a targeted municipality.

Local Development Financing Fund: Loans ranging from $50,000 to $2 million may be made for fixed assets form commercial and industrial projects located in Urban Aid communities.

Hazardous Discharge Site Remediation Loan and Grant Program: Businesses may qualify for loans of up to $1 million for remediation activities due to a closure of operations or transfer of ownership.

Petroleum Underground Storage Tank Remediation Upgrade and Closure Program: Owners/operators may qualify for 100% of the eligible project costs.

Small Business Loans: Loans and loan guarantees administered by the New Jersey Economic Development Authority's Community Development and Small Business Lending Division.

The New Jersey Redevelopment Authority (NJRA): An independent state financing agency whose mission is to focus on investing in neighborhood-based redevelopment projects. NJRA offers low and no-interest loans, loan guarantees, equity investment and technical assistance to eligible businesses and municipalities. Contact: New Jersey Redevelopment Authority, 50 W.

State Money - New Mexico

State St., P.O. Box 790, Trenton, NJ 08625; 609-292-3739; {www.state.nj.us/njra}.

New Jersey Economic Development Authority's Investment Banking Division: Loans may be available for the purchase of manufacturing equipment.

R&D Excellence Grant Program: Businesses may receive financial support for research and development in critical fields, such as healthcare (especially biomaterials, pharmaceuticals, and biotechnologies), software/information, and environmental and civil infrastructure technologies.

Very young technology enterprises may be eligible to receive seed-stage investments ranging from $50,000 to $1.5 million. Contact the managing partners of Early Stage Enterprises, LP, Mr. Ronald R. Hahn (e-mail rrhahn@aol.com) and Mr. James J. Millar (e-mail jimmillar@aol.com), or call ESE at 609-921-8896, Fax 609-921-8703. Such investments may also be available through the New Jersey Seed Capital Program.

Small Business Innovation Research Grants: Applicants for federal grants may receive technical consulting and bridge loans.

Edison Venture Fund: Provides funding assistance to high-technology companies in New Jersey. This private enterprise enjoys a close relationship with the State of New Jersey, having been selected through a competitive process to manage certain funds on behalf of the New Jersey Economic Development Authority. Contact: Edison Venture Fund, 1009 Lenox Dr. #4, Lawrenceville, NJ 08648; 609-896-1900; {www.edisonventure.com}.

New Jersey Redevelopment Authority and the New Jersey Economic Development Authority's Commercial Lending Division: Businesses and municipalities involved in urban redevelopment may be eligible for low- and no-interest loans, loan guarantees, equity investments, and technical assistance.

New Jersey Redevelopment Authority and the New Jersey Economic Development Authority's Community Development and Small Business Lending Division: Loans, loan guarantees, equity investments, and technical assistance may be available to finance investments in neighborhood-based redevelopment projects, small business lending, renovation, relocation, and/or real estate development in urban areas.

Business Relocation Assistance Grant: Provides grants to relocating companies that create a minimum of 25 new full-time jobs in New Jersey.

* Tax Incentives

For all items without a separate address, contact the New Jersey Economic Development Authority at the address listed above.

Urban Enterprise Zones: Provide significant incentives and benefits to qualified businesses located within their borders. Such benefits include sales tax to customers (3% instead of 6%), corporation tax credits for the hiring of certain employees, and subsidized unemployment insurance costs.

No net worth tax, no business personal property tax, no commercial rent or occupancy tax and no retail gross receipts tax.

Property Tax Abatements and Exemptions: Available for commercial and industrial properties in areas in need or redevelopment.

New Jobs Investment Tax Credit: Companies that make certain investments in new or expanded business facilities that are directly related to the creation of new jobs may be eligible for credits.

Manufacturing Equipment and Employment Investment Tax Credit: Certain investments made by companies for manufacturing equipment with a recovery life of four years or more are eligible for a credit.

Recognition of Subchapter S Status for Corporations: S corporations are provided a reduced corporation tax rate.

Research and Development Tax Credit for Corporation Business Tax: Businesses may be eligible for a credit for certain increased research expenditures in the state.

* Exports

For all items without a separate address, contact the New Jersey Economic Development Authority at the address listed above.

International Trade Services: Services include financing assistance, strategic advocacy in foreign markets, opportunities to network and receive information and advice regarding international commerce, and assistance in taking advantage of federal international trade programs and Foreign Trade Zones.

Export Financing: Up to a $1 million one-year revolving line of credit will be provided to finance confirmed foreign orders to assist businesses that want to enter the export market or expand export sales but are unable to do so because they cannot get the financing they need on their own.

Foreign Trade Zones: Within these zones, which are outside U.S. Customs territory, businesses may manufacture, assemble, package, process and exhibit merchandise with a substantial duty and cash flow savings.

* Women and Minorities

For all items without a separate address, contact the New Jersey Economic Development Authority at the address listed above.

New Jersey Department of Commerce and Economic Development
Division of Development for Small Businesses
and Women and Minority Businesses
CN 835
Trenton, NJ 08625
609-292-3860
Fax: 609-292-9145

Services For Businesses Owned By Women And Minorities: Businesses owned by women and minorities play an important role in the New Jersey economy. New Jersey offers a number of services to help these businesses compete and overcome the special challenges they face. These services include financial assistance, advice and instructional materials, training and education, and certification necessary to receive certain contracts.

Set Aside Contracts: State law requires that 7% of the contracts awarded by the State be given to businesses owned by minorities, and 3% to businesses owned by women. In the first half of 1998, these "set-aside contracts" amounted to more than $180 million.

Women and minorities interested in establishing franchise businesses may receive investments from the Small Business Investment Company, which works in conjunction with the New Jersey Economic Development Authority's Commercial Lending Division.

Contractors Assistance Program: Small contracting businesses owned by women or minorities may receive training courses and consultations with experienced executives of large construction companies designed to make it easier to get performance bonds and successfully bid on major construction projects. This service is provided by the New Jersey Economic Development Authority's Community Development and Small Business Lending Division.

New Jersey Development Authority For Small Businesses, Minorities' And Women's Enterprises: This office offers women and minority-owned small businesses financial, marketing, procurement, technical and managerial assistance. Loans of up to $1 million can be made for real estate, fixed asset acquisition, and working capital. Guarantees to banks are also available for fixed asset acquisition and for working capital. To be eligible, a business must be certified as a small, minority-owned or women-owned enterprise. Most of the funds are targeted to enterprises located in Atlantic City or providing goods or services to customers in Atlantic City, including but not limited to the casinos. Limited monies are available for businesses located in other parts of the state.

* Small Business Administration Offices

Francisco Marrero
2 Gateway Center, 15th Floor
Newark, NJ 07102
973-645-3580
Fax: 973-645-6265

New Mexico

Economic Development Department
Joseph M. Montoya Bldg.
1100 St. Francis Drive
Santa Fe, NM 87505-4147
505-827-0170
800-374-3061
Fax: 505-827-0407
www.edd.state.nm.us

* Business Assistance

For all items without a separate address, contact the New Mexico Economic Development Department at the address listed above.

Technology Ventures Corporation: Promotes the commercialization of technology. Offers technical, business and management assistance for its clients. Contact: Technology Ventures Corporation, 1155 University Blvd. SE, Albuquerque, NM 87106; 505-246-2882.

Technology: New Mexico offers a wide range of assistance for technology-oriented companies such as research centers, partnerships with universities, and facility use.

State Money - New Mexico

* Business Financing

For all items without a separate address, contact the New Mexico Economic Development Department at the address listed above.

ACCION: A private non-profit organization that extend microloans to small business entrepreneurs designed to help home-based and other self-employed people grow to be self sufficient. Contact: ACCION New Mexico, 219 Central NW, #620, Albuquerque, NM 87102; 505-243-8844.

Advanced Technology Program (ATP): Provides cost shared-funding to select industries for high-risk research and development projects that have the potential to launch important broad-based economic benefits to the U.S. economy.

Airport Improvement Program (AIP): Supports the development and improvement of airports in an effort to create a nationwide airport system capable of supporting the nation's civil air travel.

Albuquerque Development Capital Program: Provides loan guarantees and interest supplements for acquisition of real property, purchase of fixed assets and/or working capital purposes. Contact: City of Albuquerque, Economic Development Department, P.O. Box 1293, Albuquerque, NM 87103; 505-768-3270.

Business Participation Loans: The State Investment Council may invest a portion of the Severance Tax Permanent Fund in real property related business loans. There is a minimum of $500,000 and a maximum of $2 million.

Cibola Foundation Revolving Loan Fund: A variety of financial incentives offered to encourage economic development in Cibola County. Contact: Cibola Communities, Economic Development Foundation Inc., P.O. Box 277, Grants, NM 87020; 505-285-6604.

Community Development Loan Fund: Provides loans to businesses and organizations that have tangible benefits for low-income people. Typical loans are from $5,000 to $25,000. Contact: NM Community Development Loan Fund, P.O. Box 705, Albuquerque, NM 87103; 505-243-3196.

Community Foundation: Offers small grants, technical assistance, "capacity building" workshops, and serves as a convener around important issues for nonprofit organizations, communities and people throughout New Mexico, especially in rural areas.

FSA Farmer Programs: Guarantees loans made by agricultural lenders for family farmers and ranchers for farm ownership, improvements and operating purposes. The FSA describes a family farm as one which a family can operate and manage itself. Guarantee of up to $300,000 for farm ownership, water and soil loans; and $400,000 for operating loans. The maximum guarantee is 90%.

Industrial Development Training Program: Provides funds for classroom or on-the-job training to prepare New Mexico residents for employment. Trainee wages are reimbursed to the company at 50% during hours of training; 65% in rural New Mexico. Instructional costs involving classroom training will be reimbursed to the educational institution at 100% of all costs outlined in the training contract.

Job Training Partnership Act (JTPA): A federally funded program intended to provide job training assistance to both eligible employees and employers. Employers can receive financial reimbursement of up to 50% of the costs associated with hiring and training JTPA eligible employees.

ilagro Fund: Programs designed to promote economic development opportunities for organizations which utilize natural resources, involve small scale growers or producers, strengthen traditional skills in agriculture and production, or defend land and water rights. Funds are available to facilitate problem identification, provide training in community organizing, and to improve business skills and production techniques.

North Central New Mexico Economic Development Revolving Loan Fund: Provides loans up to $100,000 to assist small businesses in the creation and/or saving of jobs in economically disadvantaged areas. Contact: North Central New Mexico Economic Development Revolving Loan Fund, P.O. Box 5115, Santa Fe, NM 87502; 505-827-7313.

RD Housing Preservation Grants: Grants to tribes, political subdivisions and other non-profit entities to enable them to rehabilitate housing owned and occupied by very-low and low-income rural persons.

RD Rural Business Enterprise Grant Program: The purpose of the program is to support the development of small and emerging private business enterprise in rural areas under 50,000 in population, or more and adjacent urbanized areas. Priority is given to applications for projects in rural communities of 25,000 in population and under.

RD Guaranteed Business and Industry Program: The purpose of the program is to improve, develop or finance business, industry and employment, and improve the economic and environmental climate in rural communities (under 50,000 population) and non-urbanized or non-urbanizing areas. This is achieved by bolstering the existing private credit structure through the guarantee of quality loans that will provide lasting community benefits.

Severance Tax Loan Program: New Mexico can purchase up to $20 million of bonds, notes, debentures or other evidence of indebtedness, excluding commercial paper, whose proceeds are used for the establishment or expansion of business outlets or ventures located in state.

* Tax Incentives

For all items without a separate address, contact the New Mexico Economic Development Department at the address listed above.

Aerospace Research and Development Deduction: The Aerospace Research and Development tax deduction was implemented to facilitate the location of a spaceport in New Mexico.

Agriculture-Related Tax Deductions/Exemptions: Feed and fertilizer, warehousing, threshing, harvesting, growing, cultivating and processing agricultural products, agricultural products.

Compensating Tax Abatement: "Compensating tax" is an excise tax imposed for the privilege of using property in New Mexico. In New Mexico it is called gross receipts tax for purchases made within the state. For purchases made outside New Mexico and imported into the state, it is called compensating tax. Abatement of the state's portion of any sales, gross receipts, compensating or similar tax on machinery and equipment, and other movable personal property for an eligible facility. In New Mexico construction or rehabilitation of non-speculative office buildings, warehouses, manufacturing facilities, and service oriented facilities not primarily engaged in the sale of goods or commodities at retail are eligible.

Enterprise Zones: The Enterprise Zone Act is designed to stimulate the creation of new jobs and to revitalize economically distressed areas. $50,000 tax credit to property owners for the rehabilitation of qualified business facilities, technical assistance, training reimbursement, and other benefits.

Filmmakers Gross Receipts Tax Incentive: Implemented to facilitate the filming of movies, television shows and commercials in New Mexico. A qualified production company may execute nontaxable transaction certificates with its suppliers for tangible personal property or services. The suppliers may then deduct their receipts from the gross receipts tax.

Historic Preservation Tax Credit Program: Offers a maximum tax credit of 20% of the substantial rehabilitation of historic buildings for commercial, industrial and rental residential purposes, and a 10% credit for substantial rehabilitation for non-residential purposes for structures built before 1936.

Indian Employment Credit: Provides for a tax credit to employers of Indians on Indian lands to encourage economic development. The maximum credit per employee is $4,000.

Low-income Housing Tax Credit Program (LIHTC): This program can be used for new construction and/or rehabilitation of rental units. The annual credit equals a fixed percentage of the project's total cost.

Modified Accelerated Cost Recovery System: Provides for a favorable deduction for property on Indian lands to encourage economic development. Capital outlays for depreciable business or income-producing property are recoverable through the depreciation deduction allowances. A business that acquires property for use in the business is entitled to deduct the cost of the property over time for the purposes of computing income tax liability.

Cultural Property Preservation Tax Credit: Property owners are eligible to receive a personal or corporate tax credit for restoring, rehabilitating or otherwise preserving cultural properties. Specifically, a tax credit is available where historic structures are certified as having received rehabilitation to preserve and enhance their historic character. Offers a maximum tax credit of 50% of the cost of restoration, rehabilitation or preservation up to $25,000.

Gross Receipts Tax Deduction: Equipment that goes into a plant financed with industrial revenue bonds is exempt for the gross receipts or compensating tax of 5% .

Interstate Telecommunications Gross Receipts Tax Exemption: This program exempts receipts from the provision of wide area telephone services (WATS) and private communications services from the interstate telecommunications gross receipts tax. Wide-area telephone service means a telephone service that entitles a subscriber to either make or receive large volumes of communications to or from persons in specified geographical areas.

Investment Tax Credit Program: Provides a general incentive for manufacturers to locate in New Mexico and to hire New Mexicans. Equipment is eligible if essential, used directly and exclusively in a manufacturing facility, and depreciated for federal income tax purposes. The creation of new, full time jobs is required to qualify for the credit. The credit allows the manufacturer to offset the amount of compensating tax paid on eligible equipment. The credit equals the amount of compensating tax actually paid, and may be applied against compensating tax, gross receipts tax or withholding tax due.

Preferential Tax Rate for Small Wineries and Breweries: Wine produced by a small winery carries a tax of 10 cents per liter on the first 80,000 liters; 20 cents on production over that level. The basic tax rate for wine is 45 cents per liter. Beer produced by a microbrewery is taxed at 25 cents per gallon. The basic

State Money - New York

tax rate for beer is 41 cents per gallon.

Property Tax Exemption: For industry financed with industrial revenue bonds, a local government may offer a real and personal property tax exemption of up to 30 years.

Targeted Jobs Tax Credit Program (TJTC): An employer may claim a tax credit equal to 40% of the first $6,000 in wages paid to the worker during the first year of employment for a maximum credit of $2,400 per employee. For economically disadvantaged summer youth, employers may claim a tax credit equal to 40% of the first $3,000 in wages for a maximum credit of $1,200 per employee.

Tax Increment Financing: At the beginning of a project, the valuation of the project properties is summed. As the project proceeds, these properties are developed or otherwise improved, increasing their valuations. The tax proceeds flowing from the increase in valuation may be diverted to finance the project. Tax increment financing in New Mexico is available only in a designated enterprise zone.

Taxpayer's Assistance Program (TAP): Enables home buyers to qualify for a larger mortgage because of reduced tax liabilities.

Property Tax Abatement: Land, buildings and equipment associated with an eligible project are exempt from ad valorem tax, generally to promote economic development.

* Exports

For all items without a separate address, contact the New Mexico Economic Development Department at the address listed above.

Foreign Sales Corporations Tax Incentive Program: Regulations exempt from taxation part of the profit earned on exports, which can be 15% of the net income or 1.2% of gross receipts, whichever is greater.

Export-Import Bank (Eximbank) City/State Program: Assists exporters in accessing federal loan guarantees and credit insurance through the Export/Import Bank. Eximbank working capital loan guarantees may be used to finance such pre-export activities as the purchase of raw materials, finished products, labor and other services needed for processing export orders. They may also be used to cover the cost of freight, port charges and certain forms of overseas business development. Loan guarantees may be used for a specific transaction or as a revolving line of credit. There are no minimum or maximum amounts of funding.

Foreign Trade Zones: Merchandise in these zones is considered to be outside U.S. Customs territory and is subject to duty only when it leave the zones for consumption in the U.S. Market. New Mexico offers three such zones.

Export Financing Assistance: Often, even the most credit-worthy small and medium-sized businesses find that commercial banks are reluctant to approve their loan request for export financing. The New Mexico Export Finance Team (NMEFT) exists to help such businesses finance their export activities.

International Trade Division: Provides assistance to manufacturing, agricultural and other production concerns in developing their worldwide export capabilities. Services include:
- Export market development counseling
- Foreign trade shows and missions
- Foreign buying and reverse trade missions
- Identifying and disseminating overseas trade leads
- Attracting foreign businesses
- Developing, maintaining and using a database of potential domestic and international customers for New Mexico goods and services.

* Women and Minorities

For all items without a separate address, contact the New Mexico Economic Development Department at the address listed above.

Administration for Native Americans (ANA) Grant: Provides financial assistance through grants or contracts to further the three goals of the ANA: governance, economic development and social development. Technical assistance and training to develop, conduct and administer projects. Funding to public or private agencies to assist local residents in overcoming special obstacles to social and economic development. Maximum Program Benefits: Up to 80% of program cost, however, no set maximum or minimum grant amount.

BankAmerica Foundation - Community Economic Development Initiative: A special grant program targeted toward nonprofit organizations supporting community economic development and the growth of minority businesses. Maximum Program Benefits: Up to $500,000 in cash grants.

Eagle Staff Fund: Seeks to support Native grassroots and tribal organizations that are working to create Native-controlled reservation economies. Promotes economic development through technical assistance and financial resources.

EDA District, Indian and Area Planning Program: Grant assistance to defray administrative expenses in support of the economic development planning efforts of Economic Development Districts, Redevelopment Areas and Indian tribes.

BIA Indian Loan Guarantee Fund: Guaranteed loans that are made by private lenders to eligible applicants for up to 90% of the unpaid principal and interest due. Funds may be used to finance Indian-owned commercial, industrial or business activities organized for profit, provided eligible Indian ownership constitutes at least 51% of the business. Loans must benefit the economy of an Indian reservation. Also, interest subsidies might be granted when the business is incurring losses. Individual guarantees are limited to $500,000; $5.5 million maximum for tribes or organizations.

Navajo Business and Industrial Development Fund: Provides loans or loan guarantees to qualified Navajo individuals or Navajo-owned businesses. The program is intended to foster the establishment of new businesses or the expansion of existing businesses within the Navajo Nation's territorial jurisdiction. Minimum loan is $10,000; maximum loan is $100,000. Loan not to exceed 90% of purchase price of assets, or 95% of value of permanent improvements on a reservation site.

Women's Economic Self-Sufficiency Team: Provides consulting, training and support programs as well as financial assistance (loans). For more information, contact WESST Corp., 414 Silver SW, Albuquerque, NM 87102; 505-848-4760; Fax: 505-241-4766.

* Small Business Administration Offices

Ed Cadena
625 Silver Avenue, SW, Suite 320
Albuquerque, NM 87102
505-346-6764
Fax: 505-346-6711

New York

Empire State Development
One Commerce Plaza
Albany, NY 12245
518-474-7756
800-STATE-NY
www.empire.state.ny.us

633 Third Ave.
New York, NY 10017
212-803-3100

* Business Assistance

For all items without a separate address, contact the Empire State Development Office at the address listed above.

Small Business Division: Offers fast, up-to-date information on the State's economic development programs and can help in making contact with appropriate agencies in such areas as financing, job training, technical assistance, etc.

Small Business Advocacy Program: Reviews regulations affecting small business, maintains liaison with small business groups, assists business owners in the regulatory process, assists in expediting innovative business programs and projects, develops and presents workshops, seminars, conferences, and other training programs.

Technical Advisory Services; Provides free, confidential technical assistance concerning compliance to federal and state air quality requirements for small businesses.

Small Business Stationary Source Technical And Environmental Compliance Assistance Program: Provides technical assistance and advocacy services to eligible businesses in achieving environmental regulatory compliance.

Business Ombudsmen Services: Counseling and problem solving assistance to resolve complaints from small businesses concerning interactions with government authorities available to businesses employing 100 or less that are not dominant in their fields.

Entrepreneurial Assistance Program: Referrals of recipients to ESD funded assistance provides classroom instruction and individual counseling, business plan development for minorities, women, dislocated workers, public assistance recipients, public housing recipients and those seeking to start a new business or who have owned a business for five years or less.

Agricultural Business Development Assistance: Technical assistance to help locate public and private funding for food processors and agricultural producers.

State Money - New York

Contact: New York State Department of Agriculture and Markets, The Winners Circle, Albany, NY 12235; 518-457-7076.

Agricultural Ombudsman Services: Helps agricultural businesses communicate with regulatory agencies.

Food & Agricultural Industry Marketing Assistance: Marketing assistance for agricultural industries including trade shows, information distribution, and export financing.

America's Job Bank: Employers may list job openings in a statewide and national computer network.

Apprentice Training Program: Provides on-the-job training for more than 250 skilled occupations. Contact: Apprentice Training Program, Room 223, Bldg. 12, State Office Campus, Albany, NY 12240; 518-457-6820.

Business Development Office: Industrial and manufacturing companies are targeted for a variety of services.

New York State Contract Reporter: Provides listings of contracts made available for bidding by New York State agencies, public benefit corporations, and its public authorities.

Procurement Assistance: Provides technical assistance to businesses seeking to compete for contracts valued at $1,000,000 or more from the state.

Workforce Training: Empire State Development offers financial support and technical resources to companies to offset the cost of employee training.

High Technology Program: The Science and Technology Foundation maintains a mission to create and administer programs that promote scientific and technical education, industrially relevant research and development, manufacturing modernization and the capitalization of high-tech companies. Contact: New York State Science and Technology Foundation, 99 Washington Ave., Suite 1731, Albany, NY 12210; 518-473-9741.

Recycling Assistance: New York State has one of the largest concentrations of recycling companies in the world. Works with companies to demonstrate that, in addition to being an important environmental activity, recycling makes good business sense. To this end, they diagnose the research and development, capital, and marketing needs of recycling companies and tailor-make a package of technical and financial assistance. Identifies new markets and assist companies retooling to reach those markets. Assists companies to implement waste prevention practices.

Technical Assistance: New York State has developed a host of business-friendly products ranging from understanding the federal Clean Air Act and its impact on small business to ownership transition plans that can help a company grow and prosper. A hotline (800-STATE NY) puts business people directly in touch with a business ombudsman. The experts staffing this hotline are ready to answer questions. In addition, they serve as advocates for business.

Ownership Transition Services: Technical assistance.

Rural Employment Program: Recruits workers for farm, landscaping and food processing industries. Contact: Rural Employment Program, Room 282, Bldg. 12, State Office Campus, Albany, NY 12240; 518-457-6798.

Technology Development Organizations: Provides assistance to technology based companies competing for state and federal research and development grant programs, business plan review and development, management, marketing and financial packaging assistance, venture capital assistance, information systems development, technology business development training, incubator facility management and technology transfer services. Contact: Industrial Technology Programs, New York State Science and Technology Foundation, 99 Washington Ave., Suite 1730, Albany, NY 12210; 518-473-9746.

Advanced Controls for Efficiency Program (ACE): Applied research, product design, demonstration and testing, and product commercialization for individuals or enterprises with an innovative, energy-related product.

* Business Financing

For all items without a separate address, contact the Empire State Development Office at the address listed above.

Financial Services: Companies that plan to locate, expand or modernize their facilities in New York State are eligible for financial assistance. Generally, this assistance supports the acquisition of land and buildings or machinery and equipment. It also can help fund construction or renovation of buildings or the infrastructure and working capital required for the establishment or expansion of an eligible company.

Funds may be available through:
- direct loans to business for a portion of the cost of the project;
- interest rate subsidies to reduce the cost of borrowing from private or public sector financial institutions, in the form of a grant or linked deposit with the lending institution;
- loan guarantees for working capital assistance;
- assistance in the form of a loan and grant combination for a portion of the cost of an infrastructure project.

Economic Development Fund:

1. ***Industrial Effectiveness Program***: Direct technical assistance for identifying, developing and implementing improved management and production process and grants to pay the cost of feasibility studies up to $60,000.
2. ***Employee Training Assistance***: Offers skills training grant from $15,000 to $25,000.
3. ***Commercial Area Development***: Loans, loan guarantees, and grants to improve commercial buildings, commercial strips, downtown areas, and business districts from $75,000 to $100,000.
4. ***General Development***: Loans and loan guarantees for manufacturers, non-retail service firms, headquarters facilities of retail firms, retail firms in distressed areas, and businesses developing tourist attractions from $75,000 to $2,000,000.
5. ***Infrastructure Development***: Loans and grants for businesses located in distressed areas or a business that develops a tourist attraction from $25,000 to $2,000,000 for construction or renovation of basic systems and facilities.
6. ***Capital Access***: For small and medium size businesses including minority and women-owned businesses and day care centers, financing from $100,000 to $300,000.
7. ***General Development Financing***: Loans and loan guarantees for manufacturing, non-retail service firms, retail headquarters, retail firms located in distressed areas and businesses which develop recreational, cultural or historical facilities for tourist attractions. Amounts are determined case-by-case.
8. ***Competitiveness Improvement Services - Global Export Marketing Service***: Grants up to $5,000 for consulting services to assess organizational and product readiness for exporting. Grants up to $25,000 for an individual business or up to $50,000 for a business or industry group to create market development plans.

Industrial Waste Minimization Program: Technical assistance and grants up to $50,000 to assist, develop, and demonstrate energy-efficient methods to reduce, reuse, or recycle industrial wastes at the point of generation. Contact: NYS Energy Research and Development Authority, Corporate Plaza West, 286 Washington Ave. Extension, Albany, NY 12203; 518-862-1090, ext. 3206.

Environmental Finance Corporation: Grants for resource recovery facilities, solid waste disposal facilities, hazardous waste treatment facilities, Brownfields redevelopment, water supply and management facilities and sewage treatment works.

Recycling Investment Program: Technical assistance funding up to $75,000, capital project funding up to $300,000, research, development and demonstration project funding up to $100,000 for firms seeking to improve productivity and competitiveness by reducing solid waste and using recovered materials.

Energy Products Center: Product development demonstration and commercialization costs for technology-related businesses.

Retail and Office Development Assistance: Loans up to $5,000,000 for projects that retain or create significant numbers of private sector jobs in economically distressed areas.

Jobs Now Program: Worker training grant up to $10,000.

Venture Capital Fund: High Tech entrepreneurs, companies with technologies ready for market, and leading-edge enterprises each have different needs for investment capital. New York State has the seed and growth capital that will enable a high tech business to grow. The Small Business Technology Investment Fund program (SBTIF) is a source of early-stage debt and equity funding for high tech companies. Initial investments range as much as $300,000 and later stage investment up to $500,000. New York State is banking on a strong high tech future.

Transportation Capital Assistance Program: Loans up to $1,000,000 for small business enterprises and NYS-certified minority and women-owned business enterprises that have transportation-related construction contracts.

Commercial District Revolving Loans Trust Fund: Loans up to $15,000 for retail, professional or commercial service for profit businesses with 50 or fewer full-time employees.

Metropolitan Economic Revitalization Fund: Loans, capital access and linked deposits up to $5,000,000 for businesses and non-profits located in economically distressed area.

Regional Revolving Loan Trust Fund: Loans and loan guarantees up to $80,000 for businesses employing fewer than 100 people.

Small Business Technology Investment Fund: For small technology based companies, financing from $25,000 to $500,000 for seed or capital.

Job Development Authority: Loans to small and medium sized businesses in manufacturing and services from $50,000 to $1,500,000.

Jobs Now Program: Capital loans and grants to private businesses creating at least 300 new full time jobs not to exceed $10,000 per job.

Linked Deposit Program: Interest rate subsidies to a variety of businesses seeking to improve competitiveness and performance up to $1,000,000.

Commercial District Revolving Loan Trust Fund: Loans up to $20,000 to businesses with 50 or fewer employees.

State Money - New York

Empowerment Zone Program: Triple tax exempt bond financing up to $3,000,000 per zone for a variety of businesses located within a zone.

Enterprise Communities: Triple tax exempt bond financing up to $3,000,000 per community.

Economic Development through Greater Energy Efficiency: Grants and technical support for detailed engineering studies of manufacturing operations up to $50,000. Capital financing for demonstrations for energy efficient process technology up to $250,000. Contact: NYS Energy Research and Development Authority, Corporate Plaza West, 286 Washington Ave. Extension, Albany, NY 12203; 518-262-1090, ext. 3257.

Centers for Advanced Technology: Financial and technical assistance for commercially relevant research, technology transfer to industry, start up of new companies to commercialize research results, and incubator space. Amounts are determined case-by-case.

* Tax Incentives

For all items without a separate address, contact the Empire State Development Office at the address listed above.

Tax Benefits

General: New York State offers a host of tax credits to companies. For manufacturers and certain types of production operations, New York offers one of the most generous tax credits in the nation. If a company builds or expands, a new capital investment can yield up to 5% credit that can be carried-forward for 15 years. If employment increases in New York as a result of investments, a 5% tax credit could double over the following two years. To further encourage the state's strong high-technology base, they offer a credit against the corporate franchise/income tax for research and development efforts. Clean-up facilities for industrial waste or air pollution also can earn credits. At the same time, commercial and industrial plants and pollution control efforts can be eligible for partial relief from real property tax levied by counties, cities, towns, villages or school districts. They can also provide a list of taxes not imposed on New York State business. For example, there are no personal property taxes here, and they do not impose a sales tax on the purchase of production equipment.

Economic Development Zones: New York State has currently designated 52 economically distressed areas - certified as Economic Development Zones. They want to encourage the creation of jobs in these areas. In a zone they offer an investment tax credit of up to 19 percent. They can provide a tax break of up to 25% for new investors in these areas. They offer a host of benefits to make doing business easier, ranging from discounts on electric power to wage tax credits for new employees. They also have set aside Zone Equivalent Areas for special tax credits.

Empowerment Zone Program: Wage tax credits for businesses in severely distressed areas.

* Exports

For all items without a separate address, contact the Empire State Development Office at the address listed above.

Empire State Development: International market experts help a company enter and expand in the global economy. Offers a step-by-step analysis of a company's capabilities and matches them with the demands of the international marketplace. If a company has what the global marketplace needs, they will work with that company to find the niche, the spot on the globe where they can sell. Then, they will assist them in determining how to reach those markets. They provide information about tariffs, industry specifications and government regulations. They can put a company in touch with representatives, distributors, agents and strategic allies to sell a product or service abroad.

Industrial Development Agencies: IDA projects are exempt from local property taxes and mortgage recording tax. Building materials and certain purchases of capital equipment are exempt from State and local sales taxes.

Pollution Control Facilities: Facilities are exempt from local real property taxes and ad valorem levies.

Commercial and Industrial Facilities: Property tax exemptions of up to 50%.

Corporate Franchise Tax Allocation Percentage: Business corporations are subject to tax only on the portion of their activities that are deemed to be attributable to their activities in New York State.

Credits for Bank Corporation Tax: For corporations which service mortgages acquired by the New York State Mortgage Agency, the credit is equal to the amount paid for the special recording tax on mortgages recorded after 1/1/79.

- *Credits for Insurance Corporation Tax*: Credits for additional taxes of premiums written on premiums. Credit of up to 90% or retaliatory taxes paid to the state by New York domiciled or organized insurers.
- Credit equaling the amount paid in the special additional mortgage recording tax. Credit for a portion of the cost of assessments paid to the Life Insurance Company Guaranty Corporation up to $40 million or 40% of the total tax liability.

International Banking Facility: A deduction for the adjusted net income for banking corporations that establish international banking facilities in New York to accept deposits from and make loans to foreign customers.

Retail Enterprise Credit: Investment tax credit for rehabilitation expenditures of a retail facility.

Sales Tax Exemptions; Exemptions include machinery, utility services and fuels used in production, labor for installing and maintaining production equipment, anything becoming a component part of a product for sale and others.

Tax Credit for Pollution Control Expenditures: A credit of 5% for businesses constructing or improving industrial waste or air pollution control facilities.

Tax Credits Based on New Capital Investment: 5% of new capital invested in buildings used primarily in production by manufacturing, processing, assembling and certain other types of activities.

Tax Credits Based on Research and Development: 7 to 9% of qualified research and development tangible property against the corporate franchise tax.

Personal Property: New York imposes no ad valorem taxes on personal property.

* Women and Minorities

For all items without a separate address, contact the Empire State Development Office at the address listed above.

Division of Minority and Women's Business Development: Administers, coordinates, and implements a statewide program to assist the development of M/WBE's and facilitate their access to state contracting opportunities. Through the process of certification, the agency is responsible for verifying minority and women-ownership and control of firms participating in the program.

Division of Minority and Women's Business Development Lending Program: Loans up to $7,000 from the Microenterprise Loan Fund and up to $50,000 from the Minority and Women Revolving Loan Trust Fund.

* Small Business Administration Offices

Tom Bettridge
26 Federal Plaza, Room 31-08
New York, NY 10278
212-264-1450
Fax: 212-264-0038

Franklin Sciortino
111 West Huron Street, Room 1311
Buffalo, NY 14202
716-551-4305
Fax: 716-551-4418

Aubrey Rogers
26 Federal Plaza, Suite 3100
New York, NY 10278
212-264-2454
Fax: 212-264-7751

B.J. Paprocki
401 South Salina Street, 5th Floor
Syracuse, NY 13202
315-471-9393
Fax: 315-471-9288

James Cristofaro
333 East Water Street, 4th Floor
Elmira, NY 14901
607-734-1571
Fax: 607-734-4656

Bert Haggerty
35 Pinelawn Road, Suite 207
Melville, NY 11747
516-454-0750
Fax: 516-454-0769

Peter Flihan
100 State Street, Suite 410
Rochester, NY 14614

State Money - North Carolina

716-263-6700
Fax: 716-263-3146

North Carolina

Department of Commerce
Commerce Finance Center
301 N. Wilmington St.
P.O. Box 29571
Raleigh, NC 27626-0571
919-733-4977
Fax: 919-715-9265
www.commerce.state.nc.us/commerce

* Business Assistance

For all items without a separate address, contact the North Carolina Department of Commerce at the address listed above.

Retention and Expansion Programs: Professional assistance is provided for all aspects of business including environmental consultation, financing alternative, human resources consulting, marketing information, energy process surveys and other issues that impact business and industry.

Master License Application Program: Offers the business applicant a streamlined approach to applying for required business licenses.

Industrial Extension Service: Provides technical and industrial management assistance, conducts applied research, advocates industrial use of technology and modern managerial practices, as well as conducts continuing education programs for business, industry, entrepreneurs, engineers and local governments.

Biotechnology Center: Carries out a variety of programs and activities strengthening North Carolina's biotechnology community.

MCNC: A private nonprofit corporation that supports advanced education, research and technology programs to enhance North Carolina's technology infrastructure and businesses. Contact: MCNC, 3201 Cornwallis Rd., P.O. Box 12889, Research Triangle Park, NC 27709; 919-248-1800; {www.mcnc.org}.

Industrial Training Program: State funded customized job training programs for new and expanding industries that create 12 or more new jobs in a community within one year.

Small Business and Technology Development Center: Organized as an inter-institutional program of The University of North Carolina, the Small Business and Technology Development Center (SBTDC) is the primary organization through which the state of North Carolina provides counseling and technical assistance to the business community. SBTDC services are well-defined and designed to meet client needs. The primary focus is in-depth, one-on-one, confidential counseling. Assistance is provided, free of charge, to the small business owner or aspiring entrepreneur. As the only full service counseling resource statewide, the SBTDC helps with the myriad of tasks facing a business owner, including:
- assessing the feasibility of a business idea
- preparing a business plan
- finding sources of capital
- developing marketing strategies
- operations and human resource management

For more information, contact Small Business and Technology Development Center, 333 Fayetteville Street Mall, Suite 1150, Raleigh, NC 27601; 919-715-7272; 800-258-0862 (NC only); {www.sbtac.org}.

SBTDC Special Market Development Assistance:
- *Procurement Technical Assistance Program*: The SBTDC provides comprehensive assistance in selling goods and services to the federal government. Services include help in finding out about contracting opportunities, preparing bid and proposal packages, obtaining 8(a) certification, interpreting regulations, and resolving contract administration problems. An integral part of this program is PRO-BID, a computer-based bid matching service that provides accurate and timely information on procurement opportunities.
- *International Business Development*: North Carolina businesses are increasingly looking at exporting as a vehicle to increase sales and profits. The SBTDC helps successful domestic, new-to-export businesses to identify, target and then penetrate foreign markets. SBTDC counselors provide marketing research information, assist with market planning, and then identify implementation procedures.
- *The Technology Group*: Part of the SBTDC's mission is to help emerging businesses commercialize innovative new technologies, and to facilitate the transfer of technology developed within the small business and university communities. Technology Group services include assistance in maritime technology transfer, identifying markets for scientific discoveries, guiding the development of strategies to protect intellectual property and providing referrals to specialized organizations and resources.
- *Marine Trades Program*: The SBTDC's Marine Trades Program provides business development support to marine industry firms. Specific services include assistance in marketing marine products and services, complying with environmental regulations, and maintaining safe operations. The program also provides marine specific training, education and research.

* Business Financing

For all items without a separate address, contact the North Carolina Department of Commerce at the address listed above.

Industrial Revenue Bonds: Revenue Bonds have a variety of names and purposes but essentially three basic types exist. These bonds whose proper name is Small Issue Industrial Development Bonds are referred to as Industrial Revenue Bond's (IRB's). The state's principal interest in these bonds is assisting new and expanding industry while insuring that North Carolinians get good jobs at good wages. The regulations governing bond issuance are a combination of federal regulations and North Carolina statutes. The amount each state may issue annually is designated by population. There are three types of bond issuances as follows:
- Tax Exempt - Because the income derived by the bondholder is not subject to federal income tax, the maximum bond amount is $10 million in any given jurisdiction. According to federal regulations, the $10 million total includes the bond amount and capital expenditures over a six-year period going both backwards and forwards three years. The maximum any company may have is $40 million nationwide outstanding at any given period.
- Taxable - They are not exempt from federal tax (they are however exempt from North Carolina tax). The essential difference is that the Taxable bond rate is slightly higher to the borrower and not being subject to the federal volume cap, may exceed $10 million in bond amount.
- Pollution Control/Solid Waste Disposal Bond - These bonds are subject to volume cap although there is no restriction on amount, and the interest on these bonds is federally tax exempt.

Economic Development Category: Projects may involve assistance for public facilities needed to serve the target business, or loans to the private business to fund items such as machinery and equipment, property acquisition or construction. Public facility projects may provide grants of up to 75% of the proposed facility costs, with a 25% cash match to be paid by the local government applicant.

Industrial Development Fund: Purpose is to provide an incentive for jobs creation in the State's most economically distressed counties, also identified as Tier 1, 2, and 3 areas. Funds for the renovation of manufacturing buildings and the acquisition of infrastructure are made available by the Department of Commerce to eligible counties or their local units of government, which apply for the funds on behalf of their existing or new manufacturing businesses. A commitment to create jobs is executed by the benefiting firm. The amount of funds available to participating firms is determined by multiplying the number of jobs committed to be created times $4,000.00, up to a maximum of $400,000.00 or the cost of the project, whichever is less. Of course, the availability of funds also applies.

Business Energy Improvement: Program provides loans between $100,000 and $500,000 to industrial and commercial businesses located or moving to North Carolina. Loans can be financed for up to seven years at interest rates equal to 50% of the average (high and low) T-bill rate for the past year or five percent, whichever is lower. Current rate is 5%, which is the maximum. Funds are provided from a pool of $2,500,000 designated for energy related capital improvement such as cogeneration, energy saving motors, boiler improvements and low energy use lighting. A participating bank will process loans on a first-come-first-served based upon the date of receipt of a letter of credit.

Partnerships for Regional Economic Development: The counties of North Carolina have been organized into seven regional partnerships for economic development. North Carolina's regional partnerships will enable regions to compete effectively for new investment and to devise effective economic development strategies based on regional opportunities and advantages.

North Carolina SBTDC Small Business Innovation Research (SBIR): Program is a highly competitive three-phase award system which provides qualified small businesses with opportunities to propose innovative ideas that meet specific research and research and development needs of the Federal government. Phase I is a feasibility study to evaluate the proposed project's technical merit for which an awardee may receive a maximum of $100,000 for approximately six months. Phase II is the principal R&D effort which expands on the Phase I results. This two-year project may receive up to $750,000 in funding. Only

State Money - North Dakota

Phase I awardees are eligible to compete for Phase II funds. Phase III is the commercialization of the Phase II results and moves the innovation from the laboratory to the marketplace. This requires use of private sector or other non-SBIR funding. Contact: Small Business and Technology Development Center, 333 Fayetteville Street Mall, Suite 1150, Raleigh, NC 27601; 919-715-7272; 800-258-0862 (in NC); {www.sbtac.org}.

North Carolina SBTDC Small Business Technology Transfer (STTR): STTR is much like that of the Small Business Innovation Research (SBIR) program. Its unique feature is its requirement that the small business work jointly with a non-profit research institution. A minimum of 40% of the work must be performed by the small business and a minimum of 30% by the non-profit research institution. Such institutions include Federally funded research and development centers (FFRDCs), universities, university affiliated hospitals, and other non-profits. Contact: Small Business and Technology Development Center, 333 Fayetteville Street Mall, Suite 1150, Raleigh, NC 27601; 919-715-7272; 800-258-0862 (in NC); {www.sbtac.org}.

* Tax Incentives

For all items without a separate address, contact the North Carolina Department of Commerce at the address listed above.

Double-Weighted Sales Factor in Corporate Income Tax: Structured so a business in North Carolina that makes significant sales outside the state would be taxed at a lesser level than a comparable business that is located elsewhere but makes significant sales within North Carolina.

Inventory Tax Exemption: There is no local or state property tax on inventory held by manufacturers, wholesale and retail merchants or contractors.

Computer Software Tax Exemptions: There are no local or state sales taxes on custom computer programs. Additionally, there is no property tax on computer software.

Recycling Equipment: Equipment or facilities installed for the purpose of recycling solid waste or resource recovery from solid waste receives the same treatment under the tax laws as that given to pollution abatement equipment described below.

Pollution Abatement Equipment: Property used to reduce air or water pollution receives special treatment under the tax law if the Board of Environmental Management certifies that the property complies with the requirements of the Board.

OSHA Equipment: The cost of equipment and facilities mandated by the Occupational Safety and Health Act may be amortized over 60 months for income tax purposes.

Equipment to Reduce Hazardous Waste: Equipment and facilities acquired for the purpose of reducing the volume of hazardous waste generated may be amortized over a period of 60 months for income tax purposes.

Jobs Creation Tax Credit: Provides a tax credit for creating jobs based on the number of jobs created and the location of the business.

Investment Tax Credit: Available to eligible companies that invest in machinery and equipment and based on the amount of machinery purchased.

Worker Training Tax Credit: Up to a 50% credit against eligible training expenses if the firm provides training for 5 or more employees. Maximum credit is $1,000 per employee.

Research and Development Tax Credit: A line item tax credit taken by an eligible company.

Business Property Tax Credit: Equals 4.5% of tangible personal business property capitalized under the tax code, up to a maximum single-year credit of $4,500.

Central Administrative Office Tax Credit: Available to companies who have purchased or leased real property in North Carolina to be used as a central administrative office for the company. Maximum credit is $500,000.

Ports Authority Wharfage and Handling Charges: Both importers and exporters who use the North Carolina ports can apply and qualify for a tax credit up to 50% of the total state tax liability for each tax year.

Credit for Construction of Cogenerating Power Plants: Any corporation that constructs a cogenerating power plant in North Carolina is allowed a credit equal to 10% of the costs required to purchase and install the electrical or mechanical power generation equipment of that plant.

Credit for Conversion of Industrial Boiler to Wood Fuel: Any corporation that modifies or replaces an oil or gas-fired boiler or kiln and the associated fuel and residue-handling equipment used in the manufacturing process of a manufacturing business in North Carolina with a furnace capable of burning wood is permitted a credit equal to 15% of the installation and equipment costs resulting from such a conversion.

Credit for Construction of a Peat Facility: Any corporation that constructs a facility in North Carolina that uses peat as the feedstock for the productions of a commercially manufactured energy source to replace petroleum, natural gas or other nonrenewable energy sources is allowed a credit equal to 20% of the installation and equipment costs of construction.

Sales Tax Exemptions and Discounts: Available for industrial machinery and equipment; coal, coke and fuel oil used in manufacturing; electricity or piped natural gas used in connection with manufacturing; raw materials used for production, packaging, and shipping, as well as things bought for resale; motor vehicles; aircraft, boats, railway cars, and mobile offices; purchases of ingredients or component parts of manufactured products; packaging material that becomes a part of a manufactured product. Contact: NC Department of Revenue, Box 25000, Raleigh, NC 27640; 919-733-3991; {www.dor.state.nc.us/DOR/}.

* Exports

For all items without a separate address, contact the North Carolina Department of Commerce at the address listed above.

Export Outreach Program: A series of workshops designed to walk a company through every facet of the export process. In cooperation with the North Carolina Community College Small Business Network, the International Trade Division has made this program available in seven regional centers across the state. The Export Outreach Program is a hard-core, intense program where commitment, preparation and action are instilled as the basis for successful exporting. North Carolina is the only state to offer such a program, which increases the quality and competitiveness of North Carolina products.

Trade Events Program: This program consists of Catalog Shows, Trade Fairs and Trade Mission in carefully selected markets worldwide. The Trade Events Calendar is updated periodically to inform North Carolina companies of these opportunities.

International Trade Division: Because North Carolina companies are prepared and committed prior to entering international markets, North Carolina is recognized in the major trading blocs of the world as one of the most aggressive international business development states in the United States. Senior Trade Specialists of the International Trade Division represent the three major trading blocks of the world: Europe/Africa/The Middle East, The Americas, Far East.

* Women and Minorities

For all items without a separate address, contact the North Carolina Department of Commerce at the address listed above.

SBTDC Minority Business Enterprise Development: More businesses are being started by minorities than ever before. While minorities owned only 6% of North Carolina's small businesses in 1987, the number of minority-owned firms in the state jumped by 46% between 1982 and 1987 (U.S. Small Business Administration). Realizing the importance of North Carolina's minority-owned companies to future job creation and economic growth, the SBTDC is committed to providing responsive and effective support to minority business enterprises.

The SBTDC offers specialized market development assistance in the areas of government procurement, international business development, and new product and technology development. The SBTDC provides the strongest counseling resource for minority clients in the state. 25% of the 5,200 clients counseled each year are minority businesses. In addition to extensive business counseling, special focus training programs on topics such as "Equal Access to Credit" & "Minority, Women and Disadvantaged Business Enterprise Certification" are presented periodically across the state. Contact: Small Business and Technology Development Center, 333 Fayetteville Street Mall, Suite 1150, Raleigh, NC 27601; 919-715-7272; 800-258-0862 (in NC); {www.sbtdc.org}.

* Small Business Administration Offices

Lee Corneliuson
200 N. College Street, Suite A2015
Charlotte, NC 28202
704-344-6563
Fax: 704-344-6644

North Dakota

Department of Economic Development and Finance
1833 East Bismarck Expressway
Bismarck, ND 58504-6708
701-328-5300
Fax: 701-328-5320
TTY: 800-366-6888
www.growingnd.com

State Money - North Dakota

* Business Assistance

For all items without a separate address, contact the North Dakota Department of Economic Development and Finance at the address listed above.

Department of Economic Development and Finance (ED&F): This office can provide information and expertise in dealing with state, federal, and local agencies. They also have information on financing programs and other services offered by the state government.

Technology Transfer, Inc.: Serves as a liaison between ED&F, the North Dakota University System and entrepreneurs and manufacturers. The North Dakota University System provides services that help stimulate, produce and sell new ideas. Services include outreach programs designed to discover new technology; design, licensing, and patenting technical help; business development assistance; and production engineering.

North Dakota Manufacturing Technology Partnership (MTP): Approximately 400 targeted manufacturers in the state will be able to receive direct assistance from dedicated manufacturing specialists experienced in manufacturing and will be able to access other appropriate assistance through managed referrals. Manufacturers can expect benefits from improved manufacturing processes; enhanced management skills; better business practices; research and development funding and technical assistance; expanded market opportunities; defense conversion assistance; new product development resources; better trained staff; intercompany working relationships; increased revenue; and increased profit.

Community Economic Development Team: Guides communities through an intensive community inventory, a public input phase, and an ongoing process of business retention, new business start-up and recruitment. Community Services Team helps communities and counties by:
- Helping them assess the level of local interest in economic development.
- Helping them understand and assess their strengths and weaknesses.
- Identifying an organization or group of people in the community who will coordinate local development.
- Helping citizens understand the process of economic development and their role in it.
- Helping to identify community leaders and financial resources available for economic development.

Research and Information Services: A broad program to strengthen economic development efforts statewide. Its major responsibilities are:
- Responding to requests from businesses seeking to grow and wish to learn more about opportunities in North Dakota.
- Helping identify new economic development opportunities.
- Exploring ways to enhance the state's and community's climate for business growth and investment.
- Providing services that assist economic developers in conducting research, accessing and using information.
- Information Fulfillment System (IFS) which is customer driven and includes all of the systems and processes used by the Team to better manage the information needed to provide quality communications, responses and services to both external and internal clients.

Center for Innovation at University of North Dakota: Provides comprehensive, hands-on assistance for technology entrepreneurs, innovators, and manufacturers interested in starting up new ventures, commercializing new products, and licensing university technologies. Contact: Center for Innovation, UND Rural Technology Center, 4300 Dartmouth Dr., P.O. Box 8372, Grand Forks, ND 58202; 701-777-3132; {www.und.nodak.edu/dept/cibd/welcome.htm}.

Rural Technology Incubator: Located in the Center for Innovation, the Rural Technology Incubator is designed to provide a seedbed to help innovators and entrepreneurs grow their businesses. Their highly diversified staff assists startups by providing them with supportive, creative places in which to work as a team. Located next to the University of North Dakota campus, the Rural Technology Incubator offers university talent, technology, training, and technical assistance to help business startups develop and test-market new products, ideas, technologies, and ventures. Contact: Center for Innovation, UND Rural Technology Center, 4300 Dartmouth Dr., P.O. Box 8372, Grand Forks, ND 58202; 701-777-3132; {www.und.nodak.edu/dept/cibd/welcome.htm}.

Skills & Technology Training Center: Located in Fargo. A partnership between NDSU-Fargo, North Dakota State College of Science, and Wahpeton private sector leaders. Contact: Skills and Technology Training Center, 1305 19th Ave. North, Fargo, ND 58102; 701-231-6900; {www.sttc.nodak.edu}.

Job Services North Dakota: Has labor, employment, and other statistical information available. For more information, contact Job Services North Dakota, P.O. Box 5507, Bismarck, ND 58506; 800-732-9787; 701-328-2868; {www.state.nd.us/jsnd/lmi.htm}.

Publications:
North Dakota You Should See Us Now: Information on ND labor, infrastructure, taxes and quality of life targeted to primary sector site selectors.
North Dakota Tax Incentives for Business
Financing North Dakota's Future Brochure: Summary of ND commercial financing programs
Mini-Grants for Research & Development

* Business Financing

For all items without a separate address, contact the North Dakota Department of Economic Development and Finance at the address listed above.

The North Dakota Development Fund: Provides gap financing for primary sector businesses expanding or relocating in the state. Primary sector is defined as: "an individual, corporation, partnership or association which, through the employment of knowledge or labor, adds value to a product, process or service that results in the creation of new wealth." Primary sector businesses are typically considered to be manufacturing, food processing, and exported services. Types of investments include equity, debt, and other forms of innovative financing up to a limit of $300,000. One of the criteria for dollars invested is projected job creation within 24 months of funding.

Technology Transfer, Inc.: Provides leadership and funding to bring new technology developed in North Dakota to the marketplace. TTI is the only resource in North Dakota for high-risk research and development. A vital source for R&D funds, TTI invests financial resources in North Dakota companies and inventors. Individuals or companies with marketable ideas for products or manufacturing processes may use TTI funds to evaluate the product or process to find out if it has any commercial potential. They may also use TTI funds for expenses such as market research, prototyping, product testing, patenting, test marketing, and business plan development. The maximum amount allowed for each project is $100,000. TTI expects repayment through royalties if the product or process is successfully commercialized. Typically, royalties are based on gross sales, usually between 3 and 5 percent. TTI then reinvests these funds in other viable projects. If a funded project fails, TTI expects no repayment.

Agricultural Products Utilization Commission: Mission is to create new wealth and jobs through the development of new and expanded uses of North Dakota agricultural products. The commission accomplishes its mission through the administration of a grant program.

Basic and Applied Research Grants: This program centers on research efforts that focus on the uses and processing of agricultural products and by-products. Further, consideration is given to products which develop an expanded use of technology for the processing of these products.

Marketing & Utilization Grants: Funds from this category are used for the development or implementation of a sound marketing plan for the promotion of North Dakota agricultural products or by-products.

Cooperative Marketing Grants: This category encourages groups of agricultural producers to develop innovative marketing strategies.

Farm Diversification Grants: This category focuses on the diversification of a family farm to non-traditional crops, livestock or non-farm value-added processing of agricultural commodities. Traditional crops and livestock are generally defined as those for which the North Dakota Agricultural Statistics Service maintains records. The proposed project must have the potential to create additional income for the farm unit.

About The One Stop Capital Center: Located at the Bank of North Dakota, the One Stop Capital Center offers one-stop access to over twenty financing programs. Together, the five partners work with local financial institutions and economic developers to offer integrated financial packages. The One Stop Capital Center has loan officers available from each of the agencies who jointly work to streamline the financing process and provide timely service. Contact: Bank of North Dakota, 700 E. Main, 2nd Floor, P.O. Box 5509, Bismarck, ND 58506; 800-544-4674; {http://webhost.btigate.com/~onestop}.

* Tax Incentives

For all items without a separate address, contact the North Dakota Department of Economic Development and Finance at the address listed above.

No personal property tax including equipment, inventory, materials in process or accounts receivable.

Allows the entire amount of federal income tax liability to be deducted before calculating state corporate tax.

County Property Tax Exemptions: Any new or expanding business may be granted an exemption for up to five years. Other possible exemptions include: rehabilitation of buildings more than 25 years old; Geothermal, solar or wind

State Money - Ohio

energy systems.

Corporate Tax Credits: A primary sector business such as manufacturing, agricultural processing and back office operations such as telemarketing may qualify for a five-year income tax exemption. Other items that may qualify for corporate tax credits include: research expenditures within the state; seed capital investments; wages and salaries for new businesses.

Sales and Use Tax: New or expanding businesses qualify for an exemption on machinery, building materials and equipment used for manufacturing, processing or recycling. There is no sales tax on electricity, water or money when used for manufacturing purposes.

* Exports

For all items without a separate address, contact the North Dakota Department of Economic Development and Finance at the address listed above.

International Trade Program: Mission is to increase the number of jobs in North Dakota by helping companies expand their business into foreign markets. Staff counsels companies on export procedures, international marketing, banking and financing. They also provide referrals to translators, customs brokers, consultants and opportunities for participation in international trade show events. Offers a series of international business workshops, titled "Hands-On Training in International Business," to provide North Dakota businesses with the tools to target global markets and expand export opportunities.

* Women and Minorities

For all items without a separate address, contact the North Dakota Department of Economic Development and Finance at the address listed above.

Women's Business Program assists women:
- by providing counseling and technical assistance for women entrepreneurs
- by maintaining a database of women-owned businesses
- by administering the women's incentive grant program
- by certifying women-owned businesses for federal and state contracting
- by supporting the Women's Business Leadership Council
- by providing information and support through trade shows and conferences
- by serving as an information clearinghouse on economic development service providers.

For more information about Women's Business Program, contact Tara Holt, ND Women's Business Program, 418 East Broadway, Suite 25, Bismarck, ND 58501; 701-258-2251; Fax: 701-222-8071; {email: holt@btigate.com}; {www.growingnd.com/wbd_prog.html}.

Native American Program: Provides Native American individuals, businesses and tribal governments access to technical support and financial assistance. But perhaps more importantly, the NA Program advocates an improved business climate for Native American businesses and also encourages policies that address their needs. The program strives to educate all people about the unique aspects of Native American businesses. To know and understand each tribe's focus on economic development, the staff monitors the total economic development plan for each tribe. And in keeping with their philosophy that all true economic development takes place on the local level, the staff works to foster mutually beneficial relationships between Native American entrepreneurs and businesses and local development corporations and North Dakota's tribes. Finance: Provides equity gap grants to new reservation-based private businesses. Provides access to the Native American set-aside of the ND Development Fund. Assists in the development of new grant and equity participant capitol resources.

Publications:

North Dakota Women's Business Development Program Packets: Materials on programs, assistance providers and guides for ND women-owned businesses.

North Dakota Native American Program: Brochure Description of the program, services available and summary of the impact of Native American businesses in ND.

Native American Business Guide Booklet: Directory of ND Native American-owned businesses.

Grants for Native American Businesses: Booklet Directory of grants available for Native American-owned businesses.

Native American Equity Grant Program Brochure: Grant program providing "seed money" to federally recognized Indian organizations and individuals.

* Small Business Administration Offices

James Stai
657 2nd Avenue North, Room 219
Fargo, ND 58108

701-239-5131
Fax: 701-239-5645

Ohio

Ohio Department of Development
P.O. Box 1001
Columbus, OH 43216-1001
614-466-5017
800-345-OHIO
Fax: 614-463-1540
www.odod.ohio.gov

* Business Assistance

For all items without a separate address, contact the Ohio Department of Development at the address listed above.

Small Business Innovation Research (SBIR) Technical Assistance Services: Increases the number of research contracts won by Ohio companies from eleven participating federal agencies. Provides small businesses with direct, hands-on assistance in identifying research topics; guides businesses through the proposal writing process from design to review; and offers educational and technical services. Also helps companies prepare proposals for SBIR Phase I awards of up to $100,000 and Phase II awards up to $500,000.

Business Development Assistance: Assists domestic and foreign businesses with up-to-date information on sites, buildings, labor, markets, taxes and financing. Development specialists act as liaison between the companies and state/local agencies. Works to maintain and create Ohio jobs through retention and expansion of established businesses and attraction of new businesses; assists local community development organizations and acts as a liaison for communities when dealing with issues under local control.

Labor Market Information: Measurements of economic conditions. Local and national employment/labor-force data to aid in market research, business development and planning. Attracts new employers by identifying skilled workforce. Supplies free information on the training/education available to help workers meet business needs.

Ohio Data Users Center: Census and statistical data; demographic; economic; specific trade, industry and labor analyses. Develops and disseminates population estimates, projections. Provides tools for better coordinated decision-making in public/private sectors.

Ohio Procurement Technical Assistance: Free in-depth counseling, technical resources and historical contracting data, military specifications, financial guidance and advocacy services for federal procurement opportunities. Increases the federal dollars invested in Ohio; increase job and business market opportunities; increase awareness of procurement programs and opportunities.

One-Stop Business Permit Center: Supplies new entrepreneurs with information about licenses and permits required by the State of Ohio; directs callers to proper area for technical, financial and management resources; acts as advocate for licensing and permit problems.

Buy Ohio Program: Provides marketing consultation for Ohio-made products; assists with promotions, special events, and media coverage; develops buyer/seller relationships; disseminates program logo and materials. Builds consumer awareness and support for quality Ohio-made products; creates more business opportunities for Ohio companies; uses taxpayers' dollars efficiently; helps maintain jobs; develops state and local pride. No charge for consulting or start-up packet to all Ohio travel-related businesses and organizations.

Edison Technology Centers: Provides businesses with access to state-of-the-art applied research performed in-house or obtained through linkages with universities, federal laboratories and other institutions; education and training programs; plant site assessments; technical problem solving; conferences, seminars and other networking opportunities.

Edison Technology Incubators: Low-cost space that reduces operating costs during start-up phase for technology-based businesses; access to business, technical, and professional services, including legal, accounting, marketing, and financial counseling.

Federal Technology Transfer Program: "Gateway" organizations to resources of the federal laboratory system including intellectual property, engineering expertise, facilities, and equipment.

Labor Market Information: Measurements of economic conditions. Local and national employment/labor-force data to aid in market research, business development and planning.

Enterprise Ohio: Matches qualified workers to job opportunities; administers job training programs, including JTP Ohio, the Work Incentive Program and the Veterans Job Training Act.

State Money - Ohio

* Business Financing

For all items without a separate address, contact the Ohio Department of Development at the address listed above.

166 Regional Loan Program: Land and building acquisition, expansion or renovation, and equipment purchase; industrial projects preferred. Up to 40% of total eligible fixed cost ($350,000 maximum); rate negotiable for 5-15 years; equity minimum 10%, bank minimum 25%. Ohio prevailing wage rate applies.

Child Day Care Loan Program (CDCGLP): Expansion of existing day care centers and start-up of new day care centers, thus providing employment and job training opportunities for employers and employees. Encourages new child care relationships between communities, businesses and government, as well as new approaches to child care services. $15,000 per project/ no minimum.

Community Development Corporation Program: Created for the purpose of meeting the needs of a defined low- and moderate-income neighborhood or community, or target area population. Funds may be used for housing, economic development or commercial revitalization projects. Competitive grants of up to $50,000, with at least 50% of the grant being used for project implementation costs. Requires at least 2:1 ratio of other funds. As much as $25,000 of grant may be used for project development (professional services planning and administration).

Direct Loan (166 Loan): Land and building acquisition, expansion or renovation, and equipment purchase; industrial projects preferred. Up to 30% of total eligible fixed cost ($1 million maximum, $350,000 minimum), two-thirds of prime fixed rate for 10-15 years; equity minimum 10%, bank minimum 25%. In distressed areas of the State, preferential rates and terms are available. However, the Director of Development may authorize a higher loan amount or modified terms that address a unique and demonstrated economic development need. Must show repayment and management capabilities; must create one job for every $15,000 received; Ohio prevailing wage rate applies.

Labor/Management Cooperation Program: Enhances relationship between labor and management through regular meetings, seminars, conferences, and work-site labor/management training programs. Creates a stable and positive work environment by nurturing cooperative labor/management relationships and by dispelling negative labor images. Matching grants support community-based area labor/management committees, regional centers for the advancement of labor-management cooperation, and an employee stock ownership assistance program.

Linked Deposit Program: Fixed assets, working capital and refinanced-debt for small businesses, creating or retaining jobs. A similar Agricultural Linked Deposit Program provides funds for Ohio farmers to help meet planning deadlines. 3% below current lending rate fixed for 2 years (possible 2-year extension); bank may then extend term at current rates. (All other sources of funds allowable.) The Agricultural Linked Deposit Program provides up to $100,000 per farm at reduced rate, approximately 4% below borrower's current rate. Must have Ohio headquarters and no divisions out of state, create one job for every $15,000 to $25,000 received, have 150 or fewer employees, be organized for profit, and have bank loan from eligible state depository.

Ohio Enterprise Bond Fund: Land and building acquisition, construction, expansion or renovation, and equipment purchase for commercial or industrial projects between $1 million and $10 million in size. Long-term, fixed rate for up to 16 years; interest rate based on Standard & Poor's A-minus rating, for up to 90% of total project amount.

Revolving Loan Funds: Projects must create or retain jobs; 51% of all jobs must be for persons from low- and moderate-income households; federal prevailing wage rates may apply; and an environmental review covering entire project must be performed. All CDBG guidelines must be met, including documentation of all project aspects. Loan ceiling determined locally or by availability. Available to user or developer, typically at 5% to 7% fixed; flexible term. Appropriate use of federal program income funds determines participation level of community. Projects must create and/or retain jobs and help develop, rehabilitate or revitalize a participating "small city" community. Financing is usually approved for fixed assets related to commercial, industrial or infrastructure.

Ohio Coal Development Program: Financial assistance for clean coal research and development projects. Advances promising technology into the commercial market. Installed technologies will result in cleaner air, better use of by-products, greater demand for Ohio coal and the jobs associated with its production and use. Strong potential also exists for the export of the technologies. For research: up to $75,000 or two-thirds of total project costs (TPC). Pilot and demonstration scale projects: up to $5 million or one-half of TPC for a pilot project, or one-third TPC for demonstration project. Funds can be issued in the form of a grant, loan, or loan guarantee.

Small Business Innovation Research Program (SBIR) Winners' Support System: Offers SBIR winners a wide range of services including: funding between federal Phase I and Phase II awards through the Bridge Grant Program; assistance in identifying potential partners or customers through the Winners' Portfolio; assistance in securing funding for commercialization through Phase III Funding conferences; and access to a network of public and private experts through a Mentor Network.

Scrap Tire Loan and Grant Program: Financing available to scrap tire recyclers who locate or expand in Ohio and who demonstrate that they will create new/reuse scrap tire products.

Defense Adjustment Program: Provides assistance to communities and technology-based companies impacted by economic losses because of company and military base drawdowns, realignments and closures.

Coal Development Program: Financial assistance for clean coal research and development projects.

Labor/Management Cooperation Program: Matching grant support community-based area labor/management committees, regional centers for the advancement of labor-management cooperation, and an employee stock ownership assistance program.

Industrial Training Program: Up to 50% funding for orientation, training, and management program; instructional materials, instructor training.

* Tax Incentives

For all items without a separate address, contact the Ohio Department of Development at the address listed above.

Community Reinvestment Areas: Local tax incentives for businesses that expand or locate in designated areas of Ohio. Up to 100% exemption of the improved real estate property tax valuation for up to 15 years. In some instances, local school board approval may be required. Business must undertake new real estate investment.

Enterprise Zones: Local and state tax incentives for businesses that expand or locate in designated areas of Ohio. Up to 75% exemption in incorporated areas and up to 60% in unincorporated areas of the improved real estate or new tangible personal property tax valuation for up to 10 years.

Ohio Manufacturing Machinery & Equipment Investment Tax Credit: A non-refundable corporate franchise or state income tax credit for a manufacturer that purchases new machinery and equipment that is located in Ohio and is used in the production or assembly of a manufactured good. The manufacturer shall receive a 7.5% tax credit on the increase of the investment that is in excess of the three-year annual average investment on machinery and equipment.

Ohio Job Creation Tax Credit: State and municipal tax incentives are available for businesses that expand or locate in Ohio. State guidelines regulate the type of business and project eligible for the incentive. A business can receive a tax credit or refund against its corporate franchise tax based on the state income withheld on new, full-time employees. The amount of the tax credit can be up to 75% for up to ten years. The tax credit can exceed 75% upon recommendation of the Director of ODOD when there is an extraordinary circumstance. Municipalities can provide a similar arrangement with their local employee income taxes.

Targeted Jobs Tax Credit Program: Offers employers a credit against their federal tax liability for hiring individuals from nine target groups. TJTC benefits job seekers from groups that traditionally have had difficulty in obtaining jobs. When hiring from most target groups, employers may claim a credit of 40% of first year wages (up to $6,000 per employee) for a maximum credit of $2,400 per employee.

Export Tax Credit: Credits of up to 10% from pre-tax profits that result from expanded export operations with a cap of $250,000 per year.

Technology Investment Tax Credit: Taxpayers who invest in small, research and development and technology-oriented firms may reduce their state taxes by up to 25% of the amount they invest.

* Exports

For all items without a separate address, contact the Ohio Department of Development at the address listed above.

International Trade Division: Assists Ohio companies to develop export markets worldwide. Ohio's trade staff in Columbus, Tokyo, Hong Kong, Toronto, Mexico City, Sao Paulo, Brussels, and Tel Aviv provide custom-tailored assistance in international marketing and export finance and lead Ohio companies on trade missions and to the world's leading trade shows. Services include:
- Export Counseling
- Trade Shows and Trade Missions
- Electronic Trade

State Money - Oklahoma

- Export Finance
- Export Incentives
- Japan Trade Program

* Women and Minorities

For all items without a separate address, contact the Ohio Department of Development at the address listed above.

Minority Management and Technical Services: Provides assistance in management analysis, technical assistance, educational services and financial consulting. Supports overall growth and development of minority firms throughout the State. Counseling is provided at no charge.

Minority Contractor and Business Assistance Program: Provides management, technical, financial, and contract procurement assistance; loan, grant, bond packaging services. Networks with all levels of government, private businesses. Aids in economic growth and development of the minority community; increases awareness of local, state, and federal business assistance programs. Counseling is provided at no charge. Fees may be charged for some programs using federal funding.

Minority Contract Procurement Services: Assists primarily minority firms in procuring public and private sector contracts. Supports efforts of minority firms to obtain contract awards that will aid in sustaining and developing these firms. Counseling is provided at no charge.

Minority Business Bonding Program: Surety bonding assistance for state-certified minority businesses. Maximum bond pre-qualification of up to $1,000,000 per Minority Business. The bond premium for each bond issued will not exceed 2% of the face value of the bond.

Minority Direct Loan: Purchase or improvement of fixed assets for state-certified minority-owned businesses. Up to 40% of total project cost at 4.5% fixed for up to 10 years (maximum).

Ohio Mini-Loan Program: Fixed assets and equipment for small businesses. Start-up or existing business expansion. Projects of $100,000 or less. Up to 45% guarantee of an eligible bank loan. Interest rate of the State guarantee of the loan is currently 5.5%, and may be fixed for 10 years. Eligibility: Small business entrepreneurs with fewer than 25 employees, targeted 50% allocation to businesses owned by minorities and women.

Women's Business Resource Program: Assistance for start-up, expansion and management of businesses owned by women; assures equal access to state business assistance and lending programs; direction to purchase and procurement opportunities with government agencies. Researches legislation that may impact businesses owned by women. Increases start-ups and successes of women-owned businesses. No charge.

* Small Business Administration Offices

Gilbert Goldberg
1111 Superior Avenue, Suite 630
Cleveland, OH 44114
216-522-4180
Fax: 216-522-2038

Frank Ray
2 Nationwide Plaza, Suite 1400
Columbus, OH 43215
614-469-6860
Fax: 614-469-2391

Ronald Carlson
525 Vine Street, Suite 870
Cincinnati, OH 45202
513-684-2814
Fax: 513-684-3251

Oklahoma

Department of Commerce
900 North Stiles
P.O. Box 26980
Oklahoma City, OK 73126-0980
405-815-6552
800-879-6552.
Fax: 405-815-5199
www.locateok.com
www.odoc.state.ok.us/index.html

* Business Assistance

For all items without a separate address, contact the Oklahoma Department of Commerce at the address listed above.

Office of Business Recruitment: Provides comprehensive site location assistance to companies considering new investment in Oklahoma.

Business Development Division: Promotes growth by addressing the needs of existing and start-up businesses. Provides information and seminars directly to businesses. Offers business information and a referral network to assist companies through the maze of regulatory requirements and introduces local resource providers.

Site Location Planner: On CD-ROM and the web at {www.locateok.com}. Provides comprehensive site location data including available buildings, community information, state incentives, and statistical and other information.

Market Research:
- *National Trade Data Bank (NTDB)*-the U. S. Government's most comprehensive source of world trade data, consisting of more than 130 separate trade- and business-related programs (databases). NTDB offers one-stop-shopping for trade information from more than 20 federal sources.
- *The Economic Bulletin Board (EBB)* provides on-line trade leads, time-sensitive market information, and the latest statistical releases from a variety of federal agencies.
- *Country Commercial Guides (CCG)* present a comprehensive look at a particular country's commercial environment including economic, political, and market analysis.
- *Industry Sector Analyses (ISA)* are in-depth, structured reports on a broad range of industries regularly compiled by commercial specialists at U. S. embassies and consulates abroad.

Technology Partnerships: Testing of technologies developed by private business may be performed in partnership with research universities. Such institutions may devote resources such as laboratory usage and faculty time to a particular business's need in return for a portion of business's profits.

* Business Financing

For all items without a separate address, contact the Oklahoma Department of Commerce at the address listed above.

Oklahoma Finance Authorities: Provides permanent financing for real estate and equipment. Contact: Oklahoma Finance Authorities, 301 NW 63rd, Suite 225, Oklahoma City, OK 73116; 405-842-1145.

Small Business Linked Deposit Program: Provides below market interest rates for qualified small businesses and certified industrial parks through local financing sources. Contact Oklahoma State Treasurer's Office, 4545 N. Lincoln Blvd., #169, Oklahoma City, OK 73105; 405-522-4235.

Public Trust Financing: Oklahoma authorizes public trust financing for economic development purposes at the county and city level.

General Obligation Limited Tax Bonds: Revenue bonds are issued in association with a particular project.

Tax Increment Financing: Provides economic development in distressed areas for up to 25 years.

Sales Tax Financing: Oklahoma cities and counties are authorized, upon a vote of the people, to build facilities and provide other economic development benefits for businesses financed by sales tax collections.

Private Activity Bond Allocation: Generally allocations are on a first-come, first-served basis, with some size limitation.

Capital Investment Board: Facilitates investment in venture capital companies that focus on investing in quality Oklahoma companies. Contact: Oklahoma Capital Investment Board, 301 NW 63rd, Suite 520, Oklahoma City, OK 73116; 405-848-9456.

Capital Access Program: Provides a credit insurance reserve for Oklahoma banks through a fee-matching arrangement for loans enrolled in the program. Contact: Oklahoma Capital Investment Board, 301 NW 63rd, Suite 520, Oklahoma City, OK 73116; 405-848-9456.

Training for Industry: Assists qualifying businesses by paying for training for new employees.

Quality Jobs Program: Provides quarterly cash payments of up to 5% of new taxable payroll directly to a qualifying company, for up to ten years.

Small Employer Quality Jobs Program: Provides annual cash payments of 5% of taxable payroll for new employees to a qualifying company, for up to 5 years.

Enterprise Zones: The enterprise district management authorities created in some enterprise districts are empowered to establish venture capital loan programs and to solicit proposals from enterprises seeking to establish or expand facilities in the zones.

State Money - Oklahoma

* Tax Incentives

For all items without a separate address, contact the Oklahoma Department of Commerce at the address listed above.

Ad Valorem Tax Exemptions: New and expanding qualifying manufacturers, research and development companies, certain computer services and data processing companies with significant out-of-state sales, aircraft repair and aircraft manufacturing may be eligible for ad valorem exemptions.

Exempt Inventory: Oklahoma's Freeport Law exempts goods, wares, and merchandise from taxation that come into Oklahoma from outside the state and leave the state within nine months.

Pollution Control: Pollution control equipment that has been certified by the DEQ is exempt from Ad Valorem taxation.

Sales Tax Exemptions: Exemptions are available in the following areas: machinery and equipment used in manufacturing; tangible personal property used in manufacturing including fuel and electric power; tangible personal property which becomes part of the finished product; packaging materials; items sold by the manufacturer and immediately transported out of state for exclusive use in another state; machinery, equipment, fuels and chemicals used directly or in treating hazardous industrial waste, tangible personal property used in design and warehousing and located on the manufacturing site.

Aircraft Maintenance Facilities: Sales tax exemption on aircraft and parts.

Telecommunications: Exemptions apply to various services as part of an inducement to contract for wireless telecommunications services.

Sales and Use Tax Refunds: Refunds of sales/use tax are available for purchase of data processing equipment, related peripherals and telephone or telecommunications services or equipment and for construction materials.

Income Tax Credits/Exclusions: Reduces tax liability for the taxpayer that invests in qualifying property and also hires new employees. The credit is doubled for companies that locate in state Enterprise Zones.

Technology Transfer Income Tax Exemption: The taxable income of any corporation is decreased for transfers of technology to qualified small businesses located in Oklahoma not to exceed 10% of the amount of gross proceeds received by such corporation as a result of the technology transfer.

New Products Development Income Tax Exemption: Royalties earned by an inventor on products developed and manufactured in Oklahoma are exempt from state income tax.

Agricultural Commodity Processing Facility Income Tax Exclusion: Owners of agricultural commodity processing facilities may exclude a portion from taxable income based on investment.

Income Tax Credit for Investment in Oklahoma Producer-Owned Agriculture Processing: An income tax credit of 30% of investment is available to agricultural producer investors in Oklahoma producer-owned agricultural processing ventures, cooperative, or marketing associations.

Income Tax Credit for Computer/Data Processing/ Research & Development Jobs: Credit is available for a net increase in the number of full-time employees engaged in computer services, date processing or R & D. The credit allowed is $500 per employee, up to 50 employees.

Insurance Premium Tax Credit: Insurance companies which locate or expand regional home offices in Oklahoma are eligible for special tax credits against the tax imposed in the Insurance Code ranging from 15% to 50% based on number of full-time employees.

Small Business Capital Formation Tax Credit: Authorizes an income tax credit of 20% of equity investment for investors in qualified businesses.

Qualified Venture Capital Company Tax Credit: Freely transferable tax credits for investors in qualified venture capital companies.

Recycling, Reuse and Source Reduction Incentive Act: Manufacturing and service industries may receive an income tax credit of up to 20% of investment cost for equipment and installation or processes used to recycle, reuse, or reduce the source of hazardous waste. Credits are limited $50,000.

Income Tax Exemption for Interest Paid on Bonds: Interest payment received as a result of bonds issued by non-profit corporations on behalf of towns, cities, or counties for housing purposes are not subject to state income tax.

Tax Incentives on Former Indian Reservation Lands:
1. Employee Credit: Businesses located on qualified areas of former Indian reservations are eligible for a tax credit based on the increase in qualifying annual wages paid to enrolled Indian tribal members or their spouses. The credit equal 20% of the increased wages.
2. Depreciation Incentive: Provides a shorter recovery period of approximately 40% for most non-residential depreciable property being used in an active trade or business.

Work Opportunity Tax Credit Program: A tax credit is available up to $2,400 for each new hire from a target group of individuals.

Welfare-to-Work Tax Credit: Available to employers who hire individuals certified and long-term assistance recipients. The credit is as much as $8,500 per new hire.

Investment/Jobs: Allows a five-year tax credit on the greater of (1%) per year of investment in qualified new depreciable property or a credit of $500 per year per new job, doubled in an Enterprise Zone.

* Exports

For all items without a separate address, contact the Oklahoma Department of Commerce at the address listed above.

International Trade and Investment Division: Provides diverse services including hands on assistance for companies wishing to learn more about exporting to promoting Oklahoma products at trade shows throughout the world. Also works closely with the international business community to develop top of mind awareness of Oklahoma's business climate advantages. Provide confidential, reliable site location assistance, site selection assistance, tax comparisons, and incentive projections.

International Market Insights (IMI): Commercial specialists also regularly report on specific foreign market conditions and upcoming opportunities for U. S. business.

Customized Market Analysis (CMA): Provides detailed information needed to make the most efficient and beneficial export marketing decisions. CMA will give an accurate assessment of how a product or service will sell in a given market.

Trade Opportunities Program (TOP): Up-to-the-minute sales leads from around the world are prescreened and transmitted every work day to commercial specialists in U. S. embassies and consulates abroad.

Agent/Distributor Service (ADS): Customized search needed to successfully launch an export marketing campaign. Provides pertinent information on up to six prequalified potential representatives per market.

International Company Profiles (ICP): Thorough, up-to-date background checks on potential clients.

Country Directories of International Contacts (CDIC): Provides the name and contact information of importers, agents, trade associations, government agencies, etc., on a country-by-country basis.

Trade Fair Certification: Selects events in the countries and industries with the best opportunities for U. S. exporters. Only major shows within a given industry are certified-those that have proven to be well-established, high-quality events.

Foreign Trade Zones: Businesses engaged in international trade within these zones benefit from special customs procedures.

Export Finance Program: Assistance is available through a relationship with the Export-Import Bank of the United States to facilitate export financing with working capital guarantees, credit insurance and foreign buyer financing.

* Women and Minorities

For all items without a separate address, contact the Oklahoma Department of Commerce at the address listed above.

Women-owned Business Certification Program: Established to facilitate contracting capabilities for women-owned businesses with public and private sector entities.

Minority Business: Provides a forum to network with banking organizations, utility companies, state agencies and other that can be valuable resources for a business. Each month several business owners are selected to give a brief presentation about their business.

Minority Business Development Centers: A vehicle for small minority-owned businesses that are seeking help in start-up information. The centers provide assistance in business plans, procurement assistance and works with the SBA in the certified lenders program and 8(a) certification.

Oklahoma Minority Supplier Development Council (OMSDC): The mission of the OMSDC is to assist corporations and public sector agencies in creating a business environment that promotes access and increased opportunities for minority-owned businesses. The Council also helps to promote, educate and develop minority-owned businesses.

Oklahoma Consortium for Minority Business Development, Inc.: Provides a forum whereby government/private agencies and organizations may coordinate functions and activities to increase overall effectiveness in advocating and supporting the minority business community.

Minority Assistance Program, Office of Central Services: Created to increase the level of Oklahoma minority business participation in state purchases. The State has designated a percentage of contract awards to properly certified minority vendors.

Native American: Almost two-thirds of Oklahoma is considered "former Indian reservation land." Businesses located in these lands before the end of the year 2003 receive accelerated depreciation rates on capital investment. Federal employment tax credits are also available to businesses in these areas that employ American Indians or spouses.

State Money - Oregon

* Small Business Administration Offices

Ed Daum
210 Park Avenue, Suite 1300
Oklahoma City, OK 73102
405-231-5521
Fax: 405-231-4722

Oregon

Economic Development Department
775 Summer St., NE
Salem, OR 97310
503-986-0260
Fax: 503-581-5115
www.econ.state.or.us/javahome.htm

* Business Assistance

For all items without a separate address, contact the Oregon Economic Development Department at the address listed above.

Economic Development Department: This office can provide information and expertise in dealing with state, federal, and local agencies. They also have information on financing programs and other services offered by the state government.

Small Business Advocate: Entrepreneurs can find connections to a network of private sector advisers who can help them access capital. Inventors, entrepreneurs and mature companies can obtain information on how to access research and development federal grants, assessment of their technology concepts and innovative best practices from the technology transfer services supported by the department. All of Oregon's small and emerging businesses can benefit from the efforts of a public/private partnership to design and implement tools, incentives and policies that can make it easier to start and grow a company in Oregon. Small Business Advocate, Economic Development Department, 775 Summer St., NE, Salem, OR 97310; 503-986-0057.

Government Contract Acquisition Program (GCAP): Established to provide comprehensive information and assistance to Oregon small businesses desiring to compete in this market.

Impact: Provides business management, marketing and financing assistance to start-up, small businesses and existing business expansion.

Oregon Business Network: Helps Portland minority start-up businesses and established businesses in a group environment.

Oregon Downtown Development Association works to revitalize and maintain the heritage and economic health of Oregon's downtowns and older business districts.

Rural Development Initiatives: A non-profit corporation that builds the capacity of rural communities to make strategic decisions about their futures and to act on those decisions to ensure high quality of life and a vital economy.

Employment Department: Comprehensive source of qualified job applicants for new businesses in Oregon communities.

Industry Workforce Training: Provides grants to community colleges for the development and implementation of training programs for multiple firms within an industry. Employers must provide matching funds or in-kind services.

* Business Financing

For all items without a separate address, contact the Oregon Economic Development Department at the address listed above.

Capital Access Program: Offered through the Oregon Economic Development Department, is designed to increase the availability of loans to Oregon small businesses from banks. The program provides loan portfolio insurance so lenders may make loans that carry higher than conventional risks. Borrowers pay a fee of between 3% and 7% of the loan amount, which is matched by the department and contributed to a loan loss reserve account in an enrolled bank. The loans must be within soundness and safety requirements of federal and state banking regulations. A Capital Access Program loan is a private transaction between the borrower and lender. The Oregon Economic Development Department is not a party to loan negotiations or to the loan agreement. The department does not monitor the loan or require reporting from the borrower. Loan may be used for virtually any purpose, except to construct or purchase residential housing, to purchase real property that is not used for business operations of the borrower, or to refinance the principal balance of an existing loan.

Credit Enhancement Fund: Administered by the Oregon Economic Development Department, provides guarantees to enrolled banks to increase capital availability to small Oregon firms, helping them create jobs. The maximum guarantee for a loan is $500,000. The department has authority to guarantee up to $75 million of financial institution loans.

Entrepreneurial Development Loan Funds: Entrepreneurial businesses can receive loans of up to $25,000 through the Oregon Entrepreneurial Development Loan Fund.

Resource and Technology Development Fund: Equity-based capital is available for Oregon "basic-sector" businesses through the Oregon Resource and Technology Development Fund. Areas of focus include biological and biomedical services, high technology, and natural resource industries. For more information, contact Oregon Resource and Technology Development Fund, 4370 NE Halsey, Suite 233, Portland, OR 97213; 503-282-4462.

Oregon Enterprise Forum: Provides assistance to help companies that are in transition by providing mentoring services. For more information, contact Oregon Enterprise Forum, 2611 S.W. Third Ave., Suite 200, Portland, OR 97201; 503-222-2270.

Rural Development: Offers loan guarantees to banks to further business and industrial development in rural areas of the country. Loan guarantees may be made in any rural area or communities with a population of 50,000 or less. The maximum loan guarantee is $10 million. 10% equity is required. Projects must comply with certain federal requirements. Loans may be for land, facilities, equipment or working capital. Ineligible purposes include agricultural production (other federal programs are available for this purpose), hotels, motels, convention centers and tourist facilities. For more information, contact Rural Development Services, Business and Cooperative Programs, 101 SW Main, Suite 1410, Portland, OR 97204-3222; 503-414-3366.

Subordinated and Direct Loans: Subordinated loans usually fill a gap in a financing package, where commercial and private debt financing and equity have been maximized and additional funds are required to complete the financing transaction. Often these loans will "subordinate" or take a lesser security interest in the assets being financed, which will allow the senior lender first priority on project assets in the event of a default. The subordinated loan is often secured with additional assets to help collaterize its position. Direct loans and, in some limited cases, grants are available to finance businesses when the project will further the public objectives of the entity making the loan or grant.

Business Development Fund: Manufacturing, processing and regionally significant tourism projects are eligible for the Oregon Business Development Fund. The fund provides long-term, fixed rate financing for land, buildings, equipment and machinery.

Local Revolving Loan Funds: Many local and regional development groups and local governments throughout Oregon administer revolving loan funds for small business financing. In most cases, funding has been provided by the federal Department of Housing and Urban Development (HUD), the federal Economic Development Administration (EDA), the U.S. Department of Agriculture Rural Economic and Community Development Administration (RECD) or the Oregon Economic Development Department. Loan criteria may reflect some of the objectives of those funding organizations or may have special requirements of those agencies.

Oregon Port Revolving Fund Loans: Provides long-term loans to ports at below-market interest rates. Individual loans may be made to a maximum of $700,000 per project. The total outstanding loan amount any individual port can have at any one time cannot exceed $2 million. Funding may be used for port development projects (infrastructure) or to assist port-related private business development projects. The 23 legally formed Port Districts are the only entities eligible for Port Revolving Fund loans. The variety of projects eligible is very broad. These include, but are not limited to, water-oriented facilities, industrial parks, airports and eligible commercial or industrial developments. Projects must be located within port district boundaries. For more information contact Ports Division, Oregon Economic Development Department, 775 Summer Street NE, Salem, OR 97310; 503-986-0143.

Industrial Development Revenue Bonds: The Economic Development Commission may issue industrial development revenue bonds for manufacturing and processing facilities in Oregon. Industrial development bonds can finance fixed assets only, along with some limited transaction costs. If a project qualifies the bonds can be issued on a tax-exempt basis which lowers the overall cost of financing. Revenue bonds are not direct obligations of the State of Oregon. The individual or corporation on whose behalf the bonds are issued is legally obligated to repay them. An eligible company may borrow up to $10 million through the Oregon Industrial Development Revenue Bond Program. Typically, the minimum bond is for $2 million.

Small Scale Energy Loan Program: The Small Scale Energy Loan Program (SELP), administered by the Oregon Department of Energy, finances energy conservation and renewable energy projects in Oregon, through the issuance of general obligation bonds. Bond proceeds can be loaned to finance eligible

State Money - Pennsylvania

equipment costs, construction, certain design and consultation fees, some reserves, construction interest and most loan closing costs. Eligible costs are those incurred after loan approval. Land and working capital are normally not financed. Costs not part of the energy project also are not eligible. All Oregonians, Oregon businesses, nonprofit organizations, municipal corporations and state agencies can apply for loans. Eligible projects are those which conserve conventional energy, such as electricity and natural gas; or projects which produce renewable energy from geothermal or solar sources or from water, wind, biomass and some waste materials. For more information, contact Oregon Department of Energy, 625 Marion Street NE, Salem, OR 97310; 503-373-1033; 800-221-8035 (in OR).

Regional Development: Cities, counties and other governmental entities also can obtain loans and grants to help pay for construction projects. The department uses grant and loan funds to support public works, safe drinking water and housing rehabilitation projects. The department also provides funding for community facilities projects to improve or build day care, senior centers, emergency shelters and family counseling facilities, among others.

* Tax Incentives

For all items without a separate address, contact the Oregon Economic Development Department at the address listed above.

Corporate Income Tax Credits: Oregon businesses may be eligible for a number of tax credits allowed under Oregon law. Some of these business-related tax credits include:
- pollution control tax credit,
- business energy tax credit,
- research tax credit,
- reclaimed plastics product tax credit,
- dependent child care tax credit, and
- donation of computers and scientific equipment in Oregon.

Enterprise Zone Program: Created as a business incentive to create new jobs by encouraging business investment in economically lagging areas of the state. Construction of new facilities in an enterprise zone entitles a business to a 100% property tax abatement for three to five years on a new plant and most of the equipment installed.

Construction in Progress Exemption: Under Oregon law, new facilities are exempt from property taxes for up to two years while they are under construction and not in use on July 1 of the taxing year. The Construction in Progress Exemption also applies to any machinery or equipment installed in the unoccupied facility on July 1. The exemption does not apply to land. For more information, contact the county assessor or Oregon Department of Revenue, Property Tax Division, Room 256, Revenue Building, Salem, OR 97310; 503-945-8290.

Strategic Investment Program: Provides property tax exemptions for significant projects that will benefit Oregon's key industries. Properties developed under this program are exempted from local property taxes for up to 15 years on assessed value in excess of $100 million. With local government approval, participating companies pay property taxes on the first $100 million in assessed value for the approved project. This base amount ($100 million) is increased by 6% per year. Participating companies also make a direct community service payment to the local government equal to 25% of the abated amount, not to exceed $2 million per year. After local government approval, the Oregon Economic Development Commission is authorized to determine that the project is eligible for the program and determine the maximum eligible cost of real and personal property for the project.

* Exports

For all items without a separate address, contact the Oregon Economic Development Department at the address listed above.

International Division of the Oregon Economic Development Department: The international arm of state government. It provides "export ready" Oregon companies assistance in export markets, assists the Governor's Office on protocol and other assignments, and works with public and private organizations to promote Oregon in the international business community. The Division is located at One World Trade Center, Suite 300, 121 SW Salmon, Portland, OR 97204; 503-229-5625; 800-448-7512.

* Women and Minorities

For all items without a separate address, contact the Oregon Economic Development Department at the address listed above.

Southern Oregon Women's Access to Credit: Offers a business development program for new and existing business owners in Jackson, Josephine and Klamath counties. Focuses on training, mentoring and financing. Contact SOWAC, 33 N. Central Avenue, Suite #209, Medford, OR 97501; 541-779-3992; Fax: 541-779-5195.

Association Of Minority Entrepreneurs: A non-profit, tax exempt organization formed to promote and develop entrepreneurship and economic development for ethnic minorities in the State of Oregon. OAME works as a partnership between ethnic minorities, entrepreneurs, education, government and established corporate business. OAME provides a core of services to start-up and/or existing minority businesses. These services include:
- Technical Assistance
- Access To Capital/Loan Fund
- Capability And Opportunity Matching (OAME's Marketing/Clearinghouse)
- Administrative Services
- Incubator With & Without Walls Development

Contact Oregon Association of Minority Entrepreneurs, 4134 N. Vancouver, Portland, OR 97217; 503-249-7744; Fax: 503-249-2027.

Native American Business Entrepreneurs Network: Created by Northwest Indian Tribes to increase the success of private businesses owned by Native Americans. ONABEN's approach consists of technical training, access to capital, (conditional on an on-going consulting relationship), access to markets and mentors. The program is organized to integrate community resources. It assists and encourages tribes to share business development resources amongst themselves and with non-Indian neighbors. The program works where no predecessor has succeeded because it approaches business ownership as an expression of Native Americans' common values; inter-generation and community awareness, mutual respect, non-destructive harvest. Contact: ONABEN, 520 SW 6th Ave., Suite 930, Portland, OR 97204; 800-854-8289; {www.onaben.org}.

* Small Business Administration Offices

Phil Gentry
1515 South West Fifth Avenue, Suite 1050
Portland, OR 97201
503-326-5210
Fax: 503-326-5103

Pennsylvania

Department of Community and Economic Development
433 Forum Building
Harrisburg, PA 17120
800-379-7448
www.dced.state.pa.us

Governor's Action Team
100 Pine Street, Suite 100
Harrisburg, PA 17101
717-787-8199
Fax: 717-772-5419
www.teampa.com

* Business Assistance

For all items without a separate address, contact the Pennsylvania Department of Community and Economic Development at the address listed above.

Entrepreneurial Assistance Office: Established to ensure small business owners receive the support and assistance they require. The Entrepreneurial Assistance Office works to build an environment which encourages the creation, expansion and retention of small, women and minority owned businesses.

Small Business Resource Center: The single point of contact and hub of information for small businesses, answering state related and general business questions about licenses and permits. The Center has select state forms and applications available as well as other sources of information and technical assistance.

Environmental Business Advocate: Assists small businesses in complying with requirements of the Federal Clean Air Act and appropriate state regulations. Housed in the PA Department of Environmental Protection, (DEP), the EBA represents the interests of small businesses in matters affecting them with DCED and the U.S. Environmental Protection Agency.

Industrial Resource Centers: Assists companies in solving problems through the deployment of technologies.

State Money - Pennsylvania

Job Centers: Provide employers with a wide array of employment and training services.

Small Business Incubators: Sites where young businesses can start and grow. Offers businesses the opportunity to rent small units of space at a lower than market rate. Provides tenants with business development services that help to reduce costs and increase profits.

* Business Financing

For all items without a separate address, contact the Pennsylvania Department of Community and Economic Development at the address listed above.

PA Industrial Development Authority: Low-interest financing through Industrial Development Corporations for land and building acquisitions, construction and renovation resulting in the creation or retention of jobs. Amounts: Loans up to $1 million (within Enterprise Zones, $1.5 million) no more than 30 to 40% of the total eligible project costs, advanced technology projects and those in an Act 47 or within an Enterprise Zone qualify for lower interest rates.

Machinery and Equipment Loan Fund: Low-interest loan financing to acquire and install new or used machinery and equipment or to upgrade existing machinery and equipment. Amounts: Loans up to $500,000 or 50% of the total eligible project costs, whichever is less.

Small Business First: Funding for small businesses including: low-interest loan financing to small businesses for land and building acquisition and construction; machinery and equipment purchases and working capital; financing to comply with environmental regulations; for businesses involved in municipal or commercial recycling; and for those impacted by defense conversion. Amounts: $200,000 or 50% of the total eligible project costs, whichever is less. Maximum loan amount is $100,000 for working capital.

PA Infrastructure Investment Authority (PennVEST): Low-interest loans for design, engineering and construction of publicly and privately owned drinking water distribution and treatment facilities, storm water conveyance and wastewater treatment systems. Amounts: Loans up to $11 million per project for one municipality, up to $20 million for more than one municipality, up to $350,000 for design and engineering, up to 100% of the total project costs.

PA Capital Access Program: Through participating banks, loan guarantees are provided to support a wide variety of business purposes. Amounts: Loan guarantees up to $500,000.

PA Economic Development Financing Authority: An issuer of tax-exempt and taxable bonds, both in pooled transactions and stand-alone transactions. Bond funds are loaned to businesses and can be used to finance land, building, equipment, working capital and refinances. Amounts: Loans no less them $400,000 and no more than $10 million for manufacturers, no upper limits for other projects, up to 100% of project costs.

Customized Job Training: Provides grants to businesses in need of training assistance for new hires, retraining efforts and upgrading employees in an effort to retain and create jobs in Pennsylvania. Amounts: Grants up to 100% of the eligible costs for new job creations, grants up to 70% of eligible costs for job retention, grants up to 25% of the eligible costs for upgrade training. Contact: Office of Workforce and Technology Development, 464 Forum Bldg., Harrisburg, PA 17120; 717-787-4117.

Job Training Partnership Act: Up to 50% of wage rate for employees while in training.

Opportunity Grant Program: Provides grant funds to create or preserve jobs within the Commonwealth. Funds may be used for job training, infrastructure improvements, land and building improvements, machinery and equipment, working capital and environmental assessment and redemption. Amounts: No minimum or maximum grant amount.

Infrastructure Development Program: Grant and low-interest loan financing for public and private infrastructure improvements. Amounts: Loans and grants up to $1.25 million, no more than 20% of the annual appropriation for a single municipality.

Industrial Sites Reuse Program: Grant and low-interest loan financing is provided to perform environmental site assessment and remediation work at former industrial sites. Amounts: Grants and loans up to $200,000 for environmental assessment, grants and loans up to $1 million for remediation.

Rail Freight Assistance: Grants to build or repair rail lines and spurs. Amounts: Grants up to $250,000 for maintenance, up to $100,000 for construction.

Enterprise Zone Program: Grants available for loans to businesses: Planning Grant up to $50,000; Basic Grant up to $50,000; Competitive Grant: up to $250,000.

Industrial Resource Center Network: Provides financial and technical assistance to manufacturers to improve their manufacturing operations.

Seed Venture Program: Provides product development and working capital to early-stage venture companies.

Small Business First Export Loan Program: Provides short-term loans to meet the pre and post-export financing needs of small businesses. Amounts: Pre-Export loans: Up to $350,000 or 50% of total eligible project costs, whichever is less.

Post-Export loans: Loans not to exceed 80% of the face amount of the contract.

Underground Storage Upgrade Loan: Loans to assist owners of regulated storage tanks in upgrading their underground storage tank systems to meet federal Environmental Protection Agency upgrade requirements. Amounts: $500,000 or 75% of the total eligible project costs, whichever is less.

Challenge Grant Program: Provides grants ranging from $5,000 to $100,000 for research and development, technology transfer, joint research and development.

* Tax Incentives

For all items without a separate address, contact the Pennsylvania Department of Community and Economic Development at the address listed above.

Job Creation Tax Credits: A $1,000-per-job tax credit to approved businesses that agree to create jobs in the Commonwealth within three years.

Keystone Opportunity Zones: Zones in which businesses and residents will be exempt from virtually all state and local taxes.

Manufacturing, processing and research and development activities are exempt from the Capital Stock and Franchise Tax.

Pollution control devices are exempt from the Capital Stock and Franchise Tax.

Machinery and equipment used in manufacturing are exempt from the Sales and Use Tax.

Computer services are exempt from the Sales and Use Tax.

Machinery and equipment, business inventories and personal property are exempt from Pennsylvania's real property tax.

Improvements to property can be exempted from the real property tax for up to ten years.

Capital gains are taxed at a rate of 2.8%.

Films: A sales tax exemption is available for most purchases made by producers of full-length feature films.

Local Economic Revitalization Tax Assistance Act: Local municipalities, school districts and counties can offer up to 100% abatements on property taxes for up to 10 years.

Neighborhood Assistance Tax Credit: Up to 70% of the amount invested in programs that help families or communities in impoverished areas.

Employment Incentive Payments Program: Provides credits to employers that hire welfare recipients.

Enterprise Zone Credit Program: Allows corporations a tax credit of up to 20% on investments to rehabilitate or improve buildings or land in an Enterprise Zone.

* Exports

For all items without a separate address, contact the Pennsylvania Department of Community and Economic Development at the address listed above.

Headquartered in Harrisburg, the Office of International Business Development maintains offices around the world. The Office, together with the Team Pennsylvania Export Network Regions, supports Pennsylvania firms wishing to do business in the overseas market. The Office coordinates a range of trade development activities including:
- industry sector trade initiatives
- provision of market intelligence
- export financing programs
- in-country support for firms in association with the Commonwealth's overseas offices

Contact Office of International Business Development, 308 Forum Building, Harrisburg, PA 17120; 888-PA EXPORT.

* Women and Minorities

For all items without a separate address, contact the Pennsylvania Department of Community and Economic Development at the address listed above.

PA Minority Business Development Authority: Low-interest loan financing to businesses which are owned and operated by minorities. Amounts: Manufacturing, industrial, high-tech, international trade or franchise companies with loans up to $500,000 (within Enterprise Zones, $750,000) or 75% of total eligible project costs, whichever is less, retail or commercial firms loans of up to $250,000 ($350,000 in Enterprise Zones).

Minority Business Development Agency: Provides minority entrepreneurs with management and technical assistance services to start, expand, or mange a business.

National Minority Supplies Development Council: A non-profit corporation chartered in 1972 to expand business opportunities for minority owned companies, to encourage mutually beneficial economic links between minority

State Money - Rhode Island

suppliers and the public and private sectors, and to help build a stronger, more equitable society by supporting and promoting minority business development.

Pennsylvania Minority Business Development Authority: Offers low interest loan financing to businesses that are owned and operated by minorities. Maximum loan amount is $500,000 or $750,000 depending on whether the business is located in a targeted area and the nature of the business.

50 Best Women in Business: Awards program recognizes and applauds the significant contributions Pennsylvania's women business owners and leaders make to their communities, to their families and to their work.

Minority Business Advocate: Encourages the development of minority-owned businesses as part of the overall economic development strategy of the Commonwealth. Serves as an advocate for minority owned business owners in resolving issues with state agencies and interacting with other government agencies.

Women's Business Advocate: Works to assist women businesses in the development of their business, specifically assisting in resolving issues with state agencies, exploring marketing options and identifying financing strategies.

Bureau of Contract Administration and Business Development (Formerly the Minority and Women Business Enterprise Office): Benefits small, minority and women businesses. Provides the necessary resources and direction for business owners to compete for and participate in the state contracting process. Furthermore, it is the statewide agency for certification as a Minority Business Enterprise and Women Business Enterprise.

* Small Business Administration Offices

Kerry Kirkland
Robert N.C. Nix Federal Bldg.
900 Market St., 5th Floor
Philadelphia, PA 19107
215-580-2807
Fax: 215-580-2800

Tom Tolan
Robert N.C. Nix Federal Bldg
900 Market St., 5th Floor
Philadelphia, PA 19107
215-580-2700
Fax: 215-580-2800

Al Jones
1000 Liberty Avenue, Room 1128
Pittsburgh, PA 15222
412-395-6560
Fax: 412-395-6562

Vacant
100 Chesnut Street, Suite 107
Harrisburg, PA 17101
570-826-6497
Fax: 570-826-6287

7 North Wilkes-Barre Boulevard, Suite 407
Wilkes-Barre, PA 18702
717-782-3840
Fax: 717-782-4839

Rhode Island

Economic Development Corporation
One West Exchange St.
Providence, RI 02903
401-222-2601
Fax: 401-222-2102
www.riedc.com

* Business Assistance

For all items without a separate address, contact the Rhode Island Economic Development Corporation at the address listed above.

Economic Development Corporation: This office can provide information and expertise in dealing with state, federal, and local agencies. They also have information on financing programs and other services offered by the state government.

Economic Development Set Aside: The Set-Aside for Economic Development is designed to provide matching job training funds to companies that are either relocating to Rhode Island or expanding present operations in the state. The funds are used for the training of new employees through either customized training programs or on the job training.

Customized Upgrade Training to Improve Productivity: This program allows an employer to upgrade the skills of existing employees, thus improving the productivity of the business. The program awards matching grants of up to $25,000 per company through a competitive Request for Proposal process. In some cases, the company will be a fast growing firm, while others may be marginal with the training program becoming part of an overall business strategy to improve competitiveness. Businesses are urged to work through trade associations and local colleges and universities to increase the effectiveness of the training programs.

Customized Training (new hires): This type of program involves occupational skills with training provided either by the employer or by an outside trainer. The training location can be the employer's worksite or at an educational facility (or some combination). The employer makes the final decision on program design, curriculum content, and trainee selection.

First Stop Business Center: Helps businesses deal with federal, state, and local requirements and provides information and referral assistance. Contact First Stop Business Center, 100 North Main St., Providence, RI 02903; 401-277-2185; Fax: 401-277-3890; {www.state.ri.us/bus/frststp.htm}.

* Business Financing

For all items without a separate address, contact the Rhode Island Economic Development Corporation at the address listed above.

Industrial Revenue Bonds: Industrial Revenue Bonds may be used to finance qualified commercial and industrial projects. The bonds offer a competitive interest rate and state sales tax exemption on building materials that may be significant for projects involving new construction. Financing is available through the Rhode Island Industrial Facilities Corporation and covers the entire project cost. The project and the credit of the user provides the security for the bonds which may be issued on the financial strength of the user when the user is appropriately rated. The bonds may also be issued with an enhancement letter of credit from a financial institution.

Tax-Exempt "Small Issue Bonds": Under the small-issue bond provisions of the Omnibus Budget Reconciliation Act of 1993, interest on certain bonds with face amounts of less than $10 million is excluded from income if at least 95% of the bonds' proceeds is used to finance manufacturing facilities. Industrial Revenue Bonds are tax-exempt obligations of the issuer, the interest on which is exempt from federal and state income tax. The interest rate on such obligations is normally below that available for conventional mortgages.

Bond and Mortgage Insurance Program: The Program reduces the capital necessary for new manufacturing facilities, renovation of manufacturing facilities, the purchase of new machinery and equipment in financing projects up to $5,000,000.

The Small Business Loan Fund: The SBLF provides eligible Small Business Fixed Asset Loans from $25,000 to a maximum of $150,000 and Working Capital Loans to a maximum of $30,000.

Ocean State Business Development Authority: Through the SBA 504 and 7A program the Authority can provide up to 90% financing on loan requests to $2,000,000 with a participating bank. Loan proceeds may be used to purchase land, renovate, or construct buildings and acquire new and used machinery and equipment.

Seafood Revolving Loan Fund: Eligible Applicants - R. I. Seafood Industry, Dollar Limit Per Project - Maximum: $150,000, Approved Use Of Funds - New equipment. Rehabilitation of existing fishing equipment. Funds to start up non-fishing businesses.

Samuel Slater Innovation Partnership Program: Designed to provide public-sector supporting funds on a matching, cost reimbursement basis to private-sector initiated activities designed to improve the competitiveness of Rhode Island-based firms. It is designed to foster and support efforts by companies to increase their competitiveness through the development and/or better use of technology that directly and indirectly lead to an improved Rhode Island economy. By the nature of this program, the EPC is looking for creative, yet feasible, approaches to improving their industrial competitiveness through collaboration with institution of higher education and/or other firms or through the development of new technology-based businesses. A total of $1,375,000 in matching funds is available in the Innovation Partnership Program and will be awarded on a competitive, merit basis in three distinct grant programs:
- Industry-Higher Education Partnership Grants Available Funds: $750,000
- Multi-firm Collaboration Grants Available Funds: $500,000
- Technology Entrepreneur Seed Grants Available Funds: $125,000

State Money - Rhode Island

* Tax Incentives

For all items without a separate address, contact the Rhode Island Economic Development Corporation at the address listed above.

No Income Tax for Insurance Carriers.

Passive Investment Tax Exemption: A corporation's investment income may be exempt from the Rhode Island income tax if it confines its activity to the maintenance and management of its passive intangible assets, maintains an office in Rhode Island, and employs at least five persons in Rhode Island.

Telecommunication Sales Tax Exemption: Regulated investment companies with at least 500 full-time equivalent employees are exempt from the sales and use tax imposed on toll-free terminating telecommunication service.

Insurance and Mutual Holding Companies: Rhode Island allows a mutual insurance company to create a mutual holding company, owned by the policy holders exactly as they now own the mutual company. This holding company, however, would then own the actual insurance company as a stockholder, while the insurance company itself could issue stock to raise capital. The process could be controlled by the mutual holding company, which means that policyholders would be protected from any dilution of control over the majority stockholder of the company. Policyholders ownership of the insurance subsidiary would be shared with other stockholders only to the extent that they choose to issue stock to raise capital for expansion.

Captive Insurance Companies: Rhode Island allows captive insurance companies to capitalize with a letter of credit or cash as in other states.

Insurance Company Retaliatory Tax Exemption: Foreign insurance companies are exempt from gross premiums retaliatory taxes in Rhode Island when their home jurisdiction does not impose a like tax.

Income Allocation Modification for Manufacturers of Medical Instruments and Supplies (SIC Code 384) and Drugs (SIC Code 283): A Rhode Island manufacturer of Medical Instruments and Supplies or Drugs registered and certified by the United States Food and Drug Administration with a place of business outside the state may modify the numerator in the allocation formula for the current tax year.

4% Credit for Equipment and Facilities Used in Manufacturing: Manufacturers may take a 4% tax credit for new tangible personal and other tangible property that is located in Rhode Island and is principally used by the taxpayer in the production of goods by manufacturing, processing, or assembling.

Research and Development Expense Credit: A special Rhode Island credit is allowed against the business corporation taxes and Rhode Island personal income tax for qualified research expenses. The credit is computed at 22.5% of the expense as defined in Section 41 of the Internal Revenue Code for companies increasing research and development expenditures, making Rhode Island the highest in the nation. The credit drops to 16.9% for R&D expenditures above the first $25,000 of credit. Unused credit may be carried forward for up to seven years.

Rhode Island Job Training Tax Credit: A special Rhode Island credit allows companies to receive a credit of $5,000 per employee against the business corporation taxes in any three year period against the cost of offering training and/or retraining to employees. This tax credit is critically important to existing Rhode Island employers, which formerly were not provided any tax incentives for the retraining of existing employees. With this tax credit, Rhode Island businesses will be able to reduce costs, be more efficient, and add to their competitiveness.

Rhode Island Employer's Apprenticeship Tax Credit: The annual credit allowed is 50% of the actual wages paid to the qualifying apprentice or $4,800, whichever is less. The credit applies to the following trades in the metal and plastic industries: machinist, toolmaker, modelmaker, gage maker, patternmaker, plastic process technician, tool & machine setter, diesinker, moldmaker, tool & die maker, machine tool repair.

Educational Assistance and Development Credit: A credit is 8% of the contribution in excess of $10,000 made to a Rhode Island institution of higher education and the contribution is to be for the establishment or maintenance of programs of scientific research or education. "Contributions" include the cost or other basis (for federal income tax purposes) in excess of $10,000 of tangible personal property excluding sale discounts and sale-gift arrangements concerning the purchase of equipment. Amounts of unused credit may be carried over for 5 years and documentation of the credit requires a written statement from the institution.

Adult Education Tax Credit: The Rhode Island Adult Education Tax Credit allows for both a worksite and nonworksite tax credit for vocational training or basic education of 50% of the costs incurred up to a maximum of $300 per employee and $5,000 per employer per calendar year.

Child and Adult Daycare Tax Credit: Credits are available against the business corporation tax, the bank excise tax, the insurance companies gross premiums tax and the personal income tax. These credits are computed at 30% of the amount of Rhode Island licensed daycare purchased and 30% of the cost to establish and/or operate a Rhode Island licensed daycare facility whether established and/or operated by the taxpayer alone or in conjunction with others. The maximum annual credit for purchased daycare is $30,000 per year and the amounts of unused credit may not be carried forward. For daycare facilities and rents/lease foregone, the maximum total credit is $30,000 per year and amounts of unused may be carried forward for 5 years.

Tax Incentives for Employers to hire unemployed Rhode Island Residents: The incentive of 40% of an eligible employee's first year wages up to a maximum of $2,400 may be used to reduce the gross Rhode Island income of businesses and individuals that employ and retain previously unemployed Rhode Island residents.

SBA Credit for Loan Grantee Fee: A small business may take a tax credit equal to any guaranty fee they pay to the United States Small Business Administration pursuant to obtaining SBA financing.

Rhode Island Enterprise Zone Program Tax Benefits: Rhode Island offers an Enterprise Zone Program developed to revitalize distressed urban areas in Rhode Island. The program provides an aggressive and comprehensive incentive package to businesses willing to relocate or expand into the designated Enterprise Zones.

Wage Differential Tax Credit: A qualified business having a minimum of 25% Enterprise workers may receive credits against the State business corporation or personal income tax of 50% of wages and salaries paid to qualified Enterprise workers in excess of the wages and salaries paid to those employees in the prior year. Enterprise Zone businesses must increase their employment by at least 5% to qualify for the Wage Differential Tax Credit.

Resident Business Owner Tax Modification: Business owners who operate a qualified business and who live in the same Enterprise Zone are eligible for a three year modification of $50,000 from their federal adjusted gross income when computing their state income tax liability and a $25,000 modification for years four and five.

Interest Income Tax Credit: Corporations or taxpayers that make new loans to qualified Enterprise Zone businesses are eligible to receive a 10% tax credit on interest earned from the loan. The maximum credit per taxpayer is $10,000 per year.

Donation Tax Credit: A taxpayer is eligible for a credit of 20% for any cash donation against the state tax imposed for donations to public supported improvement projects in the zone.

Tax Credit Available to Certified Mill Building Owner(s): A specialized investment tax credit equal to 10% of the cost of the substantial rehab. The rehab must occur within two years following certification.

Tax Credits Available to Lenders: A credit equal to 10% of the interest earned on loans to eligible businesses. Maximum of $10,000 per taxable year. A credit equal to 100% of the interest on loans made solely and exclusively for the purpose of substantial rehab of a Certified Building. Maximum of $20,000 per taxable year.

Tax Credits Available to Eligible Businesses: Eligible businesses must meet the requirements of Enterprise Zone year end certification. A credit equal to 100% of the wages paid to new employees with a maximum credit of $3,000 per new employee.

Alternative Transportation: 50% of the capital, labor, and equipment costs incurred by businesses for construction of or improvements to any filling station that provides alternative fuel or recharging of electric vehicles and 50% of the incremental costs incurred by a taxpayer for the purchase of alternative fueled motor vehicles or for the cost of converting vehicles into alternative fueled vehicles. The amount of either of the two credits may be transferred by one taxpayer to another if the transferee is a parent, subsidiary, affiliate, or is subject to common ownership, management, and control with the transferor. A taxpayer who has not transferred a credit and whose credit exceeds its tax liability may carry forward any unused portion of the credit to one or more of the succeeding five years.

Disabled Access Credit for Small Business: The expenses must be made to enable the small business to comply with federal or state laws protecting the rights of persons with disabilities. The credit is equal to 10% of the total amount expended during the tax year in Rhode Island, up to a maximum of $1,000, for removing architectural, communication, physical, or transportation barriers; providing qualified interpreters or other effective methods of delivering aurally delivered materials to persons with hearing impairments; providing readers, tapes, or other effective means of making visually delivered materials available to persons with visual impairments; providing job coaches or other effective means of supporting workers with severe impairments in competitive employment; providing specialized transportation services to employees or customers with mobility impairments; buying or modifying equipment for persons with disabilities; and providing similar services, modifications, material or equipment for persons with disabilities.

Sales and Use Tax Exemptions: Manufacturers' machinery and equipment is exempt; Manufacturers' machinery, equipment, replacement parts and computer software used in the manufacturing process are exempt.

State Money - South Carolina

Professional Services: Services such as those provided by physicians, attorneys, accountants, engineers, and others are exempt. However, the tax applies to any tangible personal property that may be sold at retail by such professionals (i.e.--opera glasses, field glasses, etc.).

Occupational Services: Services such as provided by barbers, beauty parlors, bootblacks, cleaning and pressing shops, laundries, and similar service establishments are exempt. However, if delivery to the purchaser or his agent is consummated within, the tax applies to any tangible personal property that may be sold at retail by such establishments.

Sales in interstate commerce: A shipment by common carrier, United States mail, or delivery facilities not operated by the seller to a purchaser outside Rhode Island is not subject to the tax. If the purchaser takes delivery within the state, the tax applies.

Intangibles: Sales or transfers of intangible personal property such as stocks, bonds, accounts receivable, money, or insurance policies are exempt.

Pollution Control Equipment: Sales of air and water pollution control equipment for incorporation into or used and consumed directly in the operation of a facility or installation approved by the Rhode Island Director of Environmental Management are exempt.

Precious Metal: Sales of precious metal bullion are exempt.

Scientific Equipment: Sales of scientific equipment, computers, software and related items to a qualifying firm to be used predominantly by that firm for research and development purposes. The qualifying firm must furnish the vendor with a Rhode Island Research and Development Exemption Certificate.

Boat Sales: The sale of boats has been exempted from the state sales tax. Boats are also exempt from local property taxes.

Local Property Taxes: Intangible property is not taxed.

Inventory & Equipment Tax Exemption For Manufacturer: Manufacturers' machinery and equipment used in the production process and inventories of manufacturers in Rhode Island are exempt from property taxes.

Real Estate Property Tax Exemption/Stabilization: Any city or town in Rhode Island may exempt or stabilize the tax on real and personal property used for manufacturing, or commercial purposes, for a period not exceeding ten years. The incentive may not be used to encourage a firm to move from one municipality to another in Rhode Island.

Property Tax Exemption/Stabilization For Wholesaler's Inventory: Any city or town in Rhode Island may exempt or stabilize the tax on a wholesaler's inventory for a period of up to twenty five years. The incentive may not be used to encourage a firm to move from one municipality to another in Rhode Island.

Property Tax Exemption/Stabilization Office Equipment: Any city or town in Rhode Island may exempt or stabilize the tax on computers, telephone equipment and other office personal property for a period of up to twenty five years. The incentive may not be used to encourage a firm to move from one municipality to another in Rhode Island.

Energy Related Property Tax Exemptions: For local tax purposes, solar, wind, or cogeneration equipment shall not be assessed at more than the value of the conventional heating, cooling, or energy production capacity that would otherwise be necessary to install in the building.

Air and Water Pollution Control Equipment: Air and water pollution control equipment used to treat waste water and air contaminants produced as the result of industrial processing is exempt from local property taxes for ten years and may continue to remain exempt with municipal approval.

Hazardous Waste Equipment: Tangible personal property used for the recycling, recovery or reuse of "hazardous waste" generated by the same taxpayer on the same or adjacent property is exempt.

Capital Gains Reduction: Employees of qualified firms are exempt from paying Rhode Island Personal Income Tax on profits made from selling company stock. This law exempts current and former employees of qualified companies and their heirs from paying any state tax on capital gains resulting from the sale of stock or the purchase of stock options.

Estate and Gift Tax: An estate is required to file Rhode Island Estate Tax Form 100 with a $25 filing fee. There is no Estate Tax unless the gross value of the estate exceeds $600,000 and there is no surviving spouse. Then, the Estate Tax due is an amount equal to the Federal Credit apportioned to Rhode Island. Rhode Island has no *Gift Tax*.

Foreign Sales Corporation: Rhode Island Foreign Sales Corporations (FSC's) are exempt from the business corporation tax.

* Exports

For all items without a separate address, contact the Rhode Island Economic Development Corporation at the address listed above.

International Trade Partnership: As the official arm of state government, RIEDC is the principal liaison with foreign governments and hosts in-coming trade delegations from other countries. As the entity charged with developing the state's economic agenda, RIEDC is the partner responsible for providing business services directly to companies. These services include: development and execution of trade shows and trade missions; customized export management training and general trade assistance to Rhode Island companies.

* Small Business Administration Offices

Mark Hayward
380 Westminster Mall, 5th Floor
Providence, RI 02903
401-528-4561
Fax: 401-528-4539

South Carolina

Department of Commerce
P.O. Box 927
Columbia, SC 29202
803-737-0400
877-751-1262
Fax: 803-737-0418
www.callsouthcarolina.com

* Business Assistance

For all items without a separate address, contact the South Carolina Department of Commerce at the address listed above.

Department of Commerce: This office can provide information and expertise in dealing with state, federal, and local agencies. They also have information on financing programs and other services offered by the state government.

Enterprise Development, Inc.: Develops strategic initiatives and business resources for new capital investments. Initiatives are in the development of finances, technology and human resources.

South Carolina Research Authority: A public, self-funded, non-profit organization that works to attract and support technology-based companies in South Carolina by: encouraging collaboration between industry, government, and educational institutions; providing unique site locations in specialized research parks; offering technology management specialization. Contact: South Carolina Research Authority, P.O. Box 12025, Columbia, SC 29211; 803-799-4070; {www.scra.org}.

* Business Financing

For all items without a separate address, contact the South Carolina Department of Commerce at the address listed above.

Industrial Revenue Bonds
Jobs-Economic Development Authority (JEDA)
Small Business Administration
Economic Development Administration
Farmers Home Administration
Carolina Capital Investment Corporation: A bank consortium administered by JEDA to provide funding to small, growth oriented firms.

Taxable and Tax-Exempt Industrial Development Bonds: Bond for individual company funding range from $1 million to $10 million.

Taxable Bond Financing Program: Assists commercial business and real estate development firms with affordable long-term debt financing. Proceeds may be used to fund the acquisition, construction or renovation of buildings and land, the purchase of new or used equipment, and for working capital purposes as well as the refinancing of existing debt.

Venture Capital Funding: Loans to businesses for innovative products or processes.

* Tax Incentives

For all items without a separate address, contact the South Carolina Department of Commerce at the address listed above.

Jobs Tax Credit: Provides income tax credits for companies locating in or expanding current business in any county in South Carolina ranging from $1,500 to $4,500.

Child Care Credit: Payments made to licensed and/or registered child care facilities for the benefit of an employee are eligible for a credit against state corporate income tax not to exceed a maximum of $3,000 per employee.

Corporate Headquarters Credit: Firms establishing headquarters or expanding existing headquarters in South Carolina are eligible for credits to state corporate income taxes or corporate license fees.

State Money - South Dakota

Net Operating Loss: Net operating losses incurred may be carried forward for up to 15 years.

Credit for Former Military Employees: Offers a credit to state corporate income taxes of 10% of the first $10,000 of income per employee to firms hiring laid off defense workers.

Sales and Use Tax Exemptions: The following items are exempt for manufacturers from sales and use tax: production machinery and equipment; repair parts; materials which will become an integral part of the finished product; industrial electricity and fuels used in the manufacturing process; packaging materials.

Property Tax Exemptions: The following items are exempt from property tax: manufacturing inventory; intangible property; facilities or equipment of industrial plants designed for elimination, mitigation, prevention, treatment, abatement, or control of water, air, or noise pollution.

Other Corporate Income Tax Incentives:
- Tax credits for investments in infrastructure
- No unitary taxes on worldwide profits
- No wholesale sales taxes
- No value-added taxes
- No intangible taxes
- Five year moratorium on county ordinary property taxes for manufacturing, distribution, corporate headquarters and office facilities
- Opportunity for large investors to negotiate a fee in lieu of county property taxes

Enterprise Program: Offers tax advantages for new jobs to businesses located anywhere in the state.

* Exports

For all items without a separate address, contact the South Carolina Department of Commerce at the address listed above.

Trade Development Program: Mission is twofold: to increase awareness among South Carolina companies of world market profitability and the valuable export resources available; and to promote South Carolina companies and products to prospective overseas importers, resulting in an increased international market share and direct sales for South Carolina companies.
- Hands-on trade services include such matters as answering export-related inquiries and extending referrals to other export assistance providers. In addition, they regularly co-host trade-related conferences and seminars.
- Promotional activities include assistance to and the recruitment of companies for participation in trade shows and trade missions overseas and the hosting of visiting international trade missions sourcing South Carolina products. These activities are accomplished through staff-organized meetings with South Carolina manufacturers.
- Technological capabilities allow the trade staff to provide the most efficient service through both targeted events scheduling, and the ability to disseminate the most current international sales leads and trade-related reports to South Carolina firms with the push of a button.
- Exporters Database & Directory allows the matching of South Carolina firms with overseas requests for products, and serves as a resource for storing useful promotional information on in-state exporters. South Carolina firms may request their addition to this database, which doubles as the trade programs' mailing list, by completing an Export Questionnaire available from their office.

Export Trade and Finance Program: Assistance through financial counseling, facilitating services and lending/guarantee program.

Foreign Trade Zones: Operating with an FTZ offers several cost benefits: possible reduction or elimination of customs duty, deferral of duty payment, efficiency gains of bypassing customs through direct delivery.

* Small Business Administration Offices

Elliott Cooper
1835 Assembly Street
Room 358
Columbia, SC 29201
803-765-5339
Fax: 803-765-5962

South Dakota

Governor's Office of Economic Development
711 East Wells Ave.
Pierre, SD 57501-3369
605-773-5032
800-872-6190
Fax: 605-773-3256
www.state.sd.us/goed

* Business Assistance

For all items without a separate address, contact the South Dakota Governor's Office of Economic Development at the address listed above.

Governor's Office of Economic Development: This office can provide information and expertise in dealing with state, federal, and local agencies. They also have information on financing programs and other services offered by the state government

Workforce Development Program: Trains new employees, retrains current employees, and upgrades current employee skills.

* Business Financing

For all items without a separate address, contact the South Dakota Governor's Office of Economic Development at the address listed above.

Economic Development Finance Authority: Allows enterprises to pool tax-exempt or taxable development bonds for the purpose of constructing any site, structure, facility, service or utility for the storage, distribution or manufacturing of industrial or agricultural or nonagricultural products or the purchase of machinery and equipment used in an industrial process. Generally, the Authority will not consider loan requests for enterprises for amounts less than $300,000 and will not pool projects unless the pool volume is $1 million or more.

Revolving Economic Development and Initiative (REDI) Fund: Objective is to create "primary jobs" in South Dakota. Primary jobs are defined as "jobs that provide goods and services which shall be primarily exported from the state, gain market shares from imports to the state or meet an unmet need in the area resulting in the creation of new wealth in South Dakota. Primary jobs are derived from businesses that bring new income into an area, have a stimulative effect on other businesses or assist a community in diversification and stabilization of its economy." All for-profit businesses or business cooperatives are encouraged to apply, whether they are business start-ups, expansions, or relocations from outside South Dakota. The REDI Fund may provide up to 45% of the total project cost and requires the applicant to secure the matching funds before applying to the Board of Economic Development for the REDI Fund, including a 10% minimum equity contribution.

Bond Financing: For capital intensive projects, offers a pooled or stand-alone tax-exempt or taxable development bond issue.

* Tax Incentives

South Dakota is one of only two states with no corporate income tax, no personal income tax, no personal property tax and no business inventory tax.

* Exports

For all items without a separate address, contact the South Dakota Governor's Office of Economic Development at the address listed above.

International Trade Directory: Identifies South Dakota traders (i.e. exporters and importers) of manufactured products, agribusiness products, services and technologies. The directory also offers a list of various private companies and public agencies that are available to serve the special needs of South Dakota exporters and importers. Exporters Directory is available in hard copy upon request. Contact: Mr. Joop Bollen, South Dakota International Business Institute - NSU, 1200 S. Jay Street, Aberdeen, SD 57401-7198; 605-626-3149; Fax: 605-626-3004; {E-mail: bollenj@wolf.northern.edu}.

Foreign Direct Investment: For information on Foreign Direct Investment opportunities in South Dakota, contact one of the out-of-state development specialists at the Governor's Office of Economic Development.

* Small Business Administration Offices

Gene VanArsdale
110 South Phillips Avenue
Suite 200
Sioux Falls, SD 57104
605-330-4231
Fax: 605-330-4215

State Money - Tennessee

Tennessee

Department of Economic and Community Development
Rachel Jackson Building, 8th Floor
320 Sixth Avenue North
Nashville, TN 37243-0405
615-741-1888
Fax: 615-741-7306
www.state.tn.us

* Business Assistance

For all items without a separate address, contact the Tennessee Department of Economic and Community Development at the address listed above.

ACCE$$: The Nashville Area Chamber of Commerce, U.S. Small Business Administration and area banks started a financing program for small businesses. ACCE$$ serves the small business loan market, booking loans of $5000 and up. The program enables entrepreneurs the opportunity to present their business plans orally to a panel of bank loan officers. Panelists can qualify good credit risks immediately, improving the presenter's chances of obtaining an SBA guarantee. Regardless of the decision, small business owners receive valuable outside appraisal of their business plans. Contact: Nashville Area Chamber of Commerce, 161 Fourth Ave. N., Nashville, TN 37219; 615-259-4755; {www.nashvillechamber.com}.

Self Help: There are two self help resource centers sponsored by Nations Bank and 1st Tennessee. The centers offer information on starting a business; preparing business plans; pro forma financial statements, small business management.

- 1st Tennessee has sponsored a center at the Memphis Public Library, Main Branch, 1850 Peabody, Memphis, TN 38104; 901-725-8877. It is open library hours. Nations Bank operates their own Business Resource Center at their West End Office in Nashville and Beale Street Office in Memphis. Each center has a large business library, plus PC-based access to national magazines and newspapers. They offer videos, cassettes and slide presentations, as well as self-help guides. Entrepreneurs do not have to be bank clients to use the centers and can even schedule early evening appointments with bank staff. Contact TN Small Business Center, 3401 West End Avenue, Suite 110, Nashville, TN 37203-1069; 615-749-4088; 800- 342-8217 Ext. 4088; or Business Resource Center, 555 Beale Street, Memphis, TN 38103; 901-526-9300.
- The Tennessee Economic Development Center provides conference rooms equipped with video conferencing and multimedia capability. The demonstration room offers computers with internet access that is available for people wishing to conduct research related to business and economic development.

Manufacturing Services: Utilizes field representatives, each with extensive industrial experience and expertise, to work with Tennessee's existing industries as they strive to succeed in today's competitive marketplace. Through its Manufacturing Means Jobs Initiative the division seeks to provide businesses an environment in which to prosper and expand, creating new jobs in the process and adding strength to the state's economic growth.

Agricultural Extension Service: Assistance in areas such as research based agricultural practices, agribusiness management, small and home based businesses in a rural setting. The extension service can draw on the resources of the university for many areas of technical expertise in rural based businesses.

Consulting Services: There are several no fee consulting services available in Tennessee. Funded by federal, state, local and private sources; these services can aid business owners in a variety of ways. However, these services are in great demand. In order to maximize the effectiveness of the programs, new business owners should examine their situations to determine the most appropriate form of assistance.

For these services, contact Tennessee Economic Development Center, Bellsouth Building, 300 Commerce Street, Nashville, TN 37201-33011; 615-214-3003.

Industrial Extension:
1. University of Tennessee Center for Industrial Services: CIS is a state wide industrial extension program dedicated to helping managers of Tennessee business and manufacturing firms find solutions to technical and managerial problems they face. CIS provides information and counseling services and strives to link resources of higher education with industrial needs. Contact UT Center for Industrial Services, Suite 401 Capitol Boulevard Building, Nashville, TN 37219-1804; 615-532-8657.
2. Tennessee Technological University Center for Manufacturing Research and Technology Utilization: The Manufacturing Center was created to help improve the manufacturing productivity of state industry and to enhance instructional quality in manufacturing-related areas. The Center seeks to assist industry not only in research and development, but also in integrating manufacturing processes with a systems approach. At any given time in the Manufacturing Center, over 30 separate, but complimentary projects may be in progress. Contact Tennessee Tech Manufacturing Center, College of Business Administration, TTU Box 5077, Cookeville, TN 38505; 615-372-6634; Fax: 423-372-6249.

Management Consulting: Service Corps of Retired Executives/Active Corps of Executives is a national volunteer organization of executives (both active and retired) who can provide both counseling and training to entrepreneurs and business owners. SCORE members come from many different industries and can contribute valuable expertise in either a single counseling session or in a long term no fee consulting relationship. Counseling is available to any business and can be profitably employed by stable businesses wishing to consider long range objectives and expansion plans. SCORE/ACE is also active in conducting seminars and workshops for those interested in starting new businesses.

Small Business Incubation Centers: Incubation centers offer a low cost way for entrepreneurs to start their businesses in an office/light manufacturing environment. Offering low cost rental rates per square foot, incubators also offer shared resources such as conference rooms, utility hook ups, office copiers, some telephone support. The most valuable commodity they offer is a shared environment in which business owners can discuss common problems and reach solutions.

Small Business Information Guide: A resource manual that assists start-up and existing small businesses with issues like state and federal business taxes, business regulations and government assisted funding programs.

Industrial Training Service: Helps recruit, screen and train new employees, provide job-specific training and overall workforce development. They partner with over 40 community colleges, and technical institutes and technology centers across the state.

* Business Financing

For all items without a separate address, contact the Tennessee Department of Economic and Community Development at the address listed above.

Small And Minority Owned Telecommunications Business Assistance Program (Loan Guarantee): Designed to enhance and stimulate the growth, development and procurement opportunities for small, minority, and women owned businesses in the telecommunications industry in Tennessee.

Revolving Loan Funds: Available through nine community development corporations in Tennessee. The revolving loan fund combines funds secured from the Economic Development Administration and Farmer's Home Administration with regional funding sources to provide new or expanding businesses with financing at below market rates.

Tennessee Valley Authority Special Opportunity Counties Program: Designed to provide capital to finance projects which support the recruitment of new industry, the expansion of existing industry, the growth of small business, and the creation of new companies in the Tennessee Valley.

a) The Economic Development Loan Fund (EDLF): $20 million per year revolving loan program targeted on low interest loans to established companies relocating or expanding their operations in the Tennessee Valley. Loans are made for buildings, plant equipment, infrastructure, or property based on the capital investment leveraged, the number of jobs created, power load generated and geographic diversity. TVA Economic Development staff market the program, manage the loan review process, and manage the loan portfolio. Primary Focus: Sustained Growth.

b) Special Opportunities County Fund: $15 million revolving loan program targeted on low interest loans for companies expanding or relocating in the Tennessee Valley's most economically distressed counties. Loans are made for buildings, plant equipment, infrastructure, or property based on the capital investment leveraged and the number of jobs created. TVA Economic Development staff market the program, manage the loan review process, and manage the loan portfolio. Primary Focus: Sustained Growth.

c) Valley Management Inc.: $15 million fund designed to invest in equity or debt to finance the growth and development of socially and financially disadvantaged businesses. VMI will consider investments in start-up, growth, or established companies and finance their working capital, building, or plant equipment needs. Businesses must be located in the Tennessee Valley. Those firms who meet VMI investment criteria can apply for $100,000 to $1,000,000 to support their business. TVA Economic Development staff market the VMI program and submit projects for review by VMI management. As the principle investor in VMI, TVA Economic Development management sit on the VMI board, review investment decision making processes and return on investment. Primary focus: Initial and sustained growth.

State Money - Tennessee

d) Commerce Capital LP. A Small Business Investment Company chartered by the Department of Commerce. Administration Commerce Capital's $5 million equity fund leverages up to $90 million federal dollars for rapidly growing small business operating capital needs in the Tennessee Valley. These investments are made in both debt and equity financing for companies in health care, manufacturing, environmental services, communications and information systems. Investments range from $500,000 to $3,000,000. TVA Economic Development staff market the SBIC program to valley businesses and submit the projects for review by the Commerce Capital General Partner. A TVA representative sits on the Commerce Capital board to review investment decisions and monitor return on investment. Primary Focus: Initial growth.

e) Venture Alliance Capital Fund: $4 million venture capital fund designed to make equity investments in ideas for new products and services which create new companies in the Tennessee Valley. Venture Alliance LLC provides a world class management team which explores ideas for new companies and provides marketing and financial assistance in partnership with entrepreneurs to recommend new ventures to the VACF board of governors. The VACF provides on average up to $500,000 in capital to launch the new business and position it for later stage venture capital investment from other sources. TVA Economic Development staff market the VACF and Venture Alliance LLC management team to entrepreneurs with ideas for viable businesses. Venture Alliance management builds business plans for projects with a defined market and recommends investments to VACF board of governors. A TVA representative sits on the VACF board of governors to review investment decisions and monitor return on investment. Primary Focus: Concept and start-up firms.

Contact: Tennessee Valley Authority, P.O. Box 292409, Nashville, TN 37229; 615-882-2051.

Tennessee Child Care Facilities Program: Assists child care providers by enabling them to upgrade facilities, create or expand the number of child care slots. The Program was established to accomplish two main goals: assist child care providers in attaining higher standards of safety and environment; increase the number of child care slots especially in rural and economically distressed areas. The program also assists companies and organizations wishing to establish day care centers for employees or groups of employees. The Program has three components:
- Guarantees to lenders up to $250,000 for new construction
- Direct loans to providers up to $10,000 for upgrade of facilities
- Direct loans to providers up to $25,000 for new or addition of slots

As of spring, 1998, the guarantee portfolio totaled $2.3 million, close to its cap for prudent risk. Direct loans are subject to funding on an annual basis from different sources. Maturities as well as interest rates vary based on uses of the loans.

Rural Electric Administration (REA), Rural Economic Development Revolving Loan Program For Rural Electric And Telephone Cooperatives: Designed to promote rural economic development and job creation by providing zero interest loans to REA borrowers. The program will fund up to $100,000 per project. The maximum term of the loan is ten years at zero interest rate with a two-year deferred payment. For more information, contact your local electric utility company.

Small Business Energy Loan Program: Designed to assist in the identification, installation, and incorporation of approved energy efficiency measures onto, or into, the existing Tennessee located facilities processes, and for operations of approved applicants. The Energy Division currently maintains a loan portfolio of $4,560,000 to 115 borrowers. Approved loan requests average $39,000.

Rural Business & Cooperative Development Service Loan Guarantees: The U.S. Department of Agriculture, through the RBCDS (formerly Farmers Home Administration), guarantees term loans to non-farm businesses in rural areas; that is, localities with populations below 50,000 not adjacent to a city where densities exceed 100 persons per square mile. The Tennessee RBCDS currently maintains a loan portfolio in excess of $40,000,000 (in addition to their relending program with the Development Districts listed above) with 40 industrial borrowers. Approved loan requests average just over $1,000,000.

Small Business Investment Companies: Private investment and loan companies established to serve the small business market. They are funded with a combination of private and federal investment. SBICs assist only businesses below $6,000,000 in net worth and less than $2,000,000 in annual net income. They may prioritize investments in type (equity or loan); dollar amount, location or industry.

Occupational Safety And Health Grant: The goal of this program is to fund the education and training of employees in safe employment practices and conduct in the employer's own business for the employer's own employees; and promote the development of employer - sponsored health and safety programs in the employer's own business for the employer's own employees. Grants average in the $5000 range with some greater amounts. Contact Tennessee Department of Labor, Occupational Safety and Health Grant Program, Gateway Plaza, 2nd Floor, 710 James Robertson Parkway, Nashville, TN 37243; 800-332-2667.

Pollution Prevention Loan Program: Loans for the purchase of equipment and/or construction to complete pollution prevention activities at small and medium sized businesses.

* Tax Incentives

For all items without a separate address, contact the Tennessee Department of Economic and Community Development at the address listed above.

Personal Income: Earned income is not taxed in Tennessee; however, certain dividend and interest income received by a Tennessee resident is taxable.

Energy Fuel and Water: Reduced sales tax on manufacturers' use of energy fuel and water at manufacturing site; tax-exempt if they have direct contact with product during manufacturing process.

Pollution Control Equipment: Exempt from sales tax.

Raw Materials: Exempt from sales tax.

Industrial Machinery: Exempt from sales tax.

Work-In-Progress: Exempt from property tax.

Finished Product Inventory: Exempt from property tax.

Investment Tax Credit: Manufacturers are allowed a tax credit of 1% of the cost of industrial machinery.

Franchise Tax Jobs Credit: Allows a $2,000 or $3,000 tax credit against franchise tax liability for each new full-time employee of qualified business that increases employment by 25 or more and meets required capital investment.

Manufacturers are allowed an investment tax credit of 1% on the purchase, installation and repairs of qualified industrial machinery.

Allows excise tax credit of 1% of purchase price of equipment associated with required capital investment of $500,000 by a distribution or warehouse facility.

* Exports

For all items without a separate address, contact the Tennessee Department of Economic and Community Development at the address listed above.

Export Assistance: Five core agencies provide assistance to Tennessee firms interested in or already exporting products abroad. Tennessee Department of Economic and Community Development, International Development Group provides strategic counsel support and coordination for the expansion of Tennessee's non-agricultural business and export interests in selected international markets. Contact International Development Group, 8th Floor Rachel Jackson Building, 320 Sixth Avenue, N., 7th Floor, Nashville, TN 37243; 615-741-5870; Fax: 615-741-7306.

International Trade Centers: Export efforts focus on novice and new to exporting firms. Maintaining offices in Memphis and Knoxville, the ITC can offer one on one counseling at any SBDC office across the state. ITC counselors:
- Assists in evaluating a company's export potential.
- Assists in market research.
- Assists with market entry strategies.
- Advises on market opportunities.
- Advises on export practices.
- Advises on export procedures.

In addition to counseling, ITC sponsors continuing education seminars and workshops across the state. Those firms interested in exporting for the first time should contact the Small Business Development Center nearest them for ITC assistance. Contact SBDC - International Trade Center, University of Memphis, Memphis, TN 38152; 901-678-4174; Fax: 901-678-4072; or SBDC International Trade Center, 301 East Church Street, Knoxville, TN 37915; 423-637-4283; Fax: 423-523-2071.

Tennessee Department of Agriculture, Division of Marketing: Offers similar services as the Tennessee Export Office, however specifically catering to the Tennessee farmers and agri-business people in the state. Their services include:
- hosting foreign buyer visits from abroad
- participating in trade shows and sales missions to key agricultural market destinations
- identifying foreign import requirements and assistance in obtaining appropriate documentation
- conducting seminars highlighting agricultural exports
- disseminate trade leads and other trade information

Contact Tennessee Department of Agriculture, Division of Marketing, Ellington Agricultural Center, P.O. Box 40627, Nashville, TN 37204; 615-837-5160.

Foreign Trade Zones: Tennessee has five foreign trade zones with eight sub-zones.

State Money - Texas

* Women and Minorities

For all items without a separate address, contact the Tennessee Department of Economic and Community Development at the address listed above.

Office of Minority Business Enterprise: Facilitates the resources needed in assisting minority businesses in growth and business development by identifying sources of capital; linking successful businesses with minority businesses which need help in areas like training, quality control, supplier development or financial management; providing education and training, specialized technical assistance and identification of procurement opportunities in the public and private sectors; and publishing the Minority and Women Business Directory profiling minority businesses and their capabilities for public and private organizations which use their services or products.

Purchasing Councils: Encourages mutually beneficial economic links between ethnic minority suppliers and major purchasers in the public and private sectors. Contact Tennessee Minority Purchasing Council, Metro Center, Plaza 1 Building, 220 Athens Way, Suite 105, Nashville, TN 37225; 615-259-4699; or Mid-South Minority Purchasing Council, 4111 West Park Loop, Memphis, TN 38124; 901-678-2388.

Minority Business Development Center: Provides management, marketing, and technical assistance to increase business opportunities for minority entrepreneurs. Each center provides accounting, administration, business planning, construction, and marketing information to minority firms. The MBDC also identifies minority firms for contract and subcontract opportunities with government agencies and the private sector.

Small and Minority-Owned Telecommunications Program: Provides loan guarantees, education and training, consulting and technical assistance to help small, minority-and/or women-owned telecommunications businesses grow.

* Small Business Administration Offices

Phil Mahoney
50 Vantage Way, Suite 201
Nashville, TN 37228
615-736-5850
Fax: 615-736-7232

Texas

Department of Economic Development
P.O. Box 12728
Austin, TX 78711
512-936-0260
800-888-0511
www.tded.state.tx.us

* Business Assistance

For all items without a separate address, contact the Texas Department of Economic Development at the address listed above.

Department of Economic Development: Provides business counseling for both new and established firms. Helps firms locate capital, state procurement opportunities, state certification programs for minority and women-owned businesses, and resources management and technical assistance. An Office of Business Permit Assistance serves as a clearinghouse for permit-related information throughout the state and refers applicants to appropriate agencies for permit and regulatory needs. Publications are available containing information and resources for start-up and existing businesses.

Office of Small Business Assistance: Charged with helping the state's small businesses become more globally competitive. The Office provides information and assistance to establish, operate and expand small and historically underutilized businesses (HUBS). In addition, the Office is charged with being the focal point for comments, suggestions and information regarding HUBS and small businesses to develop and suggest proposals for changes in state and federal policies in response to this information.

Texas Manufacturing Assistance Center: Works for all Texans by enabling small manufacturers to better compete in the international marketplace. It's a manufacturing brain trust with a single mission: To improve and expand manufacturing in Texas through free technical assistance to small business manufacturers. Contact: Texas Manufacturing Assistance Center, P.O. Box 12728, Austin, TX 78711; 800-488-TMAC.

General Service Commission: To facilitate the ordering needs of the State of Texas, the General Services Commission has established procedures for procuring goods and services. Contact: General Services Commission, P.O. Box 13047, Austin, TX 78711; 512-463-3416.

Economic Development Clearinghouse: A one-stop center for information about economic development programs and technical assistance offered by state and federal agencies, local governments and other organizations. The clearinghouse's website is {www.edinfo.state.tx.us}.

Texas Marketplace: Offers businesses access to the internet including free web page, daily posting of all major procurement opportunities with the State of Texas, electronic bulletin board for posting information about commodities for sale or to buy, and other resources and government procurement opportunities. Contact: Texas Marketplace, Texas Department of Economic Development, Internet Services Group, P.O. Box 12728, Austin, TX 78711; 512-936-0236; {www.texas-one.org}.

Business & Industry Data Center (BIDC): Provides one-stop access to data, information, and analyses on the Texas economy. Contact Business and Industry Data Center, P.O. Box 12728, Austin, TX 78711; 512-936-0550; {www.bidc.state.tx.us}.

* Business Financing

For all items without a separate address, contact the Texas Department of Economic Development at the address listed above.

Linked Deposit Program: Established to encourage lending to historically underutilized businesses, child-care providers, non-profit corporations, and/or small businesses located in distressed communities by providing lenders and borrowers a lower cost of capital. Minimum loan amount is $10,000; maximum loan amount is $250,000, fixed borrower loan rate.

Capital Fund Infrastructure Program: This economic development program is designed to provide financial resources to non-entitlement communities. Funds can be utilized for public infrastructure to assist a business, which commits to create and/or retain permanent jobs, primarily for low and moderate-income persons. This program encourages new business development and expansions located in non-entitlement communities. The minimum & maximum award is $50,000 & $750,000 inclusive of administration. The award may not exceed 50% of the total project cost.

Capital Fund Real Estate Development Program: This economic development program is designed to provide financial resources to non-entitlement communities. Funds can be utilized for real estate development to assist a business that commits to create and/or retain permanent jobs, primarily for low and moderate-income persons. The minimum and maximum award is $50,000 and $750,000 inclusive of administration. The award may not exceed 50% of the total project cost.

Capital Fund Main Street Improvements Program: The Texas Capital Fund Main Street Improvements Program is designed to foster and stimulate the development of small businesses by providing financial assistance to non-entitlement cities (designated by the Texas Historical Commission as a Main Street City) for public improvements. This program encourages the elimination of slum or blighted areas. Minimum awards are $75,000. Maximum awards are $150,000. Matching funds must be provided.

Small Business Industrial Revenue Bond Program: Designed to provide tax-exempt financing to finance land and depreciable property for eligible industrial or manufacturing projects. The Development Corporation Act allows cities, counties, conservation and reclamation districts to form non-profit industrial development corporations or authorities on their behalf. Program objective is to issue taxable and tax-exempt bonds for eligible projects in cities, counties, conservation and reclamation districts. The industrial development corporation acts as a conduit through which all monies are channeled. Generally, all debt services on the bonds are paid by the business under the terms of a lease, sale, or loan agreement. As such, it does not constitute a debt or obligation of the governmental unit, the industrial development corporation, or the State of Texas.

Capital Access Fund: Established to increase the availability of financing for businesses and nonprofit organizations that face barriers in accessing capital. Through the use of the Capital Access Fund, businesses that might otherwise fall outside the guidelines of conventional lending may still have the opportunity to receive financing. The essential element of the program is a reserve account established at the lending institution to act as a credit enhancement, inducing the financial institution to make a loan. Use of proceeds may include working capital or the purchase, construction, or lease of capital assets, including buildings and equipment used by the business. There is no minimum or maximum loan amount, only a maximum amount that the state will provide to the financial institution's reserve fund.

Smart Jobs Fund: Provides grants to businesses to train their employees. Although a company is limited to $1.5 million per fiscal year, subject to certain limitations, the Fund recommends that applicants limit their applications to a

State Money - Utah

maximum of $2,500 per trainee for small businesses and $1,200 per trainee for large businesses.

Leverage Fund: An economic development bank offering an added source of financing to communities that have passed the economic development sales tax. This program allows the community to make loans to local businesses for expansion or to recruit new industries.

* Tax Incentives

For all items without a separate address, contact the Texas Department of Economic Development at the address listed above.

Enterprise Zone Program: Designed to induce capital investment and create new permanent jobs into areas of economic distress. Qualified businesses located in an enterprise zone may qualify for a variety of local and state incentives including a refund of state sales and use taxes, franchise tax reductions, and state administered program priority.

Reinvestment Zones: Zones can be created for the purpose of granting local businesses ad valorem property tax abatements on a portion of the value of real and/or tangible personal property located in the zone. Special taxation entities having jurisdiction over a reinvestment zone may participate in executed abatement agreements.

Texas does not have statewide business tax incentives. These are handled at the city and/or county level in the city/county in which a business enterprise is based.

* Exports

For all items without a separate address, contact the Texas Department of Economic Development at the address listed above.

Office of Trade and International Relations (OTIR) helps Texas companies expand their business worldwide. By providing a forum for international business exchange through international trade missions, trade shows, seminars and in-bound buyers missions, OTIR gives Texas companies the opportunity to promote their products and services to international buyers and partners. OTIR also helps to connect companies with counseling and training available through the International Small Business Development Centers and works with entities such as the U.S. Department of Commerce, the Japan External Trade Organization, the Texas consular corps and its counterparts in the Mexican border states to ensure that Texas business interests are represented abroad. The State of Texas office in Mexico City is an invaluable resource for facilitating business between Texas and Mexico. Programs include:
- Trade Missions and Trade Shows
- Export Counseling
- Partnerships
- Trade Lead Distribution
- Texas International Center
- Research Publications

* Small Business Administration Offices

Rueben Guerrero
4300 Amon Carter Boulevard
Suite 108
Fort Worth, TX 76155
817-684-5580
Fax: 817-684-5588

Carlos Mendoza
10737 Gateways West., Suite 320
El Paso, TX 79935
915-633-7007
Fax: 915-633-7005

Lavan Alexander
4300 Amon Carter Boulevard
Suite 114
Fort Worth, TX 76155
817-885-5500
Fax: 817-885-5516

Sylvia Zamponi
222 E Van Buren Street, Room 500
Harlingen, TX 78550
956-427-8625
Fax: 956-427-8537

Milton Wilson
9301 Southwest Freeway, Suite 550
Houston, TX 77074
713-773-6500
Fax: 713-773-6550

Tommy Dowell
1205 Texas Avenue, Room 408
Lubbock, TX 79401
806-472-7462
Fax: 806-472-7487

Rodney Martin
727 E Durango, 5th Floor
San Antonio, TX 78206
210-472-5904
Fax: 210-472-5936

Jesse Sendejo
606 N Carancahus, Suite 101
Corpus Christi, TX 78476
512-888-3331
Fax: 512-888-3418

Utah

Business and Economic Development Division
324 South State St., Suite 500
Salt Lake City, UT 84111
801-538-8800
Fax: 801-538-8889
www.ce.ex.state.ut.us

* Business Assistance

For all items without a separate address, contact the Utah Business and Economic Development Division at the address listed above.

Business and Economic Development Division: Provides information on regulations, sources of assistance, and other important information for starting a business.

Custom Fit Training: Provides training for new or expanding companies. A Custom Fit representative will discuss with the company the training needs anticipated and then develop a specific customized training plan to meet those needs. The required training can take place at a variety of locations including the business or a local institution. Often training is provided in both locations. The program can provide instructors from the State's learning institutions, private sector, consultants or instructors within the business. The program is designed to be flexible to meet the specific needs of the company. Contact: Utah State Office of Education, Applied Technology Division, 250 East 500 South, Salt Lake City, UT 84111; 801-538-7867; {www.usoe.k12.ut.us/ate/CF/custom.htm}.

Short Term Intensive Training (STIT): Programs are customized and designed to meet full-time job openings. Programs are usually less than one year in length and will be designed to meet the specific training needs of a company while matching needs with people seeking employment. Although potential employees must pay tuition to participate, STIT can provide qualified employees from which a company can hire. STIT gives the option of training at 50% - 70% discount of normal training costs. Funding for this program is distributed to State Colleges.

Job Service: A computerized job matching system that quickly screens applicants to ensure that they meet the qualifications set by a company. Over 16,000 active applicants are presently registered with the Salt Lake Office. Job Service personnel can save countless hours by taking all of company applications and then referring only the most qualified applicants.

Centers of Excellence Program: Supports selected research programs at Utah's universities. Programs are selected based on leading edge research activities that have projected commercial value. The primary objective is to encourage the commercialization of leading edge technologies through licensing patented technologies and by creating new companies. The Centers of Excellence Program impacts Utah's economic development by the creation of jobs, the flow of licensing royalties, the expansion of the tax base, and the leveraged use of matching fund dollars to strengthen research and development at Utah's institutions of higher learning.

Utah Partners in Education: Facilitates business/ education/ government partnerships statewide. Purpose is to find ways in which those three entities can work together to meet common needs and thereby strengthen the economy of Utah.

State Money - Vermont

Contact: Utah Partners in Education, 324 South State St., Suite 500, Salt Lake City, UT 84111; 801-538-8628; {www.utahpartnership.utah.org}.

Utah Directory of Business and Industry: A listing of more than 9,800 individual employers sorted by Standard Industrial Classification (SIC), which is a standard method for classifying what businesses or other organizations do.

Environmental Permitting: One-stop shopping for the environmental permitting process through the Department of Environmental Quality.

* Business Financing

For all items without a separate address, contact the Utah Business and Economic Development Division at the address listed above.

Utah Ventures: a privately financed venture fund focusing on investments in the life sciences and information technology in Utah, other Intermountain states and California. Utah Ventures seeks to identify the best opportunities, secure subsequent coinvestments from other venture funds and corporate investors, and works with the entrepreneur to help build the business. Contact Utah Ventures, 423 Wakara Way Suite 206, Salt Lake City, UT 84108; 801-583-5922.

Revolving Loan Funds: In an effort to create jobs and improve the business climate of a community, some cities, counties, and Associations of Governments (geographical regions) will lend money to small businesses located in their areas. The amount available to a business goes from a few thousand dollars to over $100,000. Typically, the money is used for plant and equipment, working capital, inventory or accounts receivable financing. Rates are usually less than or equal to conventional lender financing, and the term for repayment may be either short (6 months) or extended (many years). This type of financing is often used in conjunction with other lender financing since most revolving loan programs will accept a second or third position on financed assets.

Microenterprise Loan Fund (UMLF) is a tax-exempt, nonprofit corporation. It provides a modestly secured form of financing up to $10,000, with terms up to five years, to owners of startup and existing firms who do not have access to traditional funding sources, especially those who are socially or economically disadvantaged. The interest rate is prime plus 3% fixed, and the business must be located in Salt Lake County. Contact: Utah Microenterprise Loan Fund, 3595 S. Main St., Salt Lake City, UT 84115; 801-269-8408.

The Utah Technology Finance Corporation is an independent corporation of the state that makes debt investments in Utah companies. UTFC leverages state and federal funds as a catalyst in capital formation for the creations, growth, and success of Utah Businesses. UTFC offers various types of debt financing through such programs as Early Technology Business Capital, Utah Rural Loan Program, MicroLoan Program, Utah Revolving Loan Fund, Bank Participation Loan Program, and Defense Conversion Loan Program. Contact Utah Technology Finance Corporation (UTFC), 177 East 100 South, Salt Lake City, UT 84111; 801-364-4346; Fax: 801-364-4361; {www.urfc.state.ut.us}.

Industrial Assistance Fund: Can be used for relocation costs. This incentive loan can be repaid as Utah jobs created meet the IAF requirements resulting in higher quality jobs, and as Utah purchases merit enough earned credits to convert the loan to a grant. Three basic programs exist: 1) rural Utah program with funding up to $100,000 for relocation expenses; 2) Corporate Funding which is dependent on the amount of Utah purchases and wages: 3) Targeted Industries which is primarily aimed at information technology, biomedical and aerospace.

Industrial Development Bonds (IDB's): A financing tool used by private sector developers for manufacturing facilities. The federal tax code places a limit of $10.0 million per project on IDB financing.

* Tax Incentives

For all items without a separate address, contact the Utah Business and Economic Development Division at the address listed above.

No inventory or worldwide unitary taxes.

New Equipment: An exemption of sales and use taxes are available for the purchase or lease of new equipment or machinery for manufacturing facilities.

Economic Development Area/Tax Increment Financing: Tax increment financing (TIF) is utilized in areas that have been targeted for economic development. Redevelopment areas are determined by local municipalities. Portions of the new property tax generated by new development projects are returned to project developers in the form of infrastructure development, land cost write down or other appropriate means. Details of TIF are site specific. Development of a proposal is relatively simple, yet the benefits can be great.

Enterprise Zones: The act passed by the Utah State Legislature provides tax credits for manufacturing companies locating in rural areas that qualify for assistance. A $750 tax credit is given for all new job created plus a credit of $1,250 for jobs paying at least 125% of the average wage for the industry. In addition, investment tax credits are available for all investment in new plant and equipment as follows: 10% for first $100,000; 5% of next $250,000. Tax credits can be carried forward for 3 years. Enterprise Zones benefits are only available in certain non-metro counties.

Special programs such as Affirmative Action, Targeted Job Tax Credits and veterans programs are also available.

* Exports

For all items without a separate address, contact the Utah Business and Economic Development Division at the address listed above.

International Business Development Office: Programs offered include:
- Trade Representatives
- Country Information
- Market Research Reports
- Trade Lead Resource Center
- Foreign Business Directories
- Trade Shows and Exhibits

* Women and Minorities

For all items without a separate address, contact the Utah Business and Economic Development Division at the address listed above.

Offices of Ethnic Affairs: Recognizing that state government should be responsive to all citizens, and wishing to promote cooperation and understanding between government agencies and its ethnic citizens, these offices were created:
- Office Of Asian Affairs
- Office Of Black Affairs
- Office Of Hispanic Affairs
- Office Of Polynesian Affairs
- Division of Indian Affairs

Minority and Women Owned Business Source Directory: Offered by the Utah PTAC (Procurement Technical Assistance Center). The directory includes approximately 850 companies, and is the most complete such listing available. However, listings are voluntary, having been obtained through surveys, and this is not to be construed as a comprehensive catalog. There are some 4,400 minority-owned employers in the state, and 46,000 that are women-owned.

* Small Business Administration Offices

Stanley Nakano
125 S. State Street, Room 2237
Salt Lake City, UT 84138
801-524-3200
Fax: 801-524-4160

Vermont

Department of Economic Development
National Life Building, Drawer 20
Montpelier, VT 05620-0501
802-828-3221
800-341-2211
Fax: 802-828-3258
www.thinkvermont.com

* Business Assistance

For all items without a separate address, contact the Vermont Department of Economic Development at the address listed above.

Department of Economic Development: A one-stop shop ready to help with businesses to support the economic growth of the state through job creation and retention. Areas in which the Department can assist Vermont businesses are entrepreneurs; international trade; financing; government contracts; marketing; permits; site location; and training.

Regional Development Corporations: Twelve RDCs serve every geographic region of the state serving as satellites of the Department of Economic Development, and provide many of the same services. Their primary function is to coordinate job and business development activities within their geographic region.

Manufacturing Extension Center: Provides one-on-one support and services through

State Money - Vermont

Field Engineers to small and mid-sized manufacturers. Their goal is to assist Vermont manufacturers increase productivity, modernize processes, and improve their competitiveness. Ongoing training opportunities designed specifically for manufacturers are also offered. Contact: Vermont Manufacturing Extension Center, VT Technical College, P.O. Box 500, Randolph Center, VT 05061; 802-728-1432; {www.vmec.org}.

Business Assistance Network: An accessible series of resources designed to provide timely and pertinent information to businesses interested in participating in new markets for their products or services, increasing competitiveness, or building "teaming arrangements" with other businesses. The information may be accessed through the Internet at {www.state.vt.us}.

Micro Business Development Program: Promotes self-employment and business expansion opportunities for low income Vermonters. Offers free, one-to-one technical assistance and business development workshops for income eligible person.

Northeast Employment and Training Organization: Manages the Entrepreneurial Training Program which provides statewide small business management courses to enterprises of all sizes, including individuals interested in self-employment and micro businesses. Contact: Northeast Employment Training Organization, P.O. Box 186, 145 Railroad St., St. Johnsbury, VT 05819.

Government Marketing Assistance Center: Exists to design, implement, and maintain resources that promote economic expansion by providing assistance to Vermont businesses' which allow them to pursue and compete in the public procurement process and introduce them to new markets for their goods and/or services. The GMAC can provide a business with a customized search to receive Federal bid opportunities, including bids available through Electronic Data Interchange (EDI). A business must be registered to receive Federal Bids opportunities.

Vermont Business Registry: An on-line registry of businesses throughout Vermont involved in manufacturing, manufacturing support, product distribution, services, research and development, and construction.

Vermont Bid Opportunities: An electronic resource which provides businesses with a current listing of bid opportunities available through Vermont based federal, state and local governments and by the private sector purchasing organizations.

Business Calendar of Events: Lists business assistance seminars, training workshops, trade shows, etc., which are sponsored by various organizations.

The Vermonter's Guide to Doing Business: Provides information relating to public and private institutions that can assist local businesses on any aspect of successful business operation.

Department of Employment and Training: Offers a full range of workforce-related services and information through a network of 12 One-Stop Career Resource Centers.

Market Vermont Program: A cooperative effort among the Departments of Economic Development; Agriculture, food and Markets; Tourism and Marketing; Forest, Parks and Recreation; Fish and Wildlife; Historic Preservation; Vermont Life Magazine; Vermont Economic Progress Council; and Vermont Council on the Arts to identify and promote goods made, and services offered, in Vermont.

Agricultural Marketing: Provides resource for the promotion of various agricultural projects and works with commodity groups to improve market opportunities. Marketing representatives help with promotion, marketing, packaging, support publications, etc. Contact: Department of Agriculture, Development Division, 116 State St., Drawer 20, Montpelier, VT 05620; 802-828-2416.

* Business Financing

For all items without a separate address, contact the Vermont Department of Economic Development at the address listed above.

Rural Economic Activity Loans: REAL loans are available to assist rural entrepreneurs who cannot obtain adequate financing from other sources on reasonable terms to establish or expand their business. These businesses must demonstrate the potential to significantly improve or retain employment opportunities. Loans up to $25,000 may be made to fund the cost of an eligible project, but cannot exceed 75% of total project costs. For loans greater than $25,000, funds may be provided for up to 40% of fixed asset project costs and/or 50% of working capital loan projects.

Small Business Development Corporation: A non-profit corporation offering loans between $2,500 and $50,000 to assist growing Vermont small businesses who cannot access conventional sources of credit. Funds may be used to finance the acquisition of fixed assets or for working capital with restrictions.

Job Start Program: Helps develop self-employment opportunities for low and moderate income Vermonters through loans used to start, strengthen or expand small businesses. Funds may be used to purchase equipment, inventory or for working capital.

Financial Access Program: Designed to enhance opportunities for small businesses to access commercial credit utilizing a pooled reserve concept. Loans must be in an amount up to and including $200,000 made to businesses with sales less than $5 million.

Mortgage Insurance Program: Designed to aid businesses by insuring loans made by commercial banks. Proceeds may be used to insure loans made for the acquisition of land, buildings, machinery and equipment or working capital, for use in an eligible facility. Maximum is $2 million per project.

Local Development Corporation Loans: Loans to nonprofit local development corporations are available through VEDA-s Subchapter 3 program. "Spec" buildings and incubators can provided low cost, flexible leased space for businesses which prefer not to own their own facility. Loan proceeds may be used for the purchase of land for industrial parks, industrial park planning and development, and the construction or improvement of speculative buildings or small business incubator facilities.

Industrial Revenue Bonds: Designed to aid businesses through VEDA's issuance of tax-exempt, low interest bonds to provide funds for the acquisition of land, buildings, and/or machinery and equipment for use in a manufacturing facility.

Direct Loan Program: Designed to finance the establishment or expansion of eligible facilities through the acquisition, construction and installation of fixed assets. Provides attractive variable rate loans to business for the purchase of land, the purchase or construction (including renovation) of buildings, and the purchase and installation of machinery and equipment for use in an eligible facility.

For above loans, contact Vermont Economic Development Authority, 58 E. State St., Montpelier, VT 05602; 802-828-5627; {www.veda.state.vt.us}.

Vermont Sustainable Jobs Fund: The goal of the fund is to develop and support projects throughout the State leading to the creation or retention of quality jobs, and the protection and enhancement of Vermont's human and natural resources. Grants and technical assistance will be available for collaborative activity including the development of flexible manufacturing networks, business clusters, and networks. A specific area of focus will be adding value to agricultural products that use the natural resource of grass. Contact: Vermont Sustainable Jobs Fund, Inc., 58 E. State St., Montpelier, VT 05602; 802-828-5320.

Agricultural Facility and Debt Stabilization Loans: Provides loans and refinancing for family farms or agricultural facility operators.

Regional/Local Revolving Loan Funds: Existing through the state, the administration of these funds is generally a non-profit development corporation.

Business and Industrial Loan Guarantees: Designed to serve the credit needs of large rural businesses. Emphasis is placed on loan guarantees between $500,000 and $3 million, but may be issued up to $10 million.

Business and Industry Direct Loans: A limited amount of funding is available for direct business loans in designated areas of economic distress. The program is targeting loans in the $100,000 to $250,000 range.

Intermediary Relending Program: Designed to finance small and emerging business and community development projects in rural areas. Loans are made to qualified intermediaries who in turn relend to small businesses and community development organizations. Business or organizations borrowing from the intermediary must be located in a rural area. The maximum loan to an intermediary is $2 million and the maximum loan that the intermediary can relend for a project is $150,000.

Rural Business Enterprise Grant: Provides grants to public bodies and non-profit corporations for the benefit of small and emerging businesses. Grant funds may be used to establish revolving loan funds, construct facilities, provide planning, or technical assistance.

Burlington Micro Loan Program: Available for asset financing, inventory financing, and working capital to businesses located in the City of Burlington. Typical loans range from $500 to $5,000.

Green Mountain Capital, L.P.: Established as a Small Business Investment Company to provide working capital loans to rapidly growing small businesses in Vermont. Companies that qualify will probably have achieved a level of sales in excess of $1 million dollars annually. GMC does not finance start-ups.

Vermont Venture Capital Fund, L.P.: A private enterprise that seeks to invest from $100,000 to $750,000 in high-quality opportunities that have outgrown seed capital resources and are either not ready for or have exceeded the limits of commercial bank lending resources.

Planning Grant for Suspected Contaminated Site: Available in an amount not to exceed $8,000 per site, for an initial assessment of a suspected contaminated site in a downtown district that otherwise qualifies under the Community Development Block Grant program.

* Tax Incentives

For all items without a separate address, contact the Vermont Department of Economic Development at the address listed above.

Payroll Tax Credit: A firm may receive a credit against income tax liability equal to a percentage of its increased payroll costs.

State Money - Virginia

Research and Development Tax Credit: A firm may receive a credit against income tax liability in the amount of 10% of qualified research and development expenditures.

Workforce Development Tax Credit: A firm may receive a credit against income tax liability in the amount of 10% of its qualified training, education and workforce development expenditures. A 20% credit may be taken for qualified training, education and workforce development expenditures for the benefit of welfare to work participants.

Small Business Investment Tax Credit: A firm may receive a credit against income tax liability in the amount equal to 5% to 10% of its investments within the state in excess of $150,000 in plants, facilities, and machinery and equipment.

Sales and Use Tax Exemptions:
1. Sales of electricity, oil, gas and other fuels used on site directly in the production of projects or services.
2. Sales of building materials within any three consecutive years in excess of $1 million in purchase value used in the construction, renovation or expansion of facilities that are used exclusively for the manufacture of tangible personal property for sales. The threshold for sales of building materials can be reduced to $250,000 for businesses that receive approval from VEDC or are located in a designated downtown development district.
3. Machinery and equipment, including system-based software used directly in the production of products or services.

Construction In Progress Property Tax Exemption: A tax exemption for a period not to exceed two years is available for real property, excluding land, consisting of unoccupied new facilities, or unoccupied facilities under renovation or expansion that are less than 75% complete.

Brownfields Property Tax Exemption: Exempt from the statewide education property tax are real property consisting of the value of remediation expenditures incurred by a business for the construction of new, expanded or renovated facilities on contaminated property.

Rehabilitation Investment Tax Credit: A federal income tax credit is available for 20% of the costs of rehabilitating income-producing historic buildings.

Sprinkler System Rebate: A building owner who installs a complete automatic fire sprinkler system in an older or historic building that has been certified for one of the state building rehabilitation tax credits is eligible for a rebate for the cost of a sprinkler system, not to exceed $2,000.

Money Management Industry Tax Credit: An income tax credit of up to 75% for the money management industry that can be taken every year and is easy to understand and therefore claim.

Employee Training Tax Credit: An employer can claim up to $400 in tax credits per year for training qualified employees if the employer does business in a designated downtown district with the intent of providing permanent employment.

Credit For Income From Commercial Film Production: A credit shall be available against the tax imposed for that taxable year upon the taxable income received from a dramatic performance in a commercial film production during that taxable year. The credit shall be in the amount by which the Vermont tax on such income, without regard to this credit, exceeds the highest personal income tax rate in the taxpayer's state of residence, multiplied by the Vermont commercial film production income.

* Exports

For all items without a separate address, contact the Vermont Department of Economic Development at the address listed above.

Vermont World Trade Office: Assists businesses wishing to export their products and services, to expand by developing sales in new markets, and by encouraging suitable foreign companies to establish operations within the state.

VEDA Export Financing: In addition to the Export Working Capital Guarantee Program, VEDA offers a number of other loan and insurance programs for Vermont's exporting community. This includes small business credit insurance, and environmental exports program, and export credit insurance short-term multi-buyer policy, and a medium-term single-buyer policy.

Export Tax Credit: A firm which makes sales outside of Vermont may take as a credit against their income tax liability, the difference between the income tax calculated under the existing state apportionment formula and the proposed formula which double weights the sales factor and disregards throwback provision. The incentive is favorable to exporters, encouraging Vermont businesses that export to declare a greater amount of taxable income.

* Women and Minorities

For all items without a separate address, contact the Vermont Department of Economic Development at the address listed above.

Women's Small Business Program: Offers a continuum of services to women seeking to identify, start, stabilize and expand a small business. Services include: Getting Serious, a workshop to determine a business idea and whether business meets personal goals; Start-Up, a 15 week intensive course to develop a business plan and business management skills; Working Solution, topic specific workshops for micro-business owner; and a graduate association to foster ongoing networking and access to information. They also offer comprehensive skills training and the opportunity to connect with other women entrepreneurs. Grants and scholarships for training are available to income eligible women. Contact: Women's Small Business Program, Trinity College, 208 Colchester Ave., Burlington, VT 05401; 802-658-0337.

* Small Business Administration Offices

Ken Silvia
87 State Street, Suite 205
Montpelier, VT 05602
802-828-4422
Fax: 802-828-4485

Virginia

Economic Development Partnership
P.O. Box 798
Richmond, VA 23206
804-371-8100
Fax: 804-371-8112
www2.yesvirginia.org/YesVA

* Business Assistance

For all items without a separate address, contact the Virginia Economic Development Partnership at the address listed above.

Economic Development Partnership: Helps new and expanding businesses by answering questions about licensing, taxes, regulations, assistance programs, etc. The office can also locate sources of information in other state agencies, and it can identify sources of help for business planning, management, exporting, and financing.

Virginia Department of Business Assistance: A good starting point for new businesses to learn about financial programs, workshops, business planning and more. Contact Virginia Department of Business Assistance, P.O. Box 466, Richmond, VA 23218; 804-371-8200; Fax: 804-371-2142; {www.vdba.org}.

Existing Industry Division (EID): Discovers needs and identifies resources that allow existing businesses and industries to take advantage of opportunities and avoid problems. EID professionals generally call on organizations within geographic territories and discuss business conditions. Information collected is processed and analyzed for further action.

Workforce Services Division (WFS): Works with new and existing businesses and industries to recruit and train qualified workers at all skill levels for newly created jobs. The programs addressing these efforts support State and local Economic Development marketing efforts.

Workforce Services: Mission is to train and retrain Virginians for specific employment opportunities. Offers consulting, video production for training purposes, and funding.

Center for Innovative Technology: Exists to stimulate economic growth by serving technology businesses. Services include: access to 11 technology development centers; assistance with pursuing joint product development with a Virginia university and provide co-funding for projects; entrepreneurship programs designed to help early stage companies bring new products to market; assistance solving manufacturing production problems. Contact Center for Innovative Technology, 2214 Rock Hill Rd, Suite 600, Herndon, VA 20170; 800-383-2482.

Virginia's Business Development Network: Designed to provide management and technical assistance to small and medium-sized companies. Provides one-on-one counseling and group training on a variety of subjects and assists entrepreneurs with pre-business planning.

* Business Financing

For all items without a separate address, contact the Virginia Economic Development Partnership at the address listed above.

Virginia Small Business Financing Authority: Offers financing programs to provide businesses with access to capital needed for growth and expansion. Programs include:
1. *Industrial Development Bonds (IDBs) and the Umbrella IDB Program*: VSBFA issues tax-exempt and taxable revenue bonds (IDBs) statewide to

State Money - Virginia

provide creditworthy businesses with access to long term, fixed asset financing at favorable interest rates and terms. Tax-exempt IDBs may be used to finance new or expanding manufacturing facilities and exempt projects, such as solid waste disposal facilities. In addition, VSBFA offers an Umbrella IDB Program that provides a cost-effective means for businesses to sell their bonds in the public bond market, particuarly for smaller projects with limited access to this market.

2. *Virginia Economic Development Revolving Loan Fund*: This fund provides loans of up to $700,000 to bridge the gap between private debt financing and private equity for projects that will result in job creation or retention. Funding is available for fixed asset financing to new and expanding manufacturing companies and other industries that derive 50% or more of their sales outside of Virginia.
3. *Virginia Defense Conversion Revolving Loan Fund*: This fund provides loans of up to $700,000 to assist defense dependent companies seeking to expand into commercial markets and diversify their operations. Funding is available for fixed assets and working capital.
4. *Loan Guarantee Program*: This program is designed to reduce the risk to banks in making loans thereby increasing the availability of short-term capital for small businesses. Under the program, VSBFA will guarantee up to $250,000 or 50%, whichever is less, of a bank loan. Typical borrowings include revolving lines of credit to finance accounts receivable and inventory, and short-term loans for working capital and fixed asset purchases, such as office or research equipment.
5. *Virginia Capital Access Program (VCAP):* VCAP provides a form of loan portfolio insurance for participating banks through special loan loss reserve accounts which are funded by loan enrollment premiums paid by the bank/borrower and matched by the VSBFA. This allows the banks to exceed their normal risk thresholds for commercial loans of all types and, thereby, accommodate a broader array of loan requests from Virginia businesses.
6. *Export Financing*: Offers bank loans for export working capital, and continues to work in partnership with the Export-Import Bank of the United States.
7. *Child Day Care Financing Program*: VSBFA provides small direct loans to child day care providers for quality enhancement projects or to meet or maintain child care standards. Eligible loan uses include infant care equipment or equipment needed to care for children with special needs, playground improvements, vans, and upgrades or minor renovations to kitchens, bathrooms, and plumbing and electrical systems.

Contact: Virginia Small Business Financing Authority, P.O. Box 446, Richmond, VA 23218; 804-371-8254.

Financial Services Division (FSD): Identifies potential financial resources to meet the capital needs of Virginia business clients, and administers loan and guarantee programs designed to foster growth and private financing in Virginia business.

Governor's Opportunity Fund: Supports economic development projects that create new jobs and investment in accordance with criteria established by state legislation. Funds can be used for such things as site acquisition and development; transportation access; training; construction or build-out of publicly owned buildings; or grants or loans to Industrial Development Authorities.

Solar Photovoltaic Manufacturing Grants: Designed to encourage the product development and manufacture of a high technology, renewable energy source in Virginia. Any manufacturer who sells solar photovoltaic panels, manufactured in Virginia, is entitled to receive an annual grant of up to seventy-five cents per watt of the rated capacity of panel sold. Contact: Virginia Department of Mines, Minerals, and Energy, 202 N. Ninth St., Ninth Street Office Bldg., 8th Floor, Richmond, VA 23219; 804-692-3200.

Virginia Coalfield Economic Development Authority: Designed to enhance the economic base of specific areas. The Authority provides low interest loans or grants to qualified new or expanding industries through its financing program to be used for real estate purchases, construction or expansion of buildings, and the purchase of machinery and equipment. Contact: Virginia Coalfield Economic Development Authority/ The Virginia Southwest Promise, P.O. Box 1060, Lebanon, VA 24266; 540-889-0381.

Virginia Capital L.P.: A private venture capital firm. Investments that are attractive include ownership transactions and profitable, growing companies whose needs exceed senior bank debt capacity. Typical investments range between $500,000 and $1,500,000. Contact: Virginia Capital L.P., 9 South 12th St., Suite 400, Richmond, VA 23219; 804-648-4802.

Enterprise Zone Job Grants: Businesses creating new-full-time positions are eligible to receive grants of up to $500 per position ($1,000 if a zone resident fills a position). The maximum grant to any one firm is $100,000 a year for the three consecutive years in the grant period.

* Tax Incentives

For all items without a separate address, contact the Virginia Economic Development Partnership at the address listed above.

Major Business Facility Job Tax Credit: Qualified companies locating or expanding in Virginia receive a $1,000 corporate income tax credit for each new full-time job created over a threshold number of jobs

Recycling Equipment Tax Credit: An income tax credit is available to manufacturers for the purchase of certified machinery and equipment for processing recyclable materials. The credit is equal to 10% of the original total capitalized cost of the equipment.

Day Care Facility Investment Tax Credit: Corporations may claim a tax credit equal to 25% of all expenditures incurred in the construction, renovation, planning or acquisition of facilities for the purpose of providing day care for children of company employees. The maximum credit is $25,000.

Neighborhood Assistance Tax Credit: An income tax credit is provided for companies that make donations to neighborhood organizations conducting approved community assistance programs for impoverished people. The credit equals 45% of the total donation.

Clean Fuel Vehicle Job Creation Tax Credit: Businesses manufacturing or converting vehicles to operate on clean fuel and manufacturers of components for use in clean fuel vehicles are eligible to receive an income tax credit for each new full-time job created over and above the previous year's employment level. The credit is equal to $700 in the year the job is created, and in each of two succeeding years if the job is continued, for a maximum of $2,100 per job.

Clean Fuel Vehicle Tax Credit: An income tax credit is available to companies which purchase clean fuel vehicles or invest in related refueling facilities. The credit is equal to 10% of the IRS allowed deduction or credit for these purchases.

Worker Retraining Tax Credit: Employers are eligible to receive an income tax credit equal to 30% of all expenditures made by the employer for eligible worker retraining.

Property Tax Incentives: No property tax at the state level; real estate and tangible personal property are taxed at the local level. Virginia differs from most states in that its counties and cities are separate taxing entities. A company pays either county or city taxes, depending on its location. No tax on intangible property; manufacturers' inventory, manufacturers' furniture, fixtures, or corporate aircraft. Exemptions include: certified pollution control facilities and equipment; certified recycling equipment, rehabilitated commercial/industrial real estate; manufacturers' generating equipment; certified solar energy devices.

Sales and Use Tax Exemptions: Manufacturers' purchases used directly in production; items purchased for re-sale by distributors; certified pollution control equipment and facilities; custom computer software; purchases used in research and development; most film, video and audio production related purchases.

Enterprise Zones: Designed to stimulate business development in distressed urban and rural areas. Incentives include:

1. General Tax Credit: A 10 year tax credit is available against state income tax liability (80% first year and 60% in years two through ten) that results from business activity within an enterprise zone.
2. Refundable Real Property Improvement Tax Credit: A tax credit equal to 30% of qualified zone real property improvements is available to businesses that rehabilitate property or undertake new construction in an enterprise zone. The maximum credit within a five-year period is $125,000.
3. Investment Tax Credit For Large Qualified Zone Projects: Projects with an investment of at least $100 million and creating at least 200 jobs are eligible for a negotiated credit of up to 5% of total investment in real property, machinery and equipment.

* Exports

For all items without a separate address, contact the Virginia Economic Development Partnership at the address listed above.

Export Financing Assistance Program: VSBFA provides guarantees of up to the lesser of $750,000 or 90% of a bank loan for export working capital, and also works with the Export-Import Bank of the United States (Eximbank) and the U.S. Small Business Administration (SBA) to provide Virginia exporters with easier access to federal loan guarantees. In addition, VSBFA administers an Eximbank Export Credit Insurance Umbrella Policy to assist Virginia exporters in obtaining insurance on their foreign receivables.

International Market Planning: Designed to assist companies developing new export markets and increase sales. Offers international marketing research; current market analyses; specific strategies to access selected markets.

* Women and Minorities

For all items without a separate address, contact the Virginia Economic Development Partnership at the address listed above.

State Money - Washington

VWBE Certification Program: Helps Virginia's women-owned and operated companies certify themselves as WBE's to better compete in government and corporate procurement markets. In addition to being listed in the directory, certified companies will be registered in the WBE website, as well as in the Virginia Procurement Pipeline website. Certified WBE's also have the privilege of using the WBE seal on marketing materials and letterhead. They also receive information on other resources available to women-owned businesses regarding government contracting, management issues, and women's ownership. Contact: Women's Enterprise Program, P.O. Box 446, Richmond, VA 23218; 804-371-8200; {www.dba.state.va.us/SBDWBE.htm}.

* Small Business Administration Offices

Charles Gaston
Federal Building
400 North 8th Street, 11th Floor
Richmond, VA 23240
804-771-2400
Fax: 804-771-8018

Washington

Department of Community, Trade and Economic Development
906 Columbia St. SW
P.O. Box 48300
Olympia, WA 98504-8300
800-237-1233
access.wa.gov

* Business Assistance

For all items without a separate address, contact the Washington Department of Community, Trade and Economic Development at the address listed above.

Business Assistance Center:
1. *The Business Assistance Center Hotline*: A statewide, toll-free information and referral service, provides information regarding state business licensing, registration, technical assistance, other state agencies or one-to-one business counseling. To contact a person from the Business Assistance Hotline, call 800-237-1233; 360-586-4840; TDD 360-586-4852.
2. *Education & Training*: Efforts are focused on providing practical application of economic development techniques along with providing a forum for practitioners for the interchange of economic development ideas. Contact Business Assistance Center, 2001 6th Ave., Suite 2600, Seattle, WA 98121; 800-237-1233; 360-664-9501.

One-Stop Licensing Center: A convenient, one-stop system that takes care of basic registration requirements and offers information about any additional licensing.

Business Retention & Expansion Program: Works with at-risk manufacturing and processing firms to reduce the number of business closures, layoffs and failures that result in significant job loss. State and local staff provide technical and problem solving assistance for these companies.

Job Skills Program: Provides grants for customized training projects. It requires at least 50% matching support from industry which may be in the form of donated or loaned equipment, instructional time contributed by company personnel, use of company facilities or training materials.

Loan Portfolio Management: Staff evaluate and process loan applications.

Business Investment Program: Support the creation of family wage jobs by providing technical assistance and consulting services to businesses considering expansion in the state.

Downtown Revitalization Service: Encourages partnerships between business and government that revitalize a community's economy, appearance and traditional business image.

Education and Training: Works in partnership with local Economic Development Councils to provide businesses and communities with practical application of economic development techniques.

* Business Financing

For all items without a separate address, contact the Washington Department of Community, Trade and Economic Development at the address listed above.

Child Care Advantages: Provides businesses with financial and technical assistance to develop on-site or near-site child care facilities. Qualified businesses are eligible to receive direct loans, loan guarantees, or grants through the Facilities Fund to start or expand their child care facilities.

Coastal Revolving Loan Fund: This fund lends to public agencies and businesses in Jefferson, Clallam, Grays Harbor, Pacific and Wahkiakum counties. Borrowers must demonstrate job creation and private investment to qualify for loans up to $150,000. The program also provides technical assistance loans up to $50,000 for public agencies and $30,000 for businesses for feasibility studies and planning.

Industrial Revenue Bonds: Up to $10 million may be issued to finance a project. Taxable nonrecourse economic development bonds are also available through the Washington Economic Development Finance Authority.

Forest Projects Revolving Loan Fund: Provides financial assistance to small-and medium-sized forest projects companies. Loans up to $750,000 are available for secondary wood product companies and their suppliers.

Community Development Finance: Program is available to help business and industry secure long-term expansion loans. By combining private financial resources with federal and state lending assistance and local leadership, this program focuses on business expansion through community development activities.

Loan programs are available for real estate, new construction, renovation, major leasehold improvements, machinery, equipment, and working capital. Government financing for a start-up business is possible, but more difficult and requires a larger down payment by the business.

Community Economic Revitalization Board: Provides low-cost financing for public facilities improvement that are required for private development.

* Tax Incentives

For all items without a separate address, contact the Washington Department of Community, Trade and Economic Development at the address listed above.

Sales/Use Tax Exemption On Machinery And Equipment: Manufacturers and processors for hire are not required to pay the sales or use tax on machinery and equipment used directly in manufacturing operations. In addition, charges made for labor and services for installing the machinery and equipment are not subject to the sales tax.

Distressed Area Sales/ Use Tax Deferral/Exemptions: Grants a waiver of sales/use tax for manufacturing, research and development, or computer-related businesses (excluding light and power businesses) locating in specific geographical areas. In certain other locations, the sales/use taxes on qualified construction and equipment costs are waived when all qualifications are met for a specified period of time.

Sales/Use Tax Waiver: The sales and/or use taxes for businesses located in distressed areas are waived when the project is certified as operationally complete and all purchases are verified as eligible by the Department of Revenue. No repayment is required.

Areas With Employment Requirements: Deferrals are also available for certain businesses who locate in specific distressed areas and meet the employment requirements. No repayment is required on the deferred sales/use tax for these businesses after the project is operationally complete.

Distressed Area Business And Occupation Tax Credit: A program for increasing employment provides a $1,000 credit against the B&O tax for each new employment position created and filled by certain businesses located in distressed areas. A distressed county is one with unemployment rates at 20% or above.

High Technology Sales/Use Tax Deferral/Exemption: Businesses in the following research and development technology categories may be eligible for a sales/use tax deferral/exemption, if they start new research and development or pilot scale manufacturing operations, or expand or diversify a current operation by expanding, renovating or equipping an existing facility anywhere in Washington.

High Technology Business And Occupation Tax Credit: An annual credit of up to $2 million is allowed for businesses that perform research and development in Washington in specified high technology categories and meet the minimum expense requirements. The credit cannot exceed the amount of the business and occupation tax due for that calendar year. The rate for the credit is: Nonprofit corporation or association: 515% (.00515) of the expenses. For profit businesses: 2.5% (.025) of the expenses.

Investment Tax Credits for Rehabilitation of Historic Structures: Office of Archaeology and Historic Preservation helps businesses apply for a 20% investment tax credit for the certified rehabilitation of historic structures.

* Exports

For all items without a separate address, contact the Washington Department of Community, Trade and Economic Development at the address listed above.

International Trade Division: Works to expand future and existing export markets by distributing trade statistics, a bi-monthly newsletter, industry directories, organizing trade missions, participating in trade shows and managing state office in Europe, Japan, Taiwan, Tokyo, and Vladivostock.

State Money - West Virginia

Export Finance Assistance Center: Provides information and guidance on the repayment risk of financing aspects of export transactions.

* Women and Minorities

For all items without a separate address, contact the Washington Department of Community, Trade and Economic Development at the address listed above.

Linked Deposit Loan Program: Allows minority or women-owned businesses with 50 or fewer employees to apply at participating banks for reduced rate loans.

DLF Minority and Women-Owned Business Loan: Loans can be available to assist certified minority and woman-owned businesses that are located in non-metropolitan areas.

Office of Minority and Women's Business Enterprises: Mission is to enhance the economic vitality of Washington State by creating an environment which mitigates the effects of race and gender discrimination in public contracting and promotes the economic development and growth of minority and women businesses. Certifies Women's business ventures and publishes a directory.

Minority & Women Business Development: Access resources and technical assistance to start or expand a business. MWBD provides entrepreneurial training, contract opportunities, bonding assistance, export assistance, and access to capital for start-ups or expanding businesses in the minority and women's business community.

* Small Business Administration Offices

Andrew Munro
Park Place Building
1200 6th Avenue, Suite 1805
Seattle, WA 98101
206-553-5676
Fax: 206-205-4155

Bob Meredith
Park Place Building
1200 6th Avenue, Suite 1700
Seattle, WA 98101
206-553-7040
Fax: 206-553-6264

Bob Wiebe
801 West Riverside, Suite 200
Spokane, WA 99201
509-353-2808
Fax: 509-353-2829

West Virginia

West Virginia Development Office
1900 Kanawha Blvd., East
Charleston, WV 25305-0311
304-558-2234
800-982-3386
Fax: 304-558-0449
www.wvdo.org

* Business Assistance

For all items without a separate address, contact the West Virginia Development Office at the address listed above.

West Virginia Development Office: This office can provide information and expertise in dealing with state, federal, and local agencies. They also have information on financing programs and other services offered by the state government.

Business Counseling: Confidential free service is available to those exploring the option of starting or purchasing a new business and to current owners of small businesses.

Seminars and workshops: Small group training is provided in areas such as starting a business in West Virginia, the basics of business planning, accounting and record keeping, business management techniques, tax law, personnel management techniques, quality customer service, etc. Most seminars and workshops may be attended for a nominal fee.

Other services: Staff members are well networked to the business and banking community and can make referrals to state, federal, and private agencies. The staff can provide problem solving assistance, business plan assistance; financial planning assistance; loan packaging assistance; minority/woman/veterans business outreach; a minority-owned and women-owned business directory; and an employee training program called the Small Business Work Force Program. Most of these services are free of charge. In addition, the SBDC is creating a customer learning center which will allow the entrepreneur to use SBDC owned computers to generate a business plan, devise and print corporate plans, learn about the internet, and the use of Electronic Data Interchange (EDI) for the purpose of electronic commerce.

Site Selection: Industrial specialists assist out-of-state companies, existing state businesses and site location consultants with the identification of suitable locations for their proposed operations utilizing a computerized inventory.

Small Business Work Force Program: Designed to serve businesses with fewer than 20 employees that are established, viable small businesses with demonstrable growth potential. Training programs will be developed based upon a comprehensive needs analysis and the business plan.

Regional Contracting Assistance Center: A private non-profit corporation founded to create information and assistance programs to help West Virginia businesses understand, adapt to, and excel in the evolving business environment. Services include:

1. *Bid Network* which links local businesses, based on their product and/or service capabilities, to opportunities represented by internal, national, regional, and local purchasing requirements.
2. *West Virginia Information Connection*: This business resource is a modem accessible series of five interactive databases on a 24-hour basis. Using the system, businesses can utilize a searchable electronic yellow pages of West Virginia businesses to locate sources of supply or in-state marketing leads. It also offers a bid board that displays contracts available through local government and private sector purchasing organizations; a directory of West Virginia industrial plants, sites, and office buildings; a demographic file providing information on West Virginia cities and counties; and a directory or resources available through government agencies and non-profit organizations. To access the WVIC: Modem Dial: 304-344-0685 (2400 bad) 304-344-0687 (1200 baud).
3. *Information Exchange System*: A business-to-business information distribution network designed to allow West Virginians to send and receive electronic mail, distribute and collect marketing leads, and directly access the Information Connection. Through this program, West Virginians may also borrow computer modems that will allow them to electronically connect to information resources such as on-line services.
4. *Quality From The Outset*: A direct in-plant technical assistance program aimed at helping businesses improve their quality, productivity, and competitiveness. The consulting service is offered at no charge.
5. *Other Services*: Bid assistance; assistance with government contracts; market location assistance; access to a computer-assisted library of federal, military, and industry adopted standards and specifications as well as technical assistance to understand and comply with specifications and standards.

Robert C. Byrd Institute: A teaching factory to help small and medium-sized manufacturing companies increase their competitiveness through the adoption of world-class manufacturing technologies and modern management techniques. Contact Robert C. Byrd Institute, 1050 4th Avenue, Huntington, WV 25755; 304-696-6273.

* Business Financing

For all items without a separate address, contact the West Virginia Development Office at the address listed above.

Direct Loans: The WVEDA can provide up to 45% in financing fixed assets by providing low interest, direct loans to expanding state businesses and firms locating in West Virginia. Loan term is generally 15 years for real estate intensive projects and 5 to 10 years for equipment projects.

Indirect Loans: The WVEDA provides a loan insurance program and a capital access program through participating commercial banks to assist firms that cannot obtain conventional bank financing. The program insures up to 80% of a bank loan for a maximum loan term of four years.

Industrial Revenue Bonds: This provides for customized financing through the federal tax exempt industrial revenue bonds. $35 million of the state's bond allocation is reserved for small manufacturing projects.

Leveraged Technology Loan Insurance Program: This program expands the loan insurance coverage to 90% for those businesses involved in the development, commercialization, or use of technology-based products and processes.

West Virginia Capital Company Act: WVEDA administers a program that provides for debt and equity venture capital investment to small business.

For the above loans, contact: West Virginia Economic Development Authority, 1018 Kanawha Blvd., East, Suite 501, Charleston, WV 25301; 304-558-3650.

Small Business Development Loans: This program provides capital to entrepreneurs for new or expanded small business with loans from $500 to $10,000. Please contact the West Virginia Small Business Development Center.

State Money - Wisconsin

Jobs Investment Trust: A $10 million public venture capital fund that uses debt and equity investments to promote and expand the state's economy.

Training Grants: Up to $5,000 available exclusively to small businesses.

Governor's Guaranteed Work Force Program: Provides training funds to assist new employees in learning their jobs, as well as to improve and expand the skills of existing employees for companies moving to or expanding in West Virginia.

* Tax Incentives

For all items without a separate address, contact the West Virginia Development Office at the address listed above.

Super Tax Credit Program: Provides substantial tax credits for companies that create jobs in industries such as manufacturing, information processing, distribution, and destination tourism projects. A business that creates 50 jobs or more can offset up to 80% of its basic business tax liability over ten years with this credit. This innovative program is based on a formula calculated by using a job creation and a qualified investment factor. In addition, small businesses in industries previously mentioned may qualify for the credit by creating at least 10 jobs over three years.

Corporate Headquarters Relocation Credit: Available to corporations in particular industries that relocate their headquarters to West Virginia. If at least 15 jobs are created, the allowable credit is 10% of qualified investment. If the corporate headquarters relocation results in 50 or more new jobs, then the allowable credit is 50% of qualified investment. Qualified investment includes the reasonable and necessary expenses incurred by the corporation to move its headquarters to this state.

Small Business Credit: Small businesses also are eligible under the Super Tax Credit program. If ten new jobs are created, the small business is allowed 30% of it qualified investment as credit. For every job created over ten, but not over 50, the company is allowed an additional 1/2 of 1% of its qualified investment as credit.

West Virginia Capital Company Credit: Established to encourage the formation of venture capital in West Virginia. Investors in qualified capital companies are entitled to a state tax credit equal to 50% of their investment. Capital companies must have a capital base of at least $1 million but not greater than $4 million.

Warehouse Freeport Amendment: Allows goods in transit to an out-of-state destination to be exempt from local ad valorem property tax when "warehoused" in West Virginia. This exemption is specifically applicable to finished goods inventories.

Research and Development Project Credits: Manufacturers, producers of natural resources, generators of electric power and persons providing manufacturing services may qualify for the credit for research activities conducted within the state. The credit generally equals 10% of the qualified investment in depreciable personal property, wages and other expenses incurred for conducting a qualified research or development project.

Industrial Expansion and Revitalization Credit: Industrial expansion and revitalization investment by manufacturers within the state qualifies for a 10% tax credit pro-rated over a period of 10 years.

Wood Processing Tax Credit: This credit is available for new wood processing operations. The tax credit is $250 per year per full time employee for 10 years to new or expanding companies involved in the manufacture of value-added wood products. The finished product must be consumer ready.

Five For Ten Program: Provides a tax incentive to businesses that make qualified capital improvement of at least $50 million to an existing base of $100 million or more. It assesses the new capital addition at a salvage value of 5% for the first ten years.

Sales Tax Exemption: For materials and equipment used directly in manufacturing process.

Industrial Expansion or Revitalization Tax Credit: Available for manufacturers as a credit against the business franchise tax.

Major Project Appraisal: Available for expansions at facilities that have original investment of more than $100 million. This requires the property tax for capital improvements of more than $50 million be appraised at salvage value.

* Exports

For all items without a separate address, contact the West Virginia Development Office at the address listed above.

Office of International Development: Offers export counseling and trade promotion opportunities to West Virginia companies. Maintains overseas offices.

Business and Industry Development Division: The Industrial Development Division of the West Virginia Development Office, in cooperation with the Department of Commerce and SBA, cosponsors workshops in international marketing.

West Virginia Export Council: A non-profit export promotion organization committed to expanding West Virginia exports. The Council assists public sector organizations in planning, promoting, and implementing activities that assist international export efforts.

Center for International Programs: For information on this program, contact Dr. Will Edwards, Director, Marshall University, Huntington, WV 25755; 304-696-6265; Fax 304-696-6353.

* Women and Minorities

For all items without a separate address, contact the West Virginia Development Office at the address listed above.

Center for Economic Options: A non-profit statewide, community-based organization which promotes opportunities that develop the economic capacity of West Virginia's rural citizens and communities. Working with members of society who traditionally have been excluded from economic decision-making, the Center advocates equity in the workplace, coordinates alternative approaches for economic development, and works to impact the direction of public policy. The Center coordinates three strategies to accomplish these goals:

1. *Community Resources*: Coordinates a pool of facilitators and training specialists who provide technical assistance to individuals, organizations, and community groups in many areas including strategic planning, business plan development, board development, and community assessments. The program also provides workshops and resource materials on community-based development.
2. *Enterprise Development*: Promotes rural job creation through self-employment and links small-scale, sector-specific entrepreneurs in statewide production and marketing networks. The Center facilitates the development of these flexible networks and connects the business owners with information, resources, training opportunities, and markets.
3. *Public Policy*: Researches and recommends policy in several areas including worker equity, enterprise development, sustainable development, work force training, and economic equity. Through the program, consultants on establishing equity in the workplace and meeting state and federal sex equity regulations are provided.

Contact: Center for Economic Options, 601 Delaware Ave., Charleston, WV 25302; 304-345-1298.

West Virginia Women's Commission: Offers women opportunities to learn to be advocates for themselves and to work with others to address systemic change. Projects include leadership and legislative conference like the Women's Town Meeting and Women's Day at the Legislature among others. Contact West Virginia Women's Commission, Building 6, Room 637, 1900 Kanawha Boulevard, East, Charleston, WV 25305; 304-558-0070; Fax: 304-558-3240.

Minority-owned and Women-owned Business Directory: Each year the West Virginia Small Business Development Center publishes a "Minority-owned and Women-owned Business Directory" This directory is distributed to public and private purchasing agents, Chambers of Commerce, Economic Development Authorities, legislators and many privately owned businesses including contractors and all of the listees. There is no cost for the directory nor is there a charge for being included. The only requirement is that the business be located in West Virginia, be a for profit company and be 51% owned by a minority or woman.

* Small Business Administration Offices

Vacant
320 West Pike Street
Clarksburg, WV 26301
304-623-5631
Fax: 304-623-0023

Vacant
405 Capitol Street, Suite 412
Charleston, WV 25301
304-347-5220
Fax: 304-347-5350

Wisconsin

Department of Commerce (COMMERCE)
201 W. Washington Avenue
Madison, WI 53707
Business Helpline: 800-HELP-BUSiness
Fax Request Hotline: 608-264-6154
Export Helpline: 800-XPORT-WIsconsin
www.commerce.state.wi.us

State Money - Wisconsin

* Business Assistance

For all items without a separate address, contact the Wisconsin Department of Commerce (COMMERCE) at the address listed above.

Department of Commerce: The Wisconsin Department of Commerce is the state's primary agency for delivery of integrated services to businesses. Services include business financing, technical and managerial services to a wide range of businesses.

Business Development Resources: The Area Development Manager Program assists business expansions, promotes business retention, and helps local development organizations in their respective territories. Area development managers use their knowledge of federal, state, and regional resources to provide a variety of information to expanding or relocating firms. They also mobilize resources to help struggling businesses.

Brownfields Initiative Technical Assistance Program: Provides information and assistance related to brownfields redevelopment. The program can assist in the identification and resolution of regulatory issues, and electronically link prospective buyers with information on available brownfield sites.

Business Development Assistance Center: Provides assistance to small businesses. The office furnishes information on government regulations, and refers businesses to appropriate resources. Call 800-HELP BUSiness.

Dairy 2020 Initiative: A state, business, and education partnership that works to enhance the competitive edge of the Wisconsin dairy industry. Contact: Dairy 2020 Program, P.O. Box 7970, Madison, WI 53707; 608-266-7370.

Assistance with Environmental Regulations and Permits is available to manufacturers. COMMERCE can also expedite regulatory and permit clearance and resolve delays and communications problems. Businesses storing or handling flammable or combustible liquids can receive compliance assistance.

Wisconsin Health Consultation Program: Provides free assistance to employers who request help to establish and maintain a safe and healthful workplace. Health Consultants will conduct an appraisal of physical work practices and environmental hazards, will perform an ergonomics analysis, review various aspects of the employers present occupational safety and health program, and will present occupational health related training.

Industrial Recycling Assistance Program: Conducts site visits and detailed assessments to help manufacturers find the best available solutions for waste management and waste reduction problems.

Manufacturing Assessment Center: Helps small and medium manufacturers improve quality and productivity through professional assessment of operations, systems, and layouts. The center maintains a list of related seminars available throughout the country, and can arrange plant tours of leading-edge manufacturers in the state.

Plan Review Program provides plan review and consultation for structures, plumbing, elevators, HVAC, lighting, erosion control, and private onsite wastewater treatment systems. The services help designers, installers, and owners protect public safety and promote economic efficiency.

Recycling Technical Assistance Program: Helps companies switch to recycled feedstock or reduce waste generation.

Small Business Clean Air Assistance Program: Designed to help small businesses comply with standards established by the federal Clean Air Act.

Small Business Ombudsman: Provides information on government regulations and financing alternatives to small businesses, particularly entrepreneurs. Through its advocacy function, the office promotes special consideration for small businesses in Wisconsin administrative rules.

WiSCon Safety Consultation Program: Assesses current safety programs and suggests improvements; evaluates physical work practices; identifies available assistance; and provides training and education for managers and employees. The consultants do not issue citations, propose penalties, or report possible safety violations to the Occupational Safety and Health Administration.

Wisconsin TechSearch is the fee-based information outreach program of the Kurt F. Wendt Library. TechSearch offers document delivery and reference services to businesses and industry. On-line literature, patent and trademark searches are available. TechSearch provides access to the information resources of the Wendt Library, which contains outstanding collections in science and engineering, and is a US Patent and Trademark Depository Library and more than 40 libraries and information centers on the UW-Madison campus. For more information and a fee schedule, call 608-262-5913/5917 or E-mail {wtskfw@ doit.wisc.edu}.

UW-Madison Engineering Cooperative Education and Internship Program: Provides student engineering interns that can help companies undertake a variety of technical and engineering initiatives. Interns are paid commensurate with their educational level and previous experience. Advantages to the employer include developing a stronger, experienced workforce; identifying outstanding students for potential employment at graduation; evaluating an individual's performance prior to making a full-time commitment; and sharing new technology, research, and procedures.

Solid and Hazardous Waste Education Center: Provides technical assistance to businesses and communities on emissions reduction, pollution prevention, recycling, and solid waste management. The Center also offers grants that companies can use for hazardous waste reduction audits. UW- Green Bay Campus, 2420 Nicolet Dr., ES317, Green Bay, WI 54311; 920-465-2327.

* Business Financing

For all items without a separate address, contact the Wisconsin Department of Commerce (COMMERCE) at the address listed above.

Customized Labor Training Fund: Provides training grants to businesses that are implementing new technology or production processes. The program can provide up to 50% of the cost of customized training that is not available from the Wisconsin Technical College System.

Dairy 2020 Initiative: Awards grants and loans for business and feasibility planning to dairy producers and processors considering a modernization or expansion project.

Employee Ownership Assistance Loan Program: Can help a group of employees purchase a business by providing individual awards up to $25,000 for feasibility studies or professional assistance. The business under consideration must have expressed its intent to downsize or close.

Division of Vocational Rehabilitation Job Creation Program: Designed to increase employment opportunities for DVR clients by providing equipment grants, technical assistance grants, and customized assistance to companies that will hire persons with disabilities as part of a business expansion.

Major Economic Development Program: Offers low-interest loans for business development projects that create a significant economic impact.

Rural Economic Development Program: Makes individual awards up to $30,000 for feasibility studies and other professional assistance to rural businesses with fewer than 25 employees. Businesses and farms that have completed their feasibility evaluations are eligible for individual micro loans up to $25,000 for working capital and the purchase of equipment.

Technology Development Fund: Helps businesses finance Phase I product development research. Firms completing Phase I projects can receive Phase II product-commercialization funding.

Tax Incremental Financing: Helps cities in Wisconsin attract industrial and commercial growth in underdeveloped and blighted areas. A city or village can designate a specific area within its boundaries as a TIF district and develop a plan to improve its property values. Taxes generated by the increased property values pay for land acquisition or needed public works.

Brownfields Initiative: Provides grants to persons, businesses, local development organizations, and municipalities for environmental remediation activities for brownfield sites where the owner is unknown, cannot be located or cannot meet the cleanup costs.

BDI Micro Loan Program: Helps entrepreneurs with permanent disabilities and rehabilitation agencies finance business start-ups or expansions.

BDI Self-Employment Program: Helps severely disabled DVR clients start micro-businesses.

Industrial Revenue Bonds (IRBs): A means of financing the construction and equipping of manufacturing plants and a limited number of non-manufacturing facilities. The municipality is not responsible for debt service on IRBs, nor is it liable in the case of default. IRBs are also exempt from federal income tax.

Petroleum Environmental Clean-up Fund: Reimburses property owners for eligible clean-up costs related to discharges for petroleum tank systems.

Recycling Demonstration Grant Program: Helps businesses and local governing units fund waste reduction, reuse, and recycling pilot projects.

Recycling Early Planning Grant Program: Awards funds to new and expanding business plans, marketing assistance, and feasibility studies on the start-up or expansion of a recycling business.

Recycling Loan Program: Awards loans for the purchase of equipment to businesses and nonprofit organizations that make products from recycled waste, or make equipment necessary to manufacture these products.

Recycling Technology Assistance Program: Provides low cost loans to fund research and development of products or processes using recovered or recyclable materials. Eligible activities include product development and testing, process development and assessment, specialized research, and technical assistance.

Wisconsin Fund: Provides grants to help small commercial businesses rehabilitate or replace their privately owned sewage systems.

Wisconsin Housing and Economic Development Authority (WHEDA): Offers a program that buys down commercial interest rates, enabling Wisconsin lenders to offer short-term, below-market-rate loans to small, minority- or women-owned businesses. A loan guarantee program is available for firms ramping-up to meet contract demands; for firms in economically-distressed areas; and for tourism and agribusiness projects. The authority also operates a beginning farmer bond program.

Wood Utilization Program: Provides grants to the forest products industry, universities, laboratories, and industry-research partnerships for conducting research and development and in-plant trials that develop value-added products

State Money - Wyoming

from manufacturing by-products and other wood residue; develop economical solutions for environmental protection; and improve the use of available timber resources.

Community-Based Economic Development Program: Awards grants to community-based organizations for development and business assistance projects and to municipalities for economic development planning. The program helps community-based organizations plan, build, and create business and technology-based incubators, and can also capitalize an incubator tenant revolving-loan program.

* Tax Incentives

For all items without a separate address, contact the Wisconsin Department of Commerce (COMMERCE) at the address listed above.

Development Zone Program: A tax benefit initiative designed to encourage private investment and to improve both the quality and quantity of employment opportunities. The program has $21 million in tax benefits available to assist businesses that meet certain requirements and are located or willing to locate in one of Wisconsin's 20 development zones.

Enterprise Development Zone Program: This program promotes a business start-up or expansion on a particular site in any area of the state that suffers from high unemployment, declining incomes and property values, and other indicators of economic distress. The program pays on performance. Tax credits can be taken only on income generated by business activity in the zone. The maximum amount of tax credits per zone is $3 million. Up to 50 sites can be designated around the state for projects that are not likely to occur or continue unless a zone is created. Types of Credits: A business in an enterprise development zone is eligible to earn the following tax credits:

1. The jobs credit: Equal to 40% of the first $6,000 in qualified wages for the first and second years of employment of a member of a "target group."
2. The sales tax credit: Equal to the amount of sales tax paid on building materials and equipment.
3. The location credit: Equal to 2.5% of the cost of acquiring, constructing, rehabilitating, remodeling or repairing real property.
4. The investment credit: Equal to 2.5% of the cost of depreciable tangible personal property.
5. The research credit: Equal to 5% of increased expenditures on research.
6. The child care credit: Equal to expenses incurred by an employer for child care provided to children of target group members. Up to $1,200 per year per child for two years.
7. The environmental remediation credit: Equal to 7.5% of cost of the remediation of contaminated land.

Wisconsin Small Business Innovative Research (SBIR) Support Program: Coordinates resources to help businesses pursue federal SBIR grants and contracts. The federal SBIR program provides Phase I awards of up to $100,000 for feasibility studies and Phase II awards of up to $750,000 for project development.

* Exports

For all items without a separate address, contact the Wisconsin Department of Commerce (COMMERCE) at the address listed above.

COMMERCE maintains International Offices in Frankfurt, Mexico City, Seoul, Toronto and Sao Paolo. They also contract with consultants in Hong Kong/China, Japan, Singapore and Southeast Asia, Chile, Peru, and Ecuador to provide export services to state firms. Participating in a variety of promotional activities, such as trade shows and Wisconsin product exhibits, the offices forward trade leads and set up business meetings between state firms and potential clients. Overseas firms interested in sites or investment in Wisconsin can contact the offices for assistance.

Wisconsin Trade Project Program: Can help small export-ready firms participate in international trade shows. The business covers its own travel and lodging expenses. COMMERCE can then provide up to $5,000 in reimbursements to a business for costs associated with attending a trade show, such as booth rental or product brochure translation.

Trade Shows and Trade Missions: Showcase Wisconsin firms and products to prospective international clients. The Department sponsors a Wisconsin-products booth at approximately 12 international trade fairs per year, and also arranges trade and reverse investment missions abroad, many of them led by the Governor.

* Women and Minorities

For all items without a separate address, contact the Wisconsin Department of Commerce (COMMERCE) at the address listed above.

Bureau of Minority Business Development
Department of Commerce
123 W. Washington Ave.
P.O. Box 7970
Madison, WI 53707
608-267-9550
badger.state.wi.us

Certifies companies to be eligible to participate in state's minority business bid preference. Company must be at least 51% owned, controlled, and managed by minority (being a woman is not considered a minority).

Certification to participate in the state's minority business purchasing and contracting program is available to minority vendors. Interested firms may apply through the department. They are then listed in the *Annual Directory of Minority-Owned Firms*.

Marketing Assistance of various kinds is offered to minority-owned firms. Certified minority vendors are listed in the department's database for access by the purchasing community. Minority-owned firms can receive help developing marketing plans. Each year, the department sponsors the Marketplace Trade Fair to encourage business contacts between minority vendors and state and corporate buyers.

American Indian Liaison: Provides advice, training, technical assistance, and economic development information to the Wisconsin tribes, tribal communities, and American Indian entrepreneurs, and serves as state economic development liaison.

Minority Business Development Fund Revolving Loan Fund (RLF) Program: Designed to help capitalize RLFs administered by American Indian tribal governing bodies or local development corporations that target their loans to minority-owned businesses. The corporation must be at least 51-percent controlled and actively managed by minority-group members, and demonstrate the expertise and commitment to promote minority business development in a specific geographic area.

Minority Business Development Fund: Offers low-interest loans for start-up, expansion or acquisition projects. To qualify for the fund, a business must be 51-percent controlled, owned, and actively managed by minority-group members, and the project must retain or increase employment.

Minority Business Early Planning Grant Program: Provides seed capital to minority entrepreneurs for feasibility studies, business plans, and marketing plans.

Wisconsin Women's Business Initiative Corporation (WWBIC): Offers micro loans to businesses owned by women, minorities, and low-income individuals. WWBIC also offers training and technical assistance.

* Small Business Administration Offices

Eric Ness
740 Regent Street, Suite 100
Madison, WI 53715
608-264-5261
Fax: 608-254-5541

Paul Roppuld
310 West Wisconsin Avenue, Suite 400
Milwaukee, WI 53203
414-297-1178
Fax: 414-297-1377

Wyoming

Department of Commerce
2301 Central Ave.
Cheyenne, WY 82002
307-777-6303
Fax: 307-777-6005
http://commerce.state.wy.us

* Business Assistance

For all items without a separate address, contact the Wyoming Department of Commerce at the address listed above.

Division of Economic and Community Development: This office can provide information and expertise in dealing with state, federal, and local agencies. They also have information on financing programs and other services offered by the state government.

Science, Technology and Energy Authority: Helps to improve the development of research capability, stimulate basic and applied technological research and facilitate commercialization of new products and processes.

State Money - Wyoming

Mid-America Manufacturing Technology Centers: A non-profit organization that assists small and medium-sized manufacturers in becoming more competitive, improve quality, boost sales and locate production resources.

* Business Financing

For all items without a separate address, contact the Wyoming Department of Commerce at the address listed above.

The state offers a wide spectrum of public sector financial and technical assistance programs.

Wyoming Industrial Development Corporation: Matches resources in both private and public sectors that best fit the needs of business.

Workforce Training: Financial support is available for on-the-job training, classroom training, or a combination of both.

Relative Cost of Doing Business: RFA.com is an annually updated index that compares business costs in each state to the national average composed of unit labor costs, effective tax burden and energy costs. In 1998, Wyoming had the lowest costs of doing business all 50 states. Check out {www.rfa.com/free/cdb.asp}.

* Tax Incentives

For all items without a separate address, contact the Wyoming Department of Commerce at the address listed above.

No personal income tax.
No corporate income tax.
No tax on intangible assets such as bank accounts, stocks, or bonds.
No tax on retirement income earned and received from another state.
No inventory tax.
No tax on goods-in-transit or made from out-of-state.

* Small Business Administration Offices

Steve Despain
100 E. B Street, Room 4001
Casper, WY 82601
307-261-6500
Fax: 307-261-6535

＃ Small Business Development Centers

Small Business Development Centers (SBDCs) could be the best deal the government has to offer to entrepreneurs and inventors, and a lot of people don't even know about them! Where else in the world can you have access to a $150 an hour consultant for free? There are over 700 of these offices all over the country and they offer free (or very low cost) consulting services on most aspects of business including:

- how to write a business plan
- how to get financing
- how to protect your invention
- how to sell your idea
- how to license your product
- how to comply with the laws
- how to write a contract
- how to sell overseas
- how to get government contracts
- how to help you buy the right equipment

You don't even have to know how to spell ENTREPRENEUR to contact these offices. They cater to both the dreamer, who doesn't even know where to start, as well as to the experienced small business that is trying to grow to the next stage of development. In other words, the complete novice or the experienced professional can find help through these centers.

Why spend money on a consultant, a lawyer, an accountant, or one of those invention companies when you can get it all for free at your local SBDC?

Recently, I spoke with some entrepreneurs who used a California SBDC and each of them had nothing but praise for the services. A young man who dropped out of college to start an executive cleaning business said he received over $8,000 worth of free legal advice from the center and said it was instrumental in getting his business off the ground. A woman who worked in a bank started her gourmet cookie business by using the SBDC to help her get the money and technical assistance needed to get her venture up and running. And a man who was a gymnast raved about how the SBDC helped him get his personal trainer business off the ground. All kinds of businesses being started, and all kinds of compliments for the SBDC's role in assisting these entrepreneurs, in whatever they are attempting. It sounds like a solid recommendation to me.

Can something that is free be so good? Of course it can. Because most of the people who work there are not volunteers, they are paid for by tax dollars. So it's really not free to us as a country, but it is free to you as an entrepreneur. And if you don't believe me that the SBDCs are so good, would you take the word of Professor James J. Chrisman from the University of Calgary in Calgary, Alberta, Canada? He was commissioned to do an independent study of SBDCs and found that 82% of the people who used their services found them beneficial. And the businesses who used SBDCs had average growth rates of up to 400% greater than all the other businesses in their area. Not bad. Compare this to the Fortune 500 companies who use the most expensive consulting firms in the country and only experience growth rates of 5% or less. So, who says you get what you pay for?

Small Business Development Centers

Alabama
Lead Center
Office of State Director
Alabama Small Business Development Consortium
University of Alabama at Birmingham
1717 11th Ave. South
Suite 419
Birmingham, AL 35294-7645
205-934-7260
Fax: 205-934-7645

Auburn University
Small Business Development Center
108 College of Business
Auburn, AL 36849-5243

334-844-4220
Fax: 334-844-4268

University of Alabama at Birmingham
Small Business Development Center
1601 11th Ave. S.
Birmingham, AL 35294-2180
205-934-6760
Fax: 205-934-0538

Alabama Small Business Procurement System
University of Alabama at Birmingham
Small Business Development Center
1717 11th Ave. South, Suite 419
Birmingham, AL 35294-4410

205-934-7260
Fax: 205-934-7645

University of North Alabama
Small Business Development Center
P.O. Box 5248
Keller Hall, School of Business
Florence, AL 35632-0001
205-760-4629
Fax: 205-760-4813

North East Alabama Regional Small Business
Development Center
Alabama A&M University and University of
Alabama in Huntsville

Small Business Development Centers

225 Church St., NW
Huntsville, AL 35804-0168
205-535-2061
Fax: 205-535-2050

Jacksonville State University
Small Business Development Center
114 Merrill Hall
Jacksonville, AL 36265
205-782-5271
Fax: 205-782-5179

Livingston University
Small Business Development Center
212 Wallace Hall
Livingston, AL 35470
205-652-9661, ext. 439
Fax: 205-652-9318

University of South Alabama
Small Business Development Center
8 College of Business
Mobile, AL 36688
334-460-6004
Fax: 334-460-6246

Alabama State University
Small Business Development Center
915 S. Jackson St.
Montgomery, AL 36195
334-229-4138
Fax: 334-269-1102

Troy State University
Small Business Development Center
102 Bibb Graves
Troy, AL 36082-0001
205-670-3771
Fax: 205-670-3636

Alabama International Trade Center
University of Alabama
250 Bidgood Hall
Tuscaloosa, AL 35487-0396
205-348-7621
Fax: 205-348-6974

University of Alabama
Small Business Development Center
250 Bidgood Hall
Tuscaloosa, AL 35487-0397
205-348-7011
Fax: 205-348-9644

Alaska
Lead Center
Jan Fredericks
University of Alaska
Small Business Development Center
430 West 7th Ave., Suite 110
Anchorage, AK 99501
907-274-7232
Fax: 907-274-9524
Outside Anchorage: 800-478-7232

University of Alaska-Anchorage Small Business
Development Center
430 West 7th Ave., Suite 110
Anchorage, AK 99501
907-274-7232
Fax: 907-274-9524
outside Anchorage: 800-478-7232.

University of Alaska-Fairbanks
Small Business Development Center
510 Fifth Ave., Suite 101
Fairbanks, AK 99701
907-456-1701
Fax: 907-456-1873
outside Fairbanks: 800-478-1701

Southeast Alaska Small Business Development
Center
400 Willoughby St., Suite 211
Juneau, AK 99801
907-463-3789
Fax: 907-463-3929

Matanuska-Susitna Borough
Small Business Development Center
1801 Parks Highway, #C-18
Wasilla, AK 99654
907-373-7232
Fax: 907-373-2560

Kenai Peninsula
Small Business Development Center
110 S. Willow St., Suite 106
Kenai, AK 99611-7744
907-283-3335
Fax: 907-283-3913

Arizona
Lead Center
Arizona Small Business Development Center
9215 N. Black Canyon Highway
Phoenix, AZ 85021
602-943-9818
Fax: 602-943-3716

Coconino County Community College
Small Business Development Center
3000 N. 4th St., Suite 25
Flagstaff, AZ 86004
520-526-5072
Fax: 520-526-8693
1-800-350-7122

Northland Pioneer College
Small Business Development Center
P.O. Box 610
Holbrook, AZ 86025
520-537-2976
Fax: 520-524-2227

Mojave Community College
Small Business Development Center
1971 Jagerson Ave.
Kingman, AZ 86401
520-757-0894
Fax: 520-787-0836

Rio Salado Community College
Small Business Development Center
301 West Roosevelt, Suite B
Phoenix, AZ 85003
602-238-9603
Fax: 602-340-1627

Gateway Community College
Small Business Development Center
108 N. 40th St.
Phoenix, AZ 85034
602-392-5223
Fax: 602-392-5329

Yavapal College
Small Business Development Center
117 E. Gurley St., Suite 206
Prescott, AZ 86301
602-778-3088
Fax: 602-778-3109

Cochise College
Small Business Development Center
901 N. Colombo, Room 411
Sierra Vista, AZ 85635
602-459-9778
Fax: 602-459-9737
1-800-966-7943, ext. 778

Eastern Arizona College
Small Business Development Center
622 College Ave.
Thatcher, AZ 85552-0769
602-428-8590
Fax: 602-428-8462

Pima Community College
Small Business Development Center
4903 E. Broadway, Suite 101
Tucson, AZ 85709-1260
602-748-4906
Fax: 602-748-4585

Arizona Western College
Small Business Development Center
281 W. 24th St.
#152 Century Plaza
Yuma, AZ 85364
520-341-1650
Fax: 520-726-2636

Arkansas
Lead Center
Arkansas Small Business Development Center
University of Arkansas at Little Rock
Little Rock Technology Center Building
100 S. Main, Suite 401
Little Rock, AR 72201
501-324-9043
Fax: 501-324-9049

Henderson State University
Small Business Development Center
P.O. Box 7624
Arkadelphia, AR 71923
501-230-5224
Fax: 501-230-5236

University of Arkansas at Fayetteville
Small Business Development Center
College of Business - BA 117
Fayetteville, AR 72701
501-575-5148
Fax: 501-575-4013

Arkansas State University
Small Business Development Center
P.O. Box 1403
Jonesboro, AR 72467
501-932-3957
Fax:-501-932-0135

Genesis Technology Incubator--Small Business
Development Center (SBDC)
University of Arkansas Engineering Research
Center
Fayetteville, AR 72701-1201
501-575-7446
Fax: 501-575-7446

W. Arkansas Regional Office--SBDC
1109 S. 16th St.
P.O. Box 2067
Fort Smith, AR 72901
501-785-1376
Fax: 501-785-1964

Small Business Development Centers

NW Arkansas Regional Office--SBDC
818 Highway 62-65-412 N.
P.O. Box 190
Harrison, AR 72601
501-741-8009
Fax: 501-741-1905

W. Central Arkansas Regional Office--SBDC
835 Central Ave., Box 402-D
Hot Springs, AR 71901
501-624-5448
Fax: 501-624-6632

NE Arkansas Regional Office--SBDC
100 S. Main, Suite 401
Little Rock, AR 72201
501-324-9043
Fax: 501-324-9079

SW Arkansas Regional Office--SBDC
600 Bessie
P.O. Box 767
Magnolia, AR 71753
501-234-4030
Fax: 501-234-0135

SE Arkansas Regional Office--SBDC
Enterprise Center III
400 Main, Suite 117
Pine Bluff, AR 71601
501-536-0654
Fax: 501-536-7713

Arkansas State University--SBDC
Drawer 1650
State University, AR 72467
501-972-3517
Fax: 501-972-3868

Stuttgart Regional Office--SBDC
301 S. Grand, Suite 101
P.O. Box 289
Stuttgart, AR 72160
501-673-8707
Fax: 501-673-8707

California
Lead Center
California Small Business Development Center
California Department of Commerce
Office of Small Business
801 K St., Suite 1700
Sacramento, CA 95814
916-322-3502
Fax: 916-322-5084

Central Coast Small Business Assistance Center
6500 Soquel Dr.
Aptos, CA 95003
408-479-6136
Fax: 408-479-6166

Sierra College
Small Business Development Center
560 Wall St., Suite J
Auburn, CA 95603
916-885-5488
Fax: 916-823-4142

Weill Institute
Small Business Development Center
1330 22nd St., Suite B
Bakersfield, CA 93301
805-322-5881
Fax: 805-322-5663

Butte College
Tri-County Small Business Development Center
260 Cohasset Ave., Suite A
Chico, CA 95926
916-895-9017
Fax: 916-895-9099

Southwestern College
Small Business Development Center and
International Trade Center
900 Otay Lakes Rd., Bldg. 1600
Chula Vista, CA 91910
619-482-6393
Fax: 619-482-6402

Satellite Operation
Small Business Development Center
Hilltop Professional Ctr.
Suite 205, Box 4550
Clearlake, CA 95422-4550
707-996-3440
Fax: 707-995-3605

North Coast Small Business Development Center
207 Price Mall
Crescent City, CA 95531
707-464-2168
Fax: 707-445-9652

North Coast Satellite Center
529 E. St.
Eureka, CA 95501
707-465-6008
Fax: 707-445-9652

Central California Small Business Development
Center
1999 Tuolumine St., Suite 650
Fresno, CA 93721
209-275-1223
Fax: 209-275-1499

Gavilan College
Small Business Development Center
7436 Monterey St.
Gilroy, CA 95020
408-847-0373
Fax: 408-847-0393

Accelerate Technology Small Business
Development Center
Graduate School of Management
Room 230, University of California
Irvine, CA 92717-3125
714-509-2990
Fax: 714-509-2997

Greater San Diego Chamber of Commerce
Small Business Development Center
4275 Executive Square, Suite 920
La Jolla, CA 92037
619-453-9388
Fax: 619-450-1997

Export Small Business Development Center of
Southern California
110 E. 9th, Suite 669
Los Angeles, CA 90079
213-892-1111
Fax: 213-892-8232

Satellite Operation
Small Business Development Center
1632 N. St.
Merced, CA 95340
209-385-7312
Fax: 209-383-4959

Valley Sierra Small Business Development Center
1012 11th St., Suite 300
Modesto, CA 95354
209-521-6177
Fax: 209-521-9373

Napa Valley College
Small Business Development Center
1556 First St., Suite 103
Napa, CA 94559
707-253-3210
Fax: 707-253-3068

East Bay Small Business Development Center
519 17th St., Suite 210
Oakland, CA 94612
510-893-4114
Fax: 510-893-5532

Satellite Operation
Small Business Development Center
300 Esplanade Dr., Suite 1010
Oxnard, CA 93030
805-981-4633
Fax: 805-988-1862

Eastern Los Angeles County Small Business
Development Center
363 Main St., Suite 101
Pomona, CA 91766
909-629-2247
Fax: 909-629-8310

Inland Empire Small Business Development
Center
2002 Iowa Ave., Suite 110
Riverside, CA 92507
909-781-2345
Fax: 909-781-2345

Greater Sacramento Small Business Development
Center
1410 Ethan Way
Sacramento, CA 95815
916-563-3210
Fax: 916-563-3264

Silicon Valley - San Mateo County
Small Business Development Center
111 N. Market St., #150
San Jose, CA 95113
408-298-7694
Fax: 408-971-0680

San Mateo County Satellite Center
Bayshore Corporate Center
1730 S. Amphlett Blvd., Suite 208
San Mateo, CA 94402
415-358-0271
Fax: 415-358-9450

Rancho Santiago Small Business Development
Center
901 East Santa Ana Blvd., Suite 101
Santa Ana, CA 92701
714-647-1172
Fax: 714-835-9008

Redwood Empire
Small Business Development Center
520 Mendocino Ave., Suite 210
Santa Rosa, CA 95401
707-524-1770
Fax: 707-524-1772

San Joaquin Delta College
Small Business Development Center

Small Business Development Centers

814 N. Hunter
Stockton, CA 95202
209-474-5089
Fax: 209-474-5605

Solano County Small Business Development
Center
320 Campus Lane
Suisun, CA 94585
707-864-3382
Fax: 707-864-3386

Southwest Los Angeles County Small Business
Development Center
21221 Western Ave., Suite 110
Torrance, CA 90501
310-782-6466
Fax: 310-782-8607

Northern Los Angeles Small Business
Development Center
14540 Victory Blvd., Suite #206
Van Nuys, CA 91411
818-373-7092
Fax: 818-373-7740

Satellite Operation
Central California Small Business Development
Center
430 W. Caldwell, Suite D
Visalia, CA 93277
209-625-3051/3052
Fax: 209-625-3053

Colorado
Lead Center
Colorado Small Business Development Ctr.
Office of Economic Development
1625 Broadway, Suite 1710
Denver, CO 80202
303-892-3809
Fax: 303-892-3848

Adams State College
Small Business Development Center
Alamosa, CO 81102
719-589-7372
Fax: 719-589-7522

Canon City (Satellite)
402 Valley Rd.
Canon City, CO 81212
719-275-5335
Fax: 719-275-4400

Pikes Peak Community College/
Colorado Springs Chamber of Commerce
Small Business Development Center
P.O. Drawer B
Colorado Springs, CO 80901-3002
303-471-4836
Fax: 303-635-1571

Colorado Northwestern Community College
Small Business Development Center
50 College Dr.
Craig, CO 81625
970-824-7078
Fax: 970-824-3527

Delta Montrose Vocational School
Small Business Development Center
1765 U.S. Highway 50
Delta, CO 81416
970-874-8772
Fax: 970-874-8796

Community College of Denver/
Denver Chamber of Commerce
Small Business Development Center
1445 Market St.
Denver, CO 80202
303-620-8076
Fax: 303-534-3200

Fort Lewis College
Small Business Development Center
Miller Student Center, Room 108
Durango, CO 81301
970-247-9634
Fax: 970-247-7620

Morgan Community College
Small Business Development Center
300 Main St.
Fort Morgan, CO 80701
970-867-3351
Fax: 970-867-3352

Mesa State College
Small Business Development Center
304 W. Main St.
Grand Junction, CO 81505-1606
970-243-5242
Fax: 970-241-0771

Aims Community College/
Greeley and Weld Chamber of Commerce
Small Business Development Center
902 7th Ave.
Greeley, CO 80631
970-352-3661
Fax: 970-352-3572

Red Rocks Community College
Small Business Development Center
777 S. Wadsworth Blvd.
Lakewood CO 80226
303-987-0710
Fax: 303-987-1331

Lamar Community College
Small Business Development Center
2400 S. Main
Lamar, CO 81052
719-336-8141
Fax: 719-336-2448

Arapaho Community College/
South Metro Chamber of Commerce
Small Business Development Center
7901 S. Park Plaza, Suite 110
Littleton, CO 80120
303-795-5855
Fax: 303-795-7520

Pueblo Community College
Small Business Development Center
900 West Orman Ave.
Pueblo, CO 81004
719-549-3224
Fax: 719-546-2413

Stratton (Satellite)
P.O. Box 28
Stratton, CO 80836
719-348-5596
Fax: 719-348-5887

Trinidad State Junior College
Small Business Development Center
136 W. Main St.
Trinidad, CO 81082

719-846-5645
Fax: 719-846-4550

Front Range Community College
Small Business Development Center
3645 West 112th Ave.
Westminster, CO 80030
303-460-1032
Fax: 303-469-7143

Connecticut
Lead Center
Connecticut Small Business Development Center
University of Connecticut
School of Business Administration
2 Bourn Place, U-94
Storrs, CT 06269
806-486-4135
Fax: 806-486-1576

Business Regional B.C.
Small Business Development Center
10 Middle St., 14th Floor
Bridgeport, CT 06604-4229
203-330-4813
Fax: 203-366-0105

Quinebaug Valley Community College
Small Business Development Center
742 Upper Maple St.
Danielson, CT 06239-1440
203-774-1133
Fax: 203-774-7768

University of Connecticut/MBA
Small Business Development Center
1800 Asylum Ave.
West Hartford, CT 06117
860-241-4986
Fax: 860-241-4907

University of Connecticut
Small Business Development Center
Administration Building, Room 300
1084 Shennecossett Rd.
Groton, CT 06340-6097
860-449-1188
Fax: 860-445-3415

Middlesex County Chamber of Commerce
Small Business Development Center
393 Main St.
Middletown, CT 06457
860-344-2158
Fax: 860-346-1043

Greater New Haven Chamber of Commerce
Small Business Development Center
195 Church St.
New Haven, CT 06510-2009
203-782-4390 ext. 190
Fax: 203-787-6730

Southwestern Area Commerce and Industry
Association (SACIA)
Small Business Development Center
One Landmark Square
Stamford, CT 06901
203-359-3220 ext. 302
Fax: 203-967-8294

Greater Waterbury Chamber of Commerce
Small Business Development Center
101 Main St.
Waterbury, CT 06706-1042

Small Business Development Centers

203-757-8937
Fax: 203-756-9077

Eastern Connecticut State University
Small Business Development Center
83 Windham St.
Willmantic, CT 06226-2295
960-456-5349
Fax: 960-456-5670

Delaware
Lead Center
Delaware Small Business Development Center
University of Delaware
Purnell Hall, Suite 005
Newark, DE 19716
302-831-1555
Fax: 302-831-1423

Sussex County Department of Economic Development
PO Box 610
Georgetown, DE 19947
302-856-1555
Fax: 302-856-5779

Delaware State University
1200 N. Dupont Highway
Dover, DE 19801
302-678-1555
Fax: 302-739-2333

Small Business Resource & Information Center
1318 N. Market St.
Wilmington, DE 19801
302-571-1555

District of Columbia
Lead Center
District of Columbia Small Business Development Center
Howard University
6th and Fairmont St., NW, Room 128
Washington, DC 20059
202-806-1550
Fax: 202-806-1777

Small Business Clinic
720 20th St., NW
Washington, DC 20052
202-994-7463
Fax: 202-994-4946

Office of Latino Affairs
2000 14th St. NW, 2nd Floor
Washington, DC 20009
202-396-1200

George Washington University
3101 MLK Jr. Ave. SE, 3rd Floor
Washington, DC 20010
202-561-4975 ext. 3006

Marshall Heights Community Development Org.
3917 Minnesota Ave. NE
Washington, DC 20019
202-396-1200

Ward Five Community Development Corp.--SBDC
901 Newton St. NE, Suite 103
Washington, DC 20017
202-396-4106
Fax: 202-396-4106

Florida
Lead Center
Florida Small Business Development Center Network
University of West Florida
Downtown Center
19 W. Garden St., Suite 300
Pensacola, FL 32501
904-444-2060
Fax: 904-444-2070

Seminole Community College
Small Business Development Center
Seminole Chamber of Commerce
P.O. Box 150784
AltaMonte Springs FL 32715-0784
407-834-4404

Florida Atlantic University
Small Business Development Center
Building T-9
P.O. Box 3091
Boca Raton, FL 33431
407-362-5620
Fax: 407-362-5623

Brevard Community College
Small Business Development Center
1519 Clearlake Rd.
Cocoa, FL 32922
407-951-1060, ext. 2045

Small Business Development Center
46 SW 1st Ave.
Dania, FL 33304
305-987-0100

Small Business Development Center
Florida Atlantic University
Commercial Campus
1515 West Commercial Blvd., Room 11
Fort Lauderdale, FL 33309
954-771-6520
Fax: 954-776-6645

Indian River Community College
Small Business Development Center
3209 Virginia Ave., Room 114
Fort Pierce, FL 34981-5599
407-462-4796
Fax: 407-462-4796

University of South Florida
Small Business Development Center
Sabal Hall, Rooms 219 and 220
8099 College Parkway SW
Fort Myers, FL 33919
941-489-9200
Fax: 941-489-9051

University of West Florida
Fort Walton Beach Center
Small Business Development Center
1170 Martin Luther King, Jr. Blvd.
Fort Walton Beach, FL 32547
904-863-6543
Fax: 904-863-6564

Small Business Development Center
505 NW 2nd Ave., Suite D
P.O. Box 2518
Gainesville, FL 32601
352-377-5621
Fax: 352-372-4132

University of North Florida
Small Business Development Center
College of Business
4567 St. John's Bluff Rd., South
Jacksonville, FL 32216
904-646-2476
Fax: 904-646-2594

Gulf Coast Community College
Small Business Development Center
2500 Minnesota Ave.
Lynn Haven, FL 32444
904-271-1108
Fax: 904-271-1109

Florida International University
Small Business Development Center
Trailer MO1
Tamiami Campus
Miami, FL 33199
305-348-2272

Small Business Development Center
600 N. Broadway, Suite 300
Bartow, FL 33830
941-534-4370
Fax: 941-533-1247

Daytona Beach Community College--SBDC
1200 W. International Speedway Blvd.
Daytona Beach, FL 32114
904-947-3141
Fax: 904-254-4465

Minority Business Development Center
5950 W. Oakland Park Blvd., Suite 307
Fort Lauderdale, FL 33313
954-485-5333
Fax: 954-485-2514

Florida Gulf Coast University
The Midway Ctr.
17595 Tamiami Tr., Suite 200
Fort Myers, FL 33908
941-590-1053

Miami Dade Community College--SBDC
6300 NW 7th Ave.
Miami, FL 33150
305-237-1906
Fax: 305-237-1908

Seminole Community College--SBDC
100 Weldon Blvd., Bldg. R
Sanford, FL 32707
407-328-4755 ext. 3341
Fax: 407-330-4489

Small Business Development Center
110 East Silver Springs Blvd.
P.O. Box 1210
Ocala, FL 32670
352-629-8051

University of Central Florida
Small Business Development Center
P.O. Box 161530
Orlando, FL 32816-1530
407-823-5554
Fax: 407-823-3073

University of West Florida
Small Business Development Center
Building 8, 11000 University Parkway
Pensacola, FL 32514
904-474-2908
Fax: 904-474-2126

Small Business Development Centers

Florida A & M University
Small Business Development Center
1157 Tennessee St.
Tallahassee, FL 32308
904-599-3407
Fax: 904-561-2395

University of South Florida
Small Business Development Center
College of Business Administration
4202 Minnesota Ave., BSN 3403
Tampa, FL 32444
813-974-4274

Small Business Development Center
Prospect Place, Suite 123
3111 S. Dixie Highway
West Palm Beach, FL 33405
407-837-5311

Georgia
Lead Center
Georgia Small Business Development Center
University of Georgia
Chicopee Complex
1180 East Broad St.
Athens, GA 30602
706-542-6762
Fax: 706-542-6776

Small Business Development Center
Southwest Georgia District
Business and Technology Center
230 S. Jackson St.
3rd Floor, Suite 333
Albany, GA 31701-2885
912-430-4303
Fax: 912-430-3933

Small Business Development Center
University of Georgia
Chicopee Complex
1180 East Broad St.
Athens, GA 30602-5412
706-542-7436
Fax: 706-542-6823

Morris Brown College
Small Business Development Center
643 Martin Luther King Jr. Dr., NW
Atlanta, GA 30314
404-220-0205
Fax: 404-688-5985

Georgia State University
Small Business Development Center
Box 874, University Plaza
Atlanta, GA 30303-3083
706-651-3550
Fax: 706-651-1035

Small Business Development Center
1061 Katherine St.
Augusta, GA 30904-6105
706-737-1790
Fax: 706-731-7937

Small Business Development Center
1107 Fountain Lake Dr.
Brunswick, GA 31525-3039
912-264-7343
Fax: 912-262-3095

Small Business Development Center
928 45th St. North Bldg., Room 523
Columbus, GA 31904-6572

706-649-7433
Fax: 706-649-1928

DeKalb Chamber of Commerce
Small Business Development Center
750 Commerce Dr.
Decatur, GA 30030-2622
404-378-8000
Fax: 404-378-3397

Small Business Development Center
500 Jesse Jewel Parkway, Suite 304
Gainesville, GA 30501
706-531-5681
Fax: 706-531-5684

Small Business Development Center
P.O. Box 13212
401 Cherry St., Suite 701
Macon, GA 31208-3212
912-751-6592
Fax: 912-751-6607

Kennesaw State College
Small Business Development Center
1000 Chastian Rd.
Kennesaw, GA 30144-5591
770-423-6450
Fax: 770-423-6564

Clayton State College
Small Business Development Center
P.O. Box 285
Morrow, GA 30260
404-961-3440
Fax: 404-961-3428

Floyd College
Small Business Development Center
P.O. Box 1664
Rome, GA 30162-1864
404-295-6326
Fax: 404-295-6732

Small Business Development Center
450 Mall Blvd., Suite H
Savannah, GA 31406-4824
912-356-2755
Fax: 912-353-3033

Small Business Development Center
3255 S. Main St.
Statesboro, GA 30460
912-681-5194
Fax: 912-681-0648

Small Business Development Center
Valdosta Area Office
Baytree West Professional Offices
Suite 9, Baytree Rd.
Valdosta, GA 31602-2782
912-245-3738
Fax: 912-245-3741

Middle Georgia Technical Institute
Small Business Development Center
151 Osigian Blvd.
Warner Robins, GA 31088
912-953-9356
Fax: 912-953-9376

Hawaii
Lead Center
Hawaii Small Business Development Center
University of Hawaii at Hilo
200 W. Kawili St.

Hilo, HI 96720-4091
808-933-3515
Fax: 808-933-3683

Small Business Development Center - Kauai
Kauai Community College
3-1901 Kaumualii Highway
Lihue, HI 96766-9591
808-246-1748
Fax: 808-245-5102

Small Business Development Center - Maui
Maui Research and Technology Center
590 Lipoa Parkway
Kihei, HI 96753
808-875-2402

Small Business Development Center - Oahu
Business Action Center
130 N. Merchant St., Suite 1030
Honolulu, HI 96813
808-522-8131
Fax: 808-522-8135

Idaho
Lead Center
Idaho Small Business Development Center
Boise State University
College of Business
1910 University Dr.
Boise, ID 83725
208-385-1640
Fax: 208-385-3877

Idaho State University
Small Business Development Center
2300 N. Yellowstone
Idaho Falls, ID 83401
208-523-1087
Fax: 208-523-1049

Lewis-Clark State College
Small Business Development Center
500 8th Ave.
Lewiston, ID 83501
208-799-2465
Fax: 208-799-2831

Boise Satellite Office
Small Business Development Center
Boise State University
305 E. Park St., Suite 405
McCall, ID 83638
208-634-2883

Idaho State University
Small Business Development Center
1651 Alvin Ricken Dr.
Pocatello, ID 83201
208-232-4921
Fax: 208-233-0268

North Idaho College
Small Business Development Center
525 W. Clearwater Loop
Post Falls, ID 83854
208-769-3296
Fax: 208-769-3223

College of Southern Idaho
Small Business Development Center
Region IV
315 Falls Ave.
Twin Falls, ID 83303
208-733-9554, ext. 2477
Fax: 208-733-9316

Small Business Development Centers

Illinois

Lead Center
Illinois Small Business Development Center Network
Dept. of Commerce and Community Affairs
620 East Adams St., 3rd Floor
Springfield, IL 62701
217-524-5856
Fax: 217-785-6328

Waubonsee Community College/
Aurora Campus
Small Business Development Center
5 East Galena Blvd.
Aurora, IL 60506
708-892-3334, ext. 139
Fax: 708-892-3374

Southern Illinois University/Carbondale
Small Business Development Center
Carbondale, IL 62901-6702
618-536-2424
Fax: 618-453-5040

Kaskaskia College (Satellite)
Small Business Development Center
2710 College Rd.
Centralia, IL 62801
618-532-2049
Fax: 618-532-4983

Back of the Yards Neighborhood Council (Sub-Center)
Small Business Development Center
1751 West 47th St.
Chicago, IL 60609
312-523-4419
Fax: 312-254-3525

Greater North Pulaski Economic Development Corp.
Small Business Development Center
4054 West North Ave.
Chicago, IL 60639
312-384-2262
Fax: 312-384-3850

Women's Business Development Center
Small Business Development Center
8 S. Michigan, Suite 400
Chicago, IL 60603
312-853-3477
Fax: 312-853-0145

Olive-Harvey College
Small Business Development Center
10001 S. Woodlawn Dr.
Chicago, IL 60628
312-468-8700
Fax: 312-468-8086

Industrial Council of NW Chicago
Small Business Development Center
2023 West Carroll
Chicago, IL 60612
312-421-3941
Fax: 312-421-1871

Latin American Chamber of Commerce
Small Business Development Center
539 N. Kedzie, Suite 11
Chicago, IL 60647
312-252-5211
Fax: 312-252-7065

Eighteenth Street Development Corp.
Small Business Development Center
1839 S. Carpenter
Chicago, IL 60608
312-733-2287
Fax: 312-733-7315

Loop Small Business Development Center
DCCA, State of Illinois Ctr.
100 West Randolph, Suite 3-400
Chicago, IL 60601
312-814-6111
Fax: 312-814-2807

McHenry County College
Small Business Development Center
8900 U.S. Highway 14
Crystal Lake, IL 60012-2761
815-455-6098
Fax: 815-455-9319

Danville Area Community College
Small Business Development Center
28 West North St.
Danville, IL 61832
217-442-7232
Fax: 217-442-6228

Small Business Development Center
985 W. Pershing Rd., Suite F-4
305 East Locust
Decatur, IL 62526
217-875-8284
Fax: 217-875-8289

Sauk Valley College
Small Business Development Center
173 Illinois Route #2
Dixon, IL 61021-9110
815-288-5511
Fax: 815-288-5958

Southern Illinois University/Edwardsville
Small Business Development Center
Campus Box 1107
Edwardsville, IL 62026
618-692-2929
Fax: 618-692-2647

Elgin Community College
Small Business Development Center
1700 Spartan Dr.
Elgin, IL 60123
847-888-7675
Fax: 847-888-7995

Evanston Business and Technology Center
Small Business Development Center
1840 Oak Ave.
Evanston, IL 60201
847-866-1817
Fax: 847-866-1808

College of DuPage
Small Business Development Center
22nd and Lambert Rd.
Glen Ellyn, IL 60137
708-942-2600
Fax: 708-942-3789

College of Lake County
Small Business Development Center
19351 West Washington St.
Grayslake, IL 60030
708-223-3633
Fax: 708-223-9371

Southeastern Illinois College (Satellite)
303 S. Commercial
Harrisburg, IL 62946-2125
618-252-5001
Fax: 618-252-0210

Rend Lake College
Small Business Development Center
Route #1
Ina, IL 62846
618-437-5321, ext. 335
Fax: 618-437-5677

Joliet Junior College
Small Business Development Center
Renaissance Center
Room 319, 214 N. Ottawa St.
Joliet, IL 60431
815-727-6544, ext. 1313
Fax: 815-722-1895

Kankakee Community College
Small Business Development Center
101 S. Schuyler Ave.
Kankakee, IL 60901
815-933-0376
Fax: 815-933-0380

Western Illinois University
Small Business Development Center
114 Seal Hall
Macomb, IL 61455
309-298-2211
Fax: 309-298-2520

Black Hawk College
Small Business Development Center
301 42nd Ave
East Moline, IL 61244
309-755-2200 ext. 211
Fax: 309-755-9847

Maple City Business and Technology (Satellite)
Small Business Development Center
620 S. Main St.
Monmouth, IL 61462
309-734-4664
Fax: 309-734-8579

Illinois Valley Community College
Small Business Development Center
Building 11, Route 1
Oglesby, IL 61348
815-223-1740
Fax: 815-224-3033

Illinois Eastern Community College
Small Business Development Center
401 East Main St.
Olney, IL 62450
618-395-3011
Fax: 618-395-1922

Moraine Valley College
Small Business Development Center
10900 S. 88th Ave.
Palos Hills, IL 60465
708-974-5468
Fax: 708-974-0078

Bradley University
Small Business Development Center
141 N. Jobst Hall, 1st Floor
Peoria, IL 61625
309-677-2992
Fax: 309-677-3386

Rock Valley College
Small Business Development Center

Small Business Development Centers

1220 Rock St.
Rockford, IL 61102
815-968-4087
Fax: 815-968-4157

Lincoln Land Community College
Small Business Development Center
200 West Washington
Springfield, IL 62701
217-789-1017
Fax: 217-789-0958

East St. Louis
DCCA, State Office Building
10 Collinsville
East St. Louis, IL 62201
618-583-2272
Fax: 618-588-2274

Shawnee College (Satellite)
Small Business Development Center
Shawnee College Rd.
Ullin, IL 62992
618-634-9618
Fax: 618-634-9028

Governor's State University
Small Business Development Center
University Park, IL 60466
708-534-4929
Fax: 708-534-8457

Indiana
Lead Center
Indiana Small Business Development Center
Economic Development Council
One N. Capitol, Suite 420
Indianapolis, IN 46204
317-264-6871
Fax: 317-264-3102

Greater Bloomington Chamber of Commerce
Small Business Development Center
116 W. 6th St.
Bloomington, IN 47404
812-339-8937
Fax: 812-336-0651

Columbus Enterprise Development Center, Inc.
Small Business Development Center
4920 N. Warren Dr.
Columbus, IN 47203
812-372-6480
Fax: 812-372-0228

Evansville Chamber of Commerce
Small Business Development Center
100 NW Second St., Suite 200
Evansville, IN 47708
812-425-7232

Northeast Indiana Business Assistance Corporation
Small Business Development Center
1830 Wayne Terrace
Fort Wayne, IN 46803
219-426-0040
Fax: 219-424-0024

Hoosier Valley Economic Opportunity
Corporation
Small Business Development Center
1613 E. 8th St.
Jeffersonville, IN 47130
812-288-6451
Fax: 812-284-8314

Indiana University
Small Business Development Center
342 Senate Ave.
Indianapolis, IN 46204
317-261-3030
Fax: 317-261-3053

Kokomo-Howard County Chamber of Commerce
Small Business Development Center
106 N. Washington
Kokomo, IN 46901
317-457-5301
Fax: 317-452-4564

Greater Lafayette Progress, Inc.
Small Business Development Center
122 N. Third
Lafayette, IN 47901
317-742-2394
Fax: 317-742-6276

Madison Area Chamber of Commerce
Small Business Development Center
301 East Main St.
Madison, IN 47250
812-265-3127
Fax: 812-265-2923

Muncie-Delaware County Chamber
Small Business Development Center
401 S. High St.
Muncie, IN 47308
317-284-8144
Fax: 317-741-5489

Northwest Indiana Forum, Inc.
Small Business Development Center
6100 Southport Rd.
Portage, IN 46368
219-762-1696
Fax: 219-942-5806

Richmond Area Chamber of Commerce
Small Business Development Center
33 S. 7th St.
Richmond, IN 47374
317-962-2887
Fax: 317-966-0882

South Bend Chamber of Commerce
Small Business Development Center
300 N. Michigan St.
South Bend, IN 46601
219-282-4350
Fax: 219-282-4344

Indiana State University
Small Business Development Center
School of Business
Terre Haute, IN 47809
812-237-7676
Fax: 812-237-7675

Bates Office of Economic Development
132 S. Main
Batesville, IN 47006
812-933-6110

Bedford Chamber of Commerce--SBDC
1116 W. 16th St.
Bedford, IN 47421
812-275-4493

Clay County Chamber of Commerce--SBDC
Twelve N. Walnut St.
Braxil, IN 47834
812-448-8457

Clinton Chamber of Commerce--SBDC
292 N. Ninth St.
Clinton, IN 47842
812-832-3844

Chamber of Commerce--SBDC
112 N. Main St.
Columbia City, IN 46725
219-248-8131

Connersville SBDC
504 Central
Connersville, IN 47331
317-825-8328

Harrison County Development Center
The Harrison Center
405 N. Capitol, Suite 308
Corydon, IN 47112
812-738-8811

Montgomery County Chamber of Commerce--SBDC
211 S. Washington St.
Crawfordsville, IN 47933
317-654-5507

Chamber of Commerce--SBDC
125 E. Monroe St.
Decatur, IN 46733
319-724-2604

City of Delphi Community Development--SBDC
20 S. Union
Delphi, IN 46923
317-564-6692

Elkhart Chamber of Commerce--SBDC
421 S. Second St.
Elkhart, IN 46515
219-522-5453

Elwood Chamber of Commerce--SBDC
108 S. Anderson St.
Elwood, IN 46063
317-552-0180

Clinton County Chamber of Commerce--SBDC
207 S. Main St.
Frankfort, IN 46041
317-654-5507

Northlake Small Business Development Center
Firth Avenue Mall
487 Broadway, Suite 201
Gary, IN 46402
219-882-2000

Greencastle Partnership Ctr.--SBDC
Two S. Jackson St.
Greencastle, IN 46135
317-653-4517

Greensburg Area Chamber of Commerce--SBDC
125 W. Main St.
Greensburg, IN 47240
812-663-2832

Hammond Development Corp.--SBDC
649 Conkey St.
Hammond, IN 46324
219-853-6399

Blackford County Economic Development--SBDC
P.O. Box 43
Hartford, IN 47348
317-348-4944

Small Business Development Centers

Indiana Region 15 Planning Commission--SBDC
511 Fourth St.
Huntingburg, IN 47542
812-683-5699
812-683-4647

Kendallville Chamber of Commerce
Small Business Development Center
228 S. Main St.
Kendallville, IN 46755
219-347-1554

LaPorte Small Business Development Center
414 Lincolnway
LaPorte, IN 46350
219-326-7232

Dearborn County Chamber of Commerce
Small Business Development Center
213 Eads Parkway
Lawrenceburg, IN 47025
812-537-0814
Fax: 812-537-0845

Union County Chamber of Commerce
Small Business Development Center
102 N. Main St., #6
Liberty, IN 47353-1039
317-458-5976

First Citizens Band SBDC
515 N. Franklin Square
Michigan City, IN 46360
319-874-9245

Mitchell Chamber of Commerce
Small Business Development Center
First National Bank
Main St.
Mitchell, IN 47446
812-849-4441

White County Chamber of Commerce--SBDC
P.O. Box 1031
Monticello, IN 47960
219-583-6557

Mt. Vernon Chamber of Commerce--SBDC
405 E. Fourth St.
Mt. Vernon, IN 47602
812-838-3639

East Central Indiana Regional SBDC
401 S. High St.
Muncie, IN 47308
317-284-8144
Fax: 317-741-5489

Brown County Chamber of Commerce--SBDC
P.O. Box 164
Nashville, IN 47448
812-988-6647

Floyd County Private Industry Council Workforce Development Center
Small Business Development Center
3303 Plaza Dr., Suite 2
New Albany, IN 47150
812-945-2643

Jennings County Chamber of Commerce--SBDC
P.O. Box 340
North Vernon, IN 47265
812-346-2339

Private Industry Council Workforce, Orange County
326 B. N. Gospel
Paoli, IN 47464
812-723-4206

Peru Area Chamber of Commerce
Small Business Development Center
Two N. Broadway, Suite 202
Peru, IN 46970
317-472-1923

Jay County Development Corp.--SBDC
121 W. Main St., Suite A
Portland, IN 47371
219-726-9311

Park County Economic Development--SBDC
P.O. Box 296
Rockville, IN 47872
317-569-0226

Rushville Chamber of Commerce--SBDC
P.O. Box 156
Rushville, IN 47173
317-932-2222

Seymour Chamber of Commerce--SBDC
P.O. Box 43
Seymour, IN 47274
812-522-3681

Sullivan Chamber of Commerce--SBDC
Ten S. Court St.
Sullivan, IN 47882
812-268-4836

Tell City Chamber of Commerce--SBDC
Regional Federal Bldg.
645 Main St.
Tell City, IN 47586
812-547-2385
Fax: 812-547-8378

Tipton County Economic Development Corp. SBDC
136 East Jefferson
Tipton, IN 46072
317-675-7300

Porter County SBDC
911 Wall St.
Valparaiso, IN 46383
219-477-5256

Vevay/Switzerland County Foundation--SBDC
P.O. Box 193
Vevay, IN 47043
812-427-2533

Vincennes University--SBDC
P.O. Box 887
Vincennes, IN 47591
812-885-5749

Wabash Area Chamber of Commerce--SBDC
67 S. Wabash
Wabash, IN 46922
219-563-1168

Washington, Davies County SBDC
One Train Depot St.
Washington, IN 47501
812-254-5262
Fax: 812-254-2550

Purdue University SBDC
Business & Industrial Development Center
1220 Potter Dr.
West Layfayette, IN 47906
317-494-5858

Randolph County Economic Dev. Foundation--SBDC
111 S. Main St.
Winchester, IN 47394
317-584-3266

Iowa
Lead Center
Iowa Small Business Development Center
Iowa State University
College of Business Administration
Chamblynn Building
137 Lynn Ave.
Ames, IA 50010
515-292-6351
Fax: 515-292-0020

ISU Small Business Development Center
ISU Audubon Branch
Circle West Incubator
P.O. Box 204
Audubon, IA 50025
712-563-2623
Fax: 712-563-2301

University of Northern Iowa
Small Business Development Center
Suite 5, Business Building
Cedar Falls, IA 50614-0120
319-273-2696
Fax: 319-273-6830

Iowa Western Community College
Small Business Development Center
2700 College Rd., Box 4C
Council Bluffs, IA 51502
712-325-3260
Fax: 712-325-3408

Southwestern Community College
Small Business Development Center
1501 West Townline
Creston, IA 50801
515-782-4161
Fax: 515-782-4164

Eastern Iowa Community College District
Small Business Development Center
304 West Second St.
Davenport, IA 52801
319-322-4499
Fax: 319-322-8241

Drake University
Small Business Development Center
Drake Business Center
2401 University
Des Moines, IA 50311-4505
515-271-2655
Fax: 515-271-4540

Dubuque Area Chamber of Commerce
Northeast Iowa Small Business Development Center
770 Town Clock Plaza
Dubuque, IA 52001
319-588-3350
Fax: 319-557-1591

University of Iowa
Oakdale Campus
Small Business Development Center
108 Pappajohn Business Adm. Bldg.

Small Business Development Centers

Suite S-160
Iowa City, IA 52242-1000
319-335-3742
Fax: 319-335-2445

Kirkwood Community College
Small Business Development Center
2901 Tenth Ave.
Marion, IA 52302
319-377-8256
Fax: 319-377-5667

North Iowa Area Community College
Small Business Development Center
500 College Dr.
Mason City, IA 50401
515-421-4342
Fax: 515-423-0931

Indian Hills Community College
Small Business Development Center
525 Grandview Ave.
Ottumwa, IA 52501
515-683-5127
Fax: 515-683-5263

Western Iowa Tech Community College
Small Business Development Center
4647 Stone Ave.
Bldg. B, Box 265
Sioux City, IA 51102-0265
712-274-6418
Fax: 712-274-6429

Iowa Lakes Community College
Small Business Development Center
Gateway Center
Highway 71 N.
Spencer, IA 51301
712-262-4213
Fax: 712-262-4047

Southeastern Community College
Small Business Development Center
Drawer F
West Burlington, IA 52655
319-752-2731, ext. 103
Fax: 319-752-3407

Kansas
Lead Center
Kansas Small Business Development Center
Wichita State University
1845 Fairmount
Wichita, KS 67260-0148
316-689-3193
Fax: 316-689-3647

Butler County Community College
Small Business Development Center
600 Walnut
Augusta, KS 67010
316-775-1124

Neosho County Community College
Small Business Development Center
1000 S Allen
Chanute, KS 66720
316-431-2820, ext 219
Fax: 316-431-0082

Coffeyville Community College
Small Business Development Center
11th and Willow Sts.
Coffeyville, KS 67337-5064

316-252-7007
Fax: 316-252-7098

Colby Community College
Small Business Development Center
1255 S. Range
Colby, KS 67701
913-462-3984, ext. 239
Fax: 913-462-8315

Cloud County Community College
Small Business Development Center
2221 Campus Dr.
P.O. Box 1002
Concordia, KS 66901
913-243-1435
Fax: 913-243-1459

Dodge City Community College
Small Business Development Center
2501 N. 14th Ave.
Dodge City, KS 67801
316-227-9247, ext. 247
Fax: 316-227-9200

Emporia State University
Small Business Development Center
207 Cremer Hall
Emporia, KS 66801
316-342-7162
Fax: 316-341-5418

Fort Scott Community College
Small Business Development Center
2108 S Horton
Fort Scott, KS 66701
316-223-2700
Fax: 316-223-6530

Garden City Community College
Small Business Development Center
801 Campus Dr.
Garden City, KS 67846
316-276-9632
Fax: 316-276-9630

Fort Hays State University
Small Business Development Center
1301 Pine St.
Hays, KS 67601
913-628-5340
Fax: 913-628-1471

Hutchinson Community College
Small Business Development Center
815 N. Walnut, #225
Hutchinson, KS 67501
316-665-4950
Fax: 316-665-8354

Independence Community College
Small Business Development Center
College Ave. and Brookside, Box 708
Independence, KS 67301
316-331-4100
Fax: 316-331-5344

Allen County Community College
T.B.D.
Small Business Development Center
1801 N. Cottonwood
Iola, KS 66749
316-365-5116
Fax: 316-365-3284

Seward County Community College
Small Business Development Center

1801 N. Kansas
Liberal, KS 67905
316-624-1951, ext. 150
Fax: 316-624-0637

Kansas State University
Small Business Development Center
2323 Anderson Ave., Suite 100
Manhattan, KS 66502-2947
913-532-5529
Fax: 913-532-5827

Ottawa University
Small Business Development Center
College Ave., Box 70
Ottawa, KS 66067
913-242-5200, ext. 5457
Fax: 913-242-7429

Johnson County Community College
Small Business Development Center
CEC Building, Room 223
Overland Park, KS 66210-1299
913-469-3878
Fax: 913-469-4415

Labette Community College
Small Business Development Center
200 S. 14th
Parsons, KS 67357
316-421-6700
Fax: 316-421-0921

Pittsburg State University
Small Business Development Center
Shirk Hall
Pittsburg, KS 66762
316-235-4920
Fax: 316-232-6440

Pratt Community College
Small Business Development Center
Highway 61
Pratt, KS 67124
316-672-5641
Fax: 316-672-5288

KSU-Salina College of Technology
Small Business Development Center
2409 Scanlan Ave.
Salina, KS 67401
913-826-2622,
Fax: 913-826-2936

Washburn University
Small Business Development Center
101 Henderson Learning Center
Topeka, KS 66621
913-231-1010, ext. 1305
Fax: 913-231-1063

Kentucky
Lead Center
Kentucky Small Business Development Ctr.
University of Kentucky
Center for Business Development
College of Business and Economics
225 Business and Economics Building
Lexington, KY 40506-0034
606-257-7668
Fax: 606-258-1907

Ashland Small Business Development Center
Boyd-Greenup County Chamber of Commerce Building
P.O. Box 830
207 15th St.

Small Business Development Centers

Ashland, KY 41105-0830
606-329-8011
Fax: 606-325-4607

Western Kentucky University
Bowling Green Small Business Development Center
245 Grise Hall
Bowling Green, KY 42101
502-745-2901
Fax: 502-745-2902

Southeast Community College
Small Business Development Center
Room 113, Chrisman Hall
Cumberland, KY 40823
606-589-4514
Fax: 606-589-4941

Elizabethtown Small Business Development Center
238 West Dixie Ave.
Elizabethtown, KY 42701
502-765-6737
Fax: 502-769-5095

Northern Kentucky University
North Kentucky Small Business Development Center
BEP Center, Room 468
Highland Heights, KY 41099-0506
606-572-6524
Fax: 606-572-5566

Hopkinsville Small Business Development Center
300 Hammond Dr.
Hopkinsville, KY 42240
502-886-8666
Fax: 502-886-3211

University of Kentucky
Small Business Development Center
College of Business and Economics
c/o Downtown Public Library
140 Main St.
Lexington, KY 40507
606-257-7666
Fax: 606-257-1751

Bellarmine College
Small Business Development Center
School of Business
2001 Newburg Rd.
Louisville, KY 40205-0671
502-452-8282
Fax: 502-452-8288

University of Louisville
Small Business Development Center
Center for Entrepreneurship and Technology
Room 122, Burhans Hall
Louisville, KY 40292
502-588-7854
Fax: 502-588-8573

Morehead State University
Small Business Development Center
207 Downing Hall
Morehead, KY 40351
606-783-2895
Fax: 606-783-5023

Murray State University
West Kentucky Small Business Development Center
College of Business and Public Affairs
Murray, KY 42071
502-762-2856
Fax: 502-762-3049

Owensboro Small Business Development Center
3860 U.S. Highway 60 West
Owensboro, KY 42301
502-926-8085
Fax: 502-684-0714

Pikeville Small Business Development Center
222 Hatcher Court
Pikeville, KY 41501
606-432-5848
Fax: 606-432-8924

Eastern Kentucky University
Small Business Development Center
107 West Mt. Vernon St.
Somerset, KY 42501
606-678-5520
Fax: 606-678-8349

Louisiana
Lead Center
Louisiana Small Business Development Center
Northeast Louisiana University
Adm. 2-57
Monroe, LA 71209
318-342-5506
Fax: 318-342-5510

Small Business Development Center
934 3rd St., Suite 510
Alexandria,, LA 71301
318-484-2123
Fax: 318-484-2126

Capital Small Business Development Center
1933 Wooddale Blvd. Suite E
Baton Rouge, LA 70806
504-922-0998
Fax: 504-922-0999

Southeastern Louisiana University
Small Business Development Center
Box 522, SLU Station
Hammond, LA 70402
504-549-3831
Fax: 504-549-2127

University of Southwestern Louisiana
Arcadiana Small Business Development Ctr.
Box 43732
Lafayette, LA 70504
318-262-5344
Fax: 318-262-5296

McNeese State University
Small Business Development Center
College of Business Administration
Lake Charles, LA 70609
318-475-5529
Fax: 318-475-5012

Northeast Louisiana University
College of Business Administration
Monroe, LA 71209
318-342-1215
Fax: 318-342-1209

Northwestern State University
Small Business Development Center
College of Business Administration
Natchitoches, LA 71497
318-357-5611
Fax: 318-357-6810

University of New Orleans
Small Business Development Center
LA International Trade
2 Canal St., Suite 2926
New Orleans, LA 70130
504-568-8222
Fax: 504-568-8228

Loyola University
Small Business Development Center
Box 134
New Orleans, LA 70118
504-865-3496
Fax: 504-865-3347

Southern University
Small Business Development Center
College of Business Administration
New Orleans, LA 70126
504-286-5308
Fax: 504-286-5131

University of New Orleans
Small Business Development Center
Lakefront Campus
College of Business Administration
New Orleans, LA 70148
504-539-9292
Fax: 504-539-9205

Louisiana Tech University
Small Business Development Center
Box 10318, Tech Station
Ruston, LA 71271-0046
318-257-3537
Fax: 318-257-4253

Louisiana State University at Shreveport
Small Business Development Center
College of Business Administration
1 University Place
Shreveport, LA 71115
318-797-5144
Fax: 318-797-5208

Nicholls State University
Small Business Development Center
P.O. Box 2015
Thibodaux, LA 70310
504-448-4242
Fax: 504-448-4922

Maine
Lead Center
Maine Small Business Development Center
University of Southern Maine
96 Falmouth St., P.O. Box 9300
Portland, ME 04101
207-780-4420
Fax: 207-780-4810

Androscoggin Valley Council of Governments (AVCOG)
Small Business Development Center
125 Manley Rd.
Auburn, ME 04210
207-783-9186
Fax: 207-780-4810

Eastern Maine Development Corporation
Small Business Development Center
P.O. Box 2579
Bangor, ME 04402-2579
207-942-6389
Fax: 207-942-3548

Small Business Development Centers

Northern Maine Regional Planning Commission
Small Business Development Center
P.O. Box 779
2 Main St.
Caribou, ME 04736
207-498-8736
Fax: 207-493-3108

Southern Maine Regional Planning Commission
Small Business Development Center
Box Q, 255 Main St.
Sanford, ME 04073
207-324-0316
Fax: 207-324-2958

Coastal Enterprises, Inc.
Small Business Development Center
Water St., Box 268
Wiscasset, ME 04578
207-882-4340
Fax: 207-882-4456

Maryland
Lead Center
Small Business Development Center
1420 N. Charles St., Room 142
Baltimore, MD 21202
410-837-4141
Fax: 410-837-4151

Anne Arundel Office of Economic Development
Small Business Development Center
2660 Riva Rd., Suite 200
Annapolis, MD 21401
410-224-4205
Fax: 410-222-7415

Business Resource Center
Small Business Development Center
217 E. Redwood St., 10th Floor
Baltimore, MD 21202
410-333-6552
Fax: 410-333-4460

Harford County Economic Development Office
Small Business Development Center
220 S. Main St.
Bel Air, MD 21014
410-893-3837
Fax: 410-879-8043

Manufacturing and Technology
Small Business Development Center
Dingman Center for Entrepreneurship
College of Business and Management
University of Maryland
College Park, MD 20742-1815
301-405-2144
Fax: 301-314-9152

Howard County Economic Development Office
Small Business Development Center
6751 Gateway Dr., Suite 500
Columbia, MD 21043
410-313-6552
Fax: 410-313-6556

Western Region Small Business Development Center
3 Commerce Dr.
Cumberland, MD 21502
301-724-6716
Fax: 301-777-7504

Cecil Community College
Eastern Region SBDC
135 E. Main St.
Elkton, MD 21921
410-392-0597
Fax: 410-392-6225

Arundel Center N
Small Business Development Center
101 Crain Highway NW, Room 110B
Glen Burnie, MD 21601
410-766-1910
Fax: 410-766-1911

Suburban Washington Small Business Development Center
1400 McCormick Dr., Suite 282
Landover, MD 20785
301-883-6491
Fax: 301-883-6479

Eastern Shore Small Business Development Center
SubCenter
Salisbury State University
Power Professional Bldg. Suite 400
Salisbury, MD 21801
410-546-4325
Fax: 410-548-5389

Baltimore County Chamber of Commerce
Small Business Development Center
102 W. Pennsylvania Ave., Suite 402
Towson, MD 21204
410-832-5866
Fax: 410-821-9901

Carroll County Economic Development
Small Business Development Center
125 N. Court St., Room 103
Westminster, MD 21157
410-857-8166
Fax: 410-848-0003

Massachusetts
Lead Center
Massachusetts Small Business Development Center
University of Massachusetts
205 School of Management
Amherst, MA 01003
413-545-6301
Fax: 413-545-1273

University of Massachusetts at Amherst
Minority Business Assistance Center
250 Stuart St., 5th Floor
Boston, MA 02125-3393
617-287-7725
Fax: 617-287-7725

Boston College
Metropolitan Regional Small Business Development Center
96 College Rd. - Rahner House
Chestnut Hill, MA 02167
617-552-4091
Fax: 617-552-2730

Boston College
Capital Formation Service/East
Small Business Development Center
96 College Rd. - Rahner House
Chestnut Hill, MA 02167
617-552-4091
Fax: 617-552-2730

University of Massachusetts at Dartmouth
Southeastern Massachusetts Regional Small Business Development Center
200 Pocasset St.
P.O. Box 2785
Fall River, MA 02722
508-673-9783
Fax: 508-674-1929

Salem State College
North Shore Regional SBDC
197 Essex St.
Salem, MA 01970
508-741-6343
Fax: 508-741-6345

University of Massachusetts
Western Massachusetts Regional Small Business Development Center
101 State St., Suite #424
Springfield, MA 01103
413-737-6712
Fax: 413-737-2312

Clark University
Central Massachusetts Regional Small Business Development Center
950 Main St., Dana Commons
Worcester, MA 01610
508-793-7615
Fax: 508-793-8890

Michigan
Lead Center
Michigan Small Business Development Center
2727 Second Ave.
Detroit, MI 48201
313-964-1798
Fax: 313-964-3648

Ottawa County Economic Development Office, Inc.
Small Business Development Center
6676 Lake Michigan Dr.
P.O. Box 539
Allendale, MI 49401-0539
616-892-4120
Fax: 616-895-6670

Merra Specialty Business Development Center
Small Business Development Center
2200 Commonwealth, Suite 230
Ann Arbor, MI 48106-1485
313-769-4110
Fax: 313-769-4064

Huron County Economic Development Corporation (Satellite)
Small Business Development Center
Huron County Building, Room 303
Bad Axe, MI 48413
517-269-6431
Fax: 517-269-7221

Kellogg Community College
Small Business Development Center
34 W. Jackson, Suite A
Battle Creek, MI 49017
616-962-4076

Lake Michigan College
Small Business Development Center
Corporate and Community Services
2755 E. Napier
Benton Harbor, MI 49022
616-927-8179
Fax: 616-927-8103

Ferris State University
Small Business Development Center

Small Business Development Centers

330 Oak St., W115
Big Rapids, MI 49307
616-592-3553
Fax: 616-592-3539

Tuscola County Economic Development
Corporation
Small Business Development Center
194 N. State, Suite 200
Caro, MI 48723
517-673-2849
Fax: 517-673-2517

NILAC-Marygrove College
Small Business Development Center
8425 West McNichols
Detroit, MI 48221
313-945-2159
Fax: 313-864-6670

Wayne State University
Small Business Development Center
School of Business Administration
2727 Second Ave.
Detroit, MI 48201
313-577-4850
Fax: 313-577-8933

1st Step, Inc.
Small Business Development Center
2415 14th Ave., S.
Escanaba, MI 49829
906-786-9234
Fax: 906-786-4442

Genesee Economic Area Revitalization, Inc.
(Satellite)
Small Business Development Center
711 N. Saginaw St., Suite 123
Flint, MI 48503
810-239-5847
Fax: 810-239-5575

Grand Rapids Community College
Small Business Development Center
Applied Technology Center
151 Fountain NE
Grand Rapids, MI 49503
616-771-0571
Fax: 616-458-3768

Oceana Economic Development Corporation
(Satellite)
Small Business Development Center
P.O. Box 168, 100 State St.
Hart, MI 49420-0168
616-873-7141
Fax: 616-873-5914

Michigan Technological University
Small Business Development Center
Bureau of Industrial Development
1400 Townsend Dr.
Houghton, MI 49931
906-487-2470
Fax: 906-487-2858

Kalamazoo College
Small Business Development Center
Stryker Center for Management Studies
1327 Academy St.
Kalamazoo, MI 49006-3200
616-337-7350
Fax: 616-337-7415

Lansing Community College
Small Business Development Center
P.O. Box 40010
333 N. Washington Sq.
Lansing, MI 48901-7210
517-483-1921
Fax: 517-483-1675

Lapeer Development Corporation (Satellite)
449 McCormick Dr.
Lapeer, MI 48446
313-667-0080
Fax: 313-667-3541

Macomb County Business Assistance Network
115 S. Groesbeck Hwy.
Mt. Clemens, MI 48043
810-469-5118
Fax: 810-469-6787

Central Michigan University
Small Business Development Center
256 Applied Business Studies Complex
Mt. Pleasant, MI 48859
517-774-3270
Fax: 517-774-7992

Muskegon Economic Growth Alliance
Small Business Development Center
230 Terrace Plaza
P.O. Box 1087
Muskegon, MI 49443-1087
616-722-3751
Fax: 616-728-7251

Sanilac County Economic Growth (Satellite)
175 East Aitken Rd.
Peck, MI 48466
313-648-4311
Fax: 313-648-4617

St. Claire County Community College
Small Business Development Center
800 Military St., Suite 320
Port Huron, MI 48060
810-982-9511
Fax: 810-982-9531

Saginaw Future, Inc.
Small Business Development Center
301 East Genesee, Third Floor
Saginaw, MI 48607
517-754-8222
Fax: 517-754-1715

West Shore Community College (Satellite)
Business and Industrial Development
3000 N. Stiles Rd., P.O. Box 277
Scottville, MI 49454-0277
616-845-6211
Fax: 616-845-0207

Montcalm Community College (Satellite)
2800 College Dr. SW
Sidney, MI 48885
517-328-2111
Fax: 517-328-2950

Sterling Heights Area Chamber of Commerce
(Satellite)
12900 Hall Rd., Suite 110
Sterling Heights, MI 48313
810-731-5400
Fax: 810-731-3521

Northwestern Michigan College
Center for Business and Industry
1701 East Front St.
Traverse City, MI 49686

616-922-1720
Fax: 616-922-1722

Travers Bay Economic Development Corporation
Traverse City Small Business Development Center
202 E. Grandview Parkway
Traverse City, MI 49684
616-947-5075
Fax: 616-946-2565

Greater Northwest Regional CDC
2200 Dendrinos Dr., P.O. Box 506
Traverse City, MI 49685-0506
616-929-5000
Fax: 616-929-5012

Walsh/O.C.C. Business Enterprise Development
Center
1301 W. Long Lanke, Suite 150
Troy, MI 48098
810-952-5800
Fax: 810-952-1875

Saginaw Valley State University (Satellite)
Business and Industrial Development Institute
7400 Bay Rd.
University Center, MI 48710
517-790-4388
Fax: 517-790-4983

Minnesota
Lead Center
Minnesota Small Business Development Center
Department of Trade and Economic Development
500 Metro Square
121 7th Place E.
St. Paul, MN 55101-2146
612-297-5770
Fax: 612-296-1290

Customized Training Center
Small Business Development Center
Bemidji Technical College
905 Grant Ave., SE
Bemidji, MN 56601
218-755-4286
Fax: 218-755-4289

Normandale Community College
Small Business Development Center
9700 France Ave. S.
Bloomington, MN 55431
612-832-6560
Fax: 612-832-6352

Brainerd Technical College
Small Business Development Center
300 Quince St.
Brainerd, MN 56401
218-828-5302
Fax: 218-828-5321

University of Minnesota at Duluth
Small Business Development Center
10 University Dr., 150 SBE
Duluth, MN 55812
218-726-8758
Fax: 218-726-6338

Itasca Development Corporation
Grand Rapids Small Business Development Center
19 NE Third St.
Grand Rapids, MN 55744
218-327-2241
Fax: 218-327-2242

Small Business Development Centers

Hibbing Community College
Small Business Development Center
1515 East 25th St.
Hibbing, MN 55746
218-262-6703
Fax: 218-262-6717

Small Business Development Center
Rainy River Community College
1501 Hwy 71
International Falls, MN 56649
218-285-2255
Fax: 218-285-2239

Mankato State University
Small Business Development Center
P.O. Box 3367
410 Jackson St.
Mankato, MN 56001
507-387-5643
Fax: 507-387-7105

Southwest State University
Small Business Development Center
ST #105
Marshall, MN 56258
507-537-7386
Fax: 507-537-6094

Minnesota Project Innovation
Small Business Development Center
Suite 100, 111 Third Ave. S.
Minneapolis, MN 55401
612-338-3280
Fax: 612-338-3483

Small Business Development Center
University of St. Thomas
1000 LaSalle Ave., Suite MPL100
Minneapolis, MN 55403
612-962-4500
Fax: 612-962-4410

Moorhead State University
Small Business Development Center
1104 7th Ave.S
MSU Box 303
Moorhead, MN 56563
218-226-2289
Fax: 218-236-2280

Small Business Development Center
Owatonna Incubator, Inc.
P.O. Box 505
560 Dunnell Dr., Suite #203
Owatonna, MN 55060
507-451-0517
Fax: 507-455-2788

Pine Technical College
Small Business Development Center
1100 4th St.
Pine City, MN 55063
612-629-7340
Fax: 612-629-7603

Small Business Development Center
Hennepin Technical College
1820 N. Xenium Lane
Plymouth, MN 55441
612-550-7218
Fax: 612-550-7272

Pottery Bus. & Tech. Ctr.
Small Business Development Center
2000 Pottery Place Dr., Suite 339
Red Wing, MN 55066

612-388-4079
Fax: 612-385-2251

Rochester Community College
Small Business Development Center
851 30th Ave., SE
Rochester, MN 55904
507-285-7536
Fax: 507-280-5502

Dakota County Technical Institute
Small Business Development Center
1300 145th St. East
Rosemount, MN 55068
612-423-8262
Fax: 612-322-5156

Small Business Development Center
SE Minnesota Development Corp.
111 W. Jessie St.
Rushford, MN 55971
507-864-7557
Fax: 507-864-2091

St. Cloud State University
Small Business Development Center
Business Resource Center
4191 2nd St. S
St. Cloud, MN 56301-3761
612-255-4842
Fax: 612-255-4957

Minnesota Technology Inc.
Small Business Development Center
Olcott Plaza
820 N. 9th St.
Virginia, MN 55792
218-741-4251
Fax: 218-741-4249

Wadena Technical College
Small Business Development Center
222 Second St., SE
Wadena, MN 56482
218-631-1502
Fax: 218-631-2396

North/East Metro Technical College
Small Business Development Center
3300 Century Ave. N, Suite 200D
White Bear Lake, MN 55110-1894
612-779-5764
Fax: 612-779-5802

Mississippi
Lead Center
Mississippi Small Business Development Center
University of Mississippi
Old Chemistry Building, Suite 216
University, MS 38677
601-232-5001
Fax: 601-232-5650

Northeast Mississippi Community College
Small Business Development Center
Cunningham Blvd.
Holliday Hall, 2nd Floor
Booneville, MS 38829
601-728-7751
Fax: 601-728-1165

Delta State University
Small Business Development Center
P.O. Box 3235 DSU
Cleveland, MS 38733
601-846-4236
Fax: 601-846-4235

East Central Community College Small Business
Development Center
P.O. Box 129
Decatur, MS 39327
601-635-2111
Fax: 601-635-2150

Jones Jr College Small Business Development
Center
900 Court St.
Ellisville, MS 39437
601-477-4165
Fax: 601-477-4152

Mississippi Gulf Coast Community College Small
Business Development Center
Jackson County Campus
P.O. Box 100
Gautier, MS 39553
601-497-9595
Fax: 601-497-9604

Delta Community College
Small Business Development Center
P.O. Box 5607
Greenville, MS 38704-5607
601-378-8183
Fax: 601-378-5349

MS Contract Procurement Center
Small Business Development Center
3015 12th St.
P.O. Box 610
Gulfport, MS 39502-0610
601-864-2961
Fax: 601-864-2969

Pearl River Community College
Small Business Development Center
5448 U.S. Highway 49 S.
Hattiesburg, MS 39401
601-544-0030
Fax: 601-544-0032

Mississippi Valley State University Small Business
Development Center
MS Valley State University
Itta Bena, MS 38941
601-254-3601
Fax: 601-254-6704

Jackson State University
Small Business Development Center
Suite A1, Jackson Enterprise Center
931 Highway 80 West
Jackson, MS 39204
601-968-2795
Fax: 601-968-2796

University of Southern Mississippi
Small Business Development Center
136 Beach Park Place
Long Beach, MS 39560
601-865-4578
Fax: 601-865-4581

Alcorn State University SBDC
P.O. Box 90
Lorman, MS 39095-9402
601-877-6684
Fax: 601-877-6266

Meridian Community College
Small Business Development Center
910 Highway 19 N.
Meridian, MS 39307
601-482-7445
Fax: 601-482-5803

Small Business Development Centers

Mississippi State University
Small Business Development Center
P.O. Drawer 5288
Mississippi State, MS 39762
601-325-8684
Fax: 601-325-4016

Copiah-Lincoln Community College
Small Business Development Center
823 Hwy. 61 N.
Natchez, MS 39120
601-445-5254
Fax: 601-445-5254

Hinds Community College
Small Business Development Center
International Trade Center
P.O. Box 1170
Raymond, MS 39154
601-857-3537
Fax: 601-857-3535

Holmes Community College Small Business
Development Center
412 West Ridgeland Ave.
Ridgeland, MS 39159
601-853-0827
Fax: 601-853-0844

Northwest MS Comm. College Small Business
Development Center
Desoto Center
8700 Northwest Dr.
Southaven, MS 38671
601-342-7648
Fax: 601-342-7648

Southwest MS Comm. College Small Business
Development Center
College Dr.
Summit, MS 39666
601-276-3890
Fax: 601-276-3867

Itawamba Community College
Small Business Development Ctr
653 Eason Blvd.
Tupelo, MS 38801
601-680-8515
Fax: 601-842-6885

University of Mississippi
Small Business Development Center
Old Chemistry Building, Suite 216
University, MS 38677
601-234-2120
Fax: 601-232-5650

Missouri
Lead Center
Missouri Small Business Development Center
University of Missouri
Suite 300, University Place
Columbia, MO 65211
573-882-0344
Fax: 573-884-4297

Camden County Extension Center
Small Business Development Center
113 Kansas
P.O. Box 1405
Camdenton, MO 65020
573-346-2644
Fax: 573-346-2694

Southwest Missouri State University
Small Business Development Center
222 N. Pacific
Cape Girardeau, MO 63701
573-290-5965
Fax: 573-290-5005

Small Business Development Center
Chillicothe City Hall
715 Washington St.
Chillicothe, MO 64601
816-646-6920
Fax: 816-646-6811

St. Louis County Extension Center
Small Business Development Center
121 S Meramac, Suite 501
Clayton, MO 63105
314-889-2911
Fax: 314-854-6147

Boone County Extension Center
Small Business Development Center
1012 N. Hwy UU
Columbia, MO 65203
573-445-9792
Fax: 573-445-9807

University of Missouri at Columbia
Small Business Development Center
1800 University Place
Columbia, MO 65211
573-882-3597
Fax: 573-884-4297

Hannibal Satellite Center
Small Business Development Center
Hannibal, MO 63401
816-385-6550
Fax: 816-385-6568

Jefferson County Extension Center
Small Business Development Center
Courthouse, #203
725 Maple St., P.O. Box 497
Hillsboro, MO 63050
573-789-5391
Fax: 573-789-5059

Jackson County Extension Center
Small Business Development Center
1507 S. Noland Rd.
Independence, MO 64055-1307
816-252-5051
Fax: 816-252-5575

Cape Girardeau County Extension Center
Small Business Development Center
P.O. Box 408
815 Highway 25S
Jackson, MO 63755
573-243-3581 ext. 283
Fax: 573-243-1606

Cole County Extension Center
Small Business Development Center
2436 Tanner Bridge Rd.
Jefferson City, MO 65101
573-634-2824
Fax: 573-634-5463

Missouri Southern State College
Small Business Development Center
107 Mathews Hall, 3950 Newman Rd.
Joplin, MO 64801-1595
417-625-9313
Fax: 417-926-4588

Rockhurst College
Small Business Development Center
1100 Rockhurst Rd.
Kansas City, MO 64110-2599
816-926-4572
Fax: 816-926-4646

Three Rivers Community College
Small Business Development Center
Business Incubator Bldg.
3019 Fair St.
Poplar Bluff, MO 63901
314-686-3499
Fax: 314-686-5467

Washington County
102 N. Missouri
Potosi, MO 63664
573-438-2671

MO Enterprise Bus. Assistance Center
800 W 14th St., Suite 111
Rolla, MO 65401
573-364-8570
Fax: 573-341-6495

St. Louis County Extension Center
207 Marillac, UMSL
8001 Natural Bridge Rd.
St. Louis, MO 63121
314-553-5944

MO PAC--Eastern Region
975 Hornet Dr., Bldg. 279 Wing B
St. Louis, MO 63042
314-731-3533

Northeast Missouri State University
Small Business Development Center
207 East Patterson
Kirksville, MO 63501-4419
816-785-4307
Fax: 816-785-4181

Thomas Hill Enterprise Center
Small Business Development Center
P.O. Box 246
Macon, MO 63552
816-385-6550
Fax: 816-385-6568

Northwest Missouri State University
Small Business Development Center
127 S. Buchanan
Maryville, MO 64468
816-562-1701
Fax: 816-562-1900

Audrain County Extension Center
Small Business Development Center
101 N. Jefferson
4th Floor Courthouse
Mexico, MO 65265
573-581-3231
Fax: 573-581-3232

Randolph County Extension Center
Small Business Development Center
417 E. Urbandale
Moberly, MO 65270
816-263-3534
Fax: 816-263-1874

Small Business Development Center
Mineral Area College
P.O. Box 1000
Park Hills, MO 63601-1000

Small Business Development Centers

314-431-4593
Fax: 314-431-2144

Three Rivers Community College
Small Business Development Center
Business Incubator Building
3019 Fair St.
Poplar Bluff, MO 63901
314-686-3499
Fax: 314-686-5467

Washington County Extension Center
Small Business Development Center
102 N. Missouri
Potosi, MO 63664
314-438-2671
Fax: 314-438-2079

MO Enterprise Business Assistance Center
Small Business Development Center
800 W. 14th St., Suite 111
Rolla, MO 65401
314-364-8570
Fax: 314-364-6323

Phelps County Extension Center
Small Business Development Center
Courthouse
200 N. Main
P.O. Box 725
Rolla, MO 65401
314-364-3147
Fax: 314-364-0436

Center for Technology Transfer and Economic Development
University of Missouri at Rolla
Room 104, Nagogami Terrace
Rolla, MO 65401-0249
314-341-4559
Fax: 314-341-6495

Pettis County Extension Center
Small Business Development Center
1012 A Thompson Blvd.
Sedalia, MO 65301
816-827-0591
Fax: 816-826-8599

Southwest Missouri State University
Small Business Development Center
Center for Business Research
901 S. National
Springfield, MO 65804-5685
417-836-5685
Fax: 417-836-6337

St. Louis County Extension Center
207 Marillac, UMSI
8001 Nttl. Bridge Rd
St. Louis, MO 63121
314-533-5944
Fax: 314-977-7241

St. Louis University
Small Business Development Center
3750 Lindell Blvd.
St. Louis, MO 63108
314-534-7232
Fax: 314-534-7023

St. Charles County Extension Center
Small Business Development Center
260 Brown Rd.
St. Peters, MO 63376
314-970-3000
Fax: 314-970-3000

Franklin County Extension Center
Small Business Development Center
414 E. Main
P.O. Box 71
Union, MO 63084
573-583-5141
Fax: 573-583-5145

Central Missouri State
Center for Technology
Grinstead #75
Warrensburg, MO 64093-5037
816-543-4402
Fax: 816-747-1653

Howell County Extension Center
Small Business Development Center
217 S. Aid Ave.
West Plains, MO 65775
417-256-2391
Fax: 417-256-8569

Montana
Lead Center
Montana Small Business Development Center
Department of Commerce
1424 Ninth Ave.
Helena, MT 59620
406-444-4780
Fax: 406-444-1872

Billings Area Business Incubator
Small Business Development Center
115 N. Broadway, 2nd Floor
Billings, MT 59101
406-256-6875
Fax: 406-256-6877

Bozeman Human Resources Development Council
Small Business Development Center
321 E. Main, Suite 413
Bozeman, MT 59715
406-587-3113
Fax: 406-587-9565

Butte REDI
Small Business Development Center
305 W. Mercury St., Suite 211
Butte, MT 59701
406-782-7333
Fax: 406-782-9675

Haver Small Business Development Center
Bear Paw Development Corporation
P.O. Box 1549
Haver, MT 59501
406-265-9226
Fax: 406-265-3777

Flathead Valley Community College
Small Business Development Center
777 Grandview Dr.
Kalispell, MT 59901
406-756-8333
Fax: 406-786-3815

Missoula Incubator
Small Business Development Center
127 N. Higgins, 3rd Floor
Missoula, MT 59802
406-278-9234
Fax: 406-721-4584

Sidney Small Business Development Center
123 W. Main
Sidney, MT 59270

406-482-5024
Fax: 406-482-5306

Great Falls SBDC
High Plains Dev. Authority
710 First Ave. N
Great Falls, MT 59403
406-454-1934
Fax: 406-454-2995

Nebraska
Lead Center
Nebraska Small Business Development Center
Omaha Business and Tech. Ctr.
2505 N. 24th St., Suite 101
Omaha, NE 68110
402-595-3511

Chadron State College
Small Business Development Center
Administration Building
Chadron, NE 69337
308-432-6282
Fax: 308-432-6430

University of Nebraska at Kearney
Small Business Development Center
Welch Hall
19th and College Dr.
Kearney, NE 68849-3035
308-865-8344
Fax: 308-865-8153

University of Nebraska at Lincoln
Small Business Development Center
Cornhusker Bank Bldg.
11th and Cornhusker Hwy., Suite 302
Lincoln, NE 68521
402-472-3358
Fax: 402-482-0328

Mid-Plains Community College
Small Business Development Center
416 N. Jeffers, Room 26
North Platte, NE 69101
308-534-5115
Fax: 308-534-5117

University of Nebraska at Omaha
Small Business Development Center
Peter Keiwit Conference Center
1313 Farnam, Suite 132
Omaha, NE 68182-0248
402-595-2381
Fax: 402-595-2385

Peru State College
Small Business Development Center
T.J. Majors Building, Room 248
Peru, NE 68421
402-872-2274
Fax: 402-872-2422

Small Business Development Center
Nebraska Public Power Building
1721 Broadway, Room 408
Scottsbluff, NE 69361
308-635-7513
Fax: 308-635-6596

Wayne State College
Small Business Development Center
Garner Hall, 111 Main St.
Wayne, NE 68787
402-375-7575
Fax: 402-375-7574

Small Business Development Centers

Nevada

Lead Center
Nevada Small Business Development Center
University of Nevada at Reno
College of Business Administration
Room 411, Business Bldg.
Reno, NV 89577-0100
702-784-1717
Fax: 702-784-4337

Great Basin College
Small Business Development Center
1500 College Pkwy.
Elko, NV 89801
702-753-2245
Fax: 702-753-2242

University of Nevada at Las Vegas
Small Business Development Center
College of Business and Economics
Box 456011
Las Vegas, NV 89154-0611
702-895-0852
Fax: 702-895-4095

Carson City Chamber of Commerce--SBDC
1900 S. Carson St., #100
Carson City, NV 89701
702-882-1565
Fax: 702-882-4179

Incline Village Crystal Bay
Chamber of Commerce Small Business
Development Center
969 Tahoe Blvd.
Incline Village, NV 89451
702-831-4440
Fax: 702-832-1605

X Foreign Trade Zone Office SBDC
111 Grier Dr.
Las Vegas, NV 89119
702-896-4496
Fax: 702-896-8351

Small Business Development Center
19 W. Fourth St.
North Las Vegas, NV 89030
702-399-6300
Fax: 702-399-6301

Tri-County Development Authority
Small Business Development Center
P.O. Box 820
50 W. Fourth St.
Winnemucca, NV 89446
702-623-5777
Fax: 702-623-5999

New Hampshire

Lead Center
New Hampshire Small Business Development Center
University of New Hampshire
108 McConnell Hall
Durham, NH 03824-3593
603-862-2200
Fax: 603-862-4876

Keene State College
Small Business Development Center
Blake House
Keene, NH 03431
603-358-2602
Fax: 603-358-2612

Small Business Development Center
120 Main St.
Littleton, NH 03561
603-444-1053
Fax: 603-444-5463

Small Business Development Center
1000 Elm St., 14th Floor
Manchester, NH 03101
603-634-2796
Fax: 603-634-2449

Plymouth State College
Small Business Development Center
Hyde Hall
Plymouth, NH 03264
603-535-2523
Fax: 603-535-2611

Center for Economic Development
Small Business Development Center
1 Indian Head Plaza
Nashua, NH 03060
603-886-1233
Fax: 603-598-1164

First National Bank of Portsmouth
Small Business Development Center
One 3rd St., Suite 2
Dover, NH 03820
603-749-4264

Micro Enterprise Assistance Program
Small Business Development Center
Portsmouth City Hall, Room 325
P.O. Box 628
Portsmouth, NH 03802-0628
603-431-2006
Fax: 603-427-1526

New Jersey

Lead Center
New Jersey Small Business Development Center
Rutgers Graduate School of Management
University Heights
180 University Ave.
Newark, NJ 07102
201-648-5950
Fax: 201-648-1110

Small Business Development Center
Greater Atlantic City Chamber of Commerce
1301 Atlantic Ave.
Atlantic City, NJ 08401
609-345-5600
Fax: 609-345-4524

Rutgers - The State University Of New Jersey at Camden
Small Business Development Center
Business and Science Building
Second Floor
Camden, NJ 08102
609-756-6221
Fax: 609-225-6231

Brookdale Community College
Small Business Development Center
Newman Springs Rd.
Lincroft, NJ 07738
908-842-1900
Fax: 908-842-0203

Rutgers - The State University of New Jersey at Camden
Small Business Development Center
University Heights
180 University Ave.
3rd Floor, Ackerson Hall
Newark, NJ 07102
201-648-5950
Fax: 201-648-1110

Bergen Community College
Small Business Development Center
400 Paramus Rd
Paramus, NJ 07552
201-447-7841
Fax: 201-447-7495

Mercer County Community College
Small Business Development Center
P.O. Box B
Trenton, NJ 08690
609-586-4800, ext. 469
Fax: 609-890-6338

Kean College of New Jersey
Small Business Development Center
East Campus, Room 242
Union, NJ 07083
908-527-2946
Fax: 908-527-2960

Warren County Community College
Small Business Development Center
Route 57 West, Box 55A
Washington, NJ 07882-9605
908-689-9620
Fax: 908-689-7488

New Mexico

Lead Center
New Mexico Small Business Development Center
Santa Fe Community College
P.O. Box 4187
Santa Fe, NM 87502-4187
505-438-1362
Fax: 505-438-1237

New Mexico State University at Alamogordo
Small Business Development Center
1000 Madison
Alamogordo, NM 87310
505-434-5272

Albuquerque Technical Vocational Institute
Small Business Development Center
525 Buena Vista SE
Albuquerque, NM 87106
505-224-4246
Fax: 505-224-4251

New Mexico State University at Carlsbad
Small Business Development Center
P.O. Box 1090
Carlsbad, NM 88220
505-887-6562
Fax: 505-885-0818

Clovis Community College
Small Business Development Center
417 Schepps Blvd
Clovis, NM 88101
505-769-4136
Fax: 505-769-4190

Northern New Mexico Community College
Small Business Development Center
1002 N. Onate St
Espanola, NM 87532
505-747-2236
Fax: 505-747-2180

Small Business Development Centers

San Juan College
Small Business Development Center
4601 College Blvd.
Farmington, NM 87402
505-599-0528

University of New Mexico at Gallup
Small Business Development Center
P.O. Box 1395
Gallup, NM 87305
505-722-2220
Fax: 505-863-6006

New Mexico State University at Grants
Small Business Development Center
709 E. Roosevelt Ave
Grants, NM 87020
505-287-8221
Fax: 505-287-2125

New Mexico Junior College
Small Business Development Center
5317 Lovington Highway
Hobbs, NM 88240
505-392-4510
Fax: 505-392-2526

Dona Ana Branch Community College
Small Business Development Center
Box 30001, Department 3DA
Las Cruces, NM 88003-0001
505-527-7601
Fax: 505-527-7515

Luna Vocational Technical Institute
Small Business Development Center
Luna Camp, P.O. Drawer K
Las Vegas, NM 88701
505-454-2595
Fax: 505-454-2518

University of New Mexico at Los Alamos
Small Business Development Center
P.O. Box 715
901 8th St., #18
Los Alamos, NM 87544
505-662-0001
Fax: 505-662-0099

University of New Mexico at Valencia
Small Business Development Center
280 La Entrada
Los Lunas, NM 87031
505-866-5348
Fax: 505-865-3095

Eastern New Mexico University at Roswell
Small Business Development Center
P.O. Box 6000, 57 University Ave.
Roswell, NM 88201-6000
505-624-7133
Fax: 505-624-7132

Santa Fe Community College
Small Business Development Center
S. Richards Ave.
P.O. Box 4187
Santa Fe, NM 87502-4187
505-438-1343
Fax: 505-438-1237

Western New Mexico University
Southwest Small Business Development Center
P.O. Box 2672
Silver City, NM 88062
505-538-6320
Fax: 505-538-6341

Tucumcari Area Vocational School
Small Business Development Center
P.O. Box 1143
Tucumcari, NM 88401
505-461-4413
Fax: 505-461-1901

New York
Lead Center
New York Small Business Development Center
State University of New York
State University Plaza, S-523
Albany, NY 12246
518-443-5398
Fax: 518-465-4992
1-800-732-7232

State University of New York at Albany (SUNY)
Small Business Development Center
Draper Hall, Room 107
135 Western Ave
Albany, NY 12222
518-442-5577
Fax: 518-442-5582

State University of New York at Binghamton (SUNY)
Small Business Development Center
P.O. Box 6000
Binghamton, NY 13902-6000
607-777-4024
Fax: 607-777-4029

Small Business Development Center
74 N. Main St
Brockport, NY 14420
716-637-6660
Fax: 716-637-2102

Bronx Community College
Small Business Development Center
McCracken Hall, Room 14
West 181st St. and University Ave
Bronx, NY 10453
718-563-3570
Fax: 718-563-3572

Kingsborough Community College
2001 Oriental Blvd
Bldg. Tr Room 4204
Brooklyn, NY 11235
718-368-4619
Fax: 718-368-4629

Downtown Outreach Center
Small Business Development Center
395 Flatbush Ave.
Brooklyn, NY 11201
718-260-9783
Fax: 718-260-9797

State University College at Buffalo
Small Business Development Center
1300 Elmwood Ave., BA 117
Buffalo, NY 14222
716-878-4030
Fax: 716-878-4067

Cobleskill Outreach Center
Small Business Development Center
SUNY Cobleskill
Warner Hall, Room 218
Cobleskill, NY 12043
518-234-5528
Fax: 518-234-5272

Corning Community College
Small Business Development Center
24 Denison Parkway West
Corning, NY 14830
607-962-9461
Fax: 607-936-6642

Mercy College Outreach Ctr.
Small Business Development Center
555 Broadway
Dobbs Ferry, NY 10522-1189
914-674-7845
Fax: 914-693-4996

State Univ. College of Technology at Farmingdale
Small Business Development Center
Campus Commons
Farmingdale, NY 11735
516-420-2765
Fax: 516-293-5343

Marist College
Small Business Development Center
Fishkill Extension Center
2600 Route 9, Unit 90
Fishkill, NY 12524-2001
914-897-2607
Fax: 914-897-4653

SUNY Geneseo
Small Business Development Center
1 College Circle
Geneseo, NY 14454-1485
716-245-5429
Fax: 716-245-5430

Geneva Outreach Center
Small Business Development Center at Geneva
122 N. Genesee St
Geneva, NY 14456
315-781-1253

EOC Hempstead Outreach Center
Small Business Development Center
269 Fulton Ave
Hempstead, NY 11550
516-564-8672/1895
Fax: 516-481-4938

York College
Small Business Development Center
Science Building, Room 107
The City University of New York
Jamaica, NY 11451
718-262-2880
Fax: 718-262-2881

Jamestown Community College
Small Business Development Center
P.O. Box 20
Jamestown, NY 14702-0020
716-665-5754
1-800-522-7232
Fax: 716-665-6733

Kingston Small Business Development Center
1 Development Court
Kingston, NY 12401
914-339-0025
Fax: 914-339-1631

Harlem Outreach Center
Small Business Development Center
163 W. 125th St, Room 1307
New York, NY 10027
212-346-1900
Fax: 212-534-4576

Small Business Development Centers

East Harlem Outreach Center
Small Business Development Center
145 E 116th St, 3rd Floor
New York, NY 10029
212-534-2729/4526
Fax: 212-410-1359

Midtown Outreach Center
Small Business Development Center
Baruch College
360 Park Ave. S., Room 1101
New York, NY 10010
212-802-6620
Fax: 212-802-6613

Pace University
Small Business Development Center
1 Pace Plaza, Room W483
New York, NY 10038
212-346-1900
Fax: 212-346-1613

SUNY at Oswego
Small Business Development Center
Operation Oswego County
44 W. Bridge St
Oswego, NY 13126
315-343-1545
Fax: 315-343-1546

Clinton Community College
Small Business Development Center
Lake Shore Rd, Suite 9 S.
136 Clinton Point Dr
Plattsburgh, NY 12901
518-562-4260
Fax: 518-563-9759

Riverhead Outreach Center
Small Business Development Center
Suffolk County Community College
Riverhead, NY 11901
516-369-1409/1507
Fax: 516-369-3255

Small Business Development Center-SUNY
Brockport
Temple Bldg
14 Franklin St, Suite 200
Rochester, NY 14604
716-232-7310
Fax: 716-637-2182

Niagara County Community College at Sanborn
Small Business Development Center
3111 Saunders Settlement Rd.
Sanborn, NY 14132
716-693-1910
Fax: 716-731-3595

Southampton Outreach Center
Small Business Development Center
Long Island University at Southampton
Abney Peak, Montauk Highway
Southampton, NY 11968
516-287-0059/0071
Fax: 516-287-8287

The College of Staten Island
Small Business Development Center
2800 Victory Blvd.
Staten Island, NY 10314-9806
718-982-2560
Fax: 718-982-2323

SUNY at Stony Brook
Small Business Development Center
Harriman Hall, Room 109
Stony Brook, NY 11794-3775
516-632-9070
Fax: 516-632-7176

Rockland Community College at Suffern
Small Business Development Center
145 College Rd.
Suffern, NY 10901-3620
914-356-0370
Fax: 914-356-0381

Onondaga Community College at Syracuse
Small Business Development Center
Excell Bldg, Room 108
4969 Onondaga Rd.
Syracuse, NY 13215
315-492-3029
Fax: 315-492-3704

Manufacturing Technology Center
Small Business Development Center
New York Manufacturing Partnership
385 Jordan Rd
Troy, NY 12180-7602
518-286-1014
Fax: 518-286-1006

SUNY College of Technology at Utica/Rome
Small Business Development Center
P.O. Box 3050
Utica, NY 13504-3050
315-792-7546
Fax: 315-792-7554

Jefferson Community College
Small Business Development Center
Watertown, NY 13601
315-782-9262
Fax: 315-782-0901

The Small Business Resource Center
Small Business Development Center
222 Bloomingdale Rd, 3rd Floor
White Plains, NY 10605-1500
914-644-4116
Fax: 914-644-2184

North Carolina

Lead Center
North Carolina Small Business Development Center
University of North Carolina
333 Fayette St. Mall, Suite 1150
Raleigh, NC 27601
919-715-7272
Fax: 919-715-7777

Asheville Office
Small Business Development Center
34 Wall St, Suite 707
Public Services Bldg
Asheville, NC 28805
704-251-6025

Appalachian State University
Small Business Development Center
Northwestern Region
Walker College of Business
Boone, NC 28608
704-262-2492
Fax: 704-262-2027

Small Business Development Center
Central Carolina Region
608 Airport Rd., Suite B
Chapel Hill, NC 27514
919-962-0389
Fax: 919-962-3291

Small Business Development Center
Southern Piedmont Region
The Ben Craig Center
8701 Mallard Creek Rd.
Charlotte, NC 28262
704-548-1090
Fax: 704-548-9050

Small Business Development Center
Center for Improving Mountain Living
Western Carolina University, Bird Bldg.
Cullowhee, NC 28723
704-227-7494
Fax: 704-227-7422

Elizabeth City State University
Small Business Development Center
Northeastern Region
P.O. Box 874
Elizabeth City, NC 27909
919-335-3247
Fax: 919-335-3648

Fayetteville State University
Small Business Development Center
Cape Fear Region
Continuing Education Center
P.O. Box 1334
Fayetteville, NC 28302
910-486-1727
Fax: 910-486-1949

NC A&T University/CH Moore Agricultural Research Center
Small Business Development Center
Box D-22, 1602 E. Market St.
Greensboro, NC 27411
910-334-7005
Fax: 910-334-7073

East Carolina University
Small Business Development Center
Eastern Region
300 E. 1st St., Willis Bldg.
Greenville, NC 27858-4353
919-328-6157
Fax: 919-328-6992

Catawba Valley Region
Small Business Development Center
514 Hwy 321, Suite A
Hickory, NC 28601
704-345-1110
Fax: 704-326-9117

Pembroke State University
Office of Economic Development and SBTDC
Pembroke, NC 28372
910-521-6603
Fax: 910-521-6550

MCI Small Business Resource Center
800 1/2 S. Salisbury St
Raleigh, NC 27601
919-715-0520
Fax: 919-715-0518

NC Wesleyan College
Small Business Development Center
3400 N. Wesleyan Blvd
Rocky Mount, NC 27804
919-985-5130
Fax: 919-977-3701

Small Business Development Centers

University of North Carolina at Wilmington
Small Business Development Center
Southeastern Region
601 S. College Rd.
Wilmington, NC 28403
919-395-3744
Fax: 910-350-3990

Winston-Salem University
Small Business Development Center
Northern Piedmont Region
P.O. Box 13025
Winston-Salem, NC 27110
910-750-2030
Fax: 910-750-2031

North Dakota
Lead Center
North Dakota Small Business Development Center
University of North Dakota
118 Gamble Hall, Box 7308
Grand Forks, ND 58202-7308
701-777-3700
Fax: 701-777-3225

Small Business Development Center
Bismarck Regional Center
400 East Broadway, Suite 416
Bismarck, ND 58501
701-223-8583
Fax: 701-252-3843

Devils Lake Outreach Center
Small Business Development Center
417 5th St
Devils Lake, ND 58301
800-445-7232

Small Business Development Center
Dickinson Regional Center
314 3rd Ave. West, Drawer L
Dickinson, ND 58602
701-227-2096
Fax: 701-225-5116

Small Business Development Center
Fargo Regional Center
417 Main Ave.
Fargo, ND 58103
701-237-0986
Fax: 701-237-9734

Grafton Outreach Center
Red River Regional Planning Council
Small Business Development Center
P.O. Box 633
Grafton, ND 58237
800-445-7232

Small Business Development Center
Grand Forks Regional Center
The Hemp Center
1407 24th Ave. S, Suite 201
Grand Forks, ND 58201
701-772-8502
Fax: 701-775-2772

Jamestown Outreach Center
Small Business Development Center
210 10th St. SE, Box 1530
Jamestown, ND 58402
701-252-9243
Fax: 701-251-2488

Small Business Development Center
Minot Regional Center
1020 20th Ave. SW
P.O. Box 940
Minot, ND 58702
701-852-8861
Fax: 701-838-2488

Williston Outreach Center
Tri-County Economic Development Assn
Small Business Development Center
Box 2047
Williston, ND 58801
800-445-7232

Ohio
Lead Center
Ohio Small Business Development Center
Department of Development
77 S. High St., 28th Floor
Columbus, OH 43226-0101
614-466-2480
Fax: 614-466-0829

Small Business Development Center
Akron Regional Development Board
One Cascade Plaza, 8th Floor
Akron, OH 44308
216-379-3170
Fax: 216-379-3164

Ohio University
Small Business Development Center
Innovation Center
20 E. Circle Dr
Athens, OH 45701
614-593-1797
Fax: 614-593-1795

Athens Small Business Center, Inc
900 East State St.
Athens OH 45701
614-592-1188
Fax: 614-593-8283

Wood County Small Business Development Center
WSOS Community Action Commission, Inc.
P.O. Box 539
121 E. Wooster St
Bowling Green, OH 43402
419-352-7469
Fax: 419-353-3291

Wright State University
Lake Campus
Small Business Development Center
7600 State Route 703
Celina, OH 45882
419-586-0355
Fax: 419-586-0358

Cincinnati Small Business Development Center
IAMS Research Park, MC189
1111 Edison Ave.
Cincinnati, OH 45216-2265
513-948-2082
Fax: 513-948-2007

Clemont County Chamber of Commerce
Small Business Development Center
4440 Glen Este-Withamsville Rd.
Cincinnati, OH 45245
513-753-7141
Fax: 513-753-7146

Northern Ohio Mfg. Small Business Development Center
Prospect Pk. Building
4600 Prospect Ave.
Cleveland, OH 44103-4314
216-432-5364
Fax: 216-361-2900

Greater Cleveland Growth Association
Small Business Development Center
200 Tower City Center
50 Public Square
Cleveland, OH 44113-2291
216-621-3300
Fax: 216-621-4617

Columbus Small Business Development Ctr.
Columbus Area Chamber of Commerce
37 N. High St.
Columbus, OH 43215
614-225-6082
Fax: 614-469-8250

Dayton Satellite
Center for Small Business Assistance
College of Business
310 Rike Hall
Dayton, OH 45433
513-873-3503
Fax: 523-873-3545

Northwest Small Business Development Ctr.
1935 E. Second St, Suite D
Defiance, OH 43512
419-784-3777
Fax: 419-782-4649

North Central Small Business Development Center
Fremond Office
Terra Technical College
1220 Cedar St.
Freemont, OH 43420
419-332-1002
Fax: 419-334-2300

Enterprise Center Small Business Development Center
129 E. Main St
Hillsboro, OH 45132
513-393-9599
Fax: 513-393-8159

Ashtabula County Economic Development Council, Inc.
Small Business Development Center
36 West Walnut St.
Jefferson, OH 44047
216-576-9134
Fax: 216-576-5003

Kent Regional Business Alliance Small Business Development Center
Kent State Univ. Partnership
College of Business Admin., Room 302
Kent, OH 44242
216-672-2772 ext. 254
Fax: 216-672-2448

EMTEC/Small Business Development Center
Southern Area Mfg. Small Business Development Center
3171 Research Park
Kettering, OH 45420
513-259-1361
Fax: 513-259-1303

Lima Technical College
Small Business Development Center
545 West Market St., Suite 305
Lima, OH 45801-4717

Small Business Development Centers

419-229-5320
Fax: 419-229-5424

Lorain County Chamber of Commerce
Small Business Development Center
6100 S. Broadway
Lorain, OH 44053
216-233-6500
Fax: 216-246-4050

Mid-Ohio Small Business Development Center
246 E. 4th St
P.O. Box 44901
Mansfield, OH 44901
800-366-7232
Fax: 419-522-6811

Marietta College
Small Business Development Center
213 4th St
Marietta, OH 45750
614-376-4901
Fax: 614-376-4832

Marion Small Business Development Center
Marion Area Chamber of Commerce
206 S. Prospect St.
Marion, OH 43302
614-387-0188
Fax: 614-387-7722

Lakeland Community College
Lake County Economic Development Center
Small Business Development Center
750 Clocktower Dr.
Mentor, OH 44080
216-951-1290
Fax: 216-951-7336

Women's Network
1540 W. Market St., Suite 100
Akron, OH 44313
330-864-5636
Fax: 330-884-6526

Women's Entrepreneurial Growth Organization
Small Business Development Center
The University of Akron
Buckingham Bldg., Room 55
Akron, OH 44309
330-972-5179
330-972-5513

Women's Business Development Center
2400 Cleveland Ave. NW
Canton, OH 44709
216-453-3867
Fax: 216-773-2992

Kent State University/Salem Campus
Small Business Development Center
2491 State Route 45 S.
Salem, OH 44460
330-332-0361
Fax: 330-332-9256

Youngstown/Warren Small Business Development Center
Region Chamber of Commerce
180 E. Market St.
Warren, OH 44482
330-393-2565
Fax: 330-392-6040

Tuscarawas Chamber of Commerce
Small Business Development Center
330 University Dr, NE

New Philadelphia, OH 44663-9447
216-339-3391, ext. 279
Fax: 216-339-2637

Miami University Small Business Development Center
Dept. of Decision Sciences
336 Upham Hall
Oxford, OH 44046
513-529-4841
Fax: 513-529-1469

Upper Valley Joint Vocational School
Small Business Development Center
8811 Career Dr.
North County Rd. 25A
Piqua, OH 45356
513-778-8419
Fax: 513-778-9237

Portsmouth Area Chamber of Commerce
Small Business Development Center
1208 Waller St.
P.O. Box 1757
Portsmouth, OH 45662
614-353-8395
Fax: 614-353-2695

Lawrence County Chamber of Commerce
Small Business Development Center
U.S. Route 52 and Solida Rd.
P.O. Box 488
Southpoint, OH 45680
614-894-3838
Fax: 614-894-3836

Springfield Small Business Development Center, Inc.
300 E. Auburn Ave
Springfield, OH 45505
513-322-7821
Fax: 513-322-7824

Department of Development of the CIC of Belmont County
Small Business Development Center
St. Clairsville Office
100 East Main St.
St. Clairsville, OH 43950
614-695-9678
Fax: 614-695-1536

Greater Steubenville Chamber of Commerce
Small Business Development Center
630 Market St.
P.O. Box 278
Steubenville, OH 43952
614-282-6226
Fax: 614-282-6285

Northwest Ohio Women's Business Entrepreneurial Network
Small Business Development Center
Toledo Regional Growth Partnership
300 Madison Ave
Toledo, OH 43604
419-252-2700
Fax: 419-252-2724

Youngstown State University
Cushwa Center for Industrial Development
Small Business Development Center
241 Federal Plaza W.
Youngstown, OH 44503
330-746-3350
Fax: 330-746-3324

Zanesville Area Chamber of Commerce
Small Business Development Center
217 N. Fifth St.
Zanesville, OH 43701
614-452-4868
Fax: 614-454-2963

Oklahoma
Lead Center
Oklahoma Small Business Development Center Network
Southeastern Oklahoma State University
517 University
Durant, OK 74701
405-924-0277
1-800-522-6154
Fax: 405-920-7471

East Central State University
Small Business Development Center
1036 East 10th
Ada, OK 74820
405-436-3190
Fax: 405-436-3190

Northwestern State University
Small Business Development Center
709 Oklahoma Blvd
Alva, OK 73717
405-327-8608
Fax: 405-327-0560

Southeastern State University
Small Business Development Center
517 University
Durant, OK 74701
405-924-0277
Fax: 405-920-7471

Phillips University
Enid Satellite Center
100 S. University Ave.
Enid, OK 73701
405-242-7989
Fax: 405-237-1607

Langston University
Minority Assistance Center
Hwy. 33 East
Langston, OK 73050
405-466-3256
Fax: 405-466-2909

Lawton Satellite Center
Small Business Development Center
American National Bank Building
601 SW "D", Suite 209
Lawton, OK 73501
405-248-4946
Fax: 405-355-3560

Miami Satellite
215 I St. NE
Miami, OK 74354
918-540-0575
Fax: 918-540-0575

Rose State College
Procurement Specialty Center
6420 SE 15th St.
Midwest City, OK 73110
405-733-7348
Fax: 405-733-7495

Univ. of Central Oklahoma
Small Business Development Center

Small Business Development Centers

P.O. Box 1439, 115 Park Ave.
Oklahoma City, OK 73101-1439
405-232-1968
Fax: 405-232-1967

Carl Albert Junior College
Poteau Satellite Center
Small Business Development Center
1507 S. McKenna
Poteau, OK 74953
918-647-4019
Fax: 918-647-1218

Northeastern State University
Small Business Development Center
Tahlequah, OK 74464
918-458-0802
Fax: 918-458-2105

Tulsa Satellite Center
State Office Building
440 S. Houston, Suite 507
Tulsa, OK 74127
918-581-2502
Fax: 918-581-2745

Southwestern State University
Small Business Development Center
100 Campus Dr.
Weatherford, OK 73096
405-774-1040
Fax: 405-774-7091

Oregon
Lead Center
Oregon Small Business Development Center
44 W. Broadway, Suite 501
Eugene, OR 97401-3021
503-726-2250
Fax: 503-345-6006

Linn-Benton Community College
Small Business Development Center
6500 SW Pacific Blvd.
Albany, OR 97321
541-917-4923
Fax: 541-917-4445

Southern Oregon State College
Small Business Development Center
Regional Service Institute
Ashland, OR 97520
541-482-5838
Fax: 541-482-5838

Central Oregon Community College
Small Business Development Center
2600 NW College Way
Bend, OR 97701
541-383-7290
Fax: 541-383-7503

Southwestern Oregon Community College
Small Business Development Center
340 Central
Coos Bay, OR 97420
541-269-0123
Fax: 541-269-0323

Lane Community College
Small Business Development Center
1059 Willamette St.
Eugene, OR 97401
503-726-2255
Fax: 503-686-0096

Rogue Community College
Small Business Development Center
214 SW 4th St
Grants Pass, OR 97526
541-471-3515
Fax: 541-471-3589

Mount Hood Community College
Small Business Development Center
323 NE Roberts St.
Gresham, OR 97030
503-667-7658
Fax: 503-666-1140

Oregon Institute of Technology
Small Business Development Center
3201 Campus Dr., South 314
Klamath Falls, OR 97601
541-885-1760
Fax: 541-885-1855

Small Business Development Center
229 N. Bartlett
Medford, OR 97501
503-772-3478
Fax: 503-776-2224

Clackamas Community College
Small Business Development Center
7616 SE Harmony Rd.
Milwaukie, OR 97222
503-656-4447
Fax: 503-652-0389

Treasure Valley Community College
Small Business Development Center
88 SW Third Ave.
Ontario, OR 97914
541-889-2617
Fax: 541-889-8331

Blue Mountain Community College
Small Business Development Center
37 SE Dorion
Pendleton, OR 97801
541-276-6233
Fax: 541-276-6819

Portland Community College
Small Business Development Center
123 NW 2nd Ave., Suite 321
Portland, OR 97209
503-414-2828
Fax: 503-294-0725

Small Business International Trade Program
121 SW Salmon St., Suite 210
Portland, OR 97204
503-274-7482
Fax: 503-228-6350

Umpqua Community College
Small Business Development Center
744 SE Rose
Rosenburg, OR 97470
541-672-2535
Fax: 541-672-3679

Chemeketa Community College
Small Business Development Center
365 Ferry St. SE
Salem, OR 97301
503-399-5181
Fax: 503-581-6017

Clatsop Community College
Small Business Development Center
1240 S. Holladay
Seaside, OR 97138
503-738-3347
Fax: 503-738-7843

Columbia Gorge Community College
Small Business Development Center
212 Washington
The Dalles, OR 97058
541-298-3118
Fax: 541-298-3119

Tillamook Bay Community College Service District
Small Business Development Center
401 B Main St.
Tillamook, OR 97141
503-842-2551
Fax: 503-842-2555

Pennsylvania
Lead Center
Pennsylvania Small Business Development Center
University of Pennsylvania
The Wharton School
409 Vance Hall
Philadelphia, PA 19104-6374
215-898-4861
Fax: 215-898-1063

Lehigh University
Small Business Development Center
Rauch Business Center #37
Bethlehem, PA 18015
610-758-3980
Fax: 610-758-5205

Clarion University of Pennsylvania
Small Business Development Center
Dana Still Building, Room 102
Clarion, PA 16214
814-226-2060
Fax: 814-226-2636

Gannon University
Small Business Development Center
Carlisle Building, 3rd Floor
Erie, PA 16541
814-871-7714
Fax: 814-871-7383

Kutztown University
Small Business Development Center
University Center
2986 N. 2nd St.
Harrisburg, PA 17110
717-720-4230
Fax: 717-233-3181

Indiana University of PA
Small Business Development Center
Robt. Shaw Bldg.
Indiana, PA 15705
412-357-7915
Fax: 412-357-4514

St. Vincent College
Small Business Development Center
Alfred Hall, 4th Floor
Latrobe, PA 15650
412-537-4572
Fax: 412-537-0919

Bucknell University
Small Business Development Center
126 Dana Engineering Building

Small Business Development Centers

Lewisburg, PA 17837
717-524-1249
Fax: 717-524-1768

St. Francis College
Small Business Development Center
Business Resource Center
Loretto, PA 15940
814-472-3200
Fax: 814-472-3202

Temple University
Small Business Development Center
Room 6, Speakman Hall 006-00
Philadelphia, PA 19122
215-204-7282

LaSalle University
Small Business Development Center
1900 W. and Olney Ave
Philadelphia, PA 19141
215-951-1416
Fax: 215-951-1597

University of Pennsylvania
Small Business Development Center
The Wharton School
423 Vance Hall
Philadelphia, PA 19104-6374
215-898-1219
Fax: 215-898-2135

Duquesne University
Small Business Development Center
Rockwell Hall-Room 10 Concourse
600 Forbes Ave.
Pittsburgh, PA 15282
412-396-6233
Fax: 412-396-5884

University Small Business Development Center
208 Bellefield Hall
315 S. Bellefield Ave.
Pittsburgh, PA 15260
412-648-1544
Fax: 412-648-1636

University of Scranton
Small Business Development Center
St. Thomas Hall, Room 588
Scranton, PA 18510
717-941-7588
Fax: 717-941-4053

Wilkes College
Small Business Development Center
Hollenback Hall
192 S. Franklin St.
Wilkes-Barre, PA 18766-0001
717-831-4340
Fax: 717-824-2245

Rhode Island
Lead Center
Rhode Island Small Business Development Center
Bryant College
1150 Douglas Pike
Smithfield, RI 02917
401-232-6416
Fax: 401-232-6111

Salve Regina University
Small Business Development Center
Miley Hall, Room 006
Newport, RI 02840
401-849-6900
Fax: 401-847-0372

Rhode Island Small Business Development Center
Quonset P/D Industrial Park
35 Belver Ave., Room 2127
North Kingstown, RI 02852-7556
401-294-1227
Fax: 401-294-6897

Rhode Island Small Business Development Center
CCRI-Providence Campus
One Hilton St
Providence, RI 02905
401-455-6088
Fax: 401-455-6047

Bryant College
Small Business Development Center
30 Exchange Terrace, 4th Floor
Providence, RI 02903
401-831-1330
Fax: 401-454-2819

South Carolina
Lead Center
South Carolina Small Business Development Center
University of South Carolina
College of Business Administration
Columbia, SC 29208
803-777-4907
Fax: 803-777-4403

University of South Carolina
Alkan Office
Small Business Development Center
171 University Pkwy., Suite 100
School of Business
Alkan, SC 29801
803-641-3646
Fax: 803-641-3647

University of South Carolina at Beaufort
Small Business Development Center
800 Carterat St.
Beaufort, SC 29902
803-521-4143
Fax: 803-521-4198

Clemson University
Small Business Development Center
425 Sirrine Hall, College of Commerce
Clemson, SC 29634-1392
803-656-3227
Fax: 803-656-4869

University of South Carolina
USC Regional Small Business Development Center
College of Business Administration
Columbia, SC 29208
803-777-5118
Fax: 803-777-4403

Coastal Carolina
Small Business Development Center
School of Business Administration
P.O. Box 1954
Conway, SC 29526
803-349-2170
Fax: 803-349-2445

Florence Darlington Technical College
Small Business Development Center
P.O. Box 100548
Florence, SC 29501-0548
803-661-8256
Fax: 803-661-8041

Greenville Chamber of Commerce
Small Business Development Center
24 Cleveland St
Greenville, SC 29601
803-271-4259
Fax: 803-282-8549

Upper Savannah Council of Governments
Small Business Development Center
Small Business Development Center Exchange Building
222 Phoenix St., Suite 200
P.O. Box 1366
Greenwood, SC 29648
803-941-8071
Fax: 803-941-8090

University of South Carolina at Hilton Head
Small Business Development Center
Suite 300, Kiawah Bldg.
10 Office Park Rd.
Hilton Head, SC 29928
803-785-3995
Fax: 803-777-0333

South Carolina State College
Small Business Development Center
School of Business
300 College Ave
Orangeburg, SC 29117
803-536-8445
Fax: 803-536-8066

Winthrop University
Small Business Development Center
119 Thurmond Building
Rock Hill, SC 29733
803-323-2283
Fax: 803-323-4281

Spartanburg Chamber of Commerce
Small Business Development Center
P.O. Box 1636
105 N. Pine St
Spartanburg, SC 29304
803-594-5080
Fax: 803-594-5055

South Dakota
Lead Center
South Dakota Small Business Development Center
University of South Dakota
414 East Clark
Vermillion, SD 57069
605-677-5498
Fax: 605-677-5272

Small Business Development Center
226 Citizens Building
Aberdeen, SD 57401
605-626-2252
Fax: 605-626-2667

Small Business Development Center
105 S. Euclid, Suite C
Pierre, SD 57501
605-773-5941
Fax: 605-773-5942

Small Business Development Center
444 Mount Rushmore Rd., Room 208
Rapid City, SD 57701

Small Business Development Centers

605-394-5311
Fax: 605-394-6140

Small Business Development Center
200 N. Phillips, Suite 302
Sioux Falls, SD 57102
605-367-5757
Fax: 605-367-5755

Tennessee
Lead Center
Tennessee Small Business Development Center
Memphis State University
South Campus (Getwell Rd.)
Building #1
Memphis, TN 38152
901-678-2500
Fax: 901-678-4072

Chattanooga State Technical Community College
Small Business Development Center
4501 Amnicola Highway
Chattanooga, TN 37406-1097
615-697-4410 ext. 505
Fax: 615-698-5653

Southeast Tennessee Development District
Small Business Development Center
P.O. Box 4757
Chattanooga, TN 37405
423-266-5781
Fax: 423-267-7705

Austin Peay State University
Small Business Development Center
College of Business
Clarksville, TN 37044-0001
615-648-7764
Fax: 615-648-5985

Cleveland State Community College
Small Business Development Center
Business and Technology
P.O. Box 3570
Cleveland, TN 37320
423-478-6247
Fax: 423-478-6251

Small Business Development Center
Memorial Building
Room 205, 308 West 7th St.
Columbia, TN 38401
615-388-5674
Fax: 615-388-5474

Tennessee Technological University
Small Business Development Center
College of Business Administration
P.O. Box 5023
Cookeville, TN 38505
615-372-6634
Fax: 615-372-6249

Dyersburg Community College
Small Business Development Center
1510 Lake Rd.
Dyersburg, TN 38024
901-286-3201
Fax: 901-286-3271

Four Lakes Regional Industrial Development Authority
Small Business Development Center
P.O. Box 63
Hartsville, TN 37074-0063
615-374-9521
Fax: 615-374-4608

Jackson State Community College
Small Business Development Center
2046 N. Parkway St.
Jackson, TN 38305
901-424-5389
Fax: 901-425-2647

East Tennessee State University
Small Business Development Center
College of Business
P.O. Box 70, 698A
Johnson City, TN 37614-0698
423-929-5630
Fax: 423-461-7080

International Trade Center
301 E. Church Ave.
Knoxville, TN 37915
423-637-4283
Fax: 423-523-2071

Memphis State University
Small Business Development Center
320 S. Dudley St.
Memphis, TN 38104
901-527-1041
Fax: 901-527-1047

Memphis State University
Small Business Development Center
International Trade Center
Memphis, TN 38152
901-678-4174
Fax: 901-678-4072

Walters State Community College
Small Business Development Center
Business/Industrial Services
500 S. Davy Crockett Parkway
Morristown, TN 37813
423-585-2675
Fax: 423-585-2679

Middle Tennessee State University
Small Business Development Center
School of Business
1417 E. Main St.
P.O. Box 487
Murfreesboro, TN 37132
615-898-2745
Fax: 615-898-2861

Tennessee State University
Small Business Development Center
School of Business
330 10th Ave. N.
Nashville, TN 37203-3401
615-963-7179
Fax: 615-963-7160

Texas
Lead Centers
North Texas Small Business Development Center
Dallas County Community College
1402 Corinth St.
Dallas, TX 75215
214-860-5831
Fax: 214-860-5813

Houston Small Business Development Center
University of Houston
1100 Louisiana, Suite 500
Houston, TX 77002
713-752-8444
Fax: 713-756-1500

Northwest Texas Small Business Development Center
Center for Innovation
2579 S. Loop 289, Suite 114
Lubbock, TX 79423
806-745-3973
Fax: 806-745-6207

South Texas Border Small Business Development Center
University of Texas at San Antonio
1222 N. Main, Suite 450
San Antonio, TX 78205
210-558-2450
Fax: 210-558-2464

Abilene Christian University
Caruth Small Business Development Center
College of Business Administration
648 E. Highway 80
Abilene, TX 79601
915-670-0300
Fax: 915-670-0311

Alvin Community College
Small Business Development Center
3110 Mustang Rd.
Alvin, TX 77511-4898
713-338-4686
Fax: 713-388-4903

West Texas State University
Panhandle Small Business Development Center
T. Boone Pickens School of Business
1800 S. Washington, Suite 209
Amarillo, TX 79102
806-372-5151
Fax: 806-372-5261

Trinity Valley Small Business Development Center
500 S. Prairieville
Athens, TX 75751
903-675-7403
Fax: 903-675-6316

Austin Small Business Development Center
221 S. IH 35, Suite 103
Austin, TX 78767
512-473-3510
Fax: 512-443-4094

Lee College
Small Business Development Center
P.O. Box 818
Baytown, TX 77522-0818
713-425-6307
Fax: 713-425-6309

John Gray Institute/Lamar University
Small Business Development Center
855 Florida Ave.
Beaumont, TX 77705
409-880-2367
Fax: 409-880-2201

Bonham Small Business Development Center
(Satellite)
110 W. First
Bonham, TX 75418
903-583-4811
Fax: 903-583-6706

Blinn College
Small Business Development Center
902 College Ave.
Brenham, TX 77833

Small Business Development Centers

409-830-4137
Fax: 409-830-4135

Bryan/College Station Chamber of Commerce
Small Business Development Center
4001 E. 29th St.
Bryan, TX 77805
409-260-5222
Fax: 409-260-5208

Corpus Christi Chamber of Commerce
Small Business Development Center
1201 N. Shoreline
Corpus Christi, TX 78539
512-881-1888
Fax: 512-882-4256

Navarro Small Business Development Center
120 N. 12th St.
Corsicana, TX 75110
903-874-0658
Fax: 903-874-4187

International Business Center
2050 Stemmons Freeway
World Trade Center, Suite #150
P.O. Box 58299
Dallas, TX 75258
214-747-1300
Fax: 214-748-5774

Grayson Small Business Development Center
6101 Grayson Dr.
Denison, TX 75020
903-786-3551
Fax: 903-786*6284

Denton Small Business Development Center
(Satellite)
P.O. Drawer P
Denton, TX 76202
817-380-1849
Fax: 817-382-0040

University of Texas/Pan American
Small Business Development Center
1201 West University Dr.
Edinburg, TX 78539-2999
210-381-3361
Fax: 210-381-2322

El Paso Community College
Small Business Development Center
103 Montana Ave., Room 202
El Paso, TX 79902-3929
915-534-3410
Fax: 915-534-4625

Tarrant Small Business Development Center
1500 Houston St., Room 163
7917 Highway 80 West
Fort Worth, TX 76102
817-794-5900
Fax: 817-794-5952

Cooke Small Business Development Center
1525 West California
Gainesville, TX 76240
817-668-4220
Fax: 817-668-6049

Galveston College
Small Business Development Center
4015 Avenue Q
Galveston, TX 77550
409-740-7380
Fax: 409-740-7381

North Harris Community College District
Small Business Development Center
250 N. Sam Houston Parkway
Houston, TX 77060
713-591-9320
Fax: 713-591-3513

Sam Houston State University
Small Business Development Center
College of Business Administration
P.O. Box 2058
Huntsville, TX 77341-2058
409-294-3737
Fax: 409-294-3738

Kingsville Chamber of Commerce
Small Business Development Center
635 E. King
Kingsville, TX 78363
512-595-5088
Fax: 512-592-0866

Brazosport College
Small Business Development Center
500 College Dr.
Lake Jackson, TX 77566
409-266-3380
Fax: 409-265-7208

Laredo Development Foundation
Small Business Development Center
616 Leal St.
Laredo, TX 78041
210-722-0563
Fax: 210-722-6247

Kilgore College
Small Business Development Center
100 Triple Creek Dr., Suite 70
Longview, TX 75601
903-757-5857
Fax: 903-753-7920

Texas Tech University
Small Business Development Center
Center for Innovation
2579 S. Loop 289, Suite 210
Lubbock, TX 79423
806-745-1637
Fax: 806-745-6217

Angelina Community College
Small Business Development Center
P.O. Box 1768
Lufkin, TX 75902
409-639-1887
Fax: 409-639-1887

Northeast Texarkana Small Business Development
Center
P.O. Box 1307
Mt. Pleasant, TX 75455
214-572-1911
Fax: 903-572-0598

University of Texas/Permian Basin
Small Business Development Center
4901 East University
Odessa, TX 79762
915-552-2455
Fax: 915-552-2433

Paris Small Business Development Center
2400 Clarksville St.
Paris, TX 75460
214-784-1802
Fax: 903-784-1801

Collin County Small Business Development
Center
4800 Preston Park Blvd.
Plano, TX 75093
214-985-3770
Fax: 214-985-3775

Angelo State University
Small Business Development Center
2610 West Ave. N
Campus Box 10910
San Angelo, TX 76909
915-942-2098
Fax: 915-942-2096

UTSA
International Small Business Development Center
1222 N. Main
San Antonio, TX 78212
210-558-2470
Fax: 210-558-2464

Houston Community College System
Small Business Development Center
13600 Murphy Rd.
Stafford, TX 77477
713-499-4870
Fax: 713-499-8194

Tarleton State University
Small Business Development Center
Box T-0650
Stephenville, TX 76402
817-968-9330
Fax: 817-968-9329

College of the Mainland
Small Business Development Center
8419 Emmett F. Lowry Expressway
Texas City, TX 77591
409-938-7578
Fax: 409-935-5816

Tyler Small Business Development Center
1530 S. SW Loop 323, Suite 100
Tyler, TX 75701
903-510-2975
Fax: 903-510-2978

University of Houston-Victoria
Small Business Development Center
700 Main Center, Suite 102
Victoria, TX 77901
512-575-8944
Fax: 512-575-8852

McLennan Small Business Development Center
4601 N. 19th St., Suite A-15
Waco, TX 76708
817-750-3600
Fax: 817-750-3620

Wharton County Junior College
Small Business Development Center
Administration Building, Room 102
911 Boling Highway
Wharton, TX 77488-0080
409-532-0604
Fax: 409-532-2410

Midwestern State University
Small Business Development Center
Division of Business
3400 Taft Blvd.
Wichita Falls, TX 76308
817-689-4373
Fax: 817-689-4374

Small Business Development Centers

Utah

Lead Center
Utah Small Business Development Center
University of Utah
102 West 500 South, Suite 315
Salt Lake City, UT 84101
801-581-7905
Fax: 801-581-7814

Southern Utah University
Small Business Development Center
351 West Center
Cedar City, UT 84720
801-586-5400
Fax: 801-586-5493

Snow College
Small Business Development Center
345 West First North
Ephraim, UT 84627
801-283-4021
801-283-6890
Fax: 801-283-6913

Utah State University
Small Business Development Center
East Campus Building
Logan, UT 84322-8330
801-797-2277
Fax: 801-797-3317

Weber State University
Small Business Development Center
College of Business and Economics
Ogden, UT 84408-3806
801-626-7232
Fax: 801-626-7423

College of Eastern Utah
Small Business Development Center
451 East 400 North
Price, UT 84501
801-637-1995
Fax: 801-637-4102

Utah State College
Small Business Development Center
School of Management
800 W. 1200 S
Orem, UT 84058
801-222-8230
Fax: 801-225-1229

Uintah Basin Applied Technology Center
Small Business Development Center
1100 East Lagoon
P.O. Box 124-5
Roosevelt, UT 84066
801-722-4523
Fax: 801-722-5804

Dixie College
Small Business Development Center
225 South 700 East
St. George, UT 84770
801-673-4811, ext 353
Fax: 801-674-5839

Vermont

Lead Center
Vermont Small Business Development Center
Vermont Tech. College
P.O. Box 422
Randolph, VT 05060-0422
802-728-9101
Fax: 802-728-3026

Northwestern Vermont Small Business
Development Center
P.O. Box 786 NW VT SBDC
Burlington, VT 05402-0786
802-658-9228
Fax: 802-860-1899

Southwestern Vermont Small Business
Development Center
256 N. Main St.
Rutland, VT 05701
802-773-9147
Fax: 802-773-2772

Southeastern Vermont Small Business
Development Center
P.O. Box 58
Springfield, VT 05156-0058
802-885-2071
Fax: 802-885-3027

Central Vermont Small Business Development
Center
Green Mountain SBDC
P.O. Box 246
White River Jct., VT 05001-0246
802-295-3710
Fax: 802-295-3779

Brattleboro Dev. Credit Corp.
Small Business Development Center
P.O. Box 1177
Brattleboro, VT 05301-1177
802-257-7731
Fax: 802-258-3886

Addison Co. Econ. Dev. Corp
Small Business Development Center
2 Court St.
Middlebury, VT 05753
802-388-7953
Fax: 802-388-8066

Central VT Econ. Dev. Center
Small Business Development Center
P.O. Box 1439
Montpelier, VT 05601-1439
802-223-4654
Fax: 802-223-4655

Lamoille Econ. Dev. Center
Small Business Development Center
P.O. Box 455
Morrisville, VT 05661-0455
802-888-4923
Fax: 802-888-5640

Bennington Co. Industrial Corp.
Small Business Development Center
P.O. Box 357
No. Bennington, VT 05257
802-442-8975
Fax: 802-442-1101

Lake Champlain Islands
Chamber of Commerce SBDC
P.O. Box 213
No. Bero, VT 05474-0213
802-372-5683
Fax: 802-372-6104

Franklin County Industrial Dev. Corp.
Small Business Development Center
P.O. Box 1099
St. Albans, VT 05478-1099
802-524-2194
Fax: 802-527-5258

Northeastern VT Dev. Assn.
Small Business Development Center
P.O. Box 630
St. Johnsbury, VT 05819
802-748-1014
Fax: 802-748-1223

Virginia

Lead Center
Virginia Small Business Development Center
901 E. Byrd St., Suite 1800
Richmond, VA 23219
804-371-8253
Fax: 804-225-3384

VA Highland Community College
Small Business Development Center
P.O. Box 828
Abingdon, VA 24212
703-676-5615
Fax: 703-628-7576

George Mason University/Arlington Campus
Small Business Development Center
3401 N. Fairfax Dr.
Arlington, VA 22201
703-993-8128
Fax: 703-993-8130

Mt. Empire Community College
Southwest Small Business Development Center
Drawer 700, Route 23
Big Stone Gap, VA 24219
703-523-6529
Fax: 703-523-4130

New River Valley Small Business Development
Center
Donaldson Brown Center, Room 234
Virginia Tech
Blacksburg, VA 24061-0539
703-231-5278
Fax: 703-231-8850

Central Virginia Small Business Development
Center
918 Emmet St. N, Suite 200
Charlottesville, VA 22903
804-295-8198
Fax: 804-295-7066

Northern Virginia Small Business Development
Center
4260 Chainbridge Rd, Suite A-1
Fairfax, VA 22030
703-993-2131/2130
Fax: 703-993-2126

Longwood College
515 Main St
Small Business Development Center
Farmville, VA 23901
804-395-2086
Fax: 804-395-2359

Rappahannock Region Small Business
Development Center
1301 College Ave., Seacobeck Hall
Fredericksburg, VA 22401
703-899-4076
Fax: 703-899-4373

Small Business Development Centers

James Madison University
Small Business Development Center
College of Business Building, Room 523
Harrisonburg, VA 22807
703-568-3227
Fax: 703-568-3299

Lynchburg Regional Small Business Development Center
147 Mill Ridge Rd.
Lynchburg, VA 24502
804-582-6170
Fax: 804-582-6106

Small Business Development Center
Dr. William E.S. Flory
10311 Sudley Manor Dr.
Manassas, VA 22110
703-335-2500
Fax: 703-335-1700

Lord Fairfax Community College
Small Business Development Center
P.O. Box 47
Middletown, VA 22645
703-869-6649
Fax: 703-869-7881

Hampton Roads, Inc.
Small Business Development Center
P.O. Box 327
420 Bank St.
Norfolk, VA 23501
804-825-2957
Fax: 804-825-3552

Southwest Virginia Community College
Small Business Development Center
P.O. Box SVCC
Richlands, VA 24641
703-964-7345
Fax: 703-964-5788

Capital Area Small Business Development Center
403 East Grace St.
Richmond, VA 23219
804-648-7838
Fax: 804-648-7849

The Blue Ridge Small Business Development Center
310 First St., SW Mezzanine
Roanoke, VA 24011
703-983-0717
Fax: 703-983-0723

South Boston Small Business Development Center
P.O. Box 1116
515 Broad St.
South Boston, VA 24592
804-575-0044
Fax: 804-572-4087

Loudoun County Small Business Development Center
21515 Ridgetop Circle, Suite 200
Sterling, VA 22170
703-430-7222
Fax: 703-430-9562

Warsaw Small Business Development Center
P.O. Box 490
106 W. Richmond Rd
Warsaw, VA 22572
804-333-0286
Fax: 804-333-0187

Wytheville Community College
Small Business Development Center
1000 E. Main St.
Wytheville, VA 24382
703-223-4798 ext. 4798
Fax: 703-223-4850

Eastern Shore Office
P.O. Box 395
Belle Haven, VA 23306
804-442-7181

Mountain Empire Community College
Small Business Development Center
Drawer 700, Route 23 S.
Big Stone Gap, VA 24219
703-523-6529
Fax: 703-523-8139

Small Business Development Center
525 Butler Farm Rd., Suite 102
Hampton, VA 23666
804-622-6414

Washington
Lead Center
Washington Small Business Development Center
Washington State University
501 Johnson Tower
Pullman, WA 99164-4727
509-335-1576
Fax: 509-335-0949

Bellevue Community College
Small Business Development Center
3000 Landerholm Circle
Bellevue, WA 98007-6484
206-643-2888
Fax: 206-649-3113

Western Washington University
Small Business Development Center
College of Business and Economics
308 Park Hall
Bellingham, WA 98225-9073
360-650-3899
Fax: 360-650-4844

Centralia Community College
Small Business Development Center
600 West Locust St.
Centralia, WA 98531
360-736-9391
Fax: 360-753-3404

Big Bend Community College
Small Business Development Center
7662 Chanute St., Bldg. 1500
Moses Lake, WA 98837-3299
509-762-6289
Fax: 509-762-6329

Skagit Valley College
Small Business Development Center
2405 College Way
Mt. Vernon, WA 98273
360-428-1282
Fax: 360-336-6116

South Puget Sound Community College
Small Business Development Center
721 Columbia St. SW
Olympia, WA 98501
360-753-5616
Fax: 360-586-5493

South Seattle Community College
Small Business Development Center
6770 E. Marginal Way S
Seattle, WA 98106
206-764-5375
Fax: 206-764-5838

Washington State University at Seattle
Small Business Development Center
180 Nickerson, Suite 207
Seattle, WA 98109
206-464-5450
Fax: 206-464-6357

North Seattle Community College
Small Business Development Center
International Trade Institute
9600 College Way N.
Seattle, WA 98103-3599
206-527-3733
Fax: 206-527-3734

Community College of Spokane
Small Business Development Center
665 N. Riverpoint Blvd.
Spokane, WA 99202
509-358-2051
Fax: 509-358-2059

Washington State University at Tacoma
Small Business Development Center
950 Pacific Ave., Suite 300
Box 1933
Tacoma, WA 98401-1933
206-272-7232
Fax: 206-597-7305

Columbia River Economic Development Council
Small Business Development Center
100 East Columbia Way
Vancouver, WA 98660-3156
360-693-2555
Fax: 360-694-9927

Yakima Valley Community College
Small Business Development Center
P.O. Box 1647
Yakima, WA 98907
509-454-3608
Fax: 509-454-4155

Columbia Basin College
Tri-Cities SBDC
901 N. Colorado
Kennewick, WA 99336
509-735-6222
Fax: 509-735-6609

Edmonds Community College
Small Business Development Center
20000 68th Ave. W
Lynwood, WA 98036
206-640-1435
Fax: 206-640-1532

Wenatchee Valley College SBDC
P.O. Box 741
Okanogan, WA 98840
509-826-5107
Fax: 509-826-1812

Port of Walla Walla SBDC
500 Tausick Way
Walla Walla, WA 99362
509-527-4681
Fax: 509-525-3101

Small Business Development Centers

Quest Small Business Development Center
327 East Penny Rd.
Industrial Bldg. #2, Suite D
Wenatchee, WA 98801
509-662-8016
Fax: 509-663-0455

West Virginia
Lead Center
West Virginia Small Business Development Center
West Virginia Development Office
950 Kanawha Blvd.
Charleston, WV 25301
304-558-2960
Fax: 304-558-0127

Fairmont State College
Small Business Development Center
Fairmont, WV 26554
304-367-4125
Fax: 304-366-4870

Marshall University
Small Business Development Center
1050 Fourth Ave.
Huntington, WV 25755-2126
304-696-6789
Fax: 304-696-6277

West Virginia Institute of Technology
Small Business Development Center
Room 102, Engineering Building
Montgomery, WV 25136
304-442-5501
Fax: 304-442-3307

West Virginia University
Small Business Development Center
P.O. Box 6025
Morgantown, WV 26506
304-293-5839
Fax: 304-293-7061

West Virginia University at Parkersburg
Small Business Development Center
Route 5, Box 167-A
Parkersburg, WV 26101
304-424-8277
Fax: 304-424-8315

Shepherd College
Small Business Development Center
Shepherdstown, WV 25443
304-876-5261
Fax: 304-876-5117

West Virginia Northern Community College
Small Business Development Center
College Square
Wheeling, WV 26003
304-233-5900, ext. 206
Fax: 304-232-9065

College of West Virginia Small Business Development Center
P.O. Box AG
Bechkey, WV 25802
304-255-4022

Governor's Office of Community and Industrial Development SBDC
950 Kanawha Blvd. East
Charleston, WV 25301
304-558-2960
Fax: 304-558-0127

Elkins Satellite SBDC
10 Eleventh St., Suite One
Elkins, WV 26241
304-637-7205
Fax: 304-637-4902

Wisconsin
Lead Center
Wisconsin Small Business Development Center
University of Wisconsin
432 N. Lake St., Room 423
Madison, WI 53706
608-263-7794
Fax: 608-262-3878

University of Wisconsin at Eau Claire
Small Business Development Center
P.O. Box 4004
Eau Claire, WI 54702-4004
715-836-5811
Fax: 715-836-5263

University of Wisconsin at Green Bay
Small Business Development Center
460 Wood Hall
Green Bay, WI 54301
414-465-2089
Fax: 414-465-2660

University of Wisconsin at LaCrosse
Small Business Development Center
School of Business
120 N. Hall
La Crosse, WI 54601
608-785-8782
Fax: 608-785-6919

University of Wisconsin at Madison
Small Business Development Center
975 University Ave., Room 3260
Madison, WI 53706
608-263-2221
Fax: 608-263-0818

University of Wisconsin at Milwaukee
Small Business Development Center
161 W. Wisconsin Ave., Suite 600
Milwaukee, WI 53203
414-227-3240

University of Wisconsin at Oshkosh
Small Business Development Center
157 Clow Faculty Bldg.
800 Algoma Blvd.
Oshkosh, WI 54901
414-424-1453
Fax: 414-424-7413

University of Wisconsin at Stevens Point
Small Business Development Center
Main Building, Lower Level
Stevens Point, WI 54481
715-346-2004
Fax: 715-346-4045

University of Wisconsin at Superior
Small Business Development Center
29 Sundquist Hall
Superior, WI 54880
715-394-8352
Fax: 715-394-8454

University of Wisconsin at Whitewater
Small Business Development Center
2000 Carlson Bldg
Whitewater, WI 53190
414-472-3217
Fax: 414-472-4863

University of WI at Parkside SBDC
284 Tallent Hall
Kenosha, WI 53141
414-595-2189
Fax: 414-595-2513

WI Innovation Service Ctr. SBDC
Univ. of WI at Whitewater
402 McCutchan Hall
Whitewater, WI 53190
414-472-1365
Fax: 414-472-1600

Wyoming
Lead Center
Wyoming Small Business Development Center
111 West 2nd St., Suite 416
Casper, WY 82601
800-348-5207
307-234-6683
Fax: 307-577-7014

Laramie County Community College
Small Business Development Center
1400 East College Dr.
Cheyenne, WY 82007-3298
307-632-6141
800-348-5208
Fax: 307-632-6061

University of Wyoming
Small Business Development Center
P.O. Box 3620
University Station
Laramie, WY 82071-3622
307-766-3050
800-348-5194
Fax: 307-766-3406

Northwest Community College
Small Business Development Center
John DeWitt Student Center
Powell, WY 82435
307-754-6067
800-348-5203
Fax: 307-754-6069

Wyoming Small Business Development Center
P.O. Box 1168
Rock Springs, WY 82902
307-352-6894
800-348-5205
Fax: 307-352-6876

Loans / No Money

Loans for Entrepreneurs With No Money

The following is a description of loan programs available to low and moderate income individuals, minorities, Native Americans, Hispanics, refugees, unemployed individuals, welfare recipients, youths, and low and moderate income individuals who don't qualify for credit through conventional methods.

Most of these programs allow individuals (depending on the situation) to roll closing costs and fees into the amount of the loan. So you actually go to the closing with NO money in your pocket.

The aim of these programs is to stimulate economic growth through small businesses or microenterprises. Helping individuals become self-sufficient is the main focus, and also to challenge conventional methods of providing credit. All of the programs hope to demonstrate that persons with limited incomes are responsible, will repay, and can become successful if given access to knowledge and resources.

Some programs are designed just for youths, (15-21 years old), to develop their own businesses, avoid drugs and crime, sharpen academic skills and form positive attitudes about themselves and their communities. This is accomplished by utilizing the leadership, communication, management and business skills they may have acquired through affiliation with the illegal drug trade and other street activities. Loan amounts can range from $50 to $2,000 with terms from six months to two years.

The following is a small sample of many success stories that we found:

Susanna Rodriquez started making ceramic figurines for children's parties. Susanna is a former teacher's assistant who presently works in the kitchen of her small apartment. Her creations fill every free corner. She was constantly looking for ways to expand her business. One day she was in a store where the owner sold similar products. As they were comparing notes, the owner mentioned ACCION New York. After four loans as a result of working with that organization, Susanna's monthly revenue from her ceramics business has increased from $350 a month to $800 a month. In time, she hopes to open her own store. She feels that if it were not for ACCION, she would not be at the advanced stage of business that she is enjoying now.

Jeff Hess of Virginia had fished and hunted with his father since the age of five. He earned his associates degree in business and was working in an assembly plant for a moderate hourly wage, but wanted more. At the age of 24 he didn't see opportunity coming to call on him because he had no money and no credit. He and his wife, Cherylanna enrolled in the BusinessStart class at People, Inc. With this training, assistance in small business planning and a small loan, Jeff and Cherylanna were able to buy a bait shop in Honaker and turn it into Bucks and Bass, a full service hunting and fishing store. Located in prime hunting and fishing country, Bucks and Bass has nearly doubled its sales in its first year alone. Both Jeff and Cherylanna have left their jobs and run Bucks and Bass full time.

Loan Programs

Alabama

SBA Microloan Program
Birmingham Business Resource Center
110 12th Street North
Birmingham, AL 35203
E-mail: bbrc@inlinenet.net
205-250-6380
Fax: 205-250-6384

Generally this loan is open to any micro business, but it has mainly served minorities and women owned businesses. Attendance of monthly peer group meetings for technical assistance is required. The loan can be up to $7,500 with the interest rate at 10 to 13 percent. The term is determined by each case, but generally from 12 to 24 months. This is for the Jefferson County area.

Arizona

Borrowers' Circle
Self-Employment Loan Fund, Inc.
201 North Central Avenue, Suite CC10
Phoenix, AZ 85703
E-mail: Self-Employment@Juno.com
602-340-8834
Fax: 602-340-8953
TDD: 800-842-4681

The Self-Employment Loan Fund (SELF) offers assistance for those just starting a small business or that have been operational for less than six months. They use a peer lending system with a group of graduates that review the loans. Initial loans are up to $1,000 with 12 months to repay. Subsequent loans can be up to $5,000 with as many as 24 months to repay. Funding is through the U.S. Small Business Administration's Office of Women's Business Ownership, the City of Phoenix, corporations, foundations and Arizona banks.

Small Business Loan
PEEP Microbusiness and Housing Development Corporation
1100 East Hao Way, Suite 209
Tucson, AZ 85713
520-806-9513
Fax: 520-806-9515

This loan targets minority women and low-income small business owners. It is specific to the Rural Central and Southern Arizona areas. The loan is for $500 to $25,000 and the term is 60 months. It can be used for inventory, supplies, equipment and fixed assets.

Arkansas

The Good Faith Fund (GFF)
Peer Group Loan Program
2304 W. 29th Ave.
Pine Bluff, AR 71603
870-535-6233
Fax: 870-535-0741

GFF's peer-lending program is for new and emerging entrepreneurs and operates much like a community based credit union, with GFF providing the loan capital. Members join peer-lending groups, which consider and approve small business loans for their fellow member entrepreneurs. First time borrowers are eligible to borrow up to $1,200. In a "Stair-step" loan process, borrowers may secure loans of up to $7,500. Loan representatives assist interested borrowers in preparing their loan request, including cash flow projections indicating that the proposed loan use will produce increased sales and ensuring that the loan payments will be manageable. This Fund receives funding from private foundations, SBA Microloan Demonstration Program, contributions, and earnings.

Micro Loan
Good Faith Fund
2304 West 29th Street
Pinebluff, AR 71603
870-535-6233

This loan is available to people in the Delta region that would like to start a business. The amount of the loan is from $500 to $25,000. The interest rate varies depending on the loan, from 9 1/2% to 12%. Repayment must not be over 7 years.

California

Micro Enterprise Assistance Program of Orange County
18011 Skypark Circle, Suite E
Irvine, CA 92614
949-252-1380

Loans / No Money

Eligible applicants are women and ethnic minorities below the poverty level. This program receives funding from banks and private organizations. The aim of this program is to provide access to credit, training, and support so that low income individuals and their families may become self-sufficient. Loans are up to $1,500 with terms up to one year. The interest rate is prime rate plus 4%.

Self-Employment Loan Fund
Women's Economic Ventures of Santa Barbara
1136 E. Montecito St.
Santa Barbara, CA 93103
805-965-6073
Fax: 805-962-9622

This program is helping women create their own employment in a community that is currently losing jobs. Loans are from $1,000 to $25,000, with terms set by the loan officer. This fund receives funding from foundation grants, corporate and individual gifts, fees, and interest payments.

Self-Employment Microenterprise Development (SEMED)
Economic and Employment Development Center (EEDC)
241 S. Figueroa St.
Los Angeles, CA 90012
213-617-3953

Self-Employment Microenterprise Development (SEMED) assists the Southeast Asian Community in Los Angeles and surrounding counties to attain self-sufficiency. Eligible applicants are refugees admitted to the U.S. within the last five years and currently living under the national poverty level. Loans are from $2,000 to $5,000 with the term at one year. Group Lending loans are from $2,000 to $5,000 with the term at one year and the interest rate at 9.3%. SEMED receives funding from the Office of Refugee Resettlement.

The West Company
The West Enterprise Center
367 N. State St., Suite 206
Ukiah, CA 95482
707-468-3553
Fax: 707-462-8945

This program has a comprehensive approach that combines human and economic development. The aim is to stimulate the growth of economic opportunity in Northern California. Particular emphasis is on small business, economic options for low income people, and employment in the community. Eligible applicants are low income women/minorities located in Mendocino County. Loans are from $200 to $5,000 with terms from 6 to 24 months. The interest rate is at 10%. West Company receives funding from foundations, banks, utilities, CAP agency, local, state, and federal government, and donations.

Revolving Loan Fund
Tri-County Economic Development Corporation
2540 Esplanade, Suite 7
Chico, CA 95973
530-893-8732
Fax: 530-893-0820
E-mail: tcedcloan@thegrid.net
http://tricountyedc.org

The goal of this loan is to stimulate economic growth in Chico. The loan can be used for working capital, machinery, equipment, and leasehold improvements. You can apply for $2,500 to $50,000. The amount of time allowed for repayment varies with each loan. The interest rate is Prime plus 2%, or as low as 7%. For every $10,000 borrowed, one job must be created.

City of Long Beach Microenterprise Loan
City of Long Beach Business Assistance Division
200 Pine Avenue, Suite 400
Long Beach, CA 90802
562-570-3822
562-570-3800
www.ci.long-beach.ca.us/bdc

The goal of the program is to assist in the development of new businesses, to help economic growth, and to create and retain jobs. It is available to low and moderate income small business owners who cannot get conventional funding. The existing or start-up business must be located in the City of Long Beach. Funds can be used for property acquisition, machinery, equipment and moveable fixtures and working capital. The loan amount is from $5,000 to $25,000 at a fixed rate.

Micro-Loan Program
Oakland Business Development Corporation
519 17th Street, Suite 100
Oakland, CA 94612
510-763-4297
Fax: 510-763-1273
E-mail: mike@obdc.com
www.obdc.com

This loan is for small businesses located within the Seven Community Development Districts of Oakland. It can be used for working capital, inventory purchases, expansions and renovations, and contract finishing. Initially from $1,000 to $10,000 can be borrowed. After that has been repaid, up to $20,000 can be requested. The maximum term is 5 years and the interest is Prime + 3%. Eligible businesses are those in operation for one year, but 25% of funds are available for start-ups.

Entrepreneurial Resource Center Loan
2555 Clovis Avenue
Clovis, CA 93612
559-650-5050

Loans are only available to graduates of the Entrepreneurial Training Program. Funds are available from $1,000 to $5,000. The term is from 12 to 36 months depending on the loan amount.

Micro Loan Fund
Start Up: An East Palo Alto Micro-Business Initiative
1935 University Avenue
East Palo Alto, CA 94303
650-321-2193

To take advantage of this loan, entrepreneurs must graduate from the Start-Up Program. Up to $5,000 is available with a term of 5 years. Preferences are given to the residents of Palo Alto.

The Los Angeles Community Development Bank Micro Loan Program
Community Financial Resource Center
4060 S. Figueroa Street
Los Angeles, CA 90037
323-233-1900
Fax: 323-235-1686

The goal of this loan is to create jobs and to promote a positive investment environment in the Los Angeles Supplemental Empowerment Zone. It is available to micro businesses, home-based businesses and recent start-ups. Loans are from $1,000 to $25,000 and for those that have been turned down for a conventional loan. The term is 3 to 5 years at 12% fixed interest rate.

Micro Loan Revolving Loan Fund
Economic and Employment Development Corporation
2411 Figueroa Street, Suite 240
Los Angeles, CA 90012
213-617-3953

This program is available to refugees in the service area that have not been naturalized by the US. After completing a business training program, the applicant can submit a business plan and loan application. The maximum loan amount is $5,000. However, if a husband and wife apply for the same business, they could apply for $10,000. After the original has been paid back, borrowers can apply for 2 to 3 more loans and can double the loan amount. Technical assistance continues with the loan and the business is monitored on a weekly basis.

Micro Loan Fund
Interfaith Service Bureau
2117 Cottage Way
Sacramento, CA 95828
916-568-5020

This group is available for refugees that are green card holders and low income Americans. It is for those small businesses in the Sacramento area for start-up and inventory costs. After completing the training program, you may apply for a loan of up to $5,000. The maximum amount of time to repay the loan is 3 years. Funding is from private grants.

Women's Initiative Loan Fund
Women's Initiative For Self Employment
450 Mission Street, Suite 402
San Francisco, CA 94105
415-247-9473

Women's Initiative helps low-income women to learn the skills necessary to successfully start and run their businesses. After completing the training course, you can apply for a small loan. The initial loan amount is up to $1,000, and after that, up to $10,000 can be sought. The staff will work with each owner on a one-to-one basis for post loan assistance. Networking and access to experts are also available.

Small Business Micro-Lending Program
Lenders for Community Development
111 West St. John St., Suite 710
San Jose, CA 95113
408-297-9937
Fax: 408-297-4599

This loan program targets women, minority, and low-income business owners, and those businesses that are located in low-income areas. The business must have been in operation for one year and located in Santa Clara or San Mateo County. The loans range from $5,000 to $50,000 and can be used for working capital, equipment, inventory, leasehold improvements, and business acquisition.

Peer Lending Circles
West Company
306 East Redwood Ave., Suite 2
Ft. Bragg, CA 95437
707-964-7571

It is their mission to expand economic self-sufficiency and social well-being for those people that have limited access to conventional resources. The Peer Lending Circles have up to 6 members with at least 6 months of self-employment or a complete business plan. The loan amount ranges from $250 to $5,000 and the members all sign the loan note. Technical assistance is part of this program and must be continued for the term of the loan.

Loans / No Money

Colorado

Business Center for Women (BCW)
Mi Casa Resource Center for Women
571 Galapago St. 303-573-1302
Denver, CO 80204 Fax: 303-595-0422

This program assists women who are low income and Hispanic in achieving self-sufficiency. It has assisted in startup businesses and helped existing businesses expand. Loan amounts are up to a maximum of $500 for individual lending and from $500 to $5,000 for group lending. Loan terms are up to one year for individual lending; up to two years for group lending. The interest rate is at 8% for individual lending; prime rate plus 3% for group lending.

Project Success (PS)
Mi Casa Resource Center for Women
571 Galapago St. 303-573-1302
Denver, CO 80204 Fax: 303-595-0422

This program is available to women receiving welfare benefits in Denver County. The aim is to assist women who are low income and Hispanic in achieving self-sufficiency. Loans are at a maximum of $500 for individual lending and from $500 to $5,000 for group lending. Terms are up to one year for individual lending; up to two years for group lending. The interest rate is 8% for individual lending and at prime rate plus 3% for group lending.

Micro Loan
Credit for All, Inc.
2268 Birch Street
Denver, CO 80207 303-320-1955

This loan is geared towards low-income people to help them get out of poverty. Credit for All uses a pure lending model method. Five to seven small business owners approve and insure repayment of loans to peers. The first loan amount is for $500 and must be repaid in 4 months. After that, $1,000 is available and there are 8 months for repayment. If everything goes well with the first year of loans, up to $8,000 can be applied for in the second year, and so on for the following years. This is available for those within the service are of Credit for All.

Micro Loan
Colorado Capital Initiatives
1616 17th Street, Suite 371
Denver, CO 80202 303-628-5464

Basically, they provide loans to those people of good character who have difficulty obtaining conventional funding. With this program, there are 13 counties where each area makes up its own community group. Each group sets its own guidelines and standards that would best serve their region. From $500 to $30,000 is available for a loan with a maximum of 3 years for repayment. The interest rate is 1 or 2% over Prime, depending on the loan.

Small Business Loan
Colorado Enterprise Fund
1888 Sherman Street, Suite 530
Denver, CO 80203 303-860-0242
E-mail: microloans@coloradoenterprisefund.org
www.coloradoenterprisefund.org

This is available in the 10 county service are of Colorado Enterprise. It is for small businesses that need money for things like working capital and equipment. Up to $25,000 can be applied for with a term of up to 5 years. The interest rate is from 13.5% to 14.25%.

Community Enterprise Lending Initiative
Denver Small Business Development Center
1445 Market Street 303-620-8076
Denver, CO 80203 Fax: 303-514-3200

It is the mission of this program to provide counseling and loans to finance new or expanding businesses that are located in low-income, multi-ethnic areas. Also, it is for those entrepreneurs that cannot get a conventional loan. An existing business must have been in operation for at least one year. The maximum loans are $2,000 for a start-up and $15,000 for an existing company. The goal is that after this program the borrowers will be able to get conventional funding.

El Valle Microloans
San Luis Valley Christian Community Services
P.O. Box 984
309 San Juan Avenue 719-589-5192
Alamosa, CO 81101 Fax: 719-589-4330
E-mail: ccs@slvccs.org
www.slv.org/ccs

The San Luis Valley Christian Community Services (SLVCCS) wants to encourage economic development for disadvantaged individuals through support for existing and start-up business owners in the San Luis Valley. It is for those entrepreneurs that cannot get traditional bank loans. The loan amount is between $500 and $19,000 for a term of 3 years. They also have technical assistance, computer access, and network exposure.

Connecticut

Loan Programs
Hartford Economic Development Corporation
15 Lewis St. 860-527-1301
Hartford, CT 06103 Fax: 860-727-9224

This Corporation receives funding from CDBG funds, membership fees, and dues. Their aim is to create and retain jobs and tax rateable property. This program is available to AFDC recipients, low and moderate income individuals. Loans are from $1,500 to $20,000 with terms from 6 months to 7 years. The interest rate is 9%.

Trickle Up Grant
Action for Bridgeport Community Development
955 Connecticut Ave., Suite 1215 203-382-5440
Bridgeport, CT 06607 Fax: 203-382-5442

Over 75% of the recipients of the Trickle Up Grant program either have no credit or bad credit history. Entrepreneurs are given $700 in conditional start-up capital in two installments. For the first $500, they must complete a Business Plan, agree to spend a minimum of 250 hours per person over a 3 month period, and save or reinvest at least 20% of the profits in the business. At the end of three months, and when all of the requirements have been met, they can receive the final $200. Most of the recipients work out of their homes.

Delaware

Capital Works Team Success Loans
First State Community Loan Fund and YWCA of New Castle County
100 West 10th Street, Suite 1005 302-652-6774
Wilmington, DE 19801 Fax: 302-656-1272
E-mail: fsclf@diamond.net.ude.edu

This program uses the peer group lending process. The group offers support, training, and loan reviews. It is available to those businesses that are located in Delaware. The loan amounts are from $500 to $6,000. The term is 4 months to 3 years at a 12% interest rate. The group will approve the business use of the funds.

District of Columbia

Youth Microloan Fund
The Entrepreneurial Development Institute
P.O. Box 65882
Washington, DC 20035-5882 202-882-8334

This fund was established to empower disadvantaged youth to develop their own businesses, avoid drugs and crime, sharpen academic skills, and form positive attitudes about themselves and their communities. Eligible applicants are minority youths ages 17 to 21 years old. There are three levels of financing: up to $1,000, $2,500, and $5,000. Young people must have a business plan and have successfully repaid each loan before advancing to the next level. Loans carry below market interest and must be repaid within one year.

Micro Loan Fund
East of the River Community Development Corporation
4800 Nannie Helen Burroughs
Washington, DC 20019 202-397-0685

This loan is available to people in the area who want to start a small business or one that has been in existence for 2 or more years. Up to $25,000 can be applied for at 12% interest. The amount of time allowed for repayment varies depending on the loan.

Florida

SBA Microenterprise Loan Fund
Community Equity Investments, Inc. (CEII) 850-595-6234
302 North Barcelona Street 888-605-2505
Pensacola, FL 32501 Fax: 850-595-6234
E-mail: ceii2234@aol.com
http://ceii.pensacola.com

CEII provides assistance to businesses in northwest Florida and southern Alabama to help create jobs in those areas. The program has loans available for up to $25,000 for existing or start-up small businesses. The loans must be paid back within 5 years. Normally these are available to those that have had problems qualifying for a conventional loan.

Loans / No Money

Micro Loan
Florence Villa Community Development Corporation
111 Avenue R NE
Winter Haven, FL 33881
941-299-3263
Fax: 941-299-8134

Available businesses are start-up and existing that are generally owned by low to moderate-income people. The money can be used for mainly equipment. A loan of $5,000 is the maximum at 6.5% interest. The term is up to 3 years. It is only for the Polk county area.

Working Capital Program
3000 Biscayne Blvd., Suite 101A
Miami, FL 33137
305-438-1407
Fax: 305-438-1411
www.workingcapital.org

Working Capital's loans are set up in steps with each amount having a different repayment time. They start off at $500 and go in steps up to $10,000, in some cases they will go as high as $20,000. There is a 16% interest rate for processing loans. Members also can also take advantage of the business programs and network with other business owners.

Georgia

Working Capital Program
52 W. Alton St.
Atlanta, GA 30303
404-688-6884
Fax: 404-688-4009
www.workingcapital.org

Working Capital's loans are set up in steps with each amount having a different repayment time. They start off at $500 and go in steps up to $10,000, in some cases they will go as high as $20,000. There is a 16% interest rate for processing loans. Members also can also take advantage of the business programs and network with other business owners.

Micro Loan Fund
Goodwill Industries of North Georgia
2201 Glenwood Avenue
Atlanta, GA 30316
404-486-8400

This fund primarily serves Decatur and metro Atlanta. It is for women business owners that have low to moderate income. It mostly funds existing businesses, but there are some startups also. A loan from $50 to $5,000 can be applied for after completion of the Business Now training program. The term of the loan is 12 months with an interest rate that is currently 10%.

Hawaii

Refugee Enterprise Development Project
Immigrant Center
720 N. King St.
Honolulu, HI 96817
808-845-3918
Fax: 808-842-1962

This program focuses on Vietnamese and Laotian low income or welfare recipients. The objective of this program is to advance economic self-sufficiency among recently arrived refugees by providing culturally sensitive lending and support programs for the startup or expansion of microenterprise in Hawaii. Loans are from $1,500 to $5,000 with terms from 6 months to two years. The interest rate is at prime rate plus 2%, 3%, or 4%.

RED Manini MicroLoan Fund
The Immigrant Center
720 North King Street
Honolulu, HI 96817
808-845-3918
Fax: 808-842-1962
E-mail: redmanini@hotmail.com

This loan fund provides small loans, support, and technical assistance in order to help business owners to turn their talents and personal resources into economic self-sufficiency. It is for start-up and growing small businesses and to be used for inventory, supplies, furniture, fixtures, machinery, equipment, and working capital. The maximum loan is $25,000 for a maximum term of 6 years.

Idaho

JTPA Entrepreneurial Training
IDA-ORE Planning and Development Association
10624 West Executive Dr.
Boise, ID 83704
208-322-7033
Fax: 208-322-3569

JTPA receives funds from EDA revolving loan fund grant, EDA revolving loan fund interest, and JTPA training funds. Program is available to individual entrepreneurs who do not qualify for commercial credit, and who are located in rural southwest Idaho, Malheur and Harney counties. The primary motive is business and economic development in rural areas where jobs are few, and entrepreneurial activity may be the only option to support rural families. Loans are up to $10,000 with loan terms up to three years. The interest rate is at prime rate plus 5% or 12%.

Small Business Micro-Loan Program
Panhandle Area Council, Inc.
11100 Airport Drive
Hayden, ID 83835
208-772-0584

This loan is available in North Idaho to ensure growth and prosperity of the region's small businesses. Generally the loans are for businesses that have been operational for at least one year. Consideration will be given to start-up businesses. The minimum amount for a loan is $1,000 and the maximum is $25,000. The term is three to five years at a fixed interest rate. The loan can be used for the purchase or repair of equipment, purchase of inventory, and working capital.

Illinois

Community Enterprising Project
Uptown Center Hull House Association
4520 N. Beacon St.
Chicago, IL 60640
312-561-3500
Fax: 312-561-3507

Eligible applicants are low and moderate-income individuals located in Uptown, Edgewater, and Ravenswood areas. This project has assisted several new start up businesses, and others have been able to increase sales for businesses such as food industry and service businesses. Loans are from $1,000-$10,000 with terms from 1-2 years. Interest rate is at prime rate plus 6%. Receives funds from foundations, corporations, governments and individuals.

Peoria Area Micro Business Development Program
The Economic Development Council for The Peoria Area, Inc.
124 S. West Adams St., Suite 300
Peoria, IL 61602
309-676-7500
Fax: 309-676-7534

The Economic Development Council (EDC) is committed to assisting in the development of small businesses and microbusinesses and helping them overcome obstacles to growth. Eligible applicants are low and moderate-income existing or startup businesses, minorities and females. Loans are from $500 to $25,000 with terms from three to five years. The interest rate is from 5 to 12%. Receives funds from SBA Microloan Demonstration program, City of Peoria, and county of Peoria.

Self-Employment Loan Fund
Chicago Association of Neighborhood Development Organizations
123 W. Madison St., Suite 1100
Chicago, IL 60602-4589
312-372-2636
Fax: 312-372-2637

The aim of this Fund is the revitalization of all Chicago neighborhoods, retail and industrial areas. It works with community based organizations to assist low and moderate-income individuals start new business ventures. Loans are from $1,000 to $10,000 with a term of two years. Interest rate is at prime rate plus 6%. Closing costs can be included in the loan amount.

Self-Employment Training Program
Project NOW - Community Action Committee
418 19th St., P.O. Box 3970
Rock Island, IL 61201
309-793-6388
Fax: 309-793-6352

Eligible applicants are low-income county residents in the counties of Rock Island, Henry, and Mercer. Assists individuals interested in self-employment by providing training, consulting services, support services and assistance in identifying and accessing startup capital. Loans are from $1,500 to $45,000 with terms from two to four years. The interest rate is 5%. Funding comes from the Illinois Department of Commerce and Consumer Affairs.

WBDC Micro-Loan Program
Women's Business Development Center
8 S. Michigan Ave., Suite 400
Chicago, IL 60603
312-853-3477
Fax: 312-853-0145

This program has started a new initiative to strengthen the programs and services for women, and worked as an advocate on access to financing through relationship building with banks and regulators. The aim is to support women in their quest for economic self-sufficiency through entrepreneurship. Loans are up to $5,000 with terms up to one year. The interest rate is at 9%. This program receives funding from loans from various foundations and banks.

Women's Economic Venture Enterprise (WEVE)
YWCA
229 16th St.
Rock Island, IL 61201
309-788-9793
Fax: 309-788-9825

Women's Economic Venture Enterprise (WEVE) assists women in achieving economic self-sufficiency through business ownership. Eligible applicants are women of all races and income levels living in Scott County, Iowa, Rock Island County in

Loans / No Money

Illinois, and Metropolitan Quad Counties. Loans are from $200 to $3,000, terms from three months to five years. Interest rate is 2% below prime rate. WEVE receives funding from Banks, SBA, foundations, individuals, program fees and corporations.

    Women's Self-Employment Project (WSEP)
    20 N. Clark St.   312-606-8255
    Chicago, IL 60602   Fax: 312-606-9215

The Women's Self-Employment Project (WSEP) programs provide economic support and a chance for self-sufficiency to women who reside in some of Chicago's most disinvested communities. The goal of WSEP is to raise the income of low/moderate income women through a strategy of self-employment. Loans are from $100 to $10,000 with terms from four months to two years. The interest rate is at 15%. WSEP receives funding from SBA Microloan Demonstration, foundations, corporations, government contracts, individual donors, and consulting contracts.

    Self-Employment Loan Fund
    Chicago Association of Neighborhood Development Organizations (CANDO)
    123 West Madison, Suite 1100
    Chicago, IL 60602-4589   312-939-7171

This loan is generally available to low income business owners that are primarily women and minorities. It is for start-up and emerging businesses in Chicago. The loans for emerging businesses are $1,000 to $20,000 at 12.5% and repayable in 3 months to 2 years. A start-up company can apply for $1,000 to $15,000 at 10 to 12.5% interest for a term of 3 months to 2 years.

    City of Rockford Microenterprise Investment Match Program
    City of Rockford
    Illinois Community Development Department
    425 East State Street   815-987-5610
    Rockford, IL 61104   Fax: 815-967-6933
    www.ci.rockford.il.us

This program has been designed to strengthen new or young businesses owned by low and moderate-income residents in the City of Rockford. The City will provide up to four times the amount of the business' equity, or $10,000, whichever is less. Equity can include cash, previously purchased equipment, and "sweat-equity". The term is 5 years, with 20% forgiven each of the 5 years. The interest rate is 0%. Fifty-one percent of the jobs must be for low and moderate-income residents of the City. The applicant must graduate from the training program or have a business education.

    Special Initiative Funds
    ACCION Chicago
    3245 West 26th Street
    Chicago, IL 60623   773-376-9004

This loan is geared towards African Americans, women owned businesses, and geographic areas that are depressed. These loans are based on character as long as there is a cash flow in the business. The loan amount is from $500 to $25,000 with a term of 3 months to 24 months. This is for start-up and existing businesses.

    Micro Loan Program for Small Businesses
    West Cook Community Development
    1127 South Mannheim Road, Suite 1021   708-450-0100
    Westchester, IL 60559   Fax: 708-450-0655

This program is for small businesses in Western Suburban Cook County that have first been turned down by a bank for funding. It targets low to moderate-income women and minorities. The loan amount is from $2,000 to $50,000 with a term of up to 5 years. For funding, money is pooled from loans received from 20 area banks, and then in turn is loaned out from West Cook Community Development.

Indiana

    Eastside Community Fund
    Eastside Community Investments (ECI)
    26 N. Arsenal Ave.   317-637-7300
    Indianapolis, IN 46220   Fax: 317-637-7581

The aim is to loan money and provide technical assistance to both startup and existing small businesses. Preference is given to New Eastside residents or low income individuals. Loans are from $150 -$25,000; terms from three months to five years. Interest rate is 10 to 12%. This fund receives funding from SBA, Mott Foundation, state loan money, and Partners for Common Good Loan Fund.

    Rural Business Assistance Grant
    City of Madison Micro Loan Program
    P.O. Box 765
    Versailles, IN 47042   812-689-5505

This loan is funded through the U.S. Department of Agriculture (USDA). It is available to start-up or growing businesses. A maximum of $25,000 can be applied to equipment and working capital. The amount of time allowed for pay back is generally 5 to 7 years, depending on the loan, and the loan committee can decide on an extension.

    City of Madison Micro Loan Program
    SE Indiana Regional Planning Commission
    P.O. Box 765
    Versailles, IN 47042   812-689-5505

This loan is for start-up or growing small businesses in the area. The maximum of a $25,000 loan can be used for equipment and working capital. The term varies with the loan amount. Funding is from the U.S. Department of Agriculture (USDA).

Iowa

    SBA Microloan Demonstration Program
    Siouxland Economic Development Corporation
    428 Insurance Centre   712-279-6286
    Sioux City, IA 51102   Fax: 712-279-6920

Eligible applicants are low and moderate-income individuals located in Woodbury, Plymouth, Cherokee, Ida and Monona counties. This program receives referrals from local banks and community development organizations and assist in funding non-bankable individuals. Loans are from $1,500 to $25,000 with terms from 1-6 years. Funding comes from SBA grant, SEDC cash match, and other SEDC operating surplus and revenue.

    Small Enterprise Development
    Institute for Social and Economic Development
    1901 Broadway, Suite 313   319-338-2331
    Iowa City, IA 52240   Fax: 319-338-5824

This program is focused on low income, ethnic minorities, and women. Receives funds from foundations, corporations, civic and religious organizations, federal and state grants and contracts, and private contributions. The aim is to facilitate the empowerment of disadvantaged populations through the integration of social and economic development strategies. Loans are from $500 to $23,000 with terms from 6 months to five years. The interest rate is 5% for Institute's loans, and 8.5% to 15% for bank loans.

    SBA Microloan Program
    Siouxland Economic Development Corporation (SEDC)
    P.O. Box 447
    Sioux City, IA 50102   712-279-6286

Small businesses in and around the 6 counties of Sioux City can apply for this loan. The maximum amount is for $25,000 that is to be paid back in a maximum of 6 years. The interest rate is 10%. Funding is from the Small Business Association.

Kansas

    SBA Micro-Loan
    South Central Kansas Economic Development District
    209 East William, Suite 300
    Wichita, KS 67202-4012   316-262-7033
    www.sckedd.org

The goal of this loan is to stimulate the economy within the 14 county service area. A maximum of $25,000 is available for a term of 6 years. No funds may be used for the purchase of real estate. Funds are from the Small Business Association.

Kentucky

    Bluegrass Microenterprise Program
    Community Ventures Corporation
    1450 N. Broadway
    Lexington, KY 40505   606-231-0054

Upon joining the small business training program, you will have access to classes designed to help with specific areas of self-employment and business ownership. Classroom instruction is offered in business feasibility, management, marketing and financial planning. Upon completion of an approved business plan, you may be considered for inclusion in a small loan group, where loans of $500 to $2,500 are made to people operating or starting a small business.

    Community Loan Fund
    Human/Economic Appalachian Development Corp.
    P.O. Box 504   606-986-8423
    Berea, KY 40403   Fax: 606-986-1299

The Community Loan Fund is available to low income individuals and women located in Central Appalachia. Fund has provided loans to new and existing businesses in low-income communities including pilot program targeting welfare

Loans / No Money

recipients and community day care. The aim is to strengthen low-income communities. Receives funds from permanent capital, investments, grants and donations. Loans are from $100 to $25,000 with terms from one to five years. The interest rate is from 8 to 12%.

Micro-Enterprise Loan Fund
Kentucky Highlands Investment Corporation
P.O. Box 1738
London, KY 40743 — 606-864-5175

The purpose of this fund is to encourage the development of small businesses in counties of Kentucky Highlands. Expansion and start-up for profit businesses that meet the Small Business Administration's size standards are eligible. A maximum loan of $25,000 can be used for working capital and equipment. Borrowers have up to 6 years to repay with a fixed interest rate based on the loan.

SBA Micro Loan Program
Community Ventures Corporation
1458 North Broadway
Lexington, KY 40505 — 606-231-0054
Fax: 606-231-0261

This loan is open to existing micro businesses in Central Kentucky, a 20 county region. Its use is primarily for working capital and equipment. The maximum amount of the loan is for $20,000. The term is determined by the loan.

Louisiana

Micro Loan Fund
Catholic Social Services
1220 Aycock Street
Houma, LA 70360 — 504-876-0490

The area covered by this loan is the Diocese of Houma-Thibodax. A start-up business can borrow up to $1,500 and then borrow more after that loan has been paid off on time. If the business is existing, it can borrow up to $2,000 for the first loan, and more after that. The term is from 1 to 2 years.

Maine

Androscoggin Valley Council of Governments
(AVCOG)
125 Manley Rd.
Auburn, ME 04210 — 207-783-9186
Fax: 207-783-5211

The primary goal of these programs is to stimulate business investment that results in job creation and retention within the Androscoggin, Franklin, and Oxford Counties. Loans are up to $150,000. Terms are for 3-5 years at prime rate plus 1%. Eligible applicants are startups and existing businesses of all kinds.

Aroostook County Action Program, Inc. - Fleet Bank Set-Aside
P.O. Box 1116
Presque Isle, ME 04769 — 207-764-3721
Fax: 207-768-3040

This program is available to individuals who cannot obtain funding through conventional loan programs. Program is for startup and existing micro businesses, and to establish a link to conventional lending channels for each sustained business. Loans are from $1,000 to $10,000. Terms are up to five years at prime rate plus 2%.

Auburn Community Development Block Grant (CDBG) Microloan
Lewiston/Auburn Economic Growth Council
P.O. Box 1188
37 Park St.
Lewiston, ME 04240 — 207-784-0161
Fax: 207-786-4412

The Auburn Community Development Block Grant (CDBG) Microloan program is available to startup and existing businesses, manufacturing, distribution, service, non-retail, and low to moderate incomes.

Enterprise Fund
Coastal Enterprises Inc. (CEI)
P.O. Box 268
Wiscasset, ME 04578 — 207-882-7552

The aim of this fund is to help people with limited resources create their own jobs. Women-owned and child care businesses are typical examples. Loans are from $500 to $50,000. Rates are fixed market rate. Terms are up to 15 years. Funding is from the Ford Foundation, Mott Foundation, state legislative appropriation, Betterment Fund, U.S. Department of Health and Human Services, national churches, Maine Department of Economic and Community Development.

Entrepreneurs With Disabilities Loan Fund
Newmarket Tech
P.O. Box 724 — 207-287-7370
Augusta, ME 04330 — Fax: 207-287-3038

The Entrepreneurs With Disabilities Loan Fund is available to startup and existing businesses, businesses that create jobs, manufacturing, and people with mental and physical disabilities. Loans are from $500 to $2,000 and terms vary. Newmarket Tech also provides technical assistance.

Maine Centers for Women, Work and Community
46 University Dr.
Augusta, ME 04330 — 207-621-3440
Fax: 207-621-3429

This microloan is available to startup and existing businesses. Applicants must submit a written Business Plan to a committee. Loans are from $100 to $1,000. Eligible applicants are: family income below $20,000; displaced homemakers; single parents; and people in transition.

Working Capital Program
Western Mountains Alliance
P.O. Box 29
Farmington, ME 04938 — 207-778-7274
Fax: 207-778-7247

This loan is based on a peer-lending process. A potential applicant joins a business loan group of 4-10 business owners and applies directly to the group for loans. The group reviews and approves loans. All members must be current on their loans before any group member is eligible for another loan. Available to startup or businesses that projects to have a sustainable idea or product to sell or create. Loans are from $500-$5,000. Terms are four months to three years at 12%. Applicants must be a member of a peer lending group.

SBA Microloan Program
Eastern Maine Development Corporation
One Cumberland Place, Suite 300
Bangor, ME 04401 — 207-942-6389
800-339-6389
www.emdc.org

This loan is available only to counties in the area. Businesses that are starting up, expanding, or that need working capital can apply for up to $25,000. The loan includes post-loan technical support to help the owner in being successful. It must be paid back in up to 5 years.

Microloan Fund
Biddeford-Saco Area Economic Development Corporation
110 Main Street, Suite 1202
Saco, ME 04072 — 207-282-1748
Fax: 207-282-3149
E-mail: bsaedc@lamere.net
www.bsaedc.org

The loan is available to any small business in the area with emphasis on women and minorities. The maximum loan is for $25,000 at a fixed interest rate based on the market rate. One hundred percent financing is available up to $15,000. The terms of the loan vary depending on the use of the funds, but on an average are from 5 to 10 years. The Corporation is certified by the Treasury Department as CDFI.

New Ventures Loan Fund
Maine Centers for Women, Work, and Community
Stoddart House UMA
46 University Drive
Augusta, ME 043303-9410 — 207-621-3440
Fax: 207-621-3429
E-mail: wkrose@maine.edu

They established this fund to help women become economically successful. In order to apply for funds, women must graduate from New Ventures of Career/Life Planning Training. The loan is for up to $500. The term is from 3 months to one year. After that, borrowers are eligible to apply for another loan. Either start-ups or existing businesses that are low income and create jobs are eligible in the state of Maine.

NMDC Microloan Program
Northern Maine Development Commission
302 Main Street
P.O. Box 779
Caribou, ME 04736 — 207-498-8736
800-427-8736 (Maine only)
Fax: 207-493-3108

The purpose of this loan is to provide capital to women, low-income and minority small business owners that cannot get conventional loans. Money may be used for the purchase of machinery and equipment, furniture and fixtures, inventory, supplies and working capital. For loans of $7,500 and less, the interest rate is 10%. Loans over $7,500 have an interest rate of 9%. Applicants are eligible for technical assistance. Call first to be sure your business falls within the guidelines of the Small Business Administration.

Commercial Lending Program
Perquis Community Action Program
P.O. Box 1162

Loans / No Money

Bangor, ME 04402   207-973-3500

The Commercial Lending Program offers gap financing. The applicants must fall within the HUD guidelines for low income. One-third of the total amount needed can be applied for, with the maximum loan of $35,000. The term is an average of 5 to 7 years. It is available in Pennobscott and Piscataquis counties.

Androscoggin Valley Micro Loan Program
Androscoggin Valley Council of Governments
125 Manley Road
Auburn, ME 04210   207-783-9186

They call themselves the "Lender of last resorts". This loan can be used by either start-up or existing businesses for things like working capital, equipment. The loan amount is up to $40,000 with a maximum term of 7 years. Collateral, cash flow and a business plan are required. It is available to those in the 3 county service area.

Aroostook County Action Micro Loan Program
Aroostook County Action Program Inc.
P.O. Box 1166
Presque Isle, ME 04769   207-768-3033

Business owners in the Aroostook County area that meet HUD's median income guidelines can join this program. The maximum loan is $10,000 at 10% for a term of 10 years.

Maryland

Business Owners Startup Services (BOSS)
Council for Economic and Business Opportunities
800 N. Charles St., Suite 300   410-576-2326
Baltimore, MD 21201   Fax: 410-576-2498
www.cebo.com/

The aim of Business Owners Startup Services (BOSS) is to develop microenterprises via training and funding and to maintain microenterprises through technical assistance, support and funding. Eligible applicants are AFDC recipients, and residents of Housing Authority of Baltimore County. Loans are from $5,000 to $10,000, terms up to two years and interest rate is 10%. Receives funds from SBA, CDBG funds, SEID Grant, state, city, county PI and Title III contracts, and a grant from HUD.

Women Entrepreneurs of Baltimore, Inc. (WEB)
1118 Light St., Suite 202   410-727-4921
Baltimore, MD 21230   Fax: 410-727-4989

Women Entrepreneurs of Baltimore, Inc. (WEB) is a nonprofit organization, and its clients must have a viable business idea and the entrepreneurial spirit to make their business a success. WEB is committed to the economic empowerment of neighborhood women and the revitalization of Baltimore's neighborhoods. The development of microenterprise in Baltimore helps to revitalize these neighborhoods by stopping the dollar drain. The owners serve as strong role models and in some instances provide employment in their communities. Eligible applicants are economically disadvantaged women in Baltimore City. Loans are up to $500 with terms from three to six months. The interest rate is at 10%. WEB receives funding from foundations and bank contributions.

Massachusetts

Hilltown Enterprise Fund
Hilltown Community Development Corp.
432 Main Rd. #A   413-296-4536
Chesterfield, MA 01012   Fax: 413-296-4020

This fund receives funding from state and federal grants, loans from individuals, Western Massachusetts Enterprise Fund, and contributions. The aim is to promote rural cooperation and to ensure the best quality of life for all Hilltown residents. This is available to individuals with limited resources who wish to start or expand a business. Loan amounts are from $500 to $10,000 with loan terms at three years. The interest rate is 12%. For Hilltown residents only.

Microenterprise Development Program
Brightwood Development Corporation
2345 Main St.   413-734-2144
Springfield, MA 01107   Fax: 413-746-3934

This program's aim is to provide affordable housing and economic development to low and moderate income Hispanics and Puerto Ricans. Program is presently assisting eight new businesses to start in a low-income community. Loans are from $500 to $15,000. Terms are from three to five years. The interest rate is at 10%. Receives funds from the City of Springfield, Springfield Chamber of Commerce, SBA, and HUD.

Microenterprise Training and Loan Program for Refugees
Jewish Vocational Service
105 Chauncy St., 6th Floor   617-451-8147
Boston, MA 02111   Fax: 617-451-9973

Program receives funds from the Office of Refugee Resettlement and the Jewish Vocational Service. Provides refugees the opportunity to create their own jobs within the communities in which they live. Vulnerable populations, such as the disadvantaged and disabled, are the agency's priority. Loans are from $100 to $5,000 with terms from six months to three years. The interest rate is at prime rate plus 4%.

New Bedford Working Capital Network
Community Economic Development Center
166 William St.   508-999-9920
New Bedford, MA 02740   Fax: 508-990-0199

Eligible applicants are low and moderate income, racially and culturally diverse individuals. Small loans provide needed resources to these individuals who would not have funds to invest in their businesses. Loans are from $500 to $10,000 with the interest rate at 12%. Funding comes from credit through Fleet Banks, operating funds from Working Capital Institute for Cooperative Community Development, other banks, and private foundations.

Hampton City Employment and Training Consortium
Springfield Business Development Fund (SBDF)
1176 Main St.
Springfield, MA 01103   413-781-6900

Eligible applicants are low and moderate income, and minorities located in Springfield. SBDF provides secondary loans to small business for startup or expansion within the City of Springfield. It receives funding from the Small Business Administration and the Economic Development Administration. Loans are from $10,000 to $50,000 with terms from 5 to 20 years. The interest rate is at 6%.

Hilltown Enterprise Fund
Hilltown Community Development Corporation
P.O. Box 17
Chesterfield, MA 01012   413-296-4536

The Hilltown Enterprise Fund is available to the 11-town area around Hilltown for businesses that cannot otherwise get funding. Amounts from $500 to $15,000 are available at 12% interest. The terms of the loan are 6 months to 5 years, depending on the amount loaned. Funds come from local people.

Working Capital Program
Working Capital
99 Bishop Allen Drive   617-576-8620
Cambridge, MA 02139   Fax: 617-576-8623
E-mail: infor@workingcapital.org
www.workingcapital.org

Borrowers join a business loan group which control the lending process. Working Capital's loans are set up in steps with each amount having a different repayment time. They start off at $500 and go in steps up to $10,000, in some cases they will go as high as $20,000. There is a 16% interest rate for processing loans. Members also can also take advantage of the business programs and network with other business owners. This is for the greater Boston area.

Micro Loan
Twin Cities Community Development Corporation
195 Kimball Street
Fitchburg, MA 01420   978-342-9561

The goal of this fund is to increase economic development and income, and to create assets and jobs. It is available to business owners that have low to moderate incomes and do not fall within conventional loan guidelines. The business must be in operation for at least one year and located in the Fitchburg area. The loan amount is up to $50,000 with a term of 3 to 10 years. The interest rate is 12%.

Small Business Loan Fund
Dorchester Bay Economic Development Corporation
594 Columbia Road, Suite 302   617-825-4200
Dorchester, MA 02125   Fax: 617-825-3522
E-mail: DBSBAP@aol.com

This loan is open to residents or small businesses located in Dorchester. It is also available to a client that comes through a Community Development Corporation in another community. They also help with technical assistance, credit repair, financial planning, and more. The maximum loan amount is $25,000. The term is up to 5 years with a compounded interest rate.

Cambodian American League Fund
Cambodian American League of Lowell, Inc.
60 Middlesex Street

Loans / No Money

Lowell, MA 01852   978-454-3707

After a 7-week training program, small business owners must submit a business plan with their application for a loan. The loan amount is a maximum of $5,000. The loan must be paid back from one to two years, depending on the loan.

Greater Springfield Entrepreneurial Fund
Hampden County Employment and Training Consortium
1176 Main Street
Springfield, MA 01103   413-781-6900 ext. 227

This fund is available to the people in Hampden county except for the Chicopee and Chester areas. Small business owners can apply for a maximum of $25,000. It must be repaid in up to 5 years. The interest rate is 8%.

SEED Micro Loan Program
South Eastern Economic Development Corporation
88 Broadway
Taunton, MA 02780   508-822-1020

The eligible business types for this loan are manufacturing, retail, wholesale, and service. The money can be used for working capital, real estate for the use of the small business, and for machinery and equipment. The loan amount is up to $25,000 with a term up to 5 years. The interest rate is usually the market rate. The business must show potential for creating jobs, especially for low to moderate-income people. The service area of SEED is Barnstable, Bristol, Dukes, Plymouth and Nantucket counties.

Michigan

Wise Program
Ann Arbor Community Development Corp.
2008 Hogback Rd., Suite 12   313-677-1400
Ann Arbor, MI 48105   Fax: 313-677-1465

The WISE Program is to encourage small business development among women/minorities. This program assists women to become self-sufficient through self-employment. Loans are from $500 to $7,000. Terms are from 6 months to 7 years. Interest rate is prime rate plus 1%. Closing costs can be included in the amount of the loan. Receives funding from the City of Ann Arbor, Mott Foundation, U.S. Department of Health and Human Services, Michigan Women's Foundation, and the Community Foundation of Southeastern Michigan.

Lansing Community Micro-Enterprise Fund
520 West Ionia   517-485-4446
Lansing, MI 48933   Fax: 517-485-4761

To become eligible for this loan, the borrower must meet the criteria for low to moderate income and live in the City of Lansing. Or, the location of their business or residence must be within the City of Lansing where 70% or more of households are low to moderate income. They must also show that LCMF is the best loan option. The loan amount is $500 to $10,000. The term is from 12 months to 4 years at a 7% interest rate. A business training program is available, but not required.

Project Invest
Northwest Michigan Council of Governments
2194 Dendrinos Drive
P.O. Box 506   231-929-5000
Traverse City, MI 49685-0506   Fax: 231-929-5012
www.cog.mi.us

The goal of this program is to help entrepreneurs develop successful small businesses to create income and possible employment for others. To achieve this, a borrower must complete the Enterprise Development Workshops. After that, a loan of between $250 to $1,500 can be sought. Borrowers must meet with a loan advisor monthly.

Minnesota

Arrowhead Microenterprise Program
Arrowhead Community Economic Assistance Corporation
702 Third Ave. S.   218-749-2914
Virginia, MN 55792-2775   Fax: 218-749-2913

The aim of this program is to assist with startup or expansion of local businesses that increase employment opportunities, that retain existing jobs, identify and develop local skills and talents, and that provide economic opportunity for unemployed, low income and minority citizens. Loans are from $500 to $10,000. Terms are from 90 days to 10 years. The interest rate is a minimum 8%, and is adjusted annually. Receives funds from federal, state and county funds, private loans, and revenue from operations.

Business Development Services
Women Venture
2324 University Ave., Suite 200   651-646-3808
St. Paul, MN 55114   Fax: 651-641-7223

The aim of this service is to secure a stronger economic future for women through employment, career development, business development, and financial responsibility. Eligible applicants are women, with particular interest in reaching low-income women. Loans are from $50 to $25,000 with terms from three months to five years. The interest rate is at 10%. Women Venture receives funding from SBA Microloan Demonstration Grant, state and federal grants, and foundations.

Emerging Entrepreneur Development Program
Northwest Minnesota Initiative Fund
4225 Technology Dr.   218-759-2057
Bemidji, MN 56601   Fax: 218-759-2328

Although this program is available to everyone, it targets women, minorities and low-income individuals. The mission is to improve the quality of life for the people who live and work in NW Minnesota. This program provides opportunities for self-employment and the establishment of new businesses which makes it economically feasible for people to remain in the region. Loans are from $136 to $13,500, terms from one month to five years. The interest rate is 8%. Program receives funding from the SBA and The McKnight Foundation.

Northeast Entrepreneur Fund, Inc.
820 Ninth St., N., Suite 140   218-749-4191
Virginia, MN 55792   Fax: 218-741-4249

This is available to unemployed and underemployed individuals. This Fund helped to revitalize a rural region that has experienced severe economic dislocation in the last 15 years, and helped start or expand over 120 microbusinesses. The purpose is to encourage economic self-sufficiency through the growth of small businesses. Loans are from $100 to $100,000 with terms from 60 days to three years. Funds come from foundations, loans, contracts, fees, and interest.

Revolving Loan Fund (RLF)
North Star Community Development Corporation
604 Board of Trade Building
301 West First St.
Duluth, MN 55802   218-727-6690

North Star CDC is a community based economic development organization providing assistance to small businesses. Focus is placed on assisting low and moderate income individuals to achieve economic self-sufficiency. Loans are from $400 to $20,000 with the terms from 90 days to 5 years. The interest rate is 8%. Funding comes from the Community Development Block Grant. Only for those residing within the city limits of Duluth.

Self-Employment Training Opportunities (SETO)
Women Venture
2324 University Ave., Suite 200   651-646-3808
St. Paul, MN 55114   Fax: 651-641-7223

Eligible applicants are women, with particular interest in low-income women. The aim of SETO is to secure an economic future for women through employment, career development, business development, and financial responsibility. Loans are from $50 to $25,000 with terms from three months to five years. The interest rate is at 10%. Women Venture receives funding from SBA Microloan Demonstration Grant, state and federal grants, and foundations.

Child Care Provider Loan
Arrowhead Community Economic Assistance Corporation
8880 Main Street
P.O. Box 406   218-735-8201
Mountain Iron, MN 55768-0406   Fax: 218-735-8202
E-mail:aceac@rangenet.com

ACEAC's goal is to help start-up and expansion of local businesses in order to create economic opportunities for the area residents. The child care loan is offered between $300 and $7,000. Generally, repayment is from 2 to 3 years. The interest rate is 3 to 8% depending on the borrower's adjusted gross income. Priority is given to people who are open during non-traditional hours, people who care for children with disabilities, and those who operate in areas with a lack of child care. Technical support is available throughout the loan.

Micro Enterprise Loan Program
Neighborhood Development Center
651 1/2 University Avenue   651-291-2480
St. Paul, MN 55104   Fax: 651-291-2597

Small business and start-up loans are available to businesses in the cities of Minneapolis and St. Paul for up to $10,000. First, a 16-week NDC business training program must be completed. Repayment is up to 5 years at 10% interest rate. Business owners that have income below area median for their area are eligible.

Loans / No Money

Northeast Entrepreneur Fund
820 Ninth Street North
Virginia, MN 55792
218-749-4191
Fax: 218-749-5213

This fund is offered to small business owners that do not have reasonable access to other sources of money. The business must be located in, or the owner must be a resident of, the seven-county Arrowhead Region of northeast Minnesota. For a start-up or expansion of a business up to $100,000 may be requested. Repayment period varies from 30 days to 6 years. The interest is at market rate.

Revolving Loan Fund
North Star Community Development Corporation
301 West First Street, Suite 604
Duluth, MN 55802
218-727-6690

This loan is for low to moderate-income business owners. Currently, it serves the Duluth area, but it is expected to expand those boundaries soon. Up to $20,000 can be borrowed at 8% interest. The term of the loan is a maximum of 5 years.

Micro Loan
Phillips Community Development Corporation
1014 East Franklin, Suite #1
Minneapolis, MN 55404
612-871-2435
Fax: 612-871-8131

This loan is for general small businesses in the 8 neighborhood areas. The business must have been in operation for at least one year. Equity is required for a loan up to $10,000. The rate is 5 years with an interest of Prime plus 3%.

Dayton Hudson Artists Loan Fund
Resources and Counseling for the Arts
308 Prince Street, Suite 270
St. Paul, MN 55101
www.rc4arts.org
651-292-4381
Fax: 651-292-4315
TTY: 651-292-3218

This program is a community based revolving loan program for artists who cannot find traditional funding. It is available to those in the Minneapolis-St. Paul metro area. A loan of $1,000 to $5,000 with a term of 12 to 36 months can be applied for. The interest rate is 1% over Prime. The money can be used for artistic development and the artist's business development.

Micro Loan Program
Northwest Minnesota Foundation
4225 Technology Drive, NW
Bemidji, MN 56601
www.nwnf.org
218-759-2057
Fax: 218-759-2328

This loan is offered in order to help to develop small businesses and to create self-employment. It is available in the 12 extreme counties of Northwest Minnesota. Up to $20,000 can be applied for with a term of up to 5 years. This is open to either start-up or existing small businesses.

SBA Loan
Women Venture
2324 University Avenue
St. Paul, MN 55114
651-646-3808

This loan is available to help women to gain economic success. It is offered to new or existing small businesses in the 14 county service area. The amount of the loan is from $200 to $25,000 and technical assistance is given with it. The term is 30 days to 6 years with the interest up to 4 percent over prime. Fifty percent collateral is required.

Mississippi

Small Farm Loan
Alcorn State University
Small Farm Development Center
1000 ASU Drive #1080
Alcorn State, MS 39096-7500
601-877-6449
Fax: 601-877-3931

The Small Farm Loan is used to give short-term loans to small farmers. The money can be used for agriculture related expenses. The applicant must have a minimum farming experience of one year or have an educational background. Additionally, the farmer must have been turned down by 2 or more creditors. Repayment terms are from 1 to 5 years. There is a 1 to 3% service fee for approved loans, but the interest rate is 0%. Preference is given to emerging crop enterprise.

SELF Loan Fund
Economic Alternatives
P.O. Box 5208
Holly Springs, MS 38634
601-252-1575

This microloan targets low to moderate-income people. The business can be either just starting or an existing one. The loan amount is $500 to $2,500, with a 2-month grace period. The term is for not beyond 3 years with a 5% interest rate. This is available to businesses in Marshall and Benton counties. Funding is from USDA and private foundations.

Missouri

Microloan Program
First Step Fund
1080 Washington, Suite 204
Kansas City, MO 64105
816-474-5111
Fax: 816-472-4207

This loan is only for the graduates of the business training program that are members of the Alumni Group. They must also fall within the federal low to moderate income guidelines. A maximum loan for a first time borrower is $2,500; the next level of loan is up to $5,000. This money can be used for supplies and/or equipment. The average loan is 2 years. The interest rate is the prime rate. The loan is approved by the Borrowers' Group.

SBA Microloan Program
Rural Missouri, Inc.
1014 Northeast Drive
Jefferson City, MO 65109
800-234-4971
Fax: 573-635-5636

The SBA Microloan Program is for start-up and expanding businesses to provide funds for working capital, inventory, supplies, furniture, fixtures, machinery and/or equipment. The loan amount is from $500 to $25,000. The term is 1 to 5 years with an interest rate that is NY Prime plus 3%. Technical assistance is given on a one to one basis.

Montana

Action for Eastern Montana - Microbusiness Loan
2030 N. Merrill
Glendive, MT 59330-1309
406-377-3564

Action for Eastern Montana receives funds from the Montana Department of Commerce, banks, utilities, Rural Conservation and Development District, and small business donations. The mission is to help create a flourishing microbusiness climate. Eligible applicants are low income, women and minorities. Loans are from $500 to $20,000, interest rate are prime plus 2%. Closing costs/fees can be included in the loan.

Montana Microbusiness Finance Program
Montana Department of Commerce
1424 9th Ave.
Helena, MT 59620
406-444-3494
Fax: 406-444-2808

Eligible applicants are minorities, women and low income individuals. The goal is to provide disadvantaged individuals with self-employment opportunities. Loans and terms vary. Receives funds from State legislative appropriation from in-state investment fund, local capital, and operating budget.

Montana Women's Economic Development Group (WEDGO)
Women's Opportunity and Resource Development
127 N. Higgins
Missoula, MT 59802
406-543-3550
Fax: 406-721-4584

Aim is to provide business assistance services including training, consulting and capital access, targeting low and moderate income women. It works with community teams planning and implementing timber diversification strategies, and employ business assistance specialists to assist entrepreneurs. Loans are up to $35,000, terms up to five years. Interest rate is 1-2% above market rate. Receives funds from city, county, and state government, Ms. Foundation, Department of Health and Human Services, and US West Foundation. Only for residents of western Montana.

Opportunities, Inc. - Microbusiness Finance Program
Opportunities, Inc.
P.O. Box 2289
Great Falls, MT 59403
406-761-0310

Eligible applicants are those unable to receive loans from conventional sources. The purpose is to stimulate better coordination among available federal, state, local and private resources to enable low income families and individuals in rural and urban areas, to attain the skills and motivations they need to secure opportunities necessary to become self-sufficient. Loans and terms vary.

Microbusiness Loan
District 7 Human Resources Development Council
P.O. Box 2016
Billings, MT 59103
E-mail: dist7hrdc@imt.net
www.imt.net/~dist7hrdc
406-247-4710
Fax: 406-248-2943

This loan program is available to start-up and existing micro businesses in Big Horn, Carbon, Stillwater, Sweetgrass and Yellowstone Counties. The amount that can be applied for is from $500 to $35,000 with the average term being 36 months. The

Loans / No Money

money can be used for equipment, working capital, and property. There is also technical assistance and training available.

Nebraska

Rural Enterprise Assistance Project
Center for Rural Affairs
P.O. Box 406
Walthill, NE 68067
402-846-5428
Fax: 402-846-5420

The aim of this project is to demonstrate and implement programs to meet the long-term needs of existing and potential small businesses to succeed in rural areas of Nebraska. Loans are from $100 to $10,000; terms from 6 months to two years. Interest rate is prime rate plus 1% and 4%. It receives funding from the Ford Foundation, Mott Foundation, SBA Grant, The Aspen Institute, and Share Our Strength.

Rural Business Enterprise Program
Central Nebraska Community Services, Inc.
626 N Street
P.O. Box 509
Loup City, NE 68853
E-mail; cncsbd@micrord.com
308-745-0780
Fax: 308-745-0824

The goal of this loan is to maintain or increase employment in Central Nebraska. Small business loans are available from $500 to $15,000 to small and emerging businesses. The term is a maximum of 5 years at a fixed interest rate. Free consulting services are also provided.

Northeast Nebraska Microloan Fund
Northeast Nebraska Economic Development District
111 South 1st Street
Norfolk, NE 68701
www.nenedd.org/mbu.htm
402-379-1150
Fax: 402-378-9207

A For Profit Micro business in Northeast Nebraska can apply for this loan. For each $20,000 borrowed, one job must be created. And of those, at least 51% of the jobs retained must be for low to moderate-income employees. Security is required for the loan of $10,000 to $25,000, which must generally be paid back within 5 years. The interest rate is fixed by NNEDD.

Small Enterprise Economic Development Loan (SEED)
Mid-Nebraska Community Services, Inc.
16 West 11th Street
P.O. 2288
Kearney, NE 68848
308-865-5675

The borrower is asked to attempt conventional financing first. If that fails, they can apply for a loan up to $5,000. The term is a maximum of 5 years with a fixed interest rate. This is available to a 27 county area in South Central Nebraska. With the funding that comes from the USDA, the loan maximum is $15,000 within a 10 county area.

Lincoln Action Program Loan
2202 South 11th
Lincoln, NE 68502
402-471-4515

This loan targets small business owners that are in the low-income bracket. They use a pure lending peer group system. The loans are given in steps; they start small with a shorter term and when that is repaid, the next loan is larger, and so on. The maximum loan is $2,000. This is available to Lancaster County.

Micro Loan Program
New Community Development Corporation
3147 Ames Avenue
Omaha, NE 68131
402-451-2939

The goal of this program is to try and make loans available to a population that has been historically denied access to capital. The loan is available in the amounts of $100 to $10,000 for up to 36 months. Each loan level comes with a different origination fee and fixed interest rate. The eligible area is mainly North Omaha.

Rural Enterprise Assistance Project (REAP)
Center for Rural Affairs
101 Tallman
P.O. Box 406
Walthill, NE 68067
402-846-5428
Fax: 402-846-5420

REAP is designed to enhance the formation of local businesses and to invest in local people and the future of the community. Local communities form an association of members between 5 and 20 people. They meet for monthly training, support, networking and reviewing of loans. The committee can loan funds between the amounts of $100 and $10,000. This is done by step-up borrowing, with the first time amount up to $2,000. The next loan amount can be doubled up to $10,000. The interest for the first 2 loans is Prime +1%, and after that it is Prime +4%.

Micro Business Training and Development Project
Catholic Charities
Juan Diego Center
5211 South 31st Street
Omaha, NE 68107
402-731-5413

Applicants must go through the training and development program either here or at their sister agency. Generally, this is for start-up businesses, but an existing one will be considered if it has been operational for 3 years, with 3 years of tax returns. The funds available are from $250 to $1,000, but they will go up to $3,000 with sufficient reason. It may be used for inventory, operating expenses, and equipment. Available in their service area only.

Self Employment Loans Fund of Lincoln
Lincoln Partnership for Economic Development
P.O. Box 83006
Lincoln, NE 68501-3006
www.lped.com
402-436-2350
Fax: 402-436-2360

This program is available to low or moderate income business owners. They must join a Business Loan Group where the group meets monthly for assistance, networking, and loan processing. The loans are given in steps where the first amount is a maximum of $1,000. The next loan can be doubled and so on, for a maximum of $10,000. These loans are not based on credit history, but character. This program is available in Lincoln Partnership for Economic Development's (LPED) service area.

Nevada

Microloan Funds
Nevada Microenterprise Initiative
116 East 7th Street, Suite 3
Carson City, NV 89701
702-841-1420
Fax: 702-841-2221

It is the goal of the Nevada Microenterprise Initiative to strengthen the economic and quality of life of low and moderate-income business owners in the state of Nevada through training, technical assistance, and loans. For those people that cannot get commercial funding, they must attend NMI's workshop before applying for a loan. A start-up business can borrow up to $7,500, for existing or returning borrowers, the maximum loan is $25,000. The term either is up to 36 or 72 months, depending on the loan. After that, they meet with an advisor once a month.

New Hampshire

Working Capital
Microenterprise Peer Lending
New Hampshire Community Loan Fund
7 Wall St.
Concord, NH 03301
603-224-6669
Fax: 603-225-7254

This program is available to low and moderate income individuals in the Concord area. It assists underserved individuals in meeting their own basic economic needs by complementing and extending the reach of conventional lenders and public institutions. Loans are from $500 to $5,000 with the interest rate at 12%. This fund receives funding from commercial banks.

Working Capital
New Hampshire Community Loan Fund
7 Wall Street
Concord, NH 03301
603-224-6669
Fax: 603-225-7425

This program was created to increase the income and success of small business owners. They use a peer lending system where members apply for loans from their group. All members must be current on their loans for any member to apply for another loan. The available loans are from $500 to $5,000. Call for the service area covered.

Citizens Bank Women Business Owners' Loan Fund
Women's Business Center
150 Greenleaf Avenue, Unit 8
Portsmouth, NH 03801
603-430-2892

The Women's Business Center (WBC) is designed to encourage and support women in all phases of enterprise development in order to create economic development. Technical assistance and workshops must be attended in order to become a member. After that, a loan from $10,000 to $100,000 can be requested if the business is also owned by at least 51% of women. The money can be used for start-up, relocation, and working capital to expand and /or purchase equipment and/or inventory.

Working Capital
Women's Rural Entrepreneurial Network (WREN)
2013 Main Street

Loans / No Money

P.O. Box 331
Bethlehem, NH 03574
603-869-9736
Fax: 603-869-9738
E-mail: WREN@connriver.net

This program has been created to support self-employed members and to give small business loans. The peer group lending system is used so that the business owner becomes a member of the group where the loan is reviewed. The amount starts at $500 and has a $5,000 maximum. After that, there are meetings where the group gets a report as to how the loan is being used. This is for both start-up and existing businesses in the area.

New Jersey

Micro Loan
Trenton Business Assistance Corporation (TBAC)
36 Broad Street
Trenton, NJ 08608
609-396-8271
Fax: 609-396-8603
E-mail: tbacsba@earthlink.net
www.trentonj.com/tbac.html

About 70% of the funds offered by the Trenton Business Assistance Corporation (TBAC) are loaned to women and minority business owners. At least 50% of the loans are made to businesses owned by women. The loan amounts are up to $25,000 with a maximum term of 5 years. The interest rate is 10.5%. The for-profit business must be located in Mercer, Burlington, or Hunterdon counties.

New Mexico

Women's Economic Self-Sufficiency Team (WESST Corp.)
414 Silver SW
Albuquerque, NM 87102-3239
505-848-4760
Fax: 505-848-2368

The aim of Women's Economic Self-Sufficiency Team (WESST Corp.) is to help women in New Mexico achieve economic self-sufficiency through sustained self-employment. Eligible applicants are low income women and minorities located in the State of New Mexico. Loans are from $500 to $7,000 with terms from 30 days to 5 years. The interest rate is at prime rate plus 2-4%. WESST Corp. receives funding from Seton Enablement Fund, SBA Microloan Demonstration Program, and in-kind contributions.

Micro Loan Program
ACCION
#20 First Plaza NW, Suite 417
Albuquerque, NM 87102
505-243-8844

The main focus of this loan is to aid those businesses in urban or low-income areas of the Albuquerque area. Traditionally, these owners cannot get funding from banks. The loans are from $100 to $50,000. The repayment depends on the type of loan. The interest rate is from 11% to 14%. Technical assistance is also available.

New York

Adirondack Entrepreneurial Center
Adirondack Economic Development Corporation
P.O. Box 747
Saranac Lake, NY 12983
518-891-5523
Fax: 518-891-9820

The mission is to promote the development of small business. Loans are from $500 to $150,000, with flexible terms and rates. Eligible applicants are low income, women, minorities, and rural entrepreneurs. Receives funds from the Small Business Administration, Farmers Home Administration, Adirondack North County Association, NY State Urban Development Corporation, Rural Economic Development Program, and the Department of Economic Development Entrepreneurial Assistance Program.

Entrepreneurship Training Program
Worker Ownership Resource Center, Inc.
400 E. Church St.
Elmira, NY 14901
607-737-5212
Fax: 607-734-6588

This program assists low income and minority entrepreneurs to start businesses in their communities and to build personal and business assets. Eligible applicants are persons with household income below WIC guidelines and minorities. Loans are from $100 to $5,000 with terms from 6 months to two years. Interest rate is 12%. Receives funding from Diocese of Rochester, and Campaign for Human Development.

Micro-Enterprise Loan and Assistance Program
Church Avenue Merchants Block Association
885 Flatbush Ave., Suite 202
Brooklyn, NY 11211
718-287-0010
Fax: 718-287-2737

The Micro-Enterprise Loan and Assistance Program is devoted to recently arrived refugees. Goal is to enable low income persons attain self-sufficiency through microenterprise development. This program makes loans to persons who have limited or no access to capital for small businesses. Loan amounts are up to $5,000. Terms are 12 or 18 months, with an interest rate at 14%. For residents of New York City.

Minority and Women Business Development Center
Urban League of Rochester, New York, Inc.
215 Tremont St., Door #4
Rochester, NY 14608
212-803-2418

The aim is to provide training, counseling, and technical assistance to minorities and women seeking to start their own businesses. Loans are from $2,000 -$50,000; terms from 1-5 years. Interest rate is prime rate plus 1-2.5%. Receives funds from the Urban Development Corporation, and NY State Department of Economic Development Entrepreneurial Assistance Program. Only for residents of greater Rochester - Monroe County.

Neighborhood Micro-Loan Program
Ridgewood Local Development Corporation
59-09 Myrtle Ave.
Ridgewood, NY 11385
718-366-3806
Fax: 718-381-7080

The Neighborhood Micro-Loan Program serves neighborhood retailers, small manufacturers, professionals and health care providers, service businesses. and young businesses and businesses owned by minorities and women. Program is used to contract startup costs, storefront improvements, and purchase new equipment. Loan amounts and terms vary. Only for residents of the greater Ridgewood area in Queens, NY.

N.Y. State Department of Economic Development
Entrepreneurial Assistance Program
Albany-Colonie Regional Chamber of Commerce
1 Computer Dr. S.
Albany, NY 12205
518-458-9851
Fax: 518-458-1055

The purpose of this program is to promote the growth and development of minority-owned and women-owned businesses by providing technical assistance and creating access to capital, networking, and community and business leaders. Receives funds from NY State Urban Development Corp., Albany Local Development Corporation, KeyBank USA, and Town of Colonie I.D.A. Loans are from $1,000 to $5,000, terms from three to five years. Interest rate is Prime rate plus 2%.

Queens County Overall Economic Development Corporation
NY State Department of Economic Development
Entrepreneurial Assistance Program
120-55 Queens Blvd., Suite 309
Kew Gardens, NY 11424
718-263-0546
Fax: 718-263-0594

This program provides a package of services to encourage and train would be entrepreneurs; to support and assist new startup businesses in surviving the first two years of business, and assist existing businesses with their relocation and/or expansion efforts. Eligible applicants are low income and minority residents of Queens. Loans and terms vary. Funding comes from seven banks and equity investors, borough presidents, city and state agencies.

Regional Economic Development Assistance
Corporation Mini Loan Program
New York City Economic Development Corporation
110 William St.
New York, NY 10038
212-618-8900

This program is for small/startup service, retail, contractor, manufacturing businesses. Loans are available for machinery and equipment, leasehold improvements, real estate acquisition and working capital. Loans are from $5,000 to $50,000. Terms are two to five years. Interest rates are prime rate plus 1.5%.

Rural Ventures Fund
Rural Opportunities, Inc.
400 East Ave.
Rochester, NY 14607
716-340-3387
Fax: 716-340-3337

Eligible applicants are low and moderate income individuals denied access to bank credit. The aim is to promote self-sufficiency and economic independence through the creation and expansion of small businesses and microenterprises. Loans are from $3,000 to $50,000 with terms from 3 to 60 months. The interest rate is up to 15%. Funding comes from FmHA Industrial Development Grant, SBA Microloan Demonstration Program, CDBG funds, and New York State. For residents of upstate New York, primarily rural and small communities.

WORC Loan Fund
Worker Ownership Resource Center
One Franklin Square

Loans / No Money

Exchange Street
Geneva, NY 14456
www.atworc.org
315-789-5061
Fax: 315-789-0261

Worker Ownership Resource Center (WORC) funds are available to people with low to moderate income. In order to be considered for a loan, a training program through the center must be completed. Five thousand dollars is the maximum amount for first time borrowers. After half of that has been paid off on time, additional funds may be applied for. Only the interest is required during the first 3 months of a new loan. After that, repayment is normally 2 years. That may be extended for loan over $5,000. Interest is the prime lending rate at closing. The business or owner must reside in the 10 county service area.

Manhattan Loan Fund
Manhattan Borough Development Corporation
15 Park Row, Suite 510
New York, NY 10038
212-791-3660
Fax: 212-571-0873

The Manhattan Loan Fund is available to moderate-income business owners located in Manhattan. The amounts of the loan are from $5,000 to $25,000. It can be used for leasehold improvements, machinery and equipment and working capital. The terms are 6 months to 5 years at 10.5% interest.

Micro Loan Program
Project Enterprise
2303 7th Avenue
New York, NY 10030
212-690-2024

This program is for microentrepreneurs in the Brooklyn and Harlem areas that live at or below the poverty level, in order that they can increase their incomes and improve the quality of their lives. A group of peers build up a Group Savings Fund, which is used for loans to members of the group at no interest. Bi-weekly meetings must be attended. The first loan is for a maximum of $750 for 5 months or $1,500 for 12 months. After that the loan amount doubles with a maximum of $10,000. A good credit record or collateral is not needed to enroll in this program.

ACCORD Business Development Program
ACCORD Corporation
50 West Main Street
Friendship, NY 14739
E-mail: RVC_Fedz@eznet.net
716-973-2322
Fax: 716-973-3014

To be able to apply for a loan, a 10-week course or equivalent independent study must be completed. It is available to business owners that fall within HUD's low to moderate-income levels. It is for start-up or existing businesses that need money for working capital, real property, and equipment. Up to $25,000 can be applied for with the term varying. It is offered in Allegany County.

Micro Loan Program
ACCION New York
235 Havemeyer Street
Brooklyn, NY 11211
E-mail: accionnewyork@compuserve.com
www.accion.org
718-599-5170

ACCION does not require that a business be formal in their operation. It is preferred that they have been in business for at least 1 year. The loan is from $5,000 to $25,000 with a term of 3 months to 24 months. The interest is amortized on a monthly basis. This is available to businesses in New York City that cannot get conventional lending.

Appleseed Trust
MicroCredit Group of Central New York
222 Herald Place, 2nd Floor
Syracuse, NY 13202
315-424-9485
Fax: 315-424-7056

It is the mission of this program to assist low and moderate-income residents in this community to start, expand, or improve their business through training, support, and loan access. Members must join a Peer Group where they can apply for a first loan of up to $500. The money can be used for equipment, materials, or advertising and promotions. Expansions and additional loans can be sought for up to $5,000.

Trickle Up Program
121 West 27th St., Suite 504
New York, NY 10001
212-362-7958

Over 75% of the recipients of this program either have no credit or bad credit history. Entrepreneurs are given $700 in conditional start-up capital in two installments. For the first $500, they must complete a Business Plan, agree to spend a minimum of 250 hours per person over a 3 month period, and save or reinvest at least 20% of the profits in the business. At the end of three months, and when all of the requirements have been met, they can receive the final $200. Most of the recipients work out of their homes.

North Carolina

Child Care Providers
Self-Help
301 W. Main St.
Durham, NC 27701
www.self-help.org
800-476-7428
919-956-4400
Fax: 919-956-4600

This is a special loan program created by the NC Division of Child Development to help an individual get started or expand, buy indoor or outdoor equipment, upgrade buildings, and improve a particular program's quality. These loans have a below market, fixed interest rate of 5%, and no minimum/maximum loan size. Eligible applicants are anyone who runs or wants to run a registered and licensed child care program that serves or is willing to serve subsidized children.

Good Work
115 Market St. #211
Durham, NC 27702
919-682-8473
Fax: 919-687-7033

The aim is to be a resource for those who want to start or expand their small businesses. Eligible applicants are startup and small businesses. Loans are from $100-$10,000 with terms from three months to three years. Interest rate is 13%. Receives funds from Self-Help Credit Union, foundations, and churches.

Microbusiness Development
WAMY Community Action, Inc.
P.O. Box 2688
Boone, NC 28607
828-264-2421
Fax: 828-264-0952

This program allows low-income persons to begin or expand small business efforts in an area where few jobs are available. Eligible applicants are persons below poverty level located in Watauga, Avery, Mitchell and Yancey counties only. Loans are from $500 to $10,000; terms and interest rates vary.

Mountain Microenterprise Fund
29 1/2 Page Ave.
Asheville, NC 28801
828-253-2834
Fax: 828-255-7953

Eligible applicants are women and minorities, and low income persons. The aim is to create small businesses and microenterprises through a program of financial and technical assistance. Funding is from NC General Assembly, operating budget, Dogwood Fund, NC Rural Economic Development Center, and the Z. Smith Reynolds/Janirve Foundations. Loans are from $200-$25,000; terms vary.

North Carolina Microenterprise Loan Program (NCMLP)
NC Rural Economic Development Center, Inc.
4021 Carya Dr.
Raleigh, NC 27610
919-250-4314
Fax: 919-250-4325

The North Carolina Microenterprise Loan Program (NCMLP) is one of the largest microenterprise loan funds in the country. It's funded by public and private sources. It offers financing and support for the startup and expansion of small businesses for residents of the 85 counties defined as rural in NC. Borrowers have included mechanics, seamstresses, crafts people, janitorial service operators, building contractors, and retailers. Loans are from $350 to $25,000.

Northeastern Community Development Corporation
154 Highway 158 East
Camden, NC 27921
252-338-5466
Fax: 252-338-5639

The mission of this fund is to make funding available to craft artisans to startup or expand their businesses. The Fund works with low-income people who need loans to buy equipment/supplies in order to begin making crafts, or who need working capital for expanding their business. Loans are from $50 to $750 with terms from one to three months. The interest rate is prime rate plus 2%. This fund receives funding from the Ms. Foundation.

West Greenville CDC Micro Loan Program
West Greenville Community Development Corp.
706 West 5th St.
P.O. Box 1605
Greenville, NC 27835-1605
252-752-9277

Eligible applicants are women, and other high risk borrowers. The aim is to increase economic index in target counties. Loans and terms vary. Also provide business training and planning, individual business counseling, peer support, and mentoring. This program receives funding from the NC Rural Economic Development Center.

Micro Loan
Mountain Microenterprise Fund (MMF)
29 1/2 Page Avenue
Asheville, NC 28801
www.mtnmicro.org
888-389-3089

Either a secured or unsecured loan is available to those small business owners that cannot get a conventional loan through a bank. For an unsecured loan, $99-$1,500

Loans / No Money

can be applied for. The first level for a secured loan is $99 to $2,500. After that has been repaid up to $5,000 can be sought. The last level of the loan is for up to $8,000. The repayment varies from 12 months to 36 months for the larger loans. Most of the funding comes from the Rural Economic Development Center.

>Micro Loan
>Good Work, Inc.
>P.O. 25250
>Durham, NC 27702 919-682-8473

While the target of this loan is low-income minority small business owners, anyone in the service area can apply. In order to be eligible, a technical training class through the company must be completed. The loan amounts are $1,000 to $10,000. The term is from 6 to 12 years. The interest rate is 13%, but is negotiable depending on the loan size.

>Microenterprise Loan Program
>North Carolina Rural Economic Development Center
>4021 Carya Drive
>Raleigh, NC 27610 919-250-4314

The goal of this program is to help rural people become self-sufficient. It offers loans to people that could not get conventional funding in order to start-up or expand their business. Loans up to $25,000 are available. With this program, five local lending sites have group-based lending programs. The business owner joins into a group where they are involved in training and get certification. Each group controls the loan payments. This is for small businesses in the 85 rural counties of North Carolina. The local lending office should be contacted for information.

>East Carolina Microenterprise Loan Program
>315 Turner Street 252-504-2424
>Beaufort, NC 28516 Fax: 252-504-2248

It is the goal of the East Carolina Microenterprise Loan Program to loan money to microentrepreneurs in order to create more jobs in rural areas. Participants must attend business sessions and afterwards they form small groups that administer their own loans. After that they meet monthly for further training, networking and loan presentations. From $500 to $8,000 can be applied for in three stages. The terms range from 20 months to 30 months. It is available to either start-up or existing businesses in the service area.

Ohio

>Microenterprise Program
>Lima-Allen Council for Community Affairs
>405 East Market St. 419-227-2586
>Lima, OH 45801 Fax: 419-227-7626

This program is available to low income workers, displaced workers, ADC/JOBS recipients located in Allen county. The aim is to empower low income individuals through self-employment, creating self-sufficiency and alleviating poverty. Loans are up to $1,000, terms from two to five years and interest rate is at prime plus 2%. Receives funds from various financial institutions and CSBG.

>CAC Microenterprise Training Program
>Community Action Committee (CAC) of Pike County
>941 Market St.
>P.O. Box 799 740-289-2371
>Piketon, OH 45661 Fax: 740-289-4291

The program is available to low and moderate income persons. The aim is to improve economic conditions through training, small business development and support services leading to self-sufficiency. Loans are $500 to $10,000, terms three months to three years, and interest rate at prime plus 2%. Receives funds from CDC Grant Program, banks, local housing authority, and organization contributions.

>City of Cleveland Microloan Program
>City of Cleveland Department of Economic Development
>601 Lakeside Ave., Room 210 216-664-2406
>Cleveland, OH 44114 Fax: 216-664-3681

The aim is to provide financial and management support to existing and new businesses that do not have access to traditional financial sources. Eligible applicants are businesses in the City of Cleveland. Loan amounts and terms vary. Receives funds from City of Cleveland and local financial institutions.

>Columbus/Franklin County Microloan Program
>Columbus Countywide Development Corp.
>941 Chatham Lane, Suite 207 614-645-6171
>Columbus, OH 43221 Fax: 614-645-8588

This program is available to women and minority-owned businesses, day care facilities and targeted Columbus neighborhoods. The aim is to encourage the creation of small micro businesses and provide financing for small projects not available from conventional lenders. Loans are $1,000 to $25,000, terms 30 days to 6 years, and interest rate is 10.6% to 11.6%. It receives funds from SBA, Ohio Department of Development, Columbus Department of Development, and banks.

>Food Ventures Project and Product Development Fund
>ACEnet
>94 N. Columbus Rd. 740-592-3854
>Athens, OH 44701 Fax: 740-593-5451

The aim is to transform relationships within communities to allow people with low incomes to successfully enter the economic mainstream by creating opportunities for both business ownership and employment in expanding firms. Eligible applicants are low to moderate-income persons, public assistance recipients, and firms participating in ACEnet business networks in Southeastern Ohio. To promote food manufacturing businesses; funds can be a loan, royalty, or equity. Receives funds from private sources and foundations.

>HHWP Community Action Commission
>Microenterprise Development Program
>HHWP Community Action Commission
>122 Jefferson St., P.O. Box 179 419-423-3755
>Findlay, OH 45839 Fax: 419-423-4115

This program is available to low income and public assistance recipients. The aim is to create self-employment opportunities that enable low income residents to improve their living conditions and become self-sufficient. Loans are up to $5,000, terms from 3-24 months. Interest rate is prime plus 2%. Receives funds from CSBG and private foundations.

>Neighborhood Economic Development Loan Program (NEDL)
>Office of Economic Development
>City of Toledo
>One Government Center, Suite 1850 419-245-1426
>Toledo, OH 43604 Fax: 419-245-1462

The Neighborhood Economic Development Loan Program (NEDL) is available to low and moderate income target communities served by CDC housing programs. The aim is to provide commercial credit for neighborhood-based businesses and provide a competitive advantage to neighborhood commercial and industrial areas. Loan amounts and terms vary. Receives funding from City of Toledo and banks.

>Women Entrepreneurs, Inc.
>P.O. Box 2662, C-OH45201
>36 East 4th St., Suite 92 513-684-0700
>Cincinnati, OH 45201 Fax: 513-684-0779

New businesses that are started offer services to the community such as adult day care, home-bound disabled worker assistance and extra support to women in traditional industries. Receives funding from Society National Banks, Liberty National Banks, independent member/corporate contributions, and local foundations. Eligible applicants are AFDC recipients, low and moderate income individuals located in Hamilton, Clermont, Warren, Butler, Brown, Adams, Highland, Pike and Ross counties, and Northern Kentucky and Southeastern Indiana. Loans and terms vary.

>Micro Loan Fund
>Neighborhood House, Inc
>1000 Atchenson Street 614-252-4544
>Columbus, OH 43203 Fax: 614-252-7919
>E-mail: lboykin@beol.net

The purpose of this loan is to build up the empowerment zone. It is available to start-up and existing small businesses in that area, or for those business owners that live in the zone. Applications can be made for up to $7,500 for a 3 year term. The interest rate is 12%.

>Appalachian Microloan Program
>Enterprise Development Corporation 740-797-9646
>9080 Hocking Hills Drive 800-822-6096
>The Plains, OH 45780 Fax: 740-797-9659

This is for small business located in the 30 counties of Appalachia. It may be used for working capital, equipment and machinery, furniture and fixtures, inventory and supplies, and leasehold improvements. The size of the loan is $100 to $25,000. The term is flexible with a maximum of 6 years. The interest rate is from 11% to 12.75% APR. Funding is from the Small Business Administration.

>Child Care Loan
>Lima/Allen Council on Community Affairs (LACCA)
>540 South Central 419-227-2586
>Lima, OH 45804 Fax: 419-227-7626

The Child Care Loan is available to those child care providers that target low income people, infants, workers of 2nd or 3rd shifts, and disabled kids. The maximum

Loans / No Money

amount of the loan is $25,000. It must be repaid in up to 5 years and the interest is Prime + 2. The borrowers must be in the 5 county service area of LACCA.

MicroLoan Program
Hamilton County Development Company, Inc.
1776 Mentor Avenue
Cincinnati, OH 45212   513-631-8292
E-mail: lawalden@hcdc.com

This loan is open to small business owners located in one of the 8 counties of Southwest Ohio. The maximum loan for a start-up business is $7,500. For an existing business, one year or more, the amount is $15,000. The term is up to 6 years with an interest rate of 16%. Funding is provided by the Small Business Administration.

MicroLoan
Columbus Countywide Development Corporation
941 Chatham Lane, Suite 300
Columbus, OH 43221-2416   614-645-6171
E-mail: ccdc@earthlink.net   Fax: 614-645-85883

This program helps healthy growing businesses by offering financial and technical support. The maximum loan for a start-up business is $15,000. For an existing business, the loan starts at $1,000 and has a maximum of $25,000. The term depends on what the loan is being used for, but on an average is 2 years. The interest ranges from 11.6% to 10.6%. Borrowers are required to attend Technical Assistance Group meetings. This available area is in 13 counties of Central Ohio.

Pike County Microloan
CAC of Pike County, Inc.
941 Market Street
Piketon, OH 45661   740-289-2371

While they tend to serve business owners that cannot get loans from the banks, this program is also open to other entrepreneurs in Pike County. After completion of the business class, a loan for up to $10,000 can be applied for. The term is a maximum of 3 years with the interest rate of Prime plus 2.

Oregon

SBA Microloan Program
Cascades West Financial Services, Inc.
1400 Queen Avenue SE
P.O. Box 686   541-924-8480
Albany, OR 97321   Fax: 541-967-4651
E-mail: dsearle@cwcog.cog.or.us

The purpose of this microloan program is to help women, low income, minority and other business owners get loans that they could not otherwise get. The ultimate goal is to help them become eligible for conventional banking loans. The money available is up to $25,000 for up to 6 years at a fixed rate of up to 14.75%. Technical support is offered throughout the life of the loan. The business must be located in the 14 county service area of Cascades West.

Microenterprise Loan
O.U.R. Federal Credit Union
P.O. Box 11922
Eugene, OR 97440   541-485-1190

This loan is for businesses that have been operational at least 12 months and have proof of business activity. They must be members of the credit union and have participated with or in a health or human services agency in Lane County. The loan amount is a maximum of $5,000 at 13.9% interest. The term is up to 36 months.

Micro Loan
Southern Oregon Women's Access to Credit
33 North Central, Suite 209
Medford, OR 97501   541-779-3992

Start-up or expansion businesses in the Jackson County area can apply for a loan of up to $25,000. The term is 5 years with an interest rate of 3 1/2 points over prime. A written business plan must be submitted before applying for the loan. The funds can be used for working capital.

Child Care Neighborhood Network Loan Fund
Rose Community Development Corporation
7211 NE 62nd Avenue
Portland, OR 97206   503-788-0826

Through community based microenterprise development, Rose Community Development Corporation helps to increase the character of child care and secure the providers' businesses. These loans are established in order to help child care providers who have difficulty getting conventional loans. The loan amounts are $500 to $5,000 with a term between 24 and 48 months. The money may be used for business improvements, equipment or toys, and related business expenses.

Pennsylvania

Ben Franklin Enterprise Growth Fund
Ben Franklin Technology Center of Southeastern Pennsylvania
1110 Penn Center
1835 Market St., Suite 1100   215-972-0877
Philadelphia, PA 19103   Fax: 215-972-5588

Fund was established to make capital available to low income, minority, and women business owners, startups, and to help client businesses obtain credit from conventional sources in Bucks, Chester, Delaware, Montgomery, and Philadelphia counties. Loans are from $5,000 to $15,000. Interest rate is fixed at prime rate plus 3%. Closing fees are up to $350 (can be financed in the loan).

Local Enterprise Assistance Program (LEAP)
Bloomsburg University College of Business
243 Sutliff Hall   570-389-4591
Bloomsburg, PA 17815   Fax: 570-389-3892

The aim is to create opportunities for startup and self-employed business persons to earn equitable incomes and control productive resources. Dedicated to building the economic capacity of rural communities through small enterprises by providing access to credit, business training and self-management skills. Eligible applicants are the unemployed, rural microentrepreneurs, and AFDC recipients. Loans and terms vary.

Micro-Enterprise Development
Lutheran Children and Family Service
45 Garrett Rd.   610-734-3363
Upper Darby, PA 19082   Fax: 610-734-3389

This program is available to refugees in the U.S. less than five years, who are AFDC recipients, low/moderate income located in Philadelphia. Receives funding from the Office of Refugee Resettlement. Loans and terms vary.

Service for Self-Employment Training and Support (ASSETS)
Mennonite Economic Development Associates
447 S. Prince St.
Lancaster, PA 17603   717-393-6089

This program is available to low income individuals as defined by HUD guidelines. The Associates have assisted new businesses to start or expand in the most disadvantaged areas of Lancaster. The purpose is to increase personal income, create jobs, foster economic linkages, develop human potential and encourage community development through small business. Loans are from $500 to $5,000 with terms from 6 months to three years. The interest rate is prime rate.

Micro Loan
ASSETS
447 South Prince Street   717-393-6089
Lancaster, PA 17603   Fax: 717-290-7936

In order to apply for this loan, applicants must complete a 13-week training program. It is available to people with low to moderate income that live in Lancaster. Up to $5,000 can be loaned with a term of up to 3 years. The interest rate is the Prime lending rate.

Micro Loan
Community Action Development Corporation
of the Lehigh Valley
605 Turner Street
Allentown, PA 18102   610-433-5703

This program was designed to help to build up the community and to establish business owners. Before applying for the loan, the Start Your Business Program must be completed. Graduates can apply for a loan up to $5,000. The terms and interest rate of the loan vary case by case. It is available for the areas of Center City, Allenton, and South Side.

Community Capital Works
Philadelphia Development Partnership
1334 Walnut Street
Philadelphia, PA 19107   215-545-3100

Applicants must go through the customized business training to qualify for this small business loan. After that, they join a peer lending group which governs the loan. The funds are loaned in steps starting with $500. After that amount is repaid the business owner can apply for $1,000. This goes up to a maximum amount of $5,000. The amount of time to repay the loan depends on the amount. The interest rate is a 12% annual rate. Borrowers must be in the service are of PDP.

Women's Opportunities Resource Program
1930 Chestnut Street, Suite 1600
Philadelphia, PA 19103   215-564-5500

After applicants have attended the free business classes, they can apply for a loan.

Loans / No Money

The maximum amount available is $2,500 for a term of 24 months. It is intended for minority, woman, refugee and immigrant business owners. They say they are a "fund of last resort" in the 5 county area that is served.

    Enterprise Growth Fund
    Ben Franklin Technology Center
      of Southeastern Pennsylvania
    11 Penn Center
    1835 Market St., Suite 1100   215-972-6700
    Philadelphia, PA 19103   Fax: 215-972-5588

This Fund was created to make capital available to small businesses in Bucks, Chester, Delaware, Montgomery, and Philadelphia counties, so that they may be able to get conventional funding in the future. Eligible businesses are owned by credit-challenged women, minorities, low to moderate income people, and those that are located in economically distresses areas. The maximum loan is $25,000 for existing businesses and $5,000 for start-ups to be used for development and expansion.

South Dakota

    Revolving Loan Fund Program
    Northeast South Dakota Economic Corporation
    414 Third Ave. East   605-698-7654
    Sisseton, SD 57262   Fax: 605-698-3038

This program receives funding from Northwest Area Foundation, CDBG, SBA Microloan Demonstration Program, East River Electric Power Corp., and the First State Bank of Roscoe. The program addresses the economic needs of small rural communities as they relate to business development and job creation. Eligible applicants are low income, disadvantaged persons, minorities, and women. Loans are from $100 to $150,000 with terms from 6 months to 25 years. For residents of northeastern South Dakota.

Tennessee

    Community Microloan Program
    Knoxville's Community Development Corporation
    Economic Ventures, Inc.
    P.O. Box 3550   423-594-8762
    Knoxville, TN 37927-3550   Fax: 423-594-8659

This program helps individuals in getting their businesses established through financial and technical assistance. Borrowers join a peer group where they get training, support, and apply for the loans. All members must be current for one to get a loan. The loans are given in 5 stages, the first is $500 and the maximum is $10,000. Terms are from 6 months to 48 month. This is available to low to moderate-income people, women, and minorities in East Tennessee.

    Micro Loan Program
    Firestone Retirees CDC
    659 North Manassas Street, Room 106-107
    Memphis, TN 38107
    P.O. Box 80073
    Memphis, TN 38108   901-454-9524

Firestone Retirees is trying to help people in poverty to become income achievers. While they offer business training courses, it is not a requirement for a loan. The Peer Lending Group method is used with a 10-person group administering the loans. The loan amounts range from $250 to $5,000 with the term varying from 5 months to 25 months, depending on the loan. The interest rate is currently 10% and subject to change. It is available to their service area.

Texas

    Micro Loan
    ACCION El Paso
    7744 North Loop Road, Suite A
    El Paso, TX 79915   915-779-3727

This loan requires that a business has one year of experience or is a start-up in El Paso. It is for those that have limited access to bank credit. The amount loaned to a small business is $250 to $1,000, the medium business loan is for $1,000 to $3,000, and the large fund is for the maximum of $10,000. The term depends on the type of loan issued. The rate is an 18% simple interest.

    Tyler Development Fund
    Tyler Economic Development Council, Inc.
    P.O. Box 2004   903-593-2004
    Tyler, TX 75710   Fax: 903-597-0699

The goal of the Tyler Economic Development Council is to create a solid economy for small and minority business owners with low to moderate income. This fund is for those that have results within 18 months of operation and located in Smith County. The maximum amount of a loan is $50,000 with bank participation for loans over $25,000. The terms depend on the loan and the interest rate is fixed.

    MicroLoan Program
    Corporation for Economic Development
      of Harris County, Inc.
    2223 West Loop South, Suite 400   713-840-8804
    Houston, TX 77027   Fax: 713-840-8806

Their mission is to enhance the economic and community development in Harris County and the Gulf Coast Region. The target is low to moderate income people who are having trouble finding conventional funding. The amounts available for a loan are $500 to $25,000.

    MicroLoan Program
    Corporation for Economic Development
      of Harris County, Inc.
    2223 West Loop South, Suite 400   713-840-8804
    Houston, TX 77027   Fax: 713-840-8806

The goal with the Corporation for Economic Development of Harris County, Inc. (CEDHC) is to provide gap financing in order to create permanent jobs that will improve the community economically. This is available for low to moderate business owners in Harris County and the Gulf Coast Region. The loan amount is from $500 to $25,000. Technical seminars and one-on-one counseling are also offered.

Utah

    Utah Microenterprise Loan Fund
    3595 South Main Street
    Salt Lake City, UT 84115   801-269-8408

This Fund was developed to help socially and economically disadvantaged people. It is available for small businesses in Salt Lake, Davis, Summit, Toouele and Morgan Counties. Up to $10,000 can be borrowed with a term of 5 years. The interest rate varies.

Vermont

    Burlington Revolving Loan Fund
    Community and Economic Development Office
    Room 32, City Hall   802-865-7144
    Burlington, VT 05461   Fax: 802-865-7024

The aim is to create a sustainable local economy that equitably distributes costs and provides meaningful opportunities for participation by residents in essential resource allocation decisions. The fund is aimed at low and moderate-income individuals located in the Champlain Valley. Loans are from $4,000 to $100,000, terms from 3-10 years, and the interest rate is variable.

    Micro-Business Development Program
    Central Vermont Community Action Council, Inc.
    195 US Route 302/Berlin   802-479-1053
    Barre, VT 05641   Fax: 802-479-5353

The aim of this program is to eliminate poverty by opening to everyone the opportunity to live in decency and with dignity. It is aimed at low-income persons. Loans and terms vary. Closing costs can be included in the loan amount. Receives funding from the Family Foundation, HeadStart, Vermont Community Development Program, Vermont State, USDA Food Stamps, Veterans grant, and CDBG discretionary grant.

Virginia

    Eagle Staff Fund - Seed Grants
    First Nations Development Institute
    The Stores Building
    11917 Main St.
    Fredericksburg, VA 22408   540-371-5615

This Fund is dedicated to promoting economic understanding among Native people. Seed grants are to identify and develop ideas and concepts about economic development, and provide funds for training, convening meetings, and community organizing. Amounts are from $1,500 to $5,000. The applicant's proposed budget must accurately reflect the project scope.

    Northern Virginia Microenterprise Loan - SBA
    Ethiopian Community Development Council, Inc.
    1038 S. Highland St.
    Arlington, VA 22206   703-685-0510

Applicants must be opening or expanding a small business, unable to find alternative

Loans / No Money

sources of financing. Loans are up to $25,000 with the interest rate at prime rate plus 4%.

Refugee Microenterprise Loan - ORR
Ethiopian Community Development Council, Inc.
1038 S. Highland St.
Arlington, VA 22204   703-685-0510

Applicants must be refugees and political asylees in the U.S. for less than five years, and have proper documents; want to open or expand a business, and are willing to write a business plan. Loans are up to $10,000 at prime rate plus 2%.

Microloan Fund
Small Business Development Center, Inc.
147 Mill Ridge Rd.
Lynchburg, VA 24502   804-582-6170

This program is available to low to moderate-income individuals who lack access to bank or other financing. All new business owners must complete the Self-Employment Training Program prior to making application for the loan fund. (Training Program covers the basics of owning your own business). Loan amounts range from $50.00 to $10,000 with terms from 1-3 years for long term loans, and 0-12 months for short-term loans. Interest rate is prime plus 3, which is fixed at time of closing. This program is sponsored by the SBA, Virginia Department of Economic Development, Greater Lynchburg Chamber of Commerce, Virginia's Region 2000, and the City of Lynchburg. For residents of Lynchburg and these counties: Amherst, Appomattox, Bedford, and Campbell.

Business Loan Program
South Fairfax Regional Business Partnership, Inc.
6911 Richmond Highway   703-768-1440
Alexandria, VA 22306   Fax: 707-768-0547

Loans are provided for entrepreneurs that can not get conventional loans. They are for start-up or small businesses in the southeast Fairfax County. Direct loans of $3,500 to $25,000 are available with interest rates in the range of Prime + 3% to Prime + 7%. The repayment period is 3 years on an average. The funds can be used for business machinery and equipment, working capital and paying marketing expenses. The owner must be in the low or moderate-income bracket.

Micro Loan
VA Eastern Shore Economic Empowerment
  and Housing Corp.
P.O. Box 814   757-442-4509
Nassawadox, VA 23413   Fax: 757-442-7530

This loan assists low to moderate-income people to start-up or improve an existing business. The funds that may be applied for are from $500 to $50,000. The interest is 6.5% plus costs. This is only for residents of Virginia Eastern Shore.

New Enterprises Loan Fund
930 Cambria Street
Christiansburg, VA 24073   540-382-2002

This fund is available in the New River Valley of southwest Virginia. Its goal is to promote the development of micro-enterprises through training, technical assistance, loaning of funds, and follow-up support. After completing the training program, a loan from $1,000 to $25,00 can be applied for. The terms are from 1 to 4 years at an 8% interest rate. This is for both start-up and existing businesses.

Northern Neck Enterprise Program
Northern Neck Planning District Commission
153 Yankee Point Road
Lancaster, VA 22503   804-333-1900
www.nnpdc17.state.va.us

This loan is available to micro start-up or expansion businesses in the Northern Neck Area. They must have been turned down by a bank and pass the loan committee review. Up to $25,000 can be applied for and the term is up to 3 years.

MicroLoan Program
Virginia Economic Development Corporation
P.O. Box 1505   804-979-0114
Charlottesville, VA 22902-1505   Fax: 804-979-1597
E-mail: microloan.tjpd@state.va.us
www.avenue.org/Gov/TJPDC

This program is accessible to small business owners that live and operate their businesses in the Thomas Jefferson Planning District. There is an emphasis on women and minority owners. An Entrepreneur Training Course or equal training and/or experience is a requirement before applying for a loan. The maximum loan is $25,000 with a variable interest rate at Prime plus 1.5% to 5%. Collateral and a credit check are needed.

Washington

African American Community Endowment Fund
Black Dollar Days Task Force
116-21st Ave.
Seattle, WA 98122   206-323-0534

This is a new program that hopes to make its first micro-enterprise loan this year (1996). This proposed microenterprise loan fund hopes to foster an entrepreneurial spirit and encourage self-sufficiency through the growth of small business opportunities primarily in the economically depressed areas of Seattle. This micro-enterprise loan is a source of business financing for people who are unable to access capital from other sources. As this is a new program, the amount of loans, interest, etc. are not know as yet. For further information, contact the above number.

Cascadia Revolving Fund
119 1st Ave. S., Suite 100   206-447-9226
Seattle, WA 98104   Fax: 206-682-4804

This is a tax-exempt nonprofit corporation that provides loans and technical assistance to socially/environmentally based enterprises and nonprofit organizations. Loans can be up to $150,000 with variable interest rates and terms. Eligible applicants are low income women, minorities, and refugees. Receives funds from individual investors, religious orders, nonprofit corporations, earnings and individual gifts.

DownHome Washington Microloan Program
Snohomish County Private Industry Council   425-743-9669
728 134th Street SW, Bldg. A, Suite 211   425-353-2025
Everett, WA 98204   Fax: 425-742-1177
E-mail: snopic@gte.net

This program is designed for those borrowers who do not fit into the general banking guidelines. It is offered with technical assistance and available to those who have their business within the 16 county service area of the program. The loan amounts are from $500 to $25,000. Funding is from the SBA.

CASH Loan Program
Washington CASH - Community Alliance for Self-Help
410 Boston Street   206-352-1945
Seattle, WA 98109   Fax: 206-352-1899
E-mail: washcash@nwlink.com
www.washingtoncash.org

This program was established to create self-sufficiency and self-employment for low-income women, people with disabilities, and new immigrants and refugees. It uses a peer support group lending model. Each group regulates its own loans and repayment. The first loan amount is $500. After that has been successfully repaid, up to $5,000 can be applied for. A required 12-week business training course, post loan technical assistance and peer support are part of this program. It is available within CASH's service area.

Micro Loan Program
Tri-Cities Enterprise Association
2000 Logston Boulevard
Richland, WA 99052   509-375-3268
www.owt.com/tea

The Tri-Cities Enterprise Association (TEA) wants to promote the growth and development of new businesses in order to economically benefit the community. The small business loans are available to for-profit start up businesses in Benton or Franklin counties. The money can be used for working capital or acquisition of materials, supplies, furniture, fixtures or equipment. From $500 to $7,500 is available for a loan, but up to $25,000 may be considered. The average term is 18 to 36 months with up to 6 years as the maximum.

SNAP Program
Spokane Neighborhood Action Programs
212 South Wall
Spokane, WA 99201   509-456-7174
E-mail: lancaster@snapwa.org

Northwest Business Development Association
9 South Washington, Suite 215
Spokane, WA 99201   509-458-8555

This loan requires that the Technical Assistance Program be attended. Funds are available to start-up or existing businesses where the owners are in the low to medium income bracket in their area. The loan amount is up to $10,000 with repayment in a maximum of 5 years. The interest rate is Prime plus 2%. This is only for the Spokane County area. The training program is offered by SNAP and the loan comes from Northwest Business Development.

Loans / No Money

West Virginia

Monroe Neighborhood Enterprise Center
Monroe County Community Services Council
P.O. Box 403
Union, WV 24883
304-772-3381
Fax: 304-772-4014

The aim is to improve the income and self-sufficiency of low to moderate-income persons by providing loans, business training, and opportunities for microenterprises. This center receives funding from banks of Monroe, Union, West Virginia by providing lines of credit, operating funds from Neighborhood Reinvestment Corp., and Benedum Foundation. Loans are from $500 to $10,000 with terms from one to five years. Loan review committees will determine loan conditions.

Lighthouse MicroLoan
Lightstone CDC
H 363 Box 73
Moyers, WV 26815
www.lightstone.org
304-249-5200
Fax: 304-249-5310

Lightstone has developed this loan in order to help create and sustain new business development in rural areas. It is available in 10 counties in the Eastern Panhandle of West Virginia, and 2 counties in Virginia. After working with the Small Business Development Center, a loan with a maximum amount of $10,000 can be applied for. The maximum term is 5 years. This is often used by low and moderate-income entrepreneurs. They are CDFI.

Wisconsin

ADVOCAP Business Development Loan Fund
ADVOCAP, Inc.
19 W. 1st St.
Fond du Lac, WI 54935
920-922-7760
Fax: 920-922-7214

This Loan Fund is to help low income persons become self-sufficient by developing businesses that will create jobs. Loans are from $100 to $15,000. Terms are from 30 days to 6 years. Interest rate can be from 7 to 10%. Closing costs/fees can be included in the amount of the loan. Receives funding from ADVOCAP business development fund, SBA Microloan Demonstration, C.O.E. fund from agency funds. Only for residents of Fond du Lac, and Winnebago and Green Lake counties.

Business Ownership and Operations
Juneau Business High School
6415 West Mount Vernon
Milwaukee, WI 53213
414-476-5480

Program is available to 15-19 year old multi-cultural students, of which a large percentage are low income. It provides high school students with practical, hands-on experience in business ownership and operations. Provides youth with alternative career options and education in the areas of economics, citizenship and ethics. Loans are from $50 to $500 with terms at 9 months. Interest rate is 12%.

Economic Development Project
West Cap
525 2nd St.
Glenwood City, WI 54013
715-265-4271
Fax: 715-265-7031

The aim is to create opportunities that allow people to achieve self-sufficiency for themselves, their families, and their communities. Eligible applicants are low income individuals with special emphasis on women. Loans are up to $15,000. Receives funding from Farmers Home Administration and the Bremer Foundation.

Self-Employment Project
CAP Services, Inc.
1725 W. River Dr.
Stevens Point, WI 54481
715-345-5200
Fax: 715-345-6508

The aim is to mobilize public and private resources to help low income individuals to attain self-sufficiency. Loans are up to $10,000; terms up to five years. Interest rate is at 8%. Receives funds from the U.S. Office of Community Services, corporate contributions, State of Wisconsin, and CDBG funds. For residents of these counties only: Portage, Waupaca, Outagamie, Waushara, Marquette.

Small Business Loan
Wisconsin Women's Business Initiative
2745 N. Dr. Martin Luther King Jr. Drive
Milwaukee, WI 53212
www.wwbic.com
E-mail: info@wwbic.com
414-263-5450

Although this loan is open to any small start-up business in Wisconsin, women, minority and low-income entrepreneurs are targeted. Those businesses that cannot get conventional loan funding may apply for up to $25,000. The money is to be used for tangible items, but working capital will be allowed. Terms are generally from 3 to 5 years. The interest rate is a flexible one.

Job and Business Development Loan
Wisconsin Coulee Region Community Action Program
201 Melby Street
Westby, WI 54667
608-634-3104

This new fund is available to help low to moderate-income people who want to start a new business. To be able to apply for the loan, borrowers must complete the Business Program. It is offered in the 4 county area of LaCross, Monroe, Crawford and Vernon. The loan can be obtained from $100 to $500. This funding amount is expected to increase. There are 12 months to repay the loan and at this point in time, there is no interest.

Revolving Loan Fund
CAP Services
1725 West River Drive
Stevens Point, WI 54481
715-345-5200

This loan is specific to a 5 county area of Wisconsin; Marquette, Waushara, Portage, Waupaca, and Outagamie. It is available for low to moderate-income entrepreneurs or those that create jobs for low to moderate-income people. There is a maximum of $10,000 available at 8% for a maximum term of 5 years. It requires a matching conventional loan.

West CAP Child Care Loan
West Central Wisconsin Community
Action Agency, Inc. (West CAP)
119 West 6th Avenue
Menomonie, WI 54751
715-235-8525

This small business loan is available to child care providers. If the business is run out of a center, the owner must be low income to be eligible for a maximum loan of $15,000. If they are licensed or certified to work out of the home, they must target low income clients for a loan of up to $5,000. The term is up to 5 or 6 years, depending on the loan. This is available to those businesses in a seven county area.

Technical Assistance Programs for Entrepreneurs With No Money

A helping hand is just a phone call away for individuals who want to enter into a small business or microenterprise. If you fall into any of the following categories: low to moderate income, Native American, minorities, women, welfare recipients, or have little or no money, you may be eligible for a wide range of assistance. These programs are aimed to assist individuals toward self-sufficiency.

Imagine getting training, counseling, peer support and exchange, and mentoring for free to help you get the knowledge you need to start your own business. Learn how to prepare a business plan and get guidance from the best instructors in the country. One such program is NOVA, located in Arkansas. Their program has four major components: Group Training; Individual Sessions; Business Start-Up; and Networking and Mentoring.

Imagine youths able to receive effective business course training. One such program is Kidpreneur Enterprises, located in Michigan. This program is available to all youths who express an interest in owning and operating their own small business. Kidpreneur is designed to provide and instill concepts and experiences in the minds of youths.

Doors can open for entrepreneurs, like Adina Rosenthal, owner of Threadbearer, a fabric and accessory shop located on Capitol Hill. At a very young age, Adina knew she wanted to work with fabrics. At age 17, she lost the use of her right arm when she was hit by a logging truck. After receiving her degree from the Fashion Institute of Design and Merchandising she attempted to get work at various design companies only to be passed over time and time again. A friend suggested she join the Black Dollar Days' program for entrepreneurs. After completing their entrepreneurial program, Adina opened Threadbearer. She accredits her success to the assistance she received, and is still receiving, from the Black Dollar Days Task Force.

Daryl Anderson an experienced roofer, lacked the necessary skills to run a business of his own. In 1994, Daryl began his involvement with the Cottage Industry Programs offered by the Portsmouth Community Development Group (PCDG) in Montana. After a year of technical assistance, the use of an office, and hours of encouragement, Daryl and his wife Karen were able to open Quality Roofing and Siding. Daryl admits he never would have made it without PCDG's commitment to business counseling and training.

The aim of these programs is to develop a participant's confidence and skills in understanding business enterprise and to further the development of viable business ideas.

Technical Assistance Programs

Arizona

Micro Industry Credit Rural Organization
P.P.E.P. Microbusiness and Housing
  Development Corporation, Inc.
1100 E. Ajo Way, Suite 209
Tucson, AZ 85713
520-806-9513
Fax: 520-806-9515

The Micro Industry Credit Rural Organization provides business training and planning, cash flow analysis, individual business planning, and peer support. The aim is to enhance family self-sufficiency and quality of life by facilitating the development, growth, and participation of family based, micro, and small business enterprises in their local economies. It receives funding from Ford Foundation, City of Douglas, Mott Foundation, Tides Foundation, and Calvert Social Investment Fund.

Arkansas

New Opportunities for Venture Alternatives (NOVA)
Good Faith Fund (GFF)
2304 W. 29th Ave.
Pine Bluff, AR 71603
870-535-6233

New Opportunities for Venture Alternatives (NOVA) is a program funded by the Office of Community Services/Health and Human Services. It is designed to help AFDC recipients and others on public assistance work toward self-sufficiency. The program has four major components: Group training: A 12-week training program designed to enhance personal effectiveness and build basic business skills; Individual Sessions: Participants meet with business counselors and instructors, and NOVA personnel for case management and individual business counseling; Business Start-Up: Participants create a working business plan and take the steps necessary for starting their own enterprise; and Networking and Referrals: Participants are directed to other area resources that can be called upon for assistance, including governmental, educational, and social programs. Anyone who is receiving or is eligible to receive Aid to Families with Dependent Children (AFDC), Food Stamps, no or low income may participate in NOVA.

California

Arcata Economic Development Corporation
100 Ericson Court, Suite 100
Arcata, CA 95521
707-822-4616
Fax: 707-822-8982

This corporation provides services that enhance the growth and development in Arcata. Business training, business planning, individual business counseling, peer support, and exchange are available to low income women, minorities, and displaced workers.

California Indian Manpower Consortium
4153 Northgate Blvd.
Sacramento, CA 95834
916-920-0285
Fax: 916-641-6338

The aim is to promote the social, educational, and economic advancement of member tribes and Indian organizations, Indians, and other Native Americans who are unemployed and underemployed or economically disadvantaged. All programs are designed to increase self-sufficiency in rural, reservation, and urban areas. It provides business training and planning, information, and referrals.

Center for Community Futures
P.O. Box 5309
Elmwood Station
Berkeley, CA 94705
510-339-3801
Fax: 510-339-3803

This program provides business training, individual business counseling, peer support, and program development services to nonprofits seeking to begin/expand micro-business programs. The aim is to promote quality development through a training program and consulting services.

Micro Enterprise Assistance Program of Orange County
18011 Skypark Circle, Suite E
Irvine, CA 92614
949-252-1380

The Micro Enterprise Assistance Program of Orange County provides business training, peer support, and mentoring to women and minorities located in Orange County. The aim is to provide access to credit, training, and support so that they may become self-sufficient. It receives funds from bank and private contributions.

Private Industry Council
2425 Bisso Lane, Suite 200
Concord, CA 94520
925-646-5377
Fax: 925-646-5299

The Private Industry Council provides business training, individual business counseling, peer support, and mentoring to existing businesses or start-ups planning to hire low to moderate income individuals within the next 12-18 months. The aim

Technical Assistance / No Money

is to provide technical assistance and resources to small business owners, or potential owners, that will enhance their chance of business growth.

Self-Employment Microenterprise Development (SEMED)
Economic and Employment Development Center (EEDC)
241 S. Figueroa St.
Los Angeles, CA 90012   213-617-3953

Self-Employment Microenterprise Development (SEMED) provides business training and planning, individual business counseling, peer support, and mentoring to refugees admitted to the U.S. within the last 5 years and who are under the national poverty level. The aim is to assist the Southeast Asian Community to attain economic self-sufficiency and achieve a positive acculturation. Receives funding from the Office of Refugee Resettlement.

The West Company
The West Enterprise Center
367 North State St., Suite 206   707-468-3553
Ukiah, CA 95482   Fax: 707-462-8945

The West Company provides business training, individual business counseling, peer support, advanced marketing, and financial training to low income women and minorities located in Mendocino county. The aim is to stimulate the growth of economic opportunity. Emphasis is on small business. Receives funds from foundation, banks, utilities, CAP agency, local, state and federal government, donations, and fees.

Training, Network and Business Incubator
San Francisco Renaissance
275 5th St.   415-541-8580
San Francisco, CA 94103   Fax: 415-541-8589

The Training, Network and Business Incubator provides business planning, individual business counseling, peer support, and exchange and loan packaging for SEED loan to low income people, women, and minorities in San Francisco and Greater Bay Area. The aim is to increase the entrepreneurial capabilities of low and moderate income people. Works with other microenterprise development programs such as Mayor's Office, SCORE, SBA, Chamber of Commerce, Hispanic and Black Chambers of Commerce, and local banks.

Women's Economic Ventures of Santa Barbara
1216 State St., Suite 610   805-965-6073
Santa Barbara, CA 93101   Fax: 805-962-9622

This program provides business training and planning, peer support, and mentoring to low to moderate income women. The aim is to help women become self-sufficient through entrepreneurship. Receives funding from sale of real estate, foundation grants, corporate and individual gifts, and interest payments.

Colorado

Mi Casa Resource Center for Women
571 Galapago St.   303-573-1302
Denver, CO 80204   Fax: 303-595-0422

The Center provides business training and planning, individual business counseling, peer support and exchange, free continuing education seminars, and a listing in business directory to low income Hispanic women, and women receiving welfare benefits in Denver. The aim is to assist women and youth in achieving economic self-sufficiency. This Women's Center was recognized as a top site in the nation by the National Academy of Public Administration, and was given the "Outstanding Non-Profit" award by a local foundation.

Connecticut

Aid to Artisans, Inc.
14 Brick Walk Lane   860-677-1649
Farmington, CT 06032   Fax: 860-676-2170

The mission of Aid to Artisans, Inc. is to create employment opportunities for disadvantaged artisans worldwide. The services they provide are business training, product development, and marketing. Their plans are to develop more working relationships between American artisan groups and foreign artisan groups and expand our worldwide Artisans and Ecology Program.

Entrepreneurial Center for Women
Hartford College for Women
50 Elizabeth St.   860-768-5681
Hartford, CT 06105   Fax: 860-768-5622

The Center provides business training, individual business counseling, and peer support to low income women (not exclusively) located in Connecticut. The aim is to promote self-employment as a alternative through training, technical assistance, networking, personal development, and assistance with access to financing. Receives funds from fees, CDBG, SOS, Department of Social Services, and Department of Labor.

Hartford Economic Development Corporation
15 Lewis St.   860-527-1301
Hartford, CT 06103   Fax: 860-727-9224

The corporation provides business training and planning, and individual business counseling to low/moderate income individuals located in the City of Hartford. The aim is the creation and retention of jobs. Receives funds from CDBG funds, membership fees, and dues.

District of Columbia

Accion International
Department of U.S. Operations
733 15th St. NW, Suite 700   202-393-5113
Washington, DC 20005   Fax: 202-393-5115

Eligible applicants are low income microentrepreneurs, with emphasis on the Hispanic population. They provide program development support to start new affiliates; feasibility study, business plan, staff training, and board development for implementing organizations.

LEDC Microenterprise Loan Fund
Latino Economic Development Corp., Inc.
2316 18th St., NW   202-588-5102
Washington, DC 20009   Fax: 202-588-5204

This program provides business training and individual business counseling to low income entrepreneurs of Latino, African, Asian and African-American origins. The aim is to provide credit, training, and technical assistance to new small businesses, particularly those who cannot access formal lending institutions. Receives funds from First National Bank of Maryland, DC CDBG funds, National Council of LaRaza, and NationsBank.

New Enterprise Training for Profits (NET/PRO)
Venture Concepts
325 Pennsylvania Ave., SE   202-543-1200
Washington, DC 20003   Fax: 202-543-0254

The program provides business training, planning, and screening of potential entrepreneurs to all would-be entrepreneurs located in the U.S. and Canada. The aim is provide quality training to would-be and existing entrepreneurs by installing training and technical assistance capabilities.

SCORE
National SCORE Office
409 3rd St., SW
Washington, DC 20024   800-634-0245

SCORE is a nonprofit association providing free business counseling by persons who have had successful business careers as company executives or owners of businesses. They are willing to share their knowledge and experience at absolutely no charge. They are as close as your phone. SCORE has counselors in all 50 states, Puerto Rico, Guam, the Virgin Islands, and the District of Columbia.

Youth Microloan Fund
The Entrepreneurial Development Institute
P.O. Box 65882
Washington, DC 20035-5882   202-822-8334

The Youth Microloan Fund provides business training, peer support and exchange, individual business counseling, and mentoring to minority youths ages 7-21 years old located in the Washington, DC metropolitan area. The aim is to assist disadvantaged youth to develop their own businesses, avoid drugs and crime, sharpen academic skills, and form positive attitudes about themselves and their communities. Receives funds from banks, foundations, and corporations.

Georgia

Entrepreneurial Training
Grasp Enterprises
55 Marietta, Suite 2000   404-659-5955
Atlanta, GA 30303   Fax: 404-880-9561

The program provides business training and planning, individual business counseling, peer support/exchange, mentoring, and entrepreneurial lifestyle skills training to low income dislocated workers and entrepreneurs located in Greater Atlanta. The aim is to provide comprehensive services for the growth and development of small businesses. Receives funds from SBA Microloan fund, Department of Health and Human Services, local banks, City of Atlanta, and client fees.

Technical Assistance / No Money

Hawaii

Pacific Business Center Program
University of Hawaii
BUS-AD 413
2404 Maile Way
Honolulu, HI 96822   808-956-6286

The Pacific Business Center Program offers management and technical assistance to large and small businesses, entrepreneurs, government agencies, and community organizations. Through the program, the faculty, students, and some physical resources of the University of Hawaii may be accessed quickly. The program works with the faculty and students to develop proposals for more extensive projects.

Refugee Enterprise Development Project
Immigrant Center
720 North King St.   808-845-3918
Honolulu, HI 96817   Fax: 808-842-1962

The Project provides business training and planning, individual business counseling, peer support, and exchange to refugees located in Oahu. The aim is to advance economic self-sufficiency among recently arrived refugees by providing culturally sensitive lending and support programs for the startup or expansion of microenterprise in Hawaii.

Illinois

Chicago Association of Neighborhood Development Organizations
123 W. Madison St., Suite 1100   312-372-2636
Chicago, IL 60602   Fax: 312-372-2637

The Association provides business training and mentoring to low to moderate income individuals throughout Chicago. This organization is committed to the revitalization of all Chicago neighborhoods, retail, and industrial areas. Receives funding from PRC Foundation and Neighborhood Capital Corporation.

Community Enterprising Project
Uptown Center Hull House Association
4520 North Beacon St.   312-561-3500
Chicago, IL 60640   Fax: 312-561-3507

The Community Enterprising Project provides business training, individual business counseling, and peer support to low to moderate income people located in the Uptown, Edgewater, and Ravenswood neighborhoods. The aim is to help people help themselves by assisting low and moderate income residents to increase their income and overall economic capacity. Receives funds from foundations, corporations, government agencies, and individuals.

Peoria Area Micro Business Development Program
The Economic Development Council for The Peoria Area, Inc.
124 South West Adams St., Suite 300   309-676-7500
Peoria, IL 61602   Fax: 309-676-7534

The program provides business training and individual counseling to low income existing or startup businesses, minorities, and females. Aim is to assist in the development of small and microbusinesses and helping them overcome obstacles to growth. It receives funds from SBA Microloan Demonstration Program, and City and County of Peoria.

Prison Small Business Project
Self-Employment Research Project
Roosevelt University
430 South Michigan Ave.
Chicago, IL 60605   312-341-3696

The Prison Small Business Project provides business training, training materials, and mentoring to prison inmates. The aim is to develop programs and teaching materials for self employment assistance to prison inmates and ex-offenders. The Project engages in research on the topic of self employment targeted to poor people, and advocates for the low income self employed. Receives funds from grants and out-of-pocket resources.

Women's Business Development Center
8 South Michigan Ave., Suite 400   312-853-3477
Chicago, IL 60603   Fax: 312-853-0145

The Center provides business training and planning, individual business counseling, peer support, and exchange and mentoring to underemployed women located in the Chicago area. The aim is to support women in their quest for economic self-sufficiency through entrepreneurship. Receives funds from loans from various foundations and banks.

Women's Self-Employment Project
20 N. Clark St.   312-606-8255
Chicago, IL 60602   Fax: 312-606-9215

The Women's Self-Employment Project provides business training and planning, individual business counseling, peer support, and exchange to low to moderate income women located in Chicago. The aim is to raise the self-sufficiency of women through a strategy of self employment. Receives funds from SBA Microloan Demonstration, foundations, corporations, government contracts, individual donors, and consulting contracts.

Women's Economic Venture Enterprise (WEVE)
YWCA
229 16th St.   309-788-9793
Rock Island, IL 61201   Fax: 309-788-9825

The Women's Economic Venture Enterprise (WEVE) provides business training and planning, individual counseling, peer support, and mentoring to women between the ages of 18-70 located in Scott County, Iowa; Rock Island County, Illinois, and Metropolitan Quad Cities. The aim is to assist women in achieving self-sufficiency through business ownership. It receives funds from banks, SBA, foundations, program fees, individuals, and corporations.

Indiana

Eastside Community Fund
Eastside Community Investments (ECI)
26 North Arsenal Ave.   317-637-7300
Indianapolis, IN 46220   Fax: 317-637-7581

The Eastside Community Fund provides business training and planning, individual business counseling, and peer support to low income persons located near the east side of Indianapolis. The aim is to loan money and provide technical assistance to both startup businesses and existing small businesses. Receives funding from SBA, OCS, NDDP, Mott Foundation, state loan money, and the Partnership for Common Good Loan Fund.

Indiana Small Business Development Center Network
One North Capitol, Suite 1275   317-264-6871
Indianapolis, IN 46204   Fax: 317-264-2806

The Network provides business training and planning, individual business counseling, peer support, and exchange and mentoring to potential new and existing small business located in Indiana. The aim is to increase the rate of successful new business formation and to enhance and encourage existing businesses. Receives funds from SBA, Indiana Chamber of Commerce, 14 local regional economic development foundations, local churches, universities, and private corporations.

Iowa

Siouxland Economic Development Corporation (SEDC)
428 Insurance Centre   712-279-6286
Sioux City, IA 51102   Fax: 712-279-6920

The Siouxland Economic Development Corporation (SEDC) provides individual counseling, peer support, and exchange and mentoring to low to moderate income individuals located in Woodbury, Plymouth, Cherokee, Ida, and Monona counties. The aim is to further the economic development of Siouxland regions. Within the microlending program, the aim is to provide access to capital to those excluded from traditional sources and also to provide technical assistance designed to increase business success. It receives funds from SBA grant, SEDC cash match, and other SEDC operating surplus and revenue.

Small Enterprise Development
Institute for Social and Economic Development
1901 Broadway, Suite 313   319-338-2331
Iowa City, IA 52240   Fax: 319-338-5824

The program provides business training, individual business counseling, peer support, and exchange and mentoring to low income, ethnic minorities, and women. The aim is to facilitate the empowerment of disadvantaged populations through the integration of social and economic development strategies. Receives funds from foundations, corporations, civic and religious organizations, federal/state grants and contracts, and private contributions.

Kentucky

Community Loan Fund
Human/Economic Appalachian Development Corporation
P.O. Box 504   606-986-8423
Berea, KY 40403   Fax: 606-986-1299

The Fund provides business planning, individual business counseling, peer support and exchange to low income persons and women located in central Appalachia. The aim is to strengthen low income communities and foster the development of an

Technical Assistance / No Money

economy that supports its people and encourages cooperative economic structures in the workplace. Receives funds from permanent capital, grants, and donations.

Community Ventures Corporation Bluegrass
Microenterprise Program
1450 North Broadway
Lexington, KY 40506　　　　　　　　　　　　　　606-231-0054

Upon joining the small business training program, you will have access to classes designed to help with specific areas of self employment and business ownership. Classroom instruction is offered in the following areas:

Business Feasibility and Planning: Do you have a sound business idea? Do you have a product/service that customers want or need? How should you describe it? Do you have what it takes to be self-employed? An indepth look at these issues will help you decide whether or not your business idea is feasible and worth pursuing.

Marketing: A basic introduction to market research and the development of a marketing plan. A comprehensive market research analysis and customer survey will help you determine information crucial to the success of your business.

Financial Management: Learn the basics of filing/accounting systems, record keeping, cash flow, income statements, break-even analysis, personal budgeting. Technical assistance is also available to help you develop systems appropriate for your business.

Child Care Management: This training gives you the basics needed to develop a home child care business. Learn about the certification application, policies/procedures, parent handbook, activity development, communication, health, safety, sanitation/nutrition, and how to recognize child abuse.

These classes will help you determine what it takes to make a business successful, how to market your product or service, how much capital is needed to open a particular business, and most important, how to develop a comprehensive business plan.

Maine

Androscoggin Valley Council of Governments (AVCOG's)
125 Manley Rd.　　　　　　　　　　　　　　　　207-783-9186
Auburn, ME 04210　　　　　　　　　　　　　Fax: 207-783-5211

The primary goal of AVCOG's economic development programs and services is to stimulate business which results in job creation and retention. They offer information referral, seminars, workshops, individual counseling, mentoring, library resources, and computer training.

Aroostook County Action Programs, Inc.
771 Main St.　　　　　　　　　　　　　　　　　207-764-3721
Presque Isle, ME 04769　　　　　　　　　　Fax: 207-768-3040

The mission of this program is to become a reliable, consistent source of technical assistance while providing loan resources. They offer information referral, seminars, workshops, business courses, individual counseling, mentoring, library resources, and computer training to low income individuals residing in Northern Maine.

Community Concepts Inc. (CCI)
P.O. Box 278
Market Square　　　　　　　　　　　　　　　　207-743-7716
South Paris, ME 04281　　　　　　　　　　Fax: 207-743-6513

The mission of Community Concepts Inc. (CCI) is to help people in need build opportunities for a better tomorrow. Provides information referral, seminars, peer support and exchange, training, workshops, and individual counseling to low income minorities denied conventional funding located in Androscoggin and Oxford counties. Receives funding from Maine Job Start Program, SBA Microloan Demonstration Program, and CDBG funds.

Enterprise Development Fund
Coastal Enterprises, Inc.
P.O. Box 268, Water St.　　　　　　　　　　　207-882-7552
Wiscasset, ME 04578　　　　　　　　　　　Fax: 207-882-7308

The Fund provides business training, individual business counseling, peer support and exchange, mentoring, trade association organizing assistance, and policy development for state delivery system to women, low income, unemployed and refugees. Receives funding from the Ford Foundation, SBA, Mott Foundation, Betterment Fund, U.S. Department of Health and Human Services, national churches, and Maine Department of Economic and Community Development.

Greater Portland Economic Development Council
145 Middle St.　　　　　　　　　　　　　　　207-772-1109
Portland, ME 04101　　　　　　　　　　　Fax: 207-772-1179

Eligible applicants are startup businesses, businesses that create jobs, and manufacturing businesses. The Council provides seminars, information referral, workshops, individual counseling, mentoring, peer support and exchange, and library resources.

Growth Council of Oxford Hills
150 Main St.　　　　　　　　　　　　　　　　207-743-8830
South Paris, ME 04281　　　　　　　　　　Fax: 207-743-5917

The Council provides technical assistance, training and education, business resources, small business incubators, and regulatory approval assistance. All businesses are eligible who focus primarily on manufacturing, information management, and export.

Maine Centers for Women, Work and Community
46 University Dr.　　　　　　　　　　　　　　207-621-3440
Augusta, ME 04330　　　　　　　　　　　Fax: 207-621-3429

The Center provides community development and entrepreneurship training and services for displaced homemakers, single parents, and other workers in transition. Provides information referral, seminars, business training, peer support and exchange, and staff support.

New Ventures
Maine Centers for Women, Work, and Community
Stoddard House, University of Maine　　　　207-621-3433
Augusta, ME 04330　　　　　　　　　　　Fax: 207-621-3429

New Ventures provides business training, peer support, and follow-up support training to displaced homemakers, single parents, refugees, and the unemployed. The aim is to empower women to move to self-sufficiency and to support/advocate for their participation in our economy. Receives funds from Carl Perkins Vocational Education, Department of Health and Human Services, and Office of Refugee Resettlement.

Service Corps of Retired Executives (SCORE)
66 Pearl St.
Portland, ME 04101　　　　　　　　　　　　207-772-1147

SCORE matches volunteers with small businesses that need sound business advice. They provide information referral, seminars, workshops, individual counseling, and library resources to potential SBA borrowers only.

University of Maine Cooperative Extension
5741 Libby Hall, Room 106　　　　　　　　　207-581-3167
Orono, ME 04469-5741　　　　　　　　　Fax: 207-581-1387

The University of Maine Cooperative Extension provides Maine people with research based education programs in a variety of areas. It provides business management educational programs targeting home based and natural resource based businesses, educational programs in Nutrition and Health; Food Safety; Forestry and Wildlife; 4-H and Youth Development; Marine Resources; Pest Management; Sustainable Agriculture; Waste Management; and Water Quality. Provides workshops, seminars, educational publications, consultation, and technical assistance.

USM School of Applied Science/Department of External Programs
University of Southern Maine
37 College Ave.　　　　　　　　　　　　　　207-780-5439
Graham, ME 04038　　　　　　　　　　　Fax: 207-780-5129

The University of Southern Maine (USM) provides information referral, seminars, workshops, business courses, individual counseling, peer support, mentoring, computer training, and laboratory access. The aim is to develop and maintain linkages between business and industry and higher and secondary education. Eligibility would apply to a startup business, existing business, a business in manufacturing, service, or education.

Maryland

Business Owners Start-Up Services (BOSS)
Council of Economic and Business Opportunities
800 North Charles St., Suite 300　　　　　　410-576-2326
Baltimore, MD 21201　　　　　　　　　　Fax: 410-576-2498

This program provides business training and planning, individual business counseling, peer support, and mentoring to AFDC recipients, Title III dislocated workers, and residents of Housing Authority of Baltimore County. The aim is to develop microenterprises via training and funding and to maintain microenterprises through technical assistance, support, and funding. Receives funding from SBA loan via council on Economic Business Opportunities, CDBG funds, SEID Grant, state, city, county PI and Title III contracts, and grants from HUD.

Women Entrepreneurs of Baltimore, Inc.
1118 Light St., Suite 202　　　　　　　　　　410-727-4921
Baltimore, MD 21230　　　　　　　　　　Fax: 410-727-4989

Women Entrepreneurs of Baltimore, Inc. provides business training and planning, individual business counseling, peer support, mentoring, community organizing, and

Technical Assistance / No Money

outreach resource sharing to economically disadvantage women located in Baltimore City and County. The aim is to provide entrepreneurial support and training to women who have a viable business idea and the spirit to make their business a success. Receives funds from foundations and bank contributions.

Massachusetts

Berkshire Enterprises
University of Massachusetts Donahue Institute
24 Depot St.
P.O. Box 2297　　　　　　　　　　　　　　　413-448-2755
Pittsfield, MA 01201　　　　　　　　　Fax: 413-448-2749

Berkshire Enterprises provides business training, individual business counseling, and peer support and exchange to dislocated workers, low income and minorities. The aim is to assist in the creation of a positive business environment through services that aid, encourage, and advise present and future business owners and to collaborate with others having similar missions. Receives funds from ICCD-Working Capital Program, Massachusetts Industrial Services Program, and HUD-Pittsfield Enterprise Collaboration.

Brightwood Development Corporation
2345 Main St.　　　　　　　　　　　　　　413-734-2144
Springfield, MA 01107　　　　　　　Fax: 413-746-3934

The aim of the Brightwood Development Corporation is to provide affordable housing and economic development. The program provides business training courses, business planning, individual business counseling and mentoring to low and moderate income Hispanics and Puerto Ricans. It receives funds from City CDBG funds, Springfield Chamber of Commerce, SBA, and HUD.

Hilltown Enterprise Fund
Hilltown Community Development Corporation
432 Main Rd. #A　　　　　　　　　　　　413-296-4536
Chesterfield, MA 01012　　　　　　Fax: 413-296-4020

The Hilltown Enterprise Fund provides business training, counseling, and peer support to individuals with limited resources who wish to start or expand a business. The aim is to promote cooperation as a way to ensure the best quality of life for all residents; to enable them to help themselves in addressing economic and housing needs, and to create and expand opportunities for those with limited resources. Receives funds from state and federal grants, loans from individuals, Western Massachusetts Enterprise Fund, and contributions. Program is for Hilltown residents only.

Microenterprise Training and Loan Program for Refugees
Jewish Vocational Service
105 Chauncy St., 4th Floor　　　　　　617-451-8147
Boston, MA 02111　　　　　　　　　Fax: 617-451-9973

This program provides business training, individual business counseling, and peer support and mentoring to refugees who have been in the U.S. for less than five years. The aim is to provide employment, training, and career services to disadvantaged and disabled individuals. Receives funds from the Office of Refugee Resettlement and the Jewish Vocational Service.

Community Economic Development Center
166 William St.　　　　　　　　　　　　　508-979-4684
New Bedford, MA 02740　　　　　Fax: 508-990-0199

The Community Economic Development Center provides peer support and exchange, mentoring, and self-taught tutorials to low/moderate income, racially, and culturally diverse people located in SE Massachusetts. The aim is to increase the income of the self-employed by providing loans, business assistance, and a forum for peer support of self-employed, low/moderate income people in New Bedford. Receives funds from credit through Fleet Banks, funds from Working Capital-Institute for Cooperative Community Development, banks, and private foundations.

Small Business Development System (SBDS)
The Howells Group
SIS Management
930 Commonwealth Ave., South　　　　617-264-6205
Boston, MA 02215　　　　　　　　　Fax: 617-731-6531

The Small Business Development System (SBDS) provides business training and planning, mentoring, and market identification for targeted urban areas and regions to minorities, the physically disabled, and those living in low income or disadvantaged areas. The aim is to encourage the creation or expansion of microenterprises among disadvantaged populations.

The Trusteeship Institute
15 Edwards Square
Northampton, MA 01060　　　　　　　　413-259-1600

The Trusteeship Institute is a consulting firm which assists companies and organizations which seek to become employee owned and controlled. They are usually asked to provide assistance when such a firm is being created; when an Employee Stock Ownership Plan (ESOP) is being established with the ultimate goal of the employees having majority ownership and control; or when the voting rights of the ESOP stock have passed through to the employees, giving them majority control of the firm. The Institute's expertise is in the area of the conversion of firms to democratic ownership and control by their employees. They have been providing legal, financial, and training services to such firms since 1973.

Michigan

Ann Arbor Community Development Corporation
2008 Hogback Rd., Suite 12　　　　　　313-677-1400
Ann Arbor, MI 48105　　　　　　　Fax: 313-677-1465

The program assists women to become self-sufficient through self employment. The aim of this program is to encourage small business development among women and minorities, and to provide business training and planning, counseling, peer support, and exchange.

Grand Rapids Opportunities for Women (GROW)
Center for Women
25 Sheldon Blvd. SE, Suite 210
Grand Rapids, MI 49503　　　　　　　　616-458-3404

Grand Rapids Opportunities for Women (GROW) is a nonprofit organization which provides economic opportunities through self employment to women in Kent and Ottawa Counties. Women from diverse backgrounds receive self-employment training, personal consultation, peer support, and assistance in gaining access to seed money. The program provides individualized orientation, training and technical assistance, financial overview and linkages, and continuing support. It receives funds from Kent County Department of Social Services, The Michigan Women's Foundation, The Grand Rapids Foundation, Steelcase Foundation, and the Frey Foundation.

Kidpreneur Enterprises
Metropolitan Chamber of Commerce
400 N. Saginaw St., Suite 101A　　　　810-235-5514
Flint, MI 48502　　　　　　　　　　Fax: 810-235-4407

Kidpreneur is a program designed specifically for youth to provide and instill concepts and experiences in the minds of youth enabling them to become successful entrepreneurial adults. The object of the program is to work with businesses and organizations to inform the community at large of the Kidpreneur concept. Program is available to all youth that express an interest in Genesee County.

Northern Economic Initiatives Corporation
1009 West Ridge　　　　　　　　　　　　906-228-5571
Marquette, MI 49855　　　　　　　Fax: 906-228-5572

This program provides business training and planning, business counseling, and mentoring to startup and expanding small business owners. The aim is to improve the competitive position of the economy by inspiring action among value-added firms, and working to gain access to capital and markets for these Upper Peninsula firms, and developing customers, management, and emerging workforce through public and private collaboration. Receives funds from SBA Microloan Demonstration Program, Joyce Foundation, and State of Michigan.

Supportive Entrepreneurial Program
Community Action Agency of South Central Michigan
175 Main St.　　　　　　　　　　　　　　616-965-7766
Battle Creek, MI 49014　　　　　　Fax: 616-965-1152

The Supportive Entrepreneurial Program provides business training and planning, individual business counseling, and marketing assistance to low income women located in Calhoun, Barry, Branch, and St. Joseph counties. The aim is to assist women who wish to create a successful business enterprise that will lead to self-sufficiency. Receives funding from Michigan Women's Foundation (Mott) and Battle Creek Community Foundation.

Minnesota

American Institute of Small Business
7515 Wayzata Blvd., Suite 129　　　　　612-545-7001
Minneapolis, MN 55426　　　　　　Fax: 612-545-7020

The Institute provides business training, planning, business counseling, and publishing of books, videos, and software to native American Indians, Hispanics, and African-Americans. The goal is to generate jobs for Native American youth by obtaining loans to start up new businesses. Provides on-site visits with similar type businesses such as accountants, advertising agencies, and market researchers.

Technical Assistance / No Money

Arrowhead Community Economic Assistance Corporation
702 Third Ave. South
Virginia, MN 55792-2775
218-749-2914
Fax: 218-749-2913

Business planning, individual counseling, and peer support and exchange are available to unemployed and low income and minority residents located in the Taconic Tax Relief Area. The goal is to assist with the startup and expansion of local businesses that increase employment opportunities and that retain existing jobs, by developing local skills and providing economic opportunity.

Emerging Entrepreneur Development Program
Northwest Minnesota Initiative Fund
4225 Technology Dr.
Bemidji, MN 56601
208-759-2057
Fax: 208-759-2328

This program provides business planning, business counseling, peer support and mentoring to women, minorities and low income persons located in Beltrami, Clearwater, Hubbard, Kittson, Lake of the Woods, Mahnomen, Marshall, Norman, Pennington, Polk, Redlake, and Roseau. The aim is to improve the quality of life for the people who live and work in NW Minnesota by encouraging them to devise greater responses to change that will build a future with greater economic opportunity. Receives funds from SBA and the McKnight Foundation.

Northeast Entrepreneur Fund, Inc.
820 Ninth St., North, Suite 140
Virginia, MN 55792
218-749-4191
Fax: 218-741-4249

The Northeast Entrepreneur Fund provides business training and planning, individual business counseling, and peer support to unemployed and underemployed persons. The aim is to foster and encourage self-sufficiency through the growth of small business opportunities. Receives funds from foundations, loans, contracts, fees, and interest.

Self-Employment Investment Demonstration (SEID)
Minnesota Department of Human Services
444 Lafayette Rd.
St. Paul, MN 55155-3814
651-297-1316
Fax: 651-215-6388
www.dhs.state.mn.us/ecs/program/seid.htm

Minnesota operated the Self-Employment Investment Demonstration (SEID) as part of a five state demonstration project from March 1988 to September 1991. Minnesota received federal approval to continue the program for each federal fiscal year thereafter. Service providers operate the program in counties that choose to offer SEID. The aim is to serve as administrative coordinator of the program, coordinating programs run by individual service providers, provide technical services, and coordination with federal and state agencies, and private nonprofit organizations. Each service provider delivers a program that combines business training, personal effectiveness training, access to seed capital, and ongoing support for interested AFDC clients.

North Star Community Development Corporation
615 Board of Trade Building
301 West First St., Suite 604
Duluth, MN 55802
218-727-6690

North Star Community Development Corporation provides business training and planning, individual business counseling, peer support, and exchange to low and moderate income persons and public housing residents. This is a community based economic development organization providing assistance to small businesses. Focus is placed on assisting low and moderate income persons to achieve self-sufficiency. Receives funds from Community Development Block Grant, Duluth Housing and Redevelopment Authority.

Missouri

Create Your Own Job
Missouri Western State College
4525 Downs Dr.
St. Joseph, MO 64507
816-271-5830

This program provides business training, planning, and individual business counseling to anyone interested in opening a business in Northwest Missouri. The aim is to develop a participant's confidence and skills in understanding business enterprise and to further develop viable business ideas.

Montana

Action for Eastern Montana
2030 N. Merrill
Glendive, MT 59330-1309
406-377-3564

Action's mission is to help create a flourishing microbusiness climate in eastern Montana. Eligible applicants are low income, women, and minorities. They provide business training courses, business planning, individual business counseling, peer support, and mentor program. Also provides individual counseling, child care, transportation, leadership, and self-esteem courses.

Montana Women's Economic Development Group (WEDGO)
Women's Opportunity and Resource Development
127 North Higgins
Missoula, MT 59802
406-543-3550
Fax: 406-721-4584

The Montana Women's Economic Development Group provides business training, planning, and individual business counseling to low and moderate income women. Receives funds from city, county, and state government, the Ms. Foundation, Department of Health and Human Services, U.S. West Foundation, and service contracts. Only for residents of western Montana.

Opportunities, Inc.
905 1st Ave. North
Great Falls, MT 59403
406-761-0310

Opportunities, Inc. provides business training and planning, individual business counseling, peer support, and exchange and mentoring to persons unable to receive loans from conventional sources located in Cascade, Chauteau, Teton, Foale, Pondera, and Glacier. The aim is to stimulate coordination among available federal, state, local, and private resources to enable low income individuals, in rural and urban areas, to attain the skills, knowledge, and motivations they need to secure opportunities necessary to become self-sufficient. Receives funds from grants to loans from Montana Department of Commerce.

Nebraska

Rural Enterprise Assistance Project
Center for Rural Affairs
P.O. Box 406
Walthill, NE 68067
402-846-5428
Fax: 402-846-5420

The Rural Enterprise Assistance Project provides business training, business planning, individual business counseling, and peer support and exchange to low and moderate income individuals in rural Nebraska. The mission is to demonstrate and implement programs to meet the long term needs of existing and potential small businesses to succeed in rural areas. Receives funding from the Ford Foundation, the Mott Foundation, SBA Grant, the Aspen Institute, and Share Our Strength (SOS).

New Mexico

Women's Economic Self-Sufficiency Team (WESST Corp.)
414 Silver SW
Albuquerque, NM 87102-3239
505-848-4760
Fax: 505-848-2368

WESST Corp. provides business training and planning, individual business counseling, and mentoring to low income women and minorities located in the State of New Mexico. The aim is to help women achieve self-sufficiency through sustained self employment. Receives funding from Seton Enablement Fund, SBA Microloan Demonstration Program, and in-kind contributions.

New York

ACCION New York
235 Havemeyer St., 3rd Floor
Brooklyn, NY 11211
718-599-5170
Fax: 718-387-9686

ACCION was founded for the purpose of combating poverty and hunger in the poorest communities of America. It supports the economic initiatives of the poor by providing market rate loans and basic business training to family-run businesses.

Microenterprise Loan and Assistance Program
Church Avenue Merchants Block Association, Inc.
885 Flatbush Ave.
Brooklyn, NY 11226
718-287-0100
Fax: 718-287-2737

The program provides business training, individual business counseling, and peer support and exchange to refugees located in Brooklyn and New York City. The aim is to provide refugees who want to start businesses with training and loans to do so. Receives funds from the Office of Refugee Resettlement, and the U.S. Department of Health and Human Services.

Ms. Foundation for Women
120 Wall St., Floor 33
New York, NY 10005
212-742-2300
Fax: 212-742-1653

This Foundation supports the efforts of women to govern their own lives and influence the world around them. They fund and assist women's self-help organizing efforts and pursue changes in public consciousness, law, philanthropy, and social policy. Provides program planning and organizational growth to women and

Technical Assistance / No Money

nonprofit organizations assisting women to become self-sufficient through self employment. Receives funds from private and corporate foundations, individuals, and limited endowment income.

New York Department of Economic Development
Local Development Corporation of East New York
80 Jamaica Ave.   718-385-6700
Brooklyn, NY 11207   Fax: 718-385-7505

The New York Department of Economic Development provides business training and planning, individual business counseling, peer support, and mentoring to women and minority entrepreneurs located in Brooklyn. The aim is to provide microenterprise development assistance as a way to promote economic development and job creation. Receives funds from New York Urban Development Corporation and European American Bank.

New York State Department of Economic Development
Entrepreneurial Assistance Program
Queens County Overall Economic Development Corp.
120-55 Queens Blvd. #309   718-263-0546
Jamaica, NY 11424   Fax: 718-263-0594

The program provides business training and planning, individual business counseling, peer support, mentoring, seminars, and workshops to low income and minority residents of Queens. It provides a comprehensive package of services to: encourage and train would-be entrepreneurs; to support and assist startup businesses to survive the first 24 months of business; and to assist existing businesses with their relocation and/or expansion efforts. It receives funds from seven banks and equity investors, borough presidents, and city and state agencies.

Rural Venture Fund
Rural Opportunities, Inc.
400 East Ave.   716-340-3387
Rochester, NY 15607   Fax: 716-340-3337

The Rural Venture Fund provides business planning, individual business counseling, marketing analysis, and cash flow analysis to low and moderate income persons located in Western NY State who have been denied access to bank credit. The aim is to promote self-sufficiency and economic independence through the creation and expansion of microenterprises and small businesses. Receives funds from FmHA Industrial Development Grant, SBA Microloan Demonstration Program, CDBG funds, and NY State.

North Carolina

Rural Economic Development Centers, Inc.
4021 Carya Dr.   919-250-4314
Raleigh, NC 27610   Fax: 919-250-4325

It's hard to succeed in business. Being able to make a good product or offer a good service is only a start. That's why this program combines its financing with training and advice from local business counselors. The following is what you can expect: Help developing a business plan: experts will help you think through all of the decisions you need to make, such as who your customers will be and where to buy supplies; Classes and Workshops: these will cover issues you have to deal with in running your business; Support From Other Business People: many local business owners are happy to share their experiences with people in the microenterprise program. If you're in the group lending program, you will get advice and support from other group members. Expert Advice: regularly, you will go over the progress of your business with someone who can let you know what you are doing right and what you can do more effectively.

WAMY Community Action, Inc.
P.O. Box 2688   828-264-2421
Boone, NC 28607   Fax: 828-264-0952

The program provides business training, planning, and individual business counseling to persons below poverty level located in Watauga, Avery, Mitchell, and Yancey counties only. The aim is to improve economic, social, and physical conditions of low income persons. Receives funds from CDBG and repaid funds.

Northeastern Community Development Corporation
154 US Highway 158 East   252-338-5466
Camden, NC 27921   Fax: 252-338-5639

The Northeastern Community Development Corporation provides business training and planning, individual business counseling, peer support, and exchange and mentoring to Watermark members located in Northeastern North Carolina. Works with low and moderate income persons who need loans to buy equipment and supplies to begin making crafts, and those who need working capital for expanding their business. The aim is to make funding available to those with low and moderate income to startup, expand, or help their businesses in emergency situations. Receives funds from the Ms. Foundation.

North Dakota

Center for Innovation and Business Development
Box 8372, UND   701-777-3132
Grand Forks, ND 58202   Fax: 701-777-2339

The Center provides business training courses, business planning, individual business counseling, peer support and exchange, mentoring, market plans, technical evaluation, patent searches, and new product development to low and moderate income, rural small manufacturers, entrepreneurs, researchers, colleges, and universities. The aim to help manufacturers and entrepreneurs start up new ventures and bring new products and technologies to market.

Ohio

The Appalachian Center for Economic Networks (ACEnet)
94 North Columbus Rd.   740-592-3854
Athens, OH 45701   Fax: 740-593-5451

ACEnet has generated broad involvement of educational institutions, banks, social service agencies, and community groups in the development of support projects in five areas: (1) Training and Workforce Development: enables people receiving public assistance to obtain jobs in flexible manufacturing networks (FMN) firms or to start their own small businesses; (2) Access to Capital: a loan fund for very small loans; (3) Modernization and Business Assistance: introduces more current production and organizational technologies to FMN firms; (4) Telecommunications: firms are introduced to various information technologies; and (5) Market Niche Development: assists entrepreneurs in identifying niche markets and potential purchasing partners, and explores export opportunities.

The Chamber of Women's Business Initiative Program
37 North High St.
Columbus, OH 43215   614-225-6910

The Chamber provides business training and planning, business counseling, peer support, mentoring, and procurement assistance to women who are unemployed, underemployed, or receiving public assistance; women who have started their own business, or women who are interested in self employment. The aim of this program is to provide assistance in order to increase participation of women in the economy. Receives funds from federal and city funds, banks, and private foundations.

Ventures in Business Ownership
Columbiana Career Center
9364 St. Rt. 45   330-424-9561, ext. 34
Lisbon, OH 44432   Fax: 330-424-9719
(Serving Columbiana, Mahoning, Carroll counties and parts of Pennsylvania and West Virginia)

Ehove Career Center
316 West Mason Rd.   419-499-4663
Milan, OH 44846   Fax: 419-499-4076
www.ehove-jvs.k12.oh.us
(Serving Huron, Erie and Ottawa counties)

Guernsey-Noble Career Center
57090 Vocational Rd.   740-685-2516
Senecaville, OH 43780   Fax: 740-685-2518
(Serving Guernsey, Noble, Muskingum and Perry counties)

Greene County Career Center
2960 West Enon Rd.   937-426-6636
Xenia, OH 45385   Fax: 937-372-8283
(Serving Montgomery, Greene, Clark and Miami counties)

Medina County Career Center
1101 West Liberty St.   330-725-8461
Medina, OH 44256   Fax: 330-725-3842
(Serving Medina county and surrounding area)

Penta County Vocational School
30095 Oregon Rd.   419-666-1120
Perrysburg, OH 43551   Fax: 419-666-6049
(Serving Northwest Ohio)

Polaris Career Center
7285 Old Oak Blvd.   440-891-7703
Middleburg, OH 44130   Fax: 440-826-4330
www.polaris.edu
(Serving Cuyahoga county)

Technical Assistance / No Money

Upper Valley Applied Technology Center
8811 Career Dr.
Piqua, OH 45356 937-778-8419
(Serving Miami, Shelby, Darke and portions of surrounding counties)
These programs provide a 100 hour business planning and management program, and a 60 hour class-run business operation module. This is available to single parents, displaced homemakers, and single pregnant women. The aim is to provide small business training and technical assistance enabling these individuals to become independent.

Women's Business Resource Program of Southeast Ohio
20 East Circle Dr., Suite 155 740-593-0474
Athens, OH 45701 Fax: 740-593-1795
The Women's Business Resource Program of Southeast Ohio provides business training and planning, individual business counseling, peer support, networking, and mentoring to underemployed and unemployed women. The aim is to develop successful women's entrepreneurship. It receives funds from SBA, individual and corporate donations, Ohio Department of Development, and Ohio University.

Women Entrepreneurs, Inc.
36 East 4th St. #92 513-684-0700
Cincinnati, OH 45202 Fax: 513-684-0779
Women Entrepreneurs, Inc. provides business training and planning, business counseling mentoring, and certification assistance to low and moderate income people located in Cincinnati. The aim is that through community leadership, professional development, business support, and networking, Women Entrepreneurs, Inc. promotes successful entrepreneurship. The program receives funds from banks, independent member contributions, local foundations, and corporate contributions.

Women's Network Mentoring Program
526 S. Main St., Suite 221 330-379-9280
Akron, OH 44311 330-379-3454
The Women's Network Mentoring Program is available to women business owners in business for at least one year in Summit, Portage, Stark, Wayne, or Medina Counties. The aim is to stimulate the economy by encouraging the growth of small women owned businesses in the community through the provision of mentoring services. It receives funds from SBA and banks.

Pennsylvania

A Service for Self-Employment Training and Support (ASSETS)
Mennonite Economic Development Associates
447 S. Prince St.
Lancaster, PA 17603 717-393-6089
ASSETS provides business training and planning, individual business counseling, peer support, and mentoring to low income individuals as defined by HUD guidelines. The aim is to increase personal income, create jobs, foster economic linkages, develop human potential through small businesses, and provide credit and training to make small businesses profitable. It receives funds from PA Mennonite Credit Union corporate contributions, CDBG funds, and foundations.

Micro-Enterprise Development
Lutheran Children and Family Service
45 Garrett Rd.
Upper Darby, PA 19082 610-734-3363
 Fax: 610-734-3389
The program provides business training, planning, and individual business counseling to refugees, mostly Vietnamese and Russian, who have been in the U.S. less than 5 years, and are located in the Philadelphia area. The Service has a loan agreement with PNC Bank and receives assistance from lawyers and other area professionals.

Philadelphia Small Business Loan Fund
LaSalle University Small Business Development Center
1900 West Olney Ave., Box 828 215-951-1416
Philadelphia, PA 19141 Fax: 215-951-1597
The Fund provides business training, planning, and individual business counseling to applicants who have been declined by other funding sources. The aim is to provide small business financing of less than $25,000 to entrepreneurs who have been declined by a financial institution or public program. Receives funds from major corporations and six major banks within the Delaware Valley.

Rhode Island

Elmwood Neighborhood Housing Services, Inc. (N.H.S.)
9 Atlantic Ave.
Providence, RI 02907 401-461-4111
There is plenty of help and information available to get your new business started and to help you make your business successful. At Elmwood Neighborhood Housing Services, Inc. (N.H.S.), there is a full-fledged MicroBusiness Program that offers business workshops, peer lending groups, and small business loans. Programs are available to minority and disadvantaged residents of Elmwood, Upper and Lower S. Providence, West End, Reservoir Triangle, and Washington Park. Receives funds from Citizens Bank, RI Hospital Trust Bank, RI Department of Economic Development, Neighborhood Reinvestment, Hazard Trust, and the Campaign for Human Development.

South Dakota

Northeast South Dakota Energy Conservation Corporation
414 Third Ave. East
Sisseton, SD 57262 605-698-7654
The corporation provides business planning, individual business counseling, and financial record keeping to low income, disadvantaged persons, minorities, and women. The aim is to address the economic needs of small rural communities as they relate to business development. Also, the agency seeks to become directly involved in community based economic development and serve as an institution for developing an economic power base controlled by low income persons. Receives funds from Northwest Area Foundation, CDBG, SBA Microloan Demonstration Program, East River Electric Power Coop, and First State Bank of Roscoe.

Vermont

Burlington Revolving Loan Fund
Community and Economic Development Office
Room 32, City Hall
Burlington, VT 05461 802-865-7144
This Fund provides business training and planning, individual business counseling, peer support, and mentoring to low and moderate income individuals located in Champlain Valley. It receives funding from CDBG, loan money from banks, and affiliation with Working Capital.

Micro-Business Development Program
Central Vermont Community Action Council, Inc.
195 US Route 302/Berlin 802-479-1053
Barre, VT 05641 Fax: 802-479-5353
The program provides business training and planning, individual business counseling, and peer support to low income persons located in 56 towns in central Vermont. The mission is to eliminate poverty by opening to everyone the opportunity to education, training, and the ability to work. Receives funding from family foundations, HeadStart, Vermont Community Development Program, Vermont State, USDA food stamps, Veterans grant, and CDBG discretionary grant.

Virginia

Association of Farmworker Opportunity Programs
1611 N. Kent St., Suite 910 703-528-4141
Arlington, VA 22209 Fax: 703-528-4145
Business training courses, business planning, individual business counseling, and peer support are available to low income, migrant and seasonal farmworkers, minorities, and men and women. The goal is to provide a clearinghouse for the provision of information, training, support, and education, so that the lives of low income farmworkers and other rural poor can be improved.

Oweesta Program
First Nations Development Institute
The Stores Bldg.
11917 Main St. 540-371-5615
Falmouth, VA 22408 Fax: 540-371-3505
The Oweesta Program provides business planning and loan fund start up to American Indians living on reservations. The aim is to help tribes achieve financial self-sufficiency through culturally sensitive economic development; to decrease reliance on federal funding and other dependencies; and to combine direct support with national programs and policy development. Receives funds from Program Related Investments (PRIs) and individual investors.

United Community Ministries (UCM)
7511 Fordson Rd. 703-768-7106
Alexandria, VA 22306 Fax: 703-768-4788
United Community Ministries (UCM) provides business training and planning, individual business counseling, peer support, and mentoring to low and moderate income people who are clients of UCM, located in SE Fairfax County. The aim is to enable selected UCM clients to supplement, stabilize, and increase their incomes through microenterprises.

Technical Assistance / No Money

Washington

Cascadia Revolving Fund
119 1st Ave. S., Suite 100　　　　　　　　206-447-9226
Seattle, WA 98104　　　　　　　　Fax: 206-682-4804

The Fund provides business planning, business counseling, peer support, and mentoring to low income women and minorities, refugees, and displaced timber workers. It provides technical assistance and loans to both for-profit and nonprofit entrepreneurs who cannot find these services from traditional sources. They focus on low income women, minorities, rural communities, and businesses that preserve the environment. It receives funds from individual investors, religious orders, nonprofit corporations, earnings, and individual gifts.

The Inner-City Entrepreneurial Training Program (ICETP)
Black Dollar Task Force
116-21st Ave.　　　　　　　　206-323-0534
Seattle, WA 98122　　　　　　　　Fax: 206-323-4701

The Inner-City Entrepreneurial Training Program (ICETP) provides ten weeks of training to low income individuals who aspire to be entrepreneurs. Selection is based upon their income, education, and experience in the industry and their desire to start up and maintain a business. Each student is required to complete an internship with a similar business, and must write a business plan. The ICETP works with the following agencies and organizations: Seattle University Small Business Entrepreneurship Center, SBA, Department of Social and Health Services, Employment Security, Department of Vocational Rehabilitation, Representatives from the Banking and Lending Community, and the Department of Community Trade and Economic Development.

West Virginia

Center for Economic Options
601 Delaware Ave.　　　　　　　　304-345-1298
Charleston, WV 25302　　　　　　　　Fax: 304-342-0641

The Center for Economic Options provides assistance to rural entrepreneurs in developing market driven businesses, and provides technical assistance and leadership skill training to community groups. The program is available to rural residents, with emphasis on women. The aim is to promote home and community based enterprises and equal access to better paying jobs. It receives funding from foundations, corporations, and the government.

Monroe Neighborhood Enterprise Center
Monroe County Community Services Council
P.O. Box 403　　　　　　　　304-772-3381
Union, WV 24883　　　　　　　　Fax: 304-772-4014

The Center provides business training, peer support, and exchange to low to moderate income persons. The aim is to improve the income and self-sufficiency of persons by providing loans, business training, and opportunities for peer support to microenterprises. It receives funds from banks of Monroe and Union, West Virginia providing lines of credit, operating funds from Neighborhood Reinvestment Corporation, and the Benedum Foundation.

Wisconsin

Advocap, Inc.
19 W. 1st St.　　　　　　　　920-922-7760
Fond du Lac, WI 54935　　　　　　　　Fax: 920-922-7214

The aim of Advocap, Inc. is to help low income persons become self-sufficient by developing businesses. The program provides business training and planning, individual business counseling, peer support and exchange, mentoring, and loan packaging to poor and low income persons.

Business Ownership and Operations
Juneau Business High School
6415 West Mount Vernon
Milwaukee, WI 53213　　　　　　　　414-476-5480

This program provides business training and planning, individual business counseling, peer support and exchange, and mentoring to 15-19 year old multi-cultural students. Provides high school students with practical experience in business ownership and operations.

Cap Services, Inc.
5499 Highway 10 East　　　　　　　　715-345-5200
Stevens Point, WI 54481　　　　　　　　Fax: 715-345-5206

Cap Services, Inc. provides business planning, counseling, peer support, and mentoring to low income individuals. Aim is to mobilize public and private resources to enhance the ability of persons to attain self-sufficiency. Receives funds from U.S. Office of Community Services, corporate contributions, state of Wisconsin, and CDBG funds.

Economic Development Project
West Cap
525 2nd St.　　　　　　　　715-265-4271
Glenwood City, WI 54013　　　　　　　　Fax: 715-265-7031

This project provides business training, planning, and individual business counseling to low income persons, with emphasis on women located in West Central Wisconsin. Aim is to create opportunities that empower people to achieve self-sufficiency for themselves. Receives funds from Farmers Home Administration and the Bremer Foundation.

Women's Business Initiative Corporation
2745 Dr. M.L. King Dr.　　　　　　　　414-372-2070
Milwaukee, WI 53212　　　　　　　　Fax: 414-263-5456

The Women's Business Initiative Corporation provides business training, individual counseling, and mentoring to minority and low income persons. The aim is to provide business seminars, consulting services, and microloans to individuals who are owners of startup or expanding small businesses. Focus is on women who are underemployed or unemployed striving for self-sufficiency. Receives funds from SBA Microloan Demonstration Project, Wisconsin Department of Economic Development, Milwaukee County, and foundations.

Real Estate Ventures

Real Estate Ventures:
Federal Money for Housing and Real Estate

The following is a description of the federal funds available to renters, homeowners, developers, and real estate investors for housing assistance in urban and rural areas. This information is derived from the *Catalog of Federal Domestic Assistance* which is published by the U.S. Government Printing Office in Washington, D.C. The number next to the title description is the official reference for this federal program. Contact the office listed below the caption for further details. The following is a description of some of the terms used for the types of assistance available:

Loans: money lent by a federal agency for a specific period of time and with a reasonable expectation of repayment. Loans may or may not require a payment of interest.

Loan Guarantees: programs in which federal agencies agree to pay back part or all of a loan to a private lender if the borrower defaults.

Grants: money given by federal agencies for a fixed period of time and which does not have to be repaid.

Direct Payments: funds provided by federal agencies to individuals, private firms, and institutions. The use of direct payments may be "specified" to perform a particular service or for "unrestricted" use.

Insurance: coverage under specific programs to assure reimbursement for losses sustained. Insurance may be provided by federal agencies or through insurance companies and may or may not require the payment of premiums.

* Money for Conserving the Water and Soil During an Emergency

(10.054 Emergency Conservation Program (ECP))
Agricultural Stabilization and Conservation Service
U.S. Department of Agriculture
P.O. Box 2415
Washington, DC 20013   202-720-6221

Objectives: To enable farmers to perform emergency conservation measures to control wind erosion on farmlands, or to rehabilitate farmlands damaged by wind erosion, floods, hurricanes, or other natural disasters and to carry out emergency water conservation or water enhancing measures during periods of severe drought. Types of assistance: direct payments for specified use. Estimate of annual funds available: (Direct payments) $19,489,000.

* Money to Insure Your Soil and Land Remains Intact

(10.063 Agricultural Conservation Program (ACP))
Agricultural Stabilization and Conservation Service
U.S. Department of Agriculture
P.O. Box 2415
Washington, DC 20013   202-720-6221

Objectives: Control of erosion and sedimentation, encourage voluntary compliance with Federal and State requirements to solve point and nonpoint source pollution, improve water quality, encourage energy conservation measures, and assure a continued supply of necessary food and fiber for a strong and healthy people and economy. The program will be directed toward the solution of critical soil, water, energy, woodland, and pollution abatement problems on farms and ranches. Types of assistance: direct payments for specified use. Estimate of annual funds available: (Direct payment) $146,618,000.

* Money to Insure That Your Water is Clean

(10.068 Rural Clean Water Program (RCWP))
Agricultural Stabilization and Conservation Service
U.S. Department of Agriculture
P.O. Box 2415
Washington, DC 20013   202-720-6221

Objectives: To achieve improved water quality in the most cost-effective manner possible in keeping with the provisions of adequate supplies of food, fiber, and a quality environment, and to develop and test programs, policies, and procedures for control of agricultural nonpoint source pollution. Types of assistance: direct payments for specified use. Estimate of annual funds available: (Direct payments) $43,000.

* Money to Improve Your Water and Soil

(10.069 Conservation Reserve Program (CRP))
Agricultural Stabilization and Conservation Service
U.S. Department of Agriculture
P.O. Box 2415
Washington, DC 20013   202-720-6221

Objectives: To protect the Nation's long-term capability to produce food and fiber; to reduce soil erosion; to reduce sedimentation; to improve water quality; to create a better habitat for fish and wildlife; to curb production of some surplus commodities; and to provide some needed income support for farmers. Types of assistance: direct payments for specified use. Estimate of annual funds available: $1,808,578,000.

* Money to Change Your County Property Into a Wetlands

(10.070 Colorado River Basin Salinity Control Program (CRBSCP))
Agricultural Stabilization and Conservation Service
U.S. Department of Agriculture
P.O. Box 2415
Washington, DC 20013   202-720-6221

Objectives: To provide financial and technical assistance to: (1) Identify salt source areas; (2) develop project plans to carry out conservation practices to reduce salt loads; (3) install conservation practices to reduce salinity levels; (4) carry out research, education, and demonstration activities; (5) carry out monitoring and evaluation activities; and (6) to decrease salt concentration and salt loading which causes increased salinity levels within the Colorado River and to enhance the supply and quality of water available for use in the United States and the Republic of Mexico. Types of assistance: direct payments for specified use. Estimate of annual funds available: (Direct payments) $8,394,000.

* Loans to Help Your Country Property Recover From an Emergency

(10.404 Emergency Loans)
Administrator, Consolidated Farm Service Agency
U.S. Department of Agriculture
Washington, DC   202-720-1632

Objectives: To assist established (owner or tenant) family farmers, ranchers and aquaculture operators with loans to cover losses resulting from major and/or natural disasters, which can be used for annual farm operating expenses, and for other essential needs necessary to return disaster victims' farming operations to financially

Federal Money for Housing and Real Estate

sound bases in order that they will be able to return to private sources of credit as soon as possible. Types of assistance: direct loans. Estimate of annual funds available: $100,000,000.

* Money to Build Houses for Your Employees
(10.405 Farm Labor Housing Loans and Grants (Labor Housing))
Multifamily Housing Processing Division
Consolidated Farm Service Agency
U.S. Department of Agriculture
Washington, DC 20250　　　　　　　　　202-720-1604

Objectives: To provide decent, safe, and sanitary low rent housing and related facilities for domestic farm laborers. Types of assistance: project grants; guaranteed/insured loans. Estimate of annual funds available: (Loans) $16,012,000. (Grants) $11,297,000.

* Money to Buy, Fix Up or Build Houses in Small Towns
(10.410 Very Low to Moderate Income Housing Loans
(Section 502 Rural Housing Loans))
Administrator, Consolidated Farm Service Agency
U.S. Department of Agriculture
Washington, DC 20250　　　　　　　　　202-720-7967

Objectives: To assist lower income rural families through direct loans to buy, build, rehabilitate, or improve decent, safe, and sanitary dwellings and related facilities for use by the applicant as a permanent residence. Subsidized funds are available only on direct loans for low and very low income applicants. Nonsubsidized Funds (loan making) are available for very low and low income applicants who are otherwise eligible for assistance, but based on the amount of the loan requested, the interest credit assistance formula results in no interest credit. Nonsubsidized funds (loan servicing) are available to very low, low and moderate income applicants/borrowers who do not qualify for interest credit assistance for: (1) Subsequent loans for repair and rehabilitation; and (2) subsequent loan part only (repair or rehabilitation or the payment of equity) in connection with transfers by assumption or credit sales. Loan guarantees are also available to assist moderate income rural families in home acquisition. Types of assistance: direct loans; guaranteed/insured loans. Estimate of annual funds available: (Direct Loans) $1,400,000,000 (for subsidized low or moderate income loans for servicing and repairs). (Guaranteed loans) $1,000,000,000.

* Money for Nonprofits to Build Rental Houses in Small Towns
(10.415 Rural Rental Housing Loans)
Director, Multifamily Housing Processing Division
Consolidated Farm Service Agency
U.S. Department of Agriculture
Washington, DC 20250　　　　　　　　　202-382-1604

Objectives: To provide economically designed and constructed rental and cooperative housing and related facilities suited for independent living for rural residents. Types of assistance: direct loans. Estimate of annual funds available: (Direct Loans) $220,000,000.

* Money to Improve Your Water for a House in the Country
(10.416 Soil and Water Loans (SW Loans))
Administrator, Consolidated Farm Service Agency
U.S. Department of Agriculture
Washington, DC 20250　　　　　　　　　202-720-1632

Objectives: To facilitate improvement, protection, and proper use of farmland by providing adequate financing and supervisory assistance for soil conservation, water resource development, conservation and use, forestation, drainage of farmland, the establishment and improvement of permanent pasture, the development of pollution abatement and control facilities on farms, development of energy conserving measures and other related conservation measures. Types of assistance: direct loans; guaranteed/insured loans. Estimate of annual funds available: (Direct Loans) $2,894,700. (Guarantee Loans) $832,290.

* Loans and Grants to Fix Up Your House in the Country ($5,000 Grants)
(10.417 Very Low Income Housing Repair Loans and Grants
(Section 504 Rural Housing Loans and Grants))
Director, Single-Family Housing Processing Division
Consolidated Farm Service Agency
U.S. Department of Agriculture
Washington, DC 20250　　　　　　　　　202-720-1474

Objectives: To give very low income rural homeowners an opportunity to make essential repairs to their homes to make them safe and to remove health hazards to the family or the community. Types of assistance: direct loans; project grants. Estimate of annual funds available: (Loans) $25,000,000. (Grants) $25,000,000.

* Money to Conserve Soil and Water in Small Towns
(10.900 Great Plains Conservation)
Deputy Chief for Programs
Soil Conservation Service
U.S. Department of Agriculture
P.O. Box 2890
Washington, DC 20013　　　　　　　　　202-720-1868

Objectives: To conserve and develop the Great Plains soil and water resources by providing technical and financial assistance to farmers, ranchers, and others in planning and implementing conservation practices. Types of assistance: direct payments for specified use; advisory services and counseling. Estimate of annual funds available: (Grants) $2,045,000. (Salaries and expenses) $8,892,000.

* Money to Fix Up an Abandoned Coal Mine
(10.910 Rural Abandoned Mine Program (RAMP))
Deputy Chief for Programs
Soil Conservation Service
U.S. Department of Agriculture
P.O. Box 2890
Washington, DC 20013　　　　　　　　　202-720-2847

Objectives: To protect people and the environment from the adverse effects of past coal mining practices, and to promote the development of soil and water resources of unreclaimed mined lands. Types of assistance: direct payments for specified use; advisory services and counseling. Estimate of annual funds available: (Grants) $8,524,403. (Salaries and expenses) $4,854,550.

* Loans to Fix Up Houses That Are More Than One Year Old
(14.108 Rehabilitation Mortgage Insurance (203(k)))
Director, Single Family Development Division
Office of Insured Single Family Housing
U.S. Department of Housing and Urban Development
Washington, DC 20410　　　　　　　　　202-708-2720

Objectives: To help families repair or improve, purchase and improve, or refinance and improve existing residential structures more than one year old. Types of assistance: guaranteed/insured loans. Estimate of annual funds available: (Loans insured) $201,259,000.

* Loans to Buy Trailers
(14.110 Manufactured Home Loan Insurance-Financing Purchase of
Manufactured Homes as Principal Residences of Borrowers (Title I))
Director, Title I Insurance Division
U.S. Department of Housing and Urban Development　　800-733-4663
Washington, DC 20410　　　　　　　　　202-708-2880

Objectives: To make possible reasonable financing of manufactured home purchases. Types of assistance: guaranteed/insured loans. Estimate of annual funds available: Loans reported under program No. 14.142.

* Loans to Co-op Investors
(14.112 Mortgage Insurance for Construction or Substantial
Rehabilitation of Condominium Projects (234(d) Condominiums))
Policies and Procedures Division
Office of Insured Multifamily Housing Development
U.S. Department of Housing and Urban Development
Washington, DC 20410　　　　　　　　　202-708-2556

Objectives: To enable sponsors to develop condominium projects in which individual units will be sold to home buyers. Types of assistance: guaranteed/insured loans. Estimate of annual funds available: (Mortgages insured) $0.

* Loans to Homeowners Anywhere With 1 to 4 Family Units
(14.117 Mortgage Insurance-Homes (203(b)))
Director, Single Family Development Division
Office of Insured Single Family Housing

Real Estate Ventures

U.S. Department of Housing and Urban Development
Washington, DC 20410   202-708-2700
Objectives: To help people undertake home ownership. Types of assistance: guaranteed/insured loans. Estimate of annual funds available: (Mortgages insured- including funding for 14.119, 14.121, 14.163 and 14.175) $52,610,678,000.

* Loans to Buy Single Family Homes for Disaster Victims

(14.119 Mortgage Insurance-Homes for Disaster Victims (203(h)))
Director
Single Family Development Division
Office of Insured Single Family Housing
U.S. Department of Housing and Urban Development
Washington, DC 20410   202-708-2700
Objectives: To help victims of a major disaster undertake homeownership on a sound basis. Types of assistance: guaranteed/insured loans. Estimate of annual funds available: (Mortgages insured) reported under Program No. 14.117.

* Money for Low to Moderate Income Families Hurt by a Disaster or Urban Renewal

(14.120 Mortgage Insurance-Homes for Low and Moderate Income Families (221(d)(2)))
Director
Single Family Development Division
Office of Insured Single Family Housing
U.S. Department of Housing and Urban Development
Washington, DC 20410   202-708-2700
Objectives: To make homeownership more readily available to families displaced by a natural disaster, urban renewal, or other government actions and to increase homeownership opportunities for low income and moderate income families. Types of assistance: guaranteed/insured loans. Estimate of annual funds available: (Mortgages insured) $127,193,000.

* Money for Homes in Outlying Areas

(14.121 Mortgage Insurance-Homes in Outlying Areas (203(i)))
Director, Single Family Development Division
Office of Insured Single Family Housing
U.S. Department of Housing and Urban Development
Washington, DC 20410   202-708-2700
Objectives: To help people purchase homes in outlying areas. Types of assistance: guaranteed/insured loans. Estimate of annual funds available: (Mortgages insured) reported under program No. 14.117.

* Money for Homes in Urban Renewal Areas

(14.122 Mortgage Insurance-Homes in Urban Renewal Areas (220 Homes))
Director, Single Family Development Division
Office of Insured Single Family Housing
U.S. Department of Housing and Urban Development
Washington, DC 20410   202-708-2700
Objectives: To help families purchase or rehabilitate homes in urban renewal areas. Types of assistance: guaranteed/insured loans. Estimate of annual funds available: (Mortgages insured) $47,000.

* Money for Homes in Older Areas of Town

(14.123 Mortgage Insurance-Housing in Older, Declining Areas (223(e)))
For Single Family:
Single Family Development Division
Office of Insured Single Family Housing
U.S. Department of Housing and Urban Development
Washington, DC 20410   202-708-2700
For Multifamily:
Policies and Procedures Division
Office of Insured Multifamily Housing Development
U.S. Department of Housing and Urban Development
Washington, DC 20410   202-708-2556
Objectives: To assist in the purchase or rehabilitation of housing in older, declining urban areas. Types of assistance: guaranteed/insured loans. Estimate of annual funds available: (Mortgages insured - single family and multifamily) $16,794,000.

* Money to Buy a Co-op Apartment

(14.126 Mortgage Insurance-Cooperative Projects (213 Cooperatives))
Policies and Procedures Division
Office of Insured Multifamily Housing Development
U.S. Department of Housing and Urban Development
Washington, DC 20410   202-708-2556
Objectives: To make it possible for nonprofit cooperative ownership housing corporations or trusts to develop or sponsor the development of housing projects to be operated as cooperatives and to allow investors to provide good quality multifamily housing to be sold to such nonprofit corporations or trusts upon completion of construction or rehabilitation. Types of assistance: guaranteed/insured loans. Estimate of annual funds available: (Mortgages insured-including funding for 14.132) $0.

* Money to Buy a Trailer-Home Park

(14.127 Mortgage Insurance-Manufactured Home Parks (207(m) Manufactured Home Parks))
Policies and Procedures Division
Office of Insured Multifamily Housing Development
U.S. Department of Housing and Urban Development
Washington, DC 20410   202-708-2556
Objectives: To make possible the financing of construction or rehabilitation of manufactured home parks. Types of assistance: guaranteed/insured loans. Estimate of annual funds available: (Mortgages insured) Reported under program No. 14.134.

* Money to Buy a Hospital

(14.128 Mortgage Insurance-Hospitals (242 Hospitals))
Hospital Mortgage Insurance Staff
U.S. Department of Housing and Urban Development
Washington, DC 20410   202-708-0599
or
Division of Facilities Loans
U.S. Department of Health and Human Services
Rockville, MD 20857   301-443-5317
Objectives: To facilitate the affordable financing of hospitals for the care and treatment of persons who are acutely ill or who otherwise require medical care and related services of the kind customarily furnished only or most effectively by hospitals. Types of assistance: guaranteed/insured loans. Estimate of annual funds available: (Mortgages insured) $350,000,000.

* Money to Buy a Nursing Home

(14.129 Mortgage Insurance-Nursing Homes, Intermediate Care Facilities and Board and Care Homes (232 Nursing Homes))
Policies and Procedures Division
Office of Insured Multifamily Housing Development
U.S. Department of Housing and Urban Development
Washington, DC 20412   202-708-2556
Objectives: To make possible financing for construction or rehabilitation of nursing homes, intermediate care facilities and board and care homes, to allow purchase or refinancing with or without repairs of projects currently insured by HUD, but not requiring substantial rehabilitation, and to provide loan insurance to install fire safety equipment. Types of assistance: guaranteed/insured loans. Estimate of annual funds available: (Mortgages insured) $1,019,908,000.

* Money to Buy Your House if It is in a Long Term Ground Lease

(14.130 Mortgage Insurance-Purchase by Homeowners of Fee Simple Title From Lessors (240))
Director, Single Family Development Division
Office of Insured Single Family Housing
U.S. Department of Housing and Urban Development
Washington, DC 20410   202-708-2700
Objectives: To help homeowners obtain fee-simple title to the property which they hold under long-term leases and on which their homes are located. Types of assistance: guaranteed/insured loans. Estimate of annual funds available: (Mortgages insured) $0.

* Money to Buy Your Co-op

(14.132 Mortgage Insurance-Purchase of Sales-Type Cooperative Housing Units (213 Sales))
Director, Single Family Development Division
Office of Insured Single Family Housing

Federal Money for Housing and Real Estate

U.S. Department of Housing and Urban Development
Washington, DC 20410   202-708-2700

Objectives: To make available, good quality, new housing for purchase by individual members of a housing cooperative. Types of assistance: guaranteed/insured loans. Estimate of annual funds available: (Mortgages insured) Reported under program 14.126.

* Money to Buy a Condominium

(14.133 Mortgage Insurance-Purchase of Units in Condominiums (234(c)))
Director
Single Family Development Division
Office of Insured Single Family Housing
U.S. Department of Housing and Urban Development
Washington, DC 20410   202-708-2700

Objectives: To enable families to purchase units in condominium projects. Types of assistance: guaranteed/insured loans. Estimate of annual funds available: (Mortgages insured) $4,844,885,000.

* Money to Invest in Apartment Buildings for Middle Class Families

(14.135 Mortgage Insurance-Rental and Cooperative Housing for Moderate Income Families and Elderly, Market Interest Rate (221(d)(3) and (4) Multifamily - Market Rate Housing))
Policies and Procedures Division
Office of Insured Multifamily Housing Development
U.S. Department of Housing and Urban Development
Washington, DC 20410   202-708-2556

Objectives: To provide good quality rental or cooperative housing for moderate income families and the elderly and handicapped. Single Room Occupancy (SRO) may also be insured under this section (see 14.184). Types of assistance: guaranteed/insured loans. Estimate of annual funds available: (Mortgages insured excluding coinsurance) $444,913,000.

* Money to Invest in Rental Housing for the Elderly

(14.138 Mortgage Insurance-Rental Housing for the Elderly (231))
Policies and Procedures Division
Office of Insured Multifamily Housing Development
U.S. Department of Housing and Urban Development
Washington, DC 20410   202-708-2556

Objectives: To provide good quality rental housing for the elderly. Types of assistance: guaranteed/insured loans. Estimate of annual funds available: (Mortgages insured) $0.

* Money to Invest in Rental Housing in Urban Renewal Areas

(14.139 Mortgage Insurance-Rental Housing in Urban Renewal Areas (220 Multifamily))
For production information:
Policies and Procedures Division
Office of Insured Multifamily Housing Development
U.S. Department of Housing and Urban Development
Washington, DC 20410   202-708-2556
For management information:
Director, Office of Multifamily Housing Management
U.S. Department of Housing and Urban Development
Washington, DC 20410   202-708-3730

Objectives: To provide good quality rental housing in urban renewal areas, code enforcement areas, and other areas designated for overall revitalization. Types of assistance: guaranteed/insured loans. Estimate of annual funds available: (Mortgages insured) $0.

* Money to Fix Up Your Home

(14.142 Property Improvement Loan Insurance for Improving All Existing Structures and Building of New Nonresidential Structures (Title I))
Director
Title I Insurance Division
U.S. Department of Housing and Urban Development   800-733-4663
Washington, DC 20410   202-708-7400

Objectives: To facilitate the financing of improvements to homes and other existing structures and the building of new nonresidential structures. Types of assistance: guaranteed/insured loans. Estimate of annual funds available: (Loans insured including funding for programs 4.110 and 14.162) $1,289,200,000.

* Money to Fix Up Multifamily Projects

(14.151 Supplemental Loan Insurance-Multifamily Rental Housing (241(a)))
Policies and Procedures Division
Office of Insured Multifamily Housing Development
U.S. Department of Housing and Urban Development
Washington, DC 20411   202-708-2556

Objectives: To finance repairs, additions and improvements to multifamily projects, group practice facilities, hospitals, or nursing homes already insured by HUD or held by HUD. Major movable equipment for insured nursing homes, group practice facilities or hospitals may be covered by a mortgage under this program. Types of assistance: guaranteed/insured loans. Estimate of annual funds available: (Loans) $43,630,000.

* Money to Investors to Purchase or Refinance Multifamily Housing

(14.155 Mortgage Insurance for the Purchase or Refinancing of Existing Multifamily Housing Projects (Section 223(f) Insured Under Section 207))
Office of Insured Multifamily Housing Development
Policies and Procedures Division
U.S. Department of Housing and Urban Development
Washington, DC 20410   202-708-2556

Objectives: To provide mortgage insurance to lenders for the purchase or refinancing of existing multifamily housing projects, whether conventionally financed or subject to federally insured mortgages at the time of application for mortgage insurance. Types of assistance: guaranteed/insured loans. Estimate of annual funds available: (Mortgages Insured) (Excludes coinsurance) $894,910,000.

* Money to Build Housing for the Elderly That Also Provides Support Services

(14.157 Supportive Housing for the Elderly (202))
Housing for the Elderly and Handicapped People Division
Office of Elderly and Assisted Housing
U.S. Department of Housing and Urban Development
Washington, DC 20410   202-708-2730

Objectives: To expand the supply of housing with supportive services for the elderly. Types of assistance: project grants. Estimate of annual funds available: (Reservations for Capital Grants, Rental Assistance and Service Coordinators) $166,300,000.

* Money to Buy a House With Graduated Mortgage Payments

(14.159 Section 245 Graduated Payment Mortgage Program)
Director, Single Family Development Division
Office of Insured Single Family Housing
U.S. Department of Housing and Urban Development
Washington, DC 20410   202-708-2700

Objectives: To facilitate early home ownership for households that expect their incomes to rise. Program allows homeowners to make smaller monthly payments initially and to increase their size gradually over time. Types of assistance: guaranteed/insured loans. Estimate of annual funds available: (Mortgages Insured - includes 14.172) $414,624,000.

* Money to Buy a Trailer and Trailer Lot

(14.162 Mortgage Insurance-Combination and Manufactured Home Lot Loans (Title I))
Director
Title I Insurance Division
U.S. Department of Housing and Urban Development
Room B-133
Washington, DC 20410   202-755-7400

Objectives: To make possible reasonable financing for the purchase of a manufactured home and a lot on which to place the home. Types of assistance: guaranteed/insured loans. Estimate of annual funds available: (Guaranteed/Insured Loans) Reported under program No. 14.110.

Real Estate Ventures

* Money to Finance Coop Buildings
(14.163 Mortgage Insurance-Single Family Cooperative Housing (203(n)))
Director
Single Family Development Division
Office of Insured Single Family Housing
U.S. Department of Housing and Urban Development
Washington, DC 20410   202-708-2700

Objectives: To provide insured financing for the purchase of the Corporate Certificate and Occupancy Certificate for a unit in a cooperative housing project. Ownership of the corporate certificate carries the right to occupy the unit located within the cooperative project. Types of assistance: guaranteed/insured loans. Estimate of annual funds available: Reported under program No. 14.117.

* Money to Developers in Financial Trouble
(14.164 Operating Assistance for Troubled Multifamily Housing Projects (Flexible Subsidy Fund) (Troubled Projects))
Director
Office of Multifamily Housing Management
U.S. Department of Housing and Urban Development
Washington, DC 20420   202-708-3730

Objectives: To provide loans to restore or maintain the physical and financial soundness, to assist in the management and to maintain the low to moderate income character of certain projects assisted or approved for assistance under the National Housing Act or under the Housing and Urban Development Act of 1965. Types of assistance: direct payments for specified use. Estimate of annual funds available: (Reservations) $125,000,000.

* Money to Buy Houses in Areas Hurt by Defense Cuts
(14.165 Mortgage Insurance-Homes-Military Impacted Areas (238(c)))
Director
Single Family Development Division
Office of Insured Single Family Housing
U.S. Department of Housing and Urban Development
Washington, DC 20410   202-708-2700

Objectives: To help families undertake home ownership in military impacted areas. Types of assistance: guaranteed/insured loans. Estimate of annual funds available: (Mortgages Insured) $16,259,000.

* Money for Active Duty Military to Buy Houses
(14.166 Mortgage Insurance-Homes for Members of the Armed Services (Section 222))
Director
Single Family Development Division
Office of Insured Single Family Housing
U.S. Department of Housing and Urban Development
Washington, DC 20410   202-708-2700

Objectives: To help members of the armed services on active duty to purchase a home. Types of assistance: guaranteed/insured loans. Estimate of annual funds available: (Mortgages Insured) $1,776,000.

* Loans to Developers in Trouble During Their First Two Years of Operation
(14.167 Mortgage Insurance-Two Year Operating Loss Loans, Section 223(d) (Two Year Operating Loss Loans))
For program information:
Policies and Procedures Division
Office of Insured Multifamily Housing Development
U.S. Department of Housing and Urban Development
Washington, DC 20410   202-755-2556
For management information:
Director
Office of Multifamily Housing Management
U.S. Department of Housing and Urban Development
Washington, DC 20410   202-708-3730

Objectives: To insure a separate loan covering operating losses incurred during the first two years following the date of completion of a multifamily project with a HUD-insured first mortgage. Types of assistance: guaranteed/insured loans. Estimate of annual funds available: (Loans) $19,100,000.

* Money to Buy a Home Using Increased Equity Payments
(14.172 Mortgage Insurance-Growing Equity Mortgages (GEMs))
Director, Single Family Development Division
Office of Insured Single Family Housing
U.S. Department of Housing and Urban Development
Washington, DC 20410   202-708-2700

Objectives: To provide a rapid principal reduction and shorter mortgage term by increasing payments over a 10-year period, thereby expanding housing opportunities to the homebuying public. Types of assistance: guaranteed/insured loans. Estimate of annual funds available: (Mortgages insured) Reported under program 14.159.

* Money to Buy a Home Using an Adjustable Rate Mortgage
(14.175 Adjustable Rate Mortgages (ARMS))
Director
Single Family Development Division
Office of Insured Single Family Housing
U.S. Department of Housing and Urban Development
Washington, DC 20410   202-708-2700

Objectives: To provide mortgage insurance for an adjustable rate mortgage which offers lenders more assurance of long term profitability than a fixed rate mortgage, while offering consumer protection features. Types of assistance: guaranteed/insured loans. Estimate of annual funds available: Reported under 14.117.

* Money for Nonprofits to Build Houses for Lower-Income Families
(14.179 Nehemiah Housing Opportunity Grant Program (Nehemiah Housing))
Morris E. Carter, Director
Single Family Development Division
U.S. Department of Housing and Urban Development
451 7th St., SW
Washington, DC 20410   202-708-2700

Objectives: To provide an opportunity for those families who otherwise would not be financially able to realize their dream of owning a home, to increase the employment opportunities of the residents in neighborhoods where the housing is proposed and to create sound and attractive neighborhoods. Types of assistance: project grants. Estimate of annual funds available: (Grants) $16,552,000.

* Money to Invest in Houses for Those With Disabilities
(14.181 Supportive Housing for Persons with Disabilities (811))
Housing for Elderly and Handicapped People Division
Office of Elderly and Assisted Housing
U.S. Department of Housing and Urban Development
Washington, DC 20410   202-708-2730

Objectives: To provide for supportive housing and related facilities for persons with disabilities. Types of assistance: project grants. Estimate of annual funds available: (Reservations for Capital Grants and Rental Assistance) $387,000,000.

* Rental Supplements for Investors Who Provide Houses to Low Income Families
(14.182 Lower Income Housing Assistance Program-Section 8 New Construction/Substantial Rehabilitation (Section 8 Housing Assistance Payments Program for Very Low Income Families-New Construction/Substantial Rehabilitation))
For management information:
Director
Office of Multifamily Housing Management
U.S. Department of Housing and Urban Development
Washington, DC 20410   202-708-3730

Objectives: To aid very low income families in obtaining decent, safe and sanitary rental housing. Types of assistance: direct payments for specified use. Estimate of annual funds available: (Outlays for N/SR units under payment) $4,077,884,000.

* Money to Help Elderly Homeowners Convert Their Equity into a Monthly Income
(14.183 Home Equity Conversion Mortgages (255))
Director
Insured Family Development Division

Federal Money for Housing and Real Estate

Office of Single Family Housing
U.S. Department of Housing and Urban Development
Washington, DC 20410   202-708-2700

Objectives: To enable elderly homeowners to convert equity in their homes to monthly streams of income or lines of credit. Types of assistance: guaranteed/insured loans. Estimate of annual funds available: (Mortgages insured): $34,763,000.

* Money for Low Income Housing Tenants to Buy Their Building

(14.186 Mortgage Insurance-Equity Loans (241(f) Equity Loans))
For program information:
Policies and Procedures Division
Office of Insured Multifamily Housing Development
U.S. Department of Housing and Urban Development
Washington, DC 20410   202-708-2556
For management information:
Director
Office of Preservation and Property Disposition
U.S. Department of Housing and Urban Development
Washington, DC 20410   202-708-3555

Objectives: To insure a separate equity loan to owners of eligible low income multifamily properties who wish to extend the low income affordability restrictions or to insure an acquisition loan for select purchasers who will maintain such restrictions. Types of assistance: guaranteed/insured loans. Estimate of annual funds available: (Loans) $53,630,000.

* Grants to Nonprofits Who Lend Money to Low Income Families to Buy Houses

(14.240 HOPE for Homeownership of Single Family Homes (Hope 3))
Cliff Taffet
Office of Affordable Housing Programs
U.S. Department of Housing and Urban Development
Room 7168, 451 7th St., SW
Washington, DC 20410   202-708-3226

Objectives: To provide homeownership opportunities to lower income families and individuals by providing grantees with Federal assistance to finance an eligible homebuyer's direct purchase and rehabilitation of eligible single family properties or to fund the grantee's acquisition and rehabilitation of single family properties for sale and occupancy by families at affordable prices. Types of assistance: project grants. Estimate of annual funds available: (Grants) $50,000,000.

* Money for Homes That Use New Building Ideas

(14.507 Mortgage Insurance-Experimental Homes (ExTech 233-Homes))
Assistant Secretary for Policy Development
 and Research
Division of Innovative Technology
U.S. Department of Housing and Urban Development
451 7th St., SW
Washington, DC 20410   202-708-4370

Objectives: To help finance the development of homes that incorporate new or untried construction concepts designed to reduce housing costs, raise living standards, and improve neighborhood design by providing mortgage insurance. Types of assistance: guaranteed/insured loans. Estimate of annual funds available: Mortgages are insured and experimental features are guaranteed to the homeowner. No direct funding or subsidies are provided for the project.

* Money for Doctor's Offices and Hospitals That Use New Building Ideas

(14.508 Mortgage Insurance-Experimental Projects Other Than Housing (ExTech 233-Projects Other Than Housing))
Assistant Secretary for Policy Development and Research
Division of Innovative Technology
U.S. Department of Housing and Urban Development
451 7th St., SW
Washington, DC 20410   202-708-4370

Objectives: To provide mortgage insurance to help finance the development of group medical facilities that incorporate new or untried construction concepts intended to reduce construction costs, raise living standards and improve neighborhood design. Types of assistance: guaranteed/insured loans. Estimate of annual funds available: (Mortgages insured - reported under program No. 14.509).

* Money for Apartment Buildings That Use New Ideas

(14.509 Mortgage Insurance-Experimental Rental Housing (ExTech 233 - Experimental Rental Housing))
Assistant Secretary for Policy Development and Research
Division of Innovative Technology
U.S. Department of Housing and Urban Development
451 7th St., SW
Washington, DC 20410   202-708-4370

Objectives: To provide mortgage insurance to help finance the development of multifamily housing that incorporates new or untried construction concepts designed to reduce housing costs; raise living standards; and improve neighborhood design. Types of assistance: guaranteed/insured loans. Estimate of annual funds available: Mortgages are insured and experimental features are guaranteed. No funds or subsidies are available.

* Rent Supplements to Building Owners With Tenants That Have Low Incomes

(14.856 Lower Income Housing Assistance Program-Section 8 Moderate Rehabilitation (Section 8 Housing Assistance Payments Program for Very Low Income Families-Moderate Rehabilitation))
For program information:
Office of Assisted Housing
Rental Assistance Division
U.S. Department of Housing and Urban Development
Washington, DC 20410   202-708-7424

Objectives: To aid very low income families and homeless individuals in obtaining decent, safe and sanitary rental housing. Types of assistance: direct payments for specified use. Estimate of annual funds available: (Contract replacements to certificates) $54,000,000.

* More Rent Supplements for Building Owners With Tenants That Have Low Incomes

(14.857 Section 8 Rental Certificate Program (Section 8 Rental Certificates))
Office of Assisted Housing
Rental Assistance Division
U.S. Department of Housing and Urban Development
Washington, DC 20410   202-708-0477

Objectives: To aid low income families in obtaining decent, safe, and sanitary rental housing. Types of assistance: direct payments for specified use. Estimate of annual funds available: Reported under Program 14.156.

* Grants to Organizations Who Help Low Income Families Buy Houses

(14.858 HOPE for Public and Indian Housing Homeownership (HOPE for Public and Indian Housing (HOPE 1)))
Gary Van Buskirk
Homeownership Division for Public and Indian Housing
U.S. Department of Housing and Urban Development   202-708-4233
Washington, DC 20410   TDD: 202-708-9300

Objectives: To provide homeownership programs for eligible public and Indian housing residents and other low income families through the sale of eligible public and Indian housing. Types of assistance: project grants. Estimate of annual funds available: (Grants) $266,800,000.

* Money to Have Your State Buy Your Old Farm and Turn It into a Park

(15.916 Outdoor Recreation-Acquisition, Development and Planning (Land and Water Conservation Fund Grants))
Chief
Recreation Grants Division
National Park Service
U.S. Department of the Interior
P.O. Box 37127
Washington, DC 20013-7127   202-343-3700
Contact: Sam L. Hall

Objectives: To provide financial assistance to the States and their political subdivisions for the preparation of Statewide Comprehensive Outdoor Recreation Plans (SCORPs) and acquisition and development of outdoor recreation areas and facilities for the general public, to meet current and future needs. Types of assistance: project grants. Estimate of annual funds available: (Grants) $24,750,000.

Real Estate Ventures

* Grants to Build Houses on Indian Reservations
(15.141 Indian Housing Assistance)
Chief
Division of Housing Assistance
Office of Tribal Services
Room 4640, Main Interior Building
Bureau of Indian Affairs
1849 C St., NW
Washington, DC 20240　　　　　　　　　　　202-208-5427

Objectives: To use the Indian Housing Improvement Program (HIP) and Bureau of Indian Affairs resources to substantially eliminate substandard Indian housing. This effort is combined with the Indian Health Service (Department of Health and Human Services). Types of assistance: project grants (contracts); dissemination of technical information. Estimate of annual funds available: (Total HIP program costs including grant funding, self governance compact funding, salaries, and expenses) $19,083,000.

* Money for Veterans Who Want to Buy a House
(64.114 Veterans Housing-Guaranteed and Insured Loans
(VA Home Loans))
U.S. Department of Veterans Affairs
Washington, DC 20420

Objectives: To assist veterans, certain service personnel, and certain unremarried surviving spouses of veterans, in obtaining credit for the purchase, construction or improvement of homes on more liberal terms than are generally available to non-veterans. Types of assistance: guaranteed/insured loans. Estimate of annual funds available: (Closed Loans Guaranteed) $30,256,320,000.

* Loans for Disabled Veterans to Buy a House
(64.118 Veterans Housing-Direct Loans for Disabled Veterans)
U.S. Department of Veterans Affairs
Washington, DC 20420

Objectives: To provide certain severely disabled veterans with direct housing credit in connection with grants for specially adaptive housing with special features or movable facilities made necessary by the nature of their disabilities. Types of assistance: direct loans. Estimate of annual funds available: (Loans) $33,000.

* Money for Veterans to Buy Mobile Homes
(64.119 Veterans Housing-Manufactured Home Loans)
U.S. Department of Veterans Affairs
Washington, DC 20420

Objectives: To assist veterans, servicepersons, and certain unremarried surviving spouses of veterans in obtaining credit for the purchase of a manufactured home on more liberal terms than are available to non-veterans. Types of assistance: guaranteed/insured loans. Estimate of annual funds available: (Guaranteed Loans) $2,557,000.

* Loans for Native American Veterans to Buy or Build a Home
(64.126 Native American Veteran Direct Loan Program
(VA Native American Home Loan Program))
U.S. Department of Veterans Affairs
Washington, DC 20420

Objectives: To provide direct loans to certain Native American veterans for the purchase or construction of homes on trust lands. Types of assistance: direct loans. Estimate of annual funds available: (Loans): $11,202,000.

* Grants for Storm Windows or to Weatherize Your Home
(81.042 Weatherization Assistance for Low Income Persons)
Jeanne Van Viandren, Director
Weatherization Assistance Programs Division
Mail Stop CE-532
Conservation and Renewable Energy
U.S. Department of Energy
Forrestal Building
Washington, DC 20585　　　　　　　　　　　202-586-2204

Objectives: To insulate the dwellings of low income persons, particularly the elderly and handicapped low income, in order to conserve needed energy and to aid those persons least able to afford higher utility costs. Types of assistance: formula grants. Estimate of annual funds available: $230,000,000.

* Government Subsidized Flood Insurance to Homeowners
(83.100 Flood Insurance)
James M. Rose
Federal Insurance Administration
Federal Emergency Management Agency
Washington, DC 20472　　　　　　　　　　　202-646-2780

Objectives: To enable persons to purchase insurance against losses from physical damage to or loss of buildings and or contents therein caused by floods, mudflow, or flood-related erosion in the United States and to promote wise flood plain management practices in the Nation's flood-prone and mudflow-prone areas. Types of assistance: insurance. Estimate of annual funds available: $808,220,000.

* Money For Nonprofits to Provide Rural Housing Site Loans
(10.411 Rural Housing Site Loans
(Section 523 and 524 Site Loans))
Director, Single-Family Housing Processing Division
Farmers Home Administration
U.S. Department of Agriculture
Washington, DC 20250　　　　　　　　　　　202-720-1474

Objectives: To assist public or private nonprofit organizations interested in providing sites for housing, to acquire and develop land in rural areas to be subdivided as adequate building sites and sold on a cost development basis to families eligible for low and very low income loans, cooperatives, and broadly based nonprofit rural rental housing applicants. Types of assistance: direct loans. Estimate of annual funds available: (Loans) $616,000.

* Money to Fix Up Your Home in the Country
(10.433 Rural Housing Preservation Grants)
Multiple Family Housing Processing Division
Farmers Home Administration
U.S. Department of Agriculture
Washington, DC 20250　　　　　　　　　　　202-720-1606

Objectives: To assist very low and low income rural residents individual homeowners, rental property owners (single/multi-unit) or by providing the consumer cooperative housing projects (co-ops) the necessary assistance to repair or rehabilitate their dwellings. These objectives will be accomplished through the establishment of repair/rehabilitation, projects run by eligible applicants. This program is intended to make use of and leverage any other available housing programs which provide resources to very low and low income rural residents to bring their dwellings up to development standards. Types of assistance: project grants. Estimate of annual funds available: (Grants) $23,000,000.

* Money for Homes for Low Income Indian Families
(14.850 Public and Indian Housing)
Assistant Secretary for Public and Indian Housing
U.S. Department of Housing and Urban Development
Washington, DC 20410　　　　　　　　　　　202-708-0950

Objectives: To provide and operate cost-effective, decent, safe and affordable dwellings for lower income families through an authorized local Public Housing Agency (PHA) or Indian Housing Authority (IHA). Types of assistance: direct payments for specified use. Estimate of annual funds available: (Includes obligations for 14.851, 14.852, 14.853 and 14.854) $0. Indian Development: $263,000,000.

* Loans for Families With Bad Credit Histories
(14.140 Mortgage Insurance-Special Credit Risks)
For production information:
　Director, Single Family Development Division
　Office of Insured Single Family Housing
　U.S. Department of Housing and Urban Development
　Washington, DC 20410　　　　　　　　　　202-708-2700
For management information:
　Director, Single Family Servicing Division
　Secretary-Held and Counseling Services Branch
　Office of Insured Single Family Housing
　U.S. Department of Housing and Urban Development
　Washington, DC 20410　　　　　　　　　　202-708-1672

Objectives: To make homeownership possible for low and moderate income families who cannot meet normal HUD requirements. Types of assistance: guaranteed/insured loans. Estimate of annual funds available: (Mortgages insured) $13,000.

Federal Money for Housing and Real Estate

* Money to Provide Affordable Rental Housing for Low-Income Families

(14.239 HOME Investment Partnerships Program)
Gordon McKay, Director
Office of Affordable Housing Programs
Community Planning and Development
U.S. Department of Housing and Urban Development
451 7th St., SW
Washington, DC 20410   202-708-2685

Objectives: (1) To expand the supply of decent and affordable housing, particularly rental housing, for low and very low income Americans; (2) To strengthen the abilities of State and local governments to design and implement strategies for achieving adequate supplies of decent, affordable housing; (3) To provide both financial and technical assistance to participating jurisdictions, including the development of model programs for developing affordable low income housing and; (4) To extend and strengthen partnerships among all levels of government and the private sector, including for-profit and nonprofit organizations, in the production and operation of affordable housing. Types of assistance: formula grants. Estimate of annual funds available: (Grants) $1,400,000,000.

* Rental Voucher Program for Low Income Indian Families

(14.855 Section 8 Rental Voucher Program)
Office of Assisted Housing
Rental Assistance Division
U.S. Department of Housing and Urban Development
Washington, DC 20410   202-708-0477

Objectives: To aid very low income families in obtaining decent, safe, and sanitary rental housing. Types of assistance: direct payments for specified use. Estimate of annual funds available: Reported under Program 14.177.

* Money to Invest in Rental Housing for Lower Income Families

(14.856 Lower Income Housing Assistance Program-Section 8 Moderate Rehabilitation)
For program information:
Office of Assisted Housing
Rental Assistance Division
U.S. Department of Housing and Urban Development
Washington, DC 20410   202-708-7424

Objectives: To aid very low income families in obtaining decent, safe and sanitary rental housing. Types of assistance: direct payments for specified use. Estimate of annual funds available: (Contract replacements to certificates) $54,000,000.

* Loans to Investors, Builders, Developers of Affordable Housing

(14.189 Qualified Participating Entities QPE Risk Sharing Pilot Program)
Policies and Procedures Division
Office of Insured Multifamily Housing Development
U.S. Department of Housing and Urban Development
Washington, DC 20410   202-708-2556

Objectives: Under this program HUD will provide reinsurance on multifamily housing projects whose loans are originated, under-written, serviced, and disposed of by qualified participating entities (QPEs) and/or its approved lenders, up to 15,00 units through fiscal year 1994. The program is a pilot designed to assess the feasibility of risk-sharing partnerships between HUD and QPEs, including Government Sponsored Enterprises, State and local housing finance agencies, financial institutions and the Federal Housing Finance Board, in providing affordable housing for the nation. Types of assistance: guaranteed/insured loans. Estimate of annual funds available: $640,000,000.

* Money for Developers, Investors, and Builders of Low Income Housing

(14.188 HFA Rick Sharing Pilot Program)
Policies and Procedures Division
Office of Insured Multifamily Housing Development
U.S. Department of Housing and Urban Development
Washington, DC 20412   202-708-2556

Objectives: Under this program, HUD will provide full mortgage insurance on multifamily housing projects whose loans are under-written, processed, serviced, and disposed of by HFAs, up to 30,000 units through fiscal year 1995. The program is a pilot designed to assess the feasibility of risk-sharing partnerships between HUD and qualified State and local Housing Finance Agencies (HFA) in providing affordable housing for the nation. Types of assistance: guaranteed/insured loans. Estimate of annual funds available: $539,000,000.

Real Estate Ventures

State Money For Housing and Real Estate

State Initiatives

While affordable housing has long held an important place on the Federal government's policy agenda, budget cutbacks in recent years have forced the government to turn over many housing responsibilities to the states. Housing finance agencies (HFAs) have been created by states to issue tax-exempt bonds to finance mortgages for lower income first-time home buyers and to build multifamily housing.

States are involved in a host of initiatives throughout the broad spectrum of housing finance and development. Interim construction financing programs which can reduce the basic costs of lower income housing projects have been initiated in a number of states, together with innovative home ownership programs and programs directed toward rehabilitation and improved energy conservation.

States are also venturing into areas which have not received as much public sector attention until recently. By encouraging non-traditional types of housing, such as accessory units, shelters, and single room occupancy housing, states are addressing important elements of the housing market.

In Colorado, the state Housing and Finance Authority (CHFA) has issued more than $2.6 billions of bonds and notes since its establishment in 1973, providing housing for more than 47,000 families and individuals of low and moderate income; 27,200 first-time home buyers and over 20,500 rental housing units. In recent years the state has broadened CHFA's authority to allow it to develop finance programs to assist the growth of small business, help exports with insurance on goods sold overseas, and similar projects.

Colorado has done more than simply help its citizens find housing: the programs have resulted in construction employment of more than 20,000 jobs, with wages estimated at almost $20 million in new local real estate taxes and an indirect gain of $1.6 billion for the state.

Wisconsin, Maine and New York each have between 18 and 20 programs including special ones for women and minorities, for disabled persons, and for environmental hazard removal.

Maryland operates 26 programs, including those to help people with closing costs and settlement expenses. It also has special funds available for the elderly and is developing an emergency mortgage fund to help people who have fallen behind in their payments. Nonprofit developers can also tap the state for money to build low cost rental units.

Among Michigan's 29 programs and Minnesota's 25 are several for neighborhood revitalization. Minnesota also offers programs targeting the needs of urban Indians and migrant farm workers. Alaska, Oregon and Vermont offer financing for tenant acquisition of mobile home parks.

Funds are also available for persons who take steps to make their homes more energy efficient, for homeowners and landlords who remove lead paint from dwelling units, for houses without plumbing or those with plumbing that is dysfunctional, for handicapped persons, and to help landlords defray the costs of bringing low income housing into compliance with state and local housing codes. There are also funds for nonprofit organizations to acquire or renovate existing houses and apartments for use as group homes for special needs such as the mentally retarded.

In many states, elderly homeowners can look to the HFA to obtain financing and/or support services they need to remain in their homes and avoid institutionalization. Some of the states have more than one agency dedicated to housing and we have attempted to list them all here. Also, many cities and counties have quasi-federal/quasi-local "housing authorities" with additional programs. Check your local government listings for these.

The following is a complete listing of state housing programs.

Housing Offices

Alabama
Alabama Housing Finance Authority
P.O. Box 230909
Montgomery, AL 36123-0909
205-244-9200
800-325-2432

1) Mortgage Revenue Bond Program: low-rate loans for income-eligible first-time home buyers.
2) Downpayment Assistance Program: matching funds for lower income home buyers.
3) Mortgage Credit Certificate Program: provides a 20% federal tax credit on mortgage loan interest for lower income home buyers.
4) Low Income Housing Tax Credit Program: federal tax credits for owners of low income rental housing.
5) Multifamily Bond Program: tax-exempt bonds for financing multifamily projects with units affordable to low income tenants.
6) Home Program: provides additional opportunities for the production of affordable housing for low income families.

Alaska
Alaska Housing Finance Corp.
P.O. Box 101020
520 East 34th Ave.
Anchorage, AK 99510
907-561-1900

1) Home Ownership Assistance Program: interest subsidy to as low as 6%.
2) Mobile Home Loan Program: low downpayment.
3) Taxable Mortgage Program: for others than first time home buyers and veterans.
4) FmHA Guaranteed Rural Housing Loan Program: lower downpayments to those that qualify in rural Alaska's "small communities".
5) Tax Exempt Mortgage Program: loans up to $157,190 for single family and $176,996 for duplexes.
6) Second Mortgage Program: up to $99,900 for single family homes and $127,800 for duplexes can be used for home purchase or home improvement.
7) Veterans Mortgage Program: low interest loans to veterans and members of the reserve and National Guard.
8) Refinance Program: reduce monthly payments on existing loans.
9) Non-Conforming Property Program: homes which cannot be financed through traditional financing.
10) Rural Owner-Occupied or Nonowner- Occupied Loan Program: financing to qualified borrowers for the purchase, construction or rehabilitation of owner occupied or nonowner occupied housing in a "small Community in rural Alaska.
11) Section 8 New Construction and Additional Assistance: provides housing for the elderly, disabled and or handicapped in Fairbanks, Cordova, Wrangell, Seward and Anchorage.

State Money for Housing and Real Estate

12) Low to Moderate Income Home Ownership Programs: provides assistance on loans made to persons of low to moderate incomes for the purchase of owner occupied residences.
13) Refinance Program of a Non-AHFC Loan: refinancing for a loan not held by AHFC.
14) Second Mortgage Program for Health and Safety Repairs: for AHFC loan borrowers to bring property up to safety and health requirements.
15) Multifamily, Congregate and Special Needs Housing Loans: assists qualified nonprofit housing providers and for-profit companies in financing multifamily complexes for low and moderate income housing.
16) Emergency Housing Grants: grants to assist with meeting the housing needs of homeless persons.
17) Senior Housing Plan: potential borrowers may apply for financing to purchase, construct, rehabilitate or improve various kinds of housing that would meet the needs of persons 60 or older.
18) Low Income Weatherization: eligible families can receive improvements to their home resulting in a reduction of their heating bills by an average of 25 percent.

Arizona

Arizona Department of Commerce
Office of Housing and Infrastructure Development
3800 North Central, Suite 1200
Phoenix, AZ 85012
602-280-1365
TDD: 602-280-1301
Fax: 602-280-1470

1) Low Income Housing Tax Credits: federal income tax credits for owners of low income housing units.
2) Low Interest Mortgage Programs: typically below 9% interest loans for eligible Arizonans to purchase homes.
3) Arizona Housing Trust Fund: construction, housing rehabilitation, down payment, and closing cost assistance for low/moderate income home buyers.
4) Rental Rehabilitation Program: assists owners in rehabilitating rental housing for low/moderate income households.
5) HOME Program: provides help for low income families with various housing needs from rehabilitation to rental assistance.
6) Community Development Block Grant Program: develop viable communities by providing housing and a suitable living environment.

Arkansas

Arkansas Development Finance Authority
P.O. Box 8023
100 Main St., Suite 200
Little Rock, AR 72203
501-682-5900

1) HOME Program: funds are used for a variety of activities to develop and support affordable housing for low income. Eligible activities include: Tenant Based Rental Assistance, Rental Rehabilitation, and New Construction and Assistance for Homebuyers and Home Buyers.
2) Single-Family: below market rate loans to first time home buyers for the purchase of a single-family home.
3) Low Income Housing Tax Credit Program: federal tax credits for owners of low income rental housing.

California

California Housing Finance Agency
1121 L St., 7th Floor
Sacramento, CA 95815
916-322-3991

1) Multifamily Program: permanent financing for builders and developers of multifamily unit, elderly and congregate rental housing.
2) Development Loan Program: loans to small developers who have limited financial resources to complete CHFA projects.
3) Self-Help Building Assistance Program: loans to nonprofit developers to provide temporary funding for assistance with land acquisition, site development and construction.
5) Single Family Programs for Homeownership: lower interest rates, minimum down payment, a 1% origination fee, 30 year fixed rate loans, and other advantages for first-time homebuyers.
10) Rental Housing Program: provides affordable rental housing to low income families. You may obtain a list of CHFA financed apartments by county, but you must apply directly at the apartment manager's office.

California Department of Housing and Community Development
P.O. Box 952054
Sacramento, CA 94252-2050
916-322-1560

1) California Indian Assistance Program (CIAP): assists tribal organizations to obtain and administer housing, infrastructure community and economic development project funds provided by federal and state agencies.
2) California Housing Rehabilitation Program-Owner Component: low rate loans to bring homes up to code, make general improvements, or to make adaptations for handicapped.
3) Natural Disaster Assistance Program: rehabilitation loans for property damaged by natural disaster.
4) HOME Program: assist communities and community housing development organizations (CHDOs) in activities that create or retain affordable housing.
5) Mobile Home Park Assistance Program: loans and technical assistance to mobile home park resident organizations that are purchasing their park.
6) Rental Housing Construction Program: very low rate loans for development and construction costs associated with new rental housing units for low income households.
7) Family Housing Demonstration Program: very low rate loans to develop new, or rehabilitate existing, rental or co-op housing that provides on-site support programs for low-income households.
8) Permanent Housing for the Handicapped Homeless Program: partial funding to acquire, rehabilitate, and operate housing for the disabled homeless.
9) State Rental Rehabilitation Program: partial funding to rehabilitate low/moderate income rental housing in small rural communities.
10) California Energy Conservation Rehabilitation Program: grants of up to $5,000 per unit to assist energy conservation rehabilitation of low-income owner and renter farmworker housing, residential hotels, and rental housing for the elderly and handicapped.
11) Pre-Development Loan Program: low rate, 3-year loans for pre-development costs of low income housing projects.
12) PLP Natural Disaster Component: low rate, 3-year loans for pre-development costs of reconstruction or rehabilitation of subsidized housing damaged by natural disaster.
13) Emergency Housing Assistance Program: grants to provide emergency shelter for homeless households.
14) Farmworker Housing Grant Program: grants to provide owner-occupied and rental units for year-round, low income agricultural workers and to rehabilitate those damaged by natural disaster.
15) Community Development Block Grant (CDBG) Program: funds are used for housing or housing related activities and economic development.
16) Section 8 Housing Assistance Program: rental assistance payments for very low income households.
17) State (CDBG) General, Native American, and Colonials Allocations: funding for housing, community, and economic development projects serving lower income people in rural communities.
18) Senior Citizen Shared Housing Program: grants to assist seniors in obtaining shared housing or for development of group residences.

Colorado

Colorado Housing and Finance Authority
1981 Blake St.
Denver, CO 80202
303-297-7427
800-877-2432

1) Single-Family Program: lower than market interest rates available to first-time homeowners.
2) Commercial Division Programs: financial assistance provided to assist small businesses with expansion of their facilities.
3) Rental Acquisition Program: offers affordable multifamily housing for low income households.
4) Section 8 Moderate Rehabilitation Program: incentives to property owners who rehabilitate substandard rental housing for low income tenants qualifying for rent subsidies.
5) Low Income Housing Tax Credit Program: federal tax credits for owners of low income rental housing.
6) Mortgage Credit Certificates: reduction of federal income tax for home buyers.
7) Tax-Exempt Bond Program: financing for acquisition and/or rehabilitation of low income rental housing.
8) Special Needs Housing Fund: financing for housing for frail elderly, mentally ill, battered persons, runaways, etc.
9) Shelter Housing Assistance Program: financing for emergency or transitional housing.
10) Construction Loan Fund: Short-term loans to nonprofits for acquisition, rehab, construction and development costs of low income housing to be sold.
11) Housing Development Loan Fund: short-term loans to nonprofits for pre-development costs or acquisition of property for low income multifamily housing projects.
12) Special Projects Program: short-term loans to nonprofits for acquisition, rehab, or construction of projects such as group homes, shelters, co-ops, mobile home parks.
13) Rural Development Loan Program: loans for businesses in rural areas of Colorado.
14) Mortgage Revenue Bond Program: CHFA sells tax-exempt bonds and makes proceeds available to qualified home buyers under two options: Below-Market Interest Rate Program or Cash Assistance Program.
15) Recycled Funds Program: provides a limited number of mortgage loans originated by affordable housing and community reinvestment lenders.

Real Estate Ventures

Connecticut

Connecticut Housing Finance Authority
40 Cold Spring Rd.
Rocky Hill, CT 06067   203-721-9501

1) Home Mortgage Program: low interest mortgages for low and moderate income persons and families.
2) Rehabilitation Mortgages: loans to protect or improve livability or energy efficiency of a home.
3) Reverse Annuity Mortgages (RAM): allows senior citizens to convert their home's equity into monthly tax-free cash payments.
4) Market Rate Multifamily Program: below conventional-rate financing to develop or rehabilitate multifamily housing with units affordable to low income households.
5) Low Income Housing Tax Credit Program: federal tax credits for owners of low income rental housing.
6) Private Rental Investment Mortgage and Equity Program: financing for mixed-income rental developments.
7) Apartment Conversion for the Elderly: loans to homeowners 62 years of age or older for additions or conversions to their homes to create income-producing rental units.
8) Corporation for Supportive Housing Program: provides housing with special support services to people who have severe prolonged mental illness, AIDS and related disorders, chronic substance abusers, are homeless or at risk of being homeless.
9) Mortgage Revenue Bond Program: provides assistance for first time home buyers who are of low and moderate income.

Delaware

Delaware State Housing Authority
Division of Housing and Community Development
18 The Green
P.O. Box 1401
Dover, DE 19901   302-739-4263

1) Single-Family Mortgage Program: low interest loans to first-time home buyers.
2) Housing Development Funds: loans to developers of housing for low and moderate income persons and families.
3) Housing Rehabilitation Loan Program: $15,000 for ten years at 3% to fix up single-family homes.
4) Rent Subsidy Programs: money to provide subsidies for low and moderate income rental housing.
5) Public Housing Home Ownership Program: provides public housing tenants and families on the waiting list the opportunity to purchase affordable homes in residential neighborhoods.
6) Rental Rehabilitation Program: loans to cover up to 50% of rehab costs for low/moderate income housing.
7) Emergency Shelter Grants Program: to assist emergency housing shelters for the homeless.
8) Community Development Block Grants: funding to maintain or improve housing of low/moderate income households.
9) Multifamily Mortgage Revenue Bonds: financing for profit and nonprofit developers of low income housing.
10) Low Income Housing Tax Credit Program: federal tax credits for owners of low income rental housing.
11) Family Assisted Interest Rate Loans: first time homebuyers mortgage assistance at exceptionally low interest rates.
12) Second Mortgage Assistance Program: downpayment and closing cost assistance for first time homebuyers.
13) Emergency Shelter Grant Program: federal funds for local communities to rehabilitate, expand and operate shelter and transitional housing.
14) HOME Program: designed to expand affordable housing through tenant and homebuyer assistance, rehabilitation, and new construction.
15) Family Self-Sufficiency Program: designed to coordinate services that assisted housing residents need to achieve economic independence.
16) Delaware Housing Partnership Program: Second mortgages for settlement assistance to low to moderate income families purchasing homes in targeted new construction subdivisions.

District of Columbia

DC Housing Finance Agency
1275 K St., NW, Suite 600
Washington, DC 20005   202-408-0415
    Fax: 202-408-2766

1) Single-Family Purchase Program: loans to first-time home buyers with 5% down and 7.5% interest.
2) Multifamily Program: construction and permanent financing for developers of multifamily housing with at least 20% of the units designated for low income households.

District of Columbia Department of Housing and Community Development
51 N St., NE
Washington, DC 20002   202-535-1353

1) Home Purchase Assistance Program: low or no interest loans for low and moderate income home buyers.
2) First Right Purchase Assistance Program: low cost loans for low and moderate income individuals and tenant groups to exercise their right to purchase their rental housing that is being offered for sale.
3) Homestead Housing Preservation Program: repossessed properties are sold to eligible District residents at low cost and with deferred payment loans.
4) Multifamily Housing Rehabilitation Loan Program: low rate financing for construction and rehabilitation of multifamily housing.
5) Rental Rehabilitation Program: low or no interest deferred loans for rehabilitation and rent subsidies for property owners and tenants of low income housing.
6) Distressed Properties Program: tax incentives to encourage the development of new rental housing or for the rehabilitation of vacant rental housing; similar benefits for occupied properties in economic difficulty.
7) Housing Finance for the Elderly, Dependent and Disabled: loans for the development of housing for special needs households.
8) Low Income Housing Tax Credit Program: tax credits for owners of low income rental housing.
9) Single-Family Housing Rehabilitation Program: low cost financing for the rehabilitation of one to four unit low income housing in designated areas.
10) Home Improvements for the Handicapped: grants to remove barriers and improve accessibility; for homeowners or landlords on behalf of handicapped tenants.

Florida

Florida Housing Finance Agency
227 North Bronough St., Suite 5000
Tallahassee, FL 32301-1329   904-488-4197

1) First-Time Homebuyer Mortgage Revenue Bond Program: below-market rate financing for first-time home buyers with low/moderate income.
2) Home Ownership Assistance Program: $2,500 zero interest, due-on-sale loan to defer closing costs.
3) Affordable Housing Guarantee Program: below market financing for developers/home buyers of rental and for-sale housing.
4) State Apartment Incentive Loan Program: low rate financing for developers who build or rehabilitate rental housing with 20% of units for low income households and to eligible nonprofit sponsors of housing projects.
5) Low Income Housing Tax Credit Program: federal tax credits for owners of low income rental housing.
6) Rental Housing Bond Program: below-market financing to developers of rental housing with 20% for low income households.
7) Section 8 Program: federal rent subsidies for low income tenants.
8) HOME Investment Partnerships Program: provides states their opportunity to administer federally funded homeownership and rental housing programs.
9) Single Family Mortgage Revenue Bond (MRB) Program: bonds used to finance below-market interest rate mortgage loans for first time home buyers with low to middle incomes.
10) State Housing Initiatives Partnership Program (SHIP): funds for the development and maintenance of affordable housing.
11) Community Homebuyer's Program (CHBP): provides less costly Conventional financing for low and moderate income buyers.

Georgia

Georgia Residential Finance Authority
60 Executive Parkway South, Suite 250
Atlanta, GA 30329   404-679-4840

1) Single-Family Home Ownership Loan Program: 1.5% below prevailing interest rates for first-time homeowners.
2) Homeowner Rehabilitation: HOME funded loans for homeowner rehabilitation programs.
3) Nonprofit Housing Development Program: provides technical and financial assistance to nonprofit housing developers.
4) Multifamily Bond Program: below-market interest rate loans to develop or rehabilitate multifamily rental housing.
5) Low Income Housing Tax Credit Program: federal income tax credits to construct or rehabilitate low income rental housing.
6) Section 8 Existing Housing Assistance: rental assistance subsidy payments to landlords of low income individuals or families.
7) Housing Trust Fund for the Homeless: grants to homeless emergency shelters and service organizations in communities.
8) Appalachian Regional Commission: grants and loans for site development, technical assistance and others for low and moderate income housing projects.
9) HOME Investment Partnership Program: grants used to assist with state and local

State Money for Housing and Real Estate

housing concerns.
10) Emergency Shelter Grant Programs: grants to shelter facilities for building improvements and renovation.

Hawaii

Hawaii Housing Authority
1002 North School St.
P.O. Box 17907
Honolulu, HI 96817　　　　　　　　　　808-832-6020

1) Homeless Program: shelter and social services for homeless families and individuals.
2) State Rent Supplement Program: rent subsidies to tenants in approved projects.
3) Modernization and Maintenance: funds for the preservation and maintenance of existing housing.
4) Section 8 Certificate/Voucher Programs: rental housing subsidies.
5) Public Housing Projects: low rent housing for eligible families, elderly or disabled.

Housing Finance and Development Corporation
677 Queen St., Suite 300
Honolulu, HI 96813　　　　　　　　　　808-587-0597

1) Hula Mae Single Family Program: low interest loans to first-time home buyers.
2) Tax Reform: Multifamily Program: tax credits to investors in qualified low income rental housing projects.
3) Housing Finance Revolving Fund: long-term mortgage financing in geographic areas for projects where private mortgage insurers will not insure.

Idaho

Idaho Housing Agency
565 W. Myrtle
P.O. Box 7899　　　　　　　　　　　　208-331-4882
Boise, ID 83707-1899　　　　　　　TDD: 800-219-2285

1) Mortgage Credit Certificates: home buyers who have not owned a home in the last three years can claim 20% of their mortgage interest as a tax credit.
2) Single Family Mortgage Loan Program: below-market rate loans for first-time and limited-income home buyers.
3) Section 8 New Construction/Substantial Rehab Program: financing of multifamily housing affordable to very low income households via rent subsidies.
4) Section 8 Moderate Rehab Program: incentives for property owners to upgrade substandard rental units to be occupied by low income tenants qualifying for rent subsidies.
5) Section 8 Existing Certificate and Voucher Program: assistance for low income households to meet costs of rental housing.
6) Rental Rehabilitation Program: funding for private property owners to make improvements to rental units in eligible locations.
7) Low Income Housing Tax Credit Program: tax credit for owners/developers of housing for low income households.
8) Stewart B. McKinney Permanent Housing Program for Handicapped Homeless: grant funds for private nonprofit project sponsors.
9) Multifamily Housing Financing: loans for new construction or substantial rehab of multifamily housing with a percentage rented to low income tenants.
10) HOME Program: funds used for the construction and rehabilitation of affordable rental housing for low income families across the state.
11) 5/15 Low Interest Home Repair Loan Program: loans ranging from $5,000 to $15,000 are available for specific repairs under this program, with repayment terms from five to fifteen years.
12) Interest Qualifier Loan: allows borrowers to pay a lower interest rate for the first three years of their mortgage and then a one time interest increase in the fourth year for the remaining mortgage.

Illinois

Illinois Housing Development Authority
401 N. Michigan Ave., Suite 900　　　312-836-5200
Chicago, IL 60611　　　　　　　　　　800-942-8439
　　　　　　　　　　　　　　　　TDD: 312-836-5222

1) Tax Exempt Bonds: low interest loans to rehabilitate low income housing.
2) Congregate Housing Finance Program: loans for congregate housing for the elderly.
3) First Time Homebuyer Program: low interest mortgages for first-time income-eligible home buyers.
4) Affordable Housing Trust Fund: grants and loans to profit and nonprofit developers of low income housing projects.
5) HOME Program: this program is designed to expand the availability of affordable housing for low and very low income persons.
6) Tax Credits: help finance developments ranging from a single family house to a multifamily project.

Indiana

Indiana Housing Finance Authority
115 West Washington St.
Suite 1350, South Tower　　　　　　317-232-7777
Indianapolis, IN 46204　　　　　　　800-872-0371

1) First Home Program: loans to home buyers at 1 to 2 percentage points below the market rate.
2) Multifamily Program: loans for developers of low and moderate income housing.
3) Mortgage Credit Certificate Program: tax credits to families purchasing mobile homes.
4) Low Income Housing Tax Credit: federal tax credit to owners of low income rental housing.
5) Low Income Housing Trust Fund: matching funds for development of low income housing, permanent or transitional.
6) Mortgage Revenue Bonds: low interest mortgages for working families that are financed through the sale of tax-exempt bonds.
7) Equity Fund: provides financial and technical assistance to nonprofit and smaller for profit developers who want to use Low Income Tax Credits.
8) Housing Development Fund: funds to build local capacity in non-metropolitan areas.
9) HOME Program: funds used for a number of different purposes to create affordable housing.
10) First Home Program: allows qualified buyers to purchase homes using minimal amount of their own cash.

Iowa

Iowa Finance Authority
100 East Grand Ave., Suite 250
Des Moines, IA 50309　　　　　　　　515-281-4058

1) Single-Family Mortgage Loans: low interest loans to home buyers
2) Mortgage Credit Certificate Program: tax credits of up to 20% of the interest paid annually on home loans.
3) Small Business Loan Program: loans for small business.
4) Title Guaranty Program: to guaranty (insure) titles to Iowa real estate.
5) Economic Development Loan Program: for businesses exceeding the limitations of the Small Business Loan Program.
6) Targeted Area Assistance Program: assistance with origination fees and discount points.
7) Closing Cost Assistance: up to 3% or $1200 to help with closing costs of eligible buyers.
8) Low Income Housing Tax Credit Program: federal tax credits for owners of low income rental housing.
9) Housing Assistance Fund Program: funding for multifamily rehab and construction, rent subsidies, group homes, shelters, and other housing projects.
10) Homeless Shelter Assistance: funding for homeless shelters.

Kansas

Kansas Department of Commerce and Housing
700 SW Harrison, Suite 1300　　　　913-296-3481
Topeka, KS 66603　　　　　　　　　　800-752-4422

1) Tax Credits for Low Income Housing: tax credits for developers who rent to low income families.
2) Rental Rehabilitation Loan Program: loans up to $5,000 per rental unit to bring unit up to city code standard.
3) Emergency Shelter Grant Program: grants to local government agencies to provide emergency shelters for homeless households.
4) Permanent Housing for Handicapped Homeless: grants for acquisition, rehabilitation, and operation of multi-unit and group home projects for disabled homeless.
5) HOME/HOPE Program: emphasis is on assistance for first time home buyers with low to very low income.
6) Weatherization: a multi-funded program used to decrease fuel consumption in low income homes.
7) Community Service Block Grant Program: grants to community action agencies and migrant and seasonal farm worker organizations to assist low income Kansans.
8) Section 8 Rental Assistance: monthly assistance payments to project owners.
9) Emergency Community Services Homeless Funding: services are the same as the Community Service Block Grant Program with the stipulation that the target population must be homeless.
10) Rural Operation Homeless: families from specific counties who are homeless receive financial assistance toward the payment of rent.
11) Sunflower Supportive Services Program: provides supportive services for older residents of Kansas.
12) Housing Outreach Program: this program is designed to assess local community needs and to develop local resources.

Real Estate Ventures

Kentucky

Kentucky Housing Corporation
1231 Louisville Rd.
Frankfort, KY 40601
502-564-7630
800-633-8896

1) Single-Family Home Ownership: low interest loans to home buyers who currently do not own property.
2) Elderly Rural Rehabilitation Program: grants to elderly in rural areas for the installment of indoor plumbing facilities.
3) Grants to the Elderly for Energy Repairs (GEER): grants to elderly for home energy repairs.
4) Housing Trust: single-family loans for eligible low income families.
5) EPIC (Equity Partners Investing in the Commonwealth) Program: financing for eligible Kentuckians for downpayment and closing costs.
6) KHC Urban Program: initiatives to produce affordable housing in designated urban areas.
7) KHC Rural Program: loans and administrative assistance to nonprofit organizations for construction or rehab of low income housing.
8) Kentucky Appalachian Housing Program: site development grants and loans for housing developments in 49 eastern KY counties.
9) Country Home Program: low rate construction financing for families in 63 counties.
10) Field Services/Special Population Needs Emergency Fund: loans for emergency repairs for low income Kentuckians.
11) Permanent Housing for Homeless Handicapped Persons: funds for acquisition/rehabilitation of housing for homeless handicapped persons.
12) Section 8 Programs: rent subsidies and other assistance to low income households.
13) Rental Housing Finance Program: below-market financing for low income rental housing.
14) Rental Deposits Surety Program: assistance with utility and security deposits for low income households.
15) Residential Investment Program: fixed-rate mortgages for nonprofit sponsors of new rental units in rural counties.
16) Low Income Housing Tax Credits: federal tax credits for owners of low income rental housing.

Louisiana

Louisiana Housing Finance Agency
200 Lafayette St., Suite 300
Baton Rouge, LA 70801
504-342-1320

1) Single-Family: lower interest rate 8.8% for 30 yr. FHA/VA financing for first-time home buyers.
2) Multifamily: financing available for developers of low moderate income housing development.
3) Tax Credit Programs: federal and state income tax credit provisions provided to developers of low to moderate multifamily development.
4) Housing Development Action Grants: financing for multifamily housing developments.
5) ACCESS Program: qualified individuals receive a reduced rate 30 year mortgage or qualify for additional financing for up to 3.0 percent of their total mortgage loan applied towards their downpayment and closing costs.
6) HOME Assistance Program: assistance when purchasing a home for qualified individuals.
7) Builder's Program: provides take out financing of new construction or substantial rehabilitation of single-family homes made available to low and moderate income families.

Maine

Maine State Housing Authority
P.O. Box 2669
353 Water St.
Augusta, ME 04338-2669
207-626-4600
800-452-4668

1) Statewide Housing Acquisition/Rehabilitation Program (SHARP): loans to purchase and rehabilitate small (3 to 20 units) rental housing developments.
2) Fix-Me Program: low interest loans for home improvements for very low income homeowners.
3) Production Incentive Demonstration Program: financial incentive for the formation of Community Housing Development Organizations (CHDOs) and their involvement in affordable housing.
4) Home Purchase Program: low downpayment and low rate financing for first-time income-eligible home buyers.
5) Purchase Plus Improvement: home improvement loans for borrowers in the Home Purchase or Home Start programs.
6) Underground Oil Storage Tank Removal Program: grants or interest-free loans to property owners for removal and disposal of environmentally hazardous underground oil storage tanks and pipes and installation of replacements.
7) Home Equity Conversion Mortgage: supplies elderly homeowners with cash for some of the equity in their homes.
8) Home Improvement Program: low rate home improvement loans.
9) Rental Loan Program: below market rate loans for new or rehabilitated rental housing affordable to low/moderate income households.
10) Rental Rehabilitation Program: low interest deferred payment loans to repair substandard apartments.
11) Consumer Residential Opportunity Program: low rate loans for housing the mentally ill.
12) Land Acquisition Program: low rate deferred payment loans to nonprofit housing corporations to buy land for affordable housing.
13) Homeless Shelter Assistance: funding to operate or improve shelters.
14) Supportive Housing Initiative Program (SHIP): low rate, no/low down payment loans for nonprofit organizations developing housing for special needs households.
15) Low Income Housing Tax Credit: tax credits to developers of housing for low income households.
16) Section 8 New Construction: rent subsidies for low income households.
17) Section 8 Moderate Rehabilitation: rent subsidies for low income households in rehabilitated rental units.
18) Section 8 Certificates and Vouchers: rental assistance for low income tenants.
19) Low Income Heating Assistance Program: offers assistance to fuel vendors to provide heating for low income homeowners and renters.
20) Weatherization Assistance: provides energy assistance for low income homeowners.

Maryland

Department of Housing and Community Development
100 Community Place
Crownsville, MD 21032-2023
410-514-7500
800-492-7127

1) Rental Housing Production Program: loans to developers or nonprofit organizations to cover the costs of construction, rehabilitation, acquisition or related development costs through interest rate writedowns or rent subsidies.
2) Mortgage Program: below-market interest rate mortgage financing for low and moderate income home buyers.
3) Home and Energy Loan Program: below-market interest rate loans for home and energy conservation improvements for single-family homes.
4) Multifamily Home and Energy Loan Program: rehabilitation and energy conservation loans for multifamily rental projects and single scattered-site rental properties.
5) Housing Rehabilitation Program: loans to limited income homeowners, owners of multi-unit residential buildings and owners of small nonresidential properties.
6) Group Home Financing Program: low interest, no interest deferred payment loans to nonprofit organizations to purchase and modify housing for use as group homes and shelters.
7) Residential Lead Paint Abatement Program: loans to finance the abatement of lead paint in rental properties.
8) Elderly Rental Housing Program: new construction financing for rental housing for elderly citizens.
9) Rental Allowance Program: subsidies to very low income individuals with emergency needs.
10) Emergency Mortgage Assistance: assists homeowners in imminent danger of losing homes to foreclosure after loss of income due to critical circumstances.
11) Reverse Equity Program: enables low income elderly to access home equity to pay housing and other expenses that facilitate continued occupancy.
12) Settlement Expense Loan Program: low rate loans up to $5000 toward settlement expenses for low/moderate income home buyers.
13) Multifamily Bond Program: below-market financing for low income multifamily rental housing development.
14) Nonprofit Rehabilitation Program: low rate loans to nonprofit organizations to rehabilitate low income rental housing.
15) Partnership Rental Housing Program: loans for local governments and housing authorities for development or acquisition of low income rental housing.
16) Construction Loan Program: low rate financing for development of affordable single-family or multifamily housing.
17) Preferred Interest Rate Loan Program: offers preferred rates for those who qualify.
18) Housing Rehabilitation Program-Single Family: low rate financing for rehabilitation of small residential properties for low income households.
19) Accessory, Shared and Sheltered Housing Program: low rate loans to finance additions and improvements to create accessory, shared or sheltered housing for low income households.
20) Indoor Plumbing Program: low rate loans to provide indoor plumbing.
21) Energy Bank Program: matching funds to low income homeowners for energy conservation improvements.
22) Section 8 Existing Voucher Program: rent subsidies for low income households.
23) Moderate Rehabilitation Program: incentives to property owners for improvements to deteriorating housing units to be rented to households eligible for rent subsidies.

State Money for Housing and Real Estate

24) Rental Rehabilitation Program: rehab funds for property owners renting to low income households.
25) Low Income Housing Tax Credit Program: federal tax credits to owners of low income rental housing.
26) Transitional Housing and Emergency Shelter Program: provides grants to improve or create transitional housing and emergency shelters.

Massachusetts

Massachusetts Housing Finance Agency
One Beacon St.   617-854-1000
Boston, MA 02190   TDD: 617-854-1025

1) Real Estate-Owned Program: offers assistance to both lenders and borrowers.
2) General Lending: special loans for Vietnam Era Veterans, low income and minority borrowers and physically handicapped.
3) Neighborhood Rehabilitation Programs: funds for people who buy and/or rehabilitate homes in locally designated neighborhoods.
4) New Construction Set-Aside: funds for purchasers of new homes and condominiums built by specific developers.
5) Home Improvement Program: loans for owner-occupied, one- to four-family homes.
6) State Housing Assistance for Rental Productions (SHARP): interest rate subsidies to developers for production of rental housing where at least 25% are available to low income households.
7) Project TAP (Tenant Assistance Program): training for project residents for drug- and alcohol-related problems.
8) Low Income Housing Tax Credit Program: federal tax credits for owners of low income rental housing.
9) Elder Choice Program: fills the gap between independent living and a nursing home by providing a home-like setting coupled with on-site services that support the needs of frail elderly persons.
10) Mortgage Credit Certificate Program: federal tax credits for eligible first-time home buyers.
11) Mortgage Insurance Program: lower premium private mortgage insurance available to HOP- and MHFA-assisted borrowers.
12) Rental Acquisition Development Initiative: low rate financing for developers of rental properties with units affordable to low income households.
13) Supportive Services in Elderly Housing: assists elderly residents in avoiding premature placement in nursing homes by delivering affordable homemaking, health care, and other services.
14) Acquisition Set-Aside Program: allows builders to offer lower interest mortgages to eligible home buyers as a sales incentive in return for reducing cost of units.
15) Reverse Equity Mortgage Program (REM): a pilot program that allows senior citizens to use a portion of their home equity to cover expenses and meet basic needs without having to sell their homes.
16) Home Advantage Program: provides low interest rate mortgages to buyers of discounted Fannie Mae properties.
17) Get the Lead Out Program: provides loans of up to $15,000 -- some at zero percent interest for borrowers under court order to delead.

Executive Office of Communities and Development
Commonwealth of Massachusetts
100 Cambridge St., Room 1804
Boston, MA 02202   617-727-7765

1) Section 8 Certificate/Voucher Programs: rent subsidies for low income households.
2) Rental Voucher Program: rent subsidies similar to Section 8 Certificate Program.
3) Mc Kinney Emergency Community Services Homeless Grant: helps homeless individuals and those at risk of becoming homeless through eviction or foreclosure.
4) Low Income Home Energy Assistance: provides help with home heating costs for low income, elderly and handicapped clients.
5) Low Income Weatherization Assistance: funds for weatherization improvements in units occupied by low income persons.
6) Indian Affairs and Assistance: provides a broad spectrum of services to Native Americans.
7) Community Service Block Grant: provides funds for designated community action agencies to enhance the quality of life among the poor.
8) HOME: produces affordable housing units for rent or purchase by low or moderate income households.
9) Elderly Low Income Housing: provides housing for the low income elderly as well as individuals with disabilities.

Michigan

Michigan State Housing Development Authority
Plaza One, Fourth Floor
401 South Washington Square   517-373-8370
P.O. Box 30044   800-327-9158
Lansing, MI 48909   TDD: 800-382-4568

1) Single-Family Home Mortgage: low interest loans for single-family homes and condominiums.
2) Michigan Mortgage Credit Certificates: federal income tax credits that give home buyers more income to qualify for a mortgage.
3) Home and Neighborhood Improvement Loans: home improvement loans for homes over 20 years old at interest rates from 1 to 9 percent.
4) Section 8 Existing Rental Allowance Program: rent subsidies for low income persons who find their own housing in private homes and apartment buildings.
5) Moderate Rehabilitation Loans to Landlords: loans to landlords for rehabilitation of units.
6) 1% Tax Exempt Bond, Family Housing Program: offers developers 1 percent interest rate loans for constructing or rehabilitating rental housing units for families in distressed areas.
7) Housing for the Homeless: grants to organizations to operate shelters for the homeless.
8) Rehabilitation Assistance Program: provides a ten year forgivable loan to very low income families to make improvements on their homes.
9) Low Income Housing Tax Credit Program: federal tax credits for owners/developers of low income rental housing.
10) 70/30 Rental Housing Program: low interest loans to construct or rehabilitate low income rental housing.
11) Contractor's Assistance Program: provides working capital loans to small contractors who have been selected to work on rental housing projects.
12) Community Development Block Grant (Small Cities) Program: for neighborhood revitalization and improvements to infrastructure and rental housing.
13) Comprehensive Neighborhood Rehabilitation Competition: for neighborhood revitalization projects.
14) Emergency Housing Apartment Program (EHAP): pilot project; loans and grants for purchase and renovation of a homeless shelter.
15) Home Improvement Loan Program (HIP/CHIP): low cost home improvement loans.
16) Homeless Children's Fund: funds raised for shelters and transitional housing.
17) HOME Single Family Purchase Program : grants to be used to rehabilitate or construct single family homes.
18) Housing Assistance Program: targeted technical and financial assistance to local governments.
19) 21st Initiative: for neighborhood revitalization of single-family and rental housing.
20) Neighborhood Builders Alliance: targeted technical and financial assistance to local governments and nonprofits.
21) Neighborhood Housing Grant Program: assistance to nonprofits for neighborhood revitalization of single-family and rental housing.
22) Neighborhood Preservation Program (NPP): targeted technical and financial assistance for local governments sponsoring neighborhood infrastructure improvements and building preservation.
23) Pass Through Program: loans for low income rental housing development.
24) Set-Asides for Nonprofits: homebuyer assistance for low income households participating in programs of nonprofit organizations.
25) Special Housing Program: for handicapped group homes and other housing needs of the handicapped.
26) Supported Independent Living Program and Respite Program: for housing needs of the handicapped.
27) Taxable Bond Program: rental housing construction and renovation.
28) Urban Development Initiative: targeted technical assistance to local governments.
29) MSHDA Housing Initiative: low downpayment loans with liberal eligibility requirements; not restricted to first-time buyers.

Minnesota

Minnesota Housing Finance Agency
400 Sibley St.   612-296-9951
St. Paul, MN 55101   612-296-7608
    800-657-3769
    TDD: 612-297-2361

1) Indian Housing Programs: mortgage and home improvement financing for tribal housing as well as homeownership loans at below-market interest rates.
2) Innovative Housing Loan Program: no-interest and low interest loans to develop housing that is innovative in design, construction, marketing and/or financing.
3) Deferred Loan Program: interest-free loans to households with a disabled member.
4) Rental Rehabilitation Program: grants to rental property owners.
5) Rental Rehabilitation Loan Program: low interest loans to rental property owners.
6) Section 8 Housing Assistance: rents subsidies for low income renters.
7) Home Sharing Program: grants to nonprofits who assist elderly in sharing homes.
8) Purchase Plus Program: financing for both purchase and rehabilitation of existing housing for median income or below.
9) Minnesota Mortgage Program: below-market rate loans for low/moderate income first-time home buyers.

Real Estate Ventures

10) Home Ownership Assistance Fund: downpayment and monthly payment assistance to lower income MHFA mortgage recipients.
11) Urban Indian Housing Program: below-market financing for Indians in Duluth, Minneapolis and St. Paul.
12) Urban and Rural Homesteading Program: grants to organizations to acquire and rehabilitate vacant and condemned properties for sale to first-time "at risk" home buyers.
13) Deferred Loan Program: deferred payment loans to assist low income homeowners making home improvements.
14) Great Minnesota Fix-Up Fund: below-market home-improvement loans for low/moderate income credit-worthy homeowners.
15) Home Energy Loan Program: low rate loans for increasing energy-efficiency of homes; no maximum income limits.
16) Low and Moderate Income Program: property improvement loans for low/moderate income households or owners of low/moderate income rental housing in designated areas.
17) Revolving Loan Program: rehabilitation financing for low/moderate income homeowners who don't qualify for other programs.
18) Housing Trust Fund: zero-interest deferred loans for development of low income rental and co-op housing.
19) $1.00 Home Set-Aside Program: HUD lease program for nonprofit use of repossessed HUD homes to house the homeless.
20) Intermediate Care Facilities for the Developmentally Disabled: below-market financing for nonprofit sponsors to develop residential facilities for the developmentally disabled.
21) Low Income Housing Tax Credit Program: federal tax credit for owners of low income rental housing.
22) Affordable Rental Investment Fund: zero-interest deferred loans to rehabilitate small family low income rental housing.
23) Low Income Large Family Rental Housing Program: financing for construction of large rental units for low income families.
24) HOME Disaster Grant Program: provides grants to low income households for housing improvements due to weather related damages.
25) New Construction Tax Credit Mortgage/Bridge Loan Program: for construction/rehabilitation of rental units for low income households.

Mississippi

Mississippi Home Corporation
840 River Place, Suite 605
Jackson, MS 39201   601-354-6062

1) Mortgage Certificate Program: low rate financing for income-eligible first-time home buyers.
2) Low Income Housing Tax Credit Program: tax credits for owners of low income rental housing.
3) Downpayment Assistance Program: for buyers who can afford mortgage payments but not a downpayment.
4) Rental Rehabilitation Program: (under development).
5) Energy Conservation Revolving Loan Fund: (under development).

Missouri

Missouri Housing Development Commission
3770 Broadway   816-756-3790
Kansas City, MO 64111   TDD: 816-756-2744

1) Multifamily Program: low interest rate mortgages to developers of multifamily developments.
2) Single-Family Down Payment Assistance Program: below-market interest rate mortgages for first-time home buyers.
3) Neighborhood Loan Program: loans to neighborhood organizations and/or developers for acquiring and rehabilitating residential properties.
4) Home Improvements/Weatherization Loan Program: low interest loans to assist qualified homeowners in home improvements that will increase energy efficiency.
5) Affordable Housing Production Program: low interest rates to developers to stimulate production of housing for low and moderate income families and individuals.
6) RTC Home Purchase Program: low rate financing to purchase reduced cost housing.
7) HUD Repo Properties: HUD-insured low rate loans for low income households to purchase HUD-foreclosed properties.
8) Low Income Housing Tax Credit Program: tax credits for owners of low income rental housing.
9) Section 8 Programs: subsidies and financial assistance for low income tenants.
10) Operation Homeless: provides homeless households with Section 8 certificates or vouchers to secure affordable subsidized rental housing.
11) Housing Trust Fund Program: non-Section 8 rental assistance payments for low income households.
12) Housing Inventory Recycling Program: funds to facilitate purchase of foreclosed homes by lower income households.
13) FmHA Supplemental Subsidy Program: rent subsidies for low income elderly in FmHA housing projects.
14) Missouri Low Income Housing Tax Credit Program: supplements the federal Low Income Housing Tax Credit Program.
15) Risk Sharing Program: designed to produce and preserve affordable multifamily rental housing.
16) HANDS Program: provides low interest loans to officers who relocate to targeted city neighborhoods.
17) Mortgage Credit Certificate Program: certificates for home mortgage loans for low and moderate income homebuyers.
16) Equity Fund: capital for construction or renovation of housing units for lower income families.
17) Unusual Need Loan Program: designed to produce affordable rental units.
18) HOME Rental Housing Program: provides financing for the acquisition and rehabilitation of housing for low and moderate income families.
19) Flood Recovery Programs: assistance for those who wish to relocate from the flood plain.
20) Bridge Loan Program: encourages and facilitates low income housing.
21) Single Family Mortgage Revenue Bond Program: mortgage financing at interest rates below conventional market rates.

Montana

Montana Board of Housing
2001 Eleventh Ave.
Helena, MT 59620   406-444-3040

1) Single-Family Programs: low interest loans to low income families.
2) Multifamily Program: construction loans to developers of multifamily units for persons and families of lower income.
3) Homebuyers Cash Assistance Program: assist those credit worthy persons lacking the financial assistance to purchase a home under any other program.
4) Low Income Housing Tax Credit Program: federal tax credits for owners of low income housing.
5) Reverse Annuity Mortgage Loans: home-equity loans for senior 68+ homeowners.
6) Recycled Mortgage Purchase Program: assists lower income households who cannot purchase homes through the Single-Family Mortgage Program; grant funds help lower construction costs for developers, reduce home prices, create low interest loans, and assist with downpayments and closing costs.
7) Disabled Accessible Affordable Homeownership Program: assists people with disabilities to acquire affordable architecturally accessible homes enabling them to live independently.

Nebraska

Nebraska Investment Finance Authority
1033 O St., Suite 218
Lincoln, NE 68508   402-434-3900

1) Single-Family Mortgage Program: low cost loans for single family homes, townhomes, condominiums, mobile homes, and up to 4-unit dwellings.
2) Tax Credit Program: attractive interest rates for developers of rental housing for low and moderate income households.
3) Agricultural Finance Programs:
First-Time Farmer Loan: loans to purchase agricultural real estate.
FmHA: loans to refinance existing agricultural loans.
4) Low Income Housing Tax Credit Program: federal tax credits for owners of low income housing.

Nevada

Department of Commerce
Housing Division
1802 N. Carson St., Suite 154
Carson City, NV 89710   702-687-4258

1) Single Family Mortgage Purchase Program: loans to moderate income families with no previous home ownership interest within the last 3 years.
2) Industrial Development Bonds: low financing costs for new construction or expansion manufacturing projects.
3) Rural Area Housing Program: low interest mortgage loans to developers to develop affordable rental units outside metropolitan areas.

Nevada Rural Housing Authority
2100 California St.
Carson City, NV 89701   702-687-5747

New Hampshire

Housing Finance Authority
P.O. Box 5087   603-472-8623
Manchester, NH 03108   800-640-7239

State Money for Housing and Real Estate

1) Housing Expense Loan Program (HELP): provides limited financial assistance to eligible borrowers to enable them to meet a portion of the downpayment and closing costs of a single family home.
2) Single-Family Mortgage Program: low interest mortgage funds to qualifying individuals and households.
3) Multifamily Housing Program: construction loans for small rental projects for private for profit developers and nonprofit organizations.
4) Borrower Assistance Program: provides assistance to selected borrowers on the Authority's Single Family Mortgage Program who are delinquent in mortgage payments due to unexpected financial problems.
5) Affordable Housing Fund: financing primarily for nonprofit or co-op multifamily projects.
6) HOPE 3 Program: for borrowers who can afford mortgage payments but lack downpayment and closing costs.
7) Home Equity Conversion Program: loans to help seniors meet living and medical expenses while retaining ownership and residence in their own homes.
8) Section 8 Housing Programs: rental assistance for low income households.
9) Low Income Housing Tax Credit Program: tax credits for owners of low income rental housing.
10) Supportive Services Program: funding for seniors to receive services they need to remain independent.
11) Home of Your Own Program: provides homeownership opportunities for developmentally disabled people.
12) Housing Preservation Grant Program: provides funds for rehabilitation of low income, owner occupied housing in rural ares of the state.
13) HOME Rental Housing Production Program: provides funds to support the development of rental housing opportunities for low and very low income households.
14) Affordable Home Ownership Program: financing for developers of single family homes to be sold at below market cost.
15) Direct Acquisition Program: develop low income multifamily housing opportunities using existing stock.
16) Affordable Housing Fund: funds are used for the acquisition, development and preservation of low income housing.
17) Emergency Assistance Fund: funds used to correct problems which threaten the livability of property.

New Jersey

New Jersey Housing Agency
3625 Quakerbridge Rd. 609-890-8900
Trenton, NJ 08650-2085 800-NJ-HOUSE

1) Home Buyers Program: low interest loans to urban area first-time buyers with a 5% downpayment.
2) Seed Money Loan Program: funding of pre-development costs for nonprofits seeking to develop affordable housing.
3) Continuing Care Retirement Communities: construction loans and lower than market mortgage interest rates for residential communities for senior citizens.
4) Home Buyers Program: low rate financing and low downpayments for income-eligible first-time home buyers or home buyers in 41 targeted urban areas.
5) Home Buyers 100% Financing Program: for low/moderate income first-time or urban buyers.
6) Home Ownership for Performing Employees (HOPE) Program: financial assistance from sponsoring employers to reduce downpayment, closing costs and monthly payments for their employees.
7) Development Set-Aside Program: mortgage funding for purchasers of housing units in Agency-approved housing developments.
8) Multifamily Rental Housing Program: low rate financing for developers of rental housing for low/moderate income households.
9) Low Income Housing Tax Credit Program: federal tax credits for owners of low income rental housing.
10) Revolving Loan Program: financing for the production of small and medium-sized rental housing projects with units affordable to low income households.
11) Services for Independent Living Program: support services that enable senior citizens in Agency-financed housing to avoid institutionalization.
12) Boarding House Life Safety Improvement Loan Program: low rate loans to finance safety improvements in boarding homes.
13) Transitional Housing Program: financing for the construction of transitional housing for the homeless.

New Mexico

Mortgage Finance Division
P.O. Box 2047 505-843-6880
Albuquerque, NM 87103 800-444-6880

1) Mortgage Saver Program: below-market loans to first-time home buyers.
2) Multifamily Programs: financing of multifamily housing for low and moderate income tenants.

New Mexico State Housing Division
1100 St. Francis Dr.
Santa Fe, NM 87503 505-827-7124

1) Low Income Housing Tax Credit Program: federal tax credits for owners of low income rental housing.
2) State Housing Rehabilitation Program: rehabilitation grants for low income elderly, handicapped and disabled homeowners.
3) Section 8 Housing Assistance Payments Program (Voucher): rent subsidies for low income households who locate their own housing.
4) HUD Rental Rehabilitation Program: grants to rehabilitate sub-standard rental units for rental to low income tenants qualifying for rent subsidies.
5) HOME Program: expands the supply of affordable housing for low income families.

New York

State of New York
Executive Department
Division of Housing and Community Renewal
One Fordham Plaza
Bronx, NY 10458 718-563-5700

1) Special Needs Housing Program: grants to nonprofit sponsors for single room occupancy dwellings units for low income individuals.
2) Low Income Housing Trust Fund: funds to nonprofit sponsors to rehabilitate existing properties into affordable low income housing.
3) Housing Development Fund: temporary financing to nonprofit sponsors developing housing with private or government-aided mortgages
4) Rental Rehabilitation Program: up to $8,500 per unit to subsidize up to 50% of the cost of moderate rehabilitation of residential units in lower income neighborhoods.
5) Rural Preservation Program: funds to local not-for-profit organizations engaging in a variety of activities for the benefit of low and moderate income persons.
6) Rural Rental Assistance Program: monthly rent subsidy payments to owners of multifamily projects on behalf of low income tenants.
7) Turn Key/Enhanced Housing Trust Fund: financing for developers of low income rental housing.
8) Infrastructure Development Demonstration Program: grant funds for infrastructure improvements (water lines, roads, sidewalks, utility lines) that serve affordable housing projects.
9) Urban Initiative Program: funding for community preservation and improvement in designated urban areas.
10) Rural Area Revitalization Program: funding for not-for-profit organizations to make housing improvements in designated areas.
11) Housing Opportunities Program for the Elderly-RESTORE: funds for not-for-profit organizations to make emergency home repairs for elderly homeowners.
12) Shared Housing Development Program: funding for boarding houses, accessory apartments and "granny flats" in designated areas.
13) Clinton Preservation Program: financing to preserve and improve the Clinton neighborhood in NYC.
14) Low Income Housing Tax Credit Program: federal tax credits for owners of low income housing rental.
15) Neighborhood Preservation Program: funding to defray administrative costs of not-for-profit organizations performing neighborhood preservation activities.
16) Rural Home Ownership Assistance Program: funds to defray administrative costs of not-for-profit organizations assisting low income households in the acquisition, financing, and rehabilitation of affordable housing.
17) Neighborhood Redevelopment Demonstration Program: funds for planning, administration and project costs for activities that promote affordable housing or improve neighborhoods.
18) Section 8 Moderate Rehabilitation Program: incentives for property owners to upgrade substandard rental housing for tenants qualifying for rent subsidies.
19) Section 8 Existing Housing Program: rent subsidies for low income households.
20) Senior Citizen Rent Increase Exemption: exemption from rent increases for tenants 62 years of age or older who live in rent-controlled apartments in NYC and 15 other areas; landlords are compensated with certificates to pay real estate taxes or to convert to cash.
21) HOME Program: provides funds for a variety of housing needs for low income families.

New York State Housing Authority
250 Broadway
New York, NY 10007 212-306-3000

North Carolina

North Carolina Housing Finance Agency
P.O. Box 28066
Raleigh, NC 27611-8066 919-781-6115

Real Estate Ventures

1) Single-Family Mortgage Loan Program: below-market, fixed-rate loans for first-time home buyers with low/moderate income.
2) Builder Bonus Program: improves the affordability of new single family homes in nonmetropolitan counties.
3) Catalyst Home Ownership Program: encourages nonprofit organizations to develop new single family homes by providing loans and grants.
4) Mortgage Credit Certificate Program: tax-credit for first-time home buyers paying mortgage interest.
5) Home Ownership Challenge Fund: funding to nonprofits that create home ownership opportunities for low income households.
6) Maxwell/Fuller Self-Help Housing Program: zero-interest loans to nonprofits managing self-help or owner-built housing projects for low income households.
7) Multifamily Loan Program: below-market financing for developers of low/moderate income rental housing.
8) Multifamily Subsidized Program: rent subsidies for low income tenants.
9) Low Income Housing Tax Credit Program: federal tax credits for owners of low income housing.
10) Catalyst Loan Program: funding for nonprofits for front-end costs in the development of low income rental housing.
11) Housing Rehabilitation Program: rehabilitation funds for privately-owned rental housing for low income households.
12) HOME Program: provides federal funds for developing affordable housing for very low, low and moderate income households.
13) Housing Production Program: financing for new or rehabilitated housing for low income households.
14) Housing LINC Loan Fund: revolving loan fund to pay predevelopment costs for assisted living projects for the elderly.
15) Resolution Trust Corporation Clearinghouse: property information for purchasers, allowing qualified purchasers right of first refusal for single family and multifamily properties affordable to low/moderate income households.
16) Multifamily Unsubsidized Loan Program: provides mortgage financing at a lower interest rate.
17) Security and Utility Deposit Loan Program: provides loans and guarantees for security and utility deposits to help people move from homeless shelters and transitional housing into permanent housing.

North Dakota
Housing Finance Agency
P.O. Box 1535
Bismarck, ND 58502   701-328-3434

1) Housing Assistance: rental assistance program for low income renter households and mobile home space renters.
2) Single Family Program: low interest loans for low to moderate income first time home buyers.
3) Housing Assistance Program: certificates and vouchers to assist low income tenants with rent payments.
4) Moderate Rehabilitation Program: incentives for rehabilitation of substandard housing for rental to low income tenants qualifying for rent-subsidies.
5) Low Income Housing Tax Credit Program: federal tax credits for owners of low income rental housing.

Ohio
Ohio Housing Finance Agency
775 High St., 26th Floor
Columbus, OH 43266   614-466-0400

1) Seed Money Loan Program: no-interest loans to nonprofit, public and limited profit entities to arrange financing for low and moderate income rental housing developments.
2) First-Time Homebuyer Program: below-market financing for first-time home buyers.
3) Home Ownership Incentive Programs: low interest rates and downpayments for nonprofit developers of housing to meet special needs (single parents, minorities, disabled, rural, inner city).
4) Development Loan Program: financing for construction and development costs of low/moderate income housing by nonprofit and limited profit sponsors.
5) Low Income Housing Tax Credit Program: federal tax credits for owners of low income rental housing.
6) 403 Rental Housing Gap Financing Program: financial assistance to nonprofit organizations for development of low income rental housing.
7) Rental Housing Energy Conservation Program: funds to nonprofits for energy-efficient rehabilitation or new construction of low income rental housing.
8) Multifamily Rental Development Program: financing for purchase, construction, and rehabilitation of multifamily rental housing for the elderly.
9) Section 8 Rental Assistance Program: rent subsidies.
10) Downpayment Assistance Program: offers up to $2,500 in downpayment assistance for eligible homebuyers to purchase homes.

Oklahoma
Oklahoma Housing Finance Agency
P.O. Box 26720   405-848-1144
Oklahoma City, OK 73126-0720   800-256-1489

1) Single-Family Mortgage Revenue Bond Program: low rate loans to first-time home buyers.
2) Multifamily Mortgage Revenue Bond Program: funds for the purchase, construction or rehabilitation of housing for low/moderate income families.
3) Homeless Program: support for homeless families while they await funds for housing.
4) Section 8 Existing Housing Assistance Program: rent subsidies for low income tenants.
5) Section 8 Rental Rehabilitation Program: matching funds for property owners who renovate rental units for low/moderate income households.
6) Section 8 Voucher Assistance Program: rent subsidies for low income households who locate their own housing.

Oregon
Oregon Housing Agency
Housing Division
1600 State St., Suite 100
Salem, OR 97310   503-986-2000

1) Elderly and Disabled Housing Program: below-market interest rate mortgage loans for multifamily housing for elderly and disabled.
2) Family Rental Housing Program: financing for multi-unit rental housing for low income families.
3) Seed Money Advance Program: no-interest advances to nonprofits to cover pre-construction costs.
4) Low Income Housing Tax Credit: federal income tax credits to developers who construct, rehabilitate, or acquire qualified low income rental housing.
5) Single-Family Mortgage Program: below-market interest rate loans to low and moderate income Oregon home buyers.
6) Mortgage Credit Certificate Program: federal tax credit for low and moderate income Oregonians to purchase, improve or rehabilitate a single-family residence.
7) Oregon Lenders' Tax Credit Program: very low interest loans to nonprofits from qualified Oregon financial institutions for low income multifamily housing.
8) Low Income Rental Housing Fund: rental assistance for low income families.
9) Mobile Home Park Purchase Program: financial and technical assistance for tenants' associations to purchase their mobile home parks.
10) Partnership Housing Team: technical assistance to local governments and nonprofits developing low income housing.
11) Community Development Corporation Program: grants and technical assistance for local community development corporations to increase their skills in establishing low income housing.

Pennsylvania
Pennsylvania Housing Finance Agency
2101 North Front St.
Harrisburg, PA 17105   717-780-3800

1) Homeowners Emergency Mortgage Assistance Program: loans to keep delinquent homeowners from losing their homes to foreclosure.
2) PennHOMES Program: provides interim and permanent mortgage financing to developers of low income rental housing.
3) Lower Income Home Ownership Program: provides mortgage loans to low income first time homebuyers who meet income and home purchase price guidelines.
4) Rental Housing Tax Credit Program: federal income tax credits to developers of affordable rental housing.
5) Statewide Home Ownership Program: low interest financing for first-time home buyers or buyers of property in targeted areas.
6) Pennsylvania HomePlus Program: allows Pennsylvanians who are 62 or older to "convert" the equity in their property into cash.
7) Closing Cost Assistance Program: pays up to $2,000 toward closing costs for houses that are bought by participants in the Lower Income Home Ownership Program, qualified participants must have dependent children or be disabled.
8) Supportive Services Program: to help elderly residents of subsidized senior citizen rental apartments meet routine needs that enable them to remain in their own homes.

Rhode Island
Rhode Island Housing and Mortgage Finance Corporation
60 Eddy St.   401-751-5566
Providence, RI 02903   800-427-5560
        TDD: 401-421-9799

1) Home Repair: fixed rate-loans to make needed repairs on 1 to 6 unit dwellings owned or occupied by low and moderate income persons.
2) Rental Housing Production Program: tax-exempt and/or taxable bond financing for developers for projects where a minimum of 20% of the units are rented to low income tenants.

State Money for Housing and Real Estate

3) First Homes Program: low rate mortgages for income-eligible first-time home buyers.
4) Down Payment Assistance: down payment and closing cost assistance to lower income first time home buyers.
5) Energy-Efficient Homes Program: additional assistance to FIRST HOMES mortgagees if their home receives a high energy-efficiency rating.
6) HOME Program: grants and low interest loans to encourage the construction or rehabilitation of affordable housing.
7) Home Equity Conversion Mortgage Program: reverse mortgages to enable older homeowners to remain in and retain ownership of their homes.
8) Access Independence Program: provides low interest financing to cover the cost of modifying a home for persons with age or disability related permanent functional limitations.
9) Mortgage Credit Certificates: tax credit for first-time home buyers.
10) Construction Loan Program: below market rate loans to build/rehab affordable 1-4 family homes for low/moderate income persons.
11) Cooperative Housing Demonstration Program: funding packages for nonprofit organizations to develop cooperative housing.
12) Land Bank Program: below market rate loans for purchase or refinancing of undeveloped land to be used for low/moderate income housing.
13) Housing Equity Pool I and II: funds to purchase Low Income Housing Tax Credits and from developers of affordable rental housing.
14) Low Income Housing Tax Credit Program: tax credits for owners of rental housing for low income households.
15) Pre-Development Loan Program: short-term loans to cover pre-development costs for nonprofit developers.
16) Preservation Loan Fund: below-market rate loans to preserve affordability of existing subsidized rental housing.
17) Emergency Housing Assistance Program: assistance to qualified low income households facing a temporary housing crisis.
18) Employer Assisted Housing: employer resources combine with existing programs to provide affordable housing for employees.
19) Opening Doors: pilot program to assist the minority community with buying their first home.
20) Extra assistance: Lower income buyers may be eligible for deferred payment second mortgages of up to 10 percent of the purchase price of the home they buy.

South Carolina

South Carolina State Housing Finance and Development Authority
919 Bluff Rd.
Columbia, SC 29201   803-734-2000

1) Multifamily Development Programs: construction loans to construct houses for rental to low and moderate to low income persons.
2) Moderate Rehabilitation Program: mortgage financing for the upgrade of substandard rental housing.
3) Home Ownership Mortgage Purchase Program: below market rate financing for income-eligible home buyers.
4) Community Home Ownership Opportunity Partnership (CHOP): below market rate financing for purchase of affordable homes by qualified borrowers in conjunction with local communities' contributions.
5) Low Income Housing Tax Credit Program: tax credits for developers of low income rental housing.
6) Section 8 Certificates and Vouchers: rental assistance for low income households.
7) Section 8 Moderate Rehabilitation Program: rent subsidies for low income households.
9) HOME Program: affords state and local governments the flexibility to fund a wide range of low income housing activities.

South Dakota

South Dakota Housing Development Authority
P.O. Box 1237
Pierre, SD 57501   605-773-3181

1) Mortgage Assistance Program: provides down payment and closing cost assistance.
2) Mortgage Assistance Grant Program: provides an interest free second loan of up to $1,000 to assist borrowers with down payment and closing costs.
3) Single Family Homeownership Program: low rate financing for eligible single families to build, rehabilitate or buy homes.
4) Multifamily Bond Financing Program: permanent and temporary mortgage loans to finance the construction of multifamily housing.
5) Low Income Housing Tax Credit Program: federal tax credits for developers/owners of low income housing.
6) Emergency Shelter Grants Program: financing of shelters for homeless and special needs households.
7) HOME Rental Rehab Program: financing for owners of rental properties occupied by low income households.
8) Step Rate Mortgage Program: provides low interest mortgage loans to qualified, first time homebuyers.
9) HOME Programs: designed to encourage creative ways to produce housing for low income families.
10) 100 Cooperative Home Improvement Program: low interest loans for up to seven years for the improvement, repair, or addition to the borrower's home.
11) Sweat Equity Down Payment Program: provides short term sweat equity loans for outside work which cannot be completed during the fall or winter seasons.

Tennessee

Tennessee Housing Development Agency
404 James Robertson Parkway, Suite 1114   615-741-4979
Nashville, TN 37243-0900   TDD: 800-228-THDA

1) Home Ownership Program: reduced interest rate loans to low and moderate income families.
2) Veterans: permanent mortgage financing available for disabled Veterans who need specially designed homes.
3) Rental Rehabilitation: lower than market loans to owners of rental property to rehabilitate units. This program also offers a grant of up to $5000 per unit to keep the cost of rehabilitation down.
4) Owner-Built Homes: permanent financing for homes built by the owners. Sweat equity serves as the downpayment.
5) Turn Key III: subsidized rent to bring economically viable residents into personal home ownership.
6) Section 8 Rental Assistance Program: subsidy funds to low income households.
7) Technical Assistance Program: technical assistance to public and private sponsors of low and moderate income housing.
8) Low Income Housing Tax Credit: tax credits for owners of low income housing.
9) Moderate Rehabilitation Program: incentives for property owners to upgrade substandard rental units to be occupied by low income tenants qualifying for rent subsidies.
10) HOUSE Program: funding for special needs housing projects.

Texas

Texas Department of Housing and Community Affairs
P.O. Box 13941
811 Barton Springs Rd., Suite 100
Austin, TX 78711   512- 475-3800

1) Mortgage Credit Certificate Program: up to $2,000 of federal tax credits for first-time homeowners.
2) Low Income Rental Housing Tax Credit: federal tax credits for those who wish to acquire, construct, or rehabilitate rental housing for low income families.
3) Single-Family Bond Program: low rate financing for low/moderate income first-time home buyers.
4) Section 8 Housing Assistance Program: rental assistance via subsidies for low income households.
5) Multifamily Bond Program: finances below market loans to nonprofit and for profit developers of apartment projects that agree to set aside 20% for rental to low income families.
6) Down Payment Assistance Program: Assists low income families with interest free loans of up to $1,500 to be used for a downpayment on a home purchased through the First Time Homebuyer Program.
7) Home Improvement Loan Program: provides interest free loans of up to $15,000 to low and very low income homeowners for improving or protecting the livability of their residence.
8) Housing Trust Fund: assistance for persons and families of low and very low income in financing, rehabilitating and acquiring safe housing.
9) HOME Program: funds are used to address the state's most critical housing needs which include owner occupied and rental housing rehabilitation and tenant-based assistance.
10) Community Development Block Grant: assists local governments in the development of viable communities.
11) Community Development Fund: provides funds for public facility improvements and housing rehabilitation.
12) Emergency Shelter Grants Program: grants are awarded to counties and nonprofit organizations to assist with the prevention of homelessness, this includes shelters and services.
13) Permanent Housing For Handicapped and Homeless Persons: provides assistance to help establish housing for homeless individuals with mental disabilities or other handicaps.
14) Weatherization Assistance Program: helps low income households make their homes energy efficient.

Utah

Utah Housing Finance Agency
554 South 300 East   801-521-6950
Salt Lake City, UT 84147-0069   800-284-6950
                                   TDD: 801-298-9484

1) Single-Family Home Ownership Program: money to first-time home buyers or home buyers in targeted areas with required downpayment.

Real Estate Ventures

Vermont

Vermont Housing Finance Agency
One Burlington Sq.
P.O. Box 408 802-864-5743
Burlington, VT 05402 800-222-VFHA

1) Mortgage Plus: federal income tax credit for up to 20% of interest on a home loan.
2) Mortgages for Vermonters: low interest mortgages for first-time buyers.
3) Energy-Rated Homes of Vermont Mortgage Program: money to modify homes to make them energy efficient.
4) New Home Financing: low rate financing for qualified borrowers purchasing new homes.
5) Mobile Home Financing: mortgage financing for modular or permanently fixed mobile homes; financing for nonprofit or tenant acquisition of mobile home parks.
6) Perpetually Affordable Housing Program: low rate financing for nonprofit housing developers providing home ownership opportunities that will remain affordable over the long term.
7) Rural Vermont Mortgage: low rate financing for low income households in rural areas.
8) Home Energy/Improvement Loan Program: low rate loans for low/ moderate income homeowners to make energy improvements.
9) Multifamily Financing: financing to eligible housing sponsors who wish to build or renovate low/moderate income rental or cooperative housing.
10) Low Income Housing Tax Credit Program: tax credits for developers/ owners of rental housing for low income households.
11) Vermont Housing Ventures: low rate financing to cover pre-development costs of locally based nonprofit housing.
12) Housing Foundation, Inc.: purchases and preserves housing units threatened with conversion to unsubsidized stock; aids in tenant acquisition of mobile home parks.
13) Housing Vermont: develops affordable housing in partnership with nonprofit organizations throughout the state.
14) Vermont Home Mortgage Guarantee Board (VHMGB): low cost mortgage insurance for low/moderately priced housing.
15) Vermont Housing and Conservation Board: grants and loans to projects which meet both affordable housing and conservation goals.
16) ENABLE Program: low rate loans to finance modifications designed to make housing more accessible for the elderly and disabled.

Vermont State Housing Authority
P.O. Box 397
Montpelier, VT 05601-0397 802-828-3295

Virginia

Virginia Housing Development Authority
601 S. Belvedere St.
Richmond, VA 23220 804-782-1986

1) Home Mortgage Loan Program: below-market loans to eligible home buyers with required downpayment.
2) Virginia Housing Fund: flexible, below-market rate loans for lower income people.
3) Home Rehabilitation Loan Program: loans at 8% interest for 6 months to 8-year terms.
4) Targeted Area Program: below-market loans with low downpayments for purchasers of homes in designated areas.
5) Multifamily Loan Program: below-market loans to developers of low/ moderate price rental housing.
6) Low Income Housing Tax Credit Program: federal tax credits for owners of low income rental housing.
7) Rental Rehabilitation Program: grants for up to 50% of rehab costs for low income rental housing.
8) Section 8 Rent Subsidy Programs: subsidies to assist low income households in meeting rental housing costs.
9) Joint Program for Housing Persons with Mental Disabilities and Recovering Substance Abusers: below-market loans to assist nonprofit sponsors in developing supportive housing facilities.
10) Rental Assistance Programs: provide low and moderate income families and individuals with rents they can afford.
11) FHA Plus Program: assists qualified borrowers who need down payment assistance.

Washington

Washington State Housing Finance Commission
1000 Second Ave., Suite 2700 206-464-7139
Seattle, WA 98104-1046 800-767-4663

1) Streamlined Tax-Exempt Placement (STEP): provides tax-exempt financing to nonprofit and for profit organizations for new construction or purchasing of residential housing.
2) Multifamily Program: financing to developers of multifamily projects where at least 20% or more units will be rented to lower to mid-income persons, the elderly or the handicapped.
3) Low Income Housing Tax Credit Program: federal tax credits to developers/ owners of low income housing.
4) House Key Program: below market rate loans for income-eligible first time home buyers and buyers of residences in targeted areas.
5) Housing for the Elderly Program: tax-exempt financing for group homes, congregate housing, and retirement housing (non-medical).
6) Multifamily Tax Exempt Bond Financing Program: tax exempt financing for developers/owners of multifamily housing with a percentage set aside for low income households; new construction, acquisition and rehabilitation.

West Virginia

West Virginia Housing Development Fund
814 Virginia St., East 304-345-6475
Charleston, WV 25301 800-933-9843

1) Mortgage Credit Certificate Program: federal tax credit for home buyers.
2) Single Family Mortgage Program: financing for single family homes with deferred payment loans to pay downpayment and closing costs.
3) Multifamily Construction Loan Incentive Program: construction financing for sponsors of low income multifamily housing.
4) Building Revitalization/Reutilization Program: funds for rehabilitation of existing downtown residential and commercial buildings.
5) Emergency Shelters Program: financing for construction, rehabilitation, and acquisition of shelters.
6) Community Provider Financing Program: low interest loans to nonprofits for financing the acquisition or construction of health facilities.
7) Home Rehab Program: low cost loans to repair flooded homes.
8) Low Income Housing Tax Credit Program: federal tax credits for developers/ owners of low income multifamily housing.
9) Land Development Program: low rate financing for developers of raw land to support housing developments.
10) Rental Rehab Program: grants for upgrading rental units for low income households.
11) HOME Program: funding for housing for low income families.

Wisconsin

Wisconsin Division of Housing
Department of Administration
101 East Wilson St., 4th Floor
Madison, WI 53702-0001
or
P.O. Box 8944
Madison WI 53708-8944 608-266-0288

1) HOME Program: low interest, fixed rate, 30-year loans.
2) Lease Purchase Program: allows nonprofit organizations to acquire affordable single family housing and lease it to a low income home buyer who will purchase it within three years.
3) DEER Program: money to nonprofits to acquire and rehabilitate older single-family and two-family homes with special emphasis on energy conservation. Restored homes are then sold.
4) Rental Housing Programs: financing of rental housing for low and moderate income individuals and families, elderly and disabled.
5) Community Housing Alternatives Program: loans for construction, purchase or rehabilitation of projects to house those who are chronically disabled due to mental illness, development disability, physical disability, or alcohol- or other drug-related dependence, or those over 60 years of age.
6) Rental Rehabilitation Program: money for rehabilitation of rental units for low income households.
7) Low Income Housing Tax Credits: federal tax credits for low income rental housing in Wisconsin.
8) WHEDA Foundation Grants: grants to nonprofit housing project sponsors.
9) Business Development Bond Program: financing for small- and medium-sized businesses.
10) Linked Deposit Loan Program: loans to businesses that are more than 50% owned by women or minorities.
11) Multifamily Mortgage Programs: federally tax exempt and taxable financing for the development of multifamily rental housing.
12) Credit Relief Outreach Program: agricultural related families can receive interest rate reduction and loan guarantees of up to $20,000.
13) Home Improvement Loan Program: below-market financing for low/moderate income homeowners to make eligible home improvements such as energy-conserving improvements.
14) Section 8 Rent Subsidy Program: rent subsidies for low/moderate income rental households.
15) Small Business Loan Guarantee Program: funding necessary to guarantee conventional loans needed by businesses to fulfill awarded contracts.

State Money for Housing and Real Estate

16) Neighborhood Housing Program Fund: supports development and improvement of low income housing and urban and rural neighborhood revitalization.

17) Elderly Housing Program Fund: supports development and improvement of non-institutional housing facilities for frail or low income elderly persons.

18) Wisconsin Partnership for Housing Development: development financing and technical assistance to community-based organizations providing housing to low income households.

Wyoming

Wyoming Community Development Authority
123 S. Durbin St.
P.O. Box 634
Casper, WY 82602   307-265-0603

Funding for single-family homes, multifamily projects, and economic development.

1) Single Family Mortgage Program: low rate financing for first-time home buyers.

2) Section 8 Rental Assistance Program: certificates and vouchers to assist low income rental households.

3) HOME Program: funds for the development of affordable housing for low and very low income households.

4) Urban Homesteading Program: sale of deteriorating government-owned residences to "urban homesteaders" who agree to restore and live in them.

5) WCDA CDBG Revolving Loan Fund: for housing rehabilitation that benefits low/moderate income households.

6) Low Income Tax Credit Program: tax credits for owners of rental housing affordable to low income households.

Venture Capital: Finding A Rich Angel

With federal and state money getting harder to come by, and banks experiencing serious problems of their own that restrict their willingness to loan money, anyone interested in starting his own business or expanding an existing one may do well to look into venture capital. Venture capitalists are willing to invest in a new or growing business venture for a percentage of the equity. Below is a listing of some of the associations, government agencies, and businesses that have information available on venture capital.

In addition, there are Venture Capital Clubs throughout the country where entrepreneurs have a chance to present their ideas to potential investors and learn about the process of finding funds for ventures that might be long on innovative ideas for a business, but short on proven track records.

Associations

The National Venture Capital Association (NVCA)
1655 N. Fort Meyer Dr., Suite 850
Arlington, VA 22209
703-524-2549
Fax: 703-524-3940
www.nvca.org

The association works to improve the government's knowledge and understanding of the venture capital process. Staff members can answer questions about federal legislation and regulations, and provide statistical information on venture capital. NVCA members include venture capital organizations, financiers, and individuals interested in investing in new companies.

The association publishes a membership directory that includes a listing of their members with addresses, phone numbers, tax numbers and contacts. There are currently about 289 members. The directory is available for $99.

The Western Association of Venture Capitalists
3000 San Hill Rd.
Bldg. 1, Suite 190
Menlo Park, CA 94025
650-854-1322

Publishes a directory of its 130 members. The cost is $100.

National Association of Investment Companies
733 15th St. NW, Suite 700
Washington, DC 20005
202-289-4336
Fax: 202-289-4329

It is composed of specialized Small Business Investment Companies (SSBICs). The SSBIC Directory lists about 120 companies across the country including names, addresses, and telephone numbers. It also describes each company's investment preferences and policies. The 23-page publication costs $25.98.

It also publishes *Perspective*, a monthly newsletter geared toward specialized small business investment companies. This newsletter includes articles about legislation and regulations affecting SSBICs. (Note: This association was formerly called the American Association of Minority Enterprise Small Business Investment Companies (AAMESBIC)).

Technology Capital Network at MIT
201 Vassar St.
Cambridge, MA 02139
617-253-7163
Fax: 617-258-7395
www.tcnmit.org

This nonprofit corporation tries to match entrepreneurs in need of capital with venture capital sources. Investors and entrepreneurs register with the network for up to 12 months for $300.

Government Agencies

U.S. Small Business Administration
Investment Division
Washington, DC 20416

This office licenses, regulates, and funds some 350 Small Business Investment Companies (SBICs) nationwide. SBICs supply equity capital, long-term loans and management assistance to qualifying small businesses. They invest in a broad range of industries. Some seek out small businesses with new products or services, other in the field in which their management has special competency.

The office publishes the *Directory of Operating Small Business Investment Companies*, a listing by state of the names, addresses, telephone numbers and investment policies of SBICs. The directory will be sent free of charge by writing to the above address.

The U.S. Small Business Administration (SBA), Office of Business Development has videotapes and publications available on starting and managing a successful small business. For information on business development programs and services call the SBA Small Business Answer Desk at 1-800-827-5722.

Venture Capital Clubs

There are more than 150 Venture Capital Clubs worldwide where inventors can present their ideas to potential investors. At a typical monthly meeting, several entrepreneurs may give short presentations of their ideas. It is a great way for entrepreneurs and potential investors to talk informally.

The International Venture Capital Institute (IVCI)
P.O. Box 1333
Stamford, CT 06904
203-323-3143

The IVCI publishes an annual directory of domestic and international venture groups (venture capital clubs). The cost of the *1995 IVCI Directory of Domestic and International Venture Groups*, which includes contact information for all of the clubs, is $19.95.

Venture Capital Clubs

Below is a partial listing of clubs in the United States.

Alabama
Birmingham Venture Club
Chamber of Commerce
P.O. Box 10127
Birmingham, AL 35202
205-323-5461
Fax: 205-250-7669
www.birminghamchamber.com

Mobile Venture Club
c/o Mobile Area Chamber of Commerce
451 Government St.
Mobile, AL 36652
334-433-6951
Fax: 334-431-8646
www.mobcham.org
Attn: Walter Underwood

Arkansas
Venture Capital Investors
400 W. Capital
Suite 1845
Little Rock, AR 72201
501-372-5900
Fax: 501-372-8181

California
Tech Coast Venture Network
195 S. C St., Suite 250
Tustin, CA 92780
714-505-6493
Fax: 714-669-9341
www.tcvn.org
Attn: Alonzo

Orange Coast Venture Group
P.O. Box 2011
Laguna Hills, CA 92654
949-859-3646
Fax: 949-859-1707
www.ocvg.org
Attn: Gregory Beck

Community Entrepreneurs Organization
P.O. Box 9838
San Rafael, CA 94912
415-435-4461
Attn: Dr. Rick Crandall

San Diego Venture Group
750 B St., Suite 2400
San Diego, CA 92101
619-272-1985
Fax: 619-272-1986
www.sdvgroup.org

Colorado
Rockies Venture Club, Inc.
190 E. 9th Ave.
Suite 440
Denver, CO 80203
303-831-4174
Fax: 303-832-4920
www.rockiesventureclub.org
Attn: Josh

Connecticut
Connecticut Venture Group
1891 Post Rd., Suite F
Fairfield, CT 06430
203-256-5955
Fax: 203-256-9949
www.ct-venture.org

District of Columbia
Baltimore-Washington Venture Group
Michael Dingman Center for Entrepreneurship
College Park, MD 20742-7215
301-405-2144
Fax: 301-314-9152
www.rhsmith.umd.edu/dingman

Florida
Gold Coast Venture Capital Club
22783 S. State Rd. 7, #56
Boca Raton, FL 33428
561-488-4505
Fax: 561-451-4746
www.beaconmgmt.com/gcvcc

Hawaii
Hawaii Venture Group
University of Hawaii, OTTED
2800 Woodlawn Dr., Suite 280
Honolulu, HI 96822
805-533-1400
Fax: 808-524-2775
www.hawaiiventuregroup.com

Idaho
Rocky Mountain Venture Group
2300 N. Yellowstone, Suite E
Idaho Falls, ID 83402
208-526-9557
Fax: 208-526-0953
Attn: Dennis Cheney

Treasure Valley Venture Capital Forum
Idaho Small Business Development Center
Boise State University College of Business
1910 University Dr.
Boise, ID 83725
208-426-1640
Fax: 208-426-3877
www.boisestate.edu/isbdc

Iowa
Iowa City Development
ICAD Group
P.O. Box 2567
Iowa City, IA 52244
319-354-3939
Fax: 319-338-9958
Attn: Marty Kelley

Illinois
Madison Dearborn Partners
70 W. Madison, 8th Floor
Chicago, IL 60602
312-895-1000
Fax: 312-895-1001

Kentucky
Kentucky Investment Capital Network
67 Wilkinson Blvd.
Frankfort, KY 40601
502-564-4300, ext. 4315
Fax: 502-564-9758
www.state.kentucky.us
Attn: Norris Christian

Mountain Ventures Inc.
P.O. Box 1738
London, KY 40743
606-864-5175
Fax: 606-864-5194
www.ezec.gov

Louisiana
Chamber Small Business Hotline
1-800-949-7890

Maryland
Mid Atlantic Venture Association (MAVA)
2345 York Rd.
Timonium, MD 21093
410-560-5855
Fax: 410-560-1910
www.mava.org
Attn: Maryanne Gray

Massachusetts
Venture Capital Fund of New England
160 Federal St., 23rd Floor
Boston, MA 02110
617-439-4646
Fax: 617-439-4652

Michigan
Southeastern Venture Capital
The Meyering Corporation
206 30 Harper Ave.
Suite 103
Harper Woods, MI 48225
313-886-2331
Attn: Carl Meyering

Ann Arbor Chamber of Commerce
425 S. Main St.
Ann Arbor, MI 48104
734-665-4433
www.annarborchamber.org
Attn: Barb Sprague

Minnesota
The Entrepreneurs Network
4555 Erin Dr., Suite 200
Eagan, MN 55122
651-683-9141
Fax: 651-683-0584
www.ens.net

St. Paul Venture Capital
10400 Viking Drive
Suite 550
Bloomington, MN 55444
612-995-7474
Fax: 612-995-7475
www.st.paulvc.com

Missouri
Kansas City Venture Group
10551 Barkley
Suite 400
Overland Park, KS 66212
913-341-8992
Fax: 913-341-8981

Missouri Innovation Center
5650 A S. Sinclair Rd.
Columbia, MO 65203
573-446-3100
Fax: 573-446-3106

Montana
Montana Private Capital Network
7783 Valley View Rd.
Poulson, MT 59860
406-883-5677
Fax: 406-883-5677
Attn: Jon Marchi, President

Venture Capital: Finding A Rich Angel

Nebraska
Grand Island Industrial Foundation
309 W. 2nd St.
P.O. Box 1486
Grand Island, NE 68802-1486
308-382-9210
Fax: 308-382-1154
www.gichamber.com
Attn: Andrew G. Baird, II CED

New Jersey
Venture Association of New Jersey, Inc.
177 Madison Ave., CN 1982
Morristown, NJ 07960
973-631-5680
Fax: 973-984-9634
www.zanj.com
Attn: Amy or Jay Trien

New York
Long Island Venture Group
CW Post Campus
Long Island University
College of Management
Deans Office, Worth Hall
Room 309, North Blvd.
Brookville, NY 11548
516-299-3017
Fax: 516-299-2786
www.liv.edu
Attn: Carol Caracappa

New York Venture Group
605 Madison Ave., Suite 300
New York, NY 10022-1901
212-832-7300
Fax: 212-832-7338
www.nybusiness.com
Attn: Burt Alimansky

Westchester Venture Capital Network
c/o Chamber of Commerce
235 Mamaroneck Ave.
White Plains, NY 10605
914-948-2110
Fax: 914-948-0122
www.westchesterny.org

Rochester Venture Capital Group
100 Corporate Woods
Suite 300
Rochester, NY 14623

Ohio
Greater Columbus Chamber of Commerce
Columbus Investment Interest Group
37 N. High St.
Columbus, OH 43215
614-225-6087
Fax: 614-469-8250
www.columbus.org
Attn: Diane Essex

Ohio Venture Association, Inc.
1120 Chester Ave.
Cleveland, OH 44114
216-566-8884
Fax: 216-696-2582
Attn: Joan McCarthy

Oklahoma
Oklahoma Venture Forum
211 Robinson, Suite 210
P.O. Box 26788
Oklahoma City, OK 73126-0788
405-636-9736
405-270-1050
Fax: 405-416-1035
Attn: Steve Thomas

Oregon
Oregon Entrepreneur Forum
2611 Southwest Third Ave., Suite 200
Portland, OR 97201
503-222-2270
Fax: 503-241-0827
www.oes.org

Portland Venture Group
P.O. Box 2341
Lake Oswego, OR 97035
503-697-5907
Fax: 503-697-5907
Attn: Glen Smith

Pennsylvania
Enterprise Venture Capital Corporation of Pennsylvania
111 Market St.
Johnstown, PA 15901
814-535-7597
Fax: 814-535-8677

South Dakota
Dakota Ventures Inc.
P.O. Box 8194
Rapid City, SD 57709
605-348-8441
Fax: 605-348-8452
Attn. Don Frankenfeld

Texas
Capital Southwest Venture Corporation
12900 Preston Rd., Suite 700
Dallas, TX 75230
972-233-8242
Fax: 972-233-7362
www.capitalsouthwest.com

Utah
Utah Ventures
423 Wakara Way, Suite 306
Salt Lake City, UT 84108
801-583-5922
Fax: 801-583-4105

Vermont
Vermont Venture Network
P.O. Box 5839
Burlington, VT 05402
802-658-7830
Fax: 802-658-0978

Virginia
Richmond Venture Capital Club
c/o 4900 Augusta Ave.
Suite 103
Richmond, VA 23230
804-359-1139
www.ventureclub.com
Attn: Smoky Sizemore

Washington
Northwest Venture Group
P.O. Box 21693
Seattle, WA 98111-3693
425-746-1973

West Virginia
Enterprise Venture Capital Company
P.O. Box 460
Summerville, WV 26651
304-872-3000
Fax: 304-872-3040
Attn: William Bright

Wisconsin
Wisconsin Venture Network
P.O. Box 510103
Milwaukee, WI 53203
414-224-7070
www.maxnetwork.com/wvn
Attn: Paul Sweeny

International Clubs
Puerto Rico Venture Capital Club
P.O. Box 2284
Hato Rey, PR, 00919
1-809-787-9040
Attn: Danol Morales

Johannesburg Venture Capital Club
162 Anderson St.
P.O. Box 261425
EXCOM 2023 RSA
Johannesburg, South Africa, 2001
Attn: Graham Rosenthal

Cape Town Venture Capital Association
c/o Arthur Anderson and Company
12th Floor, Shell House
Capetown, South Africa, 8001
Attn: Colin Hultzer

Canada Clubs
Edmonton Chamber of Commerce
600 10123 99th St.
Edmonton, Alberta Canada, T5J 3G9
780-426-4620
Attn: Ace Cetinski

Venture Capital/Entrepreneurship
Club of Montreal, Inc.
1670 Sherbrooke St.
East Montreal (Quebec) Canada, H2L 1M5
514-526-9490
Attn: Claude Belanger

Venture Capital Clubs

Other groups with information on venture capital include:

The CPA Firm Coopers and Lybrand
1177 Avenue of the Americas   212-596-8000
New York, NY 10020   Fax: 212-596-8910
www.pwc.com

The firm publishes several publications on venture capital including *Venture Capital: The Price of Growth*, 1998, and *Venture Capital Advisory and Survey*, 1996 update. There is no charge for these publications.

Venture Economics, Inc.
22 Thompson Place
Boston, MA 02210   617-345-2504
Attn: Kelly McGow

Publications are available from:
Securities Data Publishing
40 W. 57th St., 11th Floor   212-765-5311
New York, NY 10019   Fax: 212-956-0112
Attn: Esther Miller

Venture Capital Journal, a monthly periodical that cites new issues and trends in venture capital investments. Subscription rate is $1095.

Pratt's Guide to Venture Capital Sources, an annual directory that lists 800 venture capital firms in the U.S. and Canada. It also includes articles recommending ways to raise venture capital. The cost is $385 plus shipping and taxes.

Additional Reading Material

A Venture Capital Primer for Small Business, a U.S. Small Business Administration publication that identifies what venture capital resources are available and explains how to develop a proposal for obtaining these funds ($2). SBA Publications, P.O. Box 30, Denver, CO 80201-0030. Item number FM5.

The Ernst & Young Guide to Financing for Growth. This is part of their entrepreneur series and includes bibliographical references and index. ($14.95) John Wiley & Son, 1 Wiley Dr., Somerset, NJ 08875; 800-225-5945. 1994.

Uncle Sam's Venture Capital

Uncle Sam's Venture Capital

**What Do Federal Express, Apple Computer, Staples and A Porno Shop on 42nd Street All Have In Common?
They All Used Government Venture Money To Get Started**

A few years ago I read that the government provided money to a porno shop in New York City through a program call Small Business Investment Companies (SBIC). Since 1960 these organizations have provided venture capital to over 75,000 businesses, so it's easy to see that one of those businesses might be a porno shop. Porno is a legitimate businesses in many areas of the country.

SBICs are licensed by the U.S. Small Business Administration but are privately owned and operate on a for profit basis. Their license allows companies to pool their money with borrowed money from the government in order to provide financing to small businesses in the form of equity securities or long-term debt. These government subsidized investment companies have helped Compaq, Apple, Federal Express and Staples make it to the big time. They have also helped smaller companies achieve success. They've financed Spencer and Vickie Jacobs' hot tub business in Columbus, Ohio, as well as taxi drivers in New York City who needed money to pay for the medallions which allows them to operate their own cabs.

Uncle Sam's Venture Capital Boom

In 1994, new government regulations were imposed that make it easier to become an SBIC. The budget for this program was also greatly expanded. As a result of this change, there will now be over $6 billion worth of financing available to entrepreneurs over the next several years. Now, that's not small change, even to a hotshot entrepreneur. With these new regulations and budget in place, the government expects that there will soon be 200 additional SBICs waiting to serve American entrepreneurs.

Who Gets The Money?

Basically you have to be a small business to apply for this money, and the government's definition includes companies that have less than $18 million in net worth and less than $6 million in profits. Wow, that's some small business! They seem particularly interested in businesses that offer a new product or service that has a strong growth potential. There is special consideration given to minorities and Vietnam Veterans applying for this money.

You do have to be armed with a business plan which should include the following:
   1) Identify Your Company
   2) Identify Your Product Or Service
   3) Describe Your Product Facilities And Property
   4) Detail Your Marketing Plan
   5) Describe Your Competition
   6) Describe Your Management Team
   7) Provide A Financial Statement

Where to Apply

You can apply to more than one SBIC at the same time. Each acts as an independent company and they can provide money to both local or out-of-state businesses. At the end of this section is a listing of SBA licensed Small Business Investment Companies. However, this list is growing every day so it would be wise to contact the following office to obtain a current list: Associate Administrator for Investment, U.S. Small Business Administration, Washington, DC 20416; 202-205-6510; {www.sba.gov/inv}.

States Have Venture Money, Too

It's not enough to only look at federal venture capital programs, because some state governments also have venture capital programs. More and more states continue to start new programs every month. Some states, like Maryland, see the value in the new rule changes for becoming an SBIC, and are beginning to apply to become a licensed participant of the Small Business Administration's program. Here is what is available from state governments at the time this book went to press. Be sure to check with your state to see what's new:
   1) Arkansas - Seed Capital Investment Program
   2) Connecticut - Risk Capital
      - Product Design Financing
      - Seed Venture Fund
   3) Illinois - Technology Investment Program
      - Illinois Venture Capital Fund
   4) Iowa - Venture Capital Resources Fund
   5) Kansas - Venture Capital and Seed Capital
      - Seed Capital Fund
      - Ad Astra Fund
      - Ad Astra Fund II
   6) Louisiana - Venture Capital Incentive Program
   7) Massachusetts - Venture Capital Program
   8) Michigan - Enterprise Development Fund
      - Onset Seed Fund
      - Diamond Venture Associates
      - Semery Seed Capital Fund
      - Michigan Venture Capital Fund
   9) Montana - Venture, Equity & Risk Capital
   10) New Mexico - Venture Capital Investment Program
   11) New York - Corporation for Innovation Development
   12) North Carolina - North Carolina First Flight Inc.
   13) North Carolina - Seed and Incubator Capital
   14) Pennsylvania - Seed Venture Capital
   15) South Carolina - Venture Capital Funding Program
   16) Tennessee - Venture Capital

Contact your state office of economic development in your state capital for further information on venture capital available in your state (also see the chapter entitled "State Money and Help For Your Business").

Uncle Sam's Venture Capital

Small Business Investment Companies Program Licensees

Alaska
Currently there are no SBIC Program Licensees in Alaska

Alabama
Alabama Capital Corporation SSBIC
David C. DeLaney, President
16 Midtown Park East
Mobile, AL 36606
334-476-0700
Fax: 334-476-0026

FJC Growth Capital Corporation SSBIC
William B. Noojin, Manager
200 Westside Square, Suite 340
Huntsville, AL 35801
256-922-2918
Fax: 256-922-2909

First SBIC of Alabama
David C. DeLaney, President
16 Midtown Park East
Mobile, AL 36606
334-476-0700
Fax: 334-476-0026

Hickory Venture Capital Corporation
J. Thomas Noojin, President
301 Washington St., NW, Suite 100
Huntsville, AL 35801
256-539-1931
Fax: 256-539-5130

Javelin Capital Fund
L.P. Lyle Hohnke & Joan Neuschaler, Partners
2850 Cahaba Road, Suite 240
Birmingham, AL 35223
205-870-4811
Fax: 205-870-4822

TD Javelin Capital Fund II, L.P.
Lyle Honke & Joan Neuschaler, Partners
2850 Cahaba Road, Suite 240
Birmingham, AL 35223
205-870-4811
Fax: 205-870-4822

Arkansas
Small Business Inv. Capital, Inc.
Jerry W. Davis, President
12103 Interstate 30
Mail: P.O. Box 3627
Little Rock, AR 72203
501-455-6599
Fax: 501-455-6556

Arizona
Sundance Venture Partners, L.P.
Brian Burns, General Manager
5030 E. Sunrise Drive, Suite 200
Phoenix, AZ 85044
602-785-0725
Fax: 602-785-0753

Sundance Venture Partners, L.P.
Main Office: Cupertino, CA
Gregory S. Anderson, Vice-President
5030 E. Sunrise Drive, Suite 200
Phoenix, AZ 85044
602-252-3441
Fax: 408-257-8111

Sundance Venture Partners, L.P. II
Gregory Anderson & Brian Burns, Mgrs.
5030 E. Sunrise Drive, Suite 200
Phoenix, AZ 85044
602-252-3441
Fax: 602-252-1450

California
AVI Capital, L.P.
P. Wolken, B. Weinman & B. Grossi, Mgrs.
One First St., Suite 12
Los Altos, CA 94022
650-949-9862
Fax: 650-949-8510

Allied Business Investors, Inc. SPartners
Jack Hong, President
301 W. Valley Blvd., Suite #208
San Gabriel, CA 91776
626-289-0186
Fax: 626-289-2369

Astar Capital Corp. SSBIC
George Hsu, President
9537 E. Gidley St.
Temple City, CA 91780
626-350-1211
Fax: 626-443-5874

Asian American Capital Corporation SSBIC
Jennie Chien, Manager
1251 West Tennyson Road, Suite #4
Hayward, CA 94544
510-887-6888
Fax: 510-887-6897

Aspen Ventures West II, L.P.
Alexander Cilento & David Crocket, Mgrs.
1000 Fremont Ave., Suite V
Los Altos, CA 94024
650-917-5670
Fax: 650-917-5677

Astar Capital Corp. SSBIC
George Hsu, President
9537 E. Gidley St.
Temple City, CA 91780
626-350-1211
Fax: 626-443-5874

BT Capital Partners, Inc.
Main Office: New York, NY
300 South Grand Ave.
Los Angeles, CA 90071

BankAmerica Ventures
Carla Perumean, Senior Vice President
950 Tower Lane, Suite 700
Foster City, CA 94404
415-378-6000
Fax: 415-378-6040

Bay Partners SBIC, L.P.
John Freidenrich & Neal Dempsey, Mgrs.
10600 North De Anza Blvd., Suite 100
Cupertino, CA 95014
408-725-2444
Fax: 408-446-4502

Bentley Capital SSBIC
John Hung, President
592 Vallejo St., Suite #2
San Francisco, CA 94133
415-362-2868
Fax: 415-398-8209

Best Finance Corporation SSBIC
Yong Ho Park, General Manager
3540 Wilshire Blvd., Suite 804
Los Angeles, CA 90010
213-385-7030
Fax: 213-385-7130

Calsafe Capital Corp. SSBIC
Ming-Min Su, President, Director & Mgr.
245 East Main St., Suite 107
Alhambra, CA 91801
626-289-3400
Fax: 626-300-8025

Canaan SBIC, L.P.
Main Office: Rowayton, CT
Eric Young, Manager
2884 Sand Hill Road
Menlo Park, CA 94025
415-854-8082
Fax: 415-854-8127

Capstone Ventures SBIC, L.P.
Barbara Santry & Gene Fischer, Managers
3000 Sand Hill Road
Building 1, Suite 290
Menlo Park, CA 94025
650-854-2523
Fax: 650-854-9010

Charterway Investment Corporation SSBIC
Edmund C. Lau, Chairman
9660 Flair Dr., Suite 328
El Monte, CA 91731
626-279-1189
Fax: 626-279-9062

Critical Capital Growth Fund, L.P.
Steven Sands & Allen Gold, Mgrs.
17 East Sir Francis Drake Blvd., Suite 230
Larkspur, CA 94939
415-464-5720
Fax: 415-464-5701

Draper Associates, a California LP
Timothy C. Draper, President
400 Seaport Court, Suite 250
Redwood City, CA 94063
650-599-9000
Fax: 650-599-9726

Draper-Richards L.P.
William Draper III, President
50 California St., Suite 2925
San Francisco, CA 94111
415-616-4050
Fax: 415-616-4060

Far East Capital Corp. SSBIC
Tom Wang, Manager
977 N. Broadway, Suite 401
Los Angeles, CA 90012
213-687-1361
Fax: 213-626-7497

First American Capital Funding, Inc. SSBIC
Chuoc Vota, President
10840 Warner Ave., Suite 202
Fountain Valley, CA 92708
714-965-7190
Fax: 714-965-7193

Uncle Sam's Venture Capital

Fourteen Hill Capital, L.P.
Bradley Rotter & Alan Perper, Managers
1700 Montgomery St., Suite 250
San Francisco, CA 94111
415-394-9469
Fax: 415-394-9471

Fulcrum Venture Capital Corporation SSBIC
Brian Argrett, President
300 Corporate Pointe, Suite 380
Culver City, CA 90230
310-645-1271
Fax: 310-645-1272

Hall, Morris & Drufva II, L.P.
Ronald J. Hall, Managing Director
26161 La Paz Road, Suite E
Mission Viejo, CA 92691
714-707-5096
Fax: 714-707-5121

Imperial Ventures, Inc.
Christian Hobbs, Vice President
9920 South La Cienega Blvd.
Mail: P.O. Box 92991; L.A. 90009-2991
Inglewood, CA 90009
310-417-5409
Fax: 310-417-5781

Kline Hawkes California SBIC, LP
Frank R. Kline, Manager
11726 San Vicente Blvd., Suite 300
Los Angeles, CA 90049
310-442-4700
Fax: 310-442-4707

LaiLai Capital Corp. SSBIC
Danny Ku, President
223 E. Garvey Ave., Suite 228
Monterey Park, CA 91754
626-288-0704
Fax: 626-288-4101

Magna Pacific Investments SSBIC
David Wong, President
330 North Brand Boulevard, Suite 670
Glendale, CA 91203
818-547-0809
Fax: 818-547-9303

Marwit Capital Company, L.P.
Matthew Witte, President
180 Newport Center Drive, Suite 200
Newport Beach, CA 92660
949-640-6234
Fax: 949-720-8077

New Vista Capital Fund, L.P.
Roger Barry and Frank Greene, Managers
540 Cowper St., Suite 200
Palo Alto, CA 94301
650-329-9333
Fax: 650-328-9434

Novus Ventures, L.P.
Daniel D. Tompkins, Manager
20111 Stevens Creek Blvd., Suite 130
Cupertino, CA 95014
408-252-3900
Fax: 408-252-1713

Opportunity Capital Corporation SSBIC
J. Peter Thompson, President
2201 Walnut Ave., Suite 210
Fremont, CA 94538
510-795-7000
Fax: 510-494-5439

Opportunity Capital Partners II, L.P. SSBIC
J. Peter Thompson, General Partner
2201 Walnut Ave., Suite 210
Fremont, CA 94538
510-795-7000
Fax: 510-494-5439

Pacific Mezzanine Fund, L.P.
Nathan W. Bell, General Partner
2200 Powell St., Suite 1250
Emeryville, CA 94608
510-595-9800
Fax: 510-595-9801

Pinecreek Capital Partners, L.P.
Randall F. Zurbach, President
18301 Von Karman, Suite 100
Irvine, CA 92612
949-225-4620
Fax: 949-225-4629

Positive Enterprises, Inc. SSBIC
Kwok Szeto, President
1489 Webster St., Suite 228
San Francisco, CA 94115
415-885-6600
Fax: 415-928-6363

Red Rock Ventures II
Robert Todd, Jr., Curtis K. Meyers
525 University Ave., Suite 600
Palo Alto, CA 94301
650-325-3111
Fax: 650-321-2902

San Joaquin Business Investment Group Inc. SSBIC
Eugene Waller, President
1900 Mariposa Mall, Suite 100
Fresno, CA 93721
559-233-3580
Fax: 559-233-3709

Selby Venture Partners, L.P.
Robert Marshall & James Marshall, Mgrs.
2460 Sand Hill Road, Suite 200
Menlo Park, CA 94025
650-854-7399
Fax: 650-854-7039

Sorrento Growth Partners I, L.P.
Robert Jaffe, Manager
4370 La Jolla Village Drive, Suite 1040
San Diego, CA 92122
858-452-3100
Fax: 858-452-7607

Sundance Venture Partners, L.P.
Larry Wells, Pres & CEO of GP
100 Clocktower Place, Suite 130
Carmel, CA 93923
831-625-6500
Fax: 831-625-6590

Tangent Growth Fund, L.P.
Alexander H. Schilling, Manager
180 Geary St., Suite 500
San Francisco, CA 94108
415-392-9228
Fax: 415-392-1928

TeleSoft Partners IA L.P.
Arjun Gupta, Manager
1450 Fashion Island Blvd., Suite 610
San Mateo, CA 94404
650-358-2500
Fax: 650-358-2501

UnionBanCal Venture Corporation
Robert S. Clarke, President
445 South Figueroa St.
P.O. Box 3100
Los Angeles, CA 90071
213-236-4092
Fax: 213-629-5328

Viridian Capital, L.P.
Christine Cordaro, Contact
220 Montgomery St., Suite 946
San Francisco, CA 94104
415-391-8950
Fax: 415-391-8937

VK Capital Company
Franklin Van Kasper, General Partner
600 California St., Suite 1700
San Francisco, CA 94108
415-391-5600
Fax: 415-397-2744

Walden-SBIC, L.P.
Arthur S. Berliner, Manager
750 Battery St., 7th Floor
San Francisco, CA 94111
415-391-7225
Fax: 415-391-7262

Western General Capital Corporation SSBIC
Alan Thian, President
13701 Riverside Drive, Suite 610
Sherman Oaks, CA 91423
818-907-8272
Fax: 818-905-9220

Woodside Fund III SBIC, L.P.
Vincent Occhipinti & Frank Mendicino
850 Woodside Drive
Woodside, CA 94062
650-368-5545
Fax: 650-368-2416

Colorado

CapEx L.P.
Jeffrey Ross, Manager
1670 Broadway, Suite 3350
Denver, CO 80202
303-869-4700
Fax: 303-869-4602

Hanifen Imhoff Mezzanine Fund, L.P.
Edward C. Brown, Manager
1125 17th St., Suite 1820
Denver, CO 80202
303-291-5209
Fax: 303-291-5327

Rocky Mountain Mezzanine Fund II
Edward Brown & Paul Lyons, Managers
1125 17th St., Suite 1500
Denver, CO 80202
303-291-5209
Fax: 303-291-5327

Roser Partnership III, SBIC, L.P. The
James Roser and Christopher Roser, Managers
1105 Spruce St.
Boulder, CO 80302
303-443-6436
Fax: 303-443-1885

Wolf Venture Fund III, L.P.
David O. Wolf and Elliott Husney, Managers
50 South Steel St., Suite 777

Denver, CO 80209
303-321-4800
Fax 303-321-4848

Connecticut

AB SBIC, Inc.
275 School House Road
Cheshire, CT 06410
203-272-0203
Fax: 203-250-2954

Canaan SBIC, L.P.
105 Rowayton Ave.
Rowayton, CT 06853
203-855-0400
Fax: 203-854-9117

Capital Resource Co. of Connecticut
Two Bridgewater Road
Farmington, CT 06032
860-677-1113
Fax: 860-677-5414

First New England Capital, LP
100 Pearl St.
Hartford, CT 06103
860-293-3333
Fax: 860-293-3338

Imprimis SB, LP
411 West Putnam Ave.
Greenwich, CT 06830
203-862-7074
Fax: 203-862-7374

Marcon Capital Corp.
1470 Barnum Ave., Suite 301
Bridgeport, CT 06610
203-337-4444
Fax: 203-337-4449

RFE Capital Partners, L.P.
36 Grove St.
New Canaan, CT 06840
203-966-2800
Fax: 203-966-3109

RFE Investment Partners V, L.P.
36 Grove St.
New Canaan, CT 06840
203-966-2800
Fax: 203-966-3109

RFE VI SBIC, L.P.
36 Grove St.
New Canaan, CT 06840
203-966-2800
Fax: 203-966-3109

Delaware

Blue Rock Capital, L.P.
Virginia Bonker & Paul Collison, Mgrs.
5803 Kennett Pike, Suite A
Wilmington, DE 19807-1135
302-426-0981
Fax: 302-426-0982

PNC Capital Corp.
Gary J. Zentner, President
300 Delaware Ave., Suite 304
Wilmington, DE 19801
302-427-5895
Fax: 412-762-6233

District of Columbia

Allied Investment Corporation
Kelly Anderson, Controller
1919 Pennsylvania Ave., NW
Washington, DC 20006-3434
202-973-6328
Fax: 202-331-2434

Broadcast Capital, Inc. SSBIC
John E. Oxendine, President
1700 K St., NW, Suite 405
Washington, DC 20006
202-496-9250
Fax: 202-496-9259

Capitol Health Partners, L.P.
Debora Guthrie, Manager
2620 P St., NW
Washington, DC 20007
202-342-6300
Fax: 202-342-6399

Multimedia Broadcast Investment Corp. SSBIC
Walter L. Threadgill, President
3101 South St., NW
Washington, DC 20007
202-293-1166
Fax: 202-293-1181

Women's Growth Capital Fund, LLLP
Patty Abramson & Rob Stein, Managers
1054 31st St., NW
Washington, DC 20007
202-342-1431
Fax: 202-342-1203

Florida

Capital International
Manuel Iglesias, Contact
One SE Third Ave., Suite 2255
Miami, FL 33131
305-373-6500
Fax: 305-373-6700

Market Capital Corp.
Eugene C. Langford, President
1715 W. Cleveland St.
Tampa, FL 33606
813-251-6055
Fax: 813-251-1900

PMC Investment Corporation SSBIC
Main Office: Dallas, TX
AmeriFirst Bank Building, 2nd Floor S
18301 Biscayne Boulevard N.
Miami Beach, FL 33160
305-933-5858
Fax: 305-931-3054

Western Financial Capital Corporation
Main Office: Dallas, TX
AmeriFirst Bank Building, 2nd Floor S
18301 Biscayne Boulevard N.
Miami Beach, FL 33160
305-933-5858
Fax: 305-931-3054

Georgia

Cordova Enhanced Fund, L.P.
Paul DiBella & Ralph Wright, Managers
2500 North Winds Parkway, Suite 475
Alpharetta, GA 30004
678-942-0300
Fax: 678-942-0301

EGL/NatWest Ventures USA, L.P.
Salvatore Massaro, Manager
6600 Peachtree-Dunwoody Road
300 Embassy Row, Suite 630
Atlanta, GA 30328
770-399-5633
Fax: 770-393-4825

First Growth Capital, Inc. SSBIC
Vijay K. Patel, President
P.O. Box 815
I-75 & GA 42, Best Western Plaza
Forsyth, GA 31029
912-994-9260
Fax: 912-994-1280

Wachovia Capital Associates, Inc.
Matthew J. Sullivan, Managing Director
191 Peachtree St., NE, 26th Floor
Atlanta, GA 30303
404-332-1437
Fax: 404-332-1455

Guam

Currently there are no SBIC Program Licensees in Guam

Hawaii

Pacific Century SBIC, Inc.
Robert Paris, President
130 Merchant St. 12th Floor
Mail: PO Box 2900, Honolulu HI 96846-6000
Honolulu, HI 96813
808-537-8613
Fax: 808-537-8346

Pacific Venture Capital, Ltd. SSBIC
Dexter J. Taniguchi, President
222 South Vineyard St., PH-1
Honolulu, HI 96813
808-521-6502
Fax: 808-521-6541

Idaho

Currently there are no SBIC Program Licensees in Idaho

Illinois

ABN AMRO Capital USA Inc.
Paul Widuch, Chairman
135 South LaSalle St.
Chicago, IL 60674
312-904-6445
Fax: 312-904-6376

BMO Nesbitt Burns Equity Investments
William C. Morro, President
111 West Monroe St., 20th Floor
Chicago, IL 60603
312-461-2021
Fax: 312-765-8000

Chicago Venture Partners, L.P.
John Fife, Manager
360 E. Randolph St., Suite 2402
Chicago, IL 60601
312-228-9000
Fax: 312-819-9701

Continental Illinois Venture Corp.
Christopher J. Perry, President
209 South LaSalle St.

Uncle Sam's Venture Capital

Mail: 231 South LaSalle St.
Chicago, IL 60697
312-828-8023
Fax: 312-987-0887

First Chicago Equity Corporation
David J. Vitale, President
Three First National Plaza, Suite 1330
Chicago, IL 60670
312-895-1000
Fax: 312-895-1001

Heller Equity Capital Corporation
Charles Brisman, Steven Miriani
500 West Monroe St.
Chicago, IL 60661
312-441-7200
Fax: 312-441-7208

Midwest Mezzanine Fund II, L.P.
David Gezon & Allan Kayler, Mgrs.
208 South LaSalle St., 10th Floor
Chicago, IL 60604
312-855-7140
Fax: 312-553-6647

Peterson Finance and Investment Company SSBIC
James S. Rhee, President
3300 West Peterson Ave., Suite A
Chicago, IL 60659
312-539-0502
Fax: 312-583-6714

Polestar Capital, Inc. SSBIC
Wallace Lennox, President
180 N. Michigan Ave., Suite 1905
Chicago, IL 60601
312-984-9875
Fax: 312-984-9877

Prairie Capital Mezzanine Fund, L.P.
Bryan Daniels & Stephen King, Partners
300 S. Wacker Drive, Suite 1050
Chicago, IL 60606
312-360-1133
Fax: 312-360-1193

Shorebank Capital Corporation
David Shryock, CEO
7936 S. Cottage Grove Ave.
Chicago, IL 60619
773-371-7030
Fax: 773-371-7035

Walnut Capital Corp.
Burton W. Kanter,
Chairman of the Board
Two North LaSalle St., Suite 2200
Chicago, IL 60602
312-269-1700
Fax: 312-269-1747

Indiana
1st Source Capital Corporation
Eugene L. Cavanaugh, Jr., Vice President
100 North Michgan St.
Mail: P.O. Box 1602; South Bend 46634
South Bend, IN 46601
219-235-2180
Fax: 219-235-2227

Cambridge Ventures, LP
Ms. Jean Wojtowicz, President
4181 East 96th St., Suite 200
Indianapolis, IN 46240
317-843-9704
Fax: 317-844-9815

White River Venture Partners, LP
Sam Surphin & Marc DeLong, Managers
3603 East Raymond St.
Indianapolis, IN 46203-4762
317-791-2900
Fax: 317-791-2935

Iowa
MorAmerica Capital Corporation
David R. Schroder, President
Robert A. Comey, Executive Vice President
InvestAmerica Investment Advisors, Inc.
101 2nd St. SE., Suite 800
Cedar Rapids, IA 52401
319-363-8249
Fax: 319-363-9683

North Dakota SBIC, L.P. branch
John G. Cosgriff, Manager
InvestAmerica Investment Advisors, Inc.
51 Broadway, Suite 400
Fargo, ND 58102
701-298-0003
Fax: 701-293-7819

Berthel SBIC, LLC
Berthel Fisher & Company
100 2nd St. SE
Cedar Rapids, Iowa 52407
319-365-2506
Fax: 319-365-9141

Kansas
Kansas Venture Capital, Inc.
Carol Laddish, Manager
6700 Antioch, Suite 460
Overland Park, KS 66204
913-262-7117
Fax: 913-262-3509

Kentucky
Equal Opportunity Finance, Inc. SSBIC
David A. Sattich, President
420 S. Hurstbourne Pkwy., Suite 201
Louisville, KY 40222
502-423-1943
Fax: 502-423-1945

Mountain Ventures, Inc.
L. Ray Moncrief, Exec. Vice President
P.O. Box 1738
362 Old Whitley Road
London, KY 40743
606-864-5175
Fax: 606-864-5194

Louisiana
Banc One Equity Investors, Inc.
Thomas J. Adamek, President
451 Florida St.
Mail: P.O. Box 1511
Baton Rouge, LA 70821
504-332-4421
Fax: 504-332-7377

First Commerce Capital, Inc.
William Harper, Manager
201 St. Charles Ave., 16th Floor
Mail: P.O. Box 60279
New Orleans, LA 70170
504-623-1600
Fax: 504-623-1779

Hibernia Capital Corp.
Thomas Hoyt, President
313 Carondelet St.
New Orleans, LA 70130
504-533-5988
Fax: 504-533-3873

Maine
North Atlantic Venture Fund II, L.P.
David M. Coit, Manager
70 Center St.
Portland, ME 04101
207-772-1001
Fax: 207-772-3257

Maryland
Anthem Capital, L.P.
William M. Gust, II, Manager
16 S. Calvert St., Suite 800
Baltimore, MD 21202
410-625-1510
Fax: 410-625-1735

MMG Ventures, L.P. SSBIC
Stanley W. Tucker, Manager
826 E. Baltimore St.
Baltimore, MD 21202
410-659-7851
Fax: 410-333-2552

Security Financial and Investment Corp. SSBIC
7720 Wisconsin Ave., Suite 207
Bethesda, MD 20814
301-951-4288
Fax: 301-951-9282

Spring Capital Partner
Jay Wilson, Contact
16 West Madison St.
Baltimore, MD 21201
410-685-8007
Fax: 410-727-1436

Syncom Capital Corp. SSBIC
Terry L. Jones, President
8401 Colesville Road, #300
Silver Spring, MD 20910
301-608-3207
Fax: 301-608-3307

Massachusetts
Argonauts MESBIC Corporation The-SSBIC
Kevin Chen, General Manager
929 Worcester Road
Framingham, MA 01701
508-875-6939
Fax: 508-872-3741

Ascent Venture Partner
Frank Polestra, General Partner
60 State St., 19th Floor
Boston, MA 02109
617-742-7825
Fax: 617-742-7315

BancBoston Ventures, Incorporated
Frederick M. Fritz, President
100 Federal St., 01-32-01
Mail: P.O. Box 2016, Stop 01-32-01

Uncle Sam's Venture Capital

Boston, MA 02106
617-434-2442
Fax: 617-434-1153

Caduceus Capital Health Ventures, L.P.
Bill Golden, Manager
124 Mount Auburn St., Suite 200
Cambridge, MA 02138
617-330-9345
Fax: 617-330-9349

Chestnut St. Partners, Inc.
David D. Croll, President
75 State St., Suite 2500
Boston, MA 02109
617-345-7220
Fax: 617-345-7201

Citizens Ventures, Inc.
Robert G. Garrow & Gregory Mulligan, Mgrs.
28 State St., 15th Floor
Boston, MA 02109
617-725-5635
Fax: 617-725-5630

Commonwealth Enterprise Fund Inc. SSBIC
Charles G. Broming, Fund Manager
10 Post Office Square, Suite 1090
Boston, MA 02109
617-482-1881
Fax: 617-482-7129

GMN Investors II, L.P.
James J. Goodman, Manager
20 William St.
Wellesley, MA 02481
781-237-7001
Fax: 781-237-7233

Geneva Middle Market Investors, L.P.
James J. Goodman, Manager
20 William St.
Wellesley, MA 02481
781-237-7001
Fax: 781-237-7233

Marathon Investment Partners, L.P.
10 Post Office Square, Suite 1225
Boston, MA 02110
617-423-2494
Fax: 617-423-2719

New England Partners Capital, L.P.
Robert Hanks, Prin. & Todd Fitzpatrick
One Boston Place, Suite 2100
Boston, MA 02108
617-624-8400
Fax: 617-624-8416

Northeast SBI Corp.
Joseph Mindick, Treasurer
212 Tosca Drive
Stoughton, MA 02072
781-297-9235
Fax: 781-297-9236

Norwest Equity Partners IV
Main Office: Minneapolis, MN
40 William St., Suite 305
Wellesley, MA 02181
617-237-5870
Fax: 617-237-6270

Seacoast Capital Partners, L.P.
Walt Leonard, Manager
55 Ferncroft Road
Danvers, MA 01923

978-750-1310
Fax: 978-750-1301

Transportation Capital Corp. SSBIC
Main Office: New York, NY
Jonathan Hirsch, Manager
45 Newbury St., Suite 207
Boston, MA 02116
617-536-0344
Fax: 212-949-9836

UST Capital Corp.
Arthur F. Snyder, President
40 Court St.
Boston, MA 02108
617-726-7000
Fax: 617-695-4185

Zero Stage Capital V, L.P.
Paul Kelley, Manager
Kendall Square
101 Main St., 17th Floor
Cambridge, MA 02142
617-876-5355
Fax: 617-876-1248

Zero Stage Capital VI
Paul Kelley, Gordon Baty, Stanley Fung
101 Main St., 17th Floor
Cambridge, MA 02142
617-876-5355
Fax: 617-876-1248

Michigan

Capital Fund, Inc.
Barry Wilson, President
6412 Centurion Drive, Suite 150
Lansing, MI 48917
517-323-7772
Fax: 517-323-1999

Dearborn Capital Corp. SSBIC
Michael J. Kahres, President
c/o Ford Motor Credit Corporation
P.O. Box 1729
Dearborn, MI 48121
313-337-8577
Fax: 313-248-1252

InvestCare Partners, LP
Malcolm Moss, Manager
31500 Northwest Highway, Suite 120
Farmington Hills, MI 48334
248-851-9200
Fax: 248-851-9208

Merchants Capital Partners, L.P.
Pat Beach, Dick Goff, Ross Martin, Mgrs.
24 Frank Lloyd Wright Drive
Lobby L, 4th Floor
Ann Arbor, MI 48106
734-994-5505
Fax: 734-994-1376

Motor Enterprises, Inc. SSBIC
Mark Fischer, Vice President & Treasurer
NAO Headquarters
Bldg. 1-8, Worldwide Pu
30400 Mound Road, Box 9015
Warren, MI 48090
810-986-8420
Fax: 810-986-6703

Pacific Capital, L.P.
Lois F. Marler, Vice President
2401 Plymouth Road, Suite B

Ann Arbor, MI 48105
734-747-9401
Fax: 734-747-9704

White Pines Limited Partnership I
Mr. Ian Bund, President
2401 Plymouth Road
Ann Arbor, MI 48105
734-747-9401
Fax: 734-747-9704

Minnesota

Agio Capital Partners I, L.P.
Kenneth F. Gudorf, President & CEO
First Bank Place, Suite 4600
601 Second Ave., South
Minneapolis, MN 55402
612-339-8408
Fax: 612-349-4232

Bayview Capital Partners, L.P.
Cary Musech, Manager
641 East Lake St., Suite 230
Wayzata, MN 55391
612-475-4935
Fax: 612-476-7820

Medallion Capital, Inc.
Tom Hunt, President
7831 Glenroy Road, Suite 480
Minneapolis, MN 55439-3132
612-831-2025
Fax: 612-831-2945

Mezzanine Capital Partners, Inc.
Gerald Slater and Ivar Sorenson
150 South 5th St., Suite 1720
Minneapolis, MN 55402
612-343-5540
Fax: 612-333-6118

Milestone Growth Fund, Inc. SSBIC
Esperanza Guerrero-Anderson, President
401 Second Ave. South, Suite 1032
Minneapolis, MN 55401
612-338-0090
Fax: 612-338-1172

Norwest Equity Partners IV
Robert F. Zicarelli, General Partner
222 South Ninth St.
2800 Piper Jaffray Tower
Minneapolis, MN 55402
612-667-1650
Fax: 612-667-1660

Norwest Equity Partners VI, L.P.
Daniel Haggerty, General Partner
222 South Ninth St.
2800 Piper Jaffray Tower
Minneapolis, MN 55402
612-667-1650
Fax: 612-667-1660

Norwest Equity Partners V, L.P.
John F. Whaley, Manager
222 South Ninth St.
2800 Piper Jaffray Tower
Minneapolis, MN 55402
612-667-1650
Fax: 612-667-1660

Norwest Venture Partners VI, L.P.
n/a 222 South Ninth St.
2800 Piper Jaffray Tower
Minneapolis, MN 55402

Uncle Sam's Venture Capital

612-667-1650
Fax: 612-667-1660

Norwest Venture Partners VII, L.P.
Daniel J. Haggerty, Manager
2800 Piper Jaffray Tower
Minneapolis, MN 55402

Piper Jaffray Healthcare Capital L.P.
Lloyd Buzz-Benson, Manager
222 South 9th St.
Minneapolis, MN 55402
612-342-6335
Fax: 612-342-8514

Piper Jaffray Technology Capital
Gary Blauer and Buzz Benson, Managers
222 South 9th St.
Minneapolis, MN 55402
612-342-6368
Fax: 612-342-8514

Wells Fargo SBIC, Inc.
John Whaley
2800 Piper Jaffray Tower
222 S Ninth St.
c/o Norwest Venture Capital
Minneapolis, MN 55402
612-667-1667
Fax: 612-667-1660

Mississippi

CapSource Fund, L.P.
Bobby Weatherly & James Herndon, Mgrs.
800 Woodlands Parkway, Suite 102
Ridgeland, MS 39157
601-899-8980
Fax: 601-952-1334

Sun-Delta Capital Access Center, Inc. SSBIC
Howard Boutte, Jr., Vice President
819 Main St.
Greenville, MS 38701
601-335-5291
Fax: 601-335-5295

Missouri

BOME Investors, Inc.
Gregory R. Johnson & John McCarthy, Mgrs
8000 Maryland Ave., Suite 1190
St. Louis, MO 63105
314-721-5707
Fax: 314-721-5135

Bankers Capital Corp.
Raymond E. Glasnapp, President
3100 Gillham Road
Kansas City, MO 64109
816-531-1600
Fax: 816-531-1334

CFB Venture Fund I, Inc.
James F. O'Donnell, Chairman
11 South Meramec, Suite 1430
St. Louis, MO 63105
314-746-7427
Fax: 314-746-8739

CFB Venture Fund II, LP
James F. O'Donnell, Chairman
11 South Meramec, Suite 1430
St. Louis, MO 63105
314-746-7427
Fax: 314-746-8739

Civic Ventures Investment Fund, L.P.
Bryon E. Winton, Manager
One Metropolitan Square
211 North Broadway, Suite 2380
St. Louis, MO 63102
314-436-8222
Fax: 314-436-2070

Eagle Fund I, L.P.
Scott Fesler, Operator
2301 S. Kings Highway
St. Louis, MO 63110
314-268-2512
Fax: 314-776-5200

Enterprise Fund, L.P.
Joseph D. Garea, Managing Director
150 North Meramec
Clayton, MO 63105
314-725-5500
Fax: 314-725-1732

Gateway Partners, L.P.
John S. McCarthy
8000 Maryland Ave., Suite 1190
St. Louis, MO 63105
314-721-5707
Fax: 314-721-5135

KCEP I, L.P.
William Reisler, Manager
233 West 47th St.
Kansas City, MO 64112
816-960-1771
Fax: 816-960-1777

MorAmerica Capital Corporation
Main Office: Cedar Rapids, IA
911 Main St., Suite 2424
Commerce Tower Building
Kansas City, MO 64105
816-842-0114
Fax: 816-471-7339

UMB Capital Corporation, Inc.
Noel Shull, Manager
1010 Grand Boulevard
Mail: P.O. Box 419226
Kansas City, MO 64141
816-860-7914
Fax: 816-860-7143

Montana

Currently there are no SBIC Program Licensees in Montana

Nebraska

There are no licensees for Nebraska at this time.

Nevada

Atalanta Investment Company, Inc.
L. Mark Newman, Chairman of the Board
601 Fairview Blvd.
Call Box 10,001
Incline Village, NV 89450
702-833-1836
Fax: 702-833-1890

New Hampshire

Currently there are no SBIC Program Licensees in New Hampshire

New Jersey

Acorn Technology Fund, L.P.
John B. Torkelsen, Manager
5 Vaughn Drive
Princeton, NJ 08540
609-452-7124
Fax: 609-452-2700

CIT Group/Venture Capital, Inc.
Colby W. Collier, Manager
650 CIT Drive
Livingston, NJ 07039
973-740-5429
Fax: 973-740-5555

Capital Circulation Corporation SSBIC
Judy Kao, Manager
2035 Lemoine Ave., Second Floor
Fort Lee, NJ 07024
201-947-8637
Fax: 201-585-1965

DFW Capital Partners, L.P.
Donald F. DeMuth, Manager
Glenpointe Center East, 5th Floor
300 Frank W. Burr Blvd.
Teaneck, NJ 07666
201-836-2233
Fax: 201-836-5666

Early Stage Enterprises, L.P.
Ronald Hahn and James Miller, Managers
995 Route 518
Skillman, NJ 08558
609-921-8896
Fax: 609-921-8703

Edison Venture Fund
John Martinson, Managing Partner
Ross T. Martinson, General Partner
1009 Lenox Drive, #4
Lawrenceville, NJ 08648
609-896-1900
Fax: 609-896-0066

GS Capital, L.P.
Kenneth S. Sweet, Jr., Managing Editor
Richard J. Gessner, Jr, Managing Editor
Steven D. Tobert, Managing Editor
Reginald W. Wikes, Managing Editor
Cynthia D. Gowdy, Managing Editor
435 Devon Park Drive, Suite 201
Wayne, Pa 19087
610-293-9151
Fax: 610-293-1979

MidMark Capital, L.P.
Denis Newman, Manager
466 Southern Boulevard
Chatham, NJ 07928
973-822-2999
Fax: 973-822-8911

Penny Lane Partners, L.P.
Stephen H. Shaffer, Resident Manager
One Palmer Square, Suite 309
Princeton, NJ 08542
609-497-4646
Fax: 609-497-0611

Rutgers Minority Investment Company SSBIC
Oscar Figueroa, President
180 University Ave., 3rd Floor
Newark, NJ 07102
973-353-5627

Uncle Sam's Venture Capital

Tappan Zee Capital Corporation
Jeffrey Birnberg, President
201 Lower Notch Road
Mail: P.O. Box 416
Little Falls, NJ 07424
973-256-8280
Fax: 973-256-2841

Transpac Capital Corporation SSBIC
Tsuey Tang Wang, President
1037 Route 46 East
Clifton, NJ 07013
973-470-8855
Fax: 973-470-8827

New Mexico

TD Origen Capital Fund, L.P.
J. Michael Schafer, Manager
150 Washington Ave., Suite 201
Santa Fe, NM 87501
505-982-7007
Fax 505-982-7008

New York

399 Venture Partners
William Comfort, Chairman
399 Park Ave., 14th Floor/Zone 4
New York, NY 10043
212-559-1127
Fax: 212-888-2940

American Asian Capital Corporation SSBIC
Howard H. Lin, President
130 Water St., Suite 6-L
New York, NY 10005
212-422-6880
Fax: 212-422-6880

Argentum Capital Partners II, LP
Daniel Raynor, Chairman
405 Lexington Ave., 54th Floor
New York, NY 10174
212-949-6262
Fax: 212-949-8294

Argentum Capital Partners, LP
Daniel Raynor, Chairman
405 Lexington Ave., 54th Floor
New York, NY 10174
212-949-6262
Fax: 212-949-8294

BOCNY, LLC
Shelley G. Whittington, Manager
10 East 53rd St., 32nd Floor
New York, NY 10022
504-332-7721
Fax: 504-332-7377

BT Capital Partners, Inc.
Doug Brent, Managing Director
130 Liberty St., 25th Floor
New York, NY 10006
212-250-5565
Fax: 212-250-7651

Barclays Capital Investors Corp.
Lorrie Stapleton, President
222 Broadway, 11th Floor
New York, NY 10038
212-412-5832
Fax: 212-412-7600

C.B. Capital Investors, LP
George E. Kelts, Managing Director
380 Madison Ave., 12th Floor
New York, NY 10017
212-622-3100
Fax: 212-622-3799

CIBC WG Argosy Merchant Fund 1, L.P.
Jay Levine and Jay Bloom, Contacts
425 Lexington Ave.
New York, NY 10017
212-885-4611
Fax: 212-885-4878

CIBC WMV Inc.
Robi Blumenstein, Managing Director
425 Lexington Ave., 9th Floor
New York, NY 10017
212-856-3713
Fax: 212-697-1544

CMNY Capital II, L.P.
Robert G. Davidoff, General Partner
135 East 57th St., 26th Floor
New York, NY 10022
212-909-8428
Fax: 212-980-2630

Capital Investors & Management Corp. SSBIC
Rose Chao, Manager
210 Canal St., Suite 611
New York, NY 10013
212-964-2480
Fax: 212-349-9160

Cephas Capital Partners L.P.
Clint Campbell, Jeff Holmes, Mgrs.
16 West Main St.
Rochester, NY 14614
716-231-1528
Fax: 716-231-1530

Chase Manhattan Capital, LP
George E. Kelts, Managing Director
380 Madison Ave., 12th Floor
New York, NY 10017
212-552-6275
Fax: 212-622-3799

Chase Venture Capital Associates
Jeffrey C. Walker, Managing Gen. Partner
380 Madison Ave., 12th Floor
New York, NY 10017
212-622-3060
Fax: 212-622-3750

Citicorp Venture Capital, Ltd.
William Comfort, Chairman of the Board
399 Park Ave., 14th Floor/Zone 4
New York, NY 10043
212-559-1127
Fax: 212-793-6164

Credit Suisse First Boston SB Fund I, LP
David DeNunzio & John Hennessy, Mgrs.
11 Madison Ave., 26th Floor
New York, NY 10010
212-325-2000
Fax: 212-325-2699

Bank Austria Creditanstalt SBIC, Inc.
Dennis O'Dowd, President
245 Park Ave., 32nd Floor
New York, NY 10167
203-861-1410
Fax: 203-861-1477

Dresdner Kleinwort Benson Private Equity
Christopher Wright, President
75 Wall St., 24th Floor
New York, NY 10005
212-429-2100
Fax: 212-429-2929

East Coast Venture Capital, Inc. SSBIC
Zindel Zelmanovitch, President
570 Seventh Ave., Suite 1802
New York, NY 10018
212-869-7778
Fax: 212-819-9764

East River Ventures, L.P.
Alexander Paluch & Walter Carozza
150 East 58th St., 16th Floor
New York, NY 10155
212-644-6211
Fax: 212-980-6603

Edwards Capital Corporation
Michael Kowalsky, President
437 Madison Ave.
New York, NY 10022
212-328-2110
Fax: 212-328-2125

Elk Associates Funding Corporation
Gary C. Granoff, President
747 Third Ave.
New York, NY 10017
212-421-2111
Fax: 212-759-3338

Empire State Capital Corporation SSBIC
Dr. Joseph Wu, President
170 Broadway, Suite 1200
New York, NY 10038
212-513-1799
Fax: 212-513-1892

Eos Partners SBIC II, L.P.
Steven Friedman & Brian Young, Manager
320 Park Ave., 22nd Floor
New York, NY 10022
212-832-5800
Fax: 212-832-5805

Eos Partners SBIC, L.P.
Steven Friedman, Partner
520 Madison Ave., 42nd Floor
New York, NY 10022
212-832-5814
Fax: 212-832-5815

Esquire Capital Corp. SSBIC
Wen-Chan Chin, President
69 Veterans Memorial Highway
Commack, NY 11725
516-462-6944
Fax: 516-864-8152

Exeter Capital Partners IV, L.P.
Keith Fox, Timothy Bradley, Jeff Weber
10 East 53rd St.
New York, NY 10022
212-872-1170
Fax: 212-872-1198

Exeter Equity Partners, L.P.
Keith Fox, Timothy Bradley, Jeff Weber
10 East 53rd St.
New York, NY 10022
212-872-1170
Fax: 212-872-1198

Uncle Sam's Venture Capital

Exeter Venture Lenders, L.P.
Keith Fox, Manager
10 East 53rd St.
New York, NY 10022
212-872-1170
Fax: 212-872-1198

Exim Capital Corp. SSBIC
Victor K. Chun, President
241 5th Ave., 3rd Floor
New York, NY 10016
212-683-3375
Fax: 212-689-4118

Fair Capital Corp. SSBIC
Rose Chao, Manager
210 Canal St., Suite 611
New York, NY 10013
212-964-2480
Fax: 212-349-9160

First County Capital, Inc. SSBIC
Orest Glut, Financial Manager
135-14 Northern Blvd., 2nd Floor
Flushing, NY 11354
718-461-1778
Fax: 718-461-1835

Flushing Capital Corporation SSBIC
Frank J. Mitchell, President
39-06 Union St., Room 202
Flushing, NY 11354
718-886-5866
Fax: 718-939-7761

Freshstart Venture Capital Corporation SSBIC
Zindel Zelmanovich, President
24-29 Jackson Ave.
Long Island City, NY 11101
212-361-9595
Fax: 718-361-8295

Fundex Capital Corp.
Larry Linksman, President
780 Third Ave., 48th Floor
New York, NY 10017
212-527-7135
Fax: 212-527-7134

ING Furman Selz Investments
Brian Friedman, Manager
230 Park Ave.
New York, NY 10169
212-309-8348
Fax: 212-692-9147

Genesee Funding, Inc.
Stuart W. Marsh, President & CEO
70 Linden Oaks, 3rd Floor
Rochester, NY 14625
716-383-5550
Fax: 716-383-5305

Hanam Capital Corp. SSBIC
Robert Schairer, President
38 West 32nd St., Suite 1512
New York, NY 10001
212-564-5225
Fax: 212-564-5307

Hudson Venture Partners, L.P.
Lawrence Howard & Marilyn Adler
660 Madison Ave., 14th Floor
New York, NY 10022
212-644-9797
Fax: 212-583-1849

IBJ Whitehall Capital
Peter Handy, President
One State St., 8th Floor
New York, NY 10004
212-858-2000
Fax: 212-952-1629

Ibero American Investors Corp. SSBIC
Emilio Serrano, President
104 Scio St.
Rochester, NY 14604
716-262-3440
Fax: 716-262-3441

InterEquity Capital Partners, LP
Irwin Schlass, President
220 Fifth Ave., 12th Floor
New York, NY 10001
212-779-2022
Fax: 212-779-2103

International Paper Cap. Formation, Inc. SSBIC
Main Office: Memphis, TN
John Jepsen, President
Two Manhattanville Road
Purchase, NY 10577
914-397-1578
Fax: 914-397-1909

J.P. Morgan Investment Corporation
Brian F. Watson, Managing Director
60 Wall St.
New York, NY 10260
212-483-2323
Fax: 212-648-5032

KOCO Capital Company, L.P.
Paul Echausse, President
111 Radio Circle
Mount Kisco, NY 10549
914-242-2324
Fax: 914-244-3985

LEG Partners Debenture SBIC, L.P.
Lawrence Golub, Manager
230 Park Ave., 19th Floor
New York, NY 10169
212-207-1423
Fax: 212-207-1579

LEG Partners III SBIC, L.P.
Lawrence Golub, Manager
230 Park Ave., 19th Floor
New York, NY 10169
212-207-1423
Fax: 212-207-1579

LEG Partners SBIC, L.P.
Lawrence E. Golub, Manager
230 Park Ave., 21st Floor
New York, NY 10169
212-207-1585
Fax: 212-207-1579

M & T Capital Corp.
Tom Scanlon, President
One Fountain Plaza, 9th Floor
Buffalo, NY 14203
716-848-3800
Fax: 716-848-3150

Medallion Funding Corporation SSBIC
Alvin Murstein, President
437 Madison Ave.
New York, NY 10022
212-328-2110
Fax: 212-328-2125

Mercury Capital, L.P.
David W. Elenowitz, Manager
153 East 53rd St., 49th Floor
New York, NY 10022
212-838-0888
Fax: 212-759-3897

NBT Capital Corporation
Daryl Forsythe & Joe Minor, Managers
19 Eaton Ave.
Norwich, NY 13815
607-337-6810
Fax: 607-336-8730

NYBDC Capital Corp.
Robert W. Lazar, President
41 State St.
P.O. Box 738
Albany, NY 12207
518-463-2268
Fax: 518-463-0240

NatWest USA Capital Corporation
Elliot Jones, President
660 Madison Ave., 14th Floor
New York, NY 10021
212-418-4567
Fax: 212-418-4594

Needham Capital SBIC, L.P.
John Michaelson, Manager
445 Park Ave.
New York, NY 10022
212-705-0297
Fax: 212-751-1450

Norwood Venture Corp.
Mark R. Littell, President
1430 Broadway, Suite 1607
New York, NY 10018
212-869-5075
Fax: 212-869-5331

Paribas Principal Incorporated
Steven Alexander, President
787 Seventh Ave., 32nd Floor
New York, NY 10019-8018
212-841-2000
Fax: 212-841-3558

Pierre Funding Corp. SSBIC
Elias Debbas, President
805 Third Ave., 6th Floor
New York, NY 10022
212-888-1515
Fax: 212-688-4252

Prospect Street NYC Discovery Fund, L.P.
John F. Barry
10 E. 40th St., 44th Floor
New York, NY 10016
212-448-0702
Fax: 212-448-9652

Pyramid Ventures, Inc.
Brian Talbot, Vice President
130 Liberty St., 31th Floor
New York, NY 10006
212-250-9571
Fax: 212-250-7651

RBC Equity Investments
Stephen Stewart, Manager
One Liberty Plaza
New York, NY 10002
212-428-3035
Fax: 212-858-7468

Uncle Sam's Venture Capital

Regent Capital Partners, L.P.
J. Oliver Maggard, Managing Partner
505 Park Ave., Suite 1700
New York, NY 10022
212-735-9900
Fax: 212-735-9908

SGC Partners II LLC
Steven Baronoff, President
1221 Avenue of the Americas, 8th Floor
New York, NY 10020
212-278-5400
Fax: 212-278-5387

Situation Ventures Corporation SSBIC
Sam Hollander, President
56-20 59th St.
Maspeth, NY 11378
718-894-2000
Fax: 718-326-4642

Sixty Wall St. SBIC Fund, L.P.
Brian F. Watson, Managing Director
60 Wall St.
New York, NY 10260
212-648-7778
Fax: 212-648-5032

Sterling/Carl Marks Capital, Inc.
Harvey L. Granat, President
175 Great Neck Road, Suite 408
Great Neck, NY 11021
516-482-7374
Fax: 516-487-0781

Toronto Dominion Capital U.S.A. Inc
Brian A. Rich, General Manager
31 West 52nd St.
New York, NY 10019
212-827-7000
Fax: 212-974-8429

Transportation Capital Corp. SSBIC
Michael Fanger, Pres. & Linda Miranda
437 Madison Ave.
New York, NY 10022
212-328-2110
Fax: 212-328-2125

Triad Capital Corp. of New York SSBIC
Oscar Figueroa, Manager of Rutgers Inv.
305 Seventh Ave., 20th Floor
New York, NY 10001
212-243-7360
Fax: 212-243-7647

Trusty Capital Inc. SSBIC
Yungduk Hahn, President
350 Fifth Ave., Suite 2026
New York, NY 10118
212-736-7653
Fax: 212-629-3019

T.S. Capital Corporation
James Trainor, Manager
32 Second St.
Troy, NY 12180
518-270-4914
Fax: 518-270-4904

UBS Capital, II LLC
Justin S. Maccarone, President
299 Park Ave.
New York, NY 10171
212-821-6490
Fax: 212-821-6333

United Capital Investment Corp. SSBIC
Paul Lee, President
60 East 42nd St., Suite 1515
New York, NY 10165
212-682-7210
Fax: 212-573-6352

Venture Opportunities Corporation SSBIC
A. Fred March, President
150 East 58th St., 16th Floor
New York, NY 10155
212-832-3737
Fax: 212-980-6603

Walden Capital Partners, L.P.
John Costantino & Allen Greenberg, Mgrs.
150 East 58th St., 34th Floor
New York, NY 10155
212-355-0090
Fax: 212-755-8894

Wasserstein Adelson Ventures, L.P.
Townsend Ziebold, Jr., Manager
31 West 52nd St., 27th Floor
New York, NY 10019
212-969-2690
Fax: 212-969-7879

Winfield Capital Corp.
Stanley M. Pechman, President
237 Mamaroneck Ave.
White Plains, NY 10605
914-949-2600
Fax: 914-949-7195

Women's Growth Capital Fund
1029 31st St., NW
Washington, DC 20007-1203
202-342-1431
Fax: 202-342-1203

North Carolina

Banc of America Capital Partners SBIC
Walter W. Walker, Jr., Pres.
100 N. Tryon St., 25th Floor
NCI-007-25-02
Charlotte, NC 28255
704-386-8063
Fax: 704-388-9049

Banc of America SBIC Corp.
Elyn Dortch, Sr. VP.
George Carter, Pres.
101 S. Tryon St., 18th Floor
NC-1-002-18-02
Charlotte, NC 28255
704-386-7549
Fax: 704-386-1930

BB&T Capital Partners, LLC
David Townsend & Martin Gilmore, Mgrs.
200 W. Second St., 4th Floor
Winston-Salem, NC 27101
336-733-2420
Fax: 336-733-2419

Blue Ridge Investors Ltd. Partnership
Edward C. McCarthy, Exec. VP.
300 N. Greene St., Suite 2100
Greensboro, NC 27401
336-370-0576
Fax: 336-274-4984

Capital Across America, L.P.
Whitney Johns & Chris Brown, Managers
414 Union St., Suite 2025
Nashville, TN 37219
615-254-1414
Fax: 615-254-1856

Centura SBIC, Inc.
Robert R. Anders, Jr., President
200 Providence Rd., 3rd Floor
P.O. Box 6261
Charlotte, NC 28207
704-331-1451
Fax: 704-331-1761

First Fidelity Private Capital Partners, Inc.
Tracey M. Chaffin, CFO
One First Union Center, 5th Floor
301 S. College St.
Charlotte, NC 28288-0732
704-374-4791
Fax: 704-374-6711

First Union Capital Partners, Inc.
Tracey M. Chaffin, CFO
One First Union Center, 5th Floor
301 S. College St.
Charlotte, NC 28288-0732
704-374-4791
Fax: 704-374-6711

Oberlin Capital, L.P.
Robert Shepley, Manager
702 Oberlin Rd., Suite 150
Raleigh, NC 27605
919-743-2544
Fax: 919-743-2501

Wachovia Capital Associates, Inc.
Matthew J. Sullivan, Managing Dir.
191 Peachtree St., NE, 26th Floor
Atlanta, GA 30303
404-332-1437

North Dakota

North Dakota SBIC, L.P.
Main Office: Cedar Rapids, IA
406 Main Ave., Suite 404
Fargo, ND 58103
701-298-0003
Fax: 701-293-7819

Ohio

Banc One Capital Partners, LLC
William P. Leahy, Managing Director
150 East Gay St., 24th Floor
Columbus, OH 43215
614-217-1100
Fax: 614-217-1217

Clarion Capital Corp.
Thomas E. Niehaus, Chief Financial Officer
Ohio Savings Plaza
1801 East 9th St., Suite 510
Cleveland, OH 44114
216-687-8941
Fax: 216-694-3545

Enterprise Ohio Investment Company
Steven Budd, President
8 North Main St.
Dayton, OH 45402
937-226-0457
Fax: 937-222-7035

Financial Opportunities, Inc.
Gregg R. Budoi, Manager

Uncle Sam's Venture Capital

300 Executive Parkway
West Hudson, OH 44236
330-342-6664
Fax: 330-342-6675

Key Equity Capital Corporation
David Given, President
127 Public Square, 28th Floor
Cleveland, OH 44114
216-689-5776
Fax: 216-689-3204

Key Mezzanine Capital, LLC
Stephen Stewart, Manager
10th Floor, Banc One Building
600 Superior Ave.
Cleveland, OH 44114
216-858-6090
Fax: 216-263-3577

National City Capital Corporation
William H. Schecter, President & G.M.
1965 East Sixth St., Suite 1010
Cleveland, OH 44114
216-575-2491
Fax: 216-575-9965

River Cities Capital Fund L.P.
R. Glen Mayfield, Manager
221 East Fourth St., Suite 2250
Cincinnati, OH 45202
513-621-9700
Fax: 513-579-8939

River Cities Capital Fund II, L.P.
Edwin Robinson, Contact
221 East Fourth St., Suite 2250
Cincinnati, OH 45202
513-621-9700
Fax: 513-579-8939

Oklahoma

BancFirst Investment Corporation
T. Kent Faison, Manager
101 North Broadway
Mail: P.O. Box 26788
Oklahoma City, OK 73126
405-270-1000
Fax: 405-270-1089

First United Venture Capital Corporation
John Massey and Greg Massey, Managers
1400 West Main St.
Durant, OK 74701
580-924-2256
Fax: 580-924-2228

Oregon

Northern Pacific Capital Corporation
Joseph P. Tennant, President
937 SW 14th St., Suite 200
Mail: P.O. Box 1658
Portland, OR 97207
503-241-1255
Fax: 503-299-6653

Shaw Venture Partners III, L.P.
Ralph R. Shaw, Manager
400 SW Sixth Ave., Suite 1100
Portland, OR 97204
503-228-4884
Fax: 503-227-2471

Shaw Venture Partners IV, L.P.
Ralph R. Shaw, Managing General Partner
400 SW Sixth Ave., Suite 1100
Portland, OR 97204
503-275-5710
Fax: 503-275-7565

Pennsylvania

CEO Venture Fund III, L.P.
James Colker, Manager
2000 Technology Drive, Suite 160
Pittsburgh, PA 15219
412-687-0200 ext. 236
Fax: 412-687-8139

CIP Capital L.P.
Winston Churchill, Jr., Manager
435 Devon Park Drive, Bldg. 300
Wayne, PA 19087
610-964-7860
Fax: 610-964-8136

Greater Phila. Venture Capital Corp., Inc. SSBIC
Fred S. Choate, Manager
351 East Conestoga Road, Room 203
Wayne, PA 19087
610-688-6829
Fax: 610-254-8958

GS Capital, L.P.
Kenneth S. Sweet, Jr., Managing Editor
Richard J. Gessner, Jr, Managing Editor
Steven D. Tobert, Managing Editor
Reginald W. Wikes, Managing Editor
Cynthia D. Gowdy, Managing Editor
435 Devon Park Drive, Suite 201
Wayne, Pa 19087
610-293-9151
Fax: 610-293-1979

Mellon Ventures, L.P.
Lawrence Mock & Ronald Coombs, Managers
One Mellon Bank Center, Room 3200
Pittsburg, PA 15258
412-236-3594
Fax: 412-236-3593

Meridian Venture Partners
Robert E. Brown, Jr. General Partner
The Fidelity Court Building
259 Radnor-Chester Road, Suite 140
Radnor, PA 19087
610-254-2999
Fax: 610-254-2996

Argosy Investment Partners, L.P.
Knute Albrecht, Manager
950 West Valley Road, Suite 2902
Wayne, PA 19087
610-971-9685
Fax: 610-964-9524

Liberty Ventures I, L.P.
Thomas R. Morse, Manager
441 North 5th St.
Philadelphia, PA 19123
215-928-1050
Fax: 215-928-1065

CEO Venture Fund III, L.P.
James Colker, Managing General Partner
2000 Technology Drive, Suite 160
Pittsburgh, PA 15219
412-687-3451
Fax: 412-687-8139

Mellon Ventures, L.P.
Lawrence Mock, President/CEO
Charles Billerbeck, Managing Director
One Mellon Bank Center, Room 5300
Pittsburgh, PA 15258
412-236-3594
Fax: 412-236-3593

Puerto Rico

North America Inv. Corporation SSBIC
Marcelino Pastrana Torres, President
Mercantil Plaza Bldg., Suite 813
Mail: PO Box 1831, Hato Rey Sta., PR 00919
Hato Rey, PR 00919
787-754-6178
Fax: 787-754-6181

Rhode Island

Domestic Capital Corp.
Nathaniel B. Baker, President
815 Reservoir Ave.
Cranston, RI 02910
401-946-3310
Fax: 401-943-6708

Fleet Equity Partners VI, L.P.
Robert Van Degna & Habib Y. Gorgi, Mgrs.
50 Kennedy Plaza, 12th Floor
Mail Stop: RI DE 03612C
Providence, RI 02903
401-278-6770
Fax: 401-278-6387

Fleet Venture Resources, Inc.
Robert M. Van Degna, Managing Director
50 Kennedy Plaza, 12th Floor
Mail Stop: RI DE 03612C
Providence, RI 02903
401-278-6770
Fax: 401-278-6387

Zero Stage Capital V & VI LP
Mark Thaller, Manager
40 Westminster St., Suite 702
Providence, RI 02903
401-351-3036
Fax: 401-351-3056

Zero Stage Capital V & VI LP
101 Main St., 17th Floor
Cambridge, MA 02142-1519
617-876-5355
Fax: 617-876-1248

South Carolina

Charleston Capital Corporation
111 Church St.
Post Office Box 328
Charleston, SC 29402
843-723-6464
Fax 843-723-1228

Floco Investment Company, Inc.
Highway 52, North
Scranton, SC 29561
803-389-2731
Fax 803-389-4199
Mail: P.O. Box 1629, Lake City, SC 29560

Reedy River Ventures, Limited Partnership
15 S. Main St.
Wachovia Building, Suite 750
864-232-6198

Uncle Sam's Venture Capital

Fax 864-271-8374
Mail: P.O. Box 17526, Greenville, SC 29606

South Dakota

Bluestem Capital Partners II, L.P.
Steve Kirby and Paul Schock, Managers
122 South Phillips Ave., Suite 300
Sioux Falls, SD 57104
605-331-0091
Fax: 605-334-1218

Tennessee

Capital Across America, L.P.
Whitney Johns & Chris Brown, Managers
414 Union St., Suite 2025
Nashville, TN 37219
615-254-1414
Fax: 615-254-1856

Commerce Capital, L.P.
Andrew Higgins, Pres & Rudy Ruark, V.P.
611 Commerce St., Suite 2602
Nashville, TN 37203
615-726-0202
Fax: 615-242-1407

Equitas, L.P.
D. Shannon LeRoy, President of CGP
2000 Glen Echo Road, Suite 100
Mail: P.O. Box 158838
Nashville, TN 37215
615-383-8673
Fax: 615-383-8693

International Paper Cap. Formation, Inc. SSBIC
Bob J. Higgins, V.P. and Controller
International Place II
6400 Poplar Ave.
Memphis, TN 38197
901-763-6282
Fax: 901-763-6076

Pacific Capital, L.P.
Clay R. Caroland, III, President
3100 West End Ave., Suite 1070
Nashville, TN 37203
615-292-3166
Fax: 615-292-8803

Sirrom Investments, Inc.
George M. Miller, II, President
500 Church St., Suite 200
Nashville, TN 37219
615-256-0701
Fax: 615-726-1208

Southern Venture Fund SBIC, L.P.
Don Johnston, President
310 25th Ave. North, Suite 103
Nashville, TN 37203
615-329-9448
Fax: 615-329-9237

Valley Capital Corp. SSBIC
Lamar J. Partridge, President
Suite 212, Krystal Building
100 W. Martin Luther King Blvd.
Chattanooga, TN 37402
423-265-1557
Fax: 423-265-1588

West Tennessee Venture Capital Corporation
SSBIC
Frank Banks, President
5 North Third St.
Memphis, TN 38103
901-522-9237
Fax: 901-527-6091

Texas

AMT Capital, Ltd.
Tom H. Delimitros, CGP
8204 Elmbrook Drive, Suite 101
Dallas, TX 75247
214-905-9760
Fax: 214-905-9761

Alliance Business Investment Company
Main Office: Tulsa, OK
1221 McKinney St., Suite 3100
Houston, TX 77010
713-659-3131
Fax: 713-659-8070

Alliance Enterprise Corporation SSBIC
Donald R. Lawhorne, President
North Central Plaza 1, Suite 710
12655 North Central Expressway
Dallas, TX 75243
214-991-1597
Fax: 214-991-1647

Banc One Capital Partners, L.P.
Main Office: Columbus, OH
Suzanne B. Kriscunas, Managing Director
300 Crescent Court, Suite 1600
Dallas, TX 75201

Capital Southwest Venture Corp.
William R. Thomas, President
12900 Preston Road, Suite 700
Dallas, TX 75230
972-233-8242
Fax: 972-233-7362

Catalyst Fund, Ltd. The
Richard L. Herrman, Manager
Three Riverway, Suite 770
Houston, TX 77056
713-623-8133
Fax: 713-623-0473

Chen's Financial Group, Inc. SSBIC
Samuel S. C. Chen, President
10101 Southwest Freeway, Suite 370
Houston, TX 77074
713-772-8868
Fax: 713-772-2168

First Capital Group of Texas II, L.P.
Messrs. Blanchard, Greenwood, & Locy
750 East Mulberry, Suite 305
San Antonio, TX 78212
210-736-4233
Fax: 210-736-5449

HCT Capital Corp.
Vichy Woodward Young, Jr., President
4916 Camp Bowie Boulevard, Suite 200
Fort Worth, TX 76107
817-763-8706
Fax: 817-377-8049

Houston Partners, SBIP
Glenda Overbeck, President, CGP
401 Louisiana, 8th Floor
Houston, TX 77002
713-222-8600
Fax: 713-222-8932

Jardine Capital Corp. SSBIC
Lawrence Wong, President
7322 Southwest Freeway, Suite 787
Houston, TX 77074
713-271-7077
Fax: 713-271-7577

MESBIC Ventures, Inc. SSBIC
Donald R. Lawhorne, President
North Central Plaza I, Suite 710
12655 North Central Expressway
Dallas, TX 75243
214-991-1597
Fax: 972-991-1647

Mapleleaf Capital Ltd.
Patrick A. Rivelli, Manager
Three Forest Plaza, Suite 935
12221 Merit Drive
Dallas, TX 75251
972-239-5650
Fax: 972-701-0024

NationsBanc Capital Corporation
Main Office: Charlotte, NC
901 Main St., 66th Floor
Dallas, TX 75202
214-508-0932
Fax: 214-508-0985

North Texas MESBIC, Inc. SSBIC
Allan Lee, President
9500 Forest Lane, Suite 430
Dallas, TX 75243
214-221-3565
Fax: 214-221-3566

PMC Investment Corporation SSBIC
Andrew S. Rosemore, President
18111 Preston Road, Suite 600
Dallas, TX 75252
972-349-3200
Fax: 972-349-3265

Retail & Restaurant Growth Capital, L.P.
Raymond Hemmig, Joseph Harberg, Mgrs.
10000 N. Central Expressway, Suite 1060
Dallas, TX 75231
214-750-0065
Fax: 214-750-0060

SBIC Partners II, L.P.
Nicholas Binkley & Gregory Forrest, Mgrs
201 Main St., 27th Floor
Fort Worth, TX 76102
949-729-3222
949-729-3226

SBIC Partners, L.P.
Gregory Forrest & Jeffrey Brown, Manager
201 Main St., Suite 2302
Fort Worth, TX 76102
949-729-3222
Fax: 949-729-3226

Southwest/Catalyst Capital, Ltd.
Ronald Nixon and Rick Herrman, Mgrs.
Three Riverway, Suite 770
Houston, TX 77056
713-623-8133
Fax: 713-623-0473

Stratford Capital Partners, L.P.
Michael D. Brown/John Farmer
200 Crescent Court, Suite 1650

Uncle Sam's Venture Capital

Dallas, TX 75201
214-740-7377
Fax: 214-740-7393

Stratford Equity Partners, L.P.
Michael Brown, Manager
200 Crescent Court, Suite 1600
Dallas, TX 75201
214-740-7377
Fax: 214-740-7340

United Oriental Capital Corporation SSBIC
Jai Min Tai, President
908 Town & Country Blvd., Suite 310
Houston, TX 77024
713-461-3909
Fax: 713-465-7559

Victoria Capital Corp.
Steve Selinske, Acting President
c/o Norwest Bank Texas, N.A.
16416 San Pedro
San Antonio, TX 78232
210-856-8804
Fax: 210-856-8848

Western Financial Capital Corporation
Andrew S. Rosemore, President
18111 Preston Road, Suite 600
Dallas, TX 75252
972-349-3200
Fax: 972-349-3265

Utah

First Security Bus. Investment Corp.
Louis D. Alder, Manager
15 East 100 South, Suite 100
Salt Lake City, UT 84111
801-246-5737
Fax: 801-246-5740

Utah Ventures II L.P.
Alan Dishlip & James Dreyfous, Mgrs.
423 Wakara Way, Suite 206
Salt Lake City, UT 84108
801-583-5922
Fax: 801-583-4105

Wasatch Venture Corporation
Todd J. Stevens, Secretary
1 South Main St., Suite 1400
Salt Lake City, UT 84133
801-524-8939
Fax: 801-524-8941

Wasatch Venture Fund II, LLC
Todd Stevens, Manager
1 South Main St., Suite 1400
Salt Lake City, UT 84133
801-524-8936
Fax: 801-524-8941

Virginia

Continental SBIC SSBIC
Arthur Walters, President
4141 N. Henderson Road, Suite 8
Arlington, VA 22203
703-527-5200
Fax: 703-527-3700

East West United Investment Company SSBIC
Dung Bui, President
1568 Spring Hill Road, Suite 100
McLean, VA 22102
703-442-0150
Fax: 703-442-0156

Virginia Capital SBIC
Frederick Russell & Tom Deardorff, Mgrs.
9 South 12th St., Suite 400
Richmond, VA 23219

Waterside Capital Corporation
Alan Lindauer, President
300 East Main St., Suite 1380
Norfolk, VA 23510
757-626-1111
Fax: 757-626-0114

Walnut Capital Corp.
Main Office: Chicago, IL
8000 Tower Crescent Drive, Suite 1070
Vienna, VA 22182
703-448-3771
Fax: 703-448-7751

Virgin Islands

Currently there are no SBIC Program Licensees in the Virgin Islands

Vermont

Green Mountain Capital, L.P.
Michael Sweatman, General Manager
RR 1, Box 1503
Waterbury, VT 05676
802-244-8981
Fax: 802-244-8990

Washington

Northwest Venture Partners II, L.P.
Thomas Simpson & Jean Balek-Miner, Mgrs.
221 North Wall St., Suite 628
Spokane, WA 99201
509-747-0728
Fax: 509-747-0758

Pacific Northwest Partners SBIC, L.P.
Theodore M. Wight, Manager
305-108th Ave. NE, 2nd Floor
Bellevue, WA 98004
425-455-9967
Fax: 425-455-9404

West Virginia

Shenandoah Venture Capital L.P.
Thomas E. Loehr, President
208 Capital St., Suite 300
Charleston, WV 25301
304-344-1796
Fax: 304-344-1798

WestVen Limited Partnership
Thomas E. Loehr, President
208 Capitol St., Suite 300
Charleston, WV 25301
304-344-1794
Fax: 304-344-1798

Whitney Capital Corporation
Gale Gray, CPA
707 Virginia St., East Suite 1700
Charleston, WV 25301
304-345-9400
Fax: 304-345-7258

Wisconsin

Capital Investments, Inc.
Steve Rippl, Exec. Vice-President
1009 W Glen Oaks Lane, Suite 103
Mequon, WI 53092
414-241-0303
Fax: 414-241-8451

Facilitator Capital Fund
Robert Zobel, Gustavus Taylor
5133 West Terrace Drive, Suite 204
Madison, WI 53718
608-245-3716
Fax: 608-240-1002

Future Value Ventures, Incorporated SSBIC
William P. Beckett, President
2821 N. 4th St., Suite 526
Milwaukee, WI 53212
414-264-2252
Fax: 414-264-2253

M & I Ventures L.L.C.
John T. Byrnes, President
770 North Water St.
Milwaukee, WI 53202
414-765-7910
Fax: 414-765-7850

MorAmerica Capital Corporation
Main Office: Cedar Rapids, IA
600 East Mason St., Suite 304
Milwaukee, WI 53202
414-276-3839
Fax: 414-276-1885

Wyoming

Currently there are no SBIC Program Licensees in Wyoming

Americans With Disabilities Act

Get Free Help With The Americans With Disabilities Act (ADA) Which Requires Businesses To Accommodate The Disabled

Federal law makes it illegal for businesses to discriminate against individuals with physical or mental disabilities (including AIDS). Employers are required to accommodate the disabled. Public accommodations such as restaurants, hotels, theaters, doctors' offices, pharmacies, retail stores, museums, libraries, parks, private schools, and day care centers may not discriminate on basis of disability and must accommodate the disabled customers; however, private clubs and religious organizations are exempt. All new construction must be made accessible, and alterations must be made to existing facilities to accommodate the disabled as long as the cost does not impose an undue hardship. "Undue hardship" is defined as an "action requiring significant difficulty or expense". Generally, employers with more resources would be expected to put forth greater effort and expenses to accommodate an individual with a disability.

Why Was This Law Passed?

This law was designed not only to tap into the resources of those disabled who wish to work but also to substantially reduce the outlays in federal benefits. According to the Committee on Employment of People with Disabilities' Job Accommodation Network (JAN), 17% of all reasonable accommodations cost nothing at all; 68% cost $500 or less; 84% cost $1,500 or less and only a mere 4% cost over $5,000. Accommodations are sometimes no more than a little creative management; such as flex time or placing things on lower shelves. JAN reports that 23% of businesses providing accommodations to an employee has actually saved the company between $20,001-$200,000. According to a fact sheet from the Disability Employment Leadership Roundtable, the 1991/92 U.S. Census report *Americans with Disabilities* reports that there are 49 million people with disabilities in America, comprising 19.4% of the entire United States Population.

People with disabilities who do work earn 35% less than their non-disabled co-workers. Forty times more is spent on federal public assistance than on job training for people with disabilities. Reasons cited for not working, or for not working full time:

- 40% say employers won't recognize their capabilities
- 32% say they lack the necessary training
- 31% say they'd risk losing their health benefits like Medicaid or Medicare
- 24% need a personal assistant
- 16% need special equipment for work activities

How to Get a Tax Break

Come tax time many businesses who have spent their money complying with the ADA may be pleasantly surprised to find that Uncle Sam will give some back. There are a number of disability related tax credits and deductions available from the Internal Revenue Service for providing access to customers and employees with disabilities. These credits and deductions greatly ease the burden of removing transportation, architectural, and communication barriers. Eligible small businesses (businesses with 30 or less employees during the preceding tax year or less than $1 million in gross receipts for the preceding tax year) in the amount of 50% of "eligible access expenditures" (ones required by the ADA) that exceed $250 but do not exceed $10,250 for a taxable year. A business may take the credit each year that it makes an eligible access expenditure. The Internal Revenue Service allows a deduction up to $15,000 per year for "qualified architectural and transportation barrier removal expenses."

For more information on disability-related tax provisions call the IRS at 1-800-829-1040; {www.irs.gov}.

How To Beat The New Crop Of Fear Consultants

Laws like this one that affect so many businesses, instantly spawn an entire industry of high priced consultants, lawyers, architects and other specialists who live off a business's fear of the unknown.

You don't have to pay a high priced consultant to eliminate your fears. You can get the information better than most of these consultants, and you can get it free, by going directly to the source...the government. You can also get free architectural advice, consulting help, information on funding needed construction and most any other assistance you need to help determine if you have to make changes in your business. And you can also get free help in choosing the plans, construction materials, and contractors to implement them.

What Your Business Must Do and How To Do It

The law has financed 10 Regional Disability and Business Technical Assistance Centers (DBTAC) to which businesses and individuals can turn to find out more about the law. Businesses can learn exactly what changes have to be made to their facilities. In many cases free consultants will come out to your business and identify what will have to be changed and how it can be changed in the least expensive manner.

The objectives of these centers are to help the community by:
- disseminating information;
- providing direct technical assistance;
- providing referrals for specialized information and technical assistance;
- training interested and affected parties;
- facilitating appropriate implementation of the ADA;
- facilitating successful employment outcomes for individuals with disabilities; and
- facilitating greater accessibility in public accommodations.

Americans With Disabilities Act

Call 1-800-949-4232 (this 800 number will automatically route your call to the appropriate region from which you are calling) or contact the office listed below which covers your state:

Region I (CT, ME, NH, RI, VT)
New England DBTAC
Adaptive Environments Center
374 Congress St., Suite 301
Boston, MA 02210   615-695-0085 (V/TTY)
www.adaptenv.org

Region II (NJ, NY, PR, VI)
Northeast DBTAC
United Cerebral Palsy Association
  of New Jersey
354 South Broad Street   609-392-4004 (voice)
Trenton, NJ 08608   609-392-7044 (TDD)
www.disabilityact.com

Region III (DE, DC, MD, PA, VA, WV)
Mid Atlantic DBTAC
TransCen, Inc.
451 Hungerford Dr., Suite 607
Rockville, MD 20850   301-217-0124 (V/TTY)
www.adainfo.org

Region IV (AL, FL, GA, KY, MS, NC, SC, TN)
Southeast DBTAC
United Cerebral Palsy Association, Inc.
Center for Rehabilitation Technology
490 Tenth St.
Atlanta, GA 30318   404-385-0636 (V/TTY)
www.sedbtac.org

Region V (IL, IN, MI, MN, OH, WI)
Great Lakes DBTAC
University of Illinois at Chicago/UAP
1640 West Roosevelt Road M/C627
Chicago, IL 60608   312-413-7756 (voice/TDD)
www.adagreatlakes.org

Region VI (AR, LA, NM, OK, TX)
Southwest DBTAC
Independent Living Research Utilization/
The Institute for Rehabilitation and Research
2323 S. Shepherd St., Suite 1000   713-520-0232
Houston, TX 77019   713-520-5136 (TDD)
www.ilru.org/dbtac

Region VII (IA, KS, NB, MO)
Great Plains DBTAC
ADA Project
100 Corporate Lakes Dr.
Columbia, MO 65203   573-882-3600 (V/TDD)
www.adaproject.org

Region VIII (CO, MT, ND, SD, UT, WY)
Rocky Mountain DBTAC
Meeting the Challenge, Inc.
3630 Sinton Road, Suite 103
Colorado Springs, CO 80907-5072   719-444-0268 (V/TDD)
www.ada_infonet.org

Region IX (AZ, CA, HI, NV, Pacific Basin)
Pacific DBTAC
California Public Health Institute
2168 Shattuck Ave., Suite 301   510-848-2980 (voice)
Berkeley, CA 94704   510-848-1840 (TDD)
www.pacdtac.org

Region X (AK, ID, OR, WA)
Northwest DBTAC
Washington State Governor's Committee
P.O. Box 9046   360-438-4116 (voice)
Olympia, WA 98507-9046   360-438-3167 (TDD)
www.wata.org/NWD

Publications

The following publications are available through all of the Regional Disability and Business Technical Centers:

ADA Basic Kit ($5.00)
(you have the option of ordering these separately)
   EEOC/DOJ-ADA Q&A Booklet
   EEOC-Fact Sheet on Disability Related Tax
      Provisions (Credits and Deduction)
   EEOC - ADA Employment Fact Sheet
   DOJ - ADA Fact Sheet (Title I-V)
   DOJ - ADA Public Accommodation Fact Sheet
      (Title III)
   DOJ - ADA Statutory Deadlines (Titles I - IV)
   ATBCB - ADA Accessibility Requirements Effective
      Dates, Regulations, and Enforcement (Title - IV)
   NIDRR - Regional Technical Assistance Centers List
   DBTAC - ADA Material List
   DBTAC - Mid-Atlantic ADA Center Brochure

ADA General Information
American with Disabilities Act (ADA) Public Law 101-336, July 26, 1990 ($2.50)
The ADA-A Simplified Version (MR/LD) (Q&A Format)
Q&A for Deaf and Hard of Hearing Individuals
Fact Sheet 1 - *Who Has Obligations Under Title III?*
Fact Sheet 2 - *Providing Effective Communication*
Fact Sheet 3 - *Communicating with People with Disabilities*
Fact Sheet 4 - *Tax Incentives for Improving Accessibility*
Fact Sheet 5 - *Alternatives to Barrier Removal*
Fact Sheet 6 - *Resources for More Information*
Resource List Telephone Numbers for ADA Information
ADA Information Available on Electronic Bulletin Boards
A Selected Topical Bibliography on the ADA

Title I: Employment
EEOC - *Equal Employment Opportunity for Individuals with Disabilities; Final Rule and 29 CFR Parts 1602 and 1627-- Record Keeping and Reporting Under Title VII of the Civil Rights Act of the 1962 and the ADA; Final Rule* ($1.32)
EEOC ADA Employment Poster ($1.52)
EEOC - *The ADA—Your Responsibilities as an Employer* ($1.23)
EEOC - *The ADA—Your Employment Rights as an Individual With a Disability* ($1.00)
EEOC - *How To File A Title I Complaint* ($1.00)

Americans With Disabilities Act

Employing and Accommodating Workers with Psychiatric Disabilities ($1.00)
Employment Considerations for People Who Have Diabetes ($1.00)
Working Effectively with People Who Are Blind Or Visually Impaired ($1.00)
Working Effectively with Persons Who Have Cognitive Disabilities ($1.00)
Causes Of Poor Indoor Air Quality And What You Can Do About It ($1.00)
Accommodating The Allergic Employee in The Workplace ($1.00)
Employing And Accommodating Individuals With Histories Of Alcohol And Drug Abuse ($1.00)
Working Effectively with Persons Who Are Deaf or Hard of Hearing ($1.00)
The Road to Opportunity - Employing People with Mental Retardation and the ADA ($1.00)
Entitlement to Access - A Guide to the ADA (Q&A Format, Large Resource List) ($1.23)
Job Accommodation Network (JAN assists employers and individuals with the reasonable accommodation process) ($2.00)
Complying with the ADA - A Guide for Employers ($$2.72)
Health Benefit Plans and the ADA ($1.89)
Model Plan for Implementation of Title I of the ADA - the Human Resources Perspective ($2.01)
Employment Screening, Medical Examinations, Health Insurance and the ADA ($2.74)
Reasonable Accommodation Under the ADA ($2.97)
Complying with the ADA (Interviewing, Job Descriptions and Job Qualifications, Accommodation)

Title II: State and Local Governments

DOJ - *Title II: Nondiscrimination on the Basis of Disability in State and Local Government Services: Final Rule* ($1.76)
DOJ - *Title II Technical Assistance Manual and Supplement* ($4.64)
Order Form: *Title II Technical Assistance Manual Subscription through 1996* ($1.00)
DOJ - *Title Highlights* ($1.00)
Title II Action Guide for State and Local Governments ($13.40)
ATBCB - *Americans with Disabilities Act Accessibility Guidelines (ADAAG) for Buildings and Facilities; State and Local Government Facilities; Interim Final Rule* (36 CFR 1191; 6/20/94 ($4.53)
Uniform Federal Accessibility Standards (UFAS) ($4.43)
ANSI - *Providing Accessibility and Usability for Physically Handicapped People* (A117.1-1986) ($4.00)
DOJ - *Common Questions About Title II of the ADA* (4/94) ($1.00)
Work in Progress - A Video about State and Local Government Compliance with Title II of the ADA

Title II: Transportation

You Really Can Go Places - Your Rights to Public Transportation
DOT--*Final Regulations - 49 CFR Parts 27, 37, & 38 Transportation for Individuals with Disabilities: Final Rule* ($1.32)
ATBCB Technical Assistance Manuals:
  - *High-Speed Rail Cars, Monorails, and Systems*
  - *Buses, Vans & Systems*
  - *Over-the-Road Buses & Systems*
  - *Automated Guideway Transit (AGT) Systems*
  - *Intercity Rail Cars & Systems*
  - *Commuter Rail Cars & Systems*
  - *Trams, Similar Vehicles & Systems*
  - *Rapid Rail Vehicles & Systems*
  - *Light Rail Vehicles & Systems*

Title III: Public Accommodations

DOJ - *Title Highlights* ($2.00)
DOJ - *Federal Regulation, Part III, 28 CFR Part 36, Nondiscrimination on the Basis of Disability by Public Accommodations and in Commercial Facilities: Final Rule* (includes ADAAG) ($4.00)
DOJ - *Title III ADA Technical Assistance Manual addresses the requirements of title III of the Americans with Disabilities Act* ($3.19)
Order Form: *Title III ADA Technical Assistance Manual Subscription through 1996*
ATBCB - *Accessibility Checklist for Buildings and Facilities* ($2.84)
Checklist for Existing Facilities ($2.84)
ADAAG 6.0: *Medical Care Facilities* (for Visually Impaired) ($2.84)
ADAAG 4.17: *Toilet Stalls Tech Sheet*
ADAAG 4.3.11: *Areas of Rescue Assistance Tech Sheet*
ATBCB Bulletin #1: *Detectable Warnings*
ATBCB Bulletin #2: *Visual Alarms*
ATBCB Bulletin #3: *Text Telephones*
ATBCB Bulletin #4: *Surfaces*
ATBCB Bulletin #5: *Using ADAAG*
ATBCB Bulletin #6: *Parking*
DOJ/ATBCB/DOT - *Accessibility Guidelines for Detectable Warnings: Joint Final Rule* (Federal Register; April 12, 1994)
ATBCB - *Americans with Disabilities Act Accessibility Guidelines for Buildings and Facilities; Transportation Facilities; Amendment to Final Guidelines and Part 1192; Americans with Disabilities Act Accessibility Guidelines for Transportation Vehicles; Final Guidelines* (36 CFR Part 1191)
Open for Business - A Practical Guide to the ADA
  Access Equals Opportunity Booklets:
  - Retail Stores
  - Restaurants & Bars
  - Grocery Stores
  - Car Sales & Service
  - Fun & Fitness Centers
  - Medical Offices
A Guide for Making Your Business Accessible to People with Mental Retardation
Accommodating All Guests - the ADA and the Lodging Industry
ADA Q&A for Health Care Providers
Answers to Commonly Asked Questions by Hospitals and Health Care Providers
DOE - *Removal of Architectural Barriers to the Handicapped Program: Modifications of UFA to Suit Childrens' Dimensions* ($4.04)
DOI - *Preserving the Past and Making it Accessible for People with Disabilities*
DOJ - *How to File a Title III Complaint*

Americans With Disabilities Act

Title IV: Telecommunications
FCC - *Telecommunications Relay Services (TRS)*
The ABCs of Telecommunication Relay Services (TRS)

Other Laws
DOE - *Handicapped Persons' Rights Under Federal Law - Information for Those with Rights and Responsibilities Under Section 504 of the Rehabilitation Act of 1973* (Free)
DOE *Rehabilitation Act of 1973* (Section 504) (Free)
HUD - *Final Fair Housing Accessibility Guidelines* (Federal Register 24 CFR Chapter 1; 3/6/91) (Free)
HUD - *Non-discrimination Based on Handicap in Federally-Assisted Programs and Activities; Final Rule/Delegation and Redelegation of Authority* (Federal Register 24 CFR Part 8; 6/2/88)

More Info About Laws and Requirements

If one of the regional centers listed above does not satisfy your information needs, you can always get more detail about the law and its implications by contacting one of the agencies listed below.

For technical assistance with respect to Americans with Disabilities Act Accessibility Guidelines contact:
Architectural and Transportation Barriers
  Compliance Board
1331 F Street, NW, Suite 1000   202-272-5434 (V/TDD)
Washington, DC 20004-1111   800-872-2253 (V/TDD)
www.access_board.gov

The following office specializes in State and Local Government activities:
U.S. Department of Justice
Civil Rights Division
Coordination and Review Section
P.O. Box 66560   800-514-0301 (voice)
Washington, DC 20035-6118   800-514-0383 (TDD)
www.usdoj.gov/crt/crt_home.html
    202-514-6193 (Electronic Bulletin Board)

The following office specializes in business information:
U.S. Department of Justice
Civil Rights Division
Public Access Section
P.O. Box 66738   800-514-0301 (voice)
Washington, DC 20035-6738   800-514-0383 (TDD)
www.usdoj.gov/crt/crt_home.html
    202-514-6193 (Electronic Bulletin Board)

For more information about employment contact:
Equal Employment Opportunity Commission
1801 L Street, NW   202-663-4900 (voice)
Washington, DC 20507   800-669-6820 (TDD)
www.eeoc.gov   202-663-4494 (TDD for 202 Area Code)

For additional information about transportation requirements:
Department of Transportation
400 Seventh Street, SW   888-446-4511 (voice)
Washington, DC 20590   800-877-8339 (TDD)
www.fta.dot.gov

For additional information regarding telecommunications contact:
Federal Communications Commission
445 12th Street, SW   202-418-0976 (voice)
Washington, DC 20554   202-418-0484 (TDD)
www.fcc.gov

The following organization assists employers who are looking for ways to accommodate employees or applicants with disabilities:
JAN: The President's Committee's Job Accommodation Network
918 Chestnut Ridge Rd., Suite 1
P.O. Box 6080
Morgantown, WV 25606   800-526-7234 (V/TTY)
http://janweb.icdi.wvu.edu

Franchising: How To Select The Best Opportunity

Franchising could be for you, according to a study conducted by Arthur Andersen & Company of 366 franchise companies in 60 industries. They reported that nearly 86% of all franchise operations opened in the previous five years were still under the same ownership; only 3% of these businesses were no longer in business. The U.S. Commerce Department reports that from 1971 to 1987, less than 5% of franchises were terminated on an annual basis. In contrast, a study conducted by the U.S. Small Business Administration from 1978 to 1988 found 62.2% of all new businesses were dissolved within the first six years of their operation, due to failure, bankruptcy, retirement, or other reasons. While we are sure you are beginning to entertain the idea of owning a new business, franchising is not risk free and needs to be entered into with a degree of caution. Therefore, you need to take measures to protect yourself. The following organizations and publications will help you find the right franchise for you.

Organizations

Federal Trade Commission (FTC)
Bureau of Consumer Protection
Division of Marketing Practices
Pennsylvania Avenue at 6th Street, NW
Washington, DC 20580   202-326-3128
www.ftc.gov

Buying a franchise or a business opportunity may be appealing if you want to be your own boss, but have limited capital and business experience. However, without carefully investigating a business before you purchase, you may make a serious mistake. It is important to find out if a particular business is right for you and if it has the potential to yield the financial return you expect. A Federal Trade Commission (FTC) rule requires that franchise and business opportunity sellers provide certain information to help you in your decision. Under the FTC rule, a franchise or business opportunity seller must give you a detailed disclosure document at least ten business days before you pay any money or legally commit yourself to a purchase. This document gives 20 important items of information about the business, including: the names, addresses, and telephone numbers of other purchasers; the fully-audited financial statement of the seller; the background and experience of the business's key executives; the cost required to start and maintain the business; and the responsibilities you and the seller will have to each other once you buy. The disclosure document is a valuable tool that not only helps you obtain information about a proposed business, but assists you in comparing it with other businesses. If you are not given a disclosure document, ask why you did not receive one. Some franchise or business opportunity sellers may not be required to give you a disclosure document. If any franchise or business opportunity says it is not covered by the rule, you may want to verify it with the FTC, an attorney, or a business advisor. Even if the business is not required to give the document, you still may want to ask for the data to help you make an informed investment decision.

Some Important Advice From The FTC:

1. Talk to owners. They can be valuable sources of information. The disclosure document must list the names and addresses of current owners and operators. Ask them how the information in the disclosure document matches their experiences with the company. A list of references selected by the company is not a substitute for a list of franchises or business opportunity owners.

2. Investigate claims about your potential earnings. Some companies may claim you'll earn a certain income or that existing franchisees or business opportunity purchasers earn a certain amount. Companies making earnings representations must provide you with the written basis for their claims. Be suspicious of any company that cannot substantiate its earnings representations in writing. Sellers also must tell you in writing the number and percentage of owners who have done as well as they claim you will. Keep in mind that broad sales claims about successful areas of business — "Be a part of our four billion dollar industry," for example — may have no bearing on your likelihood of success. You also have to realize that once you buy the business, you may be competing with franchise owners or independent business people with more experience.

3. Shop around: compare franchises with other business opportunities. Some companies may offer benefits not available from the first company you considered. The *Franchise Opportunities Handbook*, published annually by the U.S. Department of Commerce, describes more than 1,400 companies that offer franchises. Contact those that interest you. Request their disclosure documents and compare their offerings.

4. Listen carefully to the sales presentation. Some sales tactics should signal caution. For example, if you are pressured to sign immediately "because prices will go up tomorrow," or "another buyer wants this deal," slow down. A seller with a good offer doesn't use high-pressure tactics. Under the Rule, the seller must wait at least 10 business days after giving you the required documents before accepting your money or signature on an agreement.

5. Be wary if the salesperson makes the job sound too easy. The thought of "easy money" may be appealing, but success generally requires hard work.

6. Get the seller's promises in writing. Any oral promises you get from a salesperson should be written into the contract you sign. If the salesperson says one thing but the contract says nothing about it or says something different, the contract is what counts. If a seller balks at putting oral promises in writing, be alert to potential problems and consider doing business with another firm.

7. Consider getting professional advice. Ask a lawyer, accountant, or business advisor to read the disclosure document and proposed contract. The money and time you spend on

Franchising

professional assistance and research — such as phone calls to current owners — could save you from a bad investment decision.

Filing a Complaint

Although the FTC cannot resolve individual disputes, information about your experiences and concerns is vital to the enforcement of the Franchise and Business Opportunities Rule. The time to protect yourself is before you buy rather than after. Only fifteen states give you private rights to sue, and there is often a limited ability to recover. A franchiser knows your financial situation, and can often outwait you. Many franchise owners have no money left to hire a lawyer to try to recoup their losses.

To file a complaint with the FTC, or request a complete list of publications, contact the following addresses:

> The Consumer Response Center
> Federal Trade Commission
> Washington, DC 20580
> 202-FTC-HELP (382-4357)
> Online Complaint Form can be found at
> www.ftc.gov/ftc/complaint.htm

or

> Franchise and Business Opportunity Complaint
> Federal Trade Commission, Room 238
> Washington, DC 20580

Online

The Federal Trade Commission Online at {www.ftc.gov} offers a wide range of information and assistance for the franchisor.

Rules and Regulations of Franchising

By using this web address, {www.ftc.gov/bcp/franchise/netfran.htm}, you will be able to access vital information listed under these main topics:

Regulatory Reform: Franchise Rule Review
Before You Buy: Franchise and Business Opportunity Pamphlets
Consumer Alert: Enforcement "Sweeps" Target Business Opportunity Fraud
Your Legal Rights: Guide to the FTC Franchise Rule
Franchise Rule Text: 16 CFR Part 436
State Disclosure Requirements: Franchises and Business Opportunities
Know The Risks: Summary of Recent Enforcement Cases
How To Comply: Recent Staff Advisory Opinions
Franchise and Business Opportunity FAQS

All FTC pamphlets are available online at {www.ftc.gov/bcp/menu-fran.htm}.

State Agencies Administering Franchise Disclosure Laws

California (filing required)
Franchise Division, Department of Corporations, 1115 11th St., Sacramento, CA 95814; 916-445-7205.

Hawaii (filing required)
Franchise and Securities Division, State Department of Commerce, P.O. Box 40, Honolulu, HI 96813; 808-586-2722.

Illinois (filing required)
Franchise Division, Office of Attorney General, 500 South Second Street, Springfield, IL 62706; 217-782-4465.

Indiana (filing required)
Franchise Division, Office of Secretary of State, One N. Capitol St., Suite 560, Indianapolis, IN 46204; 317-232-6576.

Maryland (filing required)
Franchise Office, Division of Securities, 200 St. Paul Place, 20th Floor, Baltimore, MD 21202; 301-576-6360.

Michigan (notice required)
Antitrust and Franchise Unit, Office of Attorney General, 670 Law Building, Lansing, MI 48913; 517-373-7117.

Minnesota (filing required)
Franchise Division, Department of Commerce, 133 East Seventh St., St. Paul, MN 55101; 651-296-6328.

New York (filing required)
Franchise and Securities Division, State Department of Law, 120 Broadway, 23rd Floor, New York, NY 10271; 212-416-8211.

North Dakota (filing required)
Franchise Division, Office of Securities Commission, 600 East Boulevard, 5th Floor, Bismarck, ND 58505; 701-224-4712.

Oregon (no filing)
Corporate Securities Section, Department of Insurance & Finance, Labor and Industries Bldg., Salem, OR 97310; 503-378-4387.

Rhode Island (filing required)
Franchise Office, Division of Securities, 233 Richmond St., Suite 232, Providence, RI 02903; 401-277-3048.

South Dakota (filing required)
Franchise Office, Division of Securities, 910 E. Sioux Ave., Pierre, SD 57501; 605-773-4013.

Virginia (filing required)
Franchise Office, State Corporation Commission, 1300 E. Main St., Richmond, VA 23219; 804-371-9276.

Washington (filing required)
The Department of Financial Institutions, Securities Division, P.O. Box 9033, Olympia, WA 98507-9033; 360-902-8760; Fax: 360-586-5068; {www.wa.gov/dfi/securities}.

Wisconsin (filing required)
Franchise Office, Wisconsin Securities Commission, P.O. Box 1768, Madison, WI 53701; 608-266-3364; {www.wdfi.org}.

State Offices Administering Business Opportunity Disclosure Laws

California (filing required)
Consumer Law Section, Attorney General's Office, 1515 K St., Sacramento, CA 92101; 916-445-9555.

Connecticut (filing required)
Department of Banking, Securities Division, 44 Capitol Avenue, Hartford, CT 06106; 203-566-4560 ext. 8322.

Franchising

Florida (filing required)
Department of Agriculture and Consumer Services, Room 110, Mayo Building, Tallahassee, FL 32301; 904-488-2221, 800-342-2176 (in-state only).

Georgia (no filing required)
Office of Consumer Affairs, No. 2 Martin Luther King Dr., Plaza Level, East Tower, Atlanta, GA 30334; 404-656-3790.

Illinois (filing required)
Illinois Security Department, Lincoln Tower, 520 S. Second St., Suite 200, Springfield, IL 62701; 217-782-2256.

Indiana (filing required)
Consumer Protection Division, Attorney General's Office, 219 State House, Indianapolis, IN 46204; 317-232-6331.

Iowa (filing required)
Securities Bureau, Second Floor, Lucas State Office Building, Des Moines, IA 50319; 515-281-4441.

Kentucky (filing required)
Attorney General's Office, Consumer Protection Division, 209 St. Clair, Frankfort, KY 40601; 502-573-2200.

Louisiana (bond filing required)
Office of the Attorney General, Consumer Protection Division, 2610-A Woodale Blvd., Baton Rouge, LA 70804; 504-342-7900.

Maine (filing required)
Banking Bureau, Securities Division, State House, Station 121, Augusta, ME 04333; 207-624-8551.

Maryland (filing required)
Attorney General's Office, Securities Division, 200 St. Paul Pl., 20th Floor, Baltimore, MD 21202; 301-576-6360.

Michigan (notice required)
Consumer Protection Division, Department of the Attorney General, 670 Law Building, Lansing, MI 48913; 517-373-7117.

Minnesota (filing required)
Department of Commerce, Registration Division, 133 East 7th Street, St. Paul, MN 5501; 651-296-6328.

Nebraska (filing required)
Department of Banking and Finance, P.O. Box 95006, Lincoln, NE 68509; 402-471-2171, 402-471-3445.

New Hampshire (filing required)
Attorney General's Office, Consumer Protection Division, State House Annex, Concord, NH 03301; 603-271-3641.

North Carolina (filing required)
Department of Justice, Consumer Protection Division, P.O. Box 629, Raleigh, NC 27602; 919-733-3924.

Ohio (no filing required)
Attorney General's Office, Consumer Fraud and Crime Section, 25th Floor, State Office Tower, 30 East Broad Street, Columbus, OH 43266-0410; 614-466-8831, 800-282-0515 (in-state only).

Oklahoma (filing required)
Oklahoma Department of Securities, Suite 860 First National Center, 120 N. Robinson St., Oklahoma City, OK 73102; 405-280-7700; Fax: 405-280-7742; {www.securities.state.ok.us}.

South Carolina (filing required)
Secretary of State's Office, P.O. Box 11350, Columbia, SC 29211; 803-734-2169.

South Dakota (filing required)
Division of Securities, 910 E. Sioux Avenue, Pierre, SD 57501; 605-773-4013.

Texas (filing required)
Secretary of State's Office, Statutory Documents Section, P.O. Box 13563, Austin, TX 78711; 512-475-1769.

Utah (filing required)
Consumer Protection Division, 160 East 300 South, Salt Lake City, UT 84111; 801-530-6601.

Virginia (no filing required)
Consumer Affairs Office, 101 North 8th Street, Richmond, VA 23219; 804-786-0594, 800-451-1525 (in-state only).

Washington (filing required)
Department of Financial Institutions, Securities Division, P.O. Box 9033, Olympia, WA 98507-9033; 206-753-6928.

Publications

International Franchise Association (IFA)
1350 New York Avenue, NW
Washington, DC 20005-4709
202-628-8000
Fax: 202-628-0812
E-mail: ifa@franchise.org
www.franchise.org

Founded in 1960, the International Franchise Association (IFA) has more than 600 franchiser members, including thirty-five overseas in more than 60 different industries. IFA members are accepted into the organization only after meeting stringent requirements regarding number of franchises, length of time in business, and financial stability.

The IFA offers about twenty-five educational conferences and seminars yearly, including an annual convention and a legal symposium. There is a program on financing and venture capital designed to bring together franchisers and franchisees. Each year the association also sponsors several trade shows, open to the public, so that franchisers may attract potential franchisees.

The IFA has created the Institute of Certified Franchise Executives (CFE) and the IFA Educational Foundation. Both organizations are set to educate the franchiser and collect vast amounts of franchising knowledge. Between 1998 and 1999, the classes offered by the CFE more than doubled. The ICFE Brochure is available online at {www.franchise.org/edufound/cfe.paf}.

The International Franchise Association publishes the following publications, which you can order by phone: 1-800-543-1038 from 9:00 am - 4:00 pm (EST), on the IFA website {www.franchise.org/books/bookstore/bookstore.asp}, or order by fax:

Franchising

412-741-1142. You may pre-pay with a credit card through fax, phone, or web, but make sure to include all credit card information and know that all sales are final.

To Help You Franchise Your Business
How To Be A Franchisor - $8
Financial Strategies For The Growing Franchisor - $24
The Franchise Bible - $19.95
Franchise Organizations - $29.95
The Franchise Advantage: Make It Work For You - $30
The Guide To Franchising - $28.50
Target Success - $5.95

To Help You Choose A Franchise
Choosing Your Own Franchise Information - $29.95
Franchise Opportunities Guide - $15
   (The *Franchise Opportunities Guide* is also available online at {www.franchis.org/fog.asp}
The Top Franchises Available - $16.95
Investigate Before Investing - $6
The 20 Most Frequently Asked Questions About Franchising - $5
Guide to Negotiating a Business Lease - $15.95
The Franchise Bible - $19.95
Guide to Selecting the Best Entity to Own and Operate Your Business - $15.95
How To Buy and Manage A Franchise - $11
Financing Your Franchise - $18.95
The Franchise Survival Guide - $24.95

Franchisee Information
Franchising: The Bottom Line - $44.95
Public Relations For the Franchisee: How to Create Your Own Publicity - $21

For Franchisers
The Franchise Cooperatives Handbook - $45
Advisory Councils: Effective Two-Way Communications For Franchise Systems - $10
Starting Your Own Business - $12.95
The Tortoise Wins Again - $12
Multiple-Unit Franchising - $27.50
You Can't Teach a Kid to Ride a Bike at a Seminar - $23.95
The Franchise Relations Handbook - $35
Wealth Within Reach - $25
Franchising: The Business Strategy That Changed the World - $19.95

Audio/Visual Information
The UFOC Guidelines (VHS) - $145
The National Franchise Mediation Program (VHS) - $60
In Pursuit of Excellence (VHS) - $35
Franchising: How To Be In Business For Yourself, Not By Yourself (VHS) - $49.95
The Franchise Success System - Choose the Right Franchise! (audio set and workbooks) - $49.95
Target Success (audio set and workbook) - $39.95
Opportunities in Franchising (audio) - $35.00

Reference Materials
The Future of Franchising: Looking 25 Years Ahead to the Year 2010 - $10

Glossary of Franchising Terms - $4
Franchising World magazine - $18
   (call for quantity and international prices)
New! *Study of Franchised Unit Turnover* - $75
New! *International Expansion by U.S. Franchisors* - $75

Legal Information
Franchise Sales Compliance Guide - $225
Fundamentals of Franchising - $120
Building Franchise Relationships: A Guide to Anticipating Problems, Resolving Conflicts, and Representing Clients - $79.95
Mergers and Acquisitions of Franchise Companies - $69.95
The Franchise Trademark Handbook - $69.95
New! *Accounting and Tax Aspects of Franchising* - $120
International Franchising - Newly Revised 1996 Edition! - $195
International Franchising Law - $280
The Franchise Industry (CCH Tax Transactions Library) - $40
Covenants Against Competition in Franchise Agreements - $125
Franchising: An Accounting, Auditing, and Income Tax Guide - $140

Minority Business Development Agency
U.S. Department of Commerce
14th and Constitution Ave, NW, Room 5053
Washington, DC 20230
202-482-5061
Fax: 202-482-2678
www.mbda.gov

The Minority Business Development Agency (MBDA) was started in 1969 in order to provide management, technical assistance, information and advice on business matters to enterprising members of socially or economically disadvantaged individuals (though not limited to these groups of individuals). The MBDA can help to identify sources of financing and assist in the preparation of financial and bonding proposals for those looking to purchase, begin, or expand a business. The MBDA has held an annual celebration, Minority Enterprise Development Week (MED Week), since 1983. Here, over 1,000 minority owned business owners convene for networking sessions, seminars, award ceremonies, a congressional reception, trade fair, and more. MED Week is co-sponsored by the MBDA and the Small Business Administration.

The Minority Business Development Agency's website: {www.mbda.gov/rroom.html} (available in both Spanish and English) houses an electronic reading room accumulated by the MBDA Research Division as well as private providers. The library is consistently being updated.

Minority Business Development Agency Development Centers

Minority Business Development Agency of Atlanta
401 W. Peachtree St., NW., Suite 1715
Atlanta, GA 30308
404-730-3300
Fax: 404-730-3313
States Served: Alabama, Florida, Georgia, Kentucky, Mississippi, North Carolina, Puerto Rico, South Carolina, Tennessee, and the Virgin Islands

Franchising

Minority Business Development Agency of Chicago
55 E. Monroe St., Suite 1406
Chicago, IL 60603
312-353-0812
Fax: 312-353-0191
States Served: Illinois, Indiana, Iowa, Kansas, Michigan, Minnesota, Missouri, Nebraska, Ohio, and Wisconsin.

Minority Business Development Agency of Dallas
1100 Commerce St., Room 7B-23
Dallas, TX 75242
214-767-8001
Fax: 214-767-0613
States Served: Arkansas, Colorado, Louisiana, Montana, New Mexico, North Dakota, Oklahoma, South Dakota, Texas, Utah, and Wyoming.

Minority Business Development Agency of New York
26 Federal Plaza, Room 3720
New York, NY
212-264-3262
Fax: 212-264-0725
States Served: Connecticut, Delaware, Maine, New Hampshire, New Jersey, New York, Pennsylvania, Rhode Island, Vermont, Virginia, Washington, D.C., and West Virginia.

Minority Business Development Agency of San Francisco
221 Main St., Room 1280
San Francisco, CA 94105
415-744-3001
Fax: 415-744-3061
States Served: Alaska, American Samoa, Arizona, California, Hawaii, Idaho, Nevada, Oregon, and Washington.

Franchising

Top 30 Fastest Growing Franchise Companies

1. McDonald's
2. Burger King Corporation
3. Yogen Fruz Worldwide
4. 7-Eleven Convenience Stores
5. Jani-King
6. Subway
7. Baskin-Robbins USA Co.
8. Coverall North America Inc.
9. Arby's
10. Taco Bell
11. Dunkin Donuts
12. Carlson Wasgonlit Travel
13. Jazzercise Inc.
14. Blimpie Corporation
15. Mail Boxes Etc.
16. Miracle Ear Hearing Systems
17. Future Kids Inc.
18. Papa John's Pizza
19. Holiday Inn Worldwide
20. Choice Hotels International
21. Proforce USA
22. Domino's Pizza Inc.
23. KFC
24. Church's Chicken
25. Orion Food Systems Inc.
26. Great Clips Inc.
27. ReMax International
28. Super 8 Motels Inc.
29. Coldwell Bankers Res. Affil., Inc.
30. Jiffy Lube

Did You Know?...

According to the International Franchise Association:

- A new franchise opens every 8 minutes of each business day.

- 1 of every 12 businesses is a franchise.

- By the year 2000 total franchise sales could reach $1 trillion dollars.

- Franchise sales account for 40.9% of all retail sales.

- In 1992, franchise chains created approximately 21,000 new business format franchises. In contrast, more than 220,000 new businesses failed last year, resulting in over 400,000 job losses.

- According to a 1991 Gallup Poll an overwhelming 94% of franchise owners say that they are successful. Seventy-five percent of franchise owners would do it again while, only 39% of Americans would repeat their job or business.

- Based on the Gallup Poll survey, the average total investment cost, including fees and any additional expenses, was $147,570. Fifty-six percent reported total investment cost under $100,000 while 26% reported total investment cost over $100,000.

- Based on the Gallup Poll survey, the average gross income before taxes of franchisees is $124,290. Forty-nine percent reported gross income of less than $100,000 and 37% reported gross income of more than $100,000.

- By the year 2000, an astounding 35-50 percent of all retail sales will pass through a franchise chain.

Government Contracts: How to Sell Your Goods and Services To The World's Largest Buyer

If you produce a product or service, you've probably always wondered how you could offer what you produce to the biggest client in the world — the Federal government. Have you thought of the government as being a "closed shop" and too difficult to penetrate? Well, I'm happy to say that you're entirely wrong on that score. The Federal government spends over $180 billion each year on products ranging from toilet paper to paper clips and writes millions of dollars in contracts for services like advertising, consulting, and printing. Most Americans believe that a majority of those federal purchasing contracts have been eliminated over the last few years, but that's simply not true — they've just been replaced with new contracts that are looking for the same kinds of goods and services. Last year the government took action (either initiating or modifying) on over 350,000 different contracts. They buy these goods and services from someone, so why shouldn't that someone be you? To be successful doing business with the government, you need to learn to speak "governmenteze" to get your company into the purchasing loop, and I can show you how to accomplish that in just a few easy steps.

Step 1

Each department within the Federal government has a procurement office that buys whatever the department requires. Most of these offices have put together their own *Doing Business With the Department of _____* publication, which usually explains procurement policies, procedures, and programs. This booklet also contains a list of procurement offices, contact people, subcontracting opportunities, and a solicitation mailing list. Within each department there is also an Office of Small and Disadvantaged Business Utilization, whose sole purpose is to push the interests of the small business, and to make sure these companies get their fair share of government contracts. Another good resource is your local Small Business Administration Office which should have a listing of U.S. Government Procurement Offices in your state.

Step 2

Once you have familiarized yourself with the process, you need to find out who is buying what from whom and for how much. There are three ways to get this important information.

A. Daily Procurement News

Each weekday, the *Commerce Business Daily* (CBD) gives a complete listing of products and services (that cost over $25,000) wanted by the U.S. government — products and services that your business may be selling. Each listing includes the following: the product or service, along with a short description; name and address of the agency; deadline for proposals or bids; phone number to request specifications; and the solicitation number of the product or service needed. Many business concerns, including small businesses, incorporate CBD review into their government marketing activities. To obtain a subscription for $275 a year, contact: Superintendent of Documents, U.S. Government Printing Office, Washington, DC 20402; 202-512-1800; {www.gpo.gov}.

B. Federal Data Systems Division (FDSD)

This Center distributes consolidated information about federal purchases, including research and development. FDSD can tell you how much the Federal government spent last quarter on products and services, which agencies made those purchases, and what contractors did business with the government. FDSD summarizes this information through two types of reports: The FDSD standard report and the FDSD special report. The standard report is a free, quarterly compilation containing statistical procurement information in "snapshot" form for over 60 federal agencies, as well as several charts, graphs, and tables which compare procurement activities by state, major product and service codes, method of procurement, and contractors. The report also includes quarterly and year-to-year breakdowns of amounts and percentages spent on small, women owned, and minority businesses. Special reports are prepared upon request for a fee, based on computer and labor costs. They are tailored to the specific categories, which can be cross-tabulated in numerous ways. A special report can help you analyze government procurement and data trends, identify competitors, and locate federal markets for individual products or services. Your Congressman may have access to the Federal Procurement Database from his/her office in Washington, which you may be able to use for free. For more information, contact: Federal Data Systems Division, General Services Administration, 7th and D St., SW, Room 5652, Washington, DC 20407; 202-401-1529.

C. Other Contracts

For contracts under $25,000, you must be placed on a department's list for solicitation bids on those contracts. The mailing list forms are available through the Procurement Office, the Office of Small and Disadvantaged Business Utilization, or your local Small Business Association office. Last year 18.7 billion dollars was spent on these "small" purchases, so these contracts should not be overlooked. Smaller contracts, completed over the course of a fiscal year, can mean lots of revenue for your business bottom line.

Step 3: Subcontracting Opportunities

All of the federal procurement offices or Offices of Small and Disadvantaged Business Utilization (SDBU) can provide you with information regarding subcontracting. Many of the departments' prime contracts require that the prime contractor maximize small business subcontracting opportunities. Many prime contractors produce special publications which can be helpful to those interested in subcontracting. The SDBU Office can provide you with more information on the subcontracting process, along with a directory of prime contractors. Another good source for subcontract assistance is your local Small Business Administration (SBA) office, 1-800-827-5722. SBA develops subcontracting

Government Contracts

opportunities for small business by maintaining close contact with large business prime contractors and by referring qualified small firms to them. The SBA has developed agreements and close working relationships with hundreds of prime contractors who cooperate by offering small firms the opportunity to compete for their subcontracts. In addition, to complete SBA's compliance responsibilities, commercial market representatives monitor prime contractors in order to assess their compliance with laws governing subcontracting opportunities for small businesses.

Step 4: Small Business Administration's 8(a) Program

Are you a socially or economically disadvantaged person who has a business? This group includes, but is not limited to, Black Americans, Hispanic Americans, Native Americans, Asian Pacific Americans, and Subcontinent Asian Americans. Socially and economically disadvantaged individuals represent a significant percentage of U.S. citizens, yet account for a disproportionately small percentage of total U.S. business revenues. The 8(a) program assists firms in participating in the business sector and to become independently competitive in the marketplace. SBA may provide participating firms with procurement, marketing, financial, management, or other technical assistance. A Business Opportunity Specialist will be assigned to each firm that participates, and is responsible for providing the firm with access to assistance that can help the firm fulfill its business goals. SBA undertakes an extensive effort to provide government contracting opportunities to participating businesses. The SBA has the Procurement Automated Source System (PASS) which places your company's capabilities online so that they may be available to government agencies and major corporations when they request potential bidders for contracts and subcontracts. To apply for the 8(a) program, you must attend an interview session with an official in the SBA field office in your area. For more information, contact your local Small Business Administration Office, or call 1-800-827-5722 or {www.sba.gov} for the SBA office nearest you.

Step 5: Bond

A Surety bond is often a prerequisite for government and private sector contracts. This is particularly true when the contract involves construction. In order for the company to qualify for an SBA Guarantee Bond, they must make the bonding company aware of their capabilities based on past contract performance and meeting of financial obligations. SBA can assist firms in obtaining surety bonding for contracts that do not exceed $1,250,000. SBA is authorized, when appropriate circumstances occur, to guarantee as much as 90 percent of losses suffered by a surety resulting from a breach of terms of a bond.

Step 6: Publications

The Government Printing Office has several publications for sale which explain the world of government contracts. For ordering information, contact: Superintendent of Documents, Government Printing Office, Washington, DC 20402; 202-512-1800; {www.gpo.gov}.

* *U.S. Government Purchasing and Sales Directory* ($25): The Directory is an alphabetical listing of the products and services bought by the military departments, and a separate listing of the civilian agencies. The Directory also includes an explanation of the ways in which the SBA can help a business obtain government prime contracts and subcontracts, data on government sales of surplus property, and comprehensive descriptions of the scope of the government market for research and development.

* *Selling to the Military* ($14.00)

* *Women Business Owners; Selling to the Federal Government* ($3.75)

* *Subcontracting Opportunities with DOD Major Prime Contractors* ($23.00)

Step 7: What is GSA?

General Services Administration (GSA) is the Government's business agent. On an annual budget of less than half a billion dollars, it directs and coordinates nearly $8 billion a year worth of purchases, sales, and services. Its source of supply is private enterprise, and its clients include all branches of the Federal government. GSA plans and manages leasing, purchase, or construction of office buildings, laboratories, and warehouses; buys and delivers nearly $4 billion worth of goods and services; negotiates the prices and terms for an additional $2.3 billion worth of direct business between federal groups and private industry; sets and interprets the rules for federal travel and negotiates reduced fares and lodging rates for federal travelers; and manages a 92,000 vehicle fleet with a cumulative yearly mileage of over 1 billion. For a copy of *Doing Business With GSA*, *GSA's Annual Report*, or other information regarding GSA, contact: Office of Publication, General Services Administration, 18th and F Streets, NW, Washington, DC 20405; 202-501-1235. For information on GSA's architect and engineer services, such as who is eligible for GSA professional services contracts, how to find out about potential GSA projects, what types of contracts are available, and where and how to apply, contact: Office of Design and Construction, GSA, 18th and F Streets, NW, Washington, DC 20405; 202-501-1888. Information on specifications and standards of the Federal government is contained in a booklet, *Guide to Specifications and Standards*, which is available free from Specifications Sections, General Services Administration, 470 E L'Enfant Plaza, SW, Suite 8100, Washington, DC 20407; 202-619-8925.

Step 8: Bid and Contract Protests

The General Accounting Office (GAO) resolves disputes between agencies and bidders of government contracts, including grantee award actions. The free publication, *Bid Protests at GAO; A Descriptive Guide*, contains information on GAO's procedures for determining legal questions arising from the awarding of government contracts. Contact Information Handling and Support Facilities, General Accounting Office, Gaithersburg, MD 20877; 202-512-6000. For Contract Appeals, the GSA Board of Contract Appeals works to resolve disputes arising out of contracts with GSA, the Departments of Treasury, Education, Commerce, and other independent government agencies. The Board also hears and decides bid protests arising out of government-wide automated data processing (ADP) procurements. A contractor may elect to use either the GSA Board or the General Accounting Office for

Government Contracts

resolution of an ADP bid protest. Contractors may elect to have their appeals processed under the Board's accelerated procedures if the claim is $50,000 or less, or under the small claims procedure if the claim is $10,000 or less. Contractors may also request that a hearing be held at a location convenient to them. With the exception of small claims decisions, contractors can appeal adverse Board decisions to the U.S. Court of Appeals for the Federal Circuit. For more information, contact: Board of Contract Appeals, General Services Administration, 18th and F Streets, NW, Washington, DC 20405; 202-501-0720. There are other Contract Appeals Boards for other departments. One of the last paragraphs in your government contract should specify which Board you are to go to if a problem with your particular contract should arise.

Government Contracts

Free Local Help:
The Best Place To Start To Sell To The Government

Within each state there are offices that can help you get started in the federal procurement process. As stated previously, your local Small Business Administration (SBA) office is a good resource. In addition to their other services, the SBA can provide you with a list of Federal Procurement Offices based in your state, so you can visit them in person to gather valuable information. Another place to turn is your local Small Business Development Center (look under Economic Development in your phone book). These offices are funded jointly by federal and state governments, and are usually associated with the state university system in your area. They are aware of the federal procurement process, and can help you draw up a sensible business plan that will be successful.

Some states have established programs to assist businesses in the federal procurement process for all departments in the government. These programs are designed to help businesses learn about the bidding process, the resources available, and provide information on how the procurement system operates. They can match the product or service you are selling with the appropriate agency, and then help you market your product. Several programs have online bid matching services, whereby if a solicitation appears in the *Commerce Business Daily* that matches what your company markets, then the program will automatically contact you to start the bid process. The program office can then request the appropriate documents, and assist you in achieving your goal. These Procurement Assistance Offices (PAOs) are partially funded by the Department of Defense to assist businesses with Defense Procurement. For a current listing of PAOs contact:

Defense Logistics Agency
Office of Small and Disadvantaged Utilization
Bldg. 4, Cameron Station
Room 4B110
Alexandria, VA 22304-6100   703-767-1661
{www.dla.mil}, then go to the small business site

Let Your Congressman Help You

Are you trying to market a new product to a department of the Federal government? Need to know where to try to sell your wares? Is there some problem with your bid? Your Congressman can be of assistance. Because they want business in their state to boom, most Congressmen will make an effort to assist companies in obtaining federal contracts. Frequently they will write a letter to accompany your bid, or if you are trying to market a new product, they will write a letter to the procurement office requesting that they review your product. Your Congressman can also be your personal troubleshooter. If there is some problem with your bid, your Congressman can assist you in determining and resolving the problem, and can provide you with information on the status of your bid. Look in the blue pages of your phone book for your Senators' or Representatives' phone numbers, or call them in Washington at 202-224-3121.

Small Business Set-Asides

The Small Business Administration (SBA) encourages government purchasing agencies to set aside suitable government purchases for exclusive small business competition. A purchase which is restricted to small business bidders is identified by a set aside clause in the invitation for bids or request for proposals. There is no overall listing of procurements which are, or have been, set aside for small business. A small business learns which purchases are reserved for small business by getting listed on bidders' lists. It also can help keep itself informed of set aside opportunities by referring to the *Commerce Business Daily*. Your local SBA office can provide you with more information on set asides, and so can the Procurement Assistance Offices listed at the end of this section. To locate your nearest SBA office, call 1-800-827-5722 or {www.sba.gov}.

Veterans Assistance

Each Small Business Administration District Office has a Veterans Affairs Officer which can assist veteran-owned businesses in obtaining government contracts. Although there is no such thing as veterans set aside contracts, the Veterans Administration does make an effort to fill its contracts using veteran-owned businesses whenever possible. Contact your local SBA office for more information.

Woman-Owned Business Assistance

There are over 3.7 million women-owned businesses in the United States, and the number is growing each year. Current government policy requires federal contracting officers to increase their purchases from women-owned businesses. Although the women-owned firms will receive more opportunities to bid, they still must be the lowest responsive and responsible bidder to win the contract. To assist these businesses, each SBA district office has a Women's Business Representative, who can provide you with information regarding government programs. Most of the offices hold a *Selling to the Federal Government* seminar, which is designed to educate the business owner on the ins and outs of government procurement. There is also a helpful publication, *Women Business Owners: Selling to the Federal Government*, which provides information on procurement opportunities available. Contact your local SBA office or your Procurement Assistance Office (listed below) for more information.

Minority and Labor Surplus Area Assistance

Are you a socially or economically disadvantaged person who has a business? This group includes, but is not limited to, Black Americans, Hispanic Americans, Native Americans, Asian Pacific Americans, and Subcontinent Asian Americans. Socially and economically disadvantaged individuals represent a significant

Free Local Help

percentage of U.S. citizens yet account for a disproportionately small percentage of total U.S. business revenues. The 8(a) program assists firms to participate in the business sector and to become independently competitive in the marketplace. SBA may provide participating firms with procurement, marketing, financial, management, or other technical assistance. A Business Opportunity Specialist will be assigned to each firm that participates, and is responsible for providing that company with access to assistance that can help it fulfill its business goals.

Some areas of the country have been determined to be labor surplus areas, which means there is a high rate of unemployment. Your local SBA office can tell you if you live in such an area, as some contracts are set asides for labor surplus areas. For more information, contact your local Small Business Administration office (call 1-800-827-5722 for the SBA office nearest you; or online at {www.sba.gov}), or call the Procurement Assistance Office in your state (listed below).

Federal Procurement Assistance Offices

Alabama
Charles A. Hopson
University of Alabama at Birmingham
1717 11th Ave., S, Suite 419
Birmingham, AL 35294-4410
205-934-7260
Fax: 205-934-7645

Alaska
Mike Taylor
University of Alaska Anchorage
Small Business Development Center
430 W. 7th Ave., Suite 100
Anchorage, AK 99501-3550
907-274-7232
Fax: 907-274-9524

Arizona
Linda Alexius Hagerty
The National Center for AIED
National Center Headquarters
953 E. Juanita Ave.
Mesa, AZ 85204
602-545-1298
Fax: 602-545-4208

Paul R. Roddy
Aptan, Inc.
1435 N. Hayden Rd.
Scottsdale, AZ 85257-3773
602-945-5452
Fax: 602-945-4153
E-mail: aptan@pnmenet.com
www.aptan.com

Arkansas
Toni Tosch
Board of Trustees
University of Arkansas
Cooperative Extension Service
103 Page
Malvern, AR 72104
501-337-5355
Fax: 501-337-5045
E-mail: info@apacua.org
www.apacua.org

California
Lane Stafford
Riverside Community College District
3985 University Ave.
Riverside, CA 92501-3256
909-684-8469
Fax: 909-684-8369
E-mail: stafford@rccd.cc.ca.us
www.rccd.resources4u.com/pac/

Jane E. McGinnis
Action Business Center
California Central Valley PTAC
3180 Collins Dr., Suite A
Merced, CA 95348
209-385-7686
Fax: 209-383-4959
E-mail: cpc@cell2000.net
www.cell2000.net/cpc

J. Gunnar Schalin
Southwestern Community College
Contracting Opportunities Center
3443 Camino Del Rio South, Suite 116
San Diego, CA 92108-3913
619-285-7020
Fax: 619-285-7030
E-mail: sdcoc@pacbell.net
http://home.pacbell.net/sdcoc

Colorado
No PTA awarded

Connecticut
Arlene M. Vogel
Southeastern Connecticut Enterprise Region (seCTer)
190 Governor Winthrop Blvd., Suite 300
New London, CT 06320
860-701-6056
1-888-6-SECTER
Fax: 860-437-4662
E-mail: avogel@secter.org
www.secter.org/cptap/main.htm

Delaware
No PTA awarded

District of Columbia
No PTA awarded

Florida
Laura Subel
University of West Florida
Florida PTA Program
19 W. Garden St., Suite 300
Pensacola, FL 32501
850-595-6066
Fax: 850-595-6070

Georgia
Zack Osborne
Georgia Technical Research Corp.
GA Institute of Technology
400 Tenth St., CRB Room 246
Atlanta, GA 30332-0420
912-953-1460
Fax: 912-953-3169

Hawaii
No PTA awarded

Idaho
Larry Demirelli
Idaho Department of Commerce
State of Idaho
700 West State St.
Boise, ID 83720-0093
208-334-2470
Fax: 208-334-2631

Illinois
D. Lorenzo Padron
Latin American Chamber of Commerce
The Chicago Pac
2539 N. Kedzie Ave.
Chicago, IL 60647
773-252-5211
Fax: 773-252-7065
www.lacc1.com

Lois Van Meter
State of Illinois
Dept. of Commerce and Community Affairs
620 E. Adams St., Third Floor
Springfield, IL 62701
217-557-1823
Fax: 217-785-6328
E-mail: ivanmete@commerce.state.il.us
www.commerce.state.il.us

Indiana
Kathy DeGuilio-Fox
Partners in Contracting Corporation
PTA Center
6100 Southport Rd.
Portage, IN 46368
219-762-8644
Fax: 219-763-1513

A. David Schaaf
Indiana Small Business Development Corporation
Government Marketing Assistance Group
One N. Capitol Ave., Suite 1275
Indianapolis, IN 46204-2026
317-264-5600
Fax: 317-264-2806
www.isbdcorp.org

Iowa
Bruce Coney
State of Iowa
Iowa Department of Economic Development
200 E. Grand Ave.
Des Moines, IA 50309
515-242-4888
Fax: 515-242-4893
E-mail: bruce.coney@ided.state.ia.us
www.state.ia.us/sbro/ptac.htm

Kentucky
James A. Kurz
Kentucky Cabinet For Economic Development
Department of Community Development
500 Mero St.
22nd Floor Cap Plaza Tower

Government Contracts

Frankfort, KY 40601
800-838-3266
Fax: 502-564-5932
E-mail: jkurz@mail.state.ky.us
www.state.ky.us/edc/kpp.htm

Louisiana
Sherrie Mullins
Louisiana Productivity Center
University of Southwest Louisiana
P.O. Box 44172
241 E. Lewis St.
Lafayette, LA 70504-4172
318-482-6767
Fax: 318-262-5472
E-mail: sbm3321@usl.edu

Kelly Ford
Northwest Louisiana Government Procurement Center
Shreveport COC
400 Edwards St.
P.O. Box 20074
Shreveport, LA 71120-0074
318-677-2529
Fax: 318-677-2534
E-mail: kmford@iamenca.net

Maine
Michael Robinson
Eastern Maine Development Corp.
Market Development Center
One Cumberland Pl., Suite 300
P.O. Box 2579
Bangor, ME 04402-2579
207-942-6389
Fax: 207-942-3548
E-mail: mrobinson@emdc.org
www.mdcme.org

Maryland
Michael J. Wagoner, Inc.
Tri County Council For Western Maryland
111 S. George St.
Cumberland, MD 21502
301-777-2158
Fax: 301-777-2495

Massachusetts
No PTA awarded

Michigan
Sheila A. Auten
Genesee County Metropolitan Planning Commission
PTA Center
1101 Beach St., Room 223
Flint, MI 48502-1470
810-257-3010
Fax: 810-257-3185

Amy Reid
Schoolcraft College
18600 Haggerty Rd.
Livonia, MI 48152-2696
734-462-4400, ext. 5309
Fax: 734-462-4439
E-mail: 2382@softshare.com
www.schoolcraft.cc.mi.us

Michael Black
Kalamazoo Chamber of Commerce
SW & NE Michigan Technical Assistance Center
346 W. Michigan Ave.
Kalamazoo, MI 49007-3737
616-381-2977, ext. 3242

Fax: 616-343-1151
E-mail: swmitac@iserv.net

Paula Boase
Downriver Community Conference
Economic Development
15100 Northline
Southgate, MI 48195
734-281-0700, ext. 129
Fax: 734-281-3418

Janet E. Masi
Warren, Center Line
Sterling Heights Chamber of Commerce
30500 Van Dyke Ave., Suite 118
Warren, MI 48093
810-751-3939
Fax: 810-751-3995
E-mail: jmasi@wcschamber.com
www.michigantac.org

Pamela Vanderlaan
West Central Michigan Employment and Training Consortium
PTA Center
110 Elm St.
Big Rapids, MI 49307
616-796-4891
Fax: 616-796-8316

James F. Haslinger
Northwestern Michigan Council of Governments
PTA Center
P.O. Box 506
2194 Dendrinos Dr.
Traverse City, MI 49685-0506
616-929-5036
Fax: 616-929-5012

Minnesota
George Johnson
Minnesota Project Innovation, Inc.
Procurement Technical Assistance Center
100 Mill Place
Suite 100, 111 Third Ave. South
Minneapolis, MN 55401-2551
612-347-6745
Fax: 612-349-2603
E-mail: gjohnson@mpi.org
www.mpi.org

Mississippi
Richard L. Speights
Mississippi Contract Procurement Center, Inc.
1636 Poppsferry Rd., Suite 229
Biloxi, MS 39532
228-396-1288
Fax: 228-396-2520
E-mail: mprogoff@aol.com
www.mscpc.com

Missouri
Morris Hudson
The Curators of University of Missouri
Outreach & University Extension
310 Jesse Hall
Columbia, MO 65211
573-882-3597
Fax: 573-884-4297

Guy M. Thomas
Missouri Southern State College
3950 E. Newman Rd.
Joplin, MO 64801-1595
417-625-3001
Fax: 417-625-9782

Montana
James Ouldhouse
Big Sky Economic Development Authority
2722 Third Ave., North, Suite 300 West
Billings, MT 59101-1931
406-256-6871
Fax: 406-256-6877
E-mail: jewell@bigskyeda.org
E-mail: ouldhouse@bigskyeda.org

Nebraska
Jerry Dalton
Board of Regents of the University of Nebraska
Nebraska Business Development Center
1313 Farnam St., Suite 132
Omaha, NE 68182-0210
402-595-3511
Fax: 402-595-3832

Nevada
Roger Tokarz
State of Nevada
Commission on Economic Development
5151 S. Carson St.
Carson City, NV 89701
702-687-1813
Fax: 702-687-4450

New Hampshire
Joseph Flynn
State of New Hampshire
Office of Business and Industrial Development
P.O. Box 1856
172 Pembroke Rd.
Concord, NH 03302-1856
603-271-2591
Fax: 603-271-6784
E-mail: j-flynn@drred.state.nh.us
www.ded.state.nh.us/obid/ptac

New Jersey
John Fedkenheuer
County Economic Development Corp.
PTA Program
1085 Morris Ave., Suite 531
Lib Hall Center
Union, NJ 07083
908-527-1166
Fax: 908-527-1207

Dolcey Chaplin
Foundation At New Jersey Institute of Technology (NJIT)
PTA Center
University Heights
Newark, NJ 07102
973-596-3105
Fax: 973-596-5806
E-mail: chaplin@admin.njit.edu
www.nyit.edu/DPTAC

New Mexico
Charles Marquez
State of New Mexico General Services Dept.
Procurement Assistance Program
1100 St. Francis Dr., Room 2006
Santa Fe, NM 87503
505-827-0425
Fax: 505-827-0499
E-mail: cmarquez@state.nm.us

New York
Keith Cook
South Bronx Overall Economic Development Corporation

Free Local Help

370 E. 149th St.
Bronx, NY 10455
718-292-3113
Fax: 718-292-3115

Thomas M. Livak
Cattaraugus County
Department of Economic Development
Plan and Tour
303 Court St.
Little Valley, NY 14755
716-938-9111
Fax: 716-938-9431

Solomon Soskin
Long Island Development Corporation
PTA Program
255 Executive Dr.
Plainview, NY 11803
516-349-7800
Fax: 516-349-7881
E-mail: gov_contracts@lidc.org
www.lidc.org

Gordon Richards
New York City Dept. of Business Services
Procurement Outreach Program
110 William St., 2nd Floor
New York, NY 10038
212-513-6472
Fax: 212-618-8899

Roberta J. Rodriquez
Rockland Economic Development Corporation
Procurement
One Blue Hill Plaza, Suite 1110
Pearl River, NY 10965-1575
914-735-7040
Fax: 914-735-5736

North Carolina
Robert Truex
University of North Carolina at Chapel Hill
Small Business and Tech Development Center
Room 300, Bynum Hall
Chapel Hill, NC 27599-4100
919-715-7272
Fax: 919-715-7777
E-mail: rtruex@sbtdc.org

North Dakota
No PTA awarded

Ohio
Caretha Brown-Griffin
Community Improvement Corporation of Lake County Ohio
NE Ohio Government Contract Assistance Center
Lake Erie
391-W. Washington College
Painesville, OH 44077
440-357-2294
Fax: 440-357-2296
E-mail: neogcac@lcedc.org

Connie S. Freeman
Lawrence Economic Development Corporation
Procure Outreach Center
216 Collins Ave.
P.O. Box 488
South Point, OH 45680-0488
740-377-4550
Fax: 740-377-2091
E-mail: procure@zoomnet.net
www.zoomnet.net/~procure/

Oklahoma
C.L. Vache
Oklahoma Dept. of Vocational and Technical Education
Oklahoma Bid Assistance Network
1500 W. Seventh Ave.
Stillwater, OK 74074-4364
405-743-5571
Fax: 405-743-6821

Roy Robert Gann, Jr.
Tribal Government Institute
421 E. Comanche, Suite B
Norman, OK 73071
405-329-5542
Fax: 405-329-5543

Oregon
Jan Hurt
The Organization for Economic Initiatives
Government Contract Acquisition Program
99 W. 10th Ave., Suite 330
Eugene, OR 97401
541-344-3537
Fax: 541-687-4899

Pennsylvania
Joseph E. Hopkins
Mon-Valley Renaissance
CA University of Pennsylvania
250 University Ave.
California, PA 15419
724-938-5881
Fax: 724-938-4575
E-mail: wojak@cup.edu

Richard A. Mihalic
NW Pennsylvania Regional Planning and Development Commission
614 Eleventh St.
Franklin, PA 16323
814-677-4800
Fax: 814-677-7663
E-mail: nwpaptac@nwpian.org

Chuck Burtyk
PIC of Westmoreland/Fayette, Inc.
Procurement Assistance Center
531 S. Main St.
Greensburg, PA 15601
724-836-2600
Fax: 724-836-8058
E-mail: cburtyk@sgi.net

Robert J. Murphy
Johnstown Area Regional Industries
Defense PAC
111 Market St.
Johnstown, PA 15901
814-539-4951
Fax: 814-535-8677

A. Lawrence Barletta
Seda Council of Governments
RR 1, Box 372
Lewisburg, PA 17837
570-524-4491
Fax: 570-524-9190
E-mail: sedapta@seda.cog.org
www.seda.cog.org

Thomas E. Wren
University of Pennsylvania-Wharton
SE-PA PTAP
3733 Spruce St.
Vance Hall, 4th Floor
Philadelphia, PA 19104-6374
215-898-1282
Fax: 215-573-2135

David Kern
Economic Development Council of Northeast Pennsylvania
Local Development District
1151 Oak St.
Pittston, PA 18640
570-655-5581
Fax: 570-654-5137

Kerry A. Meehan
Northern Tier Regional Planning and Development Commission
Economic/Community Development
507 Main St.
Towanda, PA 18848-1697
570-265-9103
Fax: 570-265-7585
E-mail: meehan@northerntier.org
www.northerntier.org

Millicent Brown
West Chester University
Procurement Assistance Center
211 Carter Dr., Suite E
West Chester, PA 19383
610-436-3337
Fax: 610-436-2593
pac.btcwcu.org

Puerto Rico
Wilson Baez
Commonwealth of Puerto Rico
Economic Development Administration
355 Roosevelt Ave.
Hato Rey, PR 00918
787-753-6861
Fax: 787-751-6239

Rhode Island
Michael H. Cunningham
Rhode Island Development Corporation
Business Expansion Division
One W. Exchange St.
Providence, RI 02903
401-277-2601
Fax: 401-277-2102
E-mail: mcunning@riedc.com

South Carolina
John M. Lenti
University of South Carolina
Frank L. Roddey SBDC of South Carolina
College of Business Administration
Columbia, SC 29208
803-777-4907
Fax: 803-777-4403

South Dakota
No PTA awarded

Tennessee
Becky Peterson
Center for Industrial Services
University of Tennessee
226 Capitol Blvd., Suite 606
Nashville, TN 37219-1804
615-532-4906
Fax: 615-532-4937

Texas
Doug Nelson
Panhandle Regional Planning Commission

Government Contracts

Economic Development Unit
P.O. Box 9257
Amarillo, TX 79105-9257
806-372-3381
Fax: 806-373-3268

Rogerio Flores
University of Texas at Arlington
Automation and Robotics Research Institute
Office of President
Box 19125
Arlington, TX 76019
817-272-5978
Fax: 817-272-5952

Rosalie Manzano
University of Texas at Brownsville ITSC
Center for Business and Economic Development
1600 E. Elizabeth St.
Brownsville, TX 78520
956-548-8713
Fax: 956-548-8717

Carey Joan White
University of Houston, TIPS
1100 Louisiana, Suite 500
Houston, TX 77204
713-752-8466
Fax: 713-756-1515

Otilo Castellano
Texas Technical University
College of Business Administration
203 Holder
Lubbock, TX 79409-1035
806-745-1637
Fax: 806-745-6207

Thomas E. Breuer, Jr.
Angelina College
Procurement Assistance Center
P.O. Box 1768
Lufkin, TX 75902-1768
409-639-3678
Fax: 409-639-3863
E-mail: acpac@lcc.net
www.oecrc.org/acpac/

Terri L. Williams
San Antonio Procurement Outreach Program
Economic Development Department
P.O. Box 839966
San Antonio, TX 78283
210-207-3910
Fax: 210-207-3909

Frank Delgado
El Paso Community College
Resource Development
P.O. Box 20500
El Paso, TX 79998
915-831-4405
Fax: 915-831-4420

Utah

Johnny C. Bryan
Utah Department of Community and Economic Development
Utah Procurement Technical Assistance Center (UPTAC)
324 South State St., Suite 504
Salt Lake City, UT 84111
801-538-8791
Fax: 801-538-8825

Virginia

James Regan
George Mason University
Entrepreneurship Center
4400 University Dr.
Fairfax, VA 22030
703-277-7750
Fax: 703-352-8195
E-mail: ptap@gmu.edu
www.gmu.edu/gmu/PTAP

Dennis K. Morris
Crater Planning District Commission
The Procurement Assistance Center
1964 Wakefield St.
P.O. Box 1808
Petersburg, VA 23805
804-861-1667
Fax: 804-732-8972
E-mail: ptac111@aol.com

Glenda D. Calver
Southwestern Virginia Community College
Economic Development Division
P.O. Box SVCC
Richlands, VA 24641
540-964-7334
Fax: 540-964-7575
www.sw.cc.va.us/pac.html

Vermont

Greg Lawson
State of Vermont
Department of Economic Development
109 State St.
Montpelier, VT 05609
802-828-5237
Fax: 802-828-3258

Washington

Brent C. Helm
Economic Development Council of Snohomish County
728 134th St., SW
Bldg. A, Suite 219
Everett, WA 98204
425-743-4567
Fax: 425-745-5563
E-mail: ptac@snoedc.org
www.snoedc.org/patc/html

West Virginia

R. Conley Salyer
Regional Contracting Assistance Center, Inc.
1116 Smith St., Suite 202
Charleston, WV 25301
304-344-2546
Fax: 304-344-2574
www.rcacwv.com

Belinda Sheridan
Mid-Ohio Valley Regional Council
PTA Center
P.O. Box 5528
Parkersburg, WV 26105
304-428-6889
Fax: 304-428-6891
E-mail: ptac@access.mountain.net

Wisconsin

Denise Kornetzke
Madison Area Technical College
Small Business PAC
211 North Carroll St.
Madison, WI 53703
608-258-2350
Fax: 608-258-2329
http://bpac.madison.tec.wi.us

Joseph W. Hurst
Wisconsin Procurement Institute, Inc.
756 N. Milwaukee St.
Milwaukee, WI 53202
414-443-9744
Fax: 414-443-1122
E-mail: wispro@execpc.com

Wyoming

No PTA awarded in this state

Small Business Innovative Research Programs

Government Buys Bright Ideas From Inventors: Small Business Innovative Research Programs (SBIR)

The Small Business Innovative Research Program (SBIR) stimulates technological innovation, encourages small science and technology based firms to participate in government funded research, and provides incentives for converting research results into commercial applications. The program is designed to stimulate technological innovation in this country by providing qualified U.S. small business concerns with competitive opportunities to propose innovative concepts to meet the research and development needs of the Federal government. Eleven federal agencies with research and development budgets greater than $100 million are required by law to participate: The Departments of Defense, Health and Human Services, Energy, Agriculture, Commerce, Transportation, and Education; the National Aeronautics and Space Administration; the National Science Foundation; the Nuclear Regulatory Commission; and the Environmental Protection Agency.

Businesses of 500 or fewer employees that are organized for profit are eligible to compete for SBIR funding. Nonprofit organizations and foreign owned firms are not eligible to receive awards, and the research must be carried out in the U.S. All areas of research and development solicit for proposals, and the 1995 budget for SBIR is $900 million. There are three phases of the program: Phase I determines whether the research idea, often on high risk advanced concepts, is technically feasible; whether the firm can do high quality research; and whether sufficient progress has been made to justify a larger Phase II effort. This phase is usually funded for 6 months with awards up to $50,000. Phase II is the principal research effort, and is usually limited to a maximum of $500,000 for up to two years. The third phase, which is to pursue potential commercial applications of the research funded under the first two phases, is supported solely by nonfederal funding, usually from third party, venture capital, or large industrial firms. SBIR is one of the most competitive research and development programs in the government today. About one proposal out of ten received is funded in Phase I. Generally, about half of these receive support in Phase II. Solicitations for proposals are released once a year (in a few cases twice a year). To assist the small business community in its SBIR efforts, the U.S. Small Business Administration publishes the Pre-Solicitation Announcement (PSA) in December, March, June, and September of each year. Every issue of the PSA contains pertinent information on the SBIR Program along with details on SBIR solicitations that are about to be released. This publication eliminates the need for small business concerns to track the activities of all of the federal agencies participating in the SBIR Program. In recognition of the difficulties encountered by many small firms in their efforts to locate sources of funding essential to finalization of their innovative products, SBA has developed the Commercialization Matching System. This system contains information on all SBIR awardees, as well as financing sources that have indicated an interest in investing in SBIR innovations. Firms interested in obtaining more information on the SBIR Program or receiving the PSA, should contact the Office of Technology, Small Business Administration, 409 3rd St., SW, MC/6470, Washington, DC 20416, 202-205-6450.

SBIR representatives listed below can answer questions and send you materials about their agency's SBIR plans and funding:

Department of Agriculture
Dr. Charles F. Cleland, Director, SBIR Program, U.S. Department of Agriculture, Small Business Association, 409 Third St., SW, 8th Floor, Washington, DC 20416; 202-205-7777.

Department of Defense
Mr. Robert Wrenn, SBIR Program Manager, OSD/SADBU, U.S. Department of Defense, The Pentagon, Room 2A340, Washington, DC 20301-3061; 703-697-1481.

Department of Education
Mr. John Christensen, SBIR Program Coordinator, U.S. Department of Education, 555 New Jersey Ave., NW, Room 602D, Washington, DC 20208; 202-219-2050.

Department of Energy
Dr. Samuel J. Barish, SBIR Program Manager, ER-16, U.S. Department of Energy, Washington, DC 20585; 301-903-3054.

Department of Health and Human Services
Mr. Veri Zanders, SBIR Program Manager, Office of the Secretary, U.S. Department of Health and Human Services, Washington, DC 20201; 202-690-7300.

Department of Transportation
Dr. George Kobatch, DOT SBIR Program Director, DTS-22, Research and Special Program Administration, Volpe National Transportation Systems Center, U.S. Department of Transportation, 55 Broadway, Kendall Square, Cambridge, MA 02142-1093; 617-494-2051.

Environmental Protection Agency
Mr. Donald F. Carey, SBIR Program Manager, Research Grants Staff (8701), Office of Research and Development, U.S. Environmental Protection Agency, 401 M St., SW, Washington, DC 20460; 202-260-7899.

National Aeronautics and Space Administration
Mr. Harry Johnson, Manager, SBIR Office, Code CR, National Aeronautics and Space Administration Headquarters, 300 E St., SW, Washington, DC 20546-0001; 202-358-0691.

National Science Foundation
Mr. Roland Tibbetts, Mr. Ritchie Coryell, Mr. Daryl G. Gorman, Mr. Charles Hauer, Dr. Sara Nerlove, SBIR Program Managers, National Science Foundation, 4201 Wilson Boulevard, Room 590, Arlington, VA 22230; 703-306-1391.

Nuclear Regulatory Commission
Ms. Marianne M. Riggs, SBIR Program Representative, Financial Management, Procurement, and Administrative Staff, Nuclear Regulatory Commission, Washington, DC 20555; 301-415-5822.

Government Contracts

State Procurement Assistance

Have you ever wondered where the government buys all of the products that it works with each day? You might be surprised to learn that they buy from small businesses just like yours that produce products such as:

- work clothing
- office supplies
- cleaning equipment
- miscellaneous vehicles
- medical supplies and equipment

Imagine what your bottom line could look like each year if you won just ONE lucrative government contract that would provide your business with a secure income! It might even buy you the freedom to pursue other clients that you wouldn't have the time or money to go after otherwise. If your business performs well and completes a government contract satisfactorily, chances are you'll have a shot at more and maybe even bigger contracts.

The offices listed below are starting places for finding out who in the state government will purchase your products or services.

State Procurement Offices

Alabama
Finance Department
Purchasing Division
100 N. Union, Suite 192
Montgomery, AL 36104
334-242-7250
Fax: 334-242-4419
www.purchasing.state.al.us

Alaska
State of Alaska
Department of Administration
Division of General Services
P.O. Box 110210
Juneau, AK 99811-0210
907-465-2250
Fax: 907-465-2189
www.state.ak.us/local/akpages/
ADMIN/dgs/home.htm

Arizona
State Procurement Office
15 S. 15th Ave.
Suite 103
Phoenix, AZ 85007
602-542-5511
Fax: 602-542-5508
http://sporas.ad.state.az.us

Arkansas
Office of State Purchasing
P.O. Box 2940
Little Rock, AR 72203
501-324-9316
Fax: 501-324-9311

California
Office of Procurement
Department of General Services
1823 14th St.
Sacramento, CA 95814
916-445-6942
Fax: 916-323-4609
www.td.dgs.ca.gov/

Colorado
Division of Purchasing
225 E. 16th Ave.
Suite 900
Denver, CO 80203
303 866-6100
Fax: 303-894-7444
www.gssa.state.co.us

Connecticut
State of Connecticut
Department of Administrative Services
Bureau of Purchases
165 Capitol Ave.
Hartford, CT 06106
860-713-5095
Fax: 803-713-7484
www.das.state.ct.us/busopp.htm

Delaware
Purchasing Division
Purchasing Bldg.
P.O. Box 299
Delaware City, DE 19706
302-834-4550
Fax: 302-836-7642
www.state.de.us/purchase

District of Columbia
Office of Contracts and Procurement
441 4th St. NW, Suite 800
Washington, DC 20001
202-727-0252
Fax: 202-724-5673
www.ci.washington.dc.us

Florida
General Service Department
Division of Purchasing
4050 Esplanade Way
Tallahassee, FL 32399-0950
850-488-5498
http://purchasing.state.us/

Georgia
Administrative Services Department
200 Piedmont Ave., Room 1308 SE
Atlanta, GA 30334
404-656-3240
Fax: 404-651-6963
www.doas.state.ga.us

Hawaii
Purchasing Branch
Purchasing and Supply Division
Department of Accounting and General Services
Room 416, 1151 Punch Bowl St.
Honolulu, HI 96813
808-586-0575
Fax: 808-586-0570
www.state.hi.us/icsd/dags/spo.html

Idaho
Division of Purchasing
Administration Department
5569 Kendall St.
State House Mall
Boise, ID 83720
208-327-7465
Fax: 208-327-7320
www2.state.id.us/adm/purchasing

Illinois
Department of Central Management Services
Procurement Services
801 Stratton Bldg.
Springfield, IL 62706
217-782-2301
Fax: 217-782-5187
www.state.il.us/cms

Indiana
Department of Administration
Procurement Division
402 W. Washington St., Room W-468
Indianapolis, IN 46204
317-232-3032
Fax: 317-232-7213
www.state.in.us/idoa/proc

Iowa
State of Iowa
Department of General Services
Purchasing Division
Hoover State Office Building
Des Moines, IA 50319
515-281-3089
Fax: 515-242-5974
www.state.ia.us/government/dgs/
csap/purhome/business.htm

Kansas
Division of Purchasing
Room 102 North
Landon State Office Bldg.
900 SW Jackson St.
Topeka, KS 66612
785-296-2376
Fax: 785-296-7240
http://da.state.ks.us/purch

Kentucky
Purchases, Department of Finance
Room 367, Capital Annex
Frankfort, KY 40601

State Procurement Offices

502-564-4510
Fax: 502-564-7209
http://purch.state.ky.us

Louisiana
State Purchasing Office
Division of Administration
P.O. Box 94095
Baton Rouge, LA 70804-9095
225-342-8010
Fax: 225-342-8688
www.doa.state.la.us/osp/osp.htm

Maine
Bureau of Purchases
State House Station #9
Augusta, ME 04333
207-287-3521
Fax: 207-287-6578
http://janus.state.me.us/purchase

Maryland
Purchasing Bureau
301 W. Preston St.
Mezzanine, Room M8
Baltimore, MD 21201
410-767-4600
Fax: 410-333-5482
www.dgs.state.md.us

Massachusetts
Purchasing Agent Division
One Ashburton Place, Room 1017
Boston, MA 02108
617-727-7500
Fax: 617-727-4527
www.comm-pass.com

Michigan
Office of Purchasing
Mason Bldg.
P.O. Box 30026
Lansing, MI 48909
or 530 W. Ellegan, 48933
517-373-0330
Fax: 517-335-0046
www.state.mi.us/dmd/oop

Minnesota
State of Minnesota
Department of Administration
Suite 112, Administration Bldg.
50 Sherburne Ave.
St. Paul, MN 55155
651-296-6152
Fax: 651-297-3996
www.mmd.admin.state.mn.us

Mississippi
Office of Purchasing and Travel
1504 Sillers Bldg.
550 High St., Suite 1504
Jackson, MS 39201
601-359-3409
Fax: 601-359-3910
www.dfa.state.ms.us

Missouri
State of Missouri
Division of Purchasing
P.O. Box 809
Jefferson City, MO 65102
573-751-2387
Fax: 573-751-2387
www.oa.state.mo.us/purch/bids.htm

Montana
Department of Administration
Procurement Division
165 Mitchell Bldg.
Helena, MT 59620-0135
406-444-2575
Fax: 406-444-2529
www.state.mt.us/doa/ppd

Nebraska
State Purchasing Division
301 Centennial Mall S.
P.O. Box 94847
Lincoln, NE 68509
402-471-2401
Fax: 402-471-2089
www.nol.org/home/DASMAT

Nevada
Nevada State Purchasing Division
209 E. Musser St., Room 304
Blasdel Bldg.
Carson City, NV 89710
702-684-0170
Fax: 702-684-0188
www.state.nv.us/purchasing/

New Hampshire
State Purchasing Department
25 Capitol St.
State House Annex, Room 102
Concord, NH 03301
603-271-2201
Fax: 603-271-2700
www.state.nh.us/das/purchasing/index.html

New Jersey
Division of Purchase and Property
P.O. Box 039
Trenton, NJ 08625
609-292-4886
Fax: 609-984-2575
www.state.nj.us/treasury/purchase

New Mexico
State Purchasing Division
1100 St. Frances Dr., Room 2016
Joseph Montoya Bldg.
Santa Fe, NM 87503
505-827-0472
Fax: 505-827-2484
www.state.nm.us/spd

New York
Division of Purchasing
Corning Tower
Empire State Plaza, 38th Floor
Albany, NY 12242
518-474-3695
Fax: 518-486-6099
www.ogs.state.ny.us

North Carolina
Department of Administration
Division of Purchase and Contract
116 W. Jones St.
Raleigh, NC 27603-8002
919-733-3581
Fax: 919-733-4782
www.state.nc.us/pandc/

North Dakota
Central Services Division of State Purchasing
Purchasing
600 E Blvd., I Wing
Bismarck, ND 58505-0420

701-328-2683
Fax: 701-328-1615
www.state.nd.us/centserv

Ohio
State Purchasing
4200 Surface Rd.
Columbus, OH 43228-1395
614-466-4635
Fax: 614-466-2059
www.gsa.ohio.gov/gsa/ods/pur/pur.html

Oklahoma
Office of Public Affairs
Central Purchasing Division
Suite 116, Rogers Bldg.
2401 N. Lincoln
Oklahoma City, OK 73105
405-521-2110
Fax: 405-521-4475
www.dcs.state.ok.us

Oregon
General Services
Purchasing and Print Services Division
1225 Ferry St.
Salem, OR 97310
503-378-4643
Fax: 503-373-1626
tpps.das.state.or.us/purchasing

Pennsylvania
Procurement Department Secretary
N. Office Bldg., Room 414
Commonwealth and North St.
Harrisburg, PA 17125
717-787-5733
Fax: 717-783-6241
www.dgs.state.pa.us

Rhode Island
Department of Administration
Purchases Office
One Capital Hill
Providence, RI 02908-5855
401-222-2317
Fax: 401-222-6387
www.purchasing.state.ri.us

South Carolina
Materials Management Office
General Service Budget and Control Board
1201 Main St., Suite 600
Columbia, SC 29201
803-737-0600
Fax: 803-737-0639
www.state.sc.us/mmo/mmo/

South Dakota
Division of Purchasing
523 E. Capitol Ave.
Pierre, SD 57501
605-773-3405
Fax: 605-773-4840
www.state.sd.us/boa

Tennessee
Department of General Services
Division of Purchasing
Third Floor, Tennessee Towers
312 8th Ave. North
Nashville, TN 37243-0557
615-741-1035
Fax: 615-741-0684
www.state.tn.us/generalser/purchasing

Government Contracts

Texas
State Purchasing and General Services Commission
P.O. Box 13047
Austin, TX 78711
512-463-3445
Fax: 512-463-7073
www.gsc.state.tx.us

Utah
Purchasing Division
Department of Administrative Services
State Office Bldg., Room 3150
Salt Lake City, UT 84114
801-538-3026
Fax: 801-538-3882
www.purchasing.state.ut.us

Vermont
Purchasing and Contract Administration Division
128 State St., Drawer 33
Montpelier, VT 05633-7501
802-828-2211
Fax: 802-828-2222
www.bgf.state.vt.us/pca

Virginia
Department of General Services
Purchasing Division
P.O. Box 1199
Richmond, VA 23209
804-786-3842
Fax: 804-371-8936
www.dgs.state.va.us/dps

Washington
Office of State Procurement
Suite 201, General Admin Bldg.
210 11th Ave. SW
Olympia, WA 98504-1017
360-902-7400
Fax: 360-586-2426
www.ga.wa.gov/proc.htm

West Virginia
Department of Administration
Purchasing Section
Building 15
2019 Washington St. East
Charleston, WV 25305-0110
304-558-2306
Fax: 304-558-6026
www.state.wv.us/admin/purchase

Wisconsin
Division of State Agency Services
Bureau of Procurement
101 E. Wilson, 6th Floor
P.O. Box 7867
Madison, WI 53707-7867
608-266-2605
Fax: 608-267-0600
http://vendornet.state.wi.us

Wyoming
Department of Administration
Procurement Services
2001 Capitol Ave.
Cheyenne, WY 82002
307-777-7253
Fax: 307-777-5852
www.state.wy.us

Help For Inventors:
Patents, Trademarks, and Copyrights

Most inventors realize that it's vitally important to protect their idea by copyrighting it and obtaining the necessary patents and copyrights, but did you know that it's also important to look around for loans and other grants to support your business while working on your invention? If you want an idea to become an actual product, you have to invest an awful lot of your time into its research, and not just on a part time basis. Loans and grants programs for inventors help you do just that — for example, Hawaii offers low cost loans to inventors, as do other states around the country. First, let's talk about getting the necessary information concerning trademark and patent procedures.

Patent and Trademark Office

United States patent and trademark laws are administered by the Patent and Trademark Office (PTO). States also have trade secret statutes, which generally state that if you guard your trade secret with a reasonable amount of care, you will protect your rights associated with that secret. The PTO examines patent and trademark applications, grants protection for qualified inventions, and registers trademarks. It also collects, assembles, and disseminates the technological information patent grants. The PTO maintains a collection of almost 6 million United States patents issued to date, several million foreign patents, and more than 2.2 million trademarks, together with supporting documentation. Here's how to find out what you need to do to patent your idea.

What a Great Idea

To help you get started with patenting your invention, the Patent and Trademark Offices will send you a free booklet upon request called *Basic Facts About Patents*. There are three legal elements involved in the process of invention: the conception of the idea, diligence in working it out, and reducing it to practice — i.e., getting a finished product that actually works. If you have a great idea you think might work, but you need time to develop it further before it is ready to be patented, what should you do?

Protect Your Idea for $10

You can file a Disclosure Statement with the Patent and Trademark Office, and they will keep it in confidence as evidence of the date of conception of the invention or idea.

Disclosure Statement
Assistant Commissioner of Patents
Box DD
Washington, DC 20231   800-786-9199
Disclosure Office   703-308-HELP

Send an 8 1/2 x 11" drawing, a copy, signed disclosure, SASE, and a check or money order for $10 to file. Upon request, the above office will also send you a free brochure on Disclosure Statements.

This is the best way to keep the idea you are working on completely secret and yet document the date you conceived the idea. You can file the Disclosure Statement at any time after the idea is conceived, but the value of it will depend on how much information you put into it — so put as much detail into this statement as you can.

The Purpose of Documenting The Date of Conception

If someone else should try to patent your idea, filing a Disclosure Statement shows that you thought of it first, although filing this statement does not legally protect your invention. Documentation of the conception date gives you time to patent your invention, and is invaluable if you need to prove when you thought of your idea if a dispute should arise. (Note that filing a Disclosure Statement gives you limited defensive legal protection only if you follow it up with a patent in two years. Unlike a patent, it cannot be used offensively, to stop someone else from patenting the same idea.) When you go to file for a patent, if you and a competitor get into a dispute as to who was the first to invent it, the Patent and Trademark Office (PTO) will hold an Interference Proceeding. If you thought of the idea first, your Disclosure Statement will go a long way towards establishing that you were the first inventor and should therefore receive the patent for it.

Research Resources That Can Help You Turn Your Idea Into Reality

While diligently working out the details of your invention you can use the extensive resources of over 190,000 scientific and technical journals, articles, and books at the Scientific Document Library at the PTO in Crystal City, VA.

Facilitating public access to the more than 25 million cross-referenced United States patents is the job of PTO's Office of Technology Assessment and Forecast (OTAF), 703-306-2600. It has a master database which covers all United States patents, and searches are available free. An OTAF search will not result in an in-depth patent search. (More on that, and how to find classifications in the *Conducting Your Own Patent Search* section below.) OTAF extracts information from its database and makes it available in a variety of formats, including publications, custom patent reports, and statistical reports. The purpose of most of the reports generated by an OTAF search is to reveal statistical information.

Copies of the specifications and drawings of all patents are available from PTO. Design patents and trademark copies are $3 each. Plant patents not in color are $10 each, while plant patents

Help for Inventors

in color are $20 each. To make a request, you must have the patent number. For copies, contact:

Assistant Secretary and Commissioner
P.O. Box 9
ATTN: PTCS
Washington, DC 20231
Public Information Line   703-305-8716

Patenting Your Invention

To patent your invention, start by ordering the Patent Booklet called *General Information Concerning Patents*, and Application Form.

Superintendent of Documents
U.S. Government Printing Office
P.O. Box 371954
Pittsburgh, PA 15250-7954   202-512-1800

The cost is $4 and may be charged to Mastercard, VISA or Discover Card.

The application will ask you for a written description, oath, and drawing where possible. The cost to file for a patent to individuals or small businesses of under 500 employees (defined by SBA standards) is $380. It generally takes 18 months to two years for the PTO to grant a patent, and rights start the date the patent is granted. If you use your invention prior to being granted a patent, you can put "patent pending" on your product. This warns competitors that you have taken the necessary steps, but otherwise affords you no legal protection. Before embarking on the patenting process, you should conduct a patent search to make sure no one else has preceded you.

Conducting Your Own Patent Search

Before investing too much time and money on patenting your idea, you will want to see if anyone has already patented it. You may conduct the search yourself on the PTO website at {http://www.uspto.gov} or hire someone to do it for you. If you wish to hire a professional to do your patent search, consult the local yellow pages or again, search the PTO website for a roster of patent attorneys. Even if your search is not as in-depth as that of a patent attorney or a patent agent, you may still find the information that you need. You may also conduct your patent search at the Patent and Trademark Office Search Room.

Patent and Trademark Office (PTO)
Patent and Trademark Search Room
2021 South Clark Place
Crystal Plaza 3
Arlington, VA 22202   703-305-4463

For information about the Patent Depository Library Program, contact the office listed below.

Patent and Trademark Depository Library Program
U.S. Patent and Trademark Office
Crystal Park 3, Suite 461
Washington, DC 20231   Fax: 703-306-2654

You may also conduct your patent search at any of the 83 Patent Depository Libraries (PDLs) throughout the country as listed below.

Alabama
Auburn University: Ralph Brown Draughon Library, Auburn University; 334-844-1747
Birmingham: Birmingham Public Library; 205-226-3620

Alaska
Anchorage: Z.J. Lottssac Public Library, Anchorage Municipal Libraries; 907-562-7323

Arizona
Tempe: Daniel F. Noble Science and Engineering Library/Science/Reference, Arizona State University; 602-965-7010

Arkansas
Little Rock: Little Rock, Arkansas State Library; 501-682-2053

California
Los Angeles: Los Angeles Public Library; 213-228-7220
Sacramento: California State Library, Library Courts Building; 916-654-0069
San Diego: San Diego Public Library; 619-236-5813
San Francisco: San Francisco Public Library; 415-557-4500
Sunnyvale: Sunnyvale Center for Innovation, Invention & Ideas; 408-730-7290

Colorado
Denver: Denver Public Library; 303-640-6220

Connecticut
Hartford: Hartford Public Library; not yet operational
New Haven: New Haven Free Public Library; 203-946-8130

Delaware
Newark: University of Delaware Library; 302-831-2965

District of Columbia
Washington: Founders Library, Howard University; 202-806-7252

Florida
Fort Lauderdale: Broward County Main Library; 954-357-7444
Miami: Miami-Dade Public Library; 305-375-2665
Orlando: University of Central Florida Libraries; 407-823-2562
Tampa: Tampa Campus Library, University of South Florida; 813-974-2726

Georgia
Atlanta: Library and Information Center, Georgia Institute of Technology; 404-894-4508

Hawaii
Honolulu: Hawaii State Library; 808-586-3477

Idaho
Moscow: University of Idaho Library; 208-885-6235

Illinois
Chicago: Chicago Public Library; 312-747-4450
Springfield: Illinois State Library; 217-782-5659

Patents, Trademarks and Copyrights

Indiana
Indianapolis: Indianapolis-Marion County Public Library; 317-269-1741
West Lafayette: Siegesmund Engineering Library, Purdue University; 317-494-2872

Iowa
Des Moines: State Library of Iowa; 515-281-4118

Kansas
Wichita: Ablah Library, Wichita State University; 316-978-3155

Kentucky
Louisville: Louisville Free Public Library; 502-574-1611

Louisiana
Baton Rouge: Troy H. Middleton Library, Louisiana State University; 504-388-8875

Maine
Orono: Raymond H. Fogler Library, University of Maine; 207-581-1678

Maryland
College Park: Engineering and Physical Sciences Library, University of Maryland; 301-405-9157

Massachusetts
Amherst: Physical Sciences and Engineering Library, University of Massachusetts; 413-545-1370
Boston: Boston Public Library; 617-536-5400, ext. 265

Michigan
Ann Arbor: Media Union Library, The University of Michigan; 313-647-5735
Big Rapids: Abigail S. Tunme Library, Ferris State University; 616-592-3602
Detroit: Great Lakes Patent and Trademark Center, Detroit Public Library; 313-833-3379

Minnesota
Minneapolis: Minneapolis Public Library & Information Center; 612-630-6120

Mississippi
Jackson: Mississippi Library Commission; 601-359-1036

Missouri
Kansas City: Linda Hall Library; 816-363-4600
St. Louis: St. Louis Public Library; 314-241-2288, ext. 390

Montana
Butte: Montana Tech of the University of Montana Library; 406-496-4281

Nebraska
Lincoln: Engineering Library, Nebraska Hall, 2nd Floor West; 402-472-3411

Nevada
Reno: University Library, University of Nevada-Reno; 702-784-6500, ext. 257

New Hampshire
Concord: New Hampshire State Library; 603-271-2239

New Jersey
Newark: Newark Public Library; 973-733-7779
Piscataway: Library of Science and Medicine, Rutgers University; 732-445-2895

New Mexico
Albuquerque: Centennial Science and Engineering Library, The University of New Mexico; 505-277-4412

New York
Albany: New York State Library, Science, Industry and Business Library; 518-474-5355
Buffalo: Buffalo and Erie County Public Library; 716-858-7101
New York: Science, Industry and Business Library; 212-592-7000
Stony Brook: Engineering Library, State University of New York; 516-632-7148

North Carolina
Raleigh: D.H. Hill Library, North Carolina State University; 919-515-2935

North Dakota
Grand Forks: Chester Fritz Library, University of North Dakota; 701-777-4888

Ohio
Akron: Akron-Summit County Public Library; 330-643-9075
Cincinnati: The Public Library of Cincinnati and Hamilton County; 513-369-6971
Cleveland: Cleveland Public Library; 216-623-2870
Columbus: Ohio State University Libraries; 614-292-6175
Toledo: Toledo/Lucas County Public Library; 419-259-5212

Oklahoma
Stillwater: Oklahoma State University; 405-744-7086

Oregon
Portland: Paul L. Boley Law Library, Lewis & Clark College; 503-768-6786

Pennsylvania
Philadelphia: The Free Library of Philadelphia; 215-686-5331
Pittsburgh: The Carnegie Library of Pittsburgh; 412-622-3138
University Park: Pattee Library - C207, Pennsylvania State University; 814-865-4861

Puerto Rico
Mayaguez: General Library, University of Puerto Rico; 787-832-4040, ext. 3459

Rhode Island
Providence: Providence Public Library; 401-455-8027

South Carolina
Clemson: R.M. Cooper Library, Clemson University; 864-656-3024

South Dakota
Rapid City: Devereaux Library, South Dakota School of Mines and Technology; 605-394-1275

Help for Inventors

Tennessee
Memphis: Memphis & Shelby County Public Library and Information Center; 901-725-8877
Nashville: Stevenson Science and Engineering Library, Vanderbilt University; 615-322-2717

Texas
Austin: McKinney Engineering Library, The University of Texas at Austin; 512-495-4500
College Station: Sterling C. Evans Library, Texas A&M University; 409-845-3826
Dallas: Dallas Public Library; 214-670-1468
Houston: Fondren Library, Rice University; 713-527-8101, ext. 2587
Houston: South Central Intellectual Property Partnership at Rice University (SCIPPR); 713-285-5196
Lubbock: Texas Tech University; 806-742-2282

Utah
Salt Lake City: Marriott Library, University of Utah; 801-581-8394

Vermont
Burlington: Bailey/Howe Library, University of Vermont; 802-656-2542

Virginia
Richmond: James Branch Cabell Library, Virginia Commonwealth University; 804-828-1104

Washington
Seattle: Engineering Library, University of Washington; 206-543-0740

West Virginia
Morgantown: Evansdale Library, West Virginia University; 304-293-2510, ext. 5113

Wisconsin
Madison: Kurt F. Wendt Library, University of Wisconsin-Madison; 608-262-6845
Milwaukee: Milwaukee Public Library; 414-286-3051

Wyoming
Casper: Natrona County Public Library; 307-237-4935

The Patent and Trademark Library Program distributes the information to the 83 PDLs. The information is kept on CD-Rom discs, which are constantly updated, and you can use them to do a patent search. CD-Rom discs have been combined to incorporate CASSIS (Classification and Search Support Information System). CD-Rom discs do not give you online access to the PTO database. Online access is available through APS (Automated Patent Systems), and is presently available to public users of the PTO Search Room and to the 83 Patent Libraries. Each PDL with the online APS has its own rules regarding its use. To use the online APS at the PTO Search Room, you must first sign up and take a class at the Search Room. This class is held for 3 consecutive 1/2 days and is given once per month for a cost of $25. Online access costs $40 per connect hour, and the charge for paper used for printouts is an additional $.25 per sheet.

If you do not live near a PDL, several CD-Rom discs are available through subscription. You may purchase the Classification disc, which dates back to 1790, for $300; the Bibliography disc, which dates back to 1969, for $300; and the ASIST disc, which contains a roster of patent attorneys, assignees, and other information for $200. You can also conduct your patent search and get a copy of it through commercial database services such as:

MeadData Central, Nexis, Lexis: 1-800-843-6476. Patent searches are done for $25. If found, there is a charge of $5 per page of printout and $5 more if there is a drawing. Abstracts are $3. For Trademarks, the charge is $50 and $5 for the drawing. If you intend on doing many searches over time, Nexis Lexis will customize a package for you as a subscriber for approximately $250 per month.

Derwent, 1725 Duke St., Suite 250, Alexandria, VA 22314; 1-800-336-5010, 1-800-523-7668, Fax: 1-800-457-0850. Patent searches are free, but the printouts range from $3.95 to $29.50 per page plus shipping.

If you are going to do your own patent search at your local Patent Depository Library, begin with the *Manual and Index to U.S. Patent Classifications* to identify the subject area where the patent is placed. Then use the CD-Rom discs to locate the patent. CD-Rom discs enable you to do a complete search of all registered patents but do not enable you to view the full patent, with all its specific details. Lastly, view the patent, which will be kept on microfilm, cartridge, or paper. What information there is to view varies by library, depending on what they have been able to purchase. If the library you are using does not have the patent you want, you may be able to obtain it through inter-library loan.

Copies of patents can be ordered from the PTO at 703-308-9726, for $3 per copy.

To obtain a certified copy of a patent, call 703-308-9726 (Patent Search Library at the PTO). The fee is $25 and you must have the patent number. For a certified copy of an abstract of titles, the fee is $25. For a certified copy of patent assignments, with a record of ownership from the beginning until present, call 703-308-9726. The cost is $25, and to request specific assignments you must have the reel and frame number.

Trademarks

Registering a trademark for your product or service is the way to protect the recognition quality of the name you are building. The PTO keeps records on more than 2.2 million trademarks and records. Over 500,000 active trademarks are kept on the floor of the library, while "dead" trademarks are kept on microfilm. Books contain every registered trademark ever issued, starting in 1870. You can visit the Patent and Trademark Office to research a trademark. You can then conduct your search manually for no charge or use their Trademark Search System (T-Search) for $40 per hour, plus $.25 cents per page.

Assistant Commissioner of Trademarks
Trademark Search Library
2900 Crystal Dr.
Second Floor, Room 2B30
Arlington, VA 22202   703-308-9800/9805

Patents, Trademarks and Copyrights

If you can't do it yourself, you can hire someone to do the search for you. For an agent to do this, consult the local yellow pages under "Trademark Agents/Consultants" or "Trademark Attorneys". You can also locate an agent by calling your local bar association for a referral.

To conduct your own search at a Patent Depository Library use the CD-Rom disc on trademarks. It is available for purchase. The CD-Rom discs deliver patent and trademark information including full-text facsimile images and searchable text records. Images can be found in the *Official Gazette*, which contains most current and pending trademarks. Subscriptions to the *Gazette* for trademarks cost $640 per year. The *Gazette* for patents costs $711 per year. Both are issued every Tuesday and can be ordered from the U.S. Government Printing Office. You can also purchase an image file which contains pending and registered trademarks and corresponding serial or registration numbers through Thomson and Thomson by calling 1-800-692-8833. The information contained in it dates back to April 1, 1987 and is updated by approximately 500 images weekly. However, the PDL you use is likely to have an image of the trademark on microfilm or cartridge, and also have copies of the *Official Gazette*. If not, and you have the registration number, you may obtain a copy of the trademark you want for $3 from the PTO. Contact:

Assistant Commissioner of Trademarks
2900 Crystal Dr.
Second Floor, Room 2B30
Arlington, VA 22202   703-308-9800

There are also several commercial services you can use to conduct trademark searches.

Trademark Scan produced by Thomson and Thomson. It can be purchased by calling 1-800-692-8833 (ask for online services), or accessed directly via Saegis. Trademark Scan is updated three times per week, and includes state and federal trademarks, foreign and domestic. To access Trademark Scan you must already have Dialog or Saegis. Many online options are free. The Internet address is {www.thomson-thomson.com}.

Derwent, 1-800-336-5010, is a commercial service that will conduct patent searches only. The cost ranges from $100 and up with a turnaround time of 2-5 days. The Internet address is {www.derwent.com}.

Online services and database discs for both patents and trademarks are constantly being expanded. For information on an extensive range of existing and projected products, call the PTO Office of Electronic Information at 703-306-2600 and ask for the U.S. Department of Commerce, PTO Office of Information Systems' *Electronic Products Brochure*. For example, there is a Weekly Text File, containing text data of pending and registered trademarks. Information can be called up by using almost any term. It can be purchased from AvantIQ and Thomson & Thomson. You can reach AvantIQ at 1-800-320-6366, 610-584-4380, or online at {http://www.avantiq.lu/}. You can reach Thomson & Thomson at 1-800-692-8833 or online at {www.thomson-thomson.com}.

How to Register a Trademark

Get a copy of the booklet, *Basic Facts about Trademarks* from the U.S. Government Printing Office. It is free upon request from the Trademark Search Library by calling 703-308-9000. The mark you intend to use needs to be in use before you apply. The fee to register your trademark is $245. The time to process your registration can take from 12-15 months.

The Right Way to Get a Copyright

Copyrights are filed on intellectual property. A copyright protects your right to control the sale, use of distribution, and royalties from a creation in thought, music, films, art, or books. For more information, contact:

Library of Congress
Copyright Office
Washington, DC 20559
Public Information Office   202-707-3000
www.loc.gov
http://lcweb.loc.gov/copyright

If you know which copyright application you require, you can call the Forms Hotline, open 7 days per week, 24 hours per day at 202-707-9100. The fee is $20 for each registration.

The Library of Congress provides information on copyright registration procedures and copyright card catalogs which cover several million works that have been registered since 1870. The Copyright Office will research federal copyrights only for varying fees. Requests must be made in writing and you must specify exactly what information you require. Contact the Copyright Office, Reference and Bibliography, Library of Congress, 101 Independence Ave., SE, Washington, DC 20559; 202-707-6850, Public Information 707-3000.

Help for Inventors

Invention Scams: How They Work

Fake product development companies prey on amateur inventors who may not be as savvy about protecting their idea or invention as experienced inventors might be. Most of the bogus/fake companies use escalating fees.

The following is a description of how most of them operate:

- The inventor is invited to call or write for free information.

- The inventor is then offered a free evaluation of his idea.

- Next comes the sales call. The inventor is told he has a very good potential idea and that the company is willing to share the cost of marketing, etc. Actual fact, there is no sharing with these companies. Most times the inventor has to come up with the money (usually several hundred dollars or more) for a patent search and a market analysis. Neither of these are worth anything.

- Then the inventor receives a professional/impressive looking portfolio which contains no real information at all. All the paper crammed into this portfolio looks topnotch, but it's all computer generated garbage.

- Upon receiving this portfolio, the inventor is lured into signing a contract that commits him to giving the company thousands of dollars to promote/license the product. The company sends some promotional letters to fulfill their obligation, but large manufacturers simply toss them into the trash.

After all this, the inventor has spent thousands of dollars, wasted a lot of time, and gotten nowhere with his product.

How To Avoid Losing a Fortune

According to the experts, the inventor should:

- Beware of the come-ons offered by these unethical companies. Avoid using the invention brokers who advertise on TV late in the evening; in public magazines; those who offer 800 numbers; and those on public transit display signs.

- When upfront money is required, look out. There are very few legitimate consultants who insist on a retainer or hourly fee.

- Don't allow the enthusiasm of your idea to take over your inherent common sense. Talk to your patent attorney and see if he knows anything about this company. Plus, check with inventors associations in the state, and see what they have to say about this particular company.

- Demand to know what percentage of ideas the company accepts. Legitimate brokers might accept 2 ideas out of every 100. The fake companies tend to accept about 99 out of 100.

- Find out their actual success rate. Any corporation/company that will not give you their success rate (not licensing agreements) is a company to stay away from.

- Get an objective evaluation of your invention from reputable professionals. This will save you plenty of money on a bad idea.

A number of highly recommended programs are listed in the next section.

Free Help For Inventors

If you have a great idea and want to turn it into reality, don't rush out and spend what could be thousands of dollars for a private invention company and a patent attorney. You can get a lot of this help for free or at a fraction of the cost. There is a lot of help out there; university-sponsored programs, not-for-profit groups, state affiliated programs, profit-making companies, etc. Depending on the assistance and the organization, some services are free, others have reasonable fees.

Many of the inventors organizations hold regular meetings where speakers share their expertise on topics such as licensing, financing and marketing. These groups are a good place for inventors to meet other inventors, patent attorneys, manufacturers, and others with whom they can talk and from whom they can get help.

If the listings in the state-by-state section of this chapter do not prove to be useful, you can contact one of the following organizations for help.

1. Small Business Development Center
   Washington State University
   Parkplace Building
   1200 6th Ave., Suite 1700   206-553-7328
   Seattle, WA 98101   Fax: 206-553-7044
   www.sbdc.wsu.edu/franz.htm
   This service will evaluate your idea for a fee. They also provide counseling services and can assist you with your patent search.

2. Wisconsin Innovation Service Center/Technology
   Small Business Development Center
   Ms. Debra Malewicki, Director
   University of Wisconsin - Whitewater
   402 McCutchan Hall   414-472-3217
   Whitewater, WI 53190   Fax: 414-472-1600
   The only service that is guaranteed is the evaluation. However, efforts are made to match inventors with exceptional high evaluation scores with manufacturers seeking new product ideas. (Do not offer direct invention development or marketing services). WISC charges a $495 flat fee for an evaluation. The goal is to keep research as affordable as possible to the average independent inventor. Most evaluations are completed within 30 - 45 days. Those inventions from specialized fields may require more time. WISC also provides preliminary patent searches via on-line databases to client.

3. Drake University
   Small Business Development Center
   Mr. Benjamin C. Swartz, Director
   Drake Business Center   515-271-2655
   2507 University   1-800-532-1216
   Des Moines, IA 50311-4505   Fax: 515-271-1899
   www.iabusnet.org
   INVENTURE is a program of the Drake University Business Development and Research Institute designed to encourage the development of valid ideas through the various steps to becoming marketable items. INVENTURE has no paid staff. The entire panel is made up of volunteers. The administration of the program is handled by existing staff from the Small Business Development Center and the College of Business and Public Administration. They will review items from **any person** regardless of their place of residence. They will review a product idea and check it for market feasibility. INVENTURE may link individuals with business and/or financial partners.

   INVENTURE screens every product submitted, but will not consider toy/game or food items. Products are evaluated on 33 different criteria, (factors related to legality, safety, business risk, and demand analysis, to market acceptance/ competition). It normally takes up to 6 weeks to receive results of the evaluation. Evaluators are experienced in manufacturing, marketing, accounting, production, finance and investments.

   INVENTURE acts in a responsible manner to maintain confidence of an idea, but cannot guarantee confidentiality.

   For assistance with business plans, financial projections, and marketing help, you're encouraged to contact your Small Business Development Center (SBDC).

4. The Wal-Mart Innovation Network (WIN)
   Center for Business and Economic Development
   Southwest Missouri State University
   901 S. National
   Springfield, MO 65804   415-836-5671
   www.innovation-institute.com
   The WIN program is essentially an innovation evaluation service designed to provide inventors with an honest and objective third-party analysis of the risks and potential of their ideas and inventions. If the invention or new product idea passes the tough screening process, the Center will automatically send your idea to Wal-Mart for an Assessment of Marketability. Their expertise allows to provide qualified inventors with a second analysis of the marketability of their invention/new product idea. A WIN endorsement will increase the chances that others will be willing to listen. If the invention/ product idea receives a "Fully recommended" market assessment, WIN will not take the development or commercialization of your invention or idea. But, if the invention has a reasonable chance of success, WIN will supply information about the Innovation Network (IN) resources in a particular state, (Do not assume their services are free). The only advance payment charged by WIN is the $175 evaluation fee. A "fully recommended" WIN Assessment of Marketability does not obligate Wal-Mart in any way. The WIN program is limited to consumer related ideas and inventions. The only promise is an honest and objective preliminary evaluation.

5. U.S. Department of Energy
   Mail Stop EE-24
   1000 Independence Ave., SW   202-586-1478

Help for Inventors

Washington, DC 20585 Fax: 202-586-7114
www.oit.doe.gov/inventions/
Financial assistance is available at 2 levels: up to $40,000 and up to $200,000 by the Inventions and Innovations program as stated by the Office of Industrial Technologies (OIT) Department of Energy (DOE) for ideas that significantly impact energy savings and future commercial market potential. Successful applicants will find technical guidance and commercialization support in addition to financial assistance.

DOE has given financial support to more than 500 inventions with nearly 25% of these reaching the marketplace bringing in nearly $710 million in cumulative sales.

6. U.S. Environmental Protection Agency
Center for Environmental Research Information
Cincinnati, OH 45260
513-569-7562
www.epa.gov
Directory Description: Environmental Protection Agency, Office of Research and Development, 401 M Street, SW, Washington, DC 20460; 202-260-7676; Fax: 202-260-9761. The Office of Research and Development conducts an Agency wide integrated program of research and development relevant to pollution sources and control, transport and fate processes, health/ecological effects, measurement/monitoring, and risk assessment. The office provides technical reviews, expert consultations, technical assistance, and advice to environmental decision makers in federal, state, local, and foreign governments.

Center for Environmental Research Information
26 W. ML King Drive, Cincinnati, OH 45268, Calvin O. Lawrence, Director; 513-569-7562; Fax: 513-569-7566.
A focal point for the exchange of scientific/ technical information both within the federal government and to the public.

Office of Research and Development
Is responsible for working with laboratories, program offices, regions to produce information products that summarize research, technical, regulatory enforcement information that will assist non-technical audiences in understanding environmental issues. Contact Office of Research and Development, U.S. Environmental Protection Agency, 401 M St., SW, Washington, DC 20460; 202-260-5767.

Office of Exploratory Research
Robert Menzer, Acting Director, 401 M Street, SW, Washington, DC 20460; 202-564-6849, Fax: 202-260-0450.

The Office of Exploratory Research (OER) plans, administers, manages, and evaluates the Environmental Protection Agency's (EPA) extramural grant research. It supports research in developing a better understanding of the environment and its problems. Main goals are: to support the academic community in environmental research; maintain scientific/technical personnel in environmental science/ technology; to support research for the identification/solution of emerging environmental problems.

Goals are accomplished through four core programs:

1. The Research Grants Program:
Supports research initiated by individual investigators in areas of interest to the agency.

2. The Environmental Research Centers Program:
Has two components: The Academic Research Center Program (ARC) and the Hazardous Substance Research Centers Program (HSRC).

3. The Small Business Innovation Research (SBIR) Program:
Program supports small businesses for the development of ideas relevant to EPA's mission. Focuses on projects in pollution control development. Also receives 1.5% of the Agency's resources devoted to extramural Superfund research.

4. The Visiting Scientists Program:
Components are an Environmental Science and Engineering Fellows Program and a Resident Research Associateship Program. The Fellows Program supports ten mid-career post-doctoral scientists and engineers at EPA headquarters & regional offices. The Research Associateship Program attracts national and international scientists and engineers at EPA research laboratories for up to 3 years to collaborate with Agency researchers on important environmental issues.

Other programs available are:
A Minority Fellowship Program
A Minority Summer Intern Program
The Agency's Senior Environmental Employment
  Program (SEE)
The Federal Workforce Training Program
An Experimental Program to Stimulate Competitive
  Research (EPSCoR).

To learn more, contact Grants Administration, U.S. Environmental Protection Agency, 401 M St., SW, 3903R, Washington, DC 20460; 202-564-5315. The best way, though, is to search for the word "grant" at the EPA's website {www.epa.gov}.

State Sources for Inventors

Below is a listing of a variety of inventors groups, listed state by state. Some organizations listed under the state where they are located are regional or national in scope. In states where there is no specific program for inventors, the Small Business Development Centers (under the U.S. Small Business Administration) can often be of help. They are usually found at the colleges and universities. The Small Business Development Center office is located at 409 Third St., SW, Suite 4600, Washington, DC 20416; 202-205-6766; {www.sba.gov}.

Alabama

Office for the Advancement of Developing Industries
University of Alabama - Birmingham
2800 Milan Ct.
Birmingham, AL 35211   205-934-6560
www.uab.edu/oad

Inventors can receive help on the commercialization and patent processes and critical reviews of inventions in this office. Assessments can be made on an invention's potential marketability and assistance is available for patent searches. There is a charge for services.

Small Business Development Center
University of Alabama at Birmingham
9015 15th St.   205-934-6760
Birmingham, AL 35294   Fax: 205-934-0538
www.business.uab.edu/school.sbdc/seminar.html

The center offers counseling for a wide range of business issues and problems.

U.S. Small Business Administration
Business Development
2121 8th Avenue, N, Suite 200   205-731-1338
Birmingham, AL 35203-2398   Fax: 205-731-1404
www.sba.gov

This office offers counseling for a wide range of business issues and problems.

Alabama Technology Assistance Program
University of Alabama at Birmingham
1717 11th Avenue S, Suite 419   205-934-7260
Birmingham, AL 35294   Fax: 205-934-7645

This program provides general assistance/funding information. Inventors meet other inventors and investors.

Alaska

UAA Small Business Development Center of Alaska
430 W. 7th Ave., Suite 110   907-274-7232
Anchorage, AK 99501   Fax: 907-274-9524
www.sba.gov/regions/states/ak/

The SBDC provides general assistance, including free counseling to inventors on commercialization and patent processes, and arranging meetings between inventors, investors, manufacturers, and others who can be of help.

Arizona

Arizona SBDC Network
108 N. 40th Street, Suite 148   602-392-5224
Phoenix, AZ 85034   Fax: 602-392-5300

The center offers counseling for a wide range of business issues and problems.

Maricopa Community Colleges
Small Business Development Center
702 E. Osborn Rd., Suite 150   602-230-7308
Phoenix, AZ 85014   Fax: 602-230-7989
www.dist.maricopa.edu/sbdc

The center provides inventor assistance and funding information to inventors.

Arkansas

Small Business Development Center
University of Arkansas at Little Rock
100 S. Main, Suite 401   501-324-9043
Little Rock, AR 72201   Fax: 501-324-9049
www.asbdc.ualr.edu

The center offers counseling for a wide range of business issues and problems.

California

Inventors Workshop International
Inventor Center, Suite 304
3201 Corte Malpaso
Camarillo, CA 93012   805-962-5722

This foundation has chapters nationwide. They hold meetings, conduct seminars, and counsel inventors on important issues, including product development and market research. The foundation publishes journals and a guidebook. There are dues and subscription fees.

Small Business Development Center
1410 Ethan Way   916-563-3210
Sacramento, CA 95825   Fax: 916-563-2366
www.sbdc.net

The center offers counseling for a wide range of business issues and problems.

Colorado

Affiliated Inventors Foundation, Inc.
1405 Porter St., #107   719-380-1234
Colorado Springs, CO 80909   Fax: 719-380-1144

This foundation counsels inventors on commercialization and patent processes, and provides detailed information on the steps needed to reach commercialization. Preliminary appraisals, evaluations and other services are available for a fee.

Small Business Development Center
Office of Economic Development
1625 Broadway, Suite 1710   303-892-3840
Denver, CO 80202   Fax: 303-892-3848
www.state.co.us/gov_dir/oed/sbdc.html

The center offers counseling for a wide range of business issues and problems.

Connecticut

Small Business Development Center
2 Bourn Place   860-486-4135
Storrs, CT 06269-1594   Fax: 860-486-1576
www.sbdc.uconn.edu

The center offers counseling for a wide range of business issues and problems.

Delaware

Small Business Development Center
University of Delaware
102 MBNA America Hall   302-831-1555
Newark, DE 19716   Fax: 302-831-1423
www.delawaresbdc.org

The office offers management counseling and seminars on various topics, and can counsel inventors on areas such as the commercialization and patenting processes. Services are by appointment only.

Delaware Economic Development
99 Kings Highway   302-739-4271
Dover, DE 19901   Fax: 302-739-5749
www.state.de.us

Assistance is available to any applicant located in Delaware or relocating to

Help for Inventors

Delaware, who has been granted a phase I SBIR award and has submitted a Phase II SBIR application.

District of Columbia

U.S. Department of Commerce
U.S. Patent and Trademark Office   800-PTO-9199
Washington, DC 20231   703-308-4357

District of Columbia Small Business Development Center
Howard University
2600 6th St., NW, Suite 128   202-806-1550
Washington, DC 20059   Fax: 202-806-1777
The center offers counseling for a wide range of business issues and problems.

U.S. Small Business Administration
2328 19th St., NW   202-606-4060
Washington, DC 20009   Fax: 202-205-7064
www.sba.gov
This office provides general assistance and information on funding.

Florida

Small Business Development Center
1531 NW 6th St.
Gainesville, FL 32606   352-377-5621
The center offers counseling for a wide range of business issues and problems.

Small Business Development Center
University of West Florida
1170 Martin L. King, Jr. Blvd.   850-595-5480
Fort Walton Beach, FL 32547   Fax: 850-595-5487
www.sbdc.uwf.edu
The center offers counseling for a wide range of business issues and problems.

Florida SBDC Network
19 W. Garden St., Suite 300   850-595-6060
Pensacola, FL 32501   Fax: 850-595-6070
www.floridasbdc.com
The network provides general assistance; conducts market/ technical assessments; offers legal advice on patents and licensing; provides funding information; and assists in building a prototype. Inventor get to showcase their inventions and meet with other inventors and investors.

University of Central Florida
Small Business Development Center
P.O. Box 161530   407-823-3073
Orlando, FL 32816-1530   Fax: 407-823-3073
www.bus.ucs.edu.sbdc
The center provides general assistance, funding information and conducts market assessments. Inventors meet other inventors.

Georgia

Small Business Development Center
University of Georgia
Chicopee Complex
1180 East Broad Street   706-542-7436
Athens, GA 30602   Fax: 706-542-6803
The center offers counseling for a wide range of business issues and problems.

Hawaii

Small Business Development Center
University of Hawaii at Hilo
1111 Bishop St., Suite 204   808-933-3515
Honolulu, HI 96813   Fax: 808-933-3683
http://hawaii-sbdc.org
The center offers counseling for a wide range of business issues and problems.

Idaho

Idaho Research Foundation, Inc.
University of Idaho
121 Sweet Ave.
Moscow, ID 83843-2309   208-885-3548
This foundation counsels inventors on commercialization and patent processes, and provides critical reviews on inventions. Computerized data searching and marketing service is available. It takes a percentage of intellectual property royalties.

Small Business Development Center
Boise State University
1910 University Drive
Boise, ID 83725   208-426-1640
The center offers counseling for a wide range of business issues and problems.

Idaho Small Business Development Center
P.O. Box 1238
315 Falls Ave.   208-733-9554
Twin Falls, ID 83303-1238   Fax: 208-733-9316
www.csi.cc.id.us - click on community services
The center conducts market assessments and provides funding information.

Idaho Small Business Development Center
Lewis-Clark State College
500 8th Ave.   208-799-2463
Lewiston, ID 83501   Fax: 208-799-2831
www.idbsu.edu/isbdc
The center provides general assistance and funding information. They also conduct market assessments.

Idaho State University
Small Business Development Center
2300 N. Yellowstone   208-523-1087
Idaho Falls, ID 83401   Fax: 208-528-7127
The center provides general assistance and funding information, and conducts technical assessments. Inventors meet with other inventors and investors.

Illinois

Inventor's Council
431 S. Dearborn
Suite 705
Chicago, IL 60605   312-939-3329
www.donmeyer.com
This group provides a liaison between inventors and industries. It holds meetings and workshops on commercialization, evaluation, marketing, financing, etc., for U.S. and Canadian inventors. Dues are required.

Small Business Development Center
Department of Commerce and Community Affairs
620 East Adams St.
3rd Floor   217-524-5856
Springfield, IL 62701   Fax: 217-785-6328
www.commerce.state.il.us
The center offers counseling for a wide range of business issues and problems, including commercialization and patent processes.

Small Business Development Center
Evanston Business Investment Corp.
1840 Oak Avenue   847-866-1817
Evanston, IL 60201   Fax: 847-866-1808
The center provides general assistance and funding information.

Western Illinois University
Technical Center and Small Business Development Center
Seal Hall 214   309-298-2211
Macomb, IL 61455   Fax: 309-298-2520
www.wiu.edu/sbdc
The center provides general assistance; conducts market/technical assessments; provides investment and funding information; and aids in building a prototype. Inventors meet with other inventors and investors, and get the chance to showcase their inventions.

Indiana

Small Business Development Center
One North Capitol
Suite 1275   317-246-6871
Indianapolis, IN 46204   Fax: 317-264-6855
www.isbdcorp.org
The center offers counseling for a wide range of business issues and problems.

State Sources for Inventors

Iowa

Drake Small Business Development Center
2429 University Ave.   515-271-2655
Des Moines, IA 46204   Fax: 515-271-1899

This center evaluates innovations for marketability, counsels inventors on commercialization, and helps match inventors with business persons. The fee for invention assessment is $125.

Small Business Development Center
Administrative Office
Iowa State University
137 Lynn Avenue   515-292-6351
Ames, IA 50014   Fax: 515-292-0020
www.iowasbdc.org

The center offers counseling for a wide range of business issues and problems.

Kansas

Small Business Development Center
Wichita State University
Campus Box 148
1845 Fairmont   316-978-3193
Wichita, KS 67260-0148   Fax: 316-978-3647
www.twsu.edu/~ksbdc

The center offers counseling for a wide range of business issues and problems.

Kentucky

Small Business Development Center
University of Louisville
Burhans Hall, Room 137, Shelby Campus   502-852-7854
Louisville, KY 40292   Fax: 502-852-8573

This center counsels inventors on commercialization and patent processes and provides critical reviews of inventions. It provides assistance in technically refining inventions. There are no fees.

Small Business Development Center
Kentucky Small Business Development Center
Center for Business Development
College of Business and Economics Building
225 Business and Economics Building
University of Kentucky   606-257-7668
Lexington, KY 40506   Fax: 606-323-1907

The center offers counseling for a wide range of business issues and problems.

Kentucky Transportation Center
176 Oliver H. Raymond Bldg.   606-257-4513
Lexington, KY 40506   Fax: 606-257-1815
www.engrouky.edu/ktc/

The center works closely with various federal, state and local agencies, as well as the private sector to conduct research supported by a wide variety of sources.

Louisiana

Small Business Development Center
Northeast Louisiana University
College of Business Administration
700 University Avenue   318-342-5506
Monroe, LA 71209   Fax: 318-342-5510

The center offers counseling for a wide range of business issues and problems.

Louisiana Department of Economic Development
P.O. Box 94185
Baton Rouge, LA 70804-9185   225-342-3000
www.lded.state.la.us

The department provides general assistance.

Maine

Industrial Cooperation
University of Maine
5717 Corbett Hall, Room 435
Orono, ME 04469-5717   207-581-2200
www.umaine.edu/dic

This center counsels inventors on the commercialization process, provides referrals for critical reviews of inventions and for financial and patent assistance, and conducts inventors' forums. It publishes a newsletter and bulletins. The communicative services are usually free; there are fees for educational services and materials.

Sunrise County Economic Council
P.O. Box 679
Machias, ME 04654   389-255-3313

The center offers counseling for a wide range of business issues and problems.

Department of Industrial Cooperation
5711 Boardman Hall, Room 117   207-581-1488
Orono, ME 04469-5711   Fax: 207-581-2202
www.umaine.edu/dic

On March 15, 1984, the Inventors Forum of Maine, Inc. (IFM), was formed and became a nonprofit corporation in the state of Maine. It was organized to stimulate inventiveness and entrepreneurship, and to help innovators and entrepreneurs develop and promote their ideas. It allows inventors and entrepreneurs to join together, share ideas and hopefully improve the chance for success. It gives encouragement, professional expertise, evaluation assistance, confidentiality and moral support of the University of Maine's Network and the University of Southern Maine's Small Business Development Center.

The Inventors Forum of Maine generally meets on the first Tuesday evening of each month at the University of Southern Maine, Campus Center, Room A, B & C on Bedford Street in Portland. Membership is open to all. For information regarding the Inventors Forum of Maine, contact Jake Ward, 207-581-1488.

Maryland

Inventions and Innovations
Department of Energy
Forrestal Building
1000 Independence Ave., SW
Washington, DC 20585   202-586-2079
www.oit.doe.gov/inventions

The office evaluates all promising non-nuclear energy-related inventions, particularly those submitted by independent inventors and small companies for the purpose of obtaining direct grants for their development from the U.S. Department of Energy.

Small Business Development Center
MMG, Inc.   410-333-4270
Baltimore, MD 21202   Fax: 410-333-2552
www.mmggroup.com

The center offers counseling for a wide range of business issues and problems.

Massachusetts

Massachusetts Small Business Development Center
Salem State College
352 Lafayette St.
Salem, MA 01970   978-542-6345

The center offers counseling for a wide range of business issues and problems.

Small Business Development Center
205 School of Management
University of Massachusetts   413-545-6301
Amherst, MA 01003   Fax: 413-545-1273

The center provides general assistance and funding information.

Smaller Business Association of New England
252 2nd Ave.   781-890-9070
Waltham, MA 02451   Fax: 781-890-4567
www.sbane.org

The association provides general assistance and funding information.

Michigan

Small Business Development Center
2727 Second Avenue   313-226-7947
Detroit, MI 48201   Fax: 313-577-4222

The center offers counseling for a wide range of business issues and problems.

Minnesota

Minnesota Project Innovation, Inc.
111 3rd Ave. S., Suite 100   612-338-3280
Minneapolis, MN 55401-2551   Fax: 612-349-2603
www.mpi.org

Help for Inventors

This project is affiliated with the Minnesota Dept. of Energy and Economic Development, U.S. Small Business Administration, and private companies. It provides referrals to inventors for sources of technical assistance in refining inventions.

    Minnesota Inventors Congress (MIC)
    805 East Bridge Street
    P.O. Box 71   507-637-2344
    Redwood Falls, MN 56283   Fax: 507-637-8399
    www.invent1.org

The Minnesota Inventors Congress (MIC) is a nonprofit organization established in 1958 to promote creativity, innovation, entrepreneurship by assisting the inventor and entrepreneur with education, promotion and referral. It's a professional organization composed of private individuals and corporations, who are creating and developing useful technologies. MIC is for inventors at every development stage — the novice and experienced; male or female; young and old; and supporters of invention and innovation. Workshops are also available. These are for individuals with ideas or inventions not yet successfully on the market; for companies, entrepreneurs looking for such inventions or new products.

"World's Oldest Annual Invention Convention" promotes the spirit of invention and innovation. Each year a 3 day convention presents more than 200 inventions and attracts some 10,000 visitors from around the world. The MIC provides a meeting place for:

1) Inventors to showcase their new products, connecting with manufacturers/investors, product test market, educational seminars, publicity, inventors network, and $1,500 in cash awards.
2) Manufacturers, marketers, investors and licenses seeking new products.
3) Inventors, viewers and exhibitors, seeking free counsel and literature on the invention development process.
4) Public to view the latest inventions, by adults and students, purchase MarketPlace products and meet global inventors.

    Small Business Development Center
    1125 Harmon Pl.   651-962-4500
    St. Paul, MN 55403   Fax: 651-962-4508

The center offers counseling for a wide range of business issues and problems.

Mississippi

    Small Business Development Center
    Old Chemistry Building, Suite 216   601-232-5001
    University, MS 38677   Fax: 601-232-5650
    www.olemiss.edu/depts/mssbdc

The center offers counseling for a wide range of business issues and problems.

    Mississippi State University
    Small Business Development Center
    P.O. Box 5288   601-325-8684
    Mississippi State, MS 39762   Fax: 601-325-4016

The center provides general assistance; conducts market assessments; and provides funding information.

    Small Business Development Center
    Meridian Community College
    910 Highway 19 North   601-482-7445
    Meridian, MS 39307   Fax: 601-482-5803

The center provides general assistance and funding information; conducts market/technical assessments; and offers legal advice on patents and licensing. Inventors meet with other inventors and investors.

Missouri

    Missouri Innovation Center
    5658 Sinclare Rd.   573-446-3100
    Columbia, MO 65203   Fax: 573-443-3748

This group provides communications among inventors, manufacturers, patent attorneys and venture capitalists, and provides general consultations. It is sponsored by the state, city of Columbia, and the University of Missouri. There are fees for some services.

    Inventors Association of St. Louis
    P.O. Box 16544
    St. Louis, MO 63105   314-432-1291

The group holds monthly meetings, provides communications among inventors, manufacturers, patent attorneys, and venture capitalists. It publishes a newsletter. There are annual dues.

    Small Business Development Center
    University of Missouri - Columbia
    1205 University Ave.
    Suite 1800 University Pl.   573-882-7096
    Columbia, MO 65211   Fax: 573-882-9931
    www.tiger.bpa.missouri.edu/Research/Training/sbdc.homepage.htm

The center offers counseling for a wide range of business issues and problems.

Montana

    Small Business Development Center
    Montana Department of Commerce
    1424 Ninth Avenue   406-444-4780
    Helena, MT 59620   Fax: 406-444-1872
    www.state.mt.us

The center offers counseling for a wide range of business issues and problems.

Nebraska

    University of Nebraska - Lincoln
    W 191 Nebraska Hall
    Lincoln, NE 68588-0525   402-472-5600
    www.engext.unl.edu/engext.html

Upon request, the University will send a packet of information so that the individual may go to the location and conduct their own Patent and Trademark search.

    Small Business Development Center
    University of Nebraska at Omaha
    60th and Dodge Street
    CBA, Room 407   402-554-2521
    Omaha, NE 68182   Fax: 402-554-3473

The center offers counseling for a wide range of business issues and problems.

    Association of SBDCs
    3108 Columbia Pike, Suite 300
    Arlington, VA 22204   703-271-8700
    www.asbdc-us.org

Organization's name and address may be given to individual inventors for referrals.

Nevada

    Nevada Small Business Center
    University of Nevada - Reno
    College of Business Administration/032   775-784-1717
    Reno, NV 89557-0100   Fax: 775-784-4337
    www.nsbdc.org

The center provides general assistance and funding information. inventors meet with other inventors and get to showcase their inventions.

    Nevada Small Business Center
    3720 Howard Hughes Parkway, Suite 130   702-734-7575
    Las Vegas, NV 89109   Fax: 702-734-7633
    www.Nevadasbdc.com

The center provides general assistance and funding information. Inventors meet with other inventors.

New Hampshire

    Small Business Development Center
    University of New Hampshire
    108 McConnell Hall   603-862-2200
    Durham, NH 03824   Fax: 603-862-4876
    www.nhsbdc.org

The center offers counseling for a wide range of business issues and problems.

    Small Business Development Center
    OEI-MMC
    1001 Elm Street   603-624-2000
    Manchester, NH 03101   Fax: 603-647-4410
    www.nhsbdc.org

The Small Business Development Center provides general assistance and funding information, and offers legal advice on patents and licensing. Inventors meet with other inventors.

State Sources for Inventors

New Jersey

Small Business Development Center
Rutgers University
43 Bleeker St.   973-353-5621
Newark, NJ 07102-1913   Fax: 973-353-1030
www/nj.com/smallbusiness

The Small Business Development Center offers counseling for a wide range of business issues and problems.

New Mexico

Albuquerque Invention Club
P.O. Box 30062
Albuquerque, NM 87190   505-266-3541

The contact is Dr. Albert Goodman, president of the club. The club meets on a monthly basis for speakers and presentations by different inventors. Members include patent attorneys, investors, and manufacturers.

Small Business Development Center
Santa Fe Community College
6401 Richards Ave.   505-428-1343
Santa Fe, NM 87505   Fax: 505-428-1469
www.nmsbdc.org

The center offers counseling for a wide range of business issues and problems.

New York

Small Business Development Center
State University Plaza
41 State St.   518-443-5398
Albany, NY 12246   Fax: 518-443-5275
www.nys-sbdc.suny.edu

The center offers counseling for a wide range of business issues and problems.

New York State
Energy Research and Development Authority
Corporate Plaza West
286 Washington Ave. Ext.   518-862-1090
Albany, NY 12203-6319   Fax: 518-862-1091
www.nyserda.org

The office provides general assistance and investment and funding information. It assists in building a prototype.

SUNY Institute of Technology
Small Business Development Center
P.O. Box 3050   315-792-7546
Utica, NY 13504   Fax: 315-792-7554
www.sunyit.edu.sbdc/

The center provides general assistance and funding information; conducts market/technical assessments; offers legal advice on patents and licensing, and assists in building a prototype. Inventors meet with other inventors.

Small Business Technical Inv. Fund
New York State Science and Technology Foundation
99 Washington Avenue, Suite 1731
Albany, NY 12210   518-473-9741
www.empire.state.ny.us/stf/stf.htm

The program provides financing assistance for technology-based start-up companies with initial investment as much as $300,000.

North Carolina

Small Business Development Center
University of North Carolina
333 Fayetteville Street Mall, #1150   919-715-7272
Raleigh, NC 27601   Fax: 919-715-7777

The center offers counseling for a wide range of business issues and problems.

North Dakota

Center for Innovation and Business Development
University of North Dakota
University Station
Box 8372   701-777-3132
Grand Forks, ND 58202   Fax: 701-777-2339
www.innovators.net

This center conducts occasional seminars and workshops with speakers; counsels on the commercialization and patenting process; provides communications among inventors, manufacturers, and patent attorneys. There are fees for services, but the first consultation is free.

Small Business Development Center
118 Gamble Hall
University of North Dakota
Box 7308   701-777-3700
Grand Forks, ND 58202-7308   Fax: 701-777-3225
www.und.nodak.edu/dept/nsbdc/

The center offers counseling for a wide range of business issues and problems.

Ohio

Inventors Connection of Greater Cleveland
17145 Misty Lake Dr.
Strongsville, OH 44106   440-238-3083

This association meets on a regular basis and provides communication among inventors. There are no dues.

Inventors Council of Dayton
Mr. George Pierce, President
P.O. Box 611
Dayton, OH 45409   937-224-8513

This association meets on a regular basis and provides communication among inventors, manufacturers, patent attorneys, etc., and often publishes newsletters.

Docie Marketing
9855 Sand Ridge Rd.
Millfield, OH 45761   740-594-2200

This profit-making company counsels inventors on the commercialization process, provides critical review of inventions and arranges meetings between inventors and manufacturers.

Small Business Development Center
Department of Development
30 East Broad Street, 23rd Floor
P.O. Box 1001   614-466-2711
Columbus, OH 43226   Fax: 614-466-0829
www.odod.ohio.gov

The center offers counseling for a wide range of business issues and problems.

Oklahoma

Invention Development Center
8230 SW 8th Street
Oklahoma City, OK 73128   405-632-0999

The center holds regular meetings, often with speakers, publishes a newsletter, and offers counseling and technical assistance to inventors. Annual dues are $25.

Small Business Development Center
Southeastern Oklahoma State University
517 University   580-924-0277
Durant, OK 74701   Fax: 580-924-7071

The center offers counseling for a wide range of business issues and problems.

Inventors Assistance Program
395 Cordell South   405-744-8727
Stillwater, OK 74078   Fax: 405-744-7399
http://techweb.ceat.okstate.edu/ias

This is a service to help inventors navigate the process from idea to marketplace using information, education and referrals. The service itself is free.

Oregon

Eastern Oregon University
Small Business Development Center
1410 L Ave.   541-962-3391
La Grande, OR 97850   Fax: 541-962-3668

Oregon Institute of Technology
Small Business Development Center
3201 Campus Dr., South 314   541-885-1760
Klamath Falls, OR 97601   Fax: 541-885-1855

Help for Inventors

Southern Oregon University
Small Business Development Center
332 W. 6th St.   541-772-3478
Medford, OR 97501   Fax: 541-734-4813

Small Business Development Centers (SBDCs) at three state colleges and the community colleges can counsel inventors and direct them where to go for patent process, etc.

Oregon Small Business Development Center
44 W. Broadway, Suite 501   541-726-2250
Eugene, OR 97401   Fax: 541-345-6006

The center provides general assistance and funding information.

Small Business Development Center
2701 NW Vaughn St.   503-978-5080
Portland, OR 97210   Fax: 503-222-2570
www.sbdc.citysearch.com

The center provides general assistance and funding information.

Oregon State Library
State Library Building
250 Winter St., NE   503-378-4277
Salem, OR 97310   Fax: 503-588-7119
www.osl.state.or.us

Organization's name and address may be given to individual inventors for referrals.

Pennsylvania

American Society of Inventors
P.O. Box 58426
Philadelphia, PA 19102-8426   215-546-6601

Members are counseled on the commercialization and patent processes; critical reviews of inventions, and assessments of market potential are provided. The Society also offers technical assistance and referrals. There are dues.

Small Business Development Center
Bucknell University
Dana Engineering Building, 1st Floor   570-524-1249
Lewisburg, PA 17837   Fax: 570-524-1768
www.bucknell.edw/~sbdc

The center offers counseling for a wide range of business issues and problems.

Pennsylvania Small Business Development Center
Vance Hall, 4th Floor
3733 Spruce Street   215-898-4861
Philadelphia, PA 19104   Fax: 215-898-1063
www.pasbdc.org

The center provides general assistance and funding information. It also conducts market and technical assessments. It also oversees all centers in Pennsylvania.

Rhode Island

Service Corps of Retired Executives (SCORE)
c/o U.S. Small Business Administration
380 Westinghouse, Room #511
Providence, RI 02903   401-528-4571

Volunteers in the SCORE office are experts in many areas of business management and can offer advice to inventors in areas including marketing and the commercialization process.

Small Business Development Center
7 Jackson Walkway
Providence, RI 02903   401-831-1330

The center offers counseling for a wide range of business issues and problems.

Small Business Development Center
Bryant College
1150 Douglas Pike   401-232-6111
Smithfield, RI 02917   Fax: 401-232-6933
www.risbdc.org

The center provides general assistance and conducts market and technical assessments.

South Carolina

Small Business Development Center
South Carolina State University
School of Business
300 College St.
Campus Box 7176   803-536-8445
Orangeburg, SC 29117   Fax: 803-536-8066

The center offers counseling for a wide range of business issues and problems.

South Carolina Small Business Development Center
University of South Carolina
College of Business Administration   803-777-4907
Columbia, SC 29208   Fax: 803-777-4403

The center provides general assistance and funding information.

South Dakota

Business and Education Institute
Dakota State University
Madison, SD 57042   605-256-5555
www.bei.dsu.ed.com

This office can provide guidance to inventors on a wide range of issues: commercialization, patent process, marketability, etc. It has grant money available.

Small Business Development Center
University of South Dakota
School of Business
414 East Clark St.   605-677-5287
Vermillion, SD 57069-2390   Fax: 605-677-5427
www.uso.edu/brbinfo

The center offers counseling for a wide range of business issues and problems.

Tennessee

Tennessee Inventors Association
P.O. Box 11225
Knoxville, TN 37939-1225   423-539-4466
www.state.tn.us

Monthly meetings are held where a wide range of topical subjects are discussed: patenting, venture capital, marketing, etc. Workshops and invention exhibitions are held periodically.

Jackson State Community College
Small Business Development Center
2046 North Parkway Street   901-424-5389
Jackson, TN 38301   Fax: 901-425-2641

The center offers counseling for a wide range of business issues and problems.

Texas

Technology and Economic Development
DivTEEX
301 Terrow Bldg.
College Station, TX 77840-7896   409-845-3559
www.tedd.org

The organization conducts workshops, provides counseling on commercialization and patent processes, offers critical reviews of inventions on a selected basis, assesses invention's marketability, and assists with patent searches. State appropriations, federal grants and subscriptions to newsletter are available on a limited basis.

North Texas-Dallas Small Business Development Center
Dallas Community College District
1402 Corinth Street   214-860-5850
Dallas, TX 75215   Fax: 214-565-5815

The center offers counseling for a wide range of business issues and problems.

Texas Tech University
Small Business Development Center
2579 S. Loop 289, St. 114   806-745-3973
Lubbock, TX 79423   Fax: 806-745-6207
www.nwtsbdc.com

The center provides general assistance and funding information.

University of Houston
Small Business Development Center
Manufacturers Assistance Center
1100 Louisiana, Suite 500   713-752-8440
Houston, TX 77002   Fax: 713-756-1515
http://smbizsolutions.uh.edu

The center provides general assistance and funding information; conducts market and

State Sources for Inventors

technical assessments; and assists in building a prototype. Inventors meet with investors.

Utah
Utah Small Business Development Center
1627 S. State St.   801-957-3480
Salt Lake City, UT 84115   Fax: 801-957-3489
www.slcc.edu

The center provides general assistance and funding information, and conducts market and technical assessments. Inventors meet with inventors and investors.

Vermont
Economic and Development Office
State of Vermont
National Library Bldg.   802-828-3211
Montpelier, VT 05620-0501   Fax: 802-828-3258
www.state.vt.us/dca

Inventors will be counseled on the commercialization and marketing processes as well as other areas, and will be referred to other places as needed.

Small Business Development Center
60 Main St.
Suite 103   802-658-9228
Burlington, VT 05401   Fax: 802-860-1899
www.vermont.org

The center offers counseling for a wide range of business issues and problems.

Virginia
Virginia Small Business Development Center
707 E. Main St.
P.O. Box 446
Richmond, VA 23288-0446   804-371-8258
www.dba.state.va.us

The center offers counseling for a wide range of business issues and problems.

Small Business Development Center
1001 E. Market St.   804-295-8198
Charlottesville, VA 22903   Fax: 804-295-7066
http://avenue.gen.va.us/Market/SBDC

The center provides general assistance, and conducts market and technical assessments.

U.S. Department of Commerce
Patent and Trademark Office   1-800-PTO-9199
Washington, DC 20231   703-308-4357
www.uspto.gov

The office provides general assistance on patents and licensing.

Washington
Innovation Assessment Center
108 Nickerson St.
Suite 207   206-464-5450
Seattle, WA 98109   Fax: 206-464-6357
www.sbdc.wsu.edu

Part of the Small Business Development Center, this center performs commercial evaluations of inventions, counseling and provides assistance with patentability searches. There are fees for services.

Small Business Development Center
Johnson Tower, Room 501
P.O. Box 644851   509-335-6415
Pullman, WA 99164-4851   Fax: 509-335-0949
www.sbdc.wsu.edu

The center offers counseling for a wide range of business issues and problems.

Small Business Development Center
Western Washington University
308 Parks Hall   360-650-3899
Bellingham, WA 98225   Fax: 360-650-4831

The center provides general assistance, and investment and funding information.

West Virginia
Small Business Development Center
West Virginia University
912 Main St.   304-465-1434
Oak Hill, WV 25901   Fax: 304-465-8680

The center offers counseling for a wide range of business issues and problems.

West Virginia Small Business Development Office
2000 7th Ave.   304-696-6798
Huntington, WV 25703-1527   Fax: 304-696-4835
www.marshall.edu

The center provides information on investment and funding.

Wisconsin
Center for Innovation and Development
University of Wisconsin - Stout
278 Jarvis Hall
Menomonie, WI 54751   715-232-5026
http://nwmoc.uwstout.edu

The center counsels inventors on the commercialization and patent processes; provides critical reviews of inventions; assists inventors on technically refining inventions; and provides prototype development. There are fees for services.

Wisconsin Innovation Service Center
402 McCutchan Hall
UW-Whitewater   414-472-1365
Whitewater, WI 53190   Fax: 414-472-1600
www.uww.edu/business/innovate/innovate.htm

Provides early stage market research for inventors. There is a flat fee of $495 for services.

Small Business Development Center
University of Wisconsin
432 North Lake Street, Room 423   608-263-7794
Madison, WI 53706   Fax: 608-263-7830
www.uwex.edu/sbdc

The center offers counseling for a wide range of business issues and problems.

Wisconsin Department of Commerce
P.O. Box 7970   608-266-9467
Madison, WI 53707   Fax: 608-267-2829
www.commerce.state.wi.us

The office provides information on investment and funding.

Wyoming
Small Business Development Center
111 W. 2nd St., Suite 502
Casper, WY 82601   307-234-6683
www.uwyo.edu/sbdc

Dr. Leonard Holler, who works in the office, is able to help inventors on a wide range of issues including patenting, commercialization and intellectual property rights. There are fees for services.

Canada
Innovative Center
156 Columbia Street W.
Waterloo, Ontario NN 26363   519-885-5870
www.innovationcentre.ca

Provides inventors with market research, idea testing, and helps guide inventors up to the patent stage.

Home-Based Business Resources

Home-Based Business Resources

If you're looking for a $10,000 loan to start a craft business out of your home, or you would love to get a $100,000 freelance writing contract you can operate from your kitchen table, call your favorite uncle, Uncle Sam. Did you know that government offices, like the National Park Service, routinely award contracts to artists and photographers for over $50,000?

The government is likely to have all the money, help and information you will ever need for running your home-based business and what's great about these resources is that they're free. All the Fortune 500 companies rely on government programs and information sources for succeeding in their business, and you can too.

Why spend hundred of dollars hiring a lawyer to explain the trade laws that might apply to your business when you can talk to a legal expert at the Federal Trade Commission about them for the price of a phone call? Why pay for expensive crime insurance from a private carrier to protect your home office, when you might be able to get the same coverage from the federal government for a fraction of the cost? Why hire a high-priced specialist who will promise to find you customers, when the government can help you do it for free? And just because you work out of your home doesn't mean that you can't compete for lucrative government contracts just like the big companies do.

Not only can the government help you start and run your home-based business, they can even help you furnish it at bargain basement prices. By attending government surplus property auctions, you can get all the office furniture, computer equipment, and filing cabinets you need for pennies on the dollar. The Department of Defense, for example, has auctioned off office chairs for $10 and desks for $25.

Home-based businesses are among the fastest growing kinds of business in the U.S. The Small Business Administration estimates that there are about 4 million home-based businesses in the U.S. today. That represents 25% of the total number of sole proprietorship businesses in the country. And according to the American Home-Based Business Association, about 63 million Americans do some kind of work out of their home. There are a lot of people who've decided against the morning commute and fighting over the Xerox and coffee machines at the office.

The big advantage of running a business out of your home is that it keeps overhead costs to a minimum. A big overhead can be fatal to any new business venture. You don't have to spend half-a-million dollars to find out that running a fumigation or TV repair service really isn't your dream business -- no big office space to rent, no extra employees sitting around, no big insurance bills.

One of the safest ways to start a business is by starting a home-based business. And even a safer way is to take advantage of all the free help available from your Uncle Sam.

* Free Home-Based Business Start Up Guide
Office of Business Development and Marketing
Small Business Administration
Washington, DC 20416   202-205-6665
www.sba.gov

The SBA has put together a free pamphlet for those who are thinking about starting their own small business out of their homes: *How To Start A Home-Based Business*. This guide is part of the SBA's *Focus On The Facts* series of publications, which also includes information on raising capital, business planning, marketing, pricing, and exporting.

* How to Write Off Your Car and Home, and Summer Vacation As a Business Expense
Taxpayer Services
Internal Revenue Service
U.S. Department of the Treasury
1111 Constitution Ave., NW, Room 2422
Washington, DC 20224   800-829-3676
www.irs.gov

One advantage to owning a home-based business is being able to write off car expenses related to your job. For more information on guidelines for writing off your car, get a free copy of *Business Use Of A Car* (#917) explains the expenses you may deduct for the use of your car in your home-based business. And a copy of *Business Use Of Your Home* (#587) can help you decide if you qualify to deduct certain expenses for using part of your home for your business. Deductions for the business use of a home computer are also discussed. The IRS will also show you how to piggy back a vacation onto your business travel. *Travel, Entertainment, and Gift Expenses* (#463) explains what expenses you may deduct for business-related travel, meals, entertainment, and gifts for your business, along with the reporting and recordkeeping requirements for these expenses.

* Free Videos on How To Start a Business In Your Home
Office of Business Initiatives
Small Business Administration (SBA)
409 3rd St., SW
Washington, DC 20416   800-827-5722
www.sba.gov (online library of publications)
or

Oklahoma State University
Agricultural Communications
111 Public Information Building
Stillwater, OK 74078   405-744-5776

Home-Based Business Basics shows potential business owners how to do market research, handle finances, cope with legal problems, do promotions and juggle family relationships. The film is produced by a member of the County Cooperative Extension service and is available on a free loan basis at your local county cooperative extension service offices throughout the country. Call your local operator for your nearest office. Or you can purchase the film for $30 direct from the producer listed above.

* Is Your Advertising Legal?
Advertising Practices Division
Federal Trade Commission
6th and Pennsylvania Ave., NW
Washington, DC 20580   202-326-3131
www.ftc.gov

Attracting new customers through advertising is an important part of a successful business, but you'll want to do it fairly and honestly. This division of the FTC can provide you with information about how to comply with the law and avoid making deceptive advertising claims.

* Is Your Office Asbestos and Radon Free?
Office of Information and Public Affairs
Consumer Product Safety Commission
Washington, DC 20207   800-638-2772

Home-Based Business Resources

or

Radon Division (ANR-464)
Office of Radon Programs
U.S. Environmental Protection Agency
401 M St., SW
Washington, DC 20460
www.epa.gov

800-SOS-RADON
202-475-9605

If you've set your office up in your basement, you might be exposing yourself to hazardous asbestos insulation. To find out more about home asbestos and eliminating its hazards, contact the Consumer Product Safety Commission (CPSC) for a free copy of *Asbestos in the Home*. Setting up office in the basement may also make yourself vulnerable to the effects of radon gas, which often enter homes through cracks in the basement floors. To get more information on the radon risks in your area, how to test for radon, and how to protect your home, contact the EPA office above. They can send you free radon publications, along with the number of a radon expert in your state.

* Keep Up To Date On The Cheapest Way To Send Out Mail

Business Mailer Updates
P.O. Box 999
Springfield, VA 22150-0999

or

Marketing Department
Regular Mail Services Division
U.S. Postal Service
475 L'Enfant Plaza, SW
Washington, DC 20260-6336

202-268-6965

When you do business through the mail, you need to keep up on rate and classification changes when they occur. The Postal Service puts out, *Memo To Mailers*, a free monthly publication to keep you posted of any of these changes, along with other relevant postal news. To be put on the mailing list, write to the above address, or for more information about the *Memo*, contact: Communications Department, U.S. Postal Service, 475 L'Enfant Plaza, SW, Washington, DC 20260; 202-268-6874; {www.usps.gov}.

Part of having a successful home-based business is knowing how to use the mail service effectively. To help you better prepare your mail for sending, the Marketing Department of the Postal Service has put together a free booklet, *A Guide To Business Mail Preparation*. This booklet gives you information on addressing for automation, postnet bar codes, and FIM patterns, all of which prepares your mail to be processed more efficiently, economically, and accurately, which makes for happier customers.

* How Business Reply Mail Can Bring You New Customers

Rates and Classification Department
U.S. Postal Service
475 L'Enfant Plaza
Washington, DC 20260
www.usps.gov

202-268-5316

If you use the mail a lot in your business to solicit customers, you might look into using business reply mail. Under this service, you guarantee to pay the postage for all replies returned to you at the regular first class rate plus a business reply fee. To use this service, you have to pay a small annual permit charge. Contact this office for more information on setting up this service for your business mailings.

* Free Tax Consulting By The Experts

Internal Revenue Service
1111 Constitution Ave, NW
Washington, DC 20224
www.irs.gov

800-829-1040

or

Your Local IRS Office

Why pay big money to a tax attorney or accountant when you can get better information for free? Many entrepreneurs believe that you will get a more favorable answer by hiring your own expert than you would if you call the IRS, but this has not shown to be the case. The law is the law, and private studies show that your chances of saving money on your tax bill is no greater whether you go to the IRS or to a high priced consultant for help. The problem is that most people don't know how to call the IRS to get the right answer. If the person at the IRS hotline seems a little unsure of their answer or if you just want another opinion, ask the IRS person to have a specialist call you back. Within a day or two you will get a call from an IRS expert who specializes in your question. They will take as much time as you need to make sure that you get all the deductions you are entitled to.

* Free Help To Start a Home-Based Tax Preparation Business

Volunteer and Education Branch
Taxpayer Service Division
Internal Revenue Service
U.S. Dept. of Treasury
1111 Constitution Ave, NW., Room 1315
Washington, DC 20224
www.irs.gov

800-827-5722

If you want to start your own tax preparation business you don't have to pay H&R Block or some other commercial organizations $200 to take a course. You can take a free course from the best experts in the work, the IRS. Many times these courses are given by IRS auditors and this is how you really learn the inside secrets on how to avoid the wrath of the IRS computer. Courses are available every year during the Fall. In return for free training you are required to volunteer a few hours of your time during one tax season to help others prepare their returns. The rest of your time you can charge for preparing tax returns. The IRS also offers free small business workshops which assist entrepreneurs in understanding their tax obligations.

* Make Sure Your Computer Screen <u>Isn't</u> Hazardous To Your Health

Information and Consumer Affairs
Occupational Safety and Health Administration
U.S. Department of Labor
Washington, DC 20210
www.osha.gov

202-523-8148

People who run home-based businesses often spend many hours sitting in front of their computer screens doing work. If you're one of these people, you should be aware of what the U.S. Department of Labor has discovered about the hazardous of display terminals. The following two relevant publications are available free from OSHA: *Display Terminals* and *Working Safely with Display Terminals*.

* Getting The Most Out Of Your Home Computer

SBA Publications
P.O. Box 46521
Denver, CO 80201
www.sba.gov

Setting up the right computer system is very important for many home-based businesses. The SBA has a couple of publications to help you out with computer problems:

How To Get Started With A Small Business Computer. Helps you forecast your computer needs, evaluate the alternatives and select the right computer system for your business. (MP14) $2. Make check payable to the U.S. Small Business Administration.

A Small Business Guide To Computer Security. Helps you understand the nature of computer security risks and offers timely advice on how to control them. (CP3) $1.

Focus on the Facts: Buying a Computer for a Small Business. Covers most common questions about whether and what to buy in terms of home computers. Also includes a list of common computer lingo to know when selecting a computer. Free.

* Free Help In Setting Up Your Own Complaint Handling System

Marketing Practices Division
Federal Trade Commission
6th and Pennsylvania Ave., NW
Washington, DC 20580
www.ftc.gov

202-326-3128

A successful business knows how to keep consumers coming back, even after they've complained about a product or service. They way they do this is by establishing a fair and effective system of resolving customer complaints quickly and inexpensively. The FTC works to promote such procedures among businesses, and they will provide you with information to help you develop an effective consumer complaint process for your business.

Home-Based Business Resources

* How To Handle Salesmen Who Come To Your Home
Enforcement Division
Federal Trade Commission
6th and Pennsylvania Ave., NW
Washington, DC 20580   202-326-3034
www.ftc.gov

If your home-based business gets sales people coming to your door trying to sell you items you can't really decide if you want, you should be aware of the FTC's *Cooling-Off Rule*, which requires sellers to give consumers notice of their three-day cancellation rights. For more information about the *Cooling Off Rule*, including a free pamphlet that describes the law, contact the FTC.

* Free Seminars On Starting A Business At Home
Contact your County Cooperative Extension Service listed under county government in your telephone book

Most counties in the U.S. have Cooperative Extension Services that can provide you with information on how to start up and run a home-based business. Many can provide you with free publications, while others may even run free workshops or seminars on home-based business — it all depends on what your county Extension Service is doing. Most of these Services put out free newsletters that describe upcoming events, such as workshops, along with articles that might be of interest to you as a home-based business owner. Contact your Cooperative Extension Service to be put on their mailing list and for more information about their home-based business resources.

* Get Your Credit Fixed For Free
Contact your County Cooperative Extension Service listed under county government in your telephone book
or
National Foundation for Credit Counseling
8611 2nd Ave., Suite 100
Silver Spring, MD 20910   301-589-5600
www.nfcc.org

Can't get a business loan because you have bad credit? Don't spend hundred of dollars to a credit repair clinic to tell you how to do it, contact your county's Cooperative Extension Service. These Services routinely run money and budgeting workshops at no charge that can show you how to fix your credit problems and pay off your bills more efficiently. If your county Cooperative Extension Service doesn't hold money workshops, you might consider contacting the National Foundation for Credit Counseling which runs non-profit counseling services across the country, including in your state. Call them at 800-388-2227 for the service nearest you.

* Cheap Crime Insurance for Your Business Equipment
Federal Crime Insurance
P.O. Box 6301   800-638-8780
Rockville, MD 20850   301-251-1660
www.ncsi_net.com

If your home is burglarized, your home-based business could suffer large losses, such as expensive computer and telephone equipment. Residents in 13 states are eligible for a federal crime insurance program that actually subsidizes the cost of insurance to you. This means cheaper insurance premiums because the federal government is paying part of the bill for you. The following states and territories participate: AL, CA, CT, DE DC, FL, GA, IL, KS, MD, NJ, NY, PA, RI, TN, and Puerto Rico and the Virgin Islands. Contact this office for more information about the program and an application.

* The Best Way To Keep Your Customers
Office of Consumer Affairs
U.S. Department of Commerce
Washington, DC 20230   202-482-5001

Finding customers is only half the story of a successful business; you also need to know how to keep them once you have them. And to do that you need to know how to develop good customer relations through honest and effective advertising, warranties, product safety, and complaint handling procedures. Contact this office for more information on these subjects, along with getting free copies of the following publications from their series of *Consumer Affairs Guides For Business*:

Advertising, Packaging, and Labeling
Product Warranties and Servicing
Managing Consumer Complaints
Credit And Financial Issues
Consumer Product Safety

This office can also provide you with information about local small business conferences based on these consumer affairs issues.

* Choosing Day Care for Work-At-Home Families
County Cooperative Extension Service
6707 Groveton Dr.
Clinton, MD 20735   301-868-9410

If you're running your own small business or a business out of your home, you might need to consider finding good and reliable day care for your children to give you the time you need for your business. This office can send you a free copy of *How To Select Quality Day Care For Your Child*, which shows you what to look for in day care.

* How The Law Protects You If You Don't Pay Your Bills
Credit Practices Division
Federal Trade Commission
6th and Pennsylvania Ave., NW
Washington, DC 20580   202-326-3758
www.ftc.gov

If you're thinking of starting a debt collection agency, you'll need to know what the law says you can and cannot do to collect a debt for a client. The FTC can provide you with information on the *Fair Debt Collection Practices Act*, which prohibits debt collectors from engaging in unfair, deceptive, or abusive practices, such as overcharging, harassment, and disclosing consumers' debts to third parties. If you're being harassed by a debt collection agency, the FTC would like to hear about it.

* Free Legal Help On The Best Way To Treat Your Employees
Employment Standards Administration
U.S. Department of Labor, Room C4325
Washington, DC 20210   202-219-8743
www.esa.gov

One of the reasons people want to run their own businesses is that they don't like working for unfair and abusive bosses. To make sure that you don't turn into one of them, you'll need to know the federal laws that protect your employees' rights. The following free publications from the ESA will give you a good introduction to those labor laws:

Employer's Guide to Compliance with Federal Wage-Hour Laws
Federal Minimum Wage and Overtime Pay Standards
Handy Reference Guide to the Fair Labor Standards Act
Highlights of Computing Overtime Pay Under the FLSA
How the Federal Wage and Hour Laws Applies to Holidays
Employment of Apprentices
Employment of Messengers
Making EEO and Affirmative Action Work

Also see *How Labor Laws Affect Your Small Business* below for more information on this subject.

* How To Get People and Companies Who Owe You Money To Pay Up
- Local Postmaster of the U.S. Postal Service
    Call the information operator for the city in question
- State Division of Motor Vehicles
    Call your state government operator in your state capitol
- State Attorney General Office
    Call your state government operator in your state capitol
- State Office of Uniform Commercial Code
    Call your state government operator in your state capitol
- State Office of Corporations
    Call your state government operator in your state capitol
- {www.usps.gov} or {www.ftc.gov}

Before you pay an attorney big money to help you collect a bad debt, there are a number of government offices you can turn to that will help you get your money for free or for just a few dollars.

If you are looking for an individual who moved, contact the U.S. Postal Service and the state Division of Motor Vehicles. The Post Office in the city of the last know address of your deadbeat friend will give you their forwarding address and charge you only $1.00. This information is kept at most Post Offices for 18 months. And

Home-Based Business Resources

for a few dollars, almost every state government will give you the address of anyone from their file of driver licenses. Almost everyone has a drivers license.

If a business owes you money, a letter to the Attorney General in the state where the business is headquartered can easily shake lose your money. Most Attorney General offices will send the business an official letter of inquiry, and this is enough to scare any legitimate businessperson into paying their bills.

Another effective method is to use the information in government offices to shame a business into paying their bill. The Office of Corporations in every state capitol will give you the name and address of all the officers of any businesses in their state. And the state Office of Uniform Commercial Code will give you the names of all the other people this business owes money to. It is a law that anytime a business, or individual, borrows money and puts up an asset as collateral, the information is filed at the Office of Uniform Commercial Code. When you send a letter asking someone for payment, you can send copies of the letter to all these other people. And what is most effective, is that the people listed as officers of most small businesses are friend and relatives of the owner, and it can be very embarrassing for a business owner to have them know how unfairly they are treating you.

* Free Accounting Help
Contact your State Department of Economic Development Office for the Small Business Development Center near you

Accountants are expensive, especially if your small business, like most, don't have a lot of working capital to throw around. Instead of going out and hiring your own personal accountant, contact your local SBDC. Many of these centers have accounting experts who will sit down with you and help you develop your own accounting and recordkeeping systems. They can also help you work through any accounting problems that you might run into. If you don't have an SBDC near you, contact your nearest Small Business Administration Office--they work with the Service Corps of Retired Executives (SCORE) whose members can also provide you with free accounting assistance and advice.

* Entrepreneur Quiz
Superintendent of Documents
Government Printing Office
Washington, DC 20402   202-512-0000
www.access.gpo.gov

For $2.00, GPO will send you a copy of *Starting and Managing a Business from Your Home*, which contains a questionnaire to help you decide if you have the right kind of personality to be a successful entrepreneur and home-based business owner. Also included are descriptions of products and services to help you start your own home-based business, such as business planning, recordkeeping, taxes, and insurance.

* What You Need To Know When Selling Food and Medical Products
Small Business Coordinator
Food and Drug Administration
5600 Fishers Lane, Room 15-61
Rockville, MD 20857   301-827-3430
www.fda.gov

If you are going to be selling any food or drug products as part of your business, you'll need to know how to comply with the FDA's packaging and labeling regulations for these products. This office can explain FDA procedures and help you comply with their rules. Contact them for a free copy of *A Small Business Guide to the FDA*, which will give you an overview of the small business compliance program.

* How To Pick A Work-At-Home Franchise
Bureau of Consumer Protection
Federal Trade Commission
6th and Pennsylvania Ave, NW
Washington, DC 20580   202-326-3128
www.ftc.gov

or

International Franchising Association
1350 New York Ave, NW
Washington, DC 20005   202-628-8000

or

Your State Franchising Office

Just because you want to run a business out of your home, doesn't mean that you're not in a position to consider owning a franchise. Owning a franchise can mean you already have name recognition and advertising done for you. Of course, Pizza Hut isn't going to let you run a business out of your home, but others might, like lawn care companies, leak detection services, upholstery cleaners, commercial office cleaners, maid services, sewer and drain cleaning services, and many more.

The Federal Trade Commission will send you a number of free publications that will tell you what you need to know before buying a franchise. The International Franchise Association also has a number of publications on this topic, but they charge a small fee.

There are a number of state governments that require franchisors who are selling franchises in their state to file detailed background information on their company which is made available to the public. Call your state capitol operator to see if your state has such requirements, or call the Federal Trade Commission and they will tell you which states you can contact to get this information.

* Check If You And Your Employees Are Safe Working In Your Home
Information and Consumer Affairs
Occupational Safety and Health Administration
U.S. Department of Labor
Washington, DC 20210   202-219-4667
www.osha.gov

Depending on what your small business is, you might be faced with potential health and safety concerns, anything from indoor air quality to stiff joints from typing too much. OSHA has put out a series of free publications of interest to small businesses to help you remedy or avoid potential health and safety problems: *Handbook For Small Businesses, General Industry Digest, Construction Industry Digest,* and *Consultation Services For Employers*.

* Free Inspections of Your Home for Health And Safety Hazards
National Institute for Occupational Safety and Health
4676 Columbia Parkway
Cincinnati, OH 45226   800-356-4674
www.cdc.gov/niosh

The National Institute for Occupational Safety and Health (NIOSH) is responsible for conducting research to make the nation's workplaces healthier and safer by responding to urgent requests for assistance from employers, employees, and their representatives where imminent hazards are suspected. They conduct inspections, laboratory and epidemiologic research, publish their findings, and make recommendations for improved working conditions. They will also inspect any workplace for free if three employees sign a form alleging that the environment may be dangerous. Employees have the option of keeping anonymous. If any of the following applies to you, NIOSH can provide you with more information:

Do you use a video display terminal most of the day?
Are you concerned about the chemicals you are using in your dry cleaning?
Do you have tingling in your hands (carpal tunnel syndrome)?
Do you use a jackhammer most of the day and are now finding that your fingers are no longer sensitive to heat or cold?
Do you do the same motion again and again, such as on an assembly line?
Do you feel your job is causing you mental stress?
Are you having trouble hearing?

* How To Choose The Best Health Insurance Coverage
Office of Business Development and Marketing
Small Business Administration
409 3rd St., SW
Washington, DC 20416   202-205-6743
www.sba.gov

or

National Health Information Clearinghouse Hotline
P.O. Box 1133   301-565-4167
Washington, DC 20013-1133   800-336-4797

Owning your own business means that you no longer will have your health insurance taken care of the way it was when you worked for somebody else. To help you figure out the best way to find a health insurance plan best suited to your needs, the SBA has produced a free publication that's part of their *Focus on the Facts* series called *Small Business Health Insurance*. This publication covers such topics as indemnity, managed care, selecting a plan, and self insurance. Contact this office for your free copy.

Home-Based Business Resources

* How To Get Free Health Care If You Can't Afford Health Insurance
Public Health Service
Health Resource and Services Administration
U.S. Department of Health and Human Services   800-492-0359 (in MD)
Rockville, MD 20857   800-638-0742

If you can't afford health insurance and you meet certain income requirements, you may be eligible to receive free medical care under the Hill-Burton law. Under this law, hospitals and other health facilities that receive federal funding for construction and modernization must provide certain medical services at no charge to those who can't afford to pay. By calling the toll-free number above, you can find out which hospitals in your area are participating in this program, along with income eligibility requirements. If your home-based business is your only source of income, and it's making little or no profit, you may in fact be eligible for free health care.

* How Labor Laws Affect Your Small Business
Office of Small and Disadvantaged Business Utilization
U.S. Department of Labor
200 Constitution Ave., NW, Room C-2318
Washington, DC 20210   202-219-9148
www.dol.gov

Just because you run a small or home-based business doesn't mean you don't have to obey federal labor laws like larger companies do. To find out what laws apply to your small business regarding such topics as wages, overtime, pensions, and health and safety, contact this office for a free copy of the booklet, *Major Laws Administered by the U.S. Department of Labor Which Affect Small Business*. You should also contact your state's labor department to find out what state laws you should know about.

* Should You Lease Or Buy A Car For Your Business
Consumer Information Center
Pueblo, CO 81009

As a small business owner, you might have to decide whether it's better for you to lease or buy a car for the business. Using plain english, the *Consumer Guide To Vehicle Leasing* will give you an explanation of the advantages and disadvantages of buying and leasing a car, and show you how to decide what's best for you. It's available for $.50 from the Consumer Information Center.

* Get Legal Help at Little or No Cost
Contact your State Department of Economic Development Office for the Small Business Development Center near you

Many Small Business Development Centers offer free or low-cost legal advice concerning laws that you might run up against in running your small business. And since most small businesses, especially home-based businesses, have very little working capital to throw around, the last thing you want to do is spend what you do have on an expensive lawyer. They can help you with legal questions like:

When should you form a corporation?
Can my employer sue me if I take some of his business with me?

Before getting your own personal, and expensive, lawyer, contact a Small Business Development Center and see if they can give you the legal advice you need without having to spend a lot of money.

* Legal Advice On Trade Laws
Public Reference Branch
Federal Trade Commission
Washington, DC 20580   202-326-2222
www.ftc.gov

If you're not sure what business laws may apply to your new business, contact the FTC's Public Reference Branch. If you let them know what kind of business you're thinking of running, they'll be able to direct you to an expert at the FTC who specializes in the laws that you might need to know. They can send you copies of the regulations and help you comply with them. The following laws may apply to your small business. The FTC experts and their direct phone numbers are included:

Mail Order Rule, which requires companies to ship purchases made by mail when promised or give consumers option to cancel order for a refund. Elaine Kolish, 202-326-3042.

Care Labeling Rule, which requires manufacturers of textile clothing and fabrics to attach care label instructions. Steve Ecklund, 202-326-3034.

Unordered Merchandise Statute, which permits consumers to keep, as a free gift, unordered merchandise they receive through the U.S. mail. Vada Martin, 202-326-3002.

Cooling-Off Rule, which gives consumers three days to cancel sales for $25 or more made away from the seller's place of business. Brent Mickum, 202-326-3132.

Games of Chance in the Food Retailing and Gasoline Industries Rule, which requires disclosure of odds of winning prizes, the random distribution of winning prize pieces, and publication of winners' names. 216-522-4210.

Magnuson-Moss Act, which requires warranty information to be made available to consumers before making a purchase. 202-326-3128.

Holder-In-Due-Course Rule, which gives consumers certain protection when goods they buy on credit are not satisfactory. 202-326-3758.

* Avoid Mail Fraud Through The Mail
Public Affairs Branch
Postal Inspection Service
U.S. Postal Service
475 L'Enfant Plaza, SW
Washington, DC 20260   202-268-4293
or

Enforcement Division
Federal Trade Commission
6th and Pennsylvania Ave., NW
Washington, DC 20580   202-326-2996

Since many home-based businesses do business through the mail, you should be aware of the ways some con artists use the mail to steal from you. To help you, the Postal Service publishes the free booklet, *Postal Crime Prevention: A Business Guide*, which shows business owners how to protect themselves. It includes information on different types of mail fraud, check cashing precautions, guidelines for mailroom security, bombs in the mail, and other problems with mail-related crime.

If you receive merchandise through the mail that you did not order, you can keep it as a gift. Find out your rights by contacting the Federal Trade Commission and obtaining a free copy of the *Unordered Merchandise Statute*.

* Have The Government Find You Customers
Contact your State Office of Economic Development to locate a Small Business Development Center near you
or
- State Government Offices
Contact your State Government Operator located in your state capitol
or
- Federal Government Offices
Call your local U.S. Government Federal Information Center listed in your telephone directory or call the main Federal Information Center at 301-722-9000.

The government has what is indisputably the best marketing information in the world, and all the Fortune 500 companies use it to make their millions. If Citicorp uses government information to decide the best place to put up a new branch bank or for getting a list of rich people to sell trust services to, you can use the same sources to decide the best place to market a home improvement business or to get a mailing list of all the women in your neighborhood who are over 150 pounds to sell them a new diet product.

There are three basic starting places for tapping into all this huge marketing information. The best place to get free, or very-low-cost marketing consulting help is at your local Small Business Development Center (SBDC). These offices will sit down with you and help you work out the specifics on who your market is and how to reach them.

State governments offer a wide variety of market information. The division of Motor Vehicles sell information from drivers licenses and motor vehicle registrations. With this you can identify all the rich single men over 6 feet tall in your zip code. You can also get listings of doctors, lawyers, real estate agents, and even delicatessens from state licensing and regulatory offices. Or your state Census Data Center can identify those zip codes most likely to have young children who can afford orthodontist work. Your state government operator in your state capitol can help you locate the specific office that may be able to help you.

Home-Based Business Resources

Federal government offices spend hundreds of millions of dollars on marketing information rarely used by entrepreneurs. The U.S. Dept. of Agriculture can give you information on the market for thousands of products, including house plants, diets, aquaculture, and even bull sperm. The U.S. Department of Commerce can give you the latest information on hundreds of products, including golf balls, computers, toys, or biotechnology. And the U.S. International Trade Administration provides marketing information on items like video games, mushrooms, and broom handles. Your local U.S. Government, Federal Information Center can help you locate the specific office that can help you.

* The Government Will Sell Your Service or Product In Other Countries
- State Office of International Marketing
    Contact your State Office of Economic Development located in your state capitol

Don't hire a high-priced international marketing consultant if you want to see if your product or service has any opportunity of being a success in another country. Both state a federal governments are very active in offering free and low cost assistance to small businesses who wish to take advantage of markets overseas. There are programs that will provide you with free market studies for your product in any country in the world. Other programs will have embassy officials who will locate local businesses who are willing to sell your product or service in that country, and programs that will provide you with financing to sell your products overseas.

* Find A Free Government Expert On Any Topic
- Federal Government Offices
    Call your local U.S. Government Federal Information Center listed in your telephone directory or call the main Federal Information Center at 301-722-9000

It is estimated that there are approximately 700,000 experts in the federal government, each spending their careers studying some aspect of business that entrepreneurs can tap into. If you are looking for expertise on how to sell a new t-shirt idea, you can call the government's underwear expert at the U.S. International Trace Commission. This expert gets paid over $60,000 a year to study the t-shirt business, and if you treat her properly, she is available to you for the price of a telephone call. You are never going to find a private consultant who will know as much as this government expert. In fact, if you were to hire a private marketing consultant, they'd probably call a government expert to find the answer that they turn around and charge you big bucks for! You may be interested in the pasta expert at the Department of Commerce if you have a new pasta product. Or the 900 number expert at the Federal Communication Commission if you're planning to start your own Love Line.

* What Are The Rules If You Sell Your Products Through The Mail?
Enforcement Division
Federal Trade Commission
6th and Pennsylvania Ave., NW
Washington, DC 20580   202-326-2996
www.ftc.gov

Since many home-based businesses do business through the mail, you'll need to be aware of the Federal Trade Commission's (FTC) *Mail Order Rule*, which requires companies to ship purchases made by mail when promised or to give consumers the option to cancel their order for a refund. For more information on the rule and how it might apply to your business, contact the FTC.

* Free Marketing Help
    Contact your State Office of Economic Development to locate a Small Business Development Center near you

Finding out if there's a market for your products or services is the most critical part of planning a successful business. This process includes having to analyze your competition, suppliers, and new customers. The Small Business Administration (SBA) can hook you up with experts through the Service Corps of Retired Executives (SCORE) who can provide you with free advice on how to develop and execute an effective marketing plan. Don't spend a lot of money you don't have on a marketing "expert" you heard of or found in the telephone book--get it done for free through an expert at your SBA office.

* How To Set Up A Pension Plan For One Employee
Superintendent of Documents
Government Printing Office
Washington, DC 20402   202-512-0000

If you hire permanent employees, you might be interested in finding out how to set up a pension plan for them. To do this, you'll need to know more about the pension laws. For $1, GPO will send you a copy of *Simplified Employee Pensions: What Small Businesses Need to Know*, a publication specially geared toward small business owners. For more general information about the pension laws, the following office will send you a list of their free pension publications: Division of Public Information, Pension and Welfare Benefits Administration, U.S. Department of Labor, Washington, D.C. 20210; 202-254-7013; {www.access.gpo.gov}.

* 80% Discount on Office Equipment and Supplies
U.S. General Services Administration
18th and F Sts., NW
Washington, DC 20405   202-501-4906
www.gsa.gov

If you need office furniture, typewriters, computers, wastebaskets, postage meters, paper clips--practically anything you could possibly imagine--for your home-based business, but don't have much money to spend on it, the federal government might be your best buy. The General Services Administration is the federal government's housekeeper--they keep track of what supplies the government needs and doesn't need to run properly. Anything they don't need, such as overstock of office furniture and equipment, is auctioned off at rock-bottom prices. Auctions are held at GSA regional offices throughout the U.S. This office can put you on a mailing list to notify you of upcoming auctions, or you can contact the GSA office nearest you:

Atlanta
GSA, Surplus Sales Branch, 75 Spring St. SW, Atlanta, GA 30303; 404-331-0972; {www.r4.gsa.gov}.

Boston
GSA, Surplus Sales Branch, 10 Causeway St., 9th Floor, Boston, MA; 617-565-5860; {www.r1site.gsa.gov}.

Chicago
GSA, 230 S. Dearborn St., Chicago, IL 60604; {www.gsa.gov/rg05gl.htm}.

Denver
GSA, Surplus Supply Branch, Denver Federal Center, Building 41, Denver, CO 80225; 303-236-7705; {www.gsa.gov/rg08rm.htm}.

Fort Worth
GSA, Surplus Sales Branch, 819 Taylor St., Ft. Worth, TX 76102; {www.gsa.gov/rg07gsw.htm}.

Kansas
GSA, Surplus Sales Branch, 6F BPS 4400, College Blvd., Suite 175, Overland, KS 66211; {www.gsa.gov/rg06hl.htm}.

New York
GSA, Surplus Sales Branch, 26 Federal Plaza, Room 20-2016, New York, NY 10278; 212-264-3592/3593; {www.r2.gsa.gov}.

Philadelphia
GSA, Surplus Sales Branch, 9th and Market Sts., Philadelphia, PA 19107; {www.gsa.gov/rg03ma.htm}.

San Francisco
GSA, Surplus Sales Branch, 525 Market St., 32nd Floor, San Francisco, CA 94105; {www.gsa.gov/rg09pr.htm}.

Washington
GSA, Surplus Sales Branch, GSA Center, Auburn, WA 98002; {www.gsa.gov/rg10nwa.htm}.

District of Columbia
GSA, 6808 Loisdale Rd., Bldg. A, Springfield, VA 22150; 703-557-7785; {www.midatlantic.gsa.gov}.

What follows is a small list of other federal agencies that sell office furniture and supplies at auctions. Contact them for further information:

Internal Revenue Service	800-829-1040
U.S. Postal Service	202-268-2000
U.S. Customs Service	405-357-9194
Dept. of Defense	616-961-7331
U.S. Marshals Service	202-307-9237

Home-Based Business Resources

* How To Protect Yourself From Office Supply Sales Schemes
Marketing Practices Division
Federal Trade Commission
6th and Pennsylvania Ave., NW
Washington, DC 20580   202-326-3128
www.ftc.gov

One of the ways small businesses can lose money is by becoming the victims of office supply sales schemes, where your company gets billed for supplies that you never ordered or received, and you don't find out until after your check is cashed. If you think you've been the victim of such a scheme or would like information about how con artists run them, contact the Federal Trade Commission.

* How To Package and Label Your Products According To The Law
Enforcement Division
Federal Trade Commission
6th and Pennsylvania Ave., NW
Washington, DC 20580   202-326-3128
www.ftc.gov

If you're producing and selling any consumer product, you need to be aware of the *Fair Packaging and Labeling Act*, which requires consumer commodities to be accurately labeled to describe the product's identity and net quantity. For more information on how this law might apply to your products, contact the Federal Trade Commission.

* How To Price Your Product So You Make The Most Money
SBA Publications
P.O. Box 30
Denver, CO 80201-0030   800-827-5722
www.sba.gov

You've got a good product or service but don't know how much you should sell it for. The Small Business Administration's (SBA) publication, *Pricing Your Products And Services Profitably*, tells you how to do it, and includes various pricing techniques and when to use them. This publication is available on the website only.

* How To Make Your Product Safe For Your Customers
Office of Information and Public Affairs
Consumer Product Safety Commission
Washington, DC 20207   800-638-2772
www.cpsc.gov

You might think that the product you're making or selling in your home-based business is great, but it needs to meet certain government safety standards before you can sell it. You can also call the CPSC Office of Compliance at 301-504-0400. It's important that you know and follow their guidelines, because if a consumer is hurt from using your product, the CPSC has the authority to force you to recall it and correct the problem.

* How To Raise Money
Office of Business Development and Marketing
Small Business Administration
409 3rd St., SW
Washington, DC 20416   202-205-6743
www.sba.gov

Raising money to run your business is as basic a task as their is to be successful. As part of its *Focus on the Facts* series, the Small Business Administration (SBA) has put together a publication titled *How to Raise Money for a Small Business*. This fact sheet outlines the basics of raising money, where to find it, borrowing it, types of business loans, how to write a loan proposal, and SBA financial programs. Contact their website for this information.

* How To Set Up A Self-Employed Retirement Plan
Taxpayer Services
Internal Revenue Service
U.S. Department of the Treasury
1111 Constitution Ave., NW, Room 2422
Washington, DC 20224   800-829-3676
www.irs.gov

This IRS office can provide you with a free copy of *Self-Employed Retirement Plans* (#560), which discusses retirement plans (Keogh plans) for self-employed individuals, such as those running home-based businesses, and certain partners in partnerships. These retirement plans allow the self-employed to put away a certain amount of their earnings each year into a tax free account retirement account.

* Free Consultants (SCORE)
Contact your local U.S. Small Business Administration (SBA) office
or
SBA Hotline   800-827-5722

SCORE members work with local SBA offices to provide small business owners with free advice and assistance on all kinds of problems that you might run into in your day-to-day work, such as problems in accounting, marketing, business planning, and so on. Contact your local Small Business Administration office for more information on how SCORE might help you out with your special business needs.

* Hotline Helps Entrepreneurs Handle The Stress of Small Business
National Health Information Clearinghouse
P.O. Box 1133   800-336-4797
Washington, DC 20012   301-565-4167
nhic-nt.health.org

Trying to run a business out of your home can put a lot of added stress on you, your family, and marriage, especially when business isn't going very well. NHIC puts out a pamphlet titled *Healthfinder: Stress Information Resources*, which lists and describes several government agencies and private organizations that offer publications and resources on work-related stress and stress management. It's available for $2.50 by mail or get it free on the web page.

* Get A Tax Break For Hiring and Training New Employees
Employment Training Administration
Office of Public Affairs
U.S. Department of Labor, Room S-2322
Washington, DC 20210   202-219-6871

If your business employs certain types of people, such as dislocated workers or workers who have lost their jobs because of competition, your business may qualify for a federal tax credit. This Targeted Jobs Tax Credit allows businesses to write off from these taxes a portion of the salaries they pay to these special workers. This federal tax credit program is run on the state and local levels, and to find out specific information on eligibility requirements, contact your state Department of Labor or local private industry council. If you are interested in participating in this program, these offices can locate workers for you and help you through the paperwork.

This Targeted Jobs Tax Credit program can be used in conjunction with another program under the Job Training Partnership Act where the government will pay part of your employee's salary if you meet certain eligibility requirements and provide on-the-job training, such as computer or carpentry skills to the employee. Under this program, you need to hire certain disadvantaged employees, such as the handicapped, the economically disadvantaged, minorities, and the like. The office above can send you free copies of fact sheets on the Job Training Partnership Act and the Targeted Jobs Tax Credit Program.

* Tax Information For Home-Based Businesses
Taxpayer Services
Internal Revenue Service
U.S. Department of the Treasury
1111 Constitution Ave., NW, Room 2422
Washington, DC 20224   800-829-3676
www.irs.gov

Depending on the size and nature of your home-based business, there may be a lot of information you'll need to know about your federal tax responsibilities. The IRS puts out a whole series of free publications that explain the current tax laws to help you better understand them. The titles, along with brief descriptions and ordering numbers, are listed below.

Accounting Periods and Methods (#538) explains which accounting periods and methods can be used for figuring federal taxes, and how to apply for approval to change from one period or method to another.

Bankruptcy And Other Debt Cancellation (#908) explains the income tax aspects of bankruptcy and discharge of debt for individuals and small businesses.

Home-Based Business Resources

Business Expenses (#535) discusses such expenses as fringe benefits, rent, interest, taxes, insurance, and employee benefit plans. It also explains the choice to capitalize certain business expenses; amortization and depletion; and the circumstances in where expenses are and are not deductible.

Business Use Of A Car (#917) explains the expenses you may deduct for the use of your car in your home-based business.

Business Use Of Your Home (#587) can help you decide if you qualify to deduct certain expenses for using part of your home for your business. Deductions for the business use of a home computer are also discussed.

Circular E, Employer's Tax Guide (#15) explains what you'll need to know if you employ others as part of your home-based business.

Depreciation (#946) tells you how to calculate and how to write off the depreciated value of property and equipment associated with your home-based business.

Earned Income Credit (#596) discusses who may receive the earned income credit, and how to figure and claim the credit.

Tax Benefits for Work-Related Education (#508) explains how, if you take educational courses related to your home-based business, you can deduct these expenses from your taxes.

Examination of Returns, Appeal Rights, and Claims for Refund (#556) is helpful if your tax return is examined by explaining the procedures for the examination of items of partnership income, deduction, gain, loss, and credit.

Moving Expenses (#521) explains how you can deduct moving expenses when you relocate home-based business as you move.

Sales and Other Dispositions of Assets (#544) explains how to figure gain and loss on such transactions as trading or selling an asset used in a business, along with the tax results of different types of gains and losses.

Retirement Plans for Small Businesses (#560) discusses retirement plans (Keogh plans) for self-employed individuals, such as those running home-based businesses, and certain partners in partnerships.

Self-Employment Tax (#533) explains the self-employment tax (i.e., social security tax) that self-employed, home-based business owners must pay.

Tax Guide for Small Business (#334) explains the federal tax laws that apply to businesses, including the four major forms of business organizations--sole proprietorships, partnerships, corporations, and S corporations--along with the tax responsibilities for each.

Tax Information For Direct Sellers (#911) gives you helpful information if your home-based business involves "direct selling," that is, selling products to others on a person-to-person basis, such as door-to-door sales, sales parties, or by appointment in your home.

Corporations (#542) tells you what you need to know if you incorporate your home-based business.

Partnerships (#541) tells you what you'll need to know if you run your home-based business as a partnership.

Taxpayers Starting A Business (#583) shows sample records that a small business can use if it operates as a sole proprietorship. Records like these will help you prepare complete and accurate tax returns and make sure you pay only the tax you owe. It also discusses the taxpayer identification number that you must use, information returns you may have to file, and the kinds of business taxes you may have to pay.

Travel, Entertainment, and Gift Expenses (#463) explains what expenses you may deduct for business-related travel, meals, entertainment, and gifts for your business, along with the reporting and recordkeeping requirements for these expenses.

* Is Your Name Legal?
Trademark Search Library
Patent and Trademark Office
U.S. Department of Commerce
2011 Jefferson Davis Hwy., Room 2C08   800-PTO-9199
Arlington, VA 22202   703-308-9000
www.uspto.gov

Before you decide to name your new business something like Disneyland or Nutrisystem, it might be a good idea to find out if someone else already owns the trademark on the name. All registered trademarks, logos, and slogans are filed in the Trademark Search Library, and you can visit the library to research the name you want to use for your business. If you can't get to the library yourself, you can find a professional trademark specialist to hire do the search for you by looking in the telephone directory. The library staff will not do a search for you if you haven't formally applied for a trademark. However, if you do apply for a trademark, the library will tell you if the name is already taken, and if it isn't, they'll award you the trademark. Contact this office for more information on researching and applying for a trademark.

* Pay Fair
Wage and Hour Division
Fair Labor Standards
U.S. Department of Labor
200 Constitution Ave.
Washington, DC 20210   202-219-4907
www.dol.gov

Don't be caught in a pay dispute. You can learn the ins and outs of paying your employees a fair wage simply by calling the Wage and Hour Division. They can explain the rules governing minimum wage and who qualifies for time-and-a-half pay and when. This Division can even send you written material which provides more detailed information.

* How Much Should You Pay For A Typist With 2 Years Experience
Bureau of Labor Statistics
U.S. Department of Labor
Washington, DC 20210   202-691-5200
stats.bls.gov
or
Your State Department of Labor

When you run a small business, you need to know how much to pay your employees and how much to charge for your services based on average wage rates in your area of the country. The Bureau of Labor Statistics (BLS) has compiled the following *Area Wage Surveys* for major industries across the country. BLS also publishes an annual white-collar wage study, *Professional, Administrative, Technical, and Clerical Survey*. Contact this office or your Local Department of Labor Office located in your state capitol.

* What's The Law If Your Business Offers a Warranty
Marketing Practices Division
Federal Trade Commission
6th and Pennsylvania Ave., NW   877-FTC-HELP
Washington, DC 20580   202-326-3128
www.ftc.gov

If you're selling a product with a warranty, you should know about the *Magnuson-Moss Warranty Act*, which requires you to make warranty information available to consumers before making a purchase, and to honor your warranty obligations. To find out more about this law and how to comply with it, contact the Federal Trade Commission (FTC).

* Do You Need A Permit For Running A Business Out of Your Home?
Contact your local business council

Depending on what your home-based business is, you might need to get zoning permits to run your business at home. Local zoning laws exist so that residential neighborhoods aren't overrun by traffic created by having daily business going on in the area. This is especially true is a business has a steady flow of customers showing up to buy things. Your local business council will be able to tell you if your business will require a zoning permit.

* Home-Based Child Care Business
County Cooperative Extension Service
6707 Groveton Dr.
Clinton, MD 20735   301-868-9410
hw25@umail.umd.edu

If you're interested in running a child care business out of your home, you'll need some background information before you start. This office, or the Cooperative

Home-Based Business Resources

Extension Service in your own county has information on such topics as record keeping, registration and certification, rates to charge, advertising, and insurance. You'll also find a list of questions you should answer about how suitable you are for the job, such as your feelings toward children, your physical stamina, your personal family life, and much more.

* Is Your Client Sexually Harassing You?
Equal Employment Opportunity Commission
1801 L St., NW
Washington, DC 20507   800-669-3362
www.eeoc.gov

You can't have your client investigated by the government for discrimination based on sex, age, race, religion, color national origin with way you can if they are your employer or boss. But, if you do encounter such behavior you can do your part in letting them know that they would be violating federal laws if you were their employee. The office above will provide you with all the free legal advice and literature you need. And for your friends who are still employees, give them this number. This is also the office that will come out and investigate sexual harassment charges.

* Government Loans To Start Your Own Energy Conservation Business
Contact your state Economic Development Office in your state capitol
or
Your Local Small Business Administration Office

The Small Business Administration has established a separate funding program to assist entrepreneurs who provide energy production and conservation services for others. This can include engineering, architectural, consulting or other professional services specializing in specific energy measures. The funding may be in the form of direct loans or loan guarantees and can be as high as $750,000. They can be used for start-up or expansion purposes. Ask about Energy Business Loan Guarantees.

* Hotline Helps You Save On Your Trash Bill
Resource Conservation and Recovery Act Hotline
Environmental Protection Agency
401 M St, SW   703-412-9810
Washington, DC 20460   800-424-9346
www.epa.gov/epaoswer/hotline/index.htm

Recycling not only can reduce the amount of trash being sent to landfills, but can be cost-effective too. It is easy to start simple recycling programs and help is close by. Each state has a recycling office that can give you advice, direction, and information regarding the establishment of recycling efforts. Help varies from state to state but can include recycling literature to distribute to employees, lists of people who will haul away scrap paper, and speakers who will come to your business to educate your employees on recycling. The RCRA Hotline also has several free publications on recycling including: *Recycle* - provides basic information on recycling; and *Recycling Works* - explains the recycling process and takes you through examples of programs in various states.

* Free Health Inspection of Your Workplace
National Institute for Occupational Safety and Health
4676 Columbia Parkway
Cincinnati, OH 45226   800-356-4674
www.cdc.gov/niosh

The National Institute for Occupational Safety and Health (NIOSH) is responsible for conducting research to make the nation's workplaces healthier and safer by responding to urgent requests for assistance from employers, employees, and their representatives where imminent hazards are suspected. They conduct inspections, laboratory and epidemiologic research, publish their findings, and make recommendations for improved working conditions. They will inspect any workplace for free, if three employees sign a form stating that the environment may be dangerous. Employees have the option of keeping anonymous. If any of the following applies to you, NIOSH can provide you with more information:

Do you use a video display terminal most of the day?
Are you concerned abut the chemicals you are using in your dry cleaning?
Do you have tingling in your hands (carpal tunnel syndrome)?
Do you use a jackhammer most of the day and are now finding that your fingers are no longer sensitive to heat or cold?
Do you do the same motion again and again, such as on an assembly line? You could be at risk for repetitive motion-associated trauma.
Do you feel your job is causing you mental stress?
Are you having trouble hearing?

* Free Help To Make Your Company A Safe And Healthy Place To Work
Occupational Safety and Health Administration
U.S. Dept. of Labor
200 Constitution Ave, NW
Washington, DC 20210   202-219-7266
www.osha.gov

The Occupational Safety and Health Administration was created to encourage employers and employees to reduce workplace hazards and to implement new, or improve existing, safety and health programs. They provide research on innovative ways of dealing with these problems, maintain a recordkeeping system to monitor job related injuries and illnesses, and develop standards and enforce them, as well as establish training programs.

If you are concerned about the health and safety of your employees, and are having trouble establishing a safe workplace, OSHA will provide free and confidential consultation assistance.

If you have been working hard to clean up your employees' work space, and have reduced the number of injuries occurring on the job, you can be eligible for a Voluntary Protection Program award certificate.

If you are responsible for training your employees on how to work safely in a variety of situations, you can have assess to over 65 high quality, low-cost, training videos.

If you are interested in the safety record of another company, OSHA can provide you with the entire range of inspection data, including who, what, when, where and why companies are inspected and the violations that were found (Contact: Office of Management Data Systems, 202-219-7008).

If you want to take a class to learn more about how to make your workplace safe and healthy for your employees, OSHA has courses covering areas such as electrical hazards, machine guarding, ventilation and ergonomics (Contact: Safety and Health Training Institute, 708-297-4810).

An extensive list of publications is available including:
Controlling Electrical Hazards
Asbestos Standards for the Construction Industry
Hand and Power Tools
Grain Handling
Hearing Conservation
Respiratory Protection
Working Safely with Video Display Terminals
Workplace Health Programs

* Will Your Employees Get Carpal Tunnel Syndrome?
National Institute for Occupational Safety and Health
4676 Columbia Parkway
Cincinnati, Ohio 45226   800-356-4674
www.cdc.gov/niosh

Carpal Tunnel Syndrome is a tingling sensation in the hands and fingers and can be caused or aggravated by repeated twisting or awkward postures, particularly when combined with high force. The population at risk includes persons employed in such industries or occupations as construction, food preparation, clerical work, product fabrication and mining. The National Institute for Occupational Safety and Health provides free information on this syndrome including the latest developments in research, preventive recommendations, and bibliographies.

* Are Your Video Display Terminals Making Your Employees Sick?
National Institute for Occupational Safety and Health
4676 Columbia Parkway
Cincinnati, OH 45226   800-356-4674
www.cdc.gov/niosh

Over one million people each day sit down to work in front of a computer terminal, imputing and outputting information. There have been concerns about its effect on people's eyesight, its effects on pregnant women, and its potential for causing carpal tunnel syndrome. The National Institute for Occupational Safety and Health offers a free booklet describing the latest research covering all these issues.

* Free Research For Employee's Health Problems
National Health Information Center
ODPHP
P.O. Box 1133   301-565-4167

Home-Based Business Resources

Washington, DC 20013 800-336-4797
http://nhic_nt.health.org

U.S. businesses have begun implementing health education/promotion programs at worksite to help keep employees healthy and to help contain long-term health care costs. Simultaneously, groups of local businesses throughout the country have established coalitions for the purpose of implementing plans to reduce health care costs. Many of these groups view worksite health promotion programs, such as physical fitness, stress management, weight control, smoking cessation, nutrition, and drug and alcohol awareness, as an effective strategy that will contribute to achieving their goals. The National Health Information Center can provide you with publications and brochures on a wide variety of health topics, and can refer you to organizations who can help you set up programs at your place of business. This could be a one day event to test for high blood pressure, a blood donation program, free speakers, or more extensive health promotion programs.

* Cheap Office And Conference Space Overseas

Trade Information Center
U.S. Department of Commerce
Washington, DC 20230 800-USA-TRADE
www.doc.gov

If you are travelling overseas on a business trip, you may want to look into renting office space and other services through the American Embassy. Depending on the country and the space available, the embassy can provide temporary office space for as low as $25.00 per day, along with translation services, printing and other services. Meeting rooms, seminar or convention space along with promotion services, mailings, freight handling, and even catering may be available in many countries. Contact the field ITA office which is listed later in this chapter or the appropriate country desk officer at the U.S. Department of Commerce in Washington, DC.

* Free Legal Help If You Get Audited

Volunteer and Education Branch
Taxpayer Service Division
Internal Revenue Service
U.S. Department of the Treasury
1111 Constitution Ave., NW, Room 1315
Washington, DC 20224 800-829-1040
www.irs.gov

Under this program, law and graduate accounting school students are given special permission to practice before the IRS on behalf of taxpayers who cannot afford professional help. Volunteers are needed to help with the clinic operations or to serve as Student Tax Clinic Directors. Students work under the direction of their professors to handle legal and technical problems. Your local taxpayer education coordinator will inform you of tax clinics in your area.

* Fight The IRS For Free

Problem Resolution Staff
Assistant to the Commissioner
Taxpayer Ombudsman
Internal Revenue Service
U.S. Department of the Treasury
1111 Constitution Ave., NW
Washington, DC 20224 800-829-1040
www.irs.gov

A major goal of the Problem Resolution Program (PRP) is to solve tax problems that have not been resolved through normal procedures. PRP represents the interests and concerns of taxpayers within the IRS and seeks to prevent future problems by identifying the root causes of such problems. Each IRS district, service center and regional office has a Problem Resolution Officer (PRO). In resolving problems and protecting taxpayer rights, PROs have authority to intervene to assure IRS actions are correct and appropriate. Effective January 1, 1989, authority to issue Taxpayer Assistance Orders (TAOs) was granted to the Taxpayer Ombudsman. This authority was delegated to the Problem Resolution Officers, as field representatives of the Ombudsman. TAOs may be issued when, in the judgement of the Ombudsman or PRO, a taxpayer is suffering, or is about to suffer a significant hardship as a result of an IRS action or inaction. A TAO can order the function that is handling the taxpayer's case to take appropriate steps to relieve the hardship. The order can also suggest alternative actions to resolve the case. Requests for such relief may be made by taxpayers, their representatives, or by IRS employees on behalf of taxpayers. Contact the IRS toll-free information number regarding tax questions, and ask for Problem Resolution assistance.

* Find Out IF There Is Legislation That Will Affect Your Business

LEGIS
Office of Legislative Information
House Office Building Annex 2
2nd and D Streets, SW, Room 696
Washington, DC 20515 202-225-1772

The Bill Status Office can tell you within seconds the latest action on any federal legislation. Every bill and resolution for the current session as well as all House and Senate legislation dating back to 1975 are contained in LEGIS, a computerized database. When you call, it is best to give a key word or phrase (i.e., product liability, hazardous waste) which will help the congressional aides search LEGIS. This office can provide such detailed information as:

Have any bills been introduced covering a given topic?
Who is the sponsor of the bill?
How many cosponsors are there?
When was it introduced?
Which committees have the bills been referred to?
Have any hearings been held?
Has there been any floor action?
Has a similar bill been introduced in the other chamber?
Has there been any action on the other side of the Hill?
Have the House and Senate agreed to a compromise bill?
Has the bill been sent to the White House?
Has the President signed or vetoed the bill?
What is the PL (public law) number?

Telephone assistance is free, and printouts from LEGIS are available for $.20 per page but must be picked up at the Bill Status Office. However, by making arrangements with your Representative's or Senator's office, you can avoid this nominal charge and also have the printout mailed to your home or office.

Women Entrepreneurs: Special Money, Help and Programs

Women Entrepreneurs: Special Money, Help And Programs For Women Only

Did you know that the recent surge in economic growth is actually being driven by small businesses that are in large part owned by women? That's right — women are starting businesses at **twice** the rate of men, and it's probably because women are finding that their dual careers as businesswomen and mothers are not being accommodated by big business very well at all. An increasing number of women are finding that rigid corporate structures fail to make allowances for their roles as executives, wives, and mothers. Because of this inflexibility, more and more women are striking out on their own or with a partner that shares a similar philosophy, and these women are finding success on their own terms. Corporate America has held women as a group back long enough, and for that reason, women are launching their own businesses in unprecedented numbers.

When someone mentions the word "entrepreneur", most people conjure up an image of someone like Donald Trump smiling on the cover of some glossy business trade magazine. But these days, chances are that smiling face will be decidedly more feminine looking than Donald's — it might be Donna's face, as in Donna Karan, who grew her apparel business into a million dollar money maker in just a few short years. As with men, hard work and commitment to make a business work are the ingredients women are using to create their own success, and not waiting for others to hand it to them. Just look at some of these incredible statistics that the U.S. Small Business Administration has gathered on women business owners:

- Over the last 15 years, the number of women-owned businesses has almost **doubled**.

- In that same amount of time, the percentage of women-owned businesses increased by 10%, while those owned by men decreased by as much.

- Over one-third of all businesses are now owned by women.

- Women-owned businesses were awarded over $2 billion in federal prime contracts last year, compared to only $180 million ten years ago, an increase of over ten fold.

- 75% of new businesses started by women succeed, compared to only 25% of those started by men.

Since most people in the U.S. actually work for small businesses, the government has been forced to take notice of this ever-increasing trend toward women-owned businesses. Chances are your new boss or CEO is going to be a woman, not someone like Lee Iacocca. Why else would the Small Business Administration (SBA) put a women's business ownership specialist at over 100 SBA offices across the country? You don't see the Small Business Administration bending over to help men out with special programs — anyone who reads the statistics can see who's going to be the most powerful group of emerging business owners over the next couple of decades.

As you'll see in this chapter, both the Federal and state governments have created special programs to help women business owners compete and succeed like never before.

* Small Business Administration Pilot Program

The Women's Pre-Qualified Loan Program is being tested for a year in Charlotte, North Carolina, and nine other cities nationwide. This program will give the Small Business Administration greater influence on the number of loans extended to women.

This program began on June 1, 1994. Through the program, women business owners can go directly to the Small Business Administration (SBA) for a loan guarantee review, instead of being required to go to a bank first. If the woman business owner qualifies, the SBA will issue a commitment letter that she can present as part of her loan application to a bank. If the bank approves the loan, the application is returned to the SBA for final review. The SBA's decision will be based on the ability of the woman business owner to pay back the loan.

Businesses must be 51% owned and operated by women to qualify for the lending program. Only Mecklenburg County businesses qualify for Charlotte's pilot program. The pilot women's program backs loans up to $250,000. The women's program backs loans up to $250,000, and will guarantee 90% of loans up to $155,000. Bigger loans will be backed 85%. There is no cap on the number of loans that will be processed through the pilot program.

Following the guidelines for the pilot program, women applicants will go to a "facilitator", who will screen applications for the SBA for a small fee. These fees have not been established as of this printing. The program is also being tested in Albuquerque, New Mexico; Chicago, Illinois; Columbus, Ohio; Helena, Montana; Montgomery, Alabama; Louisville, Kentucky; New Orleans, Louisiana; Salt Lake City, Utah; and San Francisco, California. While there is no way to monitor the number of women applicants who are rejected at the bank level under the existing system, the pilot program will work to improve that situation.

For more information, contact the Charlotte SBA office during business hours at 200 N. College St., Suite A2015, Charlotte, NC 28202; 704-344-6463.

* Fight Suppliers Who Won't Give You Credit
Public Reference Branch
Federal Trade Commission (FTC)
Washington, DC 20580   202-326-2222

Often women who have been divorced have trouble establishing credit. And you need credit if you're going to run a business. The Federal Trade Commission (FTC) enforces the laws that prohibit creditors and credit bureaus from discriminating against women because of their sex or marital status, and they can send you the free publication, *Women and Credit Histories*. This pamphlet explains your credit rights under the law, how to get help in establishing your own credit, and what to do if you feel your credit application has been unfairly denied.

* Grants, Loans and Loan Guarantees for Women-Owned Businesses

Contact your state office of Economic Development located in your state capital.

All federal money programs aimed at small business do not discriminate between women and non-women-owned businesses. However, at the state level there are a number of specific money programs that are set aside only for women-owned businesses. The programs vary from state to state and are changing all the time so it is best to check with your State Office of Economic Development in your state capital to insure you have the latest available information. Here is a listing of what a few states offer specifically for women entrepreneurs:

- Illinois has low interest loans up to $50,000
- Iowa has grants up to $25,000 and loan guarantees up to $40,000

For Women Only

- Louisiana has loans and loan guarantee programs up to $250,000
- Minnesota offers low interest loans for up to 50% of your project
- New York offers low interest loans from $20,000 to $500,000
- Wisconsin offers low interest loans for women-owned businesses under $500,000 in sales

* Federal Government Set-Asides For Women Entrepreneurs

Contact your state office of Economic Development located in your state capital

or

Superintendent of Documents
Government Printing Office
Washington, DC 20402   202-512-1800

Many Federal government contracting offices are trying to insure that a certain percentage of their contracts go to women entrepreneurs. Most even have special offices that will help women entrepreneurs sell to their agencies. For help in selling your product or service to the government, contact your State Economic Development Office in your state capital and obtain a copy of *Women Business Owners: Selling to the Federal Government*. It is available for $3.75 from the Government Printing Office.

* 15% Set-Aside for Women Entrepreneurs

Contact your state office of Economic Development located in your state capital.

Not only is the Federal government active in insuring that women get a fair share of government contracts, but many state governments are becoming involved. Some states, like California for example, have passed laws that force their state agencies to give at least 15% of their contracts to women and minority-owned firms. Other states like Illinois, Iowa, Maine, Minnesota, Montana, New Jersey, Oregon, and Washington are among those who are active in insuring that women obtain a fair share of state government contracts. Contact your State Office of Economic Development to see how your business can take advantage of set-asides in your state.

* 28 States Offer Free Consulting To Women Only

Contact your state office of Economic Development located in your state capital.

Although every state offers free help to any person wishing to start or expand a business in their state, there are 28 states that have set up special offices just for women entrepreneurs. As an example, Colorado established a women's clearinghouse which provides hands-on assistance with business planning, marketing, financing, and government contracts. They also hold seminars at 16 locations throughout the state. Ohio offers a wide range of free services including loan packaging and marketing research. Contact your State Office of Economic Development to see what your state has to offer. If they don't have a "Women Only" office, don't let that stop you. It just means you'll have to share the help available with the men in your state.

* What To Do If You Suspect Your Bank Denied You Credit Because You Are a Woman or Divorced

Credit Practices Division
Federal Trade Commission
Washington, DC 20580   202-326-3758

Women looking for money to start up and run their businesses might run into lenders that discriminate against them simply because they are women or divorced. The Federal Trade Commission (FTC) enforces the Equal Credit Opportunity Act, which prohibits any creditor from denying credit to a consumer on the basis of sex or marital status. If you think you've been discriminated against by a lender, contact the Federal Trade Commission. While the Federal Trade Commission won't act on individual complaints, a number of complaints against the same lender may force them to investigate. If necessary, the Federal Trade Commission can take violators to court to get them to stop their illegal practices. If you want your complaint investigated and action taken immediately, contact one of the following agencies, depending on the type of lending institution involved:

National Banks
Comptroller of the Currency, Compliance Management, U.S. Department of the Treasury, Washington, DC 20219, 202-874-5000.

FDIC-Insured Banks
Division of Compliance and Consumer Affairs. 550 17th St., NW, Room F-130, Washington, DC 20429, 202-898-3535.

Savings & Loans
Office of Thrift Supervision, U.S. Department of Treasury, 1700 G St., NW, Washington, DC 20552, 202-906-6000.

State Banks
Contact your State Banking Commissioner.

* How To Select Quality Day Care For Your Child

County Cooperative Extension Service
6707 Groveton Dr.
Clinton, MD 20735   301-868-9410

If you're running your own small business or a business out of your home, you might need to consider finding good and reliable day care for your children to give you the time you need for your business. This office can send you a free copy of *How To Select Quality Day Care For Your Child*, which shows you what to look for in quality day care.

* How To Start a Child Care Business In Your Home

County Cooperative Extension Service
6707 Groveton Dr.
Clinton, MD 20735   301-868-9410

If you're interested in running a child care business out of your home, you'll need some necessary background information before you start. This office can send you a free copy of *Home-based Business: Child Care and Running a Child Care Business*, which includes information on such topics as record-keeping, registration and certification, rates to charge, advertising, and insurance. You'll also find a list of questions you should ask yourself, such as how suitable you are for the job, your feelings toward children, your physical stamina, your personal family life, and much more.

* Videos On Starting A Child Care Business

Contact your County Cooperative Extension Service listed under county government in your telephone book;

or

Video Production
Texas A & M University
107 Reed McDonald Building   409-845-2840
College Station, TX 77843   409-845-7800

Better Kid Care - Family Day Care Training is a 4-part video program in day care training. It includes the following topics: 1) Child Development, 2) Nutrition, 3) Health and Safety, and 4) Business Management. It is produced by the Texas Agricultural Extension Service and is available through their office (listed above) for a modest fee, or on a free loan basis through many County Cooperative Extension Service offices around the country. Call your local County Cooperative Extension Service for availability.

* How To Juggle The Stress of Your Business and Your Family

National Health Information Clearinghouse (NHIC)
P.O. Box 1133   301-565-4167
Washington, DC 20013-1133   800-336-4797

Trying to run a business can put a lot of added stress on you, your family, and your marriage, especially when business isn't going very well. The National Health Information Clearinghouse (NHIC) puts out a pamphlet entitled *Healthfinder: Stress Information Resources* ($1), which lists and describes several government agencies and private organizations that offer publications and resources on work-related stress and stress management.

* Free Publications For Women Business Owners

Women's Bureau
Office of the Secretary
U.S. Department of Labor
200 Constitution Ave., NW   800-827-5355
Washington, DC 20210   202-219-6652

Are you interested in how many other women business owners there are in the U.S? How about what your chances are for climbing up through various management levels? If you're interested in finding out more about women in the workforce, including trends and future projections, you might find the following free publications informative:

Alternative Work Patterns
American Indian/Alaska Native Women Business Owners

Women Entrepreneurs: Special Money, Help and Programs

Asian American Women Business Owners
Benefits to Employers Who Hire Women Veterans
Black Women Business Owners
Black Women in the Labor Force
Earning Differences Between Women and Men
Flexible Workstyles: A Look at Contingent Labor
Hispanic Origin Women Business Owners
State Maternity/Parental Leave Laws
Women Business Owners
Women in Management
Women in Skilled Trades
Women of Hispanic Origin in the Labor Force
Women on the Job: Careers in the Electronic Media
Women Who Maintain Families
Women With Work Disability
Women Workers: Outlook to 2005
Work and Family Resource Kit
Working Mothers and Their Children

* How To Get Start-Up Capital From Being Pregnant, Sexually Harassed, or From A Bad Shopping Experience

U.S. Customs Service
Fraud Division
Washington, DC 20229   800-BE-ALERT

or

Equal Employment Opportunity Commission (EEOC)
1801 L St., NW   800-669-4000
Washington, DC 20570   800-669-3362 (publications)

More people would quit what they're doing and start their own business if they had a small windfall of money to get them started. Here are two government programs that may turn a bad experience into the capital needed to begin a business.

As a business owner, there are times you may come across unscrupulous wholesalers who try to sell you some counterfeit products at cut-rate prices. Instead of risking your business by buying and reselling the bogus products, report the fraud to the U.S. Customs Service. If your complaint, which will be kept completely anonymous, leads to the seizure of counterfeit goods, you could receive a reward of up to $250,000, depending on the size of the case. What small business couldn't use some extra operating capital like that to keep it going?

So you want to start your own business because you've just been fired because you were pregnant, or wouldn't sleep with your boss to get a promotion? Before you go taking out any business loan, contact the Equal Employment Opportunity Commission (EEOC) and report how you think your former boss discriminated against you. The EEOC will investigate your complaint, and if they think there are grounds for prosecuting your former boss, they'll proceed with the case. If they prove the case, you could end up with enough money in back pay and other remedies to finance your own company.

* Health Insurance for Divorcees Who Start Their Own Business

Women Work
1625 K St. NW, #300
Washington, DC 20006   202-467-6346

Under the new law, divorced and separated women and their children can continue to receive the same health insurance coverage they had before they were divorced or separated from their husbands at the group rate. The only difference is that they must pay the premium. This law applies to all private businesses that employ more than 20 people and to federal, state, and local government plans. Depending on the reason for displacement, you may be eligible to continue coverage for up to 36 months. You must contact the health plan within 60 days of the divorce or separation to indicate that you're electing to continue coverage. If the plan refuses to honor the law, contact your state's Insurance Commissioner, and they will investigate your complaint and get you the coverage to which you're entitled. For more information on this law, contact the Women Work at the above address.

* Meet Women Entrepreneurs In Your Neighborhood For Lunch

Office of Women's Business Ownership
U.S. Small Business Administration
409 3rd St., SW
Washington, DC 20416   202-205-6673

One of the biggest problems women entrepreneurs face is breaking into the "old boys" network of successful businessmen, and important opportunities can be lost without access to these kinds of connections. To help women interested in networking with other successful business people, the U.S. Small Business Administration has a new program that pairs up a woman who is just starting out with an experienced female Chief Executive Officer running the same kind of company. This business mentor can help the novice businesswoman make connections that might otherwise take her years to make on her own. Those interested in networking should also think about joining relevant professional associations, such as the National Association of Women Business Owners at 212-922-0465 or the National Association for Female Executives at 212-645-0770, or by contacting their local Chamber of Commerce.

* Seminars On How Women Can Sell to the Government

Office of Women's Business
U.S. Small Business Administration
409 3rd St., SW
Washington, DC 20416   202-205-6673

If you're not sure how to start doing business with the government, you might consider taking a seminar sponsored by the U.S. Small Business Administration on the procurement process. These seminars will give you a complete overview on what you'll need to know and do to get involved in bidding on and landing government business contracts. For information on when these seminars are scheduled in your area, contact the office above, or the Women's Business Ownership Representative nearest you listed elsewhere in this chapter.

* Creative Financing for Women Entrepreneurs

Office of Women's Business Ownership
U.S. Small Business Administration
409 3rd St., SW
Washington, DC 20416   202-205-6673

One of the toughest parts of running a business is finding the capital resources to do it: MONEY. The Women's Business Ownership Office runs seminars on how women can use creative ways to locate financing if they've been turned down for loans by regular banks. For more information about these seminars, contact the office above or the Women's Business Ownership Representative nearest you listed elsewhere in this chapter.

* Free Mentors for New Women Entrepreneurs

Office of Women's Business Ownership
U.S. Small Business Administration
409 3rd St., SW
Washington, DC 20416   202-205-6673

How valuable would it be to your business to find a successful role model who's already gone through what's facing you as a female entrepreneur and who's willing to share her expertise with you at no charge? Through the Small Business Administration's Women's Network for Entrepreneurial Training (WNET) you can be paired up with a successful mentor who will meet with you at least once a week for an entire year, allowing you to learn from her experience and begin networking with other successful business people. If you've had your business going for at least a year and have gross receipts of at least $50,000, you can qualify for the WNET program. For more information, contact the office above or the Women's Business Ownership Representative nearest you listed elsewhere in this chapter.

* Changing Laws to Help Women Business Owners

Congressional Caucus for Women's Issues
2471 Rayburn Building
Washington, DC 20515   202-225-6740

If you think that the climate for women business owners could be improved by passing a new law, you might think of sending your ideas to the Congressional Caucus for Women's Issues. This group keeps track of the issues most important to women across the country and introduces new legislation that can help meet those needs, including those of the community of women entrepreneurs. Recently, a new law was passed that allowed federal funding for U.S. Small Business Administration Demonstration Centers that specialize in offering counseling to women interested in starting and expanding businesses. Contact this office if you have any new ideas or would simply like them to send you information about the most recent legislation currently before Congress that concerns women business owners.

Local Women's Business Ownership Representatives

For Starters:
Call Your Local Women's Business Ownership Representative

Women entrepreneurs have special needs, and the U.S. Small Business Administration recognizes those needs. That's why they've added staff members who specialize in promoting women-owned businesses in the U.S. These Women's Business Ownership (WBO) reps can help solve your unique business problems, such as how to network with other women business owners, where to find financial assistance on the state level, or how to get in on the lucrative government procurement programs, especially the ones that offer preferences to women-owned businesses. The WBO rep serving your area is your best ally in helping you cut through the red tape and direct you to free counseling and other valuable information sources.

Alabama
Susan Dunham
U.S. Small Business Administration
2121 8th Ave., North, Suite 200
Birmingham, AL 35203-2398
205-731-1334
Fax: 205-731-1404

Alaska
Joyce Courtney
U.S. Small Business Administration
222 West 8th Ave., Room 67
Anchorage, AK 99513-7559
907-271-4022
Fax: 907-271-4545

Arizona
Gail Gesell
U.S. Small Business Administration
2828 North Central, Suite 800
Phoenix, AZ 85004-1025
602-640-2316
602-640-2325
Fax: 602-640-2360

Arkansas
Valerie Coleman
U.S. Small Business Administration
2120 Riverfront, Suite 100
Little Rock, AR 72202
501-324-5871, ext. 236
Fax: 501-324-5199/5149

California
Gloria Minarik
U.S. Small Business Administration
455 Market St., 6th Floor
San Francisco, CA 94105
415-744-8491
Fax: 415-744-6812

Gilda Perez
U.S. Small Business Administration
660 J St., Suite 215
Sacramento, CA 95814-2413
916-498-6430
Fax: 916-498-6422

Delores Braswell
U.S. Small Business Administration
550 W. C St., Suite 550
San Diego, CA 92188
619-557-7250, ext. 1147
Fax: 619-557-5894

Rose Kim
U.S. Small Business Administration
200 W. Santa Ana Blvd., Suite 700
Santa Ana, CA 92703-2352
714-950-7420
Fax: 714-836-2528

Theresa Leets
U.S. Small Business Administration
330 N. Brand Blvd., Suite 1200
Glendale, CA 91203-2304
818-552-3215
Fax: 818-552-3260

Leslie Lang Lopez
U.S. Small Business Administration
2719 N. Air Fresno Dr., Suite 107
Fresno, CA 93727-1547
209-487-5791, ext. 526
Fax: 209-487-5803

Colorado
Marsha Summerlin
Cindy Cronin
U.S. Small Business Administration
721 19th St., Suite 426
Denver, CO 80202-2599
303-844-3461
Fax: 303-844-6539

Connecticut
Kathleen Duncan
U.S. Small Business Administration
330 Main St., 2nd Floor
Hartford, CT 06106
860-240-4842
Fax: 860-240-4659

Delaware
Carlotta Catullo
U.S. Small Business Administration
824 Market St., Suite 610
Wilmington, DE 19801
302-573-6380
Fax: 302-573-6060

District of Columbia
Ms. Cynthia Pope
U.S. Small Business Administration
1110 Vermont Ave. NW, 9th Floor
Washington, DC 20005
(P.O. Box 34500
Washington, DC 20043-4500)
202-606-4000, ext. 345
Fax: 202-606-4225

Florida
Judy Dunn
U.S. Small Business Administration
7825 Bay Meadows Way, Suite 100B
Jacksonville, FL 32256-7504
904-443-1900/1933
Fax: 904-443-1980

Patricia McCartney
U.S. Small Business Administration
1320 S. Dixie Hwy.
Suite 501, 3rd Floor
Coral Gables, FL 33146-2911
305-536-5833
Fax: 305-536-5058

Georgia
Dorothy Fletcher
U.S. Small Business Administration
1720 Peachtree St., NW, 6th Floor
Atlanta, GA 30309
404-853-7674
Fax: 404-853-7677

Hawaii
Doreen Ezuka
U.S. Small Business Administration
300 Ala Moana, Room 2314
Honolulu, HI 96850-4981
808-541-2971
808-541-3024
Fax: 808-541-2976

Idaho
Pat Hunt
U.S. Small Business Administration
1020 Main St., Suite 290
Boise, ID 83702-5745
208-334-9079
Fax: 208-334-9353

Illinois
Sam McGrier
U.S. Small Business Administration
500 W. Madison St., Suite 1250
Chicago, IL 60661-2511
312-353-4528/5429
Fax: 312-886-5108

Valerie Ross
U.S. Small Business Administration
511 W. Capitol St., Suite 302
Springfield, IL 62704
217-492-4416
Fax: 217-492-4867

Indiana
Ms. Betty McDonald
U.S. Small Business Administration
429 N. Pennsylvania St., Suite 100
Indianapolis, IN 46204
317-226-7272
Fax: 317-226-7259

Women Entrepreneurs: Special Money, Help and Programs

Iowa
Carolyn Tonn
U.S. Small Business Administration
215 4th Ave. SE, Suite 200
Cedar Rapids, IA 52401
319-362-6405
Fax: 319-362-7861

Deb Anderson
U.S. Small Business Administration
210 Walnut St., Room 749
Des Moines, IA 50309
515-284-4761
Fax: 515-284-4572

Kansas
Iris Newton
U.S. Small Business Administration
100 E. English, Suite 510
Wichita, KS 67202
316-269-6631
Fax: 316-269-6499

Kentucky
Carol Halfield
U.S. Small Business Administration
600 Dr. Martin Luther King, Jr. Pl.
Room 188
Louisville, KY 40202
502-582-5971
Fax: 502-582-5009

Louisiana
Loretta Puree
U.S. Small Business Administration
365 Canal St., Suite 2250
New Orleans, LA 70130
504-589-6685, ext. 231
Fax: 504-589-2339

Maine
Patricia Knowles
U.S. Small Business Administration
40 Western Ave., Room 512
Augusta, ME 04330
207-622-8242
Fax: 207-622-8277

Maryland
Martha Brown
U.S. Small Business Administration
10 S. Howard St., Suite 6220
Baltimore, MD 21201
410-962-6195
Fax: 410-962-1805

Beatrice Checket
SCORE
907 Sextant Way
Annapolis, MD 21401
410-366-8746
Fax: 410-266-8754

Massachusetts
Lisa Gonzalez
U.S. Small Business Administration
10 Causeway St., Room 265
Boston, MA 02222-1093
617-565-5588
Fax: 617-565-5598

Harry Webb
U.S. Small Business Entrepristration
1441 Main St., Room 410
Springfield, MA 01103
413-785-0268
Fax: 413-785-0267

Michigan
Catherine Gase
U.S. Small Business Administration
477 Michigan Ave., Room 515
Detroit, MI 48226
313-226-6075, ext. 404
Fax: 313-226-4769

Minnesota
Cynthia Collett
U.S. Small Business Administration
100 N. 6th St., Suite 610C
Minneapolis, MN 55403-1563
612-370-2324
612-370-2312
Fax: 612-370-2303

Missouri
U.S. Small Business Administration
911 Walnut St.
Kansas City, MO 64106
816-426-3608
Fax: 816-426-5559

Patty Ingram
U.S. Small Business Administration
323 W 8th, 5th Floor
Kansas City, MO 64105
816-374-6762
Fax: 816-374-6759

Laverne Johnson
U.S. Small Business Administration
815 Olive St., Suite 242
St. Louis, MO 63101
314-539-6600
Fax: 314-539-3785

LuAnn Hancock
U.S. Small Business Administration
620 S. Glenstone, Suite 110
Springfield, MO 65802-3200
417-864-7670
Fax: 417-864-4108

Mississippi
Charles Gillis
U.S. Small Business Administration
One Government Plaza
13th St., Suite 2909
Gulfport, MS 39501-7758
601-863-4449
Fax: 601-864-0179

Valencia Jamila
U.S. Small Business Administration
101 W. Capitol St., Suite 400
Jackson, MS 39201
601-965-5342
Fax: 601-965-5629

Montana
U.S. Small Business Administration
301 South Park Ave., Room 334
Helena, MT 59626
406-441-1081
Fax: 406-441-1090

Nebraska
Barbara Foster
U.S. Small Business Administration
11145 Mill Valley Rd.
Omaha, NE 68154
402-221-3604
Fax: 402-221-3680

Nevada
Donna Hopkins
U.S. Small Business Administration
301 E. Stewart Ave.
P.O. Box 7527
Las Vegas, NV 89125-2527
702-388-6611
Fax: 702-388-6469

New Hampshire
Sandra Sullivan
U.S. Small Business Administration
143 N. Main St.
Concord, NH 03301
603-225-1400
Fax: 603-225-1409

New Jersey
Frank Burke
U.S. Small Business Administration
Two Gateway Center, 4th Floor
Newark, NJ 07102
201-645-2434
Fax: 201-645-6265

New Mexico
Susan Chavez
U.S. Small Business Administration
625 Silver SW, Room 320
Albuquerque, NM 87102
505-766-1879
Fax: 505-766-1057

New York
Carol White
U.S. Small Business Administration
26 Federal Plaza, Room 3100
New York, NY 10278
212-264-1482
Fax: 212-264-4963

U.S. Small Business Administration
100 S. Clinton St., Room 1073
P.O. Box 7317
Syracuse, NY 13261
315-448-0428
Fax: 315-448-0410

James Cristofaro
U.S. Small Business Administration
333 E. Water St., 4th Floor
Elmira, NY 14901
607-734-8142
Fax: 607-733-4656

Donald Butzek
U.S. Small Business Administration
111 W. Huron St., Room 1311
Buffalo, NY 14202
716-551-5670
Fax: 716-551-4418

U.S. Small Business Administration
35 Pinelawn Rd., Room 207W
Melville, NY 11747
516-454-0763
Fax: 516-454-0769

Howard Daly
SCORE
431 Woodland Lane
Webster, NY 14580
716-671-4550

Local Women's Business Ownership Representatives

Marcia Ketchum
U.S. Small Business Administration
100 State St., Room 410
Rochester, NY 14614
716-263-6700
Fax: 716-263-3146

North Carolina
Cassandra Smith
U.S. Small Business Administration
200 N. College St.
Suite A2015
Charlotte, NC 28202-2173
704-344-6587
Fax: 704-344-6769

North Dakota
Marlene Koenig
U.S. Small Business Administration
657 2nd Ave. North, Room 219
Fargo, ND 58102
701-239-5131
Fax: 701-239-5645

Ohio
Rosemary Darling
U.S. Small Business Administration
1111 Superior Ave.
Suite 630
Cleveland, OH 44144
216-522-4180 ext. 128
Fax: 216-522-2038

Janice Sonnenberg
U.S. Small Business Administration
2 Nationwide Plaza
Suite 1400
Columbus, OH 43215-2542
614-469-6860
Fax: 614-469-2391

Bonnie Schenck
U.S. Small Business Administration
525 Vine St., Suite 870
Cincinnati, OH 45202
513-684-6907
Fax: 513-684-3251

Oklahoma
Joyce Jones
U.S. Small Business Administration
210 Park Ave.
Oklahoma City, OK 73102
405-231-4301
Fax: 405-231-4876

Oregon
Leann Earley
U.S. Small Business Administration
1515 SW 5th Ave., Suite 1050
Portland, OR 97207
503-326-5101
Fax: 503-326-2808

Pennsylvania
Ana Gallardo
U.S. Small Business Administration
475 Allendale Rd., Suite 201
King of Prussia, PA 19406
610-962-3800
Fax: 215-962-3743

Linda Carey
U.S. Small Business Administration
1000 Liberty Ave.
Federal Bldg., #1128
Pittsburgh, PA 15222
412-644-2780
Fax: 416-644-5446

Rhode Island
Patricia O'Rourke
U.S. Small Business Administration
380 Westminister St., 5th Floor
Providence, RI 02903
401-528-4688
Fax: 401-528-4539

South Carolina
Teresa Singleton
U.S. Small Business Administration
1835 Assembly St., Room 358
Columbia, SC 29201
803-765-5298
Fax: 803-765-5962

South Dakota
Darlene Michael
U.S. Small Business Administration
101 S. Phillips Ave.
Suite 200
Sioux Falls, SD 57104-6727
605-330-4231
Fax: 605-330-4215

Tennessee
Saundra Jackson
U.S. Small Business Administration
50 Vantage Way, Suite 201
Nashville, TN 37228-1550
615-736-5881
615-736-7935
Fax: 615-736-7232

Texas
Terry Ruiz
U.S. Small Business Administration
10737 Gateway West
Suite 320
El Paso, TX 79925
915-540-5154
Fax: 915-540-5636

Wila Lewis
U.S. Small Business Administration
9301 SW Freeway
Suite 550
Houston, TX 77074
713-773-6519
Fax: 713-773-6550

Thelma Ruelas
U.S. Small Business Administration
222 E. Van Buren St.
Suite 500
Harlingen, TX 78550
210-427-8533
Fax: 210-427-8537

Vicky Norton
U.S. Small Business Administration
1611 10th St.
Suite 200
Lubbock, TX 79401
806-472-7462
Fax: 806-472-7487

U.S. Small Business Administration
727 E. Durango, Room A527
San Antonio, TX 78206
210-472-5900
Fax: 210-472-5935

Diane Cheshier
U.S. Small Business Administration
4300 Amon Carter Blvd.
Suite 114
Ft. Worth, TX 76155
817-885-6504
Fax: 817-885-6543

Jesus Sendejo
U.S. Small Business Administration
606 N. Caranchua
Corpus Christi, TX 78476
512-888-3331
Fax: 512-888-3481

Utah
Jean Fox
U.S. Small Business Administration
125 S. State St., Room 2229
Salt Lake City, UT 84138-1195
801-524-6831
Fax: 801-524-4160

Vermont
Brenda Fortier
U.S. Small Business Administration
87 State St., Room 205
Montpelier, VT 05601-0605
802-828-4422
Fax: 802-828-4485

Virginia
Fannie Gergoudis
U.S. Small Business Administration
1504 Santa Rosa Rd.
Suite 200
Richmond, VA 23229
804-771-2765, ext. 112
Fax: 804-771-8018

Washington
Carol McIntosh
U.S. Small Business Administration
1200 Sixth Ave.
Suite 1700
Seattle, WA 98101
206-553-7310
206-553-7315
Fax: 206-553-7044

U.S. Small Business Administration
Seattle, WA 98174-1088
206-220-6520
Fax: 206-220-6570

Coralie Myers
U.S. Small Business Administration
1020 W. Riverside Ave.
Spokane, WA 99201
509-353-2800
509-353-2630
Fax: 509-353-2600

Diana Wilhite
617 N. Helena
Spokane, WA 99202
509-534-9001
Fax: 509-534-3003

West Virginia
Sharon Weaver
U.S. Small Business Administration
168 W. Main St., 6th Floor
Clarksburg, WV 26301
304-623-5631
Fax: 304-623-0023

Women Entrepreneurs: Special Money, Help and Programs

Wisconsin
U.S. Small Business Administration
212 E. Washington Ave., Room 213
Madison, WI 53703
608-264-5516
Fax: 608-264-5541

Jerry Polk
U.S. Small Business Administration
310 W. Wisconsin Ave., Suite 400
Milwaukee, WI 53203
414-297-3941
Fax: 414-297-1377

Wyoming
Beth Hink
U.S. Small Business Administration
100 E. B St., Room 4001
Casper, WY 82602-2839
307-261-6500
Fax: 307-261-6535

State Women Business Assistance Programs

The feds aren't the only ones noticing the emerging importance of female entrepreneurship in the U.S. business economy. Many states now have special programs to help new and expanding women-owned businesses get the special assistance they need to succeed. So far, almost half the states offer some kind of assistance to women business owners, from special set-aside programs to help women compete for lucrative government contracts, to nuts-and-bolts, one-on-one counseling, to special low interest loan programs, such as the ones offered by Iowa and Louisiana.

It's important to keep in mind that just because your state doesn't currently have any special programs for women entrepreneurs, that doesn't mean that they won't in the near future. In fact, many states, like Florida and Utah, now have special women's business advocates in the state capital to help bring the needs of women business owners to the attention of their legislators. We all know that many newly elected legislators happen to be women, too. This could mean new business programs for women offered in the future, so keep in touch with your state capital to keep informed on the current status of these programs.

Alabama

Office of Minority Business Enterprise (OMBE)
Alabama Development Office
401 Adams Ave.   334-242-2220
Montgomery, AL 36130   800-248-0033
http://www.ado.state.al.us

The Office of Minority Business Enterprise (OMBE) helps women and minority entrepreneurs interested in starting or expanding their businesses prepare business plans and applications for SBA loans, fill out applications for state and federal procurement opportunities, and certify women and minority-owned businesses to participate in the state purchasing programs.

Alaska

Minority Business Development Center
1577 C St.
Suite 304
Anchorage, AK 99501   907-274-5400

The Minority Business Development Center provides management and financial consulting services including loan packaging, development, marketing, investment decisions, accounting systems, and other valuable business advice.

Bureau of Indian Affairs
Alaska Area Office
P.O. Box 25520
Juneau, AK 99802-5520   907-586-7103

Indian Business Development Grants: This program provides grants to assist in the development of Native-owned enterprise that will create jobs and other economic benefits for Alaska Native communities. Priority is given to rural business development projects. For profit businesses are eligible if they are at least 51% owned and operated by individual natives. Grants to individual natives range up to $100,000 with a minimum 75% match from private and/or public sector. The applicant must demonstrate that sufficient funding is not available from other sources.

Indian Loans for Economic Development: The program provides business management, and technical and financial assistance to individual natives and Native organizations for starting, expanding, or purchasing a business enterprise whose enterprise will create jobs and have other economic benefits. Priority is given to rural business development projects. Financial assistance is in the form of guaranteed or direct loans. 20% equity is required on loans and businesses must demonstrate economic feasibility.

Arizona

Arizona Business Connection
Arizona Department of Commerce
3800 N. Central, Suite 1400
Phoenix, AZ 85012   602-280-1480
http://www.commerce.state.az.us/fr_abc.shtml

This office serves as a clearinghouse of information to assist small businesses. One-on-one counseling is available.

Arkansas

Arkansas Economic Development Commission
One Capitol Mall
Little Rock, AR 72201   501-682-1060
http://www.aedc.state.ar.us

The Minority and Small Business Development Division provides business loan packaging, contract procurement assistance, bonding information, general business counseling, seminars, workshops, and referrals to other agencies.

California

Office of Small and Minority Business
Department of General Services
1808 14th St.
Suite 100
Sacramento, CA 95814   916-322-5060
http://www.dgs.ca.gov/osmb

This office helps women-owned businesses interested in participating in the state's purchasing/contracting system, along with counseling, assistance, and protection for their interests.

Business Enterprise Program
Department of Transportation
1820 Alhambra Blvd.
Sacramento, CA 95816   916-227-9599
http://www.dot.ca.gov/hq/bep

This office offers women-owned businesses information on the certification necessary to participate in the state procurement program.

Colorado

Women's Business Office
Office of Business Development
1625 Broadway, Suite 1710   303-892-3840
Denver, CO 80202   800-592-5920 (in CO)
http://www.state.co.us/gov_dir/wbo

The Women's Business Office acts as a resource clearinghouse for women business owners. They refer callers to the appropriate state and local offices that can provide them with the hands-on assistance they need, from business planning and marketing assistance to procurement programs and financing. The program also holds business planning seminars at 16 locations throughout the state.

Delaware

Minority Enterprise Office
800 French St., 6th Floor
Wilmington, DE 19801   302-571-4093

The agency assists minority businesses in the city of Wilmington by providing technical assistance, certificate of minority businesses, and workshops. They sponsor a Minority Business Trade Fair (the largest in the Northeast) once a year. The agency works with the Wilmington Economic Development Corporation to provide financing.

Women Entrepreneurs: Special Money, Help and Programs

Florida

Florida Department of Transportation
Minority Programs Office
3717 Apalachee Pkwy, Suite G
Tallahassee, FL 32311
850-921-7370

The office develops outreach programs to recruit and inform disadvantaged business enterprises about contracting opportunities with the Department of Transportation. It also has a business support component which assesses business needs for training and technical assistance. Specific programs include classroom training, on-the-job training, conferences, seminars, workshops, and proficiency standards attainment.

Minority Business Office
Department of General Services
2012 Hartman, Room 100
Koger Executive Center
Capitol Circle SE
Tallahassee, FL 32399-0100
850-487-0915

This office is responsible for certifying minority businesses to do business with the state and for maintaining a directory of these certified businesses. The directory is available to all state agencies. They identify the concerns and unique needs of small and minority-owned businesses in Florida. It serves as a liaison between the business community, state agencies, and the legislature. It also serves as a review board for policies, procedures, and regulations as they relate to key issues of concern.

Georgia

Small and Minority Business Affairs
Georgia Department of Administrative Services
200 Piedmont Ave., SE
West Tower #1620
Atlanta, GA 30602
404-656-6315
http://www.doas.state.ga.us

The office assists small businesses in conducting business with state government, identification of coordinating offices in state agencies, and prerequisites. The Minority Subcontractors Tax Incentive is available to any company which subcontracts with a minority-owned firm to furnish goods, property, or services to the state of Georgia. The credit is for 10% of the total amount of qualified payments to minority subcontractors during the tax year, but may not exceed $100,000 per year.

Minority Business Development Agency
401 W. Peachtree, Suite 1715
Atlanta, GA 30308
404-730-3300
http://www.mbda.gov

At any of the regional offices of the Minority Business Development Agency (of the U.S. Department of Commerce), a minority owner can get help with preparing a business loan package, securing sales, or solving a management problem. The centers maintain networks of local business development organizations, assist business people in the commercialization of technologies, and coordinate other federal agency activities which assist minority entrepreneurs.

Hawaii

Honolulu Minority Business Development Center
1132 Bishop St.
1st Hawaiian Tower #1000
Honolulu, HI 96813
808-531-6232

The center provides management and technical assistance to qualified ethnic minority individuals and firms in the areas of business and financial planning, contract procurement, marketing analyses, general management, bonding, office systems, and procedures.

Illinois

Small Business Advocate
Illinois Department of Commerce and Community Affairs
State of Illinois Center
100 W. Randolph St.
Suite 3-400
Chicago, IL 60601
312-814-3540

The Small Business Advocate specializes in helping women, minorities, startups, and home-based business owners cut through the bureaucratic red tape and get the answers they need by offering information and expertise in dealing with various state, federal, and local agencies.

Small Business Assistance Bureau
Illinois Department of Commerce and Community Affairs
State of Illinois Center
620 E. Adams
Springfield, IL 62701
217-782-7500
800-252-2923 (in IL)
http://www.commerce.state.il.us

The Women's Business Advocate offers programs to women entrepreneurs through a business calendar of events, which includes conferences at which business owners have an opportunity to network. The Advocate also maintains an extensive mailing list of women entrepreneurs. Through the Women's Business Development Center of The Neighborhood Institute, women business owners can get assistance in all phases of business development.

Under the Minority and Women Business Loan Program, women business owners can get long-term, fixed rate direct financing at below market rates for loans from $5,000 to $50,000. One job must be created or retained for each $5,000 borrowed. Business owners can use the money for leasing or purchasing land and buildings, construction or renovation of fixed assets, purchase and installation of machinery and equipment, and working capital.

Under the Minority and Female Business Enterprise Program, Matchmaker Conferences are held to connect women business owners interested in landing government contracts with state and local purchasing agents.

Indiana

Small Business Development Corporation
One North Capitol, Suite 1275
Indianapolis, IN 46204
317-264-2820
http://www.isbdcorp.org

This office helps women and minority-owned small businesses with all phases of development, from management and technical assistance, to contract bidding, procurement, educational seminars and training, and financial alternatives. As part of their Procurement Program, women and minority-owned businesses receive help in seeking government services contracts.

Iowa

Targeted Small Business
Iowa Department of Inspections and Appeals
Lucas Building, 2nd Floor
Des Moines, IA 50319-0083
515-281-7250

Under the Targeted Small Business Program, women and minority-owned businesses can get help in getting certified as a targeted small business (any business 51% or more women or minority-owned), and thereby become eligible for set-aside procurement programs sponsored by the state.

Kansas

Office of Minority and Women Business
Existing Industry Development Division
Kansas Department of Commerce
700 SW Harrison
Topeka, KS 66603-3712
785-296-3805

This office helps women and minority-owned businesses with the bidding procedures for public and private procurement opportunities in Kansas. They also offer management assistance to these businesses and help identify financial resources for them.

Kentucky

Office of Minority Affairs
State Office Building
501 High St., Room 904
Frankfort, KY 40622
502-564-3601

This office certifies women and minority-owned businesses interested in participating in the procurement program for state highway-related contracts.

Kentucky Cabinet for Economic Development
67 Wilkinson Blvd.
Frankfort, KY 40601
502-564-2064
http://www.state.ky.us/edc/edchome.htm

The Small and Minority Business Division is a resource center for small and minority business owners/managers. It identifies construction contracts, procurement opportunities, and offers training programs that address the business needs of these enterprises. It focuses on new job creation and job retention by serving existing small and minority businesses in the roles of ombudsman and expediter for business growth and retention.

State Women Business Assistance Programs

Maine
Maine Department of Transportation
Division of Equal Opportunity
Employee Relations
16 State Station House
Augusta, ME 04333   207-287-3576
http://www.state.me.us/

Under the Disadvantaged/Minority/Women Business Enterprise Program, women-owned businesses can get certification to obtain government contracts. This office helps business owners with the procurement procedures used to obtain government contracts.

Massachusetts
State Office of Minority and Women Business Assistance
Department of Commerce
100 Cambridge St., Room 1305
Boston, MA 02202   617-727-8692
http://www.state.ma.us/somwba

This office helps women and minority-owned businesses get certified to participate in the state procurement programs.

Michigan
Targeted Services Division
Michigan Department of Commerce
4th Floor Law Building
P.O. Box 30225
Lansing, MI 48909   517-335-1835

This office runs Women Business Owners Services program which works largely as a referral service for women business owners. Business owners can also participate in special entrepreneurial education and procurement programs.

Minnesota
Department of Administration
Materials Management Division
112 Administrative Building
St. Paul, MN 55155   612-296-2600
http://www.mmd.admin.state.mn.us

This office certifies women-owned businesses to participate in the Small Business Program for procurement opportunities with the state. Once certified, a business earns a 6% preference on government contract bids.

Mississippi
Department of Economic and Community Development
P.O. Box 849
Jackson, MS 39205   601-359-3449
http://www.decd.state.ms.us

Under the Minority Business Enterprise Loan Program, women-owned businesses that show that they are economically disadvantaged are eligible to receive low interest loans for up to 50% of a business project's cost.

Missouri
Council on Women's Economic Development & Training
2023 St. Mary's Blvd.
P.O. Box 1684
Jefferson City, MO 65102   573-751-0810
http://www.ecodev.state.mo.us/ded/

The Council helps women small business owners through various programs, seminars, and conferences. The Missouri Council on Women's Economic Development and Training assists women in small business enterprises. The Council conducts programs, studies, seminars, and conferences. It promotes increased economic and employment opportunities through education, training, and greater participation in the labor force.

Missouri Department of Economic Development
P.O. Box 118
Jefferson City, MO 65102   314-751-3237

The Minority Business Assistance Program is designed to promote and encourage the development of minority-owned businesses in Missouri. The program provides assistance in obtaining technical and financial assistance, education programs, minority advocacy, and networking with other programs and agencies.

Montana
DBE Program Specialist
Civil Rights Bureau
Montana Department of Transportation
2701 Prospect Ave.
P.O. 201001
Helena, MT 59620-1001   406-444-6337
http://www.mdt.mt.gov

The Disadvantaged Business Enterprise and Women Business Enterprise program certifies women-owned businesses interested in bidding on and obtaining federal-aid highway construction contracts.

Nebraska
Office of Women's Business Ownership
Small Business Administration
11145 Mill Valley Rd.
Omaha, NE 68154   402-221-4691

The office directs Small Business Administration (SBA) programs to women business owners through special women's groups, seminars, networks, and other activities for women in the private sector.

New Hampshire
Office of Business and Industrial Development
Division of Economic Development
172 Pembroke Rd.
P.O. Box 856
Concord, NH 03302-0856   603-271-2591
http://ded.state.nh.us/obid

This office serves as a clearinghouse and referral center of programs for women and minority-owned businesses.

New Mexico
Economic Development Department
Joseph Montoya Building
1100 St. Francis Dr., Room 2006
Santa Fe, NM 87503   505-827-0425
http://www.edd.state.nm.us

The Procurement Assistant Program educates business owners in all phases of government contracting, and provides comprehensive technical procurement counseling for obtaining defense, federal, state, and local government contracts. It offers training seminars (hands-on workshops), and offers small, minority, and women-owned businesses the opportunity to be entered into the annual New Mexico MSBPAP Business Directory.

New York
Division of Minority and Women's Business
Department of Economic Development
1 Commerce Plaza
Albany, NY 12245   518-474-0375
or
633 Third Ave.
New York, NY 10017   212-803-2410

This office gives women and minority-owned businesses consulting and technical assistance in obtaining benefits from state programs, with a focus on business financing. They also help these businesses get the proper certification to participate in the state procurement opportunities. Additionally, this office can help these business owners obtain Federal government contracts.

New York Urban Development Corp.
Minority and Women Revolving Loan Fund
1515 Broadway
New York, NY 10036   212-930-0452

Women and minority-owned industrial, commercial, service oriented, and start-up businesses can receive low interest loans. Retail businesses are evaluated on a case-by-case basis before they qualify. Loans range from $20,000 to $500,000 and may be used for construction, renovation, leasehold improvements, acquisition of land and buildings, acquisition of an ongoing business, establishment of a nationally recognized franchise outlet, machinery and equipment, and working capital.

North Carolina
North Carolina Minority Business Development Agency
205 Fayetteville St. Mall
Raleigh, NC 27601   919-833-6122

Women Entrepreneurs: Special Money, Help and Programs

The agency provides information, referral, and support assistance to minority businesses. It offers technical referral assistance, procurement opportunities referral, management workshops and seminars, and coordination with other state and federal agencies.

North Dakota

Women's Business Program
Department for Economic Development and Finance
4182 Broadway, Suite 25
Bismarck, ND 58501 701-258-2251
http://www.growingnd.com/wbd_prog.html

These offices provide technical assistance in getting businesses started. Some of the services provided include location of funding and preparation of business plans. They also certify women businesses for federal and state contracting.

Ohio

Small Business Development Center
Ohio Department of Development
P.O. Box 1001 800-848-1300
Columbus, OH 43266-0101 614-466-4945
http://www.odod.ohio.gov/

Under the Women's Business Resource Program, women can get help for start-up, expansion and management of their businesses. The program seeks to provide women with equal access to assistance and lending programs, and helps businesswomen locate government procurement opportunities. This office also acts as a statewide center of workshops, conferences, and Women's Business Owners statistics. All of the program's services are free. This office also publishes *Ohio Women Business Leaders*, a directory of women-owned businesses in Ohio, along with other free publications.

Oklahoma

Oklahoma Department of Commerce
Small Business Division
P.O. Box 26980
Oklahoma City, OK 73126-0980 405-815-6552
http://www.odoc.state.ok.us

Under the Women Owned Business Assistance Program, businesswomen can get a variety of technical assistance, from business planning and marketing assistance, to financial information and government procurement practices.

The Minority Business Development Program provides support and assistance in the establishment, growth, and expansion of viable business enterprises. Counseling in the preparation of business plans and marketing strategies is available. The program also provides assistance for loan packaging, bid preparation, feasibility studies, and certification requirements.

Oregon

Office of Minority, Women & Emerging Small Businesses
155 Cottage St., NE
Salem, OR 97310 503-947-7976
http://www.cbs.state.or.us

This office certifies women-owned, disadvantaged, and emerging small businesses, allowing them to participate in the state's targeted purchasing programs.

Pennsylvania

Women's Business Advocate's Office
354 Forum Building
Department of Community and Economic Development
Harrisburg, PA 17120 717-787-3339
http://www.state.pa.us

The Office offers women business owners one-on-one counseling and helps them get the information they need to solve their problems in developing a business. They also will refer women business owners to the appropriate state offices and agencies that can best help them with every kind of issue, from procurement assistance to developing business and financial strategies.

Rhode Island

Office of Minority Business Assistance
Department of Economic Development
One West Exchange St.
Providence, RI 02903 401-222-6253

This office certifies women and minority-owned businesses under federal and state set-aside and goal programs and provides counseling assistance to these companies.

Tennessee

Office of Minority Business Enterprise
Department of Economic & Community Development
Rachel Jackson Building, 7th Floor
320 6th Ave. North 615-741-2545
Nashville, TN 37219-5308 800-342-8470 (in TN)
http://www.state.tn.us/ecd/smbusinf.htm

This office offers information, advocacy, referral, procurement, and other services to minority businesses in the state. They publish a directory of minority businesses, offer conferences and seminars on topics useful to business owners, and serve as a clearinghouse of important information to women and minorities. They also match vendors with potential clients and help women and minorities identify and obtain procurement opportunities.

Utah

Small Business Administration
Salt Lake District Office
125 S. State St.
Salt Lake City, UT 84138 801-524-5800

The Women's Business Ownership Program offers a series of business training seminars and workshops for women business owners and for women who want to start their own small firms. This program provides a focus on business planning and development, credit, and procurement as it relates specifically to women and their businesses.

Washington

Office of Minority and Women's Business Enterprises
P.O. Box 41160
Olympia, WA 98504-1160 360-753-9693
http://www.wsdot.wa.gov/omwbe/

This office helps women and minority-owned businesses interested in participating in state contracting opportunities by moving them through the certification process. Once certified, businesses are eligible to receive a 5% preference when bidding competitively on goods and services purchased by the state. Upon request, businesses can be placed on bid lists maintained by individual agencies, education institutions, or contractors by contacting them directly.

Wisconsin

Department of Commerce
P.O. Box 7970 800-435-7287 (in WI)
Madison, WI 53707 608-266-1018
http://badger.state.wi.us

The Women's Business Services offers assistance in gaining information about the state's loan programs available to women business owners. The office keeps track of the top 50 fastest growing and top 10 women-owned businesses in Wisconsin. They also maintain a database of women-owned businesses in the state.

Wisconsin Housing and Economic Development Authority
One South Pinckney St., #500
P.O. Box 1728 800-334-6873
Madison, WI 53701-1728 608-266-7884
http://www.wheda.state.wi.us

Under the Linked Deposit Loan Program, women or minority-owned businesses with gross annual sales of less than $500,000 can qualify for low rate loans. Loans are available under the prime lending rate for purchase or improvement of buildings, equipment, or land, but not for working capital. Business must be in manufacturing, retail trade, tourism, or agriculture packaging or processing.

Wisconsin Women Entrepreneurs
1126 S. 70th St., Suite 106
Milwaukee, WI 53214 414-358-9290

The office provides monthly programs, training, seminars, mentor committees, and a membership directory.

Commissions, Committees, and Councils
On the Status of Women

Because women so often put the needs of others before their own, they are oftentimes reluctant to seek help for themselves. Feelings of guilt, low self-esteem, depression, anger, and stress often accompany the changes that can occur during a woman's life — changes like divorce, separation, job termination or change, abuse, or sexual harassment. Never before have there been more options for women seeking help, whether it is in learning new career skills or finding a support group of other women coping with life's ups and downs that affect all of us at one time or another.

In almost every state, there are Women's Commissions and similar groups that provide direction or assistance to women. Missions and programs vary, but these groups all share the goal of working toward eliminating the inequities that affect women at home and in the workplace. Some commissions are simply advocacy groups, bringing attention to issues that affect women and working to bring about legislative changes that would improve situations that women face. Others provide information and referrals to help women get ahead — some even provide direct services to help women get the training, education, and financial help they need to succeed.

Through research, education, legislative action and special projects, the commissions are a strong voice for women's rights. Areas of interest and support include, but are not limited to:

- Child support laws
- Advancement in non-traditional jobs
- Sexual harassment
- Child care and dependent care programs
- Violence against women
- Housing
- Insurance
- Credit
- Legal rights
- Education
- Employment
- Economic equity
- Appointment of qualified women for all positions of government

Some also provide other services such as:

- Referrals and information on women's issues
- Seminars
- Workshops and/or workshop leaders
- Conferences
- Speakers bureaus
- Public forums
- Publications
- Audio-visual libraries
- Resource directories

Please don't hesitate to call your local commission. The people who work there are caring and very willing to help with just about any kind of problem. If you do not see a commission listed for your state, call the Governor's office to see if one has been established — or ask them for guidance with your problem.

Check the following list for the commission nearest you.

U.S. Department of Labor
Women's Bureau
Women's Bureau
U.S. Department of Labor
200 Constitution Ave., NW, S3311
Washington, DC 20210
800-827-5335
202-219-6631
www.dol.gov/dol/wb

National Association of Commissions for Women (NACW)
Patricia Hendel, President
127 Parkway South
New London, CT 06320
860-442-1054
Fax: 860-442-1054

Carrolena M. Key
Assistant to the President
NACW National Office
8630 Fenton St., Suite 934
Silver Spring, MD 20910
800-338-9267
301-585-8101
Fax: 301-585-3445
E-mail: nacw2@nacw.org
www.nacw.org

Alabama
Alabama Women's Commission
P.O. Box 1277
Tuscaloosa, AL 35403
205-345-7668
Jean Boutwell, elected Secretary
Bab F. Hart, Chair
www.alawomenscommission.org

Alaska
Anchorage Women's Commission
P.O. Box 196650
Anchorage, AK 99519-6650
907-343-6310
Fax: 907-343-6730
www.ci.anchorage.ak.us

Arizona
Phoenix Women's Commission
Equal Opportunity Department
251 West Washington, 7th Floor
Phoenix, AZ 85003-6211
602-261-8242
Fax: 602-256-3389

Tucson Women's Commission
240 North Court Ave.

Women Entrepreneurs: Special Money, Help and Programs

Tucson, AZ 85701
520-624-8318
Fax: 520-624-5599
E-mail: tctwc@starnet.com
Neema Caughran, Executive Director
Louisa Hernandez, Chair

Arkansas
Closed 96-99

California
California Commission on the Status of Women
1303 J St., Suite 400
Sacramento, CA 95814-2900
916-445-3173
Fax: 916-322-9466
E-mail: csw@sna.com
www.statusofwomen.ca.gov
Eileen Padberg, Chair

Colorado
Denver Women's Commission
303 West Colfax, Suite 1600
Denver, CO 80204
303-640-5826
Fax: 303-640-4627
www.denvergov.org/
Marilyn Ferran, Chair

Fort Collins City Commission on the Status of Women
c/o Human Resources, City of Ft. Collins
P.O. Box 580
Fort Collins, CO 80522
970-221-6871
970-224-6050
www.ci.fort-collins.co.us
Laurie Fonken-Joseph, Chair

Connecticut
Connecticut Permanent Commission of the Status of Women
18-20 Trinity St.
Hartford, CT 06106
860-240-8300
Fax: 860-240-8314
E-mail: pcsw@po.state.ct.us
www.cga.state.ct.us/pcswl/
Leslie Brett, Ph.D, Executive Director
Barbara DeBaptiste, Chair

Delaware
Delaware Commission for Women
4425 N. Market St.
Wilmington, DE 19802
302-761-8005
Fax: 302-761-6652
E-mail: cgomez@state.de.us
Romona S. Fullman, Esq., Director

District of Columbia
Women's Bureau
U.S. Department of Labor
200 Constitution Ave., NW
Washington, DC 20210
800-827-5335
202-219-6631
Fax: 202-219-5529
www.dol.gov/dol.wb
Delores L. Crockett, Acting Director
Lillian M. Long, Chair

Florida
Florida Commission on the Status of Women
Office of the Attorney General, The Capitol
Tallahassee, FL 32399-1050
850-414-3300
Fax: 850-921-4131
E-mail: Michele-Manning@oag.state.fl.us
http://legal.firn.edu/units/fcsw
Kate Gooderham, Chair
Susan Gilbert, Vice Chair

Georgia
GA State Commission of Women
148 International Blvd., NE
Atlanta, GA 30303
404-657-9260
Fax: 404-657-2963
E-mail: gawomen@manspring.com
www.manspring.com/~gawomen
Nellie Duke, Chair
Juliana McConnell, Vice Chair

Hawaii
Hawaii State Commission on the Status of Women
235 S. Beretaniast
Suite 401
Honolulu, HI 96813
808-586-5757
Fax: 808-586-5756
E-mail: hscsw@pixi.com
www.state.hi.us/hscsw
Alicynttikida Tasaka, Executive Director

Idaho
Idaho Commission on the Women's Program
P.O. Box 83720
Boise, ID 83720-0036
208-334-4673
Fax: 208-334-4646
E_mail: ehurlbudt@women.state.id.us
www.state.id.us/women
Linda Hurlbudt, Director
Cindy Agidius, Chair

Illinois
Governor's Commission on the Status of Women
100 W. Randolph, Suite 16-100
Chicago, IL 60601
312-814-5743
Fax: 312-814-3823
Ellen Solomon, Executive Director

Indiana
Indiana State Commission for Women
100 N. Senate Ave., N103
Indianapolis, IN 46204
317-233-6303
Fax: 317-232-6580
E-mail: icw@state.in.us
www.state.in.us/icw

Iowa
Iowa Commission on the Status of Women
Lucas State Office Building
Des Moines, IA 50319
515-281-4461
Fax: 515-242-6119
E-mail: icsw@compuserve.com
www.state.ia.us/dhr/sw
Charlotte Nelson, Executive Director
Kathryn Burt, Chair

Kansas
Wichita Commission on the Status of Women
Human Services Dept., 2nd Floor
455 North Main St.
Wichita, KS 67202
316-268-4691
Fax: 316-268-4219
Shirley Mast, Contact Person

Kentucky
Kentucky Commission on Women
614A Shelby St.
Frankfort, KY 40601
502-564-6643
Fax: 502-564-2315
E-mail: gpotter@mail.state.ky.us
www.state.ky.us/agencies/women/index.html
Genie Potter, Executive Director

Louisiana
LA Office of Women's Services
1885 Woodale Blvd., 9th Floor
Baton Rouge, LA 70806
225-922-0960
Fax: 225-922-0959
E-mail: owsbradm@ows.state.la.us
www.ows.state.la.us/
Vera Clay, Executive Director

Maine
Abolished

Maryland
Maryland Commission for Women
311 West Saratoga St., Room 232
Baltimore, MD 21201
410-767-7137
Fax: 410-333-0079
E-mail: lsajardo@dhr.state.md.us
www.dhr.state.md.us/mcw/index.html
Dr. Carl A. Silberg, Executive Director
Dr. Fran V. Tracy-Mumsford, Chair

Massachusetts
Massachusetts Governor's Advisory Committee on Women's Issues
Statehouse Governor's Office, Room 360
Boston, MA 02133
617-727-3600
Fax: 617-727-9725
Jennifer Davis Carey, Contact
Joanne Thompson, Chair

Michigan
Michigan Women's Commission
741 N. Cedar St., Suite 102
Lansing, MI 48913
517-334-8622
Fax: 517-334-8641
www.mdcr.com
Patti Garrett, Chair

Minnesota
Minnesota Commission on the Economic Status of Women
85 State Office Building
St. Paul, MN 55155
651-296-8590
Fax: 651-297-3697
E-mail: lcesw@commissions.leg.state.mn.us
www.commissions.leg.state.mn.us/
Aviva Breen, Executive Director
Becky Lourey, Chair

Mississippi
Inactive

Missouri
Missouri Women's Council
P.O. Box 1684
Jefferson City, MO 65102

Commissions, Committees, and Councils

573-751-0810
Fax: 573-751-8835
E-mail: wcouncil@mail.state.mo.us
www.womenscouncil.org
Sue P. McDaniel, Executive Director
Deborah Borchers-Ausmus, Chair

Montana
Interdepartmental Coordinating Committee for Women (ICCW)
P.O. Box 1728
Helena, MT 59624
406-444-1520
E-mail: jbranscum@state.mt.us
www.mdt.state.mt.us/iccw
Jean Branscum, Chair
Jeanne Wolf, Vice Chair

Nebraska
Nebraska Commission on the Status of Women
301 Centennial Mall South
Box 94985
Lincoln, NE 65809
402-471-2039
Fax: 402-471-5655
E-mail: ncswmail@mail.state.ne.us
www.ncsw.org
Toni Gray, Executive Director

Nevada
Nevada Women's Fund
201 W. Liberty
Reno, NV 89501
775-786-2335

New Hampshire
New Hampshire Commission on the Status of Women
State House Annex, Room 334
25 Capitol St.
Concord, NH 03301-6312
603-271-2660
Fax: 603-271-2361
E-mail: kfrey@admin.state.nh.us
www.state.nh.us/csw
Katheryn Frey, Executive Director
Molly Kelly, Chair

New Jersey
New Jersey Dept. of Community Affairs
Division of Women
101 South Broad St. CN 808
Trenton, NJ 08625-0801
609-292-8840
Fax: 609-633-6821
Elizabeth L. Cox

New Mexico
New Mexico Commission on the Status of Women
2401 12th St. NW
Albuquerque, NM 87104-2302
505-841-8920
Fax: 505-841-8926
E-mail: rdakota@nm.us.campuscwix.net
Yolanda Garcia, Info. Officer
Darlene B. Herrera, Vice Chair

New York
New York State Division for Women
633 Third Ave.
New York, NY 10017
212-681-4547
Fax: 212-681-7626
E-mail: women@women.state.ny.us

www.women.state.ny.us
Elaine Wingate Conway, Director

North Carolina
North Carolina Council for Women
526 North Wilmington St.
Raleigh, NC 27604-1199
919-733-2455
Fax: 919-733-2464
www.doa.state.nc.us/doa/cfw/cfw.htm
Juanita Bryant, Executive Director
Jane Carver, Chair

North Dakota
North Dakota Governor's Commission on the Status of Women
600 East Boulevard
Bismarck, ND 58501-0250
701-328-5300
Fax: 701-328-5320
Carol Reed, Chairman

Ohio
Ohio Women's Commission
77 S. High St., 24th Floor
Columbus, OH 43266-0920
614-466-5580
Fax: 614-466-5434
Sally Farran Bulford, Executive Director
Dr. Suzanne Crawford, Chair

Oklahoma
Oklahoma Governor's Commission on the Status of Women
101 State Capitol Bldg.
2300 North Lincoln Blvd.
Oklahoma City, OK 73105-4897
918-492-4492
Fax: 918-492-4472
Claudia Tarrington, Chair
Kathi Goebel, Senior Vice Chair

Lawton Mayor's Commission on the Status of Women
102 SW 5th St.
Lawton, OK 73501
405-581-3260
Janet Childress, Chair
Emma Crowder, Vice Chair

Tulsa Mayor's Commission on the Status of Women
c/o Department of Human Rights
200 Civic Center
Tulsa, OK 74103
918-582-0558
918-592-7818

Oregon
Oregon Commission for Women
Portland State University
Smith Center, Room M315
Portland, OR 97207
503-725-5889
Tracy Davis, Contact

Pennsylvania
Pennsylvania Commission for Women
Finance Building, Room 205
Harrisburg, PA 17120
888-615-7477
Fax: 717-772-0653
E-mail: lesbn@oa.state.pa.us
Loida Esbri, Executive Director

Puerto Rico
Puerto Rico Commission for Women's Affairs
Office of the Governor
Commonwealth of Puerto Rico
P.O. Box 11382
Fernandez Juncos Station
Santurce, PR 00910
787-722-2907
Fax: 787-723-3611
E-mail: egavilan@prtc.net
Enid M. Gavilan, Executive Director

Rhode Island
Rhode Island Advisory Commission on Women
260 W. Exchange St., Suite 4
Providence, RI 02093
401-222-6105
E-mail: tayers@doa.state.ri.us
Toby Ayers, Ph.D., Director
James M. Anthony, Chair

South Carolina
Governor's Office Commission on Women
1205 Pendleton St., Suite 306
Columbia, SC 29201
803-734-1609
Fax: 803-734-0241
Rebecca Collier, Executive Director

South Dakota
Abolished

Tennessee
Abolished

Texas
Texas Governor's Commission for Women
P.O. Box 12428
Austin, TX 78711
512-463-1782
512-475-2615
Fax: 512-463-1832
www.governor.state.tx.us/women/
Ashley Horton, Executive Director

Utah
Utah Governor's Commission for Women and Families
1160 State Office Bldg.
Salt Lake City, UT 84114
801-538-1736
Fax: 801-538-3027
E-mail: women&families@ gov.state.ut.us
www.governor.state.ut.us/women/
Michael Neider, Chair

Vermont
Vermont Governor's Commission on the Status of Women
126 State St.
Drawer 33
Montpelier, VT 05602
802-828-2851
Fax: 802-828-2930
E-mail: info@women.state.vt.us
www.state.vt.us/wom
Judith Sutphen, Executive Director

Virginia
Alexandria Council on the Status of Women
110 North Royal St., Suite 201
Alexandria, VA 22314
703-838-5030
Fax: 703-838-4976
http://ci.alexandria.va.us/ alexandria.html

Women Entrepreneurs: Special Money, Help and Programs

Norma Gattsek, Executive Director
Tara Hardiman, Chair

Arlington Commission on the Status of Women
2100 Clarendon Blvd., Suite 310
Arlington, VA 22201
703-228-3257
Fax: 703-228-3295
E-mail: publicaffairs@co.arlington.va.us
www.co.arlington.va.us/cmo
Katherine Hoffman

Fairfax City Commission for Women
10455 Armstrong St.
Fairfax, VA 22030
703-385-7894
Fax: 703-385-7811
www.ci.fairfax.va.us
Louise Armitage, Director

Fairfax County Commission for Women
12000 Government Center Pkwy., Suite 318
Fairfax, VA 22035
703-324-5720
Fax: 703-324-3959
TTY: 703-222-3504
Leia Francisco, Executive Director

Richmond Mayor's Committee on the Concerns of Women
City Hall
900 East Marshall St., Room 302
Richmond, VA 23219
804-646-5987
Nancy Ownes, Admin. Assistant
Caroline Adams, Chair

Washington
Seattle Women's Commission
c/o Seattle Office for Civil Rights
700 Third Ave, Suite 250
Seattle WA 98104
206-684-4500
Fax: 206-684-0332
E-mail: diane.pina@ci.seattle.wa.us
www.ci.seattle.wa.us/seattle/civil/swc.htm

West Virginia
West Virginia Women's Commission
Building 6, Room 637
Capitol Complex
Charleston, WV 25305
304-558-0070
Fax: 304-558-5767
E-mail: vrobinson@wvdhhr.org
www.state.wv.us/womenscom
Joyce M. Stover, Acting Executive Director
Sally Riley, Chair

Wisconsin
Wisconsin Women's Council
16 North Carroll St., Suite 720
Madison, WI 53703
608-266-2219
Fax: 608-261-2432
E-mail: Katie.Mnuk@wwc.state.wi.us
http://wwc.state.wi.us
Katie Mnuk, Executive Director

Wyoming
Wyoming State Government Commission for Women
c/o Department of Employment
Herschler Building
122 West 25th St.
Cheyenne, WY 82002
307-777-7671
http://wydoe.state.wy.us
Amy McClure, Chair

Green Entrepreneuring: Making Money While Protecting The Environment

The entrepreneur of the 2000s will not only worry about making money but will also worry about how her business operations may be affecting the environment or how the environment may be affecting her employees. Instead of hiring high priced engineers, therapists and other consultants, you can turn to the government for help and information by some of the best experts in the world. If your office is not ventilated well and is in a "sick building," the government will provide a free analysis and tell you how to solve the problem. If you have an employee worried about the effects of working in front of a computer screen, the government will send you a free study showing the latest results of research on this topic. The government will also show your business how to save money on your water, electric and commuting bills, as well as lend you money to make your business more energy efficient.

* Government Loans To Start Your Own Energy Conservation Business
Contact your state Economic Development Office
in your state capitol
or
Your Local Small Business Administration Office

The Small Business Administration has established a separate funding program to assist entrepreneurs who provide energy production and conservation services for others. This can include engineering, architectural, consulting or other professional services specializing in specific energy measures. The funding may be in the form of direct loans or loan guarantees and can be as high as $750,000. They can be used for start-up or expansion purposes. Ask about Energy Business Loan Guarantees.

* Buying Fuel Efficient Company Cars
National Alternative Fuels Hotline
Environmental Protection Agency (EPA)
9300 Lee Highway
Fairfax, VA 22031   800-423-1363
www.epa.gov/OMSWWW/cert/feguide

When purchasing company cars or vans, you can make sure that you are buying the best fuel efficient model for your needs by obtaining a free copy of EPA's annual *Mileage Guide* which contains fuel economy estimates for all new makes and models.

* Help Your Employees Carpool: It's The Law
Traffic Operations Division
Federal Highway Administration
U.S. Department of Transportation
400 7th St SW, TV-31
Washington, DC 20590   202-366-4812
or
Association for Commuter Transportation
1518 K St., NW, Suite 503
Washington, DC 20005   202-393-3497
http://tmi.cob.fsu.edu/act/main.htm

The Federal Highway Administration has several publications to get you started on what your company can do to cut down on the number of cars, fuel and pollutants used in commuting. The publications include: *Introduction to Ridesharing*, *Guidelines for Using Vanpools and Carpools*, and *The Employee Transportation Coordinator (ETC) Handbook*.

Passage of the Clean Air Act now requires companies "by law" to help their employees with carpooling. If your business is in any of the following metropolitan areas, and you have over 100 employees, then you have 2 years to increase the commuting vehicle occupancy rate by 25% for your employees. The two years begin ticking as of November 1994. After that each state will impose penalties for noncompliance. If a state does not meet their targets, they can lose federal money for highways and construction. In November 1992, the U.S. Environmental Protection Agency will send Clean Air Implementation Plans to each of the states involved. The areas affected are: Baltimore, MD; Chicago, IL; Houston, TX; Los Angeles, CA; Milwaukee, WI; New York City; Most of New Jersey; Delaware; Philadelphia, PA; San Diego, CA. The Association for Commuter Transportation can answer any further questions you may have on this topic.

* Low Interest Loans To Buy Energy Saving Equipment
Contact your State Office of Economic Development
located in your state capitol

Some state governments, like California, have established low interest loans for small businesses to purchase energy saving equipment or to use for building energy saving facilities. California offers up to $150,000 for 4 years at 5% interest.

* Encouraging Commuting By Bicycle
Bicycle-Pedestrian Program
Office of the Secretary
U.S. Dept. of Transportation
400 7th St., SW   202-366-5007
Washington, DC 20590   877-925-5245
www.bicyclinginfo.org

It takes very little effort for a business to encourage its employees to commute by bicycle. You can: provide bike racks and lockers; provide showers; pass out bike maps with information on local bike commuter routes and other bike commuters; and, support bike paths and lanes in your community as well as upgrading the access roads to your business. Information is available from this office for those interested in bicycle commuting. Also contact your state bicycling and walking coordinator at your state capitol.

* Employees Get A Tax Break For Using Public Transportation
Taxpayer Services
Internal Revenue Service (IRS)
U.S. Department of the Treasury
1111 Constitution Ave., NW, Room 2422
Washington, DC 20224   800-829-3676
or
Your Local IRS Office
www.irs.gov

It's not much, but businesses can provide their employees with $15 per month to take public transportation, and no one has to pay taxes on it. At the time of this publication, there was legislation pending that would increase the amount available as a tax deduction. This tax benefit is explained in IRS Publication #535. It's free.

* Hotline Helps You Save On Your Trash Bill
Resource Conservation and Recovery Act (RCRA) Hotline
Environmental Protection Agency
1200 Pennsylvania Ave., NW
Mail Code 5305   703-412-9810
Washington, DC 20460   1-800-424-9346
www.epa.gov/rcraonline/

Recycling not only can reduce the amount of trash being sent to landfills, but can be cost-effective too. It is easy to start simple recycling programs and help is close by. Each state has a recycling office that can give you advice, direction, and information regarding the establishment of recycling efforts. Help varies from state to state but can include recycling literature to distribute to employees, lists of people who will haul away scrap paper, and speakers who will come to your business to educate your employees on recycling. The RCRA Hotline also has several free publications on recycling including: *Recycle* - provides basic information on recycling; and *Recycling Works* - explains the recycling process and takes you through examples of programs in various states.

Green Entrepreneuring

* Local Help To Recycle Anything

If you are looking for specific information or answers to individual problems, like how to get rid of motor oil, or how to get your neighbor to recycle his plastic bottles, call your state recycling office listed below:

Alabama
Department of Environmental Management
Division of Solid and Hazardous Waste
1400 Coliseum Blvd.
Montgomery, AL 36109 — 334-271-7700

Alaska
Department of Environmental Conservation
Recycling
410 Willoughby Ave., Suite 105
Juneau, AK 99801-1795 — 907-465-5060

Arizona
Department of Environmental Quality
Division of Waste Programs
3033 N. Central Ave.
Phoenix, AZ 85012 — 602-207-4121

Arkansas
Department of Environmental Quality
P.O. Box 8913
Little Rock, AR 72219-8913 — 501-682-0602

California
California Integrated Waste Management Board (CIWMB)
8800 Cal Center Dr.
Sacramento, CA 95826-3268 — 916-255-2200

Colorado
Department of Public Health
Hazardous Material and Waste Management Division
4300 Cherry Creek Drive S
Denver, CO 80246 — 303-692-2000

Connecticut
Department of Environmental Protection
Division of Planning and Standards
79 Elm Street
Hartford, CT 06106-1632 — 860-424-3365

Delaware
Department of Natural Resources and Environmental Control
Solid Waste Management
P.O. Box 1401
Dover, DE 19903 — 302-739-4403

District of Columbia
Department of Public Works
2750 Capitol St. SE
Washington, DC 20002 — 202-645-0751

Florida
Department of Environmental Regulation
Division of Waste Management Administration
Bureau of Solid & Hazardous Waste
2600 Blairstone Road
Tallahassee, FL 32399-2400 — 850-488-0300

Georgia
Department of Natural Resources
Environmental Protection Division
4244 International Pkwy, #104
Atlanta, GA 30354 — 404-362-2692

Hawaii
Department of Health
Environmental Management Division
Solid and Hazardous Waste Branch
P.O. Box 3378
Honolulu, HI 96801-3378 — 808-586-4240

Idaho
Department of Health and Welfare
Division of Environmental Quality
1410 N. Hilton St.
Boise, ID 83706 — 208-373-0260

Illinois
Solid Waste Management Section
1021 N. Grand Ave. E
P.O. Box 19276
Springfield, IL 62794 — 217-785-8604

Indiana
Department of Environmental Management
P.O. Box 6015
Indianapolis, IN 46206-6015 — 317-232-8172

Iowa
Department of Natural Resources
Waste Management Assistance Division
502 E. 9th St.
Des Moines, IA 50319 — 515-281-4968

Kansas
Department of Health and Environment
Solid Waste Section
Bldg. 740, Forbes Field
Topeka, KS 66620 — 785-296-1601

Kentucky
Resources Conservation and Local Assistance
Division of Waste Management
14 Reilly Road
Frankfort, KY 40601 — 502-564-6716

Louisiana
Department of Environmental Quality
P.O. Box 82263
Baton Rouge, LA 70884-2263 — 225-765-0249

Maine
Department of Environmental Protection
#17 State House Station
Augusta, ME 04333 — 207-287-2651

Maryland
Department of the Environment
Recycling Services Division
2500 Broening Highway
Baltimore, MD 21224 — 410-631-3345

Massachusetts
Department of Environmental Protection
Division of Solid Waste Management
1 Winter Street, 9th Floor
Boston, MA 02108 — 617-292-5960

Michigan
Department of Environmental Quality
Waste Management Division
P.O. Box 30241
Lansing, MI 48933 — 517-335-4035

Minnesota
Pollution Control Agency
520 Lafayette Road
St. Paul, MN 55155 — 651-296-7927

Mississippi
Department of Environmental Quality
Office of Pollution Control
P.O. Box 10385
Jackson, MS 39289-0385 — 601-961-5171

Green Entrepreneuring

Missouri
Department of Natural Resources
Solid Waste Management Program
P.O. Box 176
Jefferson City, MO 65102-0176   573-526-3900

Montana
Department of Environmental Quality
Waste Management Division
P.O. Box 200901
Helena, MT 59620   406-444-5294

Nebraska
Litter Reduction and Recycling Programs
Department of Environmental Quality
P.O. Box 98922
Lincoln, NE 68509-8922   402-471-4210

Nevada
Division of Environmental Protection
Bureau of Waste Management
333 W. Nye, Capital Complex
Carson City, NV 89710   775-687-4670, ext. 3008

New Hampshire
Department of Environmental Services
Waste Management Division
6 Hazen Drive
Concord, NH 03301-2925   603-271-2900

New Jersey
Department of Environmental Protection
Division of Solid and Hazardous Waste
Bureau of Recycling and Planning
CN 414
Trenton, NJ 08625-0414   609-984-6900

New Mexico
Solid Waste Bureau
P.O. Box 26110
Santa Fe, NM 87502-6110   505-827-2775

New York
Department of Environmental Conservation
Bureau of Solid Waste Disposal
50 Wolf Road, Room 206
Albany, NY 12233-4013   518-457-5695

North Carolina
Department of Environmental Health and Natural Resources
Bureau of Solid Waste Management
P.O. Box 27687
Raleigh, NC 27611-7687   919-733-6692, ext. 256

North Dakota
Department of Health
Division of Waste Management
P.O. Box 5520
Bismarck, ND 58506-5520   701-328-5166

Ohio
Ohio Environmental Protection Agency
Division of Solid Waste
P.O. Box 1049
Columbus, OH 43216   614-644-2621

Oklahoma
Department of Environmental Quality
Solid Waste Management Services
P.O. Box 1677
Oklahoma City, OK 73101   405-702-5100

Oregon
Department of Environmental Quality
Waste Management and Clean-up
811 SW Sixth Ave.
Portland, OR 97204   503-229-5913

Pennsylvania
Department of Environmental Protection
Municipal and Residual Waste Division
P.O. Box 8471
Harrisburg, PA 17105   717-787-7381

Rhode Island
Department of Environmental Management
Office of Waste Management
235 Promenade St.
Providence, RI 02908   401-222-4700, ext. 7529

South Carolina
Department of Health and Environmental Control
Bureau of Solid and Hazardous Waste
2600 Bull Street
Columbia, SC 29201   803-896-4201

South Dakota
Department of the Environment and Natural Resources
Office of Waste Management
523 E. Capital Ave.
Pierre, SD 57501   605-773-3153

Tennessee
Department of Environment and Conservation
Office of Solid Waste Assistance
401 Church St.
L&C Tower, 14th Floor
Nashville, TN 37243-0455   615-532-0829

Texas
Department of Solid Waste Management
P.O. Box 13087
Austin, TX 78711-3087   512-239-1000

Utah
Department of Environmental Quality
Division of Solid and Hazardous Waste
P.O. Box 144880
Salt Lake City, UT 84114-4880   801-538-6170

Vermont
Department of Environmental Conservation
Division of Hazardous Materials
103 S. Main Street
Laundry Building
Waterbury, VT 05671-0407   802-241-3444

Virginia
Department of Environmental Quality
P.O. Box 10009
Richmond, VA 23240   804-698-4129

Washington
Department of Ecology
Solid Waste Services
P.O. Box 47600
Olympia, WA 95804-7600   360-407-6136
    1-800-RECYCLE

West Virginia
Division of Environmental Protection
Solid Waste Management Section
1356 Hansford St.
Charleston, WV 25301   304-558-5993

Wisconsin
Department of Natural Resources
Bureau of Solid and Hazardous Waste Management
P.O. Box 7921
Madison, WI 53707-7921   608-267-7573

Green Entrepreneuring

Wyoming
Department of Environmental Quality
Solid and Hazardous Waste Division
122 W. 25th Street
Cheyenne, WY 82002　　　　　　　　　　　307-777-7752

* Help For Your Company To "Buy Green"
Resource Conservation and Recovery Act Hotline
Environmental Protection Agency
Mail Code 5305
1200 Pennsylvania Ave., NW　　　　　　　800-424-9346
Washington, DC 20460　　　　　　　　　　703-412-9810

Your company can support recycling by examining your purchase orders to determine what items can be substituted with recycled products. Is your paper made from recycled paper? Your state recycling office may be able to direct you to vendors in your area who carry recycled products. The Resource Conservation and Recovery Act office has a free publication which provides guidance in making the switch to green.

* Light Up Your Life and Business More Efficiently
Green Lights Program
Environmental Protection Agency (EPA)
401 M St, SW
Washington, DC 20006　　　　　　　　　　888-STAR-YES
www.epa.gov/greenlights/

About 20% of the electricity used annually in the U.S. is for lighting. Lighting for industry, stores, offices, and warehouses represent more than 80% of that total. But if energy-efficient lighting were used whenever profitable, the electricity required would be cut in half, thereby reducing sulfur dioxide, nitrogen oxide, and carbon dioxide emission. Green Lights is a voluntary, non-regulatory program sponsored by the EPA to help U.S. companies realize the profit of pollution prevention by installing energy-efficient lighting designs and technologies only where they are profitable and only where they maintain or improve lighting quality. EPA provides technical support, an analysis system that will allow corporations to assess their upgrade options quickly, compiles databases of products, contractors, etc., has an independent testing program, assists in securing financing sources for the upgrading, and will publicize successful Green Lights companies.

* Your Local Utility Will Help You Save Money On Your Energy Bill
Energy Efficiency and Renewable Energy Clearinghouse
P.O. Box 3048
Merrifield, VA 22116　　　　　　　　　　　800-363-3732
www.eren.doe.gov/kids.html
or
Your Local Utility Company

Your local gas, electric, and water utility can provide you with information regarding ways to make your systems work more efficiently. They will often conduct energy or water assessments, and will advise you concerning products on the market which will help your systems run more efficiently. They can also provide you with pamphlets and brochures. Some local utilities are getting into the recycling game by offering to haul away your old refrigerator for free. They make sure the freon is safely removed and the rest is sold for scrap metal. The Department of Energy is also a good source. They have a great deal of information on energy conservation, and how to get your appliances or heating/cooling system to work more efficiently.

* Is Your Business In A "Sick Building"?
Indoor Air Quality Information Clearinghouse
Environmental Protection Agency
P.O. Box 37133
ANR-445W　　　　　　　　　　　　　　　703-893-6600
Washington, DC 20013-7133　　　　　　　1-800-438-4318
www.epa.gov/iaq/

Do you suffer from headaches and have difficulty concentrating only while you are at work? Do your eyes or nose burn? Are you dizzy or nauseous at work? You could be working in a Sick Building. The term Sick Building Syndrome (SBS) is used to describe situations where workers experience acute health or comfort effects when they are at work, but no specific illness can be identified. It can be when you are in a particular room or floor, or it may be the whole building. Symptoms of SBS can be headaches, eye, nose, or throat irritation, dizziness and nausea, difficulty in concentration, fatigue, and sensitivity to odors. The causes can be due to inadequate ventilation, chemical contaminants from indoor or outdoor sources or biological contaminants, such as molds or pollen. An indoor air quality investigation is needed to determine whether the pollutant can be removed or the ventilation rates increased. The Indoor Air Quality Information Clearinghouse can provide you with fact sheets on a wide variety of indoor air problems such as SBS, tobacco smoke, office ventilation, and air cleaners. They have a summary of Air Cleaning Devices, as well as a directory of State Indoor Air Contacts. *Building Air Quality: A Guide for Building Owners and Facility Managers* is a handbook for all air quality questions and remedies.

* How To Help Your Employees With Drug or Alcohol Problems
National Institute on Drug Abuse
6001 Executive Blvd.　　　　　　　　　　800-729-6686
Bethesda, MD 20892　　　　　　　　　　　301-443-1124
www.nida.nih.gov

Is there a problem with some of your employees' work habits? Are some coming in late or not at all? It could be that drugs or alcohol are involved. The National Institute of Drug Abuse is developing programs to eliminate illegal drug use in the workplace. Its programs include research, treatment, training and prevention activities, as well as projects related to the development of a comprehensive Drug-Free Workplace program. They will analyze and recommend Employee Assistance Programs and distribute videos available on a cost recovery basis. Other free videos include:

Drugs At Work (employee/employer versions) - presents information about the nature and scope of the alcohol and drug problem in the workplace and about the federal government's initiative to prevent and reduce the problem. The video can be purchased for $12.50.

Getting Help (employee/employer versions) - highlights the benefits of an effective employee assistance program to employees and employers through comments by business, labor, and government leaders and EPA professionals. The video can be purchased for $12.50.

Drug Testing: Handle With Care (employee/employer versions) - describes the options available for designing a drug testing component as part of a comprehensive drug-free workplace program. The video can be purchased for $12.50.

Finding Solutions - drug abuse in the workplace is portrayed as a community-wide problem. The solutions offered through education and prevention are presented as personal, workplace, and community responsibilities. The video can be purchased for $12.50.

* Free Help For Your Employees With Cholesterol, High Blood Pressure or Smoking Problems
National Heart, Lung, and Blood Institute
National Institutes of Health
Building 31, 4A-21
31 Center Drive, MSC 2480　　　　　　　301-496-4236
Bethesda, MD 20892　　　　　　　　Fax: 301-402-2405
www.nhlbi.nih.gov

This office offers a free Healthy Heart Guide dealing with high blood pressure, cholesterol, and smoking. The Guide contains literature explaining how to educate your employees on these health risks, including handouts, bibliographies, and publications lists. This information is free for the asking.

* Free Speakers and Videos To Teach Your Employees Environmental and Safety Concerns
Consumer Product Safety Commission
5401 Westbard Ave.　　　　　　　　　　800-638-2772
Washington, DC 20207　　　　　　　　　301-504-0990
www.cpsc.gov
or
Office of Field Programs
U.S. Dept. of Labor
Occupational Safety and Health Administration (OSHA)
200 Constitution Ave, NW, Room N-3101
Washington, DC 20210　　　　　　　　　202-693-1999
www.osha.gov
or
National Institute of Occupational Safety and Health (NIOSH)
4676 Columbia Parkway　　　　　　　　800-356-4674
Cincinnati, OH 45226　　　　　　　　　　513-533-8287
www.cdc.gov/niosh

Green Entrepreneuring

These government offices are willing to provide free speakers on topics covering the environment, safety hazards and accident prevention.

The National Institute of Occupational Safety and Health (NIOSH) has a catalog of videos available. The tapes deal with a variety of industrial health and safety issues. Some of the titles include:

1) *Dual Protection (Spray Painting)* - highlights the technology available to control safety and health hazards in spray painting operations
2) *Behavior Based Safety Management* - safety engineers at Proctor and Gamble present their approach to safety management
3) *It's A New Day* - shows how The Drackett Company, a household products manufacturer, manages occupational safety and health
4) *The Finest Tools (Carpal Tunnel Syndrome)* - covers the nature of cumulative trauma disorders of the hand and wrist and describes how repetitive jobs can damage a worker's body
5) *Industrial Loss Control Through Behavior Management* - illustrates behavioral solutions to industrial safety problems
6) *Asbestos Screening Process* - examines an inexpensive and simple method for identifying asbestos
7) *Vibration Syndrome* - a brief introduction to the physics of vibration, and an examination of different assessment techniques (also available from the National Technical Information Service for $110)
8) *Lifting and Analysis* - demonstrates how to calculate the parameters for safe lifting activity in specific example situations

Each of the regional Occupational Safety and Health Administration (OSHA) offices offers videos on worker safety topics. Some of the titles covered are:

1) *Basic Guide to Voluntary Compliance in Safety and Health* - develops a self inspection procedure for the correction of workplace deficiencies in accordance with Occupational Safety and Health Act Standards
2) *Facts About Vinyl Chloride* - identifies facts about working with this potentially hazardous substance
3) *I Never Had An Accident On The Job in My Life* - dramatizes accidents and potential hazards employees face in their everyday routines
4) *Eye Injuries and Eye Protection Equipment* - helps workers take steps to prevent the estimated 1,000 eye injuries that occur daily

Contact the office nearest you for further information on free videos:

Region I
(CT,MA,ME,NH,RI,VT)
133 Portland Street, 1st Floor
Boston, MA 02114   617-565-9860

Region II
(NJ, NY, Puerto Rico, Virgin Islands)
201 Varick Street
Room 670
New York, NY 10014   212-337-2378

Region III
(DC,DE,MD,PA,VA,WV)
Gateway Building, Suite 2100
3535 Market Street
Philadelphia, PA 19104   215-596-1201

Region IV
(AL,FL,GA,KY,MS,NC,SC,TN)
61 Forsyth St., SW
Atlanta, GA 30367   404-562-2300

Region V
(IL,IN,MI,MN,OH,WI)
230 South Dearborn St.
Room 3244
Chicago, IL 60604   312-353-2220

Region VI
(AR,LA,NM,OK,TX)
525 Griffin St., Room 602
Dallas, TX 75202   214-767-4731

Region VII
(IA,KS,MO,NE)
1100 Main St., Suite 800
Kansas City, MO 64105   816-426-5861

Region VII
(CO,MT,ND,SD,UT,WY)
1999 Broadway, Suite 1690
Denver, CO 80202   303-844-1600

Region IX
(American Samoa, AZ,CA,HI,NV, Guam, Pacific Trust Territories)
71 Stevenson Street
Room 415   415-975-4310
San Francisco, CA 94105   800-475-4022

Region X
(AK,ID,OR,WA)
1111 Third Avenue, Suite 715
Seattle, WA 98174   206-553-5930

* Free Hotline Helps You Save Your Energy Dollars
Energy Efficiency and Renewable Energy Clearinghouse
P.O. Box 3048
Merrifield, VA 22116   800-363-3732
www.eren.doe.gov/consumerinfo

Energy-efficient products take less energy to operate and save energy - and money - by reducing heating, cooling and lighting requirements in buildings. Renewable energy comes from sources that are easily replenished such as the sun, wind, and water. There is a section for business/work at the website that provides a wealth of information.

* Keeping Your Company Grounds Environmentally In-Tune
Cooperative State Research, Education and Extension Service
U.S. Department of Agriculture
Administration Bldg. Room 340A
Washington, DC 20250   202-720-3029
www.reeusda.gov
(to locate your local County Cooperative Extension Service)
or
General Accounting Office
P.O. Box 6015
Gaithersburg, MD 20877   202-512-6000
or
National Pesticides Telecommunications   800-858-7378
Network Hotline   800-743-3091 (in Texas)
or
Office of Pesticide Programs
U.S. Environmental Protection Agency
1200 Pennsylvania Ave., NW
Washington, DC 20460   703-305-7090
www.epa.gov/pesticides/

Look at what your maintenance staff is using to clean your offices and other work areas. Are the products dangerous or could they harm the environment, such as high phosphorous detergents? Your local County Cooperative Extension Service Office can advise you on safer substitute products. They can also provide information regarding your landscape practices, such as composting your leaves and grass clippings. They can tell you which trees (and how to plant and maintain them) will grow well around your building, and which can lower your heating and cooling bills.

The National Pesticides Telecommunication Network Hotline provides information on pesticide products, basic safety practices, health and environmental effects, and cleanup and disposal procedures. The Environmental Protection Agency's Public Information Center is also a good source of help on this topic.

* Don't Throw Out Old Paint, Batteries, Etc.
Resource Conservation and Recovery Act Hotline
U.S. Environmental Protection Agency
1200 Pennsylvania Ave., NW
Mail Code 5305   703-412-9810
Washington, DC 20460   1-800-424-9346

Green Entrepreneuring

When your maintenance staff is cleaning out the storeroom, don't let them throw leftover paint in the trash. Paint, along with batteries, lawn care products and other products can emit chemicals harmful to you and your employees. Your state recycling office or the U.S. Environmental Protection Hotline can help you properly dispose of these materials.

* Government Money For Your Business Not To Pollute
Office of Advocacy
U.S. Small Business Administration
1725 Eye St, NW, Room 414
Washington, DC 20416   1-800-827-5722
www.sba.gov

The government has special funds set aside for companies who wish to cut down on their pollution. Your local Small Business Administration office can provide you with more information about what you need to do to qualify.

* Recycle With A Tax Break
Taxpayer Services
Internal Revenue Service
1111 Constitution Ave., NW Room 2422
Washington, DC 20224   1-800-829-3676
www.irs.gov

Before you throw away your old office furniture or equipment, give it away instead and get a tax break. Local non-profit organizations, churches and even schools could use a lending hand. And the IRS will let you have a tax deduction for "gifts in kind". Request a copy of *Determining the Value of Donated Property, Pub #561* from your local IRS office or the office listed above.

* Free Updated Reports On Any Aspect Of The Environment
Capitol Hill Switchboard
Washington, DC   202-224-3121

Your U.S. Representative and Senators have instantaneous access to over 10,000 reports on current events through a computerized online network. A phone call or letter to one of your legislators is all it takes for you to tap into this rich information resource. There is no charge for these concise reports which are unquestionably the best information value because the material contained in these studies are the highlights from materials prepared by other experts in federal government agencies as well as the private sector. You can contact all legislators in Washington by calling the Capitol Hill Switchboard. The Congressional Research Service (CRS) writes these reports on a wide variety of environmental topics including:

- *Asbestos in Buildings: Current Issues*
- *Clean Air Act Issues: Motor Vehicle Emission Standards and Alternative Fuels*
- *Indoor Air Pollution*
- *Directory of Environmental and Conservation Organizations in Washington, DC*
- *Radon*
- *Hazardous Air Products*
- *Degradable Plastics*
- *Solid Waste Management*
- *Hotlines and Other Useful Government Telephone Numbers Info Pack*
- *Recycling Info Pack*
- *Acid Rain*
- *Global Climatic Changes*

* Free Health Inspection of Your Workplace
National Institute for Occupational Safety and Health
4676 Columbia Parkway
Cincinnati, OH 45226   1-800-356-4674
www.cdc.gov/niosh

The National Institute for Occupational Safety and Health (NIOSH) is responsible for conducting research to make the nation's workplaces healthier and safer by responding to urgent requests for assistance from employers, employees, and their representatives where imminent hazards are suspected. They conduct inspections, laboratory and epidemiologic research, publish their findings, and make recommendations for improved working conditions. They will inspect any workplace for free, if three employees sign a form stating that the environment may be dangerous. Employees have the option of keeping anonymous. If any of the following applies to you, NIOSH can provide you with more information:

- Do you use a video display terminal most of the day?
- Are you concerned about the chemicals you are using in your dry cleaning?
- Do you have tingling in your hands (carpal tunnel syndrome)?
- Do you use a jackhammer most of the day and are now finding that your fingers are no longer sensitive to heat or cold?
- Do you do the same motion again and again, such as on an assembly line? You could be at risk for repetitive motion-associated trauma.
- Do you feel your job is causing you mental stress?
- Are you having trouble hearing?

* Free Consultants Make Your Company A Safe And Healthy Place To Work
Occupational Safety and Health Administration (OSHA)
U.S. Dept. of Labor
200 Constitution Ave, NW
Washington, DC 20210   202-693-1999
www.osha.gov

The Occupational Safety and Health Administration was created to encourage employers and employees to reduce workplace hazards and to implement new, or improve existing, safety and health programs. They provide research on innovative ways of dealing with these problems, maintain a record keeping system to monitor job related injuries and illnesses, and develop standards and enforce them, as well as establish training programs.

If you are concerned about the health and safety of your employees, and are having trouble establishing a safe workplace, the Occupational Safety and Health Administration (OSHA) will provide free and confidential consultation assistance.

If you have been working hard to clean up your employees' work space, and have reduced the number of injuries occurring on the job, you can be eligible for a Voluntary Protection Program award certificate.

If you are responsible for training your employees in ways they can work safely in a variety of situations, you can have access to over 65 high quality, low-cost, training videos.

If you are interested in the safety record of another company, OSHA can provide you with the entire range of inspection data, including who, what, when, where and why companies are inspected and the violations that were found (Contact: Office of Management Data Systems, 202-219-7008).

If you want to take a class to learn more about ways you can make your workplace safe and healthy for your employees, OSHA has courses covering areas such as electrical hazards, machine guarding, ventilation and ergonomics (Contact: Safety and Health Training Institute, 708-297-4810).

An extensive list of publications is available including:
- *Asbestos Standards for the Construction Industry*
- *Grain Handling*
- *Hearing Conservation*
- *Respiratory Protection*

OSHA Consultation Project Directory

Alabama
Safe State Program
University of Alabama
432 Martha Parham West
P.O. Box 870388
Tuscaloosa, AL 35487
205-348-3033
http://bama.ua.edu/~deip/safest.html

Alaska
Consultation Section, ADOL/AKOSH
3301 Eagle St.
P.O. Box 107022
Anchorage, AK 99510
907-269-4957
www.labor.state.ak.us/lss/oshhome.htm

Arizona
Consultation and Training
Industrial Commission of Arizona
Division of Occupational Safety and Health
800 West Washington

Phoenix, AZ 85007
602-542-5795

Arkansas
OSHA Consultation
Arkansas Department of Labor
10421 West Markham
Little Rock, AR 72205
501-682-4522
www.state.ar.us/labor/serv01.htm

California
CAL/OSHA Consultation Service
Department of Industrial Relations
455 Golden Gate Ave., 10th Floor
San Francisco, CA 94102
415-703-5270
www.dir.ca.gov/DIR/OS&H/DOSH/consultation.html

Colorado
Colorado State University
Occupational Safety and Health Section
115 Environmental Health Building
Fort Collins, CO 80523
970-491-6151
www.bernardino.colostate.edu/enhealth/7c1.html

Connecticut
Connecticut Department of Labor
Division of Occupational Safety and Health
38 Wolcott Hill Rd.
Wethersfield, CT 06109
860-566-4550
www.ctdol.state.ct.us/osha/osha.htm

Delaware
Delaware Department of Labor
Division of Industrial Affairs
Occupational Safety and Health
4425 Market St.
Wilmington, DE 19802
302-7618219
www.state.de.us/labor/aboutdol/industrialaffairs.html

District of Columbia
DC Department of Employment Services
Office of Occupational Safety and Health
950 Upshur St., NW
Washington, DC 20011
202-576-6339

Florida
Florida Department of Labor and Employment Security
Onsite Consultation Program, Division of Safety
2002 St. Augustine Rd., Building E, Suite 45
Tallahassee, FL 32399
850-922-8955
www.safety-fl.org/consult.htm

Georgia
Georgia Institute of Technology
Onsite Consultation Program
151 6th St., NW
O'Keefe Building, Room 22
Atlanta, GA 30332
404-894-2643
www.gtri.gatech.edu/safety.htm

Hawaii
Consultation & Training Branch
Department of Labor and Industrial Relations
830 Punchbowl St.
Honolulu, HI 96813
808-586-9100
www.aloha.net/~edpso/annual.html

Idaho
Boise State University
Department of Health
Safety and Health Consultation Program
1910 University Dr.
Boise, ID 83725
208-426-3283
www.idbsu.edu/health/healthstudies/

Illinois
Illinois Onsite Consultation
Industrial Service Division
Department of Commerce & Community Affairs
State of Illinois Center, Suite 3-400
100 West Randolph St.
Chicago, IL 60601
312-814-2337
www.commerce.state.il.us/Services/Small Business/OSHA/OSHAhome.htm

Indiana
Bureau of Safety, Education and Training
Division of Labor, Room W195
402 West Washington
Indianapolis, IN 46204
317-232-2688
www.state.in.us/labor/book$.html

Iowa
Consultation Program
Iowa Bureau of Labor
2016 DMACC Boulevard
Building 17, Room 10
Ankeny, IA 50021
515-965-7162
www.state.ia.us/iwd/labor/index.html

Kansas
Kansas Consultation Program
Kansas Department of Human Resources
512 South West 6th St.
Topeka, KS 66603
785-296-7476

Kentucky
Kentucky Labor Cabinet
Division of Education and Training
1047 U.S. Highway 127, South
Frankfort, KY 40601
502-564-6895
www.state.ia.us/iws/labor/index.html

Louisiana
Consultation Program
Louisiana Department of Labor
1001 N. 23rd. St., Room 230
P.O. Box 94094
Baton Rouge, LA 70804
225-342-9601

Maine
Division of Industrial Safety
Maine Bureau of Labor Standards
Workplace Safety & Health Division
State House Station #45
Augusta, ME 04333
207-624-6460
http://janus.state.me.us/labor/consult.htm

Maryland
MOSH Consultation Services
312 Marshall Ave., Room 600
Laurel, MD 20707
410-880-4970
www.dllr.state.md.us/labor/mosh.html

Green Entrepreneuring

Massachusetts
Division of Occupational Safety and Health
Department of Workforce Development
1001 Watertown St.
West Newton, MA 02165
617-727-3982
www.state.ma.us/dos/Consult/Consult.htm

Michigan
Department of Consumer and Industry Services
7150 Harris Dr.
Lansing, MI 48909
517-322-1809
www.cis.state.mi.us/bsr/divisions/set/set_con.htm

Minnesota
Department of Labor and Industry
Consultation Division
443 LaFayette Rd.
Saint Paul, MN 55155
651-297-2393
www.doli.state.mn.us/mnosha.html

Mississippi
Mississippi State University
Center for Safety and Health
2906 North State St., Suite 201
Jackson, MS 39216
601-987-3981
www.msstate.edu/dept/csh

Missouri
Onsite Consultation Program
Division of Labor Standards
Department of Labor & Industrial Relations
3315 West Truman Blvd.
P.O. Box 449
Jefferson City, MO 65109
573-751-3403
www.dolir.state.mi.us/ls/onsite/index.html

Montana
Department of Labor and Industry
Bureau of Safety
P.O. Box 1728
Helena, MT 59624
406-444-6418
http://dli.state.mt.us/publica.htm

Nebraska
Division of Safety & Labor Standards
Nebraska Department of Labor
State Office Building, Lower Level
301 Centennial Mall, South
Lincoln, ME 68509
402-471-4717
www.dol.state.ne.us/safety/7c1.html

Nevada
Safety Consultation and Training Section
Division of Industrial Relations
Department of Business and Industry
1301 Green Valley Parkway
Henderson, NV 89104
702-486-9140
www.state.nv.us/b&i/ir/index.htm

New Hampshire
New Hampshire Department of Health & Human Services
6 Hazen Dr.
Concord, NH 03301
603-271-2024
www.state.nh.us/dhhs/ohm/dphs.htm

New Jersey
New Jersey Department of Labor
Division of Public Safety and Occupational Safety and Health
225 E. State St.
8th Floor West
P.O. Box 953
Trenton, NJ 08625
609-292-3923
www.state.nj.us/labor/consult.html

New Mexico
New Mexico Environment Department
Occupational Health and Safety Bureau
525 Camino de Los Marquez, Suite 3
P.O. Box 26110
Santa Fe, NM 87502
505-827-4230
www.nmenv.state.nm.us/env_prot.html

New York
Division of Safety and Health
State Office Campus
Building 12, Room 130
Albany, NY 12240
518-457-2238
www.labor.state.ny.us/html/employer/p469.html

North Carolina
Bureau of Consultative Services
NC Department of Labor
OSHA Division
4 West Edenton St.
Raleigh, NC 27601
919-807-2905
www.dol.state.nc.us/osha/consult/consult.htm

North Dakota
Division of Environmental Engineering
1200 Missouri Ave., Room 304
Bismarck, ND 58504
701-328-5188
www.ehs.health.state.nd.us/ndhd/environ/ee/oshc/index.htm

Ohio
Bureau of Employment Services
Division of Onsite Consultation
145 S. Front St.
Columbus, OH 43215
614-644-2246
www.state.oh.us/obes/osha.htm

Oklahoma
Oklahoma Department of Labor
OSHA Division
4001 North Lincoln Blvd.
Oklahoma City, OK 73105
405-528-1500
www.state.ok.us/~okdol/osha/index.htm

Oregon
Oregon OSHA
Department of Consumer & Business Services
350 Winter St., NE, Room 430
Salem, OR 97310
503-378-3272
www.cbs.state.or.us/external/osha/consult/consult2.htm

Pennsylvania
Indiana University Pennsylvania
Room 210 Walsh Hall
302 East Walk
Indiana, PA 15705
724-357-2396
www.iup.edu/sa/osha/index.html

Green Entrepreneuring

Rhode Island
OSHA Consultation Program
Division of Occupational Health & Radiation Control
Rhode Island Department of Health
3 Capital Hill
Providence, RI 02908
401-222-2438
www.state.ri.us/dohrad.htm

South Carolina
South Carolina Department of Labor, Licensing and Regulation
3600 Forest Dr.
P.O. Box 11329
Columbia, SC 29204
803-734-9614
www.llr.state.sc.us/oshavol.htm

South Dakota
Engineering Extension
Onsite Technical Division
South Dakota State University
West Hall, Box 510
907 Harvey Dunn St.
Brookings, SD 57007
605-688-4101

Tennessee
OSHA Consultation Services Division
Tennessee Department of Labor
710 James Robertson Parkway, 3rd Floor
Nashville, TN 37243
615-741-7036
www.state.tn.us/labor/toshcons.html

Texas
Workers' Health and Safety Division
Texas Workers' Compensation Commission
Southfield Building
400 South I H 35
Austin, TX 78704
512-804-4640
http://twcc.state.tx.us/services/oshcon.html

Utah
State of Utah Labor Commission
Workplace Safety and Health
Consultation Services
160 East 300 South
Salt Lake City, UT 84114
801-530-6901
www.labor.state.ut.us/Utah_Occupational_Safety_Hea/Consultation_Services/consultation_services.html

Vermont
Division of Occupational Safety & Health
Vermont Department of Labor and Industry
National Life Building, Drawer 20
Montpelier, VT 05602
802-828-2765

Virginia
Virginia Department of Labor and Industry
Occupational Safety and Health
Training and Consultation
13 South 13th St.
Richmond, VA 23219
804-786-6359
www.dli.state.va.us/programs/consultation.htm

Washington
Washington Department of Labor and Industries
Division of Industrial Safety and Health
P.O. Box 44643
Olympia, WA 98504
360-902-5638
www.wa.gov/lni/wicha/wisha.htm

West Virginia
West Virginia Department of Labor
Capitol Complex Building #3
1800 East Washington St., Room 319
Charleston, WV 25305
304-558-7890
www.state.wv.us/labor/sections.htm

Wisconsin
Wisconsin Department of Health and Human Services
Division of Public Health
Section of Occupational Health, Room 112
1414 East Washington Ave.
Madison, WI 53703
608-266-8579
www.dhfs.state.wi.us/dph_boh/OSHA_Cons/index.htm

Wyoming
Wyoming Department of Employment
Workers; Safety and Compensation Division
Herschler Building, 2 East
122 West 25th St.
Cheyenne, WY 82002
307-777-7786
http://wydoe.state.wy.us/wscd/osha/evtap.htm
205-348-3033

States with Approved Plans

States administering their own occupational safety and health programs through plans approved under section 18(b) of the Occupational Safety and Health Act of 1970 must adopt standards and enforce requirements that are at least as effective as federal requirements. There are currently 25 state plan states: 23 cover the private and public (state and local government) sectors and 2 cover the public sector only (Connecticut and New York). The following is a list of states with approved plans.

Alaska
Commissioner, Alaska Department of Labor, 1111 W. 8th St., Room 306, Juneau, AK 99801; 907-465-2700; {www.labor.state.ak.us/iss/oshhome.htm}.

Arizona
Director, Industrial Commission of Arizona, 800 W. Washington, Phoenix, AZ 85007; 602-542-5795; {www.ica.state.az.us/ADOSH/oshatop.htm}.

California
Director, California Department of Industrial Relations, 455 Golden Gate Ave., 10th Floor, San Francisco, CA 94102; 415-703-5650; {www.dir.ca.gov/DIR/OS&H/occupational_safety.html}.

Connecticut
Commissioner, Connecticut Department of Labor, 200 Folly Brook Blvd., Wethersfield, CT 06109; 860-566-5123; {www.ctdol.state.ct.us}.

Hawaii
Director, Hawaii Department of Labor and Industrial Relations, 830 Punchbowl Street, Honolulu, HI 96813; 808-586-8844; {www.state.hi.us/dir/niosh/}.

Indiana
Commissioner, Indiana Department of Labor, State Office Building, 402 W. Washington St., Room W195, Indianapolis, IN 46204; 317-232-2378; {www.state.in.us/labor/iosha/iosha.html}.

Iowa
Commissioner, Iowa Division of Labor Services, 1000 E. Grand Ave., Des Moines, IA 50319; 515-281-3447; {www.state.ia.us/iwd/labor/index.html}.

Kentucky
Secretary, Kentucky Labor Cabinet, 1049 U.S. Hwy, 127 South, Frankfort, KY 40601; 502-564-3070; {www.state.ky.us/agencies/labor/kyosh.htm}.

Maryland
Commissioner, Maryland Department of Labor, Licensing and Regulation, 1100 N.

Green Entrepreneuring

Eutaw St., Room 613, Baltimore, MD 21201; 410-767-2999; {www.dllr.state.md.us/labor/niosh.html}.

Michigan
Director, Michigan Department of Consumer and Industry Services, P.O. Box 30643, Lansing, MI 48909; 517-322-1814; {www.cis.state.mi.us/bsr}.

Minnesota
Commissioner, Minnesota Department of Labor and Industry, 443 Lafayette Rd., St. Paul, MN 55155; 651-296-2342; {www.doli.state.mn.us/mnosha.html}.

Nevada
Director, Division of Industrial Relations, 400 W. King St., Carson City, NV 89502; 702-687-3032; {www.state.nv.us/b&i/ir/}.

New Mexico
Secretary, New Mexico Environmental Department, Occupational Health and Safety Bureau,, 1190 St. Francis Dr., P.O. Box 26110, Santa Fe, NM 87502; 505-827-2850; {www.nmenv.state.nm.us/Ohsb/oshahome.htm}.

New York
Commissioner, New York Department of Labor, State Office Bldg., Campus 12, Room 457, Albany, NY 12240; 518-457-2741; {www.labor.state.ny.us/html/safety/saf_hlth.htm}.

North Carolina
Commissioner, North Carolina Department of Labor, 4 W. Edenton St., Raleigh, NC 27601; 919-807-7166; {www.dol.state.nc.us/osha/osh.htm}.

Oregon
Administrator, Oregon Occupational Safety and Health Division, Department of Consumer and Business Services, Labor and Industries Bldg., 350 Winter St., NE, Room 430, Salem, OR 97310; 503-378-3272, 800-922-2689; {www.cbs.state.or.us/external/osha}.

Puerto Rico
Secretary, Puerto Rico Department of Labor and Human Resources, Prudencio Rivera Martinez Bldg., 505 Munoz Rivera Ave., Hato Rey, PR 00918; 787-754-2119.

South Carolina
Commissioner, South Carolina Department of Labor, Licensing and Regulation, 110 Centerview Dr., P.O. Box 11329, Columbia, SC 29210; 803-896-4300; {www.llr.state.sc.us/OCSAFE.HTM}.

Tennessee
Commissioner, Tennessee Department of Labor,, Attn: Robert Taylor, 710 James Robertson Pkwy., Gateway Plaza, Suite "A", 2nd Floor, Nashville, TN 37243-0655; 615-741-2582; {www.state.tn.us/labor/}.

Utah
Commissioner, Industrial Commission of Utah, 160 E. 300 S, P.O. Box 146650, Salt Lake City, UT 84110; 801-530-6901; {www.labor.state.ut.us}.

Vermont
Commissioner, Vermont Department of labor and Industry, 120 State St., Montpelier, VT 05620; 802-828-2288; {www.state.vt.us/labind/vosha.htm}.

Virgin Islands
Commissioner, Virgin Island Department of Labor, 2203 Church St., Christiansted, St. Croix, VI 00820; 340-773-1994.

Virginia
Commissioner, Virginia Department of Labor and Industry, Powers-Taylor Bldg., 13 S. 13th St., Richmond, VA 23219; 804-786-2383; {www.dli.state.va.us/programs/safety.htm}.

Washington
Director, Washington Department of Labor and Industries, P.O. Box 44001, Olympia, WA 98504-4001; 360-902-4200; {www.lni.wa.gov/wisha}.

Wyoming
Occupational Safety and Health Administration, Herschler Bldg., 122 W. 25th St., Cheyenne, WY 82002; 307-777-7786; {http://wydoe.state.wy.us/wscd/osha/}.

* Manuals Show How Much Pollution Is In Your Business
National Service Center for Environmental Publications
U.S. Environmental Protection Agency
P.O. Box 42419
Cincinnati, OH 45242   800-490-9195
www.epa.gov/ncepihom/index.html

The Office of Research and Development has several publications on a wide variety of environmental topics. These manuals and guides are very technical in nature, but are an invaluable resource for your business or industry. Some of the publications include:
- *The Pesticide Formulating Industry*
- *The Paint Manufacturing Industry*
- *The Fabricate Metal Industry*
- *The Printed Circuit Board Manufacturing Industry*
- *The Commercial Printing Industry*
- *Selected Hospital Waste Streams*
- *Research and Educational Institutions*

* Free Research For Employee's Health Problems
National Health Information Center
Office of Disease Prevention and Health Promotion (ODPHP)
P.O. Box 1133   301-565-4167
Washington, DC 20013   1-800-336-4797
http://nhic_nt.health.org

U.S. businesses have begun implementing health education/promotion programs at worksites to help keep employees healthy and to help contain long-term health care costs. Simultaneously, groups of local businesses throughout the country have established coalitions for the purpose of implementing plans to reduce health care costs. Many of these groups view worksite health promotion programs, such as physical fitness, stress management, weight control, smoking cessation, nutrition, and drug and alcohol awareness, as an effective strategy that will contribute to achieving their goals. The National Health Information Center can provide you with publications and brochures on a wide variety of health topics, and can refer you to organizations which can help you set up programs at your place of business. This could be a one day event to test for high blood pressure, a blood donation program, free speakers, or more extensive health promotion programs.

* Save Water and Water Costs
National Small Flows Clearinghouse
West Virginia University
P.O. Box 6064   304-293-4191
Morgantown, WV 26506   1-800-624-8301
www.estd.wvu.edu/NSFC_homepage.html

One leaky faucet can use up to 4,000 gallons of water a month. By installing a faucet aerator you can reduce water use by 60 percent while maintaining a strong flow. Building fewer and smaller new water projects can help preserve wetlands, which naturally treat pollutants. Efficient water use means less power needed to pump and treat water and wastewater. The National Small Flows Clearinghouse or your local utility company can help you with these problems.

* Is Your Water At Work Safe To Drink Hotline
Safe Drinking Water Hotline
U.S. Environmental Protection Agency   1-800-426-4791
www.epa.gov/OGWDW

The chemicals and pesticides used every day eventually seep into our water table, thereby getting into your drinking water. Even the lead solder used to hold our pipes together becomes a hazard. The Safe Drinking Water Hotline can answer any question or concern you may have regarding your drinking water. They have an extensive list of publications, covering topics like water systems, lead, and volatile organic chemicals in your water. They can also provide you with information on ways to get your water tested as well as information on water purification techniques.

* Radon and Asbestos Can Be Silent Trouble In Your Office
Indoor Air Quality Information Clearinghouse
P.O. Box 37133   703-893-6600
Washington, DC 20013   800-438-4318
www.epa.gov/iaq/radon/

You can't feel it, taste it, or smell it, yet radon can be contaminating the air in your place of work. Asbestos was used for insulation many years ago, and now we know

Green Entrepreneuring

the danger it can cause. The Public Information Center at the U.S. Environmental Protection Agency has extensive literature on both of these topics including information on ways to remove radon and asbestos safely. They can also refer you to experts in the field that can provide you with up to the minute research.

* Video Shows What To Do About Radon

Contact your County Cooperative Extension Service
listed under county government in your telephone book
or
Cooperative Extension Service
University of Maryland System
Video Resource Center
0120 Symons Hall
College Park, MD 20742   301-405-4591

A video called *Radon: What Is It and What You Can Do About It*, explains the nature of radon and the dangers of high radon levels. It features steps toward determining radon levels as well as ways in which radon can be controlled. It is available for free from many of the local County Cooperative Extension Service Offices or for sale for $25 from the University of Maryland extension service at the address above.

* Will Your Employees Get Carpal Tunnel Syndrome?

National Institute for Occupational Safety and Health
4676 Columbia Parkway
Cincinnati, Ohio 45226   1-800-356-4674
www.cdc.gov/niosh

Carpal Tunnel Syndrome is a tingling sensation in the hands and fingers and can be caused or aggravated by repeated twisting or awkward postures, particularly when combined with high force. The population at risk includes persons employed in such industries or occupations as construction, food preparation, clerical work, product fabrication and mining. The National Institute for Occupational Safety and Health provides free information on this syndrome including the latest developments in research, preventive recommendations, and bibliographies.

* Are Your Video Display Terminals Making Your Employees Sick?

National Institute for Occupational Safety and Health
4676 Columbia Parkway
Cincinnati, OH 45226   1-800-356-4674
www.cdc.gov/niosh

Over one million people each day sit down to work in front of a computer terminal, imputing and outputing information. There have been concerns about its effect on people's eyesight, its effects on pregnant women, and its potential for causing carpal tunnel syndrome. The National Institute for Occupational Safety and Health offers a free booklet describing the latest research covering all these issues.

* State By State Listing of EPA Offices

Your State EPA office can be a gold mine of information for all your environmental needs. They have information on your state laws regarding hazardous waste, superfund sites, air pollution and drinking water. These offices also have pamphlets, brochures and fact sheets on a wide variety of topics, and can refer you to experts in your state for further information. Some examples of information the state offices provide include:
1)   A listing of superfund sites in your state as well as their current status
2)   The emergency planning and community right to know program requires anyone who stores, uses, generates or releases hazardous materials to identify the chemicals and report the locations and volume. Your state EPA office can supply you with this information.
3)   This office has publications and other information about pollution prevention for your home or office, as well as pollution prevention activities in your state.

Alabama
Environmental Management Department
1400 Coliseum Blvd.
Montgomery, AL 36110   334-271-7700
www.adem.state.al.us

Alaska
Department of Environmental Conservation
410 Willoughby Ave.
Juneau, AK 99801-1795   907-465-5060
www.state.ak.us

Arizona
Department of Environmental Quality
3033 N. Central Avenue   602-207-2300
Phoenix, AZ 85012   800-234-5677
www.adeq.state.az.us

Arkansas
Arkansas Department of Environmental Quality
8001 National Dr.
Little Rock, AR 72209   501-682-0744
www.adeq.state.ar.us

California
Environmental Protection Agency
555 Capitol Mall, Suite 525
Sacramento, CA 95814   916-445-3846
www.calepa.ca.gov

Colorado
Department of Public Health & Environment
4300 Cherry Creek Dr. S
Denver, CO 80222-1530   303-692-2000
www.cdphe.state.co.us

Connecticut
Environmental Protection Department
79 Elm St.
Hartford, CT 06106-1632   860-424-3000
http://dep.state.ct.us

Delaware
Natural Resources and Environmental Control Department
89 Kings Hwy.
Dover, DE 19901   302-739-3820
www.dnrec.state.de.us

District of Columbia
Department of Consumer and Regulatory Affairs
614 H. Street, NW, Room 505
Washington, DC 20001   202-727-7395

Florida
Department of Environmental Protection
3900 Commonwealth Blvd.
Tallahassee, FL 32399   850-488-1554
www.dep.state.fl.us

Georgia
Department of Natural Resources
4244 International Pkwy, #104
Atlanta, GA 30354   404-362-2692
www.dnr.state.ga.us

Hawaii
Department of Land and Natural Resources
1151 Punchbowl St., Room 130
Honolulu, HI 96813   808-587-0405
www.hawaii.gov/dlnr

Idaho
Environmental Quality Division
Department of Health and Welfare
1410 N. Hilton St.
Boise, ID 83706   208-373-0502
www.state.id.us/deq

Illinois
Environmental Protection Agency
325 W. Adams St., Room 300
Springfield, IL 62704   217-785-2800

Green Entrepreneuring

Indiana
Department of Environmental Management
P.O. Box 6015
Indianapolis, IN 46206-6015
www.ai.org/idem

800-451-6027
317-232-8603

Iowa
Environmental Protection Division
Department of Natural Resources
Wallace Building, 900 E. Grand Ave.
Des Moines, IA 50319
www.state.ia.us/government/dnr/index.htm

515-281-8975

Kansas
Environment Division
Department of Health and Environment
400 SW 8th St., 2nd Floor
Topeka, KS 66603
www.kdhe.state.ks.us

785-296-1500

Kentucky
Natural Resources and Environmental Protection
Capital Plaza Tower
Frankfort, KY 40601
www.nr.state.ky.us/nrhome.htm

502-564-5525

Louisiana
Department of Environmental Quality
P.O. Box 82263
Baton Rouge, LA 70884-2263
www.deq.state.la.us

225-765-0741

Maine
Environmental Protection Department
State House Station #17
Augusta, ME 04333
http://janus.state.me.us/dep/home.htm

207-287-7688

Maryland
Maryland Department of the Environment
2500 Broening Highway
Baltimore, MD 21224
www.mde.state.md.us

800-633-6101
410-631-3000

Massachusetts
Department of Environmental Protection
1 Winter St., 4th Floor
Boston, MA 02108
www.magnet.state.ma.us/dep/dephome.htm

617-292-5500

Michigan
Environmental Protection Bureau
Department of Environmental Quality
P.O. Box 30473
Lansing, MI 48909
www.deq.state.mi.us

517-373-7917

Minnesota
Pollution Control Agency
520 Lafayette Road
St. Paul, MN 55155
www.pca.state.mn.us

800-657-3864
651-296-6360

Mississippi
Environmental Quality Department
P.O. Box 20305
Jackson, MS 39289-0385
www.deq.state.ms.us

601-961-5171

Missouri
Department of Natural Resources
P.O. Box 176
Jefferson City, MO 65102-0176
www.dnr.state.mo.us

800-334-6946
573-751-5401

Montana
Department of Environmental Quality
1520 E. Sixth Avenue
Helena, MT 59620
www.deq.state.mt.us

406-444-2544

Nebraska
Department of Environmental Quality
P.O. Box 98922
Lincoln, NE 68509
www.deq.state.ne.us

402-471-2186

Nevada
Environmental Protection Division
333 W. Nye Lane
Capital Complex
Carson City, NV 89706
www.state.nv.us/ndep/index.htm

775-687-4670

New Hampshire
Department of Environmental Services
6 Hazen Drive
Concord, NH 03302
www.des.state.nh.us/descover.htm

603-271-3503

New Jersey
Department of Environmental Protection
CN 402
Trenton, NJ 08625-0414
www.state.nj.us/dep

609-292-2885

New Mexico
Environment Department
P.O. Box 26110
Santa Fe, NM 87502-6110
www.nmenv.state.nm.us

800-219-6157
505-827-2855

New York
Department of Environmental Conservation
50 Wolf Road
Albany, NY 12233-4013
www.dec.state.ny.us

518-457-5400

North Carolina
Environment, Health and Natural Resources Department
1601 MSC
Raleigh, NC 27699
www.enr.state.nc.us

877-623-6748
919-733-4984

North Dakota
Environmental Health Section
Department of Health
P.O. Box 5520
Bismarck, ND 58506-5520
www.health.state.nd.us/ndhd/environ/

701-328-5150

Ohio
Environmental Protection Agency
122 S. Front St.
Columbus, OH 43215
www.epa.state.oh.us

614-644-3020

Oklahoma
Department of Environmental Quality
707 N. Robinson
Oklahoma City, OK 73102
www.deq.state.ok.us

800-869-1400
405-702-9100

Oregon
Department of Environmental Quality
811 SW Sixth Avenue
Portland, OR 97204
www.deq.state.or.us

800-452-4011
503-229-5696

Green Entrepreneuring

Pennsylvania
Department of Environmental Protection
P.O. Box 2063
Harrisburg, PA 17105-2063   717-787-7382
www.dep.state.pa.us

Rhode Island
Department of Environmental Management
235 Promenade St.
Providence, RI 02908   401-222-6822
www.state.ri.us/dem

South Carolina
Division of Environmental Quality Control
Department of Health and Environmental Control
2600 Bull Street
Columbia, SC 29201   803-898-3900
www.state.sc.us/dhqc/eqc

South Dakota
Environment and Natural Resources Department
523 E. Capital Ave.
Pierre, SD 57501   605-773-5559
www.state.sd.us/state/executive/denr/denr.html

Tennessee
Environment and Conservation Department
401 Church St., L&C Tower, 19th Floor   888-891-TDEC
Nashville, TN 37243-0455   615-532-0091
www.state.tn.us/environment

Texas
Natural Resource Conservation Commission
P.O. Box 13087
Austin, TX 78711-3087   512-239-1000
www.tnrcc.state.tx.us

Utah
Department of Environmental Quality
P.O. Box 144810   800-458-0145
Salt Lake City, UT 84114   801-536-4400
www.eq.state.ut.us

Vermont
Vermont Agency of Natural Resources
103 S. Main St., Laundry Bldg.
Waterbury, VT 05671-0407   802-241-3600
www.anr.state.vt.us

Virginia
Department of Environmental Quality
629 E. Main St.   800-592-5482
Richmond, VA 23219   804-698-4000
www.deq.state.vt.us

Washington
Department of Ecology
P.O. Box 47600   800-RECYCLE
Olympia, WA 98504-7600   360-407-6000
www.wa.gov/ecology

West Virginia
Division of Natural Resources
1900 Kanawha Blvd.
Charleston, WV 25305   304-558-5993
www.dnr.state.wv.us

Wisconsin
Division of Environmental Protection
Department of Natural Resources
P.O. Box 7921
Madison, WI 53707-7921   608-267-7566
www.dnr.state.wi.us/Environment.html

Wyoming
Department of Environmental Quality
122 W. 25th St.
Cheyenne, WY 82002   307-777-7758
http://deq.state.wy.us

* Regional Environmental Offices Offer Help
To insure that Environmental Protection Agency (EPA) is truly responsive to the American People, it has established regional offices which cooperate with federal, state, inter-state and local agencies, industry and academic institutions, to insure that regional needs are considered and federal environmental laws implemented. They can answer your questions regarding EPA rules and regulations as well as questions on a wide variety of environmental topics.

EPA Region 1
(CT, MA, ME, NH, RI, VT)
1 Congress St.   888-EPA-7341
Boston, MA 02114   617-918-1010
www.epa.gov/regional/

EPA Region 2
(NJ, NY, Puerto Rico, Virgin Islands)
290 Broadway
New York, NY 10007-1866   212-637-3000
www.epa.gov/Region2

Field Component
Caribbean Field Office
1492 Ponce de Leon Ave.
Santurce, PR 00909   787-729-6951

EPA Region 3
(DE, MD, PA, VA, WV, DC)
1650 Arch St.
Philadelphia, PA 19103   215-814-5254
www.epa.gov/region03/

EPA Region 4
(AL, FL, GA, KY, MS, NC, SC, TN)
61 Forsyth St., SW   800-241-1754
Atlanta, GA 30303   404-562-9900
www.epa.gov/region4/reg4.html

EPA Region 5
(IL, IN, MI, MN, OH, WI)
77 West Jackson Blvd.   800-621-8431
Chicago, IL 60604   312-353-2000
www.epa.gov/Region5

Field Component
Eastern District Office
25089 Center Ridge Road
West Lake, OH 44145   216-835-5200

EPA Region 6
(AK, LA, NM, OK, TX)
1445 Ross Avenue   800-887-6063
Dallas, TX 75202-2733   214-665-2200
www.epa.gov/earth1r6/

EPA Region 7
(IA, KS, MO, NE)
901 N. 5th St.   800-223-0425
Kansas City, KS 66101   913-551-7003
www.epa.gov/rgytgrnj/

EPA Region 8
(CO, MT, ND, SD, UT, WY)
One Denver Place
999 18th Street   800-227-8917
Denver, CO, 80202-2405   303-312-6318
www.epa.gov/region08/

Green Entrepreneuring

EPA Region 9
(AZ, CA, HI, NV, American Samoa, Guam,
Trust Temtones of the Pacific)
75 Hawthorne Street
San Francisco, CA 94105   415-744-1500
www.epa.gov/region09/

Field Component
Pacific Islands Office
P.O. Box 50003
300 Ala Moana Boulevard, Room 5124
Honolulu, HI 96850   808-541-2710

EPA Region 10
(AK, ID, OR, WA)
1200 Sixth Avenue   800-424-4EPA
Seattle, WA 98101   206-553-1200
www.epa.gov/r10earth/

Videos From Uncle Sam To Help Your Business

Titles like these you're not going to find in your local video store:

Industrial Loss Control Through Behavior Management,
How To Market, Promote and Prepare a Business Plan,
How To Prepare a Balance Sheet,
How to Start a Home Based-Business, or
Always Wear the Right Stuff.

But, you will find them in the government and thousands more like them, if you know where to look. The government is not like a private business that will spend a few thousand dollars to produce a "how-to video" and then spend millions in advertising its availability. The government can easily spend millions in production costs for their videos and then not spend a nickel to let the public know about them.

Here's your chance to view some of these little-known videos. The list below is a sampling of some of the more interesting videos that should be relevant to entrepreneurs. Many of the videos are available on a loan basis. Some of the videos are available on a loan basis only to nonprofit organizations, like a local women's group or professional society, and others may be seen for a small viewing fee.

* How High Technology Will Affect Your Business

Audiovisual Communications
Public and Business Affairs, Room A903
National Institute of Standards and Technology (NIST)
Gaithersburg, MD 20899-0001   301-975-2761

The National Institute of Standards and Technology (NIST), the nation's technology laboratory, produces all kinds of videos about their research and how it can be applied to solve current industry problems. Videos are available on a free loan basis.

The videos listed below are just a sample of the audiovisuals available. Contact the office listed above for a complete listing.

The Next Generation of Enhanced Machine Controllers. Describes the Enhanced Machine Controller program that was set up to identify what interfaces are important to open architecture controllers and promote their standardization so that plug and play compatibility of manufacturing technology can be realized.

Introduction to Life-Cycle Costing: Part I, Least-Cost Energy Decisions for Buildings. Provides building design professionals with the basics needed to evaluate decisions affecting the energy use of buildings. The program is the first in a series of videotapes developed by NIST for the Department of Energy to promote the use of economic analysis to improve the long-run economy of buildings.

Color Under Energy Efficient Lighting (22m, free loan). Describes work done at the National Institute of Standards and Technology on how energy-efficient lighting systems can affect the way colors look, and provides suggestions for designing such lighting systems for commercial, industrial, and institutional buildings.

* How To Help Your Employees With Drug or Alcohol Problems

National Clearinghouse for Alcohol   800-729-6686
   and Drug Information   301-468-2600
P.O. Box 2345   Spanish: 877-767-8432
Rockville, MD 20847-2345   TDD: 800-487-4889
E-mail: info@health.org   Fax: 301-468-6433
   Online Publication form   http://www.health.org/pubs/catalog/OrderFrm.htm

Is there a problem with some of your employees' work habits? Are some coming in late or not at all? It could be that drugs or alcohol are involved. The National Institute of Drug Abuse is developing programs to eliminate illegal drug use in the workplace. Its programs include research, treatment, training and prevention activities, as well as projects related to the development of a comprehensive Drug-Free Workplace programs. They will analyze and recommend Employee Assistance Programs (EAP). Videos are available for a recovery fee of $12.50 each.

Drugs At Work (employee/employer versions) - Presents information about the nature and scope of the alcohol and drug problem in the workplace and about the federal government's initiative to prevent and reduce the problem.

Getting Help (employee/employer versions) - Highlights the benefits of an effective employee assistance program to employees and employers through comments by business, labor, and government leaders and EAP professionals.

Drug Testing: Handle With Care (employee/employer versions) - Describes the options available for designing a drug testing component as part of a comprehensive drug-free workplace program.

Finding Solutions - Drug abuse in the workplace is portrayed as a community-wide problem. The solutions offered through education and prevention are presented as personal, workplace, and community responsibilities.

America in Jeopardy: The Young Employee in the Workplace - Using interviews with recovering drug addicts, this video warns viewers that mixing drugs and work is a big mistake and encourages viewers to seek help for themselves or others.

* Worker Safety, Chemical and Physical Hazards

Various state and federal agencies have produced hundreds of videos for loan or purchase on a huge range of worker safety topics. Selected examples of specific titles are listed below, but calls to the agency offices will get you the videos that are right for your circumstances.

U.S. Department of Labor
OSHA Office of Public Affairs
200 Constitution Avenue, NW, Room N3647
Washington, DC 20210   202-693-1904

The Occupational Safety and Health Administration offers free loan videos on worker safety topics such as preventing back injuries, handling tools safely, drug abuse in the workplace, and AIDS prevention. Contact the Public Affairs Office for an up-to-date listing of available videos.

NIOSH-TV
Attn: Roger Wheeler
4676 Columbia Parkway
Mail Stop C-13   513-533-8261
Cincinnati, OH 45226   Fax: 513-533-8560
E-mail: rlw3@cdc.gov
http://www.cdc.gov/niosh/tapes.html

These tapes from the National Institute for Safety and Health tend to be rather technical, intended for engineers, scientists, managers and teachers. Just a small

Videos From Uncle Sam To Help Your Business

sample of titles includes, *As It Should Be Done (Blood Borne Pathogens), Biological and Animal Hazards, Chemical Procurement and Inventory Control, Confined Space Entry, Evaluation of Industrial Hoods, Filter Mounting Procedure, Fire Prevention and Control, Hazard Communication for Small Business Professionals, Industrial Loss Control Through Behavior Management,* and *Legal Aspects of Laboratory Safety.* For a complete listing, call NIOSH-TV or visit the website {http://www.cdc.gov/niosh/tapes.html}. To order, send a written request by post, fax or E-mail to Roger Wheeler at the above address.

    The National Ag Safety Database
    http://www.cdc.gov/niosh/nasd/video/avhome.html

Don't let the "ag"—short for agriculture—put you off this resource, which lists hundreds of video tapes on topics such as back safety, handling chemicals, fire safety, first aid, gun safety, hearing conservation, horticulture and landscape maintenance safety, ladder safety, chain saw safety, welding safety, personal protective equipment, supervising for safety, and worker's compensation. This online catalog includes a brief description of each tape and how to borrow or purchase it.

    Electronic Library of Construction Safety and Health
    http://www.cdc.gov/niosh/elcosh.html

Access to important information on construction worker safety should become considerably easier after August 2000, when this website is expected to be completed. Modeled after the National Ag Safety Database, this electronic catalog will point the way toward print and video resources for the construction industry. In the meantime, you can contact the library's creators c/o Center to Protect Workers' Rights, 5th Floor, 111 Massachusetts Ave., NW, Washington, DC 20001; 202-962-8490.

    National Audiovisual Center
    National Technical Information Center
    Technology Administration
    U.S. Department of Commerce   800-553-6847
    Springfield, VA 22161   703-605-6000
    http://www.ntis.gov/about.htm

With more than 9,000 audiovisual and media productions grouped into more than 600 individual subject headings, the National Audiovisual Center (NAC) provides centralized access to federally developed training and education materials. Although this service is designed for purchasing materials, many agencies loan videos upon request. You can use the database to search topics, then contact the public affairs office of the agency that produced it and request a loan. Here are just two of the videos found searching "safety."

    Finest Tools. Produced by the National Institute for Occupational Safety and Health Public Health Service, this video covers the nature of cumulative trauma disorders of the hand and wrist, e.g., carpal tunnel syndrome. Dr. Lynne Moody describes how repetitive jobs can damage a worker's body. Dan Habes describes how to analyze a job to determine how stressful it is. The video also shows practical examples of how jobs can be altered to stress the worker less. NTIS order number AVA09952-VM00INA.

    Accident Prevention through Equipment Guarding. Produced by the Mine Safety and Health Administration, Arlington, VA, this video shows the need for proper safety guards on industrial equipment such as conveyors, drive units, motor shafts, and other machinery with exposed gears, pulleys, belts, and hazardous moving parts. Various types of safety guarding devices are shown, with emphasis on proper installation, maintenance and repair. Emphasizes the advantages of a well-planned safety guarding program aimed at increasing awareness and worker involvement. NTIS Order Number AVA07787-VNBIINA.

* Starting a Small Business, Keeping Records, and Paying Taxes

Both the Small Business Administration and the Internal Revenue Service have made a major shift in how they provide information for their customers, with older audiovisual materials being replaced by online publications and CD-ROMs. Together, the two federal agencies have created one *free* CD-ROM that includes information business persons should know before going into business, and tax information needed for operating a business, expanding a business, and closing, selling or changing a business structure. This CD-ROM contains all of the IRS business forms and publications, plus information on how to electronically file and pay your taxes. You can order your free copy of the "Small Business Resource Guide" CD-ROM online at {http://www.irs.gov/bus_info/sm_bus/smbus-cd.html} or call IRS at 800-829-3676. Please ask for IRS Publication 3207 when ordering your copy.

The Small Business Administration has produced a series of videos that may be viewed at any of the more than 30 Business information Centers (BICs) across the country. To find the location of the BIC nearest you, call the SBA's Office of Business Initiatives at 202-205-6665, or find a listing online by visiting the website {www.sba.gov/gopher/Local-Information/BIC}. Please be sure to call ahead before you visit a BIC, since not all the centers will have all the tapes in stock.

    Marketing: Winning Customers With a Workable Plan. Take advantage of this easy-to-follow course and develop the marketing plan designed to meet your goals. Developed by two of the country's leading small business marketing experts, this hands-on program offers a step-by-step approach to writing the best possible marketing plan for your business. #VT01

    The Business Plan: Your Road Map to Success. Learn the essentials of developing a business plan that will lead you to capital, growth and profitability. This video teaches you what to include, what to omit, and how to get free help from qualified consultants when developing your business plan. #VT02.

    Promotion Solving the Puzzle. Master the components that make a successful promotional campaign — advertising, public relations, direct mail and trade shows. This videotape shows you how to put the pieces together. Learn how to choose the best advertising medium for your needs, and much more. #VT03.

    Home-Based Business: A Winning Blueprint. This practical program examines the essentials of operating within a productive and profitable home-based business — from designing your home office and avoiding isolation to networking strategies and building an image that gets you taken seriously. #VT04.

    Basics of Exporting. This videotape shows you how to open the doors to international markets. This tape provides information on getting your goods overseas, payment mechanisms, selling and distributing overseas, international marketing and sources of financial assistance. #VT05.

* How To Inspect A Home Before You Invest
    School of Architecture-Building Research Council
    University of Illinois at Urbana-Champaign
    1 East St. Mary's Road
    Champaign, IL 61820   800-336-0616
    http://www.arch.uiuc.edu/brc/

From Roof to Foundation follows a building inspection expert on a home tour, and shows examples of what to look for when considering buying a home. The film is produced by a member of the County Cooperative Extension service and is available on a free loan basis at local county cooperative extension service offices throughout the country. Call your local operator for your nearest office. You may purchase this 30-minute video for $29.95 from the Building Research Council.

* Financial Planning to Rattlesnakes — Local Cooperative Extension Services Could Have It On Tape

    Contact Your Local County Cooperative Extension Service

Hundreds of helpful videos are available on a free loan basis through your local County Government Cooperative Extension Service. The available programs differ from state to state, and you should contact your local office to see what titles are available to you. Listed below are some of the titles produced by various extension service offices:

- *Risk Management*
- *Types of Investments*
- *Investment Series: The Fundamentals (Part I)*
- *Investment Series: The Fundamentals (Part II)*
- *Family and Economic Well Being: 5 Critical Issues*
- *The Choice is Yours: Housing Options for Seniors Today*
- *Packing Your Home To Sell*
- *You're Accountable: How To Select and Use Financial Accounts*
- *Cake Decorating*
- *Bread Baking*
- *Microwave Cooking*
- *Removing Rattlesnakes from Human Dwellings*
- *Pruning Walnut Trees For Profit*
- *How To Calibrate a Manure Spreader*
- *Baby Pig and Sow Management*
- *Getting Rid of Stinky Neighbors - Skunk Control in Residential Areas*

Videos From Uncle Sam To Help Your Business

However, don't stop looking just because your local extension service doesn't have what you need. The U.S. Department of Agriculture's Extension Services offers "E-answers," a searchable website that gives you access to research-based information available from Land Grant universities around the nation. Searchable topics include agriculture, forestry, fishing, family/consumer issues, lawn and garden, child development, 4-H/youth, environment, public policy, economics, water quality and communities. "E-Answers" can also take you directly to ordering information for the many publications and audiovisual materials available nationwide. Search this website at {http://www.e-answers.org}.

* Business Training from Cornell University

Cornell University Resource Center
7 Business and Technology Park   607-255-2080
Ithaca, NY 14850   Fax: 607-255-9946
http://www.cce.cornell.edu/publications/catalog.html

Cornell University's Cooperative Extension Service offers literally *hundreds* of videos on business-related topics available for rent or purchase. Rental fees are usually in the $10-$15 range per title, including shipping. Special collections include more than 200 titles in "Industrial and Labor Relations," and the 100 titles in the "Southeast Asia" collection would be invaluable to anyone considering doing business in that part of the world. The faculty at Cornell has produced an original video series on business-related topics, which are also available for sale or rent. You may be able to find some of the titles listed below in your local cooperative extension service office. Shipping for purchases costs $1 per order. New York State residents need to include 8 percent sales tax or provide a tax exempt number.

Counseling Skills for Financial Managers. Used to train budget counselors and others who help people solve financial problems. Counseling basics include types of approaches and a review of basic skills. Shows a budget counselor working with a client at the initial interview. Discusses motivating clients to return, helping clients identify alternatives, dealing with distressed clients, and more. 52 min. Video 325VCSFM. $24.95.

Suburban Deer Management: Voices, Views, Visions. Explains the causes of deer overpopulation, describes health and safety concerns and property damage, explains the positive and negative effects and controversy of various solutions, and suggests ways to determine the best solutions for individual communities. 28 min. Video 147VSDM. $19.95.

Always Wear the Right Stuff! Pesticide users can reduce the risk of pesticide problems and contamination by wearing certain protective clothing and equipment. Spanish appears after English on the same videotape. Video 329VAWTRS (English: 26 min./Spanish: 34 min.). $19.95.

Compost: Because a Rind is a Terrible Thing to Waste. Detailed guidance for large institutions and businesses to implement food scrap composting through source separation of scraps and composting either on-site or collection for composting elsewhere. A 65-page manual includes worksheets, and describes the experiences and cost savings realized in nine case studies. A 30-minute video shows how source separation and composting are done. A 7-minute tape describes the benefits and is aimed at convincing decision-makers in the business or institution. ISBN 1-57753-158-2. Video 174VCBRWPKG (Manual with both videos). $35.00.

* Hundreds of Business-Related Videos From a Single Government Source

National Audiovisual Center
National Technical Information Center
Technology Administration
U.S. Department of Commerce   800-553-6847
Springfield, VA 22161   703-605-6000
http://www.ntis.gov/about.htm

With more than 9,000 audiovisual and media productions grouped into more than 600 individual subject headings, the National Audiovisual Center (NAC) provides centralized access to federally developed training and education materials. A quick search yielded titles such as *Child Care and Facility Management, Consumer Tax Video—Employee or Independent Contractor?, Sales Promotion,* and *Labor and Employment Practices.* Although this service is designed for purchasing materials, many agencies loan videos upon request. You can use the database to search topics, then contact the public affairs office of the agency that produced it and request a loan. You can obtain a free catalog of new and best-selling titles by calling the 800 number listed above, or search the entire catalog online.

* Help for Home-Based Businesses

OSU Ag Communications
Room 116, PIO Building
Stillwater, OK 74078-6041   405-744-5398
http://agweb.okstate.edu/pearl/video

Some of these videos may be available for loan to Oklahoma residents from local cooperative extension services. They are available for purchase for $24.95 each, which includes shipping and handling within the United States.

Using Computers in a Home-Based Business. The viewer is given a general introduction to computers. The video was produced for home-based business owners, but could be used as a starting point for anyone who is thinking of buying a computer. It covers general computer applications and how to start a search for a computer system. (VT 353, 15 min.).

Home-Based Business: Putting It All Together. Business experts — a certified public accountant, attorney, professional writer and home-based business owners — give advice and relate experiences on researching the market, developing a plan, keeping simplified records for taxes, creating a business image, legal structures and constraints, and family/business interactions. (TC 34, 90 min.).

Mapping Your Marketing Future. This videoconference features successful business operators/owners sharing their knowledge and insight on how to successfully market home-based and micro-based businesses. In addition to two "case studies", the program features a panel discussion with five business owners, plus a question and answer session from the original, live telecast of the program. Emphasis is given to the four "P's" of marketing: positioning, production, pricing and promotion. (TC 153, 1 hour).

First Steps for Job Hunters and Career Changers. Ready to start a job hunt? Begin your search with this video, as you learn the basics about the job search process. Six sections show you how: 1) The Job Search, 2) Assessing Job Skills, 3) Your Resume, 4) The Job Application, 5) The Job Interview, and 6) Starting the Job. Advice is given to those employed in production agriculture as they identify skills which can be used in non-farm jobs. (VT 83, 69 min.).

Money and Help To Companies Which Want To Use or Sell Technology

It is not uncommon today for many small technology-based businesses to fail simply because the owners aren't aware of the state programs that could significantly reduce their crucial, first year start-up costs. If a new company needs some kind of technical service assistance for which private consulting firms charge large amounts of money, chances are that an appropriate state program is available to do it for much less. Why pay consulting firms thousands of dollars of your hard-to-come-by start-up capital for financial planning and product refinement when free or low cost help is available? Many states have programs that will provide assistance at no cost or at reduced rates simply because your company is a technology-oriented small business.

It is no secret that successful businesses are run by people who either know all the right information themselves or know where to find it. So, before your company spends a dime on technical problem-solving in Maryland, for example, you should know to call the Technology Extension Service, which just may be able to solve the problem for free. Or, before you spend hundreds of dollars for preliminary patent searches in Wisconsin, you should know to call the University-Industry Research program, which can do it for about $15. But, to save the money, you need to know where to get this important information.

To keep up with the rapidly growing advanced technology-based industries in the U.S., over half of the states have developed program offices that cater to the special needs of these businesses. Aside from administering the individual programs, these offices often act as information clearinghouses and referral services for those interested in any of their state's technology-related services. Instead of having to go to ten different offices for information on such programs as technical assistance, business planning, and technology transfer, these central offices provide, in many cases, one-stop information shopping.

Since many of these offices are closely associated with their state's Department of Economic Development, you can get information on, let's say, technical assistance, venture capital, product marketing strategies, and managerial assistance all in the same place.

Unfortunately, many states do not yet have such umbrella organizations to oversee and coordinate their state technology initiatives, and your state may be one of them. If that's the case, don't automatically assume that there are no special programs for technology-oriented businesses in your state. Start at your state's Department of Economic Development or Commerce, or Small Business Association to find out what programs are offered to address your particular needs. You also might try your state universities, which may have technology-oriented and business assistance programs. Also, call the Department of Commerce, 202-482-6014, for information on a clearinghouse for state and local initiatives on productivity, technology, and innovation technology administration.

Following are some brief descriptions of the programs most often offered:

Seed Capital
Although its funding policies vary from state to state, Seed Capital is usually awarded in the form of a grant to especially promising new business ideas that demonstrate strong potential for creating jobs and broadening the state economic base. Through the program, companies can often use this capital to leverage financial support from other resources as well. On the other hand, some businesses may obtain seed capital on a dollar-for-dollar basis whereby the state program fund will match the capital that the business has raised through other resources. Note, however, that some state programs consider seed capital and venture capital one and the same.

Venture Capital
Venture Capital programs often provide financing specifically for technology-oriented businesses through networks which match entrepreneurs with investors. Some states, such as Michigan and Missouri, have developed computerized matching services whereby individuals with specific investment interests can be matched with the appropriate entrepreneurs. Other states have compiled venture capital directories and formal venture referral networks to accomplish a similar matching process. Also see the *State Money* and *Venture Capital* Sections.

Small Business Innovative Research Grants
Small Business Innovation Research (SBIR) programs provide assistance to companies of 500 employees or less that wish to tap into the lucrative federal research and development funding annually available for the development and commercialization of new products. Each year federal agencies publish a list of specific topics they would like researched, and small businesses submit proposals in response to these solicitations to obtain the SBIR funding. Since the composition of these proposals is highly technical and complex, many of these state SBIR programs will walk small businesses through the procurement process, showing them successful proposal strategies that have worked in the past. A Small Business Association pamphlet titled, *Proposal Preparation for Small Business Innovation Research*, is also available at your local Small Business Administration office. Also see the *State Money* Section.

Technology Transfer
Technology Transfer programs establish contacts between businesses and university researchers to facilitate the transfer of new technologies from the lab to industry. This collaboration can, in turn, help solve technical problems and create new economic opportunities. For example, a business will contact a tech transfer office, such as the Center for Innovative Technology in Virginia or the New Jersey Commission on Science and Technology, to discuss its problem. The office will then use its technology resource networks with universities, private industry, and federal agencies to locate potential solutions, which are then related back to the business. Tech transfer can also take other forms, such as

State Level Technology Assistance Programs

gaining access to state-of-the art technical information through database searches, buying or leasing necessary technology-oriented equipment, or using technical consulting resources.

A detailed listing of the state technology transfer programs follows this listing of the state technology information offices.

Technical And Managerial Assistance
Many states' technical and managerial assistance programs provide short-term assistance to businesses with specific technological problems. Much like technology transfer, technical assistance programs, such as PENNTAP in Pennsylvania, are designed to target and solve problems using the most up-to-date technology at little or no cost. Many of these technical consultants, for example, can redesign facilities, analyze manufacturing costs, refine computer systems, and much more.

Incubator Programs
Businesses often fail during their critical early stages. Incubator programs are geared toward avoiding this high failure rate by reducing start-up costs. Like the Center for the Advancement of Developing Industries in Alabama, these incubators provide office, laboratory, and manufacturing space at significantly reduced rates to qualifying start-up companies that exhibit a strong potential for growth. The incubator services to these companies often include technical and managerial assistance, access to university expertise and technology, financial backing, and business and finance planning.

If the following technology development offices do not have the specific information you need, they can most likely refer you to someone who does. And since many of these technology programs are new, it is not uncommon for one office to say no to your inquiry while another will say yes. Persistence is one of the greatest money savers.

State Offices Offering Technology-Oriented Assistance

Alabama
Office for the Advancement of Developing Industries (OADI), University of Alabama at Birmingham, UAB Station, Birmingham, AL 35294; 205-934-6566, Fax: 205-934-6563; {www.uab.edu/oadi/index.htm}. OADI provides information on the following: seed and venture capital; technology transfer; incubator facilities; legal, financial, business, and technical assistance; and conferences and seminars.

Alaska
Alaska Science and Technology Foundation, (ASTF), 4500 Diplomacy Dr., Suite 515, Anchorage, AK 99501-3555; 907-272-4333, Fax: 907-274-6228; {www.astf.org}. This Foundation assists in taking a good technical idea to application or commercialization. Grants are awarded on a competitive basis and grantees are expected to contribute time, effort and resources.

Arkansas
Arkansas Science and Technology Authority (ASTA), 100 Main Street, Suite 450, Little Rock, AR 72201; 501-324-9006, Fax: 501-324-9012; {www.state.ar.us/asta/index.html}. ASTA provides information on the following for young technology-based businesses: incubator facilities, research grants, seed capital investment, SBIR funding, and technology transfer.

California
Engineering Technology Transfer Center, 3716 S. Hope St., Suite 200, Los Angeles, CA 90007-4344; 800-642-2872, 213-743-2353, Fax: 213-746-9043; {www.usc.edu/dept/engineering/TTC/NASA/index.html}

Colorado
University of Colorado Business Advancement Centers (UCBAC), 3333 Iris Ave., Boulder, CO 80301; 303-444-5723, Fax: 303-447-8748; {www.colorado.edu/cubac/}. UCBAC can provide information on the following: SBIR funding, financial planning, marketing and feasibility studies, government contract procurement, technology transfer, and technical expertise.

Connecticut
Connecticut Innovations Inc., 999 West St., Rocky Hill, CT 06067; 860-563-5851, Fax: 860-563-4877; {www.ctinnovations.com}, provides information on the following programs and services: business plan development; technical, managerial, and marketing assistance; new product funding; start-up, expansion, and research and development grants; private sector financing and venture capital funds; access to university technical expertise; state hi-tech business profiles; employee education and training; incubator facilities; and educational forums and conferences.

Florida
Southern Technology Applications Centers (STAC), 1900 SW 34th St., Suite 206, Gainesville, Fl 32608; 352-294-STAC, Fax: 352-294-7802; {www.state.fl.us/stac/}. STAC will provide information on their following programs: technology transfer, entrepreneurial assistance, SBIR funding, venture capital, incubator facilities, workshops and seminars, and extensive technical information.

Georgia
Advanced Technology Development Center (ATDC), 430 Tenth Street, N.W., Suite N-116, Atlanta, GA 30318; 404-894-3575, Fax: 404-894-4545; {www.atdc.org}. ATDC's assistance programs include the following services: business planning and management; financing, marketing, and manufacturing strategy development; accounting, financial, and legal services; access to Georgia Tech research and development equipment and services, including computing systems; on-campus space for labs, research and development, office, and light manufacturing uses; and access to university technical consultants.

Hawaii
Hawaii High Technology Development Corporation (HTDC), 300 Kahelu Avenue, Suite 35, Honolulu, HI 96789; 808-625-5293, Fax: 808-625-6363. HTDC provides information on the following programs: business planning and assistance, technical assistance, and incubator facilities. HTDC also publishes the *Hawaii HiTech Journal*, and *Hawaii HiTech Business Directory*, which covers state technology-related economic growth.

Indiana
Indiana Business of Modernization and Technology Corporation, One North Capitol Avenue, Suite 925, Indianapolis, IN 46204; 317-635-3058, Fax: 317-231-7095; {www.bmtadvantage.org}. This corporation provides support to qualifying technology-based companies through three major programs: 1) technological counseling and assistance; 2) business and financial counseling development; and 3) funding support. Programs are also provided for small and medium size industries.

Iowa
Center for Industrial Research and Service (CIRAS), ISU Research Park, Suite 500, 2501 North Loop Drive, Ames, IA 50010-8286; 515-294-3420, Fax: 515-294-4925; {www.ciras.iastate.edu}. CIRAS assists manufacturing and processing firms by providing information in technical and management areas which include manufacturing, engineering, management, marketing, and database access.

Kansas
Kansas Technology Enterprise Corporation (KTEC), 214 W. 6th, Topeka, KS 66603; 785-296-5272, Fax: 785-296-1160; {www.ktec.org}. KTEC provides information on its following programs: seed capital investment and SBIR funding; the Kansas Technology Resource Database, which will provide information on research objectives, facilities, equipment, consulting services, training programs, market sources; technology expositions and conferences; and technology transfer.

Kentucky
Kentucky Business & Technology Branch, Kentucky Cabinet for Economic Development, 500 Mero Street, 22nd Floor, Frankfort, KY 40601; 502-564-4252,

Money and Help To Companies Which Want To Use Or Sell Technology

Fax: 502-564-3256; {www.edc.state.ky.us/kydec/biztech.html}. This office provides information on the following: newly developing technologies, technology transfer, technical expertise, access of research and development contracts, business development funds, and seminars and workshops on emerging technologies.

Louisiana
The Louisiana Business and Technology Center (LBTC), South Stadium Drive, Louisiana State University, Baton Rouge, LA 70803-6100; 225-334-5555, Fax: 225-388-3975; {www.bus.lsu.edu/btc/}. The Louisiana Business and Technology Center (LBTC) is a high-tech incubator offering start-up assistance to new high-tech companies. It operates a Small Business Institute, a Management Assistance Office, and a Technology Utilization Office at NASA-Stennis Space Center. The LBTC offers technology transfer and utilization as well as technical and business expertise. It is linked with experts in engineering, agriculture, basic sciences, micromachining, and biomedics. Services include space, office support, grant writing, financial counseling, business planning and marketing planning.

Maine
Maine Science and Technology Foundation (MSTF), State House Station #147, Augusta, ME 04333; 207-621-6350, Fax: 207-621-6369; {www.mstf.org}. The Maine Science and Technology Foundation (MSTF) offers technology support and can refer companies to its three branches for electronics, bio-technology, and aquaculture for technical assistance and development.

Maryland
Division of Business Resources Department, 217 E. Redwood St., 12th Floor, Baltimore, MD 21202; 410-333-6990, Fax: 410-333-1836; {www.mdbusiness.state.md.us}. Contact: John Hamilton. This office provides information on the following: venture capital, incubator facilities, SBIR funding, national and international technologies markets, and technical assistance. The Challenge Grant program is also provided.

Massachusetts
Massachusetts Technology Development Corporation (MTDC), 148 State Street, 9th Floor, Boston, MA 02109; 617-723-4920, Fax: 617-723-5983; {www.mtdc.com}. The Massachusetts Technology Development Corporation (MTDC) directly provides some financing in the areas of equity, working capital, and product development. There are also high-tech task forces (one each for bio-tech, enviro-tech and medi-tech) which nurture high-tech companies as well as the Small Business Development Centers which provide free consulting and start-up advice to entrepreneurs.

Center for Technology Commercialization, 1400 Computer Drive, Westboro, MA 01581-5043; 508-870-0042, Fax: 508-366-0101; {www.ctc.org}.

Michigan
Michigan Economic Development Corporation, 201 N. Washington Square, Lansing, MI 48913; 517-373-9808; {http://medc.state.mi.us}. The Michigan Economic Development Corporation oversees the following technology programs: seed capital, research and development grants, technology transfer, technical consulting, product development and testing services, computer assistance, and technical training.

Minnesota
Minnesota Technology, Inc. (MTI), 111 3rd St., Suite 400, Minneapolis, MN 55401; 612-373-2900, 800-325-3073, Fax: 612-373-2901; {www.minnesota_technology.org}. Minnesota Technology, Inc. (MTI) can provide information on the following: SBIR, economic development grants, technology transfer, product development, marketing assistance, incubator facilities, employee training, and much more. MTI also distributes a hi-tech company directory, a state technology economic impact report, the state software technology commission report, and others.

Mississippi
Enterprise for Technology, John C. Stennis Space Center, Bldg. 1103, Stennis Space Center, MS 39529-6000; 601-688-3144, 800-746-4699, Fax: 601-688-1064. Enterprise for Technology provides access to technology developed by federal agencies housed at NASA's John C. Stennis Space Center and various federal laboratories. It also gives assistance in applying for Small Business Innovation Research (SBIR) grants.

Missouri
Office of Productivity, Department of Economic Development, P.O. Box 118, Jefferson City, MO 65102, 573-526-1366, Fax: 573-751-7385; {www.ecodev.state.mo.us/technology}. High Tech oversees the SBIR/Hi-Tech programs, which distributes information on the following programs: business planning and financing, marketing assistance, venture capital network, technical and managerial assistance, product design, and employee training. High Tech distributes directories of in-state hi-tech companies and venture capital firms. High Tech also provides assistance to four innovation centers that deal with new product development and other aspects concerning start-up ventures. It also provides three centers in Advanced Technology in the areas of manufacturing, telecommunications, and plant bio-technology.

Nebraska
Engineering Extension, W191 Nebraska Hall, University of Nebraska-Lincoln, Lincoln, NE 68588-0535; 402-472-5600, toll free in Nebraska 1-800-332-0265, Fax: 402-472-0015; {www.engext.unl.edu/ET/EngExt.html}. The Engineering Extension provides the following services: provides consultants for short-term diagnostic assistance; helps in finding sources of technical and scientific information; assists in providing information about new technologies. Other services are also provided.

Nevada
The Center for Business and Economic Research at the University of Nevada Las Vegas, 4505 Maryland Pkwy, Las Vegas, 89154 NV; 702-895-3191, Fax: 702-895-3606; {www.unlv.edu/Research_Centers/cber/}. The center encourages technology transfer through the collection of data, analysis of issues, and dissemination of finds on the business and economic environment of Nevada. It also studies markets, economic and fiscal impacts, financial feasibility and specific management issues.

New Hampshire
The University of New Hampshire, Vice President for Research and Public Service, 108 Thompson Hall, Durham, NH 03824; 603-862-1997, Fax: 603-862-3617; {www.unh.edu/orps/}, has various programs and offices which assist high technology companies, some of which are the Biomedical Engineering Center, Biotechnology Resource Group, Computer-Aided Design Laboratory, and Partnership for Technology and Management Training.

New Jersey
New Jersey Commission on Science and Technology, 28 West State Street, CN 832, Trenton, NJ 08625; 609-984-1671, Fax: 609-292-5920; {www.state.nj.us/scitech}. The commission oversees the following programs for hi-tech businesses: managerial and technical assistance, venture capital network, business planning, product design, incubator facilities, technology transfer, and entrepreneurial seminars.

New Mexico
Office of Science & Technology, State of New Mexico Economic Development Department, P.O. Box 20003, Santa Fe, NM 87504; 505-827-0549, Fax: 505-827-0588; {www.edd.state.nm.us/TECHNO/index.html}. TED provides support services to businesses through the State Technical Assistance Resource System (STARS) a reference service which can be accessed via touch-tone phone. The service can lead you to the best starting place to gain the assistance desired. It also provides a national database of specialty experts and industry organizations which can be called upon for specific problem solving assistance. Also included is a One-Stop Shop for information on all state and local licensing requirements, taxation, and regulations which may affect a business.

New York
New York State Science and Technology Foundation, 30 S. Pearl St., Albany, NY 12245; 518-292-5700; {www.empire.state.ny.us/stf/stf.htm}. The Foundation administers the Regional Technology Development Organization Program, which encourages economic development through the following: technology transfer, product development, venture capital sources, technical and managerial assistance, incubator facilities, application assistance, and sponsored conferences and seminars on technology development.

North Carolina
North Carolina Technological Development Authority, Inc. (NCTDA), 2 Davis Drive, or P.O. Box 13169, Research Triangle Park, Raleigh, NC 27709; 919-990-8558, Fax: 919-558-0156; {www.nctda.org}. The NCTDA can provide information

State Level Technology Assistance Programs

on the following: SBIR funding, incubator facilities, technical and managerial assistance, research and development funding, and technology transfer.

North Dakota
Wally Kerns, Center for Innovation and Business Development, University of North Dakota, Room 118, Gamble Hall, P.O. Box 7308, Grand Forks, ND 58202; 701-777-3132, Fax: 701-777-3225; {www.innovators.net}. This office administers program to assist technology based companies. They provide management assistance and facilitate technology transfer.

Ohio
Thomas Edison Program (TEP), 77 S. High Street, 26th Floor, Columbus, OH 43266; 614-466-3086, Fax: 614-644-5758; {www.odod.state.oh.us/tech/edison/default.htm}. TEP oversees the following programs: matching seed capital funding, incubator facilities, technology transfer, technical training, venture capital, business assistance resources, technical expertise, research and development funding, and seminars.

Great Lakes Industrial Technology Center, 25000 Great Northern Corporate Center, Suite 450, Cleveland, OH 44070-5310; 440-734-0094, Fax: 440-734-0686; {www.battelle.org/glitec}.

Oklahoma
Oklahoma Center For The Advancement of Science and Technology (OCAST), 4545 N. Lincoln Blvd., Suite 116, Oklahoma City, OK 73105; 405-524-1357, Fax: 405-521-6501; {www.ocast.state.ok.us}. OCAST provides information on their following programs: seed capital, research and development funding, technical expertise, technology transfer, SBIR funding, and venture capital.

Pennsylvania
Office of Technology Development, Pennsylvania Department of Commerce, 352 Forum Building, Harrisburg, PA 17120; 717-787-4148; {www.dced.state.pa.us}. This office oversees the Ben Franklin Partnership, which provides information on the following programs: technology transfer and assistance, technical expertise, SBIR funding, incubator facilities, and financial planning.

Mid-Atlantic Technology Applications Center, 3400 Forbes Ave., Fifth Floor, Pittsburgh, PA 15260; 412-383-2500, Fax: 412-383-2595; {www.mtac.pitt.edu/www/}.

Rhode Island
Rhode Island Economic Development Corporation, One West Exchange St., Providence, RI 02903; 401-222-2601, Fax: 401-222-2102; {www.riedc.com}. This agency has two programs it administers to aid technology based companies. The Applied Research Grant Program provides grants to businesses to do research with other institutions within the state. Only major research projects that have commercial potential and have a minimum combined business and research budget of $200,000 qualify. The State Support Small Business Innovation Research Program provides counseling and financial incentives for companies interested in submitting proposals to the Federal Small Business Innovation Program.

Tennessee
Tennessee Resource Valley (TRV), P.O. Box 23770, Knoxville, TN 37933-1184; 423-694-6772, Fax: 423-694-6429; {www.trv.org}. TRV provides information on the following programs: venture capital, SBIR workshops, technology transfer, technical and managerial assistance, technical training, and networking services.

Texas
Texas Technology and Economic Development, 310 Wisanbaker Engineering Research Center, Texas A&M, College Station, TX 77843-8000; 409-845-2913, Fax: 409-845-3559; {www.teexweb.tamu.edu}. This office provides information on the following: technology transfer and commercialization, patent licensing, venture capital, access to technological databases, prototype testing and evaluation, and business planning and assistance.

Utah
Weber State University, Community and Economic Partnerships (CEP), Ogden, UT 84408-4001; 801-626-6344, Fax: 801-626-7970; {http://weber.edu/sbdc}. This office provides the business community with a variety of programs that have working relationships with business, industry, government, and other organizations such as the following: Center for Aerospace Technology, Center for Business and Economic Training and Research and the Center for Chemical Technology, Technology Assistance Center and Environmental Research.

Virginia
Center for Innovative Technology (CIT), CIT Tower, 2214 Rock Hill Road, Suite 600, Herndon, VA 22070-4005; 703-689-3000, Fax: 703-689-3041; {www.cit.org}. The Center for Innovative Technology (CIT) provides information on their following programs: technology development funding, technology transfer, technical problem assistance, business planning, financing and marketing assistance, incubator facilities, patent licensing, and conferences and seminars for entrepreneurs.

Washington
Washington Technology Center (WTC), University of Washington, Sluke Hall, FJ-15, Seattle, WA 98195; 206-685-1920, Fax 206-543-3059; {www.watechcenter.org}. The Washington Technology Center (WTC) provides information on its following programs: acquisition of federal research and development contracts and funding (SBIR), technical and managerial assistance, technology transfer, and technology seminars and workshops.

West Virginia
West Virginia Robert C. Byrd Institute for Advanced Flexible Manufacturing Systems, 1050 Fourth Ave., Huntington, WV 25755; 304-696-3092, Fax: 304-696-6280; {www.rcbi.org}. The Institute provides computer facilities for training, networking and demonstration; it has an advanced telecommunications network to transfer data from computer to machine tools. It also facilitates research and development in the areas of computer engineering, design, and manufacturing, electronics, computer hardware and software, and engineering applications.

Wisconsin
University-Industry Relations, University of Wisconsin-Madison, 1215 WARF Office Building, Room 215, 610 Walnut Street, Madison, WI 53705; 608-263-2840, Fax: 608-263-2841; {www.wisc.edu/uir}. This program provides information on the following: technology transfer, technical and scientific information services, seminars for business and industry, patent licensing, managerial and technical assistance, and SBIR funding.

Wyoming
State/Science, Technology and Energy Authority (STEA) Director, STEA University of Wyoming, P.O. Box 3295, UW Station, Laramie, WY 83071; 307-766-6797, Fax: 307-766-6799; {www.stea.org}. The State/Science, Technology and Energy Authority (STEA) helps businesses involved with advanced technology move from research and development to the marketplace. Some financing is provided through state dollars for applied research.

Free Technology Help: Futuristic Solutions To Today's Business Problems

The federal government is not the only one helping businesses solve their technology-oriented problems:

A $17,000 Savings on Software: A Pittsburgh company, having trouble gathering information on some computer software and hardware they needed to purchase, contacted the Pennsylvania Technical Assistance Program (PENNTAP) for help. As a result, the company ended up saving $17,000, and months of searching, on a computer system they chose based on the suggestions from one of PENNTAP's computer specialists who visited the firm and gathered the necessary information for them.

Laser Company Gets Market Study: Tigart Laser, a small laser machine shop in Indianapolis, asked the Technical Assistance Program at Purdue University for advice on improving its industrial marketing to new customers. TAP completed a study of the company's strengths and potential markets and made recommendations, all of which were implemented. Since then, sales have increased by 18%, three employees were added, and negotiations are under way for the purchase of a new $170,000 six-axis laser cutting machine.

These success stories are just two examples of how companies can benefit from the different state-level technology transfer programs across the country. The state level programs are similar to the federal government's technology transfer program which requires federal labs to conduct research that responds to industry and governmental problems. Many states with major research universities now have technology transfer programs. These programs help private businesses tap into the great economic potential of the technology being developed at their state research laboratories. By having a "window in" and "window out" of the research and technical expertise available at research institutions, these programs can seek out businesses that use the technologies they have developed. They are also able to locate technologies in their labs based on requests from private industry.

Using University Research Projects

The commercial application of university-generated research projects and expertise is a rapidly growing phenomenon. In the past, research projects developed at universities often sat on the shelf after completion. Many states have taken initiatives to get projects that are patentable intellectual properties into the market place where they can do the greatest good. After all, the states have poured a lot of their money into these university research programs, and they see no reason why they shouldn't try to convert some of that investment into tangible economic benefits for their businesses.

Helping Both Business and Research Communities

This transfer of technical innovations and expertise from the lab to private industry usually involves a two-sided process:

1) Helping university researchers identify companies that can use their technologies, and

2) Helping companies that need specific types of technologies identify the appropriate university expertise to develop and/or apply them.

The goal, then, of many of these state-based technology transfer programs is to maintain an active system of communication between the universities and industry. In this way industry knows what the university labs have to offer, and the university labs know what kinds of technology industry is interested in developing. It's through this back and forth dialogue, effective transfer of information can take place.

Definition of Technology Transfer

You will find that the definition of "technology transfer" changes from program to program, and from state to state. It is not as simple as the phrase suggests: the transfer of technology from one place to another, from the laboratory to industry. It can mean everything from research and development to database search services, depending on what state program you consult. But for the purposes of this survey, we will confine our definition of technology transfer to the following categories:

Technical Assistance
Modeled after the Department of Agriculture's Cooperative Extension Service, many states have created programs to help your company solve short-term, technology-related problems at no charge or substantial discount. Many of the states that have such programs provide the assistance through a network of offices that serve specific regional areas of the state. The Technical Extension Service in Maryland, for example, has field representatives who provide on-site technical assistance to companies within their six or so designated regional areas. Some states consider such services "technology transfer" because they involve transferring the expertise and knowledge of university-based faculty to private sector businesses. Usually, this type of technology assistance and application involves the use of already existing and proven technologies to solve particular problems. Also note that these services are usually limited to in-state companies. Here are some *examples*:

Honda Clone Discovers Better Plastic: In New Jersey, a small manufacturer had created a plastic clone part for Honda automobile carburetors that he could sell much cheaper than the ones produced by Honda. Unfortunately, the plastic part he designed corroded when exposed to petroleum products. He contacted the Technical Extension Program at the New Jersey Commission on Science and Technology, and they helped him choose a better plastic polymer that wouldn't corrode.

Free Chemist Helps Ticket Maker: In Montana, a woman who owned a ticket making business was having trouble with her

State-Based Technology Transfer Programs

inking process. She contacted the University Technical Assistance Program at Montana State University. They arranged for a chemist to consult with her and remedy the problem for no charge.

Candy Firm Gets New Plant Layout: A candy manufacturer in Georgia was concerned about the high rejection rate of its products that were coming out broken, so they contacted the Industrial Extension Program at Georgia Tech. After appraising the problem, an expert suggested a new layout for cooling and handling the candy which remedied the problem.

Technical Expertise Referral Services

Many of the states' technology transfer programs, such as Michigan's Technology Transfer Network and the Connecticut Technical Assistance Center, will act as referral services that match up companies that have technology-based problems with experts with the appropriate background to solve those problems. These services can differ slightly from the technical extension programs in that they often end up in a contractual arrangement for the necessary consultation between the two parties. Here are some *examples*:

Windmill Saves Electricity for Restauranteur: A Virginia restauranteur with a seaside location wanted to reduce his $34,000 annual electricity bill by installing a windmill to generate some of his power. He contacted the Center for Innovative Technology (CIT) for a feasibility assessment for selection and installation of his windmill. The CIT member gathered the necessary information, demonstrated the feasibility and operating methods, and helped the owner secure the correct government permits. The windmill is expected to provide a 35% return on the initial $12,000 investment, and will supply 8% of the electricity for the restaurant.

Automated Printing System: A Michigan textile company that needed help in designing an innovative printing system using lasers contacted the Michigan Technology Transfer Network (TTN). TTN's staff found two university experts who, after meeting with the company, wrote a project design proposal which was then developed into a prototype model. The new automated printing system is expected to substantially lower the company's printing costs and raise its manufacturing efficiency.

Solves a Smelly Business Problem: In Wisconsin, a manufacturer of door panels for automobiles had received numerous complaints from the neighboring community about an unpleasant odor that his plant was emitting. Facing a major shutdown of operations, the owner contacted the University-Industry Research Program at the University of Wisconsin. They quickly located an expert who made recommendations to reduce the offensive odor and also helped the company undertake plans to relocate in an area further away from communities with families living in them.

University-Industry Joint Research and Development

Some states have programs which help link up companies having technical problems that cannot be solved with already existing technologies with capable university-based researchers. Together they conduct research and develop an answer to the problem. The resulting products are then transferred from the lab to industry under licensing agreements that are worked out between the companies and the university researchers. Here are some *examples*:

$80,000 Grant For Tool Company: Master Machine Tool Inc., a small company in Hutchinson, Kansas, received a $80,000 grant from the Kansas Technology Enterprise Corporation to undertake a joint research and development project with a university faculty member. Together they developed a high speed cutting device to be used in welding and painting. The company projects a $20 to $40 million increase in revenues over the next 2-3 years.

Food Company Lowers Cholesterol: A food manufacturer in Minnesota developed a food product that they believed has a cholesterol lowering quality to it. The Office of Research and Technology Transfer at the University of Minnesota helped the company locate a faculty member at the medical school who was interested in further researching the properties and commercial potential of this innovative product.

Airplane Manufacturer Makes Rivetting Rosy: A large airplane manufacturer in Washington State was having problems with their automated riveters. They were putting good rivets into poorly drilled holes, which was causing unwanted metal fatigue in the assembled parts. The company contacted the Washington Technology Center whose researchers designed and developed an automatic hole gate censor for the automatic riveters which wouldn't allow a riveter to put a rivet in a hole that wasn't perfectly drilled. WTC then negotiated a licensing agreement with the airplane manufacturer for its use.

Centers of Excellence

Some states, such as Utah, Colorado, and Ohio, have developed research centers that receive funding from state and private industry to undertake designated research and development projects that address the state's industrial needs and plans. The technologies developed at these centers are available to private companies that are either subscribers to the centers or that provide research and development matching funds. Each center has its own licensing and purchasing agreements with its industry sponsors. Here is an *example*:

Biotechnology in Colorado: The Colorado Institute For Research in Biotechnology, a partnership of three Colorado universities and 20 private biotechnology company sponsors, conducts research and development in response to the mutual needs of both partners, and transfers the resulting innovations to the private companies for commercial use.

Currently, about 35 states have offices, many of which are located at the state universities, that assist companies in identifying the appropriate kinds of technology they may need. If your state is not listed, it doesn't necessarily mean you cannot gain access to innovative technologies developed in the state universities. Many research universities have informal networks to get their innovative, patentable ideas into the private sector. Try contacting their research offices to see if they can help you. Also, most of the states that do have technology transfer programs, such as Minnesota, Wisconsin, and Ohio, are willing to allow companies from other states to license their new technologies as long as companies from their own state have had the opportunity to do so first.

Also, many universities have developed databases of their faculty members' professional profiles which can be searched, often times

Free Technology Help

at no cost to you. You will find a listing of the offices that will conduct these searches for you in our new edition of the *State Data and Database Finder*. Of course, if you still can't get the technology you are looking for, you can always get involved in the federal technology transfer program through their regional offices. For the location of the NASA Applications Center nearest you, contact the Federal Laboratory Consortium (FLC), U.S. Department of Agriculture, 3865 South Building, Washington, DC 20250; 202-447-7185.

State-Based Technology Transfer Programs

Alabama
Alabama Development Office, 401 Adams Ave., Montgomery, AL 36130; 800-248-0033; {www.ado.state.al.us}; E-mail: {idinfo@www.ado.state.al.us}. The Alabama Development Office provides technical and management training as well as financing through industrial revenue bonds (IRBs). The Alabama Development Office's Research Division prepares cost and feasibility studies for clients as well as cost analyses of labor, transportation, utilities, and state and local taxes. The division prepares studies, reports, and promotional brochures containing information on natural resources, quality of life, demographics, economics, and technology. It also maintains a comprehensive industrial research library.

Alaska
Alaska Science and Technology Foundation (ASTF), 4500 Diplomacy Dr., Suite 515, Anchorage, AK 99508; 907-272-4333, Fax: 907-274-6228; {www.astf.org}, E-mail: {info@astf.org}. This Foundation assists in taking a good technical idea to application or commercialization. Grants are awarded on a competitive basis and grantees are expected to contribute time, effort and resources.

Arkansas
Arkansas Science and Technology Authority (ASTA), 100 Main Street, Suite 450, Little Rock, AR 72201; 501-324-9006, Fax: 501-324-9012; {www.state.ar.us/asta}. By maintaining contacts with Arkansas' research universities, federal labs, and its business community, ASTA is able to coordinate the transfer of technologies available for technical problem solving as well as commercialization to the businesses that need them. After discussing its technology needs with ASTA, a business will be directed toward the appropriate university experts to solve the problem.

Arkansas Industrial Development Commission (AIDC), One State Capitol Mall, Little Rock, AR 72201; 501-682-7322, Fax: 501-682-2703. The AIDC was established in 1955 and is guided by an advisory board of 16 commissioners appointed by the governor. The agency publishes the *Manufacturers Exchange Bulletin*, which contains a "bulletin board" of information for small manufacturers.

Colorado
Business Research and Information Network (BRAIN), University of Colorado Business Advancement Center, 5353 Manhattan Circle, Suite 202, Boulder, CO 80303; 303-554-9493, Fax: 303-554-9605; {www.colorado.edu/cubac}. For CO companies needing technical problem solving assistance and access to state-of-the-art technologies, BRAIN will conduct searches of the NASA Industrial Application Center's (NIAC) databases. For technical information not available through computer searches, the BRAIN office will contact experts at NASA Field Centers, Federal Labs, and universities, and relay the answers to the problem back to the client.

Colorado Advanced Technology Institute (CATI), 11515 Quiuas Way, Denver, Co 80234; 303-460-9503, Fax: 303-409-3237; {www.sni.net/~pub/cati.html}. CATI oversees the funding of five state research centers at which joint university-industry research and development projects are undertaken. Each of the centers, along with their corporate partners, determine the areas they wish to target for their research and development projects. Colorado businesses wishing access to the technologies developed at these centers must pay subscription or membership fees, along with any licensing or purchasing charges.

Connecticut
Connecticut Innovations, Inc., 999 West St., Rocky Hill, CT 06067; 860-563-5851, Fax: 860-563-4877; {www.ctinnovations.com}. Connecticut Innovations, Inc. acts as a referral agency to coordinate the linking up of industry and university technology. After a company contacts the office and discusses their technology needs, they will then make the necessary connections with university experts that solve the problem. This program can also work the other way, by finding appropriate industries that can use technologies with commercial potential developed by university researchers.

Florida
Florida Manufacturing Technology Center, 390 North Orange Ave., Suite 1300, Orlando, FL 32801; 407-316-4619, Fax: 407-316-4586; {http://www.fmtc.org/}. FMTC draws from a pool of professional resources, including manufacturing specialists and experts in the fields of technology, education, and government to improve productivity, enhance quality assurance, develop your workforce, improve plant layout, create market niches, launch new products, comply with environmental issues, implement new technology, state Internet sites, or upgrade business information systems. FMTC is non-profit, partially funded by government and private grants and awards. Fee-based.

Georgia
Economic Development Laboratory (EDL), GTRI, Georgia Institute of Technology, Atlanta, GA 30332; 404-894-2000, 894-6100 {www.edi.gatech.edu}. Attn: Dr. David Swanson. The Economic Development Laboratory (EDL) provides free on-site, short-term assistance to manufacturing companies with technology-based problems. They will also conduct free database searches and document retrievals for the most up-to-date information that can help companies solve their problems. Businesses can also contact the EDL office if they are looking for new, already existing technologies they would like implemented into their companies.

Advanced Technology Development Center (ATDC), 430 10th Street, NW, Suite N-116, Atlanta, GA 30318; 404-894-3575, Fax: 404-894-4545; {www.atdc.org}. The ATDC encourages high technology growth in the state by supporting technology-based entrepreneurs and small businesses, and by helping existing businesses with new product development.

Georgia Tech Research Institute, Georgia Institute of Technology, Atlanta, GA 30332-0800; 404-894-3411, Fax: 404-894-9875; {www.gtri.gatech.edu/}. The Engineering Extension Program provides technical services through its field offices throughout the state.

Idaho
Science and Technology Committee/SBIR Support Services State Advisory Council: c/o Karl Tueller, Chairman; Idaho Department of Commerce, 700 West State St., 6th Floor, Boise, ID 83720-2700; 208-334-2470, Fax: 208-334-2631; {www.idoc.state.id.us}. By maintaining contacts with both the university and business community, the Science and Technology committee helps to promote the transfer of technologies for commercialization to businesses that need them.

Illinois
Technology Grant Challenge Program (TGC), 100 W. Randolph St., Chicago, Il 60601; 312-814-7179, Fax: 312-814-2320; {www.commerce.state.il.us}. TGC promotes the commercialization of new ideas and products that will contribute to the state's economic growth. TGC does this by linking Illinois' businesses with the appropriate research expertise. Areas covered include feasibility studies, prototype development and testing, technical problem solving, identification of manufacturers to produce new products, and commercialization of new technologies.

Governor's Commission on Science and Technology, 100 West Randolph, Suite 3-400, Chicago, IL 60601. The Governor's Commission on Science and Technology was founded in 1983. The commission promotes public/private collaborative and cooperative research ventures and projects.

Indiana
Technical Assistance Program (TAP), Purdue University, 1284 Civil Building, Room G175, West Lafayette, IN 47907-1284; 317-494-6258, Fax: 317-494-9187; {http://tap.www.ecn.purdue.edu}. TAP offers free, limited technical assistance to Indiana companies in the following areas: product development, manufacturing processes, and management. TAP experts will use existing technologies already available to their staff to solve business problems involving product design, quality control, and operational cost strategies. Assistance is also provided for small and medium size industries.

State-Based Technology Transfer Programs

Iowa
Center for Industrial Research and Service (CIRAS), 2272 Howe Hall, Suite 2620, Ames, IA 50011-2272; 515-294-3420, Fax: 515-294-4925; {www.ciras.iastate.edu}. The Center provides businesses with technology transfer through linkage with faculty researchers, data base searches, and federal laboratories.

Kansas
Kansas Technology Enterprise Corporation (KTEC), 214 West 6th Street, 1st Floor, Topeka, KS 66603; 785-296-5272, Fax: 785-296-1160; {www.ktec.com}. The Kansas Technology Enterprise Corporation (KTEC) offers manufacturing assistance for automation problems and provides subsidized technology audits and feasibility studies. If a business wishes to purchase existing technologies developed at the universities, they must pay for it themselves through a agreement with the licenser. If a company has a specific technology need which cannot be addressed by existing technologies, KTEC offers research matching grants to develop that technology.

Division of Business Development, Kansas Department of Commerce, 700 SW Harrison, Suite 1300, Topeka, KS 66603; 785-296-5298, Fax: 785-296-3490; {http://kansascommerce.com}. The Division of Business Development promotes the growth, diversification, and retention of business and industry in Kansas. The division provides assistance both directly and through a statewide business assistance network, channeling appropriate resources for business technical help and other related problems.

Kentucky
Kentucky Office of Business and Technology (OBT), Cabinet for Economic Development, Capital Plaza Tower, Frankfort, KY 40601; 502-564-4252, Fax: 502-564-5932; {www.thinkkentucky.com/kyedc/entrance.html}. The Office of Business and Technology (OBT) links businesses with sources of technology information, expertise, and opportunities by identifying newly developed technologies, technical problem solving experts, and research and development contracts. After discussing their technical needs with OBT's staff, a business will be directed toward the appropriate sources of innovative technologies to solve the problem.

Louisiana
Office of Technology Transfer, Louisiana State University Business and Technology Center, Room 146 A, South Stadium Drive, Baton Rouge, LA 70803; 504-388-6941; Fax: 504-388-4925. The Office of Technology Transfer helps take new ideas, inventions or discoveries and solicits commercial interest as well as negotiates contracts with prospective clients. The office also assists in determining the patentability of new products.

Office of Intellectual Property, 203 David Boyd Hall, Baton Rouge, LA 70803-6100; 225-388-6941, Fax: 225-388-4925; {www.lsu.edu/guests/wwwott/public_html/index.html}

Maine
Maine Science and Technology Foundation, 87 Winthrop St., Augusta, ME 04330; 207-621-6350, Fax: 207-621-6369. The Foundation helps industry introduce technical innovation by providing researchers in the fields of biomedical technology, metals electronics and aquaculture.

Maryland
Engineering Research Center (ERC), University of Maryland, Potomac Building 092, College Park, MD 20742; 301-405-3906, Fax: 301-403-4105; {www.erc.umd.edu}. ERC oversees two programs which involve the transfer of technology from the university to industry: The Technology Extension Service (TES) provides Maryland-based businesses with free, short-term technical problem solving services, including problem identification, direct technical assistance, plant modernization planning, new product evaluation, and more. The other program, the Maryland Industrial Partnerships (MIPS), provides matching funds for joint industry-university research and development projects having commercialization potential that can produce economic benefits for the state. The company has to be involved in a Hi-Technology business or industry.

Massachusetts
Center for Applied Special Technology, 39 Cross St., Peabody, MA 01960; 978-531-8555, Fax: 978-531-0192; {www.cast.org}. CAST is unique in its approach to the transfer of manufactory technology into new forms of work organization into industries. After a business contacts CAST with a technical problem, the Center brings together all the parties involved -- management, workers, and university-based technical experts -- to analyze and decide on the appropriate solution. CAST acts as a matching service by linking up the companies with the appropriate technical consultants. Small and medium sized industries and companies can save from 30% to 50% on consultation fees by using CAST's services.

Michigan
Michigan Economic Development Corporation, 201 N. Washington Square, 4th Floor, Lansing, MI 48913; 517-373-9808; {http://medc.michigan.org}. The Michigan Economic Development Corporation oversees Michigan's Great Technology website, a portal for information about the impact of Michigan's technology on the state, nation and world. The major initiatives of the Great Technology website include Great Stories, Great Capital, Great Events, Great Links, Great Research, and Great Forum.

Michigan Technology Transfer Centers:
Technology Management Office, University of Michigan, Wolverine Tower Room 2071, 3003 S. State St., Ann Arbor, MI 48109-1280; 734-763-0614, Fax: 734-936-1330; {www.tmo.umich.edu}, E-mail: {info@mail.tmo.umich.edu}.

Technology Transfer Office, Wayne State University, 4032 Faculty/Administration Building, 656 West Kirby, Detroit, MI 48202; 313-577-5541, Fax: 313-577-3626.

Michigan Technological University, Attn. Intellectual Properties, 1400 Townsend Dr., Houghten, MI 49931; 313-487-2228; {www.mtu.edu/index.html}.

Western Michigan University, Business Development Services, Kalamazoo, MI 49008; 616-387-2714; {www.wmich.edu}.

Minnesota
Patents and Technology Marketing, University of Minnesota, University Gateway, Suite 450, 200 Oak St., SE, Minneapolis, MN 55455; 612-624-0550, Fax: 612-624-6554; {www.ptm.umn.edu}. This office seeks out companies that can use the patented innovations developed at the university. It also responds to requests from private businesses by locating appropriate technologies developed at their labs. The office will also help link up businesses with faculty expertise for technical problem solving arrangements and joint research and development projects.

Mississippi
Institute for Technology Development (ITD), 700 North State Street, Suite 500, Jackson, MS 39202; 601-960-3600, Fax: 601-960-3605. In the transfer of technology, ITD assists in two ways: it locates projects for interested companies at university research and development facilities with commercial potential and helps implement them. ITD also identifies key problem areas in industry needing innovative technology and initiates research and development projects to respond to those needs. Part of this communication between the lab and industry is accomplished through TechNet, a program which seeks out in-state manufacturers that can profit from existing technology, and then helps them apply it in a practical manner.

Missouri
Office of Productivity, MO Department of Economic Development, P.O. Box 118, Jefferson City, MO 65102-0118; 573-526-1366, Fax: 573-751-7385; {http://www.ecodev.state.mo.us/technology}. This office seeks to increase the wealth of Missouri manufacturers and technology-based business ventures by improving their ability to compete in a global economy through a series of state programs and networks with other organizations in Missouri, which also exist to assist Missouri businesses.

Center for Technology and Business Development, Grinstead Building, Room 009, Central Missouri State University, Warrensburg, MO 64093; 660-543-4402; {http://153.91.1.141/SBDC/centech/tech.htm}. The Center assists companies in solving their technology-based problems by providing the following: access to technical consultants, prototype analysis and improvement, new product development, plant layout assistance, access to published technical information, energy audits, and the transfer of university-researched technologies into the marketplace.

Montana
Montana Science and Technology Alliance (MSTA), 1424 9th Ave., Helena, MT 59620; 406-444-2778, Fax: 406-444-1585; {http://commerce.mt.gov}. The Montana Science and Technology Alliance (MSTA) oversees the Technology Review and Transfer Program which give university researchers who have developed technologies that they feel have commercial potential the opportunity to present those projects to

Free Technology Help

a review board. The board then assesses commercial potential, need for further research, and appropriateness for venture financing.

Montana State University, Research Creativity and Technology Transfer, 304 Montana Hall, Bozeman, MT 59717; 406-994-2752; {www.montana.edu/wwwvr/technotransfer.html}. The IPATNT Office assists faculty with the disclosure, patenting and licensing of processes, products or creative works that may have commercial potential. It also seeks sponsored research from private industry and helps outside users gain access to University facilities, services and specialized equipment.

Census and Economic Information Center, Department of Commerce, 1424 Ninth Avenue, Helena, MT 59620; 406-444-2896, Fax: 406-444-1518; {http://commerce.mt.gov/ceic}. The Census and Economic Information Center (CEIC) is the lead agency of the Montana State Data Center. The CEIC serves as a central location for businesses, government agencies, and the general public to obtain population and economic information for research, planning, and decision-making purposes.

Nebraska

Engineering Extension, W191 Nebraska Hall, University of Nebraska-Lincoln, P.O. Box 880535, Lincoln, NE 68588-0535; 402-472-5600, toll free in NE 800-332-0265, Fax:402-472-0015; {www.nuengr.unl.edu/ET/EngExt.html}.The Extension provides engineering assistance to Nebraska manufacturing companies, and promotes technology transfer within the state from the university and various other sources to the manufacturing segment.

Nevada

The Center for Business and Economic Research at the University of Nevada Las Vegas, 4505 Maryland Pkwy, Las Vegas, NV 89154; 702-895-3191, Fax: 702-895-3606; {www.univ.edu/Research_Centers/cber}, encourages technology transfer through collection of data, analysis of issues, and dissemination of finds on the business and economic environment of Nevada. It also studies markets, economic and fiscal impacts, financial feasibility or specific management issues. The Office of Technology Liaison, University of Nevada-Reno, Mail Stop 326, Reno, NV 89557; 702-784-6869, Fax: 702-784-6064, serves as a focal point for strengthening the university/industry partnership by providing research funding and patent search.

New Hampshire

The University of New Hampshire, Research and Technical Assistance Center, McConnell Hall, Durham, NH 03824-3593; {http://orbit.unh.edu/cber}, provides interfaces with business and industry to transfer technology through its various departments and programs.

New Jersey

New Jersey Technology Council, 1001 Briggs Road, Suite 280, Mt. Laurel, NJ 08054; 856-787-9700, Fax: 856-787-9800; {http://www.njtc.org/}. The New Jersey Technology Council provides networking information and other services to the state's technology businesses.

New Mexico

Office of Science and Technology, P.O. Box 20003, Santa Fe, NM 87504-5003; 505-827-0549, Fax: 505-827-0588; {http://www.edd.state.nm.us/TECHNO/index.html}. The Office of Science and Technology has a very clear and concise mission: to be the state's advocate for high technology-based business start-ups. Teamed with such partners as the Governor's Science and Technology Advisory Council, federal and state labs in New Mexico, state universities, and private agencies with similar interests, the Office is able to provide services vital to the entrepreneur, or reference to those organizations most likely to be able to help.

New York

Central New York Technology Development Organization, 1201 E. Fayette St., Syracuse, NY 13210; 315-425-5144, Fax: 315-233-1259; {http://www.tdosolutions.com/services.htm}. The Central New York Technology Development Organization offers the Industrial Technology Extension Services (ITES) program to small and medium-sized manufacturers in the give-county Central New York Region. As partial funding is provided by the New York State Science and Technology Foundation, the majority of the work ITES performs is low in cost. The ITES program is tightly integrated with the federally sponsored MEP program. Consultations on issues like management, technology, training, and operations as well as information on low-cost funding or grants are provided by ITES.

North Carolina

Industrial Extension Service (IES), College of Engineering, North Carolina State University, Box 7902, Raleigh, NC 27695-7902; 919-515-2358, Fax: 919-515-6159; {www.ies.ncsu.edu}. IES uses the resources of NCSU to provide short-term assistance in the following areas free of charge or on a cost recovery basis: problem identification, quality assurance, metalworking production and inventory control, work simplification, energy audits, plant layout, computer aided design, and much more. Using the expertise of the university, IES also acts as a referral service for companies needing long-term consulting assistance.

North Carolina Biotechnology Center, P.O. Box 13547, Research Triangle Park, NC 27709;919-541-9366,Fax:919-990-9544; {www.ncbiotech.org}. The North Carolina Biotechnology Center was established in 1981 to support biotechnology research and development statewide through research, programmatic activities, new facilities, meetings, and commercial ventures. It encourages technology transfer between universities, industry and small businesses.

Research Triangle Institute, P.O. Box 12194, Research Triangle Park, NC 27709; 919-541-6000; {www.rti.org}. The Research Triangle Institute is a nonprofit consulting research and development firm of approximately 900 employees. The institute conducts contract research involving physical, life, and social sciences.

North Carolina Board of Science and Technology, 116 W. Jones St., Box 1326, Mail Service Center, Raleigh, NC 27699-1326; 919-733-6500, Fax: 919-715-3775; {http://www.governor.state.nc.us/govoffice/science/main.html}. The North Carolina General Assembly established the North Carolina Board of Science and Technology (the board) in 1963 to encourage, promote and support scientific, engineering and industrial research applications in North Carolina.

North Dakota

Center for Innovation and Business Development, 4300 Dartmouth Dr., Grand Forks, ND 58202; 701-777-3132, Fax: 701-777-2339; {www.innovators.net}. Through the University of North Dakota School of Engineering and Mines and the Department of Industrial Technology, the Center can help companies identify and analyze technology-based problems and then provide solutions in the following areas: computer aided design, quality control, safety and energy evaluations, prototype development, and more.

Technology Transfer Center, North Dakota State University, Civil Engineering Bldg., Room 201H, Fargo, ND 58105; 701-231-7051, Fax: 701-231-7195; {http://hardhat.cme.ndsu.nodak.edu/tttcent}. The Technology Transfer Center was established at North Dakota State University, Fargo to enable North Dakota firms to use the most advanced technologies available. It provides to North Dakota businesses Control Data Corporation's access to worldwide computer software.

Ohio

Ohio Department of Development, 77 S. High Street, P.O. Box 1001, Columbus, OH 43216-1001; 800-848-1300, 614-466-2480, Fax: 614-644-5167; {http://www.odod.state.oh.us/tech/}. The Ohio Department of Development Technology Division offers a comprehensive array of programs designed to stimulate, create and support opportunities for economic development across Ohio. Many of their services are without charge. Through the Thomas Edison Program, businesses can gain access to technologies developed at the Edison Technology Centers by becoming a center partner through membership fees or jointly funding the research and development at the centers.

Ohio State University Office for Technology, 960 Kenny Rd., Columbus, OH 43210; 614-292-4540,Fax:614-292-8907; {http://www.techtransfer.rf.ohio-state.edu/}. The Ohio State University Office for Technology packages and licenses to industry intellectual property developed at the Ohio State University.

Oklahoma

Oklahoma Center for the Advancement of Science and Technology (OCAST), 4545 N. Lincoln Blvd., Suite 116, Oklahoma City, OK 73105; 405-524-1357; {www.ocast.state.ok.us}. OCAST oversees three programs that involve technology transfer. When state funding is approved, the Centers of Excellence will conduct joint university-industry research and development that must culminate in the transfer of the resulting innovations to private businesses. The Applied Research program also encourages university-industry collaboration that will result in commercially viable products. The Oklahoma Technical and Research Network is a database that will link up companies with the appropriate technical experts to conduct joint research and development and on-site consultation.

State-Based Technology Transfer Programs

Rural Enterprises, Inc., Durant, OK 74702; 405-924-5094, out of state toll free 800-658-2823, Fax: 405-920-2745; {www.ruralenterprises.com}. Rural Enterprises, Inc. (REI) is a nonprofit industrial development corporation and national demonstration model headquartered in Durant. It provides financial services, technology transfer, new product evaluation, and other resources to rural businesses.

Oregon

Technology Transfer Services (TTS), 1238 University of Oregon, Eugene, OR 97403-1238; 541-346-3176, Fax: 541-346-5215; {http://darkwing.uoregon.edu/~techtran}. Contact: Lynnore Stevenson. TTS coordinates the funding and contractual aspects of the technology transfer program - patent rights, licensing agreements, research and development contracts, and so on.

Pennsylvania

Pennsylvania Technical Assistance Program (PENNTAP), 117 Technology Center, University Park, PA 16802; 814-865-0427, Fax: 814-865-5909; {www.penntap.psu.edu}. PENNTAP provides free, short-term technical problem solving assistance by linking up businesses with the appropriate expertise. PENNTAP staff members assemble the most up-to-date information concerning the problem and presents the most practical solutions to the company in easy to understand terminology.

Ben Franklin Partnership, Department of Commerce, 352 Forum Bldg., Harrisburg, PA 17120; 717-787-4147, Fax: 717-772-5080; {www.dced.state.pa.us}. The Ben Franklin Partnership (BFP) programs promote entrepreneurial assistance services, which include: linking research, financial, and human resources; assisting in the preparation of business plans and feasibility studies; and providing small business incubator and technology transfer services.

South Carolina

South Carolina Manufacturing Extension Partnerships 1136 Washington Street, Suite 300, Columbia, SC 29202; 803-252-6976; {http://www.scmep.org/}. The South Carolina Manufacturing Extension Partnerships is the primary resource for South Carolina manufacturers, providing them with valuable technological, workplace, and business solutions that improve their industrial competitiveness.

South Dakota

South Dakota Governor's Office of Economic Development, 711 E. Wells Ave., Pierre, SD 57501-3369; 605-773-5032, 800-872-6190, Fax: 605-773-3256; {www.state.sd.us/state/executive/oed}, works with the Centers for Innovation, Technology and Enterprise (CITEs), located on each state-supported university campus to provide university-industry linkage.

Tennessee

Center for Industrial Services, Suite 606, 226 Capitol Boulevard Building, Nashville, TN 37219-1806; 615-532-8657, Fax: 615-532-4937; {www.cis.utk.edu}. Attn: T.C. Parsons. By drawing on university resources, the Center for Industrial Services (CIS) provides TN manufacturers and industries with free, short- term technical problem solving services in the following areas: product design and refinement, environmental impact assessments, waste reduction, quality control, computer systems, and more. CIS also helps small companies identify and implement new technologies that would be useful to their operations.

Texas

University of Texas, College of Engineering, ECJ 10.310, Austin, TX 78712; 512-232-1810, Fax: 512-471-3955; {http://www.engr.utexas.edu/cr/}. The Corporate Relations office of the University of Texas helps companies develop strategies for partnering with the College of Engineering to achieve specific goals for the benefit of the company, the students, and the faculty. The office strives to match a company's interests with the needs of the College to maximize a company's visibility and recognition on the UT Austin campus.

Technology and Economic Development, Texas Engineering Extension Service, Texas A&M University System, College Station, TX 77843-8000; 409-845-2907, 800-541-7149, Fax: 409-845-3559; {http://teexweb.tamu.edu}. The Texas Engineering Extension Service offers a broad range of technical assistance and technology transfer services for public and private sector organizations. TEEX helps businesses adapt to new technologies and provides customized business solutions that improve productivity and achieve results.

Utah

Centers of Excellence Program, Community and Economic Development, 324 S. State, Suite 500, Salt Lake City, UT 84111-7380; 801-538-8770, Fax: 801-538-8773; {www.dced.state.ut.us/techdev/coep.html}. The Centers receive state funding, which is matched by industry at least on a two to one basis, to develop technologies in targeted areas important to the state's industrial needs. To obtain access to technologies developed at the Centers, UT businesses must become program members, which involves offering matching research and development funds to the projects. Fees for transferred technologies depend on technology patents.

Utah has several offices which assist with technology transfer:
University of Utah's Technology Transfer Office, 615 Arapeen Drive, Suite 110, Salt Lake City, UT 84108; 801-581-7792, Fax: 801-581-7538; {www.tto.utah.edu}.

Utah State University Research and Technology Park, 1770 North Research Park Way, Suite 120, North Logan, UT 84341-1941; 435-797-9600, Fax: 435-797-9605; {http://www.usu.edu/research.htm}.

Brigham Young University, Technology Transfer Office, Provo, UT 84602; 801-378-4636 (switchboard); {http://acadvp.byu.edu/ORCA/TTHOME.HTM}.

Weber State University, Technology Assistance Center, Weber State University, Ogden, UT 84408; 801-626-7514 (Rick Orr), 801-626-6000 (switchboard); {http://www.weber.edu}.

Vermont

Vermont Department of Economic Development, Office of Technology, National Life Building, Drawer 20, Montpelier, VT 05620-0501; 800-VERMONT, 802-828-3080, Fax: 802-828-3258; {http://www.thinkvermont.com}. The Office of Technology works closely with several organizations on technology transfer.

Experimental Program to Stimulate Competitive Research (EPSCoR), Cook Building, University of Vermont, Burlington, VT 05405; 802-656-7969; {http://epscor.uvm.edu/}. The Vermont EPSCoR office is headquartered on the University of Vermont campus and involves research and transfer activities at nine colleges and universities in the state of Vermont.

Virginia

Center for Innovative Technology (CIT), 2214 Rock Hill Rd., Suite 600, Herndon, VA 22070; 703-689-3000, Fax: 703-689-3041; {www.cit.org}. CIT, in conjunction with the Virginia Community College system, provides free, short-term technical assistance to VA businesses. A company contacts a regional technology assistance transfer office to discuss their problem. The office, in turn, finds potential solutions from existing technologies and then presents them to the company. CIT also coordinates active industry involvement in research and development conducted at universities that demonstrates practical, commercial potential.

Washington

Washington Technology Center, 300 Fluke Hall, Box 352140, Seattle, WA 98195; 206-685-1920, Fax: 206-543-3059; {www.watechcenter.org}. Located at the state's major research universities, the Washington Technology Center's (WTC) labs conduct research and development projects for companies with specific technology oriented needs, and works out licensing agreements for the use of the new innovations. Companies wanting use of technologies already developed from WTC labs can do so through licensing agreements.

Wisconsin

University-Industry Research Relations (UIR), University of Wisconsin-Madison, 1215 WARF Building, 610 Walnut Street, Madison, WI 53705; 608-263-2840, Fax: 608-263-2841; {www.wisc.edu/uir}. Businesses with technical problems can contact University-Industry Research Relations (UIR), which will search their faculty databases for the appropriate expert to solve the problem. The company and expert then work out any consulting contractual arrangements on their own. UIR's search services are done at no charge.

Transfer of UWM technology to business and industry increases economic development in southeastern Wisconsin. Staff in the office act as a liaison between industry and the University in two ways: (1) initiating collaborative research and development programs and (2) assisting in faculty/researcher consulting agreements. Contact Kenneth C. Lerner, in Research Services and Administration, Mitchell 272, Milwaukee, WI 53201; 414-229-6302; {http://www.uwm.edu/Dept/RSA/center/patents.html}.

2,000 Productivity Specialists Offer *Free* Analysis

Lorrie Browing got help to find the best way to move her homemade beef jerky business out of her kitchen and into a real facility. A Texas wood products company turned their $35,000 loss disposing of sawdust into a $15,000 profit by selling it as animal bedding for horse stable floors.

The U.S. Department of Commerce has established 70 not-for-profit centers that will analyze your program and help you determine the best way to solve your problem. The analysis is free but there is a charge for follow up work. They have been established to help small and medium size manufacturers increase their potential for success. They can help companies cope with a changing environment, decrease manufacturing costs or discover ways to use new technology.

To identify your local center, contact Manufacturing Extension Partnership, National Institute of Standards and Technology, Gaithersburg, MD 20899; 800-637-4634; {www.mep.nist.gov}.

Alabama
Alabama Technology Network
One Perimeter Park South
Suite 486 North Tower
Birmingham, AL 35243
205-968-3455
Fax: 205-969-2228
www.atn.org

Alaska
Industry Network Corporation-Alaska
1155 University Blvd., SE
Albuquerque, NM 87106
505-843-4250
800-716-6462
Fax: 505-843-4255
www.mfg-inc.com

Arizona
Industry Network Corporation-Arizona
1155 University Blvd., SE
Albuquerque, NM 87106
505-843-4250
800-716-6462
Fax: 505-843-4255
www.mfg-inc.com

Arkansas
Arkansas Manufacturing Extension Network
100 Main St., Suite 450
Little Rock, AR 72201
501-324-9006
Fax: 501-324-9012
www.tecnet.org/amen

California
California Manufacturing Technology Center
13430 Hawthorne Blvd.
Hawthorne, CA 90250
310-263-3060
Fax: 310-676-8630
www.cmtc.com

Corporation for Manufacturing Excellence
48001 Fremont Blvd.
Freemont, CA 94538
510-249-1480
Fax: 510-249-1499
www.manex.org

San Diego Manufacturing Extension Center, Inc.
9663 Tierra Grande St., Suite 204
San Diego, CA 92126
619-530-4890, ext. 1201
619-530-4898
www.sanmec.org

Colorado
Mid-America Manufacturing Technology Center
10561 Barkley, Suite 602
Overland Park, KS 66212
913-649-4333
800-653-4333
Fax: 913-649-4498
www.mamtc.com

Connecticut
Connecticut State Technology Extension Program
185 Main St., Suite 408
New Britian, CT 06051
860-832-4600
Fax: 860-832-4620
www.connstep.org

Delaware
Delaware Manufacturing Extension Partnership
Delaware Technology Park
One Innovation Way, Suite 301
Newark, DE 19711
302-452-2520
Fax: 302-452-1101
www.delmep.org

Florida
Florida Manufacturing Technology Center
390 North Orange Ave.
Suite 1300
Orlando, FL 32801
407-316-4633
Fax: 407-316-4586
www.fmtx.org

Georgia
Georgia Manufacturing Extension Partnership
Georgia Institute of Technology
223 O'Keefe Bldg.
Atlanta, GA 30332
404-894-8989
Fax: 404-894-8194
www.edi.gatech.edu

Hawaii
Industry Network Corporation-Hawaii
1155 University Blvd., SE
Albuquerque, NM 87106
505-843-4250
800-716-6462
Fax: 505-843-4255
www.mfg-inc.com

Idaho
Idaho TechHelp
Boise State University
1910 University Dr.
Boise, ID 83725
208-426-3689
888-IDTEXHLP
Fax: 208-426-3877
www.techhelp.org

Illinois
Chicago Manufacturing Center
3333 West Arthington
Chicago, IL 60624
773-265-2020
Fax: 773-265-8336
www.cmcusa.org

Illinois Manufacturing Extension Center
404 Jobst Hall
Bradley University
Peoria, IL 61625
309-677-4632
Fax: 309-677-3289
www.imex1.org

Indiana
Indiana Business Modernization and Technology Corporation
One North Capitol Ave., Suite 925
Indianapolis, IN 46204
317-635-3058
800-877-5182
Fax: 317-231-7095
www.bmtadvantage.org

Iowa
Iowa Manufacturing Technology Center
Des Moines Area Community College
ATC Bldg., 3E
2006 S. Ankeny Blvd.
Ankeny, IA 50021
515-965-7125
Fax: 515-965-7050
www.tecnet.org/iowamtc

Kansas
Mid-America Manufacturing Technology Center
10561 Barkley, Suite 602

2,000 Productivity Specialists Offer Free Analysis

Overland Park, KS 66212
913-649-4333
800-653-4333
Fax: 913-649-4498
www.mamtc.com

Kentucky
Kentucky Technology Service
167 W. Main St., Suite 500
Lexington, KY 40507
606-252-7801
Fax: 606-252-7900

Louisiana
Louisiana Manufacturing Extension Partnership of Louisiana
P.O. Box 44172
241 E. Lewis St.
Lafayette, LA 70504
318-482-6767
Fax: 318-262-5472
http://lpc.usl.edu/mepol

Maine
Maine Manufacturing Extension Partnership
87 Winthrop St.
Augusta, ME 04330
207-623-0680
Fax: 207-623-0779
www.mainemep.org

Maryland
Maryland Technology Extension Service
University of Maryland Engineering Research Center
Potomac Bldg. 092, Room 2104
College Park, MD 20742
301-405-3883
301-403-4105
www.erc.umd.edu

Massachusetts
Massachusetts Manufacturing Partnership
Corporation for Business, Work and Learning
The Schrafft Center
529 Main St.
Boston, MA 02129
617-727-8158
800-667-6347
Fax: 617-242-7660
www.mmpmfg.org

Michigan
Michigan Manufacturing Technology Center
P.O. Box 1485
2901 Hubbard Rd.
Ann Arbor, MI 48106
734-769-4472
800-292-4484
Fax: 734-213-3405
www.iri.org/mmtc

National Metal Finishing Resource Center
National Center for Manufacturing Sciences
3025 Boardwalk Dr.
Ann Arbor, MI 48108
313-995-4911
Fax: 313-995-1150
www.nmfrc.org

Minnesota
Minnesota Technology, Inc.
111 Third Ave., South, Suite 400
Minneapolis, MN 5540
612-338-7722

Fax: 612-339-5214
www.minnesotatechnology.org

Mississippi
Mississippi Polymer Institute and Pilot Manufacturing Extension Center
P.O. Box 10003
Hattiesburg, MS 39406
601-266-4607
Fax: 601-266-5635
www.psrc.usm.edu/MPI

Mississippi Technology Extension Partnership
Bldg. 1103, Suite 146K
Stennis Space Center, MS 39529
228-688-3535
800-746-4699
Fax: 228-688-1426
www.technet.org/mtep

Missouri
Mid-America Manufacturing Technology Center
800 W. 14th St., Suite 111
Rolla, MO 65401
573-364-8570
800-956-2682
Fax: 573-364-6323
www.tecnet.org/mamtc

Mid-America Manufacturing Technology Center
10561 Barkley, Suite 602
Overland Park, KS 66212
913-649-4333
800-653-4333
Fax: 913-649-4498
www.mamtc.com

Montana
Montana Manufacturing Extension Center
313 Roberts Hall
Montana State University
Bozeman, MT 59717
406-994-3812
Fax: 406-994-3391
www.coe.montana.edu/mmec

Nebraska
Nebraska Manufacturing Extension Partnership
301 Centennial Mall South, 4th Floor
Lincoln, NE 68509
402-471-3755
Fax: 402-471-4374
http://nics.ded.state.ne.us

Nevada
Industry Network Corporation-Nevada
1155 University Blvd., SE
Albuquerque, NM 87106
505-843-4250
800-716-6462
Fax: 505-843-4255
www.mfg-inc.com

New Hampshire
Manufacturing Extension Partnership of New Hampshire
Millyard Technology Park
25 Pine Street Extension
Nashua, NH 03060
603-594-1188
Fax: 603-594-9146
www.nhmep.org

New Jersey
New Jersey Manufacturing Extension Partnership
New Jersey Institute of Technology

University Heights
GITC Suite 3200
Newark, NJ 07102
973-642-7099
Fax: 973-596-6056
www.njmep.org

New Mexico
Industry Network Corporation-New Mexico
1155 University Blvd., SE
Albuquerque, NM 87106
505-843-4250
800-716-6462
Fax: 505-843-4255
www.mfg-inc.com

New York
New York Manufacturing Extension Partnership
New York Science and Technology Foundation
99 Washington Ave., Suite 1730
Albany, NY 12210
518-486-7384
Fax: 518-473-6876

New York Manufacturing Extension Partnership
Hudson Valley Technology Development Center
33 Westage Business Center
Suite 130
Fishkill, NY 12524
914-896-6934
Fax: 914-896-706
www.hvtdc.org

New York Manufacturing Extension Partnership
Alliance for Manufacturing and Technology
61 Court St., 6th Floor
Binghamton, NY 13901
607-774-0022
Fax: 607-774-0026
http://amt-mep.org

New York Manufacturing Extension Partnership
Industrial Technology Assistance Corporation
253 Broadway, Room 302
New York, NY 10007
212-240-6920
Fax: 212-240-6879
www.itac.org

New York Manufacturing Extension Partnership
Western New York Technology Development Center
1576 Sweet Home Rd.
Amherst, NY 14228
716-636-3626
Fax: 716-636-3630
www.wnytdc.org

New York Manufacturing Extension Partnership
High Technology of Rochester
Five United Way
Rochester, NY 14604
716-327-7930
Fax: 716-327-7931
www.monroe.edu/rochproj/ htr.html

New York Manufacturing Extension Partnership
Center for Economic Growth
One Key Corporation Plaza, Suite 600
Albany, NY 12207
518-465-8975
Fax: 518-465-6681

New York Manufacturing Extension Partnership
Central New York Technology Development Organization

2,000 Productivity Specialists Offer Free Analysis

1201 E. Fayette St.
Syracuse, NY 13201
315-425-5144
Fax: 315-475-8460
www.cnytdor.org

New York Manufacturing Extension Partnership
CI-TEC
Box 8561, Peyton Hall
Potsdam, NY 13699
315-268-3778
Fax: 315-268-4432
www.northnet.org.citec/

New York Manufacturing Extension Partnership
Long Island Forum for Technology
P.O. Box 170
Farmingdale, NY 11735
516-755-3321
Fax: 516-755-9264
www.lift.org

New York Manufacturing Extension Partnership
Mohawk Valley Applied Technology Commission
207 Genessee St., Room 1604
Utica, NY 13501
315-793-8050
Fax: 315-793-8057
www.borg.com/~mvatc

New York Manufacturing Extension Partnership
National Center for Printing, Publishing and Imaging
Rochester Institute of Technology
111 Lomb Memorial Dr.
Rochester, NY 14623
716-475-2100
Fax: 716-475-5250

North Carolina
North Carolina Manufacturing Extension Partnership
900 Capability Dr.
Raleigh, NC 27695
919-515-5408
Fax: 919-515-8585
www.les.ncsu.edu

North Dakota
North Dakota Manufacturing Technology Partnership
Institute for Business and Industry Development
NDSU-Hastings Hall
P.O. Box 5256
Fargo, ND 58105
701-231-1001
Fax: 701-231-1007
www.growingnd.com/man_part_prog.htm

Ohio
Great Lakes Manufacturing Technology Center
Prospect Park Bldg.
4600 Prospect Ave.
Cleveland, OH 44103
216-432-5300
Fax: 216-432-5510
www.camp.org

Plastics Technology Development Center
GLMTC Manufacturing Outreach Program
Prospect Park Bldg.
4600 Prospect Ave.
Cleveland, OH 44103
216-432-5340
Fax: 216-432-2900
http://ptdc01.bd.psu.edu

Miami Valley Manufacturing Extension Center
1111 Edison Dr.
Cincinnati, OH 45216
513-948-2000
800-345-4482
Fax: 513-948-2109
http://iams.org/mvmec/ mvmec.htm

Lake Erie Manufacturing Extension Partnership
1700 N. Westwood Ave.
Toledo, OH 43607
419-534-3705
Fax: 419-531-8465
www.eisc.org

Oklahoma
Oklahoma Alliance for Manufacturing Excellence
525 S. Main St., Suite 210
Tulsa, OK 74105
918-592-0722
Fax: 918-592-1417
www.okalliance.com

Oregon
Oregon Manufacturing Extension Partnership
29353 Town Center, Loop East
Wilsonville, OR 97070
503-650-7350
800-MEP-4MFG
Fax: 503-682-4494
www.omep.org

Pennsylvania
North/East Pennsylvania Manufacturing Extension Partnership
125 Goodman Dr.
Bethlehem, PA 18015
610-758-5599
800-343-6732
Fax: 610-758-4716

Northeastern Pennsylvania Industrial Resource Center
75 Young St.
Wilkes Barre, PA 18706
717-819-8966
800-654-8960
Fax: 717-819-8931

Manufacturers' Resource Center
125 Goodman Dr.
Bethlehem, PA 18015
610-758-5599
800-343-6732
Fax: 610-758-4716

Mid-Pennsylvania Manufacturing Extension Partnership
MANTEC Inc.
The Manufacturers' Technology Center
227 W. Market St.
P.O. Box 5046
York, PA 17405
717-843-5054
888-843-5054
Fax: 717-854-0087
www.mantec.org

Industrial Modernization Center
Farm Complex
RR #5, Box 220-62A
Montoursville, PA 17754
717-368-8361
800-326-9467
Fax: 717-368-8452
www.imcpa.com

Southwestern Pennsylvania Industrial Resource Center
200 Technology Dr.
Pittsburgh, PA 15219
412-687-0200
Fax: 412-687-5232

Northwest Pennsylvania Industrial Resource Center
Uniflow Center
1525 East Lake Rd.
Erie, PA 16511
814-456-6299
Fax: 814-459-6058

Delaware Valley Industrial Resource Center
2905 Southhampton Rd.
Philadelphia, PA 19154
215-464-8550
Fax: 215-464-8570
www.technet.org/dvirc

Plastics Technology Development Center
C/o Penn State-Erie
Behrend College
Station Rd.
Erie, PA 16563
814-898-6132
Fax: 814-898-6006
http://ptdc01.bd.psu.edu

Rhode Island
Rhode Island Manufacturing Extension Services
229 Waterman St.
Providence, RI 02906
401-621-5710
Fax: 401-621-5702
www.rimes.org

South Carolina
South Carolina Manufacturing Extension Partnership
1136 Washington St.
Suite 300
Columbia, SC 29201
803-252-6976
Fax: 803-254-8512
www.scmep.org

South Dakota
South Dakota Manufacturing Extension Partnership Center
Governor's Office of Economic Development
711 E. Wells Ave.
Pierre, SD 57501
605-773-5653
Fax: 605-773-3256

Tennessee
Tennessee Manufacturing Extension Partnership
University of Tennessee
Center for Industrial Services
226 Capitol Blvd.
Suite 606
Nashville, TN 37219
615-532-8657
Fax: 615-532-4937
www.cis.utk.edu

Texas
Texas Manufacturing Assistance Center
1700 Congress Ave.
Suite 200
Austin, TX 78701
512-936-0234
800-488-TMAC

512-936-0433
www.tmac.org

Utah
Utah Manufacturing Extension Partnership
UT MEP at UVSC
800 W. 1200 S.
Orem, UT 84058
801-764-7221
Fax: 801-764-7222
www.mep.org

Vermont
Vermont Manufacturing Extension Center
Vermont Technical College
P.O. Box 520
Randolph Center, VT 05061
802-728-1432
Fax: 802-728-1456
www.vmec.org

Virginia
Virginia's A.L. Philpott Manufacturing Extension Partnership
P.O. Box 5311
645 Patriot Ave.
Martinsville, VA 24112
540-666-8890
Fax: 540-666-8892
www.vpmep.org

Washington
Washington Manufacturing Services
2333 Seaway Blvd.
Everett, WA 98271
425-267-0173
800-637-4634
Fax: 425-267-0175
www.tecnet.org/wms

West Virginia
West Virginia Manufacturing Extension Partnership
P.O. Box 6070
Morgantown, WV 26506
304-293-3800 Ext. 810
Fax: 304-293-6751

Wisconsin
Northwest Wisconsin Manufacturing Outreach Center
University of Wisconsin-Stout
278 Jarvis Hall
Menomonie, WI 54751
715-232-2397
Fax: 715-232-1105
http://nwmoc.uwstout.edu

Wisconsin Manufacturing Extension Partnership
2601 Crossroads Dr., Suite 145
Madison, WI 53718

608-240-1740
Fax: 608-240-1744
www.mep.org

Wyoming
Mid-America Manufacturing Technology Center
10561 Barkley
Suite 602
Overland Park, KS 66212
913-649-4333
800-653-4333
Fax: 913-649-4498
www.mamtc.com

National
National Center for Printing, Publishing and Imaging
Rochester Institute of Technology
111 Lomb Memorial Dr.
Rochester, NY 14623
716-475-2100
Fax: 716-475-5250

National Metal Finishing Resource Center
National Center for Manufacturing Sciences
3025 Boardwalk Dr.
Ann Arbor, MI 48108
313-995-4911
Fax: 313-995-1150
www.nmfrc.org

Company Intelligence

Company Intelligence: How To Find Information On Any Company

When many researchers are doing investigations on companies they often rely only on two major information sources:

Public Companies = U.S. Securities and Exchange Commission Filings

Privately Held Companies = Dun & Bradstreet Reports

Although many people still depend heavily on the Securities and Exchange Commission (SEC) and Dun & Bradstreet (D & B), these two resources have severe limitations. The Securities and Exchange Commission has information on approximately only 10,000 public companies in the United States. However, according to the IRS and the U.S. Bureau of the Census (both agencies count differently), there are between 5,000,000 and 12,000,000 companies in the country. So you can see that the SEC represents only a small fraction of the universe. Also, if you are interested in a division or a subsidiary of a public corporation and that division does not represent a substantial portion of the company's business, there will be no information on their activities on file at the SEC. This means that for thousands of corporate divisions and subsidiaries, it is necessary to look beyond the SEC.

D & B Won't Jail You for Not Telling the Truth but the Government Will

The problems with Dun & Bradstreet reports are more significant than the shortcomings of company filings at the SEC. The main drawback is that D & B reports have been established primarily for credit purposes and are supposed to indicate the company's ability to pay its bills. Therefore, you will find information from current creditors about whether a business is late in its payments, which may or may not be a useful barometer to evaluate the company.

If there is additional financial information in these reports, you should also be aware of who in the company provides D & B with information and their motives. The information contained in these reports does not carry the legal weight of the company information registered with the Securities and Exchange Commission. If a company lies about any of the information it turns over to the SEC, a corporate officer could wind up in jail. Dun & Bradstreet, however, collects its information by telephoning a company and asking it to provide certain information voluntarily. The company is under no obligation to comply and, equally important, is under no obligation to D & B to be honest. Unlike the government, Dun & Bradstreet cannot prosecute.

If a competitor or someone was interested in acquiring Information USA, Inc., for example, the first likely step would be to obtain any financial data about this privately held company. In this hypothetical case, Information USA, Inc. might be interested in such a sale or perhaps want to impress the competition.

Consequently, the information supplied to Dun & Bradstreet most likely would be the sanitized version which I would want outsiders to see. My only dilemma would be in remembering what half truths we told D & B last year so that our track record would appear consistent. However, Information USA, Inc. would not, and does not, play such games with its financial information filed with the Maryland Secretary of State.

This is why resourceful researchers are starting to appreciate the value of the thousands of non-traditional information sources such as public documents and industry experts.

Starting at the Securities and Exchange Commission

First find out whether the company you are gathering intelligence about is a public corporation. If it is, you should get your hands on copies of the company's Securities and Exchange Commission (SEC) filings. The fastest way to make this determination is to call:

Primark Financial Information Division
5161 River Road Building 60   301-951-1300
Bethesda, MD 20816   800-638-8241
www.disclosure.com

The price depends on which document you wish to have retrieved. The range is between $18 to $38 per document. If the company in question files with the Securities and Exchange Commission, the least you should do is to obtain a copy of the Annual Report, known as 10-K. This disclosure form will give you the most current description of the company's activities along with their annual financial statement.

Financial Statements in Addition to the Annual Report

In addition to the 10-K you may also want to see the company's most current financial statements by obtaining copies of all 10-Q's filed since their last 10-K. 10-Q's are basically quarterly financial statements which will bring you up-to-date since the last annual report.

The two other documents which may be of immediate interest are the 8-K's and the Annual Report to Stockholders. An 8-K will disclose any major developments that have occurred since the last annual report, such as information about a takeover or major lawsuit. The Annual Report to Stockholders, the glossy quasi-public relations tool that is sent to all those who own stock in the company, can provide another component in assembling a company's profile. The most interesting item in this report, which is not included in the 10-K Annual Report, is the message from the president. This message often provides insights about the company's future plans.

How To Find Information On Any Company

Obtaining Copies of SEC Documents

The fastest way to get Securities and Exchange Commission (SEC) documents is through one of the many document retrieval companies which provide this service. In addition to the firm mentioned above, other companies that specialize in quickly obtaining corporate SEC filings include:

1) FACS Info Service, Inc.
   157 Fisher Avenue
   Eastchester, NY 10709
   914-779-6900
   Fax: 914-779-7038

2) Federal Document Retrieval, Inc. (Disclosure)
   SEC Building
   601 Indiana Ave., 8th Floor
   Washington, DC 20001
   202-347-2824

3) Research Information Services
   717 D Street, NW
   Washington, DC 20004
   202-737-7111
   Fax: 202-737-3324

4) Prentice Hall Legal and Financial Services
   1090 Vermont Ave., NW, Suite 430
   Washington, DC 20005
   202-408-3120
   Fax: 202-408-3142

5) Washington Service Bureau
   655 15th Street NW, Room 275
   Washington, DC 20005
   202-508-0600
   Fax: 202-508-0694

6) Washington Document Service
   400 7th Street NW, Suite 300
   Washington, DC 20001
   202-628-5200
   Fax: 202-626-7628

7) Vickers Stock Research Corp.
   600 S Street NW, Suite 504
   Washington, DC 20004
   202-626-4951

You can also go to one of the four major Securities and Exchange Commission Document Rooms to see any public filing. These reference rooms are located in Washington, DC, New York City, Chicago, and Los Angeles.

If the company headquarters or main office is located in the area served either by the Atlanta, Boston, Denver, Fort Worth, or Seattle regional offices, the 10-K and other documents can be examined at the appropriate SEC office. For the exact location of any of the regional offices mentioned contact:

Office of Public Affairs
U.S. Securities and Exchange Commission
450 5th Street NW, Stop 1-2
Washington, DC 20549
www.sec.gov
202-942-0020

One way to obtain free copies of these reports is to call the company and tell them you are a potential investor. Many public corporations are set up to respond to these inquiry.

Before you order any of these SEC filings, it is wise to ask for the total number of pages contained in each of the documents you want to obtain. Most of these document retrieval firms charge by the page, and no doubt, you don't want to be surprised if a company's amendment to its 10-K happens to run 500 pages in length.

Once you have obtained the SEC documents you can then explore the additional sources described below.

Clues at the State Level About Privately Held Companies Plus Divisions and Subsidiaries of Public Corporations

The following sources are designed primarily to help you gather information on privately held companies or those divisions and subsidiaries of public corporations which are not contained in documents filed with the U.S. Securities and Exchange Commission. However, the sources described here will enhance your work in collecting data on all types of companies. If the company in question is not publicly owned, the next step is to turn your attention to the appropriate state government offices. All companies doing business in any state leave a trail of documentation there. The number of documents and the amount of detail vary widely depending upon the state regulations and the type of company.

One of the main reasons you should begin your search with the state government is that it may take longer to retrieve the information from the state offices than from other checkpoints which are described in this Section.

Puzzling Together Bits of Information

Remember that only the U.S. Securities and Exchange Commission documents provide you with information on your competitor or acquisition candidate. All other government documents are generated to comply with some law or policy, such as pollution control, consumer protection, or tax collection. Because of this, government bureaucrats who collect and analyze these documents have no idea just how valuable the information can be to you. Do not expect that the data contained in other government documents will be presented in a way that automatically will suit your particular needs. Furthermore, no single document will provide all the information about a corporate entity that you are seeking.

The strategy is to get any information you can because each piece might contribute to your overall information mosaic. Although a full profit and loss statement will be out of reach, the office of uniform commercial code can tell you to whom the company owes money and provide a description of the corporation's assets. The state office of corporations may not give you the total sales figure, but if the company's headquarter is out of state, it may tell you the corporation's total sales in that state and what percentage this is of its total. With a little bit of algebra you can estimate the total sales. If it were as easy as making one phone call and getting complete financial information on any company, everyone would be doing it. Your competitive advantage lies in getting information that other people don't know about, or are too lazy to get.

In the event you intend to dig around at the state level, the following three offices are a must. They offer the biggest potential for the least amount of effort:

1) Office of Corporations
Every corporation, whether it is headquartered or has an office in a state, must file some information with a state agency. The

Company Intelligence

corporations division or office of corporations usually is part of the office of the Secretary of State. When a company incorporates or sets up an office in the state, it must file incorporation papers, or something similar. This provides, at a minimum, the nature of the business, the names and addresses of officers and agents, and the amount of capital stock in the company. In addition to this registration, every company must file some kind of annual report. These annual reports may or may not contain financial data. Some states require sales figures, and others ask just for asset figures.

2) Office of Uniform Commercial Code

Any organization, and for that matter, any individual, which borrows money and offers an asset as collateral, must file within the state at the office of uniform commercial code. A filing is made for each loan and each of the documents is available to the public. To obtain these documents is a two step process. First, one must request a search to see if there are any filings for a certain company. The fee for a search is usually under $10. Such a search will identify the number of documents filed against the company. You then will have to request copies of each of these documents. The cost for each document averages only a few dollars. This office of uniform commercial code usually is located in, or near to, the same office of corporations.

3) State Securities Office

The U.S. Securities and Exchange Commission in Washington, DC regulates only those corporations which sell stock in their company across state lines. There is another universe of corporations which sells stock in their companies only within state lines. For such stock offerings, complete financial information is filed with the state securities regulator. These documents are similar to those filed at the U.S. Securities and Exchange Commission. But, remember, that the documents vary from one state to the next and, equally important, the requirement of filing an annual report differs from state to state. Usually a telephone call to the office in charge can tell you whether a particular company has ever offered stock intrastate. If so, you are then in a position of getting copies of these filings. Usually the Secretary of State's office can refer you to the state's securities regulator.

Finding the Right State Office

Because of the multitude of differences between the 50 state governments, expect to make half a dozen calls before you locate the right office. Several starting places are described below with the simplest ones listed first.

1) State Government Operator

The AT&T information operator can give you the telephone number for the state government operator, and then in turn you can ask for the phone number of the specific government office.

2) State Department of Commerce

Now that every state is aggressively trying to get companies to expand or relocate to their state, these departments can serve as excellent starting points, because they are familiar with other government offices which regulate business. Many times these departments have established a "one-stop office" with a separate staff on call to help a business find whatever information it needs.

3) State Capital Library

By asking the state government operator to connect you to the state capital library, a reference librarian can identify the state agency which can best respond to your queries.

4) Directories

If you intend to dig around various state government offices on more than just an infrequent basis, you might consider purchasing a state government directory. Usually the state office of Administrative Services will sell you a directory, or you might want to contact the state bookstore. If you want to purchase a directory that covers all 50 states, consider:

State Executive Directory
Carroll Publishing Company
4701 Sangamore Rd., Suite S-155
Bethesda, MD 20816   301-263-9800
www.carrollpub.com
(Price is $300 per year plus shipping and handling.)

Tracking the Trail of Company Information in Other State Offices

The three offices described earlier are only the starting places for information on companies. There are dozens of other state agencies that are brimming with valuable bits of data about individual corporations; however, these sources require a bit more care because they can be used only under certain circumstances or require extra resourcefulness.

1) Utility and Cable TV Regulators

Utility companies are heavily regulated by state agencies, and as a result, there is a lot of financial and operational information that is accessible. Most people know that gas and electric companies fall into this category, but you may not be aware that this also applies to water companies, bus companies, rail systems, telephone companies, telecommunication companies, and cable TV operators.

2) Other State Regulators

State government is very similar to the federal government in that its function is to regulate many of the activities of the business community. In those states where state laws and enforcement are very effective, Uncle Sam relies on those states to enforce the federal laws. For example, the U.S. Food and Drug Administration will use the records from the state of New Jersey for information on pharmaceutical manufacturers instead of sending out its own team of federal data collectors. The U.S. Environmental Protection Administration will use state records in those states that have strict environmental statutes rather than using its own resources.

3) Financial Institutions

Banks, savings and loans, credit unions and other financial institutions all file information with the state bank regulator. Many of these organizations are also regulated by federal agencies so what you get from the state office often will be a copy of the form filed with the federal government.

4) Environment Regulators

Almost every state has an office which regulates pollutants in the air, water and ground. Such departments are similar to the U.S. Environmental Protection Agency in Washington, DC and monitor whether any new or old business is polluting the environment. If

How To Find Information On Any Company

the company you are investigating has plans to build a new plant in the state, get ready to collect some valuable information. Before construction can begin, the company must file information with the state environmental protection agency. These documents will detail the size of the plant, what kind of equipment it will use, and how much this equipment will be used. With such information, other manufacturers in the same business can tell exactly what the capacity and estimated volume of the plant will be. Sometimes there will be three separate offices with authority over air, water or solid waste. Each will collect basically the same information, and they can be used, one against each other, to ensure that you get all the information you need.

5) **Department of Commerce/Economic Development**
As mentioned earlier, each state is now actively trying to attract and develop business development within the state. The state's office of economic development or department of commerce is normally charged with this responsibility. To attract business to the state, this agency has to know all about existing business throughout the state, which all translates into who is doing what, how successful they are, and how large the company is. At a minimum, the economic development office can probably provide you with information on the number of employees for a given company. They will also be aware what other government offices in the state keep records about the industry or company which interests you. The experts at this state agency are similar to the 100 industry analysts at the U.S. Department of Commerce and can serve as excellent resources for collecting government information on an industry.

6) **State Government Contractors**
Although many states are not accustomed to sharing information with researchers, you should be able to obtain details about any purchase the state makes. If the company in question sells to the state, you should get copies of their contracts. Just like the federal government which makes all this procurement information available, the state which spends public funds guarantees that the public has a right to know how the money is being spent. You may have to enforce your rights under the state law which is equivalent to the federal Freedom of Information Act.

7) **Minority and Small Business**
Many states maintain special offices which track minority firms and other small companies. These offices can be helpful by identifying these businesses and may also be able to tell you the size or products of a given business. The small business office and possibly a separate minority business division normally fall under the state department of commerce.

8) **Attorney General**
The state Attorney General's office is the primary consumer advocate for the state against fraudulent practices by businesses operating within the state. So, if the company you are investigating is selling consumer services or products, it would be worth the effort to check with this office. In some states the attorney generals have begun to concentrate on certain areas. For example, the office in Denver specializes in gathering information on companies selling energy saving devices, and the one in New York investigates companies with computerized databases which provide scholarship information.

9) **Food and Drug Companies**
Any company which produces, manufactures or imports either food or drug products is likely to come under the jurisdiction of the state food and drug agency. This office makes routine inspections of facilities and the reports are generally accessible; however, a Freedom of Information Act request is sometimes necessary.

County and Local Sources

County and local sources can prove to be the biggest bucket of worms as far as information sources go. Unlike state government offices where there are 50 varieties to choose from, there are over 5,000 different jurisdictions at the local level. Here are some basic checkpoints that can enhance your information gathering efforts.

Local Newspapers: Business Editors

The local newspaper can provide the best leads for anything you are investigating at the local level. It is perhaps the best source mentioned in this book. A well placed telephone call to the business editor or the managing editor, if there is not a business section, can prove to be most useful. In smaller towns, and even in suburbs of larger cities where there are suburban newspapers, a local business generates a good deal of news. A local reporter often knows the company like no one else in the country. The company executives usually are more open with the local media because they like to show off about how big they are, how much the company is growing, etc. A reporter is also likely to know company employees who can corroborate or refute the executive's remarks.

Ask the local newspaper if you can get copies of all articles written about the company in question. After you review them, call the reporter to see what additional information may be stored in his or her head.

Other Checkpoints

It is worth fishing for information in a number of other places, including agencies and private organizations.

1) **Chamber of Commerce**
Talking to someone on the research staff or the librarian can help you identify sources within the community about a company. A friendly conversation with Chamber executives can also provide insight into a company's financial position and strategies.

2) **Local Development Authority**
Many local communities, counties, and regional areas have established development authorities to attract business and industry to their area. They operate pretty much the same as the state department of economic development described above, and as a result, collect a large amount of data about the businesses in their area.

3) **Local Courts**
Civil and criminal court actions can provide excellent source material for company investigations. Perdue Chicken Company, a private corporation in Maryland, revealed its annual sales figures while fighting Virginia sales tax in the courts. A recent search revealed four financial-related suits filed against a large

Company Intelligence

privately held political campaign fund raising firm in McLean, Virginia. If you are not in close proximity to the court, it may be worthwhile to hire a local freelance reporter or researcher. In most jurisdictions there are chronological indexes of both civil and criminal cases which are kept by the clerk of the court. These indexes record all charges or complaints made, the names of the defendants and plaintiffs in the event of civil cases, the date of the filing, the case number, and the disposition if one has been reached. Armed with the case number you can request to see the case files from the clerk.

Company Information at the Office of Federal Regulators

The federal offices identified in the preceding section on market studies are also excellent sources for information on companies. Industry specialists within the federal government are likely to have information on companies or can refer you to other sources which may have just the information you need.

The 26 government agencies listed here are those that are involved with regulating industries and/or the companies within those industries. The information held at each federal office varies from agency to agency; however, most of the offices maintain financial or other information that most researchers would consider sensitive.

Airlines, Air Freight Carriers, and Air Taxis
Office of Community and Consumer Affairs
U.S. Department of Transportation
400 7th Street SW, Room 10405
Washington, DC 20590
www.dot.gov/ost/
202-366-2220/5957

Airports
Airport Section
National Flight Data Center, Room 634
Federal Aviation Administration, ATM-612
800 Independence Avenue SW
Washington, DC 20591
www.faa.gov/aviation.htm
202-267-9311

Bank Holding Companies and State Members of the Federal Reserve System
Freedom of Information Act Office
Board of Governors of the Federal Reserve System
20th St. and Constitution Ave. NW, Room B1122
Washington, DC 20551
www.bog.frb.fed.us
202-452-3684

Banks, National
Communications Division
Comptroller of the Currency
250 E St., SW
Washington, DC 20219
www.occ.treas.gov
202-874-4700

Barge and Vessel Operators
Financial Analysis, Tariffs
Federal Maritime Commission
800 N. Capitol St., NW
Washington, DC 20573
www.fmc.gov
202-523-5876

Cable Television System Operators
Cable TV Branch
Federal Communications Commission
445 12th St., SW, Room 3-C830
Washington, DC 20554
www.fcc.gov/csb
202-418-7200

Colleges, Universities, Vocational Schools, and Public Schools
Office of Educational Research and Improvement
U.S. Department of Education
555 New Jersey NW, Room 600
Washington, DC 20208-5530
www.ed.gov/offices/OERI/
202-219-2050

Commodity Trading Advisors
National Futures Association
200 W. Madison St., Suite 1600
Chicago, IL 60606-3447
Attn: Compliance Dept.
www.nfa.futures.org
800-621-3570
Fax: 312-781-1467

Consumer Products
Consumer Protection Division
U.S. Consumer Product Safety Commission
4330 East-West Highway
Bethesda, MD 20814
www.cpsc.gov
301-504-0621

Electric and Gas Utilities and Gas Pipeline Companies
Federal Energy Regulatory Commission
888 First St., NE
Washington, DC 20426
www.ferc.fed.us
202-208-0200

Exporting Companies
Bureau of Export Administration
Exporter Counseling Division
U.S. Department of Commerce
14th and Constitution Avenue, Room 1099
Washington, DC 20230
www.bxa.doc.gov
202-482-4811

Federal Land Bank and Production Credit Associations
Farm Credit Administration
1501 Farm Credit Drive
McLean, VA 22102-5090
www.fca.gov
703-883-4000

Foreign Corporations
World Traders Data Report
U.S. Department of Commerce
Washington, DC 20230
www.stat-usa.gov/tradtest.nsf
202-482-4204

Government Contractors
Federal Procurement Data Center
General Services Administration
7th and D Streets, SW, Room 5652
Washington, DC 20407
http://fpds.gsa.gov
202-401-1529

Hospitals and Nursing Homes
National Center for Health Statistics
6525 Belcrest Rd.
Hyattsville, MD 20782
www.cdc.gov/nchs/
301-436-8500

Land Developers
Office of Interstate Land Registration
U.S. Department of Housing and Urban Development
451 7th Street SW, Room 9146
Washington, DC 20410
www.hud.gov
202-708-0502

Mining Companies
Mine Safety and Health Administration
U.S. Department of Labor

How To Find Information On Any Company

4015 Wilson Boulevard
Arlington, VA 22203
www.msha.gov
703-235-1452

Non-Profit Institutions
U.S. Internal Revenue Service
Freedom of Information Reading Room
1111 Constitution Ave. NW, Room 1563
P.O. Box 388, Ben Franklin Station
Washington, DC 20044
www.irs.gov
202-622-5164

Nuclear Power Plants
Director, Office of Nuclear Reactor Regulation
U.S. Nuclear Regulatory Commission
Washington, DC 20555
www.nrc.gov
301-415-7163

Pension Plans
Division of Inquiries and Technical Assistance
Office of Pension and Welfare Benefits Programs
U.S. Department of Labor
200 Constitution Avenue NW, Room N5619
Washington, DC 20210
www.dol.gov/dol/pwba
202-219-8776

Pharmaceutical, Cosmetic and Food Companies
Associate Commissioner for Regulatory Affairs
U.S. Food and Drug Administration
5600 Fishers Lane, Room 14-90
Rockville, MD 20857
www.fda.gov/ora/ora_home_page.html
301-827-3101

Pesticide and Chemical Manufacturers
U.S. Environmental Protection Agency
Office of Prevention Pesticides and Toxic Substances
401 M Street, SW (7101)
Washington, DC 20460
www.epa.gov/internet/oppts/
202-260-2902

Radio and Television Stations
Mass Media Bureau
Federal Communications Commission
445 12th St., SW, Room 2-C334
Washington, DC 20554
www.fcc.gov/mmb/
202-418-2600

Savings and Loan Associations
Office of Thrift Supervision
1700 G Street NW
Washington, DC 20552
www.ots.treas.gov
202-906-6000

Telephone Companies, Overseas Telegraph Companies, Microwave Companies, Public Land and Mobile Service
Common Carrier Bureau
Federal Communications Commission
445 12th St., SW
Washington, DC 20554
www.fcc.gov/ccb/
202-418-1500

Suppliers and Other Industry Sources

If all of the above sources fail to provide information you need on a given company, your last resort is to go directly into the industry and try to extract the information by talking with insiders.

Although your telephone is an essential and perhaps the best research tool, there are two other reference sources that will help you track down industry specialists:

1) **Trade Associations** are identified in *Encyclopedia of Associations* - (Gale Research Inc., 27500 Drake Rd., Farmington Hills, MI 48331; 248-699-4253; {www.gale.com});

2) **100 Industry Analysts** at the U.S. Department of Commerce. Government Industry Analysts who cover industries such as athletic goods, dairy products or truck trailers.

Your first step is to begin casting around for someone in the industry who knows about the company in question. When hunting for an expert, it is essential that you remain determined and optimistic about eventually finding one or several individuals who will be "information jackpots."

People who know their industry will be able to give you the details you need about any company (i.e., its size, sales, profitability, market strategies). These sources probably will not be able to give you the precise figure that is on the balance sheet or profit and loss statement, but they will offer a very educated guess which is likely to be within 10 to 20% of the exact figure. And usually this estimate is good enough for anyone to work with.

The real trick is finding the right people -- the ones who know. Talk to them and get them to share their knowledge with you.

Where Else to Look for Industry Experts

Industry experts are not concentrated in Washington, DC but are located all over the world, so you need to exercise some common sense to figure out where to find them. Here are some general guidelines.

1) **Industry Observers**
These are specialists on staff at trade associations, think tanks, and at the U.S. Department of Commerce and other government agencies. Anyone who concentrates on an industry has familiarity with the companies that comprise that industry.

2) **Trade Magazines**
You will find that there is at least one magazine which reports on every industry. The editors and reporters of these trade publications are also well acquainted with individual companies.

3) **Suppliers**
Most industries have major suppliers which must know about the industry they service and the companies within that industry. For example, the tire manufacturers anticipate every move among auto makers well before any other outsiders. Suppliers also have to know the volume of every manufacturer to whom they sell their product because of the obvious repercussions on the supplier's business. Every company is like this, even Information USA, Inc. We are basically a publisher, and if you talk to our printers, you would get a pretty good picture of exactly what we are doing.

Company Case Studies and Databases

1) **Company Case Studies For As Little As $2 Each**
Case studies of major and minor companies, as well as subsidiaries of public companies, can provide valuable competitive intelligence. These cases are identified in an $10 publication titled *Catalog of Teaching Materials*.

Company Intelligence

HBS Publications Division
Operations Department   617-783-7400
Boston, MA 02163   Fax: 617-783-7555
www.hbsp.harvard.edu

2) Government and Commercial Databases

ABI/Inform, Disclosure, and Management Contents are just a few of the online databases which provide quick access to information about all types of companies. Additional leads for gathering information about companies can be derived from diverse databases maintained by the U.S. government, many of which are identified in the *Federal Database Finder* (Information USA, Inc.).

Complete Financials on Franchising Companies

Franchising companies, whether public or privately held, must file detailed financial information in 14 different states. These state statutes create excellent opportunities for gathering competitive and marketing data as outlined below.

Inside Information

If the company of interest is a franchise organization, a great deal of financial information for their average franchisee is available in addition to their corporate profit and loss statements and balance sheets. A typical table of contents for a filing includes:

* biographical information on persons affiliated with the franchisor
* litigation
* bankruptcy
* franchisees' initial franchise fee or other initial payment
* other recurring or isolated fees and payments
* the franchisee's initial investment
* obligations of the franchisee to purchase or lease from designated sources
* obligations of the franchisee to purchase or lease in accordance with specifications or from approved suppliers
* financing arrangements
* obligations of the franchisor: other supervision, assistance or services
* territorial rights
* trademarks, service marks, trade names, logotypes and commercial symbols
* patents and copyrights
* obligation of the franchisee to participate in the actual operation of the franchise business
* restrictions on goods and services offered by the franchisee
* term, renewal, termination, repurchase, modification, assignment and related information
* agreements with public figures
* actual, average, projected or forecasted franchisee sales, profits and earnings
* information regarding franchises of the franchisor
* financial statements
* contracts
* standard operating statements
* list of operational franchisees
* estimate of additional franchised stores
* company-owned stores
* estimate of additional company-owned stores
* copies of contracts and agreements

Market Information and Franchising Trends

The franchise information packets often include information on the results of their market studies which establish the need for their product or service. These can provide valuable market information as well as forecasts for potential markets. Is the ice cream boom over? A quick check into Ben and Jerry's forecast for future stores will give you a clue of what the experts think.

Franchise companies are often the first to jump into current trends and fads in the U.S., for example, ice cream shops and diet centers. You can get an instant snapshot of such a trend by reviewing the marketing section of a franchise agreement.

Career Opportunities

If you ever wondered how much it would cost to open up your own bookstore, restaurant, video store, or most any other kind of venture, you can get all the facts and figures you need without paying a high-priced consultant or tipping your hand to your current employer. Just take a look at a franchise agreement from someone in a similar line of business. You can even discover the expected salary level.

New Business for Suppliers

If you are looking to sell napkins, Orange Julius or computer services to Snelling & Snelling, their franchise statements will disclose what kind of agreements they currently have with similar suppliers.

State Checkpoints for Franchising Intelligence

To obtain franchise agreements from the 15 states that require such disclosure, simply call one or more of the offices listed below and ask if a specific company has filed. Copies of the documentation are normally sent in the mail with a copying charge of $.10 to $.50 per page.

California
Department of Corporations, 1115 11th Street, Sacramento, 95814, 916-445-7205. Fee is 30 cents per page. Send blank check stating $25 limit. They will call with price for orders exceeding that amount.

Hawaii
Department of Commerce and Consumer Affairs, Business Registration Department, 1010 Richards Street, Honolulu, 96813, P.O. Box 40, Honolulu, 96810, 808-586-2722. Fee is 25 cents per page.

Illinois
Franchise Division, Office of Attorney General, 500 South Second Street, Springfield, 62704, 217-782-4465. Charge is a $40 flat fee per company franchise.

Indiana
Franchise Division, Secretary of State, 302 West Washington Street, Room E-111, Indianapolis, 46204, 317-232-6576. Fee is 10 cents per page plus handling charges.

Maryland
Assistant Attorney General, Maryland Division of Securities, 200 St. Paul Place, 21st Floor, Baltimore, 21202-2020, 410-576-6360. Maryland does not make copies. Suggests contacting Documents-To-Go, 800-879-4949.

Michigan
Antitrust and Franchise Unit, Office of Attorney General, 670 Law Building, Lansing, MI 48913; 517-373-7117.

Minnesota
Minnesota Department of Commerce, Enforcement Division, 133 East Seventh Street, St. Paul, 55101, 651-296-6328. Contact Ann Hagestad at 612-296-6328. Fee is 50 cents per page.

New York
Bureau of Investor and Protection Securities, New York State Department of Law, 120 Broadway, New York, 10271, 212-416-8211. Fee is 25 cents per page.

North Dakota
Franchise Examiner, North Dakota Securities Commission, 600 East Blvd., Fifth Floor, Bismarck, 58505, 701-328-2910. Documents are open for the public to inspect and copy, but this office does not provide copies as a service.

Oregon
Department of Insurance and Finance, Corporate Securities Section, Division of Finance and Corporate Securities, 21 Labor and Industries Bldg., Salem, 97310, 503-378-4387. Oregon does not keep franchise documents on file.

Rhode Island
Securities Section, Securities Division, 233 Richmond Street, Suite 232, Providence, 02903-4237, 401-222-3048. Special request form must be used. Fee is 15 cents per page copy and $15 an hour per search time.

South Dakota
Franchise Administrator, Division of Securities, State Capitol, Pierre, 57501, 605-773-4013. Fee is 50 cents per sheet.

Virginia
Franchise Section, Division of Securities and Retail Franchising, 1300 E. Main Street, Richmond, 23219, 804-371-9276. Fee is $.50 per page.

Washington
Department of Financial Institutions, Securities Division, P.O. Box 9033, Olympia, 98507-9033, 360-902-8760; {www.wa.gov/dfi/securities}. No charge for orders under 30 pages, then 10 cents for each page thereafter, plus tax.

Wisconsin
Franchise Investment Division, Wisconsin Securities Commission, PO Box 1768, 101 East Wilson Street, Madison, 53701, 608-266-3414/3364; {www.wdfi.org}. Wisconsin does not provide copies of franchise agreements. One must come in person or hire private service.

Company Intelligence

Every Company Has To File With The State

State documents on 9,000,000 public and private companies have hit the computer age. Thirty states already offer online access to their files and others intend to follow suit within the next year. Computerized records are such a major issue with state officials who administer corporate division offices that they have placed online access on their annual convention agenda. Furthermore, 27 states will make their complete files available on magnetic tape, and, I should say, at bargain prices. And if you are not computerized, all but a few states offer free telephone research services. Here are a dozen ways to ferret out current information on companies:

- a list of companies by SIC code within a given state or county
- names and addresses of a company's officers and directors
- a list of all new companies incorporated in a given week or month
- the location of any company with a single phone call
- a mailing list of 300,000 companies for $100
- the availability of a given company name
- a complete list of non-profit organizations
- a list of companies by city, zip, date of incorporation, or size of capital stock
- a mailing list of limited partnerships
- a listing of companies on which a given individual is an officer or board member
- a listing of trademarks for a given state
- which companies in a given state are subsidiaries of a given company

Financial Data and Other Documents on File

Although there are variations, almost all states maintain the following documents for every company doing business in their state: Certificate of Good Standing; Articles of Incorporation; Reinstated Articles of Incorporation; Articles of Amendment; Articles of Merger; Articles of Correction; Articles of Dissolution; Certificate of Incorporation; Certificate of Authority; and Annual Report (which contains list of officers and directors).

All states require corporations to file the original Articles of Incorporation, a yearly annual report and amendments to the Articles of Incorporation. Clerks can provide you with certifications of good standing stating that the corporation has complied with the regulation to file a yearly annual report. A certificate of good standing does not assure financial stability, and is only a statement that the corporation has abided by the law. You may obtain a statement of name availability if you are searching for a name for your new corporation. Most states require prepayment for copies of documents. You can mail them a blank check stipulating the amount not to exceed a certain amount. You may want to call the phone information number for details before sending in your written request.

Only a few states require financial information in their annual reports. However, every state requires companies to list the value of the capital stock in their Articles of Incorporation. Some states, such as Massachusetts used to require financial data in the past, so it may be useful to request annual reports of previous years.

Data on Six Different Types of Companies

The types of companies required to file documents with the state include: Domestic Companies (those incorporated within the state), Foreign Companies (those incorporated in another state, but doing business in the state), Partnerships, Limited Partnerships, Non-Profit Organizations, Business Names (incorporated and non-incorporated firms). It should be emphasized here that all public and private companies as well as subsidiaries of public corporations are required to reveal this information.

Company Information Available in Numerous Formats

Each state provides information about corporations in some or all of the following formats:

1) Telephone, Mail and Walk-In Services:
Telephone information lines have been established in all but one state to respond to inquiries regarding the status of a specific corporation. New Jersey and North Dakota charge for phone service. The NJ Expedite Service allows you to receive information over the phone and charge the cost of the service to your credit card. Another option for New Jersey company information is to have it sent via Western Union's electronic mail service.

Telephone operators can verify corporate names, identify the resident agent and his address, the date of incorporation, the type of corporation (foreign, domestic, etc.), and the amount of capital stock. Often these operators can either take your request for documents on file pertaining to a corporation or they can refer you to the appropriate number. Names of officers and directors are never given over the phone. This information is usually contained in a company's annual report, copies of which can be requested by phone or letter.

These state telephone lines tend to be quite busy. It is not unusual for the larger offices of a corporation to answer over 1,200 inquiries a day. Persistence and patience are essential on your part. Requests for copies of documents usually require prepayment. You can mail them a blank check stipulating the amount not to exceed a certain amount. You may want to call the phone information number for details before sending in your written request.

Walk-in service, with access to all documents, is an option in every state. However, if you do not want to do the research yourself, almost every state can suggest private firms which will obtain the pertinent data for you.

2) Mailing Labels:
The following six states will print mailing labels of companies on file: Arizona, Idaho, Maine, New Mexico, Mississippi, and

Every Company Has To File With The State

Nebraska. However, over half the states will sell you a computer tape of their files, from which mailing labels can be generated easily by a good mailhouse or service bureau.

3) Computer Tape Files:
Currently 27 states will provide you with magnetic tapes of their corporate files. The cost is very reasonable, and in many cases the state will require the user to supply blank tapes.

4) Custom Services:
Many of the states provide custom services with outputs ranging from computer printouts and magnetic tape files to statistical tables. Such services are a valuable way to obtain specific listings of corporations such all non-profit corporations or all companies within a given SIC code. Most states that offer this option compute cost by figuring time, programming time, and printing expense.

5) New Companies:
Almost all of the states offer some type of periodic listing of newly formed companies. As a rule, these can be purchased on a daily, weekly, or monthly subscription basis.

6) Microfiche and Microfilm:
Eleven of the states will also sell you copies of their documents on microfiche or microfilm at a nominal fee.

7) Online Access:
As mentioned earlier, thirty states now provide online access to their files, and other states are in the active planning stages. The states currently with online systems include: Alabama, Alaska, Arizona, Arkansas, Colorado, Florida, Georgia, Hawaii, Idaho, Illinois, Indiana, Iowa, Kansas, Louisiana, Massachusetts, Michigan, Minnesota, Mississippi, Missouri, Nevada, New Mexico, North Carolina, Oklahoma, Pennsylvania, South Carolina, Texas, Utah, Virginia, and Vermont.

State Corporation Divisions

Alabama
Division of Corporation, Secretary of State, 4121 Carmichael Road, Montgomery, AL 36106 or P.O. Box 5616, Montgomery, AL 36103-5616, 334-242-5324, Fax: 334-242-4993; {www.sos.state.al.us}. Selected Publications: Guide to Incorporation. Phone Information: 334-242-5324. Office is not completely computerized yet, but can do word search or partial name search by officer, incorporator, or serving agent. Copies of documents on File: Available by written request for $1 per page plus $5 for certified copies. Can provide information over the phone at no cost. Mailing Labels: No. Magnetic Tape: No. Microfiche: No. New Corporate Listings: No. Custom Searches: Can do word or partial name search. Printout of search results by mail is free. Online Access: Yes. Number of active corporations on File: Figures Not Available

Alaska
State of Alaska, Division of Banking, Securities and Corporation, Corporation Section, P.O. Box 110808, Juneau, AK 99811-0808, 907-465-2530, Fax: 907-465-3257; {www.commerce.state.ak.us}. Selected Publications: None. Phone information: 907-465-2530. Copies of Documents on File: Complete corporate record (Articles of Incorporation, annual report, amendments, etc.) Cost $30, certified copies add $5, list of officers and directors cost $1, Certificate of Status cost $10. Mailing Labels: No. Magnetic tape: no, only diskettes. Copy of complete master file excluding officers and directors is priced at $100. Monthly supplements are an additional $10. Microfiche: No, only disk and e-mail. New corporate listings: yes. Custom Searches: yes. Online Access: Yes. Number of active corporations on file: 25,172.

Arizona
Arizona Corporations Division, Records Division, Secretary of State, 1200 W. Washington, Phoenix, AZ 85007 or P.O. Box 6019, Phoenix, AZ 85005, 602-542-3026, Fax: 602-542-4100; {www.cc.state.az.us}. Selected Publications: Sample packet with forms and statutes mailed for $8. Guideline booklets will be available soon. Phone Information : 602-542-3026. Copies of Documents on File: Cost 50 cents per page, $5 for certified copies. Mailing Labels: No. Magnetic Tape: Master File $400, issued monthly. Requester must supply blank tape. Microfiche: All corporations statewide $75. New Corporate Listing: Monthly Listing of New Domestic Companies for $200 plus $200 for new foreign listings. Custom searches: Yes, request in writing or in person. Can search by company name, agent name or officer name. Online Access. There is a charge for filing online. Contact business connection for forms 602-280-1480. Available through Information America, Dunn and Bradstreet and other commercial services. Number of corporations on file: 100,000

Arkansas
Secretary of State, Corporations Division, State Capitol Building, Room 058, Little Rock, AR 72201, 501-682-5151, Fax: 501-682-3437; {http:\\sos.state.ar.us}. Selected Publications: None. Phone Information: 501-682-5151. Copies of Documents on file: Call 501-371-3431 for copies at 50 cents per page plus $5 for certified copies. Domestic companies $50, Foreign companies $300. Mailing labels: No. Magnetic Tape: Master file 2 cents per name. Microfiche: No. New corporate Listing: Statistics only. Custom Searches. Categories include foreign, domestic, profit, and non-profit corporations. Cost: 2 cents per name, 50 cents per page. Online Access: Yes. Number of active corporations on file: 1,000,000

California
Corporations, Supervisor of Records, Secretary of State, 1500 11th Street, CA 95814-5701, 916-653-6814, {www.ss.ca.gov}. Selected Publications: Corporations Checklist Booklet. Request must be in writing and cost is $5. Phone Information: 916-653-6814. Copies of Documents on File: Articles of Incorporation: cost is $1 for first page, 50 cents for each additional page plus $5 for certified copies, Certificate of status $6, Statement of officers $5 and $10 for certified copies (written requests only). You must pay in advance or send blank check not to exceed $20. Send requests to secretary of state, Attention RIC unit. Mailing Labels: No. Magnetic Tape: Yes, Master copy $17,600 annually. Call 916-653-8905 for information. Hard copy $14,000.13. Microfiche: No. Custom Searches: Computer generated listing of Active Stock ($17,030), Active Non-Stock ($422). Active Non-Stock by Classification $150 per list. Management Services Division, Information Systems Section, 1230 J Street, Suite 242, Sacramento, CA 95814. All orders must be submitted in writing. Basic cost of magnetic tape copy is $1.02 per 1,000 names. Basic cost of same run, for custom search, printed on paper, is $4.13 per 1,000 names. $150 minimum is applied to both. Online Access: Yes. Number of Corporations on File: 2,000,000.

Colorado
Corporate Division, Secretary of State, 1560 Broadway, Suite 200, Denver, CO 80202, 303-894-2251, Fax: 303-894-2251; {www.state.co.us/gov_dir\sos}. Selected Publications: Corporate Guide. Copies of Documents on File: Cost is 50 cents per page, plus $10 for certification. Mailing Labels: No. Magnetic Tape: Available for $500 for complete set of five. Tapes must be purchased individually. Categories: Foreign and Domestic. Microfiche: available at $1 a sheet (includes Summary of Master Computer File, must be purchased in its entirety). New Corporate Listings: Reporting Service costs $200 a year. Weekly list of New Corporations. Written requests only. Custom searches: Yes. Categories: Foreign and Domestic available on a cost recovery basis. The minimum fee is $50. Online Access: Available. Fee is $300 for 3 months or $1,000 per year. Number of Corporations on File: 235,000.

Connecticut
Office of Secretary of State, Division of Corporations, 30 Trinity Street, Hartford, CT 06106; Fax: 860-509-6068; {www.state.ct.us/sots}. Selected Publications: None, but to get a copy of Connecticut General Statutes, call 860-509-6190. Phone Information: 860-509-6001. Copies of Documents on File: Fees are $20 regardless of number of pages, $25 for certified. Written requests only. Mailing Labels: No. Magnetic Tape: Copy of master database of corporations $300. Requester must provide tapes. Microfiche: No. New Corporate Listing: No. Custom Searches: No. Online Access: Yes. Number of Corporations on File: over 200,000

Delaware
Delaware Department of State, Division of Corporations, Secretary of State, P.O. Box 898, Dover, DE 19903, 302-739-3073, Fax: 302-739-3812; {www.state.de.us\corp}. Selected Publications: Incorporating in Delaware. Phone Information: 302-739-3073. Copies of Documents on File: (for domestic only) Available at $1 per page $20 for certification. Short forms $20 and $100 for long forms of good standing. Certificate of incorporation $50 minimum, amendment certificate $100

Company Intelligence

minimum, change of registered agents $75. Requests may be faxed to 302-739-3812, but written requests are preferred. Requests must be paid for in advance, add county fee and send a check. Call for number of pages. Documents filed prior to 1983 are not on computer and must be requested in writing. They offer same day or 24-hour expedited services to file or retrieve certified documents. Same day request completed and released by 5pm, when requested by 2pm. Additional fee is $20. Mailing Labels: No. Magnetic Tape: No. Microfiche: No. New Corporate Listings: No. Custom Searches: Yes, domestic corporations only. Number of Active Corporation on File 397,829.

District of Columbia
Corporations Division, Consumer and Regulatory Affairs, 941 N. Capitol NE, 1st Floor, Washington, DC 20002, 202-442-4430, Fax: 202-442-4523; {www.dcra.org}. Selected Publications: Guideline and Instruction Sheet for Profit, Non-Profit, Foreign, or Domestic. Phone Information: 202-442-9453. Copies of Documents on File: Available for $25 each (all copies certified). Mailing Labels: Will be available in near future. Profit and non-profit lists updated quarterly. Magnetic Tape: No. Microfiche: No. New Corporate Listings No. Custom Searches: Computer searches on registered agents are available. Online Access: Yes. Number of Active Corporations on File: 50,000.

Florida
Division of Corporations, Secretary of State, PO Box 6327, Tallahassee, FL 32314, 850-487-6000, Fax: 850-487-6012; {www.sunbiz.org}. Selected Publications: Copy of the Law Chapter 607 (corporate law). Forms included. (Publications on laws of non-profit corporations and limited partnerships also available.) Phone Information: 904-488-9000. Limit of up to 3 inquiries per call. $10 charge to receive hard copy of microfiche on the corporations, no charge for faxing copies. Copy of Documents on File: Available at $1 per page if you do it yourself. Written requests must be paid for in advance: $1 for non-certified annual report; $10 for plain copy of complete file; $8.75 per 8 pages and $1 each additional, for any certified document including complete file. Microfiche: Yes. Contact Frank Reinhart or Ed Bagnell at Anacomp, 850-488-1486. Magnetic Tape: No. New Corporate Listings: No. Custom Searches: 850-488-1486. Online Access: Available through on CompuServe, 800-848-8199, address written request to Attn: Public Access, division of Corporations, 904-487-6866. Ask for a CompuServe intro-pak. Charge for connect time online is $24 per hour, plus $12.50 per hour additional corporate access fee. Both are prorated by time used. CompuServe can be contacted directly at South eastern Information Systems, P.O. Box 6867, Tallahassee, FL 32314, Attn: Keith Meyer, 904-656-4500. As of February, 1992, Anacomp will handle. Contact Eileen Self, 904-487-6073 for service. Number of active Corporations on File: 691,000.

Georgia
Division of Business Services and Regulation, Secretary of State, Suite 315, West Tower #2, Martin Luther King Drive, SE, Atlanta, GA 30334, 404-656-2185, Fax: 404-651-9059; {www.sos.state.ga.us}. Selected Publications: None, but information package on how to file sent upon request. Phone Information: 404-656-2817. Copies of Documents on File: Available for a minimum of $10 and all copies certified. Bills will be sent for orders over $10. Mailing Labels: No. Magnetic Tape: No. Microfiche: No. New Corporate Listings: through Georgia Net at 404-651-8692. Cost is $1,000 for a one time listing, if you want to receive a monthly or weekly update, cost is $600. Lists are on magnetic tape. Custom Searches: No. Online Access: Yes Number of Active Corporations on File: 350,000

Hawaii
Business Registration Division, Department of Commerce and Consumer Affairs, 1010 Richards Street, PO Box 40, Honolulu, HI 96810, 808-586-2744, Fax: 808-586-2733; {www.hawaii.gov/bedt./start.html}. Selected Publications: None. Phone Information: 808-586-2727. Copies of Documents on File: Available at 25 cents per page, plus $10 per page for certified copies. Expedited service available for $10 fee plus 25 cents per sheet, plus $1 per page. Mailing Labels: No. Magnetic Tape: No. Microfiche: No. New Corporate Listing: Weekly printout available but only for walk-ins. Custom Searches: No. Online Access: Yes. Downloading information from database available through FYI at 808-586-1919. Number of Active Corporations on File: 45,000

Idaho
Corporate Division, Secretary of State, Room 203, Statehouse, Boise, ID 83720, 208-334-2300, Fax: 208-334-2847; {www.idsos.state.id.us}. Selected Publications: Idaho Corporation Law. Phone Information: 208-334-2300. Copies of Documents on File: Available at 25 cents per page, $2 for certified copies. Mailing Labels: Very flexible and may be combined with custom search. Fee is $10 for computer base, 25 cents for first 100 pages, 10 cents for next 500 pages and 5 cents per page thereafter. Magnetic Tape: available for $20 per tape if you supply the tape. They will supply diskette for additional $10. Microfiche: Available for $10, 50 cents for each additional copy of same. Custom Searches: Yes. You supply the tapes or they will supply them at cost. New Corporate Listing: No, but published weekly in The Idaho Business Review. Online Access: Available though Data Share program. Call computer department 208-334-5354. Number of Active Corporations on File 200,000.

Illinois
Corporations Division, Centennial Building, Room 328, Springfield, IL 62756, 217-782-6961, Fax: 217-782-4528; {www.sos.state.il.us}. Selected Publications: Guide for Organizing (Domestic, Non-Profit, or Foreign). Phone Information: 217-782-7880. Copies of Documents on File: available at $5 per page up to first 10 pages; 50 cents for each page thereafter. Mailing Labels: No. Magnetic Tape: yes. Categories: Domestic and Foreign cost $1,500; Not-for-Profit cost $1,500. You must supply tape. Microfiche: Available for $171. New Corporate Listings: Daily list of newly formed corporations costs $185 per year; Monthly List priced at $105 per year. Contact Sharon, 217-782-4104 for more information. Custom Searches: No. Other: Certified List of Domestic and Foreign Corporations (Address of Resident Agent included) costs $38 for two volume set. Online Access: Yes.

Indiana
Office of Corporation, Secretary of State, E018, 302 West Washington Street, Indianapolis, IN 46204, 317-232-6582, Fax: 800-726-8000; {www.state.in.us/sos}. Selected Publications: Guide Book. Request by calling 800-726-8000. Phone Information: 317-232-6576. Copies of Documents on File: Available at $1 per page and $15 to certify. May pay in advance or be billed. Mailing Labels: No. Magnetic Tape: No. Microfiche: No. New Corporate Listings: Daily Listing is published monthly for $20 a month. Custom Searches: No. Online Access: Available: Yes. Number of Active Corporations on file: 200,000.

Iowa
Corporate Division, Secretary of State, Hoover State Office Building, Des Moines, IA 50319, 515-281-5204, Fax: 515-242-6566; {www.sos.state.ia.us}. Selected Publications: Iowa Profit Corporations. Phone Information 515-281-5204. Copies of Documents on File: available at $1 per page; certified copies cost $5. Mailing Labels: No. Magnetic Tape: No. Master file is available on CD-Rom for $200. Microfiche: No. New Corporate Listings: No. Custom Searches: Yes. Searches by name of corporation or partial name. Online Access: Available through Dial Up Program. Contact Sheryl Allen 515-281-5247. Cost is $175 per year, plus telephone charges. Number of Active Corporations on File: 200,000.

Kansas
Corporate Division, Secretary of State, Capitol Building, Second Floor, 300 SW 10th Avenue, Topeka, KS 66612-1594, 785-296-7456, Fax: 785-296-4570; {www.kssos.org}. Selected Publications: None. Will send out forms with instruction sheets. Phone Information: 785-296-4564. Copies of Documents on File: Available at 50 cents per page plus $7.50 . Certificate of Good Standing $7.50, Letter of Good Standing $5, Written Record Search $5. Magnetic Tape: Yes. Master file is available. Microfiche: No. Other: New Corporate Listings: No. Custom Searches: Yes, but they cannot search for . Online Access: Available through Info Network Kansas, 785-296-5143. Number of Active Corporations on File: 66,000.

Kentucky
Corporate Division, Secretary of State, Room 154, Capitol Building, 700 Capitol Avenue, PO Box 718, Frankfort, KY 40601, 502-564-2848, Fax: 502-564-4075; {www.sos.state.ky.us}. Selected Publications: None. Phone Information: 502-564-2848. Copies of Documents on File: Call 502-564-7330 to obtain number of copies in advance. Cost is 50 cents per page; $5 for certified copies. Computer screen print out is $1. Mailing label: No. Magnetic Tape: No. CD Rom available for free and they can send it to you for free. Microfiche: No. New Corporate Listings: available for $50 a month. Custom Searches: Yes, partial name search. Online Access: Yes. Number of Active Corporations on File: 400,000.

Louisiana
Corporate Division, Secretary of State, 3851 Essen Lane, Baton Rouge, LA 70809, 225-925-4704, Fax: 225-925-4410; {www.sec.state.la.us}. Selected Publications: Corporate Law Book ($10). Phone Information: 225-925-4704. Copies of Documents on File: Available starting at $10 for certified articles only. Cost for complete file, including amendments is $20. Mailing Label: No. Magnetic Tape: No. Microfiche: No. New Corporate Listing: Weekly Newsletter at no charge. Requester must supply self addressed stamped envelope. Custom Searches: Yes, can search by agents and individual names. Online Access: Dial Up Access, 225-922-1475. Cost is $360 per year. Number of Active Corporations on File: 120,000.

Maine
Information and Report Section, Bureau of Corporations, Secretary of State, 101 State House Station, Augusta, ME 04333-0101, 207-287-4195, Fax: 207-287-5874; {http://janus.state.me.us}. Selected Publications: None at this time. Phone

Every Company Has To File With The State

Information: 207-287-4195. Copies of Documents on File: Available for $2 per page, plus $5 for certified copies. Mailing Labels: No. Magnetic tape: No. Microfiche: No. New Corporate Listings: Monthly Corporations Listing costs $10. Send written request to Audrey Dingley or call 207-287-4188. Custom Searches: Yes, by corporation name. Online Access: Yes. Number of Active Corporations on File 46,000.

Maryland

Corporate Charter Division, Department of Assessments and Taxation, 301 W. Preston Street, Baltimore, Maryland 21201, 410-767-1330, Fax: 410-333-5873; {www.dat.state.md.us/bfsd}. Selected Publications: Information Guides for Filing and other issues are available. Phone Information: 410-225-1330. Copies of Documents on File: Available for $1 per page, plus $6 for certified copies. There is a $20 expediting fee. Certificate of good standing $6, Articles of Incorporation $20. Mailing Labels: No. Magnetic Tape: available on 6 tapes for $75 each. Contact Dale Brown of Specprint in Timonium, 410-561-9600. Microfiche: No. New Corporate Listings: Monthly corporate Computer Printout costs $25 a month. Custom Searches. Yes. They can search for names, agents, principal offices, and documents filed by the corporation. Online Access: Yes. Number of Active Corporations on File: 300,000.

Massachusetts

Corporate Division, Secretary of State, 1 Ashburton Place, Boston, MA 02108, 617-727-9640; {www.state.ma.us/sec/cor}. Selected Publications: Compendium of Corporate Law ($15). Phone Information: 617-727-9640. Copies of Documents on File: available for 20 cents per page, $12 for certified copies. Mailing Labels: No. Magnetic Tape: Cost is $300 for copy of master file and record layout. Requester must supply tapes. Microfiche: No. New Corporate Listings: Semi-monthly Filings cost $15; Quarterly Filings cost $50; bi-weekly printout cost $15. Custom Searches: available on a cost recovery basis. Online Access: Direct Access program. Cost is $149 annually. Connect time is 40 cents per minute. Number of Corporations on File: 375,000.

Michigan

Corporation Division, Corporation and Securities Bureau, Michigan Department of Commerce, PO Box 30054, 6546 Mercantile, Lansing, MI 48909, 517-334-6302, Fax: 517-334-8048; {www.cis.state.mo.us/corp}. Selected Publications: None. Phone Information: 517-334-6311. Call 517-334-6905 for automated form request line. Copies of Documents on File: available at a minimum of $6 for 6 pages or less, $1 for each page thereafter. Certified copies cost $10. (Request a price list.) Mailing Labels: No. Magnetic Tape: No. Microfiche: Available for $145. New Corporate Listings: Monthly Listing ranges at about $100 per month (each month is priced differently). Custom Searches: No. Online Access: Available through KnowX (www.knowx.com), a division of Information America, 800-235-4008. You can pay for these online searches by credit card or prepaid account. Price varies. To view all records of a corporation, $15. Other prices range from $1 to $6. Number of Corporations on File: 251,000.

Minnesota

Corporate Division, Secretary of State, 180 State Office Building, 100 Constitution Avenue, St. Paul, MN 55155, 651-296-2803; {www.sos.state.mn.us}. Selected Publications: Guide to Starting a Business in Minnesota. Phone Information: 651-296-2803. Copies of Documents on File: Available for $3 per copy, $8 for certified copies. Request copies by sending a letter, indicating your address or fax number. Mailing Labels: No. Magnetic Tape: Yes, on 9 tapes for $11,250 annually and $710 per month. Microfiche: No. New Corporate Listings: Daily Log costs 25 cents per page. Custom Searches: Available on a cost recovery basis. Categories same as for mailing labels. Online Access: Yes. Number of Corporations on File: 194,500

Mississippi

Office of Corporations, Secretary of State, PO Box 136, Jackson, MS 39205, 601-359-1350, Fax: 601-359-1499; or street address: 202 N. Congress, Suite 601, Jackson, MS 39205; {www.sos.state.ms.us}. Selected Publications: None. Phone Information: 601-359-1627. Copies of Documents on File: $1 per page plus $10 for certified copies. Mailing Labels: No. Magnetic tape: No. Microfiche: No. New Corporate Listings: No. Custom Searches: Available to limited extent. Printout costs $2 per page. Online Access: Yes. Number of Active Corporations on File: 80,000.

Missouri

Corporate Division, Secretary of State, 600 W. Main and 208 State Capitol, PO Box 778, Jefferson City, MO 65102, 573-751-4936, Fax: 573-751-5841; {http://mosl.sos.state.mo.us}. Selected Publications: Corporation Handbook (free). Phone Information: 573-751-4153. Copies of Documents on File: available at 50 cents per page plus $10 for certified copies. Mailing Labels: No. Magnetic Tape: No. Microfiche: No. New Corporate Listings: not usually, but can be set up on special request. Custom Searches: Yes, on website. Online Access: Yes. Number of active Corporations on File: 192,000.

Montana

Corporate Division, Secretary of State, Capitol Station, Helena, MT 59620, 406-444-3665, Fax: 406-444-3976; {www.state.mt.us/sos}. Selected Publications: None. Phone Information: 406-444-3665. Copies of Documents on File: available for 50 cents per page; $3 for certification. Prepaid accounts are available for obtaining certificates and other information. Mailing Labels: No. Magnetic Tape: No. Microfiche: No. New Corporate Listings: No. Custom Searches: No but can search by name of corporation only. Online access: Yes. Number of Active Corporations on File: 33,000

Nebraska

Corporate Division, Secretary of State, State Capitol, Lincoln, NE 68509, 402-471-4079, Fax: 402-471-3666; {www.nol.org/home\SOS}. Selected Publications: None. Phone Information: 402-471-4079. Copies of Documents on File: Available for $1 per page, $10 for certified copies. Fax your requests and they will bill you, or request over the phone. Mailing Labels: No, but database is available on floppy or CD-Rom. Magnetic Tape: Contact Nebraska Online at 800-747-8177. Microfiche: No. New Corporate Listings: also available through Nebraska Online. Custom Searches: No: Online Access: Yes. Number of Active Corporations on File: 50,000.

Nevada

Office of Corporations, Secretary of State, Capitol Complex, Carson City, NV 89710, 702-684-5708, Fax: 702-684-5725; {www.sos.state.nv.us}. Selected Publications: Guidelines. Phone Information: Corporate Status call 900-535-3355, $3.50 per call. Copies of Documents on File: available for $1 per page, $10 for certified copies. Prepayment required (they will not send a bill). Mailing Labels: No. Magnetic Tape: Copy of master file available, 702-684-5715. Corporations takes 2 tapes which requester supplies. Cost per tape is $25. Microfiche: No. New Corporate Listings: Monthly Listing of New Corporations costs $20 a month. Custom Searches: yes. Cost determined at time of request. Other: A listing of corporations on file, the "Alpha Listing", which includes names of active and inactive corporations can be fully downloaded for $100. Available on reel tape only. Contact Timothy Horgon. Online access: Yes. Number of active Corporations on File: 60,000.

New Hampshire

Corporate Division, Secretary of State, State House, Room 204, Concord, NH 03301, 603-271-3244. Selected Publications: None. Phone Information: 603-271-3246. Copies of Documents on File: Available for $1 per page, plus $5 for certified copies, and $25 expedited services. Annual report can be faxed to you for $10. Mailing Labels: No. Magnetic Tape: No. Microfiche: Complete listing of all registrations. No breakdown by type of entity (updated monthly). Annual Subscription costs $200. New Corporate Listings: Monthly Subscriber List costs $25 plus postage. Custom Searches: No. Online Access: No. Number of Active Corporations on File: 33,000.

New Jersey

Commercial Recording Division, Secretary of State, 820 Bear Tavern Road, West Trenton, NJ 08628, (Mailing address: CN 308), 609-530-6400, Fax: 609-530-6433; {http:\\accessnet.state.nj.us}. Selected Publications: Corporate Filing Packet. Phone Information: General Information call 609-530-6400; Forms call 609-292-0013; Expedite Service call 609-984-7107. There is a charge for standard information, $15 look-up fee for each verbal or fax request plus $10 expedited service fee. User may pay with Visa, Master Card or Discover. Requests may be sent by Fax at 609-530-6433. Copies of Documents on File: available for $1 per page plus $25 for certified copies (except for LLCs and Non-Profit corporations, which cost $15 to certify). Mailing Labels: No. Magnetic Tape: No. Microfiche: No. New Corporate Listings: No. Custom Searches: Yes. Each request is reviewed on individual basis. Requester is billed for computer time. Online Access: Yes. Number of Active Corporations on File: 436,314.

New Mexico

State Corporation Commission, PO Drawer 1269, Santa Fe, NM 87504-1269, 505-827-4502, Fax: 505-827-4502; {www.nmprc.state.nm.us}. Selected Publications: None. Phone Information: 505-827-4504. Copies of documents on File: Available for $1 per page, minimum $10, plus additional $25 for certified copies. Mailing Labels: No. Magnetic Tape: No. Microfiche: No. New Corporate Listings. Yes. Monthly listings available. Requester must send manilla self-addressed envelope, with postage worth $1.70 each, for as many listings as you would like. Online Access: Custom Searches: Yes, call their information line, 505-827-4509. They provide free printouts of certificates of good standing, officers and agent names. Number of Active Corporations on File: Over 100,000.

New York

New York State, Department of State, Division of Corporations, 41 State Street, Albany, NY 12231, 518-474-0050; {http:\\www.dos.state.ny.us/corp\corpwww.html}. Copies of Documents on File: Available for $5 per document, $10 for certified copies. Call 900-835-2677 to obtain information on a filed corporation or status of

Company Intelligence

a corporation. To receive copies of documents on file, send in a letter of request. Mailing Labels: No. Magnetic Tape: No. Microfiche: No. New Corporate Listing: Report of Corporations is printed daily and mailed out every other day. It is available in the Daily Report through subscription only, for $125 per year, $75 for 6 months or $40 for 3 months. Online Access: Yes. Number of Corporations on File: 1,200,000.

North Carolina

Division of Corporation, Secretary of State, 300 N. Salisbury Street, Raleigh, NC 27603-5909, 919-733-4201, Fax: 919-733-1837; {www.state.nc.us/secstate}. Selected publications: North Carolina Business Corporation Guidelines, North Carolina's Non-Profit Corporation Handbook. Phone Information 919-733-4201. Copies of Documents on File: available for $1 per page, $5 for certified copies. You can leave a message with your requests by calling 888-246-7630. Mailing Labels: No. Magnetic Tape: Available on cost recovery basis. To make a request write Bonnie Elek. Categories: All active corporations, foreign, domestic, non-profit, and profit. Microfiche: No. New Corporate Listings: Available for $20 per month and issued in hard copy only. Custom Searches: Yes. Categories: Type of Corporation, Professional Corporations, Insurance Corporations, Banks, and Savings and Loans. Online Access: Available. Number of Active Corporations on File: 400,000.

North Dakota

Corporation Division, Secretary of State, Capitol Building, 600 E. Boulevard Ave., Bismarck, ND 58505, 701-328-2900, Fax: 701-328-2992; {www.state.nd.us/sec}. Selected Publications:. Phone Information: 701-328-2900. Copies of Documents on File: $5, $25 for certified copies, $1 additional for every four pages. Written or phone requests accepted. Fax on demand service will send you the forms you need, 701-328-0120. Mailing Labels: No. Magnetic Tape: No. Microfiche No. New Corporate Listings: Monthly Corporation list costs $35-$37 per month. Custom Searches: No. Online Access: Yes. Number of Active Corporations on File: 22,500.

Ohio

Corporation Division, Secretary of State, 30 East Broad Street, 14th Floor, Columbus, OH 43266-0418, 614-466-4980, Fax: 614-466-3899. Selected Publications: Corporate Checklist. Phone Information: Corporate Status call 614-466-3910; Name Availability call 614-466-0590. Copies of Documents on File: contact 614-466-1776. Available for $1 per page, $5 for certified copies. Mailing Labels: No. Magnetic Tape: available for $125 for 6,250 corporation names, thereafter the cost is 2 cents per corporate name with a maximum of 25,000 names. Microfiche: No. New Corporate Listing: List is updated daily. $48 flat fee, plus 5 cents a page and 3 cents a line. Depends on how recent or old a list you would like. Custom Searches: Yes. Categories: location (county), Foreign, Domestic, Profit, Non-Profit. Online Access: No. Number of Active Corporations on File: 400,000.

Oklahoma

Corporations, Secretary of State, 101 State Capitol Building, Oklahoma City, OK 73105, 405-521-3911, Fax: 405-521-3771; {www.state.ok.us/~sos}. Selected Publications: Forms and Procedures to Incorporate. Phone Information: 900-555-2424 for record search. Charge is $3 per call. Copies of Documents on File: available for $1 per page, $10 for certified copies. Mailing Labels: No Magnetic Tape: $500 per tape. Requester must supply 3490 type cartridges . Contact Vicky Mitchell, 405-521-3257. Microfiche: No. New Corporate Listings: Hard Copy costs $150 a month, with Amendments it is $250 a month plus postage. Custom Searches: Yes, date of incorporation and registered agent information is provided. Online Access: Yes. Number of Corporations on File: 224,159.

Oregon

Corporation Division, Department of Commerce, 255 Capitol St., NE, Suite 151, Salem, OR 97310-1327, 503-986-2200, Fax: 503-986-2346; {www.sos.state.or.us/corporation/corp.hp.html}. Selected Publications: None. Phone Information: 503-986-2200. Copies of Documents on File: Available for $5 for all documents in a corporation's file except annual report. Annual reports are an additional $5. Certification fee is $15. Business Registry on diskette or e-mail is $15 per month or $150 per year. Mailing Labels: No. Magnetic Tape: Complete master file costs $200. Requester must provide tape. Microfiche: No. New Corporate Listings: Statistical Report of New Corporations is available for $15 per monthly issue. $150 per year. Custom Searches: Yes, minimum charge is $50. Online Access: Yes. Mead Data, Information America and Dunn and Bradstreet also have database. Number of Active Corporations on File: 73,000.

Pennsylvania

Corporation Bureau, 308 N. Office Building, Harrisburg, PA 17120, 717-787-1057, Fax: 717-783-2244; {www.dos.state.pa.us/corp.htm}. Selected Publications: Corporate Guide. Phone Information: 717-787-1057. Copies of Documents on File: Available for $2 per page, $12 search fee, $28 for certified copies. Mailing Labels: No. Magnetic Tape: Copy of master file available for $3500 startup fee. Monthly, you will be charged $48.12 for each tape received. This is the only way to receive the master file. It is not currently on disk or CD-Rom. Microfiche: No. New Corporate Listings: County or area listing available for cents per name. Custom Searches: Yes. Categories: Non-Profit, Domestic, Foreign county location, Limited partnerships, Fictitious name, Trademarks, Foreign Non-profits, Cooperatives, Professional Corporations cents per name. Online Access: Online Searches will be available in the future. Available from Information America at 404-892-1800; Prentice-Hall, Legal and Financial Services at 518-458-8111; or Mead Data Central at 513-865-6800. Number of Corporations on File: 616,000.

Rhode Island

Corporations Division, Secretary of State, 100 North Main Street, Providence, RI 02903, 401-222-3040, Fax: 401-222-1309; {www.state.ri.us}. Selected Publications: Instruction sheet, The Rhode Island Law Manual (Free). Phone Information: 401-222-3040. Staff will look up two corporations per call. Copies of Documents on File: Available for 50 cents per page, $5 for certified sheet. Mailing Labels: No. Magnetic Tape: Yes, master file is available. Microfiche: No. New Corporate Listings: Not usually provided. New corporate listings are published weekly in The Providence Journal, Sunday Business Section. Send a letter requesting weekly printouts. Custom Searches: No. Online Access: Yes. Number of Active Corporations on File: 90,000.

South Carolina

Division of Corporation, Secretary of State, PO Box 11350, Columbia, SC 29211, 803-734-2158, Fax: 803-734-2164. Selected Publication: None. Phone Information: 803-734-2158. Copies of Documents on File: available for $1 for first page, 50 cents thereafter. $3 for certified copies. Mailing Labels: No. Magnetic Tape: No. Microfiche: No. New corporate Listing: Yes. Custom Searches: No. Online Access: Yes. Number of Active Corporations on File: 250,000.

South Dakota

Corporate Division, Secretary of State, 500 East Capitol, Pierre, SD 57501, 605-773-4845; Fax: 605-773-4550; {www.state.sd.us/stat/e/executive/sos.htm}. Selected Publications: None. Phone Information: 605-773-4845. Copies of Documents on File: Available for 50 cents per page plus $5 for certification. Mailing Labels: No. Magnetic Tape: No. Microfiche: No. New Corporate Listings: No. Custom Searches: No. Online Access: No. Number of Active Corporations on File: 30,000.

Tennessee

Office of Secretary of State, Services Division, Suite 1800, James K. Polk Building, Nashville, TN 37243-0306, 615-741-2286, Fax: 615-741-7310; {www.state.tn.us/sos/}. Selected Publications: None. Phone Information: 615-741-2286. Copies of Documents on File: All available information on a corporation is available for $20. Mailing Labels No. Magnetic Tape: Yes. Categories: All Corporations on file, Foreign, Domestic Profit, Non-Profit, Banks, Credit Unions, Cooperative Associations. Charge of an additional $2 for each tape supplied. Cost, done on a cost recovery basis, is determined at time of request. Contact Mr. Thompson at 615-741-0584. Microfiche: No. New Corporate Listings: Monthly New Corporation Listing on a cost recovery basis of 25 cents per page, 8 names per page. Call 615-741-1111. Custom Searches: Yes. Online Access: Yes. Number of Active Corporations on File: 100,000.

Texas

Corporation Section, Statute Filing Division, Secretary of State, PO Box 13697, Austin, TX 78711, 512-463-5586, Fax: 512-463-5709; {www.sos.state.tx.us}. Selected Publications: Filing Guide to Corporations. Phone Information: 512-463-5555. Copies of Documents on File: Available for $35; for names and all filings of corporations. Certification is $10 plus $1 for each additional page. $5 for express services. Business entity information, excluding individual names is $3 per call, 10 cents for each page after 20 pages. Mailing Labels: No. Magnetic Tape: No. Microfiche: Names of officers and directors available. Cost determined at time of request. New Corporate Listings: Weekly Charter Update costs $27.50 per week. Custom Searches: No. Online Access: Available through Information America 404-892-1800. Number of Active Corporations on File: Not Available.

Utah

Corporations and UCC, Division of Business Regulations, P.O. Box 45801, 160 East 300 South Street, Second Floor, Salt Lake City, UT 84145-0801, 801-530-4849, Fax: 801-530-6111 or 801-530-6438; {www.commerce-state.ut.us}. Selected Publications: Doing Business in Utah; A Guide to Business Information (available online). Phone Information: 801-530-4849. Copies of Documents on File: Available for 30 cents a page plus $10 for certified copies. Mailing Labels: No. Magnetic Tape: No. Microfiche: No. New Corporate Listing: Updated every ten days. You can obtain by calling their information line. Custom Searches: Yes. Cost includes printing charge of 30 cents per page. Online Access: Available through Datashare. Call 801-538-3440. It gives you access to their database online. You need to obtain a log in name and password by signing up. Number of Active Corporations on File: 40,000.

Every Company Has To File With The State

Vermont
Corporate Division, Secretary of State, 109 State Street, Montpelier, VT 05609-1104, 802-828-2386, Fax: 802-828-2853; {www.sec.state.vt.us}. Selected Publications: None. Phone Information: 802-828-2386. Copies of Documents on File: Available for $1 per page, $5 for certified copies. Send the $5 certification fee in advance. They will bill you for the copies. Mailing Labels: No. Magnetic Tape: No. Microfiche: No. Corporate Listings: Yes. Monthly New Corporations an Trade names on diskette cost $6 plus 1 cent per name. Total cost is never more than $15. Out-of-State Corporations, $50 for complete list. Custom Searches: Yes. Categories: Foreign, Domestic, Non-profits, by date of registration. Cost is 1 cent per name plus $6 to run list. Online Access: Yes. Number of Active Corporation on File: 24,000.

Virginia
Clerk of Commission, State Corporation Commission, Secretary of State, 1330 East Main Street 23219, 804-371-9733, Fax: 804-371-9654; {www.state.va.us/scc}. Selected Publications: Business Registration Guide. Phone Information: 804-371-9733. Copies of Documents on File. Available for $1 per page, $3 for certified copies. Mailing Labels: No. Magnetic Tape: Yes. They provide you tapes for $1,000 a month and you do not have to provide blank tapes. Microfiche: No. New Corporate Listings: No. Custom Searches: Yes. Online Access: Available through Direct Access. You will dial into their database for free to obtain the information you need. Call 804-371-9733 to ask for a password. Number of Active Corporations on File: 160,000.

Washington
Corporate Division, Secretary of State, 2nd Floor Republic Bldg., 505 Union Ave. Mail Stop PM-21, Olympia, WA 98504, 360-753-7115, Fax: 360-586-5629; {www.secstate.wa.gov}. Selected Publications: None. Phone Information: 360-753-7115. Copies of Documents on File: Fees are $1 for the first page and 20 cents thereafter. Certification is $10. Mailing Labels: No Magnetic Tape: No. Microfiche: Cost is $10 a month. New Corporate Listings: No. Custom Searches: No. Online Access: Yes. Number of Active Corporations on File: 145,000.

West Virginia
Corporate Division, Secretary of State, Room 139 West, State Capitol, Charleston, WV 25305, 304-558-8000, Fax: 304-558-9000. Selected Publications: None. Phone Information: 304-558-8000. Copies of Documents on File: Available for 50 cents per page, $10 for certified copies. Mailing Labels: No. Magnetic Tape: No. Microfiche: No. New Corporate Listing: Monthly Report costs $5 a month or $50 per year. Custom Searches: yes. Cost is $1 for first hour and $5 for every hour thereafter, prorated. Online Access: No. Number of Active Corporations on File: 39,000.

Wisconsin
Corporate Division, Secretary of State, PO Box 7846, Madison, WI 53707; Street address: 345 West Washington Avenue, 3rd Floor, Madison, WI 53703, 608-266-3590, Fax: 608-267-6813; {www.wdfi.org}. Selected Publications: Chapter 180 Statutes Book ($4). Phone Information: 608-266-3590. Copies of Documents on File: For simple copy request must be in writing. Fee is $2. Requests for certified copies may be phoned in. Fee is $5. Mailing Labels: No. Magnetic Tape: No. Microfiche: Yes. Monthly new Corporations costs $12 per month. New Corporate Listing: Yes (see Microfiche entry). Minimum cost is $10 per week. Custom Searches: Yes. Online Access: yes. Number of Active Corporations on File: 130,708.

Wyoming
Corporate Division, Secretary of State, State of Wyoming, Capitol Building, Cheyenne, WY 82002, 307-777-7311; Fax: 307-777-5339; {http:\\soswy.state.wy.us}. Selected Publications: Wyoming Business Corporation Act (available free on website). Phone Information: 307-777-7311. Copies of Documents on File: available for 50 cents for first 10 pages then 15 cents per page, $3 for certified copies. Mailing Labels: No. Magnetic Tape: No. Microfiche: No. New corporate Listings: yes: $300/yr for monthly listing of both foreign and domestic corporations, or $150 each. Custom Searches: Yes: Categories: Foreign, Domestic, Statutory trust, Non-profit and Profit, Limited Partnership, Limited Liability, Trade names and Trademarks. Listing of all active profit corporations can be purchased for $25 on diskette. They can e-mail it to you at no cost. Contact Jeanie Sawyer, 307-777-5334. Online Access: Yes. Number of Active Corporations on File: 33,000.

Company Intelligence

Who Owes Money To Whom

Any public or private company, organization, and for that matter, individual, that borrows money and offers an asset as collateral, must file with the state at the Office of Uniform Commercial Code (UCC). A filing is made for each loan and each of the documents is available to the public. To obtain these documents is a two-step process. The first step is to request a search to see if there are any filings for a certain company. The fee for such a search usually is under $10. You will next want to request copies of each of these documents. The cost for each document averages only a few dollars. This Office of Uniform Commercial Code is part of the state government and usually is located near or in the same office as the Office of Corporations which falls under the Secretary of State.

The initial search of records will provide:
- the number of listings under one name;
- the file number for each of the listings;
- the date and time of filing; and
- the name and address of the debtor.

Each UCC filing will disclose:
- a description of the asset placed as collateral; and
- the name and address of the secured party.

This disclosure not only provides insights into the financial security of an individual or organization, but it can also give a picture of their assets. Remember, this information is available on any public or private company or individual. The next time your brother-in-law asks you for money for a new business venture, it probably is worth the investment of a few dollars for a UCC search to see whether your relative owes money to others.

Most states will ask if you would like certified or non-certified information. Certification means that they will stand by the accuracy of the information if it is used in a court or other legal proceeding. For most cases, business researchers will not need the extra procedure of certification.

Farm Loan Filings

The Food and Security Act of 1986 is a law that involves filings on crop and livestock loans. Not all states have adopted this law. However, those which have must set up an automated central filing system under the Office of Uniform Commercial Code. Many states have not adopted the law because of the expense involved in setting up the system. Under this system the office must be able to provide information on filings in 24 hours. The purpose of the system is to notify those who purchase crops from growers if the farmer has already offered that crop as collateral.

UCC Request Forms

Some states provide you with current information about recent filings over the telephone, but others will only accept your request on a standard UCC Form. Still others will respond if you send your request in writing but will give you a discount if your query is on an official UCC Form. Most states use UCC Form 11 for requesting information. Copies of UCC Forms for all 50 states are available by calling Forms, Inc. (800-854-1080). The cost for forms is as follows: 9 or less, $1 each; 10-49, $.75 each; 50-99, $.65 each; 100 and over, $.55 each.

Online Access

Although you have to pay for most direct access to the UCC office files, a few are free, e.g., Virginia. With online capabilities you can usually search by such categories as: personal or commercial debtor, type of amendments, name of secured party, name of assigned party, and type of collateral. The following states offer online access to their files: Alabama, Colorado, Florida, Illinois, Iowa, Kansas, Massachusetts, Mississippi, Montana, New Mexico, Nebraska, Oregon, Pennsylvania, South Carolina, South Dakota, Texas, Utah, Vermont, Washington, and Wyoming. Many states allow you to search on the Secretary of State's website to see if a person has filed with their office and to find the date of filing.

Exceptions

In Georgia the Uniform Commercial Code filings are maintained by the Clerk of the Superior Court. Florida does not conduct UCC searches through their office any longer. All searches are online.

Uniform Commercial Code Offices

Alabama
Uniform Commercial Code Division, Secretary of State, 4121 Carmichael Rd. Suite 200, Montgomery, AL 36106; 334-242-5231 (mailing address: P.O. Box 5616, Montgomery, AL 36103); {www.sos.state.al.us}. Searches: There are no phone searches. Requests must be submitted in writing. The charge is $5 for name searches submitted on Alabama Form UCC-11, $7 for searches submitted by letter and $1 for each additional listing. Copies of Documents: Available for $1 per page. All documents are certified. Farm Filings: Call 334-242-5231. A list of new farm filings is published every month. Online Access: Searches will soon be available online at the website listed above.

Alaska
Uniform Commercial Code Division, Central Filing System, 3601 C St., Suite 1140-A, Anchorage, AK 99503-5947; 907-269-8899; {www.commerce.state.ak.us}. Searches: There are no phone or online searches. Requests must be submitted in writing on letterhead or on an Alaska Form UCC-11. The charge is $15 per name search for a copy search, and $5 per name search for an information search. Information searches state only whether loans have been filed with the UCC Division and the filing date. Send your check payment with your request. Copies of Documents: Individual copies are $2 each. To have copies certified, pay $5 per document. Requests are processed in the order they are received. Farm Filings: Maintained by the District Recorder's Office.

Arizona
Uniform Commercial Code Department, Secretary of State, 7th Floor, 1700 W. Washington, Phoenix, AZ 85007; 602-542-6178; {www.cc.state.az.us}. Searches: Requests must be submitted in writing on Arizona Form UCC-3 or UCC-11. The charge is $6 per name plus 50 cents per listing for copying fee. Send blank check with stated limit or $6 and they will call you with the additional amount for copies. When they receive it they will release the documents. Copies of Documents: Available for 50 cents per page. Farm Filings: Maintained by the County Recorder.

Who Owes Money To Whom

Arkansas
Uniform Commercial Code, Secretary of State, State Capitol Building, Room 25, Little Rock, AR 72201; 501-682-5078, Fax: 501-682-3500; {www.sosweb.state.ar.us/ucc.html}. Searches: Requests must be submitted in writing in a letter or on an Arkansas Form UCC-11. You can send it by fax or mail. The charge is $5 per debtor name or data search. Copies of Documents: Available for $6 for the first page. Each additional page is $.50 per page, up to 100 pages. They will bill you for copies. Farm Filings: Maintained by this office. Same price and search request structure.

California
Uniform Commercial Code Division, Secretary of State, P.O. Box 942835, Sacramento, CA 94235-0001 (Street Address: 1500 11th Street, Room 255, Sacramento, CA); 916-653-6814; {www.ss.ca.gov}. Searches: Request must be submitted in writing on a letter, a California Form UCC-3 or Form UCC-11. Charge is $10 per name. One name per request only. Copies of Documents: Available for $1 for the first page and 50 cents for every additional page. All documents are certified. Send payment with your request. If you are not sure of the cost, you may submit a blank check and state "not to exceed $35" on the check. Make it payable to the Secretary of State. Farm Filings: If you do not find them at the state level, remember some are filed with the county government (there is no standard procedure in California).

Colorado
Uniform Commercial Code Division, Secretary of State, 1560 Broadway, Suite 200, Denver, CO 80202; 303-894-2200; Fax: 303-894-2242; {www.state.co.us/gov_dir/sos}. Searches: Written requests for hard copies must be on a Form UCC-11 or in the form of a letter. The form may belong to any state or even be a national form. It does not matter. Your letter should have your name, address, phone and fax number. The cost is $16.50 per search and $1 for certificates. Copies for $1.25 per page. Searches usually last 24-48 hours. Copies of Documents: Available for $1.25 per page. You can use their website to find out if any information on a certain person has been filed with the UCC office. Farm Filings: Maintained at the County Court Recorder. Online Access: Call the Central Indexing System at 303-894-2175.

Connecticut
Uniform Commercial Code Division, Secretary of State, 30 Trinity St., P.O. Box 150470, Hartford, CT 06106; 860-509-6004; {www.state.ct.us}. Searches: Request must be submitted in writing. The charge is $25 for requests submitted on a Connecticut Form UCC-11. You can also write a letter and send the same amount by check. Requests cannot be faxed in because you cannot pay with credit cards. Copies of Documents: The charge for the first three pages is $5, each additional page is $1. The new CONCORD system allows UCC searches to be conducted on a self-serve basis. There is no charge to use the computers in the Customer Service Center at 30 Trinity Street. You can access business filings and UCC liens. Farm Filings: Maintained in this office. Online Access: Searches can be completed in your personal office by establishing access to the UCC office's system. You will need to complete a Remote Access Customer Data Sheet and submit a check for $500. The contact person is David Pritchard, VIII, 860-509-6165.

Delaware
Uniform Commercial Code Section, P.O. Box 793, Dover, DE 19903 (Street Address: 401 Federal Street, John D. Townsend Building, Suite 4, , Dover, DE 19901); 302-739-4279 (Choose 4 for UCC recorded message, choose 0 for a UCC service representative); Fax: 302-739-3812; {www.state.de.us/corp}. Searches: Requests must be submitted in writing on UCC-11 Form. You can send in your request on a letter (non-standard) but they will charge you $10 for not filling out the proper form. The cost is $25 per each debtor's name search. To have your documents certified, you will need to pay $25 more. Send your requests by fax or mail. Credit cards and checks are acceptable forms of payment. Copies of Documents: Available for $2 per page, $5 minimum. Expedited services are available. 24 hour service costs $25, same day service is $50 and priority is $75. Farm Filings: Maintained by this office. Send a written request or fill out a UCC-11. To find out if any liens have been filed with the UCC section, without receiving any documents or further information, call 900-555-CORP. This service is $10 and the charge will appear on your phone bill.

District of Columbia
Recorder of Deeds, 515 D Street NW, Washington, DC 20001; 202-727-5374; {www.dcra.org}. Searches: Requests must be submitted in writing. No special form is required. The charge is $30 for each secured party and must be paid in advance. Copies of Documents: Available for $2.25 per page, plus $2.25 per page for certification. Farm Filings: Maintained in this office.

Florida
Uniform Commercial Code Division, Department of State, P.O. Box 6327, Tallahassee, FL 32314 (Street Address: 409 East Gaines Street, Tallahassee, FL 32399); 850-487-6055; {www.sunbiz.org}. UCC searches are no longer available through the office. All the information is online at the above website address at no cost to you. If you are seeking searches on loans before 1997, write to the UCC division.

Georgia
The State of Georgia does not maintain Uniform Commercial Code Filings. They are filed at the county level.

Hawaii
Uniform Commercial Code, Bureau of Conveyances, P.O. Box 2867, Honolulu, HI 96803; 808-587-0154; {www.hawaii.gov/bedt/start.html}. Searches: Requests must be submitted in writing or on a Hawaii Form UCC-3. The UCC office does not provide forms; you can buy them through Conrad or simply write a letter requesting your search. The search charge is $25 per debtor name for a certificate, and $5 extra for every financing statement shown on the report. Copies of Documents: Available for $1 per page. They will bill you. Farm Filings: Maintained by this office. Online Access: No.

Idaho
Secretary of State, Uniform Commercial Code Division, State House, Boise, ID 83720; 208-334-3191; {www.idsos.state.id.us}. Searches: Information may be requested by phone or in writing. The charge is $6 for one lien, and $10 for two or more liens if the requests are in writing. When a UCC-4 is filled out, the cost is $4. To retrieve information on a person's liability status only, the cost is $4. The cost is $10 for more than one lien. Farm Filings: Yes, fill out a UCC-4. A 24-hour Expedited Service is available for all searches for $10. Online Access: No

Illinois
Uniform Commercial Code Division, Secretary of State, Howlett Building, Room 30, Springfield, IL 62756; 217-782-7518; {www.sos.state.il.us}. Searches: All requests must be in writing. The charge is $10 per data name search. Copies of Documents: The charge is $1 per page. Farm Filings: If you do not find them at the state level, remember, some are filed with the county government. (There is no standard procedure in Illinois.) Payment for searches and copies may be charged to VISA or MasterCard. Microfilm: Copies of all documents filed within the month are available on a subscription basis. Call 217-785-2238 for pricing information.

Indiana
Uniform Commercial Code Division, Secretary of State, 302 West Washington Street, Room E 018, Indianapolis, IN 46204; 317-232-6393; {www.state.in.us/sos}. Searches: All searches must be requested in writing on an Indiana Form UCC-11 only. You cannot fax your request because they need the original copies of the form for filing purposes. The cost depends on the number of pages that result from your search. They will bill you after the search is complete. Copies of Documents: The charge is 50 cents per page and $1 for certification. Farm Filings: If incorporated they are filed both at this office and the county recorder where the land is located. If the farm is not incorporated, the filing is placed at the county recorder's office only. Online Access: Not available.

Iowa
Uniform Commercial Code Division, Secretary of State, Second Floor, Hoover Building, Des Moines, IA 50319; 515-281-5204, Fax: 515-242-6556; {www.sos.state.ia.us}. Searches: The cost of a phone search is $5, plus $1 for a printout. The charge for a non-standard request is $6 and $5 for requests submitted on an Iowa Form UCC-11. Copies of Documents: The fee is $1 for each copy requested. All copies of liens are certified. Farm Filings: Maintained by this office. (Monthly updating may be obtained from Iowa Public Record Service, 515-223-1153.) Online Access: Available through the website listed above.

Kansas
Uniform Commercial Code Division, Secretary of State, Second Floor, State Capitol, Topeka, KS 66612; 785-296-1849; {www.kssos.org}. Searches: Phone requests are accepted with VISA or MC or from those holding a prepaid account with the UCC. The charge for phone requests is $15 per name for verbal information. The charge for written requests is $8. Turnaround time for searches is 48-72 hours. Copies of Documents: The charge is $1 per page. There is no additional charge for certification of name searches. Printouts are $1 per page. Farm Filings: This office has handled farm filings since 1984. Filings prior to that year are maintained by the County Register of Deeds.

Kentucky
Uniform Commercial Code Division, Office of Secretary of State, State Capitol Bldg., Capitol Avenue, Frankfort, KY 40601; 502-564-2848; {www.sos.state.ky.us}. Searches: All searches of UCC filings must be conducted in person by requester or by outside agencies. Law firms or Kentucky Lender's Assistance, 606-278-6586, may

Company Intelligence

do it for you. Kentucky Lender's Assistance currently charges $16 per debtor name for searches at the Secretary of State's office. In addition to the agency fee, the UCC charges 10 cents per page for plain copies, with $1 minimum; and $5 for certification. Farm Filings: Filings are maintained by the County Circuit Court. Online Access: You can also conduct searches at {commonwealth.com}.

Louisiana
Uniform Commercial Code Division, Louisiana Secretary of State, P.O. Box 94125, Baton Rouge, LA 70804-9125; 225-342-5542, Fax: 225-342-0316; {www.sec.state.la.us/ucc-1.htm}. Searches: Requests should be submitted in writing on a UCC-11 or on letterhead. The certificate costs $15 per debtor name searched. If more than 10 statements are reflected on your search results, you will be charged $1 per statement. Copies of Documents: $1 per page, with a minimum request of $3. Farm Filings: Maintained at the Parish (county) level. Online Access: For direct access to UCC files, the annual charge is $400 per use password. Call 225-922-1475 for more information.

Maine
Uniform Commercial Code Division, Secretary of State, State House Station 101, Augusta, ME 04333; 207-287-4177, Fax: 207-287-5874; {http://janus.state.me.us}. Searches: All requests must be submitted in writing in a letter or on a Form UCC-11. State whether plain or certified copies are desired. The charge is $5 per name search. Copies are $2 per page plus $5 for certification. Attachments are 50 cents per page. They will bill you. For expedited service, an additional $5 fee guarantees a 24 hour turnaround time. Farm Filings: Maintained by this office. Online Access: No.

Maryland
Uniform Commercial Code Division, State Department of Assessments and Taxation, 301 West Preston Street, Baltimore, MD 21201; 410-767-1340; {www.dat.state.md.us/bsfd}. Searches: The State of Maryland does not conduct searches. You will have to hire a search company like Hylinf Infoquest (410-728-4990) or Harbor City Research (410-539-0400). Otherwise, try your search online through their web address listed above. Copies cost $1 per page. Cost to certify a document is $6. Farm Filings: Maintained by this office. Online Access: No.

Massachusetts
Uniform Commercial Code Division, Secretary of State, Room 1711, 1 Ashburton Place, Boston, MA 02108; 617-727-2860; {www.state.ma.us/sec/gov/}. Searches: Requests must be submitted in writing on a Form UCC-11 (any state's form is acceptable). The charge is $5 for an information computer printout and $15 for computer printout with face page and up to 15 pages. They will call you if pages exceed this limit. All fees must be paid in advance. Copies of Documents: Charge is $2 per page and $3 for certification. Farm Filings: Maintained in Town Clerk's Office.

Michigan
Uniform Commercial Code Section, P.O. Box 30197, Lansing, MI 48909-7697; 517-322-1495; {www.cis.state.mo.us/corp}. Searches: Requests submitted on a Michigan Form UCC-11 are $3 per data name search. UCC-11 is the official search request form. Letterhead is also acceptable; include the data name you are searching, request for copies, and contact information. All requests are processed in the order received. Copies of Documents: $1 per page for copies of financing statements. Expedited searches are $25 in addition to other charges. For this service, you must prepay $25 and a $3 base fee by check addressed to the State of Michigan. If received before 11am, the search is completed the same day. When received after 11 am, the search will be completed by 3pm the next business day. Farm Filings: Filings are maintained by the County Recorder of Deeds. Online Access: No.

Minnesota
Uniform Commercial Code Division, Secretary of State, 100 Constitution Avenue, St. Paul, MN 55155; 651-296-2434; {www.sos.state.mn.us}. Searches: There are no telephone searches. Requests must be submitted in writing and include a self-addressed, stamped envelope. The charge for a request submitted on a Minnesota Form UCC-11 is $15. Non-standard forms are $20 (other than the UCC-11). You may call the automated forms fax library to request forms at the number listed above. There is a limit of four pages of attachments per filing. The cost for financing statements for the first two data names is $15. Each additional statement is $15. The initial search fee includes 10 copies. Each additional copy will be filled. Copies of Documents: Available for 50 cents per page. Charge for certified copies is a $5 plus 50 cents for each page. Farm Filings: Available from the County Recorder of Deeds or the UCC Division.

Mississippi
Uniform Commercial Code Division, Secretary of State, 202 N. Congress St., #601, Jackson, MS 39201; 601-359-1614; {www.sos.state.ms.us}. Searches: The charge for written requests submitted on Mississippi Form UCC-11 is $5. The charge for non-standard forms is $10. Copies of Documents: They will bill you for the exact amount of copies made. Farm Filings: Maintained by this office. Use a Form 1-F. Price structure is the same. Other: Master list of all farm registrations available for $2040. Master list by type is $500 per crop. Online Access: Call 601-359-1548. The initial charge is $250 plus 10 cents per transaction, per page. The office is working on providing free searches through their webpage, so look for that soon.

Missouri
Uniform Commercial Code Division, Secretary of State, P.O. Box 1159, Jefferson City, MO 65102 (Street Address: Missouri State Info Center, 600 West Main Room 302, Jefferson City, MO 65101); 573-751-2360; {http://mosl.sos.state.mo.us}. Searches: Information searches will be given over the phone, but you will have to follow up in writing. These searches are not certified and are free of charge. The charge for written requests is $13 per certificate. Copies of Documents: $13 plus 50 cents per copy after 10 pages. You may request a search with copies for $26, which will cover both the search and copies up to 10 pages. After 10 pages, copies are 50 cents. Farm Filings: Maintained by the County Recorder.

Montana
Uniform Commercial Code Bureau, Secretary of State, Capitol Station, P.O. Box 202801, Helena, MT 59620; 406-444-3665, Fax: 406-444-3976; {www.state.mt.us/sos}. Searches: Searches can be conducted over the phone or by fax if you have a prepaid account. The cost is $7 per debtor name. If you do not have an account, you must send in a written request. There are no restrictions on the form on which you put in your request. Requests are usually completed in 14 days. Copies of Documents: Available for 50 cents a page. Farm Filings: Maintained in this office. For total listing of crop you are interested in, fill out a Buyer's Registration Form for crops you want on the list.

Nebraska
Uniform Commercial Code Division, P.O. Box 95104, 301 Centennial Mall S., Lincoln, NE 68509; 402-471-4080; {www.nol.org/home/SOS}. Searches: You may request your search by phone and they will mail or fax you the documents. If they mail it to you, it is $3.50 for the search and $1 per copy. By fax, the search is $5 and $2 per page for copies. Any additional search results, such as financing statements, cost $1.50 per page. Copies of Documents: Available for $1 per page. Farm Filings: Maintained by the same office, same pricing. Online Access: Available through Nebraska Online; 800-747-8177.

Nevada
Uniform Commercial Code Division, Secretary of State, 200 North Carson Street, Carson City, NV 89701-4201; 775-684-5708; {www.sos.state.nv.us}. Searches: Only written requests for information will be accepted. The charge is $15 for a request submitted on a Nevada Form UCC-3, and $20 for any non-standard request forms. For an additional $25 your request will be expedited. Copies of Documents: Available for $1 per page. You may request certified copies. Farm Filings: Maintained at the office of the County Recorder.

New Hampshire
Uniform Commercial Code Division, Secretary of State, State House, 107 North Main Street, Room 204, Concord, NH 03301; 603-271-3277. Fax: No. Searches: Requests must be submitted in writing by letter or on a Form UCC-11 or UCC-11A, and must contain a self-addressed, stamped envelope in which requested documents will be mailed. Requests will not be processed without an enclosed SASE. The charge for a request submitted on a New Hampshire Form UCC-11 is $5. The charge for a request submitted on a letter or non-standard form is $7. Copies of Documents: Available for $2 per copy. Farm Filings: Maintained by this office. Microfiche: Available from New England Micrographics. Contact Nick Brattan, 603-625-1171. Online Access: No.

New Jersey
Uniform Commercial Code Division, State Department, State Capitol Building, CN303, Trenton, NJ 08625; 609-530-6426, Fax: 609-530-0688; {http://accessnet.state.nj.us}. Searches: Requests must be submitted in writing with the exact name and address of debtor or on a New Jersey Form UCC-11. Payment must accompany request. You may fax your request if you have a prepaid UCC account or you will be paying with Visa or MasterCard. The charge is $35 per name search. All documents are certified. Expedited service allows your search to be completed in 8 1/2 working hours. The requester must include their FedEx account number with the request. Copies of Documents: $1 per page. Farm Filings: Maintained by the county and the state. At the county level you will want to check with the County Recorder. Online Access: No.

Who Owes Money To Whom

New Mexico
Uniform Commercial Code Division, Bureau of Operations, Secretary of State, Executive Legislative Building, Room 400, Santa Fe, NM 87503; 505-827-3600; {www.sos.state.nm.us}. Searches: Certification is $8. Copies cost $1 per page. The State of New Mexico does not conduct searches, but they will provide you with a list of companies that are authorized to do so. Call Bureau of Operations for a list, 505-827-3608. Farm Filings: This office located at the same address will conduct a search for an Agricultural Eddective Financing Statement for $15. They have a master list of farm filings for registered buyers. It costs $300 or $75 per quarter. There is a $30 registration fee. Contact Ben Vegil, 505-827-3609 or fax your request to 505-827-3611. Online Access: No.

New York
Uniform Commercial Code Division, Secretary of State, 41 State Street, 2nd Floor, Albany, NY 12231; 518-474-4763; {www.dos.state.ny.us/corp}. Searches: There are no phone or online searches. Requests must be submitted in writing. For requests submitted on a New York Form UCC-11 the charge is $7. For requests submitted on non-standard forms the charge is $12. Copies of Documents: Available for $1.50 per page. Farm Filings: Maintained by both the state and the County Recorder. Online Access: No.

North Carolina
Uniform Commercial Code Division, Secretary of State, 300 N. Salisbury St., Raleigh, NC 27611; 919-733-4205; {www.state.nc.us/secstate/}. Searches: Requests must be submitted in writing. Signature for the requester is required, therefore make the request on Form UCC-11 or North Carolina Form UCC-11. The charge is $15 per data name. Search fee must be sent with request. All requests are handled in 10-14 days. Copies of Documents: They will let you know the cost depending on the number of pages from the search. Farm Filings: Maintained by this office and County Recorder. Online Access: The web address listed above allows you to see if the office has anything on file for a certain person and the date the filing was made. Other: Microfilm listings can be purchased for $50 per roll.

North Dakota
Uniform Commercial Code Division, Secretary of State, Main Capitol Building, 600 Boulevard Avenue East, Bismarck, ND 58505; 701-328-2900; {www.state.nd.us/sec}. Searches: Requests may be phoned in or submitted in writing preferably on a North Dakota UCC-11. Letters and nonstandard forms also accepted. The charge is $7. Copies of Documents: Available for $5 for the first three pages and $1 a page for additional pages. Send a blank check to pay for your copies, stating a "not to exceed" amount. Farm Filings: The Central Notice staff will take requests for searches over the phone for crop and livestock filings. The initial search fee is $7. The charge is $15 for documents. Online Access: Yes. There is a $50 one-time registration fee; and it costs $120 for unlimited access.

Ohio
Uniform Commercial Code Division, Secretary of State, 30 E. Broad Street, 14th Floor, Columbus, OH 43215; 614-466-9316, Fax: 614-466-2892. Searches: Phone requests for information are not certified and are free of charge. Limit is 3 requests per phone call. Written requests may be submitted on a non-standard letter form, Form UCC-11 or on an Ohio Form UCC-11. Specify if you would like copies or information alone, and if you want a search of any and all addresses. The charge is $9 per debtor name search. The first 34 pages from your search are free, the 35th page is $1.05. All documents after that are 3 cents per page. All copies are certified and they will bill you. It takes 4-6 weeks for these searches to be conducted. A two week expedite service is available for an additional $10. Copies of Documents: Available for $1 per page. They will bill you. Farm Filings: Maintained by the County Recorder. Online Access: No.

Oklahoma
Uniform Commercial Code Office, Oklahoma County Clerk, 320 Robert S. Kerr, Room 105, Oklahoma City, OK 73102; 405-278-1521; {www.state.ok.us/~sos}. Searches: Requests must be submitted in writing on letterhead or a Form UCC-11. Be sure to include the debtors name and address and your contact information. The charge is $5; send a check with your request. Credit card payments are not accepted. Copies of Documents: Available for $1 per page. They will bill you for copies. The charge for certification is $1 per page. Farm Filings: Maintained by Secretary of State's Office, 405-521-2474. They will charge you $6 per EFS found. Even if no EFS is found, they will provide a no-record result for $6. Online Access: No.

Oregon
Uniform Commercial Code Division, Secretary of State, 255 Capitol St., NE, Salem, OR 97310; 503-986-2200, Fax: 503-373-1166; {www.sos.state.or.us}. Searches: Requests must be phoned in using Visa or MasterCard, charged to an established prepaid UCC account or submitted in writing by letter, or on Form UCC-11. The charge for requests on a UCC-11 is $10 per debtor name for an information search. An information search with copies is $15. Copies of Documents: $5 per name search. Certification with a state seal costs $10. Farm Filings: Maintained by this office. Price structure is the same as a UCC search; $10 per name search. You may subscribe annually for monthly reports by agricultural product code. Microfilm cost is $50 for the first 5 products, and each additional product costs $10. A paper report is $500 per product. Online Access: Searches are available through the Secretary of State's webpage listed above. Online searches for UCC information are free.

Pennsylvania
Uniform Commercial Code Division, Corporation Bureau, Department of State, P.O. Box 8721, Harrisburg, PA 17105-8721; 717-787-8712, Fax: 717-783-2244; {www.dos.state.pa.us/corp.htm}. Searches: Requests for searches must be paid in advance by check or money order only and submitted in writing on a Pennsylvania Form UCC-11 or letterhead. The charge is $12 per data name search and $28 to certify your documents. Send separate checks for each search. When using a non-Pennsylvania form there is a $28 additional filing fee. They accept the national financing statement form at the required Pennsylvania fee. Processing time for searches is 3-4 working days, and for copies, 6-7 working days. Copies of Documents: Available for $2 per page. Farm Filings: Maintained by this office. Pennsylvania is a dual filing state so you may perform searches on the county level. Online Access: No.

Rhode Island
Uniform Commercial Code Division, Secretary of State, 100 North Main Street, Providence, RI 02903; 401-222-2521; {www.state.ri.us}. Searches: They suggest that you stop by the office, fill out the required form, and have your search conducted immediately. You could also submit your request in writing on Form UCC-11 or letterhead. The charge is $5. Copies of Documents: Available for 50 cents per copy. Call for number of pages. Farm Filings: Maintained by the City Recorder of Deeds or the Corporation Division, 401-222-2560.

South Carolina
Uniform Commercial Code Division, Secretary of State, P.O. Box 11350, Columbia, SC 29211; 803-734-2175. Searches: Requests must be submitted in writing on Form UCC-11, or preferably South Carolina Form UCC-4. Letters are not accepted. The charge is $5 per debtor name. No priority or expediting service is available. All requests are completed in the order received. Copies of Documents: Available for $2 for the first page, $1 for each page thereafter. They will bill you for copies. Farm Filings: Maintained by the UCC office and County Recorder. The UCC office will need to search by name to obtain collateral information. Online Access: A program called Direct Access allows you to conduct your searches online. Call the office for more information.

South Dakota
Central Filing System, Secretary of State, 500 E. Capitol, Pierre, SD 57501; 605-773-4422, Fax: 605-773-4550; {www.state.sd.us/state/executive/sos.htm}. Searches: Telephone information provided at no charge. Requests for searches are accepted by fax from those with prepaid deposit accounts or credit cards. Written requests are accepted on any UCC standard request form or letterhead. The charge is $10. Copies of Documents: Available for $1 per page. They will bill you and all copies are certified. Farm Filings: Maintained by this office. Online Access: Available by subscription. Cost is $240 per year for 200 transactions and 10 cents per transaction thereafter.

Tennessee
Uniform Commercial Code Section, Secretary of State, J.K. Polk Bldg., 505 Deaderick St., Suite 1800, Nashville, TN 37243-0306; 615-741-3276; {www.state.tn.us/sos/}. Searches: Requests must be submitted in writing, preferably on a Tennessee Form UCC-11. Indicate if you want information or information plus copies. The charge is $12 even if the search shows no listing. Send the $12 fee with request. Copies of Documents: Available for $1 per copy. Do not send money with request for copies. They will bill you. The only form of payment is by check; they cannot accept credit card payments and faxes. It takes 48 hours to complete your request after their office receives it. Farm Filings: Maintained by this office and County Recorder. Online Access: No.

Texas
Uniform Commercial Code, Secretary of State, P.O. Box 13193, Austin, TX 78711-3193; 512-475-2705; {www.sos.state.tx.us}. Searches: The charge for a search requested by phone is $25. They accept credit cards if you place your order over the phone. The charge for written requests submitted on Texas Form UCC-11 is $10. You may fax your request if you have a prepaid account to 512-475-2812. The charge for written requests submitted on a letterhead or non-standard form is $25. Copies of Documents: Available for $1.50 per page with a $5 minimum charge. The charge for certification is an additional $10. Farm Filings: Maintained by the above

Company Intelligence

office. Online Access: Direct Access allows you to link your computer to their files to conduct a search. You are charged per search you conduct. Call the UCC office for more information about Direct Access.

Utah
Uniform Commercial Code Division, Secretary of State, UCC Division, Box 146705, Salt Lake City, UT 84114-6705; 801-530-4849, Fax: 801-530-6438; {www.state.ut.us}, E-mail: {orders@br.state.ut.us}. Searches: Written request may be on letter, UCC-11 or Utah Form UCC-2. You may mail, fax or e-mail your request, and credit card payments are accepted. The charge is $10 per debtor name. On your request, state if you will be needing copies. Copies of Documents: Available for 30 cents per page. They will bill you. Certification: No additional charge. An expedited service is available for $25 if documents are needed sooner than ten days. 24-hour services are also available. Farm Filings: Central Filings maintains these files. Phone requests are accepted but there is a limit of three requests per call. Online Access: To obtain instant access to statewide UCC information, contact DATASHARE, 801-530-6012, or write to 160 East 300 South, 2nd Floor, Box 146705, Salt Lake City, UT 84114-6705.

Vermont
Uniform Commercial Code, Secretary of State, 81 River Street, Montpelier, VT (Mail to 109 State Street, Montpelier, VT 05609-1104)); 802-828-2386, Fax: 802-828-2853; {www.sec.state.vt.us}. Make checks payable to Vermont Secretary of State. Searches: Requests for searches may be submitted in writing. The charge is $10 per debtor name when you fill out a UCC-11 and $15 if you write a letter. Copies of Documents: Available for $2 for regular copies and $5 for different paper sizes. Certification fee is $5. Farm Filings: Central Filings maintains these files. Contact the above address. Online Access: You can search their website for information about a debtor.

Virginia
Uniform Commercial Code Division, Office of the Clerk, State Corporation Commission, P.O. Box 1197, Richmond, VA 23209 (Street Address: 1300 East Main Street, Richmond, VA 23209); 804-371-9733; {www.state.va.us/scc}. Searches: Requests must be submitted in writing on letterhead or Form UCC-11. The charge is $6 per debtor name. Copies of Documents: Available for $1 per page for the first 2 pages, 50 cents for each page afterwards. There is an additional charge of $6 for certification. Farm Filings: Maintained by this office and the County Recorder. Online Access: Direct Access to debtor information, secured party information and date and time of filing is available at no charge by applying for a user password from the clerk's office. Application forms can be downloaded from their website at the address listed above.

Washington
Uniform Commercial Code Division, Department of Licensing, 405 Black Lake Blvd., Olympia, WA 98502 (Mailing Address: P.O. Box 9660, Olympia, WA 98507); 360-753-2523, Fax: 360-586-1404; {www.wa.gov/dol/bpd/uccfront.htm}. Searches: Requests must be submitted in writing. Indicate if you want information or information and copies. The charge is $17.70 for an information search. Copies of Documents: Available for $25. This includes search fee, plus copies of all documents for one debtor. Credit cards, checks, money orders, and prepaid accounts are acceptable payment forms. Farm Filings: Maintained in this office. Microfilm: Copies of each days filings are available for $20 per roll, per day plus shipping and handling fees. Online Access: Contact Darla Gehrke for information on how to set up a prepaid account. Minimum deposit is $200 and monthly access costs $18 per month.

West Virginia
Uniform Commercial Code Division, Secretary of State, 1900 Kanawha, Bldg. 1, Room 131W, Charleston, WV 25305-0770; 304-558-6000; {www.state.wv.us/sos}. Searches: Phone requests for information are accepted. The charge is $5. They will bill you. Written requests are preferred. The charge is $3 if Form UCC-11 is used, $5 for all others. Copies of Documents: Available for 50 cents per page. The charge for certification is $5. Farm Filings: Maintained by this office. Online Access: No.

Wisconsin
Uniform Commercial Code Division, Department of Financial Institutions, P.O. Box 7847, Madison, WI 53707; 608-266-3087; {www.wdfi.org}. Searches: Phone searches are available for $10 per name. The charge for written requests is $10 per debtor name. Copies of Documents: Available for $1 per document. Farm Filings: Maintained by the County Register of Deeds. The UCC division cannot search by collateral but only by name. Online Access: The UCC division is currently working on a contract for a private company to provide access to searches online.

Wyoming
Uniform Commercial Code, Secretary of State, State Capitol Building, Cheyenne, WY 82002; 307-777-5372; {www.soswy.state.wy.us}. Searches: Requests may be faxed to 307-777-5988 if you have a prepaid account. You may also write a letter and send a check by mail. The charge is $5 for each name. Copies of Documents: Available for 50 cents per page up to 10 pages, and 15 cents per page for 11 or more pages. Farm Filings: Maintained by this office. Cost is $5 per debtor name. Online Access: You can conduct searches through the State of Wyoming's Dial Up Mainframe program. It costs $50 per year to register plus phone and usage costs. Call the UCC division to register.

Companies That Only Sell Stock In One State

State Securities Offices Offer Company Information, Mailing List of Brokers and More

The offices of state security regulators offer financial data on thousands of companies which are not required to file with the U.S. Securities and Exchange Commission as well as the names, addresses, financial data, and consumer information on thousands of stockbrokers and broker-dealers.

State regulation of the sale of securities in the U.S. began in 1911 when the Kansas legislature passed the first securities law. North Carolina enacted a law the same year; Arizona and Louisiana did so in 1912. By 1919, 32 states had followed suit. Now, all states and the federal government have laws regulating the sale of corporate securities, bonds, investment contracts and stocks.

The reason for these laws is simple enough: they protect the public, unfamiliar with the intricacies of investing, against deceitful promoters and their often worthless stocks. This is the same type of function that the U.S. Securities and Exchange Commission performs in Washington, DC. The United States covers companies trading stocks across state boundaries, and the states cover companies trading stocks within their state. The laws — called Blue Sky laws — prevent speculative schemes "which have no more basis than so many feet of blue sky," according to the Commerce Clearing House Blue Sky Law Reports.

The Blue Sky Law is usually administered by each state's Securities Commission or Securities Division. Securities to be sold within a state must register with this office. If the issuer is a corporation, for example, it must submit the following information:

- articles of incorporation
- purpose of proposed business
- names and addresses of officers and directors
- qualifications and business history of applicant
- detailed financial data

Each state, however, has numerous exemptions. Securities issued by national banks, savings and loan associations, non-profit organizations, public utilities, and railroads are usually exempt from the Blue Sky laws, as are securities listed on the stock exchange, those issued by companies registered with the U.S. Securities and Exchange Commission, and those issued by foreign governments with which the U.S. has diplomatic relations.

Securities offices also require broker-dealer firms, the agents (or sales representatives), and investments advisers wanting to work in the state to file applications.

Agents wanting to work in one or more states now apply for registration by filing with National Association of Securities Dealers' Central Registration Depository (CRD). To keep the CRD current, agents must submit all pertinent employment and application changes. All state securities offices are hooked up to the CRD through computer terminals and use them to monitor agents registered or applying to register in their jurisdictions as well as any complaints filed against individuals.

Most states will also use the system for registration of broker-dealer firms. Information kept in the repository will include registration applications, amendments to applications, complaints on file, and so forth. The purpose is to reduce the amount of paperwork for the states and to promote more uniformity.

The system is not set to accept broker-dealers' audited financial statements or annual reports so applicants will have to continue to file in the states requiring them. The broker-dealer phase of the CRD is now in operation. Several states are now trying to determine what, if any, information they will require broker-dealers to file with their securities divisions. Most of those states that have made a decision said they will continue to require annual financial reports to be filed with their offices.

Below are the names, addresses and telephone numbers for the state securities offices. Most of these offices will routinely provide information over the phone on whether specific companies, agents, or broker-dealers are registered in their states. Requests for more detailed information may have to be submitted in writing.

Securities Offices

Alabama
Securities Commission, 770 Washington Ave., Suite 570, Montgomery, AL 36130; 334-242-2984, 800-222-1253.

Alaska
Division of Banking, Securities and Corporations, Department of Commerce and Economic Development, State Office Building #94, P.O. Box 110807, Juneau, AK 99811-0807; 907-465-2521; {www.dced.state.ak.us/bsc/secur.htm}.

Arizona
Securities Division, Arizona Corporation Commission, 1300 West Washington St., Suite 201, Phoenix, AZ 85007; 602-542-4242; {www.ccsd.cc.state.az.us}.

Arkansas
Securities Department, Heritage West Building, Third Floor, 201 East Markham, Little Rock, AR 72201; 501-324-9260.

California
Securities Regulation Division, Department of Corporations, 980 9th St., Suite 500, Sacramento, CA 95814; 916-445-7205; {www.corp.ca.gov}.

Colorado
Division of Securities, Department of Regulatory Agencies, 1580 Lincoln, Suite 420, Denver, CO 80203; 303-894-2320; {www.dora.state.co.us/securities}.

Connecticut
Securities and Business Investments Division, Department of Banking, Securities and Business, 260 Constitution Plaza, Hartford, CT 06106; 860-240-8299, 800-831-7225; {www.state.ct.us/dob}.

Delaware
Division of Securities, Dept. of Justice, 8th Floor, Civil Division, 820 N. French St., Wilmington, DE 19801; 302-577-8424.

Company Intelligence

District of Columbia
Division of Securities, DC Public Service Commission, P.O. Box 37378, Washington, DC 20001; 202-727-8000.

Florida
Division of Securities and Investor Protection, Department of Banking and Finance, Office of Comptroller, The Capitol, LL-22, Tallahassee, FL 32399-0350; 850-488-9805, 800-848-3792; {www.dbf.state.fl.us/index.html}.

Georgia
Business Services and Regulations, Office of Secretary of State, Suite 802 West Tower, Two Martin Luther King Dr., Atlanta, GA 30334; 404-656-2894; {www.sos.state.ga.us/securities}.

Hawaii
Business Registration Division, Department of Commerce and Consumer Affairs, 1010 Richards St., P.O. Box 541, Honolulu, HI 96810; 808-586-2744.

Idaho
Securities Bureau, Department of Finance, 700 West State St., Boise, ID 83720-2700; 208-332-8004; {www2.state.id.us/finance/dof.htm}.

Illinois
Securities Department, Office of Secretary of State, 520 S. Second St., Springfield, IL 62701; 217-782-2256, 800-628-7937; {www.sos.state.il.us/depts/securities/sec_home.html}..

Indiana
Securities Division, Office of Secretary of State, 302 W. Washington, Room E-111, Indianapolis, IN 46204; 317-232-6688; {www.ai.org/sos}.

Iowa
Securities Bureau, Office of Commissioner of Insurance, Lucas State Office Bldg., 2nd Floor, Des Moines, IA 50319; 515-281-4441; {www.state.ia.us/government/com/ins/security/security.htm}.

Kansas
Office of Securities Commissioner, 618 S. Kansas, 2nd Floor, Topeka, KS 66603-3804; 785-296-3307, 800-232-9580; {www.cjnetworks.com/~ksecom/}.

Kentucky
Division of Securities, Department of Financial Institutions, 477 Versailles Rd., Frankfort, KY 40601; 502-573-3390, 800-223-2579; {www.dfi.state.ky.us}.

Louisiana
Securities Commission, 3445 N. Causeway, Suite 509, Metairie, LA 70002; 504-846-6970.

Maine
Securities Division, Bureau of Banking, Department of Professional and Financial Regulation, State House Station 121, Augusta, ME 04333; 207-576-6360; {www.state.me.us/pfr/sec/sechome2.htm}.

Maryland
Division of Securities, Office of Attorney General, 200 St. Paul Place, 21st Floor, Baltimore, MD 21202-2020; 410-576-6360; {www.oag.state.md.us/securities}.

Massachusetts
Securities Division, Department of Secretary of State, 1719 John W. McCormack Bldg., One Ashburton Place, Boston, MA 02108; 617-727-3548, 800-269-5428; {www.magnet.state.ma.us/sec/sct/sctidx.htm}.

Michigan
Corporation and Securities Bureau, Department of Commerce, 6546 Merchantile Way, Lansing, MI 48909; 517-334-6200; {www.commerce.state.mi.us/corp}.

Minnesota
Registration and Licensing Division, Department of Commerce, 133 East 7th Street, St. Paul, MN 55101; 651-296-4026; {www.commerce.state.mn.us}.

Mississippi
Securities Division, Office of Secretary of State, P.O. Box 136, Jackson, MS 39205; 601-359-6371; {www.sos.state.ms.us}.

Missouri
Office of Secretary of State, 600 West Main, Jefferson City, MO 65101; 573-751-4136; {http://mosl.sos.state.mo.us/sos-sec/sossec.html}.

Montana
Securities Department, State Auditor's Office, 126 North Sanders, Room 270, Helena, MT 59620; 406-444-2040, 800-332-6148; {www.mt.gov/sap}.

Nebraska
Bureau of Securities, Department of Banking and Finance, 1200 N Street, The Atrium #311, Lincoln, NE 68508; 402-471-3445; {www.ndbf.org}.

Nevada
Securities Division, Office of Secretary of State, 555 E. Washington, Las Vegas, NV 89101; 702-486-2440; {http://sos.state.nv.us}.

New Hampshire
Department of State, Bureau of Securities Regulation, State House, Room 204, Concord, NH 03301-4989; 603-271-1463.

New Jersey
Bureau of Securities, 153 Halsey Street, 6th Floor, Newark, NJ 07101; 973-504-3600; {www.state.nj.us/lps/ca/bos.htm}.

New Mexico
Securities Division, Regulation and Licensing Department, 725 St. Michaels Dr., P.O. Box 25101, Santa Fe, NM 87501; 505-827-7140.

New York
Bureau of Investor Protection and Securities, Department of Law, 120 Broadway, 23rd Fl., New York, NY 10271; 212-416-8200; {www.oag.state.ny.us}.

North Carolina
Securities Division, 300 N Salisbury St., Room 302, Raleigh, NC 27603; 919-733-3924, 800-688-2910; {www.state.nc.us/secstate/sec.htm}.

North Dakota
Securities Commissioner's Office, State Capitol Building, 5th Floor, 600 East Boulevard Ave., Bismarck, ND 58505; 701-328-2910.

Ohio
Division of Securities, Department of Commerce, 77 S. High St, 22nd Fl., Columbus, OH 43266-0548; 614-644-7465, 800-788-1194; {www.securities.state.oh.us}.

Oklahoma
Department of Securities, 120 N. Robinson, Suite 860, Oklahoma City, OK 73102; 405-280-7700; www.state.ok.us/~osc/}.

Oregon
Division of Finance and Corporate Securities, Department of Insurance and Finance, 21 Labor and Industries Bldg., Salem, OR 97310; 503-378-4140; {www.cbs.state.or.us/external/dfcs/index.html}.

Pennsylvania
Securities Commission, Division of Licensing and Compliance, 1010 North Seventh St., 2nd Floor, Harrisburg, PA 17102-1410; 717-787-8061, 800-600-0007; {www.state.pa.us/Pa_Exec/Securities}.

Rhode Island
Securities Division, Department of Business Regulation, 233 Richmond St., #232, Providence, RI 02903-4232; 401-222-3048.

South Carolina
Securities Division, Department of State, P.O. Box 11549, Columbia, SC 29211; 803-734-9916; {www.scattorneygeneral.org}.

South Dakota
Division of Securities, Department of Commerce and Regulation, 118 W. Capitol, Pierre, SD 57501-2017; 605-773-4013; {www.state.sd.us/dcr/securities/}.

Tennessee
Division of Securities, Department of Commerce and Securities, Volunteer Plaza, Suite 680, 500 James Robinson Pkwy., Nashville, TN 37243; 615-741-5905; {www.state.tn.us/commerce/securdiv.html}.

Companies That Only Sell Stock In One State

Texas
State Securities Board, P.O. Box 13167, Austin, TX 78711; 512-305-8300; {www.ssb.state.tx.us}.

Utah
Securities Division, Department of Business Regulation, P.O. Box 146760, Salt Lake City, UT 84114; 801-530-6600; {www.commerce.state.ut.us/web/commerce/secint/index.htm}.

Vermont
Securities Division, Department of Banking and Insurance, 89 Main Street, Drawer 20, Montpelier, VT 05620-3101; 802-828-3301; {www.state.vt.us/bis}.

Virginia
Division of Securities and Retail Franchising, State Corporation Commission, PO Box 1197, Richmond, VA 23209; 804-371-9051, 800-552-7945; {www.state.va.us/scc/division/srf/index.htm}.

Washington
Securities Division, Department of Licensing, PO Box 9033, 405 Black Lake Blvd., SW, 2nd Floor, Olympia, WA 98507-9033; 360-902-8760; {www.wa.gov/dfi/securities}.

West Virginia
Securities Division, State Auditor's Office, Room W-118, State Capitol, Charleston, WV 25305; 304-558-2257; {www.wvauditor.com}.

Wisconsin
Office of Commissioner of Securities, 101 East Wilson St., P.O. Box 1768, Madison, WI 53701; 608-266-1064; {www.wdfi.org}.

Wyoming
Securities Division, Office of the Secretary of State, Capitol Building, Cheyenne, WY 82002; 307-777-7370; {http://soswy.state.wy.us}.

State Licensing Offices

Buried within each state government are several, and sometimes dozens, of offices where individuals as well as business establishments must register in order to perform certain types of services and commercial activities. State laws require accountants, architects, concert promoters, employment agencies, podiatrists and numerous other professionals to register. The data derived from these regulatory boards provide unique opportunities for researchers and marketing executives to obtain demographic data, mailing lists and even competitive information.

Mailing Lists

Mailing lists offer the biggest potential from these offices. The unusual as well as the mundane are available in a variety of formats. Many of these lists are not accessible commercially, but you can get them from the states inexpensively and usually without restrictions. In other words, you can purchase a state list once, and use it over and over again. Commercial list brokers will never let you do this. Here is a sampling of available mailing lists:

- 1 cent per name for all dentists in Kentucky;
- Free directory of real estate agents in Arizona;
- $40 for a list of all nurses in Colorado;
- A mailing list of all contractors in Arkansas for $10;
- 2 cents per name for all swimming pool dealers in Florida;
- A listing of librarians in Georgia;
- 4 cents a name for all the psychologists in California;
- $100 for a computer tape of all accountants in Florida;
- $1.45 per 1,000 names for all medical practices in Illinois;
- Free list of all attorneys in Maine.

Almost every state provides mailing labels in the form of cheshire or pressure sensitive labels. In many cases, the charge is nominal.

Common Lists and Specialized Rosters

Every state maintains a variety of standard rosters. Some states keep as few as 20 lists and others have over 100. Names of licensed professionals and business establishments available from most every state include:

- medical professionals
- accountants
- real estate agents and brokers
- veterinarians
- barbers
- insurance agents
- architects
- nursing homes
- cosmetologists
- hearing aid dealers
- social workers
- lawyers

After reviewing the rundown of all 50 states and District of Columbia licensing boards, you will be amazed at the variety of lists that are within easy reach. In most cases you can obtain printouts for such licensed services as:

- burglar alarm contractors in Maine
- tow truck operations in Minnesota
- hat cleaners in Ohio
- ski areas in Michigan
- day care centers in New York
- security guards in New Hampshire
- outfitters in Colorado

Computer Tapes and Diskettes: Selections and Sorting Options

Many states can provide the information on magnetic tape and some are beginning to offer data on IBM PC compatible diskettes. Almost every state will allow you to select names by zip code or county whether the licensee is active or inactive. Some states will allow you to select certain demographic characteristics, such as years of formal education.

Markets and Demographics

With a little creativity and resourcefulness, the information at licensing boards can provide pertinent clues in formulating a market profile. For example, you can determine:

- which counties have the highest concentration of psychologists;
- what is the average number of years of schooling for real estate agents in certain zip codes;
- which zip codes have experienced the fastest growth for accountants for the past 10 years;
- the number of out-of-state licensed paralegals;
- which counties have the most podiatrists or veterinarians
- how many insurance agents there are in a given county.

Some states have the capability of performing historical analysis, while others will supply you with the raw data.

Competitive Intelligence

Depending upon the type of business you are investigating, pertinent competitive information may be ferreted from state licensing boards. For example, if you are a dentist, mobile home dealer, nursing home administrator or real estate broker, you could plot how many competitors you are up against in a given zip code or county. Or, you may be able to determine how many opticians work for an eye care chain, or tax consultants for a given tax preparer.

Organization of Licensing Boards

Approximately half of the states have a central office which is responsible for all licensed professions. For such states it is a

State Licensing Offices

relatively easy process to obtain information because it is all generated from a single source. However, the other states make this task difficult. Typically, each separate independent board maintains information for one profession. The only connection these agencies have to the state government is that their board members are appointed by the governor.

States With Restrictions

Some states have restrictions on the use of their lists of licensed professionals. California, District of Columbia, Hawaii, Louisiana, New Hampshire, North Dakota, and Oklahoma do not release information. Alabama and North Carolina will only release the number of professionals, not their names. Minnesota will only release information if action has been taken against a professional or business. And in Iowa, Montana, New York, and Rhode Island, the data may not be used for commercial purposes.

State Licensing Boards

Besides issuing licenses to professionals so they can do business, the following offices act as consumer watchdogs to make sure that those with licenses do business fairly and ethically. Not only will these offices investigate complaints against licensed professionals, they also have the ability to revoke or suspend the licenses if the professional repeatedly acts unprofessionally or unethically. Each state listing includes the professionals licensed in that state, including health professionals, along with their different licensing offices where noted.

Alabama
State Occupational Information Coordinating Community (SOICC), 401 Adams Ave., P.O. Box 5690, Montgomery, AL 36103-5690; 334-242-2990. Licensing boards and professions: accountants, aircraft personnel, architects, auctioneers, audiologists, speech pathologists, bar pilots, water transportation personnel, boxer and wrestler trainers, classroom teachers, coal mine foremen/mine electricians, cosmetologists, counselors, dentists, dental hygienists, chiropractors, doctors of medicine, physician's assistants, surgeon's assistants, school bus drivers, embalmer/funeral directors, engineer-in-training and professional engineers, land surveyors, fire fighters, foresters, general contractors, hearing aid specialists, heating and air conditioning contractors, insurance agents, interior designers, landscape architects, landscape horticulturist/planters, lawyers, pest control operators and fumigators, tree surgeons, law enforcement personnel, nurses, nursing home administrators, optometrists, pharmacists, physical therapists, physical therapist assistants, plumbers, podiatrists, polygraph examiners, psychologists, real estate brokers, security salespersons, social workers, veterinarians.

Alaska
Division of Occupational Licensing, Department of Commerce and Economic Development, State of Alaska, P.O. Box 110806, Juneau, AK 99811-0806; 907-465-2534; {www.commerce.state.ak.us/occ.home.htm}. Licensing boards and professions: architects, engineers, land surveyors, audiologists, barbers and hairdressers, chiropractors, collection agencies, construction contractors, concert promoters, dental professionals, dispensing opticians, electrical administrators, geologists, guides, hearing aid dealers, marine pilots, physicians, morticians, naturopaths, nursing, nursing home administrators, optometrists, pharmacists, physical therapists, psychologists, public accountants, veterinarians.

Arizona
Arizona Department of Revenue, Registrar of Contractors, 800 W. Washington, Phoenix, AZ 85007; 602-542-1525, ext. 7605; {www.rc.state.az.us}. Licensing boards and professions: pharmacists, physical therapists, podiatrists, psychologists, chiropractors, dentists, teachers, homeopathic specialists, veterinarians, medical examiners, radiologic technicians, naturopathic physicians, nurses, opticians, optometrists, osteopaths, barbers, cosmetologists, real estate brokers, contractors, technical registrars, insurance agents, physician assistants, nursing care administrators.

Arkansas
Boards and Commissions, Governor's Office, State Capitol Building, Little Rock, AR 72201; 501-682-3570. Licensing boards and professions: architects, abstracters, accountants, barber examiners, funeral directors, contractors, cosmetologists, dental examiners, electricians, speech pathologists, audiologists, nurses, pharmacists, real estate brokers, veterinary engineers, land surveyors, athletic trainers, chiropractors, collection agencies, counselors, embalmers, foresters, landscape architects, manufactured home builders, physicians, opticians, optometrists, podiatrists, psychologists, sanitarians, social workers, soil classifiers, therapy technologists.

California
State of California, Department of Consumer Affairs, 400 R Street, Sacramento, CA 95814; 916-445-1254, 800-952-5210 (toll-free in CA); {www.dca.ca.gov}. Licensing boards professions: professional engineers, cosmetologists, fabric care technicians, physical therapists, medical quality assurance, physician's assistants, chiropractors, acupuncture specialists, accountants, psychologists, registered nurses, pharmacists, architects, funeral directors, embalmers, landscape architects, veterinarians, animal health technicians, home Furnishings decorators, collection and investigative agents, dentists, dental auxiliaries, barbers, behavioral scientists, optometrists, shorthand reporters, structural pest control operators, athletic trainers, vocational nurses, psychiatric technicians, osteopaths, electronic repair dealers, personnel services, geologists and geophysicists, dispensing opticians/contact lens examiners, respiratory care specialists, nursing home administrators, podiatrists, hearing aid dispensers, speech pathologists, audiologists, tax preparers.

Colorado
Department of Regulatory Agencies, State Services Building, 1560 Broadway, Suite 1550, Denver, CO 80202; 303-894-7855; {www.dora.state.co.us}. Licensing Board/Professions: accountants, architects, barbers, cosmetologists, chiropractors, dentists, electricians, engineers, hearing aid dealers, insurance agents, land surveyors, mobile home dealers, nurses, nursing home administrators, optometrists, outfitters, pharmacists and pharmacies, physical therapists, physicians, plumbers, psychologists, realtors, ski lift operators, social workers, veterinarians.

Connecticut
Occupational Licensing Division, Department of Consumer Protection, 165 Capitol Avenue, Hartford, CT 06106; 860-566-2825, 800-842-2649 (toll-free in CT); {www.dcp.state.ct.us/licensing}. Licensed Occupations: electricians, plumbers, heating and cooling specialists, well drillers, elevator installers, home improvement contractors, arborists, TV and radio repair specialists. Licensed Health Professions: Department of Health Services, 150 Washington St., Hartford, CT 06106; 203-566--7398. Physicians, dentists, optometrists, osteopaths, naturopaths, homeopaths, chiropractors, psychologists, registered nurses, licensed practical nurses, dental hygienists, registered physical therapists, hypertrichologists, audiologists, speech pathologists, podiatrists, hairdressers, barbers, embalmers, funeral directors, sewer installers/ cleaners, registered sanitarians, nursing home administrators, hearing aid dealers, opticians, veterinarians, occupational therapists. Other Licensed Professions: Contact Professional Licensing Division, 165 Capitol Avenue, Room G1, Hartford, CT 06106, 203-566-1814: architects, landscape architects, engineers, engineers-in--training, land surveyors, pharmacists, patent medicine distributors, mobile manufactured home parks.

Delaware
Division of Professional Regulation, P.O. Box 1401, O'Neil Building, Dover, DE 19903; 302-739-4522. Complaints in writing only. Licensed Professionals: architects, accountants, landscape architects, cosmetologists, barbers, podiatrists, chiropractors, dentists, electricians, adult entertainment, physicians, nurses, real estate brokers, land surveyors, private employment agencies, athletic (wrestling and boxing), deadly weapons dealers, nursing home administrators, funeral directors, social workers, speech pathologists, hearing aid dealers, audiologists, psychologists, veterinarians, optometrists, occupational therapists, pharmacists, river boat pilots.

District of Columbia
Department of Consumer and Regulatory Affairs, 614 H Street NW, Room 108, Washington, DC 20001; 202-727-7080. Licensing Board/Professions: accountants, architects, barbers, cosmetologists, dentists, dieticians, electricians, funeral directors, physicians, nurses, nursing home administrators, occupational therapists, optometrists, pharmacists, physical therapists, plumbers, podiatrists, engineers, psychologists, real estate agents, refrigeration and air conditioning specialists, social workers, steam and other operating engineers, veterinarians.

Florida
Florida Department of Business and Professional Regulation, 1940 N. Monroe St., Tallahassee, FL 32399-075; 850-488-6602 [{www.state.fl.us/dbpr}. Licensing boards and professions: accountants, architects, barbers, chiropractors, cosmetologists,

Company Intelligence

dentists, dispensing opticians, electrical contractors, professional engineers and land surveyors, landscape architects, funeral directors and embalmers, medical examiners, hearing aid dispensers, naturopathics, nursing home administrators, nurses, optometrists, osteopaths, pharmacists, pilot commissioners, podiatrists, psychologists, real estate brokers, veterinarians, acupuncture technicians, radiological health technicians, laboratory services, entomology specialists, emergency medical personnel.

Georgia
Examining Board Division, Secretary of State, 166 Pryor Street, SW, Atlanta, GA 30303; 404-656-3900; {www.sos.state.ga.us/ebd/default.htm}. Licensing boards and professions: accountants, architects, athletic trainers, auctioneers, barbers, chiropractors, construction industry, cosmetologists, professional counselors, social workers, marriage and family therapists, dietitians, dentists, engineers, land surveyors, foresters, funeral directors/embalmers, geologists, hearing aid dealers and dispensers, landscape architects, librarians, physicians, nurses, nursing home administrators, occupational therapists, dispensing opticians, optometrists, pharmacists, physical therapists, podiatrists, polygraph testers, practical nurses, private detectives and security agencies, psychologists, recreation specialists, sanitarians, speech pathologists, audiologists, used car dealers, used motor vehicle dismantlers, rebuilders, and salvage dealers, veterinarians, water and wastewater treatment plant operators and laboratory analysts.

Hawaii
Office of the Director, Department of Commerce and Consumer Affairs, P.O. Box 3469, Honolulu, HI 96801; 808-586-2850 {www.hawaii.gov/dcca/dcca.html}. Licensing boards and professions: accountants, acupuncture specialists, barbers, boxers, chiropractors, contractors, cosmetologists, dental examiners, detectives and guards, electricians and plumbers, elevator mechanics, engineers, architects, land surveyors, landscape architects, hearing aid dealers and fitters, massage specialists, physicians, motor vehicle Industry, motor vehicle repair technicians, naturopaths, nurses, nursing home administrators, dispensing opticians, optometrists, osteopaths, pest control operators, pharmacists, physical therapists, psychologists, real estate brokers, speech pathologists, audiologists, veterinarians, embalmers/funeral directors, collection agencies, commercial employment agencies, mortgage and collection servicing agents, mortgage brokers and solicitors, port pilots, time sharing and travel agents.

Idaho
State of Idaho, Department of Self-Governing Agencies, Bureau of Occupational Licenses, Owyhee Plaza, 1109 Main, #220, Boise, ID 83702; 208-334-3233. Licensing boards and professions: accountants, athletic directors, bartenders, engineers, land surveyors, dentists, geologists, physicians, architects, barbers, chiropractors, cosmetologists, counselors, dentists, environmental health specialists, hearing aid dealers and fitters, landscape architects, morticians, nursing home administrators, optometrists, podiatrists, psychologists, social workers, outfitters and guides, pharmacists, public works contractors, real estate brokers.

Illinois
State of Illinois, Department of Professional Regulations, 320 W. Washington, Third Floor, Springfield, IL 62786; 217-785-0800; {www.state.il.us/dpr}. Licensed professions: athletic trainers, architects, barbers, cosmetologists, chiropractors, collection agencies, controlled substance specialists, dentists and dental auxiliaries, polygraph testers, detectives, embalmers, funeral directors, land sales, land surveyors, physicians, nurses, nursing home administrators, occupational therapists, optometrists, pharmacists, physical therapists, podiatrists, boxing and wrestling, engineers, psychologists, accountants, real estate brokers and salespersons, roofing contractors, shorthand reporters, social workers, structural engineers, veterinarians.

Indiana
Indiana Professional Licensing Agency, Indiana Government Center S., 302 W. Washington Street, Room E-034, Indianapolis, IN 46204; 317-232-2980; {www.state.in.us/pla}. Licensing boards and professions: accountants, architects, auctioneers, barbers, beauticians, boxers, engineers and land surveyors, funeral directors, plumbers, real estate agents, TV-radio and watch repair technicians. Licensed health professionals: Indiana Health Professional Bureau, One America Square #1020, Indianapolis, IN 46282; 317-232-2960 for the following medical specialties: chiropractors, dentists, health facility administrators, nurses, optometrists, pharmacists, sanitarians, speech pathologists, audiologists, psychologists, veterinarians, hearing aid dealers, podiatrists, physical therapists.

Iowa
Bureau of Professional Licensing, Iowa Department of Health, 1918 SE Hulsizer, Ankeny, IA 50021; 515-281-3183; {www.state.ia.us/government/com/prof/pld1.htm}. Licensed professionals: dietitians, funeral directors and embalmers, hearing aid dealers, nursing home administrators, optometrists, ophthalmology dispensers, podiatrists, psychologists, physical and occupational therapists, occupational therapist assistants, social workers, speech pathologists and audiologists, respiratory care therapists, barbers, cosmetologists, chiropractors, nurses, physicians, dentists, pharmacists, veterinarians. Other licensed professionals: Professional Licensing Regulation Division, Department of Commerce, 1918 SE Hulsizer, Ankeny, IA 50021; 515-281-7400: accountants, engineers and land surveyors, landscape architects, architects, real estate agents.

Kansas
Governor's Office, State Capitol, 2nd Floor, Topeka, KS 66612; 785-296-3232. Licensing boards: abstracters, accountants, adult home administrators, operating engineers, plumbers and pipefitters, carpenters, electrical workers, attorneys, barbers, cosmetologists, court reporters, dentists and dental auxiliaries, educators, emergency medical services, healing arts specialists, hearing aid dispensers, insurance agents, land surveyors, embalmers/funeral directors, nurses, optometrists, pharmacists, physical therapists, podiatrists, private schools, real estate agents, engineers, architects, landscape architects, veterinarians.

Kentucky
Division of Occupations and Professions, P.O. Box 456, Frankfort, KY 40602-0456; 502-564-3296; {www.state.ky.us/agencies/finance/occupations}. Licensing boards and professions: hearing aid dealers, nurses, private schools, psychologists, social workers, speech and audiologists. Other licensed professionals: Kentucky Occupational Information Coordinating Committee, 275 E. Main St., Two Center, Frankfort, KY 40621; 502-564-4258: accountants, agriculture specialists, architects, auctioneers, bar examiners, barbers, chiropractors, dentists, hairdressers, cosmetologists, emergency medical technicians Services, radiation and product safety specialists, insurance agents, medical licensure supervisors, natural resources and environmental protection specialists, nursing home administrators, ophthalmic dispensers, optometric examiners, pharmacists, physical therapists, podiatrists, polygraph examiners, professional engineers and land surveyors, real estate agents, veterinarians.

Louisiana
First Stop Shop, Secretary of State, P.O. Box 94125, Baton Rouge, LA 70804; 504-922-2675, 800-259-0001; {www.sec.state.la.us}. Licensing boards and professions: acupuncture assistants, adoption agencies, adult day care administrators, agricultural consultants, alcoholic beverages solicitors, ambulatory surgical centers, arborists, archaeological investigators, architects, auctioneers, barbers, beauticians, bedding and furniture upholsterers, beer distributors, blind business enterprise operators, blood alcohol analysts, embalmers/funeral directors, accountants, shorthand reporters, chiropractors, pesticide applicators, driving school instructors, sewage/construction contractors, cotton buyers, waste-salvage oil operators, cut flower dealers, dairy product retailers, day care centers, fuels dealers, dentists, drug manufacturers, egg marketers, electrolysis technicians, embalmers, emergency medical technicians, employment service agencies, family support counselors, grain dealers, hearing aid dealers, hemodialysis clinics, home health centers, horticulturists, independent laboratories, sewage system installers, insurance, landscape architects, nurses, lime manufacturers, liquefied gas distributors, livestock dealers, maternity homes, mental and substance abuse clinics, midwives, nursing home administrators, nursery stock dealers, occupational therapists, optometrists, pesticide dealers, pharmacists, physical therapists, physicians, physicians, plant breeders, plumbers, podiatrists, solid waste processors, seafood distributors, psychologists, radiation therapists, radio and television repair technicians, radiologic technologists, real estate brokers, sanitarians, social workers, speech pathologists and audiologists, veterinarians, voice stress analysts.

Maine
Department of Professional and Financial Regulation, State House Station 35, Augusta, ME 04333; 207-624-8500; {www.state.me.us/pfr/pfrhome.htm}. Licensing boards and professions: veterinarians, itinerant vendors, consumer credit protection services, insurance agents, athletic trainers, real estate agents, geologists and soil scientists, solar energy auditors, hearing aid dealers and fitters, accountants, arborists, barbers, commercial drivers, education instructors, speech pathologists and audiologists, auctioneers, electricians, funeral directors, foresters, dietitians, nursing home administrators, oil and solid fuel installers, substance abuse counselors, mobile home parks, river pilots, physical therapists, plumbers, psychologists, social workers, radiological technicians, occupational therapists, respiratory care therapists, nurses, dentists, chiropractors, osteopaths, podiatrists, physicians, engineers, attorneys.

Maryland
Division of Occupational and Professional Licensing, Department of Labor, Licensing and Regulation, 500 N. Calvert St., Baltimore, MD 21202; 410-230-6000; {www.dllr.state.md.us}. Licensed professionals: architects, master electricians, engineers, foresters, hearing aid dealers, landscape architects, pilots, plumbers, land surveyors, public accountants, second hand dealers, precious metal and gem dealers, pawnbrokers, real estate agents and brokers, home improvement contractors, barbers and cosmetologists. Referral to the licensing agency for collection agencies, mortgage brokers and insurance agents can be provided by the office listed above. Other licensed professions: Boards and Commissions, Department of Health and Dental

State Licensing Offices

Hygiene, 4201 Patterson Ave., Baltimore, MD 21215; 410-764-4747: audiologists, chiropractors, dentists, dietitians, electrologists, medical examiners, morticians, nurses, nursing home administrators, optometrists, occupational therapists, pharmacists, physical therapists, podiatrists, professional counselors, psychologists, environmental sanitarians, speech pathologists, social workers, well drillers, water work and waste system operators.

Massachusetts
Division of Registration, 239 Causeway St., Boston, MA 02114; 617-727-3074; {www.state.ma.us/reg}. Licensing boards and professions: electrologists, gas fitters, hairdressers, health officers, landscape architects, licensed practical nurses, nursing home administrators, optometrists, physician's assistants, podiatrists, pharmacists, plumbers, psychologists, real estate brokers, registered nurses, sanitarians, speech pathologists, audiologists, social workers, tv-repair technicians, physical therapists, occupational therapists, athletic trainers, architects, barbers, barber shops, certified public accountants, chiropractors, dental hygienists, dentists, dispensing opticians, pharmacies, electricians, embalmers, engineers, veterinarians, cosmetologists, and real estate appraisers.

Michigan
Michigan Department of Consumer and Industry Services, P.O. Box 30650, Lansing, MI 48909; 517-373-1820; {www.cis.state.mi.us}. Licensing board and professions: accountants, architects, barbers, athletic control (wrestlers and boxers), builders, carnival amusement rides, cosmetologists.

Minnesota
Office of Consumer Services, Office of Attorney General, 1400 NCL Tower, 445 Minnesota Street, St. Paul, MN 55101; 651-296-2331. Licensing boards and professions: abstracters, accountants, adjusters, alarm and communications contractors, architects, assessors, attorneys, auctioneers, bailbondsmen, barbers, beauticians, boiler operators, boxing related occupations, brokers, building officials, burglar installers, chiropractors, clergy, cosmetologists, dentists, dental assistants, dental hygienists, private detectives, electricians, energy auditors, engineers, financial counselors/financial planners, funeral directors/embalmers/morticians, hearing aid dispensers, insurance agents, investment advisors, landscape architects, land surveyors, midwives, notary publics, nursing home administrators, optometrists, osteopathic physicians, pawnbrokers, peace officers, pharmacists, physical therapists, physicians, surgeons, physician's assistants, high pressure pipefitters, plumbers, podiatrists, practical nurses, precious metal dealers, process servers, psychologists, real estate brokers, registered nurses, rehabilitation consultants, sanitarians, securities brokers, tax preparers, teachers, tow truck operators, transient merchants, veterinarians, water conditioning contractors and installers, water and waste treatment operators, water well contractors/explorers/engineers. Information will be released only if action has been taken against a professional or business.

Mississippi
Secretary of State, P.O. Box 136, Jackson, MS 39205; 601-359-3123; {www.sos.state.ms.us}. Licensing boards and professions: agricultural aviation pilots, architects, landscape architects, athletic trainers, funeral directors, chiropractors, dentists, physicians, nurses, nursing home administrators, optometrists, pharmacists, physical therapists, psychologists, veterinarians, barbers, cosmetologists, engineers and land surveyors, foresters, polygraph examiners, public accountants, public contractors, real estate agents, accountants, lawyers, dental hygienists, audiologists, embalmers, professional counselors, and speech pathologists.

Missouri
Division of Professional Registration, Department of Economic Development, 3605 Missouri Blvd., Jefferson City, MO 65109; 573-751-0293; {www.ecodev.state.mo.us/pr}. Licensing boards and professions: accountants, architects/engineers/land surveyors, athletic trainers, barbers, chiropractors, cosmetologists, professional counselors, dentists, embalmers/funeral directors, healing arts specialists, employment agencies, hearing aid dealers/fitters, nurses, optometrists, podiatrists, pharmacists, real estate agents, veterinarians, insurance agents, nursing home administrators, lawyers, dental hygienists, physicians, physical therapists, speech pathologists and audiologists, psychologists.

Montana
Professional and Occupational Licensing, Business Regulation, Department of Commerce, 111 N. Jackson St., Helena, MT 59620; 406-444-3737; {www.com.state.mt.us/License/POL/index.htm}. Licensing boards and professions: accountants, acupuncturists, architects, athletic trainers, barbers, beer distributors, chiropractors, cosmetologists, dental hygienists, dentists, denturists, electricians, electrologists, employment Agencies, engineers and land surveyors, hearing aid dispensers, insurance, landscape architects, lawyers, librarians, medical doctors, morticians, nurses, nursing home administrators, occupational therapists, operating engineers (boiler), optometrists, osteopathic physicians, pawnbrokers, physical therapists, plumbers, podiatrists, polygraph examiners, private investigators, contractors, radiologic technologists, real estate brokers and salesmen, sanitarians, securities brokers and salesmen, social workers and counselors, speech pathologists and audiologists, taxidermists, tourist campground and trailer courts, veterinarians, water well drillers.

Nebraska
Bureau of Examining Boards, Nebraska Department of Health, P.O. Box 95007, Lincoln, NE 68509; 402-471-2115; {www.hhs.state.ne.us}. Licensing boards and health professions: athletic trainers, advanced emergency medical technicians, audiologist/speech pathologists, cosmetologists, chiropractors, dentists/dental hygienists, embalmers/funeral directors, hearing aid dealers and fitters, pharmacists, podiatrists, optometrists, physical therapists, nurses, nursing home administrators, massage specialists, occupational therapists, professional counselors, psychologists, respiratory care specialists, social workers, sanitarians, veterinarians. For other licensing boards and professions, contact the NE state operator at 402-471-2311 to be connected with the board that licenses the following professions: accountants, engineers/architects, barbers, abstracters, appraisers, land surveyors, landscape architects.

Nevada
State of Nevada Executive Chamber, 4600 Kietezke Lane, Building B, Suite 113, Reno, NV 89502; 702-688-1800, 800-326-5202; {www.state.nv.us/st_boards.htm}. Licensing boards and professions: accountants, architects, athletic trainers, audiologists and speech pathologists, barbers, chiropractors, contractors, cosmetologists, dentists, engineers and land surveyors, funeral directors and embalmers, hearing aid specialists, homeopaths, landscape architects, liquefied petroleum gas distributors, marriage and family counselors, physicians, naturopathic healing arts specialists, nurses, dispensing opticians, optometrists, oriental medicine, osteopaths, pharmacists, physical therapists, podiatrists, private investigators, psychologists, shorthand reporters, taxicab drivers, veterinarians.

New Hampshire
SOICC of New Hampshire, Economic and Labor Market Information Bureau, New Hampshire Employment Security, 32 S. Main St., Concord, NH 03301; 603-228-4370; {www.nhes.state.nh.us}. Licensing boards and professions: accountants, emergency medical technicians, engineers/architects/land surveyors, attorneys, auctioneers, insurance (bailbondsmen), barbers, cosmetologists, chiropractors, court reporters, dentists, drivers education Instructors, electricians, funeral directors/embalmers, engineers, physicians, private security guards, lobbyists, nurses, nursing home administrators, occupational therapists, optometrists, psychologists, pesticide control operators, pharmacists, plumbers, podiatrists, real estate agents, teacher agents, veterinarians, water supply and pollution control operators.

New Jersey
Director, Division of Consumer Affairs, 124 Halsey St., Newark, NJ 07102; 973-504-6200; {www.state.nj.us/lps/ca/home.htm}. Licensing boards and professions: accountants, architects, barbers, beauticians, dentists, electrical contractors, marriage counselors, plumbers, morticians, nurses, ophthalmic dispensing technicians, optometrists, pharmacists, physical therapists, professional engineers and landscape surveyors, professional planners, psychological examiners, shorthand reporters, veterinarians, public movers and warehousemen, acupuncture specialists, landscape architects, athletic trainers, hearing aid dispensers, chiropractors, opthomologists.

New Mexico
Regulation and Licensing Department, 2055 Pacheco St., Suite 300, Santa Fe, NM 87504; 505-476-7100; {www.rld.state.nm.us}. Licensing boards and professions: accountants, architects, athletic promoters, barbers, chiropractors, cosmetologists, dentists, engineers and land surveyors, landscape architects, physicians, nurses, nursing home administrators, occupational therapists, optometrists, osteopaths, pharmacists, physical therapists, podiatrists, polygraphers, private investigators, psychologists, realtors, thanatopractice, veterinarians.

New York
New York State Education Department, Division of Professional Licensing, Cultural Education Center, Empire State Plaza, Albany, NY 12230; 518-474-3817, 800-442-8106 (toll-free in NY); {www.nysed.gov/prof/profhome.htm}. Licensed professionals: acupuncturists, architects, audiologists, certified shorthand reporters, chiropractors, dentists, landscape architects, land surveyors, massage therapists, physicians, osteopaths, nurses, occupational therapists, ophthalmic dispensers, optometrists, pharmacists, physical therapists, podiatrists, engineers, psychologists, public accountants, social workers, speech pathologists, veterinarians.

North Carolina
Department of the Secretary of State, P.O. Box 29622, Raleigh, NC 27626; 919-733-4161; {www.secstate.state.nc.us/blio/blocc.htm}. Licensing boards and professions: architects, auctioneers, barbers, boiler operators, accountants, chiropractors, cosme-

Company Intelligence

tologists, registered counselors, dental, electrical contractors, foresters, general contractors, hearing aid dealers and fitters, landscape architects, landscape contractors, marital and family therapists, physicians, navigators and pilots, morticians, nurses, nursing home administrators, opticians, optometrists, osteopaths, pesticide operators, pharmacists, physical therapists, plumbers and heating specialists, podiatrists, practicing psychologists, private protective services, professional engineers and land surveyors, public librarians, real estate, refrigeration technicians, sanitarians, social workers, speech and language pathologists, structural pest control operators, veterinarians, waste water treatment operators, water treatment facility operators.

North Dakota

North Dakota Legislative Council Library, 600 East Boulevard Avenue, Bismarck, ND 58505; 701-224-2916. Licensing boards and professions: abstracters, accountants, architects, athletic trainers, audiologists and speech pathologists, barbers, chiropractors, cosmetologists, dentists, dietitians, electricians, embalmers, emergency medical services, engineers and land surveyors, hearing aid dealers and fitters, massage therapists, physicians, nurses, nursing home administrators, occupational therapists, optometrists, pharmacists, physical therapists, plumbers, podiatrists, private investigators, private police security, psychologists, real estate agents, respiratory care specialists, social workers, soil classifiers, veterinarians, water well contractors.

Ohio

State of Ohio, Department of Administrative Services, Division of Computer Services, 30 East Broad St., 40th Floor, Columbus, OH 43215-0409; 614-466-2000. Licensed professionals: wholesale distributors of dangerous drugs, terminal distributors of dangerous drugs, pharmacists, accountants, barbers, barber shops, beauty shops, managing cosmetologists, cosmetologists, manicurists, architects, landscape architects, practical nurses, registered nurses, surveyors, engineers, surveyors, dentists, dental hygienists, osteopaths, physicians, podiatrists, chiropractors, midwives, embalmers, funeral directors, embalmer and funeral directors, hat cleaners, dry cleaners, public employment agencies, auctioneers, private investigators, auctioneers.

Oklahoma

Governor's Office, State Capitol, Oklahoma City, OK 73105; 405-521-2342 or State Information Operator, 405-521-2011. Licensing board and professions: accountants, real estate agents, physicians, foresters, medico-legals, nursing homes, nurses, optometrists, osteopaths, physicians, pharmacists, polygraph examiners, psychologists, shorthand reporters, social workers, speech pathologists, veterinarians, landscape architects, architects, chiropractors, cosmetologists, dentists, embalmers and funeral directors. For other licensed professionals, contact Occupational Licensing, OK State Health Department, 1000 North East, 10th Street, Oklahoma City, OK 73117; 405-271-5217: barbers, hearing aid dealers, electricians, water and waste treatment plant operators.

Oregon

Oregon Secretary of State, Corporations Division, 255 Capitol St., NE, Suite 151, Salem, OR 97310; 503-986-2200. Licensing boards and professions: accountants, architects, barbers and hairdressers, builders, contractors, collection agencies, debt consolidators, geologists, landscape architects, landscape contractors, and TV/radio service dealers, engineering examiners, fire marshals, insurance agents, maritime pilots, real estate agents, tax practitioners.

Pennsylvania

Bureau of Professional and Occupational Affairs, 618 Transportation and Safety Building, Harrisburg, PA 17120-2649; 717-787-8503, or 800-822-2113 (toll-free in PA); {www.dos.state.pa.us/bpoa/bpoa.html}. Licensing boards and professions: accountants, architects, auctioneers, barbers, cosmetology, funeral directors, landscape architects, professional engineers, real estate agents. For licensed health professions, contact Bureau of Professional and Occupational Affairs, Secretary of State, 618 Transportation and Safety Building, Harrisburg, PA 17120; 717-783-1400: dentists, physicians, nurses, nursing home administrators, occupational therapists, optometrists, osteopaths, pharmacists, physical therapists, podiatrists, psychologists, speech-language and hearing specialists, veterinarians, navigators.

Rhode Island

Rhode Island Occupational Information Coordinating Commission, 10 Friendship Street, Providence, RI 02908; 401-272-0830; {www.dlt.state.ri.us/webdev/lmi/rioicc/rioicchm.html}. Licensing boards and professions: nurses aides, psychologists, respiratory therapists, sanitarians, speech pathologists, veterinarians, physical therapists, plumbers, podiatrists, prosthetists, nurses, nursing home administrators, occupational therapists, opticians, optometrists, osteopaths, physician assistants, embalmers/funeral directors, hairdressers, cosmetologists, manicurists, massage therapists, physicians, midwives, acupuncturists, athletic trainers, audiologists, barbers, barber shops, chiropractors, dentists, dental hygienists, electrologist, architects, coastal resource management, engineers and land surveyors.

South Carolina

South Carolina Department of Labor, Licensing, and Regulation, P.O. Box 11329, Columbia, SC 29211; 803-896-4363; {www.llr.state.sc.us/boards.htm}. Licensing boards and professions: accountants, architects, auctioneers, barbers, morticians, chiropractors, contractors, cosmetologists, dentists, engineers, environmental systems (well diggers), foresters, funeral services, landscape architects, physicians, nurses, nursing home administrators, occupational therapists, opticians, optometrists, pharmacists, physical therapists, professional counselors, marriage and family therapists, psychologists, real estate agents, sanitarians, home builder, social workers, speech pathologist/audiologists, veterinarians, athletic trainers (boxing and wrestling), geologists.

South Dakota

Department of Commerce and Regulation, 118 E. Capitol Ave., Pierre, SD 57501-5070; 605-773-3178; {www.state.sd.us/dcr/dcr.html}. South Dakota Medical and Osteopath Examiners, 1323 S. Minnesota Avenue, Sioux Falls, SD 57105; 605-336-1965. Licensing boards and professions: physicians, osteopaths, physician's assistants, physical therapists, medical corporations, emergency technicians, abstracters, accountants, barbers, chiropractors, cosmetologists, electricians, engineers/architects, funeral directors, hearing aid dispensers, medical/osteopaths, nurses, nursing home administrators, optometrists, pharmacists, plumbers, podiatrists, psychologists, real estate agents, social workers, veterinarians.

Tennessee

Division of Regulatory Boards, Department of Commerce and Insurance, 500 James Robertson Parkway, Nashville, TN 37243; 615-741-3449; {www.state.tn.us/commerce}. Licensing boards and professions: accountants, architects and engineers, auctioneers, barbers, collection services, contractors, cosmetologists, funeral directors and embalmers, land surveyors, motor vehicle salesmen and dealers, personnel recruiters, pharmacists, polygraph examiners, real estate. For other licensed health professionals, contact Division of Health Related Professions, Department of Health and Environment, 283 or 287 Plus Park Blvd Complex, Nashville, TN 37247-1010; 615-367-6220: dentists, dental hygienists, podiatrists, physicians, physician's assistants, osteopaths, optometrists, veterinarians, nursing home administrators, dispensing opticians, chiropractors, social workers, hearing aid dispensers, registered professional environmentalists, marital and family counselors, speech pathology/audiologists, occupational and physical therapists, x-ray technicians, registered nurses, licensed practical nurses.

Texas

Department of Licensing and Regulation, P.O. Box 12157, Austin, TX 78711; 512-463-6599, 800-803-9202 (toll-free in TX); {www.licence.state.tx.us}. Licensing boards and professions: accountants, architects, barbers, cosmetologists, morticians, educators, public safety, chiropractors, psychologists, dentists, real estate agents, engineers, veterinarians, insurance agents, land surveyors, landscape architects, fitting and dispensing of hearing aids, private investigators and private security agencies, polygraph, Vocational nurses, nursing home administrators, physicians, optometrists, structural pest control operators, pharmacists, physical therapists, plumbers, podiatrists, professional counselors, dietitians, speech-language pathology and audiology.

Utah

Division of Occupational and Professional Licensing, Department of Commerce, Heber M. Wells Building, 160 East 300 South, P.O. Box 45802, Salt Lake City, UT 84145-0805; 801-530-6628; {www.commerce.state.ut.us}. Licensing boards and professions: accountants, architects, barbers, cosmetologists, electrologists, chiropractors, podiatrists, dentists, dental hygienists, embalmers, funeral directors, pre-need sellers, engineers, land surveyors, physicians, surgeons, Naturopaths, registered nurses, licensed practical nurses, nurse midwives, nurse anesthetists, nurse specialists, prescriptive practice specialist, IV therapists, optometrists, osteopaths, pharmacists, pharmacies, manufacturing pharmacies, shorthand reporters, veterinarians, health facility administrators, sanitarians, morticians, physical therapists, psychologists, clinical social workers, conduct research on controlled substance, marriage and family therapists, master therapeutic recreational specialists, speech pathologists, audiologists, occupational therapists, hearing aid specialists, massage therapists, massage establishments, acupuncture practitioners, physician assistants, dieticians, contractors.

Vermont

Office of Professional Regulation, Secretary of State, Pavilion Office Building, Montpelier, VT 05609; 802-828-2363; {http://vtprofessionals.org}. Licensing boards and professions: accountants, architects, barbers, boxing control, chiropractors, cosmetologists, dentists, engineers, funeral directors/embalmers, land surveyors, medical board (physicians, podiatrists, real estate brokers, veterinarians, physical therapists, social workers, physician assistants, motor vehicle racing, nurses, nursing

State Licensing Offices

home administrators, opticians, optometrists, osteopaths, pharmacies, pharmacist, psychologists, private detectives, security Guards, radiological technicians.

Virginia
Virginia Department of Professional and Occupational Regulation, 3600 W. Broad St., Richmond, VA 23230; 804-367-8500; {www.state.va.us/dpor/indexie.html. Licensed professions: accountants, architects, auctioneers, audiologists, barbers, boxers, contractors, commercial driver training schools, employment agencies, professional engineers, geologists, hairdressers, harbor pilots, hearing aid dealers and fitters, landscape architects, nursing home administrators, librarians, opticians, polygraph examiners, private security services, real estate brokers, speech pathologists, land surveyors, water and wastewater works operators, wrestlers. For licensed health professions, contact receptionist, Health Professionals: 804-662-9900. The office listed above can provide you with phone numbers for the following licensing boards: dentists, funeral directors/embalmers, physicians, medical/legal assistants, nurses, optometrists, pharmacists, psychologists, professional counselors, social workers, veterinarians.

Washington
Department of Licensing, Department of Health, P.O. Box 9020, Olympia, WA 98507-7860; 360-902-3600; {www.wa.gov/dol/main.htm}. Licensed professions: acupuncturists, auctioneers, architects, barbers, camp club registration/salespersons, chiropractors, cosmetology schools/ instructors, cosmetologists, manicurists, collection agencies, debt adjusters/agencies, dentists, dental hygienists, drugless therapeutic-naturopaths, employment agencies/managers, professional engineers, engineers-in-training, land surveyors, engineering corporations/partnerships, escrow officers/agents, firearms dealers, embalmers, apprentice embalmers, funeral directors, funeral establishments, hearing aid dispensers/trainees, land development registration, landscape architects, massage operators, midwives, notary publics, nursing home administrators, occularists, occupational therapists, dispensing opticians, optometrists, osteopaths, osteopathic physician/ surgeon, osteopathic physician assistants, physicians, surgeons, physician's assistants, limited physician, podiatrists, practical nurses, psychologists, physical therapists, real estate (brokers, salespersons, corporations, partnerships, branch offices), land development representatives, registered nurses, timeshare registration and salespersons, veterinarians, animal technicians.

West Virginia
Secretary of State, State Capitol, Charleston, WV 25305; 304-558-6000; {www.state.wv.us/sos}. Licensing boards and professions: accountants, architects, barbers, beauticians, chiropractors, dentists, and dental hygienists, embalmers and funeral directors, engineers, foresters, hearing-aid dealers, landscape architects, land surveyors, law examiners, physicians, practical nurses, registered nurses, nursing home administrators, occupational therapists, optometrists, osteopaths, pharmacists, physical therapists, psychologists, radiologic technicians, real estate agents, sanitarians, state water resources, veterinarians.

Wisconsin
Department of Regulation and Licensing, P.O. Box 8935, Madison, WI 53708; 608-266-7482; {http://badger.state.wi.us/agencies/drl}.Licensed professions: accountants, animal technicians, architects, architects, engineers, barbers, bingo organizations, morticians, chiropractors, cosmetologists, distributors of dangerous drugs, dental hygienists, dentists, interior designers, private detectives, drug manufacturers, electrologists, professional engineers, funeral directors, hearing aid dealers/fitters, land surveyors, manicurists, physicians, surgeons, nurse midwives, registered nurses, licensed practical nurses, nursing home administrators, optometrists, pharmacists, physical therapists, physician's assistants, podiatrists, psychologists, raffle organizations, real estate brokers, beauty salons, electrolysis salons, veterinarians.

Wyoming
Governor's Office, State Capitol, Cheyenne, WY 82002; 307-777-7434. Licensing boards and professions: funeral directors and embalmers, health service administrators, buyers and purchasing agents, shorthand reporters, medical record technicians, accountants and auditors, claims adjusters, appraisers, engineers, architects, surveyors, interior designers and decorators, medical laboratory workers, dental laboratory technicians, opticians, radiological technicians, respiratory technicians, quality control inspectors, security salespeople, insurance agents, real estate agents, physicians, physician's assistants, chiropractors, pharmacists, occupational therapists, activity therapists, physical therapists, speech pathologist and audiologist, veterinarian, optometrist, dietitians, dentists, dental hygienists, registered nurses, licensed practical nurses, emergency medical technicians, nurse's aides, medical assistants, counselors, lawyers, legal assistants, cosmetologists and barbers.

Company Intelligence

State Company Directories

Market Info, Mailing Lists, Databases Available from State Company Directories

Would you like to know what kind of computing systems and software 24,000 manufacturing firms in California use? Or where to find out what materials 7,000 manufacturers in North Carolina need for their manufacturing processes? Or which of 2,700 manufacturers in Nevada have contracts with the federal government? You can get quick answers to these questions and more in the state directories of manufacturing companies.

These directories contain valuable information concerning what products are bought, sold, and distributed in each state. At the very least, each directory lists the companies' names, addresses, phone numbers, products, and SIC codes, and is cross-referenced by company name, location, and SIC code/product. So, if you want to find out which companies in Tennessee manufacture a certain type of electronic component and where they are located, all you have to do is look it up in the product index. If you want to find out what manufacturing firms are operating in a certain town or county, the geographic index will tell you. These directories can be invaluable for targeting new market areas, monitoring industry trends, developing more effective mailing lists, and much more.

The directories are generally put out by the individual state's Chamber of Commerce or Department of Economic Development and private publishing companies. The price and sophistication of these directories vary from state to state. While some, like Montana's may offer only the basic information mentioned above, others, like the New Jersey directory, will also include key personnel, CEO, parent company, employment figures, import/export market, and more. Prices range from $36 for Utah's directory, all the way to $179 for California's directory. Most of the prices listed below include shipping and handling, and state sales tax where applicable.

Many of these directories are also available in database formats and differ widely in cost. While there are some real bargains, such as Montana's directory for over 3,000 firms on diskette for $50, some, like California's of over 69,000 will cost you $995.

List of State Company Directories

Alabama
Alabama Development Office, Research and Communications Division, 401 Adams Avenue, Montgomery, AL 36104; 800-248-0033, 334-242-0400, Fax: 334-353-1212; {www.ado.state.al.us}, E-mail: {info@www.state.al.us}. $55. Over 6,000 businesses included, which list the company name, address, contact name, phone number, SIC code, product description, number of employees, and the year the firm was established. A number of them also include fax numbers, high-tech status, plant size and sales volume. Cross referenced by alphabet, geography, product(SIC code), export, parent company and product index. $150 for ASCII files, shipped on 3.5" diskette or as an e-mail attachment.

Alaska
Harris InfoSource Company, 2057 East Aurora Road, Twinsburg, OH 44087; 800-888-5900, 330-425-9000, Fax: 800-643-5997; {www.harrisinfo.com}, E-mail: {webmaster@harrisinfo.com}. *Alaska Industrial Directory:* $46, CD-ROM Databases: $215 (1+ employees), $120 (20+ employees). Approximately 980 firms with contacts for 1,718 executives are included. Some of the data included is the company address, phone number, employment size, geographic area, plant size, SIC code, estimated annual sales, and import/export. It is cross-referenced by geographic, alphabetic, product and SIC code information.

Arizona
Greater Phoenix Chamber of Commerce, Bank Center Plaza, 201 North Central Avenue, 27th Floor, Phoenix, AZ 85073; 602-254-5521, Fax: 602-495-8913; {www.phoenixchamber.com}, E-mail: {info@phoenixchamber.com}. *Arizona Industrial Directory:* $90 (non-member), $80 (member). More than 8,400 manufacturers, distributors and wholesalers with addresses, phone numbers, name of principals, number of employees, SIC codes and market areas. They are cross referenced by products and services, alphabet section, geographical section, and international trade section.

Arkansas
Arkansas Department of Economic Development, Research Department, One Capitol Mall, Little Rock, AR 72201; 800-ARKANSAS, 501-682-1121; {www.1800arkansas.com}. $75. Approximately 2,400 companies listed with name, address, phone, contact person, parent company, products and SIC code. Cross-referenced by company name, location, and product (SIC code).

California
Harris InfoSource Company, 2057 East Aurora Road, Twinsburg, OH 44087; 800-888-5900, 330-425-9000, Fax: 800-643-5997; {www.harrisinfo.com}, E-mail: {webmaster@harrisinfo.com}. *California Manufacturers Directory:* $179. CD-ROM Databases: $995 (1+ employees), $695 (20+ employees). Approximately 69,000 firms with contacts for 165, 658 executives are included. Some of the data included is the company address, phone number, employment size, geographic area, plant size, SIC code, estimated annual sales, and import/export. It is cross-referenced by geographic, alphabetic, product and SIC code information.

Colorado
Business Research Division, University of Colorado, Campus Box 420, Boulder, CO 80309; 303-492-8227. *Colorado Manufacturers Directory:* $80, diskette: $400. About 5,000 companies listed with name, address, phone number, CEO, employee size, market area, product, and SIC code. Cross referenced by name, location and SIC code.

Connecticut
Connecticut Business and Industry Association, 350 Church Street, Hartford, CT 06103-1106; 860-244-1900, Fax: 860-278-8562; {www.cbia.com}. *Connecticut Manufacturers Directory:* $70 (CBIA members), $87 (non-members), CD-ROM database: $320 (members), $300 (non-members). Over 6,730 companies are included with SIC codes, geography, products, and company size. Cross-referenced alphabetically, geographically, by SIC code and product. CD-ROM includes business credit scores, links to company headquarters and parent companies, and geo-coded database.

Delaware
Harris InfoSource Company, 2057 East Aurora Road, Twinsburg, OH 44087; 800-888-5900, 330-425-9000, Fax: 800-643-5997; {www.harrisinfo.com}, E-mail: {webmaster@harrisinfo.com}. *Delaware Manufacturers Directory:* $50, CD-ROM: $299 (1+ employees), $199 (20+ employees). Included are over 1,000 firms and 2,000 executives with addresses, phone numbers, locations, employment size, plant size, estimated annual sales, SIC code and import/export designation. Cross-referenced by alphabet, SIC code, geographic and product.

Florida
Harris InfoSource Company, 2057 East Aurora Road, Twinsburg, OH 44087; 800-888-5900, 330-425-9000, Fax: 800-643-5997; {www.harrisinfo.com}, E-mail: {webmaster@harrisinfo.com}. *Florida Manufacturers Directory:* $139, CD-ROM database: $619 (1+ employees), $415 (20+ employees). Over 17,000 companies and 37,000 executives with the address, phone number, employee size, SIC code, geographic area, plant size, estimated annual sales, and import/export information. Cross-referenced geographically, alphabetically, SIC codes and product.

State Company Directories

Georgia
Georgia Department of Industry, Trade and Tourism, Research Division, 285 Peachtree Center Avenue, NE,, Suite 1000 & 1100, Atlanta, GA 30303-1230; 404-656-3619, Fax: 404-656-3567; {www.georgia.org}. *Georgia Manufacturers Directory:* $65. Information on over 9,400 companies and their products. Included are the name, address, phone, market area, parent company, employee figures, and SIC codes. Cross-referenced by company name, location, and SIC code.

Hawaii
Harris InfoSource Company, 2057 East Aurora Road, Twinsburg, OH 44087; 800-888-5900, 330-425-9000, Fax: 800-643-5997; {www.harrisinfo.com}, E-mail: {webmaster@harrisinfo.com}. *Hawaii Industrial Directory:* $46, CD-ROM Databases: $215 (1+ employees), $120 (20+ employees). Approximately 1,250 firms with contacts for 2,1444 executives are included. Some of the data included is the company address, phone number, employment size, geographic area, plant size, SIC code, estimated annual sales, and import/export. It is cross-referenced by geographic, alphabetic, product and SIC code information.

Idaho
Harris InfoSource Company, 2057 East Aurora Road, Twinsburg, OH 44087; 800-888-5900, 330-425-9000, Fax: 800-643-5997; {www.harrisinfo.com}, E-mail: {webmaster@harrisinfo.com}. *Idaho Manufacturers Registry:* $75, CD-ROM database: $300 (1+ employees), $205 (10+ employees), $165 (20+ employees). Over 17,000 companies and 37,000 executives with the address, phone number, employee size, SIC code, geographic area, plant size, estimated annual sales, and import/export information. Cross-referenced geographically, alphabetically, SIC codes and product.

Illinois
Harris InfoSource Company, 2057 East Aurora Road, Twinsburg, OH 44087; 800-888-5900, 330-425-9000, Fax: 800-643-5997; {www.harrisinfo.com}, E-mail: {webmaster@harrisinfo.com}. *Illinois Manufacturers Directory:* $174, CD-ROM database: $739 (1+ employee), $ 415 (20+ employees). Information on over 21,000 firms and 58,000 executives along with SIC codes, number of employees, plant size, location, estimated annual sales, and import/export. It is cross-referenced geographically, alphabetically, by SIC code and product.

Indiana
Harris InfoSource Company, 2057 East Aurora Road, Twinsburg, OH 44087; 800-888-5900, 330-425-9000, Fax: 800-643-5997; {www.harrisinfo.com}, E-mail: {webmaster@harrisinfo.com}. *Indiana Manufacturers Directory:* $117, CD-ROM database: $619 (1+ employees), $519 (10+ employees), $415 (20+ employees). It includes about 11,000 companies and 30,432 executive contacts. Some of the data included is the company employee size, geographic area, plant size, SIC code, estimated annual sales, and import/export. It is cross-referenced by geographic, alphabetic, product and SIC code information.

Iowa
Harris InfoSource Company, 2057 East Aurora Road, Twinsburg, OH 44087; 800-888-5900, 330-425-9000, Fax: 800-643-5997; {www.harrisinfo.com}, E-mail: {webmaster@harrisinfo.com}. *Official Iowa Manufacturers Directory:* $87, CD-ROM Databases: $375 (1+ employees), $230 (20+ employees). Approximately 6,499 firms with contacts for 13,733 executives are included. Some of the data included is the company address, phone number, employment size, geographic area, plant size, SIC code, estimated annual sales, and import/export. It is cross-referenced by geographic, alphabetic, product and SIC code information.

Kansas
Harris InfoSource Company, 2057 East Aurora Road, Twinsburg, OH 44087; 800-888-5900, 330-425-9000, Fax: 800-643-5997; {www.harrisinfo.com}, E-mail: {webmaster@harrisinfo.com}. *Kansas Manufacturers Register:* $49, CD-ROM database: $375 (1+ employees), $260 (20+ employees). Over 3,623 companies and 7,155 executives with the address, phone number, employee size, SIC code, geographic area, plant size, estimated annual sales, and import/export information. Cross-referenced geographically, alphabetically, SIC codes and product.

Kentucky
Department of Economic Development, Maps Sales, 133 Holmes Street, Frankfort, KY 40601; {www.thinkkentucky.com/kyedc/entrance.html}, E-mail: {harris@mis.net}. *Kentucky Directory of Manufacturers:* $87, CD-ROM $375 (1+ employees), $210 (20+ employees). Approximately 5,900 firms with name, address, phone, CEO, year established, employee count, products and SIC code. Cross-referenced alphabetically by firm name, geographically by city, and by products manufactured.

Louisiana
Louisiana Department of Economic Development, Office of Policy and Research, P.O. Box 94185, Baton Rouge, LA 70804-9185; 225-342-9009; {www.lded.state.la.us/new/home.htm}. *Directory of Louisiana Manufacturers:* $75, CD-ROM database: $325. Nearly 5,000 companies includes name, address, phone, contact, employee number, gross sales, product and SIC code. Cross-referenced geographically, alphabetically, by SIC code and product.

Maine
Tower Publishing Company, 588 Saco Road, Standish, ME 04084; 800-969-8693, Fax: 207-642-5463; {www.ime.net/tower/index.html}, E-mail: {tower@ime.net}. *Maine Manufacturing Directory:* $55. Listed are 2,200 companies with employee sizes, gross sales, SIC code, product descriptions, year established, full mailing, and plant addresses. There are 3,154 key executives, and 667 companies with import/export information. They are cross-referenced by alphabet, geography and SIC code.

Maryland
Harris InfoSource Company, 2057 East Aurora Road, Twinsburg, OH 44087; 800-888-5900, 330-425-9000, Fax: 800-643-5997; {www.harrisinfo.com}, E-mail: {webmaster@harrisinfo.com}. *Maryland Manufacturing Directory:* $81, CD-ROM: $375 (1+ employees), $210 (20+ employees). About 6,000 firms and 12, 810 executives are included with SIC codes, number of employees, plant size, location, estimated annual sales, and import/export. It is cross-referenced geographically, alphabetically, by SIC code and product.

Massachusetts
Harris InfoSource Company, 2057 East Aurora Road, Twinsburg, OH 44087; 800-888-5900, 330-425-9000, Fax: 800-643-5997; {www.harrisinfo.com}, E-mail: {webmaster@harrisinfo.com}. *Massachusetts Manufacturers Directory:* $117, CD-ROM: $415 (1+ employees), $340 (20+ employees). Over 10,000 companies and 22,000 executives with address, phone number, employee size, SIC code, geographic area, plant size, estimated annual sales, and import/export information. Cross-referenced geographically, alphabetically, SIC codes and product.

Michigan
Harris InfoSource Company, 2057 East Aurora Road, Twinsburg, OH 44087; 800-888-5900, 330-425-9000, Fax: 800-643-5997; {www.harrisinfo.com}, E-mail: {webmaster@harrisinfo.com}. *Michigan Industrial Directory:* $169, CD-ROM: $739 (1+ employees), $579 (10+ employees), $415 (20+ employees). This directory includes about 18,000 companies and over 47,000 executive contacts with estimated annual sales, plant size, location, employee count, SIC code, and import/export information. Cross-referenced geographically, alphabetically, by SIC code and product.

Michigan Chamber of Commerce, 600 South Walnut Street, Lansing, MI 48933; 517-371-2100, Fax: 517-371-7228; {www.michamber.com}. *Michigan Directory of Business CD,* $295. It covers 40,000 business with 10 and more employees, 78,000 individuals by title. Information included is company name and address, CEO, number of employees, SIC codes, phone numbers and congressional district.

Minnesota
Harris InfoSource Company, 2057 East Aurora Road, Twinsburg, OH 44087; 800-888-5900, 330-425-9000, Fax: 800-643-5997; {www.harrisinfo.com}, E-mail: {webmaster@harrisinfo.com}. *Directory of Minnesota Manufacturers:* $117, CD-ROM $515 (1+ employees), $ 389 (10+ employees), $260 (20+ employees). Listing of 10,191 companies, 21,591 executives includes company employment size, SIC code, geographic area, plant size, estimated annual sales, import/export, name, address, and phone. Cross-referenced by geography, alphabet, SIC code and product.

Mississippi
Mississippi Manufacturers Association, 720 North President Street, Jackson, MS 39202, P.O. Box 22607, Jackson, MS 39225-2607; 601-948-1222, Fax: 601-948-1475; {www.mma-web.org}. *Mississippi Directory of Manufacturers:* $76 (members receive 20% off). There are approximately 3,600 companies with 7,057 key executives. Cross-referenced by company name, SIC code and product.

Missouri
Harris InfoSource Company, 2057 East Aurora Road, Twinsburg, OH 44087; 800-888-5900, 330-425-9000, Fax: 800-643-5997; {www.harrisinfo.com}, E-mail: {webmaster@harrisinfo.com}. *Missouri Manufacturing Directory:* $117, CD-ROM: $619 (1+ employees), $479 (10+ employees), $340 (20+ employees). Included are 9,761 firms and 22,803 executives with addresses, phone numbers, locations, employment size, plant size, estimated annual sales, SIC code and import/export designation. Cross-referenced by alphabet, SIC code, geographic and product.

Montana
Department of Commerce, Economic Development Division, Office of Trade and International Development, 1424 9th Avenue, Helena, MT 59620; 406-444-4392; {http://commerce.state.mt.us}. *Montana Manufacturers Directory:* $50 (for paper or

Company Intelligence

diskette). Around 3,000 companies includes name, address, phone number, owner, products and SIC code. Cross-referenced alphabetically, geographically, by products and SIC code.

Nebraska
Nebraska Department of Economic Development, P.O. Box 94666, Lincoln, NE 68509; 402-471-3784, 800-426-6505; {www.ded.state.ne.us}. *Nebraska Directory of Manufacturers:* $50, CD-ROM $150 (includes a book also). Includes information on over 2,000 businesses with phone numbers, addresses, web addresses, SIC code, and listings by communities.

Nevada
Gold Hill Publishing Company, P.O. Drawer F, Virginia City, NV 89440; 702-847-0222, Fax: 702-847-0327; {www.nevadaweb.com}, E-mail: {goldhill@nevadaweb.com}. *Nevada Industrial Directory:* Listing of over 7,300 companies includes SIC codes, telephone number, fax number, up to 4 top executives, physical mailing address, e-mail and web address, annual sales, number of employees, and square footage occupied. It also identifies importers, exporters and federal contractors.

New Hampshire
Tower Publishing, 588 Saco Road, Standish, ME 04084; 800-969-8693, Fax: 207-648-5463; {www.ime.net/tower}, E-mail: {tower@ime.net}. *New Hampshire Manufacturing Directory:* $55. Listing 3,022 companies, 4,416 key executives, employee size, gross sales, product description, year established, full mailing and plant address. It also includes 988 companies with import/export information, 1,109 companies with square footage, 277 web addresses, and 422 e-mails. Cross-reference sections are alphabetical, geographical and by SIC code.

New Jersey
Manufacturer's News Incorporated, 1633 Central Street, Evanston, IL 60201; 847-864-7000; {www.mninfo.com}. *New Jersey Manufacturer's Directory:* $107, EZ Select disk: $299, EZ Select Unlimited disk: $490, Omni Disk: $545. Listing of over 11,000 companies with mailing and physical address, phone, fax and 800 number, e-mail and web addresses, annual sales, plant square footage, number of employees, distribution area, and name and titles of key executives. Cross-referenced by product name, city location, SIC code and parent company.

New Mexico
Center for Economic Development and Research Assistance, New Mexico State University, Business Complex Room 143, Las Cruces, NM 88003-0001; 505-646-6315, Fax: 505-646-7037. *New Mexico Manufacturers Directory:* $50. Listing of over 1,500 companies with mailing address, phone, employee size, location, and key people contact.

New York
Harris InfoSource Company, 2057 East Aurora Road, Twinsburg, OH 44087; 800-888-5900, 330-425-9000, Fax: 800-643-5997, {www.harrisinfo.com}, E-mail: {webmaster@harrisinfo.com}. *New York Manufacturing Directory:* $145, CD-ROM: $725 (1+ employees), $559 (10+ employees), $399 (20+ employees). Included are 18,754 firms and 39,170 executives with addresses, phone numbers, locations, employment size, plant size, estimated annual sales, SIC code and import/export designation. Cross-referenced by alphabet, SIC code, geographic and product.

North Carolina
Harris InfoSource Company, 2057 East Aurora Road, Twinsburg, OH 44087; 800-888-5900, 330-425-9000, Fax: 800-643-5997, {www.harrisinfo.com}, E-mail: {webmaster@harrisinfo.com}. *North Carolina Manufacturing Directory:* $123, CD-ROM: $525 (1+ employees), $429 (10+ employees), $340 (20+ employees). Included are 11,486 firms and 27,832 executives with addresses, phone numbers, locations, employment size, plant size, estimated annual sales, SIC code and import/export designation. Cross-referenced by alphabet, SIC code, geographic and product.

North Dakota
North Dakota Department of Economic Development and Finance, 1833 East Bismarck Expressway, Bismarck, ND 58504, 701-328-5300, TTY: 800-366-6088, Fax: 701-328-532; {www.growingnd.com}. *North Dakota Directory of Manufacturers and Food Processors:* $50 (book or 3.5" diskette). Approximately 850 companies listed with name, address, phone, contact person, number of employees, products and SIC code. Cross-referenced by location, SIC code, and name.

Ohio
Harris InfoSource Company, 2057 East Aurora Road, Twinsburg, OH 44087; 800-888-5900, 330-425-9000, Fax: 800-643-5997, {www.harrisinfo.com}, E-mail: {webmaster@harrisinfo.com}. *Ohio Manufacturers Directory:* $174, CD-ROM $739 (1+ employees), $415 (20+ employees). Listing of 22,260 companies, 62,268 executives includes company employment size, SIC code, geographic area, plant size, estimated annual sales, import/export, name, address, and phone. Cross-referenced by geography, alphabet, SIC code and product.

Oklahoma
Oklahoma Department of Commerce, Data and Statistics, P.O. Box 26980, Oklahoma City, OK 73126-0980; 405-815-5183, 800-879-6552. *Oklahoma Manufacturer's Directory:* $81, CD-ROM: $345 (1+ employees), $210 (20+ employees). Listing of 5,999 companies and 11,690 key executives with the company name, address, location, estimated annual sales, product, number of employees, plant size and import/export information. Cross-referenced by company, SIC code, SIC code description, city and county.

People out of state should contact Harris InfoSource Company at, 2057 East Aurora Road, Twinsburg, OH 44087; 800-888-5900, 330-425-9000, Fax: 800-643-5997, {www.harrisinfo.com}, E-mail: {webmaster@harrisinfo.com}.

Oregon
Harris InfoSource Company, 2057 East Aurora Road, Twinsburg, OH 44087; 800-888-5900, 330-425-9000, Fax: 800-643-5997, {www.harrisinfo.com}, E-mail: {webmaster@harrisinfo.com}. *Oregon Manufacturers Directory:* $110, CD-ROM $485 (1+ employees), $345 (10+ employees), $270 (20+ employees). A listing of 7,669 companies and 16,095 key executives is included with each companies mailing address, phone number, location, product, number of employees, SIC code, plant size, and estimated annual sales, import/export information. Cross referenced by alphabet, geography, SIC code and product.

Pennsylvania
Harris InfoSource Company, 2057 East Aurora Road, Twinsburg, OH 44087; 800-888-5900, 330-425-9000, Fax: 800-643-5997, {www.harrisinfo.com}, E-mail: {webmaster@harrisinfo.com}. *Pennsylvania Manufacturers Directory:* $169, CD-ROM $739 (1+ employees), $410 (20+ employees). Listing of 20,060 companies includes name, address, phone, 49,538 key executives, employee size, SIC code, location, plant size, estimated annual sales, and import/export destination. Cross-referenced by alphabet, geography, SIC code and product.

Rhode Island
Rhode Island Economic Development Corporation, One West Exchange Street, Providence, RI 02903, 401-222-2601, Fax: 401-222-2102; {www.riedc.com}, E-mail: {riedc@riedc.com}. *Rhode Island Manufacturers Directory:* $64, CD-ROM database: $260 (1+ employees), $179 (20+ employees).

South Carolina
South Carolina Department of Commerce, P.O. Box 927, Columbia, SC 29202; 803-737-0238; {www.callsouthcarolina.com}. *South Carolina Industrial Directory:* $65, CD-ROM $199. Listing of 3,800 companies with name, address, phone number, CEO, location, product line, parent company, and SIC code. Cross-referenced by alphabet, county, SIC code, and parent company.

South Dakota
Governor's Office of State Economic Development, Capitol Lake Plaza, Pierre, SC 57501; 605-773-5032. *South Dakota Directory of Manufacturers:* $50 plus $3 for shipping. Listings on around 5,286 companies including name, address, phone number, trade name, location, marketing area, number of employees, CEO, products and SIC code. Cross-referenced by company name, location and SIC code.

Tennessee
M. Lee Smith Publishers and Printers, P.O. Box 5094, Brentwood, TN, 37024-5094; 800-274-6774; {www.mleesmith.com}, E-mail: {custserv@mleesmith.com}. *Directory of Tennessee Manufacturers:* $92, disk: $395. Includes over 5,600 manufacturers detailing each of their key prospects, supply sources, potential markets and the names and titles of the decision makers. There is also the company location, mailing address, phone number, products and raw materials by SIC code, area of distribution, years in business, number of employees, annual sales, and parent company information included. Charge varies for diskette, magnetic tape or cheshire and pressure sensitive labels.

Texas
Manufacturer's News Incorporated, 1633 Central Street, Evanston, IL 60201; 847-864-7000; {www.mninfo.com}. *Texas Manufacturer's Directory:* $159, EZ Select disk: $399, EZ Select Unlimited disk: $670, Omni Disk: $745. Listing of over 18,000 companies with detailed profiles that include addresses, phone numbers, fax numbers, web addresses, e-mails, annual sales, plant square footage, number of employees, distribution areas, and the names and titles of key executives. Cross-referenced by company name, product name, location, SIC code, and parent company.

State Company Directories

Utah
Utah Department of Community and Economic Development, 324 South State Street, 5th Floor, Salt Lake City, UT 84111; 877-488-3233; {www.dced.state.ut.us/dbi}. *Utah Directory of Business and Industry:* $36 CD-ROM: $75. Information on 10,000 companies including name, address, phone number, employee figures, products and SIC code. Cross-referenced by company name and SIC code.

Vermont
Tower Publishing, 588 Saco Road, Standish, ME 04084; 800-969-8693, Fax: 207-648-5463; {www.ime.net/tower}, E-mail: {tower@ime.net}. *Vermont Manufacturing Directory:* $55. Listing 2,308 companies, 3,002 key executives, employee size, gross sales, product description, year established, full mailing and plant address. It also includes 604 companies with import/export information, 383 companies with square footage, 516 toll-free numbers, and 1,661 fax numbers. Cross-reference sections are alphabetical, geographical and by SIC code.

Virginia
Virginia Chamber of Commerce, 9 South 5th Street, Richmond, VA 23219; 804-644-1607; {www.vachamber.com}. *Virginia Industrial Directory:* $65 (member)/$85 (non-member), CD-ROM or disk: $355 (member)/$395 (non-member). Over 7,000 manufacturing companies are listed with name, address, phone number, CEO, employee figure, parent company, products and SIC code. Cross-referenced by county, city, SIC code and product.

Washington
Greater Seattle Chamber of Commerce, 1301 Fifth Avenue, Suite 2400, Seattle, WA 98101-2603; 206-389-7200, TDD/TTY: 206-389-7248, Fax: 206-389-7288; {www.seattlechamber.org}. *Washington Manufacturers Register:* $85 (members)/$110 (non-member). Listing 8,100 manufacturing companies with name and title of CEO, owner, and key executives. Also the company name, address, phone and fax number, annual sales, number of employees, year established, products, SIC codes, export/import data, web site and e-mails. Cross-referenced by location, SIC code, product, and alphabet.

West Virginia
Harris InfoSource Company, 2057 East Aurora Road, Twinsburg, OH 44087; 800-888-5900, 330-425-9000, Fax: 800-643-5997, {www.harrisinfo.com}, E-mail: {webmaster@harrisinfo.com}. *West Virginia Manufacturing Directory:* $67, CD-ROM: $87. Included are 2,629 firms and 5,673 executives with addresses, phone numbers, locations, employment size, plant size, estimated annual sales, SIC code and import/export designation. Cross-referenced by alphabet, SIC code, geographic and product.

Wisconsin
WMC Service Corporation, P.O. Box 352, 501 East Washington Avenue, Madison, WI 53701-0352; 608-258-3400, 8000-258-3400, Fax: 608-258-3413; {www.wmn.org}. *Wisconsin Manufacturer Directory:* $119, CD-ROM $595 (1+ employees), $345 (20+ employees). Approximately 9,709 company profiles and 21,748 key executive contacts with name, address, phone, year established, employee count, parent company, computer brand used, products, SIC code, parent company, and out-of-state affiliates. Cross-referenced by SIC code, product, GEO indexes, and alphabet listing.

Wyoming
Wyoming Business Council, 214 West 15th, Cheyenne, WY 82002; 307-777-2800, 800-262-3425, Fax: 307-777-2838; {http://wyomingbusiness.org}. *Wyoming Manufacturers Directory:* $57. Listings on over 1,100 companies with name, address, phone, CEO, market area, number of employees, and SIC code.

Company Intelligence

Company Background Reports Free From Better Business Bureaus

If you are looking for information on a private or public company, and the company sells goods and services to consumers, you would be wise to check with the local Better Business Bureau in the city closest to the company's headquarters. A recent investigation into a patent research firm by our staff turned up a comprehensive report which outlined the company's activities, officers, claims and problems. For example, it revealed that the state of Wisconsin had filed a suit against the company. Moreover, it also outlined the company's response to the lawsuit.

The Better Business Bureaus (BBB) around the country provide this service **free** to consumers who may be interested in dealing with any given company. Simply call, and the local BBB will search its files for any information about the company in question. If the report is brief and straightforward, they will read it over the telephone. If it is more complex, like the report on the patent research company, a copy of it will be sent to you free of charge.

Listed below are the telephone numbers for the Better Business Bureaus in the U.S. and Canada. (CC# = call charged to the consumer's credit card.)

Better Business Bureau Directory

Alabama
Birmingham, AL 35205
    1210 S. 20th St., P.O. Box 55268; 205-558-2222
Cullman, AL 35057
    1528 Peachtree Lane; 205-775-2917
Dothan, Al 36301
    118 Woodburn; 334-794-0492
Florence, AL 35630
    121A Court St.; 800-239-1642 (24 hrs)
Huntsville, AL 35801-5549
    107 Lincoln St., NE; 205-533-1640
Mobile, AL 36602-3295
    100 N. Royal St.; 334-433-5494, 800-544-4714 (So. AL only)
Montgomery, AL 36104-3559
    60 Commerce St., Suite 806; 334-262-5606

Alaska
Anchorage, AK 99503-3819
    2805 Bering St., Suite 2; 907-562-0704
Fairbanks, AK 99707
    P.O. Box 74675; 907-451-0222

Arizona
Phoenix, AZ 85014-4585
    4428 N. 12th St.; 602-264-1721; 877-291-6222
Tucson, AZ 85719
    3620 N. 1st Ave., Suite 136; Inquiries 502-888-5353, Complaints 502-888-5454, 800-696-2827 (So. AZ only)

Arkansas
Little Rock, AR 72204-2605
    1415 S. University; 501-664-7274, 800-482-8448 (AR only)

California
Bakersfield, CA 93301-4882
    705 Eighteenth St.; 805-322-2074
Colton, CA 92324-0814
    315 N. La Cadena; 900-505-1000 ($.95/min. 24 hrs.), CC# 909-426-0813 ($2.75/call)
Encino, CA 91316
    17609 Ventura Blvd., Suite LL03; 818-386-5510
Fresno, CA 93711
    2519 W. Shaw, #106; 559-222-8111
Los Angeles, CA 90020-2538
    3727 W. 6th St., Suite 607; CC# 909-426-0813 ($2.75/call); 900-505-1000 ($.95/min. 24 hrs.)
Millbrae, CA 94030
    510 Broadway, Suite 200; 650-552-9222
Monterey, CA 93940-2717
    494 Alverado St., Suite C; 408-372-3149
Oakland, CA 94612-1584
    510 16th St., Suite 550; 510-238-1000 (24 hrs)
Placentia, CA 92870
    550 W. Orangethorpe Ave., 900-505-1000
Sacramento, CA 95814-6997
    400 S St.; 916-443-6843
San Diego, CA 92123
    5050 Murphy Canyon, Suite 110; 858-496-2131 (24 hrs)
San Jose, CA 95125
    2100 Forest Ave.; 408-278-7400
Santa Barbara, CA 93102
    213 Santa Barbara St., P.O. Box 129 (93101); 805-963-8557
Stockton, CA 95202
    11 S. San Joaquin St., Suite 803; 209-948-4880
Torrance, CA 90502
    20280 S. Vermont, Suite 201; 310-771-1447

Colorado
Colorado Springs, CO 80907-5454
    3022 N. El Paso, P.O. Box 7970 (80933-7970); 719-636-1155
Denver, CO 80222-4350
    1780 S. Bellaire, Suite 700; Inquiries 303-758-2100, Complaints 303-788-2212, TDD 303-758-4786
Fort Collins, CO 80525-1073
    1730 S. College Ave., Suite 303; 970-484-1348, Cheyenne 307-778-2809
Pueblo, CO 81003-3119
    119 W. 6th St., Suite 203; 719-542-6464

Connecticut
Wallingford, CT 06492-2420
    821 N. Main St. Ext.; 203-269-2700

Delaware
Wilmington, DE 19802
    1010 Concord Ave.; 302-594-9200

District Of Columbia
Washington, DC 20005-3410
    1411 K St., NW, 10th Floor; 202-393-8000

Florida
Altamonte Springs, FL 32174
    151 Wymore Rd., Suite 100; 407-621-3300
Clearwater, FL 34620
    5830 142nd Ave. N., Suite B; 727-535-5522

Better Business Bureaus

Fort Meyers, Fl 33901
    2710 Swamp Cabbage Ct.; CC# 305-625-0307 ($.95/min.), 900-225-5222 ($.95/min., 24 hrs.)
Jacksonville, FL 32211
    7820 Arlington Expressway, Suite 147; 904-721-2288
Pensacola, FL 32501
    921 E. Gadsen St.; 805-429-0002
Port St. Lucie, FL 34954-5579
    1950 Port St. Lucie Blvd., Suite 211; 561-878-2010
West Palm Beach, FL 33409
    2924 N. Australia Ave.; 561-842-1918, Martin City 561-337-2083

Georgia
Albany, GA 31701
    101 1/2 S. Jackson; 912-883-0744
Atlanta, GA 30303-3075
    100 Edgewood Ave., Suite 1012; 404-688-4910, Chattanooga 612-266-6144
Augusta, GA 30901
    301 7th St., P.O. Box 2085 (30903-2085); 706-722-1574
Columbus, GA 31901
    208 13th St., P.O. Box 2587; 706-324-0712, 706-324-0713
Macon, GA 31201
    277 M.L. King Blvd.; 912-742-7999
Savannah, GA 31405
    6606 Abercon St., Suite 108-C, P.O. Box 13956 (91416-0956); 912-354-7521, 912-354-7522

Hawaii
Honolulu, HI 96814-3801
    1132 Bishop St.; 808-536-6956

Idaho
Boise, ID 83702-5320
    9619 Emerald; 208-342-4649
Idaho Falls, ID 93404-5926
    1575 South Blvd.; 208-523-9754

Illinois
Chicago, IL 60611
    330 N. Wabash Ave.; CC# 312-832-0500 ($3.80/call), 900-225-5222 ($.95/min. 24 hrs.)
Peoria, IL 61615-3770
    3024 West Lake; 309-688-3741
Rockford, IL 61104-1001
    810 E. State St., 3rd Floor; CC# 815-953-8967 ($3.80/call), 900-225-5222 ($.95/min., 24 hrs.)

Indiana
Elkhart, IN 46514-2988
    722 W. Bristol St., Suite H-2, P.O. Box 405; 219-262-8996
Evansville, IN 47716-2265
    1139 Washington Square; 812-473-0202
Fort Wayne, IN 46802-3493
    1203 Webster St.; 219-423-4433, 800-552-4631 (IN only)
Indianapolis, IN 46204-3584
    Victoria Center, 22 E. Washington St., Suite 200; 317-488-2222
Merrillville, IN 46410
    6111 Harrison St., Suite 101; 219-980-1511
South Bend, IN 46637-3360
    207 Dixie Way N., Suite 130; 219-277-9121, 800-439-5313 (N. IN only)

Iowa
Bettendorf, IA 52722-4100
    852 Middle Rd., Suite 290; 319-355-6344
Des Moines, IA 50309-2375
    505 5th Ave., Suite 615; 515-243-8137
Sioux City, IA 51101
    505 Sixth St., Suite 417; 712-252-4501

Kansas
Topeka, KS 66607-1190
    501 Southeast Jefferson, Suite 24; 785-232-0454
Wichita, KS 67211
    328 Laura; 316-263-3146

Kentucky
Lexington, KY 40511
    1460 Newtown Pike; 606-259-1008
Louisville, KY 40203-2186
    844 S. Fourth St.; 502-583-6546 (24 hrs), 800-388-2222 (24 hrs; S. IN & KY only)

Louisiana
Alexandria, LA 71303
    5220-C Rue Verdun; 318-473-4494
Baton Rouge, LA 70802
    748 Main St.; 225-346-5222
Houma, LA 70364
    3038 Park Ave.; 504-868-3456
Lafayette, LA 70506
    100 Huggins Rd., P.O. Box 30297; 318-981-3497
Lake Charles, LA 70605
    3941-L Ryan St., P.O. Box 7314; 318-478-6253
Monroe, LA 71201-7380
    141 Desiard St., Suite 808; 318-387-4600
New Orleans, LA 70130-5843
    1539 Jackson Ave., Suite 400; 504-581-6222 (24 hrs), 504-528-9277
Shreveport, LA 71105-2122
    3612 Youree Drive, 318-868-5146

Maine
Portland, ME 04103-2648
    812 Stevens Ave., 207-878-2715

Maryland
Baltimore, MD 21211-3215
    2100 Huntingdon Ave.; CC# 410-347-3990 ($3.80/call), 900-225-5222 ($.95/min., 24 hrs.)

Massachusetts
Boston, MA 02116-4344
    20 Park Plaza, Suite 820; 617-426-9000, 800-422-2811 (802 area only)
Springfield, MA 01103-1402
    293 Bridge St., Suite 320; 413-734-3114
Worcester, MA 01608-1900
    32 Franklin St., P.O. Box 16555; 508-755-2548

Michigan
Grand Rapids, MI 46503-3001
    40 Pearl, NW, Suite 354; 616-774-8236, 800-884-3222 (W. MI only, 24 hrs)
Southfield, MI 48076-7751 (Detroit)
    30555 Southfield Rd., Suite 200; 248-644-9100 (24 hrs)

Minnesota
Minneapolis/St. Paul 55116-2600
    2706 Gannon Rd., 651-699-1111, Complaints 800-646-6222

Mississippi
Jackson, MS 39206
    4915 I-55 N, P.O. Box 12745; 601-987-8282

Missouri
Kansas City, MO 64106-2418
    306 E. 12th St., Suite 1024; 816-421-7800
St. Louis, MO 63110-1400
    12 Sunnen Dr.; 314-645-3300 (24 hrs)
Springfield, MO 65806-1326
    205 Park Central E., Suite 509; 417-862-4222, 800-497-4222 (SW MO only)

Montana
none

Nebraska
Lincoln, NE 68510-1670
    3633 O St., Suite 1; 402-436-2345
Omaha, NE 68134-6022
    2237 N. 91st Ct.; 402-391-7612

Company Intelligence

Nevada
Las Vegas, NV 89146
 5595 W. Spring Mountain Rd.; 702-320-4500
Reno, NV 89502
 991 Bible Way, P.O. Box 21269; 775-322-0657

New Hampshire
Concord, NH 03301-3483
 410 S. Main St., Suite 3; 603-224-1991

New Jersey
Parsippany, NJ 07054 (Newark)
 400 Lanidex Plaza; 973-581-1313
Toms River, NJ 08753-8239
 1721 Route 37 East; 732-270-5577
Trenton, NJ 08690-3596
 1700 Whitehorse-Hamilton Sq., #D-5; 609-588-0808
Westmont, NJ 08108-0303
 16 Maple Ave., P.O. Box 303; 856-854-8467

New Mexico
Albuquerque, NM 87110-3657
 2625 Pennsylvania NE, Suite 2050; 505-346-0110, 800-873-2224 (NM only)
Farmington, NM 87401-5855
 308 N. Locke; 505-326-6501
Las Cruces, NM 88001-3548
 201 N. Church, Suite 330; 505-524-3130

New York
Buffalo, NY 14202
 741 Delaware Ave.; CC# 716-881-5222 ($3.80/call), 900-225-5222 ($.95/min., 24 hrs.)
Farmingdale, NY 11735
 266 Main St.; CC# 212-533-6200 ($3.80/call), 900-225-5222 ($/95/min., 24 hrs.)
New York, NY 10010
 257 Park Ave., S.; CC# 212-533-6200 ($3.80/call), 900-225-5222 ($.95/min., 24 hrs.)
White Plains, NY 10603
 30 Glenn St.; CC# 212-533-6200 ($3.80/call), 900-225-5222 ($.95/min., 24 hrs.)

North Carolina
Asheville, NC 28801-2111
 1200 BB&T Bldg.; 828-253-2392
Charlotte, NC 28209-3650
 5200 Park Rd., Suite 202; 704-527-0012 (24 hrs)
Greensboro, NC 27410-4895
 3608 W. Friendly Ave.; 336-852-4240 (24 hrs)
Raleigh, NC 27604-1080
 3125 Poplarwood Ct., Suite 308; 919-872-9240, 800-222-0950 (E NC only)
Sherrills Ford, NC 28673
 P.O. Box 69; 828-478-5622
Winston-Salem, NC 27101-2728
 500 W. 5th St., Suite 202; 336-725-8348

North Dakota
Minneapolis/St. Paul 55116-2600
 2706 Gannon Rd., 651-699-1111, Complaints 800-646-6222

Ohio
Akron, OH 44303-2111
 222 W. Market St.; 330-253-4590
Canton, OH 44703-3135
 1434 Cleveland Ave., NW, P.O. Box 8017; 800-362-0494 (OH only), 330-454-9401
Cincinnati, OH 45202-2097
 898 Walnut St.; 513-421-3015
Cleveland, OH 44115-1299
 2217 E. 9th St., Suite 200; 216-241-7678
Columbus, OH 43215-1828
 1335 Dublin, Suite 30A; 614-486-6336
Dayton, OH 45402-1828
 40 W. Fourth St., Suite 1250; 937-222-5825
Lima, OH 45802-0269
 112N, N. West St., P.O. Box 269; 419-223-7010, 800-462-0468
Toledo, OH 43606
 3103 Executive Parkway, Suite 200; 419-531-3116
Youngstown, OH 44501-1495
 600 Mahoning Bank Bldg., P.O. Box 1495; 330-744-3111, Lisbon 216-424-5522, Warren 216-394-0628

Oklahoma
Oklahoma City, OK 73102-2400
 17 S. Dewey; Inquiries 405-239-6081
Tulsa, OK 74136-3327
 6711 S. Yale, Suite 230; 918-492-1266

Oregon
Portland, OR 97204
 333 SW Fifth Ave., Suite 300; 503-226-3981, 800-488-4166 (OR/SW WA only)

Pennsylvania
Bethlehem, PA 18018-5789
 528 N. New St.; 610-866-8780
Lancaster, PA 17602-2852
 29 E. King St., Suite 322; CC# 717-291-1151 ($3.80/call), 900-225-5222 ($.95/min., 24 hrs.)
Philadelphia, PA 19103-0297
 1608 Walnut St.; CC# 215-448-3870 ($3.80/call), 215-985-9313, 900-225-5222 ($.95/min., 24 hrs.)
Pittsburgh, PA 15222-2511
 300 Sixth Ave., Suite 100-UL; 412-456-2700
Scranton, PA 18503-2204
 129 N. Washington Ave., P.O. Box 993; 570-342-9129, 570-655-0445

Puerto Rico
San Juan, PR 00936-3488
 1608 Bori St., P.O. Box 363488; 787-756-5400

Rhode Island
Warwick, RI 02888
 120 Lavan St.; Inquiries 401-785-1212, Complaints 401-785-1213

South Carolina
Columbia, SC 29205
 2330 Devine St., P.O. Box 8326; 803-254-2525
Greenville, SC 29601
 307-B Falls St.; 864-242-5052
Myrtle Beach, SC 29577-1601
 1601 N. Oak St., Suite 403; 843-626-6881

South Dakota
Sioux City, IA 51101
 505 Sixth St., Suite 417; 712-252-4501

Tennessee
Blountville, TN 37617-1178
 P.O. Box 1178, TCA #121; 423-325-6616
Chattanooga, TN 37402-2614
 1010 Market St., Suite 200; 423-266-6144
Knoxville, TN 37919
 2633 Kingston Pike, Suite 2, P.O. Box 17036; 423-522-2552
Memphis, TN 38120
 6525 Quail Hollow, Suite 410, P.O. Box 17036; 901-759-1300
Nashville, TN 37219-1778
 201 Fourth Ave. N., Suite 100; 615-250-4222 (24 hrs)

Texas
Abilene, TX 79605-5052
 3300 S. 14th St., Suite 307; 915-691-1533
Amarillo, TX 79101-3408
 724 S. Polk, P.O. Box 1905; 806-379-6222
Austin, TX 78741-3854
 2101 S. IH35, Suite 302; 512-445-2911 (24 hrs)
Beaumont, TX 77701-2011
 550 Fannin St., Suite 100; 409-835-5348
Bryan, TX 77802-4413
 4346 Carter Creek Pkwy., 409-260-2222

Better Business Bureaus

Corpus Christi, TX 78412
    4301 Ocean Dr.; 361-852-4949
Dallas, TX 75201-3093
    2001 Bryan St., Suite 850; CC# 214-220-2000 ($3.80/call), 900-225-5222 ($.93/min., 24 hrs.)
El Paso, TX 79901
    State National Plaza, Suite 1101; 915-577-0191
Fort Worth, TX 76102-5978
    1612 Summit Ave., Suite 260; 817-332-7585 (24 hrs)
Houston, TX 77007
    525 Katy Freeway, Suite 500; CC# 713-867-4946 ($3.80/call), 713-868-9500, 900-225-5222 ($.95/min., 24 hrs.)
Longview, TX 75604
    2002 Judson, Suite 107; 903-758-3222
Lubbock, TX 79401-3410
    916 Main St., Suite 800; 806-763-0459 (24 hrs)
Midland, TX 79711-0206
    P.O. Box 60206; 915-563-1880 800-592-4433 (TX only)
San Angelo, TX 76904
    3121 Exec. Office, P.O. Box 3355; 915-949-2989
San Antonio, TX 78217-5296
    1800 NE Loop 410, Suite 400; 210-828-9441
Tyler, TX 75701
    3600 Old Bullard Rd., Suite 400, P.O. Box 6652; 903-581-5704
Waco, TX 76701
    2210 Washington Ave.; 254-755-7772
Weslaco, TX 78599-0069
    609 International Blvd., P.O. Box 69; 956-968-3678
Wichita Falls, TX 76308-2830
    4245 Kemp Blvd., Suite 900; 800-388-1778

Utah
Salt Lake City, UT 84115-5382
    1588 S. Main St.; 801-892-6009 (24 hrs), 800-456-3907 (UT only)

Vermont
see Boston, MA 002116-4344
    800-422-2811 (802 area only)

Virginia
Fredericksburg, VA 22408
    11903 Main St.; 540-373-9872
Norfolk, VA 23509-1499
    586 Virginian Dr.; 757-531-1300
Richmond, VA 23219-2332
    701 E. Franklin, Suite 712; 804-648-0016 (24 hrs)
Roanoke, VA 24011-1301
    31 W. Campbell Ave.; 540-342-3455

Washington
Kennewick, WA 99336-3819
    101 N. Union, #105; 509-783-0892
Seatac, WA 98188
    4800 S. 188th St., Suite 222, P.O. Box 68926; 206-431-2222, 900-225-2222
Spokane, WA 99204
    508 W. Sixth Ave., Suite 401; 509-445-4200
Yakima, WA 98901
    401 Liberty Bldg.; 509-248-1326

West Virginia
Canton, OH 44703-3135
    1434 Cleveland Ave., NW, P.O. Box 8017; 800-362-0494 (OH only), 330-454-9401

Wisconsin
Milwaukee, WI 53203-2478
    740 N. Plankinton Ave.; Inquiries 414-273-1600, Complaints 414-273-0123

Wyoming
Fort Collins, CO 80525-1073
    1730 S. College Ave., Suite 303; 970-484-1348, Cheyenne 307-778-2809
Idaho Falls, ID 93404-5926
    1575 South Blvd.; 208-523-9754

International Bureaus

National Headquarters For Canadian Bureaus
Markham, Ontario L3R 6C9
    115 Apple Creek Blvd.; 905-415-1750

Alberta
Calgary, AB T2H8
    7330 Fisher St., SE Suite 257; 403-531-8780
Edmonton, AB T5K 2L9
    514 Capital Pl., 9707 110th St.; 403-482-2341

British Columbia
Vancouver, BC V6B 2M1
    788 Beatty St., Suite 404; 604-682-2711
Victoria, BC V8W 1V7
    201-1005 Langley St.; 604-386-6348

Manitoba
Winnipeg, MB R3B 2K3
    301-365 Hargrave St., Room 301; 204-989-9010

Newfoundland
St. John's, NF A1E 2B6
    360 Topsail Rd., P.O. Box 516; 709-364-2222

Nova Scotia
Halifax, NS B3J 3J8
    1888 Brunswick St., Suite 601; Inquiries 902-422-6581, Complaints 902-422-6582

Ontario
Hamilton, ON L8N 1A8
    100 King St., E; 905-526-1112
Kitchener, ON N2G 4L5
    354 Charles St., E; 519-579-3080
London, ON N6A 5C7
    200 Queens Ave., P.O. Box 2153; 519-673-3222
Ottawa, ON K1P 5N2
    130 Albert St., Suite 603; 613-237-4856
Windsor, ON N9A 5K6
    500 Riverside Dr. W; 519-258-7222

Quebec
Montreal, PQ H3A 1V4
    2055 Peel St., Suite 460; 514-286-9281

Saskatchewan
Regina, SA S4P 1Y3
    302-2080 Broad St., 306-352-7601

Market Studies, Demographics, And Statistics

Existing Market Studies

Finding information about a market, whether it is a comprehensive market study or a single fact or figure, seems to be one of the most common challenges for business researchers. And how one handles this problem can depend upon a number of variables, including time and money. Since it is virtually impossible to map out a research strategy for all possible circumstances, presented here is a collection of some obvious and not so obvious sources to help with such an effort. If you are under the gun to get the most information in the shortest amount of time, the good old telephone is the efficient method (refer to the section entitled *The Art of Getting A Bureaucrat To Help You*).

Traditional Published Sources

If you want to begin with traditional published sources, start with a local library that is oriented toward the business community. A nearby university with a business school or a large public library can be a good starting place. Many business libraries offer free or low-cost telephone research service. For example, the Brooklyn Public Library's Business Library, 280 Cadman Plaza West, Brooklyn, NY 11201, 718-623-7000, 800-266-6696 in New York; {www.brooklynpubliclibrary.org/business/business.htm} will answer brief questions over the telephone and hold your hand in identifying information sources if you visit in person.

If you are not familiar with traditional published information sources, using the services of a research librarian can be an efficient way to get at exactly what is there that you need. If you are in a hurry, see what you can get over the telephone. If time is not critical, it will be worth visiting the library to become acquainted with local resources, because if these reference sources are not useful to you now, most likely they will be in the future. Many of the questions we answer for clients at a rate of $100 an hour can be answered for free by a local reference librarian.

Computerized Databases And Data Sources

Currently there are an estimated 3,000 to 5,000 computerized databases available to the public. Some publications which identify online databases include:

1) *Gale Directory of Databases, Volume 1: Online Databases* by Gale Group, 27500 Drake Road, Farmington Hills, MI 48331; 248-699-4253, 800-477-GALE, Fax: 800-414-5043; {www.galegroup.com}, E-mail: {galeord@galegroup.com} ($265 for two issues per year.)

2) *Gale Directory of Databases, Volume 2: Portable Databases* by Gale Group, 27500 Drake Road, Farmington Hills, MI 48331; 248-699-4253, 800-477-GALE, Fax: 800-414-5043; {www.galegroup.com}, E-mail: {galeord@galegroup.com} ($175 for two issues per year.)

Almost all major vendors maintain databases which contain marketing information. A review of any of the four books cited above will help you pinpoint databases which may be helpful, or you can call BRS, Dialog and other database vendors directly. Some of the more popular databases which contain marketing information on a wide variety of industries are basically indexes and abstracts of current trade and business periodicals. Included in this category are:

- ABI/INFORM
- Management Contents
- NewsNet
- Industry Data Sources

If you are a first time user of databases, it may be wise to have someone else do your searching. Companies called Information Brokers are in this line of business. The best way to find such brokers is to contact your local reference librarian. They are in a good position to tell you what retrieval services exist locally.

If you have trouble with this method, you may find help by calling Dialog Information Services, Customer Service at 800-334-2564, 919-462-8600, Fax: 919-462-9890, {www.dialog.com}. This major database vendor maintains a list of organizations which provide this service. Dialog can narrow down your options according to what city you are in and what subjects you want searched. There is no charge for referrals.

Be sure to inquire whether a nearby public, academic or specialized library performs online retrieval services. If they do, it is probably going to be much cheaper. For example, the Brooklyn Business Library {www.brooklynpubliclibrary.org} will do **database searches and charge only for direct out-of-pocket costs**. An information broker is likely to cost you three to four times more.

If you have a PC with a modem but have been reluctant to access the more complicated business databases, you may want to contact Winstar Telebase. Two of their products available are **WinStar Business Research Center** {www.hoovers.telebase.com} and **Brainwave** {www.brainwave.telebase.com}. Some of the databases that will be available to you include the Encyclopedia of Associations, Industry News, MG Financial/Stock Statistics, Market and Product News, and Market Intelligence. These products use over 500 databases. By using these two products, you can obtain corporation profiles, credit reports, patents, market research, customer size, and stay on top of market trends.

WinStar Telebases, Inc.
1150 First Avenue, Suite 820
King of Prussia, PA 19406
610-945-2420
Fax: 610-945-2460

Existing Market Studies

In order to find relevant market studies which have already been published, several checkpoints should be covered:

Existing Market Studies

1) The databases described above are likely to cover the news of currently released market studies.

2) Many industries have market research firms which specialize only in that industry. To identify these firms contact one or all of the following:

- an industry analyst at the U.S. Department of Commerce, Office of the Assistant Secretary for Trade Development at 202-482-1461, 800-USA-TRADE; {www.ita.doc.gov/td/td_home/tdhome.html}, E-mail: {TIC@ita.doc.gov}

- a specialist at an industry trade association (see *Encyclopedia of Associations* published by Gale Group, 27500 Drake Road, Farmington Hills, MI 48331; 800-347-4353 {www.galegroup.com}, available in most libraries);

- relevant trade magazines which can be identified by either one of the first two choices.

3) Contact those organizations which publish market studies on many industries, for example:

- Frost and Sullivan, Inc., 2525 Charleston Rd., Mountain View, CA 94043; 650-961-9000, Fax: 650-961-5042, {www.frost.com}, E-mail: {webmaster@frost.com}.

- Decision Resources, Inc., 1100 Winter Street, Waltham, MA 02154; 781-487-3700, E-mail: {carbone@dresources.com}.

- International Resource Development Inc., P.O. Box 1716, New Canaan, CT 06840, 203-966-2525;

- Creative Strategies Research International, 901 Campisi Way, Suite 370, Campbell, CA 95008; 408-371-3333, {www.creativestrategies.com}.

- BusinessCommunications Co. Inc., 25 Van Zant St., Norwalk, CT 06855, 203-853-4266;

4) Review the major databases and publications which index available market studies for sale. These include:

- FINDEX: its database or book identifies studies available from Wall Street investment firms and management consulting firms, contact: Kalorama Information, 7200 Wisconsin Avenue, Suite 601, Bethesda, MD 20814. Call 1-877-4FINDEX (toll-free) for a free catalogue or table of contents of Market Research Reports;

- INVESTEXT: its database provides full text of research reports produced by Wall Street and regional investment banking companies. Contact: Thompson Financial Network, Investext, 22 Thompson Place, Boston, MA 02210, 617-856-2704, 1-800-662-7878, Fax: 617-330-1986; {www.investext.com} and

- *Industry Trends and Analysis:* provides access to the non-exclusive publications of Decision Resources, Inc. an affiliate of Arthur D. Little, Inc. Includes references and selected full-text items covering industry forecasts, strategic planning, company assessments, and emerging technologies. Contact: Decision Resources, Inc., 1100 Winter St., Waltham, MA 02154, 781-487-3700.

Market Studies From Associations

Many trade associations conduct market studies about their member organizations and/or industries. These reports may or may not be included in the databases and other sources described above. It is worth contacting relevant associations directly to ensure that you have not missed an important report. To identify a relevant association use Gale's *Encyclopedia of Associations* (see reference above). This book is well indexed and available at most libraries. The proper association can normally be identified with a simple phone call to the reference desk or visit to a local library. If you cannot find what you need in this encyclopedia, the American Society of Association Executives may be of help.

Information Central
American Society of Association Executives
1575 I Street, NW   202-626-2723
Washington, DC 20005-1168   Fax: 202-371-8825
www.asaenet.org/main   TDD: 202-626-2803

You should be aware that some associations will not sell their studies to non-members. However, there are some ways you can circumvent this problem.

1) Join the association; some memberships are relatively inexpensive.

2) Access thanks to antitrust laws; the association may be violating antitrust laws if it does not make the study available to non-members. This does not mean the organization cannot charge you a whole lot more than they do for its members. And, you must keep in mind that the ultimate action in pursuing this strategy is to take the association to court. But it is worth trying because many associations are very concerned about the antitrust laws, and simply mentioning that you are going to check with your legal counsel about possible antitrust violations may be enough to shake free the report.

If you want to investigate further about how an association may be violating antitrust laws, obtain a copy of *Association Law Handbook, 3rd Edition*, ($110 for members, $135 for non-members), *Anti-Trust Guide for Association Members*, ($2.20 for members, $3.30 for non-members), or *Association Liability*, ($44 for members, $66 for non-members) from American Society of Association Executives, plus $5.25 for regular UPS or first class postage and handling on all orders (see address above). This book explores association executives' worries and ways to avoid possible antitrust problems.

A $1,500 Market Study For Free

Many business researchers are unaware of the fact that if a high priced market study carries a copyright, like a Frost and Sullivan study, it may be **available for free** at the Library of Congress in Washington, DC, online at {www.loc.gov}. The Library receives two copies of all copyrighted material and usually adds these reports to its collection. The problem is that these companies are aware that people use the Library of Congress to see these studies and, as a result, they often wait for the last possible legal moment before filing their copyright. This can be 3 months or more after the study is published which means that it may take several more months before it gets into the collection.

Market Studies, Demographics and Statistics

Here are examples of how much money you can save by using this approach. Recently, we searched the Library of Congress catalog under "digital" and found 79 reports, studies and publications, including the following:

- *The Digital Telecommunications Market*
- *Digital and Analog Control Value* market studies published by Frost and Sullivan, Inc.

Other studies found included:

- *Universe Service and Digital Communications*
- *Performance Analysis of Digital Transmission Systems*
- *Case Study in the Economic and Technical Aspects of Digital Transmission*
- *Two-way Business Communications*
- *International Conference on Digital Satellite*
- *Scientific Visualization: the New Eyes of Science*

If you get to Washington, it will certainly be worth your time to visit the Library of Congress and discover market studies in your area of interest.

The Library is basically set up for visiting researchers, so it may be a bit more difficult, but not impossible, to see these studies if you do not come to Washington. However, you can arrange to obtain these studies through an interlibrary loan. The best way to do this is to identify the title of the study and then telephone the Reference Section at the Library of Congress to see if it is in their collection (telephone number noted below). If it is, then ask how to arrange an interlibrary loan. Any local library will also be happy to work with you on this matter.

If you do not know the title of a particular market study, it will be a bit harder to work remotely. The Library is not set up to do this sort of general reference work over the telephone. You can try calling the telephone reference number below to see what kind of assistance you can get to such an inquiry. If you do not get the help you need, call the office of your U.S. Representative or Senator (simply phone the Capitol Hill switchboard at 202-224-3121). What you should request is a list of Library of Congress holdings covering a specific subject area of interest. Requesting the titles of all Frost and Sullivan reports would not be of value because the publisher's name is not always an index term. **How successful you are at getting the Library to help may depend a lot on when you call and on how good you are at working with people over the telephone** (refer to the section entitled *The Art Of Getting A Bureaucrat To Help You*). Keep in mind that the Library is open weekdays 8:30 am until 9:30 pm Eastern standard time, AND Saturdays from 8:30 am to 5:30 pm.

Reference Referral Service
Library of Congress
101 Independence Ave., SE
Washington, DC 20540   202-707-5522 (general public)
www.loc.gov   202-707-2905 (news media queries)

The Library of Congress is not the only collection that contains copies of expensive market studies which can be viewed on sight or through an interlibrary loan. Practically every major federal agency has a library which collects studies in those fields within its mandate. The National Library of Medicine (www.nlm.nih.gov) contains hundreds of market studies relating to health care;

the U.S. Department of Energy (www.doe.gov) has studies about the oil and gas industry; the U.S. Department of Defense (www.defenselink.mil) maintains surveys of the aerospace industry, etc. If you cannot figure out which government agency is responsible for certain industries, either one of the following books can help:

1) *U.S. Government Manual*, ($21, Superintendent of Documents, U.S. Government Printing Office, Washington, DC 20402-9325, 202-783-3238; {www.access.gpo.gov/su_docs/aces/desc016.html}); or

2) *Lesko's Info-Power III*, by Matthew Lesko, ($39.95, 1996 Information USA), available at local bookstores and public libraries, or call 1-800-UNCLE-SAM.

If you don't have time to locate either of these books, the following free resources are designed to help you learn how the government can help you:

- The district or Washington office of your Member of Congress;

- Local Federal Information Center which is part of the General Services Administration, (800-688-9889, TTY: 800-826-2996; {http://fic.info.gov}) or

- Washington, DC Directory Assistance at 202-555-1212. These operators are equipped to identify phone numbers of major agencies.

Free Government Market Studies

The federal government serves as a major repository of market studies it generates. Not only are these reports likely to be available at very reasonable prices, such surveys also offer powerful information opportunities by virtue of the fact that most people are unaware of their availability. And, unlike market studies produced by commercial organizations which may invest 6 to 12 man-months on a project, a government sponsored effort is likely to represent several man-years worth of investment. The value for the money is unbeatable. The seven major government institutions which produce market studies are described below.

U.S. Congress

Each year the United States Congress conducts several thousand hearings which either analyze proposed legislation or oversee existing laws. In the same way that the government seems to affect every facet of our lives, the Congress seems to get involved in most every aspect of business. For instance, take the time when six franchise agreements from privately held companies became part of public testimony at hearings before the Senate Commerce Committee. Everyone in the industry said this information was proprietary and not available to anyone outside the companies in question.

In order to convince you of the broad range of areas probed by the Congress, listed below are a sampling of subject headings we recently found under the letter "C" in the index of bills for a recent session of Congress:

Existing Market Studies

- Campaign Financing
- Congressional Campaign Finance Reform
- Communications Decency Act
- Cellular Phones
- Children's Sleepwear
- China
- Chinese Embassy Bombing
- Columbine High School Shooting
- Copyright Licensing
- Cox Report
- Crime Bill/Juvenile Crime
- Cuba
- Cybersquatting

An important aspect of a congressional hearing is that the committee in charge is usually very thorough in covering a subject. The best experts in the world normally present testimony or submit written comments. Committee staffers identify all available information sources and collect the latest research. Many times the committee will even commission a research study on the subject. Documentation from committee hearings normally exists in a number of formats which are described next.

1) **Published reports:** It often takes 6 months to one year after the date of the hearing before the report is published. Sometimes the printed committee or subcommittee hearings can be obtained free from the professional staffers or the full committee documents clerk. More popular transcripts on controversial subjects are frequently available for sale from the Government Printing Office (Superintendent of Documents, Washington, DC, 202-512-1800).

2) **Unedited transcripts:** Debates are published the following day in the *Congressional Record* {www.access.gpo.gov/su_docs/aces/aces/50.html}. The Senate only has official reporters for debates. For unedited transcripts of Senate committee or subcommittee hearings, contact the committee to see what commercial transcription service they employed.

House committee transcripts, if available, can be purchased from the Government Printing Office's ACCESS system. The Government Printing Office can be reached by phone at 202-512-1800 or by fax at 202-512-2250. The web address is {www.access.gpo.gov}. The Committees listed below have some form of electronic transcripts available at their web pages. At some of the websites, you can listen to or view the hearings as they happen.

Agriculture	http://agriculture.house.gov/
Budget	www.house.gov/budget
Education & the Workforce	www.house.gov/ed_workforce
Banking and Financial Services	www.house.gov/banking
International Relations	www.house.gov/international_relations
Judiciary	www.house.gov/judiciary
Science	www.house.gov/science
Ways and Means	www.house.gov/ways_means
Resources	www.house.gov/resources
Rules	www.house.gov/rules
Veterans	http://veterans.house.gov
Joint Economic Committee	www.house.gov/jec

Committees that sometimes make transcripts available for public purchase are:

Armed Services	www.house.gov/hasc
Commerce	www.house.gov/commerce
Small Businesses	www.house.gov/smbiz
Select Committee on Hunger	
Government Reform	www.house.gov/reform

The remaining House committees do not publicly release transcripts of their hearings.

3) **Prepared testimony presented by witnesses:** These formal statements sometimes are made available before the hearing date, but usually a limited number of copies are distributed at the hearings. If you are trying to get this documentation and cannot wait until the hearing is printed, contact the committee or subcommittee staffer responsible for the hearing or call the witness directly to request a copy. These statements sometimes are made available before the hearing date and usually only a limited number of copies are distributed at the hearings. Both oral and written statements will comprise the published hearing record.

4) **Studies commissioned by congressional committees:** Such studies are usually conducted by the Congressional Research Service (CRS) of the Library of Congress. If copies are available, they can be obtained only through a Member of Congress. (More details about CRS reports are provided later in this Section.)

5) **Formal comments about proposed legislation sent to the committee by interested parties, including government agencies:** Such comments often are included in the published hearing and also are contained in the committee report on the bill. Moreover, they became part of the committee files and usually can be viewed in the committee office.

There are a number of options for finding out if hearings have been held on a specific topic. However, since there is no centralized list of all congressional hearings, you should expect to make a dozen or so calls.

1) **Bill Status Office: 202-225-1772**
This can be the fastest source because by accessing the LEGIS computerized database, congressional staffers can tell you over the phone if legislation has been introduced on a specific topic. In addition to telling you which committees are working on the legislation, they can give you the status of a bill, who sponsored the measure, when it was introduced, and the status of similar bills. Although this congressional database is limited because it does not cover investigative or "oversight" hearings, it is still quite inclusive since the information goes back to 1975. If a committee held a hearing on a subject because of proposed legislation, it is also likely to be responsible for oversight hearings on that subject. Telephone assistance is free and printouts are available for a $5 minimum, 20 cents per page. If you cannot easily arrange to have the printout picked up by messenger, you may want to ask your Representative or Senator's office to have it sent to you (and that way you can avoid the charge). Contact: Office of Legislative Information and Status, B106 Cannon House Office Bldg., Washington, DC 20515.

2) **Congressional Committees: 202-224-3121**
Contacting a committee or subcommittee directly is another way to identify relevant hearings. However, the problem with this approach is that there are approximately 300 from which to choose. You must prepared to make a few calls before landing on

Market Studies, Demographics and Statistics

target. The advantage to this method is that if the committee you call does not cover a particular subject area, it is usually very helpful in suggesting the appropriate committee. Keep in mind that the jurisdictions of many committees overlap, so it is necessary to check with all those committees when searching for valuable market information. If you do not get help, ask the Capitol Hill Switchboard at the number noted above to transfer you to the House or Senate Parliamentarian. These offices are very knowledgeable about the jurisdictions of all the committees. And, of course, you can also ask your Member of Congress to help identify the right committees. You can also search online at {www.house.gov} and {www.senate.gov}, list Committees and link to their sites.

3) **Congressional Caucuses: 202-224-3121**
The Steel Caucus, The Textile Caucus, and several dozen other "informal" study groups composed of House Members and Senators frequently produce reports on particular industries.

4) **Congressional Information Service: 301-654-1550**
This commercial firm indexes and provides copies of all published committee hearings. This service, *CIS Index*, has its limitations because some hearings are never published or are published a long time after the hearing has been held. Remember that copies of unpublished documentation can be obtained by using the methods described above. The complete service costs approximately $3,240 per year or $1,040 for the annual index. Most libraries are subscribers to this service. Contact: Congressional Information Service, Inc., 4520 East-West Highway, #800, Bethesda, MD 20814; 800-638-8380; {www.cispubs.com}, E-mail: {cisinfo@lexis-nexis.com}

5) **The C.Q. Weekly Report: 202-887-8500**
Congressional Quarterly publishes *The C.Q. Weekly Report*, which lists all printed committee and subcommittee hearings. It contains an analysis of the week's current and pending legislative and political activity, including voting records and legislative, oversight and investigative activities released during the past week. Annual subscription is $1299 and it is also available online for $2,500 for 12 hours of online time. A hardbound *Almanac*, available for $370, is a compendium of a particular session's activity. To order, call 1-800-432-2250, ext. 279. Contact: Congressional Quarterly, Inc., 1414 22nd Street NW, Washington, DC 20037; {www.cq.com}, E-mail: {customerservice@cq.com}.

U.S. International Trade Commission

Part of the function of this agency is to study the volume of imports in comparison to domestic production and consumption. As a result, it produces close to 100 market studies each year on topics ranging from ice hockey sticks to clothespins. Some of the studies released recently and available at {www.usitc.gov} include:

- Dairy Products
- Fertilizers
- Canned Fish
- Adhesives, Glues & Gelatin
- Non-Rubber Footwear
- Magnesium
- Wool
- Telecommunication Equipment
- Barbed Wire
- CD-Rom Controllers

If you are interested in publications produced prior to 1984, this office has the *Publications and Investigations of the United States Tariff Commission and the United States International Trade Commission* list. It is for in-house use only, but may be viewed at the Docket Room. This office will send you a free copy of *Lists of Selected Publications of the United States International Trade Commission*, which contains a list of reports that are now in print. You can also request to be placed on a list to be notified of future studies. Call 202-205-2000 to add your name to the mailing list. Free copies of any of the above publications can be ordered 24 hours a day, seven days a week by calling 202-205-1809 (recording), or contact:

Docket Room
Office of the Secretary
U.S. International Trade Commission
500 E Street SW, Room 112
Washington, DC 20436   202-205-2799

Congressional Research Service: Reports

The Congressional Research Service (CRS) is an important research arm of the Library of Congress and conducts custom research for the Members of Congress on **any subject**. When a congressional committee plans hearings on a subject such as the insurance industry, often the Congressional Research Service will churn out a background report on the industry. Here are examples of some current studies which may be of interest to the business community:

- *Welcome to Cyberia: An Internet Overview*
- *Speechwriting in Perspective: A Brief Guide to Effective and Persuasive Communication*
- *Africa Trade & Development Initiative*
- *Air Quality and Transportation Enhancement Provisions*
- *Current Economic Conditions and Selected Forecasts*
- *Managed Health Care*
- *V chip and TV Rating*
- *Cloning, Where Do We Go From Here?*
- *Great Lakes Water Quality*
- *Farm Economic Relief*
- *Organic Foods*
- *Automobile and Light Truck Fuel Economy*
- *Banking and Finance*

Free copies of these reports can be obtained only by contacting the Washington or district office of your Senator or Representative. The Congressional Research Service also publishes an index to all its reports. Although this *Index* is free, it can be difficult to obtain. If your legislator's office tells you they cannot get you an *Index*, ask to have a copy sent to the district office so you can review it at your Member's local office. Oddly enough, the reports are easier to get than the CRS Index. You can simply call your Member of Congress through the Capitol Hill Switchboard at 202-224-3121 or put your request in writing:

U.S. Senate
Washington, DC 20510
www.senate.gov/~dpc/crs

Existing Market Studies

U.S. House of Representatives
Washington, DC 20515
www.house.gov

Congressional Research Service: Current Issue Briefs

Each day the Congressional Research Service updates over 400 studies, called Current Issue Briefs. These reports are designed to keep Members of Congress informed on timely topics. Listed below is a sampling of subjects covered.

- *Airbus Industries: An Economic and Trade Perspective*
- *Banking, Securities, and Insurance*
- *Inflation: Causes, Costs, and Current Statutes*
- *FDA and NIH: Selected Public Health Issues*
- *Prohibiting Television Advertising of Alcoholic Beverages*
- *The European Union's Ban on Hormone-Treated Meat*
- *Mars: The Search for Life*
- *Stratospheric Ozone Depletion*
- *Awards of Attorneys Fees by Federal Courts*
- *Food Stamp Reform*
- *Clean Water Issues*
- *National Information Infrastructure*

To receive a complete list of all Current Issue Briefs, you must contact the office of your Representative or Senator.

Every month the Congressional Research Service publishes *Update* which includes a list of new and updated issue briefs of current interest. Briefs that are no longer of intense public or congressional interest are listed in the *Archived Issue Briefs List*. These publications, along with copies of the Issue Briefs listed above, are available only by making arrangements through your Member of Congress in the same manner as described above.

PennyHill Press has the current Congressional Research Index available for $198 per year.
Penny Hill Press
6440 Wiscasset Road   301-229-8229
Bethesda, MD 20816   Fax: 301-229-6988
http://pennyhill.com
E-mail: congress@pennyhill.com

U.S. Commerce Department
International Trade Administration

Each year the International Trade Administration (ITA) {www.ita.doc.gov} at the U.S. Department of Commerce investigates dozens of products from certain countries for possible violations of Anti-Dumping laws or the use of unfair subsidies under countervailing duty laws. These statutes have been established to protect domestic manufacturers from unfair foreign competition.

When the government conducts an investigation, the resulting file, that is open to public inspection, usually contains a complete report of the industry in question. The final determination of an investigation is published in *The Federal Register*. A few of the products the ITA has investigated since 1999 include:

- Brake Rotors
- Petroleum Wax Candles
- Porcelain-On-Steel Cookware
- Sugar and Syrups
- Electric Cutting Tools
- Paint Brushes
- Chrome Plated Lug Nuts
- Refrigeration Compressors
- Bulk Aspirin
- Paper Clips

A complete listing of cases of industries studied by the ITA is available upon request. Copies of documentation from any of the above investigations are available for 10 cents per page if you make the copies yourself, 15 cents per page if they make the copies. They may be downloaded for free from their website.

Central Records Unit
International Trade Administration
U.S. Department of Commerce
14th & Constitution Avenue NW
Room B-009
Washington, DC 20230   202-482-1248

General Accounting Office

The General Accounting Office (GAO) {www.gao.gov} conducts special audits, surveys and investigations at the request of the U.S. Congress. It produces as many as 600 reports annually, many of which identify market opportunities. Below are just a few of their recent reports which have marketing potential.

- *Pesticides: Use, Effects, and Alternative to Pesticides in School*
- *Contract Management: A Comparison of DOD and Commercial Airline Purchasing Practices*
- *Financial Management: Increased Attention Needed to Prevent Billions in Improper Payments*
- *International Trade: Improvements Needed to Track and Archive Trade Agreements*
- *Mass Transit: Use of Alternative Fuels in Transit Buses*
- *Risk-Focused Bank Examinations: Regulators of Large Banking Organizations Face Challenges*
- *Superfund: Information on the Program's Funding and Statutes*
- *The Year 2000 Computing Crisis*
- *Alaskan North Slope Oil: Limited Effects of Lifting Export Ban on Oil and Shipping Industries and Consumers*
- *Evolving Mission Favors Resource Protection Over Production*
- *Farmer Mac: Revised Charter Enhances Secondary Market Activity, but Growth Depends on Various Factors*
- *Nuclear Waste: Process to Remove Radioactive Waste From Savannah River Tanks Fail to Work*
- *International Monetary Fund: Trade Policies of IMF Borrowers*
- *Federal Research: Evaluation of Small Business Innovation Research Can Be Strengthened*

The first copy of a report is available free of charge and additional copies can be obtained for $2 each. You can also receive a free annual index of available GAO reports, a free

Market Studies, Demographics and Statistics

monthly catalog of current reports, and a free printout from a database which contains all titles and document numbers. For further information or for any of the above contact the General Accounting Office. The pickup address is: 700 4th Street NW, Room 1100, Washington, DC 20548; 202-512-6000. The mailing address is: U.S. General Accounting Office, P.O. Box 37050, Washington, DC 20013; TDD: 202-512-2537; {www.gao.gov/cgi_bin/ordtab.pl}. Fax requests to 202-512-6061.

Federal Trade Commission

Besides the antitrust activities of the U.S. Department of Justice, the Federal Trade Commission (FTC) {www.ftc.gov} also has the authority to investigate certain industries or companies for possible antitrust violations. Recent FTC investigations have targeted particular industries.

- Gas Station Industry
- Telemarketing Industry
- Dietary Supplement Industry
- Telecommunications Industry
- Foreign Anti-Trust
- Home Equity Loans
- Cat & Dog Food Industry
- Franchise
- Funeral Industry
- Apparel Industry

You can inquire to determine whether a specific company has been probed by the Commission. The investigation itself is confidential, but much results in documentation that is public record and available for 12 cents per page. Recent FTC reports and publications are:

- *A Business Person's Guide to Federal Warranty Law*
- *Environmental Marketing Claims*
- *Selling on the Internet: Prompt Delivery Rules Alert*
- *Thinking of Buying a Business Opportunity?*
- *Measurements of Market Power in Long Distance Telecommunications*
- *A Generic Copy Test of Food Health Claims in Advertising*

The Federal Trade Commission (FTC) will mail copies of reports they have on hand to you free of charge. They also maintain copies on their website. Contact:

Consumer Response Center
Federal Trade Commission (FTC)
600 Pennsylvania Avenue NW, Room H-130
Washington, DC 20580-0001   202-326-2222
Consumer Response Center   877-FTC-HELP (toll-free)
www.ftc.gov

Nine Federal Statistical Agencies

Everyone Is Selling Demographic Data That's Available Free

Almost everyone who sells demographic data is getting it from a public source and repackaging it for the convenience of the customer. A few years ago we were looking for demographic data on the use of health care facilities and were told by all the experts in the business that the Association of Blue Cross and Blue Shield Companies was the only place to obtain this data. After finally locating the office in the Association which produced this information, we were told it would cost us $50. At the time we were feeling a little poor, so we decided to check sources in the federal government. Soon we located an office at the Social Security Administration in Baltimore that actually collected the pertinent data which Blue Cross requested periodically. The statistician at the Social Security Administration said he would be happy to give us the data for free and, equally important, his information was more current than the data contained in the Blue Cross report because the Association had not yet asked him for the latest figures.

Many times it may be worth buying information from private firms, but there are times when it may not. In any case, you owe it to your organization to check on the availability of public demographic data from the primary non-commercial sources.

Nine Major Federal Statistical Agencies

The federal government is the place where you should definitely begin. Without a doubt it is the largest collector of demographic data in the world. Over $1 billion dollars are spent to amass the decennial census which counts all the noses and toilets in the country. Although budget cuts have reduced some federal data collection activities, more data still are generated by departments and agencies in Washington than you could imagine or could ever put to use. **Actually federal spending cutbacks have been more harmful to the dissemination of the information rather than the collection of demographic and statistical data.** Nowadays it is somewhat more difficult to determine what data are available and where to find it.

There are nine major federal statistical agencies which are listed below. Contact the ones you feel may be of some help in your data search. When you call, ask to speak to the data expert who concentrates on the specific issue you are investigating. If the expert tells you that his or her agency does not collect the exact data you require, remember that this government specialist probably can tell you who might have the information. These statisticians stay current by reading all pertinent journals and attending international conferences. Most likely they can tell you which organizations and individuals to contact.

Plotting The Baby Boom

Recently we were trying to obtain the forecast of births in the U.S., and in particular, first births (how many first born sons and daughters). The Bureau of the Census {www.census.gov} and the National Center for Health Statistics {www.cdc.gov/nchs} were very cooperative in giving us this data quickly. Equally helpful was a statistician at the Census Bureau who recommended an expert at the Urban Institute in Washington, DC {www.urban.org} who studied how much money parents spend on their children. A call to this expert produced a free report just published by the Institute, which showed that the average family spends over 50% more on their first child than they do on their second or third. This report, together with federal data on the boom in first births, proved to our client that the outlook for the baby products industry was on a large upswing.

The federal agencies noted here can probably provide much of the demographic data you need and also suggest sources elsewhere in the government as well as experts in the private sector.

1) Agriculture and Food Statistics
   National Agriculture Statistics Service
   Director, Estimates Division
   U.S. Department of Agriculture
   14th and Independence Avenue SW
   Washington, DC 20250   202-720-3896
   Hotline   800-727-9540
   www.usda.gov/nass
   E-mail: nass@nass.usda.gov

2) Economic and Demographic Statistics
   Bureau of the Census
   U.S. Department of Commerce
   Data User Service Division   888-249-7295
   Customer Service   301-763-4100
   Washington, DC 20233   Fax: 301-763-4794
   www.census.gov

3) Crime Statistics
   Uniform Crime Reporting Section
   Federal Bureau of Investigations (FBI)
   7th & D Streets, NW   888-UCR-NIBR
   Washington, DC 20535   202-324-3000
   www.fbi.gov/ucr

4) Economics-National, Regional and International
   Bureau of Economic Analysis
   U.S. Department of Commerce   202-606-9900
   Washington, DC 20230   TDD: 202-606-5335
   www.bea.doc.gov

5) Education Statistics
   National Center for Education Statistics
   Office of Educational Research and Improvement
   555 New Jersey Avenue NW   202-219-1828
   Washington, DC 20208-5574   800-424-1616

6) Health Statistics
   National Center for Health Statistics
   Center for Disease Control
   6525 Belcrest Road

Market Studies, Demographics and Statistics

       Hyattsville, MD 20782   301-458-4636
       www.cdc.gov/nchs/about.htm

7) Employment, Prices, Living Conditions, Productivity, and Occupational Safety and Health
    Bureau of Labor Statistics
    Division of Information Services
    2 Massachusetts Ave., NE, Room 2860
    Washington, DC 20212
    http://stats.bls.gov
    E-mail: blsdatastaff@bls.gov
    Information   202-606-5886
    Publications   313-353-1880, option 0
    Fax on Demand   202-606-6525
    TDD: 202-606-5897

8) Import and Export Statistics
    Trade Reference Room
    U.S. Industry Trade Outlook
    U.S. Department of Commerce
    Herbert Hoover Building   202-482-2185
    14th and Constitution Ave., NW Fax: 202-482-4614
    Washington, DC 20230   TDD: 202-482-4512
    www.ita.doc.gov/tradestats
    E-mail: Marva_Thompson@ita.doc.gov

9) World Import and Export Statistics
    Office of Trade and Economic Analysis
    Trade Development, HCHB 2815   202-482-3126
    Washington, DC 20230   Fax: 202-482-4614
    www.ita.doc.gov/tradestats
    E-mail: Kemble_Stokes@ita.doc.gov

Tips For Finding Federal Data

We have found that one of the best sources for identifying data in the federal government is a publication titled the *Statistical Abstract of the United States*. Do not expect to find the precise data you need in this book. What you will discover is an invaluable index to hundreds of data tables on literally thousands of subjects. Below each table is the name of the agency which produced the data. This means that if you are trying to locate how many left-handed monkeys there are in the United States, you can refer to the index under monkey and turn to the appropriate table. What you are likely to find is a table that contains data on all the monkeys in the country and not how many are left-handed. You can then look at the bottom of the table and see what office compiled the numbers. If you call the office directly, someone there can probably track down the information you need in their files (in this case of monkeys, it may be difficult). Remember this *Abstract* contains only a small fraction of data available from any government office, but it serves as an excellent starting point for identifying which federal office collects what kind of information. The latest edition can be purchased from the U.S. Government Printing Office online at {www.access.gpo.gov} (noted earlier).

Another way to uncover opportunities in the vast federal repository is to obtain a copy of the forms that are filled out in the data collection phase. For example, if you are selling toothpaste, you may see that those who completed the long census form in the last decennial census stated what kind of toothpaste they use. This may not be printed in any report offered by the Census Bureau, but that does not mean you cannot get this data. The Bureau can do a special search for you and charge you on a cost recovery basis. This is true with any federal agency. What you should do is request copies of the data collection forms for any survey you think may be of interest to you. If you are in a consumer-related business, you should at least get a copy of the long form used in the decennial census.

Hotlines For Monitoring The Economy And Your Markets: Listen To Tomorrow's News Today

Why wait for tomorrow's *Wall Street Journal* to find out the latest economic statistics that will affect your business? You can find out today by calling the U.S. Department of Commerce Hotline. This is the same message that the *Wall Street Journal* listens to before going to press. If you want to know when the best time is to convert your adjustable rate mortgage to a fixed rate mortgage, you don't have to wait until your mortgage banker gives you the information at the end of the month. You can plot the trends daily by calling the Mortgage Rate Hotline at the Federal National Mortgage Association. This is where your mortgage banker gets the information, and you can be a month ahead of him.

Banks and Savings and Loans, Information on Failed Banks
Federal Deposit Insurance Corporation
800-276-6003
www.fdic.gov

Banks and Savings and Loans, Obtaining a Financial Statement on Your Bank
Federal Deposit Insurance Corporation
800-276-6003
www.fdic.gov

Banks, Aggregate Reserves of Depository Institutions
Thursday, Federal Reserve Board
202-452-3206
www.bog.frb.fed.us

Banks, Assets and Liabilities of Insured Domestically Chartered and Foreign Banks
Friday, Federal Reserve Board
202-452-3206
www.bog.frb.fed.us

Benefits, Employment Costs
Middle of Month, Bureau of Labor Statistics
202-606-7828 - 24 hour hotline
202-691-6199
www.bls.gov/cpshome.htm

Construction
Beginning of Month, Department of Commerce
301-457-3030
www.esa.doc.gov

Consumer Price Index
Middle of Month, Bureau of Labor Statistics
202-606-7828 - 24 hr hotline
202-691-7000
www.bls.gov

Credit, Consumer Installment
5th Working Day of Month; Federal Reserve Board
202-452-3206
www.bog.frb.fed

Earnings, Hourly and Weekly
Beginning of Month; Bureau of Labor Statistics
202-606-7828 - 24 hr hotline
202-691-6378
www.bls.gov

Earnings, Real
Middle of Month, Bureau of Labor Statistics
202-606-7828 - 24 hr hotline
202-691-6555
www.bls.gov

Economic News
GNP, Trade Figures, Housing Starts, and Other Economic Figures, Department of Commerce
202-482-2235
www.bea.doc.gov

Economic News Highlights
Department of Commerce
202-482-2235
www.doc.gov

Economic News Weekend Preview
Department of Commerce
202-482-2235
www.bea.doc.gov

Employment Situation
Beginning of Month, Bureau of Labor Statistics
202-606-7828 - 24 hr hotline
202-691-6378
www.bls.gov/cpshome.htm

Foreign Exchange Rates
Monday, and 1st of Month, Federal Reserve Board
202-452-3206
www.bog.frb.fed.us

Foreign Trade
End of Month, Department of Commerce
202-393-4100
www.doc.gov

Gross National Product
End of Month, Department of Commerce
202-482-2235
www.bea.doc.gov

Housing, New Home Sales
Beginning of Month, Department of Commerce
301-457-3030
www.esa.doc.gov

Housing Starts
Middle of Month, Department of Commerce
301-457-1321
www.esa.doc.gov

Hours Worked In A Week
Beginning of Month, Bureau of Labor Statistics
202-606-7828 - 24 hr hotline
202-691-5611
www.bls.gov/lprhome.htm

Income, Personal
End of Month, Department of Commerce
202-482-2235
www.bea.doc.gov

Market Studies, Demographics And Statistics

Industrial Production and Capacity Utilization
Middle of Month, Federal Reserve Board
202-452-3206
www.bog.frb.fed.us

Interest Rates, Selected
Monday, Federal Reserve Board
202-452-3206

International Trade, Merchandise Trade
Middle of Month, Department of Commerce
301-457-2311
www.esa.gov

Inventories and Sales, Manufacturing and Trade
Middle of Month, Department of Commerce
202-482-3727
www.esa.doc.gov

Leading Economic Indicators
Beginning of Month, Department of Commerce
202-609-9900
www.bea.doc.gov

Loans and Securities at All Commercial Banks
3rd Week of Month, Federal Reserve Board
202-452-3206

Merchandise Trade
Middle of Month, Department of Commerce
202-606-9900
www.bea.doc.gov

Money Stock and Debt Measures
Thursday, Federal Reserve Board
202-452-3206
www.bog.frb.fed.us

Mortgage Rates, Adjustable Rate Information
Middle of Month, Federal Housing Finance Board
202-408-2940
www.fhfb.gov

Mortgage Rates, National Average Contract Rate For Purchase of Previous Occupied Homes By Combined Lenders
Middle of Month, Federal Housing Finance Board
202-408-2940
www.fhfb.gov

Mortgage Rates, 30-Year Fixed Rate Yields
Continually Updated, Federal National Mortgage Association
1-800-752-7020, 202-752-0471 ext. 3
www.fanniemae.com

Mortgage Rates, Fixed Intermediate Term Yields
Continually Updated, Federal National Mortgage Association
1-800-752-7020, 202-752-0471 ext. 4
www.fanniemae.com

Mortgage Rates, Adjustable Yields
Continually Updated, Federal National Mortgage Association
1-800-752-7020, 202-752-0471 ext. 5
www.fanniemae.com

Payroll for Industry
Beginning of Month, Bureau of Labor Statistics
202-606-7828

Personal Income and Outlays
End of Month, Bureau of Labor Statistics
202-606-7828

Plant and Equipment Expenditures
Middle of Month, Department of Commerce
202-898-2453

Producer Price Index
Middle of Month, Bureau of Labor Statistics
202-606-7828 - 24 hr hotline
202-691-7888
http://stats.bls.gov/pp.com.htm

Production and Capacity Utilization, Industrial
Middle of Month, Federal Reserve Board
202-452-3206
www.bog.frb.fed.us

Productivity and Cost
Beginning of Month, Bureau of Labor Statistics
202-606-7828 - hotline
202-691-5607
www.bls.gov/lprhome.htm

Retail Trade, Advance Report for Previous Month
Middle of Month, Department of Census
301-457-3030
www.esa.doc.gov

Salaries and Wages Information
Middle of Month, Bureau of Labor Statistics
202-606-7828 - 24 hr hotline
202-691-6569

Sales and Inventories, Manufacturing and Trade
Middle of Month, Department of Commerce
202-393-4100

Treasury Bill Auction Results
Department of the Treasury
202-874-4400 ext. 221
www.ustreas.gov

Treasury Bill, Notice of Next Auction
Department of the Treasury
202-874-4400 ext. 211
www.ustreas.gov

Treasury Note and Bond Auction Results
Department of the Treasury
202-874-4400 ext. 222
www.ustreas.gov

Treasury Note and Bond, Notice of Next Auction
Department of the Treasury
202-874-4400 ext. 212

Treasury Securities, How To Purchase Notes, Bonds and Bills
Continually Updated, Department of the Treasury
202-874-4400 ext. 251
www.ustreas.gov

Unemployment Rates
Beginning of Month, Department of Labor Statistics
202-606-7828

Wholesale Trade
Middle of Month, Department of Commerce
301-457-3030
www.esa.doc.gov

Wages and Salaries Information
Beginning of Month, Department of Labor Statistics
202-606-7828

State Data Centers

Approximately 1,300 organizations nationwide receive data from the U.S. Bureau of the Census and in turn disseminate the information to the public free of charge or on a cost recovery basis. These organizations are called state data centers and serve as ideal information sources for both local and national markets. The centers listed in this report are the major offices for each state. If you are looking for national markets, start with a center in your state. If you are searching for local market data, contact the center located in the relevant area.

Demographics and Target Market Identification

State data center offices are most frequently used for obtaining information on target markets. For instance, the Army and Navy used such services to identify which areas are populated with large numbers of teenagers in order to open recruiting offices and focus their advertising campaign. Avon door-to-door sales reps used state data center generated demographic maps to identify homes with highest potential. L.L. Bean relied on a center to determine large Hispanic populations for a special promotion of outdoor recreational products. These offices could provide current data including:

- The age distribution within a given county;
- Moving patterns for particular geographical areas;
- The number of wells and mobile homes in 85 counties;
- How many gravel pits in the state of Montana;
- Counties with the highest rate of illegitimate children;
- Analysis of why certain stores in an auto parts chain are doing better than others;
- Demographic profile of a person in need of child care;
- The top 25 markets by zip code;
- The number of male secretaries in a dozen contiguous counties.

Forecasting Future Markets

The biggest opportunities often lie in knowing the future of a market. Many of the state data centers have developed specific software for analyzing Census and other data to project growth of specific markets. Here is a sampling of what some centers can do:

- Population projections for every three years to the year 2020 (done by California center);
- State population changes by the year 2000;
- What year the white population will not be in the majority;
- The number of teenagers by the next century;
- Series of economic indicators for plotting future economic health in state (Oklahoma center provides such data).

Site Location

Another major area of interest is in providing information to companies considering relocating into a state. Because most states are aggressively trying to attract business, numerous customized services receive a high priority. Local centers can provide information such as the number of fast food restaurants in the area and the best location for another one. And some states, like Arkansas, have special site evaluation software which can manipulate Census data to show the demographic characteristics for market radiuses which are 2, 5 or 10 miles from a given site. Oklahoma and other states have free data sheets covering every community in their state which are loaded with specifics for choosing a location. Their reports contain data on:

- Distance from major cities
- Population: past and future
- Climate
- Municipal services
- Utilities
- Labor market analysis
- List of major manufacturers
- List of major employers
- Transportation
- Commercial services
- Major freight lines and truck terminals
- Educational facilities
- Financial institutions
- Tax structure
- Housing and churches
- Medical facilities
- Retail business in city
- Industrial financial assistance
- Water analysis report
- Recreational facilities
- Wholesale business in city
- Items deserving special consideration

Professional and Personal Relocation

The same services that are intended to help businesses relocate also can be useful to individuals and professionals. For example, if you are looking for a place to start an orthodontics practice, a local data center could determine which counties and cities have the most affluent families with young people -- a prime market for braces. Also, if you get an offer for a new job in another city, obtaining a data sheet on the local community like the one described above provides insight into the types of housing, schools, churches, and recreational facilities available.

Business Proposals Plus Loan and Grant Applications

If you are looking for money for either a grant, a loan or even venture money, data centers can provide the information needed for proposal writing. Grantors must have information such as what percent of people live below poverty line, and banks want to know current business patterns for a new enterprise when seeking a loan. These sorts of data can be obtained easily from these centers.

Market Studies, Demographics and Statistics

Level of Detail

Because the data centers use information from other sources in addition to the Bureau of Census, the level of detail will vary according to subject area as well as the state and office contacted. Much of the Census data can be provided at the state, county, city, census tract and block group level (which is normally even smaller than a zip code). Data according to zip code are also available for many categories of information. All states also have the public use micro data sample, which do not contain aggregate data, but actual questionnaire information filled out by respondents. They can be manipulated into any kind of special detail required.

Custom Work, Workshops and Other Services

A lot of work performed by the data centers is customized in nature. The organizations collect data from other federal and state sources to enhance their Census information. Many have arrangements with other state data centers to send any computer file needed to do special analysis. This is how local centers can provide national information or inter-market comparisons. Some centers will even perform custom census projects for clients, which means raw data collection for market research.

Free and low cost workshops about services and information opportunities are sponsored in some areas for potential users. These workshops are important at the local level because in the past they were readily available from the Bureau of Census, but recent budget cuts have reduced their frequency and increased their price. Because of the centers' familiarity of census data, these offices are excellent starting places for almost any information search.

Formats

Data centers offer some of the most sophisticated formats you are likely to find from public organizations. They all provide computer tapes, off-the-shelf reports, custom reports from computer analysis, and quick answers over the telephone. Most are also set up to provide custom analysis and/or raw data on computer diskettes, and some — like Ohio — have developed a PC database from which they can generate standard reports and download onto diskettes. Colorado and other states are beginning to make data accessible online.

Prices

Although the U.S. government provides most of the data to these centers, the feds do not interfere with fee schedules. Most offices try to give out information free, but some charge on a cost recovery basis. Some states do not charge for the first so many pages of a report but charge a nominal fee for additional pages. Some say they have a minimum fee of $20 for customized computer runs. It is interesting that these centers sell you computerized data cheaper than the U.S. Bureau of the Census in Washington. In contrast to the Bureau's fee of $140, Illinois and Georgia only charge $50 for a data tape file, and in Florida, the cost is $15 for a file.

In the dozens of interviews we conducted with these centers about the complicated market research reports they have provided to clients, the highest figure we found they ever charged was $2,000. That amount of money would buy virtually nothing from most marketing consultants.

State Data Centers

Below is a roster of data centers in all 50 states as well as the District of Columbia, Puerto Rico and Virgin Islands. Some of these Census Bureau information providers are based in state departments and agencies, universities, business colleges, and libraries.

Alabama

Center for Business and Economic Research
University of Alabama
P.O. Box 870221
Tuscaloosa, AL 34587-0221
205-348-6191
http://www.cba.ua.edu/~cber/

Alabama Department of Economic and
Community Affairs
Office of State Planning
P.O. Box 5690
401 Adams Ave.
Montgomery, AL 36103-5690
334-242-5525
http://alaweb.asc.edu/govern/adeca.html

Alabama Public Library Service
6030 Monticello Dr.
Montgomery, AL 36130
334-213-3900
http://www.apls.state.al.us/

Alaska

Alaska State Data Center
Research and Analysis
Department of Labor
P.O. Box 25501
Juneau, AK 99802-5501
907-465-4500
http://www.state.ak.us/local/akpages/labor/research/research.htm

Office of Management and Budget
Division of Policy
Pouch AD
Juneau, AK 99811-0020
907-465-4660
http://www.gov.state.ak.us/omb/akomb.htm

Department of Education
Division of Libraries and Museums
Alaska State Library
Government Publications
P.O. Box 110571
Juneau, AK 99811-0571
907-465-2927
http://www.educ.state.ak.us/lam/library.html

Dept. of Community and Regional Affairs
Division of Municipal and Regional Assistance
P.O. Box 112100
Juneau, AK 99811-2100
907-465-4700
http://comregaf.state.ak.us/default.htm

Institute for Social and Economic Research
University of Alaska
3211 Providence Dr.
Anchorage, AK 99508
907-786-7710
http://www.iser.uaa.alaska.edu/home.htm

Arizona

Arizona Department of Economic Security
Mail Code 045Z
1789 W. Jefferson St.
Phoenix, AZ 85007-3202
602-542-4296
http://www.de.state.az.us/

Center for Business Research
College of Business Administration
Arizona State University
Box 874406
Tempe, AZ, 85287-4406
602-965-3961
http://www.cob.asu.edu/seid/cbr/

College of Business Administration
Northern Arizona University
Box 15066
Flagstaff, AZ 86011-5066

State Data Centers

520-523-3657
http://www.cba.nau.edu/website/index.html

Research Library
Department of Library Archives and Public Records
1700 W. Washington, 2nd Floor
Phoenix, AZ 85007
602-542-4035
http://www.dlapr.lib.az.us/

Economic and Business Research Program
College of Business and Public Administration
University of Arizona
McClelland Hall 204
Tucson, AZ 85721-0108
602-621-2155
http://www.bpa.arizona.edu/programs/ebr/

Arkansas
State Data Center
University of Arkansas-Little Rock
2801 S. University
Little Rock, AR 72204
501-569-8530
http://www.aiea.ualr.edu/csdc/default.html

Arkansas State Library
1 Capitol Mall
Little Rock, AR 72201
501-682-2864
http://asl.lib.ar.us/

Research and Analysis Section
Arkansas Employment Security Division
P.O. Box 2981
Little Rock, AR 72203
501-682-3159
http://www.ark.org/esd/ask_esd.html

California
State Census Data Center
Department of Finance
915 L St.
Sacramento, CA 95814
http://www.dof.ca.gov
916-445-3878

Sacramento Area COG
3000 S Street, Suite 300
Sacramento, CA 95816
916-457-2264
http://www.sacog.org/

Association of Bay Area Governments
P.O. Box 2050
Oakland, CA 94604-2050
510-464-7937
http://www.abag.ca.gov

Southern California Association of Governments
818 W. 7th St., 12th Floor
Los Angeles, CA 90017-3435
213-236-1800
http://www.scag.ca.gov/

San Diego Association of Governments
Wells Fargo
401 B St., Suite 800
San Diego, CA 92101
619-595-5300
http://www.sandag.cog.ca.us/

State Data Center Program
University of California-Berkeley
2538 Channing Way
Berkeley, CA 94720-5100
510-642-6571
http://ucdata.berkeley.edu

Association of Monterey Bay Area Governments
445 Reservation Rd., Suite G
P.O. Box 838
Marina, CA 93933
408-883-3750

Colorado
Division of Local Government
Colorado Department of Local Affairs
1313 Sherman St., Room 521
Denver, CO 80203
303-866-2156
http://www.dlg.oem2.state.co.us/demog/demog.htm

Business Research Division
Graduate School of Business Administration
Campus Box 420
University of Colorado-Boulder
Boulder, CO 80309-0420
303-492-8227
http://www-bus.colorado.edu/brd/

Agriculture and Resource Economics
Colorado State University
C-307 Clark Bldg.
Fort Collins, CO 80523-1172
907-491-5706

Connecticut
Policy Development and Planning Division
Connecticut Office of Policy and Management
450 Capitol Ave.
P.O. Box 341441
Hartford, CT 06134-1441
860-418-6230
http://www.state.ct.us/opm

Government Documents
Connecticut State Library
231 Capitol Ave.
Hartford, CT 06106
860-566-3614
http://csl.ctstate.edu/

Connecticut Department of Economic Development, Research, Planning, and Information Systems
505 Hudson St.
Hartford, CT 06106
860-270-8174
http://www.state.ct.us/ecd/

Capitol Region Council of Governments
221 Main St.
Hartford, CT 06106
860-522-2217

Delaware
Delaware Economic Development Office
99 Kings Highway
P.O. Box 1401
Dover, DE 19901
302-739-4271
http://www.state.de.us/dedo/

College of Urban Affairs and Public Policy
University of Delaware
Graham Hall, Room 286
Academy St.
Newark, DE 19716
302-831-8406
http://www.ude/edu/

District of Columbia
Data Services Division
Mayor's Office of Planning
Presidential Bldg., Room 570
415 12th St., NW
Washington, DC 20004
202-727-6533

Metropolitan Washington Council of Governments
777 N. Capitol St., NE, Suite 300
Washington, DC 20002-4201
202-962-3200
http://www.mwcog.org

Florida
Florida State Data Center
Executive Office of the Governor
REA/OPB, The Capitol, Room 1604
Tallahassee, FL 32399-0001
Ms. Valerie Jugger
850-487-2814

Center for the Study of Population
Institute for Social Research
654 Bellemy Bldg., R-93
Florida State University
Tallahassee, FL 32306-4063
850-644-7101
http://mailer.fsu.edu/~popctr

State Library of Florida
R.A. Gray Bldg.
Tallahassee, FL 32399-0250
850-487-2651
http://stafla.dlis.state.fl.us/

Bureau of Economic Analysis
Florida Department of Commerce
107 W. Gaines St.
315 Collins Bldg.
Tallahassee, FL 32399-2000
Mr. Nick Leslie
850-487-2971

Georgia
Div. of Demographic and Statistical Services
Georgia Office of Planning and Budget
270 Washington St., SW
Atlanta, GA 30334
404-656-3820
http://www.opb.state.ga.us/

University of Georgia Libraries
Government Documents
6th Floor
Athens, GA 30602
706-542-3472
http://www.libs.uga.edu/

State Data and Research Center
Georgia Institute of Technology
GCATT Bldg.
250 14th St., NW
Atlanta, GA 30318
404-894-6698
http://www.gatech.edu/sdrc/

Hawaii
Hawaii State Data Center
Department of Business, Economic Development, and Tourism
#1 Capitol District Bldg.
250 S. Hotel St., 4th Floor
Honolulu, HI 96813
Mailing Address: P.O. Box 2359
Honolulu, HI 96804

Market Studies, Demographics and Statistics

808-586-2493
http://www.hawaii.gov/dbedt/sdcrpt.html

Information and Communication Services Division
State Department of Budget and Finance
Kalanimoku Bldg.
P.O. Box 0150
1151 Punchbowl St.
Honolulu, HI 96813
808-568-1940
http://www.hawaii.gov/icsd/dbf/dbf.html

Idaho

Idaho Department of Commerce
700 W. State St.
P.O. Box 83720
Boise, ID 83720-0093
208-334-2470
http://www.idoc.state.id.us/

Institutional Research
Room 319, Business Bldg.
Boise State University
1910 University Drive
Boise, ID 83725
208-385-1613
http://www.idbsu.edu/

The Idaho State Library
325 W. State St.
Boise, ID 83702
208-334-2150
http://www.lili.org/isl/

Center for Business Research and Services
Campus Box 8044
Idaho State University
Pocatello, ID 83209
208-236-3049
http://www.isu.edu/departments/cbr/

Illinois

Illinois Bureau of the Budget
108 Statehouse
Springfield, IL 62706
217-782-4520
http://www.state.il.us/budget/

Census and Data Users Services
Department 4690
Research Services Bldg., Suite A
4950 Illinois State University
Normal, IL 61790-4950
309-438-7771
http://www.ilstu.edu/depts/cadus/cadus.htm

Center for Governmental Studies
Northern Illinois University
Social Science Research Bldg.
138 N. 3rd St.
DeKalb, IL 60115
815-753-0922/0934
http://www.cgs.niu.edu/

Regional Research and Development Services
Southern Illinois University at Edwardsville
P.O. Box 1456
Edwardsville, IL 62026-1456
618-692-3500
http://www.rrds.siue.edu/

Chicago Area Geographic Information Study
Department of Geography (M/C 092)
1007 W. Harrison St., Room 2102
University of Illinois at Chicago
Chicago, IL 60607-7138

312-996-6367
http://www.cagis.uic.edu/

Northeastern Illinois Planning Commission
Research Services Department
222 S. Riverside Plaza
Suite 1800
Chicago, IL 60606-6097
312-454-0400
http://www.nipc.cog.il.us/

Indiana

Indiana State Library
Indiana State Data Center
140 N. Senate Ave.
Indianapolis, IN 46204
317-232-3733
http://www.statelib.lib.in.us/www/rl/sdcment.html

Indiana Business Research Center
Indiana University
School of Business
1309 E. 10th St., Room 416
Bloomington, IN 47405-1701
812-855-5507
http://www.iupui.edu/it/ibrc/ibrc.html

Indiana Business Research Center
801 W. Michigan
B.S. 4015
Indianapolis, IN 46202-5151
317-274-2205

Research Division
Indiana Department of Commerce
1 N. Capitol, Suite 700
Indianapolis, IN 46204
317-232-8959
http://www.ai.org/doc/index.html

Iowa

State Library of Iowa
Old Historical Bldg.
E. 12th and Grand
Des Moines, IA 50319
515-281-4350
http://www.silo.lib.ia.us/st-data.html

Center for Social and Behavioral Research
University of Northern Iowa
Cedar Falls, IA 50614-0402
319-273-2105
http://csbsnt.csbs.uni.edu/dept/csbr

Census Services
Iowa State University
303 East Hall
Ames, IA 50011-1070
515-294-8337
http://www.exnet.iastate.edu/pages/soc/census/

Iowa Social Science Institute
University of Iowa
123 N. Linn St.
Brewery Square
345 Shaeffer Hall
Iowa City, IA 52242
319-335-2371
http://www.uiowa.edu/~issi/

Bureau of Planning, Research and Evaluation
Department of Education
Grimes State Office Bldg.
Des Moines, IA 50319-0146
515-281-4730
http://www.state.ia.us/educate/pre/index.html

Kansas

State Library
State Capitol Bldg.
300 W. 10th St.
Room 343-N
Topeka, KS 66612-1593
785-296-3296
http://skyways.lib.ks.us/kansas/ksl/

Division of the Budget
State Capitol Bldg.
300 SW 10th St.
Room 152-E
Topeka, KS 66612-1504
785-296-2436
http://www.ink.org/public/kansasbudget/

Institute for Public Policy and Business Research
607 Blake Hall
The University of Kansas
School of Business
Lawrence, KS 66045-2960
785-864-3701
http://kufacts.cc.ukans.edu/cwis/units/ippbr/

Center for Economic Development and Business Research
1845 Fairmont
Wichita State University
Wichita, KS 67260-0121
316-978-3225
http://www.twsu.edu/~cedbrwww/index.html

Population and Research Laboratory
202 Ahern St.
Department of Sociology
Kansas State University
Manhattan, KS 66506
785-532-6865
http://www.ksu.edu/sasw/

Kentucky

Urban Studies Institute
College of Business and Public Administration
University of Louisville
Louisville, KY 40292
502-852-7990
http://www.louisville.edu/cbpa/sdc/

Governor's Office of Policy and Management
New Capitol Annex, Room 284
Frankfort, KY 40601
502-564-7300
http://www.state.ky.us/agencies/gopm/gopm.htm

State Library Division
Department for Libraries and Archives
300 Coffeetree Rd.
P.O. Box 537
Frankfort, KY 40601
502-564-8300
http://www.kdla.state.ky.us/

Louisiana

State Census Data Center
P.O. Box 94095
1051 N. 3rd St.
Baton Rouge, LA 70804
504-342-7410
http://www.state.la.us/state/census/census.htm

Division of Business and Economic Research
University of New Orleans
Lake Front
New Orleans, LA 70148

State Data Centers

504-286-6980
http://www.uno/edu/

Division of Business Research
Louisiana Tech University
College of Business and Administration
P.O. Box 10318
Ruston, LA 71272
318-257-3701
http://www.cab.latech.edu/

Louisiana State Library
P.O. Box 131
Baton Rouge, LA 70821-0131
504-342-4913
http://smt.state.lib.la.us/statelib.htm

Louisiana Population Data Center
Department of Sociology
Room 126, Stubbs Hall
Louisiana State University
Baton Rouge, LA 70803-5411
Mr. Charles Tolbert
504-388-1646
http://www.lapop.lsu.edu/

Center for Business and Economic Research
Northeast Louisiana University
Monroe, LA 71209-0101
318-342-1215
http://leap.nlu.edu/

Maine

University of Southern Maine
School of Business
Center for Business and Economic Research
118 Bedford St.
Portland, ME 04104-9300
207-780-4187
http://www.usm.maine.edu/~cber/

Maine State Library
Cultural Bldg.
State House Station 64
Augusta, ME 04333-0064
207-287-5600
http://www.state.me.us/msl/mslhome.htm

Maryland

Maryland Department of State Planning
301 W. Preston St., Room 1101
Baltimore, MD 21201
Mr. Robert Dadd
Ms. Jane Traynham
410-225-4450
http://www.inform.umd.edu:8080/ums+state/md_resources/msdc/

University of Maryland
UMCP McKeldin Library
College Park, MD 20742
301-405-9169
http://itd.umd.edu/ums/umcp/gov/govt.docs.htm

Enoch Pratt Free Library
Resource Center
Maryland Room
400 Cathedral St.
Baltimore, MD 21201-4484
410-396-1789
http://pratt.lib.md.us/

Small Business Development Center
7100 Baltimore Ave., Suite 401
College Park, MD 20740
301-403-8300

Massachusetts

Massachusetts Institute for Social and Economic Research
128 Thompson Hall
Box 37515
University of Massachusetts
Amherst, MA 01003-7515
413-545-3460
http://www.umass.edu/miser/

Massachusetts Institute for Social and Economic Research
Box 219
Saltonstall State Office Bldg.
Room 1103
Boston, MA 02133-0219
617-727-4537
http://www.umass.edu/miser

Whelden Memorial Library
P.O. Box 147
West Barnstable, MA 02668-0147
508-362-2262

University of Massachusetts
Documents Library
100 Morrissey Blvd.
Boston, MA 02125-3393
617-287-5932
http://www.lib.umb.edu/

Michigan

Michigan Information Center
Department of Management and Budget
Demographic Research and Statistics
P.O. Box 30026
Lansing, MI 48909
517-373-7910
http://www.state.mi.us/dmb/mic/

MIMIC/Center for Urban Studies
Wayne State University
Faculty/Administration Bldg.
656 W. Kirby
Detroit, MI 48202
313-577-8996
http://www.cus.wayne.edu/mimic/ mimhome.htm

The Library of Michigan
Government Documents Service
P.O. Box 30007
717 W. Allegan St.
Lansing, MI 48909
517-373-1580
http://www.libofmich.lib.mi.us/

Minnesota

State Demographer's Office
Minnesota Planning
300 Centennial Office Bldg.
658 Cedar St.
St. Paul, MN 55155
612-296-2557
http://www.mnplan.state.mn.us/demography/index.html

Machine Readable Data Center
University of Minnesota
309 19th Ave., South
Minneapolis, MN 54555
612-624-6370
http://www.mrdc.umn.edu/

Children, Families and Learning Educational Resources Center
Department of Education
550 Cedar St. SE
501 Capitol Square Bldg.
St. Paul, MN 55101
612-296-6684
http://children.state.mn.us/libry/edures.htm

Mississippi

Center for Population Studies
The University of Mississippi
Bondurant Hall, Room 3W
University, MS 38677
601-232-7288
http://www.olemiss.edu/depts/population_studies/

Division of Research and Information Systems
Department of Economic and Community Development
1200 Walter Sillas Bldg.
P.O. Box 849
Jackson, MS 39205
601-359-3593
http://www.decd.state.ms.us/

Missouri

Missouri State Library
600 W. Main St.
P.O. Box 387
Missouri State Census Data Center
Jefferson City, MO 65102
573-526-7648
http://www.oseda.missouri.edu/mscdc/

Missouri Small Business Development Centers
300 University Place
Columbia, MO 65211
314-882-0344
http://www.missouri.edu/~sbdwww/

Office of Administration
124 Capitol Bldg.
P.O. Box 809
Jefferson City, MO 65102
314-751-2345
http://www.state.mo.us/oa/bp/plngrsrc.htm

Urban Information Center
University of Missouri-St. Louis
8001 Natural Bridge Rd.
211 Lucas Hall
St. Louis, MO 63121
314-516-6035
http://www.oseda.missouri.edu/uic/

Office of Social and Economic Data Analysis
University of Missouri-Columbia
224 Lewis Hall
Columbia, MO 65211
314-882-7396
http://www.oseda.missouri.edu/index.html

Geographic Resources Center
University of Missouri-Columbia
16 Stewart Hall
Columbia, MO 65211
314-882-2324
http://www.msdis.missouri.edu/

Montana

Census and Economic Information Center
Montana Department of Commerce
P.O. Box 200501
1424 9th Ave.
Helena, MT 59620-0501
406-444-2896
http://commerce.mt.gov/ceic/

Market Studies, Demographics and Statistics

Montana State Library
1515 E. 6th Ave.
Capitol Station
Helena, MT 59604-1800
406-444-3004
http://msl.mt.gov/

Bureau of Business and Economic Research
University of Montana
School of Business Administration
Missoula, MT 59812-1110
406-243-5113
http://www.business.umt.edu/

Research and Analysis Bureau
Employment Policy Division
Montana Department of Labor and Industry
P.O. Box 1728
Helena, MT 59624
406-444-4831
http://jsd.dli.mt.gov/lmi/lmi.htm

Nebraska

Center for Public Affairs Research
Nebraska State Data Center
Peter Kiewit Conference Center, #232
University of Nebraska at Omaha
Omaha, NE 68182
402-595-2311
http://cid.unomaha.edu/~wwwpa/cpar/cparhome.html

Governor's Policy Research Office
P.O. Box 94601
State Capitol, Room 1319
Lincoln, NE 68509-4601
402-471-2414

Federal Documents Librarian
Nebraska Library Commission
The Atrium, 1200 N. St., Suite 120
Lincoln, NE 68508-2023
402-471-2045
http://www.nlc.state.ne.us/

The Central Data Processing Division
Department of Administration Services
Nebraska Department of Economic Development
301 Centennial Mall S., Lower Level
P.O. Box 95045
Lincoln, NE 68509-5045
402-471-4855
http://www.careerlink.org/emp/neb/

Nebraska Department of Labor
550 S. 16th St.
P.O. Box 94600
Lincoln, NE 68509-4600
402-471-4189
http://www.dol.state.ne.us/

Natural Resources Commission
301 Centennial Mall South
P.O. Box 94876
Lincoln, NE 68509-4876
402-471-3964
http://www.nrc.state.ne.us/

Nevada

Nevada State Data Center
Nevada State Library
Capitol Complex
100 Stewart St.
Carson City, NV 89710
702-687-8326
http://www.clan.lib.nv.us/docs/nsla/sdc/sdc.html

New Hampshire

Office of State Planning
2-1/2 Beacon St.
Concord, NH 03301-4497
603-271-2155
http://webster.state.nh.us/osp/ospweb.htm

New Hampshire State Library
20 Park St.
Concord, NH 03301-6303
603-271-2392
http://webster.state.nh.us/nhsl/index.html

New Jersey

New Jersey Department of Labor
Division of Labor Market and Demographic Research
P.O. Box 388
Trenton, NJ 08625-0388
609-984-2595
http://www.state.nj.us/labor/lra/njsdc.html

New Jersey State Library
U.S. Documents Office
185 W. State St.
P.O. Box 520
Trenton, NJ 08625-0520
609-292-6259
http://www.state.nj.us/statelibrary/

Data and Statistical Services
Social Science Reference Center
Princeton University
87 Prospect Ave.
Princeton, NJ 08544
609-258-6052

Rutgers University
Urban Planning and Policy Development
33 Livingston Ave., Suite 301
New Brunswick, NJ 08901-1987
908-932-3822
http://www.policy.rutgers.edu/uppd/

New Mexico

Economic Development Department
P.O. Box 20003
Santa Fe, NM 87504-5003
505-827-0182
http://www.edd.state.nm.us/

New Mexico State Library
325 Don Gaspar Ave.
P.O. Box 1629
Santa Fe, NM 87501-2777
505-827-3852
http://www.stlib.state.nm.us/

Bureau of Business and Economic Research
University of New Mexico
1920 Lomas NE
Albuquerque, NM 87131-6021
505-277-6626
http://www.unm.edu/~bber

Department of Economics
New Mexico State University
Box 30001, Dept. 3CQ
Las Cruces, NM 88003-8001
Dr. Kathleen Brook
505-646-2112
http://cbae.nmsu.edu/departments/economics/

New York

Division of Policy and Research
Department of Economic Development
1 Commerce Plaza, Room 905
99 Washington Ave.
Albany, NY 12245
518-474-1141
http://205.232.252.23/nysdc/

Cornell University
CISER Data Archive
201 Caldwell Hall
Ithaca, NY 14853
607-255-4801
http://www.ciser.cornell.edu/

Nelson A. Rockefeller Institute of Government
411 State St.
Albany, NY 12203-1003
518-443-5522
http://rockinst.org

New York State Library
6th Floor, Cultural Education Center
Empire State Plaza
Albany, NY 12230
518-474-3940
http://www.nysl.nysed.gov/

Office of Real Property Services
16 Sheridan Ave.
Albany, NY 12210-2714
518-486-5446
http://www.orps.state.ny.us/

North Carolina

North Carolina Office of State Planning
116 W. Jones St.
Raleigh, NC 27603-8003
919-733-3270
http://www.ospl.state.nc.us/

Division of State Library
109 E. Jones St.
Raleigh, NC 27601-2807
919-733-3270
http://www.dcr.state.nc.us/ncslhome.htm

Institute for Research in Social Science
University of North Carolina
Manning Hall CB 3355
Chapel Hill, NC 27599-3355
919-962-0512
http://www.unc.edu/depts/irss/

Center for Geographic Information
Office of State Planning
301 N. Wilmington St.
Suite 700
Raleigh, NC 27601
919-733-2090
http://www.cgia.state.nc.us/

North Dakota

North Dakota State Data Center
North Dakota State University
Morrill Hall, Room 224
P.O. Box 5636
Fargo, ND 58105-5636
701-231-8621
http://www.sdc.ag.ndsu.nodak.edu/

Office of Intergovernment Assistance
State Capitol, 14th Floor
600 E. Boulevard Ave.
Bismarck, ND 58505-0170
701-328-2094
http://www.state.nd.us/intergov/index.html

State Data Centers

Department of Geography
University of North Dakota
Box 9020
Grand Forks, ND 58202
701-777-4246
http://www.und.nodak.edu/dept/geog/mainpage.html

North Dakota State Library
Liberty Memorial Bldg.
604 East Blvd.
Bismarck, ND 58505-0800
701-328-4622
http://www.sendit.nodak.edu/ndsl/

Ohio

Office of Strategic Research
Ohio Department of Development
P.O. Box 1001
77 High St., 27th Floor
Columbus, OH 43216-0101
614-466-2115
http://www.odod.ohio.gov/osr/

State Library of Ohio
65 S. Front St.
Columbus, OH 43215-4163
614-644-7061
http://winslo.ohio.gov/

Cleveland State University
Northern Ohio Data and Information Service
The Urban Center
1737 E. Euclid Ave., Room 45
Cleveland, OH 44115-2440
216-687-2209
http://cua6.csuohio.edu/~ucweb/nodis/nodis.htm

Ohio State University Extension
Data Center
Information Services Department
2120 Fyffe Rd.
Columbus, OH 43210-1084
614-292-1868
http://www.ag.ohio-state.edu/~dataunit/index.html

University of Cincinnati
Southwest Ohio Regional Data Center
Institute for Policy Research
P.O. Box 210132
Cincinnati, OH 45221-0132
513-556-5077
http://www.ipr.uc.edu/sordc/index.htm

Oklahoma

Oklahoma State Data Center
Oklahoma Department of Commerce
6601 Broadway Extension
(Mailing address) P.O. Box 26980
Oklahoma City, OK 73126-0980
405-841-5184
http://www.odoc.state.ok.us/osdc.htm

Oklahoma Department of Libraries
200 NE 18th St.
Oklahoma City, OK 73105
405-521-2502
http://www.state.ok.us/~odl/

Center for Economic and Management Research
The University of Oklahoma
307 W. Brooks, Room 4
Norman, OK 73019-0450
405-325-2931
http://origins.ou.edu/

Oregon

Oregon State Library
State Library Bldg.
250 Winter St., NE
Salem, OR 97310
503-378-4277
http://www.osl.state.or.us/

Center for Population Research and Census
School of Urban and Public Affairs
Portland State University
P.O. Box 751
Portland, OR 97207-0751
503-725-5159
http://www.upa.pdx.edu/cprc

Oregon Housing and Community Services
Department
1600 State St., Suite 100
Salem, OR 97310-0161
503-986-2000
http://www.hcs.state.or.us/

Geographic Information Systems
Department of Energy Bldg.
155 Cottage St., NE
Salem, OR 97310
503-378-4036
http://www.sscgis.state.or.us/

Pennsylvania

Pennsylvania State Data Center
Institute of State and Regional Affairs
Pennsylvania State University at Harrisburg
777 W. Harrisburg Pike
Middletown, PA 17057
717-948-6336
http://www.hbg.psu.edu/psdc/psdchome1.1.htm

Pennsylvania State Library
Forum Building
Box 1601
Harrisburg, PA 17105
717-787-2327
http://www.cas.psu.edu/docs/pde/libstate.html

Rhode Island

Rhode Island Department of State Library Services
300 Richmond St.
Providence, RI 02903
401-222-2726
http://www.dsls.state.ri.us/

Social Science Data Center
Brown University
P.O. Box 1916
Providence, RI 02912
401-863-3459

Rhode Island Department of Administration
Office of Municipal Affairs
One Capitol Hill
Providence, RI 02908-5873
401-222-6493
http://webster.doa.state.ri.us/

Office of Health Statistics
Rhode Island Department of Health
3 Capitol Hill, Room 407
Providence, RI 02908-5097
401-222-2550
http://www.health.state.ri.us/

Rhode Island Department of Education
Assessment Office
255 Westminister St.
Providence, RI 02903-3900
401-222-3126
http://instruct.ride.ri.net/

Rhode Island Economic Development Corporation
7 Jackson Walkway
Providence, RI 02903
401-222-2601
http://www.riedc.com/

South Carolina

Division of Research and Statistical Services
South Carolina Budget and Control Board
1000 Assembly St., Suite 425
P.O. Box 12444
Columbia, SC 29211
803-734-3793
http://www.state.sc.us/drss/

South Carolina State Library
1500 Senate St.
P.O. Box 11469
Columbia, SC 29211
803-734-8666
http://www.state.sc.us/scsl/

South Dakota

Business Research Bureau
School of Business, Patterson Hall
University of South Dakota
414 E. Clark
Vermillion, SD 57069
605-677-5287
http://www.usd.edu/brbinfo/brb/home.htm

Documents Department
South Dakota State Library
800 Governors Dr.
Pierre, SD 57501-2294
605-773-3131
http://www.state.sd.us/state/executive/deca/st_lib/st_lib.htm

Labor Market Information Center
South Dakota Department of Labor
420 S. Roosevelt, Box 4730
Aberdeen, SD 57402-4730
605-626-2314
http://www.state.nd.us/dol/lmic/lmihp.htm

Office of Administration Services
South Dakota Department of Health
445 E. Capitol Ave.
Pierre, SD 57501-3185
605-773-3693
800-738-2301
http://www.state.sd.us/state/executive/doh/doh.html

South Dakota State University
Rural Sociology Department
Scobey Hall 226, Box 504
Brookings, SD 57007-1296
605-688-4132
http://www.sdstate.edu/

Tennessee

Economic and Community Development
Research Division
320 6th Ave. N, 8th Floor
Rachel Jackson Bldg.
Nashville, TN 37243-0405
Mr. Charles Brown
615-741-1676
http://www.state.tn.us/ecd/

Market Studies, Demographics and Statistics

Center for Business and Economic Research
College of Business Administration
University of Tennessee
Room 100, Glocker Hall
Knoxville, TN 37996-4170
615-974-5441
http://cber.bus.utk.edu/

Texas

Texas State Data Center
Department of Economic Development
P.O. Box 12728
Capitol Station
Austin, TX 78701
512-936-0223
http://www.tded.state.tx.us/

State Data Center
Department of Rural Sociology
Texas A & M University System
Special Services Bldg.
College Station, TX 77843-2125
409-845-5115/5332
http://www-txsdc.tamu.edu/

Texas State Library and Archive Commission
P.O. Box 12927
Capitol Station
Austin, TX 78711
512-463-5455
http://www.tsl.state.tx.us/

Utah

Office of Planning and Budget
Room 116, State Capitol
Salt Lake City, UT 84114
801-538-1550
http://www.governor.state.ut.us/dea/sdc/

University of Utah
Bureau of Economic and Business Research
1645 E. Campus Center Dr., Room 401
Salt Lake City, UT 84112
801-581-6333
http://www.business.utah.edu/bebr/

Dept. of Community and Economic Development
324 S. State St., Suite 500
Salt Lake City, UT 84111
801-538-8700
http://www.dced.state.ut.us/

Department of Workforce Services
140 E. 300 S.
P.O. Box 45249
Salt Lake City, UT 84145-0249
801-536-7813
http://dwsa.state.ut.us/labor/index.asp

Vermont

Office of Policy Research and Coordination
Pavilion Office Bldg.
109 State St.
Montpelier, VT 05602
802-828-3326

Center for Rural Studies
University of Vermont
207 Morrill Hall
Burlington, VT 05405-0106
802-656-3021
http://crs.umv.edu/

Vermont Department of Libraries
109 State St.
Montpelier, VT 05609-0601
802-828-3261
http://dol.state.vt.us/

Vermont Travel Department
134 State St.
Montpelier, VT 05601-1471
802-828-3237
http://www.travel-vermont.com/

Virginia

Virginia Employment Commission
703 E. Main St.
Richmond, VA 23219
804-786-1485
http://www.state.va.us/vec/vec.html

Wheldon Cooper Center for Public Service
University of Virginia
918 Emmet St. N., Suite 300
Charlottesville, VA 22903-4832
804-982-5585
http://www.virginia.edu/~cpserv/

Virginia State Library
Documents Section
800 E. Broad St.
Richmond, VA 23219-1905
804-692-3500
http://lco.vsla.edu/

Washington

Forecasting Division
Office of Financial Management
450 Insurance Bldg.
Box 43113
Olympia, WA 98504-3113
360-586-0599
http://www.wa.gov/ofm/

Puget Sound Regional Council
1011 Western Ave., Suite 500
Seattle, WA 98104-1035
206-464-7090
http://www.psrc.org/

Social Research Center
Department of Rural Sociology
Washington State University
Pullman, WA 99164-4006
509-335-8623
http://www.ruralsoc.wsu.edu/

Department of Sociology
Demographic Research Laboratory
Western Washington University
Bellingham, WA 98225-9081
360-650-3176
http://www.ac.wwu.edu/~drl/

Department of Employment Security
LMEA
P.O. Box 46000
Olympia, WA 98507-6000
360-438-4804
http://www.wa.gov/esd/

CSSCR
University of Washington
145 Savery Hall, DK 45
Box 353345
Seattle, WA 98195
206-543-8110
http://augustus.csscr.washington.edu/

West Virginia

West Virginia Development Office
Research and Strategic Planning Division
Capitol Complex
Bldg. 6, Room 553
Charleston, WV 25305
304-558-4010
http://www.wvdo.org/research/

Reference Library
West Virginia State Library Commission
1900 Kanawha Blvd. East
Cultural Center
Charleston, WV 25305
304-558-2045
http://www.wvlc.wvnet.edu/

Office of Health Services Research
WVU Health Science Center
Medical Center Dr.
P.O. Box 9145
Morgantown, WV 26506-9145
304-293-1086
http://www.hsc.wvu.edu/

Bureau of Business and Economic Research
College of Business and Economics
West Virginia University
P.O. Box 6025
Morgantown, WV 26506-6025
304-293-7832
http://www.wvu.edu/~colbe/serve/
bureau/index.htm

Wisconsin

Department of Administration
Demographic Services Center
101 E. Wilson St., 6th Floor
P.O. Box 7868
Madison, WI 53707-7868
608-266-1927
http://www.doa.state.wi.us/deir/boi.htm

Applied Population Laboratory
Department of Rural Sociology
University of Wisconsin
1450 Linden Dr., Room 316
Madison, WI 53706
608-262-1515
http://www.ssc.wisc.edu/poplab/
aplhome.htm

Wyoming

Survey Research Center
University of Wyoming
P.O. Box 3925
University Station
Laramie, WY 82071-3925
307-766-2025
http://www.uwyo.edu/a&s/src/index.htm

Department of Administration and Information
Economic Analysis Division
Emerson Bldg. 327E
Cheyenne, WY 82002-0060
307-777-7504
http://eadiv.state.wy.us/eahome.htm

State Labor Information Centers

Labor market information departments are an overlooked resource within state governments. These little-known offices can provide current, customized data such as:

- which cities have the highest concentration of restaurants or credit agencies;
- how many Hispanic males were living in Bridgeport, Connecticut in 1987;
- which zip codes have the fastest growing population of working women in managerial positions;
- the name, address and size of each new business or business expansion in a given state;
- which U.S. counties offer the highest entry level salaries for market research analysts.

Two reasons for tapping state government labor offices for market and demographic data are that in most cases the information is free and less than one year old.

Sources of Data

The primary function of each state labor information office is to collect data in conjunction with the federal government in order to produce employment, unemployment, occupational and wage information. The most interesting data sources are state unemployment contribution forms filled out by every employer in the state. This form is filed quarterly revealing total wages and number of employees for companies by SIC code in each city and county.

In addition, each state compiles data showing future manpower needs within the state. By studying labor trends, economic conditions and school enrollments, these agencies project the future supply and demand for up to 1,000 different occupations. Many offices also supplement their information with data from the U.S. Bureau of Census as well as other state data collection agencies to provide additional studies and forecasts.

More Current than Federal Data

If you are a user of the Census Bureau's *County Business Patterns*, you are aware that the latest information available is nearly two years old. But, are you aware that right now you can obtain basically the same information from most states that was collected only six months ago? This information is 18 months more current than Census data? If you are looking for personal income figures by state, county or city, the latest available data from the federal government dates back two years. Moreover, the majority of personal income is made up of wage data which is available from most states much more recently.

Also remember that all data, such as state unemployment information, are passed on to the federal government for publication, but are available from state governments several weeks before being released from Washington.

State Data More Detailed, Cheaper and More Accessible than Federal Data

Unemployment rate data are released by the U.S. Bureau of Labor Statistics for approximately 150 major cities. However, the state of Connecticut alone can provide unemployment data for 169 cities. If you are looking for salary by type of occupation, the Bureau of the Census covers about 400 occupations in their data. But state governments will cover up to one thousand occupations based on data which can be up to three years more current.

Federal policies combined with the public's increased reliance on traditional federal data sources have caused many of major federal statistical agencies to increase prices and to decrease services. In contrast, using state labor information centers is like walking into virgin data territory. Almost everything is still free from these offices, and state employees are eager to do a lot of free research for those who call. In a conversation I had with the labor information office in Ohio, the director recounted how a local bank requested demographic data for a few dozen zip codes in a three state area. Not only did the state office assemble this information but also gave it to the bank on diskettes...all for free.

Multiple Uses of Labor Market Data

State labor data provide an endless array of uses, but here are some of the primary applications.

1) Marketing:
The marketing information available from the states is overwhelming. The data cover both the consumer and industrial markets. It can be used for determining your current market size as well as identifying new or emerging marketing opportunities. For example, you can find:

- monthly employment and average wages by SIC code, by county;
- annual employment for up to 1,000 occupations, by county, by SIC code;
- which counties have the highest concentration of hairdressers making over $20,000 per year;
- how many bartenders are working in a given city;
- how many hotels with fewer than 100 employees operate in a given city;
- what are the fastest growing jobs or industries in any county or city;
- one year projections (1987) of demographic data for each city and county; or
- five to ten year projections of industries and occupations by city and county.

Many labor market information centers also offer special market studies to cover specific industries which may be important within the state. You can get free studies covering the hospital industry, ski industry, finance industry and many high-tech related industries.

Market Studies, Demographics and Statistics

2) Company Information:
These offices can tell you how many companies in a given SIC code are located in any county or city. States also can provide the median salary and average starting salary for up to 1,000 different jobs, and can even tell you how many people are employed in all these companies by type of job. Many states keep information on any company which is a newcomer to the state or undertaking major business expansion. And, almost every state can give you the number of employees for any manufacturer in the state.

3) Business Location:
Whether you are establishing a new plant, a real estate business, or fast food franchise, these offices can help you locate the best location with regard to labor availability, customer availability and competition. The state labor experts can furnish specifics on how many college graduates, typists or computer programmers with three years of experience are looking for work in any given area. Or, how many are unemployed and looking for work, or how many are working for other companies in the area and their salaries. You can discover what wages are being paid by your competitors in the area for these jobs. Some states volunteer to provide information on union activity in any area. Some states can give you an indication of the work ethic of potential employees. Work ethic can be quantified by showing the number of days off taken by specific employees in certain industries. And if your customers are going to be consumers or businesses in the area, these labor market specialists can share estimates on your potential clientele.

4) Employee Development:
If you are worried about the availability of skilled employees for the future growth of your business, these offices can forecast for you the exact number of people who will be available from school training programs and other employers. This can help you determine if your business will have to move to another location or begin an in-house training program to ensure a plentiful supply of trained labor.

5) Labor Negotiations:
You can find out what the average entry wage for a typist is in your area or what the average fringe benefit package looks like for businesses in your industry. What is the maximum amount of days off allowed for sick leave in your industry? How many companies in your industry offer paid dental care? Answers to these, and other employee benefit questions, can be useful leverage in negotiating employee benefit packages.

6) Affirmative Action, EEOC and Government Contracts:
Organizations which have to comply with EEOC and affirmative action criteria can get all the data necessary from these offices. Labor force data for any area can pinpoint how many women, Hispanics, etc., are in the labor force for various occupations. Such data can be compared with a company's current employee demographics. This information can be useful when seeking government contracts. Also, remember that many government contracts are set aside for those companies in high unemployment areas. This data, too, can be obtained from these offices to see if you qualify.

7) Economic Analysis:
If you are interested in any local area economic forecasting or economic monitoring, this is an ideal place to start. All of these offices have monthly and quarterly newsletters which plot economic health down to the city and county level. If your business is dependent on the economic conditions of a specific region, state, city or county, this approach is an easy way to keep your finger on the pulse of what is happening.

8) Careers and Job Search:
An important function of each of these offices is to provide career and job counseling information. If you are looking for a job, each office has access to a state database which identifies available job openings throughout the state. They project which jobs will in demand in the next 10 to 20 years. And more importantly, the future supply is projected for these positions so that you can more easily spot important opportunities. Moreover, you can obtain the starting salaries and median wages for approximately 1,000 occupations in hundreds of industries. Many states give out free books designed for job seekers, as well as information on how to participate in training programs and vocational education opportunities.

9) Computer Formats and Special Services:
You must remember that no two states operate in the same manner or generate identical data. Although many offer the same reports, some may break down the data into 2-digit SIC codes and others into 4-digit SIC codes. What you must never forget is that although one state may NOT provide the data in the format you need, this does not rule out the possibility when dealing with other states. A few states now have their data online and more are beginning to offer diskettes and computer tapes. But if a state labor office says it does not provide computer readable formats, you may be able to convince them to let you be the first. These offices all seem to be very flexible and not heavily encumbered in bureaucracy.

Be sure to investigate any special services which may be offered by the state. Some offer free sources on how to interpret and use labor data and others provide customized affirmative action reports.

State Labor Offices

Alabama
Department of Industrial Relations, Research and Statistics Division, 649 Monroe Street, Montgomery, AL 36131; 334-242-8859; Fax: 334-242-2543; {www.dir.state.al.us/lmi}; {E-mail: ddyer@dir.state.al.us}; Selected Publications: *Alabama Workforce, Occupational Trends, Occupational Employment Statistics, Alabama Labor Market News, Nonagricultural Wage & Salary Employment, Affirmative Action Data, Annual Average Labor Force Estimates, LMI Bulletin, Selected Labor Market Information*. Publications are downloadable at website for free. Most research assistance is free.

Alaska
Department of Labor, Research and Analysis, P.O. Box 25501, Juneau, AK 99802-5501; 907-465-4500; Fax: 907-465-2101; {www.labor.state.ak.us/research/research.htm}; Selected Publications: *Alaska Economic Trends, Alaska Population Overview, Employment & Earning Report, Residency Analysis of Alaska's Workers by Firm, 2000 Alaska Occupational Table, Nonfatal Occupational Injuries and Illnesses, UI Actuarial Study and Financial Handbook, Employment and Earnings of Participants in Selected Alaska Training Programs*. Many publications are available for download at web site at no charge. Research assistance is free.

Arizona
Department of Economic Security, Research Administration, 1789 West Jefferson 1 NW, Phoenix, AZ 85007, Site Code 733A, P.O. Box 6123, Phoenix, AZ 85005; 602-542-3871; Fax: 602-542-6474; {www.de.state.az.us/links/economic/webpage/index.html}, {E-mail: wgdand@de.state.az.us}; Selected Publications: *Arizona Economic Trends, 1999-2000, Workforce Development Planning Information, 1996-2006, Occupational Forecasts, LMI Directory, Occupation/Business Licensing*

State Labor Information Centers

Requirements, Arizona Forecasts, Arizona Economic Profiles, Arizona Historical Labor Force and Nonfarm Jobs Data, Special Unemployment Report. Publications are free at web site. Research assistance is available for free.

Arkansas
Employment Security Department, Labor Market Information Section, #2 State Capitol Mall, Little Rock, AR 72201; P.O. Box 2981, Little Rock, AR 72203; 501-682-3198;TDD:800-285-1131;{www.state.ar.us/esd/labormarketinformation.htm}; Selected Publications: *Labor Market Information for Arkansas Counties, Industrial and Occupational Trends, Arkansas Affirmative Action Data, Covered Employment and Earnings, The Future Awaits, Arkansas Career Watch, Labor Force Statistics, Employment Outlook, Occupational Outlook Handbook, 1996-2006, Industrial Occupational Employment Projections.* Publications free at web site. Research assistance is free.

California
Employment Development Department, Labor Market Information Division, 7000 Franklin Boulevard, #1100 Sacramento, CA 95823; 916-262-2162; Fax: 916-262-2443;{www.calmis.cahwnet.gov}; {E-mail:lmid.webmaster@edd.ca.gov}; Selected Publications: *State of the State's Labor Markets, Labor Supply in Information Technology Occupations, California Labor Market Bulletins, California Occupational Guides Set, Labor Market Condition in California.* There is a charge for some publications. Research assistance is free of charge.

Colorado
Department of Labor & Employment, Labor Market Information, 1515 Arapahoe Street, Tower 2, Suite 300, Denver, CO 80202-2117; 303-620-4856; {http://lmi.cdle.state.co.us}; Selected Publications: *Labor Force Conditions, Labor and Industry Focus, Consumer Price Index, Occupational Wage Data, Employment & Wages, Employment Outlook, Occupational Supply/Demand, Annual Planning Information, Affirmative Actions Statistics.* A number of the publications are free. There is no charge for research assistance.

Connecticut
Department of Labor, Office of Research, 200 Folly Brook Boulevard, Wethersfield, CT 06109-1114; 860-263-6275; Fax: 860-263-6263; {www.ctdol.state.ct.us/lmi}; {E-mail: dol.lmi@po.state.ct.us}; Selected Publications: *Choices Today...A High Performance Workforce Tomorrow, Connecticut Labor Market Information At-A-Glance, Connecticut Data for Affirmative Action Plans, The Connecticut Economic Digest, Connecticut Forecast 2006: A Look at Today's and Tomorrow's Industries and Occupations, Connecticut Labor Situation, Connecticut Occupational Employment and Wages, Connecticut Labor Situation, Work Stoppages in Connecticut.* Publications can be downloaded for free at their web site. There is no charge for research assistance as long as it is not very time consuming.

Delaware
Office of Occupational & Labor Market Information, Delaware Department of Labor, 4425 North Market Street, Wilmington, DE 19802, P.O. Box 9965, Wilmington, DE 19809-0965; 800-452-1589; 302-761-8069; Fax: 302-761-6598; {www.oolmi.net}; {E-mail: esimon@state.de.us}; Selected Publications: *Occupational Outlook Handbook, Delaware Stepping Stones, Delaware Tomorrow, Delaware Careers, Delaware Career Compasses, Delaware Wages, Delaware Jobs, Delaware Snapshot, Monthly Labor Review, Future Labor Market Trends, 1996-2006, Marketing Labor Market Information: The WIA Imperative, New Castle County Labor Market, Occupational & Industrial Projections, Affirmative Action Statistics.* Publications can be downloaded for free from their web site. They will guide you in the right direction to help with research.

District of Columbia
Employment Services Department, Labor Market Information, Room 201, 500 C Street, NW, Washington, DC 20001; 202-724-7214; {http://209.122.85.51/lmi.html}; {E-mail: roeslch@bls.gov}. Selected Publications: *Labor Force, Employment & Unemployment Statistics, Industry Employment Statistics, Occupational Employment Statistics, D.C.'s Top 200 Employers, LMI for Affirmative Action Planning, Demand Occupations.* Publications are available for free download from their web site. They will assist with research.

Florida
Department of Labor and Employment Security, Office of Labor Market Statistics, Suite 200, Hartman Building, 2012 Capital Circle, SE, Tallahassee, FL 32399-2151; 850-488-1048; {http://lmi.floridajobs.org}; {E-mail: LMIWEB@fdles.state.fl.us}. Selected Publications: *Labor Market Review, Florida Occupation Profiles, Florida Fact Sheet-Older Workers in Florida, Florida Trends, Florida Employment Outlook 2006, Fact Sheet-Women Workers in Florida.* Publications can be downloaded for free from their web site. Contact them with research questions.

Georgia
Department of Labor, Labor Information Systems, 148 International Boulevard, NE, Atlanta, GA 30303; 404-656-3177; {www.dol.state.ga.us/lmi}; {E-mail: lmi@dol.state.ga.us}; Selected Publications: *Civilian Labor Force Estimates, Georgia Economic Indicators, Labor Market Trends, Statistical Digest of Georgia's Economy, Nonagricultural Employment, Georgia Occupational Trends in Brief: Projections to 2006, Licensed and Certified Occupation in Georgia, Planning for Tomorrow: Industry and Occupation Outlook.* Publications are free. Research assistance is also free.

Hawaii
Department of Labor and Industrial Relations, Research and Statistics Office, P.O. Box 3680, Honolulu, HI 96811; 808-586-9021; Fax: 808-586-9022; {www.state.hi.us/dlir/rs/loihi}; {E-mail: loihi@rs.dlir.state.hi.us}; Selected Publications: *Employment Outlook for Industries and Occupation, Hawaii Labor Market Information Directory, Labor Area News, Labor Force Data Book, Labor Force Information For Affirmative Action Programs, Licensed Occupations in Hawaii, Occupational Employment and Wages in Hawaii, Occupations in Demand at Hawaii Workforce Development Division.* Publications free while they last. Research assistance is available at no charge.

Idaho
Department of Employment, Research and Analysis Bureau, 317 Main Street, Boise, ID 83735; 208-334-6170; {www.doe.state.id.us/lmi/id-lmi.htm}; {E-mail: jfackrel@loabor.state.id.us}; Selected Publications: *Affirmative Action Statistics, Basic Economic Data, Distribution of Covered Workers in Idaho by Industry, Economic Profiles, Idaho Demographic Profile, Idaho Employment, Labor Force in Idaho, Occupational Employment Statistics, Affirmative Action Statistics.* Most publications are available at web site for download.

Illinois
Department of Employment Security, Research and Analysis, 7-North, 401 South State Street, Chicago, IL 60605; 312-793-9223; Fax: 312-793-2192; {http://lmi.ides.state.il.us}; {E-mail: lmi@ides.state.il.us}; Selected Publications: *Affirmative Action Data, LMI Directory, Illinois Employment-industry Summary, Illinois Labor Market Review, Occupational Wage Report, Occupational Projections: 2006, Where Workers Work, Occupational Employment Statistics: Wage Data.* Publications are available at no charge. Research assistance is free.

Indiana
Department of Workforce Development, Labor Market Information, IGCSE211, 10 North Senate Avenue, Indianapolis, IN 46204-2277; 317-232-1920; Fax: 317-232-8480; {www.dwd.state.in.us/labor_market.shtm}; Selected Publications: *Affirmative Action, Occupational Projections Long Term, Labor Surplus Area, Indiana Employment Review, Annual Covered Employment Payrolls, Civilian Labor Force Estimates, Employment and Wage Survey.* Publications are free. Research assistance is free.

Iowa
Workforce Development, Labor Market Information Bureau, 1000 East Grand Avenue, Des Moines, IA 50319; 515-281-6642; Fax: 515-281-8203; {www.state.ia.us/iwd/ris/lmi/index.html}; {E-mail:iwd.lmi@iwd.state.ia.us}; Selected Publications: *Iowa Condition of Employment, Iowa Occupational Projection 1996-2005, Iowa Job Outlook 1994-2005, Iowa Licensed Occupations, Labor Market Information, Affirmative Action Data.* Publications are free. There is no charge for research assistance.

Kansas
Department Of Human Resources, Labor Market Information Services, 401 SW Topeka Boulevard, Topeka, KS 66603; 785-296-5058; Fax: 785-296-5286; {http://laborstats.hr.state.ks.us}; {E-mail: laborstats@hr.state.ks.us}: Selected Publications: *Kansas Monthly Employment Review, Unemployment Insurance Claims, Kansas Wage Survey 1999 Edition, Occupational Outlook 2005, Job Opportunities in Kansas, Quarterly Employment and Wages, Labor Market Information Catalog, Affirmative Action Reports.* Publications can be obtained for free. Research assistance is available at no cost.

Kentucky
Department for Employment Services, Labor Market Information, 275 East Main Street, CHR Building and FL., Frankfort, KY 40621; 502-564-7976; 800-542-8840; Fax: 502-564-2937; {www.state.ky.us/agencies/wforce/des/lmi/lmi.htm}; {E-mail: des.labor@mail.state.ky.us}; Selected Publications: *Kentucky Career Outlook and Job Opportunities, Current Employment Statistics, Kentucky Occupational Outlook to 2006, Kentucky Total and Nonwhite Population and Labor Force Data by County, Occupational Employment Statistics.* There is no charge for publications. They will give guidance in research.

Market Studies, Demographics and Statistics

Louisiana
Department of Labor, Office of Employment Security, Research and Statistics Unit, P.O. 94094, Baton Rouge, LA 70804-9094; 504-342-3141; Fax: 504-342-9193; {www.ldol.state.la.us/lmipage.htm}; {E-mail:webmaster@www.ldol.state.la.us}; To view publications online, go to {http://leap.ulm.edu}; Selected Publications: *Employees by Major Industries, Employment Projection, Female Labor Force, Labor, Occupation and Commuting, Minority Labor Force, Non-agriculture Wage and Salary Employment, Occupations of Job Applicants, Employment Projection.* Publications are free. Research assistance is available for no cost.

Maine
Maine Department of Labor, Labor Market Information Services, 20 Union Street, Augusta, ME 04330-6826; 207-287-2271; Fax: 207-287-2947; {http://janus.state.me.us/labor/lmis/frdef.htm}; {E-mail:lmi.me@state.me.us}; Selected Publications: *Hot Jobs in Maine, Occupational Profiles for Hot Jobs in Maine, Gaining Good Jobs in Maine, Careers in Maine For College Graduates, Labor Market Digest, Maine Employment Statistical handbook, Maine Occupational Wages, Technical Services Monographs, Maine, Labor Force and Unemployment Statistics, Employment and Wages by Area and by Industry, Nonfarm Wage and Salary Employment.* There is a charge for a few of the publications. Research assistance is available for free.

Maryland
Department of Labor, Licensing and Regulation, Office of Labor Market Analysis and Information, 1100 North Eutaw Street, Room 601, Baltimore, MD 21201; 410-767-2250; Fax: 410-767-2219; {www.dllr.state.md.us/lmi/index.htm}; {E-mail: lmai@dllr.state.md.us}; Selected Publications: *Affirmative Action Data, Business Services Industries-An Inside Look, Civilian Labor Force, Employment and Unemployment by Place of Residence, Civilian Claims Processed for Unemployment Insurance Benefits, Health Services Industry in Maryland, Labor Market in Review, Labor Market Indicators, Maryland High Technology, Maryland Industrial Profile, Occupation and Wage Highlights by Industry, People to Jobs, 1992-2005.* There is no charge for publications. Research assistance is offered for no charge.

Massachusetts
Division of Employment and Training, Labor Market Information, 19 Saniford Street, Boston, MA 02114; 617-626-6562; {www.detma.org/lmi.htm}; {E-mail: detlmi@detma.org}; Selected Publications: *State Labor Force Statistics, Local Area Labor Force Statistics, Occupational Wages by Service Delivery Area, Labor Market Information Report, The Massachusetts Job Outlook Through 2006, Employment and Wages by Industry and Area.* Publications can be downloaded at their web site at no cost. No fee for research.

Michigan
Department of Career Development, Office of Labor Market Information, 201 North Washington Square, Lansing, MI 48913; 517-241-4000; Fax: 517-373-0314; {www.michlmi.org}; Selected Publications: *Occupational Employment Forecasts 1994-2005, Industry Employment Forecasts 1994-2005, Michigan's Economic Situation at a Glance, Covered Employment and Wage Statistics, Labor Market Area Labor Force and Industrial Employment Trend Series, Occupational Employment Outlook, Industrial Employment Outlook, Local Area Unemployment Statistics.* Publications are available at no charge. Research assistance is free.

Minnesota
Department of Economic Security, Research and Statistics Office, 390 North Robert Street, St. Paul, MN 55101; 651-296-6545; 888-234-1114; Fax: 651-282-5429; {www.des.state.mn.us/lmi}; {E-mail: lmi@ngwmail.des.state.mn.us}; Selected Publications: *Beyond 2000: Information Technology Workers in Minnesota, Minnesota Economic Trends, Minnesota Job Outlook 1996-2006, Minnesota Wage Distribution Report, Trends in Minnesota: Job Service Openings and Reemployment Insurance Characteristics, Minnesota Careers What Could Your Next Job Be?, Minnesota Employment Review, Employment Outlook, Employment Hours and Earnings.* No charge for most publications. Research under 1/2 is free; otherwise it is $50/hour.

Mississippi
Employment Security Commission, Labor Market Information Department, P.O. Box 1699, Jackson, MS 39215-1699; 601-961-7424; {www.mesc.state.ms.us/lmi/index.html}; {E-mail: lmi-info@mesc.state.ms.us}; Selected Reports: *Annual Manpower Reports, Mississippi's Bearfacts, Economic Profile, Farm Income and Expenditures, LMI for Affirmative Action Programs, Annual Labor Force Statistics, Labor Market Trends, Fringe Benefit Survey, Business Population, Occupational employment Statistics Survey Report, Personal Income by Major Sources, Unemployment Insurance Activities.* Publications and research assistance are free.

Missouri
Department of Economic Development, Division of Workforce Development, 1716 Four Seasons, Suite 101, Jefferson City, MO 65101-1815; 573-751-4962; {www.works.state.mo.us/lmi/index.htm}; {E-mail: wfd@state.mo.us}; Selected Publications: *Labor Market Information, Economic Overview for Missouri, Personal Income, Occupational Wage and Employment Information, Labor Surplus Areas, Industry Employment and Earnings/Wages, Industry/Occupation Projections, Labor Force and Unemployment, Occupational Injuries and Illness Statistics.* Publications and research assistance are free.

Montana
Office of Research and Analysis, Job Service Division, P.O. Box 1728, Helena, MT 59624; 406-444-2430; 800-633-0229; TDD: 406-444-0532; Fax: 406-444-0532; {http://rad.dli.state.mt.us}; {E-mail: questions4RAD@state.mt.us}; Selected Publications: *Statistics-in-Brief, Montana Employment and Labor Force Trends, Workforce Information Newsletter, Montana Annual Labor Market Planning Information, Profile of Montana Worker, Montana Occupational Injuries and Illnesses, Informational Wage Rates by Wage and Occupation, Job Projections for Montana's Industries and Occupations, Nonagricultural Wage and Salary Employment.* Publications are free unless noted (none at their site were noted); No custom research for individual, but they will direct you to any information that they are aware of.

Nebraska
Department of Labor, Labor Market Information, 550 South 16th Street, P.O. Box 94600, Lincoln, NE 68509; 402-471-2600; Fax: 402-471-9867; {www.dol.state.ne.us/nelmi.htm}; {E-mail: pbaker@dol.state.ne.us}; Selected Publications: *Nebraska Licensed Occupations 1999-2000, Nebraska Labor Market Review, Nebraska Underemployment Study, Affirmative Action 1999, Economic Trends, A Monthly Review of LMI, Disability Data for Nebraska, Employment Projections by Occupation, Estimates of Hours and Earnings, Nebraska Employment Projections 1996-2006, Nebraska Quarterly Business Conditions.* A majority of the publications are free. There is no charge for research assistance, unless it is very time consuming and requires a lot of computer time.

Nevada
Department of Employment, Training and Rehabilitation, Information Development and Processing Division, Research and Analysis Bureau, 500 East Third Street, Carson City, NV 89713; 775-684-0450; {www.state.nv.us/detr/lmi}; {E-mail: lmi@govmail.state.nv.us}; Selected Publications: *Nevada Affirmative Action Data, Nevada Employment and Payrolls, Nevada Occupational Employment and Projections 1996-2006, Nevada OES Wage Data, Industrial Employment Data, Nevada Employment AT A Glance, Quarterly Economic Indicators, Nevada Labor Force Statistics.* All publications can be downloaded for free at their site. There is no charge for research assistance.

New Hampshire
Employment Security Department, Economic Analysis and Research and Labor Market Information Bureau, 32 South Main Street, Concord, NH 03301; 603-224-3311; Fax: 603-228-4172; {www.nhworks.state.nh.us/lmipage.htm}; {E-mail: webmaster@nhes.state.ne.us}; Selected Publications: *Economic Conditions in New Hampshire, Summary of New Hampshire Economy, Vital Signs: Economic and Social Indicators for New Hampshire, Profile of New Hampshire and its Eighteen Labor Market Areas, New Hampshire Occupational Employment and Wages, New Hampshire Affirmative Action 1999, New Hampshire Employment Projections by Industry and Occupation 1996-2006, 1998 New Hampshire Benefits.* Most publications can be viewed at the web site. Research assistance is available for no cost.

New Jersey
Labor Department, Office of Labor Planning and Analysis, John Fitch Plaza CN056, Trenton, NJ 08625; 609-292-7376; {www.wnjpin.state.nj.us/OneStopCareerCenter/LaborMarketInformation/lmilist.htm}; Selected Publications: *Economic Indicators, Employment and the Economy, Income Security Fast Cards, Labor Force Estimate, Occupational Safety and Health Survey Results, Projection 2006, unemployment Insurance Developments in New Jersey, Employment Projection: Industry and Occupation, Guide to Labor Demand Occupation, Labor Force by Sex and Race, New Jersey Occupational Wages, Licensed Occupations.* There is a charge for some publications or research assistance.

New Mexico
Department of Employment Security, Economic Research and Analysis, 401 Broadway, NE, Albuquerque, NM 87102; 505-841-8645; {www3.state.nm.us/dol/dol_lmi.html}; Selected Publications: *New Mexico Labor Market Review, New Mexico Annual, Social and Economic Indicators, Hours and Earnings Estimates, Nonagricultural Wage and Salary Employment, Affirmative Action Information,*

State Labor Information Centers

Civilian Labor Force Employment and Unemployment Rate, Nonagricultural Wage and Salary Employment By Industry, New Mexico 2006, Employment Projections, New Mexico Labor Market Review. All publications are free. They can be contacted for assistance in research.

New York
Department of Labor, Division of Research and Statistics, Building #12 State Campus, Albany, NY 12240; 518-457-1130; {www.labor.state.ny.us/html/businf.htm}; Selected Publications: *Affirmative Action Data, Agricultural Employment Bulletin, Comparison of Key Unemployment Insurance Statistics, Directory of Labor Market Information, Employment in New York State, Labor Area Summary Resident Employment Status of the Civilian Labor Force, Work Injuries and Illnesses Resulting in Lost Worktime, Private Industry, Collective Bargaining Settlements in New York State, Occupational Projections for New York State and Regions, Nonfarm Payroll Employment, Estimates by Industry, Current Employment/Unemployment Statistics.* Most publications available at no cost. Usually no charge for research assistance, unless it requires significant computer use.

North Carolina
Employment Security Commission, Labor Market Information, 700 Wade Avenue, Raleigh, NC 27605; 919-733-2936; Fax: 919-733-8662; {www.esc.state.nc.us}; {E-mail: cottrell.bob@exc.state.nc.us}; Selected Publications: *Current Employment Statistics, Employment and Wages in North Carolina, North Carolina Largest Employers, Company Policies and Fringe Benefits, Labor Supply and Wage Rates, Wage Rates in Selected Occupations, Labor Market Information Directory, Occupations Requirement License in North Carolina.* Publications and research assistance are available for free.

North Dakota
Job Service, Research and Statistics, P.O. box 5507, Bismarck, ND 58506, 701-328-2868; 800-732-9787; TTY: 800-366-6888(relay ND); Fax: 701-328-4193; {www.state.nd.us/jsnd/lmi2.htm}; {E-mail: jsndweb@state.nd.us}; Selected Publications: *Annual Planning Report, Benefits Survey, Employment and Wages, Labor Market Advisor, Projections, Ups and Down the River: The 1997 Flood Impact on Employment and Wages in Grand Forks County, Where Will the Jobs Be in 2006?, Current Economic Conditions, Census at a Glance, Wage Survey.* Both publications and research assistance are free.

Ohio
Bureau of Employment Services, Labor Market Information Division, 145 South Front Street, P.O. Box 1618, Columbus, OH 43216; 614-466-4636; {http://lmi.state.oh.us/home.htm};{E-mail: ewaldk@obes.state.oh.us};SelectedPublications: *Covered Employment and Payrolls, Equal Employment Opportunity/Affirmative Action, IPEDS Earned Degree Report, Labor Force Estimates, Labor Market Projections, Labor Market Review, Leading Indicators, Occupational Employment Statistics, Unemployment Industry Wage Survey.* No charge for publications. Research assistance is available for no charge.

Oklahoma
Employment Security Commission, Economic Analysis, P.O. Box 52003, Oklahoma City, OK 73105; 405-557-7261; Fax: 405-525-0139; {www.oesc.state.ok.us/lmi/default.htm}; {E-mail: lmi@oesc.state.ok.us}; Selected Publications: *A World of Information at Your Fingertips, County Employment and Wage Data, Great Plains General Business Index, Handbook of Employment Statistics, Labor Force Information for Affirmative Action Programs, Oklahoma Economic News, Oklahoma Labor Force Data, Workforce Oklahoma Occupational Outlook 2005, Oklahoma Labor Market Information Annual Summary.* Publications are free. Research assistance is also free.

Oregon
Employment Division, Research and Statistics, 875 Union NE, Salem, OR, 97311; 503-378-8656; Fax: 503-373-7515; {http://olmis.emp.state.or.us/OLMISHOM.HTML}; Selected Publications: *Around the State, CES Annual Tables, Consumer Price Index, Covered Employment and Payroll, Farm Labor Bulletin, Hispanics in Oregon's Workforce, Industry Projections, Labor Force by Race and Gender, Local Labor Trends, Occupational Projections, Resident Oregon Labor Force and Unemployment by Area.* Publications are available at no charge. Research assistance is free.

Pennsylvania
Department of Labor and Industry, Center for Workforce Information and Analysis, Commonwealth of Pennsylvania, Harrisburg, PA 17121; 877-4WF-DATA (493-3282); {www.lmi.state.pa.us}; {E-mail: info-lmi@dli.state.pa.us}; Selected Publications: *Labor Market Information Regional Forums, Occupational Wage Survey, Pennsylvania Labor Force, Pennsylvania Workforce 2005, Pennsylvania Unemployment Compensation Statistics, Employment and Wages by County and Industry, Pennsylvania's Insured Unemployed, Labor Market Information for Affirmative Action Programs, Annual Planning Information, Nontraditional Jobs for Women.* Publications are free. Research assistance is free of charge if it is not extremely time consuming.

Rhode Island
Department of Labor and Training, Labor Market Information Division, 101 Friendship Street, Providence, RI 02903; 401-222-3706; Fax: 401-222-2731; {www.det.state.ri.us/webdev/lmi/Lmihome.htm}; {Email:mferreira@dlt.state.ri.us}; Selected Publications: *Affirmative Action Data for Rhode Island, Characteristics of the Insured Unemployed, Covered Employment and Wages, Establishment Employment in Rhode Island, Nonfarm Employment, Hours and Earnings, Occupational Wages, Rhode Island 2006- A Positive Outlook on Tomorrow's Workforce, Labor Market Information for Rhode Island Planners.* Publications are free. There generally is not a charge for research assistance.

South Carolina
Employment Security Commission, Labor Market Information Division, P.O. Box 995, Columbia, SC 29202; 803-737-2660; {www.sces.org/lmi/index.htm}; {E-mail: blisbon@sces.org}; Selected Publications: *Labor Force Data by Race and Sex, Labor Market Review, Occupational Distribution of the Labor Force, South Carolina Economic Indicators, South Carolina Industry and Occupation Projections, Labor Force and Industry, Employment Trends, Occupational Employment Statistics, Wage Survey, Affirmative Action.* Most publications are free. There is no charge for research assistance.

South Dakota
Department of Labor, Labor Market Information Center, P.O. Box 4730, 420 South Roosevelt Street, Aberdeen, SD 57402-4730; 605-626-2314; Fax: 605-626-2322; {www.state.sd.us/lmic/index.htm}; {E-mail: Phil.George@state.sd.us}; Selected Publications: *South Dakota Labor Bulletin, South Dakota Workers and Pay Covered by Unemployment Insurance, South Dakota Benefits Publications, South Dakota Career Wonders, South Dakota Occupational Outlook Handbook, Labor Availability Studies, South Dakota Affirmative Action, Reading the Career Signs in South Dakota 1996-2006, Career Planning Focus.* Most publications are free. Research assistance is free.

Tennessee
Department of Employment Security, Labor Market Information, Davy Crockett Tower-11th Floor, 500 James Robertson Parkway, Nashville, TN 37245-1040; 615-741-1729;{www.state.tn.us/labor-wfd/lmi.htm};{E-mailmherron@mail.state.tn.us}; Selected Publications: *Data to Affirmative Action Plans, Labor Force Estimates Summary, Labor Market Report Dateline, Annual Averages-Labor Force and Nonagricultural Employment Estimates, Occupational Wage Survey, Industrial and Occupational Outlook 2006.* Publications and research assistance are available at no charge.

Texas
Texas Workforce Commission, Labor Market Department, 101 East 15th Street, Suite 103A.2, Austin, TX 78778-0001; 512-491-4922; {www.twc.state.tx.us/lmi/lmi.html}; {E-mail: lmi@twc.state.tx.us}; Selected Publications: *Labor Market Information Spotlight, Texas Labor Market Review, Texas Labor Market Monograph Services, Current Employment Estimates, Covered Employment and Wages, Occupational Wage Data, Estimated Hours and Earnings, Industry Staffing Patterns, Affirmative Action Data.* Publications are free. Normally, there is no charge for the research data provided.

Utah
Department of Workforce Services, Workforce Information, 140 East 300 South, P.O. Box 45249, Salt Lake City, UT 84145-0249; 801-526-9456; Fax: 801-526-9238; {http://wi.dws.state.ut.us}; {E-mail: wsadmwi.grobert@state.ut.us}; Selected Publications: *Utah Labor Market Report, Utah Occupational Wages, Utah Job Outlook Statewide and Service Delivery Area 1998-2003, Utah Equal Employment Opportunity Information, Key Labor Market Information, Occupations in Demand at Utah Department of Workforce, Utah Employers, Employment and Wages by Size Demographic and Economic Profiles.* The publications are free. Research assistance is available at no charge.

Vermont
Department of Employment and Training, Labor Market Information, P.O. Box 488, 5 Green Mountain Drive, Montpelier, VT 05601; 802-828-4202; 800-253-0195; TDD: 800-253-0191; Fax: 802-828-4050; {www.det.state.ut.us/lmi}; Selected Publications: *Affirmative Action Summary, Directory of Labor Market Information, Employment and Wages-Covered by Unemployment Insurance, Job Creation and Destruction Report, Occupational Employment and Wage Survey, Vermont Industrial*

Market Studies, Demographics and Statistics

and Occupational Projections, The Vermont Labor Market Employment and Wages by County. The publications are free. Research assistance is also free.

Virginia
Virginia Employment Commission, 703 East Main Street, Richmond, VA 23219; 804-786-8223; {www.vec.state.va.us/lbrmkt/lmi.htm}; Selected Publications: *Occupational Wages, Occupational Employment and Projections, Labor Supply and Demand, Occupational Employment by Industry, Current Employment Statistics, Industry Employment and Projections, Staffing Patterns, Education/Training Completers, Labor Force Employment and Unemployment.* Publications and research are free.

Washington
Employment Security Department, Labor Market Economic Analysis Branch, P.O. Box 9046, Olympia, WA 98507-9046; 800-215-1617; Fax: 360-438-4109; {www.wa.gov/esd/lmea}; {E-mail: lmi@esd.wa.gov}; Selected Publications: *Affirmative Action Information, Annual Demographic Information, Annual Labor Market Economic Report, Agricultural Work Force in Washington State, Labor Area Summaries, Labor Market Information Review, Occupational Outlook, Washington Labor Market.* Many publications can be downloaded for free from their site, but there is a charge for ordering hard copies. Research assistance is free.

West Virginia
Bureau of Employment Programs, Research, Information and Analysis, 112 California Avenue, Charleston, WV 25305; 304-558-2660; Fax: 304-558-1343; {www.state.wv.us/bep/lmi}; {E-mail: perryle@wvnvm.wvned.edu}; Selected Publications: *Economic Summary, Affirmative Action, Employment and Wages, West Virginia Employment and Earning Annual Summary, West Virginia Metropolitan Statistical Areas Annual Planning Information for FY 2000, Occupational Projections 2000, Employment and Earnings Trends, West Virginia Bureau of Employment Programs, West Virginia Youth and the Labor Market, West Virginia County Profiles.* There is not a charge for publications or research assistance.

Wisconsin
Department of Workforce Development, Division of Workforce Excellence, 201 East Washington Avenue, P.O. Box 7946, Madison, WI 53707-7946; 608-267-9613; {www.dwd.state.wi.us/dwelmi}; Selected Publications: *A Wisconsin Employers' Guide for Recruitment and Retention Survival in the Late 20th And Early 21st Century, Affirmative Action Data for Wisconsin, Civil Labor Force Estimates, Labor Market Information, Wisconsin Commuting Patterns, Wisconsin Economic Indicators, Wisconsin Projections 1996-2006, Labor Force, Industries, and Occupations.* Most publications are available for no charge. Research assistance is free.

Wyoming
Employment Security Commission, Department of Employment/Research and Planning, 122 West 25th Street, Cheyenne, WY 82002; 307-265-6732; Selected Publications: *County Fact Sheets, Covered Employment, Licensed Occupations, Projections, Research and Planning News, Unemployment Insurance Statistics, Wyoming Labor Force Trends, Wage Survey.* Publications are free. Research assistance that takes 2 hours and less is free of charge.

State Statistical Abstracts

For years researchers have been aware of the importance of keeping around the latest edition of the *Statistical Abstract of the United States* (available for $32 in paperback and $38 in hardback from Superintendent of Documents, U.S. Government Printing Office, P.O. Box 371954, Pittsburgh, PA 15250-7954, 202-512-1800). Now if you are interested in local or regional opportunities, trends, or markets, every state government offers their own *State Statistical Abstract* or something comparable. Most of the states produce their abstract on an annual basis.

Tables and graphs are used to illustrate the performance of the economy. Where comparisons can be made, state, regional, and national data can be compared. Market analysts, businesses and researchers will find the following kinds of information in a statistical abstract:

- how many of Fortune magazine's top 500 companies have manufacturing plants in the state;
- the number of jobs directly or indirectly related to exports;
- largest sources of personal income;
- number of people employed in agricultural/non-agricultural jobs;
- how a state ranks in population and land size;
- number of acres of forest land;
- number of airports, number privately owned;
- number of registered aircraft;
- changes in population-age distribution;
- percentage of 17- and 18-year-olds graduating from high school;
- number of state universities, vocational schools;
- number of vehicle registrations;
- crime rates; and
- traffic fatalities.

Similar to the *Statistical Abstract of the U.S.* in providing important data in charts and tables, these state abstracts offer important leads to more detailed sources of information. Although the specific charts and tables may not offer the exact detail of data you require on a particular topic, they will identify the offices which generate this type of information. By contacting the specific office, you are likely to get the precise data you require. They can't publish everything they have in a single statistical abstract, but they can dig the information out of their files for you.

Statistical Abstract Offices

Alabama
University of Alabama
Center for Business and Economic Research
Box 870221
Tuscaloosa, AL 35487
205-348-6191
http://cber.cba.ua.edu/
Publication: *Economic Abstract of Alabama*. 1997. 488 pp.

Alaska
Department of Commerce and Economic Development
Division of Trade & Development
P.O. Box 110804
Juneau, AK 99811-0804
907-465-2017
Publication: *The Alaska Economy Performance Report*. 1996.

Arizona
University of Arizona
Economic and Business Research
College of Business and Public Administration
McClelland Hall 204
Tucson, AZ 85721-0001
520-621-2155
Fax: 520-621-2150
Publications: *Arizona Statistical Abstract: A 1993 Data Handbook*. 616 pp.
Arizona Economic Indicators. 52 pp. Biennial.
Arizona's Economy. 20 pp. (Quarterly newsletter and data).

Arkansas
University of Arkansas at Little Rock
Institute for Economic Advancement, Economic Research
2801 South University
Little Rock, AR 72204
501-569-8550
Publication: *Arkansas State and County Economic Data*. 1997. 16 pp. (Revised annually).

University of Arkansas at Little Rock
Institute for Economic Advancement
Census State Data Center
Little Rock, AR 72204
501-569-8530
Publication: *Arkansas Statistical Abstract, 1998*. 700 pp. (Revised biennially).

California
Department of Finance
915 L Street, 8th Floor
Sacramento, CA 95814
916-322-2263
www.dof.ca.gov/html/fs_data/stat-abs/sa_home.htm
Publication: *California Statistical Abstract, 1997*.

Pacific Data Resources
P.O. Box 1922
Santa Barbara, CA 93116-1922
800-422-2546
Publication: *California Almanac, 6th ed*. Biennial. 275 pp.

Colorado
University of Colorado
Government Publications Library
Boulder, CO 80309
303-492-8834
www.colorado.edu/libraries/govpubs/online.htm
Publication: *Colorado by the Numbers*, online version only

Connecticut
Connecticut Department of Economic & Community Development
505 Hudson St.
Hartford, CT 06106
860-270-8165
Publication: *Connecticut Market Data*. Fall/winter 1998. (Diskette also available.)
Connecticut Town Profiles, 1996-97. 340 pp.

Delaware
Delaware Economic Development Office
99 Kings Highway
Dover, DE 19901
302-739-4271
www.state.de.us/dedo/index.htm
Publication: *Delaware Statistical Overview, 1997*.

Market Studies, Demographics and Statistics

District of Columbia
Office of Planning
Data Management Division
Presidential Bldg., Suite 500
415 12th St., NW
Washington, DC 20004
202-727-6533
Publication: *Socio-Economic Indicators by Census Tract*. 221 pp.
Socio-Economic Indicators of Change by Census Tract, 1980-1990. 146 pp.

Office of Policy and Evaluation
Executive Office of the Mayor
1 Judiciary Square, Suite 920
441 4th St., N.W.
Washington, DC 20001
202-727-6979
Publication: *Indices--A Statistical Index to DC Services, Dec. 1994-96*. 331 pp.

Florida
University of Florida
Bureau of Economic and Business Research
Box 117145
Gainesville, FL 32611-7145
352-392-0171
Publications: *Florida Statistical Abstract, 1997*. 31st ed. 800 pp. Also available on diskette.
Florida County Perspectives, 1997. One profile for each county. Annual.
Florida County Rankings, 1997.
Florida and the Nation, 1998.

Georgia
University of Georgia
Selig Center for Economic Growth
Terry College of Business
Athens, GA 30602-6269
706-542-4085
www.selig.ga.edu/
Publication: *Georgia Statistical Abstract, 1997-98*. 500 pp.

University of Georgia
College of Agricultural and Environmental Sciences
Athens, GA 30602-4356
706-542-8938
Fax: 706-542-8934
Publication: *The Georgia County Guide*. 1998. 17th ed. Annual. 200 pp.

Hawaii
Hawaii State Department of Business
Economic Development & Tourism
Research and Economic Analysis Division
Statistics Branch
P.O. Box 2359
Honolulu, HI 96804
Inquiries 808-586-2481
Copies 808-586-2424
www.hawaii.gov/dbedt/
Publication: *The State of Hawaii Data Book 1997: A Statistical Abstract*. 30th ed. 700 pp.

Idaho
Department of Commerce
700 West State St.
Boise, ID 83720-0093
208-334-2470
www.idoc.state.id.us
Publications: *County Profiles of Idaho, 1998*.
Idaho Community Profiles, 1997.
Idaho Facts, 1998.
Idaho Facts Data Book, 1995.
Profile of Rural Idaho 1998.

University of Idaho
Center for Business Development and Research
Moscow, ID 83844-3227
208-885-6611
Publication: *Idaho Statistical Abstract, 4th ed*. 1996.

Illinois
University of Illinois
Bureau of Economics and Business Research
430 Commerce West
1206 South Sixth Street
Champaign, IL 61820
217-333-2331
www.cba.uiuc.edu/research/OfficeofResearch/abstract.html/98abstract.htm
Publication: *Illinois Statistical Abstract*. 1998. 855 pages.

Indiana
Indiana University
Indiana Business Research Center
School of Business
801 W. Michigan BS4015
Indianapolis, IN 46202-5151
317-274-2204
www.iupui.edu/it/ibrc/
Publication: *Indiana Factbook, 1998-99*. 393 pages.

Iowa
Public Interest Institute
600 N. Jackson Street
Mount Pleasant, IA 52641
319-385-3462
Publication: *1996 Statistical Profile of Iowa*.

Kansas
University of Kansas
Institute for Public Policy and Business Research
607 Blake Hall
Lawrence, KS 66045-2960
785-864-3701
www.ukans.edu/cwis/units/IPPBR/ksdata/ksdata.shtml
Publication: *Kansas Statistical Abstract, 1997*. 32nd ed. 1998.

Kentucky
Kentucky Cabinet for Economic Development
Division of Research
500 Mero Street, Capital Plaza Tower
Frankfort, KY 40601
502-564-4886
Publication: *Kentucky Deskbook of Economic Statistics*. 34th ed. 1998.

Louisiana
University of New Orleans
Division of Business and Economic Research
New Orleans, LA 70148
504-280-6240
Publication: *Statistical Abstract of Louisiana*. 10th ed. 1997

Maine
Maine Department of Economic and Community Development
State House Station 59
Augusta, ME 04333
207-287-2656
http://janus.state.me.us/spo/
Publication: *Maine: A Statistical Summary*. (Updated periodically).

Maryland
Regional Economic Studies Institute (RESI)
Towson University
Towson, MD 21252-7097
410-830-3778
Publication: *Maryland Statistical Abstract*. 1997. 356 pp.

Massachusetts
Massachusetts Institute for Social and Economic Research
Box 37515, University of Massachusetts
Amherst, MA 01003-7515
413-545-3460
Fax: 413-545-3686
www.umass.edu/miser/dataop/
Publications: *Population Estimates for Massachusetts Cities and Towns*. 1995.
Projection of the Population, Mass., Cities and Towns, Years 1990-2010.
Journey to Work in Mass., 1990.

State Statistical Abstracts

Michigan
Michigan Information Center
Department of Management & Budget
Demographic Research and Statistics
P.O. Box 30026
Lansing, MI 48909

Minnesota
Department of Trade and Economic Development
Business and Community Development Division
500 Metro Square Building
St. Paul, MN 55101
651-297-1291
Publication: *Compare Minnesota: An Economic and Statistical Factbook, 1994-95.* 165 pp. *Economic Report to the Governor: State of Minnesota, 1992.* 148 pp.

Office of State Demographer
Minnesota Planning
300 Centennial Bldg.
St. Paul, MN 55155
651-296-2557
Publications: *Minnesota Population and Household Estimates, 1997.* Available diskette in Lotus, dBase or ASCII formats.
Minnesota Population Projections, 2025.

Mississippi
Mississippi State University
College of Business and Industry
Division of Research
P.O. Box 5288
Mississippi State, MS 39762
601-325-3817
601-325-3571
Publication: *Mississippi Statistical Abstract.* 1997. 554 pp.

Missouri
University of Missouri
Business and Public Administration Research Center
Columbia, MO 65211
573-882-4805
Publication: *Statistical Abstract for Missouri, 1997 Biennial.* 256 pp.

Montana
Montana Department of Commerce
Census and Economic Information Center
1424 9th Ave.
Helena, MT 59620
406-444-2896
http://commerce.state.mt.us/ceic/
Statistical reports from the Montana County Database. (Separate county and state reports available by subject section as well as complete reports by county and state, updated periodically.)

Nebraska
Department of Economic Development
Division of Research
Box 94666
Lincoln, NE 68509
402-471-3784
www.ded.state.ne.us
Publication: *The Nebraska Databook.* 1997-1998. 300 pp. (Available only on Internet).

Nevada
Department of Administration
Budget and Planning Division
209 East Musser Street, Suite 200
Carson City, NV 89710
702-687-4065
Publication: *Nevada Statistical Abstract.* 1996. Biennial. 225 pp.

New Hampshire
Office of State Planning
2 1/2 Beacon St.
Concord, NH 03301-4497
603-271-2155
Publications: *Current Estimates and Trends in New Hampshire's Housing Supply. Update: 1996.* 32 pp.
1996 Population Estimates for New Hampshire Cities and Towns
New Hampshire Population Projections for Counties by Age & Sex, Apr. 1997, 2000-2020.

New Jersey
New Jersey State Data Center
NJ Department of Labor
P.O. Box 388
Trenton, NJ 08625-0388
609-984-2595
Publication: *New Jersey Source Book, 1993.* 156 pp.

New Mexico
University of New Mexico
Bureau of Business and Economic Research
1919 Lomas N.E.
Albuquerque, NM 87131-6021
505-277-6626
Fax: 505-277-2773
www.unm.edu/%7Ebber/
Publications: *County Profiles. 1997.* 72 pp.
Community Profiles for selected New Mexico Cities.
Population Projections for the State of New Mexico, 1997.

New York
Nelson A. Rockefeller Institute of Government
411 State Street
Albany, NY 12203-1003
518-443-5522
http://rockinst.org/
Publication: *New York State Statistical Yearbook, 1997.* 21st ed. 582 pp.

North Carolina
Office of Governor
Office of State Planning
116 West Jones Street
Raleigh, NC 27603-8003
919-733-4131
Publication: *Statistical Abstract of North Carolina Counties, 1991.* 6th edition. (No longer being published).

North Dakota
North Dakota State University
Department of Agricultural Economics
North Dakota State Data Center
Fargo, ND 8105
701-231-7980
www.sdc.ag.ndsu.nodak.edu/
Publications: *Population Bulletins*, periodic.
Economic Bulletins, periodic.
Economic Briefs, periodic

Ohio
Department of Development
Office of Strategic Research
P.O. Box 1001
Columbus, OH 43216-1001
614-466-2115
Research products and services. (Updated continuously.)

The Ohio State University
School of Public Policy and Management
1775 College Road
Columbus, OH 43210-1399
614-292-8696
Publication: *Benchmark Ohio, 1993.* Biennial. 300 pp.

Oklahoma
University of Oklahoma
Center for Economic and Management Research
307 West Brooks Street, Room 4
Norman, OK 73019

Market Studies, Demographics and Statistics

405-325-2931
Publication: *Statistical Abstract of Oklahoma, 1997*. Annual. 441 pp.

Oregon
Secretary of State
Business Services Division
Publication Services Bldg.
2555 Capital Street, NE, Suite 180
Salem, OR 97310
503-986-2234
Publication: *Oregon Blue Book, 1997-1998*. Biennial. 476 pp.

Pennsylvania
Pennsylvania State Data Center
Institute of State and Regional Affairs
Penn State Harrisburg
777 West Harrisburg Pike
Middletown, PA 17057-4898
717-948-6336
Publication: *Pennsylvania Statistical Abstract, 1998*. 301 pp.

Rhode Island
Rhode Island Economic Development Corporation
1 West Exchange Street
Providence, RI 02903
401-222-2601
Fax: 401-222-2102
Publication: *Rhode Island 1990 Census of Population and Housing Summary*. May 1994. *The Rhode Island Economy*. July, 1998.

South Carolina
Budget and Control Board
Office of Research and Statistical Services
R. C. Dennis Building, Room 425
Columbia, SC 29201
803-734-3781
Publication: *South Carolina Statistical Abstract: 1997*. 440 pp.

South Dakota
University of South Dakota
State Data Center
Business Research Bureau
Vermillion, SD 57069-2390
605-677-5287
Publication: *1997 South Dakota Community Abstracts*. 400 pp.

Tennessee
University of Tennessee at Knoxville
Center for Business and Economic Research
100 Glocker
Knoxville, TN 37996-4170
615-974-6075
Publication: *Tennessee Statistical Abstract, 1996-97*. 16th ed. 807 pp. Biennial.

Texas
Dallas Morning News
Communications Center
P.O. Box 655237
Dallas, TX 75265-5237
214-977-8261
Publication: *Texas Almanac, 1998-99*. 672 pp.

Texas State Data Center
Department of Rural Sociology
Texas A&M University
College Station, TX 77843-2125
409-845-5332
http://txsdc.tamu.edu/

Utah
University of Utah
Bureau of Economic and Business Research
1645 East Campus Center Drive
Salt Lake City, UT 84112-9302

801-581-6333
Publication: *Statistical Abstract of Utah, 1996*. (Centennial.)

Utah Foundation
10 West 100 South, Suite 323
Salt Lake City, UT 84101-1544
801-364-1837
Publication: *Statistical Review of Government in Utah*. 1997.

Vermont
Labor Market Information
Department of Employment and Training
5 Green Mountain Drive, P.O. Box 488
Montpelier, VT 05601-0488
802-828-4202
Publication: *Demographic and Economic Profiles*. Annual. Regional County reports also available.

Center for Rural Studies
University of Vermont
207 Morrill Hall
Burlington, VT 05405
802-656-0258
http://crs.uvm.edu/

Virginia
University of Virginia
Weldon Cooper Center for Public Service
918 Emmet Street, North Suite 300
Charlottesville, VA 22903-4832
804-982-5585
Publication: *Virginia Statistical Abstract, 1996-97*, biennial. 950 pp.

Washington
Washington State Office of Financial Management
Forecasting Division
P.O. Box 43113
Olympia, WA 98504-3113
360-902-0599
Publication: *Washington State Data Book, 1997*. 300 pp.
Population Trends for Washington State. Annual. 48 pages.

West Virginia
West Virginia University
College of Business and Economics
Bureau of Business and Economic Research
P.O. Box 6025
Morgantown, WV 26506-6026
304-293-7831
Publications: *West Virginia Statistical Abstract, 1995*. Biennial. 400 pp.
County Data Profiles. Annual. 50 pp.
Census Data Profiles. Decennial. 30 pp.
West Virginia Economic Outlook. Annual. 50 pp.

West Virginia Research League, Inc.
P.O. Box 11176
Charleston, WV 25339
304-346-9451
Publication: *Economic Indicators*. 1995. 215 pp.
The 1997 Statistical Handbook. 94 pp.

Wisconsin
Wisconsin Legislative Reference Bureau
P.O. Box 2037
Madison, WI 53701-2037
608-266-7098
Publication: *1997-1998 Wisconsin Blue Book*. 950 pp. Biennial.

Wyoming
Department of Administration and Information
Division of Economic Analysis
327 E. Emerson Building
Cheyenne, WY 82002-0060
307-777-7504
Publication: *The Equality State Almanac 1997*. 120 pp.

State Forecasting Agencies

State planning offices can provide vast quantities of local market information, demographic data, and company intelligence--more than you would believe possible. Every state has a bureau equivalent to a planning office to assist the Governor in charting future economic change. Of course, the quantity of information varies from one state to the next as does the sophistication in methods of gathering and analyzing data. However, most information is generated to support decision making for policies and legislative initiatives which will affect the current and future status of the state economy. These blueprints for the future usually include plans for attracting new businesses and industries as well as improving the quality of housing, education and transportation.

It should be noted that there is a wide disparity in the research and strategic focus of these state planning offices. The position of this function within the state bureaucratic structure often provides clues about the scope of its mission. In most states this forecasting operation is housed in the Department of Economic Development or in a separate policy office under the Governor's office. However, in our survey of all fifty states, we discovered this crucial function in unexpected places. In South Carolina, for example, there is a special Commission on the Future within the Lieutenant Governor's office, and in Texas, a comparable office falls under the jurisdiction of the state comptroller.

Business Expansion and Economic Outlook

If you currently do business in a state or intend to establish a business there, it would be wise to learn about the Governor's long-term strategy. Keep in mind that no one is more concerned about the state's future than this elected official. If your company sells to farmers, inquire at the planning office about the Governor's agricultural policies. If your firm relies on high tech complementary business, see whether there is a plan to attract high tech companies. Or, if you are interested in consumer markets, be aware of demographic projections conducted by the planning agency for the state as well as for specific regions and counties. Many states appear to be charting future population patterns on a regular basis as is evident with the sampling of publications noted here.

Nebraska: *Nebraska Databook*
Louisiana: *Vision 2000*
Montana: *Population Projections*
Michigan: *Trends in Agriculture*

Demographics and Market Studies

Most of these offices are aware of the current demographic situation within their state. They also continually monitor the major industries in the state as well as emerging industries. Their data are usually derived from a combination of federal, state and locally generated information. Sometimes these offices are part of the state data center program run by the U.S. Bureau of the Census. Demographic studies as well as state statistical abstracts are readily available.

Alabama: *Economic Outlook*
Arizona: *Community Profiles*
Illinois: *Community Profiles*
Minnesota: *Counties and Townships Demographics Estimates*
Oklahoma: *Demographic State of the State*
Utah: *Utah Economic and Demographic Profiles*

These state planning offices often produce in-depth market studies on diverse topics, for example:

Arizona: *Economic Impact Study of Major League Baseball Team on State of Arizona*
Nebraska: *Profit Opportunities in Nebraska for Manufacturers of Pet Food*
New York: *NY State's Technology Driven Industries: Biotechnology and Pharmaceuticals*
Oregon: *Annual Economic Impact Report for Oregon Travel*
South Carolina: *Plastics in South Carolina*
Utah: *Skier Visit Analysis*

Company Information and Industry Directories

Many of these offices are responsible for maintaining information on the companies which are located within their state. It is not unusual for the state to collect the following data on every manufacturer and corporation:

- Name of company;
- Address and telephone number;
- Names of principal officers;
- Types of products or services produced;
- Number of employees; and
- Sales estimate.

You stand to learn more about a company, especially its financial picture, if the business in question received some type of economic assistance from the state. After all, once a company takes taxpayer money, the public has a right to know. There is a number of companies that fall into this category. We have received a list of over 100 firms which obtained financial assistance from Pennsylvania in a single year.

Other handy resources available from many state planning offices are company directories. Many of them concentrate on one industry sector.

Arizona: *Arizona Housing Resource Directory*
Iowa: *Targeted Small Business Directory*
Kansas: *Kansas Minority Owned and Women Owned Businesses*
Oregon: *Annual Economic Impact Report for Oregon Travel*
New Hampshire: *Manufacturers Database*
North Carolina: *International Firms Directory*

Market Studies, Demographics and Statistics

Databases and Special Services

Because these planning agencies share their forecasts and statistical data with other offices with the state government, often the data are readily available to the public, usually for free or on a cost recovery basis. Already many have established customized databases, some of which permit direct online access. Examples include:

- New Jersey Business Resource Center (one stop shop for information)

- Louisiana Information Clearinghouse

- Massachusetts Electronic Atlas (ability to map different data)

- Oklahoma's Oklahoma Resources Integrated General Information Network System

- Nebraska Databook

- Connecticut Economic Information System

- Utah GOPB online database

State Planning Offices

The address and telephone numbers are included for the primary planning offices in each state as well as the District of Columbia. The publications listed with the office do not represent the entire universe of hardcopy data available. These titles are included only when the office is capable of providing us with a current listing. There are states which have publication, but do not have any sort of a catalog. For those states you must request data under specific topic headings.

Alabama
Center for Business and Economic Research, University of Alabama, Box 870221, Tuscaloosa, AL 35487; 205-348-6191, Fax: 205-348-2951; {www.cba.ua.edu/~cber}, E-mail: {uacber@cba.ua.edu}. *Economic Abstract of Alabama* (price not available at this time), *Alabama Economic Outlook* ($18), *Alabama Business* (newsletter), *Alabama State Data Center News* (quarterly newsletter), *Alabama Retail Sales 1997-1998, The Alabama Economy: Critical Issues for the 1900's, Alabama Population Projections 1990-2015.*

Alaska
State Planning Office, P.O. Box 110804, Juneau AK, 99811, 550 West 7th Avenue, Suite 1770, Anchorage, AK 99501-3510, 907-269-8110, Fax: 907-269-8125; {www.dced.state.ak.us/trade}, E-mail: {Rudy_Tsukada@dced.state.ak.us}. *Summary of Alaska's 1998 Exports, Alaska's Top Export Partners 1st half of 1999, Alaska's Top Export Commodities 1st half of 1999, Alaska Economy Performance Report '98, Economic Indicators Brochure 1998, Establishing a Business in Alaska, Alaska Business Facts Brochure 1998, Halibut Farming, Forest Products Industry Brochure, Alaska Mineral Commission Report, Seafood Export Opportunity - Korea, Seafood Export.*

Arizona
Department of Commerce, 3800 North Central, Suite 1500, Phoenix, AZ 85012; 602-280-1300, Fax: 602-280-1302; {www.commerce.state.az.us}, E-mail: {webmaster@az.commerce.com}. *A State Meant for Success, Arizona Community Profiles* ($15), *Arizona Economic Development Directory, Relocation Information Packet, Small Business Book, Arizona Directory of Minority/Women-Owned Small Businesses* ($11), *Business Assistance Center Promotional Brochure, Arizona Statistical Review, Doing Business in Indian Country, The Greater Arizona Advantage, Aerospace in Arizona, Food, Fiber and Natural Products in Arizona, Transportation and Logistics: An Arizona Advantage, Manufacturing and Metal Fabrication in Arizona, Optics in Arizona, Arizona Economic Development Organizational Structure and Funding Report* ($7), *Common Questions about Planning Newsletter, Facilitators Handbook* ($2), *General and Comprehensive Plan Booklet, Planning and Zoning Handbook* ($15), *Rural Economic Development Initiatives, Public Participation Booklet, Alternative Transportation Fuels Incentives, Arizona Energy Patterns and Trends 1960-1990* ($3), *Bright Idea Series: Energy and the Environment, Energy Policy Updates, Revolving Energy Loans for Arizona, Sunsmart: An Energy Handbook for Desert Dwellers, Strategic Assessment* (Volume IV, $20), *Arizona High Technology Directory, Townhall/Public Forum Reports, Strategic Framework* (Volume VI, $10), *Home Investment Partnerships Program: Program Summary and Application Guide for Development Projects, News from the HOME Investment Partnerships Program, Grant Administration Handbook* ($5/10), *Arizona Environmental Handbook* ($5/$10), *Procurement and Contracting Handbook* ($5/$10), *CDBG "Building Blocks for Better Communities", 20 Questions about Community Development Block Grants, Property Management Business* ($10), *Revolving Loan Funds* ($10), *Rural Arizona Continuum of Care, Arizona Housing Resource Directory, Prison Cities Housing Development Fund, Arizona Directory of Exporters* (annual: $35), *Film in Arizona, Arizona Baseball: An Oasis in the Desert, Job Training for Arizona Business, Make it EZ! Put Your Business in an Arizona Enterprise Zone, School to Work Briefing Papers, Arizona Employment Program Summary.*

Arkansas
Institute For Economic Advancement, University of Arkansas at Little Rock, 2801 South University Avenue, Little Rock, AR 72204; 501-569-8519, Fax: 501-569-8538; {www.aiea.ualr.edu}, E-mail: {dabullwinkle@ualr.edu}. *Arkansas Statistical Abstract, A Profile of Pulaski County, A Profile of Madison County, Economic Impact of Arkansas Volunteers, A Report on the Economy, A Target Industry Study For SE Arkansas, Arkansas State and County Economic Data, Technology Assessment of the SW Region, Industrial Incentive Programs: Arkansas and Neighboring States.*

California
California Trade and Commerce Agency, Office of Economic Research, 801 K Street, Suite 1700, Sacramento, CA 95814; 916-322-3539; {http://commerce.ca.gov/california/economy}, E-mail: {gpochy@commerce.ca.gov}. *California Economic Review, California: An Economic Profile, California Small Business, Foreign Direct Investment In California, The California Multimedia Industry, The California Entertainment Technology Industry, The California Apparel and Fashion Design Industry, The California Wine Industry, County Agriculture.*

Colorado
Office of Economic Development, Research and Special Projects Division, 1625 Broadway, Suite 1710, Denver, CO 80202; 303-892-3840; {www.state.co.us/gov_dir/oed.html}. *Colorado Data Book.*

Connecticut
Department of Economic and Community Development, 505 Hudson Street, Hartford, CT 06106-7107; 860-270-8000; {www.state.ct.us/ecd}, E-mail: {DECD@po.state.ct.us}. *Construction Report-Housing Production and Permit, Industry Clusters-Progress Report, DECD Resource Catalog, Connecticut Economic Conference Board/Report of the Governor and General Assembly 1999, Connecticut Market Data 1999, Connecticut Economic Digest* (monthly), *DECD Annual Report, Connecticut Town Profiles, Connecticut Vacation Guide 1999, The Connecticut Economy* (quarterly), *The Connecticut Tourism News, Partnership for Growth: Connecticut's Economic Competitiveness Strategy-At a Glance.*

Delaware
Delaware Economic Development Office, State of Delaware, Executive Department, 99 Kings Highway, P.O. Box 1401, Dover, DE 19903; 302-739-4271, Fax: 302-739-5749; {www.state.de.us/dedo}, E-mail: {mreardon@state.de.us}. *Statistical Overview of Delaware, Delaware Reuse Guide for Businesses and Consumers, Delaware Quick Look, Delaware Dateline* (newsletter), *Delaware Main Street, Economic Impact of the Wilmington Blue Rocks Baseball Team, List of Summary Visitor Profile: Sussex County, Rehoboth, Bethany, Lewes, Delaware Quality Award Overview, Delaware Population Consortium 1999 Annual Report, Delaware's Cities By Population, Delaware Property Tax Rates, Delaware Tax Incentives.*

District of Columbia
Office of Planning, 801 North Capitol Street, NW, 4th Floor, Washington, DC 20002; 202-442-7600.

Florida
Bureau of Economic and Business Research, University of Florida, P.O. Box 117145, Gainesville, FL 32611-7145; 352-392-0171, Fax: 352-392-4739; {www.bebr.ufl.edu}, E-mail: {info@bebr.ufl.edu}. *Concurrency Management Systems in Florida* ($15), *Cuban Immigration and Immigrants in Florida and the US* ($9), *Economic Impacts*

State Forecasting Agencies

of *Local Government Comprehensive Plans* ($17), *Building Permit Activity in Florida* ($10 annual summary), *Commercial Properties in Florida* ($1999 CD ROM), *Consumer Confidence Index, County Perspective* ($20 per county), *Florida and the Nations* ($20), *Florida County Ranking* ($24.95), *Florida Economic Database* ($6.75 per data series), *Florida Estimates of Population* ($20), *The Florida Long-term Economic Forecast* ($54.95-$94.95), *Florida Population Studies* ($9), *Florida Statistical Abstract* ($39.95), *Gross and Taxable Sales Report* ($10 per county per month), *BEBR Migration Releases* ($20 or $25), *NAL 1997 Florida Property Tax Assessor's File* ($199 each), *Housing Starts* ($25), *Special Population Reports* ($8 each). They offer customized survey services that include telephone and mail surveys of Florida customers. It is priced by the clients needs.

Georgia
Department of Industry Trade and Tourism, Economic Development, 285 Peachtree Center Avenue; 404-656-3573; {www.georgia.org}, E-mail: {business@georgia.org}. Services: GIS Data Clearinghouse.

Hawaii
Department of Business, Economic Development and Tourism, Business Resource Center, P.O. Box 2359 Honolulu, HI 96804, No. 1 Capitol District Building, 250 South Hotel Street, 4th Floor, Ewa Wing, HI 96813; 808-586-2423, Fax: 808-587-2790; {www.hawaii.gov/dbedt}, E-mail: {library@dbedt.hawaii.gov}. *State of Hawaii Databook, Leading Economic Indicator Report, Quarterly Statistical and Economic Report, Population Estimate Reports from the U.S. Bureau of the Census, Information Extracted by the Hawaii State Data Center, Housing Unit Estimates for Hawaii Military Personnel and Dependents in Hawaii, Tourism Looks to the Future, DBET Selected Economic Activities: State of Hawaii, The Economic Impacts of Shipboard Gaming and Pari-mutuel Horse Racing in Hawaii, 1999 State of Hawaii Facts and Figures, Foreign Investment Activities in Hawaii and the U.S. 1954-1998, Hawaii Economy; A Periodic Economic Report, Organizations, Academic Institutions and Government Agencies in Hawaii, Energy Efficiency Policy and Technology Transfer: A Hawaii-Philippine Case Study, Measuring the Economic Impact of Tourism, The Emerging Cruise Ship Market. Biotechnology in Hawaii: A Blueprint for Growth, Directory of Ocean R&D Businesses, Organizations, Academic Institutions and Government Agencies in Hawaii, Energy Efficiency Policy and Technology Transfer: A Hawaii-Philippine Case Study, Measuring the Economic Impact of Tourism, The Emerging Cruise Ship Market.*

Idaho
Department of Commerce, Economic Development, 700 West State Street, P.O. Box 83720, Boise, ID 83720; 208-334-2470; {www.idoc.state.id.us}, E-mail: {info@idoc.state.id.us}. *Community Profiles, County Profiles, Profile of Rural Idaho, Idaho Facts, Idaho at a Glance, Starting a Business in Idaho, Population of Idaho Cities, Population of Counties, Total Sales-Fiscal (94-99) years, Lodging Sales, Service Sales-Fiscal (94-99) Years, Retail Sales (94-99) Years, Workforce Development Training Fund, Idaho Exporters Guide, Idaho International Trade Directory, Idaho and the CE Mak, Industry bulletins, Advantage Handbook, ICDBG Application Handbook, Downtown Handbook, ICDBG Grant Administration Manual, CDBG Status Report.*

Illinois
Department of Commerce and Community Affairs, 620 East Adams, Springfield, IL 62701; 217-782-7500, TDD: 217-785-0211, Fax: 217-524-3701; {www.commerce.state.il.us}. *Quarterly Economic Indicators, Population Projections, Highlights on the Illinois Economy, Community Profiles, Economic Bulletin, Illinois Coal Fact Sheet, OCDM Program Profile FY 2000 Infrastructure Request for Proposal, The Illinois Coal Industry, Coal Technology Profiles, Understanding Electric Utility Restructuring, Export Markets for Illinois, Coal Development and Testing of Commercial Scale Coal Water Slurry-Fired Combustion System, Gas-Reburning-Sorbent Injection at Hennepin and Lakeside Power Stations, Moving Bed Copper Oxide Desulfurzation Denitrification Process, Rochelle Municipal Utilities TCS Micronized Coal System, Does My Business Need an Air Pollution Central Permit?.*

Indiana
Indiana Economic Development Council, One North Capitol Avenue, Suite 425, Indianapolis, IN 46204-2224; 317-631-0871, Fax: 317-231-7067. *IEDC Annual Report, Break Away Growth, IEDC Newsletter, Strategic Plan Fact Finder, Capitol Markets Report 99, Growth Companies 99, INvesting IN INdiana, Indiana Benchmarks, State Rankings.*

Iowa
Department of Economic Development, 200 East Grand Avenue, Des Moines, IA 50303; 515-242-4700, Fax: 515-242-4809; {www.state.ia.us/government/ided}, E-mail: {info@ided.state.ia.us}. IDED Study on the impact of the state's machinery and equipment tax phaseout, *Iowa Beat, Iowa Destination, Smart Sites* (quarterly newsletter), *Iowa Developments* (bi-monthly publication), *Iowa Business Sphere* (bi-monthly newsletter), *Iowa Directory of Exporters, Food Products Directory Companies, Iowa Grain Products Directory, Iowa Economy-News and Trends* (sign-up for e-mail updates), *Small Business Resource Guide, Targeted Small Business Directory, Regulatory Liaison, Entre News* (newsletter), *Iowa Travel Guide, Iowa Transportation Map, The Digest, Statistical Profile of Iowa* (quarterly).

Kansas
Department of Commerce and Housing, 700 SW Harrison Street, Suite 1300, Topeka, KS 66603-3172; 785-296-3481; {www.kansascommerce.com}, E-mail: {webmaster@kdoch.state.ks.us}. *Community Development Resource Directory, Data Book* (sections on distribution, manufacturing, and service), *Developing Kansas Quarterly Newsletter, Kansas Aerospace Directory, Kansas Agribusiness Directory, Kansas Consolidated Plan Executive Summary, Kansas Department of Commerce and Housing FY 99 Annual Report, Kansas Film Production Guide, Kansas International Trade Resource Directory, Kansas! Magazine* (quarterly subscription), *Kansas Minority-Owned and Women Owned Business Directory, Steps to Success: A Guide to Starting a Business in Kansas* ($3.50), *Travel and Event Guide.*

Center for Economic Development and Business Research, 1845 Fairmont, 2nd Floor, Devlin Hall, Wichita State University, Wichita, KS 67260-0121; 316-978-3225, Fax: 316-978-3950; {www.twsu.edu/~cedbrwww/index.html}. *Kansas Economic Report, Kansas Economic Indicators, New Business and Expansion Report.*

The University of Kansas, Institute for Public Policy and Business Research, 607 Blake Hall, Lawrence, KS 66045-2960; 785-864-3701, Fax: 785-864-3701 {www.ukans.edu/cwis/units/ippbr/ippbr.shtml}. *Kansas Business Review, Kansas Statistical Abstract, Kansas Economic Outlook, Research Reports, County Profiles.*

Kentucky
Cabinet for Economic Development, 2400 Capital Plaza Tower, 500 Mero Street, Frankfort, KY 40601; 800-626-2930, Fax: 502-564-3256; {www.edc.state.ky.us}. *Annual Report, Strategic Plan, Kentucky Directory of Manufacturers* ($87), *The Kentucky Deskbook of Economic Statistics, The Kentucky International Trade Directory* ($20), *The Kentucky Facts Book, Community Brochures* ($5), *County Profiles.*

Center for Business and Economic Research, 335-BA Carol Martin Gatton College of Business and Economics Building, University of Kentucky, Lexington, KY 40506-0034; 606-257-7675, Fax: 606-257-7671; {http://gatton.gws.uky.edu/cber.htm}, E-mail: {cber@pol.uky.edu}. *2000 Kentucky Annual Economic Report.*

Louisiana
Department of Economic Development, P.O. Box 94185, Baton Rouge, LA 70804-9185; 225-342-3000; {www.lded.state.la.us}, E-mail: {webmaster@lded.state.la.us}. *Economic Indicators, International Trade Data, Port Profiles, Demographics, Parish Profiles, Industrial Data, Economic Impact of the Music Industry Analyzed by City, The State of Music in Louisiana June 1998.*

Maine
State Planning Office, 38 State House Station, 184 State Street, Augusta, ME 04333; 207-287-3261, Fax: 207-287-6489; {http://janus.state.me.us/spo}. Publications: *Making the Connection in Maine, Issues Facing Maine Economy, Report Card on Poverty in Maine, Retail Sales Annual Review, The Maine Economy: Year-End Review and Outlook, State of the Maine Coast, Sustaining Island Communities: An Economic Development Guide, The Cost of Sprawl, Land for Maine's Future Board Biennial Report, Environmental Programs, Issues in Shoreland Zoning, Forestry in the Shoreland Zone, Strategic Planning/Performance Budget, Patterns of Development Initiative, Atlantic Salmon Plan, Population, Demographic and Housing, Population Estimates, Income and Poverty, Maine's Strategic Planning Initiative, A Guide to Common Maine Organisms Along the Coast of Maine, Sea and Shore: Maine's Shared Resources in the International Year of the Ocean.*

Maryland
Department of Business and Economic Development, 217 East Redwood Street, Baltimore, MD 21202; 410-333-6947, 800-541-8549; {www.mdbusiness.state.md.us}. *Maryland Business Review, Annual Report, Economic Pulse* (monthly report), *Financing Programs and Business Incentives, The Magnitude and Impact of the Technology Industry in Maryland, Policy and Program Recommendations For a Maryland Technology Incubator Program, SBED Annual Report, Brief Economic Facts, Trade Secrets: The Export Answer Book.*

Massachusetts
Department of Economic Development, One Ashburton Place, Room 2101, Boston, MA 02108; 617-757-1130, 617-727-8380, Fax: 617-727-4426; {www.magnet.state.

Market Studies, Demographics and Statistics

ma.us/econ}, E-mail: {econ@state.ma.us}. *Key Economic Indicators, Municipal Profiles, Municipal Employment Data, Municipal Tax Rates, Local Financial Data, Laborforce/Unemployment Rate, Employment in Industries, Commonwealth Communities, Massachusetts Production Guide, The Massachusetts Film Office Fee-Free Location Book.*

Michigan
Economic Development Corporation, 201 North Washington Square, 4th Floor, Lansing, MI 48913; 517-373-9808; {http://medc.michigan.org}. *Trends in Michigan Agriculture, Building the Michigan Life Sciences Corridor, State Smart: Michigan, Gold Collar Jobs, Economic Development Job Training Grants, Michigan Economic Diversification Study, New Businesses Created in Michigan, Cyber-State, Gross State Product, County Profiles, Population Estimates, County Business Patterns, Detailed Economic Data by Kind of Business, Selected Population and Housing Characteristics, Social and Economic Data, Detailed Agricultural Data For State and County Level Geography* ($50), *Michigan Manufacturers Profile* (price varies), *Michigan Construction Industries Profile, Census of Agricultural Data, Social and Economic Data.*

Minnesota
State Planning Agency, 658 Cedar Street, St. Paul, MN 55155; 612-296-3985; {www.mnplan.state.mn.us}, E-mail: {minnesota.planning@mnplan.state.mn.us}. *Hogs and Bumper Crops Boost Farm Sales in 1977, East Grand Forks Area Population Most Affected By 1977 Flood, Turn of the Century: Minnesota's Population in 1900 and Today, Estimates of Immigrants Populations in Minnesota, Minnesota Labor Shortages are Likely to Continue, Minnesota School Enrollment Projected to Peak in 1999-2000, Smart Signals: Property Tax Reform for Smart Growth, Smart Signals: An Assessment of Progress Indicators, Cash Flows: Minnesota's Fiscal Geography, Staying Within Our Means, Choosing a Consultant for Local Planning, Sustainable Communities and Land Use, Economics and Incentives, 1999 Children's Report Card, Suffer the Children, Ideas for Welfare Reform Minnesota Homicides, Tracking Crimes: Analyzing Minnesota Criminal History Records, Governor's Workforce Development Framework: Making Minnesota a World Competitor in the 21st Century, Balancing the Books: Affording College in Minnesota, Class Schedule: New Approaches in Minnesota Schools, Degrees of Excellence: Higher Education in Minnesota, A Course for the Future: Higher Educational and Economic Development, Educating Spending, Smart Signals: Economic for Lasting Progress, Preparing for Minnesota Water Plan 2000, Progress, EQB Monitor* (bi-weekly), *Scoping Document: Generic Environmental Impact Statement on Animal Agriculture, 1999 Annual Report: The Minnesota Governor's Council on Geographic Information, Positional Accuracy Handbook: Using the National Standard for Spatial Data Accuracy to Measure and Report Graphic Data Quality, Status Report: Priority GIS Data, Making Plans: Community Based Plannings-First 2 Years, The Initiative Funds of Minnesota, Regional Development Commissions, Minnesota Issue Watch* (electronic newsletter).

Mississippi
Department of Economic Development, Communications Office, P.O. Box 849, Jackson, MS 39205; 601-359-3449, Fax: 601-359-5505; {www.mississippi.org/decd/homepage.htm}. *Mississippi Department of Economic and Community Development: An Overview, Mississippi Finance Programs, Mississippi: We Can Do That, Industry Publications (Telecommunications, Chemical, Plastics, Forestry and Pharmaceutical), Mississippi Spec Express, International Overview Brochure, Export Financing Brochure, Quality of Life, International Services, 1997-98 Whirlpool Manufacturing States Comparative Report Slide, Videos: Harmonies: A Mississippi Overture, Mississippi On The Move, On the Move in Mississippi, Move It To Mississippi, Mississippi: Center of the Americas.*

Missouri
Department of Economic Development, P.O. Box 118, 301 West High, Room 770, Jefferson City, MO 65102; 573-751-9064; {www.ecodev.state.mo.us}. *1999 Economic Overview, Community Development Program Information Booklet, Missouri Business and Economic News, Missouri Stock Price Index, Community Profiles.* Services: Product Finder, Buildings Query, Business Location and Expansion Service.

Montana
Census and Economic Information Center, Department of Commerce, 1424 9th Avenue, Helena, MT, 59602; 406-444-2896, Fax: 406-444-1518; {http://commerce.state.mt.us/ceic}, E-mail: {CEIC@state.mt.us}. *Business Locations Assistance, County Business Patterns, Economic Censuses, Major Employers in Selected Montana Cities/Counties, Minority and Women Owned Businesses-Montana, Montana Companies 100 Million Dollars and Over, Top Ten Employers, Montana at a Glance, Montana by the Numbers, Population Projections, Montana County Statistical Reports, Bear Facts, Economic Census, Export Data.*

Nebraska
Department of Economic Development, 301 Centennial Mall South, P.O. Box 94666, Lincoln, NE 68509; 402-471-3111, 800-426-6505, TDD: 402-471-3441, Fax: 402-471-3778; {www.ded.state.ne.us}, E-mail: {alw@neded.org}. *Nebraska Databook, Nebraska Quarterly Business Conditions Survey, Recent Nebraska Economic Trends, Nebraska's Economic Performance, Summary of New and Expanding Business Survey-1999, Nebraska Travel and Tourism Facts, Nebraska Exports by Industry, Nebraska Communities with a Local Sales Tax, Nebraska Tax Exempt Organizations.*

Nevada
Center for Business and Economic Research, University of Nevada, Las Vegas, 4505 Maryland Parkway, BEH 205, Box 456002, Las Vegas, NV 89154-6002; 702-895-3191, Fax: 702-895-3606; {www.unlv.edu/Research_Center/cber}, E-mail: {cber@nevada.edu}. *Economic Outlook 2000, Clark County Population Forecasts, Southern Nevada Business Directory, 1999 Historical Prospectives of Southern Nevada, We, the Southern Nevada, Migration Statistics Summary, Statistical Summary of Housing Market Conditions, Quarterly Housing Market Condition, 2000 Nevada Kids Count Data Book.*

New Hampshire
Division of Economic Development, Business and Industrial Development, 172 Pembroke Road, P.O. Box 1856, Concord, NH 03302-1856; 603-271-2591, Fax: 603-271-6784; {www.ded.state.nh.us/obid}, E-mail: {dedinfo@dred.state.nh.us}. Services: OBID Industrial Property Database, New Hampshire Manufacturers Database, Community Economic Development Web Crawler. Publications: *Why Relocate to New Hampshire, State to State Comparisons, General Fact Sheet Information, Property and Community Information.*

New Jersey
Department of Commerce and Economic Development, Economic Research, P.O. Box 824, Trenton, NJ 08625-0824; 609-777-0885; {www.state.nj.us/commerce/dcedhome.htm}. Services: Business Resource Center. Publications: *Annual Report Dredging Project, Facilitation Task Force: Policy and Procedures, Foreign Trade Zones, Let George Do It, New Jersey Filmography.*

New Mexico
Economic Development Department, 1100 St. Francis Drive, Santa Fe, NM 87503; 505-827-0236, Fax: 505-827-0211; {www.edd.state.nm.us}, E-mail: {orlinda@edd.state.nm.us}. *1999 Annual Report, Action Plan, Factbook, 1998 Export Summary, New Mexico Industrial Building/Site Inventory.*

New York
Empire State Development, State Data Center, 30 South Pearl Street, Albany, NY 12245; 518-292-5300, Fax: 518-292-5806, Fax-on-Demand: 518-292-5844; {www.empire.state.ny.us/nysdc}, E-mail: {esdwebmaster@empire.state.ny.us}. *The Economic Impact of Empire State Development's Top 100 Projects, New York State's Technology-Driven Industries: Biotechnology and Pharmaceuticals, 1990 Census Profiles, 1985-1990 Migration, Current Population Survey, Population Estimates, Economic Census Data, Business Fact Book, Price Indexes, County Business Patterns, Gross State Product, Productivity, New Business Incorporations in New York State 1984-August 1999* (monthly), *F.W. Dodge's Value of Construction Contracts in New York State 1992-August 1999* (monthly), *Government Information Quarterly, Employment/Labor Force/Wages, 1998 State Personal Income Data, County Personal Income Data.*

North Carolina
Department of Commerce, 301 North Wilmington Street, Raleigh, NC 27020-0571; 919-733-7651; {www.commerce.state.nc.us}. *Executive Summary-A Guide to Incorporating Your Business in North Carolina, Financial Advantages, State and Local Taxes, 1999 Economic Development Resource Guide, International Firms Directory, State Comparisons, County Profiles, Regional Information, Industry Profiles, North Carolina Economic Trends: a Quarterly Report on Key Economic Indicators, Population Estimates and Projections.*

North Dakota
Department of Economic Development and Finance, 1833 East Bismarck Expressway, Bismarck, ND 58504; 701-328-5300, Fax: 701-328-5320; {www.growingnd.com/index.html}, E-mail: {ndedf@state.nd.us}. *North Dakota You Should See Us Now...Details for Business and Industry, North Dakota You Should See Us Now...Imaging Piece, State of North Dakota New Business Registration Form, North Dakota Directory of Manufacturers and Food Processors, North Dakota Tax Incentives for Business, Financing North Dakota's Future, North Dakota Development Fund/Regional Rural Development Revolving Loan Fund, North Dakota Manufacturing Technology Partnership, Where to Find Information for Value-Added Production Possibilities-A Guide for North Dakotans, North Dakota Rural Development Council, Mini-Grants for Research and Development, Large North*

State Forecasting Agencies

Dakota Highway Maps, North Dakota International Trade Program Services, Developing Success-Simplifying the Filing Process, North Dakota Women's Business Development Program Packets, North Dakota Native American Program, Native American Business Guide, Native American Businesses, Grants for Native American Businesses, Native American Equity Grant Program.

Ohio
State of Ohio, Department of Development, Office of Strategic Research, P.O. Box 1001, Columbus, OH 43216; 614-466-2115, 800-848-1300, ext. 2115; {www.odod.state.oh.us/osr}. *Ohio Economic Overview, Ohio's Economy: A Chartbook* ($15), *Ohio Gross State Product* ($15), *Exports with Ohio As State of Origin of Movement* ($20), *Major Ohio Employers*, ($5), *Ohio Business Expansions and Attractions* ($25), *Foreign Companies with Operations in Ohio* ($40), *Ohio Women and Minority Owned Business Enterprises* ($10), *Ohio Industry Series* ($20-25), *Ohio Job Creation Tax Credit Program* ($10), *Enterprise Zone Reports* ($10), *Population by Race and Governmental Unit* ($15), *Net Migration by Age and Sex for State and Counties* ($10), *1990-2015 County Population, Data Line Ohio* ($20 annual subscription), *Ohio Statistical Abstract* ($25).

Oklahoma
Department of Commerce, 6601 Broadway, P.O. Box 26980, Oklahoma City, OK 73126-0980; 405-841-9770, 800-879-6552; {www.odoc.state.ok.us}. *Aerospace Manufacturer's Business and Incentives Tax Guide, Demographic State of the State, Folio* (newspaper), *Indian Land Tax Incentive, Marketing Materials, Oil and Gas Directory, Oklahoma's Resource Directory, Oklahoma Community Developer, Oklahoma Entrepreneur Portfolio, Oklahoma Capital Review.*

Data & Statistics: 800-652-8779, 405-815-5284; E-mail: {info@odoc.state.ok.us}. *Agricultural Overview, Business Overview, Business Reports, Construction Overview, Demographics, Education, Finance, Insurance and Real Estate, Forecast on the Oklahoma and National Economies, Foreign Trade Overview, Government Abstract, Income Summary, Labor Force Review, Manufacturing Overview, Mining Overview, National Economic Review, Oklahoma Services Overview, Transportation, Communications and Utilities, Wage and Salary Employment Overview.*

Demographic Forum: 405-815-5184; E-mail: {jeff-wallace@odoc.state.ok.us}. *State Data Center, County Population Estimates, City Population Estimates, State Estimates, Population Projections, Income, Poverty and Wages, GIS Links, 1990 Census, 1997 Economic Census, Kids Count Factbook, ORIGENS database, Student Information.*

Industrial Parks: 405-815-5144; E-mail: {donna_brown@odoc.state.ok.us}. Listed by City.

Community Profiles: 800-879-6552. Listed by City.

Manufacturers Directory: 405-815-5183. 2000 Edition.

Oregon
Art Announcements ($1.50, 503-986-0088), *Arts Commission News* (503-986-0088), *Arts Sponsors in Oregon* ($7, 503-986-0088), *Doing Business in Oregon-New 1999 Edition* (503-986-0160), *Top 25 Private Sector Employers in Oregon as of May 1998* (503-986-0150), *Community Development in Oregon: Applicants Handbook for the Oregon Community Development Block Grant Program* (503-986-0122), *Developing Communities in Oregon, Project Awards by County* (503-986-0122), *Oregon Enterprise Zone Information* (503-986-0140), *Oregon Film Location Brochure* (503-229-5832), *Oregon Film and Video Relocation Packet* (503-229-5832), *Natural Resource Agencies Permits and Licensing Directory* (503-986-0200), *Oregon Ports Brochure* (503-986-0243), *Economic Profile of Oregon* ($3.50, 503-986-0111), *Oregon County Economic Indicators, 1992-2997* ($3.50, 503-986-0111), *Summary of Oregon Taxes* (503-986-0150), *Ad Conversion Studies* ($10, 503-986-0000), *Annual Economic Impact Reports for Oregon Travel* ($10, 503-986-0000), *Oregon Tourism Commission Marketing Plan, 1995-97* ($5, 503-986-0000), *Plan for the Tourism Industry* ($5, 503-986-0000), *Travel Industry Employment in Oregon* ($10, 503-986-0000), *Guide and Workbook for Dislocated Workers in Oregon* (800-282-6514).

Pennsylvania
Department of Community and Economic Development, 455 Forum Building, Harrisburg, PA 17120; 717-787-3003; {www.dced.state.pa.us}, E-mail: {DCED@dced.state.pa.us}. *Business Resource Network; Entrepreneur's Guide.*

South Carolina
Department of Commerce, P.O. Box 927, Columbia, SC 29202; 803-737-0238, Fax: 803-727-0418; {www.callsouthcarolina.com}, E-mail: {webrequests@commerce.state.sc.us}. *Automotive and Related Industry, Labor Availability in South Carolina, Plastics in South Carolina, Manufacturing Excellence, South Carolina's Advantages for European Manufacturers, Corporate Office Facilities, SC Community Profiles, Legal Issues for Investors in SC, SC Department of Commerce Annual Report, South Carolina Commerce Magazine* (quarterly), *Resource Guide for Existing Industry, International Films in South Carolina, Metal Working Companies in South Carolina, Directory of Exports from South Carolina* (803-737-0238), *Distribution and Transportation in South Carolina* ($20, 803-737-0238), *South Carolina Industrial Directory* ($65, 803-737-0238), *SC Business Incentives, SC Property Tax Rates for 1998 by County, 1999 Tax Incentives for Economic Development, Strategic Plan for South Carolina.*

South Dakota
Governor's Office of Economic Development, Capitol Lake Plaza, 711 East Wells Avenue, Pierre, SD 57501-3369; 605-773-5032; {www.state.sd.us/oed}. *South Dakota Profile, South Dakota Communities, South Dakota Made, Manufacturing-Economic Indicators, Agriculture-Economic Indicators, Industrial Parks and Properties, Marketing Checklist.*

Tennessee
Department of Economic and Community Development, Rachel Jackson Building, 320 6th Avenue North, Nashville, TN 37243-0405; 615-741-2626, Fax: 615-532-8715; {www.state.tn.us/ecd}, E-mail: {srhea@mail.state.tn.us}. *County Profiles, Community Datasheets, Transportation Overview, Manufacturing Profiles* (specify profile topic), *Annual Investment Figures, Population Figures, List of Corporate Headquarters in Tennessee, Tennessee by Vital Statistics Categories.*

Texas
Comptroller of Public Accounts, P.O. Box 13528, Capitol Station, Austin, TX 78711-3528; 512-463-4000; {www.window.state.ts.us}, E-mail: {research@cpa.state.tx.us}. *Texas School Performance Review Reports, Challenging the Status Quo, Texas Performance Review Reports, Texas and 2000, Community Reinvestment in Texas, Special Economic Reports, Tax Publications, Audit Manuals, Property Tax Reports, Tax Exemptions and Tax Incidence, 2000-01 Certifications Revenue Estimate, Texas Revenue History by Source, Texas Expenditure History by Function, Texas 1999 State Expenditure by County, 1998 Comprehensive Annual Financial Report, 1999 Annual Cash Report, State Accounting Materials, Bond Appendix, Financial Management Review, Economic Development Corporation Report, Sheriffs and Constables Fees Manual, E-Newsletter* (twice-a-month), *Fiscal Notes, Texas Innovator* (monthly newsletter), *Keeping an Eye on Texas, Texas: Where We Stand, Tax Policy News, Statewise* (monthly news), *Local Sales and Use Tax Reports, Statement* (property tax issues newsletter), *City and County Financial Management Newsletter, Texas Economic Update, State Economic Forecast, Texas Fast Forward.*

Utah
Governor's Office of Planning and Budget, Demographic and Economic Analysis, 116 State Capitol, Salt Lake City, UT 84114; 801-538-1027, Fax: 801-538-1547; {www.governor.state.ut.us/gopb}, E-mail: {lhillman@gov.state.ut.us}. *Utah Annual Report of the State Olympic Officer Relating to the 2002 Olympic Winter Games, Utah Data Guide, Federal Land Payment in Utah, Scenario Analysis: Executive Summary, Utah Skier Visit Analysis, 2002 Olympic Winter Games: Economic, Demographic and Fiscal Impacts, 2002 Olympic Winter Games: Estimated Local Government Olympic Revenues, Baseline Scenario, Utah Ski Database, QGET Data Book, Tourism Potential in Garfield and Emery Counties, Utah Population Estimated Methodology, Employment and Population Impacts of Circle Four Farms: Four Development Scenarios, Race and Ethnicity Data, Micron's Utah Valley Plant: The Economic Projection Model System, Utah in the 1990's: A Demographic Perspective.*

Vermont
Department of Economic Development, Agency of Commerce and Community Development, National Life Building, Drawer 20, Montpelier, VT 05620-0501; 800-VERMONT, 802-828-3080, Fax: 802-828-3258; {www.thinkvermont.com}. *1999 Report by the Vermont Economic Progress Council, 2000 Report on Economic Advancement Tax Incentives, The Guide to Doing Business in Vermont, Vermont Wood Manufacturers Association Listing.*

Virginia
Virginia Economic Development Partnership, P.O. Box 798, Richmond, VA 23218-0798, 901 East Byrd Street, Richmond, VA 23219-4068; 804-371-8100, 800-828-1120, Fax: 804-371-8112; {www.yesvirginia.org}. *The Virginia Strategy, Guide to Establishing a Business, Guide to Local Taxes on Business, Guide to Business Incentives.*

Washington
Washington State, Community Trade and Economic Development, Office of Economic Development, 906 Columbia Street, SW, P.O. Box 48300, Olympia, WA 98504-8300, 760-586-1924, 800-237-1233, Fax: 760-586-0873; {www.cted.was.gov}. *1991-98 Travel Impacts and Visitor Volume, Building Your Hometown's Future,*

Market Studies, Demographics and Statistics

Business and Job Retention Program Biennium Report, Business Opportunities in Washington State, Community Development Block Grant Float Loans, Canadian Travel to Washington State, Child Care Advantages, Coastal Loan Fund, Community Economic Revitalization Board 1996 Legislative Report, Development Loan Fund, Economic Development Plan-Columbia River Gorge National Scenic Area, Economic Impacts and Net Economic Values Associated with Non-Indian Salmon and Sturgeon Fisheries 1998, Employment and Sales Growth in Washington State, Employee-Ownership Companies: A Comparative Analysis, Washington Entrepreneur's Guide, Guide for Small Businesses, How Are Your Company's Vital Signs, Infrastructure Financing for Small Communities in Washington State, How to Create Jobs Now and Beyond 2000, Learning to Lead: A Primer on Economic Development Strategies, Certified Minority and Women Owned Businesses, Minority and Women's Business Development Program, Regional Economic Diversification Studies for National Forest Areas of Washington State 1990-91, The RACE to RECRUIT: Strategies for Successful Business Attraction, The Brownsfields Resource Guide, Washington State Lodging Tax Report, Washington State Tourism Bulletin, Washington State Visitor Profile, Wealth and Income consequences of Employee Ownership: A Comparative Study for Washington State.

West Virginia

West Virginia Development Office, Research and Strategic Planning, Capitol Complex, Building 6 Room 553, 1900 Washington Street, East, Charleston, WV 25305-0311; 304-558-2234, Fax: 304-558-0449; {www.wvdo.org}, E-mail: {wvdo@wvdo.org}. *1998 Annual Report West Virginia Council for Community and Economic Development, Target Industry Brochures, West Virginia Portfolio, the Polymer Alliance Zone, West Virginia (CD ROM), 1990 Decennial Census Reports and Maps, 1995-1996 West Virginia Statistical Abstract, Annual Survey of Manufacturers, County Business Patterns.*

West Virginia Bureau of Business and Economic Research, College of Business and Economic, WV University, P.O. Box 6025, Morganstown, WV 26506; 304-293-5834; {www.be.wvu.edu/serve/bureau/index.htm}, E-mail: {moore@be.wvu.edu.directory}. *West Virginia Economic Outlook* ($15), *Eastern Panhandle Region Outlook 1998-2003* ($10), *Parkersburg MSA Outlook 1998-2003*, ($10), *North Central Region Outlook 1998-2003* ($10), *Preston County Outlook 1998-2003* ($10), *Harrison, Marion and Monogalia County Outlook 1998-2003* ($10), *Charleston MSA Outlook 1998-2003* ($10), *Economic Prospects of the Central West Virginia Chemical Industry* ($20), *Economic Impact of Mountaineer Race Track and Gaming Resort FY 1998* ($20), *The 11th Annual West Virginia County Data Profiles* ($12-350), *Economic Impact of WVHTCF Member Companies and Federally Supported Facilities in North Central WV 1996-1997* ($10), *West Virginia Economic Outlook Long-Term Forecast 1998-2008* ($15), *Aspects of the Polymer Alliance Zone* ($15), *Economic Impact of Historic Preservation in W.V.* ($20), *Potomac Highlands Region Labor Market Study* ($15), *Economic Impact of the Wood Products Industry: West Virginia 1995* ($15), *The State of Manufacturing in West Virginia-1995* ($10), *Economic Impacts of Retirees and Retirement Communities* ($10), *Business and Economic Review Subscription* (free).

Wisconsin

Department of Commerce, 201 W. Washington Avenue, P.O. Box 7970, Madison, WI 53703; 608-266-1018, Fax Request Hotline: 608-264-6154 (24 Hours); {www.commerce.state.wi.us}. *Going into Business in Wisconsin: An Entrepreneur's Guide* ($5), *A Start-Up Guide for International Business, Directory of Local Development Partners* ($4), *Financial Resources for Businesses and Communities, Growing A Business? There's Help, Technical Resources for Businesses and Communities, Technology Resources for Businesses in Wisconsin* ($3.50), *Wisconsin's 1998-99 Minority-Owned Businesses Directory* ($15), *Business Tax Chronology, Community Economic Profiles* (specify Community), *County Economic Profiles* (specify County), *Recycling Market Development Programs, Wisconsin Economic Profile, What a Difference a Decade Makes!, Wisconsin Community Preparedness Manual.*

Wyoming

Department of Administration and Information, Division of Economic Analysis, 327 East Emerson Building, 2001 Capitol Avenue, Cheyenne, WY 82002-0060; 307-777-7504, Fax: 307-777-5852; {http://eadiv.state.wy.us}. *Outlook 2000: Joint Economic and Demographic Forecast to 2008, Wyoming Cost of Living Index, Wyoming and all Counties Income, Employment and Gross State Product, Wyoming Sales, Use and Lodging Tax Revenue Report, Wyoming State Data Center Newsletter, Consensus Revenue Estimating Group-Monthly Report, Consensus Revenue-State Revenue Forecast, Equality State Almanac, Monthly Wyoming Economic Conditions, Wyoming 1999, Just the Facts, 1990 Census of Wyoming Population and Housing, Population Estimates and Forecasts, Wyoming GIS Resources Page, Wyoming Housing Database Information.*

State Division of Motor Vehicles

State Division of Motor Vehicles

Back in 1990, when I published the first edition of this book, you could, for example, purchase a list that included the names and addresses of all the males aged 16-40 who drove sport utility vehicles and lived in the upscale suburbs of your city. Wouldn't those names be great to know if you sold ski equipment or were setting up a clinic to treat sports injuries? Especially if you could buy the list for less than $500!

It used to be as easy as making a few phone calls and sending a check to your state's division of motor vehicles, but not any more. Now, don't get me wrong, you may still be able to get information from your DMV, but it's not going to be as complete or up-to-date as it once was.

When you get your driver's license or renew your license tags, you give the state a gold mine of information--not just your name and address, but also your age, sex, medical information, weight, social security number, and even a photograph. Your vehicle registration tells what make, model, and year car you drive.

This data is used in countless ways by direct marketers and researchers for compiling statistics. The government uses it for all sorts of transportation studies and auto pollution reports. Manufacturers access the data for recalls and warranty programs, while insurance companies, financial institutions, and other businesses thrive on this cross sectioning of the driving public. In the early 1990s, New York State alone made about $17 million a year selling this information to commercial databases, which in turn, sorted and sold data to direct marketers, private investigators and journalists.

However, a growing number of people nationwide began to complain that it was wrong for the state to require its residents to provide information for the purpose of licensing, then have the government turn around and sell facts that tell a lot about you to organizations that had nothing to do with your authorization to drive.

Privacy advocates gained the spotlight in Los Angeles, when, in 1989, a stalker came to the home of sitcom star Rebecca Schaeffer and shot her to death when she answered the door. Her murderer had obtained her address from the California Department of Motor Vehicles.

In 1994, Congress passed the Driver's Privacy Protection Act (DPPA), which gave states until 1997 to devise a system in which drivers could prevent the states from selling personal data for commercial purposes. Most states chose an "opt-out" statement, which a driver could sign to forbid the sale of his or her personal information. In Kansas, almost one third of the state's drivers chose to close their records to the public during the first months of the program. Nevertheless, that still left a huge pool of driver and vehicle information accessible to the public.

Congress put the pressure on DMVs again in October 1999 when it amended the DPPA, adding even tighter measures. As a result, after June 1, 2000, the states may not sell any information in driver and vehicle databases for commercial purposes unless the driver has specifically given his permission, or "opted in," to the sale of personal information. A group of states, led by South Carolina, appealed to the U.S. Supreme Court, but in January 2000 the court ruled that the DPPA was constitutional, thus removing the last obstacle to enforcement of the DPPA.

What does this mean for the many organizations that use DMV databases?

* Existing databases, i.e., those sold for commercial purposes before June 1, 2000, can still be used, but over time their accuracy will diminish as drivers change addresses and purchase new vehicles.
* You'll still be able to search for information on any driver who has given permission for his personal information to be released.
* There are still lots of exceptions to the privacy rules. For example, states are still required to release information to government agencies and others for use in court or law enforcement, for insurers investigating claims, for research purposes if personal information is not published or used to contact individual drivers, and for alerting vehicle owners to auto recalls, polluting auto emissions, or other safety issues.
* Much of this information will continue to be available from other sources, although it will not be as easy and inexpensive to acquire.
* Some states already restrict access to these databases and have not sold information for commercial use for many years.

Information derived from a state's automobile owner registration databases is usually available in two formats--magnetic tape or computer printouts. Most states prefer sending you a tape for larger files, while printouts are allowed for shorter sorts. In addition, some states offer mailing labels for an additional charge. The most likely sorting options include: an entire state file; all vehicles within a county; vehicle type (two-door, four-door, four-wheel drive) by state or county; and vehicle make or year by state or county.

Driver's license information can usually be extracted to provide name and license number; name, license number, and address; and a variety of other variables such as age and gender.

Motor Vehicle Offices

Alabama

Drivers: Alabama Department of Public Safety, Drivers License Division, P.O. Box 1471, Montgomery, AL 36172; 334-242-4400. This data is not released for commercial purposes. Individuals may retrieve information. A form is required and it must be notarized. The cost is $5.75 per request. {http://www.dps.state.al.us}

Registered vehicles: Alabama Department of Revenue, Motor Vehicle Division, P.O. Box 327610, Montgomery AL 36132; 334-242-9000. This data is not released for commercial purposes. Individuals may retrieve information. A form is required. The cost is $15 per individual record. {http://www.ador.state.al.us/motorvehicle/MVD_MAIN.html}

Market Studies, Demographics And Statistics

Arizona
Drivers and registered vehicles: Arizona Motor Vehicles Division, 1801 W. Jefferson St., Phoenix, AZ 85007; 602-255-0072; {http://www.dot.state.az.us/MVD/mvd.htm} The Arizona drivers data is not available for commercial purposes. Individuals can retrieve information. Request must be made in writing with complete name, license number and date and birth. The cost is $3 for a 39-month check, $5 for a five-year check. The database for Arizona owners contains owner's name and address, plus make, model, year, tag and license numbers for 3,667,819 cars and 489,664 other vehicles. A mailing list is available for $3,500, or a computer tape can be purchased and data sorted by name and address. Tapes cost $30 per 1,000 names received. Contact Bill Foutch 602-712-4667.

Arkansas
Drivers and registered vehicles: Arkansas Office of Motor Vehicle Registration, P.O. Box 1272, Little Rock, AR 72203; 501-682-7060; {http://www.state.ar.us/dfa/motorvehicle/driverservices.html} License information is protected under the state's Privacy Act. A release must be signed by the license holder before data can be released. The cost is $1 per request. The Arkansas Automobile Owners database contains the owner's name and address, plus make, model, year and license number for more than 15 million automobiles and approximately 300,000 other vehicles including motorcycles and boats. No data tapes are released. Records are open for public inspection at the office only.

California
Drivers and registered vehicles: Department of Motor Vehicles, Office of Information Services, Public Operations, Unit-G199, P.O. Box 944247, Sacramento, CA 94244-2470; {http://www.dmv.ca.gov/dmv.htm}. Vehicle, vessel, driver license and identification (ID) card records are open to public inspection. Confidential information, such as social security numbers and residence addresses, may only be disclosed to a court or law enforcement agency when they are authorized by a specific federal or state statute. To request information, complete a Vehicle/Vessel Registration Information Request form (INF 70-R/2) for a vehicle or vessel record or a Driver License/Identification Card Record Request form (INF 70-D/2) for a driver license or ID card record. Mail your request with the appropriate fees ($5 per request) to the above address.

Colorado
Drivers and registered vehicles: Driver Services Division, 1881 Pierce St., Lakewood, CO 80214; 303-205-5823, 303-205-5745, 303-205-5762. Unless someone has requested confidentiality, you can search for the state's drivers license database by name or drivers license number for $2.20 per request using Form DR 2489. (You can pull this form off the Internet at http://www.state.co.us/gov_dir/revenue_dir/MV_dir/driverforms.html.) You can purchase lists of a minimum of 1,000 names for a $60 non-refundable request for services plus $35 per hour on a cartridge or $25 in media or paper form. Every additional 1,000 names costs another $35 or $25 respectively. The $60 request for services fee will be applied to the cost of a project if your request is approved.

Connecticut
Drivers and registered vehicles: Connecticut State Department of Motor Vehicles, 60 State Street, Wethersfield, CT 860-263-5154. {http://dvmct.org/copypg.htm}.

Delaware
Drivers and registered vehicles: Delaware Motor Vehicles Division, P.O. Box 698, Dover, DE 19903; 302-744-2500. Information on drivers' names, addresses, and other information is available, along with vehicle owners' names, addresses, and vehicle make, model, year, title number and expiration date. The cost is $11.50 per 1,000 records, with a minimum charge of $350 to be paid up front.

District of Columbia
Drivers and registered vehicles: DC DMV, Driving Records office, 301 C Street NW, Room 1000, Washington, DC 20001; 202-727-5000, 202-727-5692; {http://dvm.dcgov.org/body_driver_records.htm}. The DC DMV will only release information to the following individuals: the driver of record with identification; the driver's representative (such as a spouse) with written authorization from the driver, and a copy of the driver's proof of identification; law enforcement representatives with documentation showing a connection to an investigation; government entities as part of an established activity requiring records, such as security clearances or investigations; attorneys with written authorization for releasing records from their clients; insurance company representatives with written authorization from their clients as part of an investigation; individuals or entities requesting information as part of the freedom of information act. The cost is $5 per record.

Florida
Vehicle Registration: Division of Motor Vehicles, Data Listings Unit, Room A126B, MS 73, 2900 Apalachee Parkway, Tallahassee, FL 32399; 850-488-6710; {http://hsmv.state.fl.us/othercomp.html}. You can find out a tremendous amount of information if you know a vehicle's tag number, decal number, title number or vehicle identification number: owner name and address, owner's date of birth, owner's sex, lienholder's name and address, lien date, tag number, title number, previous state of registration, decal expiration, vehicle identification number, year, make, body type, vehicle weight, tag issue date, title issue date, use, and odometer status. Fees range from 50¢ to $15, depending upon how much information is requested. You can purchase microfiche files providing the name, city of residence, date of birth and title number(s) for motor vehicles, boats and motor homes titled in the state of Florida. The cost is 20¢ per card, plus a $4.50 shipping and handling fee. You can also purchase listings of all vehicles registered in the state of Florida sorted by make of vehicle, model type, model year, county of residence or class code. Data are available on computer tape or printout. Purchase requires a $50 deposit, which is applied to the cost of 1¢ per record. Lists of licensed auto, recreational vehicle, or mobile home manufacturers or dealers. Add $4.50 for shipping and handling.

Georgia
Drivers and vehicle registration: Department of Public Safety, 959 East Confederate Avenue, Atlanta, GA 30316; 404-657-9300; {www.ganet.org/dps/drivers}. Georgia does not release driver information for commercial purposes. A Georgia Motor Vehicle Record may be purchased in person at the or at your local Georgia State Patrol post. Proper identification will be required. If obtaining a motor vehicle record other than your own, a notarized authorization form from the licensee, naming the person authorized to receive record, the full name, date of birth and Georgia driver's license number of the licensee is required. Three-year records cost $5, five-year records are $7. By mail, send a notarized letter requesting either a three-year or five-year MVR, and include you full name (as it appears on your driver's license), driver's license number, date of birth and complete mailing address to: Georgia Department of Public Safety, MVR Unit, Post Office Box 1456, Atlanta, Georgia 30371-2303. Requests made through the mail must have the licensee's signature notarized.

Hawaii
Hawaii does not release information. Division of Motor Vehicles and Licenses, 2455 S. Beretainia St., Honolulu, HI 96814. 808-973-2700.

Idaho
Drivers and registered vehicles: Idaho Transportation Department, Economics and Research Section, P.O. Box 7129, Boise, ID 83707-1129. 208-334-8741. {www2.state.id.us/idt/dmv/DS.htm}. Information may not be purchased for commercial use. The Idaho drivers database provides name, address, sex, date of birth, license type, expiration date, and county of origin for approximately 1 million Idaho drivers. Data may be selected by sex, age, county of residence.. Idaho owners database provides the registered owner, address, make, model, year, issue and expiration dates of approximately 1.3 million records. Data can be sorted by registration type and county of residence. The cost is $75 plus computer and shipping charges. Computer tape or printouts are available.

Illinois
Drivers: Illinois Secretary of State, Drivers Services Division, 2701 S. Dirkson Parkway, Springfield, IL 62723; 217-782-1970. The Illinois drivers database contains the name, address, owner's sex, make, model and year of more than 6 million passenger cars and 2 million other vehicles. Data can be sorted by various categories and provided on a computer tape for $200 plus $20 per 1,000 names, or on a printout for 50¢ per page (15,000 names or less). Information may not be purchased for commercial use.

Registered vehicles: Illinois Secretary of State, Centennial Building, Room 114, Springfield, IL 62756; 217-782-0029. The Illinois Automobile Owners database provides owner's name and address, make, model, and year of more than 6 million passenger cares and more than 2 million other vehicles. Complete records are available. Data can be sorted by various categories and provided on a computer tape for $200 plus $20 per 1,000 names, or on a printout for 50¢ per page (15,000 names or less). Information may not be purchased for commercial use.

State Division of Motor Vehicles

Indiana
Drivers: Indiana Bureau of Motor Vehicles, 100 N. Senate Avenue, Indianapolis, IN 46204; 317-232-2798. Although this information is not released for commercial purposes, individuals may request information in writing using State Form #43511 (available on the Internet at {http://www.state.in.us/bmv/info/forms/43511.pdf}). The cost is $4 per license.

Iowa
Drivers and registered vehicles: Iowa Department of Transportation, Driver Services, Park Fair Mall, 100 Euclid Avenue, P.O. Box 9204, Des Moines, IA 50306; 515-244-8725, 515-237-3110, 800-532-1121; {www.dot.state.ia.us/mvd/ovs/records.htm}. Unsorted data for more than 2.5 million drivers and vehicle information are available for $550. Purchaser must provide 20 blank tapes or 14 mainframe cartridges.

Kansas
Kansas offers two options for accessing drivers records and vehicle registration. Data is not released for commercial purposes. You may request information in person by appearing at the following office with the name and date of birth or license plate number of the person you are searching. The cost is $5 per request. Topeka Drivers License Bureau, 37th and Burlingame, Topeka, KS 66609; 785-296-5671 or 785-296-3621.

Or, you can access this information on-line by subscribing to the Information Network of Kansas (INK), signing a certificate promising you won't use the information for solicitation or marketing, and setting up an account with INK to pay a fee for each record you look up. For more information, contact Information Network of Kansas, 534 S. Kansas Avenue, Suite 1210, Topeka, KS 66603-3406; 800-4-KANSAS (800-452-6727); {www.ink.org/public/mrv}, {www.ink.org/public/about-ink/subscribe.html}.

Kentucky
Drivers: Any information must be requested by letter. Address to Ed Roberts, Commissioner, Department of Administrative Services, Room 903, State Office Building, 501 High Street, Frankfort, KY 40622.

Registered vehicles: Kentucky Transportation Cabinet, Division of Motor Vehicle Licenses, State Office Building, Room 205, Frankfort, KY 40622; 502-564-3298. Database: Kentucky Automobile Owners-provides owner's name and address along with make, model and year for more than 2 million vehicles. Data can be sorted by various categories. Computer tapes and printouts available for 2¢ per name plus programming costs ($510). Mailing labels can be purchased for $3.50 per 1,000 plus programming costs.

Louisiana
Drivers and registered vehicles: Department of Public Safety and Corrections, Office of Motor Vehicles, P.O. Box 64886, Baton Rouge, LA 70896; 225-925-6146, 225-925-4017; {http://www.dps.state.la.us/omv/home.html}. The Louisiana Drivers database provides name, address, height, weight, sex, and date of birth for more that 2.7 million drivers. The Louisiana Owners database provides owners' name, address, make, model and year, date of acquisition, new or used, and color for 4.5 million vehicles. Data can be sorted by various categories. Computer tapes or printouts are available. The cost is 3¢ per record, plus $500.

Maine
Drivers and registered vehicles: Information is available from Informe. Contact Informe, 1 Market Square, Station 101, Augusta ME 04330; 877-212-6500. You can reach the Maine Motor Vehicle Division at 101 Hospital Street, Station 29, Augusta, ME; 207-624-9264; {www.state.me.us/sos/bmv/dlc/dlchmpg.htm}. The Maine Drivers database provides name, address, date of birth, and sex of 800,000 drivers. The Maine Automobile Owners database contains the owner's name, address, and date of birth, along with make, model, year and identification number for 700,000 registered vehicles. The cost is 3¢ per record if you order the entire database. Sorted data costs 1¢ per record. Data can be sorted by variables and can be purchased on computer tape, printouts, or mailing labels.

Maryland
Drivers and registered vehicles: Maryland Motor Vehicle Division, 6601 Ritchie Highway, Room 200, Glen Burnie, MD 21062; 410-768-7665; {http://mva.state.md.us/}. The Maryland Drivers database contains name, address, date of birth, height, weight, and identification number of more than 2 million drivers. The Maryland Automobile Owners database provides owner's name and address along with make, manufacturer, and year for nearly 3 million passenger cars and 3 million other vehicles. Some insurance information is included, such as company and policy number. Data can be sorted by variables and is available on computer tape. The cost is $500 for the first 10,000 records and 5¢ for each additional record.

Massachusetts
Drivers and registered vehicles: Massachusetts Registry of Motor Vehicles, Production Control Department, 100 Nashua Street, Boston, MA 02114; 617-660-4330; {www.state.ma.us/rmv/privacy/faq.htm}. Searches cost $2,500 initially. The appropriate forms must be filled out and approved along with $2,500 payment. Detailed estimates will be provided. Data is delivered on cartridges.

Michigan
Drivers and registered vehicles: Michigan Department of State, Information Services Division, 208 N. Capitol Avenue, Lansing, MI 48918; 517-241-2782; {www.sos.state.mi.us/bdvr}. Any information other than your own records must be requested using a form provided by the division. Allow two weeks for delivery and up to four weeks for microfilm requests. The Michigan Drivers database provides names, addresses, date of birth, and sex for more than 6.8 million drivers. Data can be sorted by sex, date of birth, county, state, city and zip code. The Michigan automobile owners database provides owner's name and address with year, license number, made and model for 8.3 million registered vehicles. You can purchase sorted data for $64 per 1,000 names or unsorted data for $16 per 1,000. There is a $500 minimum charge. Data can be purchased on computer tape or printout.

Minnesota
Drivers and registered vehicles: Minnesota Department of Public Safety, Driver and Vehicle Services, Suite 191, 445 Minnesota St., St. Paul, MN 55101; 651-297-1714, 651-296-6911; {www.dps.state.mn.us/dvs/Records/general.htm}. The Minnesota Drivers database provides, name, address and sex for 3.4 million drivers. The Minnesota Automobile Owners database provides the owner's name and address along with the make, model and year for 5.4 million vehicles. The two databases can be purchased in their entirety for $5,000 each. Sorted data can cost as little as $300 for drivers and $250 for registration. You can access records by computer dial-up connection, computer listings or tapes.

Mississippi
Drivers: Mississippi Department of Public Safety/Data Processing, P.O. Box 950, Jackson, MS 39205; Drivers information: 601-987-1337; Vehicle registration: 601-923-7461. The Mississippi Drivers database contains the name, address, date of birth, race and sex of more than 1.9 million drivers.

Registered vehicles: Mississippi State Tax Commission Network, P.O. Box 960, Room 220, Jackson, MS 39205; 601-923-7461. The Mississippi Automobile Owners database provides a complete file, including the owner's name and address, make, model and year for 1.6 million registered vehicles. Custom information costs $300; an entire database costs $600. You must provide your own reels or tapes. Information may not be used for commercial purposes.

Missouri
Drivers and registered vehicles: Missouri Department of Revenue, Information Services Bureau, P.O. Box 41, Jefferson City, MO 65105; 573-751-0474; {http://dor.state.mo.us/}. The Missouri Drivers database contains the name, address, sex, date of birth, height, weight, eye color, restrictions, license number, class and county for 6 million drivers. The Missouri Owners database provides the name and address of registered owners, plus make, model, year, number of cylinders, type of fuel, license number, license expiration date and year for more than 10 million cars and other vehicles. Databases are ordered separately. There is a processing fee of $35 per database, plus a fee for programming time (typically about three or four hours) at $35 per hour. Records cost $4.30 per 1,000 up to 50,000 records. The cost drops to 30¢ per 1,000 beyond 50,000. Information can be recorded magnetic tape, CDs, or, for very small files, 3.5" diskettes. Paper and label printouts are also available.

Montana
Drivers: Records and Driver Control Bureau, 2nd Floor, Scott Hart Building, P.O. Box 201430, 303 N. Roberts, Helena, MT 59620; 406-444-3288; {www.doj.state.mt.us/mvd/recdriv.htm}. Information may be available for non-commercial purposes with authorization.

Market Studies, Demographics And Statistics

Registered vehicles: Montana Motor Vehicle Division, 1032 Buckskin Drive, Deerlodge, MT 59722; 406-846-6000. The Montana Automobile Owners database provides the owner's name and address along with year, make, model, body, color, serial number, and second owner for more than 1 million registered vehicles. Data is available on computer tape or printout. Montana charges a $300 set up fee, plus $30 for the first 1,000 records on diskette and every 1,000 thereafter. Printouts are $40 for each 1,000 records. Yearly updates are free after the initial purchase.

Nebraska
Nebraska does not release driver or registered vehicle information. Vehicles and Driver Records Division, State Office Building, 301 Centennial Mall South, Lincoln, NE 68509; 402-471-3909, 402-471-3906; {www.nol.org.home/DMV/index.htm}.

Nevada
Drivers and registered vehicles: Nevada Department of Motor Vehicles, 555 Wright Way, Carson City, NV 89711; 775-684-4830; {www.state.nv.us/dmv_ps}. The Nevada drivers database provides name, address, date of birth, height, and weight for more than one million drivers. Data can be sorted by county, zip code, date of birth and make of car. The Nevada owners database provides the owner's name and address along with make, model and year for more than 1 million vehicles. Data can be selected by county, zip code, or make of car. Data is available on computer tape or printout (up to 1 million names). Mailing labels are available for an additional fee. Cost is $2,500 for the entire file or $15 per 1,000 records for a partial listing. You must apply to purchase information; sometimes the sale of information is approved for commercial purposes.

New Hampshire
Drivers and registered vehicles: New Hampshire Department of Safety, Data Processing, 10 Hazen Drive, Concord, NH 03305; 603-271-2314. The New Hampshire Drivers database contains address, date of birth, gender, license type, endorsements (i.e., tanker, passenger, hazardous materials, double or triple trailer), and expiration date. The New Hampshire Owners database contains the owner's name and address along with make, model and year for more than 800,000 cars and 500,000 other vehicles. Data can be sorted by zip code, model or make. Printouts, mailing labels, and tapes all cost $150 plus 3¢ per record. The entire file costs $3,000. Estimates for sorts can be provided. All requests to purchase data must be in writing.

New Jersey
Drivers and registered vehicles: Motor Vehicle Services. Certified Information Unit, CN 146, Trenton, NJ 08666; 609-292-4102; {www.state.nj.us/mvs}. Requests must be in writing. The price per page is $10 per certified copy, $8 per uncertified copy. There are approximately 8 records per page.

New Mexico
Drivers and registered vehicles: New Mexico Taxation and Revenue Department, Motor Vehicle Division, P.O. Box 1028, Santa Fe, NM 87504-1028; 505-827-2294; {www.state.nm.us/tax/mvd_home.htm}. Data is not released.

New York
Drivers and registered vehicles: Department of Motor Vehicles, Data Preparation, ESP, Swan St., Albany, NY 12228; 518-473-5483; {www.nydmv.state.ny.us/abstract.htm}. Data is not released for commercial purposes.

North Carolina
Drivers and registered vehicles: North Carolina Division of Motor Vehicles, 1100 New Bern Avenue, Raleigh, NC 27697; 919-715-7000; {www.dmv.state.nc.us}. Data is not released for commercial purposes.

North Dakota
Drivers: North Dakota Drivers License and Traffic Safety Division, 608 East Boulevard Avenue, Bismarck, ND 58505-0700; 701-224-2725; {www.state.nd.us/dot/dnv.html}. The North Dakota drivers database provides name, address, date of birth and license number for 450,000 drivers. Special sort/extraction is available. The cost is $9 per 1,000 names with a $250 minimum. Mailing labels are also available for an extra fee.

Registered vehicles: North Dakota Department of Transportation, Motor Vehicle Service Division, 608 East Boulevard, Bismarck, ND 58505; 701-224-2725. The North Dakota automobile owners database provides owners' name, address, make, model. year, license number and expiration date for more than 360,000 cars and 390,000 other vehicles. Data can be sorted by variables and provided on computer tape for $50 plus $40 per 1,000 names. Mailing labels are available for an extra fee.

Ohio
Drivers and registered vehicles: Ohio Bureau of Motor Vehicles, Data Services, P.O. Box 16520, Columbus, OH 43266-0020; 614-752-7695; {www.state.oh.us/odps/division/bmv/bmv.html}. The Ohio drivers database includes the name, address, gender, date of birth, height, weight, hair color, eye color, zip code and some medical restrictions for more than 7.4 million drivers. The Ohio automobile owners database provides owners' name, address, make, model, year, license number, and expiration date for more than 9 million vehicles. Data can be sorted. It is available on computer tape for 75¢ per record, on diskette or CD for $23 for 10,952 records or less. Mailing labels are 8¢ each.

Oklahoma
Drivers and registered vehicles: Oklahoma Tax Commission, Motor Vehicles Division, 2501 N. Lincoln Boulevard, Oklahoma City, OK 73194; 405-425-2300 (drivers license), 405-521-3538 (vehicle registration); {www.dps.state.ok.us/dls}. For $1 the Tax Commission will match a name to a tag number. No other driver information is available. To request a name and tag number match, write to Bob Ricks, Commissioner, P.O. Box 11415, Oklahoma City, Oklahoma, OK 73136.

Oregon
Drivers and registered vehicles: Oregon Department of Transportation, Motor Vehicle Division, Records Policy Unit, 1905 Lana Avenue, N.E., Salem, OR 97314; 503-945-8906, 503-945-7950; {www.odot.state.or.us/dvm/index.htm}. The Oregon Drivers database contains the name, address, age, gender, and date of birth for more than 2 million drivers. The Oregon automobile owners database includes the owners name and address along with make, model, and year, for more than 2 million registered vehicles. Unsorted data is available for $700 for each database. It is available on cartridge or tape.

Pennsylvania
Drivers and registered vehicles: Bureau of Drivers License Information, Box 58691, Harrisburg, PA 17106; 717-787-2158; {www.dmv.state.pa.us/home/index}. Pennsylvania does not release records.

Rhode Island
Drivers and registered vehicles: Department of Motor Vehicles, State Office Building, Providence, RI 02903; 401-277-2064. Rhode Island does not release records.

South Carolina
Drivers and registered vehicles: South Carolina Highway Department, Public Transportation, P.O. Box 1498, Columbia, SC 29216-0028; 803-737-2004; {www.state.us/dps/dmv}. Drivers' records are not released. The South Carolina automobile owners database contains the name, address, city, state, zip, birth date, registration issue date, gender, class, endorsements and restrictions for 4.3 million auto owners. The records department does not sort the data. You must purchase the entire database for $5,000. Data is provided on tape or cartridges.

South Dakota
Drivers and registered vehicles: Division of Motor Vehicles, 118 W. Capitol St., Pierre, SD 57501; 605-773-3545; {www.state.sd.us/state/executive/der/dl/sddriver.htm}. Although you can purchase both the driver and registered vehicle databases, 50 percent of licensed South Dakota drivers have requested that their names be withheld from database sales. Each database costs somewhere in the range of $342 to $2,155 for a printed version, or $335 to 706 for a version on tape or cartridge. The maximum number of records you can purchase is 700,000. You must apply for permission to purchase the databases and receive authorization from the South Dakota DMV. To request an application form, write to the Division of Motor Vehicles, 445 E. Capitol Avenue, Pierre, SD 57501.

State Division of Motor Vehicles

Tennessee
Drivers and registered vehicles: Department of Safety Information System, 150 Foster, Nashville, TN 37249; 615-251-5322; {www.state.tn.us/safety}. The Tennessee drivers database contains the name address, date of birth, gender and physical characteristics of 4.1 million drivers. The Tennessee automobile owners database contains the owners name, address, model, make, year and tag number for 5 million vehicles. Data can be sorted by category. Computer processing costs $427.20 per CPU hour. Data is available on microfiche for 95¢ each, printouts for 60¢ per 1,000 lines, cartridges for $5 each, and diskettes for $2 each. Sale is subject to approval. Contact the Department of Safety Information for the necessary application form.

Texas
Drivers: Texas Department of Public Safety, Attn: L.I. and V.I., P.O. Box 4087, Austin, TX 78773; 512-424-2186; {www.dot.state.tx.us/vtinfo.htm}. The Texas drivers database provides the name, address, date of birth, and license number for more than 19 million drivers. Data can be sorted by category. The database costs $1,600 unsorted and is available on magnetic tape or cartridge.

Registered vehicles: Texas Department of Transportation, Division of Motor Vehicles, 40th and Jackson, Austin, TX 78779; 512-465-7611; {www.dot.state.tx.us/vtinfo.htm}. The Texas automobile owners database contains the owners name and address along with make, model, year, previous owner, and lien holder for 14 million vehicles. Sorting is not available. The database is sold in full. The cost is $17,156 up front or in weekly updates for $138 each over the course of a year.

Utah
Drivers: Department of Public Safety, Drivers License Division, 4501 S. 2700 West, 3rd Floor, P.O. Box 30560, Salt Lake City, UT 84130-0560; 801-965-4437. Utah does not release its drivers data base.

Vehicle registration: Utah State Tax Commission, Technical Management Division, 210 N 1950 W., Salt Lake City, UT 84134. The Utah automobile owners database provides owners name and address along with make, model and year for 1.9 million vehicles. Purchasing the database requires a $53 set-up fee, plus $200-300 for a CD (programmed to be sortable by the purchaser), $300 for a tape, or $1,000 for a printout.

Vermont
Drivers and registered vehicles: Vermont Department of Motor Vehicles, 120 State Street, Montpelier, VT 05603; 802-828-5432; {www.aot.state.vt.us/dmv/Miscellaneous/DVMhome/Vermont_DMV_Homepage.htm}. The Vermont drivers database contains the name, address, physical characteristics, license number and date of birth for 513,000 drivers. The Vermont automobile owners database provides the owners name and address along with make, model and year for 875,000 vehicles. The cost is $1 per record.

Virginia
Drivers and registered vehicles: Dealer and Information, P.O. Box 7412, Richmond, VA 23269; 804-367-1519; {www.dmv.state.va/webdoc/citizen/records/release.html}. Virginia does not release records.

Washington
Drivers and registered vehicles: Department of Licensing, Highways/Licensing Building, P.O. Box 3090, Olympia, WA 98507; 306-902-3726; {www.wa.gov/dol}. Driver records are not available. The Washington automobile owners database contains the owners name and address along with the make, model, year and class of vehicle. The database can be sorted alphabetically by the owners name or county.

West Virginia
Drivers and registered vehicles: West Virginia Department of Motor Vehicles, Bldg. 3, Room 113, Charleston, WV 25317; 304-558-2723. The West Virginia drivers database provides the name, address, height, weight, race, gender, and date of birth for 1.4 million drivers. The automobile owners database contains the owners name and address plus make, model and year for 1.4 million passenger cars and 246,000 other vehicles. Data cannot be sorted. The entire file must be purchased on computer tape for $2,200.

Wisconsin
Drivers and registered vehicles: Wisconsin Department of Transportation, 4802 Sheyboygan Avenue, P.O. Box 7918, Madison, WI 53711; 608-266-2353; {www.dot.state.wi.us/dmv/records.html}. As of April 2000, Wisconsin will not longer sell its driver or vehicle owner databases.

Wyoming
Drivers: Wyoming Department of Transportation, Attn: Driver Control, P.O. Box 1708, Cheyenne, WY 82003; 307-777-4710; {http://wydotweb.state.wy.us/Docs/Licenses/DriverServices.html}. The Wyoming drivers database provides the name, address, date of birth, Social Security number, status, expiration and issue date for 500,000 drivers. Magnetic tape costs $1 per record with a minimum charge of $100.

Registered vehicles: Wyoming Department of Transportation, Licensing Station, 5300 Bishop Boulevard, Cheyenne, WY 82009; 307-777-4810. The Wyoming automobile owners database is not available for purchase.

Selling Overseas: Foreign Markets

If you've found that the domestic market for your product or service is dwindling, it's time to consider broadening your sales base by selling overseas. Hey, it's not as complicated as you might think. There is a lot of information available to us in this country about other countries that isn't even available in that particular country. In other words, we have access to things like marketing trend reports on countries like Turkey that business people in Turkey can't even get hold of! Important expertise and assistance for new and more experienced exporters continue to increase at both the federal and state level.

That widget that you invented in your garage so many years ago is now found in every hardware store in this country — why shouldn't it be in every French hardware store? Or the line of stationery that sold so well for you in this country could definitely be a hit in British stores that specialize in selling fine writing papers. So how do you go about finding what countries are open to certain imports and what their specific requirements are? If you're smart, you go to the best source around — the government — and make it work for you.

Polypropylene In Countries That Don't Even Count People

A few years ago a Fortune 500 company asked us to identify the consumption of polypropylene resin for 15 lesser developed countries. It was a project they had been working on without success for close to a year. After telexing all over the world and contacting every domestic expert imaginable, we too came up empty handed. The basic problem was that we were dealing with countries that didn't even count people, let alone polypropylene resin.

Our savior was a woman at the U.S. Commerce Department named Maureen Ruffin, who was in charge of the World Trade Reference Room. Ms. Ruffin and her colleagues collect the official import/export statistical documents for every country in the world as soon as they are released by the originating countries. Although the data are much more current and more detailed than those published by such international organizations as the United Nations, the publications available at this federal reference room are printed in the language of origin. Because none of the 15 subject countries manufacture polypropylene resin, Ms. Ruffin showed us how to get the figures by identifying those countries which produce polypropylene and counting up how much each of them exported to the countries in question. To help us even further, she also provided us with free in-house translators to help us understand the foreign documents.

Exporter's Hotline

The Trade Promotion Coordinating Committee has established this comprehensive "one-stop shop" for information on U.S. Government programs and activities that support exporting efforts. This hotline is staffed by trade specialists who can provide information on seminars and conferences, overseas buyers and representatives, overseas events, export financing, technical assistance, and export counseling. They also have access to the National Trade Data Bank.

Trade Information Center 800-USA-TRADE
infoserv2.ita.doc.gov/tic.nsf

U.S. Department of Commerce 202-482-0543
Washington, DC 20230 Fax: 202-482-4473
TDD: 800-833-8723
www.doc.gov

Country Experts

If you are looking for information on a market, company or most any other aspect of commercial life in a particular country, your best point of departure is to contact the appropriate country desk officer at the U.S. Department of Commerce. These experts often have the information you need right at their fingertips or they can refer you to other country specialists that can help you.

U.S. and Foreign Commercial Services (FCS)
International Trade Administration
U.S. Department of Commerce, Room 2810
Washington, DC 20230 202-482-5777
Fax: 202-482-5013
www.ita.doc.gov/uscs

All the Department of Commerce/US & FCS field offices around the country are listed later in this chapter. (You will also find a separate roster of international trade offices maintained by the states.)

ITA Country Desk Officers

A
Afghanistan	202-482-2954	2029B
Albania	202-482-4915	3413
Algeria	202-482-1870	2039
Angola	202-482-4228	3021
Anguilla	202-482-2527	3021
Antigua/Barbuda	202-482-2527	3021
Argentina	202-482-1548	3021
Aruba	202-482-2527	3020
Australia	202-482-3696	2036
Austria	202-482-2920	3039
Armenia	202-482-2354	3318
Azerbaijan	202-482-2354	3318

B
Bahamas	202-482-2527	3021
Bahrain	202-482-5545	2039
Baltic States	202-482-3952	3318
Bangladesh	202-482-2954	2029B
Barbados	202-482-2527	3021
Belarus	202-482-2354	3318
Belgium	202-482-5401	3042
Belize	202-482-2527	3021

Country Experts

Benin	202-482-4228	3317
Bermuda	202-482-2527	3021
Bhutan	202-482-2954	2029B
Bolivia	202-482-1659	3029
Botswana	202-482-4228	3317
Brazil	202-482-3871	3017
Brunei	202-482-3875	2308
Bulgaria	202-482-4915	3413
Burkina Faso	202-482-4388	3317
Burma	202-482-3875	2308
Burundi	202-482-4388	3317

C

Cambodia	202-482-3875	2308
Cameroon	202-482-5149	3317
Canada	202-482-3103	3033
Cape Verde	202-482-4388	3317
Caymans	202-482-2527	3021
Central Africa Republic	202-482-4388	3020
Chad	202-482-4388	3317
Chile	202-482-1495	3017
China	202-482-2462	2317
Colombia	202-482-1659	3025
Comoro Islands	202-482-4564	3317
Congo	202-482-5149	3317
Costa Rica	202-482-2527	3021
Cuba	202-482-2527	3021
Cyprus	202-482-3945	3044
Czechoslovakia	202-482-2645	3143

D

D'Jibouti	202-482-4564	3317
Denmark	202-482-3254	3413
Dominica	202-482-2527	3021
Dominican Republic	202-482-2527	3021

E

Ecuador	202-482-1659	3025
Egypt	202-482-4441	2039
El Salvador	202-482-2527	3020
Equatorial Guinea	202-482-4228	3317
Ethiopia	202-482-4564	3317
European Community	202-482-5278	3036

F

Finland	202-482-3254	3413
France	202-482-8008	3042

G

Gabon	202-482-5149	3317
Gambia	202-482-4388	3317
Germany	202-482-2434	3409
Ghana	202-482-5149	3317
Greece	202-482-3945	3042
Grenada	202-482-2527	2039
Guadaloupe	202-482-2527	3021
Guatemala	202-482-2528	3021
Guinea	202-482-4388	3317
Guinea-Bissau	202-482-4388	3317
Guyana	202-482-2527	3021

H

Haiti	202-482-2521	3021
Hong Kong	202-482-3832	2317
Hungary	202-482-2645	3413

I

Iceland	202-482-3254	3037
India	202-482-2954	2029
Indonesia	202-482-3875	2308
Iran	202-482-1870	2039
Iraq	202-482-4441	2039
Ireland	202-482-2177	3039
Israel	202-482-1870	2039
Italy	202-482-2177	3045
Ivory Coast	202-482-4388	3317

J

Jamaica	202-482-2527	3021
Japan	202-482-2425	2318
Jordan	202-482-1857	2039

K

Kenya	202-482-4564	3317
Korea	202-482-4957	2308
Kuwait	202-482-1860	2039
Kazakhstan	202-482-2354	3318
Kyrgyzstan	202-482-2354	3318

L

Laos	202-482-3875	2308
Lebanon	202-482-1860	2039
Lesotho	202-482-4220	3317
Liberia	202-482-4388	3317
Libya	202-482-5545	2039
Luxembourg	202-482-5401	3046

M

Macau	202-482-2462	2317
Madagascar	202-482-4504	3317
Malawi	202-482-4228	3317
Malaysia	202-482-3815	2308
Maldives	202-482-2954	2029B
Mali	202-482-4388	3317
Malta	202-482-3748	3049
Martinique	202-482-2527	3021
Mauritana	202-482-4388	3317
Mauritius	202-482-4564	3317
Mexico	202-482-0300	3028
Mongolia	202-482-2462	2317
Montserrat	202-482-2527	3314
Morocco	202-482-5545	2039
Mozambique	202-482-5148	3317
Moldova	202-482-2354	3318

N

Namibia	202-482-4228	3317
Nepal	202-482-2954	2029B
Netherlands	202-482-5401	3039
Netherlands Antilles	202-482-2527	3021
New Zealand	202-482-3647	2308
Nicaragua	202-482-2521	3021
Niger	202-482-4388	3317
Nigeria	202-482-4288	3317
Norway	202-482-5149	3037

Selling Overseas: Foreign Markets

O
Oman	202-482-1870	2039

P
Pacific Islands	202-482-3647	2308
Pakistan	202-482-2954	2029B
Panama	202-482-2527	3020
Paraguay	202-482-1548	3021
People/China	202-482-3583	2317
Peru	202-482-2521	2038
Philippines	202-482-3875	2038
Poland	202-482-2645	3413
Portugal	202-482-4508	3044
Puerto Rico	202-482-2527	3021

Q
Qatar	202-482-1070	2039

R
Romania	202-482-2645	6043
Russia	202-482-2354	3318
Rwanda	202-482-4388	3317

S
Sao Tome & Principe	202-482-4338	3317
Saudi Arabia	202-482-4652	2039
Senegal	202-482-4388	3317
Seychelles	202-482-4564	3317
Sierra Leone	202-482-4388	3317
Singapore	202-482-3875	2038
Somalia	202-482-4564	3317
South Africa	202-482-5498	3317
Spain	202-482-4508	3045
Sri Lanka	202-482-2954	2029B
St. Bartholomy	202-482-2527	3021
St. Kitts-Nevis	202-482-2527	3021
St. Lucia	202-482-2527	3021
St. Martin	202-482-2527	3021
St. Vincent Grenadines	202-482-2527	3021
Sudan	202-482-4564	3317
Suriname	202-482-2527	3021
Swaziland	202-482-5148	3317
Sweden	202-482-4414	3037
Switzerland	202-482-2920	3039
Syria	202-482-4441	2039

T
Taiwan	202-482-4957	2308
Tajikistan	202-482-2354	3318
Tanzania	202-482-4228	3317
Thailand	202-482-3875	2038
Togo	202-482-5149	3317
Trinidad/Tobago	202-482-2527	3021
Tunisia	202-482-1860	2039
Turkey	202-482-5373	3045
Turkmenistan	202-482-2354	3318
Turks & Caicos Islands	202-482-2527	3021

U
Uganda	202-482-4564	3317
Ukraine	202-482-2354	3318
United Arab Emirates	202-482-5545	2039
United Kingdom	202-482-3748	3045
Uruguay	202-482-1495	3021

V
Venezuela	202-482-4303	3029
Vietnam	202-482-3875	2038
Virgin Islands (UK)	202-482-2527	3021

Y
Yemen, Rep of	202-482-1870	2039
Yugoslavia	202-482-2615	3413

Z
Zaire	202-482-5149	3317
Zambia	202-482-4228	3317
Zimbabwe	202-482-4228	3317

State Department Country Experts

If you need information that is primarily political, economic or cultural in nature, direct your questions first to the State Department Country Desk Officers. An operator at the number listed below can direct you to the appropriate desk officer.

U.S. Department of State
2201 C Street, NW
Washington, DC 20520   202-647-4000
www.state.gov

Foreign Specialists At Other Government Agencies

The following is a listing by subject area of other departments within the federal government which maintain country experts who are available to help the public:

1) **Foreign Agriculture:**
Foreign Agriculture Service, Agriculture and Trade Analysis Division, U.S. Department of Agriculture, Room 732, 1301 New York Ave., NW, Washington, DC 20005, 202-219-0700; {www.fas.usda.gov}.

Food Safety and Inspection Service, International Programs, U.S. Dept. of Agriculture, Room 341-E, 14th and Independence Ave., SW, Washington, DC 20250-3700, 202-720-3473; {www.fsis.usda.gov}.

Animal and Plant Health Inspection Service, Import-Export, U.S. Department of Agriculture, 6505 Bellcrest Rd., Hyattsville, MD 20782, 301-436-8590; {www.aphis.usda.gov}.

2) **Energy Resources:**
Office of Export Assistance, U.S. Department of Energy, 1000 Independence Ave., SW, Washington, DC 20585, 202-586-7997; {www.doe.gov}.

Office of Fossil Energy, U.S. Dept. of Energy, 1000 Independence Ave., SW, Washington, DC 20585, 202-586-6503; Fax: 202-586-5146; {www.fe.doe.gov}.

3) **Economic Assistance to Foreign Countries:**
Business Office, U.S. Agency for International Development, 320 21st St. NW, Washington, DC 20523, 703-875-1551; {gaia.usaid.gov}.

Money For Selling Overseas

4) **Information Programs and Cultural Exchange:**
U.S. Information Agency, 301 4th St. SW, Washington, DC 20547, 202-619-4700; Fax: 202-619-6988; E-mail: {inquiry@usia.gov}; {www.usia.gov}.

5) **Metric:**
Office of Metric Programs, National Institute of Standards and Technology, 100 Bureau Drive, Building 411, Room A146, Gaithersburg, MD 20899, 301-975-6259; {ts.nist.gov/ts}.

6) **Telecommunications Information:**
Bureau of International Communications and Information Policy, U.S. Department of State, Washington, DC 20520, 202-647-5212.

7) **Fisheries:**
Office of Trade and Industry Services, Fisheries Promotion and Trade Matters, National Marine Fisheries Service, 1315 East-West Highway, Silver Spring, MD 20910, 301-713-2379; {www.nmfs.gov}.

Money for Selling Overseas

1) **State Government Money Programs:**
Some state government economic development programs offer special help for those who need financial assistance in selling overseas. See the section presented later in this chapter entitled *State Government Assistance To Exporters*.

2) **Export-Import Bank Financing (Eximbank):**
The Export-Import Bank facilitates and aids in the financing of exports of United States goods and services. Its programs include short-term, medium-term, and long-term credits, small business support, financial guarantees, and insurance. In addition, it sponsors conferences on small business exporting, maintains credit information on thousands of foreign firms, supports feasibility studies of overseas programs, and offers export and small business finance counseling. To receive *Marketing News* Fact Sheets, or the *Eximbank Export Credit Insurance* booklet, or the Eximbank's *Program Selection Guide*, contact: Export-Import Bank, 811 Vermont Ave. NW, Washington, DC 20571, 202-566-4490, 1-800-424-5201; Fax: 202-566-7524; {www.exim.gov}.

3) **Small Business Administration (SBA) Export Loans:**
This agency makes loans and loan guarantees to small business concerns as well as to small business investment companies, including those which sell overseas. It also offers technical assistance, counseling, training, management assistance, and information resources, including some excellent publications to small and minority businesses in export operations. Contact your local or regional SBA office listed in the blue pages of your telephone book under Small Business Administration, or Small Business Administration, Office of International Trade, 409 3rd St., SW, Washington, DC 20416, 202-205-6720; {www.sbaonline.sba.gov/oit/finance}.

4) **Overseas Private Investment Corporation (OPIC):**
This agency provides marketing, insurance, and financial assistance to American companies investing in 140 countries and 16 geographic regions. Its programs include direct loans, loan guarantees, and political risk insurance. OPIC also sponsors U.S. and international seminars for investment executives as well as conducts investment missions to developing countries. The Investor Services Division offers a computer service to assist investors in identifying investment opportunities worldwide. A modest fee is charged for this service and it is also available through the Lexis/Nexis computer network. OPIC has supported investments worth nearly $112 billion, generated $56 billion in U.S. exports, and helped to create 230,000 American jobs. Specific Info-Kits are available identifying basic economic, business, and political information for each of the countries covered. In addition, it operates:

> Program Information Hotline
> Overseas Private Investment Corporation
> 1100 New York Ave., NW
> Washington, DC 20527
> 202-336-8799 (Hotline)
> 202-336-8400 (General Information)
> 202-336-8636 (Public Affairs)
> 202-336-8680 (Press Information)
> 202-408-9859 (Fax)
> E-mail: {info@opic.gov}
> www.opic.gov

5) **Agency for International Development (AID):**
The Agency for International Development was created in 1961 by John F. Kennedy. AID offers a variety of loan and financing guarantee programs for projects in developing countries that have a substantial developmental impact or for the exportation of manufactured goods to AID-assisted developing countries. Some investment opportunities are region specific, which include the Association of Southeast Asian National, the Philippines, and Africa. For more information contact the Office of Investment, Agency for International Development, 515 22nd St. NW, Room 301, Washington, DC 20523-0231, 703-875-1551; {www.info.usaid.gov}.

6) **Grants to Train Local Personnel**
The Trade and Development Agency has the authority to offer grants in support of short-listed companies on a transaction specific basis. These are usually in the form of grants to cover the cost of training local personnel by the company on the installation, operation, and maintenance of equipment specific to bid the proposal. The average grant awarded is $320,000. Contact: 703-875-4357; Fax: 703-875-4009.

7) **Consortia of American Businesses in Eastern Europe (CABEE):**
CABEE provides grant funds to trade organizations to defray the costs of opening, staffing, and operating U.S. consortia offices in Eastern Europe. The CABEE grant program initially began operations in Poland, the Czech Republic, Slovikia, and Hungary, targeting five industry sectors: agribusiness/agriculture, construction/housing, energy, environment, and telecommunications. Contact: CABEE, Department of Commerce, 14th and Constitution Avenue, Room 1104, Washington, DC 20230, 202-482-5004; Fax: 202-482-1790; {www.ita.doc.gov/oetca}.

8) **Consortia of American Businesses in the Newly Independent States (CABNIS):**
This program was modeled after CABEE and stimulates U.S. business in the Newly Independent States (NIS) and assist the region in its move toward privatization. CABNIS is providing grant funds to nonprofit organizations to defray the costs of

Selling Overseas: Foreign Markets

opening, staffing, and operating U.S. consortia offices in the NIS. Contact: CABNIS, Department of Commerce, 14th and Constitution Avenue, Washington, DC 20230, 202-482-5004; {www.ita.doc.gov/export_admin/brochure.html - info}. For financing and a listing of grantees, contact {www.itaiep.doc.gov/bisnis/finance/cabnis.htm}.

Marketing Data, Custom Studies, and Company Information

Further information on any of the following services and products can be obtained by contacting a U.S. Department of Commerce/US & FCS field office listed later in this chapter, or by contacting the US & FCS at: United States and Foreign Commercial Services, U.S. Department of Commerce, Room 3810, HCH Building, 14th and Constitution Ave., NW, Washington, DC 20230, 202-482-4767 or call 1-800-USA-TRADE.

1) **International Industry Experts:**
A separate Office of Trade Development at the Commerce Department handles special marketing and company problems for specific industries. Experts are available in the following international market sectors:

Technology and Aerospace Industries:	202-482-1872
Office of Automotive Affairs:	202-482-0554
	www.ita.doc.gov/auto
Basic Industries:	202-482-0614
Capital Goods and International Construction:	202-482-5023
Environmental Technologies Exports	201-482-5225
Office of Computers and Business Equipment	202-482-0952
	infoserv2.ita.doc.gov/ocbe/ocbehome.nsf
Telecommunications:	202-482-4466
	infoserv2.ita.doc.gov/ot/home.nsf
Service, Industries and Finance:	202-482-5261
Textiles, Apparel and Consumer Goods:	202-482-3737
	otexa.ita.doc.gov

You can also talk to industry desk officers at the Department of Commerce. They can provide information on the competitive strengths of U.S. industries in foreign markets from abrasives to yogurt. They are listed in the "Experts" section at the end of this book and have "COMMERCE" after their name. You can call the Department of Commerce at 202-482-2000 (main office) or 1-800-872-8723 (trade information) to locate specific industry analysts. You can also contact them online at {www.ita.doc.gov/ita_home/itatdhom.html}.

2) **Trade Lists:**
Directories of overseas customers for U.S. exports in selected industries and countries: They contain the names and product lines of foreign distributors, agents, manufacturers, wholesalers, retailers, and other purchasers. They also provide the name and title of key officials as well as telex and cable numbers, and company size data. Prices range up to $40 for a list of a category.

3) **Country Statistics:**
There are multiple ways to get up to date statistics for most countries worldwide. The Census Bureau maintains a listing of country statistics on its website: {www.census.gov/main/www/state_int.html}.

InfoNation is another easy to use database for quick statistical information for every country that is a member of the United Nations. Maintained by the U.N., InfoNation is a very helpful site for being able to easily compare statistics using its two-step database. Contact InfoNation at {www.un.org/Pubs/CyberSchoolBus/infonation/e_infonation.htm}.

4) **Demographic and Social Information:**
The Center for International Research compiles and maintains up to date global demographic and social information for all countries in its International Data Base (IDB). Last year, the IDB represented 227 countries and areas worldwide. The IDB has all vital information available for easy download from its website. The only requirements are that your machine must be a PC compatible, 386 computer (or higher). Contact: Systems Analysis and Programming Staff, 301-457-1403; Fax: 301-457-1539; E-mail: {idb@census.gov}; {census.gov/pub/ipc/www/idbnew.html}.

5) **Customized Export Mailing Lists:**
Selected lists of foreign companies in particular industries, countries, and types of business can be requested by a client. Gummed labels are also available. Prices start at $35.

6) **World Traders Data Reports:**
Background reports are available on individual firms containing information about each firm's business activities, its standing in the local business community, its creditworthiness, and overall reliability and suitability as a trade contact for exporters. The price is $100 per report.

7) **Agent Distributor Service (ADS):**
This is a customized search for interested and qualified foreign representatives on behalf of an American client. U.S. commercial officers overseas conduct the search and prepare a report identifying up to six foreign prospects which have personally examined the U.S. firm's product literature and have expressed interest in representing the firm. A fee of $250 per country is charged. Contact them online at {www.ita.doc.gov/uscs/uscsads.html}.

8) **New Product Information Service:**
This service is designed to help American companies publicize the availability of new U.S. products in foreign markets and simultaneously test market interest in these products. Product information which meets the criteria is distributed worldwide through Commercial News USA and Voice of America broadcasts. A fee is charged for participation.

9) **Customized Market Analysis (CMA):**
At a cost of $800 to $13,500 per country per product, these studies are called "Comparison Shopping Service". They are conducted by the U.S. Embassy foreign commercial attaches and can target information on quite specific marketing questions such as:

- Does the product have sales potential in the country?
- Who is the supplier for a comparable product locally?
- What is the going price for a comparable product in this country?
- What is the usual sales channel for getting this type of product into the market?
- What are the competitive factors that most influence purchases of these products in the market (i.e., price, credit, quality, delivery, service, promotion, brand)?

Marketing Data

- What is the best way to get sales exposure in the market for this type of product?
- Are there any significant impediments to selling this type of product?
- Who might be interested and qualified to represent or purchase this company's products?
- If a licensing or joint venture strategy seems desirable for this market, who might be an interested and qualified partner for the U.S. company?

10) **Special Opportunities in the Caribbean Basin and Latin America:**
Under the Caribbean Economic Recovery Act of 1983, the government has established special incentives for American firms wishing to do business with Latin American and Caribbean Basin companies. Seminars, workshops, business development missions, business counseling, as well as marketing and competitive information are available.

Latin America/Caribbean Business Development Center
U.S. Department of Commerce
Room 1235   202-482-0841
Washington, DC 20230   Fax: 202-482-5364

11) **New Markets in Eastern European Countries (EEBIC):**
The Eastern Europe Business Information Center is stocked with a wide range of publications on doing business in Eastern Europe. These include lists of potential partners, investment regulations, priority industry sectors, and notices of upcoming seminars, conferences, and trade promotion events. The center also serves as a referral point for programs of voluntary assistance to the region.

Eastern Europe Business Information Center
U.S. Department of Commerce
Room 7412   202-482-2645
Washington, DC 20230   Fax: 202-482-4473

12) **Exporting to Japan: Japan Export Information Center (JEIC)**
The Japan Export Information Center (JEIC) provides business counseling services and accurate information on exporting to Japan. The JEIC is the point of contact for information on business in Japan, market entry alternatives, market information and research, product standards and testing, tariffs, and non-tariff barriers. The center maintains a commercial library and participates in seminars on various aspects of Japanese business. Contact: Japan Export Information Center, U.S. Department of Commerce, Room 2320, Washington, DC 20230; 202-482-2425; Fax:202-482-0469;{www.ita.doc.gov/regional/geo_region/japan/jeic.html}.

13) **Office of Export Trading Company Affairs**
The Office of Export Trading Company offers various information as well as promoting the use of export trading companies and export management companies; offers information and counseling to businesses and trading associations regarding the export industry; and administers the Export Trade Certificate of Review program which provides exporters with an antitrust "insurance policy" intended to foster joint export activities where economies of scale and risk diversification are achieved. Contact: Office of Export Trading Company Affairs, 202-482-5131; Fax: 202-482-1790.

14) **U.S.-Asia Environmental Partnership**
US-AEP is a comprehensive service to help U.S. environmental exporters enter markets in the Asia/Pacific region. It is a coalition of public, private and non-governmental organizations which promotes environmental protection and sustainable development in 34 nations in the Asia/Pacific area. Contact: U.S.-Asia Environmental Partnership, 1720 I St., NW, Suite 700, Washington, DC; 202-835-0333; Fax: 202-835-0366; E-mail: {usasia@usaep.org}; {www.usaep.org}.

15) **Business Information Service for the Newly Independent States (BISNIS)**
BISNIS provides "one stop shopping" for U.S. firms interested in doing business in the Newly Independent States (NIS) of the former Soviet Union. Information is available on commercial opportunities in the NIS, sources of financing, up to date lists of trade contacts as well as on U.S. Government programs supporting trade and investment in the region. BISNIS publishes a monthly bulletin with information on upcoming trade promotion events, practical advice on doing business with NIS and other topics. Contact: BISNIS, U.S. Department of Commerce, Room 7413, 202-482-4655; Fax: 202-482-2293.

16) **Technical Assistance with Transportation Concerns**
The Department of Transportation provides technical assistance to developing countries on a wide range of problems in the areas of transportation policy, highways, aviation, rail and ports. It also supports AID in the foreign aid development program. Contact:
International Transportation and Trade: Bernard Gillian,
    202-366-4368; Fax: 202-366-7417
Federal Aviation Administration: 202-267-3173;
    Fax: 202-267-5306; {www.faa.gov}
Federal Highway Administration: Kennith Wylde, 202-366-0605;
    Fax: 202-366-9626; {www.fhwa.dot.gov}
Federal Railroad Administration: Ilona Williams, 202-493-6130;
    Fax: 202-493-6171; {www.fra.gov}
Maritime Administration: 202-366-5773; Fax: 202-366-3746;
    {marad.dot.gov}
Office of International Aviation: Paul Gretch, 202-366-2423.

17) **"First Business"**
The "First Business" television program is a half-hour long monthly televised business program sent by satellite to more than 100 countries highlighting innovation and excellence in U.S. business. The program consists of segments on new products, services, and processes of interest to overseas buyers and promising research. "First Business" is produced by Worldnet Television, a division of the International Broadcasting Bureau. Contact: Worldnet Television, 202-619-1783; Fax: 202-205-2967; E-mail: {worldnet@ibb.gov}.

18) **Environmental Technology Network for Asia (ETNA):**
ETNA matches environmental trade leads sent from U.S.-Asia Environmental Partnership (USAEP) Technology Representatives located in 11 Asian countries with appropriate U.S. environmental firms and trade associations that are registered with ETNA's environmental trade opportunities database. U.S. environmental firms receive the trade leads by Broadcast Fax system within 48 hours of leads being identified and entered electronically from Asia. Companies may register online to join ETNA's 2400 firms and associations. Contact: 800-818-9911; Fax: 202-835-8358; {www.usaep.org/ouractiv/etna.htm}.

Selling Overseas: Foreign Markets

19) **Automated Trade Locator Assistance System:**
The SBAtlas is a market research tool which provides free of charge two types of reports: product-specific and country-specific. The product report ranks the top 35 import and export market for a particular good or service. The country report identifies the top 20 products most frequently traded in a target market. This service is free of charge. Contact: SBAtlas is available through SBA district offices, Service Corps of Retired Executives (SCORE) office, and Small Business Development Centers, to get the address and phone number to the nearest office call 1-800-U-ASK-SBA.

20) **Export Contact List Service (ECLS):**
This database retrieval service provides U.S. exporters with names, addresses, products, sizes and other relevant information on foreign firms interested in importing U.S. goods and services. Similar information is also available on U.S. exporters to foreign firms seeking suppliers from the U.S. Names are collected and maintained by Commerce district offices and commercial officers at foreign posts. Contact your nearest district Commerce office located in this book or call 1-800-USA-TRADE.

Trade Fairs and Missions

Trade fairs, exhibitions, trade missions, overseas trade seminars, and other promotional events and services are sponsored by the Export Promotion Services Group, U.S. and Foreign Commercial Services, U.S. Department of Commerce, 14th and E Streets, NW, Room 2810, Washington, DC 20230, 202-482-6220. This office or one of its field offices which are listed later in this chapter can provide additional details on these activities.

1) **Industry-Organized, Government-Approved Trade Missions:**
Such missions are organized by trade associations, local Chambers of Commerce, state trade development agencies, and similar trade-oriented groups that enjoy U.S. Department of Commerce support.

2) **Catalog Exhibitions:**
Such exhibitions feature displays of U.S. product catalogs, sales brochures, and other graphic sales materials at American embassies and consulates or in conjunction with trade shows. A Department of Commerce specialist assists in the exhibition. Call 202-482-3973; Fax: 202-482-2716.

3) **Video Catalog:**
This catalog is designed to showcase American products via video tape presentation. This permits actual product demonstrations giving the foreign buyer an opportunity to view applications of American products. Federal specialists participate in these sessions. Call 202-482-3973; Fax: 202-482-0115.

4) **U.S. Specialized Trade Missions:**
These missions are distinct from those mentioned above since the U.S. Department of Commerce plans the visits and accompanies the delegation. They are designed to sell American goods and services as well as establish agents or representation abroad. The Department of Commerce provides marketing information, advanced planning, publicity, and trip organization. Call 1-800-USA-TRADE.

5) **U.S. Seminar Missions:**
The objective here is to promote exports and help foreign representation for American exporters. However, unlike trade missions, these are designed to facilitate the sales of state-of-the-art products and technology. This type of mission is a one to two day "seminar" during which team members discuss technology subjects followed by private, sales-oriented appointments. Call 1-800-USA-TRADE.

6) **Matchmaker Trade Delegations:**
These Department of Commerce-recruited and planned missions are designed to introduce new-to-export or new-to-market businesses to prospective agents and distributors overseas. Trade Specialists from Commerce evaluate the potential firm's products, find and screen contacts, and handle logistics. This is followed by an intensive trip filled with meetings and prospective clients and in-depth briefings on the economic and business climate of the countries visited. Contact: 202-482-3119; Fax: 202-482-0178; {www.ita.doc.gov/uscs/uscsmatc.html}.

7) **Investment Missions:**
These events are held in developing countries offering excellent investment opportunities for U.S. firms. Missions introduce U.S. business executives to key business leaders, potential joint venture partners, and senior foreign government officials in the host country. Call Investment Missions, 202-336-8799; Fax: 202-408-5155.

8) **Foreign Buyer Program:**
This program supports major domestic trade shows featuring products and services of U.S. industries with high export potential. Government officials recruit on a worldwide basis qualified buyers to attend the shows. Call Export Promotion Services, 202-482-0481; Fax: 202-482-0115.

9) **Trade Fairs, Solo Exhibitions, and Trade Center Shows:**
The Department of Commerce organizes a wide variety of special exhibitions. These events range from solo exhibitions representing U.S. firms exclusively at trade centers overseas to U.S. pavilions in the largest international exhibitions. Call 1-800-USA-TRADE.

10) **Agent/Distributor Service (ADS):**
Looking for overseas representatives to expand your business and boost your export sales? Commerce will locate, screen, and assess agents, distributors, representatives, and other foreign partners for your business. Contact: 1-800-USA-TRADE; {www.ita.doc.gov/uscs/uscsads.html}.

11) **Trade Opportunities Program (TOP):**
The Trade Opportunities Program (TOP) provides companies with current sales leads from international firms seeking to buy or represent their products or services. TOP leads are printed daily in leading commercial newspapers and are also distributed electronically via the U.S. Department of Commerce Economic Bulletin Board. Call 1-800-STAT-USA, 202-482-1986; Fax: 202-482-2164; {www.ita.doc.gov/uscs/uscstop.htm}.

12) **Gold Key Service:**
This customized service is aimed at U.S. firms which are planning to visit a country. Offered by many overseas posts, it combines several services such as market orientation briefings, market research, introductions to potential partners, and interpreters for meetings, assistance in developing a sound market strategy, and

Other Services

an effective followup plan. Gold Key Service is available in 70 of the world's best export markets for fees ranging from $150-$600. Call 1-800-USA-TRADE; {www.ita.doc.gov/uscs/uscsgold.html}.

Special Programs for Agricultural Products

The following programs are specifically aimed at those who wish to sell agricultural products overseas. Agricultural exporters should also be sure not to limit themselves only to programs under this heading. Programs listed under other headings can also be used for agricultural products.

1) **Office Space for Agricultural Exporters:**
The Foreign Agriculture Service (FAS) maintains overseas agricultural trade offices to help exporters of U.S. farm and forest products in key overseas markets. The facilities vary depending on local conditions, but may include a trade library, conference rooms, office space, and kitchens for preparing product samples. Contact: Foreign Agriculture Service, U.S. Department of Agriculture, 14th and Independence Ave. SW, Washington, DC 20250, 202-720-7420; Fax: 202-205-9728; {www.fas.usda.gov}.

2) **Foreign Market Information:**
A special office serves as a single contact point within the Foreign Agriculture Service for agricultural exporters seeking foreign market information. The office also counsels firms which believe they have been injured by unfair trade practices. Contact: Trade Assistance and Promotion Office, U.S. Department of Agriculture, 14th and Independence Avenue, SW, Washington, DC 20250, 202-720-7420; Fax: 202-720-3229.

3) **Export Connections:**
The AgExport Action Kit provides information which can help put U.S. exporters in touch quickly and directly with foreign importers of food and agricultural products. The services include trade leads, a *Buyer Alert* newsletter, foreign buyer lists, and U.S. supplier lists. This bi-weekly newsletter, distributed by USDA's overseas offices, can introduce your food and agricultural products to foreign buyers around the world. *Buyer Alert* reaches more than 15,000 importers in 75 countries. Last year, *Buyer Alert* helped generate confirmed export sales of $100 million. Contact: AgExport Connection, Ag Box 1052, U.S. Department of Agriculture, FAS/AGX, Washington, DC 20250, 202-690-3421; Fax: 202-690-4374. Export Kit: {www.fas.usda.gov/egexport.html}. Buyer Alert: {www.fas.usda.gov/agexport/banews.html}

Export Regulations, Licensing, and Product Standards

Talk to ELVIS — Bureau of Export Administration (BXA)
BXA is responsible for controlling exports for reasons of national security, foreign policy, and short supply. Licenses on controlled exports are issued, and seminars on U.S. export regulations are held domestically and overseas. Contact: Bureau of Export, U.S. Department of Commerce, 14th St. and Pennsylvania Ave., Room 2705 (for mail), Room 1099 (for visitors), Washington, DC 20230; 202-482-4811; Fax: 202-482-3617; {www.bxa.doc.gov}; or BXA Western Regional Office, 3300 Irvine Ave., Suite 345, Newport Beach, CA 92660; 949-660-0144; 949-660-9347.

Export license applications may be submitted and issued through computer via the Export License Application and Information Network (ELAIN). The System for Tracking Export License Application (STELA) provides instant status updates on license applications by the use of a touch-tone phone.

The Export Licensing Voice Information (ELVIS) is an automated attendant that offers a range of licensing information and emergency handling procedures. Callers may order forms and publications or subscribe to the *Office of Export Licensing (OEL) Insider Newsletter*, which provides regulatory updates. While using ELVIS, a caller has the option of speaking to a consultant.

Office of Export Licensing	202-482-8536
	Fax: 202-482-3322
ELAIN	202-482-4811
STELA	202-482-2752
ELVIS	202-482-4811
Export Seminars	202-482-6031

The National Institute of Standards and Technology provides a free service which will identify standards for selling any product to any country in the world. This federal agency will tell you what the standard is for a given product or suggest where you can obtain an official copy of the standard.

National Center for Standards and Certification
National Institute of Standards and Technology
Building 820, Room 164
Gaithersburg, MD 20899   301-975-4040
                           Fax: 301-926-1559

Cheap Office and Conference Space Overseas

If you are travelling overseas on a business trip, you may want to look into renting office space and other services through the American Embassy. Depending on the country and the space available, the embassy can provide temporary office space for as low as $25 per day, along with translation services, printing, and other services. Meeting rooms, seminar or convention space along with promotion services, mailings, freight handling, and even catering may be available in many countries. Contact the Department of Commerce/US & FCS field office which is listed later in this chapter, or the appropriate country desk officer at the U.S. Department of Commerce in Washington, DC.

Other Services, Resources, and Databases

The following is a description of some of the additional services and information sources that can be useful to anyone investigating overseas markets:

1) **Help in Selling to Developing Nations:**
The U.S. Agency For International Development (AID) provides information to U.S. suppliers, particularly small, independent enterprises, regarding purchases to be financed with AID funds. U.S. small businesses can obtain special counseling and related services in order to furnish equipment, materials, and services to AID-financed projects. AID sponsors Development Technologies Exhibitions, where technical firms in the U.S. are matched up with those in lesser developed countries for the purpose of

Selling Overseas: Foreign Markets

forming joint ventures or exploring licensing possibilities. AID provides loans and grants to finance consulting services that support project activities related to areas such as agriculture, rural development, health, and housing. Contact: Information Center, U.S. Agency for International Development, Ronald Reagan Bldg., Washington, DC 20523, 202-712-4810; Fax: 202-216-3524; {www.info.usaid.gov}.

2) **Foreign Demographic Profiles:**
The Government Printing office has a publication called the CIA *World Factbook*. Produced annually, this publication provides country-by-country data on demographics, economy, communications, and defense. The cost is $29 (GPO: 041-015-00173-6). Order by contacting Superintendent of Documents, Government Printing Office, Washington, DC 20402; 202-512-1800.

3) **Counseling and Licenses:**
The Office of Exporter Services is responsible for counseling exporters, conducting export control seminars, processing license applications and commodity classifications, and for publishing changes to the Export Administration Regulations. The Office of Exporter Service is an office of the Department of Commerce. To contact the main office: Eileen Albanese, 202-482-0436; Fax: 202-482-3322. Export Counseling Division: Laverne Smith, 202-482-4811; Fax: 202-482-3617.

4) **Help With Selling Commodities Abroad:**
The Foreign Agricultural Service is charged with maintaining and expanding export sales of U.S. agricultural commodities and products. Staff can provide information on foreign agricultural production, trade and consumption, marketing research including areas of demand for specific commodities in foreign countries, and analyses of foreign competition in agricultural areas. Other services include financing opportunities, contributing to export promotion costs, and testing market assistance. This office also handles U.S. representation to foreign governments and participates in formal trade negotiations. Contact: Foreign Agricultural Service, U.S. Department of Agriculture, 14th and Independence Ave., S.W., Room 4647, South Building, Washington, DC 20250, 202-720-7420; {www.fas.usda.gov}.

5) **International Prices:**
Export price indexes for both detailed and aggregate product groups are available on a monthly basis. Price trends comparisons of U.S. exports with those of Japan and Germany are also available. Contact: International Prices Division, Bureau of Labor Statistics, U.S. Department of Labor, 2nd Massachusetts Ave., NE, Room 3955, Washington, DC 20212, 202-606-7100.

6) **Identifying Overseas Opportunities:**
The International Trade Administration (ITA) of the Commerce Department assists American exporters in locating and gaining access to foreign markets. It furnishes information on overseas markets available for U.S. products and services, requirements which must be fulfilled, economic conditions in foreign countries, foreign market and investment opportunities, etc. Operations are divided into four major areas:

- **International Economic Policy:** promotes U.S. exports geographically by helping American businesses market products in various locations abroad and by solving the trade and investment problems they encounter. This office is staffed by Country Desk Officers knowledgeable in marketing and business practices for almost every country in the world. Contact: Office of International Economic Policy, ITA, U.S. Department of Commerce, Washington, DC 20230, 202-482-3022; {infoserv.ita.doc.gov}.

- **Export Administration:** supervises the enforcement provisions of the Export Administration Act, and administers the Foreign Trade Zone Program. Personnel in its export enforcement and its administration, policy, and regulations offices can offer technical advice and legal interpretations of the various export legislation which affect American businesses. Assistance in complying with export controls can be obtained directly from the Exporter Counseling Division within the Bureau of Export Administration (BXA) Office of Export Licensing in Washington, DC, 202-482-4811; Fax: 202-482-3617; {www.bxa.doc.gov}.

BXA also has field offices that specialize in counseling on export controls and regulations:
Western Regional Office 949-660-0144
Northern California
  Branch Office 408-998-7402

- **Trade Development:** advises businesses on trade and investment issues, and promotes U.S. exports by industry or product classifications. Offices offer assistance and information on export counseling, statistics and trade data, licensing, trading companies, and other services. Contact: Office of Trade Development, ITA, U.S. Department of Commerce, Washington, DC 20230, 202-482-1461; Fax: 202-482-5697.

- **U.S. and Foreign Commercial Service:** provides information on government programs to American businesses, and uncovers trade opportunities for U.S. exporters. They also locate representatives and agents for American firms, assist U.S. executives in all phases of their exporting, and help enforce export controls and regulations. They operate through 47 district offices located in major U.S. cities and in 124 posts in 69 foreign countries. In addition, a valued asset of the U.S. and Foreign Commercial Services is a group of about 525 foreign nationals, usually natives of the foreign country, who are employed in the U.S. embassy or consulate and bring with them a wealth of personal understanding of local market conditions and business practices. U.S. exporters usually tap into these services by contacting the Department of Commerce/US & FCS field office in their state (listed later in this chapter), or Office of U.S. and Foreign Commercial Service, U.S. Department of Commerce, Washington, DC 20230; 1-800-USA-TRADE.

Or contact regional directors at:
Africa, Near East 202-482-4925
Asia and Pacific 202-482-5251
Europe 202-482-5638
Japan 202-482-4527

7) **Latest News on Foreign Opportunities:**
In addition to technical reports on foreign research and development, National Technical Information Service sells foreign market airgrams and foreign press and radio translations. A free video is available explaining NTIS services. Contact: National

Other Services

Technical Information Service, U.S. Department of Commerce, 5285 Port Royal Rd., Springfield, VA 22161, 703-605-6000; Fax: 703-605-6900; {www.ntis.gov}.

8) Planning Services for U.S. Exporters:
In its effort to promote economic development in Third World countries, the Trade and Development Program finances planning services for development projects leading to the export of U.S. goods and services. A free pamphlet is available that describes the planning services offered by the Trade and Development Program. To obtain a copy, contact: U.S. Trade and Development Program, Department of State, Room 309 SA-16, Washington, DC 20523-1602, 703-875-4357.

9) Terrorism Abroad:
Assistance is available to companies doing business abroad to assess current security conditions and risk in certain cities and countries which may pose a threat. Over 1600 U.S. companies are already affiliated with the OSAC. The OSAC has numerous publications on security guidelines available from its website at {ds.state.gov/osacmenu.cfm}. Contact: Overseas Security Advisory Council (OSAC), U.S. Department of State, Washington, DC 20522-1003, 202-663-0533; Fax: 202-663-0868; E-mail: {osca@dsmail.state.gov}.

10) Trade Remedy Assistance Office (TRAO):
The Center provides information on remedies available under the Trade Remedy Law. It also offers technical assistance to eligible small businesses to enable them to bring cases to the International Trade Commission. Contact: ITC Trade Remedy Assistance Center, U.S. International Trade Commission, 500 E St. SW, Washington, DC 20436, 202-205-2200; Fax: 202-205-2139.

11) International Expertise:
Staff in the following offices will prove helpful as information sources regarding the international scope of their respective subject areas:

Economics:
International Investment, Bureau of Economic Analysis, U.S. Department of Commerce, 1441 L St., NW, Washington, DC 20230, 202-606-9800; {www.bea.doc.gov}.

Productivity and Technology Statistics:
Bureau of Labor Statistics, U.S. Department of Labor, 2 Massachusetts Ave., NE, #2150, Washington, DC 20212, 202-606-5654; Fax: 202-606-5679; {www.bls.gov}.

Investments and Other Monetary Matters:
Office of Assistant Secretary for International Affairs, U.S. Department of the Treasury, 1500 Pennsylvania Ave., Washington, DC 20220, 202-622-2000; Fax: 202-622-6415.

Population:
International Program Center, Bureau of Census, U.S. Department of Commerce, Room 205, Washington Plaza, Washington, DC 20233, 301-457-1403.

Population Reference Bureau, Inc., 1875 Connecticut Ave., NW, Suite 520, Washington, DC 20009, 202-483-1100; Fax: 202-328-3937; E-mail: {popref@prb.org}; {www.igx.org/pub}.

Country Development:
Inter-American Development Bank, 1300 NY Ave., NW, Washington, DC 20577, 202-623-1000; E-mail: {pic@iadb.org}; {www.iadb.org}.

International Monetary Fund, 700 19th St. NW, Washington, DC 20431, 202-623-7000; Fax: 202-623-6278; E-mail: {publicaffairs@ifm.org}; {www.imf.org}.

World Bank, 1818 H St. NW, Washington, DC 20433, 202-477-1234; Fax: 202-522-1159; {worldbank.org}.

12) National Trade Data Bank (NTDB):
This is a "one-stop" source for export promotion and international trade data collected by 17 U.S. government agencies. Updated each month and released on CD-ROM, the Data Bank enables a user with an IBM-compatible personal computer equipped with a CD-ROM reader to access over 100,00 trade documents. It contains the latest Census data on U.S. imports and exports by commodity and country; the complete Central Intelligence Agency (CIA) *World Factbook*; current market research reports compiled by the U.S. and Foreign and Commercial Service; the complete Foreign Traders Index which has over 60,000 names and addresses of individuals and firms abroad interested in importing U.S. products; and many other data services. It is available for free at over 900 Federal Depository Libraries and can be purchased for $35 per disc or $360 for a 12-month subscription. Contact: Economics and Statistics Administration, U.S. Department of Commerce, Washington, DC 20230, 202-482-1986; Fax: 202-482-2164; {www.state.usa.gov/tradtest.nsf}.

13) Global Demographics:
The International Program Center at the Census Bureau compiles and maintains up-to-date global demographic and social information for all countries in its International Data Base, which is accessible to U.S. companies seeking to identify potential markets overseas. Contact Systems Analysis and Programming Staff, 301-457-1403.

14) International Energy Database:
The Office of Fossil Energy forwards prospective energy-related leads to the Agency for International Development (AID) for inclusion in its growing trade opportunities database in an effort to reach an extended audience seeking energy-related trade opportunities. For more information on the Fossil Energy-AID Database contact: The Office of Fossil Energy, U.S. Department of Energy, 1000 Independence Ave. SW, Washington, DC 20585, 202-586-6503; Fax: 202-586-5146; {www.fe.doe.gov}.

15) Online Economic Bulletin Board (EBB):
This computer-based electronic bulletin board, is an online source for trade leads as well as the latest statistical releases from the Bureau of Census, the Bureau of Economic Analysis, the Bureau of Labor Statistics, the Federal Reserve Board, and other federal agencies. Subscribers pay an annual fee, plus cost per minute. Contact: EBB, Office of Business Analysis, U.S. Department of Commerce, Washington, DC 20230, 202-482-1986; {www.ita.doc.gov/uscs/uscsebb.html}.

16) Free Legal Assistance:
The Export Legal Assistance Network (ELAN) is a nationwide group of attorneys with experience in international trade who

Selling Overseas: Foreign Markets

provide free initial consultations to small businesses on export related matters. Contact: Export Legal Assistance Network, Small Business Administration, 1667 K St., NW, Suite 1100, Washington, DC 20006; 202-778-3080; Fax: 202-778-3063; {www.fita.org/elan}.

17) Global Learning:
U.S. Department of Education, Business and International Education Programs. The business and international education program is designed to engage U.S. schools of business language and area programs, international study programs, public and private sector organizations, and U.S. businesses in a mutually productive relationship which will benefit the Nation's future economic interest. Approximately $3.6 million annually is available to assist U.S. institutions of higher education to promote the Nation's capacity for international understanding. Typical grantee activities include executive seminars, case studies, and export skill workshops. For more information contact: Office of Higher Education Programs, U.S. Department of Education, 600 Independence Avenue, SW, Washington, DC 20202; 202-401-9778.

18) Export Counseling — SCORE:
The Small Business Administration can provide export counseling to small business exporters by retired and active business executives. The Service Corps of Retired Executives (SCORE) is an overly active organization with over 12,400 volunteers and 389 SCORE chapters. Members of SCORE, with years of practical experience in international trade, assist small firms in evaluating their export potential and developing and implementing basic export marketing plans. Two of SCORE's most helpful programs are its weekly low cost workshops and its e-mail counseling. For more information, contact your local Small Business Administration (SBA) office listed in the government pages of your telephone book, or National SCORE Office, Washington, DC 20024; 800-634-0245; Fax: 202-205-7636; E-mail: {score@sba.gov}; {www.score.org}.

19) Department of Energy — Office of International Affairs and Energy Emergencies:
The Department of Energy (DOE) promotes U.S. exports of energy goods, services, and technology primarily through participation in The Committee on Renewable Energy Commerce and Trade, and The Coal and Clean Technology Export Program. The following is a list of the Department of Energy's programs and the corresponding telephone numbers to call for more information.

Committee on Renewable Energy Commerce and Trade (CORECT): Through the concept of "one-stop shopping" potential exporters can receive comprehensive advice on potential markets, financing and information on export guidelines. Call the Office of Conservation and Renewable Energy, 202-586-8302; Fax: 202-586-1605.

Coal and Technology Export Program (CTEP): The Coal and Technology Export Program (CTEP) serves as a reservoir for international information on U.S. coal and coal technologies, as the Department of Energy's intra-departmental coordinator, and as the USG inter-agency liaison for coal companies and technology firms. Call 202-586-7297.

The Export Assistance Initiative: This entity in the Bureau of International Affairs has been designed to help identify overseas opportunities for U.S. companies, identify and attempt to alleviate discriminatory trade barriers, and identify possible financing alternatives for U.S. companies. Call 202-586-1189.

20) Fax Retrieval Systems
A number of offices offer documents on demand, delivered directly to a fax machine 24 hours a day. These automated systems each have a menu of available documents which can be sent to a fax machine by dialing from a touch-tone phone and following directions. Below is a list of offices who offer this program:

Uruguay Round Hotline: This fax retrieval system is located at the International Trade Administration and has information on the GATT agreement. Document #1000 is the menu of available information packets. A series of prompts will allow you to enter: 1, 1, 2, 2. This system allows retrieval for information on the Uruguary Round, service sector reports, state opportunities reports, industry sector highlight reports, and tariff and harmonization decisions. 1-800-USA-TRADE.

Center for Eastern European Business Information Center (CEEBIC): This fax system has 5 main menus. Menu document #1000 has export and financing information. Document #2000 has a menu of documents relating to export and investment opportunities and upcoming trade events. A listing of Eastern European country information is available on menu document #3000. Document menus #4000 and #5000 have information on the *Eastern Europe Business Bulletin*, and the *Eastern Europe Looks For Partners* publications; 202-482-5745.

Business Information Service for the Newly Independent States: There are 3 menus available through BISNIS. Menu number 1, document #0001 has trade and investment opportunities and trade promotion information. Menu number 2, document #0002 has industry and country specific information, and financing alternatives. Menu number 3, document #0003, has information on BISNIS publications; 202-482-3145.

Office of Mexico: The main menu for Mexico is document #0101. There is also a menu of labeling and standards requirements (document #8404). Information on documents relating to the certificate of origin and rules of origin under NAFTA is document #5000. A complete NAFTA tariff schedule is on document #6000. Begin by selecting "1" when prompted. 202-482-4464 or 202-482-1495.

Office of Canada: The main menu for Canada is document #0101. The fax retrieval system offers menus on NAFTA rules of origin, customs information, and tariff schedules. 202-482-1495 or 202-482-4464.

Office of Africa, Near East, and South Asia: A list of documents covering the nations of North Africa and the Middle East is document #0100. Africa is #3000 and South Asian countries is #4000; 202-482-1064.

Helpful Publications

Overseas Private Investment Corporation: This system has information on OPIC project finance and political risk insurance programs; 202-336-8700.

Office of Latin America and Caribbean Basin: This fax retrieval system is maintained by the ITA. Select "2", Index Code: 1 to receive country fact sheets, key contacts, tariff and duty information, and trade programs. This system covers Southern Cone, Andean, Central American and Caribbean Basin countries. 202-482-2521.

21) International Visitors Program

Foreign individuals or groups are brought to the U.S. for about one month. The programs feature visits by business leaders and foreign government officials who have the opportunity to meet with their U.S. counterparts. Contact: Office of International Visitors, U.S. Information Agency, 301 4th St., SW, Room 255, Washington, DC 20547; 1-800-650-9822; Fax: 202-205-0792.

Read All About It: Helpful Publications

The Government Printing Office (GPO) has many titles to choose from. For a listing, contact the GPO (listed below) by mail, or phone and ask for the Foreign Trade and Tariff Subject Bibliography (SB-123; 021-123-00405-1).

Government Printing Office
Superintendent of Documents
Washington, DC 20402   202-512-1800
www.access.gpo.gov/su_docs

Basic Guide to Exporting:
This publication outlines the sequence of steps necessary to determine whether to, and how to, use foreign markets as a source of profits. It describes the various problems which confront smaller firms engaged in, or seeking to enter, international trade, as well as the types of assistance available. It also provides a guide to appraising the sales potential of foreign markets and to understanding the requirements of local business practices and procedures in overseas markets. The booklet is available for $13 (GPO: 003-009-00604-0) from: Superintendent of Documents, U.S. Government Printing Office, Washington, DC 20402, 202-512-1800; Fax: 202-512-2250.

Commercial News USA:
This publication describes a free export promotion service that will publicize the availability of your new product to foreign markets of more than 150 countries, and test foreign market interest in your new product. There is a small fee. Contact Commercial News USA: Associated Publications International, 317 Madison Ave., New York, NY 10017; 212-490-3999; Fax: 212-986-7864; {www.cnews.com}.

Export Programs: A Business Directory of U.S. Government Resources:
This guide provides an overview of U.S. government export assistance programs and contact points for further information and expertise in utilizing these programs. Contact: Trade Information Center, U.S. Department of Commerce, Washington, DC 20230, 1-800-872-8723.

Business America:
The principal Commerce department publication for presenting domestic and international business news. Each monthly issue includes a "how to" article for new exporters, discussion of U.S. trade policy, news of government actions that may affect trade, a calendar of upcoming trade shows, exhibits, fairs, and seminars. The annual subscription is $47 in the U.S., $4 for any single copy. (GPO: 703-011-0000-4-W). Contact: Superintendent of Documents, Government Printing Office, Washington, DC 20402, 202-512-1800.

Key Officers of Foreign Service Posts: A Guide for Business Representatives:
Lists the names of key State and Commerce officers at U.S. embassies and consulates. Cost is $3.75 per copy (GPO: 044-000-0299-3). Contact: Superintendent of Documents, Government Printing Office, Washington, DC 20402, 202-512-1800.

Export Trading Company (ETC) Guidebook:
This Guidebook is intended to assist those who are considering starting or expanding exporting through the various forms of an ETC. The Guidebook will also facilitate your review of the ETC Act and export trading options and serve as a planning tool for your business by showing you what it takes to export profitably and how to start doing it. Cost is $15 (GPO: 003-009-00523-0). Contact: Superintendent of Documents, Government Printing Office, Washington, DC 20402, 202-512-1800.

Foreign Labor Trends:
Published by the Department of Labor, these are a series of reports, issued annually, that describe and analyze labor trends in more than 70 countries. The reports, which are prepared by the American Embassy in each country, cover labor-management relations, trade unions, employment and unemployment, wages and working conditions, labor and government, international labor activities, and other significant developments. Contact: Office of Foreign Relations, Room S 5006, 200 Constitution Ave., NW, Washington, DC 20210, 202-523-6257, 202-219-6257. This publication is also available from the GPO for $1.50-$2.00.

ABC's of Exporting:
This is a special issue of Business America which takes you step by step through the exporting process. It explains the federal agencies and how they can help, as well as providing a directory of export sources. This publication is free and is available by contacting: Trade Information Center, U.S. Department of Commerce, Washington, DC 20230, 1-800-872-8723.

Ag Exporter:
Monthly magazine published by the U.S. Department of Agriculture's Foreign Agricultural Service (FAS). The annual subscription cost is $27 (GPO: 701-027-00000-1). Contact: Superintendent of Documents, Government Printing Office, Washington, DC 20402; 202-512-1800.

AID Procurement Information Bulletin:
This publication advertises notices of intended procurement of AID-financed commodities. The subscription cost is free. Contact: USAID's Office of Small and Disadvantaged

Selling Overseas: Foreign Markets

Business Utilization/Minority Resource Center, Washington, DC 20523-1414; 703-875-1551.

Breaking into the Trade Game: A Small Business Guide to Exporting:

The Small Business Administration has created this comprehensive guide to exporting. A must have for all exporters, new and experienced. This guide is available from the SBA website: {www.sba.gov/oit/txt/finance/pubs.html}.

U.S. Department of Commerce/ US & FCS Field Offices

Trade experts from the US & FCS are available to help you from 47 district offices and 21 branch locations throughout the U.S. The ITA trade specialists are also available at any of the 51 District Export Councils nationwide to assist U.S. firms export.

Alabama
Birmingham: 2015 Second Ave., North, Room 302, 35203, 205-731-1331; Fax: 205-731-0076.

Alaska
Anchorage: 4201 Tudor Center Dr., World Trade Center, Suite 319, 99508-5916, 907-271-6237; Fax: 907-271-6242.

Arizona
Phoenix: 230 N. First Ave., Room 3412, 85025, 602-379-3285; Fax: 602-379-4324.

Arkansas
Little Rock: 425 West Capitol Ave., TCBY Tower Building, Suite 700, 72201, 501-324-5794; Fax: 501-324-7380.

California
Los Angeles: 11000 Wilshire Blvd., Room 9200, 90024, 310-575-7105; Fax: 310-575-7220.
Newport Beach: 3300 Irvine Ave., Suite 305, 92660, 714-660-1688; Fax: 714-660-8039.
San Diego: 6363 Greenwich Drive, 92122, 619-557-5395; Fax: 619-557-6176.
San Francisco: 250 Montgomery St., 14th Floor, 94104, 415-705-2310; Fax: 415-705-2297.

Colorado
Denver: 1625 Broadway, Suite 680, 80202, 303-844-3246; Fax: 303-844-5651.

Connecticut
Hartford: 450 Main St., Room 610-B, 06103, 203-240-3530; Fax: 203-240-3473.

District of Columbia
Served by Gaithersburg, MD, ITA office.

Delaware
Served by Philadelphia, PA, District Office.

Florida
Miami: 2224 Federal Bldg., 51 SW First Ave., 3130, 305-536-5268, Fax: 305-536-4765.
Clearwater: 128 North Osceola Ave., 34617, 813-461-0011; Fax 813-449-2889.
Tallahassee: 107 W. Gaines St., Collins Bldg., Room 366G, 32399, 904-486-6469; Fax: 904-487-1407.
Orlando: 200 E. Robinson St., Suite 695, 32801, 407-648-6235; Fax: 407-648-6756.

Georgia
Atlanta: 4360 Chamber-Dunwoody Road, Suite 310, 30341, 404-452-9101; Fax: 404-452-9105.
Savannah: 120 Barnard St., A-107, 31401, 912-652-4204; Fax: 912-652-4241.

Hawaii
Honolulu: 300 Ala Moana Blvd., Room 4106, Federal Building, 96850, 808-541-1782; Fax: 808-541-3435.

Idaho
Boise: 700 W. State St., 2nd Floor, Boise, 83720, 208-334-3857; Fax: 208-334-2787.

Illinois
Chicago: 55 E. Monroe, Room 1406, 60603, 312-353-4450; Fax: 312-886-8025.
Rockford: 515 N. Court St., P.O. Box 1747, 61110-6247, 815-987-8123; Fax: 815-987-8122.
Wheaton: Illinois Institute of Technology, 201 E. Loop Dr., 60187; 312-353-4332, Fax: 312-353-4336.

Indiana
Indianapolis: 11405 N. Pennsylvania St., Penwood One, Suite 106, Carmel, IN 46032, 317-582-2300; Fax: 317-582-2301.

Iowa
Des Moines: 210 Walnut St., Room 817, 50309, 515-284-4222; Fax: 515-284-4021.

Kansas
Wichita: 151 North Volutsia, 67214-4695, 316-269-6160; Fax: 316-683-7326.

Kentucky
Louisville: 601 W. Broadway, Room 636B, 40202, 502-582-5066; Fax: 502-582-6573.

Louisiana
New Orleans: Two Canal St., 431 World Trade Center, 70130, 504-589-6546; Fax: 504-589-2337.

Maine
Augusta: 77 Sewall St., Suite 59, 04330, 207-622-8249; Fax: 207-626-9156.

Maryland
Baltimore: 431 U.S. Custom House, 40 S. Gay St., 21202, 410-962-3560; Fax: 410-962-7813.
Gaithersburg: National Institute of Standards and Technology, Building 411, Room A102, 20899, 301-975-3904; Fax: 301-948-4360.

Massachusetts
Boston: World Trade Center, Suite 307, 02210, 617-565-8563; Fax: 617-565-8530.

Michigan
Detroit: 477 Michigan Ave., 1140 McNamara Bldg., 48226, 313-226-3650; Fax: 313-226-3657.
Grand Rapids: 300 Monroe NW, Room 408, 49503, 616-456-2411; Fax: 616-456-2695.

Minnesota
Minneapolis: 110 S. 4th St., Room 108, 55401, 612-348-1638; Fax: 612-348-1650.

Mississippi
Jackson: 201 W. Capitol St., Suite 310, 39201-2005, 601-965-4388, Fax: 601-965-5386.

Missouri
St. Louis: 8182 Maryland Ave., Suite 303, 63105, 314-425-3305; Fax: 314-425-3381.
Kansas City: 601 E. 12th St., Room 635, 64106, 816-426-3141; Fax: 816-426-3140.

Montana
Served by Portland ITA office.

Nebraska
Omaha: 11133 O St., 68137, 402-221-3664; Fax: 402-221-3668.

Nevada
Reno: 1755 E. Plumb Lane, #152, 89502, 702-784-5203; Fax: 702-784-5343.

New Hampshire
Served by the Boston ITA office.

New Jersey
Trenton: 3131 Princeton Pike Building 6, Suite 100, 08648, 609-989-2100; Fax: 609-989-2395.

State Government Assistance to Exporters

New Mexico
Albuquerque: 625 Silver Ave. SW, Third Floor, 87102, 505-766-2070; Fax: 505-766-1057.

New York
Buffalo: 111 W. Huron St., Room 1312, Federal Building, 14202, 716-846-4191; Fax: 716-846-5290.
Rochester: 111 East Ave., 14604, 716-263-6480; Fax: 716-325-6505.
New York: 26 Federal Plaza, Room 3718, 10278, 212-264-0634; Fax: 212-264-1356.

North Carolina
Greensboro: 400 W. Market St., Suite 400, 27401, 919-333-5345; Fax: 919-333-5158.

Ohio
Cincinnati: 9504 Federal Building, 550 Main St., 45202, 513-684-2944; Fax: 513-684-3200.
Cleveland: 668 Euclid Ave., Room 600, 44114, 216-522-4750; Fax: 216-522-2235.

Oklahoma
Oklahoma City: 6601 Broadway Extension, Room 200, 73116, 405-231-5302; Fax: 405-841-5245.
Tulsa: 440 S. Houston St., Suite 505, 74127, 918-581-7650; Fax: 918-581-2844.

Oregon
Portland: Suite 242, One World Trade Center, 121 SW Salmon St., 97204, 503-326-3001; Fax: 503-326-6351.

Pennsylvania
Pittsburgh: 1000 Liberty Ave., Room 2002, 15222, 412-644-2850; Fax: 412-644-4875.
King of Prussia: 475 Allendale Rd., Suite 202, 19406, 215-962-4980; Fax: 215-951-7959.

Puerto Rico
San Juan: Room G-55 Federal Building, Chardon Ave. 00918, 809-766-5555; Fax: 809-766-5692.

Rhode Island
Providence: 7 Jackson Walkway, 02903, 401-528-5104; Fax: 401-528-5067.

South Carolina
Columbia: 1835 Assembly St., Suite 172, 29201, 803-765-5345; Fax: 803-253-3614.
Charleston: 9 Liberty St., Room 128, 29424, 803-765-5345; Fax: 803-253-3614.

South Dakota
Served by Omaha, Nebraska, District Office.

Tennessee
Nashville: 404 James Robertson Pkwy., Suite 114, 37219, 615-736-5161; Fax: 615-736-2454.
Memphis: 22 N. Front St., Suite 200, 38103, 901-544-4137; Fax: 901-575-3510.
Knoxville: 301 E. Church Ave., 37915, 615-545-4637.

Texas
Dallas: 1100 Commerce St., Room 7A5, 75258, 214-767-0542; Fax: 214-767-8240.
Austin: 410 E. 5th St., Suite 414A, Box 12728, 78711, 512-472-5059; Fax: 512-320-9424.
Houston: 2625 Federal Bldg., 575 Rusk St., 77002, 713-229-2578; Fax: 713-229-2203.

Utah
Salt Lake City: Suite 105, 324 S. State St., 84111, 801-524-5116; Fax: 801-524-5886.

Vermont
Served by the Boston ITA office.

Virginia
Richmond: 400 N. Eighth St., Suite 8010, 23240, 804-771-2246; Fax: 804-771-2390.

Washington
Seattle: 3131 Elliott Ave., Suite 290, 98121, 206-553-5615; Fax: 206-553-7253.

West Virginia
Charleston: 405 Capitol St., Suite 807, 25301, 304-347-5123; Fax: 304-347-5408.

Wisconsin
Milwaukee: 517 E. Wisconsin Ave., Room 596, 53202, 414-297-3473; Fax: 414-297-3470.

Wyoming
Served by Denver, Colorado, District Office.

State Government Assistance to Exporters

Last year state governments spent approximately $40,000,000 to help companies in their state sell goods and services overseas. This figure increased almost 50% over the previous two years. During the same period of time, federal monies devoted to maximizing companies' export capabilities remained virtually constant. This is another indicator of how the states are fertile sources of information and expertise for large and small businesses.

The underlying mission of these offices is to create jobs within their state. Usually their approach is to help companies develop overseas marketing strategies or to offer incentives to foreign companies to invest in their state. The major state trade development programs and services are outlined below.

1) **Marketing Research and Company Intelligence:**
All of the states can provide some degree of overseas marketing information. The level of detail will depend upon the resources of the state. Thirty-five states (except for California, Hawaii, Idaho, Kansas, Maryland, Minnesota, Nebraska, Nevada, New Jersey, New York, South Dakota, Texas, Washington, West Virginia, and Wyoming) say they will do customized market studies for companies. Such studies are free or available for a small fee. For example, the Commonwealth of Virginia will do an in-depth market study for a company and charge $1,000. They estimate similar surveys done by the private sector cost up to $20,000. Virginia relies on MBA students and professors within the state university system who get credit for working on such projects.

Even if a state does not perform customized studies, the trade office within a Department of Economic Development will prove to be an ideal starting place for marketing information. Some states which do not undertake comprehensive studies for prospective exporters will do a limited amount of research for free. These offices can also point to outside sources as well as the notable resources at the federal level which may be able to assist. And those states with offices overseas also can contact these foreign posts to identify sources in other countries. Moreover, many of the offices have people who travel abroad frequently for companies and also work with other exporters. Such bureaucrats can be invaluable for identifying the exact source for obtaining particular market or company intelligence.

2) **Company and Industry Directories:**
Many states publish directories which are helpful to both exporters and researchers. Some states publish export/import directories which show which companies in the state are exporters and what they sell as well as which are importers and what they buy. Because many of the trade offices are also interested in foreign investment within their state, many publish directories or other reference sources disclosing which companies in their state are foreign owned, and by whom. Other state publications may

Selling Overseas: Foreign Markets

include export service directories which list organizations providing services to exporters such as banks, freight forwarders, translators, and world trade organizations. Some also publish agribusiness exporter directories, which identify agricultural-related companies involved in exporting.

3) Free Newsletters:
All but four states (i.e., Florida, Kentucky, Ohio, and North Carolina) generate international newsletters or publish a special section within a general newsletter on items of interest to those selling overseas. These newsletters are normally free and cover topics like new trade leads, new rules and regulations for exports, and details about upcoming overseas trade shows. Such newsletters can also be a source for mailing lists for those whose clients include exporters. We haven't specifically investigated the availability of such lists, but remember that all states have a law comparable to the federal Freedom of Information Act which allows public access to government data.

4) Overseas Contacts:
Finding a foreign buyer or an agent/distributor for a company is one of the primary functions of these state offices. How they do this varies from state to state. Many sponsor trade fairs and seminars overseas to attract potential buyers to products produced in their state. The more aggressive trade promotion offices may organize trade missions and escort a number of companies overseas and personally help them look for buyers or agents. Many will distribute a company's sales brochures and other literature to potential buyers around the world through their overseas offices. Some states work with the federal government and explore general trade leads and then try to match buyers with sellers. Others will cultivate potential clients in a given country and contact each directly.

5) Export Marketing Seminars:
Many of the states conduct free or modestly priced seminars to introduce companies to selling overseas. Some of the courses are held in conjunction with the regional International Trade Administration office of the U.S. Commerce Department. The course may be general in nature, for example, *The Basics of Exporting*, or focused on specific topics such as *International Market Research Techniques*, *Letters of Credit*, *Export Financing*, or *How to do Business with Israel*.

6) State Grants and Loans for Exporters:
Many states offer financial assistance for those wishing to export. Some states even provide grants (money you do not have to pay back) to those firms which cannot afford to participate in a trade mission or trade fair. This means that they provide money to those companies which are just trying to develop a customer base overseas. More typically the state will help with the financing of a sale through state-sponsored loans and loan guarantees, or assistance in identifying and applying for federal or commercial export financing.

7) Trade Leads Databases:
Because these offices provide mostly services, there are not many opportunities for them to develop databases. However, their trade leads program is one area where a number of offices have computerized their information. These databases consist of the names and addresses along with some background information on those overseas companies which are actively searching or might be interested in doing business with companies within the state. The number of leads in such a system could range from several hundred to five or ten thousand. None of these states seem to have made such information available on machine readable formats to those outside the office. But, in light of state Freedom of Information statutes, it may be worth making a formal inquiry if you have an interest. The states which have computerized their trade leads include: Alabama, Arkansas, Arizona, California, Colorado, Connecticut, Delaware, Florida, Georgia, Hawaii, Illinois, Indiana, Iowa, Maine, Michigan, Maryland, Minnesota, Mississippi, Missouri, Nebraska, New Jersey, New York, North Carolina, North Dakota, Ohio, Oklahoma, Oregon, New Hampshire, Pennsylvania, Puerto Rico, Rhode Island, South Dakota, Tennessee, Texas, Utah, Virginia, Washington, West Virginia, and Wisconsin.

State International Trade Offices

The foreign cities in parentheses after the telephone number are those locations where the state maintains a trade office.

Alabama
International Development and Trade Division, Alabama Development Office, 401 Adams Ave., Montgomery, AL 36130, 334-242-0400, 800-248-0033; Fax: 334-353-1330; E-mail: {idinfo@ado.state.al.us}; {www.ado.state.al.us/trade.htm}. (Stuttgart, **Germany**; Seoul, **Korea**; Tokyo, **Japan**; Jerusalem, **Israel**).

Alaska
Office of International Trade, Department of Commerce and Economic Development, 550 W. 7th Ave., Suite 1770, Anchorage, AK 99501, 907-269-8110; Fax: 907-269-8125; {www.commerce.state.ak.us/trade}. (Tokyo, **Japan**; Seoul, **Korea**; Taipei, **Taiwan**; Sakhalinsk, **Russia**).

Arizona
International Trade and Investment Division, Department of Commerce, 3800 N. Central, Suite 1500, Phoenix, AZ 85012, 602-280-1371; Fax: 602-280-1305; {www.commerce.state.az.us/itrade/itrade.shtml}. (Hermosillo, **Mexico**; Mexico City, **Mexico**; Tokyo, **Japan**; Taipei, **Taiwan**; London, **UK**; Munich, **Germany**).

Arkansas
International Marketing, Arkansas Industrial Commission, One State Capitol Mall, Little Rock, AR 72201, 501-682-2460; Fax: 501-324-9856; {www.1800arkansas.com}. (Brussels, **Belgium**; Tokyo, **Japan**; Mexico City, **Mexico**; Kuala Lumpur, **Malaysia**).

California
California State World Trade Commission, 801 K St., Suite 1926, Sacramento, CA 95814, 916-324-5511; Fax: 916-324-5791 (Tokyo, **Japan**; London, **UK**; **Hong Kong**; Frankfurt, **Germany**; Mexico City, **Mexico**; Taipei, **Taiwan**; Jerusalem, **Israel**; Seoul, **Korea**; Johannesburg, **South Africa**).

Export Development Office, One World Trade Center, Suite 990, Long Beach, CA 90831, 562-590-5965; Fax: 562-590-5958; E-mail: {expdev@commerce.ca.gov}, {commerce.ca.gov/international}.

Colorado
International Trade Office, Department of Commerce and Development, 1625 Broadway, Suite 900, Denver, CO 80202, 303-892-3850; Fax: 303-892-3820; E-mail: {ito@governor.state.co.us};www.state.co.us/gov_dir/govnr_dir/ITO/intl_trade_gov.htm}. (Tokyo, **Japan**; London, **UK**; Guadalajara, **Mexico**).

Connecticut
International Division, Department of Economic and Community Development, 505 Hudson St., Hartford, CT 06106, 203-258-4285; Fax: 203-529-0535; {www.state.ct.us/ecd/international/}. (Tokyo, **Japan**; Taipei, **Taiwan**; Hong Kong; Mexico City, **Mexico**).

Delaware
Delaware Development Office, International Trade Section, 820 French St., Carvel State Building, 3rd Floor, Wilmington, DE 19801, 302-577-8464; Fax: 302-577-8499; {www.state.de.us/dedo/departments/trade/intnt.htm}.

State International Trade Offices

District of Columbia
D.C. Office of International Business, 717 14th St. NW, Suite 1100, Box 4, Washington, DC 20005, 202-727-1576; Fax: 202-727-1588.

Florida
Office of International Affairs, Florida Department of State, The Capitol, Tallahassee, FL 32399-0250; 850-414-1727; Fax: 850-414-1734; E-mail: {intrel@mail.dos.state.fl.us};{oir.dos.state.fl.us}.(Toronto,**Canada**;Taipei, **Taiwan**; Seoul, **Korea**; Frankfurt, **Germany**; Tokyo, **Japan**; London, **UK**; Sao Paulo, **Brazil**; Mexico City, **Mexico**).

Georgia
International Trade Division, Suite 1100, 285 Peachtree Center Ave., Atlanta, GA 30303, 404-656-3571; Fax: 404-651-6505; {www.georgia.org}. (Brussels, **Belgium**; Tokyo, **Japan**; Toronto, **Canada**; Seoul, **Korea**; Mexico City, **Mexico**; **Malaysia**; Sao Paulo, **Brazil**; Shang Hai, **China**; Jerusalem, **Israel**; Johannesburg, **South Africa**; Taipei, **Taiwan**).

Hawaii
Business Development and Marketing Division, Department of Business and Economic Development, P.O. Box 2359, Honolulu, HI 96804, 808-587-2584; Fax: 808-587-3388; {www.hawaii.gov/dbedt/trade/greg.html}. (Tokyo, **Japan**; Taipei, **Taiwan**).

Idaho
Division of International Business, Department of Commerce, 700 W. State St., 2nd Floor, Boise, ID 83720, 208-334-2470; Fax: 208-334-2783; {www.idoc.state.id.us/information/exportinfo/index2.htm}. (Guadalajara, **Mexico**; Taipei, **Taiwan**; Tokyo, **Japan**; Seoul, **Korea**).

Illinois
International Business Division, Illinois Department of Commerce and Community Affairs, 100 W. Randolph St., Suite 3-400, Chicago, IL 60601, 312-814-7179; Fax: 312-814-2370{www.commerce.state.il.us/Services/International/International.htm}. (Brussels, **Belgium**; Causeway Bay, **Hong Kong**; Tokyo, **Japan**; Warsaw, **Poland**; Mexico City, **Mexico**; Budapest, **Hungary**).

Illinois Export Council and Illinois Export Development Authority, 321 N. Clark St., Suite 550, Chicago, IL 60610; (Export Council) 312-793-4982; (Development Authority) 312-793-4995.

Indiana
International Marketing, Department of Commerce, One North Capitol, Suite 700, Indianapolis, IN 46204, 317-232-8845; Fax 317-232-4146; {www.state.in.us/doc/indiresidents/intmarket}. (Tokyo, **Japan**; Mexico City, **Mexico**; Toronto, **Canada**; Taipei, **Taiwan**; Beijing, **China**; Seoul, **Korea**; Amsterdam, **Netherlands**).

Iowa
Department of International Trade, Iowa Department of Economic Development, 200 East Grand Ave., Des Moines, IA 50309, 515-242-4743; Fax: 515-242-4918; E-mail: {international@ided.state.ia.us};{www.state.ia.us/government/ided/intl}.(Frankfurt, **Germany**; Tokyo, **Japan**).

Kansas
Kansas Department of Commerce, 700 SW Harrison St., Suite 1300, Topeka, KS 66603,785-296-4027;Fax:785-296-5763;{kansascommerce.com/0306international.html}. (Tokyo, **Japan**; Brussels, **Belgium**; Sydney, **Australia**; **UK**).

Kentucky
International Trade, Cabinet for Economic Development, 2400 Capitol Plaza Tower, 500 Mero St., Frankfort, KY 40601, 502-564-2170; Fax 502-564-7697; {www.edc.state.ky.us/kyedc}. (Tokyo, **Japan**; Brussels, **Belgium**).

Louisiana
Office of International Marketing, P.O. Box 94185, Baton Rouge, LA 70804-9185, 225-342-4319; Fax: 225-342-5389; {www.lded.state.la.us}. (Mexico City, **Mexico**; Taipei, **Taiwan**; **Netherlands**; Frankfurt, **Germany**).

Maine
International Trade Center, 511 Congress St., Portland, ME 04101, 207-541-7400; Fax: 207-541-7420, {www.mitc.com}.

Maryland
U.S. Export Assistance Center, World Trade Center, 401 East Pratt St., 7th Floor, Suite 2432, Baltimore, MD 21202, 410-962-4539; Fax: 410-962-4529. (Brussels, **Belgium**; Yokohama, **Japan**; **Hong Kong**)

Massachusetts
The Massachusetts Export Center, Fishpier West, Building 2, Boston, MA 02210, 617-478-4133; Fax: 617-478-4135; {www.state.ma.us/export}. (Berlin, **Germany**; Jerusalem, **Israel**; Tokyo, **Japan**; London, **UK**; Guangzhou, **PRC**; Budapest; Taipei, **Taiwan**).

Massachusetts Trade Office State Transportation Building, 10 Park Plaza, Suite 3720, Boston, MA 02116, 617-367-1830; Fax: 617-227-3488; E-mail: {moiti@state.ma.us}; {www.magnet.state.ma.us/moiti/}.

Michigan
International Trade Division, International Trade Authority, Michigan Department of Commerce, P.O. Box 30105, Lansing, MI 48909, 517-373-6369; Fax: 517-335-2521; {michigansbdc.org/intlrsrc.html}. (Toronto, **Canada**; **Hong Kong**; Brussels, **Belgium**; Tokyo, **Japan**; Mexico City, **Mexico**; Harvae, **Zimbabwe**).

Minnesota
Minnesota Trade Office, 1000 Minnesota World Trade Center, 30 E. 7th St., St. Paul, 55101, 800-657-3858, 612-297-4222; Fax: 651-296-1290; E-mail: mto@state.mo.us}; {www.dted.state.mo.us}. (Oslo, **Norway**; Stockholm, **Sweden**; London, **UK**; Paris, **France**; Frankfurt, **Germany**; **Hong Kong**; Osaka, **Japan**; Budapest, **Hungary**; Tokyo, **Japan**; Taipei, **Taiwan**).

Mississippi
Department of Economic and Community Development, P.O. Box 849, Jackson, MI 39205, 601-359-6672; Fax: 601-359-3605 (Seoul, **Korea**; Frankfurt, **Germany**; Taipei, **Taiwan**).

Missouri
International Trade, Department of Economic Development, 301 W. High St., Room 720C, P.O. Box 118, Jefferson City, MO 65102, 573-751-4855, Fax: 573-526-1567; E-mail:{missouri@mail.state.mo.us}, {www.ecodev.state.mo.us/intermark}.(Tokyo, **Japan**; Dusseldorf, **Germany**; Seoul, **Korea**; Taipei, **Taiwan**; Guadalajara, **Mexico**; London, **UK**).

Montana
International Trade Office, Montana Department of Commerce, 1424 9th Ave., Helena, MT 59620, 406-444-4112; Fax: 406-444-2903; {www.state.mt.us}, {commerce.state.mt.us}. (Taipei, **Taiwan**; Kumamoto, **Japan**).

Nebraska
Department of Economic Development, 301 Centennial Mall South, P.O. Box 94666, Lincoln, NE 68509, 402-471-3111; Fax: 402-471-3778; {international.ded.state.ne.us}.

Nevada
Commission of Economic Development, 108 E. Proctor St., Capital Complex, Carson, NV 89710, 775-687-4325; Fax: 775-687-4450; {www.state.nv.us/businessop}.

New Hampshire
International Trade Resource Center, Department of Resources and Economic Development, 601 Spaulding Turnpike, Suite 29, Portsmouth, NH 03801, 603-334-6074; Fax: 603-334-6110; {www.ded.state.nh.us/oic/trade}.

New Jersey
Division of International Trade, Department of Commerce and Economic Development, 20 West State St., 12th Floor, Trenton, NJ 08625, 609-633-3606; Fax: 609-633-3672; {www.nj.njbrc.org}. (Tokyo, **Japan**; London, **UK**; Mexico City, **Mexico**).

New Mexico
Trade Division, Economic Development, 1100 St. Francis Dr., Joseph Montoya Building, Santa Fe, NM 87501, 505-827-0307; Fax: 505-827-0263; {www.edd.state.nm.us/TRADE}. (Mexico City, **Mexico**).

New York
International Division, Department of Trade and Economic Development, 1515 Broadway, 51st Floor, New York Department of Economic Development, New York, NY 10036, 212-827-6200; Fax: 212-827-6279 (Tokyo, **Japan**; London, **UK**; Milan, **Italy**; Toronto and Montreal, **Canada**; **Hong Kong**; Frankfurt, **Germany**).

Selling Overseas: Foreign Markets

North Carolina
International Division, Dept. of Commerce, 430 N. Salisbury St., Raleigh, NC 27611, 919-733-7193; Fax: 919-733-0110; {www.commerce.state.nc.us/commerce/itd}. (Dusseldorf, **Germany**; Hong Kong; Tokyo, **Japan**; London, **UK**; Dubai, **United Arab Emirates**; Toronto, **Canada**).

North Dakota
International Trade Specialist, Department of Economic Development and Finance, 1833 E. Bismarck Expressway, Bismarck, ND 58504, 701-328-5300; Fax: 701-328-5320; {www.growingnd.com/itp_prog.html}.

Ohio
International Trade Division, Department of Development, 77 S. High St., P.O. Box 1001, Columbus, OH 43216, 614-466-5017; 614-463-1540; E-mail: {itd@odod.ohio.gov}, {ohiotrade.tpusa.com}. (Brussels, **Belgium**; Tokyo, **Japan**; Hong Kong; Toronto, **Canada**; Mexico City, **Mexico**; Israel).

Oklahoma
International Trade Division, Oklahoma Department of Commerce, 700 N. Greenwood Ave., Suite 1400, Tulsa, OK 74106, 405-594-8116, Fax: 405-594-8413; {www.odoc.state.ok.us/HOMEPAGE/internat.nsf}. (Seoul, **Korea**; Mexico City, **Mexico**; Singapore; Antwerp, **Belgium**; Ho Chi Mnh City, **Vietnam**; Beijing, **China**; Taipei, **Taiwan**).

Oregon
International Trade Division, Oregon Economic Development Department, One World Trade Center, Suite 300, 121 Salmon St., Portland, OR 97204, 503-229-5625; Fax: 503-222-5050; {www.econ.state.or.us/intl/it.html}. (Tokyo, **Japan**; Seoul, **Korea**; Taipei, **Taiwan**).

Pennsylvania
Department of Commerce, Office of International Trade, 464 Forum Building, Harrisburg, PA 17120, 717-787-7190, 888-PA-EXPORT, Fax: 717-234-4560; {www.dced.state.pa.us/PA_Exec/DCED/international/officeof.htm}. (Frankfurt, **Germany**; Tokyo, **Japan**; Brussels, **Belgium**; Toronto, **Canada**).

Puerto Rico
Fomexport, P.O. Box 362350, San Juan, PR 00936-2350, 809-758-4747, ext. 2785, Fax: 809-764-1415; {www.ddec.govpr.net}.

Rhode Island
International Trade Office, Department of Economic Development, 7 Jackson Walkway, Providence, RI 02903, 401-277-2601; Fax: 401-277-2102; {www.sec.state.ri.us/bus/REIX.htm}. (Mexico City, **Mexico**).

South Carolina
International Business Development, South Carolina State Department of Commerce, P.O. Box 927, Columbia, SC 29202, 803-737-0400; Fax: 803-737-0818; {www.callsouthcarolina.com/InternationalTrade.htm}. (Tokyo, **Japan**; Frankfurt, **Germany**; Seoul **Korea**; London, **UK**).

South Dakota
South Dakota International Business Institute, 1200 S. Jay St., Aberdeen, SD 57401, 605-626-3098, Fax: 605-626-3004; {www.state.sd.us/goed}.

Tennessee
Tennessee Export Office, Department of Economic and Community Development, Rachel Jackson Building, 320 Sixth Ave. North, 7th Floor, Nashville, TN 37219, 615-741-5870, 800-342-8470, 800-251-8594; Fax: 615-741-5829.

Texas
Office of International Marketing, Texas Department of Commerce, 410 E. 5th St., 3rd Floor, Austin, TX 78701, 512-472-5059, Fax: 512-320-9674. (Mexico City, **Mexico**; Frankfurt, **Germany**; Tokyo, **Japan**; Taipei, **Taiwan**; Brussels, **Belgium**; Seoul, **Korea**).

Utah
International Business Development Office, 324 S. State St., Suite 500, Salt Lake City, UT 84111, 801-538-8737, Fax: 801-538-8889; {international.state.ut.us}. (Tokyo, **Japan**).

Vermont
Vermont World Trade Office, 60 Main St., Suite 102, Burlington, VT 05401, 802-865-0493, 800-305-8321, Fax: 802-860-0091; {www.vermontworldtrade.org}.

Virginia
Virginia Economic Development Partnership, P.O. Box 798, 901 E. Byrd St., Richmond, VA 23218, 804-371-8123, Fax: 804-371-8860, E-mail: {exportva@vedp.state.va.us}, {www.exportvirginia.org}. (Tokyo, **Japan**; Frankfurt, **Germany**; Hong Kong; Mexico City, **Mexico**)

Washington
Domestic and International Trade Division, Department of Trade and Economic Development, 2001 Sixth Ave, 26th Floor, Seattle, WA 98121, 206-956-3131; Fax: 206-956-3151; {www.trade.wa.gov}. (Tokyo, **Japan**; Canada; Shanghai, **China**; Paris, **France**; Primorski Krai, **Russian Federation**; Taipei, **Taiwan**).

West Virginia
West Virginia Department of Development, Capitol Complex Bldg. 6, Room 517, 1900 Kanawha Blvd., Charleston, WV 25305, 304-558-2234; Fax: 304-558-1957; {www.wvdo.org/international}. (Tokyo, **Japan**; Nagaya, **Japan**; Munchen, **Germany**; Taipei, **Taiwan**).

Wisconsin
Bureau of International Business Development, Department of Development, P.O. Box 7970, 201 W. Washington Ave., Madison, WI 53707, 608-267-0587; Fax: 608-266-5551; {www.commerce.state.wi.us/Com-International.html}. (Frankfurt, **Germany**; Hong Kong; Mexico City, **Mexico**; Toronto, **Canada**; Tokyo, **Japan**; Seoul, **Korea**; South Korea).

Wyoming
International Trade Office, Department of Commerce, 4th Floor N., Barrett Building, Cheyenne, WY 82002, 307-777-7576; Fax: 307-777-5840.

Overseas Travel: Business or Pleasure

The following sources and services will be helpful to anyone who is on business or vacation in any foreign country:

1) Travel Overseas on Government Expense:
The U.S. Speakers program will pay experts, who can contribute to foreign societies' understanding of the United States, to travel abroad and participate in seminars, colloquia, or symposia. Subjects relevant to the program include economics, international political relations, U.S. social and political processes, arts and humanities, and science and technology. To see if you qualify contact: U.S. Speakers, Office of Program Coordination and Development, U.S. Information Agency, 301 4th St. SW, Room 550, Washington, DC 20547, 202-619-4764.

2) Citizens Arrested Overseas:
The Arrest Unit at the State Department monitors arrests and trials to see that American citizens are not abused; acts as a liaison with family and friends in the United States; sends money or messages with written consent of arrestee; offers lists of lawyers; will forward money from the United States to detainee; tries to assure that your rights under local laws are observed. The Emergency Medical and Dietary Assistance Program includes such services as providing vitamin supplements when necessary; granting emergency transfer for emergency medical care; and short-term feeding of two or three meals a day when arrestee is detained without funds to buy his or her own meals. Contact: Arrests Unit, Citizens Emergency Center, Overseas Citizens Service, Bureau of Consular Affairs, U.S. Department of State, 2201 C St. NW, Room 4817, Washington, DC 20520, 202-647-5225; Fax: 202-647-5226; {travel.state.gov/arrest.html}.

3) Citizens Emergency Center:
Emergency telephone assistance is available to United States citizens abroad under the following circumstances:

Arrests: 202-647-5225; (see details above)

Overseas Travel

Deaths: 202-647-5225; {travel.state.gov/deathrep.html}; notification of interested parties in the United States of the death abroad of American citizens; assistance in the arrangements for disposition of remains.

Financial Assistance: 202-647-5225; {travel.state.gov/money.html}; repatriation of destitute nationals, coordination of medical evacuation of non-official nationals from abroad; transmission of private funds in emergencies to destitute United States nationals abroad when commercial banking facilities are unavailable (all costs must be reimbursed).

Shipping and Seamen: 202-647-5225; {travel.state.gov/where.html}; protection of American vessels and seamen.

Welfare and Whereabouts: 202-647-5225; {travel.state.gov/where.html}; search for nonofficial United States nationals who have not been heard from for an undue length of time and/or about whom there is special concern; transmission of emergency messages to United States nationals abroad. The Welfare and Whereabouts website lists all of the questions that will need to be answered upon calling the service. For other help contact: Overseas Citizen Services, Bureau of Consular Affairs, U.S. Department of State, 2201 C St. NW, Washington, DC 20520, 202-647-5225.

4) **Country Information Studies:**
For someone who wants more than what the typical travel books tell about a specific country, this series of books deals with more in-depth knowledge of the country being visited. Each book describes the origins and traditions of the people and their social and national attitudes, as well as the economics, military, political and social systems. For a more complete listing of this series and price information, contact: Superintendent of Documents, Government Printing Office, Washington, DC 20402, 202-512-1800.

5) **Foreign Country Background Notes:**
Background Notes on the Countries of the World is a series of short, factual pamphlets with information on the country's land, people, history, government, political conditions, economy, foreign relations, and U.S. foreign policy. Each pamphlet also includes a factual profile, brief travel notes, a country map, and a reading list. *Background Notes* is also available online at {www.state.gov/www/background_notes/index.html}. Contact: Public Affairs Bureau, U.S. Department of State, Room 4827A, 2201 C St. NW, Washington, DC 20520, 202-647-2518 for a free copy of *Background Notes* for the countries you plan to visit. This material is also available from the: Superintendent of Documents, U.S. Government Printing Office, Washington, DC 20402, 202-512-1800. Single copies cost from $1.25 to $2.50. Order online at {accessgpo.gov/su_docs/sale/prf/prf.html}.

6) **Foreign Language Materials:**
The Defense Language Institute Foreign Language Center (DLIFC) has an academic library with holdings of over 100,000 books and periodicals in 50 different foreign languages. These materials are available through the national interlibrary loan program which can be arranged through your local librarian. Contact: {pom_www.army.mil}.

7) **Foreign Language Training:**
The Foreign Service Institute is an in-house educational institution for foreign service officers, members of their families and employees of other government agencies. It provides special training in 50 foreign languages. Its instructional materials, including books and tapes, are designed to teach modern foreign languages. Instruction books must be purchased from Superintendent of Documents, U.S. Government Printing Office, Washington, DC 20402, 202-512-1800; {www.gpo.gov}. Tapes must be purchased from the National Audiovisual Center, National Archive, NTIS, Springfield, VA 22161, 1-800-788-6282 or 703-487-8400; {www.ntis.gov/nac}.

8) **Free Booklets for Travelers:**
The following booklets and guides are available free of charge:

Travel Information: Your Trip Abroad:
Contains basic information such as how to apply for a passport, customs tips, lodging information, and how American consular officers can help you in an emergency. Contact: Publications Distribution, Bureau of Public Affairs, U.S. Department of State, 2201 C St. NW, Room 5815A, Washington, DC 20520, 202-647-9859.

Customs Information:
Provides information about custom regulations both when returning to the U.S. as well as what to expect when traveling to different parts of the world. Contact: Customs Office, P.O. Box 7118, Washington, DC 20044; {www.customs.ustreas.gov}.

Visa Requirements of Foreign Governments:
Lists entry requirements of U.S. citizens traveling as tourists, and where and how to apply for visas and tourist cards. For Americans attempting to gain visas in other countries, Consular Affairs maintains a listing of the requirements for acquiring a visa in each country and which countries are not currently not accepting visas. Contact online at {travel.state.gov/foreignentryreqs.html}. Contact: Passport Services, Bureau of Consular Affairs, U.S. Department of State, 1425 K St. NW, Room G-62, Washington, DC 20524, 202-647-0518; E-mail: {usvisa@state.gov}; {travel.state.gov/visa_services.html}

9) **Passport Information:**
U.S. citizens and nationals can apply for passports at all passport agencies as well as those post offices and federal and state courts authorized to accept passport applications. Due to the cost of maintaining passport services, the National Passport Information Center created a fee-financed call center with two options. 900-225-5674 charges 35 cents per minute for all calls. 888-362-8668 charges a flat rate of $4.95 per call. To avoid these charges, the NPIC has created a detailed website containing passport applications, statistics, information on how to add pages, replace a lost or stolen passport, renew an old passport, and get a listing of fees for services as well as all post offices handling passport affairs.

10) **Travel Warnings:**
Before traveling, it is always a good idea to be aware of any travel warnings for your destination. All travel warnings, general warnings, and public announcements are listed by country and are available on the Bureau of Consular Affairs website at {travel.state.gov/travel_warnings.html}. These warnings may also be heard by telephone at any time by dialing 202-647-5225, or by utilizing an automated fax retrieval system at 202-647-3000.

Legislation

Legislation:
How To Monitor Federal Legislation

The U.S. Congress is accustomed to answering questions and sharing information with the public. Here is how you can quickly learn about any bill or resolution pending before the House of Representatives or Senate:

Free Legislation Database

This Bill Status Office can tell you the latest action on any federal legislation within seconds. Every bill and resolution for the current session as well as all House and Senate legislation dating back to 1975 are contained in LEGIS, a computerized database. When you call, it is best to give a key word or phrase (i.e., product liability, hazardous waste) which will help the congressional aides search LEGIS. This office can provide such detailed information as:

Have any bills been introduced covering a given topic?
Who is the sponsor of the bill?
How many co-sponsors are there?
When was it introduced?
Which committees have the bills been referred to?
Have any hearings been held?
Has there been any floor action?
Has a similar bill been introduced in the other chamber?
Has there been any action on the other side of the Hill?
Have the House and Senate agreed to a compromise bill?
Has the bill been sent to the White House?
Has the President signed or vetoed the bill?
What is the PL (public law) number?

Telephone assistance is free, and printouts from LEGIS are available for $.20 per page with a $5 minimum, but must be picked up at the Bill Status Office. However, by making arrangements with your Representative's or Senator's office, you can avoid this nominal charge and also have the printout mailed to your home or office. Contact: LEGIS, Office of Legislative Information, B106 Cannon House Office Building, Washington, DC 20515; 202-225-1772.

Bill Sponsor's Legislative Assistant

The aide to the Senator or Representative who is the sponsor of a particular bill is the best person to contact next. The Bill Status Office can tell you the sponsor, and the Capitol Hill Switchboard at 202-224-3121 can transfer you to the appropriate office; then ask to speak to the person in charge of the particular bill. Usually, this congressional aide will offer to send you a copy of the bill, a press announcement, and other background information. Don't lose this opportunity to get your first of many predictions about the likelihood of the bill becoming law.

Committee Staff

Committees and subcommittees are the real work centers of the Congress. After you touch base with the Bill Status Office (LEGIS), it is wise to double-check that information with the House or Senate committees which have jurisdiction over the legislation you are tracking. The Capitol Hill Switchboard at 202-224-3121 can connect you with any committee. Once you reach the committee staffer who handles the bill in question, you are now in a position of obtaining the following information:

Are hearings expected to be held?
Has the subcommittee or committee chair promised a vote on the measure?
What is the timetable for committee "markup" and consideration of amendments?
What is the Administration's position on the legislation?
Has the committee filed its report on the bill?
Is there any action on a similar proposal on the other side of the Hill?

You can get free copies of House bills, resolutions, and House committee reports by sending a self-addressed mailing label to the House Document Room, B106 Cannon House Office Building, Washington, DC 20515; 202-226-5200. Similarly, you can direct your requests for Senate documents to the Senate Document Room, Senate Hart Bldg., Room B-04, Washington, DC 20510; 202-224-7860. Public laws, often called slip laws, can be obtained from either the House or Senate Document Rooms, but call the Bill Status Office to get the public law number. You can get printed copies of hearings by contacting the committee which conducted the inquiry, but expect several months lag time before it becomes available.

If the legislation you are concerned about is scheduled for action on the floor of the House or Senate, you can monitor its activity by the hour by listening to the following recorded messages:

House of Representatives Cloakroom
    Democrat   202-225-7400
    Republican   202-225-2020

Senate Cloakroom
    Democrat   202-224-8541
    Republican   202-224-8601

Play Constituent

Your Representative's or Senator's office also can help with your questions about specific bills, particularly when you have difficulty getting through to committee or subcommittee staffers. Remember that Members of Congress are eager to serve their constituents, especially for simple requests such as sending you copies of bills or new public laws. The Capitol Hill Switchboard Operator at 202-224-3121 can connect you with the Washington office of your Representative and Senators.

How To Monitor Federal Legislation

Additional Tools for Monitoring Federal Legislation

There are sophisticated variations of the free LEGIS database described above. One reason for the growth of commercial databases is that direct online access to LEGIS is limited to Members of Congress and their staff. The following databanks cover every bill or resolution pending before the current session:

* Electronic Legislative Search System
This online system tracks all current federal legislation (as well as all 50 states) and also provides introductory bill summaries and legislative histories. Contact: Commerce Clearinghouse, 4025 W. Peterson Avenue, Chicago, IL 60646, 312-583-8500.

* Washington Alert Service
This database covers all bills introduced in the U.S. Congress and includes information on committee schedules, release of committee reports and other documents, all recorded votes as well as full text of the publication, *CQ Weekly Report*. Contact: Congressional Quarterly, 1414 22nd Street, NW, Washington, DC 20037; 800-432-2250, 202-887-6279; {www.oncongress.cq.com}.

There are plenty of specialized trade publications designed to help lobbyists stay apprised of developments on the Hill. Online access is available to some of these newsletters, for instance, the Bureau of National Affairs' *Daily Tax Report* and *Money and Politics* (BNA, 1231 25th St., NW, Washington, DC 20037; 800-253-0332 or 202-452-4200; {www.bna.com}). Another example is Budgetrack, a database produced by the editors of *Aviation Week and Space Technology*, which monitors the budget for the U.S. Defense Department and NASA from presidential submission to final congressional action (Budgetrack is available online from Data Resources, Inc., 1750 K St., NW, Washington DC 20006).

The American Enterprise Institute {www.aei.gov}, the Brookings Institution {www.brook.edu}, and other Washington-based think tanks generate position papers on specific legislative initiatives and often will share their information with the public. Other useful outside sources which can shed light on activities on the Hill are both small, specialized trade associations and large ones, for example, the National Paint and Coating Association {www.paint.org} and the U.S. Chamber of Commerce {www.uschamber.com}. How successful you are at getting these organizations to help you depends in large measure on how good you are on the telephone.

Congressional Experts

An estimated 4,000 legislative assistants and committee aides fall into the category of "professional staff." Because these congressional aides often draft bills and amendments and play a critical role in the negotiations with special interest groups, they are valuable sources of information, but some are much more open and candid than others. When dealing with these experts, remember they are at the beck and call of an elected official. It doesn't hurt to appeal to their egos and offer to call them when they aren't quite so busy.

Investigations and Special Reports

There are approximately 20 congressional committees and subcommittees which do not have legislative authority but serve as watchdogs with responsibility for reviewing existing laws. Some examples include the Senate Permanent Subcommittee on Investigations, House Select Committee on Aging, the Joint Economic Committee, and the House Science and Technology Subcommittee on Investigations and Oversight. These congressional panels conduct full-scale hearings on a wide range of subjects. A complete listing of these committees appears in the U.S. Congress Committees section. Some hearings conducted by the House Energy and Commerce Subcommittee on Oversight and Investigations during the 105th Congress include the following examples:

> "Medicaid Fraud and Abuse: Assisting State and Federal Responses"
> "Problems with EPA's Brownfields Cleanup Revolving Loan Fund Program"
> "Paducah Gaseous Diffusion Plant: An Assessment of Worker Safety and Environmental Contamination"

Many of these committees will put you on their mailing lists to receive notices of upcoming hearings as well as their *Committee Calendar*, which lists all of the hearings held during the previous year.

Congressional Caucuses

Approximately 100 non-legislative caucuses formed by Members of Congress serve as in-house think tanks. Some of these coalitions, such as the Congressional Clearinghouse on the Future, provide information to the public. The House Steel Caucus, the Senate Coal Caucus, the Congressional Port Caucus, and others work to get their particular legislative initiatives through the Congress. The staff directors of these organizations can be good sources because these congressional aides have access to all government studies and also have close contact with industry and special interests that the caucus is going to bat for.

Many of these "informal groups" dissolve after work on its legislative priorities is completed, so you should expect that these organizations come and go. A list of these organizations appear next in U.S. Congress Committees section. Note that the Capitol Hill Switchboard at 202-224-3121 or your Member of Congress can help you find out if a particular special interest caucus exists. A list of the current caucuses appears in the U.S. Congress Committee section.

Federal Agencies Legislative Affairs Offices

Every federal department and agency has an office which makes the Administration's case for the President's proposed budget or legislation. These offices within the executive branch usually are termed the "Offices of Legislative Affairs," which concentrate on particular bills. This is in contrast to an agency's own Office of Congressional Relations, which tends to respond to requests made by lawmakers or their staff. The office of legislative affairs also makes available written testimony by agency officials who appeared as witnesses at congressional hearings.

Legislation

Arms of Congress

In addition to the 47 House and Senate committees, the following four organizations produce volumes of information and reports to aid lawmakers. These studies and recommendations by these arms of Congress are available to the public.

* **Congressional Budget Office**
    Ford House Office Building
    2nd and D Streets SW
    Washington, DC 20515   202-226-2600
    www.cbo.gov

Scorekeeping reports, special studies and other economic assessments are all available free to the public.

* **Congressional Research Service (CRS)**
    Library of Congress
    101 Independence Ave., SE
    Washington, DC 20540   202-707-5008
    www.loc.gov
    E-mail: lcweb@loc.gov

Congressional Research Service (CRS) studies cover practically every current event topic. You must arrange to get copies of any CRS publications through your Member of Congress.

* **General Accounting Office**
    Office of Public Affairs Room 7049
    441 G Street NW
    Washington, DC 20548   202-512-4800
    www.gao.gov

Reports and audit information about every government program.

Tracking State Legislation

Bill Status Information

Most state legislatures maintain an office responsible for providing bill status information to the public. In Ohio, for example, a bank of telephone reference experts answer questions about current or past legislation on any given subject. The researchers rely on their own files and also have access to a computerized database updated by the Senate Clerk's office. Usually these offices can search their databases or indexes in several ways, by keyword or phrase, by specific subject, or by state senator or representative.

About half of the legislatures can send you this information in the form of a computer printout free of charge. In those states which do not operate a central bill status office, it is necessary to contact the Clerk of the House for information on bills pending before the House and similarly a call to the Secretary or Clerk of the Senate for updates on legislation pending before that body. Many legislatures have toll-free numbers which can be accessed only if you are calling from inside the state. Most of the State House hotlines operate just during the regular session of the legislature and, as you might expect, some of the "800" numbers change from one session to the next.

Your initial call to the bill status office will lead you to the appropriate committees, and if no action has been taken on a particular bill, this legislative information office can provide you with the sponsor of the legislation whom you can call directly for more details.

Copies of Bills and Other Legislative Documents

In most states, the legislative information office can send you copies of bills. Indiana is the only state that charges $.10 per page if the bill is more than 10 pages long. All states print the bills at the time of introduction. Over half reprint the amended legislation after committee action, and about two-thirds of all chambers print the legislation after the floor vote. Unlike the U.S. Congress, legislative documentation is skimpy when it comes to committee hearings as well as floor debate. Only about a third of all legislative bodies tape all committee sessions. You can make arrangements with the Clerk's office to listen to the tapes, and some states, like the Minnesota House, sell audio tapes of committee meetings and floor debates for $12.50 per copy. For copies, call 612-296-3398.

Advanced Strategy for Monitoring One or All 50 State Legislatures

Coverage of a state legislature can be substantially enhanced in many ways; some are inexpensive and others can be costly:

* **Clipping Service**:
Newspapers, especially those published in the state capital, can prove to be a cost effective way of staying informed provided the issues of concern are controversial or significant enough to capture the attention of the local media.

* **Local Chamber of Commerce**:
This organization may offer information about certain issues it is following on behalf of the business community.

* **Stringers**:
Often expensive, but there may be no substitute for hiring someone who is in frequent contact with legislators and is a familiar face in the document rooms and statehouse corridors.

* **Governor's Legislative Liaison Office**:
On major legislative initiatives and politically "hot" issues, try telephoning this office.

* **National Conference of State Legislators (NCSL)**:
Although this organization serves legislators, the staff will respond to requests from the public. The Conference maintains a list of reports and studies by investigative committees in all 50 states. Access to its in-house database may be possible in the future. This national organization of state legislators and legislative staff aims to improve the quality and effectiveness of state legislators, to ensure states a strong, cohesive voice in the federal decision-making process and to foster interstate communication and cooperation. Contact either of the two offices at 1560 Broadway, Suite 700, Denver, CO 80202; 303-830-2200, Fax: 303-863-8003; or 444 North Capitol St., NW, Suite 515, Washington, DC 20001; 202-624-5400, Fax: 202-737-1069, {www.ncsl.org}.

* **Council of State Governments/State Information Center**:
This arm of the Council of State Governments publishes several useful directories, including *The Book of States*, *Administration Officials* and *Legislative Leadership Committees and Staff*. Its database may soon be available to the public. Contact: State Information Center, Council of State Governments, 2760 Research Park Drive, P.O. Box 11910, Lexington, KY 40578; 606-244-8000, Fax: 606-244-8001, {www.statesnews.org}.

* **Commerce Clearing House (CCH)**:
CCH offers the "State Legislative Reporting Service" as well as the Electronic Legislative Search System. The Reporting Service allows you to select only those legislatures you are interested in, whereas the online search system tracks all current legislation in all 50 states. Contact: CCH, 4025 West Peterson Avenue, Chicago, IL 60646; 312-583-8500, 800-TELL-CCH.

* **Information for Public Affairs**:
This private firm offers online access to its database containing the status of legislation pending before the current session of all 50 state legislatures. Contact: IPA, 2101 K St., Sacramento, CA 95816; 916-444-0840.

* **Other Private Legislative Reporting Services**:
Legi-Tech Corporation and other firms specialize in tracking one or two statehouses. About half of the legislatures are covered by such information brokers.

Legislation

Reports and Resources Available from State Legislatures

A trend among state legislatures is the creation of special investigative committees which have responsibility for oversight and often the power to subpoena. These watchdogs usually have permanent full-time staff and produce reports throughout the year. Frequent contact with these committees is necessary to stay informed about their activities.

Here is a sampling of reports issued by the Virginia Joint Legislative Audits and Review Committee:

The Impact of Digital TV on Public Broadcasts in Virginia
Review of Air Medevac Services in Virginia
Competitive Procurement of State Printing Contracts
Alternatives to Stabilize Regional Criminal Justice Training
   Academy Membership
Review of Undergraduate Student Financial Aid in
   Virginia's Public Institutions
Activities to Identify Water Toxic Problems and Inform
   the Public
The Feasibility of Converting Camp Pendelton to a State
   Park
Review of the Health Regulatory Board
Virginia's Welfare Reform Initiative
Review of the Functional Area of Health and Human
   Resources

Even those legislatures that compress their work into 60 or 90 day sessions are active year-round. Information about hearings, meetings, and reports produced throughout the Interim can be provided by each state house legislative information office.

State Legislatures: Bill Status Information Offices

You will find more than 50 information offices listed here because some state houses do not have one centralized legislature reference office.

Alabama
Senate Bill Status, 11 S. Union, Room 716, New State House, Montgomery, AL 36130-4600; 334-242-7800, 800-499-3051. This office can respond to questions about all Senate bills and refer you to the appropriate committee, document room, etc.

House Bill Status, 11 S.Union, Room 512, New State House, Montgomery, AL 36130-4600; 334-242-7600, 800-499-3052, {www.legislature.state.al.us/ALIShome.html}. This office can provide information on all bills pending before the House of Representatives and can refer you to the appropriate committees, document rooms, etc.

Alaska
Legislative Information, 130 Seward St., Suite 313, Juneau, AK 99801-2197; 907-465-4648, TDD: 907-465-2864, {www.legis.state.ak.us/home}. This office can provide information on the status of House and Senate bills. It can do subject searches by accessing a database but at this time Legislative Information cannot provide computer printouts. Copies of bills will be sent out by this office.

Arizona
Information Desk, House of Representatives, State House, 1700 West Washington Street, Phoenix, AZ 85007; 520-628-6593, {www.azleg.state.az.us}. This Information Desk is the best starting point to learn the status of all bills pending before the House of Representatives. This office will refer you to the appropriate committees, document room, etc.

Senate Information Desk, State House, 1700 West Washington Street, Phoenix, AZ 85007; 520-628-6596. This Information Desk maintains current information on all bills pending before the Arizona Senate. This office will refer you to the appropriate committees, document rooms, etc.

Arkansas
Office of Legislative Counsel, State Capitol Building, Room 315, Little Rock, AR 72201; 501-682-1937, {www.arkleg.state.ar.us}. This office can provide status information on all legislation pending before the House of Representatives and the Senate. It has scheduling information and can you refer you to the appropriate committees, document rooms, etc.

California
Office of the Chief Clerk, State Assembly, State Capitol, Room 3196, Sacramento, CA 95814; 916-319-2856, {www.leginfo.ca.gov/index.html}. This office can respond to questions regarding legislation pending before the State Assembly and Assembly committees. This office can refer you to the appropriate offices in the State Capitol such as the document rooms.

Secretary of the Senate, State Capitol, Room 3044, Sacramento, CA 95814; 916-445-4251. This office can provide information about bills pending before the Senate and the Senate committees. The Secretary of the Senate also will refer you to appropriate offices in the State Capitol such as where to obtain copies of Senate bills.

Colorado
Legislative Information Center, 200 E. Colfax Ave., Room 022, Denver, CO 80203; 303-866-3055, {www.state.co.us/gov_dir/stateleg.html}. This office can provide information on the status of both House and Senate bills. The Legislative Information Center also can send you copies of bills as well as mail out status sheets which target on bills pertaining to a specific subject.

Connecticut
Bill Information Room, Law and Legislative Reference Dept., State Library Bldg., 231 Capitol Avenue, Hartford, CT 06106; 860-566-4544, {www.cga.state.ct.us}. This office can provide information about both House and Senate bills and send you copies of bills. Besides doing a key word or subject search, this office can mail you a printout of all legislation pertaining to one topic.

Delaware
Division of Research, Legislative Counsel, Legislative Hall, Dover, DE 19901; 302-739-4114; 800-282-8545, {www.state.de.us/research/assembly.htm}. This office can provide status information on both House and Senate bills and send you copies of bills. It can access a legislative computerized database and do searches for free. The toll-free number operates year-round.

Florida
Legislative Information Division, 111 W. Madison St., Room 704, Tallahassee, FL 32399-1400; 850-488-4371; 800-342-1827, {www.leg.state.fl.us}. This office can provide status information on all House and Senate bills. It can send you single copies of up to 10 bills and mail out printouts of all House and Senate bills pertaining to a specific subject.

Georgia
Clerk of the House, 309 State Capitol, Atlanta, GA 30334; 404-656-5015, {www.ganet.org/services/leg}. This office can provide up-to-date information on all House bills and send you copies of House bills. The Clerk of the House also will search its database to tell you all legislation that has been introduced on a specific topic.

Secretary of the Senate, State Capitol, Room 353, Atlanta, GA 30334; 404-656-5040; 800-282-5803. This office can respond to questions about all bills pending before the Georgia Senate. The Secretary of the Senate can send you copies of Senate bills and search its database for legislation pertaining to a specific subject.

Hawaii
Clerk of the House, State Capitol of Hawaii, Room 027, Honolulu, HI 96813; 808-586-6400, {www.capitol.hawaii.gov}. This office can respond to questions about bills

Tracking State Legislation

pending before the House and refer you to the appropriate offices in the State Capitol such as the document room.

Clerk of the Senate, State Capitol of Hawaii, Room 010, Honolulu, HI 96813; 808-586-6720. This office can provide status information on all legislation pending before the Hawaii Senate. It can refer you to the appropriate offices in the State Capitol such as the document room.

Idaho
Legislative Services Research and Information, 700 W. Jefferson, State Capitol, Room 108, P.O. Box 83720, Boise, ID 83720-0054; 208-334-2475, {ww2.state.id.us/legislat/legislat.html}. This office can give you information on the status of all House and Senate bills. It also can send you copies of bills as well as a printout of all legislation pertaining to a specific topic.

Illinois
Clerk of the House, State Capitol Building, Room 424, Springfield, IL 62706; 217-782-6010; 800-252-6300, {www.legis.state.il.us}. This office can respond to questions about both House and Senate bills, and provide you with copies of bills. The Clerk's office can send you printouts, for example, a list of all bills sponsored by one legislator.

Indiana
Legislative Information, Legislative Services Agency, 302 State House, Indianapolis, IN 46204; 317-232-9856, {www.state.in.us/legislative/index.html}. The agency can give you bill status information and do searches by bill number, subject or legislator. Legislative Information can send you copies of bills but charge $.15 per page.

Iowa
Legislative Information Office, State Capitol, Room 16, Des Moines, IA 50319; 515-281-5129, {ww2.legis.state.ia.us/GA/786A/legislation}. This office can provide information on all House and Senate bills and send you copies of bills. It can access a computerized database and mail you a printout of all legislation pertaining to a specific subject.

Kansas
Legislative Reference, State Library, State Capitol Third Floor, 343-N, Topeka, KS 66612; 913-296-2149; 800-432-3924, {http://skyways.lib.ks.us/ksleg/KLRD/klrd.htm}. This office can tell you the status of all current House and Senate legislation as well as provide bill histories. Legislative Reference can send you copies of bills and voting records.

Kentucky
Bill Status, State Capitol Annex, Room T-3, Frankfort, KY 40601; 502-564-8100; 800-776-9158, {www.lrc.state.ky.us/home.htm}. This office can provide information on House and Senate bills pending before the legislature. It can also send you copies of bills.

Louisiana
Legislative Research Library, House of Representatives, P.O. Box 94012, Baton Rouge, LA 70804-9012; {www.legis.state.la.us/welcome.htm}; Senate Docket 504-342-2365; House Docket 504-342-1986. During the session, call the toll-free PULS Line, 800-256-3793 (if out-of-state, 504-342-2456) for bill status information and to have them send you copies of House and Senate bills. When the legislature is not in session, contact the Legislative Research Library, 504-342-4914.

Maine
Legislative Information Office, State House Station 100, Room 314, Augusta, ME 04333; 207-287-1692, TTY: 207-287-6826, {http://janus.state.me.us/legis}. This office can respond to questions about House and Senate bills and do key word or subject searches of its database.

Maryland
Legislative Information Desk, Dept. of Legislative Reference, 90 State Circle, Annapolis, MD 21401; 410-946-5400; 800-492-7122, {http://mlis.state.md.us#bill}. This office can provide status information on all House and Senate bills and send you copies of bills. It also can provide you with a printout of all bills which pertain to a specific subject area.

Massachusetts
Citizen Information Service, 1 Ashburton Place, 16th Floor, Boston, MA 02108; 617-727-7030, 800-392-6090, {www.magnet.state.ma.us/legis/legis.htm}. This office can provide bill status information and supply copies of bills but you must know the bill number. To obtain bill numbers and other information contact the Clerk of the House which is listed below.

Clerk of the House, House of Representatives, State House, Boston, MA 02133; 617-722-2356. This office can respond to questions about House bills and will refer you to the document room and other appropriate offices within the State House. For Senate bills, contact the Senate Clerk at 617-722-1276.

Michigan
Clerk of the House, State Capitol, Lansing, MI 48909; 517-373-0135, {www.milegislativecouncil.org}. This office can provide information on the status of House bills and can do searches of its database to identify legislation which pertains to a specific subject. It will refer you to the House document room for copies of bills.

Secretary of the Senate, P.O. Box 30036, Lansing, MI 48909-7536; 517-373-2400. This office can provide Senate bill status information and also can send you copies of bills.

Minnesota
House Index Office, State Capitol Building, Room 211, St Paul, MN 55155; 612-296-6646, {www.leg.state.mn.us/leg/legis.htm}. This office can tell you the status of all House bills but will refer you to the Chief Clerk's office (612-296-2314) for copies of all House bills. It can search its database to identify all bills that pertain to a specific subject.

Senate Index Office, State Capitol Building, Room 231, St Paul, MN 55155, 612-296-2887. This office can provide bill status information on all Senate legislation and will refer you to the Secretary of the Senate if you want to obtain copies of bills. It can search its database and identify all bills pertaining to a specific subject.

Mississippi
House Docket Room, PO Box 1018, New Capitol Room 305, Jackson, MS 39215; 601-359-3358, {www.ls.state.ms.us/index.html}. This office can tell you the status of all House bills and send you copies of proposed laws pending before the House.

Senate Docket Room, PO Box 1018, New Capitol Room 308, Jackson, MS 39215; 601-359-3229. This office can respond to questions about bills pending before the Mississippi Senate and send you copies of Senate bills.

Missouri
House Information Bill Status, State Capitol, Room 307B, Jefferson City, MO 65101; 314-751-3659, {www.moga.state.mo.us}. This office can provide information on bills pending before the House and will refer you to the appropriate offices within the State Capitol such as the document room.

Senate Research, State Capitol Room B-9, Jefferson City, MO 65101; 314-751-4666. This office can respond to questions about bills pending before the Senate and will refer you to the appropriate offices such as the document room.

Montana
Legislative Counsel, State Capitol, Room 138, Helena, MT 59620; 406-444-3064, 800-333-3408, {www.mt.gov/leg/branch/branch.htm}. The in-state toll-free number may change in subsequent sessions of the Montana legislature. The Legislative Counsel office can respond to inquiries year-round and send you copies of bills.

Nebraska
Hotline, Office of the Clerk, State Capitol, Room 2018, Lincoln, NE 68509; 402-471-2709; 800-742-7456, {www.unicam.state.ne.us/index.htm}. This office operates an in-state hotline during the session that can provide information on all bills pending before this unicameral legislature. The Clerk can respond to questions year-round.

Legislation

Nevada
Chief Clerk of the Assembly, Legislative Building, 401 S. Carson St., Carson City, NV 89710; 702-687-5739, {www.leg.state.nv.us}. This office can provide information about the status of bills pending before the Assembly. The Chief Clerk will refer you to the appropriate offices in the State Capitol such as the documents room or the Clerk of the Senate.

New Hampshire
State Library Reference and Information Services, 20 Park Street, Concord, NH 03301; 603-271-2239, {www.state.nh.us/gencourt/legcourt.html}. This office can respond to questions about House and Senate bills pending before the legislature. It can send you copies of bills and search its database for bills pertaining to specific subject areas. Senate Clerk Office, Senate Chamber-State Office, 107 North Main Street, Concord, NH 03301, 603-271-3420.

New Jersey
Office of Legislative, Services-Bill Room, Executive Statehouse, Room #6, Statehouse CN 068, Trenton, NJ 08625; 609-292-6395; 800-792-8630, {www.njleg.state.nj.us}. This office can provide information about House and Senate legislation and send you copies of bills. It will refer you to other offices within the State House if necessary.

New Mexico
Legislative Counsel, State Capitol, Room 311, Santa Fe, NM 87501; 505-986-4600, {http://legis.state.nm.us/directory}. This office can provide bill status information on House and Senate legislation. It will refer you to the appropriate offices within the State Capitol such as the document room.

New York
Public Information Office, Room 202 LOB 2nd Floor Empire State Plaza, Albany, NY 12248; 518-455-4218, 800-342-9860, {http://assembly.state.ny.us}. This office can provide information on the status of House and Senate bills and send you copies of bills. It may refer you to your local library if you want a search done to identify all bills which pertain to a specific subject.

North Carolina
State Legislative Building, Legislative Library, Raleigh, NC 27601; 919-733-7779, {www.ncga.state.nc.us}. This office can provide information about House and Senate bills and will refer you to the appropriate offices within the State Capitol such as where to obtain copies of bills.

North Dakota
Legislative Counsel Library, State Capital, 2nd Floor, Bismarck, ND 58505; 701-328-2916, {www.state.nd.us/lr}. This office can provide information about House and Senate bills year-round and will refer you to appropriate offices in the State Capitol. The legislature maintains an in-state toll-free number during the biannual session.

Ohio
Legislative Information, State House, Columbus, OH 43266-0604; 614-466-8842; 800-282-0253, {www.legislature.state.oh.us}. This office can provide information on the status of House and Senate legislation and do subject searches. This telephone bank of researchers will route your requests (i.e., copies of bills). In-state toll-free access is available throughout the year.

Oklahoma
Chief Clerk, House of Representatives, State Capitol Bldg., Oklahoma City, OK 73105; 405-521-2711, 800-522-8502, {www.lsb.state.ok.us}. This office can respond to questions about bills pending before the House and Senate. It will refer you to the appropriate offices within the State Capitol.

Oregon
Legislative Library, State Capitol S-347, Salem, OR 97310; 503-378-8871, 800-332-2313, {http://landru.leg.state.or.us/comm/pro.htm}. This office can provide information on House and Senate bills year-round. During the biannual session the legislature offers an in-state toll-free number for bill information.

Pennsylvania
Legislative Reference Bureau, History Room, Main Capitol Building, Room 648, Harrisburg, PA 17120-0033; 717-787-2342, {www.legis.state.pa.us}. This office can provide information on House and Senate bills be consulting its card index and computerized database. It will refer you to the appropriate offices, for example, where to obtain copies of bills.

Rhode Island
Legislative Information Line, State House, Room #2, Providence, RI 02903; 401-751-8833; {www.rilnstate.ri.us}. This office can provide you with information on the status of House and Senate bills and send you copies of bills. It will refer you to the appropriate legislators or committees.

South Carolina
Legislative Information Systems, Room 112, Blatt Building, 1105 Pendleton St., Columbia, SC 29201; 803-734-2923, 800-922-1539, {www.lpitr.sc.us}. This office can respond to inquiries about House and Senate bills and will refer you to the appropriate offices such as where to obtain copies of bills. It can do subject searches but is unable to send out a printout.

South Dakota
Public Information Clerk, Legislative Research Counsel, State Capitol Building, 500 East Capitol, Pierre, SD 57501; 605-773-4498, {www.state.sd.us/state/legis/lrc.home}. They can provide information on the status of House and Senate bills. They can access a computerized database and do a search to identify legislation which pertains to a specific subject.

Tennessee
Office of Legislative Services, Room G-20, War Memorial Bldg, Nashville, TN 37243; 615-741-3511, 800-342-1003, {www.legislature.state.tn.us}. This office can provide information on House and Senate bills and will send you copies of bills. It can identify all legislation pending on specific subjects.

Texas
Legislative Reference Library, P.O. Box 12488, Capitol Station, Austin, TX 78711; 512-463-1252, {www.capitol.state.tx.us}. This office can provide information on the status of all House and Senate bills. It can search its database to identify all legislation which pertains to a specific subject. It will refer you to the appropriate offices such as the document room. The in-state toll-free access number changes yearly.

Utah
Legislative Research and General Counsel, 436 State Capitol, Salt Lake City, UT 84114; 801-538-1032, {www.lc.state.utah.us}. This office can respond to questions about House and Senate bills. It will refer you to the appropriate offices within the State Capitol.

Vermont
Vermont Legislative Counsel, 115 State St., Montpelier, VT 05633-5301; 808-828-2231, {www.leg.state.vt.us}. This office responds to House and Senate Bill Status questions. They will refer you to the appropriate offices.

Virginia
Legislative Information, House of Delegates, P.O. Box 406, Richmond, VA 23218; 804-786-6530, {http://legis.state.va.us}. This office can provide information on House and Senate bills and can send you copies of bills. It can consult a printed index which is updated daily to identify bills which pertain to a specific subject.

Washington
House Workroom, Legislative Building, Third Floor Capitol Campus, P.O. Box 40600, Olympia, WA 98504-0600; 360-786-7780; 800-562-6000, {http://wsl.leg.wa.gov/wsladin}. This office can provide information on the status of bills pending before the House. It can also provide copies of bills. The toll free number (out of state should call 360-786-7763) is in operation only during the session.

Senate Workroom, Legislative Building AS32, Third Floor Capitol Campus, P.O. Box 40482, Olympia, WA 98504-0482; 360-786-7592; 800-562-6000. This office can

Tracking State Legislation

provide information on bills pending before the Senate and can supply you with copies of bills. An in-state toll-free number (out of state call 360-786-7763) provides both House and Senate bill information but only during the session.

West Virginia

Clerk of the House, House of Delegates, 1900 Kanawha Blvd. E, Bldg.1, Room M212, Charleston, WV 25305-0470; 304-340-3200, {www.legis.state.wv.us}. This office can respond to questions about legislation pending before the House of Delegates and House committees. It will refer you to the appropriate offices in the State Capitol such as where to obtain legislative documents.

Clerk of the Senate, 1900 Kanawha Blvd. E, Bldg., Room M-211, Charleston, WV 25305-0470; 304-357-7800. This office can provide information on the status of bills pending before the Senate. It will refer you to the appropriate offices in the State Capitol.

Wisconsin

Legislative Reference Bureau, 100 N. Hamilton St., POB 2037, Madison, WI 53701-2037; 608-266-0341; 800-362-9472, {www.legis.state.wi.us}. The legislature operates a Legislative Hotline during the session (if calling from inside Madison, dial 608-266-9960). The Legislative Reference Bureau can respond to questions year-round will refer you to the document room, etc.

Wyoming

Legislative Service Office, State Capitol Building, Room 213, Cheyenne, WY 82002; 307-777-7881, 800-342-9570 within Wyoming, {http://legisweb.state.wy.us}. When the Wyoming legislature is not in session it is necessary to contact this office. During the session, bill status questions are best directed to the two offices noted below.

Senate Information Clerk, State Capitol Building, Cheyenne, WY 82002; 307-777-6185. This office can respond to questions about the status of bills pending before the Senate. It will refer you to the Bill Room to obtain copies of bills.

House Information Clerk, Bill Status, State Capitol Building, Cheyenne, WY 82002; 307-777-6185; 800-342-9570 (in state only). This office can provide current information on legislation pending before the House. It will refer you to the proper offices in the State Capitol, for instance, the Bill Room.

Government Auctions and Surplus Property

Government Auctions and Surplus Property: Federal Auctions

Whether you're looking for a good bargain on equipment to furnish your home office, or whether you're interested in a low overhead business of buying government property and reselling it, all you need is here. Year round, the federal government offers hundreds of millions of dollars worth of property and goods — from animals to real estate — at remarkable prices. The Customs Service sells seized property — jewelry, camera, rugs — anything brought in from another country. The Internal Revenue Service (IRS) auctions off everything imaginable — boats, cars, businesses. The U.S. Postal Service sells unclaimed merchandise, including lots of books.

There is one story to inspire: a New Yorker bought surplus parachutes from the Pentagon and became a supplier selling clothesline cord. If you are looking for a business, try the Small Business Administration, which sells equipment and businesses it has acquired through foreclosure. Want a good deal on a house? U.S. Department of Housing and Urban Development offers repossessed homes — sometimes for practically nothing — on government foreclosures. There are also many people who go to the U.S. Postal Service auctions and buy bin loads of videos, CDs, and other goodies, and make nice money reselling them at flea markets.

Very few people know about these unique bargains because the federal government doesn't advertise them. Described below are 30 of Uncle Sam's Red Tag Specials. Contact the appropriate offices for more information. And remember, if you don't find what you want, stay at it. This is ongoing, and new merchandise and property are coming in all the time.

* Burros and Horses: Bureau of Land Management

Nevada State Office
Bureau of Land Management
U.S. Department of the Interior 800-417-9647
850 Harvard Way 775-861-6583
Reno, NV 89520-0006 Fax: 775-861-6711
www.blm.gov/whb/

Or contact your local Bureau of Land Management office. The "Adopt-a-Horse" program is aimed at keeping wild herds at in the West at manageable levels, and allows individuals around the country to purchase a wild horse for $125 or a burro for $75. The animals usually have their shots. Aside from the purchase price you only need pay for shipping. If you live west of the Mississippi, call the Program Office above to find out which of the 12 adoption satellites are nearest you. Representatives of the BLM travel around the country, so you don't have to travel to Wyoming to participate. The only qualifications for adoption are that you have appropriate facilities to house the animal, that you are of legal age in your state, and that you have no record of offenses against animals. The horses and burros may not be used for any exploitative purposes such as rodeos or races, nor may they be re-sold. Upon adoption, you sign an agreement to that effect, and no title of ownership is given until one year after an adoption. Animals are usually from two to six years in age, and must be trained. The offices listed above have a brochure called *So You'd Like to Adopt a Wild Horse or Burro* on the "Adopt-a-Horse" program that gives more details.

Alaska
Alaska State Office, 222 W. 7th Ave., #13, Anchorage, AK 99513-7599; 907-271-5555.

Arizona
Phoenix District Office, 2015 W. Deer Valley Rd., Phoenix, AZ 85027; 602-580-5500.
Kingman Resource Area, 520-692-4400.

California
California State Office, Federal Building, Room E-2807, 2800 Cottage Way, Sacramento, CA 95825-1889; 916-979-2800.
Bakersfield District Office, 661-391-6049.
Ridgecrest, CA, 619-446-6064, 800-951-8720.
Susanville District Office, 530-257-5381.
Clear Lake Resource Area, 707-468-4055.

Colorado
Canon City District Office, 3170 E. Main St., Canon City, CO 81212; 719-269-8500.

Idaho
Boise District Office, 3948 Development Ave., Boise, ID 83705-5389; 208-384-3300.

Montana, North Dakota, South Dakota
Montana State Office, 5001 Southgate Dr., Billings, MT 59107-6800; 406-896-5222.

Nevada
National Wild Horse and Burro Center, Palomino Valley, P.O. Box 3270, Sparks, NV 89432; 775-475-2222.

New Mexico, Kansas, Oklahoma, Texas
Oklahoma Resource Area, 221 N. Service Rd., Moore, OK 73160-4946; 405-794-9624, 800-237-3642.

Oregon, Washington
Burns District Office, HC74-12533, Highway 20 West, Hines, OR 97738; 541-573-4400.

Utah
Salt Lake City District Office, 2370 South 2300 West, Salt Lake City, UT 84119; 801-977-4300.

Wyoming, Nebraska
Rock Springs District Office, P.O. Box 1869, Highway 191 North, Rock Springs, WY 82902-1869; 307-382-5350.
Elm Creek, NE, 308-856-4498.

AL, AR, FL, GA, KY, LA, MS, NC, SC, TN, VA
Jackson District Office, 411 Briarwood Dr., Suite 404, Jackson, MS 39206; 601-977-5430, 888-274-2133.
Cross Plains, TN, 615-654-2180, 800-376-6009.

CT, DE, DC, IL, IN, IA, ME, MD, MA, MI, MN, MO, NH, NJ, NY, OH, PA, RI, VT, WV, WI
7450 Boston Blvd., Springfield, VA 22153; 800-370-3936.

* Christmas Trees, Seedling, Wooden Poles and Posts:
U.S. Department of the Interior
Bureau of Land Management
Bureau of Land Management
Division of Forestry
1849 C Street, NW
Washington, DC 20240 202-653-8864

Federal Auctions

or
U.S. Forest Service (USDA) 202-208-3435
  202-205-1389

Contact your local Bureau of Land Management (BLM), U.S. Department of Interior. In the 11 Western states, the Bureau of Land Management has a program for obtaining low-cost Christmas trees from Federal lands. By contacting your local BLM office, you may obtain a permit for a nominal fee (usually $10) to cut a tree for your own use. You will be given a map with directions as to which are permissible areas for tree-cutting. Non-profit organizations may also qualify. Non-profit may get free use permits and cut larger amounts. Trees must be for their own use and may not be resold at fundraisers.

In addition, under the Minor Forest Products program, you may collect or cut specified small trees for use as poles or posts; or, you may obtain cactus or plant seedlings from areas of natural growth where there are abundant supplies -- again at a very low cost. These items are free for non-profit organizations for their own use. Permits for commercial usage may also be available. Cost depends on market value. Below are the addresses and phone numbers of Regional Bureau of Land Management Offices.

Alaska
222 W. 7th Ave. #13, Anchorage, AK 99513-5076; 907-271-5076.

Arizona
222 N. Central Ave., Phoenix, AZ 85004; 602-417-9200.

California
2800 Cottage Way, E-2841, Sacramento, CA 95825; 916-978-4400.

Colorado
2850 Youngfield St., Lakewood, CO 80215-7076; 303-239-3670.

Eastern States
7450 Ballston Blvd., Springfield, VA 22153; 703-440-1713.

Idaho
1387 S. Vinnell Way, Boise, ID 83709; 208-373-4000.

Montana
5001 Southgate Dr., P.O. Box 36800, Billings, MT 59107-6800; 406-896-5000.

Nevada
1340 Financial Blvd., Reno, NV 89520-0006; 775-861-6400.

New Mexico
1474 Rodeo Road, P.O. Box 27115, Santa Fe, NM 87502-0115; 505-438-7514.

Oregon
1515 SW 5th Ave., P.O. Box 2965, Portland, OR 97208-2965; 503-952-6027.

Utah
324 South State Street, Suite 301, P.O. Box 45155, Salt Lake City, UT 84145-0155; 801-539-4021.

Wyoming
5353 Yellowstone Rd., P.O. Box 1828, Cheyenne, WY 82009; 307-775-6011.

* Federal Deposit Insurance Corporation (FDIC)

Federal Deposit Insurance Corporation
550 17th St. NW 800-934-FDIC
Washington, DC 20429 202-393-8400
www.fdic.gov
or
Northeast Service Center
(CT, ME, MA, NH, NJ, NY, PA, RI, VT)
101 E. River Dr. 800-873-7785
East Hartford, CT 06108 860-291-4000
or
Field Operations Branch
(All other states and DC)
1910 Pacific Ave.
Dallas, TX 75201 888-206-4662

The FDIC sells at auctions the furnishings and equipment of failed commercial banks. Consult the blue pages in your phone directory for the regional FDIC office nearest you. Each regional office handles their own personal property disposal. Professional auctioneers are contracted to auction off the accumulation of desks, calculators, chairs, computers and other furnishings that banks normally have. These auctions will be advertised in the auction section or classifieds of local newspapers.

The FDIC also holds open for offers costly commercial property and real estate. For a full catalog of these listings across the country, which also includes homes over $250,000. Check out their website. About 97 percent of the listings are commercial offerings such as hotels, offices, and industries. Sales of commercial real estate are advertised nationally by the FDIC in such papers as *The Wall Street Journal*. Call for information on how to be placed on a mailing list.

* FHA Money May Be Waiting for You

Support Service Center
U.S. Department of Housing and Urban Development
P.O. Box 23699
Washington, DC 20026-3699
www.hud.gov/wsrefund/html/page1.html
HUD Locator 1-800-697-6967
  202-708-1422

If you or someone in your family has successfully paid off a mortgage on a house, there may be money waiting for you at the U.S. Department of Housing and Urban Development (HUD). HUD oversees the Federal Housing Administration (FHA) which insures mortgages that your bank lends to house buyers. Each year FHA predicts how many people will default on their loans, and based on that prediction, they calibrate how much mortgage insurance home buyers will pay during that year. If it turns out that there are fewer loan defaults than FHA predicted, those borrowers that have continued to pay their mortgages have what are called "Mutual Mortgage Dividend" checks coming to them upon completion of the loan agreement. Call 703-235-8117 if you think you are due a one time mortgage insurance premium refund or a distributive share.

Another way you may qualify for an FHA insurance refund is to have taken out, say, a 30 year mortgage and paid the entire FHA insurance premium up front instead of in installments over the entire period of the loan. If you have completed the loan agreement in less than 30 years, you may have money coming back to you since you didn't use the insurance for the entire 30 years you've already paid for. In most cases, though, you have to carry a loan for at least 7 years to qualify for a dividend, and the longer you have a loan, the more likely it is that you will qualify for a dividend check.

In these cases where you prepay all of your mortgage insurance premium up front, your bank should let you know that you may eventually be eligible for a mutual mortgage refund upon fulfillment of the loan agreement. Also, after you have paid off your loan, your bank should notify HUD, who in turn should notify you if you have any refund coming, usually within six months. However, if HUD cannot locate you, they will add your name to a list of other individuals who cannot be located but have HUD money coming to them.

Through the Freedom of Information Act many individuals have gotten their hands on copies of this list from HUD and gone around the country tracking down the people and charging them fees to recover this HUD money. Depending on the size of the original loan, your dividend refund could be several thousand dollars, and since some of these "bounty hunters" may ask for up to 50% of the refund just for making a phone call that you could make yourself, you could be losing out on a substantial sum of money by letting them do it. In fact, all you have to do to get the same list the bounty hunters are using is to call 703-235-8117. The staff will mail to you an "information package" which contains the names of all the mortgagors in the state in which you reside (or request the list for), forms and basic information you would need to apply for a refund.

If you feel you may have money coming to you, or if a member of your family who took out a mortgage is now deceased and you are an heir, try to locate the original loan contract number, and then make a few calls. To apply for a refund you will need the loan number and FHA case number, which you can find on the Recorded Deed of Purchase, kept at your local county courthouse.

* Firewood: U.S. Forest Service

U.S. Forest Service
Timber Management
U.S. Department of Agriculture
14th and Independence Ave. SW
Box 96090
Washington, DC 20090-6090
Operations and Technology Information 202-205-0855/0893

Contact your nearest National Forest Office (listed below) to find out about the firewood program and to learn which national forest is near you. Also, ask these regional offices about firewood from state forestry organizations and private timber

Government Auctions and Surplus Property

companies. Ask about availability of firewood before you make the trip. In any National Forest, you may pick up downed or dead wood for firewood for a nominal charge of $5 per cord, $10 minimum fee, after requesting a permit from the Forest of your choice. You may phone to request the permit, and must have it in your possession while collecting the wood. The Forest Service allows you to gather 2-10 cords worth of wood. Six cords are equal to 12 pick-up truck loads. Wood may not be collected for commercial purposes. All permits to cut wood are issued locally, so you must purchase permits directly from the district ranger. Regional offices do not sell permits.

Northern Region I
Federal Building, 200 East Broadway St., P.O. Box 7669, Missoula, MT 59807; 406-329-3316. Includes Northern Idaho and Montana.

Rocky Mountain Region II
740 Simms Ave., P.O. Box 25127, Lakewood, CO 80225; 303-275-5450. Includes Colorado, Nebraska, South Dakota, Eastern Wyoming.

Southwestern Region III
Federal Building, 517 Gold Ave. S.W., Albuquerque, NM 87102; 505-842-3306. Includes New Mexico, Arizona.

Intermountain Region IV
Federal Building, 324 25th St., Ogden, UT 84401; 801-625-5605. Includes Southern Idaho, Nevada, Utah, and Western Wyoming.

Pacific Southwest Region V
1325 Club Dr., Vallejo, CA 94592; 707-562-USFS. Includes California, Hawaii, Guam, Trust Territories of the Pacific Islands.

Pacific Northwest Region VI
333 SW First Avenue, P.O. Box 3623, Portland, OR 97208-3623; 503-808-2202. Includes Oregon and Washington.

Southern Region VIII
1720 Peachtree Rd. NW, Atlanta, GA 30367; 404-347-4177. Includes Alabama, Arkansas, Florida, Georgia, Kentucky, Louisiana, Mississippi, North Carolina, Puerto Rico and the Virgin Islands, South Carolina, Tennessee, Texas, Virginia.

Eastern Region IX
310 West Wisconsin Ave., Room 500, Milwaukee, WI 53203; 414-297-3600. Includes Illinois, Indiana, Ohio, Michigan, Minnesota, Missouri, New Hampshire, Maine, Pennsylvania, Vermont, West Virginia, Wisconsin, and Fingerlakes section of New York.

Alaskan Region X
Federal Office Building, 709 West Ninth St., P.O. Box 21628, Juneau, AK 99802-1628; 907-586-8863. Abundance of wood results in extensive free-use permits.

* Homes: Department of Agriculture

Rural Housing and Community Development Service
14th and Independence Ave., SW
Room 5334-S
Washington, DC 20250   202-720-1474/1577
www.rurdev.usda.gov

Contact your local Rural Housing and Community Development Service (formerly Farmers Home Administration FmHA) Office. There are 1900 around the country. The Rural Housing and Community Development Service, part of the Department of Agriculture, makes low-interest loans available to qualified applicants to purchase homes or farms in rural areas (among other things). Rural settings are small towns with a population under 10,000. Check to see if the locale you are interested in qualifies. Sometimes areas of up to 25,000 in population are approved. Rural Housing and Community Development Service (RHCDS) is also charged with disposing of properties that are foreclosed. First, they make any necessary repairs to the properties, then offer them for sale to people who have the same qualifications as those applying for RHCDS loans (based on income, credit worthiness and other criteria). Eligible applicants also qualify to purchase the properties at special low RHCDS interest rates (as low as 1%). If no eligible applicants purchase a property, it is then put up for sale to the general public at competitive prices. If the property is not sold within 10 days, it may be reduced by 10%. Sales to the general public may be through RHCDS offices or through private real estate brokers. RHCDS "eligible applicants" must reside on the property purchased; but if no such eligible buyers are available, other buyers may use it for investment or rental purposes. A separate program applies for farms. This program is designed to serve people of modest income and good credit who don't have enough to make a down payment on a home. Credit evaluation is done on the most recent 12 months. Bankruptcy is not looked at after 36 months. The current loan budget is one-third of what is was in the 70s. This program is being changed to eventually act as insurers to guarantee loans from professional lenders. Applicants may work in a city if their home is rural. The address and telephone number for your local county office may be obtained by calling or writing the applicable state office listed below.

Alabama
Rural Housing and Community Development Service, Sterling Center, Office Bldg., 4121 Carmichael Rd., Suite 601, Montgomery, Al 36106-3683; 334-279-3400.

Alaska
Rural Housing and Community Development Service, 800 W. Evergreen, Suite 201, Palmer, AK 99645; 907-745-2176.

Arizona
Rural Housing and Community Development Service, Phoenix Corporate Center, 3003 N. Central Ave., Suite 900, Phoenix, AZ 85012; 602-280-8700.

Arkansas
Rural Housing and Community Development Service, P.O. Box 2778, 700 W. Capitol, Little Rock, AR 72203; 501-301-3200.

California
Rural Housing and Community Development Service, 430 G St., Davis, CA 95616; 530-792-5800.

Colorado
Rural Housing and Community Development Service, 655 Parfet St., Room E100, Lakewood, CO 80215; 303-236-2801.

Connecticut
See Massachusetts

Delaware, Maryland
Rural Housing and Community Development Service, P.O. Box 400, 4611 S. DuPont Hwy., Camden, DE 19934-9998; 302-697-4300.

Florida
Rural Housing and Community Development Service, P.O. Box 147010, 4440 NW 25th Pl., Gainesville, FL 32614-7010; 352-338-3400.

Georgia
Rural Housing and Community Development Service, Stephens Federal Bldg., 355 E. Hancock Ave., Athens, GA 30610; 706-546-2162.

Hawaii
Rural Housing and Community Development Service, Federal Bldg., Room 311, 154 Waianuenue Ave., Hilo, HI 96720; 808-933-3000.

Idaho
Rural Housing and Community Development Service, 9173 Barnes, Suite A1, Boise, ID 83709; 208-378-5630.

Illinois
Rural Housing and Community Development Service, Illini Plaza, Suite 103, 1817 S. Neil St., Champaign, IL 61820; 217-398-5235.

Indiana
Rural Housing and Community Development Service, 5975 Lakeside Blvd., Indianapolis, IN 46278; 317-290-3100.

Iowa
Rural Housing and Community Development Service, 873 Federal Blvd., 210 Walnut St., Des Moines, IA 50309; 515-284-4663.

Kansas
Rural Housing and Community Development Service, P.O. Box 4653, 1200 SW Executive Dr., Topeka, KS 66604; 785-271-2700.

Kentucky
Rural Housing and Community Development Service, 771 Corporate Dr., Suite 200, Lexington, KY 40503; 606-224-7300.

Louisiana
Rural Housing and Community Development Service, 3727 Government St., Alexandria, LA 71302; 318-473-7920.

Federal Auctions

Maine
Rural Housing and Community Development Service, P.O. Box 405, 444 Stillwater Ave., Suite 2, Bangor, ME 04402-0405; 207-990-9160.

Maryland
See Delaware

Massachusetts, Connecticut, Rhode Island
Rural Housing and Community Development Service, 451 West Street, Amherst, MA 01002; 413-253-4302.

Michigan
Rural Housing and Community Development Service, 3001 Coolidge Rd., Room 200, East Lansing, MI 48823; 517-324-5100.

Minnesota
Rural Housing and Community Development Service, 410 Farm Credit Service Bldg., 375 Jackson St., St. Paul, MN 55101-1853; 651-602-7800.

Mississippi
Rural Housing and Community Development Service, Federal Bldg., Suite 831, 100 W. Capitol St., Jackson, MS 39269; 601-965-4318.

Missouri
Rural Housing and Community Development Service, Parkdade Center, Suite 235, 601 Business Loop 70 West, Columbia, MO 65203; 573-876-0976.

Montana
Rural Housing and Community Development Service, Unit 1, Suite B, 900 Technology Blvd., Bozeman, MT 59715; 406-585-2580.

Nebraska
Rural Housing and Community Development Service, Federal Building, Room 308, 100 Centennial Mall N, Lincoln, NE 68508; 402-437-5551.

Nevada
Rural Housing and Community Development Service, 1390 S. Curry St., Carson City, NV 89703-5405; 702-887-1222.

New Hampshire
Rural Housing and Community Development Service, Concord Center, Suite 218, Box 317, 10 Ferry St., Concord, NH 03301; 603-223-6045.

New Jersey
Rural Housing and Community Development Service, Tarnsfield Plaza, Suite 22, 790 Woodlane Rd., Mt. Holly, NJ 08060; 609-265-3600.

New Mexico
Rural Housing and Community Development Service, 6200 Jefferson St., NE, Room 255, Albuquerque, NM 87109; 505-761-4950.

New York
Rural Housing and Community Development Service, The Galleries of Syracuse, 441 S. Salina St., Suite 357, Syracuse, NY 13202; 315-477-6433.

North Carolina
Rural Housing and Community Development Service, 4405 Bland Rd., Suite 260, Raleigh, NC 27609; 919-873-2000.

North Dakota
Rural Housing and Community Development Service, Federal Building, Room 208, 220 E. Rosser, P.O. Box 1737, Bismarck, ND 58502; 701-530-2037.

Ohio
Rural Housing and Community Development Service, Federal Bldg., Room 507, 200 N. High St., Columbus, OH 43215; 614-255-2500.

Oklahoma
Rural Housing and Community Development Service, 100 USDA, Suite 108, Stillwater, OK 74074; 405-742-1000.

Oregon
Rural Housing and Community Development Service, 101 SW Main, Suite 1410, Portland, OR 97204; 503-414-3300.

Pennsylvania
Rural Housing and Community Development Service, One Credit Union Place, Suite 330, Harrisburg, PA 17110-2996; 717-237-2299.

Puerto Rico
Rural Housing and Community Development Service, New San Juan Office Building, Room 01, 159 Carlos E. Chardon Street, Hato Rey, PR 00918-5481; 787-766-5095.

Rhode Island
See Massachusetts

South Carolina
Rural Housing and Community Development Service, Strom Thurmond Federal Building, Room 1007, 1835 Assembly Street, Columbia, SC 29201; 803-765-5163.

South Dakota
Rural Housing and Community Development Service, Federal Building, Room 308, 200 Fourth St., SW, Huron, SD 57350; 605-352-1100.

Tennessee
Rural Housing and Community Development Service, 3322 West End Ave., Suite 300, Nashville, TN 37203-1071; 615-783-1300, 800-342-3149.

Texas
Rural Housing and Community Development Service, Federal Bldg., Suite 102, 101 South Main, Temple, TX 76501; 254-742-9710.

Utah
Rural Housing and Community Development Service, Wallace F. Bennett Federal Bldg., 125 S. State St., Room 5438, Salt Lake City, UT 84138; 801-524-4230.

Vermont
Rural Housing and Community Development Service, City Center, 3rd Floor, 89 Main St., Montpelier, VT 05602; 802-828-6000.

Virginia
Rural Housing and Community Development Service, Culpeper Bldg., Suite 238, 1606 Santa Rosa Rd., Richmond, VA 23229; 804-287-1550.

Washington
Rural Housing and Community Development Service, 1835 Black Lake Blvd., SW, Suite B, Olympia, WA 98512; 360-704-7740.

West Virginia
Rural Housing and Community Development Service, 75 High St., Morgantown, WV 26505-7500; 304-291-4793.

Wisconsin
Rural Housing and Community Development Service, 4949 Kirschling Ct., Stevens Point, WI 54481; 715-345-7600.

Wyoming
Rural Housing and Community Development Service, Federal Bldg., Room 1005, 100 East B, P.O. Box 820, Casper, WY 82602; 307-261-6300.

* Homes: Department of Housing and Urban Development

Property Disposition Division
U.S. Department of Housing and Urban Development (HUD)
451 7th St. SW, Room 9172
Washington, DC 20410-4000   202-708-0740
www.hud.gov
HUD Locator   202-708-1422
Multi-Family Property Dispositions   202-708-3343
Single-Family Property Dispositions   202-708-0740

HUD homes are properties HUD owns as a result of paying the balance on foreclosed FHA insured home mortgages. Any qualified buyer can purchase a HUD home. Generally, your monthly mortgage payment should be no more than 29% of your monthly gross income. Many HUD homes require only a 3% down payment. You can move into some HUD homes with a $100 down payment. HUD will pay the real estate brokers commission up to the standard 6% of the sales price. HUD may also pay your closing costs. HUD homes are priced at fair market value. Consult your local newspapers for HUD listings; or, your regional HUD office, listed below; or, the real estate broker of your choice.

HUD's Property Disposition facilities are located within state offices and various coordinator's offices around the country. Contact your state office for details (see listing below). Frequently, HUD will advertise upcoming auctions of foreclosed properties in a local newspaper. The properties may be apartments, condominiums,

Government Auctions and Surplus Property

or various kinds of single-family homes. The condition of these properties varies widely, including some that are little more than shells; and that, of course, affects the price. Some may be located in less than desirable neighborhoods; but others may end up being bargains, either as investments or personal residences. Bids are placed through private real estate brokers, who then submit them to HUD. Some offers for HUD homes are made to the seller and there may be negotiations. Offers for other HUD homes are done by bids placed during an "Offer Period." If you bid the full asking price, it may be accepted immediately. Otherwise, all the bids are opened at the close of the "Offer Period." The highest bidder wins. Contact the participating broker of your choice to show you the property and submit your bid. HUD broker contracted services are free to prospective buyers. Earnest money is a flat scaled fee ranging from $500-$2000 and must accompany the bid. Bidders must furnish their own financing. HUD stresses that properties sell "as is," so HUD will not make any repairs. It is up to a potential buyer to determine the value and condition, although the listings will state major problems.

Newspaper ads list houses that will be available for the next ten days, as well as others that did not sell in previous auctions. Listings include addresses, number of bedrooms and bathrooms, and suggested prices. Remember that HUD contracts are binding and non-negotiable: once your bid has won, there's no turning back. For a step by step buying guide to purchasing HUD owned homes, call the HUD Homeline, 1-800-767-4483, and request the brochure, *A Home of Your Own*. To learn about other programs at HUD that may be useful to you, call 202-708-0685.

Alabama
Heager Hill, State Coordinator, HUD-Alabama State Office, Beacon Ridge Tower, Suite 300, 600 Beacon Parkway West, Birmingham, AL 35209-3144; 205-290-7617.

Arizona
Terry Goddard, State Coordinator, HUD-Arizona State Office, Two Arizona Center, 400 N. 5th St., Suite 1600, Phoenix, AZ 85004-2361; 602-379-4434.

Arkansas
Bobbie J. (BJ) McCoy, Acting State Coordinator, HUD-Arkansas State Office, TCBY Tower, Suite 900, 425 W. Capitol Ave., Little Rock, AR 72201-3488; 501-324-5401.

Alaska
Arlene Patton, State Coordinator, HUD-Alaska State Office, University Plaza Bldg., 949 E. 36th Ave., Suite 401, Anchorage, AK 99508-4135; 907-271-4170.

California
Arthur Agnos, Secretary's Representative, HUD-California State Office, Philip Burton Federal Bldg. and U.S. Courthouse, 450 Golden Gate Ave., P.O. Box 36003, San Francisco, CA 94102-3448; 415-436-6532.

Colorado
Anthony Hernandez, Secretary's Representative, HUD-Colorado State Office, 633 17th St., Denver, CO 80202-3607; 303-672-5440.

Connecticut
Robert S. Donovan, Acting State Coordinator, HUD-Connecticut State Office, One Corporate Center, Hartford, CT 06103; 860-240-4844.

Delaware
David Sharbaugh, Acting State Coordinator, HUD-Delaware State Office, 824 Market St., Suite 850, Wilmington, DE 19801-3016; 302-573-6300.

District of Columbia
Jessica Franklin, State Coordinator, HUD-District of Columbia Office, Union Center Plaza, Phase II, 820 First St., NE, Suite 300, Washington, DC 20002-4205; 202-275-9206.

Florida
Jose Cintron, State Coordinator, 909 SE First Ave., Miami, FL 33131; 305-536-5678.

Georgia
Davey L. Gibson, Secretary's Representative, HUD-Georgia State Office, 40 Marietta St., Atlanta, GA 30303; 404-331-4111.

Hawaii
Gordon Y. Furutani, State Coordinator, HUD-Hawaii State Office, Seven Waterfront Plaza, 500 Ala Moana Blvd., Suite 500, Honolulu, HI 96813-4918; 808-522-8175.

Idaho
Gary Gillespie, Acting State Coordinator, HUD-Idaho State Office, Park IV, 800 Park Blvd., Suite 220, Boise, ID 83712-7743; 208-334-1990.

Illinois
Edwin Eisendrath, Secretary's Representative, HUD-Illinois State Office, Ralph Metcalfe Federal Bldg., 77 W. Jackson Blvd., Chicago, IL 60604-3507; 312-353-5680.

Indiana
William Shaw, State Coordinator, HUD-Indiana State Office, 151 N. Delaware St., Indianapolis, IN 46204-2526; 317-226-7034.

Iowa
William McNarney, State Coordinator, HUD-Iowa State Office, Federal Bldg., 210 Walnut St., Room 239, Des Moines, IA 50309-2155; 515-284-4573.

Kansas
Joseph O'Hern, Secretary's Representative, HUD-Kansas-Missouri State Office, Gateway Tower II, 400 State Ave., Room 200, Kansas City, KS 66101-2406; 913-551-5462.

Kentucky
State Coordinator, HUD-Kentucky State Office, 601 W. Broadway, P.O. Box 1044, Louisville, KY 40201-1044; 502-582-5251.

Louisiana
Jason Gamlin, State Coordinator, HUD-Louisiana State Office, Hale Boggs Federal Bldg., 9th Floor, 501 Magazine St., New Orleans, LA 70130-3099; 504-589-7201.

Maine
Richard Young, Acting State Coordinator, HUD-Maine State Office, 202 Harlow St., Bangor, ME 04402; 207-945-0468.

Maryland
Harold Young, Acting State Coordinator, HUD-Maryland State Office, City Crescent Bldg., 10 S. Howard St., 5th Floor, Baltimore, MD 21201-2505; 410-962-2520.

Massachusetts
Mary Lou Crane, Secretary's Representative, HUD-Massachusetts State Office, Thomas P. O'Neill, Jr. Federal Building, 10 Causeway St., Room 375, Boston, MA 02222-1092; 617-565-5236.

Michigan
Regina F. Solomon, State Coordinator, HUD-Michigan State Office, Patrick V. McNamara Federal Bldg., 477 Michigan Ave., Detroit, MI 48226-2592; 313-226-7900.

Minnesota
Thomas Feeney, State Coordinator, HUD-Minnesota State Office, 220 Second St., South, Minneapolis, MN 55401-2195; 612-370-3288.

Mississippi
Thomas Cooper, Acting State Coordinator, HUD-Mississippi State Office, Dr. AH McCoy Federal Bldg., 100 W. Capitol St., Room 910, Jackson, MS 39269-1096; 601-965-4700.

Missouri
Roy Pierce, HUD-St. Louis Office, 1222 Spruce St., #3207, St. Louis, MO 63103; 314-539-6560.

Montana
Richard Brinck, State Coordinator, HUD-Montana State Office, Federal Office Bldg., Drawer 10095, 301 South Park, Room 340, Helena, MT 59626-0095; 406-441-1298.

Nebraska
Terry Gratz, State Coordinator, HUD-Nebraska State Office, Executive Tower Centre, 10909 Mill Valley Rd., Omaha, NE 68154-3955; 402-492-3103.

Nevada
Paul Pradia, State Coordinator, HUD-Nevada State Office, Atrium Bldg., 333 N. Rancho Dr., Suite 700, Las Vegas, NV 89106-3714; 702-388-6500.

New Hampshire
David B. Harrity, State Coordinator, HUD-New Hampshire State Office, Norris Cotton Federal Bldg., 275 Chestnut St., Manchester, NH 03103-2487; 603-666-7682.

New Jersey
Diane Johnson, State Coordinator, HUD-New Jersey State Office, One Newark Center, 13th Floor, Newark, NJ 07102-5260; 973-622-7619.

Federal Auctions

New Mexico
Michael R. Griego, State Coordinator, HUD-New Mexico State Office, 625 Silver Ave., SW, Suite 100, Albuquerque, NM 87102; 505-346-6463.

New York
Diane Johnson, Acting Secretary's Representative, HUD-New York State Office, 26 Federal Plaza, New York, NY 10278-0068; 212-264-1161.

North Carolina
James Blackmon, State Coordinator, HUD-North Carolina State Office, Koger Bldg., 2306 W. Meadowview Rd., Greensboro, NC 27407-3707; 336-547-4001.

North Dakota
Keith Elliot, Acting State Coordinator, HUD-North Dakota State Office, Federal Building, 657 2nd Ave., North, P.O. Box 2483, Fargo, ND 58108-2483; 701-239-5040.

Ohio
Deborah C. Williams, State Coordinator, HUD-Ohio State Office, 200 N. High St., Columbus, OH 43215-2499; 614-469-2540.

Oklahoma
Katie Worsham, Acting State Coordinator, HUD-Oklahoma State Office, 500 Main St., Oklahoma City, OK 73102; 405-553-7500.

Oregon
Mark Pavolka, Acting State Coordinator, HUD-Oregon State Office, 400 SW 6th Ave., Suite 700, Portland, OR 97204-1632; 503-326-2561.

Pennsylvania
Karen A. Miller, Secretary's Representative, HUD-Pennsylvania State Office, The Wanamaker Bldg., 100 Penn Square East, Philadelphia, PA 19107-3390; 215-656-0600.

Puerto Rico
Maria Teresa Pombo, Acting State Coordinator, HUD-Caribbean Office, New San Juan Office Bldg., 159 Carlos E. Chardon Ave., San Juan, PR 00918-1804; 809-766-6121.

Rhode Island
Nancy Smith, State Coordinator, HUD-Rhode Island State Office, 10 Weybosset St., 6th Floor, Providence, RI 02903-3234; 401-528-5352.

South Carolina
Choice Edwards, State Coordinator, HUD-South Carolina State Office, Strom Thurmond Federal Bldg., 1835 Assembly St., Columbia, SC 29201-2480; 803-765-5592.

South Dakota
Dwight Peterson, State Coordinator, HUD-South Dakota State Office, 2400 West 49th St., Suite I-201, Sioux Falls, SD 57105-6558; 605-330-4223.

Tennessee
Ginger Van Ness, State Coordinator, HUD-Tennessee State Office, 235 Cumberland Bend Dr., Suite 200, Nashville, TN 37228-1803; 615-736-5213.

Texas
Stephen Weatherford, Secretary's Representative, HUD-Texas State Office, 801 Cherry St., P.O. Box 2905, Fort Worth, TX 76113-2905; 817-978-9000.

Utah
John Milchick, State Coordinator, HUD-Utah State Office, 257 Tower, 257 East 200 South, Suite 550, Salt Lake City, UT 84111-2048; 801-524-3574.

Vermont
William Peters, Acting State Coordinator, HUD-Vermont State Office, Federal Building, 11 Elmwood Ave., Room 244, P.O. Box 879, Burlington, VT 05402-0879; 802-951-6290.

Virginia
Mary Ann Wilson, State Coordinator, HUD-Virginia State Office, The 3600 Centre, 3600 West Broad Street, P.O. Box 90331, Richmond, VA 23230-0331; 804-278-4507.

Washington
Bob Santos, Secretary's Representative, HUD-Washington State Office, Seattle Federal Office Bldg., 909 First Ave., Suite 200, Seattle, WA 98104-1000; 206-220-5101.

West Virginia
Fred Roncaglione, State Coordinator, HUD-West Virginia State Office, 405 Capitol St., Suite 708, Charleston, WV 25301-1795; 304-347-7036.

Wisconsin
Delbert F. Reynolds, State Coordinator, HUD-Wisconsin State Office, Henry S. Reuss Federal Plaza, 310 W. Wisconsin Ave., Suite 1380, Milwaukee, WI 53203-2289; 414-297-3214.

Wyoming
William Garrett, Acting State Coordinator, HUD-Wyoming State Office, 4225 Federal Office Bldg., 100 East B St., P.O. Box 120, Casper, WY 82602-1918; 307-261-6251.

* Homes: H.O.P.E. 3

U.S. Department of Housing and Urban Development
Office of Community Planning and Development
Office of Affordable Housing Programs
451 7th St., SW
Washington, DC 20410-7000   202-708-3226
www.hud.gov/progdesc/hope3fin.html

The HUD Urban Homesteading Program has been replaced by the HOPE 3 Program. It is designed to provide homeownership for low income families and individuals. The funds will be distributed to the 10 HUD regions and awarded to local governments and non-profit organizations on a competitive bidding basis. It will generally provide down payment assistance for groups to acquire or rehabilitate affordable low income housing. Call your regional HUD office to find out who has been awarded grants, and then contact them directly to see what is available.

You qualify for housing help through HOPE 3 under the Low Income Family Housing Act if you are a first time homebuyer and are below 80% of the median income in your area. You may also qualify if you have not owned a home in 3 years. You must also meet the affordability criteria -- which requires that the cost of principal interest, taxes and insurance for the home comes to no more than 30% of your income. Since the program is new, the quality of public dissemination of information about these programs remains to be seen. These programs are instituted to help you, so don't be afraid to be persistent in asking for information about what HOPE 3 programs are available in your area from the Community Planning and Development Office at the Field or Regional HUD office nearest you.

* Homes: Veterans Administration

U.S. Veterans Administration (VA)
1120 Vermont Ave., NW
Washington, DC 20420   202-418-4270
www.vba.va.gov/bln.loan.homes.htm

Contact the local Veterans Administration Office in your state, or a real estate broker. Watch newspaper ads in local papers for listings of foreclosed properties. The "For Sale" signs on VA foreclosed properties are distinctive. The National Veterans Administration office in Washington, DC is not directly involved in handling the sales; for any inquiries you will be referred to a real estate broker or local VA office.

The Veterans Administration sells foreclosed properties through private real estate brokers. Properties are frequently advertised in local newspapers, giving information such as address, number of bedrooms and bathrooms, particular defects in the property, and price. Almost any real estate agent can show you the property. No broker has an exclusive listing for any of these properties. Local VA offices are the best source of information on the procedures involved in purchasing these properties. Regional offices publish lists of foreclosed properties with descriptions in multiple listing code and phone numbers to call about the property. In some cases, they will also directly send you lists of properties currently available in your area. These offices will mail out a list each time you write in a request, but unless you are a broker, they will not send the list for foreclosures to you on a monthly basis. You can, however, have the agent of your choice put on the mailing list. Others will not mail lists to you, but allow you to pick up the list from their office and/or will refer you to a broker. In either case, you must go through an agent to purchase the house, since they have the keys to the premises, and the process is very much like a regular real estate transaction. The listing has the price on it the VA wants. It will also state if the VA is willing to entertain a lower price. Houses come "as is" with no guarantees, so it is important to inspect them carefully. Some are located in less than desirable neighborhoods, but there are bargains to be had as well. For the most part VA financed homes are mainstream suburban, not inner city. They are often found in neighborhoods located in economically hard hit areas -- such as the Southwest. Prices may drop on homes that are not sold in a certain period of time. VA financing is possible. Also, if you plan on VA financing, in cases of a tie, the other bidder gets

Government Auctions and Surplus Property

priority for cash offers (pre-approved financing through a commercial lender.) You must state at the time of the bid whether you intend to use VA financing or have found your own.

There are two basic avenues to arrange financing. You can be pre-qualified by lenders and then go shopping. More commonly, the real estate broker you are working with will tell you what is available in the mortgage market. The usual way it works is that you find a broker, find a house, bid on it, wind the bid and then the broker helps you to find financing.

If you should win a bid on a VA foreclosed home but be unable to procure financing, some regional offices will put the home up for bid again. Others hold backup offers and will contact the next highest bidder if the original successful bidder is unable to complete the purchase. Most listings offer to sell financing at the current rate of interest for GI loans, even if the buyer is not a GI. A purchaser who is a GI can get these rates without using his GI benefits. Call the office listed above if you have questions. They will direct you to the appropriate department of your regional office. If you are a GI and wish to find out about a Certificate of Eligibility, whereby you can purchase a home worth up to $203,000 without a down payment, call 202-418-4270, ext. 3308 or your regional office. To discuss VA loan qualifications generally, call 202-827-1000 or your regional office.

Purchase is done through a sealed bidding process. Earnest money requirements are 1 percent of the purchase price, and are nonrefundable if the bid is accepted. This is a salvage program designed to recover what it can of the cost to the VA for purchasing the property, within a reasonable amount of time after foreclosure -- usually around 6 months.

* Miscellaneous Property: U.S. Customs Service

E.G.& G. Dynatrend
3702 Pender Dr., Suite 400
Fairfax, VA 22030   703-273-7373
www.treas.gov/auctions/customs

E.G.& G. Dynatrend, under contract with the U.S. Customs Service, auctions forfeited and confiscated general merchandise, including vehicles, on a nationwide basis. Items include everything from vessels--both pleasure and commercial--to aircraft, machinery, clothes (in both commercial and individual quantities), jewelry, household goods, precious stones, liquor, furniture, high technology equipment, and infrequently, real estate. Public auctions and sealed and open bid methods are all used. Items are sold only by lot and number of items in a lot vary from one to many. You must bid on the entire lot.

The U.S. Customs Public Auction Line is 703-351-7887. Call it to subscribe to the mailing list of locations and dates of sales, to obtain general information about the custom sales program, dates of sales in your region or information about real estate sales. For $50 dollars per year you can subscribe to a mailing list of items to be auctioned nationwide; or you may subscribe to a list limited to one region of the country for $25. You will then receive fliers with descriptions of items available in upcoming auctions. There are two regions: states east of the Mississippi River, and states west of the Mississippi River. Send your name, address, telephone number, and a money order to the above address. Allow six to eight weeks for the first flier to arrive. The fliers will then arrive three weeks prior to the viewing period and will tell you when and where the items are available for inspection and details of auction procedures. Catalogs are also available a week before the sale with additional details. For sealed bids, a deposit in cashier's check for the total bid must be submitted along with the bid. Make the cashier's check payable to U.S. Customs Service/E.G.& G. Dynatrend, Agent. Indicate sale number on cashier's check and outside on the envelope.

U.S. Customs auctions are held every nine weeks in the following eight cities: Los Angeles, CA; Laredo, TX; Nogales, AZ; Miami, FL; Edinburg, TX; Houston, TX; Chula Vista, CA (San Diego, CA area); El Paso, TX; and Yuma, AZ. Other auctions are scheduled at different times at various other cities also.

* Miscellaneous Property: U.S. Department of Defense

The Defense Reutilization Marketing Service (DRMS)
Federal Center
74 N. Washington   888-352-9333
Battle Creek, MI 49017-3092   1-800-GOVT-BUY
www.drms.com

Imagine what kinds of items are used, then discarded by a government department as big as the Defense Department: literally everything from recyclable scrap materials and weapons accessories, to airplanes, ships, trains, and motor vehicles; to wood and metalworking machinery, agricultural equipment, construction equipment, communications equipment and medical, dental and veterinary supplies. Not to forget photographic equipment, chemical products, office machines, food preparation and serving equipment, musical instruments, furs, tents, flags, and sometimes live animals such as goats and horses. No activated items with military applications are included. Neither are real estate or confiscated items such as sports cars or luxury goods.

Goods sold are either surplus or not usable by other government agencies. First priority is given to designated groups which qualify for donations. The rest is then put up for public sale. By contacting the Defense Reutilization Marketing Service at the above address or telephone, you can receive a booklet called *How to Buy Surplus Personal Property* which explains what Department of Defense has for sale and how to bid for it. The Defense Department also lists notices of Sealed Bid property sales in the *Commerce Business Daily*, available from the Superintendent of Documents, Government Printing Office, Washington, DC 20402-9325; 202-512-1800.

Sales are conducted by regional Defense Reutilization and Marketing Region (DRMR) sales offices which coordinate sales in their geographical area. Local sales are by auction, spot bid, or on a retail basis. Auctions are held where there are relatively small quantities of a variety of items. Spot bids are made through forms submitted in the course of a sale - usually when the property is something with a high demand or interest. The retail sales offer small quantities at fixed, market-level prices. There are 180 retail sales outlets, on military bases.

Large quantities of goods are usually sold by sealed bid, which you submit by mail, along with a deposit, on a form you obtain in a catalog which describes the items. (You receive the catalogs once you are on the mailing list). Recyclable materials are sold through the Resource Recovery Recycling Program or through the Hazardous Property Program. Call the above listed number for further details. You can be put on a mailing list to receive advance notice of DOD sales in your region, but if you don't make any bids after two notifications it will probably be removed unless you make an additional request to remain on the list. You can also be placed on a National Bidders List for sales throughout the country. People under age 18 and members of the U.S. Armed Forces, including civilian employees, are not eligible to participate in these sales.

You can also take advantage of DOD sales if you live outside the United States. The DOD booklet, *How to Buy Surplus Personal Property*, lists addresses for various regions in Europe and the Pacific.

* Miscellaneous Property: General Services

Administration Property
Personal Property Sales Center
U.S. General Services Administration
1941 Jefferson Davis Hwy.
Arlington, VA 22202   703-305-7814/7240
http://pub.fss.gsa.gov/property/

Contact your local General Services Administration (GSA) office listed below. The GSA disposes of surplus property for most of the government agencies, and has items ranging from vehicles and scrap metals, to office furniture, office and industrial equipment, data processing equipment, boats, medical equipment, waste paper and computers; as well as aircraft, railroad equipment, agricultural equipment, textiles, food waste, photographic equipment, jewelry, watches, and clothing.

Some regional offices have no mailing list. Instead, there is a number they will give you to call that is a recorded message of all upcoming events. It will give the time, date, and location of the auction and type, such as warehouse, vehicles or office furniture. Other regions allow you to have your name placed on a mailing list to receive advance notices of auctions at no cost. Catalogs list the specific items and their condition. Sales are conducted as regular auctions, spot auctions (where bids are submitted on-the-spot in writing) and by sealed bid (written on a form and mailed in). For auctions and spot bids, you will have two days prior to the sale to view and inspect property, and one week prior for sealed bids. For sealed bid items you receive a catalog, once your are on the mailing list, describing the merchandise. If your region does not have a mailing list, you may pick up catalogs at the office or the sale. Announcements come out as property is accumulated, with March to October being the busiest period. The highest bidder wins in all cases.

Prices may range from way below wholesale for some items to close-to-market prices for others, especially automobiles and boats. Cars tend to be common American-made brands, such as Tempos, Citations, and Reliances. Cars are auctioned when they are three years old or have reached 60,000 miles, whichever occurs first, and are usually sold at a fair market price. Seized cars may be newer and of a foreign make. A Mercedes-Benz was recently sold at a National Capitol Region auction. Payment may be by cash, cashier's checks, money orders, traveler's checks,

Federal Auctions

government, or credit union checks; but any personal or business checks must be accompanied by an Informal Bank Letter guaranteeing payment. Full payment must be made by the following day, and bidders are responsible for removal of all property. To bid in GSA auctions, you must register at the site and obtain a bidder number. Once you are on the bidders mailing list, you must bid at least once while receiving five mailings or your name will be removed from the list. Then you must contact the appropriate office again to continue receiving mailings.

Some listings for a GSA sale in Bismarck, North Dakota included the following items: miscellaneous kitchen equipment, meat slicers, coffee makers, cameras, film, binoculars, screens, paper, postage meter, nuts and bolts, typewriters, lettering set, mailboxes, lamps, and a streetlight.

For information about GSA auctions in your area, contact one of the regional offices listed below:

National Capitol Region (Washington DC and vicinity)
6808 Loisdale Rd., Building A, Springfield, VA 22150; 703-557-7785, or 703-557-7796, for a recording.

Region I (Boston)
GSA, Surplus Sales Branch, 10 Causeway St., Room 1079, Boston, MA, 02109; 617-565-5700, Auction Hotline Recording, 617-565-6045 or 800-755-1946.

Region II (New York)
GSA Surplus Sales Branch, 26 Federal Plaza, Room 20-116, New York, NY, 10078; 212-264-4824, or 212-264-4823, for a recording.

Region III (Philadelphia)
GSA Surplus Sales Branch, P.O. Box 40657, Philadelphia, PA 19107-3396; 215-656-3939 or 215-656-3400 for a recording.

Region IV (Atlanta)
GSA Surplus Sales Branch, Attn: 4PR, 401 West Peachtree St., Room 3015, Atlanta, GA 30365-2550; 404-331-0972, recording 404-331-5133 or 800-473-7836.

Region V (Chicago)
230 S. Dearborn St., Chicago, IL 60604; 312-353-6061 office, 800-755-1946 or 312-353-0246 hotline for a recorded announcement.

Region VI (Kansas)
GSA Surplus Sales Branch (6FB), 4400 College Blvd., Suite 175, Overland Park, KS 66211; 816-823-3700.

Region VII (Ft. Worth)
GSA Surplus Sales Branch (2PR), 819 Taylor St., Room 9A33, Ft. Worth, TX 76102-6105; 817-978-2331 or 800-833-4317.

Region VIII (Denver)
GSA Surplus Sales Branch (7FBP-8), Denver Federal Center, Building 41, Room 253, P.O. Box 22506-DSC, Denver, CO 80225-0506; 303-236-7705 for recording or 303-236-7702.

Region IX (San Francisco)
GSA Surplus Sales Section 9PR, 450 Golden Gate Ave., 4th Floor East, San Francisco, CA 94102; 888-GSA-LAND.

Region X (Washington)
GSA Surplus Sales Branch GSA Center (9PR-F), 400 15th St., SW, Room 1138, Auburn, WA 98001-6599; 253-931-7566 for a recording or 800-814-6205.

* Miscellaneous Property: Internal Revenue Service

Office of Special Procedures
Internal Revenue Service (IRS)
U.S. Department of the Treasury
1111 Constitution Ave., NW
Washington, DC 20224   202-622-6938

No information concerning auctions is available from this office. Contact your local district office to see if they maintain a mailing list to receive information on upcoming auctions. If not, this information can be found in your local newspaper. Check the classified section for a listing of IRS seized property to be sold. The listing will give phone number and details. The property sold by the IRS is seized from delinquent taxpayers rather than being used or surplus government property. Many kinds of merchandise are put up for auction, including real estate, vehicles, and office and industrial equipment. Sales are by both sealed bids and public auction.

Regarding property sales, the IRS warns that land may still be redeemed by the original owner up to 180 days AFTER you, the bidder, purchase it at an auction; and therefore no deed is issued until this time period has elapsed. Buildings on land being sold by the IRS are NOT open for inspection by a potential buyer unless permission is granted by the taxpayer/owner.

Payment may be by cash, certified check, cashier's check, or money order. In some cases, full payment is required the day of the sale. Otherwise, a 20% down payment (or $200, whichever is greater) is needed to hold the property, with the balance due at a specified time from the date of the sale, not to exceed one month.

* Miscellaneous Property: U.S. Marshals Service

U.S. Marshals Service
Seized Assets Division
U.S. Department of Justice
600 Army-Navy Drive
Arlington, VA 22202   202-307-9087
www.usdoj.gov/marshals/assets/assets.html

Contact your local Sunday newspaper for auction notices in the legal section, or the nearest U.S. Marshals Office under U.S. Department of Justice. Usually the Marshals Office is located in the Federal Building of a city. The U.S. Marshals Service or a contracted commercial sales or auction service may handle disposal of the property. Sales are always listed every third Wednesday in *USA Today* newspaper.

In 1991, the Drug Enforcement Agency managed 1.4 billion dollars worth of property from convicted drug dealers. The U.S. Marshals Service, which holds crime-related property accumulated in Federal drug-related and other confiscations, auctions much of this off to the public through 94 offices around the country. Items sold include everything from entire working businesses, to cars, houses, copiers, jewelry, rare coin and stamp collections, apartment complexes, and restaurants. The government is not giving these properties away by any means, but bargains are possible as well as opportunities to purchase some exotic goodies. Confiscated viable businesses are managed by the Service until the time of the auction in order to keep up or increase the businesses' value.

Auctions are not scheduled regularly, but occur when items accumulate. Auctions may be conducted by private auctioneers or the Marshals Service itself. No mailing list is kept to notify you individually, and there is no national listing of items, since new properties are seized daily and adjudication of drug-related cases may take years. Payment at these auctions is by cash, certified check, or special arrangements when large amounts of money are involved. One note, the Marshals Service checks out people paying for large items with cash to make sure the government is not re-selling things to drug dealers. The Marshals Service also auctions off property seized by the Drug Enforcement Agency and the Federal Bureau of Investigation.

* Miscellaneous Property: U.S. Postal Service

Claims and Inquiry Office
U.S. Postal Service
475 L'Enfant Plaza, S.W.
Washington, DC 20260-0001   202-636-1500
www.usps.gov
Vehicle Management Facility   202-832-0176

Contact the Mail Recovery Centers listed below for undeliverable goods; or your local Postmaster for Vehicle Maintenance Facilities and surplus property auctions. To receive advance notice of the auctions you can write to a Mail Recovery Center and request that your name be put on the auction sales mailing list. To be on all of them, you must write to each one separately. Usually 10 days before the auction, you will be notified by postcard of the time, date and place. Viewing inspections are usually held 2 hours before the auction begins.

The Postal Service holds auctions of unclaimed merchandise which includes a wide range of property — from electronic and household items — to clothes, jewelry, linens, toys, all types of equipment, and lots of books. Sales are handled through the Mail Recovery Centers throughout the country listed below. However, any high value items such as art works, are sold at the New York auction. Contact your local Postmaster to ask about their auctions of surplus property and used vehicles. There are 225 post office vehicle maintenance facilities throughout the country. Their addresses and phone numbers are all listed at the back of the Zip Code Directory kept at post offices. The used vehicle sales can be good bargains, since the vehicles are somewhat fixed up, painted, and occasionally in good condition. Some jeeps, for instance, may sell for between $1200 and $1500. Recently a man bought 15 jeeps for $100 each at auction. Vehicles that do not sell off the storage lot are auctioned. Sometimes cars such as Pintos can be picked up for as little as $750. The sales conducted by the 225 Vehicle Maintenance Facilities around the country are usually fixed price sales, but 5 or 6 times per year auctions have been held at larger cities.

Government Auctions and Surplus Property

The mail recovery items are usually sold in lots of similar goods, with the volume or quantity varying widely. Prices depend on what the goods are and the number of people bidding at a particular auction. There may be a minimum bid required, such as $20; and often cash is the only acceptable payment. Bidders are responsible for removing the items purchased.

A flier for a Postal Service auction of unclaimed and damaged merchandise in St. Paul, Minnesota advised that only those already on an established check register may pay by check; otherwise, cash is required. It also advised that potential bidders to bring their own containers — boxes, crates, and bags — for packing. The Postal Service in San Francisco, California, announced that books, jewelry, sound recordings, speakers, and cabinets, as well as miscellaneous merchandise would be available.

Central Region
U.S. Postal Service Mail Recovery Center, 443 E. Fillmore Ave., St. Paul, MN 55107-9617; 651-293-3083. Includes Minnesota, Michigan, Wisconsin, North Dakota, South Dakota, Nebraska, Iowa, Illinois, Northern New Jersey, New Hampshire, Maine, Vermont, Rhode Island, Massachusetts, Kansas, Missouri, Connecticut, and New York.

Southern Region
U.S. Postal Service Mail Recovery Center, 730 Great Southwest Parkway, Atlanta, GA 30336-2496; 404-344-1625. Includes Georgia, Florida, Louisiana, Tennessee, Arkansas, Mississippi, Oklahoma, part of Texas, Alabama, Mississippi, Virgin Islands, and Puerto Rico.

Western Region
U.S. Postal Service Mail Recovery Center, 390 Main St., 4th Floor, San Francisco, CA 94105-9602; 415-543-1826. Auctions are held at 228 Harrison St., San Francisco, CA. Includes: Alaska, Oregon, Idaho, California, Washington, Nevada, Utah, Arizona, New Mexico, part of Texas, Hawaii, Wyoming, Colorado, Montana, Guam, and Samoa.

* Natural Resources Sales Assistance
Office of Government Contracting
Small Business Administration (SBA)
409 Third Street SW, 8th Floor　　　　　　　　　1-800-827-5722
Washington, DC 20416　　　　　　　　　　　　　202-205-6460
www.sba.gov/GC/sales.html

The federal government sells surplus property and natural resources, such as timber. SBA works with government agencies which are selling the property and resources to assure that small businesses have an opportunity to buy a fair share of them. Occasionally natural resources that the federal government is releasing on the market are made available. Small fuel companies and producers may get the option to buy their fair share of federal government coal leases. The royalty oil program enables small and independent refineries to buy oil at valuations set by the federal government — which is in excess of spot market prices. Agricultural leases may be had for land on which to graze cattle or grow crops. This SBA program is designed to ensure that small businesses get their fair share of real and personal federal property put on the market. Don't expect bargains. To find out what SBA Natural Resources Sales Assistance programs are in your area, contact your nearest SBA office. For information on other SBA services, call 1-800-827-5722 (recorded listing from which you can order brochures.)

* Real Estate: General Services Administration
Property Sales
General Services Administration (GSA)
Office of Real Estate Sales
Washington, DC 20406　　　　　　　　　　　　　1-800-GSA-1313
http://propertydisposal.gsa.gov

Call this toll-free number for national listing of properties and to receive a booklet describing the GSA real estate program. Then contact local GSA office for the area you are interested in. You can also obtain the list by calling the Property Disposal Division, 202-501-2075. The phone number of the local GSA office to contact will be provided on the list that is mailed to you free of charge upon request. If you have a computer equipped with a modem, you can access the Federal Real Estate Bulletin Board for information on real estate sales. Set you communications software to 8 data bits, no parity, and 1 stop bit. Dial 800-776-7872 or 202-501-6510.

* Real Estate: Small Business Administration (SBA)
U.S. Small Business Administration
Portfolio Management Division
409 Third Street, SW
Washington, DC 20416　　　　　　　　　　　　　202-205-6481
www.sba.gov/assets.html
Recording from which to order brochures　　　　1-800-827-5722

Contact your local SBA office located in 10 Regional Offices around the country, or any of the 68 District Offices. SBA does not maintain a mailing list. No district or regional SBA office is aware of what the other offices are offering. The SBA auctions off properties of people who have defaulted on home loan payments in SBA-sponsored programs. Listings of auctions are printed in local newspapers, usually in the Sunday edition in the classified section. Merchandise is identified as SBA property and sold by brokers, none of whom have the exclusive listing, or by private auctioneers. The auctioneers are chosen on a rotating basis. SBA attempts to sell to the highest bidder, but may reject a winning bid if too low. Sales are infrequent. Do not expect bargains. Items sold range from office furniture and equipment to buildings or entire bakeries, drycleaners, or other businesses. There may be parts or whole businesses available. The auctioneer may have an entire auction of SBA items, or a mixture of things from various sources. You may request to bid by sealed bid if you desire; and a deposit is required. Payment is by cash or certified check. If you are interested in certain categories of merchandise, you might want to be placed on the mailing list of one or more auctioneers who specialize in that particular type of item, such as farm equipment, for example. Since the SBA is often the guarantor of bank loans, SBA auctions are relatively infrequent and bargains are not easy to find.

* Ships: Maritime Administration
U.S. Department of Transportation
Office of Ship Operations
Maritime Administration
400 7th St., SW, Room 7324
Washington, DC 20590　　　　　　　　　　　　　202-366-5111
www.marad.dot.gov

When the government decides that a merchant ship is no longer needed or useable, it may put that ship up for sale by auction, through a sealed bid procedure. A ten percent deposit is required. It is sold to the highest bidder for its scrap value. Contact the above address to be put on the auction mailing list. When ships are available, you will receive descriptions of the ships and information on the bidding procedure

Donations to Non-Profit Organizations

* Art Exhibits
Smithsonian Institution
1100 Jefferson Dr., SW, Room 3146   202-357-3168
Washington, DC 20560   Fax: 202-357-4324
www.si.edu/organiza/offices/sites/start.htm

The Smithsonian can bring art to you, whether you live in a major metropolitan area or a rural one. The Smithsonian Institute Traveling Exhibition Service (SITES) sponsors approximately 65 different exhibits at any given time in museums and other locations around the country. The participation fee will range from $100 to $100,000. The exhibitions range from popular culture, to fine arts, photography, science, historical exhibits, or topics of interest to children. The collections are from other museums and institutions, and are most frequently sent to other museums, libraries, historic homes, or even schools and community centers. More than half the locations are in rural settings. SITES estimates that more than 11 million people view the exhibits it circulates in this program. The bigger exhibits that require special security arrangements go only to museums equipped to handle them. If interested, call the above number for the SITES *Updates* catalog.

* Books
Library of Congress
Anglo-American Acquisitions Division
101 Independence Ave., SE
Washington, DC 20540   202-707-9514
http://lcweb.loc.gov/acq/surplus.html

Government agencies, educational institutions, and other non-profit organizations may qualify to obtain free books from the U.S. Library of Congress. The books are largely technical and legal works, but from time to time contains entire collections from military installation lending libraries that have been closed. There is no way to tell what books will be available. Stock is constantly changing. Books are first offered on a competitive bidding basis. If they are not sold, they become available on a donation bidding basis. Commercial book dealers may compete in this bidding against non-profit organizations. The proceeds sustain the Book Preservation Program. Someone from the organization must choose which books are desired. He or she must have a letter from the organization or appropriate Congressional representative stating that the person it selected to choose the books acts for a non-profit organization. The Library will ship the books UPS at the organization's expense or the organization may supply the Library with pre-addressed franking labels. Congressional offices will help educational institutions such as universities and schools obtain these labels. Non-profit organizations may submit bids to purchase books. The Library will contact the organization if the bid is unacceptably low and give the bidder one chance to raise it. There is no limit on the number of books a group may order.

* Department of Housing and Urban Development (HUD)
HUD USER
451 7th Street SW, Room 814
Washington, DC 20743   800-245-2691
www.hud.gov

To find out about the over 100 programs HUD offers to assist low and moderate income housing groups and individuals, obtain *Programs of HUD* by calling 202-708-1420.

* Food and Surplus Commodities
USDA Food Distribution Programs
  or Food Distribution Division
Food and Nutrition Service
3101 Park Center Drive, Room 503
Alexandria, VA 22302   703-305-2888
www.fns.usda.gov/fdd

Non-profit groups with tax-exempt status may apply for surplus commodities held by the Agriculture Department, such as grain (usually flour), oils, and sometimes milk and cheese. The large quantities of surplus cheese and milk that existed a couple of years ago are largely depleted. The items available depend somewhat on which foods are currently in surplus. Contact your state distribution agency, frequently the state Department of Agriculture, Department of Education, or Administrative Services, or the above address.

* Foreign Gifts
General Services Administration
Crystal Mall Building #4
1941 Jefferson Davis Highway, Room 800
Washington, DC 20406   703-308-0745
http://pub.fss.gsa.gov/property

Non-Presidential gifts worth over $200 from foreign countries to U.S. government agencies or their representatives may be displayed by the recipient in his government office, then purchased by him at an officially assessed value. If the gift is not purchased, it may end up in a State Surplus Property office, where the general public can get a chance to buy it. Watches and jewelry are commonly available, along with books, sculptures, and various artifacts. But the souvenir from Anwar Sadat to Jimmy Carter during the Middle East peace talks goes to the U.S. Archives and possibly later to the Jimmy Carter Library.

When gifts are reported to the GSA, they first go through the federal screening cycle. Federal agencies have the first chance to purchase items at retail value price. If none exercise that option, the recipient may purchase the item. If the item remains unsold, it enters the donation screening cycle. It may then be used for display purposes at state agencies such as libraries or museums. After that, it may be sold to the public at auction. At public auction, anyone can purchase the item. Non-profits have no special footing. Items are disposed of by GSA in basically the same way as other surplus and excess property.

Items desired by non-profit organizations should be requested through your local Surplus Property Office, which can then contact the GSA about a donation. You can find a list of foreign gifts given to government agencies published yearly in the *Federal Register*, State Department, Chief of Protocol, Washington, DC, 202-647-4169.

* Interagency Council on the Homeless
Office of Special Needs Assistance Programs
U.S. Department of Housing and Urban Development
451 Seventh Street, SW, Room 7262
Washington, DC 20410   202-708-1480
www.hud.gov

This is a coordinating counsel of 16 different federal agencies, headed by the HUD Secretary. It works with state and local governments and private organizations on homeless-related efforts. Call for information on homeless activities. For information on financing rehabilitation or support services, contact HUD's Office of Special Needs Assistance Program at 202-708-4300.

Title V of the McKinney Act is the "Federal Surplus Property Program." You can call 1-800-927-7588 to get answers about the Title V Program and properties 24 hours per day. Under this program, federally owned surplus or unused property may be deeded, leased or made available on an interim basis at no cost to homeless providers such as states, local governments and non-profit organizations. To find out about eligible properties, ask to be put on the mailing list that tells you of properties in your area as they are published by contacting your nearest field HUD office.

* Miscellaneous Property
Director, Property Management Division
Office of Property Disposal
Federal Supply Service
Washington, DC 20406   703-308-0745
http://propertydisposal.gsa.gov

Or contact your local State Office of Surplus Property. The General Services Administration (GSA) will donate items it handles to qualifying nonprofit organizations which request it. Items are "as is" and range from tools, office machines, supplies and furniture, clothes, hardware, medical supplies to cars, boats, and planes. Your State Agency for Surplus Property, also called Office of Purchasing, Property Control, or General Services, makes the determination whether your group qualifies, then contacts the GSA to obtain it. There may be a charge of 2% of the value and a fee for handling and service. Groups eligible can include public agencies, and non-profit educational, public health, elderly, or homeless organizations.

Government Auctions and Surplus Property

* Travel Aboard an Icebreaker

Ice Operations Division
U.S. Coast Guard Headquarters
2100 2nd Street, SW
Washington, DC 20593   202-267-1450
www.uscg.mil/lantarea/iip/home.html

The Coast Guard evaluates scientific projects to determine if they qualify. The group that qualifies as a primary user, because it is willing to pay for fuel and part of maintenance and helicopter costs on resupply trips, may send a scientist they select to ride along with one of the two Coast Guard Icebreakers that travel to the Arctic and Antarctica. At present, the National Science Foundation (4201 Wilson Blvd., Arlington, VA 22230, 703-306-1070) is the primary user. Other interested parties who wish to send scientists or observers, such as scientific or environmental groups must obtain the consent of the primary user for that trip. Most travelers are sponsored by government or educational organizations, but the Coast Guard is interested in any appropriate, professional project and will consider other applications as well. They can also be flexible on their itinerary to accommodate projects. Sometimes scientists on short missions may travel at no cost. In addition, special expeditions are commissioned, such as the one in 1992 by the U.S. Geological Survey. If interested, contact the primary user.

State Government Auctions

The following is a descriptive listing of state government offices which offer auctions or donations of surplus property.

Alabama

Alabama Surplus Property, P.O. Box 210487, Montgomery, AL 36121, 334-277-5866; {www.adeca.state.al.us}. Alabama auctions off a variety of items about three times per year, including office equipment, heavy machinery (such as milling machines and drill presses), and vehicles, including cars, trucks, boats, and tractors. Trailers, medical equipment, tires, dossiers, and lathes are also sold. The state advertises upcoming auctions in the classified section of local newspapers. Upon written request made to the above address, you can be put on a mailing list. You will then be notified 2 or 3 weeks in advance of each upcoming auction, but you won't receive a list of items. Lists of items can be picked up at the above office 2 days before the auction. Payment can be by cash, cashier's check, or personal check with a bank letter of credit. Items are available for viewing two days prior to the auction. No bids by mail.

Alaska

Surplus Property Management Office, 2400 Viking Dr., Anchorage, AK 99501, 907-279-0596. The Juno office is 907-465-2172. Call it for general information and mailing list information. Alaska's Division of General Services and Supply sells surplus office equipment, including furniture and typewriters, every Wednesday from 8:30 am to 3:30 pm in a garage sale fashion with prices marked for each item. For items costing over $1000, cash or cashiers checks are required. Vehicles, at various locations throughout the state, are sold during sealed bid or outcry auctions twice a year, in the spring and fall. Payment is by cashiers check after you have been notified of your winning bid.

Arizona

Office of Surplus Property, 1537 W. Jackson St., Phoenix, AZ 85007, 602-542-5701. About three times per year, usually in January, May, and September, Arizona auctions off everything from vehicles to miscellaneous office equipment and computers. Items are sold by lots rather than individually; and prices, especially cars, can be below blue book price, depending upon opening bids. Vehicles range from empty frames to Jaguars. A mailing list is maintained. You can have it sent to you for no charge. Individual cities and county governments in Arizona also hold their own surplus auctions.

Arkansas

State Marketing and Redistribution Office, 8700 Remont Rd., North Little Rock, AR 72118, 501-835-3111. Arkansas conducts both sealed bid and retail, fixed price sales of surplus items. On Wednesdays, between 7:30 am and 3:00 pm, buyers may view and purchase items, which include office machines, tables, and tires, valued at under $500. Larger, more valuable items, including vehicles, medical equipment, mobile homes, and machine shop and automotive supplies, are sold by sealed bid. You can have your name placed on the mailing list for various categories such as computers, autos and miscellaneous equipment. You must bid three times to keep your name on the mailing list. The state also conducts sealed bids by mail. The bid fee is $1. No personal checks are accepted for sealed bids. All items are sold "as is," with no refunds or guarantees implied or stated.

California

Department of General Services, Procurement Division, 1421 N. Market Blvd., Sacramento, CA 95834; 916-928-4633. The Department of General Services Reutilization disposes of salvage and surplus personal property from California state agencies. The property is made available to other state agencies, political subdivisions, and assistance organizations for a predetermined service and handling fee. If the property is not picked up by an eligible entity, private citizens and the general public are invited to purchase the property in a cash and carry, first come, first served basis. (Cash, check, Visa or MasterCard).

State of California, Office of Fleet Administration, 1421 Richards Blvd., Sacramento, CA 95814, 916-327-9196 (recorded message), 916-327-2085.. Once a month on Wednesdays, the General Services Department of the state holds open bid auctions at Sacramento or Los Angeles State Garages of surplus automobiles previously owned by state agencies. Vehicles can be viewed from 8:30 am to 9:30 am. The auction begins at 9:30 am. Vehicles may include sedans, cargo and passenger vans, pick-ups (mostly American-made). Auctions are occasionally advertised in the newspapers. Minimum bid prices are set for exceptionally nice cars. Only state agency vehicles are sold. Payment is by cash, cashiers check, or certified check. Successful bidders have up to five working days to pay for and pick up the cars (the following Friday). Out-of-state checks are frowned upon. Prices vary greatly, and some vehicles have required minimum bids.

California Highway Patrol, Used Vehicle Sales Office, 3300 Reed Ave., W. Sacramento, CA 95605, 916-371-2270. Minimum bids are stated on a recorded telephone message (916-371-2284). The auction is by sealed bids which are opened at 3:00 pm daily; winners may be present or notified by telephone. Payment is by cashiers check, certified check, or, money order only -- no personal checks or cash accepted. Bids may be submitted and inspection is available between 8:00 am and 3:00 pm.

Colorado

Department of Correctional Industries, State Surplus Agency, 4200 Garfield Street, Denver, CO 80216, 303-321-4012. Several times a year, Colorado auctions off its surplus property, including motor vehicles. Auctions are pre-announced in newspaper ads, and a mailing list is also maintained. To be put on the mailing list, call the above number. The auctions of state property are held the third Thursday of every month. If you are on the mailing list, you will receive a notice the weekend before the auction with a brief description of the items. Non-profit organizations have first choice of state surplus items, which can include typewriters, desks, computers, file cabinets, hospital beds, and much more. Payment may be made by cash, money order or personal checks with two IDs.

Connecticut

State and Federal Property Distribution, Department of Administrative Services, 165 Capital Ave., Room 420, Hartford, CT 06106; 860-713-5158. Property auctions are scheduled monthly.

60 State St. Rear, Wethersfield, CT 06109, 860-566-7018, or 860-566-7190. Items vary from day to day. Vehicles are auctioned separately 8 or 9 times per year, with ads in the 4 largest newspapers and on 2 radio stations giving advance notice. There is no mailing list. These auctions are usually on the second Saturday of the month. Vehicles may be viewed one hour prior to the auction. Buyers may also purchase a brochure with vehicle descriptions when they pay the $3 registration fee. You may go Monday-Friday, noon to 3:45 to view and purchase smaller items in their warehouse.

Delaware

Division of Purchasing Surplus Property, P.O. Box 299, Delaware City, DE 19706, 302-834-7645, ext. 226. Twice a year, in May and in September, Delaware publicly auctions off vehicles, office furniture, and other surplus or used property. Vehicles include school buses, paddle boats, vans, pick-up trucks, heavy equipment, and sedans. Prices depend on the condition of the item and how many people are bidding for it. Vehicles may be inspected prior to the auction. You may get on a mailing list to be advised of upcoming auctions. A flyer with information and conditions of payment will be sent to you.

District of Columbia

District of Columbia, State Agency, Department of Administrative Services, 2100 Adams Pl. NE, 2nd Floor, Washington, DC 20218; 202-576-6472.

District of Columbia Dept. of Public Works, 5001 Shepard Parkway, SW, Washington, DC 20032, 202-645-4227. DC holds vehicle auctions every 1st and 3rd Tuesday of every month. Vehicles include cars, trucks, buses, ambulances, and boats. Inspection and viewing is available at 7:00 am, one hour prior to the 8:00 am open bid auction. $100 cash must be paid to attend the auction. Prices and conditions of vehicles vary greatly. No mailing list is kept. Auctions are posted 45 days in advance in the *Washington Times*. A $100 cash entry fee must be paid to attend an auction. This fee will be credited toward the purchase price, and is refunded if no car is purchased. Cars must be paid for in full at the auction by certified or cashier's check. Twice a year confiscated bikes and property found inside of cars go to auction.

Government Auctions and Surplus Property

Florida
Department of Management Services, Division of Motor Pool Bureau of Motor Vehicles, 813B Lake Bradford Rd., Tallahassee, FL 32304, 850-488-5178. Approximately once per month, somewhere in Florida, items are auctioned for the state. Descriptive information and viewing schedules are published in newspapers. Surplus items, including motorcars, heavy equipment and boats are sold. Automobile auctions take place anywhere from 7 to 15 times per year, with dates set 4 to 6 weeks in advance at various auction locations throughout the state. The auctions are advertised. Some industrial equipment is also included, along with various kinds of used and confiscated vans, trucks, and cars. Pleasure and fishing boats are also auctioned. Items may be viewed prior to the auction. Call 800-342-2666 (in state) to be placed on a mailing list.

Georgia
State of Georgia, Dept. of Administrative Services, Purchasing Division, Surplus Property Services, 1050 Murphy Ave., SW, Atlanta, GA 30310, 404-756-4800. Georgia auctions vehicles, including sedans, wagons, trucks, vans, buses, and cement mixers. The state also auctions shop equipment, generators, typewriters, copiers, computers, tape recorders, and other office equipment, as well as audio-visual equipment, cameras, electronic equipment, and air conditioners. They keep a mailing list and also advertise the auctions in local newspapers. Merchandise may be inspected by pre-registered bidders two days before an auction. Vehicles may be started up, but not driven. For auctions, items are payable with cash only. Items must be paid for on the day of sale. Auctions are held every three months at different locations.

Hawaii
Surplus Property Branch, 729 Kakoi St., Honolulu, HI 96819; 808-831-6757. Auctions are held periodically. Contact this office to learn what is available and where the auction will be held.

Idaho
Bureau of Federal Surplus Property, 6941 South Supply Way, P.O. Box 83720, Boise, ID 83720; 208-327-7471. The property is donated to units of state and local government and to certain, eligible, nonprofit health and educational entities, programs for the elderly and for the homeless. No auctions are held.

Division of Purchasing, 208-327-7465. In 1991 the Idaho state legislature dissolved centralized public auctions. Each state agency now holds its own auction or has a commercial auctioneer handle its surplus. If an agency decides to auction cars through sealed bids, it must advertise in 3 newspapers for 10 days. To find out if, when, and what an agency is disposing of through auction, contact that agency directly.

Illinois
Central Management Services, Division of Property Control, 3550 Great Northern Ave., Springfield, IL 62707, 217-785-6903. Two or three times per year this office auctions vehicles and property. Auctions are held at the address listed above. Auctions are always held on Saturdays. Property includes office equipment, desks, chairs, typewriters, restaurant equipment, calculators, cameras, refrigerators, and filing cabinets. Scrap metal and equipment not easily moved are sold by sealed bid. The office maintains a mailing list which costs $20/year to subscribe. Notices of auctions and bids are mailed out 3 weeks prior to the auction. The auctions are also advertised in advance in local newspapers. All the cars auctioned have a minimum mileage of 75,000 miles and were driven by state employees. Prices vary widely, but below-market prices are available. Illinois auctions off vehicles by open bid auctions. (Confiscated cars are sold at federal auctions and may present greater possibility for a bargain.) Payment is made by cash, cashiers or certified check, or personal check with bank letter.

Indiana
State of Indiana, Department of Administration, Federal Surplus Property, 6400 E. 30th St., Indianapolis, IN 46219, 317-591-5321. Indiana holds auctions as items accumulate through open cry auctions to the highest bidder. During the summer months, the state sells surplus from the Department of Transportation and the Department of Natural Resources. A mailing list is maintained. Auctions are advertised the first Thursday of every month in the *Indianapolis Star*. The auction date and selected auctioneer changes every year during July. Call the above office in May to obtain the new schedule. Sealed bids must contain 100% deposit. Payment is by cash, certified check, cashiers check, or money order. No personal checks or letters of credit are accepted. Items vary and are all state surplus.

Iowa
Iowa Federal Surplus Property, Department of General Services, Fairgrounds Distribution Center, Des Moines, IA 50319; 515-262-9810. Auctions are held periodically. You can inspect goods the day prior to the sale and the morning of the sale. Contact this office to see when the next auction will be held.

Department of Natural Resources, Wallace State Office Bldg., Des Moines, IA 50319, 515-281-5145. The Department of Natural Resources holds an auction when and if a sufficient number of items have accumulated, on the second Saturday of every May. Items disposed of include boats, fishing rods, tackle boxes, guns, and other fishing and hunting equipment, as well as office equipment. Payment is by cash or check with appropriate identification. There is no mailing list, but auctions are advertised in local newspapers.

Vehicle Dispatchers Garage, 301 E. 7th, Des Moines, IA 50319, 515-281-5121. The Vehicle Dispatchers Garage holds auctions, if there is sufficient accumulation, three to four times per year at 9:00 am on Saturdays. The state disposes of approximately 500 vehicles yearly through these auctions. They mostly sell patrol cars, pickups and trucks. All have at least 81,000 miles of travel on them, and prices vary widely. A deposit of $200 is required on the day of the sale, with full payment due by the following Wednesday. Payment may be made by cash or check with an accompanying letter of credit guaranteeing payment by the issuing institution. Viewing is possible Friday all day and Saturday morning prior to the sale. There is a mailing list. Auctions are advertised in the local papers.

Kansas
Kansas State Surplus Property, P.O. Box 19226, Topeka, KS 66619-0226, 785-296-2351, Fax: 785-296-4060. The State Surplus Property office sells sedans, snow plows, and everything they have, from staples to bulldozers. Property is first offered to other state agencies at set prices for 30 days. Whatever is left over is opened to public sale at the same prices. Prices tend to be competitive. Items are sold at set prices, with a catalog available containing descriptions of items and where they are located. Confiscated vehicles are not sold to the public. They are disposed of by county courthouses, usually to county agencies. To obtain copies of catalogs describing sealed bid items, write to the above address. It will be sent to you for 6 months, after which time your name will be purged unless you re-request it.

Kentucky
Kentucky Office of Surplus Property, 514 Barrett Ave., Frankfurt, KY 40601, 502-564-4836. Kentucky holds public auctions on Saturdays every two or three months. Items may include vehicles, desks, chairs, calculators, typewriters, file cabinets, tape recorders, electronic equipment, couches, beds, and lawnmowers, to name a few. Merchandise may be viewed the day before an auction. The office maintains a mailing list and also advertises upcoming auctions in local newspapers two to three weeks before the sale. Some items are auctioned by sealed bids. Property is payable by cash, certified check, or money order.

Louisiana
Division of Administration, Louisiana Property Assistance Agency, 1635 Foss Dr., Baton Rouge, LA 70804-9095, 225-342-7860. Public auctions are held on the second Saturday of every month at 9:00 am at 1502 North 17th St. Items may be viewed at the warehouse from 8:00 am to 4:30 pm the week before. Property sold ranges from medical and office equipment, to boats, shop equipment, typewriters, file cabinets, pinball machines, bicycles, televisions, adding machines, and chairs, and vehicles. All items are sold "as is" and "where is." Payment is required in full the day of the auctions, but no personal or company checks are accepted. In addition, all merchandise must be removed within five days after the sale. Auctions are conducted by a different auctioneer each year, depending on who wins the bid for the annual contract.

Maine
Office of Surplus Property, Station 95, Augusta, ME 04333, 207-287-2923. Five or six times per year, Maine publicly auctions off vehicles on the grounds of the Augusta Mental Health Institute. You must register to be able to bid. Vehicles may include police cruisers, pick-up trucks, snowmobiles, lawn mowers, and heavy equipment, such as large trucks, graders, and backhoes. Inspection is allowed between 7:30 am and 10:00 am the day of the auctions, which are always held on Saturdays. The impound yard opens at 7:00 am. Vehicles may be started up but not driven. Personal checks (local banks only), money orders, certified checks, and cash are all accepted. Exact date, place, and time of auctions are announced in local newspapers, but there is no mailing list. Payment is due for both vehicles and other items the day of the auction or sale.

Maryland
Maryland State Agency for Surplus Property, P.O. Box 122, 8037 Brock Bridge Rd., Jessup, MD 20794, 410-540-4066. Office furniture and the like are sold or donated to non-profit organizations or state agencies, and vehicles are sold to dealers only. The state maintains a warehouse for surplus property at the above address. After a certain length of time, items that do not go to non-profits or state agencies become

State Government Auctions

available to the public at set prices at its retail store. Checks are acceptable up to $500.

Massachusetts
Massachusetts State Purchasing Agency, Department of Procurement and General Services, Surplus Property, One Ashburton Place, Room 1017, Boston, MA 02108, 617-720-3146. About six times per year, Massachusetts holds public auctions of surplus property. Bidders must register in the morning by filling out a card. The State Purchasing Agency places ads in The Boston Globe on the Sunday and Wednesday prior to each of the auctions, which are normally held on Saturdays. Vehicles are usually auctioned after about 60 or so accumulate. Vehicles sold include sedans, wagons, vans, and pick-ups with an average age of 7 years. The average car has over 100,000 miles. Conditions range from good to junk. Viewing is available the day before the auction from 9:00 am to 4:00 pm. Purchases are "as is". No start-ups allowed. The state does not auction other surplus property, in general, but occasionally special auctions are held for boats, parts from the Department of Public Works, and most recently, helicopters.

Michigan
State of Michigan, Department of Management and Budget, State Surplus Property, P.O. Box 30026, 12 Martin Luther King Blvd., Lansing, MI 48913, 517-335-9105. The state auctions off all kinds of office furniture, household goods, machinery, livestock, and vehicles, such as sedans, buses, trucks, and boats. Auctions are held at different locations for different categories of property. The State Surplus Property Office sends out yearly calendars with auction dates and information. Contact them at the above address to have it sent to you. Double check dates because additions or changes may occur. Auctions are also published in the local newspapers. Payment may be made by cash or check and should include the 6% state sales tax. No refunds are made. Inspections of merchandise are available either the day before from 8:00 am to 3:00 pm or the morning of an auction from 8:00 am to 9:30 am. Vehicles may be started but not driven. Auctions begin at 10:00 am. Items must be paid in full on the day of sale by cash or in state check. Buyer has 3 working days to remove the property.

Minnesota
Minnesota Surplus Operations Office, 5420 Highway 8, New Brighton, MN 55112, 651-639-4023; Hotline: 612-296-1056. The hotline is updated with any changes in the auction schedule. Minnesota holds about 15 auctions per year at different locations around the state. They sell vehicles such as old patrol cars, passenger cars, trucks, vans, and trucks, as well as heavy machinery, boats, snowmobiles and outboard motors. The state also auctions off furniture, office equipment, kitchen equipment, tools, and confiscated items such as vehicles, computers, jewelry, car stereos and radios, and other personal effects. Many of these items are sold under market price. You may be put on a mailing list to receive a calendar for the schedule of upcoming auctions for the year. Auctions are advertised in the locale where they occur by radio, TV, and in Minneapolis and St. Paul newspapers. Inspection of property is held from 8:00 am to 9:30 am, an hour and a half before the auction begins; and payment is by personal check for in-state residents, cash, or money order.

Mississippi
Mississippi Office of Surplus Supply, P.O. Box 5778, Jackson, MS 39288; 601-939-2050. Auctions are held periodically. Contact the office to learn when the next auction will be held.

Department of Public Safety, Support Services, P.O. Box 958, Jackson, MS 39205, 601-987-1500. The state cars that are auctioned are mostly patrol cars, and only occasionally vans and other types of vehicles. State cars are usually wrecked or old. Most have at least 100,000 miles on them. Recent average prices have ranged from $1200 to $1500. The state is keeping cars longer, so less are being sold. These agency cars and others from the Department of Wildlife and Fisheries, military bases, Narcotics Division, and U.S. Marshal's Office -- which includes confiscated cars -- are auctioned the first Tuesday of every month by Mid South Auctions, 6655 N. State St., Jackson, MS 39213, 601-956-2700. Call to be put on the mailing list. Many car dealers as well as the public attend these auctions, so prices are competitive. Bargains are still possible. Payment must be in cash or cashiers check -- no personal checks. The balance is due the day of the auction. Cars are available a few days before the auction.

Missouri
State of Missouri, Surplus Property Office, Materials Management Section, P.O. Drawer 1310, 117 N. Riverside Dr., Jefferson City, MO 65102, 573-751-3415. At various times throughout the year, Missouri holds regular public auctions every 6-8 weeks, as well as sealed bid auctions of merchandise located at various places in the state. The wide range of items include clothing, office equipment and vehicles. No confiscated or seized vehicles or other items are sold. You can be put on a mailing list to receive notices of upcoming auctions, plus they are advertised in local newspapers. For regular auctions, inspection is available the day before or on the day of the auction; and sealed bid items may be viewed two or three days before the deadline. Items may be sold by lot or individually. Payment may be made by cash or personal check.

Montana
Property and Supply Bureau, 930 Lyndale Ave., Helena, MT 59620-0137, 406-444-4514. Montana holds a vehicle auction once a year, of about 300 state vehicles. Contact the above to get on the mailing list. The auctions are by open cry and sealed bid. All items are from state surplus; nothing is seized or confiscated. These auctions are advertised in local newspapers prior to the auction. In addition, the state offers other property for sale each month on the second Friday of the month at set prices. The sales include items such as office supplies, computers, chairs, tables, and vehicles including trucks, vans, sedans, highway patrol cars, and more. Payment can be by cash, certified or business check, or bank check.

Nebraska
Nebraska Office of Administrative Services, Material Division, Surplus Property, P.O. Box 94661, Lincoln, NE 68509, 402-471-2677. Three or four times a year, Nebraska auctions off office furniture, computers, couches, and more. Separate auctions are held for vehicles and heavy equipment -- also about three or four times per year. Auctions are advertised in newspapers and on radio, and a mailing list is also kept. Sealed bids for property such as scrap iron, wrecked vehicles, guard posts, and tires are taken. Items are available for viewing two days prior to the auctions, which are held on Saturdays at 5001 S. 14th St. All items are sold "as is". Payment, which can be made by cash or check, must be in full on the day of the auction.

Nevada
Nevada Purchasing Division, Kinkead Bldg., Room 304 Capitol Complex, 209 E. Muzzer, Carson City, NV 89710, 702-687-4070. The sales and auction are located at the warehouse at 2250 Barnett Way, Reno, NV 89512; 702-688-1161. About once a year, Nevada holds a sale on the second Saturday in August of such items as calculators, desks, cabinets, tables and chairs. Office equipment is released for sale to the public at a set price. The sale is held to clear the warehouse, and is on a first come, first serve basis, with minimum prices to cover service and handling marked on the property. Very few vehicles are confiscated. Most are surplus turned in by other state agencies for resale. Vehicles and motorcycles are auctioned. Public auctions are not served by mailing lists but are advertised in the newspapers. You can be put on a mailing list to receive notice of sealed bid sales of 19 categories of merchandise, including heavy equipment, boats, and planes. Once you have requested to place your name on the mailing list, if you do not subsequently bid on two consecutive occasions, it will be removed. Payment is by cash or local check with proper I.D. No out of state checks accepted. For vehicles, you can put down a 5% deposit with 5 days to complete payment. The county, city and University of Nevada also advertise and hold public auctions.

New Hampshire
Office of Surplus Property, 12 Hills Ave., Concord, NH 03301, 603-271-2602. New Hampshire holds two auctions per year of vehicles and other equipment, such as office furniture and machines, and refrigerators. Vehicles, which include cruisers, pickups, vans, and sometimes confiscated vehicles may be viewed the day before the auction, while other merchandise can be viewed on the same day just before the auction. Vehicles may be started but not driven. A mailing list is maintained, and ads are also placed in local newspapers prior to the auctions. Acceptable payment includes cash and certified funds.

New Jersey
New Jersey State Agency for Surplus Property, 152 U.S. Highway 106 South, Building 15F, Somerville, NJ 08876; 908-685-9562. Auctions are held periodically. Contact the office to learn when the next auction will be held.

New Jersey Purchase and Property Distribution Center, CN-234, Trenton, NJ 08625-0234, 609-530-3300. New Jersey auctions used state vehicles such as vans, various types of compacts, and occasionally boats, buses and heavy equipment. Frequency of auctions depends on availability which currently averages once per month. Vehicles may be inspected and started up the day before the auction from 9:00 am to 3:00 pm. Payment is by cash, money order, or certified check. No personal checks. A 10% deposit is required to hold a vehicle. The successful bidder has 7 calendar days to complete payment and remove the vehicle by Friday. If an item is left after that, even if paid in full, a $20 per day storage fee is charged. After one week, the vehicle is forfeited. To be advised of auctions, put your name on the mailing list by writing the address above. Phone calls are not accepted. A recent vehicle auction in New Jersey offered a variety of Dodge and Chevy vehicles, ages ranging from three to thirteen years, with mileages from 50,000 to 130,000. Other surplus items are not put up for public auction, but are offered to other state agencies.

Government Auctions and Surplus Property

New Mexico

New Mexico Federal Property Assistance Program, 1990 Siringo Rd., Santa Fe, NM 87505; 505-827-4603; Auctions are held periodically. Contact the office to learn when the next auction will be held.

New Mexico Highway and Transportation Department, SB-2, 7315 Cerrillos Road, P.O. Box 1149, Santa Fe, NM 87504-1149, 505-827-5580. About once a year, on the last Saturday of September, New Mexico auctions off vehicles, including sedans, loaders, backhoes, snow removal equipment, pick-ups, vans, four-wheel drives, and tractors. They have some office equipment as well. The items come from state agencies. You may place your name on a mailing list to receive the exact date of the auction and descriptions of merchandise up for bidding. A public entity auction is held first. The published list of items to be publicly auctioned consists of what is left over. Everything is open auction; there are no sealed bids. Items may be inspected the day before the auction. Payment is by cash, checks with proper I.D., money orders, or cashier's checks. No credit cards.

Department of Public Safety, State Police Division, Attn: Major W.D. Morrow, P.O. Box 1628, Santa Fe, NM 87504; 505-827-9001. The above holds a public auction on the second Saturday in July at 4491 Cerrillos Road. Write the office above to be put on the mailing list. It is also advertised in local newspapers. Items sold include everything from calculators to cars. They come from seizures and surplus from other agencies. The vehicles may be viewed and started up the Friday before the auction. Payment may be by cash, money order, cashier's check or personal check with bank letter of guarantee.

New York

State of New York Office of General Service, Bureau of Surplus Property, Building #18, W.A. Harriman State Office Building Campus, Albany, NY 12226, 518-457-3264. The Office of General Services holds auctions continuously in locations around the state. The items are so numerous that the state finds it necessary to sell them by category. You can designate which categories you are interested in on the mailing list application. Items are sold as they become available. Sales are advertised one week in advance in local newspapers. These items include surplus and used office equipment, scrap material, agricultural items (even unborn cows). Most categories such as medical, photographic, institutional and maintenance equipment are sold through sealed bids, usually in lots of varying size. To participate in a sealed bid, you place your name on a mailing list for items in seven different categories, then make your bid by mail. Send the sealed bids to Bureau of Surplus Property Distribution, Building 18, State Office Building, Albany, NY 12226. The highest bidder wins and is notified by mail. Mailings give as much information as possible about the items being auctioned; but state officials stress that merchandise is sold "as is" and "where is". They advise viewing property in person before making a bid. A ten percent deposit is required with each sealed bid. Vehicles are sold by public auction and may include cars, trucks, buses, tractors, bulldozers, mowers, compressors, plows, sanders, and other highway maintenance and construction equipment. Large items are sold individually, and smaller equipment, such as chain saws, is more likely to be sold in lots. These auctions take place about 55 times per year. It is always possible that enough surplus may not accumulate to warrant an auction. The state warns that just because an auction is scheduled is no guarantee that it will occur. Payment may be made by certified check or cash. A ten percent deposit will hold a vehicle until the end of the day.

North Carolina

State Surplus Property, P.O. Box 26567, Raleigh, NC 27611, 919-733-3885. North Carolina sells through sealed bids surplus state merchandise including vehicles and office equipment every Tuesday. Office equipment includes furniture, typewriters, desks, and chairs. For a fee of $15 you can be placed on a mailing list to receive weekly advisories of what is for auction, with a description of the item and its condition. Otherwise, if you visit the warehouse in person, you can pick up free samples of bid listings and look at lists of prices that items sold for in previous auctions. The warehouse is located on Highway 54 - Old Chapel Hill Road. Payment is by money order or certified check, and you have 15 days to pay for your merchandise and 15 days to pick it up. Items may be inspected two weeks before an auction from Monday to Friday between 8:00 am and 5:00 pm. On Tuesdays, the warehouse is closed between 1:00 pm and 3:00 pm when the bids are opened and the public is then invited to attend. The state may reject bids that are too low. Vehicles vary greatly in type and condition.

North Dakota

Surplus Property Office, P.O. Box 7293, Bismarck, ND 58507, 701-328-9667. Once a year, usually in August or September, the Office of Surplus Property auctions through open bidding surplus office furniture and equipment, as well as vehicles and scrap materials. The auction is advertised the two days before and merchandise may be viewed the morning of the auction. The auction is held at Igo Industrial Park. Cash, cashiers checks, or money orders are acceptable forms of payment. Personal or business checks are accepted only with a bank letter of credit.

Ohio

Office of State and Federal Surplus Property, 4200 Surface Road, Columbus, OH 43228, 614-466-4485. Ohio holds public auctions and sealed bid sales on a wide range of office machines and equipment, and furniture. There are no sealed bids on vehicles. No mailing list is maintained. Call or write for the information. When you attend an auction, you can fill out a label that will be used to notify you of the next auction. Vehicle auctions are held three to four times a year, depending on the amount accumulated. Inspections are available the day before. Vehicles may include sedans, trucks, vans, 4x4s, boats, mowers, tractors, and chain saws. No seized or confiscated items are sold. At the time of the auction, a 25% down payment is required, with the balance due by the following Monday (auctions are held on Saturdays). For the sealed bid auctions, payment must be by money order or certified check.

Oklahoma

Oklahoma Property Distribution Division, 3100 North Creston, P.O. Box 11355, Oklahoma City, OK 73136; 405-425-2700. Auctions are held periodically. Contact the office to learn when the next auction will be held.

Central Purchasing, Dept. Central Services, B-4, State Capitol, Oklahoma City, OK 73105, 405-521-3046; general information only for public auctions, 405-521-3835; for general information and information on sealed bids, 405-521-2110. Oklahoma auctions vehicles as they accumulate. Vehicles often have from 80,000 to 120,000 miles on them and it is rare for a car to be rated as fair -- which means it is in running condition. They are usually bought by wholesalers. State agency cars are commonly sold, but occasionally seized or confiscated cars are sold. Agencies most likely to have auctions are: Department of Human Services (occasionally vehicles and other items, but they usually take their cars to public auctions); Wildlife Department (vehicles); Department of Public Safety (vehicles); and the Department of Transportation (vehicles). The Department of Transportation has four auctions per year. Vehicles are usually not in good condition. The state advises that you contact each agency separately for details. The auctions are not always advertised in newspapers, but some agencies, such as the Department of Transportation (405-521-2550) have mailing lists.

Oregon

Department of General Services, Surplus Property, 1655 Salem Industrial Drive NE, Salem, OR 97310, 503-378-4711 (Salem area). Oregon auctions both vehicles and other equipment, such as office furniture. Merchandise may include snow plows, horse trailers, computer equipment, desks, chairs, tires or shop equipment. Some items are in excellent condition, and bargains may be found. Items come from state agency surplus and confiscations. On rare occasions exotic items such as a Porsche and hot tub have been sold. Public sales are held every Friday at set prices. Sealed bid sales are held separately. The frequency of auctions depends on the amount of items to be disposed. The numbers of vehicles for sale is increasing. Cars are also sold every week at set prices. For info call the 24 hour information line that is always kept current, 503-373-1392, ext. 400. Ads are also placed on radio and in local newspapers in the areas where the auction will be held, giving the date and location of the auction. The procedure is to register and obtain a bidder number, which you hold up when you are making a bid. The forms may be obtained at the auction site. At the same time as you register, you must show some form of identification. The conditions and terms of sale are always listed. At the public sales if you pay by Mastercard or Visa, title is immediately released. You can also pay 10% down at the auction site and pay the balance at the office with Mastercard or Visa in 3 days. A mailing list is maintained.

Pennsylvania

General Services Department, Bureau of Vehicle Management, P.O. Box 1365, 2221 Forster Street, Harrisburg, PA 17105, 717-787-9724, ext. 3205. About 10 times per year, depending on the number of cars accumulated, the DGS auctions off all kinds of vehicles. Many have mileages under 100,000, and ages commonly range from 1979 to 1986. There are about 200 cars at each auction. They are mostly used state agency cars that have been replaced, but up to 3 seized cars are also sold each year. An inspection period begins two weeks before an auction on Monday through Friday from 9:00 am to 5:00 pm at the storage facility located at 22nd & Forster Sts. in Harrisburg. Inspection period ends 2 days before the auctions. Each car has a form detailing its condition. It will state if the car must be towed. All cars are sold "as is". Cars are started up the day of the auction, which is open cry. If you request an application, you may have your name put on a mailing list for advance advisories of auctions for a period of six months. A $100 deposit is required (cash only) if you win a bid, with full payment due within five working days by cashier's check, certified check, or postal money order. No personal or company checks accepted.

State Government Auctions

Bureau of Supplies and Surplus, Department of General Services, P.O. Box 1365, 2221 Forster Street, Harrisburg, PA 17105, 717-787-4083. The Bureau of Supplies and Surplus of the General Services Department sells such items as mainframe computers and off-loading equipment, office furniture and machines, including typewriters, desks, chairs, sectional furniture, filing cabinets, copy machines, dictaphones, and calculators. This merchandise is first offered to other state agencies, then municipalities, and is then put up for public sale after five days. There is no mailing list for notification of upcoming auctions, but ads are placed in the local newspapers in the area where an auction will be held and in the *Pennsylvania Bulletin*. Property is sold at set prices. You may call to find out what items are currently for sale, or visit the warehouse which sells mostly office equipment such as computers, desks, chairs and file cabinets, between 10:00 am and 2:45 pm Monday through Friday.

Rhode Island

Department of Administration, Division of Purchase, 1 Capitol Hill, Providence, RI 02908, 401-222-5801. Rhode Island's Division of Purchase auctions off its surplus vehicles and office equipment, as well as other items, through sealed bid to a list of buyers who are usually in the business. Most of the cars sold have no plates and must be towed. They are sold primarily to wholesalers. Office equipment and supplies are primarily sold to suppliers. If the state ever does hold a public auction, it advertises two or three times in the local papers.

South Carolina

Surplus Property Office, Division of General Services, 1441 Boston Avenue, West Columbia, SC 29170, 803-896-6880. South Carolina sells items ranging from vehicles, to office and heavy equipment. Property is collected in monthly cycles and offered first to state agencies before being put up for sale to the public. No mailing list is kept for it, but you can visit the warehouse on 1441 Boston Ave., in West Columbia, which is open between 8:00 am and 4:30 pm Monday through Friday. Prices are tagged; there is no auction. Every 6 to 8 weeks, the General Services Division holds public auctions of items by lot for State, Federal, and Wildlife Department property. A mailing list is kept for advance advisories and property descriptions. There is a $15 fee, payable by check or money order, to receive the mailings annually. Items can be inspected two days prior to the sale. You are advised to make notes of the numbers of property you are interested in, then to check back to inquire if it is still available, since state agencies have first choice.

South Carolina Public Transportation Department, 1500 Shop Road, P.O. Box 191, Columbia SC 29202, 803-737-6635, for general information; 803-737-1488, for mailing list. About every five weeks, the South Carolina Department of Public Transportation holds auctions of its used and surplus vehicles, which include everything from patrol cars, trucks, and passenger cars, to highway equipment. To have your name put on a mailing list of upcoming auctions, call the number above. Payment is by cash, check or money order. Banking information will be requested for personal checks. Vehicles may be viewed from 9:00 am to 4:30 pm on the Tuesday before the auctions, which are always held on Wednesdays at 10 am. Vehicles are also available for viewing the day of the auction from 8 am - 10 am. You may start up the cars. The bidding is open. Usually about 100 cars are sold at each auction.

South Dakota

South Dakota Federal Property Agency, Bureau of Administration, 20 Colorado Ave., SW, Huron, SD 57350; 605-353-7150. Federal Surplus Property handles surplus Federal Government property and late model federal vehicles. This property is available to public agencies and certain nonprofit agencies within South Dakota for their use.

Bureau of Administration, State Property Management, 500 E. Capital, Pierre, SD 57501-3221, 605-773-4935. Twice a year, in the spring and fall, the Department of Transportation holds on its premises public auctions for office equipment and vehicles, including pick-ups. Most vehicles have over 85,000 miles on them and sell for well under market price. The cars usually sell for under $5000. Most are surplus or have been replaced at state agencies. A few are from seizures or confiscation. You may visually inspect the vehicles prior to the auction, but you may not enter them. However, during the auction, the vehicles are started and demonstrated. Auctions and special sales are located wherever the most property has accumulated in the state. Call or write the above office to have your name put on the mailing list. There is no charge. Terms are up to the auctioneer. Title is released only after checks clear, or immediately if accompanied by a bank letter.

Tennessee

Department of General Services Property Utilization, 6500 Centennial Boulevard, Nashville, TN 37243-0543, 615-350-3373. Tennessee auctions surplus vehicles, and machinery of various kinds -- milling machines, lathes, welders, and metal working equipment. The vehicles are of all types, including dump trucks, pick-ups, sedans, and station wagons. Auctions are held in Jackson, Dandridge, Nashville, and Chattanooga when property accumulates. A mailing list is kept, and auctions are advertised in local newspapers. Items are available for inspection the day before the auction. Keys are in the car, and start ups are allowed. Register at no charge the morning of the auction. Payment can be in cash, cashier's checks, or certified check. The state also conducts sealed bids usually 12 times a year and most commonly on office furniture.

Texas

General Services Commission, P.O. Box 13047, Austin, TX 78711-3047, 512-463-4739. Every two months, Texas auctions off vehicles, office furniture and machines, and highway equipment. You must apply to be put on the mailing list, which will give you a brief description of items available at the next auction (call 512-463-3416). It will also tell you the location of the auction, which changes often. You may call the agency selling the property to arrange to inspect it; however, merchandise that is on site is available for inspection two hours before the auction. Items are mostly used state property, although some is confiscated as well. You must register to bid beforehand. Most registrations take place the day of the auction, beginning at 7:00 am. Payment on a winning bid is due at the end of the auction. Cash, cashiers check, certified check, money order, bank draft with Letter of Credit, or personal or company check with Letter of Credit are acceptable forms of payment. Items sold on site must be removed the day of the sale. For off-site items, 30 days are usually allowed for removal. Texas also holds sealed bid auctions, where you make a bid by mail. First, you indicate what category of property you are interested in, and they will send you bid forms and descriptions of items in that category. Sealed bid participants are notified by letter if winning bids and the exact amount due. Deposits for non-winners are returned. Also, each of the Texas state agencies hold local sales, for which each has its own mailing list and advertises in the local papers.

Utah

Utah State Surplus Office, P.O. Box 141152, Salt Lake City, UT 84114, 801-576-8280. Utah auctions vehicles and office furniture, as well as heavy equipment, whenever property accumulates. Most items are sold by public auction, although sealed bid auctions are sometimes held as well. Mail-in bids are accepted if you can't attend in person. A 10% deposit is required. It is refunded unless you win the bid. Most of the public auctions are held in Salt Lake City at the address above, although some are occasionally held in other parts of the state. You may request your name be put on a mailing list to receive advance notice of auctions and a description of the items. Auctions are usually held on Saturdays. Property may be viewed the Thursday and Friday prior to an auction. Acceptable forms of payment are cash, cashier's check, and personal checks up to $100 with two forms of I.D. Checks over $100 must have a letter of guarantee from the bank. No business checks are accepted. Items must be removed and payments must be made in full on the day of the auction.

Vermont

Vermont Central Surplus Property Agency, RD #2, Box 520, Montpelier, VT 05602, 802-828-3394. Vermont sells low-priced surplus office furniture and machines on retail basis between 8:00 am and 4:00 pm Tuesday-Friday at the warehouse on Barre Montpelier Rd. Items include desks, chairs, file cabinets, and book shelves. Twice a year, vehicles, which may include police cruisers, dump trucks, and pick-ups, are sold by public auction, on a Saturday in late May and September. A mailing list is kept to advise you in advance of upcoming auctions. To have your name placed on it, contact the auctioneer. Local newspapers also advertise them. Vehicles may be inspected the Friday before an auction. The auctions are open bid, "as is", and "where is". There are no hold backs. The highest bid, even if it is far below market value, will take the item. A 25% deposit is due the day of the sale. The balance is due in 2 days, by the following Tuesday by 3:00 pm. Payment is up to the auctioneer, a private contractor. Usually, checks must be bank-certified, and a deposit is required to hold any vehicle not paid for in full the day of the auction.

Virginia

State Surplus Property, P.O. Box 1199, Richmond, VA 23209, 804-236-3675. Virginia auctions everything but land. It sells vehicles, office equipment and furniture, computers, tractors, bulldozers, dump trucks, pick-ups, and vans. Some of the cars are in good condition. Scrap metal, tires, and batteries are sold separately. Auctions may be held on any day of the week except Sunday. Sales are by both public auction and sealed bid. Agencies have the discretion to decide which way their surplus is sold. There may be sealed bid offerings every week, and as many as two auctions per week. Twice a year there are auctions for cars only. The rest are mixed. Items are occasionally seized, such as jewelry. Auction sites are at various locations around the state. You may call or write to place your name on a mailing list for both public auctions and sealed bid auctions. For sealed bid, there are usually 100 to 200 items available. Inspections are encouraged. They are allowed the day before the auction and again for a couple of hours on the day of the auction. For sealed bid items, you may call for more details on the items offered for sale or to make an appointment to inspect the items.

Government Auctions and Surplus Property

Washington
Washington State Agency for Surplus Property, 1222 46th Ave., East, Fife, WA 98424; 253-597-3726. The State Surplus Retail Store sells individual units of pre-priced, used equipment. Items for sale typically include computers, printers, fax machines, tables, desks, chairs, chain saws and a wide range of other types of equipment. Every other month, on a Saturday, they offer pre-owned state vehicles and equipment at their public auto auction. Vehicles offered for sale to the highest bidder include sedans, pick-ups, vans, four wheel drive vehicles, and the occasional drug seizure specialty item. Equipment items include dump trucks, graders, tractors, flatbeds, loaders, shop equipment, buses, and other miscellaneous equipment.

Office of Commodity Redistribution, 2805 C St. S.W., Building 5, Door 49, Auburn, WA 98001-7401, 206-931-3931, Fax: 206-931-3946. Washington holds auctions of used state vehicles, conducts "silent bids" (auctions where the bids are written rather than spoken), and also sells surplus materials by sealed bid (bids are placed through the mail) via catalogs. The vehicles are auctioned five times a year and include all kinds of used state conveyances, from patrol cars, to trucks and passenger cars, most having over 100,000 miles. There are few new luxury or confiscated type vehicles. The "silent bids" are held once a month, and include large quantities of office furniture sold by the pallet, with the exception of typewriters, which are sold individually. You may visit the warehouse to inspect the items beforehand. Payment may be made by cashiers check, money order, or cash, but no personal checks. For the sealed bids, you may request a catalog of merchandise, which includes everything from vehicles, to scrap material, office equipment, computers, clothes, cleaning fluids, tools, and pumps. Periodically the store at the central warehouse is open to the public where items may be purchased at set prices for cash. For any of these sales, you may request to be put on the mailing list at the address above.

West Virginia
West Virginia State Agency Surplus Property, 2700 Charles Ave., Dunbar, WV 25064, 304-766-2626. Contact the above to be put on the mailing list. Statewide sealed bids have a separate mailing list you must specifically request. For sealed bids, prospective buyers can inspect only by going to the site. Each month, West Virginia auctions such items as chairs, desks, telephones, computers, typewriters, office equipment and furniture, and other miscellaneous property, as well as vehicles. They are all auctioned at the same auction. The vehicles are in varying conditions. The auctions are always held on a Saturday. Inspection is available the week before the auction from 8:30 am to 4:30 pm. On auction day, the gate opens at 9:00 am. Miscellaneous property is sold until 12:00 noon. Then all the cars are sold. If time allows, any remaining miscellaneous property is auctioned. Payment may be by personal check, business check, or certified check, but no cash. Payment is due in full the same day. For sealed bids, payment is due 7-10 days after a bid has won.

Wisconsin
Wisconsin Division of Federal Property, One Foundation Circle, Waunakee, WI 53597; 608-849-2449. Auctions are held periodically. Contact the office to learn when the next auction will be held.

Wisconsin Department of Administration, P.O. Box 7880, Madison, WI 53707, 608-266-8024. The Department of Administration holds vehicle auctions approximately eight times a year -- usually with around 100 vehicles, including passenger vehicles, vans, trucks, and station wagons, all of different makes and models. Most are in running condition. Cars that need towing are rare and clearly designated. The vehicles are usually at least four years old, or have at least 70,000 miles on them. The auctions begin on Saturday at 10:00 am. Cars may be inspected the Friday before from 1:00 pm to 6:00 pm. The public may also inspect and start up the cars from 8:00 am to 10:00 am on the morning of the auction. Cars may be started but not driven. You may have your name placed on a mailing list for advance notice of auctions; however, the auctions are also advertised in local newspapers. There are no sealed bids. Payment is by cash, personal check, cashiers check, or money order. No credit cards. The full amount is due the day of the auction. Occasionally, if the auctioneer is consulted at pre-registration, a small delay for bank loan arrangements are pre-approved so that the prospective buyer can bid.

Wyoming
Wyoming Surplus Property, Department of Administration and Information, 2045 Westland Rd., Cheyenne, WY 82002; 307-777-7901. Auctions are held periodically. Contact the office to learn when the next auction will be held.

State Motor Pool, 723 West 19th Street, Cheyenne, WY 82002, 307-777-7247. Although it first donates most of its surplus property to other state agencies, Wyoming does auction its remaining surplus vehicles, which may include pick-ups, vans, sedans, and jeeps, and also tires. Although most have high mileage -- from 80,000 to 100,000 miles, the majority are dependable vehicles. You can have your name placed on a mailing list to receive advance notices of auctions, which are held when items accumulate. On the average, two or three auctions are held each year. The state also advertises in local newspapers. Inspection of the vehicles is available between 3:00 pm and 5:00 pm the Friday before the auction, which is usually held on Saturdays and begins at 10:00 am. No start ups are allowed. Anything known to be wrong with the car will be on the list handed out at the auction, or sent if you are on the mailing list. Payment depends on the auctioneer who is a private contractor. Usually, cash or check with proper I.D. are acceptable. Some cars go for well below market value, but others may bid up in price, depending on the mood of the crowd.

Unclaimed Property: Does The Government Owe You Money?

In the United States today, experts believe that about $5 billion in unclaimed money is collecting dust in state Abandoned Property offices. Some of the monetary items that end up in a state's possessions after being declared abandoned by the holding institution include:

- forgotten bank accounts
- uncashed stock dividends
- insurance payments
- safe deposit boxes
- utility deposits
- travelers checks
- money orders

People move away, lose track of investments, or die, and the accounts or funds, after a set amount of time — frequently five years — are reported to the state Treasurer's Escheats, Comptroller's, or Revenue office. The state then tries to track down the owners and return the money.

If you think financial property may be held by your state, the first step is to contact the appropriate office (a state by state list follows) to find out whether your name is listed. Or, in the case of the estate of a deceased person, the listing would be under his/her name. You will then fill out a claim form which you must return together with the required identification or proof of ownership. Requirements for proving ownership may vary according to the amount of the claim and the complications involved, but frequently states will ask for such things as copies of driver's licenses, social security numbers, and bank account numbers and passbooks. Most require that the information be notarized. A few states have limitations on how long they keep abandoned property before turning it over to state coffers, but most keep it indefinitely. Some also pay interest on the money if the property was originally interest-bearing.

Honest Finders vs. Vultures

The states currently owe money from abandoned property to an estimated one in ten people in the country, according to attorney David Epstein. But many states do not have the resources to investigate every case, and do little more than advertise names of owners in local newspapers. The resulting gap is sometimes filled by professional "finders" or "heir searchers" who find the owners themselves and charge a fee or commission in exchange for returning it. They can obtain lists, legally in most cases but sometimes surreptitiously, of the names of the owners from the state offices, then conduct their own search. Some finders have charged commissions of 60% to 100%. The price of one finders fee in a past Colorado case was 30% of the dividends and all the shares of stock! Finders can, however, perform a valuable service by reuniting people with money that would have been lost to them forever. Because of cases where these finders have charged excessive fees to people for returning their own money, and because of the strain their demands have put on some already over-burdened state offices, the finders have a shady reputation in some quarters. One state office, for example, refers to them as "bounty hunters," and another calls them "vultures." Many state offices feel that the finders infringe on the owner's right to have their money returned with no charge involved, which is the goal of the state.

The National Association of Abandoned Property Administrators says that since the states never find 100% of the owners, there is a place for honest finders. For example, if a state is unable to locate the owner of a sizable property that he didn't even know about, and a finder does the job, then a service has been performed. Many states, such as Texas, limit the amount of commission a finder may charge; and others have confidentiality laws that prevent them from aiding finders in any way.

One of the biggest obstacles states face is obtaining the cooperation of the banks, insurance companies, and other institutions in reporting properties to them. Despite laws that govern how a holding institution should deal with dormant accounts, they are often low priority items in a business. A state must sometimes work hard to convince them that it is best qualified to return the money. Some states are passing laws that would penalize lax holding companies by charging them a fee.

With billions of dollars in property sitting around out there, clearly many people have an interest in what happens to it. Finders, keepers, states and businesses all have something at stake, and the losers will be those who fail to take advantage of the services that the states offer.

State Listing of Unclaimed Property Offices

Alabama
Unclaimed Property Division
P.O. Box 302520
Montgomery, AL 31632
334-242-9614
http://agencies.state.al.us/treasurer/

Alaska
Department of Revenue
Unclaimed Property Unit
P.O. Box 110420
Juneau, AK 99811
907-465-4653
www.revenue.state.ak.us/iea/ property/index.htm

Arizona
Department of Revenue
Unclaimed Property Unit
1600 West Monroe
Phoenix, AZ 85007
602-542-4643
www.revenue.state.az.us/uclprop.htm

Arkansas
Auditor of State
Unclaimed Property Division
1400 West 3rd, Suite 100
Little Rock, AR 72201
501-682-9174
800-252-4648
www.unclaimed.org/ar.htm

Unclaimed Property: Does The Government Owe You Money?

California
Division of Collections
Bureau of Unclaimed Property
P.O. Box 942850
Sacramento, CA 94250
916-445-8318
800-992-4647
www.sco.ca.gov

Colorado
Unclaimed Property Division
1560 Broadway, Suite 1225
Denver, CO 80202
303-894-2443
www.treasurer.state.co.us

Connecticut
Unclaimed Property Unit
Office of State Treasurer
55 Elm ST.
Hartford, CT 06106
860-702-3050
www.state.ct.us/ott

Delaware
Delaware State Escheater
P.O. Box 8931
Wilmington, DE 19899
302-577-3349
www.state.de.us/govern/agencies/revenue/escheat.htm

District of Columbia
Office of the Comptroller
Unclaimed Property Unit
415 12th St., NW, Room 408
Washington, DC 20004
202-727-0063

Florida
Department of Banking and Finance
Abandoned Property Division
101 East Gaines St.
Tallahassee, FL 32399
850-488-0357
www.dbf.state.fl.us/index.html

Georgia
Department of Revenue
Property Tax Division
Unclaimed Property
270 Washington St., Room 404
Atlanta, GA 30334
404-656-4244
www2.sate.ga.us/departments/dor/ptd/

Hawaii
Unclaimed Property Section
P.O. Box 150
Honolulu, HI 96810
808-586-1589

Idaho
Unclaimed Property Division
P.O. Box 36
Boise, ID 83722
208-334-7623
www.unclaimed.org/id.htm

Illinois
Unclaimed Property Division
Department of Financial Institutions
500 Iles Park Place
Springfield, IL 62718
217-785-6995
www.state.il.us/dfi/

Indiana
Attorney General's office
Unclaimed Property Division
402 West Washington, Suite C-531
Indianapolis, IN 46204
317-232-6348
www.state.in.us/atty_gen/index.html

Iowa
Treasurer
Unclaimed Property Division
State Capitol Bldg.
Des Moines, IA 50319
515-281-5367

Kansas
Unclaimed Property Division
900 Jackson
Suite 201
Topeka, KS 66612
913-296-4165
www.treasurer.state.ks.us

Kentucky
Unclaimed Property Branch
Kentucky State Treasury Department
Suite 183
Capitol Annex
Frankfort, KY 40601
502-564-4722
www.state.ky.us/agencies/treasury/homepage.htm

Louisiana
Louisiana Department of Revenue and Taxation
Unclaimed Property Section
P.O. Box 91010
Baton Rouge, LA 70821
504-925-7407
www.rev.state.la.us

Maine
Treasury Department
Abandoned Property Division
39 State House Station
Augusta, ME 043333
207-287-6668

Maryland
Unclaimed Property Section
301 West Preston St.
Baltimore, MD 21201
410-225-1700
www.comp.state.md.us/main.htm

Massachusetts
Abandoned Property Division
1 Ashburton Place, 12th Floor
Boston, MA 02108
617-367-0400
www.magnet.state.ma.us/treasury

Michigan
Department of Treasury
Abandoned and Unclaimed Property Division
Lansing, MI 48922
517-335-4327
www.treas.state.mi.us/unclprop/unclindx.htm

Minnesota
Minnesota Commerce Department
Unclaimed Property Section
133 East 7th St.
St. Paul, MN 55101
612-296-2568
www.commerce.state.mn.us

Unclaimed Property: Does The Government Owe You Money?

Mississippi
Unclaimed Property Division
P.O. Box 138
Jackson, MS 39205
601-359-3600
www.treasury.state.ms.us

Missouri
Unclaimed Property Section
P.O. Box 1272
Jefferson City, MO 65102
573-751-0840
www.sto.state.mo.us/ucp/unclprop.htm

Montana
Abandoned Property Section
Department of Revenue
Mitchell Bldg.
Helena, MT 59620
406-444-2425
www.state.mt.us/revenue.rev.htm

Nebraska
Unclaimed Property Division
P.O. Box 94788
Lincoln, NE 68509
402-471-2455
www.nebraska.treasurer.org

Nevada
Unclaimed Property Division
2501 East Sahara Ave.
Suite 304
Las Vegas, NV 89104
702-486-4140
www.state.nv.us/b&i/up/

New Hampshire
Abandoned Property Division
Treasury Department
25 Capitol St., Room 205
Concord, NH 03301
603-271-2649
www.state.nh.us/treasury/

New Jersey
Department of the Treasury
Property Administration
CN 214
Trenton, NJ 08646
609-984-8234
www.state.nj.us/treasury/taxation/index.html

New Mexico
Department of Revenue & Taxation
Special Tax Programs and Services
P.O. Box 25123
Santa Fe, NM 87504
505-827-0767
www.state.nm.us/tax/

New York
Office of Unclaimed Funds
Alfred E. Smith Bldg., 9th Floor
Albany, NY 12236
518-474-4038
www.osc.state.ny.us

North Carolina
Escheat & Unclaimed Property
325 North Salisbury St.
Raleigh, NC 27603
919-733-6876
www.treasurer.state.nc.us/Treasurer/

North Dakota
Unclaimed Property Division
State Land Department
P.O. Box 5523
Bismarck, ND 58506
701-328-2805
www.land.state.nd.us

Ohio
Division of Unclaimed Funds
77 South High St.
Columbus, OH 43266
614-466-4433
www.com.state.oh.us

Oklahoma
Oklahoma Tax Commission
Unclaimed Property Section
2501 Lincoln Blvd.
Oklahoma City, OK 73194
405-521-4275
www.kocotv.com/5oys/fortune.html

Oregon
Unclaimed Property Unit
775 Summer St., NE
Salem, OR 87310
503-378-3805, ext. 450

Pennsylvania
Pennsylvania State Treasury
Office of Unclaimed Property
P.O. Box 1837
Harrisburg, PA 17105
800-222-2046
www.treasury.state.pa.us

Rhode Island
Unclaimed Property Division
P.O. Box 1435
Providence, RI 02901
401-277-6505
www.state.ri.us/treas/moneylst.htm

South Carolina
State Treasurer's Office
Unclaimed Property Division
P.O. Box 11778
Columbia, SC 29211
803-734-2629

South Dakota
Unclaimed Property Division
500 East Capitol Ave.
Pierre, SD 57501
605-773-3378
www.state.sd.us/state/executive/treasurer/prop.htm

Tennessee
Unclaimed Property Division
Andrew Jackson Bldg., 9th Floor
Nashville, TN 37243
615-741-6499
www.state.tn.us/treasury/treasury.htm

Texas
Comptroller of Public Accounts
Unclaimed Property Section
P.O. Box 12019
Austin, TX 78711
512-463-3120
www.window.state.tx.us/comptrol/unclprop/unclprop.html

Unclaimed Property: Does The Government Owe You Money?

Utah
State Treasurer's office
Unclaimed Property Division
341 South Main St., 5th Floor
Salt Lake City, UT 84111
801-533-4101
www.treasurer.state.ut.us

Vermont
Abandoned Property Division
State Treasurer's Office
133 State St.
Montpelier, VT 05633
802-828-2301
www.cit.state.vt.us/treasurer/

Virginia
Division of Unclaimed Property
Department of Treasury
P.O. Box 2478
Richmond, VA 23218
804-225-2393
www.trs.state.va.us/

Washington
Unclaimed Property Section
Department of Revenue
P.O. Box 448
Olympia, WA 98507
360-586-2736
www.wa.gov/dor/unclaim/

West Virginia
West Virginia State Treasurer
1900 Kanawha Blvd., East
State Capitol Bldg. 1, Room E-145
Charleston, WV 25305
304-558-5000
www.wvtreasury.com

Wisconsin
Unclaimed Property Division
State Treasurer's Office
P.O. Box 2114
Madison, WI 53701
608-267-7977
http://badger.state.wi.us/agencies/ost

Wyoming
Unclaimed Property Division
State Treasurer's Office
1st Floor West, Herschler Bldg.
122 West 25th St.
Cheyenne, WY 82008
307-777-5590
www.state.wy.us/~sot/unc_prop.html

Federal Tax Help

Free Tax Help

Federal Tax Help

Why pay money to expensive tax preparers, accountants, and attorneys when you can get better services and information directly from the government? The government has dozens of free tax help programs very few people know about. There is a special section at the end of this chapter for state tax assistance.

Interesting Facts

In 1996, the total taxes paid by individuals was 4 times the amount paid by corporations, or one-half the total revenue collected. In 1992, individual taxpayers claimed 86 million of the 89 million refunds issued and their refunds averaged $1,027. Since 1982, there have been 14,859 contributions to reduce the Public Debt totaling 9.2 million dollars. The percent of total returns audited is 1.38%. The percent of returns audited that result in disputed penalties is 3.8%.

* Amending Your Tax Return

IRS Service Center
(listed elsewhere in this book)
www.irs.ustreas.gov

If you find that you did not report income on your tax form, did not claim deductions or credits you could have claimed, or you claimed deductions or credits that you should not have claimed, you can correct your return by filing a Form 1040X, *Amended U.S. Individual Income Tax Return*. Generally, this form must be filed within three years from the date of your original return or within two years from the date you paid your taxes, whichever is later. File Form 1040X with the IRS Service Center in your area, listed elsewhere in this book.

* Collection

Office of the Assistant Commissioner
Internal Revenue Service (IRS)
1111 Constitution Ave., NW, Room 7238
Washington, DC 20224   202-622-5430

Collection is responsible for securing delinquent Federal tax returns and for collecting taxes where the amount owed is not in dispute, but remains unpaid. The Service Center Collection Branch (SCCB) is Collection's first point of contact with taxpayers who are delinquent in filing returns and paying taxes. They send notices to taxpayers and act on the replies. The SCCB also reviews selected Forms W-4, Employee's Withholding Allowance Certificate, to determine whether employees have the correct amount of tax withheld from their wages and directs employers to increase the amount withheld when appropriate.

* Corporation Tax Statistics

Statistics of Income Division
Internal Revenue Service (IRS)
P.O. Box 2608   202-874-0410
Washington, DC 20013-2608   Fax: 202-874-0964
www.irs.ustreas.gov/prod/tax_stats/index.html

The following Statistics of Income reports and tapes can be purchased from the Superintendent of Documents, P.O. Box 371954, Pittsburgh, PA 15250-6954; 202-512-1800, Fax: 202-512-1716.

Corporation Source Book, 1995, Publication 1053, $175. This document presents income statement, balance sheet, tax and selected other items, by major and minor industry groups and size of total assets. The report, which underlies the *Statistics of Income — Corporation Income Tax Returns* publication, is part of an annual series and can be purchased for $175 (issues prior to 1982 are for sale at $150 per year). A magnetic tape containing the tabular statistics for 1989 can be purchased for $1,500.

Studies of Tax-Exempt Organizations, 1986-1992, Publication 1416. This publication presents 22 articles from *Statistics of Income* studies on tax-exempt organizations. The articles emphasize important issues within the non-profit sector, and also include several other articles previously unpublished in the *SOI Bulletin*, as well as papers published in proceedings of the American Statistical Association and the Independent Sector Research Forum. Topics featured are non-profit charitable organization s (primarily charitable, educational, and health organizations), private foundations and charitable trusts, and unrelated business income of exempt organizations. Current price is $26.

Statistics of Income, 1995, Individual Tax Returns, Publication 1304 (S/N 048-004-023-95-4). This report presents information on sources of income, exemptions, itemized deductions, and tax computations, with the data presented by size of adjusted gross income, and marital status. Current price is $13.

Statistics of Income, 1994, Corporation Income Tax Returns, Publication 16 (S/N 048-004-02386-5). This report presents information on receipts/deductions, net income, taxable income, income tax, tax credits, and assets/liabilities, with the data classified by industry, accounting period, size of total assets, and size of business receipts. Current price is $17.

The Statistic of Income (SOI) Bulletin, Quarterly Publication 1136 (S/N 748-005-00000-5). Provides the earliest published annual financial statistics from the various types to tax and information returns filed with the Internal Revenue Service. The *Bulletin* also includes information from periodic or special analytical studies of particular interest to tax administrators. Historical data is provided for selected types of taxpayers, as well as state data and gross internal revenue collections. Current price is $29 annually or $18 for single copies.

Studies of International Income and Taxes, 1984-1988, Publication 1267. This report presents information from 13 *Statistics of Income* studies in the international area (many of them previously published in the *SOI Bulletin*), including foreign activity of U.S. corporations, activity of foreign corporations in the United States, foreign controlled U.S. corporations, statistics related to individuals, trusts and estates, and data presented by geographical area or industrial activity, as well as other classifiers. Current price is $26.

* District Court and Claims Court

United States Claims Court
717 Madison Place NW
Washington, DC 20005   202-219-9657

Generally, the District Court and the Claims Court hear tax cases only after you have paid the tax and filed a claim for credit or refund. You may file a claim for a credit or refund if you think that the tax you paid is incorrect or excessive. If the claim is rejected, they will inform you unless you signed a Form 2297, Waiver of Statutory Notification of Claim Disallowance. If no action has taken place on a claim after 6 months from the date you filed it, you may then file suit for a refund. You must file suit for credit no later than 2 years after you have been informed that you were rejected or you file form 2297. For more information on filing a suit, write to the above address or the Clerk of the U.S. District Court listed below for your area.

United States District Courts

Alabama
Northern: 140 U.S. Courthouse, 1729 5th Ave. N, Birmingham, AL 35203
Middle: P.O. Box 711, Montgomery, AL 36101
Southern: Box 11, U.S. Courthouse, 113 St. Joseph St., Mobile, AL 36602

Alaska
222 W. 7th Ave., #4, Anchorage, AK 99513-7564

Arizona
Room 1400, U.S. Courthouse & Federal Bldg., 230 N. 1st Ave., Phoenix, AZ 85025

Arkansas
Eastern: P.O. Box 869, Little Rock, AR 72203-0869
Western: P.O. Box 1523, Fort Smith, AR 72902

Free Tax Help

California
Northern: P.O. Box 36060, 450 Golden Gate Ave., San Francisco, CA 94102
Eastern: 2546 U.S. Courthouse, 650 Capitol Mall, Sacramento, CA 95814
Central: 312 N. Spring St., Los Angeles, CA 90012
Southern: 940 Front St., San Diego, CA 92189

Colorado
Room C-145, U.S. Courthouse, 1929 Stout St., Denver, CO 80294

Connecticut
141 Church St., New Haven, CT 06510

Delaware
Lockbox 18, 844 King St., Wilmington, DE 19801

District of Columbia
U.S. Courthouse, 3rd & Constitution Ave. NW, Washington, DC 20001

Florida
Northern: 110 E. Part Ave., Tallahassee, FL 32301
Middle: P.O. Box 53558, Jacksonville, FL 32201-3558
Southern: 301 N. Miami Ave., Miami, FL 33128-7788

Georgia
Northern: 2211 U.S. Courthouse, 75 Spring St. SW, Atlanta, GA 30335
Middle: P.O. Box 128, Macon, GA 31202
Southern: P.O. Box 8286, Savannah, GA 31412

Hawaii
P.O. Box 50129, Honolulu, HI 96850

Idaho
550 W. Fort St., Box 039, Boise, ID 83724

Illinois
Northern: 219 S. Dearborn St., Chicago, IL 60604
Central: P.O. Box 315. Springfield, IL 62705
Southern: P.O. Box 249, 750 Missouri Ave., E St. Louis, IL 62202

Indiana
Northern: 102 Federal Bldg., 204S Main St., South Bend, IN 46601
Southern: Room 105, U.S. Courthouse, 46 E. Ohio St., Indianapolis, IN 46204

Iowa
Northern: 313 Federal Bldg. & U.S. Courthouse, 101 1st St., SE, Cedar Rapids, IA 52401
Southern: 200 U.S. Courthouse, E 1st St. SE, Des Moines, IA 50309

Kansas
204 U.S. Courthouse, 401 N. Market St., Wichita, KS 67202

Kentucky
Eastern: P.O. Box 741, Lexington, KY 40586
Western: 231 U.S. Courthouse, 601 W. Broadway, Louisville, KY 40202

Louisiana
Eastern: C-11 U.S. Courthouse, 500 Camp St., New Orleans, LA 70130
Middle: P.O. Box 2630, Baton Rouge, LA 70821
Western: 500 Fannin St., Room 106, Shreveport, LA 71101

Maine
P.O. Box 7505 DTS, Portland, ME 04112

Maryland
101 W. Lombard St., Baltimore, MD 21201

Massachusetts
Room 1515, John McCormick Post Office & Courthouse, Boston, MA 02108

Michigan
Eastern: Room 133, U.S. Courthouse, 231 W. Lafayette Blvd., Detroit, MI 48226
Western: 452 Federal Bldg., 110 Michigan St. NW, Grand Rapids, MI 49503

Minnesota
708 Federal Bldg., 316 N. Robert St., St. Paul, MN 55101

Mississippi
Northern: P.O. Box 727, Oxford, MS 38655
Southern: 245 E. Capitol St., Suite 416, Jackson, MS 39201

Missouri
Eastern: 1114 Market St., U.S. Court & Custom Bldg., St. Louis, MO 63101
Western: Room 201, U.S. Courthouse, 811 Grand Ave., Kansas City, MO 64106

Montana
5405 Federal Bldg., 316 N. 26th St., Billings, MT 59101

Nebraska
P.O. Box 129 DTS, Omaha, NE 68101

Nevada
300 Las Vegas Blvd. S, Las Vegas, NV 89101

New Hampshire
P.O. Box 1498, Concord, NH 03301

New Jersey
U.S. Post Office & Courthouse, Box 419, Newark, NJ 07102

New Mexico
P.O. Box 689, Albuquerque, NM 87103

New York
Northern: James T. Foley U.S. Courthouse, P.O. Box 1037, Albany, NY 12201
Southern: U.S. Courthouse, Foley Square, New York, NY 10007
Eastern: 225 Cadman Plaza E., Brooklyn, NY 11201
Western: 304 U.S. Courthouse, 68 Court St., Buffalo, NY 14202

North Carolina
Eastern: P.O. Box 25670, Raleigh, NC 27611
Middle: P.O. Box V-1, Greensboro, NC 27402
Western: 309 U.S. Courthouse, 100 Otis St., Asheville, NC 28801-2611

North Dakota
P.O. Box 687, Bismarck, ND 58502

Ohio
Northern: 102 U.S. Courthouse, 201 Superior Ave. NE, Cleveland, OH 44114
Southern: 260 U.S. Courthouse, 85 Marconi Blvd., Columbus, OH 43215

Oklahoma
Northern: 411 U.S. Courthouse, 333 W. 4th St., Tulsa, OK 74103
Eastern: P.O. Box 607, Muskogee, OK 74401
Western: 3210 U.S. Courthouse, 200 NW 4th St., Oklahoma City, OK 73102

Oregon
503 Gus J. Solomon U.S. Courthouse, 620 SW Main St., Portland, OR 97205

Pennsylvania
Eastern: 2609 U.S. Courthouse, Independence Mall St., 601 Market St., Philadelphia, PA 19106
Middle: P.O. Box 1148, Scranton, PA 18501
Western: P.O. Box 1805, Pittsburgh, PA 15230

Puerto Rico
P.O. Box 3671, San Juan, PR 00904

Rhode Island
119 Federal Bldg. & U.S. Courthouse, Providence, RI 02903

South Carolina
P.O. Box 867, Columbia, SC 29202

South Dakota
220 U.S. Courthouse & Federal Bldg., 400 S. Phillips Ave., Sioux Falls, SD 57102

Tennessee
Eastern: P.O. Box 2348, Knoxville, TN 37901
Middle: 800 U.S. Courthouse, 801 Broadway, Nashville, TN 37203
Western: 950 Federal Bldg., 167 N. Main St., Memphis, TN 38103

Federal Tax Help

Texas
Northern: Room 14A20, U.S. Courthouse, 1100 Commerce St., Dallas, TX 75242-1496
Southern: P.O. Box 61010, Houston, TX 77208
Eastern: 309 Federal Bldg. & U.S. Courthouse, 211 W. Ferguson St., Tyler, TX 75702
Western: Hemisfair Plaza, 655 E. Durango Blvd., San Antonio, TX 78206

Utah
204 U.S. Courthouse, 350 S. Main St., Salt Lake City, UT 84101

Vermont
P.O. Box 945, Burlington, VT 05402

Virginia
Eastern: P.O. Box 21449, 200 S. Washington St., Alexandria, VA 22320
Western: P.O. Box 1234, Roanoke, VA 24006

Washington
Eastern: P.O. Box 1493, Spokane, WA 99210
Western: 308 U.S. Courthouse, 1010 5th Ave., Seattle, WA 98104

West Virginia
Northern: P.O. Box 1518, Elkins, WV 26241
Southern: P.O. Box 1493, Charleston, WV 25329

Wisconsin
Eastern: 362 U.S. Courthouse, 517 E. Wisconsin Ave., Milwaukee, WI 53202
Western: P.O. Box 432, Madison, WI 53701

Wyoming
P.O. Box 727, Cheyenne, WY 82001

* Earned Income Credit
Taxpayer Service Division
Internal Revenue Service (IRS)
1111 Constitution Ave., NW   800-829-1040
Washington, DC 20224   202-874-1470
www.irs.ustreas.gov

The Earned Income Credit (EIC) is a special credit for workers with a child or children who live with them. In general, you may qualify even if you do not claim your child as your dependent. Your earned income and adjusted gross income must each be less than $30,580. You may be entitled to a refundable credit of up to $3,816. For more information, call 1-800-TAX-FORM (1-800-829-3676) to get a copy of Publication 596, *Earned Income Credit*, or visit the IRS website.

* Electronic Tax Filing
Electronic Filing Division
Internal Revenue Service (IRS)
1111 Constitution Ave., NW   800-829-1040
Washington, DC 20224   202-927-2400
www.irs.ustreas.gov

Electronic returns take a much shorter time to process because there are fewer steps in electronic processing which saves time. Within 48 hours of transmission, your filer or professional transmitter will be notified electronically by the IRS that your return has been received and accepted. Computers automatically check for errors and missing information, thus allowing minor errors to be corrected in days instead of weeks. The processing time is minimized, allowing you to get your refund much faster. Refunds will be issued within three weeks from the time the IRS accepts your return. Now, even filers who owe money can file their returns electronically, by transmitting the completed return and mailing the payment due before April 15. Taxpayers in 35 states and the District of Columbia will now be able to file their federal and state tax returns electronically in one transmission to the IRS. The IRS will then forward the state data to the appropriate state tax authority. This option is available statewide in Alabama, Arizona, Arkansas, Colorado, Connecticut, Delaware, District of Columbia, Georgia, Idaho, Illinois, Indiana, Iowa, Kansas, Kentucky, Louisiana, Maryland, Michigan, Mississippi, Missouri, Montana, Nebraska, New Jersey, New Mexico, New York, North Carolina, Ohio, Oklahoma, Oregon, Pennsylvania, Rhode Island, South Carolina, Utah, Virginia, West Virginia, and Wisconsin. To get Form 8453-OL, *U.S. Individual Income Tax Declaration for Electronic Filing*, call 1-800-TAX-FORM (1-800-829-3676), or get one from a transmitter. You can also visit the IRS website at {www.irs.ustreas.gov}.

* Employee Plans and Exempt Organizations
Exempt Organizations Technical Division
Internal Revenue Service (IRS)
U.S. Department of the Treasury
Washington, DC 20224   202-622-8100

The Employee Plans function administers the tax laws governing pension plans by issuing letters determining whether a plan qualifies under the law, examining returns to ensure that plans are complying with the law, and publishing rulings to clarify the law. Speakers address various practitioner groups across the country to highlight new Employee Plans developments and receive insights first-hand from practitioners. This office also handles exempt organizations, and administers the tax laws governing these organizations and private foundations. The IRS monitors whether sponsors of charitable fundraising events are providing accurate information on the extent to which contributions are deductible. The IRS educates the soliciting organizations and conducts a special examination program to decrease the abusive and misleading fundraising practices of some charities. Publication 1391, *Deductibility of Payments made to Charities Conducting Fundraising Events*, is part of an on-going educational program that includes speeches, taxpayer assistance workshops, and revisions to forms and publications. IRS has established a telephone hotline to help charities make a determination of the value of premiums offered in fundraising activities and to help charities answer questions from donors on the deductibility of contributions made. Charitable organizations engaging in misleading or abusive practices are referred for examination.

* Estate and Gift Tax
Office of Passthroughs and Special Industries
Internal Revenue Service (IRS)
1111 Constitution Ave., NW, Room 5427
Washington, DC 20224   202-622-3000

This office will help you on matters pertaining to the regulations of estate and gift tax. This office is most often used by lawyers who are helping people manage estates, but they will answer people's questions or direct them to appropriate sources for more information.

* Foreign Language Assistance in Tax Preparation
Taxpayer Services International
Internal Revenue Service (IRS)
U.S. Department of the Treasury
950 L'Enfant Plaza
Washington, DC 20024   202-874-1332
www.irs.ustreas.gov

Interpreters are available at the IRS in the major foreign languages to assist taxpayers who do not speak English. Written requests for help may be sent to the above office, and IRS interpreters will respond to the questions, but only in English. Requests are received only for obtaining solutions to specific tax problems and not for the preparation of tax returns.

Volunteer Income Tax Assistance (VITA) centers in local area often have foreign interpreters if the population in that area warrants them. Contact your local IRS office in the white pages of your phone directory or your area's Taxpayer Education Coordinator, listed elsewhere in this book, for information.

Many of the IRS forms are also available in Spanish. They are:

1SP	*Your Rights as a Taxpayer*
556SP	*Examination of Returns, Appeal Rights, and Claims for Refund*
579SP	*How to Prepare the Federal Income Tax Return*
584SP	*Nonbusiness Disaster, Casualty, and Theft Loss Workbook*
596SP	*Earned Income Credit*
594SP	*Understanding the Collection Process*
850	*English-Spanish Glossary of Words and Phrases Used in Publications Issued by the Internal Revenue Service.*

* Foreign Tax Credits
Assistant Commissioner (International)
950 L'Enfant Plaza South, SW
CP:IN:D:CS
Washington, DC 20024   Fax: 202-874-5440

If you need information or assistance in the guidelines for foreign tax credit allowed for income taxes paid to foreign governments, contact this office. Income in this situation is taxed by both the United States and the foreign country. Publication 514, *Foreign Tax Credit for Individuals*, from the IRS describes in detail the tax credit, who is eligible, and how to calculate the credit.

Free Tax Help

* Free Courses on How To Prepare Taxes

Volunteer and Education Branch
Taxpayer Service Division
Internal Revenue Service (IRS)
U.S. Department of the Treasury
1111 Constitution Ave., NW, Room 1046   800-829-1040
Washington, DC 20224   202-283-0197
www.irs.ustreas.gov

The Volunteer Income Tax Assistance (VITA) is a program within the IRS where training is provided to volunteers to help people prepare basic tax returns for older, handicapped and non-English speaking taxpayers. The volunteers serve in the community at neighborhood centers, libraries, churches and shopping malls. The IRS provides free instruction and materials and trains volunteers to prepare Forms 1040 EZ, 1040A, and the basic 1040. New volunteers generally receive four-to-five days instruction; experienced individuals, a one-to-two day refresher. There is also self-instruction. Training is usually available December through January at convenient locations. In exchange for the free training, VITA asks that you spend several hours a week on VITA from January 1 through April 15. To join VITA in your area, just call the Taxpayer Education Coordinator at the number listed below.

Taxpayer Education Coordinators
General number; 800-829-1040

Alabama
600 S. Maestri Place, Stop 21, New Orleans, LA 70130

Alaska
915 Second Ave., MSW 180, Seattle, WA 98174

Arizona
210 E. Earil, Stop 4040 PHX, Phoenix, AZ 85012-2623; 602-207-8618

Arkansas
700 West Capitol, Stop 6030, Little Rock, AR 72201-3271; 501-324-5332

California
Los Angeles: 300 N. Los Angeles St., Room 5119, Los Angeles, CA 90012; 213-894-4574
San Francisco: 1301 Clay St., Suite 15205, Oakland, CA 94612-5210; 510-637-2473
Laguna Niguel: 24000 Avia Road, Room 3361, Laguna Niguel, CA 92677; 714-360-2094
Sacramento: 1301 Clay St., Suite 15206, Oakland, CA 94612; 510-637-2473
San Jose: 55 S. Market St., Stop HQ-6300, San Jose, CA 95113; 408-291-8123

Colorado
600 17th St., Stop 6610-DEN, Denver, CO 80202; 303-446-1659

Connecticut
135 High St., Stop 116, Hartford, CT 06103-1185; 203-240-4149

Delaware
31 Hopkins Plaza, #1206, Baltimore, MD 21201; 410-962-2222

District of Columbia
31 Hopkins Plaza, Room 1208, Baltimore, MD 21201; 410-962-2222/2402

Florida
Jacksonville: 400 W. Bay St., 6th Floor, Jacksonville, FL 32202-0045; 904-232-2514
Ft. Lauderdale: One N. University Dr., Stop 6030, Building 1, Room 270, Ft. Lauderdale, FL 33324-2019; 954-423-7621

Georgia
Peachtree Summit Bldg., 401 W. Peachtree St. NW, Room 531, Stop 902D, Atlanta, GA 30365; 404-331-3408

Guam
Taxpayer Service Division, PDN Building, Room 902, Agana, Guam 96910; 671-472-7471

Hawaii
915 Second Ave., MSW 180, Seattle, WA 98174

Idaho
600 17th Street, Stop 6610DEN, Denver, CO 80202-2490; 303-446-1659

Illinois
230 S. Dearborn St., Room 1710, 6602 CHI, Chicago, IL 60604-1132; 312-886-5544

Indiana
P.O. Box 44211, Room 573, Stop 66, Indianapolis, IN 46244; 317-226-6543

Iowa
310 W. Wisconsin Ave., Stop 6712 MIL, Milwaukee, WI 53203-2221; 414-297-3302

Kansas
1222 Spruce St., Stop 1022 STL, St. Louis, MO 63103; 316-352-7610 (KS residents), 314-539-3660

Kentucky
801 Broadway, MDP46, Nashville, TN 37203; 615-736-2280, 502-582-6259 (KY residents)

Louisiana
Stop 21, 600 S. Maestro Place, New Orleans, LA 70130; 504-558-3011

Maine
JFK Federal Building, 15 Sudbury St., Stop 40726, Boston, MA 02203; 617-565-4325, 207-622-8328 (ME residents)

Maryland
31 Hopkins Plaza, Room 615A, Baltimore, MD 21201; 410-962-2222

Massachusetts
JFK Federal Bldg., Room 760, 15 New Sudbury St., Stop 40726, Boston, MA 02203; 617-565-4325

Michigan
P.O. Box 330500, Stop 45, Detroit, MI 48232-6500; 313-628-3950

Minnesota
316 North Robert St., Stop 6610 STP, St. Paul, MN 55101-1474; 612-290-3320, ext. 222

Mississippi
600 S. Maestri Place, Stop 21, New Orleans, LA 70130; 504-558-3011, 601-965-4142 (MS residents)

Missouri
1222 Spruce St., Stop 1022 STL, St. Louis, MO 63108; 314-539-3660

Montana
600 17th Street, Stop 6610 DEN, Denver, CO 80202-2490; 303-446-1659

Nebraska
310 W. Wisconsin Ave., Stop 6712 MIL, Milwaukee, WI 53203-2221; 414-297-3302, 402-221-3501 (NE residents)

Nevada
210 E. Earil Dr., Stop 4040 PHX, Phoenix, AZ 85012-2623; 602-207-8333, 702-455-1029 (NV residents)

New Hampshire
JFK Federal Bldg., 15 New Sudbury, Stop 40726, Boston, MA 02203; 617-454-4325, 603-433-0519 (NH residents)

New Jersey
P.O. Box 668, Newark, NJ 07101-9788; 973-645-6690

New Mexico
210 E. Earil Dr., Stop 4040 PHX, Phoenix, AZ 85012-2623; 602-207-8333, 505-766-2537 (NM residents)

New York
Manhattan: P.O. Box 3036, Church Street Station, New York, NY 10008-3036; 212-436-1021
Brooklyn: 10 Metrotech Ctr., 625 Fulton St., Brooklyn, NY 11202-0013; 718-488-2908
Buffalo: P.O. Box 606, Buffalo, NY 14225-0606; 716-686-4777

North Carolina
320 Federal Pl., Room 120, Greensboro, NC 27401; 919-378-2193

North Dakota
316 N. Robert St., Stop 6610 STP, St. Paul, MN 55101-1474; 612-290-3320

Ohio
550 Main St., Room 5417, Cincinnati, OH 45201; 513-684-2828

Oklahoma
55 N. Robinson, Stop 1040-OKC, Oklahoma City, OK 73102; 405-297-4125

Oregon
915 Second Ave., MSW 180, Seattle, WA 98174; 206-220-5776, 503-326-6565 (OR residents)

Pennsylvania
600 Arch St., Room 4425, Philadelphia, PA 19106; 215-597-6710

Puerto Rico
Mercantil Plaza Bldg., GF, Taxpayer Service Division, Room GF-05, Ponce De Leon Ave., Stop 17 1/2, Hato Rey, PR 00917; 809-759-4560

Rhode Island
135 High St., Stop 116, Hartford, CT 06103-1185; 860-240-4149, 401-528-4276 (RI residents)

South Carolina
320 Federal Place, Room 120, Greensboro, NC 27401; 336-378-2193, 803-253-3031 (SC residents)

South Dakota
316 N. Robert St., Stop 6610 STP, St. Paul, MN 55101-1474; 612-290-3320, 605-226-7230 (SD residents)

Tennessee
801 Broadway, Room 481, MDP 46, Nashville, TN 37203-3836; 615-736-2280

Texas
Austin: 300 E. 8th St., M/C 6610 AUS, Austin, TX 78701; 512-499-5439
Houston: 8701 S. Gessner, Stop 6610HAL, Houston, TX 77074; 713-721-7070
Dallas: 1100 Commerce St., M/C 6610 DAL, Dallas, TX 75242; 214-767-1428

Utah
600 17th St., Stop 6610 DEN, Denver, CO 80202-2490; 303-446-1659, 801-524-6095 (UT residents)

Vermont
JFK Federal Bldg., 15 New Sudbury St., Stop 40726, Boston, MA 02203; 617-565-4325, 802-860-2089 (VT residents)

Virginia
400 N. Eighth St., Room 10-502, Richmond, VA 23240; 804-771-2289

Washington
915 Second Ave., MSW 180, Seattle, WA 98174; 206-220-5776

Federal Tax Help

West Virginia
400 N. Eighth St., Room 10-502, Richmond, VA 23240; 804-771-2289, 304-420-6612 (WV residents)
Wisconsin
Stop 6712 MIL, 310 W. Wisconsin Ave., Milwaukee, WI 53203-2221; 414-297-3302
Wyoming
600 17th St., Stop 6400 DEN, Denver, CO 80202-2490; 303-446-1659

* Free Legal Help if You Get Audited
Volunteer Assistance and Compliance Education Program
Internal Revenue Service (IRS)
U.S. Department of the Treasury
1111 Constitution Ave., NW   800-829-1040
Room 1046   202-283-0197
Washington, DC 20224   Fax: 202-622-3190
www.irs.ustreas.gov

Under this program, some law and graduate accounting school students are given special permission to practice before the IRS on behalf of taxpayers who cannot afford professional help. Students work under the direction of their professors to handle legal and technical problems on a host of tax issues. Your local taxpayer education coordinator will inform you of tax clinics in your area. You can also visit the IRS website listed above.

* Free Tax Forms at Your Library
Volunteer Assistance and Compliance Education Program
Internal Revenue Service (IRS)   800-829-1040
1111 Constitution Ave., NW, Room 1046   202-283-0197
Washington, DC 20224   Fax: 202-622-3190
www.irs.ustreas.gov

The IRS supplies over 45,000 libraries, technical schools, prisons, banks, post offices, and other facilities with free tax forms and instructions. Most participating libraries have a "Master Copy" of the most frequently requested IRS tax forms. If you need forms or publications listings, from your fax machine — not your desk phone — call 703-368-9694 for 24 hour tax service. You can also visit the IRS website at {www.irs.ustreas.gov}.

* Future Tax Legislation
House Bill Status Office - "LEGIS"
B-106 Cannon
Legislative Resource Center
Washington, DC 20515   202-225-1772

The House Bill Status Office is responsible for developing IRS legislative proposals, tracking pending legislation, analyzing and implementing new legislation, and preparing responses to General Accounting Office reports.

For further information regarding tax laws that have been introduced, or for an assessment of future laws, contact the following offices. Ask to speak with the person monitoring changes in the tax provision you are calling about.

U.S. Department of the Treasury, Legislative Affairs, 15th and Pennsylvania Ave., NW, Washington, DC 20224; 202-622-0576
Senate Committee on Finance, 219 Dirksen Senate Office Building, Washington, DC 20510; 202-224-4515, Fax: 202-228-0554
House Committee on Ways and Means, 1102 Longworth House Office Building, Washington, DC 20515; 202-225-3625
Joint Committee on Taxation, 204 Dirksen Senate Office Building, Washington, DC 20510; 202-224-5561

* Hotline for Tax Aspects of Retirement Plans
Employee Plans Technical and Actuarial Division
Internal Revenue Service (IRS)
U.S. Department of the Treasury
Room 6550, CP:E:EP
1111 Constitution Ave., NW
Washington, DC 20224   Fax: 202-622-5797
                         Retirement and Pension: 202-622-6074/6075
                                        Actuarial: 202-622-6076

The above numbers are hotlines to attorneys within this division that are there to discuss tax questions relating to retirement and pension plans, such as 401(k) and 501(c)3. Attorneys are available to answer retirement and pension questions Monday through Thursday from 1:30 to 3:30 p.m., and more technical actuarial questions from pension plan administrators Monday through Thursday from 2:30 to 4:00 p.m.

* How the Public Rates the Internal Revenue Service
Communications Division
Internal Revenue Service (IRS)
1111 Constitution Ave. NW, Room 007
Washington, DC 20224   202-622-4010
www.irs.ustreas.gov

Every three years, an independent company conducts a Public Opinion Survey to rate the perception of the IRS in the eyes of the public. Public Opinion Surveys are one of many studies conducted by the Research Department. Other areas include, but are not limited to, studies on alternative filing methods, identifying fraudulent returns, and reducing the burden of paperwork for the taxpayer. If you are interested in keeping up with the latest findings, you can subscribe to the *Internal Revenue Bulletin*. This bulletin announces official IRS rulings, Treasury decisions, Executive orders, legislation, and court decisions pertaining to Internal Revenue matters. he price is $140 per year (S/N 748-004-0009). Individual copies dating from 1988 to the present are available at a cost from $4 to $65. To order the *Internal Revenue Bulletin*, contact: Superintendent of Documents, U.S. Government Printing Office, Washington, DC 20402. To place a credit card order, call 202-512-2250. To obtain copies of research studies, contact the office listed above. Past and current issues are available on the IRS website for free at {www.irs.ustreas.gov}. Click on "Tax Info For You", and then "Internal Revenue Bulletin".

* How to Protect Older Americans From Overpayment
Special Committee on Aging
U.S. Senate
Dirksen Building G-31
Washington, DC 20510   202-224-5364

This is a free information paper updated yearly, which is designed to assure that older Americans claim every legitimate income tax deduction, exemption, and tax credit. This publication is very easy to understand and provides many examples and checklists. Also included is a section of income tax items which will change in the following year. To get a free copy of this publication, contact the above address.

There are also many free publications available from the IRS that you should read. They include:

502 *Medical and Dental Expenses*
523 *Selling Your Home*
524 *Credit for Elderly or the Disabled*
525 *Taxable and Nontaxable Income*
554 *Tax Information for Older Americans*

* Individual Income Tax Statistics
Statistics of Income Division
Internal Revenue Service (IRS)
1301 Constitution Ave., NW
Washington, DC 20004   202-622-2000
www.irs.gov/prod/tax_stats/index.html/

Statistical data on *Individual Income Tax Returns* is now available from IRS Statistics of Income Division. This report contains data on sources of income, adjusted gross income, exemptions, deductions, taxable income, income tax, modified income tax, tax credits, self-employment tax, and tax payments. You can review all the tables and statistics at {www.irs.gov/prod/tax_stats/index.html/}.

* Individual Tax Model
Statistics of Income Division
Internal Revenue Service (IRS)
1301 Constitution Ave., NW
Washington, DC 20004   202-874-0700
www.irs.gov/prod/tax_stats/index.html/

State tax officials determine rate structure and revenue yields through the use of *Individual Tax Model*. Public use tape files are available from the office above that include this tax model.

* Information for Tax Practitioners
Forms Distribution Centers
P.O. Box 25866
Richmond, VA 23289   800-829-3676

The IRS provides the following information to keep practitioners up-to-date:: The free *Director's Newsletter* will inform you of changes in the tax laws. The IRS also sponsors workshops to bring practitioners up to date on tax changes that occurred during the previous year. Package X: *Information Copies of Federal Tax Forms*

Free Tax Help

contains copies of 70 of the most popular forms with instructions for preparing them. For additional information, visit the IRS website at {www.irs.ustreas.gov}.

* In-House IRS Audit Manuals
Internal Revenue Service (IRS)
Attn: Freedom of Information
c/o Ben Franklin Station
P.O. Box 795   202-622-5164
Washington, DC 20044   Fax: 202-622-5165
www.irs.ustreas.gov

Tax audit manuals used by IRS staff and other in-house manuals are available to the public. Contact the office above for arrangements to use particular materials. For the latest information, visit the IRS website at {www.irs.ustreas.gov}.

Available IRS Technical Manuals:
Organization and Staffing, (1100, $45.90)
General Management (1200, $22.20)
Policies of the Internal Revenue (1218, $10.80)
Delegation (1229, $23.10)
Internal Management Document System (1230, $19.20)
Disclosure of Official Information (1272, $64.20)
Problem Resolution Program (1279, $30.30)
Travel (1763, $31.20)
General (4000, $24.30)
Classification, Screening and Identification of Tax Returns, Claims and Information Items (4100, $17.70)
Classification (41(12)0, $10.50)
Income Tax Examinations (4200, $68.70)
Tax Audit Guidelines for Internal Revenue Examiners (4231, $30.00)
Techniques Handbook for Specialized Industries (4232)
  1. Insurance ($15.45)
  2. Auto Dealers ($2.25)
  3. Textiles ($4.50)
  4. Timbers ($5.70)
  5. Brokerage Firms ($13.50)
  6. Railroads ($13.50)
  7. Construction ($20.10)
  8. Oil and Gas ($43.80)
  9. Financial Institutions ($5.70)
  10. Public Utilities ($11.70)
  11. Barter Exchanges ($0.45)
  13. Retail ($22.20)
Tax Audit Guidelines, Individuals, Partnerships, Estates and Trusts, and Corporations (4233, $24.60)
Currency and Banking Reports (4234)
Techniques Handbook for In-Depth Examinations (4235, $26.40)
Examination Tax Shelters (4236, $24.60)
Report Writing Guide for Income Tax Examiners (4372, $8.40)
Processing Income Estate & Gift Tax Cases After Examination (4400, $21.00)
Handbook for Quality Measurement (4419, $6.90)
Collateral Income, Estate and Gift Tax Procedures (4500, $46.50)
Employment Tax Procedures (4600, $13.80)
Excise Tax Procedures (4700, $12.90)
Management, Reports and Regional Review (4800, $28.20)
Examination Reports (4810, $18.90)
AIMS – use of Forms and Special Handling Procedures (48(13)1, $31,80)
AIMS – District Office and Service Center Processing (48(13)2, $66.60)
AIMS – Audit Information Management Reports (48(13)3, $7.20)
Examination Uniform Issue Codes (48(14)0, $2.10)
Miscellaneous (4900, $2.10)
Handbook for Examination Group Managers (4(10)20, $20.10)
Handbook for Examination Branch Managers (4(10)30, $9.00)
General Procedural Guidelines (5100, $71.70)
Collection Quality Review System (CQRS) (5190, $4.80)
Delinquent Return Procedures (5200, $32.10)
Balance Due Account Procedures (5300, $52.05)
Service Center Collection Branch Procedures (5400, $129.30)
Service Center Collection Function Procedures (5415, $14.70)
Automated Collection Function Procedures (5500, $76.80)
Automated Collection System Managers (5512, $23.55)
Field Function Techniques and Other Assignments (5600, $60.30)
Group Managers Handbook (56(20)0, $10.20)
Field Branch Chief's Handbook (56(30)0, $8.10)
Special Procedures (5700, $74.70)
Offers in Compromise (57(10)0, $7.05)
Special Procedures Function Managers (57(15)0, $9.00)
Legal Reference Guide for Revenue Officers (57(16)0, $38.40)
Records and Reports (5800, $11.40)
Collection Reports for Field Managers (5890, $4.80)
Collection Support Function (5900, $40.80)
Collection Support Function Managers (5918, $10.50)
Employment Tax Examinations (5(10)00, $17.70)
Revenue Officer Examiner Group Managers (5(10)(10)0, $5.40)
Technical Review for Employment Tax Examinations (5(10)(20)0, $3.00)
Employment Tax Examination (ETE) Support Operation (5(10)(30)0, $19.20)
Taxpayer Service (6810, $66.60)
Accounts Resolution (6830, $55.50)
Exempt Organizations (7751, $72.30)
Private Foundations (7752, $41.70)
Employee Plans Master File (7810, $7.20)
Exempt Organizations Business Master File (7820, $30.00)
Examination Procedures (7(10)00, $78.30)
Employee Plans Examination Guidelines (7(10)54, $27.60)
Exempt Organizations Exam. Guides Handbook (7(10)(69), $22.20)
Actuarial Guidelines (7(10)5(10), $6.30)
Handbook for Special Agents (9881, $139.20)
Internal Audit Handbook, ((10)260, $22.80)
Inspector's Handbook ((10)311, $74.70)
Taxpayer Service (Part VI, $16.80)
Appeals (Part VIII, $61.20)
Criminal Investigation (Part IX, $75.30)
Inspection (Part X, $13.65)
Technical (Part XI, $43.50)
Penalties Handbook (Part XX, $70.65)

Chief Counsel Directive Manuals
Administrative (Part 30, $111.90)
Criminal Tax (Part 31, $37.95)
Disclosure Litigation (Part 32, $12.75)
General Legal Service (Part 33, $25.20)
General Litigation (Part 34, $45.75)
Tax Litigation (Part 35, $176.55)
Employee Plans and Exempt Organization Division (Part 36, $4.20)
Interpretative (Part 37, $8.25)
Legislation and Regulation Division (Part 38, $3.60)
Technical/Rulings (Part 39, $38.85)
Data Processing (Part 40, $9.00)
International (Part 42, $13.05)

Employee Plans Training Program - Phase I (4210-001, $60.45)
Employee Plans EP/EO CPE Operational Topics for FY 1989 (4213-002, $12.15)
Employee Plans EP/EO CPE Technical Topics for 1989 (4213-003, $18.75)
Employee Plans EP/EO CPE Technical Topics for 1989 (4213-005, $4.04)
Employee Plans CPE Technical Topics for 1990 (4213-007, $52.80)
Employee Plans CPE Technical Topics for 1990 (4213-009, $15.30)
Employee Plans CPE Technical Topics for 1998 (4213-018, $51.30)
Employee Plans Phase II Examination Training Coursebook (4215-001, $28.50)
Employee Plans Training Program - Phase III (4220-001, $51.60)
Exempt Organizations Continuing Professional Education Technical Instruction Program for 1986 (4277-020, $43.80)
Exempt Organizations Continuing Professional Education Technical Instruction Program for 1987 (4277-025, $44.70)
Exempt Organizations Continuing Professional Education Technical Instruction Program for 1988 (4277-028, $37.65)
Exempt Organizations EP/EO CPE Operational Topics for 1989 (4277-031, $10.05)
Exempt Organizations Continuing Professional Education Technical Instruction Program for 1989 (4277-032, $43.35)
Exempt Organization Continuing Professional Education Technical Instruction Program for 1989 Index (4277-033, $9.00)
Exempt Organization Continuing Professional Education Technical Instruction Program for 1990 (4277-039, $68.85)
Exempt Organizations Continuing Professional Education Technical Instruction Program for 1990 and Index (4277-040, $6.60)
Update of Exempt Organizations Technical Topics for 1990 (no charge)
Exempt Organizations Continuing Professional Education Technical Instruction Program for 1992 (4277-041, $55.00)
Exempt Organizations Continuing Professional Education Technical Instruction Program for 1992 Index (4277-042, $7.05)
Exempt Organizations Continuing Professional Education Technical Instruction Program for 1993 (4277-043, $79.95)
Exempt Organizations Continuing Professional Education Technical Instruction Program for 1993 Index (4277-044, $7.35)

Federal Tax Help

Exempt Organizations Continuing Professional Education Technical Instruction Program for 1994 (4277-045, $55.20)

Exempt Organizations Continuing Professional Education Technical Instruction Program for 1994 Index (4277-046, $8.10)

Exempt Organizations Continuing Professional Education Technical Instruction Program for 1995 (4277-047, $54.60)

Exempt Organizations Continuing Professional Education Technical Instruction Program for 1996 (4277-048, $75.00)

Exempt Organizations Continuing Professional Education Technical Instruction Program for 1997 (4277-049, $69.00)

Exempt Organizations Continuing Professional Education Technical Instruction Program for 1999 (4277-050, $60.45)

* Internal Revenue Bulletin

Superintendent of Documents
Government Printing Office
Washington, DC 20402
To place a credit card order   202-512-2250

The *Internal Revenue Bulletin* announces official Internal Revenue Service rulings, Treasury decisions, Executive Orders, legislation, and court decisions pertaining to Internal Revenue matters. The price is $140 per year (S/N 748-004-0009). Individual copies dating from 1988 to the present are available at a cost from $4 to $65.

* International Tax Assistance

Assistant Commissioner (International)
Internal Revenue Service (IRS)
950 L'Enfant Plaza, SW
CP:IN:D:CS
Washington, DC 20024   202-874-5440

The International Office plays the lead role in devising strategies to assure that worldwide revenues due the United States are assessed and collected. International maintains a high number of taxpayer service visits to U.S. embassies and consulates to help U.S. taxpayers living abroad and in U.S. territories and possessions. Year-round taxpayer assistance by IRS staff at 7 overseas posts is supplemented by these visits. The specialists in this office will offer technical assistance concerning questions relating to foreign taxes and tax credits. Refer also to Publications 54, *Tax Guide for U.S. Citizens and Resident Aliens Abroad*, and 514, *Foreign Tax Credits for Individuals*. International's Office of International programs administers 35 income tax treaties, 16 estate tax treaties and 7 gift tax treaties worldwide. These treaties provide for relief from double taxation, exchanges of information, routine sharing of information, and simultaneous examinations. During the past year, this office successfully completed negotiations in 122 cases for U.S. taxpayers who requested relief from double taxation. To obtain Publication 776, *Overseas Tax Package*, contact one of the international IRS offices listed below, or write to Forms Distribution Center, P.O. Box 25866, Richmond, VA 23289. You can also visit the IRS website at {www.irs.ustreas.gov}.

IRS International Offices:

Bonn: United States Embassy/IRS, Deichmanns Ave 29, 53179 Bonn, Federal Republic of Germany; 49-228-339-2119, Fax: 49-228-339-2810

London: United States Embassy, 24/31 Grosvenor Square, London, England W1A-1AE; 44-71-408-8077, Fax: 44-171-495-4224

Mexico City: United States Embassy-IRS, Apartado Postal 88-BIS, Delegacion Cuauhtemoc, 06500 Mexico, D.F., Mexico; 52-5-211-0042, ext. 3557 or 3559, Fax: 52-5-208-2494

Paris: United States Consulate, 2, rue St. Florentin, 75001 Paris, France; 33-1-4312-2555, Fax: 33-1-4312-4752

Rome: American Consulate/Rome, Via Veneto, 121, 2nd Floor, Rome, Italy 00187; 390-6-4674-2560, Fax: 39-6-4674-2223

Singapore: American Embassy, 27 Napier Road, Republic of Singapore 258508; 65-476-9413, Fax: 65-476-9030

Tokyo: United States Embassy, IRS, 10-5 Akasaka, 1-chome, Minato-ku, Tokyo 107 Japan; 81-3-3224-5466, Fax: 81-3-3224-5274

* IRS Assistance Through the Media

Media Relations Division
Internal Revenue Service (IRS)
U.S. Department of the Treasury
1111 Constitution Ave., NW
Washington, DC 20224   202-622-4000
www.irs.gov

The IRS can provide you with a variety of print and audiovisual tax information materials to inform the public of current tax issues and assistance. Printed media such as news releases, question and answer columns, public service advertisements and informational graphics are available to news media through the IRS Public Affairs Office.

One popular item that the IRS produces is the "Tax Supplement" which contains articles and graphics in clipsheet format ready for paste up and printing. During the tax filing season, the IRS produces special clinics for broadcast on radio and public television stations. These segments are broadcast nationally and may also include call-in segments. Some shows are also produced in other languages.

* IRS Collection of Delinquent Child Support Payments

Chief Operations Officer
Internal Revenue Service (IRS)
U.S. Department of the Treasury
1111 Constitution Ave, NW
Washington, DC 20224   202-622-5430

If you are delinquent in child support and alimony payments, student or agricultural loans, or government funded mortgages, the IRS has a Debt Offset Program that flags tax forms of those delinquent in these and other areas of government loans. Your refund would be reduced by the amount of money you owe for back support payments or on a government loan. The IRS notifies you in writing of the actions they have taken, explaining why your tax refund is less than you anticipated.

* IRS Collections and Returns

Office of the Assistant Commissioner
Internal Revenue Service (IRS)
U.S. Department of the Treasury
1111 Constitution Ave., NW
Washington, DC 20224   202-622-5430

This office is responsible for the processing of collection and returns within the IRS tax system. Statistics generated from this office are available in the *Commissioner's Annual Report*, available from the Government Printing Office, Washington, DC 20402, 202-512-1800, for $3.50 (S/N 048-004-02280-9).

* IRS Community Outreach Assistance

Volunteer Assistance and Compliance Education Program
Internal Revenue Service (IRS)
U.S. Department of the Treasury
1111 Constitution Ave., NW
Room 2706   800-829-1040
Washington, DC 20224   202-283-0197

IRS employees and volunteers provide free tax help in coordination with local groups. The help is offered at places of business, community or neighborhood centers, libraries, colleges, and other popular locations. Within the Community Outreach program, line-by-line help with your income tax forms is provided. Tax information seminars are also held, including discussions, films or videotapes, and a question and answer period. The programs are aimed at particular interest groups, such as low-to-middle income people interested in preparing their own returns, or small business owners needing free tax assistance. Contact the taxpayer education coordinator in your area for additional information.

* IRS Criminal Investigation

Assistant Commissioner
Criminal Investigation
Internal Revenue Service (IRS)
U.S. Department of the Treasury
c/o Ben Franklin Station
Washington, DC 20044   202-622-6190

The mission of criminal investigation within the IRS is to encourage and achieve the highest possible level of voluntary compliance with the law by conducting investigations and recommending criminal prosecutions when warranted. Special agents target their efforts in the areas such as organized crime, narcotics trafficking, money laundering, questionable refund schemes, and tax shelters, of both domestic and international scope.

* IRS Private Letter Rulings and Information Letters

Chief Counsel
Internal Revenue Service (IRS)
Employee Plans Rulings
Assistant Commissioner (EP/EO)
Attn: OP:E:EP:T
P.O. Box 14073

Free Tax Help

    Ben Franklin Station
    Washington, DC 20044

or

    Exempt Organizations Rulings
    Internal Revenue Service (IRS)
    Assistant Commissioner (EP/EO)
    Attn: E:EO
    P.O. Box 120
    Ben Franklin Station
    Washington, DC 20044

If your tax situation warrants special interpretation on a particular tax deduction you would like to take, you can ask the Internal Revenue Service (IRS) for a private letter ruling. The cost of a Private Letter Ruling can vary in price. Send these requests to the addresses listed above. Requests can also be hand delivered to The Courier Desk, 1111 Constitution Avenue, NW, Washington, DC.

Determination Letters are also issued by the IRS to businesses and organizations regarding questions related to employee pension plans and tax-exempt status. The procedure for submitting information for a Determination Letter is similar to filing for a Private Letter Ruling. There is a fee for Determination Letters.

General Information Letter are frequently issued by the IRS and are not as formal as the two other letters previously mentioned. Simply write a letter to either the IRS district office in your area or to the IRS national office with your question that requires clarification. Requests for Information Letters should be sent to Internal Revenue Service, EP/EO Division, Customer Service, P.O Box 2508, Cincinnati, OH 45201; 877-829-5500, Fax: 513-684-5936.

For more information, get Publication 1375, *Revenue Procedures for Issuing Rulings*, or Publication 1380, *Revenue Procedure 94-23*.

* IRS Research Efforts

    Research Division
    Assistant Secretary for Tax Policy
    U.S. Department of the Treasury
    Washington, DC 20220   202-874-0561

Internal Revenue Service (IRS) research efforts emphasize voluntary compliance, trend identification, and analysis. The IRS published estimates and projections of gross income owed but not voluntarily paid for individuals and corporations for selected years from 1973 through 1992. An analysis is also being completed on the net tax gap, the amount of income tax owed but not paid either voluntarily or involuntarily.

One of the primary objectives is to provide high quality service to taxpayers. IRS began conducting taxpayer opinion surveys in its functions that have direct contact with taxpayers to get initial or baseline measurements of taxpayer perceptions about the quality level of IRS service. A report has also been released on a new method for estimating taxpayer paperwork burden associated with preparation, recordkeeping, obtaining and learning materials, and filing forms associated with tax preparation.

IRS completed a second major study of the effects of refund offsets for non-tax debts on subsequent taxpayer behavior. IRS learned that taxpayers are more likely to file balance-due returns or not to file in the subsequent year.

* IRS Service Centers

    Service Center Directors
    Deputy Commissioner, Operations
    Internal Revenue Service (IRS)
    U.S. Department of the Treasury
    1111 Constitution Ave, NW
    Washington, DC 20224   202-622-4255

The following is a listing of the Internal Revenue Service Centers where taxpayers must mail their tax forms. If an addressed envelope comes with your return, the IRS asks that you use it. If you do not have one, or if you have moved during the year, mail your return to the Internal Revenue Service Center for the place where you live. No street address is needed.

Service Center Offices:

Andover, MA	617-727-4392
Atlanta, GA	404-656-6286
Austin, TX	512-462-7025
Austin Compliance Center	512-326-0816
Brookhaven (Holtsville), NY	516-654-6886
Cincinnati, OH	606-292-5316
Fresno, CA	209-488-6437
Kansas City, MO	816-926-6828
Memphis, TN	901-365-5419
Ogden, UT	801-625-6374
Philadelphia, PA	215-969-2499

District Offices

Ohio Key District

The Ohio Key District has jurisdiction over exemption applications.
Internal Revenue Service
EP/EO Division, Customer Service
P.O. Box 2508   877-829-5500
Cincinnati, OH 45201   513-684-5936

Northeast Key District

The Northeast Key District has jurisdiction over organizations in Connecticut, Maine, Massachusetts, Michigan, New Hampshire, New Jersey, New York, Ohio, Pennsylvania, Rhode Island, and Vermont.
Internal Revenue Service
EP/EO Division, Customer Service
P.O. Box 1680
Brooklyn, NY 11201   718-488-2333

Southeast Key District

The Southeast Key District has jurisdiction over organizations in Alabama, Delaware, District of Columbia, Florida, Georgia, Indiana, Kentucky, Louisiana, Maryland, Mississippi, North Carolina, South Carolina, Tennessee, Virginia and West Virginia.
Internal Revenue Service
EP/EO Division, Customer Service
P.O. Box 13163
Baltimore, MD 21203   410-962-6058

Mid-States Key District

The Mid-States Key District has jurisdiction over organizations in Arkansas, Illinois, Iowa, Kansas, Minnesota, Missouri, Nebraska, North Dakota, Oklahoma, South Dakota, Texas, and Wisconsin
Internal Revenue Service
EP/EO Division, Customer Service
1100 Commerce, Microloan Contact: 4926 DAL
Dallas Texas 75242   800-829-1040 (toll free)

Western Key District

The Western Key District has jurisdiction over organizations in Alaska, Arizona, California, Colorado, Hawaii, Idaho, Montana, Nevada, New Mexico, Oregon, Utah, Washington, and Wyoming.
Internal Revenue Service
EP/EO Division, Customer Service
300 N. Los Angeles, #4310
MS 7043
Los Angeles, CA 90012   213-894-2289

* IRS Speakers and Customized Seminars

    Volunteer Assistance and Compliance Education Program
    Internal Revenue Service (IRS)
    1111 Constitution Ave., NW
    S.A.L. Bldg., Room 1046   202-283-0197
    Washington, DC 20224   800-829-1040
    www.irs.ustreas.gov

The Internal Revenue Service (IRS) provides trained speakers for area civic organizations and other interested groups. This service is provided through the IRS's Community Outreach Tax Education (Outreach) program. Outreach sessions can also offer group tax return preparation assistance. For more information, contact your local Taxpayer Education Coordinator. You can also visit the IRS website. Go to "Taxpayer Help and Education".

* IRS Special Enrollment Agents

    Director of Practice
    Internal Revenue Service (IRS)
    U.S. Department of the Treasury
    1111 Constitution Ave., NW
    Washington, DC 20224   202-684-1891
    www.irs.ustreas.gov

Enrolled agents are persons (other than attorneys and certified public accountants) who have been licensed by the Internal Revenue Service (IRS) to prepare taxes and

Federal Tax Help

who can represent you before the IRS in matters connected with your rights, privileges, and liabilities under laws or regulations administered by the IRS. These special agents are able to prepare and file documents and communicate with the IRS on your behalf, as well as represent you at conferences, hearings and meetings with the IRS.

To locate an enrolled agent, check the yellow pages of your telephone directory under Tax Return Preparation. To purchase a list of IRS enrolled agents, contact National Technical Information Service, 5285 Port Royal Rd., Springfield, VA 22161, 800-553-6847, 888-584-8332 (customer service), Fax: 703-605-6900. You can also visit the IRS website at {www.irs.ustreas.gov}.

* IRS Technical-Advice Memorandums
Internal Revenue Service (IRS)
U.S. Department of the Treasury
1111 Constitution Ave., NW
Washington, DC 20224   877-777-4778
www.irs.ustreas.gov

If you are audited by the IRS and are in disagreement with the IRS agent over interpretation of a tax law, you can ask the agent to request a technical-advice memorandum for you. These memorandums must be requested through the IRS district offices. The national office then makes the final determination. Dollar amounts cannot be disputed through these memorandums, only the interpretation of the tax laws and procedures. Call 202-622-5164, the Freedom of Information Reading Room, for additional information. You can also visit the IRS website.

* IRS Walk-In Service Centers
Volunteer Assistance and Compliance Education Program
Internal Revenue Service (IRS)
U.S. Department of the Treasury
1111 Constitution Ave., NW, Room 1046   800-829-1040
Washington, DC 20224   202-283-0197
www.irs.ustreas.gov

Assisters are available in most IRS offices throughout the country to help you prepare your own return. In this way you will be given the opportunity to learn how to research and prepare your own tax return. An assister will "walk through" a return with you and a number of other taxpayers either individually or in a group setting. If you want help with your tax return, you should bring in your tax package, forms W-2 and 1099, and any other information (such as a copy of last year's return) that will help the assister to help you. At most IRS offices you can also get tax forms, publications, and help with questions about IRS notices or bills. For more information, contact your local Taxpayer Education Coordinator. You can also visit the IRS website.

* Learn What's New in Taxes
Volunteer Assistance and Compliance Program
Internal Revenue Service (IRS)
U.S. Department of the Treasury
1111 Constitution Ave., NW, Room 1046   800-829-1040
Washington, DC 20224   202-283-0197
www.irs.ustreas.gov

Tax professionals can learn recent tax law changes at Practitioner Institutes, which will enhance the professional quality of the services they provide. These institutes are sponsored by qualified educational institutions, state and local governments, and professional and other non-profit organizations. Contact your local Taxpayer Education Coordinator regarding these institutes. You can also visit the IRS website at {www.irs.ustreas.gov}.

* Let the IRS Compute Your Taxes
District Offices
Internal Revenue Service (IRS)
U.S. Department of the Treasury
1111 Constitution Ave., NW   202-622-3190
Washington, DC 20224   800-829-1040
www.irs.ustreas.gov

If you wish, the IRS will complete the calculation for your taxes. They will figure the tax that you owe and even some of your credits (if you have any) whether you use Form 1040, 1040A or 1040EZ. Certain conditions must be met for the IRS to perform this service for you. Publication 17, *Your Federal Income Tax for Individuals* will guide you through this process. To get Publication 17, contact your local IRS office or call the toll-free number 1-800-TAX-FORM (1-800-829-3979). You can also visit the IRS website.

* Money Waiting for You: Unclaimed Refunds
Department of Revenue
Income and Taxpayer Assistance
441 4th St., NW   800-829-1040
Washington, DC 20001   202-726-6104

Each year the IRS has approximately $62 million in undelivered refunds (averaging about $627 per check) waiting to be claimed. You can call the IRS to investigate if one of these checks might be yours. To see if there are any old refund checks waiting for you, contact your local IRS office or call you State Comptroller Office or State Office for Unclaimed Money.

* Obtaining Prior Year Tax Returns
Service Center Directors
Chief Operations Officer
Internal Revenue Service (IRS)
U.S. Department of the Treasury
1111 Constitution Ave, NW   800-829-1040
Washington, DC 20224   202-622-4255
www.irs.ustreas.gov

It is possible to obtain a copy of your previously filed and processed tax returns for at least six years by completing Form 4506, *Request for Copy of Tax Form*, and mailing it to the Service Center where you filed the return. There is no charge to get a copy of Form W-2; however, to get copies of your returns you will be charged $23 for each year you request. You may request up to four returns for four years on one Form 4506 provided that everything you ask for was filed at the same IRS Service Center. It will take approximately 60 days to get the copies of the forms that you requested, so be patient.

If you don't need a photocopy of the entire return, the IRS will furnish information to you such as taxable income, gross income, number of exemptions, etc., for free. Note RTVUE on the Form 4506 to distinguish it from a normal photocopy request. Within two weeks, you will get a computer printout of the information you requested.

* Penalties and Interest
Volunteer Assistance and Compliance
Education Program
1111 Constitution Ave., NW
Room 1046   800-829-1040
Washington, DC 20224   202-283-0197

The IRS will charge you interest on taxes not paid by their due date and on penalties imposed for failure to file, negligence, fraud, substantial valuation overstatements, and substantial understatements of tax. You will be penalized for late filing, late payment of tax, and filing an incomplete return. Publication 17, *Your Federal Income Tax for Individuals*, details additional circumstances under which you may be charged penalties. Publication 594, *Understanding the Collection Process*, discusses the collection process in more detail.

* Practitioner Services
Volunteer Assistance and Compliance Education Program
Taxpayer Service Division
Internal Revenue Service (IRS)
1111 Constitution Ave., NW
S.A.L. Bldg.   800-829-1040
Washington, DC 20224   202-283-0197

The IRS provides a free monthly *Director's Newsletter* to tax professionals, and anyone else interested in staying informed about tax law changes. You can request a single copy or ask to be placed on their mailing list for future copies. Be prepared to answer a few general questions, like name, address, type of business you do, and telephone number.

* Small Business Tax Education Course
Volunteer Assistance and Compliance Education Program
Taxpayer Service Division
Internal Revenue Service (IRS)
U.S. Department of the Treasury
1111 Constitution Ave., NW, Room 1046   800-829-1040
Washington, DC 20224   202-283-0197
www.irs.ustreas.gov

Over 1,200 junior colleges and universities in both rural and urban areas offer courses, workshops, and seminars sponsored by the IRS for tax education of those in small businesses. As a community service, some courses are offered free or at a

Free Tax Help

nominal charge, while others, offered through an educational facility, may include costs for course materials, in addition to tuition. These courses will inform you about your tax rights and responsibilities, including which taxes you are responsible for and which you are not, how to fill out various business or employment tax forms correctly, and when to withhold money from employees and when it is not necessary. For more information, contact the Taxpayer Education Coordinator in your area. You can also visit the IRS website. Go to "Taxpayer Help and Education".

* Statistics of Income Bulletin

Statistics of Income Division
Internal Revenue Service (IRS)
P.O. Box 2608   202-874-0410
Washington, DC 20013-2608   Fax: 202-874-0964

The *Statistics of Income Bulletin* provides the earliest published annual financial statistics from the various types of tax and information returns filed with the Internal Revenue Service. The *Bulletin* also includes information from periodic or special analytical studies of particular interest to tax administrators. In addition, historical data is provided for selected types of taxpayers, as well as State data and gross internal revenue collections. The *SOI Bulletin* is published quarterly and is available from the Superintendent of Documents, Government Printing Office, Washington, DC 20402; 202-512-1800. The subscription is $29 annually, $18 for single copies.

* Student Tax Clinics

Volunteer Assistance and Compliance Education Program
Internal Revenue Service (IRS)
111 Constitution Ave. NW, Room 7207   202-283-0197
Washington, DC 20224   Fax: 202-622-3190

Student Tax Clinics have been set up around the country to assist taxpayers who would not normally have the funds to obtain counsel when faced with a tax audit or examination. Some law and graduate accounting students are given special permission by the IRS Director of Practice to come before the IRS on behalf of taxpayers who can't afford professional assistance. Students work under the direction of their professors in handling legal/technical problems on a host of tax issues. If you are interested in starting a Student Tax Clinic or if you want general information on clinics in your area, you should contact the above office, or contact one of the current tax clinic participants listed below.

The American University, Washington College of Law, Washington, DC, Prof. Janet A. Spragens, 202-274-4144
Illinois Institute of Technology, Chicago-Kent College of Law, Chicago, IL, Gerald Brown, Assoc. Clinical Professor of Law, 312-906-5050
Widener University School of Law, (Formerly Delaware Law School), Wilmington, DE, I. Jay Katz, Esq., 302-478-5280
University of Denver College of Law, Graduate Tax Program, Denver, CO, Mark Vogel, Director, 303-871-6239
Georgia State University, College of Law, Atlanta, GA, Prof. Ronald W. Blasi, 404-651-2096
University of Illinois at Urbana-Champaign, Department of Accountancy, Champaign, IL, Prof. Eugene Willis, 217-333-0857
Loyola University of Chicago (low income only), School of Law, Chicago, IL, Patrick T. Sheehan, 312-915-7176
University of Minnesota Law School, Minneapolis, MN, Kathryn J. Sedo, Professor, 612-625-5515
University of Nebraska-Lincoln, College of Law, Lincoln, NE, William H. Lyons, Adjunct Prof. of Law, 402-472-1246
University of North Texas, College of Business Administration, Denton, TX, John E. Price, Assoc. Prof., 817-565-3097
San Jose State University, College of Business-Accounting and Finance, San Jose, CA, Pat James, Tax Lecturer, 408-924-3460
Southern Methodist University School of Law, Dallas, TX, 214-768-2562
Villanova University School of Law, Villanova, PA, Prof. Marcus Schoenfeld, 215-519-4231

* Tax Analysis

Assistant Secretary for Tax Policy
U.S. Department of the Treasury
Room 3108
Washington, DC 20220   202-622-0120

This departmental office within Treasury analyzes tax programs and legislation and looks for alternative programs depending on the current economic climate. Advisors are available in many areas, such as economic modeling, revenue estimating, international taxation, individual taxation, business taxation, and depreciation analysis.

* Tax Assistance for the Military

Taxpayer Services, International
Internal Revenue Service (IRS)
U.S. Department of the Treasury
950 L'Enfant Plaza
Washington, DC 20024   202-287-4311

The IRS sends trained instructors to military bases here and overseas to train personnel on tax procedures. Through the VITA program, these military personnel then organize internal training sessions to assist others in the preparation of their tax returns. Those chosen to be instructors often have experience in taxation or accounting. If your tax situation is complex, the Legal Assistance offices at military bases can assist you. United States embassies and consulates are also accessible for those in need of their services.

The following international telephone numbers are the local numbers of the 14 U.S. Embassies and consulates with full-time permanent staff from the IRS. Please check with your telephone company for any country or city codes required if you are outside the local dialing area. The Nassau and Ottawa numbers include the United States area codes.

Bonn, West Germany	339-2119
Caracas, Venezuela	285-4641
London, England	408-8076 or 408-8077
Mexico City, Mexico	525-211-0042, ext. 3559
Nassau, Bahamas	809-322-1181
Ottawa, Canada	613-238-5335
Paris, France	4296-1202
Riyadh, Saudi Arabia	488-3800, ext. 210
Rome, Italy	4674-2560
Sao Paulo, Brazil	881-6511, ext. 287
Singapore	338-0251, ext. 245
Sydney, Australia	261-9275
Tokyo, Japan	3224-5466

Publication 3, *Tax Information for Military Personnel*, may also be useful to you. Write to your area's IRS forms and publications distribution center, listed elsewhere, for a copy or call 800-424-3676.

* Tax Audits

Freedom of Information
Internal Revenue Service (IRS)
c/o Ben Franklin Station
P.O. Box 795
Washington, DC 20044   202-622-5164

If the IRS selects your return for examination, you may be asked to produce records such as canceled checks, receipts or other supporting documents to verify entries on your return. Not all examinations result in changes in tax liability. If the examination of your return shows that you overpaid your tax, you will receive a refund. If the examination of your return shows that you owe additional tax, payment is expected.

If you don't agree with the Examiner's findings, you have the right to appeal them. Publication 556, *Examination of Returns, Appeal Rights, and Claims for Refund* will give you an overview of the examination process. You may find it helpful to get Publication 1, *Your Rights as a Taxpayer*, Publication 17, *Your Federal Income Tax For Individuals*, Publication 594, *Understanding the Collection Process* and Publication 334, *Tax Guide for Small Business*.

If you are an individual or a corporation, and you disagree with the IRS over the amount of money that is owed, you then must petition for a hearing before the United States Tax Court. This is an independent court and not a part of the IRS and therefore (in theory at least) an impartial judge. Cases fall under two categories: Small Tax Cases, normally under $10,000, and Regular Procedure, for cases over $10,000. All decisions in Small Tax Cases are final, while Regular Procedure Cases can be appealed. However, cases under $10,000 can be filed under the Regular Procedure. You might want to consider this alternative so that you have the ability to appeal a decision if you disagree with the verdict.

In Small Tax Cases, if the decision is in your favor, (in whole or in part), the Government cannot appeal to a higher court to change that decision. The same holds true if the Tax Court decides in favor of the IRS: you cannot appeal. Any decision in Regular Procedure cases may be appealed.

The U.S. Tax Court can provide you with the following information:
- Pamphlet - *Election of Small Tax Case Procedure & Preparation of Petitions*, which lists the places for hearing Small Tax Cases and instructions for filing
- Pamphlet - *United States Tax Court*

Federal Tax Help

- Designation of Place of Trial. Its Origins and Functions
- Pre-printed Petition

At any point in the collection process, you can ask to meet or speak with a manager who will then review your case. You can represent yourself or have an attorney, certified public accountant, enrolled agent or any person enrolled to practice before the Internal Revenue Service represent you at that meeting.

If a tax problem will cause you a significant hardship such as loss of housing, utility shut off, an inability to obtain food, to keep your job or to buy necessary medication, contact the Taxpayer Assistance number, 1-800-829-1040. Tell them that you want to apply for a Taxpayer Assistance Order (Form 911, *Application for Taxpayer Assistance Order to Relieve Hardship*). An IRS representative will take the following information over the telephone and forward it to the Problem Resolution Office. Or you may send a completed Form 911 or letter detailing the following information directly to the Problem Resolution Office in your area:

- Your name and social security number or employer identification number
- Your address and zip code
- Your daytime telephone number and the hours you can be reached
- The time, place, and kind of problem associated with payment
- Your previous attempts to solve the problem and the offices you contacted
- The type of tax return and year(s) involved

If you owe the IRS money and want to make payments, you can fill out Form 9465, *Installment Agreement Request* and send it to the IRS. You can send your request along with your tax return. At that time, they will decide whether or not you qualify to make installment payments.

CAUTION: While you are making installment payments, the IRS will continue to charge your account with interest and penalties on the unpaid balance of taxes you owe, plus interest on the unpaid balance of penalties and interest you owe. Interest rates are currently 9% and the late payment penalty is 1/2% per month. You may be able to arrange a commercial loan at a bank or other lending institution for less than the IRS interest and penalty rate if you shop around. Obviously it's best to pay an outstanding tax bill as quickly as possible, to avoid accumulating interest charges.

* Tax Counseling for the Elderly

Volunteer Assistance and Compliance Education Program
Taxpayer Service Division
Internal Revenue Service (IRS)
U.S. Department of the Treasury
1111 Constitution Ave., NW, Room 7207   800-829-1040
Washington, DC 20224   202-622-3190

Tax Counseling for the Elderly (TCE) provides free tax help to people aged 60 or older, especially those who are disabled or who have special needs. Volunteers who provide tax counseling are often retired individuals who are associated with non-profit organizations that receive grants from the IRS. The grants are used to help pay out-of-pocket expenses for the volunteers to travel wherever there are elderly who need help, whether they are homebound, in retirement homes, or at special TCE sites. Sites are located conveniently in neighborhood centers, libraries, churches and other places in the community. Contact your local taxpayer education coordinator for programs in your area.

* Tax Court

United States Tax Court
400 Second St., NW
Washington, DC 20217   202-606-8754
www.irs.ustreas.gov

If your taxes are delinquent, the Internal Revenue Service will issue you a delinquency notice, whether you are a consumer or a corporation. If you wish to contest the delinquency, a petition for a hearing can be filed with the U.S. Tax Court. This court is an independent court and not part of the IRS. The court's decision is final and cannot be appealed.

* Tax Data

U.S. Treasury Department
Statistics of Income Division
Internal Revenue Service (IRS)
1301 Constitution Ave., NW
Washington, DC 20004   202-622-2000
www.irs.gov/prod/tax_stats/index.html/

Statistical data on *Individual Income Tax Returns* is available from the IRS Statistics of Income Division. This report contains data on sources of income, adjusted gross income, exemptions, deductions, taxable income, income tax, modified income tax, tax credits, self-employment tax, and tax payments. Classifications are by tax status, size of adjusted gross income, marital status, and type of tax computation.

Additional unpublished information from individual income tax returns, classified by size of adjusted gross income, is available on a reimbursable basis. The Statistics of Income Division also makes the results of its studies available to the general public in the form of electronic databases, electronic bulletin boards, and the Internet. You can review all the tables and statistics at {www.irs.gov/prod/tax_stats/index.html/}.

* Tax Education for High School Students

Volunteer Assistance and Compliance Education Program
Internal Revenue Service (IRS)
U.S. Department of the Treasury
1111 Constitution Ave., NW, Room 1046   800-829-1040
Washington, DC 20224   202-283-0197

If you are a teacher who wants to develop a course on the tax system, you can obtain free course materials from the Internal Revenue Service (IRS). The IRS offers several programs that may fit your needs, including "Taxes in U.S. History", "Understanding Taxes", and "Taxes and You". People who are home schooling should contact their Home Schooling Resource Centers or local library (if available) to borrow these kits.

* Tax Exempt Organizations

Exempt Organizations
Internal Revenue Service (IRS)
U.S. Department of the Treasury
1111 Constitution Ave., NW, Room 6411
Washington, DC 20224   202-622-8100

This office within the IRS sets the qualifications of organizations seeking a tax exempt status. Compliance with the law is also monitored. For a listing of the names of exempt organizations, subscribe to *Cumulative List of Organizations* (S/N 948-013-00000-2), as legislated through Section 170(c) of the Internal Revenue Code (Publication 78). The subscription is $91 annually, and is available from the Superintendent of Documents, P.O. Box 371954, Pittsburgh, PA 15250-7954; 202-512-1800, Fax: 202-512-2250.

* Tax Help for the Hearing Impaired

Taxpayer Services Division
Internal Revenue Service (IRS)
U.S. Department of the Treasury
1111 Constitution Ave, NW
Washington, DC 20224   TDD: 800-829-4059
www.irs.ustreas.gov

Toll-free telephone tax assistance is available for the hearing impaired. In order to call this toll-free number, you must have access to TDD (telecommunication device for the deaf) equipment. The hours of operation are:

- January 1 through April 2 - 8:00am to 6:30pm EST
- April 3 through April 15 - 9:00am to 7:30pm EDT
- April 16 through October 29 - 9:00am to 5:30pm EDT
- October 30 through December 31 - 8:00am to 4:30pm EST.

Residents of all states, including Alaska, Hawaii, Puerto Rico and the U.S. Virgin Islands can call the toll-free number. Some Volunteer Income Tax Assistance sites have interpreters to assist the hearing impaired.

* Tax Help on Audio and Video Cassettes

Audio/Visual Branch
Public Affairs Division
Internal Revenue Service (IRS)
U.S. Department of the Treasury
1111 Constitution Ave., NW   800-829-1040
Washington, DC 20224   202-622-7541

The IRS provides local libraries with audio cassettes and videocassettes, for loan to the public, on how to fill out Forms 1040EZ, 1040A, 1040, and Schedules A and B. These tax tapes contain simple, step-by-step instructions to the forms and tax tips. Contact this office or your local library for more information.

* Tax Information for Older Americans

Special Committee on Aging
U.S. Senate
Dirksen Building G-31
Washington, DC 20510   202-224-5364

Free Tax Help

Tax Information for Older Americans is a free publication, which presents an introduction to the basic provisions of the Tax code benefiting older Americans. It is designed to address the needs of older Americans with moderate income. In addition to emphasizing issues directly affecting senior citizens, the Tax Guide also discusses this year's tax forms to better help taxpayers fully understand the entire process. It also identifies numerous Internal Revenue service publications and prerecorded telephone messages which give more detailed information on the subjects discussed. Forms are available by calling 1-800-TAX-FORM (1-800-829-3676) or by visiting the IRS website at {www.irs.ustreas.gov}.

* Tax Information in Braille

National Library Service of the Blind and Physically Handicapped
1291 Taylor St., NW
Washington, DC 20542
800-424-8567
202-707-5100
TDD: 800-829-4059

IRS materials are available in Braille through the 56 regional and 89 subregional libraries throughout the United States. In addition to tax publications and forms that are in Braille, the libraries also carry several tax related books available in Braille. Anyone who is unable to read or use standard printed materials as a result of temporary or permanent visual or physical limitations may take advantage of this service.

Internal Revenue Service Libraries

Alabama
Regional Library
Alabama Regional Library for the Blind and Physically Handicapped
Alabama Public Library Service
6030 Monticello Drive
Montgomery, AL 36130
Librarian: Mrs. Fara L. Zaleski
Phone: 334-213-3906
In-WATS: 1-800-392-5671
TDD: 334-213-3900
Fax: 334-213-3993

Subregional Libraries
Library for the Blind and Handicapped
Public Library of Anniston and Calhoun County
P.O. Box 308
Anniston, AL 36202
Librarian: Mrs. Deenie M. Culver
Phone: 256-237-8501
Fax: 256-238-0474

Department for the Blind and Physically Handicapped
Houston-Love Memorial Library
P.O. Box 1369
Dothan, AL 36302
Librarian: Mrs. Myrtis Merrow
Phone: 334-793-9767
TDD: 334-793-9767
Fax: 334-793-6645

Huntsville Subregional Library for the Blind and Physically Handicapped
P.O. Box 443
Huntsville, AL 35804
Librarian: Mrs. Joyce L. Smith
Phone: 256-532-5980; 256-532-5981
TDD: 256-532-5968
Fax: 256-532-5994

Library and Resource Center for the Blind and Physically Handicapped
Alabama Institute for Deaf and Blind
705 South Street, P.O. Box 698
Talladega, AL 35161
Librarian: Mrs. Teresa Lacy
Phone: 205-761-3287; 205-761-3288
In-WATS: 1-800-848-4722
Fax: 205-761-3337

Tuscaloosa Subregional Library for the Blind and Physically Handicapped
Tuscaloosa Public Library
1801 River Road
Tuscaloosa, AL 35401
Librarian: Mrs. Barbara B. Jordan
Phone: 205-345-3994
TDD: 205-345-3994
Fax: 205-752-8300

Alaska
Regional Library
Alaska State Library
Talking Book Center
344 West Third Avenue, Suite 125
Anchorage, AK 99501
Librarian: Ms. Patricia Meek
Phone: 907-269-6575
TDD: 907-269-6575
Fax: 907-269-6580

Arizona
Regional Library
Arizona State Braille and Talking Book Library
1030 North 32nd Street
Phoenix, AZ 85008
Librarian: Ms. Linda A. Montgomery
Phone: 602-255-5578
In-WATS: 1-800-255-5578
Fax: 602-255-4312

Arkansas
Regional Library
Library for the Blind and Physically Handicapped
One Capitol Mall
Little Rock, AR 72201-1081
Librarian: Mr. John J.D. Hall
Phone: 501-682-1155
TDD: 501-682-1002
Fax: 501-682-1529

Subregional Libraries
Library for the Blind and Handicapped, Northwest
Ozarks Regional Library
217 East Dickson Street
Fayetteville, AR 72701
Librarian: Ms. Rachel Anne Ames
Phone: 501-442-6253
Fax: 501-442-6254

Fort Smith Public Library for the Blind and Handicapped
61 South Eighth Street
Fort Smith, AR 72901
Librarian: Ms. Kelly Hamlin
Phone: 501-783-0229
TDD: 501-783-5129
Fax: 501-782-8571

Library for the Blind and Handicapped, Southwest
CLOC Regional Library
P.O. Box 668
Magnolia, AR 71753
Librarian: Ms. Susan Walker
Phone: 870-234-1991
Fax: 870-234-5077

California (Southern)
Regional Library
Braille Institute Library Services
741 North Vermont Avenue
Los Angeles, CA 90020
Librarian: Dr. Henry C. Chang
Phone: 323-663-1111, ext. 500; 323-660-3880
In-WATS: 1-800-808-2555
TDD: 323-660-3880
Fax: 323-663-0867

California (Northern)
Regional Library
Braille and Talking Book Library
California State Library
P.O. Box 942837
Sacramento, CA 94237-0001

Federal Tax Help

Librarian: Miss Donine Hedrick
Phone: 916-654-0640
In-WATS: 1-800-952-5666
Fax: 916-654-1119

Subregional Libraries
Fresno County Public Library
Talking Book Library for the Blind
770 North San Pablo
Ted Wills Community Center
Fresno, CA 93728-3640
Librarian: Ms. Deborah Janzen
Phone: 209-488-3217
In-WATS: 1-800-742-1011
TDD: 209-488-1642
Fax: 209-488-1971

Library for the Blind and Print Handicapped
San Francisco Public Library
Civic Center, 100 Larkin Street
San Francisco, CA 94102
Librarian: Mr. Martin Magid
Phone: 415-557-4253
Fax: 415-557-4205

Colorado
Regional Library
Colorado Talking Book Library
180 Sheridan Boulevard
Denver, CO 80226-8097
Librarian: Ms. Barbara Goral
Phone: 303-727-9277
In-WATS: 1-800-685-2136
Fax: 303-727-9281

Connecticut
Regional Library
Connecticut State Library
Library for the Blind and Physically Handicapped
198 West Street
Rocky Hill, CT 06067
Librarian: Ms. Carol A. Taylor
Phone: 860-566-2151
In-WATS: 1-800-842-4516
Fax: 860-566-6669

Delaware
Regional Library
Delaware Division of Libraries
Library for the Blind and Physically Handicapped
43 South DuPont Highway
Dover, DE 19901
Librarian: Mrs. Anne E. Norman
Phone: 302-739-4748
In-WATS: 1-800-282-8676
TDD: 302-739-4748
Fax: 302-739-6787

District of Columbia
Regional Library
District of Columbia Regional Library for the Blind
 and Physically Handicapped
901 G Street NW, Room 215
Washington, DC 20001
Librarian: Ms. Grace J. Lyons
Phone: 202-727-2142
TDD: 202-727-2145
Fax: 202-727-1129

Florida
Regional Library
Florida Bureau Braille and Talking Book Library Service
420 Platt Street
Daytona Beach, FL 32114-2804
Librarian: Mr. Donald John Weber
Phone: 904-239-6000
In-WATS: 1-800-226-6075
TDD: 1-800-226-6079
Fax: 904-239-6069

Subregional Libraries
Talking Book Service
Manatee County Branch Library
6081 26th Street, West
Bradenton, FL 34207
Librarian: Ms. Candace Conklin
Phone: 941-742-5914
TDD: 941-742-5951
Fax: 941-749-7189

Brevard County Library System
Talking Books Library
308 Forrest Avenue
Cocoa, FL 32922-7781
Librarian: Ms. Kay Briley
Phone: 407-633-1810; 407-633-1811
TDD: 407-633-1811
Fax: 407-633-1838

Broward County Talking Book Library
100 South Andrews Avenue
Ft. Lauderdale, FL 33301
Librarian: Mrs. Joann Block
Phone: 954-357-7555
TDD: 954-357-7413
Fax: 954-357-7420

Talking Book Library
Jacksonville Public Libraries
1755 Edgewood Ave. West, Suite 1
Jacksonville, FL 32208-7206
Librarian: Ms. Elsie Oishi
Phone: 904-765-5588
TDD: 904-768-7822
Fax: 904-768-7404

Pinellas Talking Book Library for the Blind and Physically Handicapped
12345 Starkey Road, Suite L
Largo, FL 33773-2629
Librarian: Mr. Greg Carlson
Phone: 813-538-9567
TDD: 813-538-8949
Fax: 813-538-8731

Talking Book Library of Dade and Monroe Counties
Miami-Dade Public Library System
150 NE 79th Street
Miami, FL 33138-4890
Librarian: Mr. Barbara L. Moyer
Phone: 305-751-8687
In-WATS: 1-800-451-9544
TDD: 305-758-6599
Fax: 305-757-8401

Lee County Talking Book Library
13240 N. Cleveland Ave.
N. Ft. Myers, FL 33903-4855
Librarian: Ms. Ann Bradley
Phone: 941-995-2665
In-WATS: 800-854-8195
TDD: 941-995-2665
Fax: 941-995-1681

Orange County Library System
Talking Book Section
101 East Central Boulevard
Orlando, FL 32801
Librarian: Ms. Sally Fry
Phone: 407-425-4694, ext. 421 or 422
TDD: 407-425-5668
Fax: 407-316-8435

West Florida Regional Library
Subregional Talking Book Library

Free Tax Help

200 West Gregory Street
Pensacola, FL 32501
Librarian: Ms. Blanche C. Hooper
Phone: 850-435-1760
Fax: 850-432-9582

Talking Books
Palm Beach County Library Annex
7950 Central Industrial Drive, Suite 104
Riviera Beach, FL 33404-9947
Librarian: Pat Mistretta
Phone: 561-845-4600
Fax: 407-845-4640

Hillsborough County Talking Book Library
Tampa-Hillsborough County Public Library System
900 North Ashley Drive
Tampa, FL 33602-3788
Librarian: Ms. Jeannette Martin
Phone: 813-273-5727; 813-273-3609
TDD: 813-273-3610
Fax: 813-273-5728

Georgia
Regional Library
Georgia Library for the Blind and Physically Handicapped
1150 Murphy Avenue SW
Atlanta, GA 30310
Librarian: Mr. Dale Snair
Phone: 404-756-4619
In-WATS: 1-800-248-6701
Fax: 404-756-4618

Subregional Libraries
Albany Library for the Blind and Handicapped
Dougherty County Public Library
300 Pine Avenue
Albany, GA 31701
Librarian: Mrs. Kathryn R. Sinquefield
Phone: 912-430-1920
In-WATS: 800-337-6251
TDD: 912-430-1911
Fax: 912-430-4020

Athens Talking Book Center
Athens-Clarke County Library
2025 Baxter Street
Athens, GA 30606
Librarian: Ms. Paige Burns
Phone: 706-613-3655
In-WATS: 800-531-2063
TDD: 706-613-3655
Fax: 706-613-3660

Talking Book Center
Augusta-Richmond County Public Library
425 Ninth Street
Augusta, GA 30901
Librarian: Mr. Gary Swint
Phone: 706-821-2625
Fax: 706-724-5403

Bainbridge Subregional Library for the Blind and Physically Handicapped
Southwest Georgia Regional Library
301 S. Monroe Street
Bainbridge, GA 31717
Librarian: Ms. Susan Whittle
Phone: 912-248-2680
In-WATS: 1-800-795-2680
TDD: 912-248-2665
Fax: 912-248-2670

Talking Book Center
Brunswick-Glynn County Regional Library
208 Gloucester Street
Brunswick, GA 31523
Librarian: Mrs. Betty Ranson
Phone: 912-267-1212

Subregional Library for the Blind and Physically Handicapped
Talking Book Center
W.C. Bradley Memorial Library
1120 Bradley Drive
Columbus, GA 31906-2800
Librarian: Ms. Dorothy Bowen
Phone: 706-649-0780, ext. 22 or 23
In-WATS: 1-800-652-0782
TDD: 706-649-0974
Fax: 706-649-1914

Oconee Regional Library
Library for the Blind and Physically Handicapped
801 Bellevue Avenue
P.O. Box 100
Dublin, GA 31040
Librarian: Ms. Susan S. Williams
Phone: 912-275-5382
In-WATS: 1-800-453-5541
TDD: 912-275-3821
Fax: 912-272-0524

Hall County Library
Library for the Blind and Physically Handicapped
127 North Main Street
Gainesville, GA 30505
Librarian: Ms. Sandra Whitmer
Phone: 770-532-3311, ext. 136
In-WATS: 1-800-260-1598
Fax: 770-532-4305

La Fayette Subregional Library for the Blind and Physically Handicapped
301 South Duke Street
La Fayette, GA 30728
Librarian: Mr. Charles Stubblefield
Phone: 706-638-2992
In-WATS: 1-888-506-0509
Fax: 706-638-4028

Macon Subregional Library for the Blind and Physically Handicapped
Washington Memorial Library
1180 Washington Avenue
Macon, GA 31201-1790
Librarian: Ms. Rebecca M. Sherrill
Phone: 912-744-0877
In-WATS: 1-800-805-7613
TDD: 912-744-0877
Fax: 912-742-3161

Rome Subregional Library for the Blind and Physically Handicapped
Sara Hightower Regional Library
205 Riverside Parkway, NE
Rome, GA 30161-2911
Librarian: Ms. Diane Mills
Phone: 706-236-4618
In-WATS: 1-888-263-0769
TDD: 706-236-4618
Fax: 706-236-4631

Subregional Library for the Blind and Physically Handicapped
309 Main Street
Garden City, GA 31408
Librarian: Ms. Linda Stokes
Phone: 912-652-3644
In-WATS: 1-800-342-4455
TDD: 912-652-3635
Fax: 912-652-3641

Subregional Library for the Blind and Physically Handicapped
South Georgia Regional Library
300 Woodrow Wilson Dr.
Valdosta, GA 31602-2592
Librarian: Ms. Beverly Speck peters
Phone: 912-333-5210
In-WATS: 1-800-246-6515
Fax: 912-245-6483

Federal Tax Help

Guam
(see Hawaii)

Hawaii
Regional Library
Hawaii State Library
Library for the Blind and Physically Handicapped
402 Kapahulu Avenue
Honolulu, HI 96815
Librarian: Ms. Fusako Miyashiro
Phone: 808-733-8444
In-WATS: 1-800-559-4096
TDD: 808-733-8444
Fax: 808-733-8449

Subregional Library
Guam Public Library for the Blind and Physically Handicapped
Nieves M. Flores Memorial Library
254 Martyr Street
Agana, GU 96910
Librarian: Ms. Christina Scott Smith
Phone: 671-475-4753/475-4754
Fax: 671-477-9777

Idaho
Regional Library
Idaho Regional Library
Idaho State Talking Book Library
325 West State Street
Boise, ID 83702
Librarian: Mr. Kay H. Salmon
Phone: 208-334-2117
In-WATS: 1-800-233-4931
TDD: 1-800-377-1363
Fax: 208-334-2194

Illinois
Regional Library
Illinois Regional Library for the Blind and Physically Handicapped
1055 West Roosevelt Road
Chicago, IL 60608-1591
Librarian: Ms. Barbara Perkis
Phone: 312-746-9210
In-WATS: 1-800-331-2351
Fax: 312-746-9192

Subregional Libraries
Southern Illinois Talking Book Center
c/o Shawnee Library System
607 Greenbriar Road
Carterville, IL 62918-1600
Librarian: Ms. Marcia Sorensen
Phone: 618-985-8375
In-WATS: 1-800-455-2665
TDD: 618-985-8375
Fax: 618-985-4211

Harold Washington Library Center
Talking Book Center
400 S. State Street, Room 5N7
Chicago, IL 60605
Librarian: Ms. Mamie Grady
Phone: 312-747-4001
In-WATS: 1-800-757-4654
Fax: 312-747-1609

Talking Book Center of Northwest Illinois
P.O. Box 125
Coal Valley, IL 61240
Librarian: Ms. Karen Odean
Phone: 309-799-3137
In-WATS: 1-800-747-3137
Fax: 309-799-7916

Voices of Vision
Talking Book Center
DuPage Library System
127 South First Street
Geneva, IL 60134
Librarian: Ms. Linda Jaeger
Phone: 630-208-0398
In-WATS: 1-800-227-0625
Fax: 708-208-0399

Mid-Illinois Talking Book Center
Alliance Library System
845 Brenkman Drive
Pekin, IL 61554
Librarian: Ms. Eileen Sheppard
Phone: 309-353-4110
In-WATS: 1-800-426-0709
Fax: 309-353-8281

Mid-Illinois Talking Book Center
Alliance Library System
515 York
Quincy, IL 62301
Librarian: Ms. Eileen Sheppard
Phone: 217-224-6619
In-WATS: 1-800-537-1274
TDD: 217-224-6619
Fax: 217-224-9818

Indiana
Regional Library
Indiana State Library
Special Services Division
140 North Senate Avenue
Indianapolis, IN 46204
Librarian: Ms. Lissa Shanahan
Phone: 317-232-3684
In-WATS: 1-800-622-4970
TDD: 317-232-7763
Fax: 317-232-3728

Subregional Libraries
Bartholomew County Public Library
536 Fifth Street
Columbus, IN 47201
Librarian: Ms. Wilma J. Perry
Phone: 812-379-1277
Fax: 812-379-1275

Blind and Physically Handicapped Services
Elkhart Public Library
300 South Second
Elkhart, IN 46516-3184
Librarian: Mrs. Pat Ciancio
Phone: 219-522-2665, ext. 52

Talking Books Services
Evansville-Vanderburgh County Public Library
22 South East Fifth Street
Evansville, IN 47708-1694
Librarian: Mrs. Barbara Shanks
Phone: 812-428-8235
Fax: 812-428-8215

Northwest Indiana Subregional Library for the Blind
  and Physically Handicapped
Lake County Public Library
1919 West 81st Avenue
Merrillville, IN 46410-5382
Librarian: Ms. Renee Lewis
Phone: 219-769-3541, ext. 323/390
TDD: 219-769-3541
Fax: 219-769-0690

Iowa
Regional Library
Library for the Blind and Physically Handicapped
Iowa Department for the Blind
524 Fourth Street
Des Moines, IA 50309-2364

Free Tax Help

Librarian: Ms. Catherine M. Ford
Phone: 515-281-1389/1333
In-WATS: 1-800-362-2587
TDD: 515-281-1355
Fax: 515-281-1378; 515-281-1263

Kansas
Regional Library
Kansas State Library
Kansas Talking Book Service
ESU Memorial Union
1200 Commercial
Emporia, KS 66801
Librarian: Ms. Patti Lang
Phone: 316-343-7124
In-WATS: 1-800-362-0699
Fax: 316-343-7124

Subregional Libraries
Talking Book Service
CKLS Headquarters
1409 Williams
Great Bend, KS 67503
Librarian: Ms. Joanita Doll Masden
Phone: 316-792-2393
In-WATS: 1-800-362-2642
Fax: 316-793-7270

South Central Kansas Library System
Talking Book Subregional
901 North Main
Hutchinson, KS 67501
Librarian: Ms. Karen Socha
Phone: 316-663-5441, ext. 129
In-WATS: 1-800-234-0529, ext. 129
Fax: 316-663-1215

Manhattan Public Library Talking Book Service
N. Central Kansas Libraries System
629 Poyntz Ave.
Manhattan, KS 66502
Librarian: Ms. Marion Rice
Phone: 785-776-4741, ext. 152
In-WATS: 1-800-432-2796, ext. 152
Fax: 785-776-1545

Talking Books
Northwest Kansas Library System
2 Washington Square
P.O. Box 446
Norton, KS 67654-0446
Librarian: Ms. Clarice Howard
Phone: 785-877-5148
In-WATS: 1-800-432-2858
TDD: 787-877-5148; 1-800-432-2858
Fax: 785-877-5697

Talking Books
Topeka and Shawnee County Public Library
1515 West 10th Street
Topeka, KS 66604
Librarian: Ms. Suzanne Bundy
Phone: 785-231-0574
In-WATS: 1-800-432-2925
TDD: 785-233-3277
Fax: 785-231-0579

Wichita Public Library
Talking Books Department
223 South Main
Wichita, KS 67202
Librarian: Mr. Brad Reha
Phone: 316-262-0611
In-WATS: 1-800-362-2869
TDD: 316-262-3972
Fax: 316-262-4540

Kentucky
Regional Library
Kentucky Library for the Blind and Physically Handicapped
300 Coffee Tree Road
P.O. Box 818
Frankfort, KY 40602
Librarian: Mr. Richard Feindel
Phone: 502-564-8300
In-WATS: 1-800-372-2968
Fax: 502-564-5773

Subregional Libraries
Northern Kentucky Talking Book Library
502 Scott Street
Covington, KY 41011
Librarian: Ms. Julia Allegrinc
Phone: 606-491-7610
Fax: 606-655-7960

Talking Book Library
Louisville Free Public Library
301 West York Street
Louisville, KY 40203
Librarian: Mr. Tom Denning
Phone: 502-574-1625
TDD: 502-574-1621
Fax: 502-574-1657

Louisiana
Regional Library
Louisiana State Library Section for the Blind
 and Physically Handicapped
701 N. Fourth Street
Baton Rouge, LA 70802
Librarian: Mrs. Jennifer Anjier
Phone: 504-342-4944; 504-342-4943
In-WATS: 1-800-543-4702
Fax: 504-342-3547

Maine
Regional Library
Library Services for the Blind and Physically Handicapped
Maine State Library
State House Station 64
Augusta, ME 04333-0064
Librarian: Ms. Benita D. Davis
Phone: 207-287-5650; 207-947-8336
In-WATS: 1-800-452-8793; 1-800-762-7106
Fax: 207-287-5624

Maryland
Regional Library
Maryland State Library for the Blind and Physically Handicapped
415 Park Avenue
Baltimore, MD 21201-3603
Librarian: Ms. Sharon McFarland
Phone: 410-333-2668
In-WATS: 1-800-964-9209
TDD: 410-333-8679; 1-800-934-2541
Fax: 410-333-2095

Subregional Libraries
Special Needs Library
Montgomery County Department of Public Libraries
6400 Democracy Boulevard
Bethesda, MD 20817
Librarian: Ms. Charlette Stinnett
Phone: 301-897-2212
TDD: 301-897-2217

Massachusetts
Regional Library
Braille and Talking Book Library
Perkins School for the Blind
175 North Beacon Street
Watertown, MA 02172
Librarian: Ms. Patricia Kirk

Federal Tax Help

Phone: 617-972-7240
In-WATS: 1-800-852-3133
Fax: 617-972-7363

Subregional Library
Talking Book Library
Worcester Public Library
3 Salem Square
Worcester, MA 01608-2074
Librarian: Mr. James Izatt
Phone: 508-799-1730; 508-799-1661
In-WATS: 1-800-762-0085
TDD: 508-799-1731
Fax: 508-799-1658/1713

Michigan (Except Wayne County)
Regional Library
Library of Michigan
Service for the Blind and Physically Handicapped
Box 30007
Lansing, MI 48909
Librarian: Ms. Maggie Bacon
Phone: 517-373-5614
In-WATS: 1-800-992-9012
TDD: 517-373-1592
Fax: 517-373-5865

Subregional Libraries
Northland Library Cooperative
316 East Chisholm Street
Alpena, MI 49707
Librarian: Ms. Catherine Glomski
Phone: 517-356-1622
In-WATS: 1-800-446-1580
Fax: 517-354-3939

Washtenaw County Library for the Blind and Physically Handicapped
P.O. Box 8645
Ann Arbor, MI 48107-8645
Librarian: Ms. Margaret Wolfe
Phone: 734-971-6059
Fax: 734-971-3892

Macomb Library for the Blind and Physically Handicapped
16480 Hall Road
Clinton Township, MI 48038-1140
Librarian: Ms. Linda Champion
Phone: 810-286-1580
TDD: 810-286-9940
Fax: 810-286-0634

Oakland County Library for the Blind and Physically Handicapped
1200 N. Telegraph, Dept. 482
Pontiac, MI 48341-0482
Librarian: Ms. Betty Ramey
Phone: 248-858-5050
In-WATS: 1-800-774-4542 (residents only)
TDD: 248-452-2247
Fax: 248-452-9145

Mideastern Michigan Library for the Blind and Physically Handicapped Talking Book Center
G-4195 West Pasadena Avenue
Flint, MI 48504
Librarian: Ms. Carolyn Nash
Phone: 810-732-1120
Fax: 810-732-1715

Kent District Library for the Blind and Physically Handicapped
Grandville Branch Library
4055 Maple Street, SW
Grandville, MI 49418
Librarian: Ms. Cathy Nois
Phone: 616-530-6219
TDD: 616-530-6219
Fax: 616-530-6222

Upper Peninsula Library for the Blind and Physically Handicapped
1615 Presque Isle Avenue
Marquette, MI 49855
Librarian: Ms. Suzanne Dees
Phone: 906-228-7697
In-WATS: 1-800-562-8985
TDD: 906-228-7697
Fax: 906-228-5627

Muskegon County Library for the Blind and Physically Handicapped
97 E. Apple Ave.
Muskegon, MI 49442
Librarian: Miss Sheila D. Miller
Phone: 616-724-6257
TDD: 616-722-4103
Fax: 616-724-6675

St. Clair County Library
Blind and Physically Handicapped Library
210 McMorran Boulevard
Port Huron, MI 48060
Librarian: Ms. Kathleen Wheelihan
Phone: 810-982-3600
In-WATS: 1-800-272-8572
Fax: 810-987-7327

Grand Traverse Area Library for the Blind and Physically Handicapped
322 Sixth Street
Traverse City, MI 49684
Librarian: Mrs. Evelyn Wethy
Phone: 616-922-4824
TDD: 616-922-4843
Fax: 616-922-0901

Michigan (Wayne County Only)
Regional Library
Wayne County Regional Library for the Blind and Physically Handicapped
30555 Michigan Ave.
Westland, MI 48186-5310
Librarian: Mr. Frederick Hawkins
Phone: 734-727-7300
In-WATS: 1-888-968-2737
TDD: 734-727-7330
Fax: 734-727-7333

Subregional Library
Downtown Detroit Subregional Library for Blind and Physically Handicapped
Detroit Public Library
3666 Grand River Avenue
Detroit, MI 48208
Librarian: Ms. Deborah Seunagal
Phone: 313-833-5494
TDD: 313-833-5492
Fax: 313-965-1977

Minnesota
Regional Library
Minnesota Library for the Blind and Physically Handicapped
P.O. Box 68
Highway 298
Faribault, MN 55021
Librarian: Ms. Nancy Walton
Phone: 507-332-3279
In-WATS: 1-800-722-0550
Fax: 507-332-3260

Mississippi
Regional Library
Mississippi Library for the Blind and Physically Handicapped
5455 Executive Place
Jackson, MS 39206-4104
Librarian: Ms. Ranye Puckett
Phone: 601-354-7208
In-WATS: 1-800-446-0892
TDD: 601-354-6411
Fax: 601-354-6077

Free Tax Help

Missouri
Regional Library
Wolfner Library for the Blind and Physically Handicapped
P.O. Box 387
Jefferson City, MO 65102
Librarian: Ms. Elizabeth Eckles
Phone: 573-751-8720
In-WATS: 1-800-392-2614
TDD: 1-800-347-1379
Fax: 573-526-2985

Montana
Regional Library
Montana Talking Book Library
1515 East Sixth Avenue
Helena, MT 59620-1800
Librarian: Ms. Christie O. Briggs
Phone: 406-444-2064
In-WATS: 1-800-332-3400
TDD: 406-444-5431
Fax: 406-444-5612

Nebraska
Regional Library
Nebraska Library Commission
Talking Book and Braille Service
The Atrium
1200 N Street, Suite 120
Lincoln, NE 68508-2006
Librarian: Mr. David Oertli
Phone: 402-471-4038
In-WATS: 1-800-742-7691
TDD: 402-471-4038; 1-800-742-7691
Fax: 402-471-6244

Nevada
Regional Library
Nevada State Library and Archives
Regional Library for the Blind and Physically Handicapped
Capitol Complex, 100 N. Stewart Street
Carson City, NV 89710
Librarian: Ms. Kerin E. Putnam
Phone: 702-687-5154
In-WATS: 1-800-922-9334
TDD: 702-687-8338
Fax: 702-687-8311

Subregional Library
Las Vegas-Clark County Library
Talking Book Program
1401 East Flamingo Road
Las Vegas, NV 89119
Librarian: Mrs. Mary Anne Morton
Phone: 702-733-1925
Fax: 702-733-1567

New Hampshire
Regional Library
New Hampshire State Library
Library Services to Persons with Disabilities
117 Pleasant Street
Concord, NH 03301-3852
Librarian: Ms. Eileen Keim
Phone: 603-271-3429
In-WATS: 1-800-491-4200
Fax: 603-226-2907 (Sept.-May)
Fax: 603-271-6826 (June-Aug.)

New Jersey
Regional Library
New Jersey Library for the Blind and Handicapped
2300 Stuyvesant Avenue
P.O. Box 501
Trenton, NJ 08625-0501
Librarian: Ms. Vianne Connor
Phone: 609-530-4000
In-WATS: 1-800-792-8322 (English);
1-800-582-5945 (Spanish)
TDD: 609-633-7250
Fax: 609-530-6384

New Mexico
Regional Library
New Mexico State Library
Talking Book Library
1209 Camino Carlos Rey
Santa Fe, NM 87501-2777
Librarian: Mr. John Brewster
Phone: 505-476-9770
In-WATS: 1-800-456-5515
Fax: 505-827-3888

New York (Except New York City and Long Island)
Regional Library
New York State Library for the Blind and Visually Handicapped
Cultural Education Center
Empire State Plaza
Albany, NY 12230
Librarian: Ms. Jane Somers
Phone: 518-474-5935
In-WATS: 1-800-342-3688
TDD: 518-474-7121
Fax: 518-474-5786

New York (New York City and Long Island)
Regional Library
Andrew Heiskell Library for the Blind and Physically Handicapped
The New York Public Library
40 West 20th Street
New York, NY 10011-4211
Librarian: Ms. Kathleen V. Rowan
Phone: 212-206-5400
TDD: 212-206-5458
Fax: 212-206-5418

Subregional Libraries
Talking Books Plus
Outreach Services
Suffolk Cooperative Library System
627 North Sunrise Service Road
Bellport, NY 11713
Librarian: Ms. Julie Klauber
Phone: 516-286-1600; 516-286-4685 (answering service)
TDD: 516-286-4546
Fax: 516-286-1647

Talking Books
Nassau Library System
900 Jerusalem Avenue
Uniondale, NY 11553
Librarian: Ms. Dorothy Puryear (acting)
Phone: 516-292-8920
Fax: 516-481-4777

North Carolina
Regional Library
North Carolina Library for the Blind and Physically Handicapped
State Library of North Carolina
Department of Cultural Resources
1811 Capital Boulevard
Raleigh, NC 27635
Librarian: Ms. Francine I. Martin
Phone: 919-733-4376
In-WATS: 1-800-662-7726 (North Carolina only)
TDD: 919-733-1462
Fax: 919-733-6910

North Dakota
North Dakota State Library
Talking Book Services
604 E. Boulevard
Bismarck, ND 58505
Librarian: Ms. Stella Cone
Phone: 701-328-1477

Federal Tax Help

In-WATS: 1-800-843-9948
TDD: 1-800-892-8622
Fax: 701-328-2040

Ohio (Southern Ohio)
Regional Library
The Public Library of Cincinnati and Hamilton County
Library for the Blind and Physically Handicapped
800 Vine Street, Library Square
Cincinnati, OH 45202-2071
Librarian: Ms. Donna Foust
Phone: 513-369-6999
In-WATS: 1-800-582-0335
TDD: 533-369-3372; 513-369-3384
Fax: 513-369-3111

Ohio (Northern Ohio)
Regional Library
Library for the Blind and Physically Handicapped
Cleveland Public Library
17121 Lake Shore Boulevard
Cleveland, OH 44114-4006
Librarian: Ms. Barbara T. Mates
Phone: 216-623-2911
In-WATS: 1-800-362-1262
Fax: 216-623-7036

Oklahoma
Regional Library
Oklahoma Library for the Blind and Physically Handicapped
300 NE 18th Street
Oklahoma City, OK 73105
Librarian: Ms. Geraldine Adams
Phone: 405-521-3514; 405-521-3833
In-WATS: 1-800-523-0288
TDD: 405-521-4672
Fax: 405-521-4582

Oregon
Regional Library
Oregon State Library
Talking Book and Braille Services
250 Winter Street, NE
Salem, OR 97310-0645
Librarian: Ms. Donna Benson
Phone: 503-378-3849; 503-224-0610 (Portland only; toll free)
In-WATS: 1-800-452-0292 (except Portland)
TDD: 503-378-4276
Fax: 503-588-7119

Pennsylvania (Eastern Pennsylvania)
Regional Library
Library for the Blind and Physically Handicapped
Free Library of Philadelphia
919 Walnut Street
Philadelphia, PA 19107
Librarian: Ms. Vickie Lange Collins
Phone: 215-925-3213
In-WATS: 1-800-222-1754
Fax: 215-928-0856

Pennsylvania (Western Pennsylvania)
Regional Library
Library for the Blind and Physically Handicapped
The Carnegie Library of Pittsburgh
The Leonard C. Staisey Building
4724 Baum Boulevard
Pittsburgh, PA 15213-1389
Librarian: Mrs. Sue O. Murdock
Phone: 412-687-2440
In-WATS: 1-800-242-0586
Fax: 412-687-2442

Puerto Rico
Regional Library
Puerto Rico Regional Library for the Blind
  and Physically Handicapped
520 Ponce de Leon Avenue
San Juan, PR 00901
Librarian: Ms. Igri Enriquez
Phone: 787-723-2519
In-WATS: 1-800-981-8008
Fax: 787-721-8177

Rhode Island
Regional Library
Talking Books Plus
Office of Library and Information Services
One Capitol Hill
Providence, RI 02908
Librarian: Mr. Richard G. Leduc
Phone: 401-222-5800
In-WATS: 1-800-734-5141
TDD: 401-222-2726
Fax: 401-222-4195

South Carolina
Regional Library
South Carolina State Library
Department for the Blind and Physically Handicapped
301 Gervais Street
P.O. Box 821
Columbia, SC 29202-0821
Librarian: Ms. Guynell Williams
Phone: 803-898-5900
In-WATS: 1-800-922-7818
TDD: 803-734-7298
Fax: 803-898-5907

South Dakota
Regional Library
South Dakota Braille and Talking Book Library
State Library Building
800 Governors Drive
Pierre, SD 57501-2294
Librarian: Mr. Daniel W. Boyd
Phone: 6075-773-3131
In-WATS: 1-800-423-6665
TDD: 605-773-4194
Fax: 605-773-4950

Tennessee
Regional Library
Tennessee Library for the Blind and Physically Handicapped
Tennessee State Library and Archives
403 Seventh Avenue North
Nashville, TN 37243-0313
Librarian: Miss Mary Lou Markham
Phone: 615-741-3915
In-WATS: 1-800-342-3308
TDD: 1-800-848-0298
Fax: 615-532-8856

Texas
Regional Library
Texas State Library
Talking Book Program
P.O. Box 12927
Austin, TX 78711-2927
Librarian: Ms. Jenifer O. Flaxbart
Phone: 512-463-5458
In-WATS: 1-800-252-9605
TDD: 512-463-5449
Fax: 512-463-5436

Utah
Regional Library
Utah State Library Division
Program for the Blind and Physically Handicapped
2150 South 300 West, Suite #16
Salt Lake City, UT 84115-2579
Librarian: Mr. Gerald A Buttars
Phone: 801-468-6789
In-WATS: 1-800-662-5540 (Utah)

Free Tax Help

1-800-453-4293 (Western states)
Fax: 801-468-6767

Vermont
Regional Library
Vermont Department of Libraries
Special Services Unit
RD #4, Box 1870
Montpelier, VT 05602
Librarian: Mr. S. Francis Woods
Phone: 802-828-3273
In-WATS: 1-800-479-1711
Fax: 802-828-2199

Virgin Islands
Regional Library
Virgin Islands Library for the Visually and Physically Handicapped
3012 Golden Rock
Christiansted, St. Croix, VI 00820
Librarian: vacant
Phone: 809-772-2250
Fax: 809-772-3545

Virginia
Regional Library
Virginia State Library for the Visually and Physically Handicapped
395 Azalea Avenue
Richmond, VA 23227-3623
Librarian: Ms. Barbara McCarthy
Phone: 804-871-3661
In-WATS: 1-800-552-7015
TDD: 804-371-3661; 1-800-552-7015
Fax: 804-371-3508

Subregional Libraries
Fairfax County Public Library Access Services
12000 Government Center Pkwy., Suite 123
Fairfax, VA 22035-0012
Librarian: Ms. Jeanette A. Studley
Phone: 703-324-8380
TDD: 703-324-8365
Fax: 703-324-8366

Alexandria Library
Talking Book Service
826 Slaters Lane
Alexandria, VA 22314
Librarian: Mrs. Loni McCaffrey
Phone: 703-838-4298
TDD: 703-838-4568
Fax: 703-838-4614

Talking Book Service
Arlington County Department of Libraries
1015 North Quincy Street
Arlington, VA 22201
Librarian: Ms. Roxanne Barnes
Phone: 703-228-6333
TDD: 703-228-6320
Fax: 703-228-6336

Fredericksburg Area Subregional Library
Central Rappahannock Regional Library
1201 Caroline Street
Fredericksburg, VA 22401
Librarian: Ms. Nancy Schiff
Phone: 540-372-1144
In-WATS: 1-800-628-4807
TDD: 540-371-9165
Fax: 540-373-9411

Hampton Subregional Library for the Blind
 and Physically Handicapped
4207 Victoria Boulevard
Hampton, VA 23669
Librarian: Ms. Mary Sue Woolard
Phone: 757-727-1900

TDD: 757-727-1900
Fax: 757-727-1151

Library for the Blind and Physically Handicapped
Newport News Public Library System
110 Main Street
Newport News, VA 23601
Librarian: Ms. Sue Baldwin
Phone: 757-591-4858
TDD: 757-591-4858
Fax: 757-591-7425

Roanoke City Public Library Talking Book Services
Outreach Services, Melrose Branch
2607 Salem Turnpike, Northwest
Roanoke, VA 24017-5397
Librarian: Mrs. Rebecca Cooper
Phone: 540-853-2648
In-WATS: 1-800-528-2342
Fax: 540-853-1030

Talking Book Center
Staunton Public Library
1 Churchville Ave.
Staunton, VA 24401
Librarian: Mr. Oakley Pearson
Phone: 540-885-6215
In-WATS: 1-800-995-6215
Fax: 540-332-3906

Special Services Library
Virginia Beach Public Library
930 Independence Boulevard
Virginia Beach, VA 23455
Librarian: Ms. Susan Head
Phone: 757-464-9175
TDD: 757-464-9175
Fax: 757-464-7606

Washington
Regional Library
Washington Library for the Blind and Physically Handicapped
2021 9th Avenue
Seattle, WA 98121-2783
Librarian: Ms. Jan Ames
Phone: 206-615-0400
In-WATS: 1-800-542-0866
TDD: 206-615-0419
Fax: 206-615-0437

West Virginia
Regional Library
West Virginia Library Commission
Services for the Blind and Physically Handicapped
Cultural Center
1900 Kanawha Boulevard
Charleston, WV 25305
Librarian: Ms. Donna Calvert
Phone: 304-558-6016
In-WATS: 1-800-642-8674
Fax: 304-558-6016

Subregional Libraries
Services for Blind and Physically Handicapped
Kanawha County Public Library
123 Capitol Street
Charleston, WV 25301
Librarian: Ms. Dixie Smith
Phone: 304-343-4646, ext. 264
TDD: 304-343-4646
Fax: 304-348-6530

Services for the Blind and Physically Handicapped
Cabell County Public Library
455 Ninth Street Plaza
Huntington, WV 25701
Librarian: Ms. Suzanne L. Marshall

Federal Tax Help

Phone: 304-528-5700
TDD: 304-528-5700
Fax: 304-528-5739

Parkersburg and Wood County Public Library
Services for the Blind and Physically Handicapped
3100 Emerson Avenue
Parkersburg, WV 26104-2414
Librarian: Mr. Michael Hickman
Phone: 304-420-4587, ext. 5
In-WATS: 1-800-642-8674
Fax: 304-420-4589

West Virginia School for the Blind Library
301 East Main Street
Romney, WV 26757
Librarian: Ms. Cynthia S. Johnson
Phone: 304-822-4894
Fax: 304-822-4896

Ohio County Public Library
Services for the Blind and Physically Handicapped
52 16th Street
Wheeling, WV 26003-3696
Librarian: Mrs. Lori Nicholson
Phone: 304-232-0244
Fax: 304-232-6848

Wisconsin
Regional Library
Wisconsin Regional Library for the Blind and Physically Handicapped
813 West Wells Street
Milwaukee, WI 53233-1436

Librarian: Ms. Marsha Valance
Phone: 414-286-3045
In-WATS: 1-800-242-8822
TDD: 414-286-3548
Fax: 414-286-3102

Wyoming
Eligible readers of Wyoming receive library service from the regional library in Salt Lake City, Utah.

Machine Lending Agency
State Department of Education
Services for Visually Impaired
Hathaway Building, Room 144
Cheyenne, WY 82002
Phone: 307-777-7274
Fax: 307-777-6234

U.S. citizens residing in foreign countries receive library service from:
Network Service Section
National Library Service for the Blind and Physically Handicapped
Library of Congress
Washington, DC 20542
Librarian: Mr. Yealuri Rathan Raj
Phone: 202-707-9261
Fax: 202-707-0712
TDD: 202-707-0744

* Tax Matters Digest System
Superintendent of Documents
Government Printing Office   202-512-1800
Washington, DC 20402   Fax: 202-512-2250

The *Bulletin Index - Digest System* contains the *Finding List* and *Digests* of all permanent tax matters published in the Internal Revenue System. Each subscription service consists of a basic manual and cumulative supplements for an indefinite period.

Service No. 1 - Income Taxes, 1953-1987. ($42) (S/N 948-001-00000-4)
Service No. 2 - Estate and Gift Taxes, 1953-1986. ($17) (S/N 948-002-00000-1)
Service No. 3 - Employment Taxes, 1953-1986. ($17) (S/N 948-003-00000-7)
Service No. 4 - Excise Taxes, 1953-1986. ($17) (S/N 948-004-00000-3)

* Taxpayer Service
Director, Taxpayer Revenue Service
1111 Constitution Ave. NW, Room 7331
Washington, DC 20224   202-624-4224

The Taxpayer Service Division offers advisory services, counseling and training. The purpose is to give information and guidance on income tax matters. Apart from "800" numbers and information offices, IRS offers training for volunteer programs, films, seminars and other services. Special educational programs are available to assist small business, as well as elementary and secondary school teachers, adult education classes and colleges. Special procedures become effective for victims of natural disasters. Eligible applicants and beneficiaries are individuals with questions on tax returns, and groups interested in the tax system.

* Tax Returns Prepared Free for Low Income, Elderly and Handicapped
Volunteer Assistance and Compliance Education Program
Taxpayer Service Division
Internal Revenue Service (IRS)
U.S. Department of the Treasury
1111 Constitution Ave., NW, Room 7207   800-829-1040
Washington, DC 20224   202-283-0197
www.irs.ustreas.gov

The Volunteer Income Tax Assistance (VITA) Program offers free tax help to people who cannot afford professional assistance. Volunteers, trained by the IRS, help prepare basic tax returns for taxpayers with special needs, including persons with disabilities, those with a low to limited income, non-English speaking persons and elderly taxpayers. Assistance is provided at community and neighborhood centers, libraries, schools, shopping malls, and at other convenient locations. Many locations also offer electronic filing.

Volunteers may take part in various VITA program activities, such as directly preparing returns, teaching taxpayers to prepare their own returns, managing a VITA site, or arranging publicity. Volunteers generally include college students, law students, members of professional business and accounting organizations, and members of retirement, religious, military, and community groups. The IRS provides VITA training materials and instructors. Training is conducted at a time and location convenient to volunteers and instructors. Generally, these sessions are offered in December through January each year.

The emphasis in VITA is to teach taxpayers to complete their own tax returns. A volunteer's role becomes that of an instructor rather than a preparer. VITA volunteers will teach taxpayers to prepare their own Forms 1040EZ, 1040A, 1040, and W-4. Assistance with state and local returns can also be provided. If complicated questions or returns are introduced, professional assistance will be provided or the taxpayer will be referred to one of the IRS publications for guidance. Contact your local taxpayer education coordinator for additional information on programs in your district. You can also visit the IRS website.

* Tax Workshops for Small Businesses
Volunteer Assistance and Compliance Education Program
Taxpayer Service Division
Internal Revenue Service (IRS)
U.S. Department of the Treasury
1111 Constitution Ave., NW
S.A.L. Building, Room 1046   800-829-1040
Washington, DC 20224   202-283-0196

Small businesses usually need help getting started and taxes are one important aspect of successful entrepreneurship. The Small Business Tax Education Program (STEP) offers programs designed to help people understand their federal tax obligations. These workshops explain withholding tax responsibilities and the completion of employment tax returns. Contact the Taxpayer Education Coordinator in your area for information regarding the meeting time and place.

* Taxpayer Publications
Forms Distribution Center
P.O. Box 25866
Richmond, VA 23289   800-829-3676
www.irs.ustreas.gov

The IRS publishes over 100 free taxpayer information publications on various subjects. To order forms and publications, call toll-free 1-800-TAX-FORM (1-800-829-3676), or contact your local IRS office. If you need forms or publications listings, from your fax machine — not your desk phone — call 703-368-9694 for 24 hour tax service. To get paper tax forms and publications, call 1-800-TAX-FORM.

Free Tax Help

For tax forms on CD-ROM, call 1-877-CDFORMS (1-877-233-6767). You can also visit the IRS website at {www.irs.ustreas.gov}.

* The Buck Stops Here

Office of the Taxpayer Advocate
Internal Revenue Service (IRS)
U.S. Department of the Treasury
1111 Constitution Ave., NW
Room 3017, C:TA   877-777-4778
Washington, DC 20224   202-622-4318

For prompt assistance solving tax problems that have not been resolved through normal procedures, contact your local Problem Resolution Center. These offices have been set up by Congress specifically to fight the IRS on your behalf, and their help is absolutely FREE. They know the laws because they are part of the office that writes them. They also have direct access to IRS computers enabling them to oftentimes stop the IRS from hassling you in any way. Besides resolving thousands of routine matters each day as advocates of the taxpayer, Problem Resolution Centers also perform many services that are far beyond the call of duty.

Problem Resolution Centers

Office of the Taxpayer Advocate
1111 Constitution Avenue, NW
Room 3017, C:TA
Washington, DC 20224
Fax: 202-622-4318

Alabama
801 Tom Martin Dr., Room 268-PR
Birmingham, AL 35211
Fax: 205-912-5632

Alaska
P.O. Box 101500
Anchorage, AK 99510
or
949 East 36th Ave.
Fax: 907-271-6824

Arizona
210 E. Earll Street
Stop 1005 PX
Phoenix, AZ 85012-2623
Fax: 602-207-8250

Arkansas
700 West Capital Ave.
Stop 100fLIT
Little Rock, AR 72201
Fax: 501-324-5183

California
Laguna Niguel District
P.O. Box 30207
Laguna Niguel, CA 92607-0207
or
24000 Avila Rd.
Laguna Niguel, CA 92656
Fax: 949-360-2463

Los Angeles District
P.O. Box 4531791
Los Angeles, CA 90053
or
300 N. Los Angeles St., Room 4352
Los Angeles, CA 90012
Fax: 213-894-6365

Sacramento District
P.O. Box 2900
Stop SA 5043
Sacramento, CA 95812
or
4330 Watt Ave.
North Highlands, CA 95660
Fax: 916-974-5902

San Francisco District
1301 Clay St. #1540S
Oakland, CA 94612
Fax: 510-637-2715

San Jose District
P.O. Box 100
Stop HQ0004
San Jose, CA 95103
or
55 S. Market St., Room 900
San Jose, CA 95113
Fax: 408 494-8065

Colorado
P.O. Box 1302
Stop 1005 DEN
Denver, CO 80201
or
600 17th St., Stop 1005
Denver, CO 80202-2490
Fax: 303-446-1011

Connecticut
135 High St. (Stop 219)
Hartford, CT 06103
Fax: 860-240-4023

Delaware
409 Silverside Rd.
Wilmington, DE 19809
Fax: 302-791-4511

District of Columbia
P.O. Box 1553
Room 620A
Baltimore, MD 21203
or
31 Hopkins Plaza, Room 620A
Baltimore, MD 21201
Fax: 410-962-9340

Florida
Ft. Lauderdale District
P.O. Box 17167
Plantation, FL 33318
or
One North University Dr.
Room A-312
Plantation, FL 33324
Fax: 954-423-7685

Jacksonville District
P.O. Box 35045
Stop D:PRO
Jacksonville, FL 32202
or
400 West Bay St., Room 116
Jacksonville, FL 32202
Fax 904-232-2266

Georgia
P.O. Box 1065
Stop 202-D, Room 1520
Atlanta, GA 30370
or
401 West Peachtree St., NW
Summit Building
Stop 202-D, Room 1520
Atlanta, GA 30365
Fax: 404-730-3438

Hawaii
300 Ala Moana Blvd., Room 2104
Box H-405
Honolulu, HI 96850-4992
Fax: 808-541-3379

Federal Tax Help

Idaho
550 West Fort St.
Box 041
Boise, ID 83727
Fax: 208-334-9663

Illinois
Chicago District
230 S. Dearborn St.
Room 3214, Stop 1005-CHI
Chicago, IL 60604
Fax: 312-886-1564

Springfield District
320 West Washington St.
Springfield, IL 62701
Fax: 217-527-6332

Indiana
P.O. Box 44687 (Stop 11)
Indianapolis, IN 46244
or
575 N. Pennsylvania St., Stop 11
Indianapolis, IN 46204
Fax: 317-226-6222

Iowa
210 Walnut St., Stop 1005
Des Moines, IA 50309-2109
Fax: 515-284-6645

Kansas
271 West Third Street North
Stop 1005 WIC
Wichita, KS 67202
Fax: 316-352-7212

Kentucky
600 Dr. Martin Luther King Jr. Place
Federal Bldg., Room 363
Louisville, KY 40202
Fax: 502-582-6463

Louisiana
600 South Maestri Place
Stop 12
New Orleans, LA 70130
Fax: 504-558-3250

Maine
68 Sewall St., Stop 1010
Augusta, ME 04330
Fax: 207-622-8458

Maryland
P.O. Box 1553
Room 620A
Baltimore, MD 21203
or
31 Hopkins Plaza, Room 620A
Baltimore, MD 21201
Fax: 410-962-9340

Massachusetts
P.O. Box 9112 JFK Bldg.
Boston, MA 02203
Fax: 617-565-4959

Michigan
P.O. Box 330500 (Stop 7)
Detroit, MI 48232-6500
or
McNamara Federal Building
477 Michigan Ave., Room 2492
Detroit, MI 48226-2597
Fax: 313-226-3502

Minnesota
316 N. Robert St., Stop 1005
St. Paul, MN 55101
Fax: 651-290-4236

Mississippi
100 W. Capitol St., Stop 31
Jackson, MS 39269
Fax: 601-965-5251

Missouri
P.O. Box 66776
Stop 1005 STL
St. Louis, MO 63166
or
Robert A. Young Bldg.
1222 Spruce St.
Mail Stop 1005 STL
St. Louis, MO 63103
Fax: 314-539-2362

Montana
Federal Building
301 S. Park
Helena, MT 59626-0016
Fax: 406-441-1035

Nebraska
106 S. 15th St.
(Stop 1005 OMA)
Omaha, NE 68102
Fax: 402-221-3051

Nevada
4750 W. Oakey Blvd., Room 303
Las Vegas, NV 89102
Fax: 702-455-1216

New Hampshire
P.O. Box 720
Portsmouth, NH 03802
or
Federal Office Bldg.
80 Daniel St.
Portsmouth, NH 03801
Fax: 603-433-0739

New Jersey
P.O. Box 1143
Newark, NJ 07102
or
970 Broad St.
Newark, NJ 07102
Fax: 973-645-3323

New Mexico
5338 Montgomery Blvd., ME
Stop 1005 ALB
Albuquerque, NM 87109-1311
Fax: 505-837-5519

New York
Albany District
Leo O'Brien Federal Bldg., Room 617
Clinton Ave. & N. Pearl St.
Albany, NY 12207
Fax: 518-431-4697

Brooklyn District
G.P.O. Box R
Brooklyn, NY 11202
or
10 Metro Tech Center
625 Fulton St.
Brooklyn, NY 11201
Fax: 718-488-3100

Free Tax Help

Buffalo District
P.O. Box 500
Niagara Square Station
Buffalo, NY 14201
or
111 West Huron Street
Thaddeus J. Dulski FOB
Buffalo, NY 14202
Fax: 716-551-5473

Manhattan District
P.O. Box 408
Church Street Station
New York, NY 10008
or
290 Broadway, 7th Floor
New York, NY 10007
Fax: 212-436-1900

North Carolina
320 Federal Place, Room 125
Greensboro, NC 27401
Fax: 919-378-2495

North Dakota
P.O. Box 8
Fargo, ND 58107
or
657 Second Ave., N
Stop 1005-FAR
Fargo, ND 58107
Fax: 701-239-5104

Ohio
Cincinnati District
550 Main St., Room 7010
Cincinnati, OH 45202
Fax: 513-684-6417

Cleveland District
P.O. Box 99709
Cleveland, OH 44199-0709
or
1240 E. Ninth Street
Cleveland, OH 44199-2002
Fax: 216-522-2947

Oklahoma
55 N. Robinson
Stop 1005 OKC
Oklahoma City, OK 73102-9229
Fax: 405-297-4056

Oregon
1220 S.W. 3rd Ave., O-405
Portland, OR 97204
Fax: 503-326-5453

Pennsylvania
Philadelphia District
P.O. Box 12010
Philadelphia, PA 19106
or
600 Arch St., Room 7214
Philadelphia, PA 19106
Fax: 215-597-7341

Pittsburgh District
P.O. Box 705
Pittsburgh, PA 15230
or
1000 Liberty Ave., Room 1102
Pittsburgh, PA 15222
Fax: 412-395-4769

Rhode Island
380 Westminster St.
Providence, RI 02903
Fax: 401-528-4312

South Carolina
1835 Assembly St.
Room 571, MDP 03
Columbia, SC 29201
Fax: 803-253-3910

South Dakota
115 4th Ave., Southeast
Stop 1005-ABE
Aberdeen, SD 57401
Fax: 605-226-7270

Tennessee
P.O. Box 1107 Stop 22
Nashville, TN 37202
or
801 Broadway, Stop 22
Nashville, TN 37203
Fax: 615-736-7489

Texas
Austin District
300 E. 8th St.
Stop 1005-AUS
Austin, TX 78701
Fax: 512-499-5687

Dallas District
1100 Commerce St.
MC1005DAL
Dallas, TX 75242
Fax: 214-767-0040

Houston District
1919 Smith St.
Stop 1005 HOU
Houston, TX 77002
Fax: 713-209-3708

Utah
50 South 200 East
MS 1005
Salt Lake City, UT 84111
Fax: 801-779-6957

Vermont
Courthouse Plaza
199 Main St.
Burlington, VT 05401
Fax: 802-860-2006

Virginia
P.O. Box 10113
Room 5502
Richmond, VA 23240
or
400 N. 8th St.
Richmond, VA 23240
Fax: 804-771-2008

Washington
915 Second Ave.
Stop W-405
Seattle, WA 98174
Fax: 206-220-6047

West Virginia
P.O. Box 1040, Room 1004
Parkersburg, WV 26102
or
425 Juliana St.
Parkersburg, WV 26101
Fax: 304-420-6682

Federal Tax Help

Wisconsin
310 W. Wisconsin Ave., Room M-28
Stop 1005-MIL
Milwaukee, WI 53203
Fax: 414-297-3362

Wyoming
5353 Yellowstone Rd., Room 206A
Cheyenne, WY 82009
Fax: 307-633-0811

* Treasury's Learning Vault

www.irs.ustreas.gov
The Office of IRS Historian has been closed, but the IRS has established a website called The Learning Vault. For interesting information, facts and historical data, visit the IRS website at {www.irs.ustreas.gov}. Go to "About Treasury". For a really great kids section, visit the IRS website and go to "Educational".

* Voicing Opinions of IRS Tax Laws

Secretary of the Treasury
U.S. Department of the Treasury
Room 3330
Washington, DC 20220   202-662-5000

or

Assistant Secretary for Tax Policy
U.S. Department of the Treasury
1500 Pennsylvania Ave., NW
Room 1000   202-622-0120
Washington, DC 20220   202-622-0050

If you have a personal recommendation for changing a federal tax law, you may send written comments to the address above. The letter must include the section within the Internal Revenue Code in which the portion of the law appears. Please send an original and eight copies of the correspondence.

If you wish to comment on how to improve a tax form or instruction booklet, you may address correspondence to the Chairman of the Tax Form Coordinating Committee, Internal Revenue Service, Room 5577, 1111 Constitution Ave. NW, Washington, DC 20224 or The Office of Management and Budget, 17th and Pennsylvania Ave. NW, Paperwork Reduction Project, Washington, DC 20503.

You may also want to contact your congressman or senator to draw attention to a particular issue. Their opinions and subsequent votes can indeed be influenced by hearing from a significant number or irate constituents. The Capitol Hill switchboard number is 202-224-3121. You may write to them at: The Honorable (your senator's name), U.S. Senate, Washington, DC 20515 or The Honorable (your representative's name), U.S. House of Representatives, Washington, DC 20515.

You can also write or call the House subcommittee, the Senate subcommittee and the Joint committee, (whose main task is reviewing tax laws and procedures) at : The Senate Committee on Finance, 219 Dirksen Senate Office Building, Washington, DC 20510, 202-224-4515; The Committee on Ways and Means, U.S. House of Representatives, 1102 Longworth House Office Building, Washington, DC 20515, 202-225-3625; and Joint Committee on Taxation, 204 Dirksen Building, Washington, DC 20515, 202-224-5561.

* Wage Reporting

Office of the Assistant Commissioner
Internal Revenue Service (IRS)
U.S. Department of the Treasury
1111 Constitution Ave., NW
Washington, DC 20224   202-622-5430

The combined annual wage reporting system was designed to assist employers in the reporting of taxes. For more assistance in this area, contact your local field office listed in your phone directory or the office above.

* Where To File: Mailing Address

If an addressed envelope came with your return, please use it. If you do not have one, or if you moved during the year, mail your return to the Internal Revenue Service Center for the place where you live. No street address is needed.

Florida, Georgia, South Carolina
Use this address: Atlanta, GA 39901

New Jersey, New York (New York City and counties of Nassau, Rockland, Suffolk, and Westchester)
Use this address: Holtsville, NY 00501

New York (all other counties), Connecticut, Maine, Massachusetts, New Hampshire, Rhode Island, Vermont
Use this address: Andover, MA 05501

Illinois, Iowa, Minnesota, Missouri, Wisconsin
Use this address: Kansas City, MO 64999

Delaware, District of Columbia, Maryland, Pennsylvania, Virginia
Use this address: Philadelphia, PA 19255

Indiana, Kentucky, Michigan, Ohio, West Virginia
Use this address: Cincinnati, OH 45999

Kansas, New Mexico, Oklahoma, Texas
Use this address: Austin, TX 73301

Alaska, Arizona, California (counties of Alpine, Amador, Butte, Calaveras, Colusa, Contra Costa, Del Norte, El Dorado, Glenn, Humboldt, Lake, Lassen, Mendocino, Modoc, Napa, Nevada, Placer, Plumas, Sacramento, San Joaquin, Shasta, Sierra, Siskiyou, Solano, Sonoma, Sutter, Tehama, Trinity, Yolo, and Yuba), Colorado, Idaho, Montana, Nebraska, Nevada, North Dakota, Oregon, South Dakota, Utah, Washington, Wyoming
Use this address: Ogden, UT 84201

California (all other counties), Hawaii
Use this address: Fresno, CA 93888

Alabama, Arkansas, Louisiana, Mississippi, North Carolina, Tennessee
Use this address: Memphis, TN 37501

American Samoa
Use this address: Philadelphia, PA 19255

Guam
Use this address: Commissioner of Revenue and Taxation
                                    855 West Marine Dr
                                    Agana, GU 96910

Puerto Rico (or if excluding income under section 933), Virgin Islands (Nonpermanent residents)
Use this address: Philadelphia, PA 19255

Virgin Islands (Permanent residents)
Use this address: V.I. Bureau of Internal Revenue
                                  Lockharts Garden No. 1A
                                         Charlotte Amalie,
                                      St. Thomas, VI 00802

Foreign country: U.S. citizens and those filing Form 2555 or Form 4563
Use this address: Philadelphia, PA 19255

All A.P.O. or F.P.O. addresses
Use this address: Philadelphia, PA 19255

Free Tax Help

Tax Hotlines

In addition to telephone hotlines, the IRS has added more ways to help you find answers to your questions:

Website: www.irs.ustreas.gov
Questions: 1-800-829-1040
Tele-Tax Topics: 1-800-829-4477
Fax by Phone: 703-368-9694 (for forms and publications)
Publication 910: *Guide to Free Tax Service*

Toll-free telephone tax assistance is available in all 50 states, the District of Columbia, Puerto Rico, and the Virgin Islands. Certain cities listed here have local numbers to call as well. But if it's a long distance call for you, use the toll-free number! Try calling early in the morning or later in the week for prompt service. You'll encounter fewer busy signals that way.

Before You Call:
When you call an IRS office, it will save you time if you have:

1. The tax form, schedule, or notice to which your question relates.
2. The relevant facts about your particular situation. Keep your comments concise and to the point.
3. The name of any IRS publication or other source of information that you used to look for the answer.

Before You Hang Up:
If you do not fully understand the answer you receive, or you feel the representative may not fully understand your question, the representative needs to know this. He or she will be happy to take the additional time required to be sure they have answered your question fully and in the manner which is most helpful to you.

By law, you are responsible for paying your fair share of Federal income tax. If the IRS should make an error in answering your question, you are still responsible for the payment of the correct tax. Should this occur, however, you will not be charged any penalty. To make sure that IRS representatives give accurate and courteous answers, a second IRS representative sometimes listens in on telephone calls. No record is kept of any taxpayer's identity.

Alabama
1-800-829-1040

Alaska
Anchorage 907-271-6877
Elsewhere 1-800-829-1040

Arizona
Phoenix 602-640-3933
Elsewhere 1-800-829-1040

Arkansas
1-800-829-1040

California
1-800-829-1040

Colorado
1-800-829-1040

Connecticut
1-800-829-1040

Delaware
1-800-829-1040

District of Columbia
1-800-829-1040

Florida
Jacksonville 904-232-3440
Elsewhere 1-800-829-1040

Georgia
Atlanta 404-522-0050
Elsewhere 1-800-829-1040

Hawaii
1-800-829-1040

Idaho
1-800-829-1040

Illinois
Chicago 312-886-9183
Elsewhere 1-800-829-1040

Indiana
1-800-829-1040

Iowa
Des Moines 515-283-0523
Elsewhere 1-800-829-1040

Kansas
1-800-829-1040

Kentucky
1-800-829-1040

Louisiana
1-800-829-1040

Maine
1-800-829-1040

Maryland
1-800-829-1040

Massachusetts
1-800-829-1040

Michigan
1-800-829-1040

Minnesota
St. Paul 651-296-3781
Elsewhere 1-800-829-1040

Mississippi
1-800-829-1040

Tax Hotlines

Missouri
1-800-829-1040

Montana
1-800-829-1040

Nebraska
1-800-829-1040

Nevada
1-800-829-1040

New Hampshire
1-800-829-1040

New Jersey
1-800-829-1040

New Mexico
1-800-829-1040

New York
Brooklyn 718-488-2080
Manhattan 212-436-1011
Nassau 516-571-1500
Staten Island 718-488-2080
Suffolk 516-571-1500
Elsewhere 1-800-829-1040

North Carolina
1-800-829-1040

North Dakota
1-800-829-1040

Ohio
1-800-829-1040

Oklahoma
1-800-829-1040

Oregon
1-800-829-1040

Pennsylvania
1-800-829-1040

Puerto Rico
1-800-829-1040

Rhode Island
1-800-829-1040

South Carolina
1-800-829-1040

South Dakota
1-800-829-1040

Tennessee
1-800-829-1040

Texas
1-800-829-1040

Utah
1-800-829-1040

Vermont
1-800-829-1040

Virginia
Richmond 804-649-2631
Elsewhere 1-800-829-1040

Washington
1-800-829-1040

West Virginia
1-800-829-1040

Wisconsin
1-800-829-1040

Wyoming
1-800-829-1040

Telephone Assistance Services for Hearing Impaired Taxpayers Who Have Access to TDD Equipment:

Hours of Operation:
8:00 am to 6:30 pm EST
(January 1 - April 2)

9:00 am to 7:30 pm EDT
(April 3 - April 15)

9:00 am to 5:30 pm EDT
(April 16 to October 29)

8:00 am to 4:30 pm EST
(October 30 to December 31)

All locations in U.S., including Alaska, Hawaii, Virgin Islands, and Puerto Rico
1-800-829-4059

Free Tax Help

Recorded Messages

What is Tele-Tax?

Recorded Tax Information provides recorded answers to over 140 frequently asked questions. You can hear up to three topics on each call you make. Automated Refund Information is available so you can check the status of your refund.

How Do I Use Tele-Tax?

To call Tele-Tax, use the toll-free number: 1-800-829-4477. Tele-Tax topic numbers and subjects are listed below. These topic numbers are effective January 1, 1998. While touch tone service is available 24 hours a day, seven days a week, rotary or pulse dial service is usually available Monday through Friday, during regular office hours. Select by number the topic you want to hear. For the directory of topics, listen to topic #123. You can also visit the IRS website at {www.irs.ustreas.gov}.

Automated Refund Information

Be sure to have a copy of your tax return available since you will need to know the first social security number shown on your return, the filing status, and the exact amount of your refund. Then, call the toll-free phone number and follow the recorded instructions. While touch tone service is available 24 hours a day, seven days a week, rotary or pulse dial service is usually available Monday through Friday, during regular office hours. IRS updates refund information every 7 days. If you call to find out about the status of your refund and do not receive a refund mailing date, please wait 7 days before calling back.

Toll-Free Tele-Tax Number
1-800-829-4477

Tele-Tax Topic Numbers and Subjects

IRS Help Available:
101 IRS services: Volunteer tax assistance programs, toll-free telephone, walk-in assistance, and outreach programs
102 Tax assistance for individuals with disabilities and the hearing impaired
103 Small Business Tax Education Program (STEP): Tax help for small businesses
104 Problem Resolution Program: Help for problem situations
105 Public libraries: Tax information tapes and reproducible tax forms.

IRS Procedures:
151 Your appeal rights
152 Refunds: How long they should take
153 What to do if you haven't filed your tax return (nonfilers)
154 Form W-2: What to do if not received
155 Forms and publications: How to order
156 Copy of your tax return: How to get one
157 Change of address: How to notify IRS
158 Ensuring proper credit
159 Hardship application

Collection:
201 The collection process
202 What to do if you can't pay your tax

203 Failure to pay child support and other federal obligations
204 Offers in compromise
205 Innocent spouse relief

Alternative Filing Methods:
251 1040PC tax return
252 Electronic filing
253 Substitute tax forms
254 How to choose a tax preparer
255 Telefile

General Information:
301 When, where, and how to file
302 Highlights of 1998 tax changes
303 Checklist of common errors when preparing your tax return
304 Extensions of time to file your tax return
305 Recordkeeping
306 Penalty for underpayment of estimated tax
307 Backup withholding
308 Amended returns
309 Roth IRS contribution
310 Education IRA contribution
311 Power of attorney information

Filing Requirements, Filing Status, and Exemptions:
351 Who must file?
352 Which form: 1040, 1040A, or 1040EZ?
353 What is your filing status?
354 Dependents
355 Estimated tax
356 Decedents

Types of Income:
401 Wages and salaries
402 Tips
403 Interest received
404 Dividends
405 Refund of state and local taxes
406 Alimony received
407 Business income
408 Sole proprietorship
409 Capital gains and losses
410 Pensions and annuities
411 Pensions: The general rule and the simplified general rule
412 Lump-sum distributions
413 Rollovers from retirement plans
414 Rental income and expenses
415 Renting vacation property and renting to relatives
416 Farming and fishing income
417 Earnings for clergy
418 Unemployment compensation
419 Gambling income and expenses
420 Bartering income
421 Scholarships and fellowships grants
422 Nontaxable income
423 Social Security and equivalent railroad retirement benefits
424 401(k) plans
425 Passive activities: Losses and credits
426 Other income
427 Stock options
428 Roth IRA distributions

Adjustments to Income:
451 Individual Retirement Arrangements (IRAs)
452 Alimony paid
453 Bad debt reduction
454 Tax shelters
455 Moving expense
456 Student loan interest deduction

Recorded Messages

Itemized Deductions:
- 501 Should I itemize?
- 502 Medical and dental expenses
- 503 Deductible taxes
- 504 Home mortgage
- 505 Interest expense
- 506 Contributions
- 507 Casualty losses
- 508 Miscellaneous expenses
- 509 Business use of home
- 510 Business use of car
- 511 Business travel expenses
- 512 Business entertainment expenses
- 513 Educational expenses
- 514 Employee business expenses
- 515 Disaster area losses (including flood losses)

Tax Computation:
- 551 Standard deduction
- 552 Tax and credits figured by IRS
- 553 Tax on a child's investment income
- 554 Self-employment tax
- 555 Five- or ten-year averaging for lump-sum distributions
- 556 Alternative minimum tax
- 557 Tax on early distributions from traditional IRA

Tax Credits:
- 601 Earned income credit (EIC)
- 602 Child and dependent care credit
- 603 Credit for the elderly or the disabled
- 604 Advance earned income credit
- 605 Education credits
- 606 Child care tax credits
- 607 Adoption credits
- 608 Social security tax credits

IRS Notices and Letters:
- 651 Notices: What to do
- 652 Notice of under-reported income C CP2000
- 653 IRS notices and bills and penalty and interest charges

Basis of Assets, Depreciation and Sale of Assets:
- 701 Sale of your home: General – after May 6, 1997
- 702 Sale of your home: How to report gain – before May 7, 1997
- 703 Basis of assets
- 704 Depreciation
- 705 Installment sales

Employer Tax Information:
- 751 Social security and Medicare withholding rates
- 752 Form W-2: Where, when and how to file
- 753 Form W-4: Employee's Withholding Allowance Certificate
- 754 Form W-5: Advance Earned Income Credit
- 755 Employer identification number (EIN): How to apply
- 756 Employment Taxes for household employees
- 757 Form 941: Deposit requirements
- 758 Form 941: Employer's Quarterly Federal tax return
- 759 Form 940/940EZ: Deposit requirements
- 760 Form 940/940EZ: Employer's Annual Federal Unemployment tax return
- 761 Tips: Withholding and reporting
- 762 Independent contractor vs. employee

Magnetic Media Filers: 1099 Series and Related Information Returns (For electronic filing of individual returns, listen to Topic 252):
- 801 Who must file magnetically
- 802 Applications, forms and information
- 803 Waivers and extensions
- 804 Test files and combined federal and state filing
- 805 Electronic filing of information returns

Tax Information for Aliens and U.S. Citizens Living Abroad:
- 851 Resident and nonresident aliens
- 852 Dual status alien
- 853 Foreign earned income exclusion: General
- 854 Foreign earned income exclusion: Who qualifies?
- 855 Foreign earned income exclusion: What qualifies?
- 856 Foreign tax credit
- 857 IRS individual taxpayer ID number Form W7
- 858 Alien tax clearance

Tax Information for Puerto Rico Residents (in Spanish):
- 901 Who must file a U.S. income tax return in Puerto Rico
- 902 Deductions and credits for Puerto Rico filers
- 903 Federal employment taxes in Puerto Rico
- 904 Tax assistance for residents of Puerto Rico

Other Tele-Tax Topics in Spanish:
- 951 IRS services: Volunteer tax assistance, toll-free telephone, walk-in assistance, and outreach programs
- 952 Refunds: How long they should take
- 953 Forms and publications: How to order
- 954 Highlights of 1998 tax changes
- 955 Who must file?
- 956 Which form to use
- 957 What is your filing status?
- 958 Social security and equivalent railroad retirement benefits
- 959 Earned income credit (EIC)
- 960 Advance earned income credit
- 961 Alien tax clearance

Free Tax Help

IRS Tax Forms and Publications

The Internal Revenue Service publishes many free publications to help you "make your taxes less taxing." The publications listed in this section give general information about taxes for individuals, small businesses, farming, fishing, and recent tax law changes. Forms and schedules related to the subject matter of each publication are indicated after each listing. All federal income tax forms are listed in numerical order after this state-by-state roster.

To order forms and publications, call toll-free 1-800-TAX-FORM (1-800-829-3676), or contact your local IRS office. If you need forms or publications listings, from your fax machine — not your desk phone — call 703-368-9694 for 24 hour tax service. To get paper tax forms and publications, call 1-800-TAX-FORM. For tax forms on CD-ROM, call 1-877-CDFORMS (1-877-233-6767). You can also visit the IRS website at {www.irs.ustreas.gov}. To send for forms through the mail, write to the appropriate state address below. Two copies of each form and one copy of each set of instructions will be sent.

Forms Distribution Centers

IRS Forms and Publications Distribution
Forms Distribution Center
P.O. Box 25866
Richmond, VA 23289

Tax forms and publications can be obtained by calling the toll-free number. To send for forms through the mail, write to the state IRS address listed below. Two copies of each form and one copy of each set of instructions will be sent.

Alabama
P.O. Box 8903
Bloomington, IL 61703

Alaska
Rancho Cordova, CA 95743-0001

Arizona
Rancho Cordova, CA 95743-0001

Arkansas
P.O. Box 8903
Bloomington, IL 61703

California
Rancho Cordova, CA 95743-0001

Colorado
Rancho Cordova, CA 95743-0001

Connecticut
P.O. Box 85074
Richmond, VA 23261-5074

Delaware
P.O. Box 85074
Richmond, VA 23261-5074

District of Columbia
P.O. Box 85074
Richmond, VA 23261-5074

Florida
P.O. Box 85074
Richmond, VA 23261-5074

Georgia
P.O. Box 85074
Richmond, VA 23261-5074

Hawaii
Rancho Cordova, CA 95743-0001

Idaho
Rancho Cordova, CA 95743-0001

Illinois
P.O. Box 8903
Bloomington, IL 61703

Indiana
P.O. Box 8903
Bloomington, IL 61703

Iowa
P.O. Box 8903
Bloomington, IL 61703

Kansas
P.O. Box 8903
Bloomington, IL 61703

Kentucky
P.O. Box 8903
Bloomington, IL 61703

Louisiana
P.O. Box 8903
Bloomington, IL 61703

Maine
P.O. Box 85074
Richmond, VA 23261-5074

Maryland
P.O. Box 85074
Richmond, VA 23261-5074

Massachusetts
P.O. Box 85074
Richmond, VA 23261-5074

Michigan
P.O. Box 8903
Bloomington, IL 61703

Minnesota
P.O. Box 8903
Bloomington, IL 61703

Mississippi
P.O. Box 8903
Bloomington, IL 61703

IRS Tax Forms and Publications

Missouri
P.O. Box 8903
Bloomington, IL 61703

Montana
Rancho Cordova, CA 95743-0001

Nebraska
P.O. Box 8903
Bloomington, IL 61703

Nevada
Rancho Cordova, CA 95743-0001

New Hampshire
P.O. Box 85074
Richmond, VA 23261-5074

New Jersey
P.O. Box 85074
Richmond, VA 23261-5074

New Mexico
Rancho Cordova, CA 95743-0001

New York
P.O. Box 85074
Richmond, VA 23261-5074

North Carolina
P.O. Box 85074
Richmond, VA 23261-5074

North Dakota
P.O. Box 8903
Bloomington, IL 61703

Ohio
P.O. Box 8903
Bloomington, IL 61703

Oklahoma
P.O. Box 8903
Bloomington, IL 61703

Oregon
Rancho Cordova, CA 95743-0001

Pennsylvania
P.O. Box 85074
Richmond, VA 23261-5074

Puerto Rico
P.O. Box 85074
Richmond, VA 23261-5074

Rhode Island
P.O. Box 85074
Richmond, VA 23261-5074

South Carolina
P.O. Box 85074
Richmond, VA 23261-5074

South Dakota
P.O. Box 8903
Bloomington, IL 61703

Tennessee
P.O. Box 8903
Bloomington, IL 61703

Texas
P.O. Box 8903
Bloomington, IL 61703

Utah
Rancho Cordova, CA 95743-0001

Vermont
P.O. Box 85074
Richmond, VA 23261-5074

Virgin Islands
V.I. Bureau of Internal Revenue
Lockharts Garden No. 1A
Charlotte Amalie
St. Thomas, VI 00802

Virginia
P.O. Box 85074
Richmond, VA 23261-5074

Washington
Rancho Cordova, CA 95743-0001

West Virginia
P.O. Box 85074
Richmond, VA 23261-5074

Wisconsin
P.O. Box 8903
Bloomington, IL 61703

Wyoming
Rancho Cordova, CA 95743-0001

Foreign Addresses
Forms Distribution Center
P.O. Box 85074
Richmond, VA 23261-5074

Forms Distribution Center
Rancho Cordova, CA 95743-0001

Taxpayers with mailing addresses in foreign countries should send the order blank to either address. Send letter requests for other forms and publications to: Forms Distribution Center, P.O. Box 85074, Richmond, VA 23261-5074.

Free IRS Publications and Forms

The forms and schedules related to the subject matter of each publication are indicated after each listing.

1 Your Rights as a Taxpayer
To ensure that you always receive fair treatment in tax matters, you should know your rights. This publication clarifies your rights at each step in the tax process.

1SP Derechos del Contribuyente (Your Rights as a Taxpayer)
Spanish version of Publication 1.

3 Tax Information for Military Personnel (Including Reservists Called to Active Duty)
This publication gives information about the special tax situations of active members of the Armed Forces. It includes information on items that are includible in and excludable from gross income, alien status, dependency exemptions, sale of residence, itemized deductions, tax liability, and filing returns.
Forms 1040, 1040A, 1040EZ, 1040NR, 1040X, 1310, 2106, 2688, 2848, 3903, 3903F, 4868 and W-2.

4 Student's Guide to Federal Income Tax
This publication explains the federal tax laws that are of particular interest to high school and college students. It describes the student's responsibilities to pay taxes, how to file returns, and how to get help.
Forms 1040EZ, W-2 and W-4.

Free Tax Help

5 Appeals Rights and Preparation of Protests for Unagreed Cases
This publication provides information on your examination appeal rights and how to prepare a protest if you disagree with the findings of an IRS agent in an examination report.

17 Your Federal Income Tax
This publication can help you prepare your individual tax return. It takes you step by step through each part of the return, and explains the tax laws in a way that will help you better understand your taxes so that you pay only as much as you owe and no more.
The tax table, tax rate schedules, and earned income credit tables are included in this publication.
Forms 1040, 1040A, 1040EZ, Schedules A, B, D, E, EIC, R, SE, Forms W-2, 2106, 2119, 2441, 3903.

225 Farmer's Tax Guide
This publication discusses the kind of farm income you must report and the different deductions you can take.
Form 1040, Schedules A, D, F, SE, and Forms 4136, 4562, 4684, 4797, 6251.

334 Tax Guide for Small Business
This book explains some federal tax laws that apply to businesses and the tax responsibilities of the four major forms of business organizations: sole proprietorship, partnership, corporation, and S corporation.
Schedule C (Form 1040), Schedule K-1 (Forms 1065 and 1120S), Forms 1065, 1120, 1120-A, 1120S, 4562.

595 Tax Guide for Commercial Fishermen
This publication is intended for sole proprietors who use Schedule C (Form 1040) to report profit or loss from fishing. This guide does not cover corporations or partnerships. Schedule C (Form 1040), Forms 1099-MISC, 4562, 4797.

910 Guide to Free Tax Services

More Free Tax Publications

The following publications supplement the general ones previously listed. They provide a few more details on specific topics and are shown in numerical order.

15 Circular E, Employer's Tax Guide
Forms 940, 941, and 941E.

51 Circular A, Agricultural Employer's Tax Guide
Form 943.

54 Tax Guide for U.S. Citizens and Resident Aliens Abroad
This publication discusses the tax situations of U.S. citizens and resident aliens who live and work abroad. In particular, it explains the rules for excluding income and excluding or deducting certain housing costs.
Forms 1040, Schedule SE (Form 1040), 1116, 2555 and 2555-EZ.

80 Circular SS, Federal Tax Guide for Employers in the Virgin Islands, Guam, American Samoa, and the Commonwealth of the Northern Mariana Islands
Forms 940, 941SS, and 943.

179 Circular PR, Guia Contributiva Federal Para Patronos Puertorriquenos (Federal Tax Guide for Employers in Puerto Rico)
Forms W-3PR, 940PR, 941PR, 942PR, and 943PR.

349 Federal Highway Use Tax on Heavy Vehicles
This publication explains which trucks, truck-tractors, and buses are subject to the federal highway use tax on heavy motor vehicles, and how to figure and pay any tax due on the taxable vehicle. Form 2290.

378 Fuel Tax Credits and Refunds
This publication explains the credit or refund allowable for the federal excise taxes paid on certain fuels, and the income tax credit available for alcohol used as a fuel.
Forms 843, 4136 and 6478.

448 Federal Estate and Gift Taxes
Forms 706 and 709.

463 Travel, Entertainment, and Gift Expenses
Some business-related travel, entertainment, gift and local transportation expenses may be deductible.
Form 2106.

501 Exemptions, Standard Deduction, and Filing Information
Form 2120 and 8332.

502 Medical and Dental Expenses
Explains which medical and dental expenses are deductible, how to deduct them and how to treat insurance reimbursements you may receive for medical care.
Schedule A (Form 1040).

503 Child and Dependent Care Expenses
You may be able to take a credit if you pay someone to care for your dependent who is under age 13, your disabled dependent, or your disabled spouse. For purposes of the credit, "disabled" refers to a person physically or mentally not capable of self-care. Tax rules covering benefits paid under a dependent care assistance plan are also explained.
See Publication 926, which explains the employment taxes you may have to pay if you are a household employer.
Schedule 2 (Form 1040A), and Form 2441.

504 Divorced or Separated Individuals
Form 8332.

505 Tax Withholding and Estimated Tax
Forms W-4, W-4P, W-4S, 1040-ES, 2210, and 2210F.

508 Educational Expenses
Some work-related educational expenses may be deductible.
Form 2106 and Schedule A (Form 1040).

509 Tax Calendars for 1999

510 Excise Taxes for 1998
This publication covers in detail the various federal excise taxes reported on Form 720. These include environmental taxes; facilities and service taxes on communication and air transportation; fuel taxes; manufacturers taxes; vaccines; tax on heavy trucks, trailers and tractors; luxury taxes; and tax on ship passengers. It briefly describes other excise taxes and tells which forms to use in reporting and paying the taxes.
Forms 11-C, 637, 720, 730, 6197, 6627, 8743, and 8807.

513 Tax Information for Visitors to the United States
This publication briefly reviews the general requirements of U.S. income tax rules for foreign visitors who may have to file a U.S. income tax return during their visit. Most visitors who come to the United States are not allowed to work in this country. Check with the Immigration and Naturalization Service before taking a job.
Forms 1040C, 1040-ES (NR), and 2063.

514 Foreign Tax Credit for Individuals
If you paid foreign income tax, you may be able to take a foreign tax credit or deduction to avoid double taxation. This publication explains which foreign taxes qualify and how to figure your credit or deduction. Form 1116.

515 Withholding of Tax on Nonresident Aliens and Foreign Corporations
This publication provides information for withholding agents who are required to withhold and report tax on payments to nonresident aliens and foreign corporations. Includes information on required withholding upon the disposition of a U.S. real property interest by a foreign person. Also includes three tables listing U.S. tax treaties and some of the treaty provisions that provide for reduction of or exemption from withholding for certain types of income. Forms 1001, 1042 and 1042S, 1078, 4224, 8233, 8288, 8288-A, 8288-D, 8709, 8804, 8805, 8813, and W 8.

516 Tax Information for U.S. Government Civilian Employees Stationed Abroad

IRS Tax Forms and Publications

517 Social Security and Other Information for Members of the Clergy and Religious Workers
This publication discusses social security and Medicare taxes for ministers and religious workers. It explains the income tax treatment of certain income items.
Forms 1040, 2106, 4029, and 4361, Schedule C-EZ and SE (Form 1040).

519 U.S. Tax Guide for Aliens
This comprehensive publication gives guidelines on how to determine your U.S. tax status and figure your U.S. tax.
Forms 1040, 1040C, 1040NR, 2063, and Schedule A (Form 1040).

520 Scholarships and Fellowships
This publication explains the tax laws that apply to U.S. citizens and resident aliens who study, teach or conduct research in the United States or abroad under scholarships and fellowship grants. Forms 1040A and 1040EZ.

521 Moving Expenses
This publication explains whether or not certain expenses of moving are deductible. For example, if you changed job locations last year or started a new job, you may be able to deduct your moving expenses. You also may be able to deduct expenses of moving to the United States if you retire while living and working overseas or if you are a survivor or dependent of a person who died while living and working overseas.
Forms 3903, 3903F, 4782.

523 Selling Your Home
This publication explains how to treat any gain or loss from selling your main home.
Form 2119.

524 Credit for the Elderly or the Disabled
You may be able to claim this credit if you are 65 or older, or if you are retired on permanent and total disability.
Schedule R (Form 1040) and Schedule 3 (Form 1040A).

525 Taxable and Nontaxable Income

526 Charitable Contributions
Schedule A (Form 1040), Form 8283.

527 Residential Rental Property
This publication explains rental income and expenses and how to report them on your return. It also discusses the sale of rental property and other special rules that apply to rental activity.
Schedule E (Form 1040), and Forms 4562 and 4797.

529 Miscellaneous Deductions
This publication discusses expenses you may be able to take as miscellaneous deductions on Schedule A (Form 1040), such as employee business expenses and expenses of producing income. It does not discuss other itemized deductions, such as the ones for charitable contributions, moving expenses, interest, taxes, or medical and dental expenses.
Schedule A (Form 1040), Form 2106.

530 Tax Information for First-Time Homeowners

531 Reporting Tip Income
This publication explains how tip income is taxed as well as the rules for keeping records and reporting tips to your employers. It focuses on employees of food and beverage establishments, but recordkeeping rules and other information may also apply to other workers who receive tips, such as hairdressers, cab drivers and casino dealers. (See Publication 1244.)
Forms 4070 and 4070A.

533 Self-Employment Tax
Payment of self-employment tax is explained. This is a social security and Medicare tax for people who work for themselves. Schedule SE (Form 1040).

534 Depreciation of Property Placed in Service Before 1987
Form 4562.

535 Business Expenses

536 Net Operating Losses
Form 1045

537 Installment Sales
Some sales arrangements provide for part or all of the selling price to be paid in a later year. These are installment sales. If you finance the buyer's purchase of your property instead of having the buyer get a loan or mortgage from a bank (or other lender), you probably have an installment sale.
Form 6252.

538 Accounting Periods and Methods

541 Tax Information on Partnerships
Forms 1065 and Schedules K, and K-1 (Form 1065).

542 Tax Information on Corporations
Forms 1120 and 1120A

544 Sales and Other Dispositions of Assets
This publication explains how to figure gain and loss on various transactions, such as trading, selling, or exchanging an asset used in a trade or business. It explains capital and noncapital assets and the tax results of different types of gains and losses.
Schedule D (Form 1040) and Forms 4797 and 8824.

547 Business and Nonbusiness Disasters, Casualties, and Thefts
This publication explains when you can deduct a disaster, casualty, or theft loss occurring from events such as hurricanes, earthquakes, tornadoes, fires, floods, vandalism, loss of deposits in a bankrupt or insolvent financial institution, and car accidents. It also explains how to treat the reimbursement you receive from insurance or other sources.
Form 4684.

550 Investment Income and Expenses
Forms 1099-INT and 1099-DIV, 4952, 6781, and 8815, and Schedules B and D (Form 1040).

551 Basis of Assets
This publication explains how to determine the basis of property, which is usually its cost.

552 Recordkeeping for Individuals

553 Highlights of 1998 Tax Changes

554 Older Americans Tax Guide
Schedules B, D, and R (Form 1040), and Forms 1040, 1040A and 2119.

555 Federal Tax Information on Community Property
This publication may help married taxpayers who reside in a community property state-- Arizona, California, Idaho, Louisiana, Nevada, New Mexico, Texas, Washington or Wisconsin. If you file a separate tax return, you should understand how community property laws affect the way you figure your tax before completing your federal income tax return.

556 Examination of Returns, Appeal Rights, and Claims for Refund
Forms 1040X and 1120X

556SP Revision de las Declaraciones de Impuesto, Derecho de Apelacion y Reclamaciones de Reembolsos (Examination of Returns, Appeal Rights, and Claims for Refund)
(Spanish version of Publication 556).
Forms 1040X and 1120X.

557 Tax-Exempt Status for Your Organization
This publication discusses the rules and procedures that apply to organizations seeking and retaining exemption from federal income tax under section 501(a) of the internal Revenue Code of 1986.
Forms 990, 990EZ, 990PF, 1023, and 1024.

Free Tax Help

559 Survivors, Executors, and Administrators
This publication can help you report and pay the proper federal income tax if you are responsible for settling a decedent's estate. It answers many questions that a spouse or other survivor faces when a person dies.
Forms 1040, 1041, and 4810.

560 Retirement Plans for the Self-Employed
Plans discussed include Simplified Employee Pensions (SEPs) and Keogh (H.R. 10) plans.
Forms 5305-SEP and 5500EZ.

561 Determining the Value of Donated Property
Form 8283.

564 Mutual Fund Distributions
This publication discusses the tax treatment of distributions paid or allocated to an individual shareholder of a mutual fund, and explains how to figure gain or loss on the sale of mutual fund shares. Forms 1040, Schedules B and D (Form 1040), and Form 1099-DIV.

570 Tax Guide for Individuals with Income from U.S. Possessions
This publication is for individuals with income from American Samoa, Guam, the Commonwealth of the Northern Mariana Islands, Puerto Rico, or the U.S. Virgin Islands. Forms 4563, 5074, and 8689.

571 Tax-Sheltered Annuity Programs for Employees of Public Schools and Certain Tax-Exempt Organizations
This publication explains the rules concerning employers qualified to buy tax-sheltered annuities, eligible employees who may participate in the program, and the amounts that may be excluded from income. Form 5330.

575 Pension and Annuity Income (Including Simplified General Rule)
This publication explains how to report this income and discusses the special tax treatment you may be able to get for lump-sum distributions from pension, stock bonus, or profit-sharing plans. It also discusses rollovers from qualified retirement plans. Forms 1040, 1040A, 1099-R and 4972.

578 Tax Information for Private Foundations and Foundation Managers
Form 990-F.

579SP Como Preparar la Declaracion de Impuesto Federal (How to Prepare the Federal Income Tax Return)
Forms 1040, 1040EZ, 1040A, 1040A (Espanol) and Schedules 1, 2, and EIC (Form 1040A (Espanol)).

583 Taxpayers Starting a Business
Schedule C (Form 1040), and Form 4562.

584 Nonbusiness Disaster, Casualty, and Theft Loss Workbook

584SP Registro de Perdidas Personales Causadas por Hechos Fortuitos (Imprevisto) o Robos
(Spanish version of Publication 584)

587 Business Use of Your Home
Form 8829.

589 Tax Information on S Corporations
Forms 1120S and Schedule K-1 (Form 1120S).

590 Individual Retirement Arrangements (IRAs)
This publication explains the rules for IRAs as well as the penalties for not following them. An IRA is a personal savings plan that offers you tax advantages to set aside money for your retirement. It also discusses simplified employee pension (SEP) plans. Forms 1040, 1040A, 5329, 8606.

593 Tax Highlights for U.S. Citizens and Residents Going Abroad
A brief overview of various U.S. tax provisions that apply to U.S. citizens and resident aliens who live or work abroad and expect to receive income from foreign sources.

594 Understanding the Collection Process
This booklet explains your rights and duties as a taxpayer who owes federal taxes. It also explains how the IRS fulfills its legal obligation to collect these taxes.

594SP Comprendiendo el Proceso de Cobro (Understanding the Collection Process
(Spanish version of Publication 594.)

596 Earned Income Credit
If you work and have a child living with you, you may qualify for the earned income credit. This publication discusses who may receive the credit, how to figure and claim the credit, and how to receive advance payments of the credit. Forms W-5, 1040, 1040A and Schedule EIC.

596SP Credito por Ingreso del Trabajo (Earned Income Credit)
(Spanish version of Pub. 596).

597 Information on the United States-Canada Income Tax Treaty
This publication reproduces the text of the U.S.-Canada income tax treaty, and explains its key provisions. It discusses certain tax problems that may be encountered by Canadian residents who temporarily work in the United States.

598 Tax on Unrelated Business Income of Exempt Organizations
This publication explains the tax provisions that apply to most tax-exempt organizations that regularly operate a trade or business that is not substantially related to its exempt purpose. Generally, a tax-exempt organization with gross income of $1,000 or more from an unrelated trade or business must file a return and pay any taxes due. Form 990-T.

686 Certification for Reduced Tax Rates in Tax Treaty Countries
This publication explains how U.S. citizens, residents, and domestic corporations may certify to a foreign country that they are entitled to tax treaty benefits.

721 Tax Guide to U.S. Civil Service Retirement Benefits
Forms 1040 and 1040A.

850 English-Spanish Glossary of Words and Phrases Used in Publications Issued by the Internal Revenue Service

901 U.S. Tax Treaties
This publication discusses the reduced tax rates and exemptions from U.S. taxes provided under U.S. tax treaties with foreign countries. It is intended for residents of those countries who receive income from U.S. sources, but may be useful to U.S. citizens and residents with income from abroad.
Forms 1040NR and 8833.

904 Interrelated Computations for Estate and Gift Taxes
Forms 706 and 709.

907 Information for Persons with Disabilities
Schedules A and R (Form 1040), and Form 2441.

908 Bankruptcy and Other Debt Cancellation
Forms 982, 1040, 1041, 1120.

909 Alternative Minimum Tax for Individuals
Forms 6251, and 8801.

IRS Tax Forms and Publications

911 Tax Information for Direct Sellers
A direct seller is a person who sells consumer products to others on a person-to-person basis, such as door-to-door, at sales parties, or by appointment in someone's home. Information on figuring your income from direct sales and the kinds of expenses you may be able to deduct is provided.
Form 4562 and Schedules C and SE (Form 1040).

915 Social Security Benefits and Equivalent Railroad Retirement Benefits
Forms SSA-1042S and RRB-1042S, SSA-1099 and RRB-1099, Social Security Benefits Worksheets, and Notice 703.

917 Business Use of a Car
Form 2106.

919 Is My Withholding Correct for 1999?
Explains Form W-4 to help you make sure the right amount of tax is withheld from you pay.
Form W-4.

924 Reporting of Real Estate Transactions to IRS
This publication informs sellers of certain real estate about the information they must provide to the real estate reporting person in order that the reporting person can complete the Form 1099-S that must be filed with the IRS.

925 Passive Activity and At-Risk Rules
Form 8582.

926 Employment Taxes for Household Employers
You may be a household employer if you have a babysitter, maid, gardener or other person who works at your house. This publication explains what taxes to withhold and pay, and what records to keep.
Forms W-2, W-3, W-5, 940, 940-EZ, and 942.

929 Tax Rules for Children and Dependents
This publication explains filing requirements and the standard deduction amount for dependents. It also explains when and how a child's parents may include their child's interest and dividend income on their return, and when and how a child's interest, dividends and other investment income is taxed at the parents' tax rate.
Forms 8615, and 8814.

936 Home Mortgage Interest Deduction
Form 1040 and Schedule A (Form 1040).

937 Employment Taxes and Information Returns
This publication explains your tax responsibilities and reporting requirements if you have employees.
Forms W-2, W-4, 940, 941, and 1099-MISC.

938 Real Estate Mortgage Investment Conduits (REMICS) Reporting Information (And Other Collateralized Debt Obligations (CDOs))
This publication discusses reporting requirements for issuers of real estate mortgage investment conduits (REMICS) and collateralized debt obligations (CDOs) and contains a directory of REMICs and CDOs to assist brokers and middlemen with their reporting requirements.

939 Pension General Rule (Nonsimplified Method)
This publication covers the nonsimplified General Rule for the taxation of pensions and annuities, which must be used if the Simplified General Rule does not apply or is not chosen. For example, the nonsimplified method must be used for payments under commercial annuities. The publication also contains needed actuarial tables.

945 Tax Information for Those Affected by Operation Desert Storm

946 How to Begin Depreciating your Property

947 Power of Attorney and Practice Before the IRS
This publication explains who can represent a taxpayer before the IRS and what forms or documents are used to authorize a person to represent a taxpayer.
Forms 2848 and 8821.

950 Introduction to Estate and Gift Taxes
An easy-to-read publication that briefly outlines some of the topics covered in Publication 448, Federal Estate and Gift Taxes.

953 International Tax information for Businesses
Covers topics of interest to U.S. citizens and resident aliens with foreign investments and nonresident aliens who want to invest in U.S. businesses.

954 Tax Incentives for Empowerment Zones and Other Distressed Communities
This publication is for business owners who want to find out whether they qualify for certain tax incentives. These incentives are intended to help empowerment zones, enterprise communities, and other distressed communities.

957 Reporting Back Pay and Special Wage Payments to the Social Security Administration
The Social Security Administration (SSA) has special rules for back pay awarded by a court or government agency under a statute (a law) to enforce a worker's protection law. The SSA also has rules for reporting special wage payments made to employees after they retire. These rules enable the SSA to correctly compute an employee's benefits under the social security earnings test. These rules are for social security coverage and benefit purposes only.

967 IRS Will Figure Your Tax For You
You can have the IRS figure your tax on Form 1040EZ, Form 1040A, or Form 1040 if you mail your return by April 15, 1999. If you paid too much, you will receive a refund. If you did not pay enough, you will receive a bill for the balance. To avoid interest or penalty for late payment you must pay the bill within 30 days of the date of your bill or by the due date for your return, whichever is later. The IRS will also figure the credit for the elderly or the disabled and earned income credit.

968 Tax Benefits for Adoptions
This publication explains two new tax benefits available to offset the expenses of adopting a child. These benefits begin in 1997. The first part of the publication is for persons who have recently adopted a child, are in the process of adopting a child, or are considering adopting a child. The second part is for employers who provide adoption assistance payments to workers.

969 Medical Savings Accounts
This publication explains Medical Savings Accounts (MSAs). MSAs were created to help self-employed individuals and employees of certain small employers meet the costs of medical care.

971 Innocent Spouse Relief
In certain cases, a spouse is relieved of responsibility for tax, interest, and penalties on a joint tax return.

1004 Identification Numbers Under ERISA

1045 Information for Tax Practitioners

1212 List of Original Discount Instruments
This publication explains the tax treatment of original issue discount (OID) by brokers and other middlemen and by owners of OID debt instruments.

1244 Employee's Daily Record of Tips (Form 4070-A) and Employee's Report of Tips to Employer (Form 4070)
Forms 4070 and 4070-A.

1437 Procedures for Electronic and Magnetic Media Filing of US Income Tax Return for Estates and Trusts

1542 Per Diem Rates
This publication is for employers who pay a per diem allowance to employees for business travel away from home, on or after January 1, 1998, within the continental United States.

1544 Reporting Cash Payments of Over $10,000 (Received in a Trade or Business)
Explains when and how persons in a trade or business must file a Form 8300 when they receive cash payments of more than $10,000 from one buyer. It also discusses the substantial penalties for not filing the form. Form 8300.

Free Tax Help

1546 How To Use the Problem Resolution Program of the IRS

1915 Understanding Your IRS Individual Taxpayer Identification Number
An ITIN, or Individual Taxpayer Identification Number, is a tax processing number that became available on July 1, 1996, for certain nonresident and resident aliens, their spouses, and their dependents. The ITIN is only available to individuals who cannot get a Social Security Number (SSN).

2053 Quick and Easy Access to IRS Tax Help and Forms/Fax Forms List:

2183 IRS Customer Service Standards Annual Report 1997
The employees of the Internal Revenue Service want to provide good service and this annual report demonstrates how we are achieving our goal to become a customer-focused organization.

2188 Tax Item, Request for IRS to Figure Taxable Part of Annuity
If you are a retiree, or the survivor of an employee or retiree, and you cannot determine how much of the annuity you receive is taxable, you can ask the Internal Revenue Service to figure the amount for you.

3079 Gaming Publication for Tax-Exempt Organizations
All exempt organizations conducting or sponsoring gaming activities, whether for one night out of the year or throughout the year, whether in their primary place of operation or at remote sites, must be aware of the federal requirements.

3106 Overview of Imaging Reimbursements Program for Gasoline Station Owners

3114 Checks Compliance
A compliance check is a review conducted by the IRS, under Title 26 of the Internal Revenue Code, to determine whether a business owner (or individual) is adhering to record keeping and information reporting requirements.

3125 An Important Message For Taxpayers With IRAs

3204 Automotive Manufacturers Incentive Program
Did you know that incentive payments paid by an automotive manufacturer whether directly to individual salespersons or through a dealer are taxable income?

Numerical List of Federal Tax Return Forms and Related Forms

Timber/Forest Industries Schedules
Supplement to income tax return for taxpayers claiming a deduction for depletion of timber and for depreciation of plant and other timber improvements.
IT-IRC sec. 631; Regs. sec. 1.611-3: IT-IRC sec. 6012

Package X
Informational Copies of Federal Income Tax Forms
A three-volume set that contains most of the principal income tax and information return forms. It is the primary form reference for tax practitioners.

CT-1
Employer's Annual Railroad Retirement and Unemployment Repayment Tax Return
Used to report employees' and employers' taxes under the RRTA and RURT.
Emp-IRC secs. 3201, 3202, 3221, 3321, 3322, and 6011; Regs. secs. 31.6011(a)-2, 31.6011(a)-3A, 31.6302(c)-2 and 31.6302-3T; Separate instructions

CT-2
Employee Representative's Quarterly Railroad Tax Return
Used to report employee representative's tax under the RRTA and RURT.
Emp-IRC secs. 3211, 3321, and 6011; Regs. secs. 31.6011(a)-2 and 31.6011(a)-3A

W-2
Wage and Tax Statement
Used to report wages, tips and other compensation, allocated tips, employee social security and Medicare tax, Federal, state or city income tax withheld; and to support credit shown on individual income tax return.
Emp-IRC sec 6051; Regs secs 1.6041-2 and 31.6051-1; Circular E; Separate instructions

W-2AS
American Samoa Wage and Tax Statement
Used to report wages, tips, and other compensation, employee social security and Medicare tax, Samoan income tax withheld, and to support credit shown on American Samoa individual income tax return.
Emp-IRC sec. 6051; Regs. sec. 31.6051-1, Circular S

W-2c
Statement of Corrected Income and Tax Amounts
Used to correct previously filed Forms W-2, W-2AS, W-2CM, W-2GU, and W-2VI. Also used to correct Form W-2P for years ending before 1991.
Emp-IRC sec. 6051; Reg. sec. 1.6041-2 and 31.6051-1

W-2c PR
Corrected Withholding Statement
Used to correct previously filed Forms 499R-2/W-2PR. Emp-IRC sec. 6051; Regs. sec. 1.6041-2 and 31.6051.1

499R-2/W-2PR
Puerto Rico Withholding Statement
Used to report social security wages, tips, and social security and Medicare tax withheld for employees in Puerto Rico.
Emp-IRC sec. 6051; Regs. sec. 31.6051-1; Circular PR

W-2G
Certain Gambling Winnings
Used to report gambling winnings and any taxes withheld.
IT-IRC secs. 3402(q) and 6041; Temp. Regs. sec. 7.6041-1 and Regs. sec. 31.3402(q)-1(f); See separate Instructions for Forms 1099, 1098, 5498, and W-2G.

W-2GU
Guam Wage and Tax Statement
Used to report wages, tips and other compensation, employee social security and Medicare tax, Guam income tax withheld, and to support credit shown on individual income tax return. Emp-IRC sec. 6051; Regs. sec. 31.6051-1; Circular SS

W-2VI
U.S. Virgin Islands Wage and Tax Statement
Used to report wages, tips and other compensation, employee social security and Medicare tax, VI income tax withheld, and to support credit shown on individual income tax return. Emp-IRC sec. 6051; Regs. secs. 1.6041-2 and 31.6051-1; Circular SS

W-3
Transmittal of Income and Tax Statements
Used by employers and other payers to transmit Forms W-2 to the Social Security Administration. W-2 magnetic media filers use transmittal Form 6559. Emp-IRC sec. 6011; Reg. sec. 31.6051-2

W-3c
Transmittal of Corrected Income and Tax Statements
Used by employers and other payers to transmit corrected income and tax statements (Forms W-2c).
Emp-IRC sec. 6011; Reg. 31.6051-2

W-3SS
Transmittal of Wage and Tax Statements
Used by employers to transmit Forms W-2AS, W-2CM, W-2GU, and W-2VI.
Emp-IRC sec. 6011; Reg. sec. 31.6051-2; Circular SS

W-4
Employee's Withholding Allowance Certificate
Completed by employee and given to employer so that proper amount of income tax can be withheld from wages. Also used by employee to claim exemption from

IRS Tax Forms and Publications

withholding by certifying that he or she had no liability for income tax for preceding tax year and anticipates that no liability will be incurred for current tax year. Emp-IRC secs. 3402(f), 3402(m) and 3402(n); Regs. secs. 31.3402(f)5)-1 and 31.3402(n)-1; Circular E

W-4P
Withholding Certificate for Pension or Annuity Payments
Used to figure amount of Federal income tax to withhold from periodic pension or annuity payments or to claim additional withholding or exemption from withholding for periodic or nonperiodic payments. Emp-IRC sec. 3405

W-4S
Request for Federal Income Tax Withholding from Sick Pay
Filed with a third party payer of sick pay to request Federal income tax withholding. Emp-IRC sec. 3402(o); Regs. sec. 31.3402(o)-3

W-5
Earned Income Credit Advance Payment Certificate
Used by employees to request advance payment of part of the basic earned income credit. IRC sec. 3507

W-8
Certificate of Foreign Status
Used by foreign persons to notify payers of mortgage interest recipients, middlemen, brokers, or barter exchanges that they are exempt foreign persons not subject to certain U.S. information return reporting or backup withholding rules. IRC secs. 3406, 6042, 6044, 6045, and 6049, 6050H and 6050N; Temp. reg. 35a.9999

W-9
Request for Taxpayer Identification Number and Certification
Used by a person required to file certain information returns with IRS to obtain the correct taxpayer identification number (TIN) of the person for whom a return is filed. Also used to claim exemption from backup withholding and to certify that the person whose TIN is provided is not subject to backup withholding because of failure to report interest and dividends as income. Emp.IRC sec. 3406; Temp. Regs. secs. 35a.3406-1, 35a.9999-1, 35a.9999-2, and 35a.9999-3

W-10
Dependent Care Provider's Identification and Certification
Used by taxpayers to certify that the name, address, and taxpayer identification number of their dependent care provider is correct. IRS secs. 21, 129.501(a), 501(c)3

SS-4
Application for Employer Identification Number
Used by employers and other entities to apply for an identification number. Emp-IRC Regs. sec. 31.6011(b)-1, 301.6109-1

SS-4 PR
Solicitud de Numero de Identificacion Patronal
Used by employers and other entities in Puerto Rico to apply for an identification number. A variation of Form SS-4. Emp-IR Regs. sec. 31.6011(b)-1, 301.6109-1

SS-8
Determination of Employee Work Status for Purposes of Federal Employment Taxes and Income Tax Withholding
Used by employers and workers to furnish information to the IRS in order to obtain a determination as to whether a worker is an employee for purposes of Federal employment taxes and income tax withholding. Emp-IRC sec. 3121; Regs. sec. 31.3121(d)-1, 31.3401(c)-1 and (d)-1

SS-16
Certificate of Election of Coverage Under the Federal Insurance Contributions Act
Used by religious orders or autonomous subdivisions, whose members are required to take a vow of poverty, to certify election of social security and Medicare coverage for services the members perform.
Emp-IRC sec. 3121(r); Regs. sec. 31.3121(r)-1

11-C
Occupational Tax and Registration Return for Wagering
Used to report taxes due under IRC sections 4401 and 4411, and as an application for registry and wagering activity. Upon approval of the return, the Service will issue a Special Tax Stamp. Ex-IRC secs. 4411 and 4412; Regs. secs. 44.4412 and 44.4901

56
Notice Concerning Fiduciary Relationship
Used by persons to notify IRS that they are acting in fiduciary capacity for other persons.
IT-IRC sec. 6903; Regs. sec. 301.6903-1

637
Application for Registration
Used as an application and certificate; by manufacturers, refiners or importers who buy taxable articles tax-free for further manufacture of taxable articles, or for resale direct to a manufacturer for such purpose. The original of the application is validated and returned as the Certificate of Registry by the District Director. Ex-IRC secs. 4052, 4064(b)(1)(c), 4101, 4221, and 4661; Regs. secs. 48.4101-1, 48.4222(a)-1, and 48.4222(d)-1; Separate instructions

706
United States Estate (and Generation-Skipping Transfer) Tax Return
Used for the estate of a deceased United States resident or citizen with a date of death after December 31, 1992.
E&G-IRC sec. 6018; Regs. sec. 20.6018-1; Separate instructions

706-A
United States Additional Estate Tax Return
Used to report recapture tax under special use valuation.
E&G-IRC sec. 2032A; Separate instructions

706CE
Certificate of Payment of Foreign Death Tax
Used to report credit against United States estate tax for estate inheritance, legacy, or succession tax paid to a foreign government.
E&G-IRC sec. 2014; Regs. sec. 20.2014-5

706GS(D)
Generation-Skipping Transfer Tax Return for Distributions
Used by distributees to report generation-skipping transfer tax on taxable distributions from trusts subject to the tax.
E&G-IRC sec. 2601; Temp Regs. sec. 26.2662-1(b)(1); Separate instructions

706GS(D-1)
Notification of Distribution from a Generation-Skipping Trust
Used by trustees to report certain information to distributees regarding taxable distributions from a trust subject to the generation-skipping transfer tax.
E&G-IRC sec. 2601; Temp. Regs. sec. 26.2662-1(b)(1); Separate instructions

706GS(T)
Generation-Skipping Transfer Tax Return for Terminations
Used by trustees to report generation-skipping transfer tax on taxable terminations of trusts subject to the tax.
E&G-IRC sec. 2601; Temp. Regs. sec. 26.2662-1(b)2); Separate instructions

706NA
United States Estate (and Generation-Skipping Transfer) Tax Return, Estate of nonresident not a citizen of the United States
Used for United States nonresident alien decedent's estate to be filed within 9 months after date of death.
E&G-IRC sec. 6018; Regs. sec. 20.6018-1(b); Separate instructions

Free Tax Help

706-QDT
U.S. Estate Tax Return for Qualified Domestic Trusts
Used by trustee or designated filer to report estate tax on distribution from qualified domestic trust or on property in trust at death of surviving spouse.
E&G-IRC sec. 2056A. Separate instructions

709
United States Gift (and Generation-Skipping Transfer) Tax Return
Used to report gifts of more than $10,000 made after December 31, 1992 (or, regardless of value, gifts of a future interest in property).
E&G-IRC sec. 6019; Regs. sec. 25.6019-1; Separate instructions

709-A
United States Short Form Gift Tax Return
Used to report gifts of more than $10,000 but not more than $20,000 if the gifts are nontaxable by reason of gift splitting.
E&G-IRC secs. 6019, 6075; Regs. sec. 25.6019-1

712
Life Insurance Statement
Used with Form 706 or 709.
E&G-IRC secs 6001 and 6018; Regs secs 20.6001-1, 20.6018-4(d), 25.6001-1(b)

720
Quarterly Federal Excise Tax Return
Used to report excise taxes due from retailers and manufacturers on sale or manufacture of various articles; taxes on facilities and services; taxes on certain products and commodities (gasoline, coal, etc); and Inland waterways taxes.
Ex-IRC sec. 6011; Separate instructions

730
Tax on Wagering
Used to report taxes due under IRC section 4401.
Ex-IRC sec. 4401; Regs. sec. 44.6011(a)-1

843
Claim for Refund and Request for Abatement
Used to claim refund of taxes (other than income taxes) which were illegally, erroneously or excessively collected; or to claim amount paid for stamps unused or used in error or excess; and for a refund or abatement of interest or penalties assessed.
Misc-IRC secs. 6402, 6404, 6511, 6404(e), and 6404(f); Regs. secs. 31.6413(c)-1, 301.6402-2, and 301.6404-1; Separate instructions

851
Affiliations Schedule
Used with Form 1120 by parent corporation for affiliated corporations included in consolidated tax return. IT-IRC sec. 1502; Regs. sec. 1.1502-75(h)

926
Return by a U.S. Transferor of Property to a Foreign Corporation, Foreign Trust or Estate, or Foreign Partnership
Used to report transfers of property by a U.S. person to a foreign partnership, trust or estate, or corporation, and pay any excise tax due on the transfer. Also used to report section 6038B information. IT-IRC sec. 1491, 6038B; Regs. sec. 1.1491-2

928
Fuel Bond
Used to post bond for excise tax on fuel and gasoline. Ex-IRC sec. 4101

940
Employer's Annual Federal Unemployment (FUTA) Tax Return
Used by employers to report Federal unemployment (FUTA) tax.
Emp-IRC sec 6011; IRC Chapter 23; Regs sec 31.6011(a)-3; Circular A; Circular E; Circular SS; Separate instructions

940-EZ
Employer's Annual Federal Unemployment (FUTA) Tax Return
Used by employers to report Federal unemployment (FUTA) tax. This form is a simplified version of Form 940. EMP-IRC sec. 6011; IRC Chapter 23; Regs. sec. 31.6011(a)-3; Circular A; Circular E; Circular SS

940PR
Planilla Para La Declaracion Anual Del Patrono-La Contribucion Federal Para el Desempleo (FUTA)
Used by employers in Puerto Rico. A variation of Form 940.
Emp-IRC sec. 6011; IRC Chapter 23; Regs. sec. 31.6011(a)-3; Circular PR

941
Employer's Quarterly Federal Tax Return
Used by employer to report social security and Medicare taxes and income taxes withheld, advance earned income credit (EIC), and back up withholding.
Emp-IRC secs. 3101, 3111, 3402, 3405 and 3406; Regs. secs. 31.6011(a)-1 and 31.6011(a)-4; Circular E

Sch. A (Form 941)
Record of Federal Backup Withholding Tax Liability
Used to report backup withholding liability when treated as a separate tax for depositing purposes. Emp-IRC secs. 3406, 6302; Regs. secs. 31.6302 and 35a.9999-3

Sch. B (Form 941)
Employer's Record of Federal Tax Liability
Used by employers required to deposit on a semiweekly basis to report employment tax liability. Emp-IRC sec. 6302(g)

Anexo B (Forma 941-PR)
Registro suplementario de la obligacion contributive federal Del Patrono
Used by employers in Puerto Rico. A variation of Schedule B (Form 941).
Emp-IRC sec. 6302(g)

941c
Supporting Statement to Correct Information
Used by employers as a supporting statement for employment tax adjustment.
Emp-IRC secs. 6205 and 6402; Regs. secs. 31.6011(a)-1, 31.6205-1, and 31.6402(a)-2; Circulars A, E, and SS

941c PR
Planilla Para La Correccion De Informacion Facilitada Anteriormente En Complimiento Con La Ley Del Seguro Social del Seguro Medicare
Used by employers in Puerto Rico. A variation of Form 941c. Emp-IRC Chapter 21; Regs secs 31.6011(a)-1 and 31.6205-1, 31.6402(a)-2; Circular PR

941E
Quarterly Return of Withheld Federal Income Tax and Medicare Tax
Used by State and local government employers and by other organizations that are not liable for social security taxes. A variation of Form 941.
Emp-IRC secs. 3121(u) and 3402

941-M
Employer's Monthly Federal Tax Return
Used by employers to report withheld income tax and social security taxes (because they have not complied with the requirements for filing quarterly returns, or for paying or depositing taxes reported on quarterly returns). Emp-IRC sec. 7512; Regs. sec. 31.6011(a)-5

941 PR
Planilla Para La Declaracion Trimestral Del Patrono-La Contribucion Federal al Seguro Social al Seguro Medicare
Used by employers in Puerto Rico. A variation of Form 941. Emp-IRC secs. 3101 and 3111; Regs. sec. 31.6011(a)-1; Circular PR

941-SS
Employer's Quarterly Federal Tax Return
Used by employers in Virgin Islands, Guam, the Northern Mariana Islands, and American Samoa. A variation of Form 941. Emp-IRC secs. 3101 and 3111; Regs. sec. 31.6011(a)-1; Circular SS

IRS Tax Forms and Publications

943
Employer's Annual Tax Return for Agricultural Employees
Used by agricultural employers to report social security, Medicare, and income taxes withheld. Emp-IRC secs. 3101, 3111 and 3402; Regs. sec. 31.6011(a)-1 and 31.6011(a)-4; Circular A

943A
Agricultural Employer's Record of Federal Tax Liability
Used by agricultural employers who have a tax liability of $3,000 or more during any month. Emp-IRC sec. 6302; Regs. sec. 6302(c)-1; Circular A

943 PR
Planilla Para La Declaracion Anual De La Contribucion Del Patrono De Empleados Agricolas
Used by agricultural employers in Puerto Rico. A variation of Form 943. Emp-IRC secs 3101 and 3111; Regs sec 31.6011(a)-1, 31.6011(a)-4; Circular PR

943A-PR
Registro De La Obligacion Contributiva Del Patrono Agricola
Used by agricultural employers in Puerto Rico. A variation of Form 943A. Emp-IRC sec. 6302; Regs. sec. 31.6302(c)-1; Circular PR

952
Consent to Fix Period of Limitation on Assessment of Income Taxes
Used when complete liquidation of a subsidiary is not accomplished within the tax year in which the first liquidating distribution is made. The receiving corporation is required to file this consent with its return for each tax year which falls wholly or partly within the period of liquidation. IT-IRC sec. 332; Regs. sec. 1.332-4

966
Corporate Dissolution or Liquidation
Used (under IRC section 6043(a)) by corporations within 30 days after adoption of resolution or plan of dissolution, or complete or partial liquidation. (An information return.) IT-IRC sec. 6043(a)

970
Application to Use LIFO Inventory Method
Used to change to the LIFO inventory method provided by section 472. IT-IRC sec. 472; Regs. sec. 1.472-3

972
Consent of Shareholder to Include Specific Amount in Gross Income
Used by shareholders of a corporation who agree to include in their gross income for their taxable year a specific amount as a tax dividend. IT-IRC sec. 565

973
Corporation Claim for Deduction for Consent Dividends
Used by corporations that claim a consent dividends deduction. Accompanied by filed consents of shareholders on Form 972. IT-IRC sec. 561

976
Claim for Deficiency Dividends Deduction by a Personal Holding Company, Regulated Investment Company, or Real Estate Investment Trust
Used by a personal holding company, regulated investment company, or real estate investment trust to claim a deficiency dividends deduction. IT-IRC sec. 547 and 860; Regs. sec. 1.547-2(b)(2) and 1.860-2(b)(2)

982
Reduction of Tax Attributes Due to Discharge of Indebtedness
Used by a taxpayer who excludes from gross income under section 108 any amount of income attributable to discharge of indebtedness. Also used as a consent of a corporation to adjustment of basis of its property under regulations prescribed under IRC section 1082(a)(2).
IT-IRC secs. 108, 1017, and 1082

990
Return of Organization Exempt From Income Tax Under section 501(c) of the Internal Revenue Code (except black lung benefit trust or private foundation) or Section 4947(a)(1) charitable trust.
Used by organizations exempt under IRC section 501(a) and described in Code section 501(c), other than private foundations. (An information return.) Also used by nonexempt section 4947(a)(1) charitable trusts not treated as a private foundation. IT-IRC sec. 6033; Regs. sec. 1.6033-1(a)(2); Separate instructions

Sch. A (Form 990)
Organization Exempt Under 501 (c)(3) (Supplementary Information)
Used by organizations described in IRC section 501(c)(3), 501(e), 501(f), and 501(k), and section 4947(a)(1) charitable trusts (other than private foundations filing Form 990-PF). Attach to Form 990 or 990EZ. IT-IRC sec. 6033; Separate instructions

990-BL
Information and Initial Excise Tax Return for Black Lung Benefit Trusts and Certain Related Persons
Used by Black Lung Benefit Trusts exempt under Section 501(c)(21) as an information return. Also used by these trusts and certain related persons for attaching Schedule A (Form 990-BL) when taxes under sections 4951 or 4952 are due. IT/EX-IRC sec. 501 (c)(21); Chapter 42; Separate instructions

990-C
Farmers' Cooperative Association Income Tax Return
Used by Farmers' Cooperative Marketing and Purchasing Association.
IT-IRC secs. 521, 1381, 1382, 1383, 1385, 1388, and 6012; Regs. secs. 1.522-1, 1.1381-1, 2, 1.1382-1, 2, 3, 4, 5, 6, 7, 1.1383-1, 1.1385-1, 1.1388-1, and 1.6012-2(f); Separate instructions

990-EZ
Short Form Return of Organization Exempt Form Income Tax Under Section 501(c) of the Internal Revenue Code
Used by organizations exempt under IRC section 501(a) with gross receipts less than $100,000 and total assets of less than $250,000 at end of year. IT-IRC sec. 6033; Regs. sec. 1.6033-1(a)(2); Separate instructions

990-PF
Return of Private Foundation or Section 4947(a)(1) Charitable Trust Treated as a Private Foundation
Used to figure and pay the excise tax on investment income. It is also used as a substitute for the nonexempt section 4947(a)(1) charitable trusts income tax return when trust has no taxable income. IT/Ex-IRC sec. 6033; IRC Chapter 42; Separate instructions

990-T
Exempt Organization Business Income Tax Return
Used by exempt organization with unrelated business income of $1,000 or more (under IRC section 511). IT-IRC secs. 511 and 6012; Regs. secs. 1.6012-2(e) and 1.6012-3(a)(5); Separate instructions

990-W
Estimated Tax on Unrelated Business Taxable Income for Tax-Exempt Organizations
Used as a worksheet by tax-exempt trusts and tax-exempt corporations to figure their estimated tax liability. Tax-exempt trusts and corporations should keep it for their records. IT-IRC sec. 6655

1000
Ownership Certificate
Used by a citizen, resident individual, fiduciary, partnership, or nonresident partnership all of whose members are citizens or residents who have interest in bonds of a domestic or resident corporation (containing a tax-free covenant and issued before January 1, 1934). IT-IRC sec. 1461; Regs. sec. 1.1461-1(h)

Free Tax Help

1001
Ownership, Exemption, or Reduced Rate Certificate
Used by a nonresident alien individual or fiduciary, foreign partnership, foreign corporation or other foreign entity, nonresident foreign partnership composed in whole or in part of nonresident aliens (applies to IRC section 1451 only), or nonresident foreign corporation (applies to Code section 1451 only), receiving income subject to withholding under Code section 1441, 1442, or 1451.
IT-IRC sec. 1461; Regs. sec. 1.1461-1(i)

Package 1023
Application for Recognition of Exemption
Used to apply for exemption under section 501(a) IRC as organizations described in section 501(c)3-(also sections 501(e) and (f)). Includes 3 copies of Form 872-C. IT-IRC sec. 501; Regs. sec. 1.501(a)-1(a)(3)

Package 1024
Application for Recognition of Exemption Under Section 501(a) or Determination Under Section 120
Used by organizations to apply for exemption under IRC section 501(a) (as described in Code sections 501(c)(2),(4), (5), (6), (7), (8), (9), (10), (12), (13), (15), (17), (19), (20) and (25). (Also used to apply for a determination as a qualified plan under section 120.)
IT-IRC secs. 501, 120; Regs. sec. 1.501(a)-1(a)3

1028
Application for Recognition of Exemption
Used by farmers, fruit growers, or similar associations to claim exemption under IRC section 521.
IT-IRC sec. 521; Regs. sec. 1.521-1, Separate instructions

1040
U.S. Individual Income Tax Return
Used by citizens or residents of the United States to report income tax. (Also see Form 1040A, and 1040EZ.)
IT-IRC secs. 6012 and 6017; Regs. secs. 1.6012-1 and 1.6017-1; Pub. 17; Separate instructions

Sch. A and B (Form 1040)
Itemized Deductions and Interest and Dividend Income
Used to report itemized deductions (medical and dental expense, taxes, contributions, interest, casualty and theft losses, moving expenses, miscellaneous deductions subject to the 2% AGI limit, and other miscellaneous deductions).
IT-IRC secs. 67, 68, 163, 164, 165, 166, 170, 211, 212, 213, and 217; Pub. 17; See the separate instructions for Form 1040.

Sch. B and A (Form 1040)
Interest and Dividend Income and Itemized Deductions
Used to list gross dividends received and interest income, claim the exclusion of interest from series EE U.S. Saving Bonds issued after 1989, and to answer questions about foreign accounts and foreign trusts. IT-IRC secs. 6012, 61, and 116; Pub. 17; See the separate Instructions for Form 1040.

Sch. C (Form 1040)
Profit or Loss From Business
Used to figure profit or (loss) from business or professions.
IT-IRC sec. 6017; Regs. sec. 1.6017-1; Pubs. 17 and 334; See separate instructions for Form 1040.

Sch. C-EZ (Form 1040)
Net Profit From Business
Used by individuals having gross receipts under $25,000 and expenses under $5,000.
IT-IRC sec. 6017; Reg. sec. 1.6017-1

Sch. D (Form 1040)
Capital Gains and Losses
Used to report details of gain (or loss) from sales or exchanges of capital assets; to figure capital loss carryovers from 1990 to 1991, and to reconcile Forms 1099-B for bartering transactions with amounts reported on the tax return.
IT-IRC secs. 1202-1223, 6045; Pubs. 17 and 334; See the separate Instructions for Form 1040.

Sch. D-1 (Form 1040)
Continuation Sheet for Schedule D (Form 1040)
Used to attach to Schedule D (Form 1040) to list additional transactions on lines 1a and 8a.
IT-IRC secs. 1202-1223, 6045

Sch. E (Form 1040)
Supplemental Income and Loss
Used to report income from rents, royalties, partnerships, S corporations, estates, trusts, REMICs, etc.
IT-IRC secs. 6012 and 6017; Regs. secs. 1.6012-1 and 1.6017-1; Pub. 17; See separate Instructions for Form 1040.

Sch. EIC (Forms 1040 and 1040A)
Earned Income Credit
Used to figure the earned income credit and provide required identifying information for qualifying children.
IT-IRC sec. 32; Pub. 17 and 596

Sch. F (Form 1040)
Profit or Loss From Farming
Used to figure profit or (loss) from farming.
IT-IRC sec. 6012; Regs. sec. 1.61-4; Pub. 225; See the separate Instructions for Form 1040.

Sch. R (Form 1040)
Credit for the Elderly or the Disabled
Used to figure credit for the elderly and for individuals under age 65 who retired on permanent and total disability and received taxable disability income.
IT-IRC sec. 22; Publications 17 and 524; Separate instructions

Sch. SE (Form 1040)
Self-Employment Tax
Used to figure self-employment tax.
IT-IRC secs. 1401 and 1402; See the separate Instructions for Form 1040.

1040A
U.S. Individual Income Tax Return
Used by citizens and residents of the United States to report income tax. (Also see Form 1040 and 1040EZ.)
IT-IRC sec. 6012; Regs. sec. 1.6012-1; Publication 17; Separate instructions

Sch. 1 (Form 1040A)
Interest and Dividend Income for Form 1040A Filers
Part I is used by Form 1040A filers to report interest income (if more than $400) and for claiming the exclusion of interest from series EE U.S. savings bonds issued after 1989. Part II is used by Form 1040A filers to report dividends received (if more than $400).
IT-IRC sec. 61; Publication 17

Sch. 2 (Form 1040A)
Child and Dependent Care Expenses for Form 1040A Filers
Used by Form 1040A filers to figure the credit for child and dependent care expenses and/or the exclusion of employer-provided dependent care benefits.
IT-IRC secs. 21 and 129; Regs. sec. 1.44A-1; Pub. 17 and 503

Sch. 3 (Form 1040A)
Credit for the Elderly or the Disabled for Form 1040A Filers
Used by Form 1040A filers to figure the credit for the elderly (age 65 or older) or the disabled (under 65 who retired on permanent disability and received taxable disability benefits).
IT-IRC sec. 22; Pub. 17 and 524; Separate instructions

1040C
U.S. Departing Alien Income Tax Return
Used by aliens who intend to depart from the U.S., to report income received, or expected to be received for the entire taxable year, determined as nearly as possible by the date of intended departure. (Also see Form 2063.)
IT-IRC sec. 6851; Regs. sec. 1.6851-2; Pub. 519; Separate instructions

IRS Tax Forms and Publications

1040-ES
Estimated Tax for Individuals
Used to pay income tax (including self-employment tax and alternative minimum tax) due (the tax that is more than the tax withheld from wages, salaries, and other payments for personal services). It is not required unless the total tax is more than withholding (if any) by $500 or more. IT-IRC sec. 6654

1040-ES (Espanol)
Contribucion Federal Estimada Del Trabajo Por Cuenta Propia-Puerto Rico
Used in Puerto Rico. The payment vouchers are provided for payment of self-employment tax on a current basis. IT-IRC sec. 6654

1040-ES (NR)
U.S. Estimated Tax for Nonresident Alien Individuals
Used by nonresident aliens to pay any income tax due in excess of the tax withheld. It is not required unless the total tax exceeds withholding (if any) by $500 or more. IT-IRC sec. 6654

1040EZ
Income Tax Return for Single Filers With No Dependents
Used by citizens and residents of the United States to report income tax. (Also see Form 1040 and Form 1040A.) IT-IRC sec. 6012; Reg. sec. 1.6012-1; Pub. 17; Separate instructions

1040NR
U.S. Nonresident Alien Income Tax Return
Used by all nonresident alien individuals, whether or not engaged in a trade or business within the United States, who file a U.S. tax return. Also used as required for filing nonresident alien fiduciary (estate and trusts) returns.
IT-IRC secs. 871 and 6012; Pub. 519; Separate instructions

1040 PR
Planilla Para La Declaracion De La Contribucio n Federal Sobre El Trabajo Por Cuenta Propia-Puerto Rico
Used in Puerto Rico to compute self-employment tax in accordance with IRC Chapter 2 of Subtitle A, and to provide proper credit to taxpayer's social security account. IT-IRC secs. 6017 and 7651; Regs. sec. 1.6017-1; Circular PR

1040SS
U.S. Self-Employment Tax Return-Virgin Islands, Guam, American Samoa and the Commonwealth of the Northern Mariana Islands
Used to compute self-employment tax in accordance with IRC Chapter 2 of Subtitle A, and to provide proper credit to taxpayer's social security account. IT-IRC secs. 6017 and 7651; Regs. sec. 1.6017-1; Circular SS

1040X
Amended U.S. Individual Income Tax Return
Used to claim refund of income taxes, pay additional income taxes, or designate dollar(s) to a Presidential election campaign fund.
IT-IRC secs. 6402, 6404, 6511, and 6096; Separate instructions

1041
U.S. Fiduciary Income Tax Return
Used by a fiduciary of a domestic estate or domestic trust to report income tax and alternative minimum tax. IT-IRC sec. 6012; Regs. secs. 1.671-4, 1.6012-3(a), and 1.6041-1; Separate instructions

Sch. D (Form 1041)
Capital Gains and Losses
Used to report details of gain (or loss) from sales or exchanges of capital assets. IT-IRC sec. 6012; Regs. sec. 1.6012-3(a)

Sch. J (Form 1041)
Trust Allocation of an Accumulation Distribution (Under IRC section 665)
Used by domestic complex trusts to report accumulation distributions. IT-IRC secs. 665, 666, and 667

Sch. K-1 (Form 1041)
Beneficiary's Share of Income, Deductions, Credits, etc.
Used to report each beneficiary's share of the income, deductions, credits, and distributable net alternative minimum taxable income from the estate or trust. IT-IRC sec. 6012; Regs. secs. 1.6012-3(a)

1041-A
U.S. Information Return-Trust Accumulation of Charitable Amounts
Used by a trust that claims a contribution deduction under IRC section 642(c), or by a trust described in Code section 4947(a)2). (An information return.)
IT-IRC secs. 6034 and 6104; Regs. sec. 1.6034-1

1041-ES
Estimated Income Tax for Fiduciaries
Used to figure and pay estimated tax for fiduciaries.
IT-IRC sec. 6654

1041-T
Allocation of Estimated Tax Payments to Beneficiaries
Used by an estate or trust to make an election under section 643(g) allocate an estimated tax payment to beneficiaries.
IT-IRC sec. 643(g)

1042
Annual Withholding Tax Return for U.S. Source Income of Foreign Persons
Used by withholding agents to report tax withheld at source on certain income paid to nonresident aliens, foreign partnerships, or foreign corporations not engaged in a trade or business in the U.S.
IT-IRC secs. 1441, 1442, 1461; Regs. secs. 1.1441-1 and 1.1461-2(b); Separate instructions

1042S
Foreign Person's U.S. Source Income Subject to Withholding
Used by a withholding agent to report certain income and tax withheld at source for foreign payees. (An information return.)
IT-IRC sec. 1461; Regs. sec. 1.1461-2(c); Separate instructions

1045
Application for Tentative Refund
Used by taxpayers (other than corporations) to apply for a tentative refund from the carryback of a net operating loss, unused general business credit, or overpayment of tax due to a claim of right adjustment under section 1341(b)(1).
IT-IRC sec. 6411; Regs. sec. 1.6411-1; Separate instructions

1065
U.S. Partnership Return of Income
Used by partnerships as an information return.
IT-IRC sec. 6031 and 6698; Regs. secs. 1.761-1(a), 1.6031-1, and 1.6033-1(a)(5); Separate instructions

Sch. D (Form 1065)
Capital Gains and Losses
Used to show partnership's capital gains and losses.
IT-IRC 6031

Sch. K-1 (Form 1065)
Partner's Share of Income, Credits, Deductions, Etc.
Used to show partner's share of income, credits, deductions, etc.
IT-IRC secs. 702 and 6031; Separate instructions

1066
U.S. Real Estate Mortgage Investment Conduit Income Tax Return
Used to report income, deductions, gains and losses, and the tax on net income from prohibited transactions, of a real estate mortgage investment conduit (REMIC).
IT-IRC secs. 860D, 860F(e); Separate instructions

Free Tax Help

Sch. Q (Form 1066)
Quarterly Notice to Residual Interest Holder of REMIC Taxable Income or Net Loss Allocation
Used to show residual interest holder's share of taxable income (or net loss), excess inclusion, and section 212 expenses. IT-IRC sec. 860G(c)

1078
Certificate of Alien Claiming Residence in the United States
Used by an alien claiming residence in the U.S., for income tax purposes. Filed with the withholding agent.
IT-IRC secs. 871 and 1441; Regs. secs. 1.1441-5 and 1.871-3,4

1096
Annual Summary and Transmittal of U.S. Information Returns
Used to summarize and transmit Forms W-2G, 1098, 1099-A, 1099-B, 1099-DIV, 1099-G, 1099-INT, 1099-MISC, 1099-OID, 1099-PATR, 1099-R, 1099-S, and 5498.
IT-IRC secs. 408(i), 6041, 6041A, 6042, 6043, 6044, 6045, 6047, 6049, 6050A, 6050B, 6050D, 6050E, 6050H, 6050J, and 6050N

1098
Mortgage Interest Statement
Used to report $600 or more of mortgage interest (including points) from an individual in a trade or business. IT-IRC sec. 6050H; Regs. sec. 1.6050H-2; See the separate Instructions for Forms 1099, 1098, 5498, 1096, and W-2G

1098E
Student Loan Interest Statement
Statement used by lending institutions to report interest paid on student loans. A student may be able to deduct loan interest on their tax returns if the interest payments were made during the first 60 months the interest payments were required.

1098T
Tuition Payment Statement
Statement made by colleges and universities to report receiving qualified tuition and related expenses on a student's behalf.

1099-A
Acquisition or Abandonment of Secured Property
Used by lenders to report acquisitions by such lenders or abandonments of property that secures a loan.
IT-IRC sec. 6050J; Temp. Regs. sec. 1.6050J-1T; See the separate Instructions for Forms 1099, 1098, 5498, and W-2G

1099-B
Proceeds From Broker and Barter Exchange Transactions
Used by a broker to report gross proceeds from the sale or redemption of securities, commodities or regulated futures contracts, or by a barter exchange to report the exchange of goods or services. IT-IRC sec. 6045; Regs. sec. 1.6045-1; See the separate instructions for Forms 1099, 1098, 5498, 1096, and W-2G

1099C
Cancellation of Debt
If a Federal government agency, financial institution, or credit union cancels or forgives a debt you owe of $600 or more, this form must be provided to you,.

1099-DIV
Dividends and Distributions
Used to report dividends and distributions. IT-IRC secs. 6042 and 6043; Regs. secs. 1.6042-2 and 1.6043-2; See the separate instructions for Forms 1099, 1098, 5498, and W-2G

1099-G
Certain Government Payments
Used to report government payments such as unemployment compensation, state and local income tax refunds, credits, or offsets, discharges of indebtedness by the Federal Government, taxable grants, and subsidy payments from the Department of Agriculture.
IT-IRC secs. 6041, 6050B, 6050D, and 6050E; Regs. secs. 1.6041-1, 1.6050B-1, 1.6050D-1, and 1.6050E-1; See the separate Instructions for Forms 1099, 1098, 5498, and W-2G

1099-INT
Interest Income
Used to report interest income.
IT-IRC secs. 6041 and 6049; Regs. secs. 1.6041-1, 1.6049-4, and 1.6049-7; See the separate Instructions for Forms 1099, 1098, 5498, and W-2G

1099-MISC
Miscellaneous Income
Used to report rents, royalties, prizes and awards, fishing boat proceeds, payments by health, accident and sickness insurers to physicians or other health service providers, fees, commissions or other compensation for services rendered in the course of the payer's business when the recipient is not treated as an employee, direct sales of $5,000 or more of consumer products for resale, substitute payments by brokers in lieu of dividends or tax-exempt interest, and crop insurance proceeds.
IT-IRC secs. 6041, 6041A, 6045(d), 6050A and 6050N; Regs. secs. 1.6041-1, 1.6045-2, and 1.6050A-1; See the separate Instructions for Forms 1099, 1098, 5498, and W-2G

1099-OID
Original Issue Discount
Used to report original issue discount.
IT-IRC sec. 6049; Regs. secs. 1.6049-4; 1.6049-7; Temp. Regs. secs. 1.6049-5T; See the separate Instructions for Forms 1099, 1098, 5498, and W-2G

1099-PATR
Taxable Distributions Received From Cooperatives
Used to report patronage dividends.
IT-IRC sec. 6044; Regs. sec. 1.6044-2; See the separate instructions for Forms 1099, 1098, 5498, and W-2G

1099-R
Distributions From Pensions, Annuities, Retirement or Profit-Sharing Plans, IRAs, Insurance Contracts, Etc.
Used to report total distributions from profit-sharing, retirement plans and individual retirement arrangements, and certain surrenders of insurance contracts. Replaces Form W-2P.
IT-IRC sec. 402, 408, and 6047; Temp Regs. sec. 35.3405-1; Regs. secs. 1.408-7 and 1.6047-1; See the separate Instructions for Forms 1099, 1098, 5498, and W-2G

1099-S
Proceeds From Real Estate Transactions
Used by the person required to report gross proceeds from real estate transactions.
IT-IRC sec. 6045(e); Regs. sec. 1.6045-4; See the separate Instructions for Forms 1099, 1098, 5498, and W-2G

1116
Foreign Tax Credit (Individual, Fiduciary, or Nonresident Alien Individual)
Used to figure the foreign tax credit claimed for the amount of any income, war profits, and excess profits tax paid or accrued during the taxable year to any foreign country or U.S. possession.
IT-IRC secs. 27, 901, and 904; Pub. 514; Separate instructions

1118
Foreign Tax Credit-Corporations
Used to support the amount of foreign tax credit claimed on corporation income tax returns. IT-IRC secs. 901 through 906; Separate instructions

Sch. I (Form 1118)
Reduction of Oil and Gas Extraction Taxes
Used to compute the section 907(a) reduction for a corporation that is claiming a foreign tax credit with respect to any income taxes paid, accrued, or deemed to have been paid during the tax year with respect to foreign oil and gas extraction income. IT-IRC sec. 907

Sch. J (Form 1118)
Separate Limitation Loss Allocations and Other
Adjustments Necessary to Determine Numerators of Limitation Fractions, Year-End Recharacterization Balances and Overall Foreign Loss Account Balances

IRS Tax Forms and Publications

Used to show the adjustments to separate limitation income or losses in determining the numerators of the limitation fractions for each separate limitation; the year-end balances of separate limitation losses that were allocated among other separate limitations (in the current year or in prior years) that have yet to be recharacterized; and the balances in the overall foreign loss accounts at the beginning of the tax year, any adjustments to the account balances, and the balances, in the overall foreign loss accounts at the end of the tax year.
IT-IRC sec. 904(f)

1120
U.S. Corporation Income Tax Return
Used by a corporation to report income tax. (Also see Form 1120-A.)
IT-IRC sec. 6012; Regs. secs. 1.1502-75(h), and 1.6012-2; Separate instructions

Sch. D (Form 1120)
Capital Gains and Losses
Used with Forms 1120, 1120-A, 1120-DF, 1120-IC-DISC, 1120-F, 1120-FSC, 1120-H, 1120L, 1120-ND, 1120-PC, 1120-POL, 1120-REIT, 1120-RIC, 990-C and certain Forms 990-T to report details of gain (or loss) from sales or exchanges of capital assets.
IT-IRC secs. 1201 and 1231

Sch. PH (Form 1120)
U.S. Personal Holding Company Tax
Used to figure personal holding company tax; filed with the income tax return of every personal holding company.
IT-IRC secs. 541, 6012, and 6501(f); Separate instructions

1120-A
U.S. Corporation Short-Form Income Tax Return
Used by a corporation to report income tax.
IT-IRC sec. 6012; Regs. sec. 1.6012-2; Separate instructions

1120F
U.S. Income Tax Return of a Foreign Corporation
Used by foreign corporations to report income tax.
IT-IRS secs. 881, 882, 884, 887, and 6012; Separate instructions

1120-FSC
U.S. Income Tax Return of a Foreign Sales Corporation
Used by foreign sales corporations to report income tax. IT-IRC secs. 922, 6011(c), and 6012; Separate instructions

Sch. P (Form 1120-FSC)
Transfer Price or Commission
Used to compute transfer price or commission under IRC sections 925(a)(1) and (2).
IT-IRC sec. 6011(c)

1120-H
U.S. Income Tax Return for Homeowners Associations
Used by homeowner associations to report income tax. (An annual return.) IT-IRC secs. 528, 6012; and Reg. sec. 1.528-8

1120-IC-DISC
Interest Charge Domestic International Sales Corporation Return
Used by domestic corporations that make the election under IRC section 992(b) to be a domestic international sales corporation.
IT-IRC secs. 6011(c) and 6072(b); Separate instructions

Sch. K (Form 1120-IC-DISC)
Shareholder's Statement of IC-DISC Distributions
Used to report deemed and actual distributions from an IC-DISC to shareholders and to report deferred DISC income and certain other information to shareholders.
IT-IRC sec. 6011(c)

Sch. P (Form 1120-IC-DISC)
Intercompany Transfer Price or Commission
Used to compute intercompany transfer prices or commissions under IRC section 994(a)(1) and (2).
IT-IRC sec. 6011(c)

Sch. Q (Form 1120-IC-DISC)
Borrower's Certificate of Compliance with the Rules for Producer's Loans
Used by an IC-DISC to establish that the borrower is in compliance with the rules for producer's loans.
IT-Regs. sec. 1.993-4(d)

1120L
U.S. Life Insurance Company Income Tax Return
Used by life insurance companies to report income tax.
IT-IRC secs. 801 and 6012; Reg. sec. 1.6012-2; Separate instructions

1120-ND
Return for Nuclear Decommissioning Funds and Certain Related Persons
Used by nuclear decommissioning funds to report income, expenses, transfers of funds to the public utility that created it and to figure the taxes on income plus penalty taxes on trustees and certain disqualified persons.
IT-IRC sec. 468A; Separate instructions

1120-PC
U.S. Property and Casualty Insurance Company Income Tax Return
Used by nonlife insurance companies to report income tax.
IT-IRC secs. 527 and Regs. sec. 1.6012-6(b)

1120-POL
U.S. Income Tax Return for Certain Political Organizations
Used by certain political organizations to report income tax.
IT-IRC secs. 527 and Regs. sec. 1.6012-6(b)

1120-REIT
U.S. Income Tax Return for Real Estate Investment Trusts
Used by real estate investment trusts to report income tax.
IT-IRC secs. 856 and 6012; Separate instructions

1120-RIC
U.S. Income Tax Return for Regulated Investment Companies
Used by regulated investment companies to report income tax.
IT-IRC secs. 851 and 6012; Separate instructions

1120S
U.S. Income Tax Return for an S Corporation
Used by S corporations that have made the election prescribed by IRC section 1362.
IT-IRC sec. 6037; IRC Subchapter S; Regs. sec. 1.6037-1; Separate instructions

Sch. D (Form 1120S)
Capital Gains and Losses and Built-in Gains
Used by corporations that have made the election prescribed by IRC section 1362. Sch. D is used to report details of gains (and losses) from sales, exchanges or distribution of capital assets and to figure the tax imposed on certain capital gains and certain built-in gains.
IT-IRC secs. 1201 and 1231; and IRC Subchapter S; Separate instructions

Sch. K-1 (Form 1120S)
Shareholder's Share of Income, Credits, Deductions, Etc.
Used to show shareholder's share of income, credits, deductions, etc. A copy is filed with Form 1120S, a copy is for S corporation records, and a copy is given to each shareholder along with the separate shareholders' instructions.
IT-IRC sec. 6037; Separate instructions

1120-W
Corporation Estimated Tax
Used as a worksheet by corporations to figure estimated tax liability; not to be filed. Corporations should keep it for their records.
IT-IRC sec. 6655

Free Tax Help

1120X
Amended U.S. Corporation Income Tax Return
Used by corporations to amend a previously filed Form 1120 or Form 1120-A. IT-Regs. sec. 301.6402-3

1122
Authorization and Consent of Subsidiary Corporation to be Included in a Consolidated Income Tax Return
Used as the authorization and consent of a subsidiary corporation to be included in a consolidated income tax return. IT-IRC sec. 1502; Regs. sec. 1.1502-75(h)

1127
Application for an Extension of Time for Tax Payments
The District Director may approve additional time for you to pay your tax if you can show that it will cause you undue hardship to pay on the date it is due.

1128
Application to Adopt, Change, or Retain a Tax Year
Used to obtain approval of a change, adoption or retention of a tax year. IT-IRC sec. 442; Regs. secs. 1.442-1(b) and 1.1502-76; Separate instructions

1138
Extension of Time for Payment of Taxes by a Corporation Expecting a Net Operating Loss Carryback
Used by a corporation expecting a net operating loss carryback to request an extension of time for payment of taxes.
IT-IRC sec. 6164

1139
Corporation Application for Tentative Refund
Used by corporations to apply for a tentative refund from the carryback of a net operating loss, net capital loss, unused general business credit, or overpayment of tax due to a claim or right adjustment under section 1341(b)(1).
IT-IRC sec. 6411

1310
Statement of Person Claiming Refund Due a Deceased Taxpayer
Used by claimant to secure payment of refund on behalf of a deceased taxpayer.
IT-IRC sec. 6402; Regs. sec. 301.6402-2(e); Pubs. 17 and 559

1363
Export Exemption Certificate
Used by shipper or other person to suspend liability for the payment of the tax for a period of 6 months from the date of shipment from the point of origin. The original is filed with the carrier at time of payment of the transportation charges and the duplicate is retained with the shipping papers for a period of 3 years from the last day of the month during which the shipment was made from the point of origin. May also be used as a blanket exemption certificate, with approval of District Director.
Ex-IRC secs. 4271 and 4272; Temp Regs. Part 154.2-1

2032
Contract Coverage Under Title II of the Social Security Act
Used to make an agreement pursuant to IRC section 3121(l).
Emp-IRC sec. 3121(l); Regs. sec. 36.3121(l)(1)-1

2063
U.S. Departing Alien Income Tax Statement
Used by a resident alien who has not received a termination assessment, or a nonresident alien who has no taxable income from United States sources.
IT-IRC sec. 6851(d); Regs. sec. 1.6851-2; Rev. Rul. 55-468; C.B.1955-2, 501; Pub. 519

2106
Employee Business Expenses
Used by employees to support deductions for business expenses. IT-IRC secs. 62, 162, and 274; Instructions for Form 1040, Pub. 463; Separate instructions

2119
Sale of Your Home
Used by individuals who sold their principal residence whether or not they bought another one. Also used by individuals 55 or over who elect to exclude gain on the sale of their main home.
IT-IRC secs. 121 and 1034; Pub. 17; Separate instructions

2120
Multiple Support Declaration
Used as a statement disclaiming as a dependent an individual to whose support the taxpayer and others have contributed.
IT-IRC sec. 152(c); Regs. sec. 1.152-3(c); Pub. 17

2210
Underpayment of Estimated Tax by Individuals and Fiduciaries
Used by individuals and fiduciaries to determine if they paid enough estimated tax. The form is also used to compute the penalty for underpayment of estimated tax.
IT-IRC sec. 6654; Regs. secs. 1.6654-1 and 1.6654-2; Separate instructions

2210F
Underpayment of Estimated Tax by Farmers and Fishermen
Used by qualified farmers and fishermen to determine if they paid enough estimated tax. Used only by individuals whose gross income from farming or fishing is at least two-thirds of their gross annual income. (All other individuals should use Form 2210.) The form is also used to compute the penalty for underpayment of estimated tax.
IT-IRC sec. 6654; Reg. secs. 1.6654-1 and 1.6654-2

2220
Underpayment of Estimated Tax by Corporations
Used by corporations (including S corporations) to determine if they paid enough estimated tax. The form is also used to compute the penalty for underpayment of estimated tax.
IT-IRC sec. 6655; Separate instructions

2290
Heavy Vehicle Use Tax Return
Used to report tax due on use of any highway motor vehicle which falls within one of the categories shown in the tax computation schedule on the form or meets certain weight limitations.
Ex-IRC sec. 4481; Regs. sec. 41.6011(a)-1(a)

2350
Application for Extension of Time to File U.S. Income Tax Return
Used by U.S. citizens and certain resident aliens abroad, who expect to qualify for special tax treatment to obtain an extension of time for filing an income tax return.
IT-IRC secs. 911 and 6081; Regs. sec. temporary 5b.911-6(b), 1.911-7(c), and 1.6081-2; Pub. 54

2438
Regulated Investment Company Undistributed Capital Gains Tax Return
Used to report tax payable on or before 30th day after close of company's taxable year. A copy is filed with Form 1120-RIC. (An annual return.)
IT-IRC sec. 852(b)(3); Regs. sec. 1.852-9

2439
Notice to Shareholder of Undistributed Long-Term Capital Gains
Used as an annual statement to be distributed to shareholders of a regulated investment company. (Copy to be attached to Form 1120-RIC.)
IT-IRC sec. 852(b)(3)(D)(i); Regs. sec. 1.852-9

2441
Child and Dependent Care Expenses
Used to figure the credit for child and dependent care expenses and/or the exclusion of employer-provided dependent care benefits. (To be attached to Form 1040.) IT-IRC sec. 21 and 129; Regs. sec. 1.44A-1; Pubs. 17 and 503; Separate instructions

IRS Tax Forms and Publications

2553
Election by A Small Business Corporation
Used by qualifying small business corporations to make the election prescribed by IRC section 1362. IT-IRC sec. 1362; Separate instructions

2555
Foreign Earned Income
Used by U.S. citizens and resident aliens who qualify for the foreign earned income exclusion and/or the housing exclusion or deduction. (To be filed with Form 1040.) IT-IRC secs. 911 and 6012(c); Regs. secs. 1.911-1 and 1.6012-1; Pub. 54; Separate instructions

2555-EZ
Foreign Earned Income Exclusion
Used by citizens and resident aliens who qualify for the foreign earned income exclusion. IT-IRC secs. 911 and 6012(c); Regs. secs. 1.911-1 and 1.6012-1; Separate instructions

2688
Application for Additional Extension of Time To File U.S. Individual Income Tax Return
Used to apply for an extension of time to file Form 1040. IT-IRC sec. 6081; Regs. sec. 1.6081-1(b)(5); T.D.6436

2758
Application for Extension of Time To File Certain Excise, Income, Information, and Other Returns
Used to apply for an extension of time to file certain returns listed on the form. A separate Form 2758 must be filed for each return. IT-IRC sec. 6081; Regs. sec. 1.6081-1(b)

2848
Power of Attorney and Declaration of Representative
Used as an authorization for one person to act for another in any tax matter (except alcohol and tobacco taxes and firearms activities). IT-Title 26, CFR, Part 601

3115
Application for Change in Accounting Method
Used to secure approval for change in accounting method. IT-IRC sec. 446(e); Regs. sec. 1.446-1(e); Separate instructions

3206
Information Statement by United Kingdom Withholding Agents Paying Dividends From United States Corporations to Residents of the U.S. and Certain Treaty Countries
Used to report dividends paid by U.S. corporations to beneficial owners of dividends paid through United Kingdom nominees. Used when the beneficial owners are residents of countries other than United Kingdom with which the U.S. has a tax treaty providing for reduced withholding rates on dividends. IT secs. 7.507 and 7.508 of T.D. 5532

3468
Investment Credit
Used by individuals, estates, trusts, and corporations claiming an investment credit made up of the rehabilitation, energy and reforestation credits. Also see Form 3800. IT-IRC secs. 38, 46, 47, 48, and 50; Separate instructions

3491
Consumer Cooperative Exemption Application
Used by certain consumer cooperatives that are primarily engaged in retail sales of goods or services generally for personal, living or family use to apply for exemption from filing Form 1099-PATR. IT-IRC sec. 6044(c); Regs. sec. 1.6044-4

3520
U.S. Information Return-Creation of or Transfers to Certain Foreign Trusts
Used by a grantor in the case of an inter vivos trust, a fiduciary of an estate in the case of a testamentary trust, or a transferor to report the creation of any foreign trust by a U.S. person or the transfer of any money or property to a foreign trust by a U.S. person. IT-IRC sec. 6048; Regs. secs. 16.3-1

3520-A
Annual Return of Foreign Trust with U.S. Beneficiaries
Used to report the operation of foreign trust that has U.S. beneficiaries. IT-IRC sec. 6048; Regs. sec. 404.6041

3800
General Business Credit
Used to summarize the credits that make up the general business credit to determine the tax liability limitation of the credits for the year. Included are any carryback or carryover of the credits. IT-IRC secs. 38 and 39; Separate instructions

3903
Moving Expenses
Used to figure the deduction for expenses incurred from an employment-related move to a new location in the United States or its possessions. IT-IRC sec. 217; Regs. sec. 1.217; Pub. 521; Separate instructions

3903F
Foreign Moving Expenses
Used by U.S. citizens or resident aliens moving to a new principal workplace outside the United States or its possessions. IT-IRC 217(h); Pub. 521; Separate instructions

4029
Application for Exemption from Social Security and Medicare Taxes and Waiver of Benefits
Used by members of qualified religious groups to claim exemption from social security and Medicare taxes. IT-IRC sec. 1402(g)

4136
Credit for Federal Tax Paid on Fuels
Used by individuals, estates, trusts, or corporations, including S corporations and domestic international sales corporations, to claim credit for Federal excise tax paid on the number of gallons of fuels used for exempt purposes. Also used to claim the one-time credit allowed owners of qualified diesel-powered highway vehicles. Ex-IRC secs. 34, 4041, 4081, 4091, 6420, 6421, and 6427

4137
Social Security and Medicare Taxes on Unreported Tip Income
Used by employees who received tips subject to social security and Medicare taxes but failed to report them to employer and to report any unreported allocated tips shown on the Form W-2. IT/Emp-IRC sec. 3102; Regs. sec. 31.3102-3(d) and 31.6011(a)-1(d)

4224
Exemption From Withholding of Tax on Income Effectively Connected With the Conduct of a Trade or Business in the United States
Used to secure, at the time of payment, the benefit of exemption from withholding of the tax on certain income for nonresident alien individuals and fiduciaries, foreign partnerships, and foreign corporations. IT-IRC secs. 1441 and 1442; Regs. sec. 1.1441-4

4255
Recapture of Investment Credit
Used by individuals, estates, trusts, or corporations to figure the increase in tax if regular, rehabilitation, or energy property was disposed of or ceased to qualify before the end of the property class life or life years used to figure the credit. IT-IRC sec. 50

4361
Application for Exemption from Self-Employment Tax for Use by Ministers, Members of Religious Orders and Christian Science Practitioners
Used by members of qualified religious groups to claim exemption from tax on self-employment income. IT-IRC sec. 1402(e)

Free Tax Help

4461
Application for Approval of Master or Prototype Defined Contribution Plan
Used by employers who want an opinion letter for approval of form of a master or prototype plan.
IT-IRC secs. 401(a), and 501(a)

4461-A
Application for Approval of Master or Prototype Defined Benefit Plan
Used by employers who want an opinion letter for approval of form of a master or prototype plan.
IT-IRC secs. 401(a) and 501(a)

4461-B
Application of Master or Prototype Plan, or Regional Prototype Plan Mass Submitter Adopting Sponsor
Used by mass submitters who want approval on a plan of adopting sponsoring organization or sponsor.
IT-IRC secs. 401(a) and 501(a)

4466
Corporation Application for Quick Refund of Overpayment of Estimated Tax
Used to apply for a "quick" refund of overpaid estimated tax. (Must be filed before the regular tax return is filed.) IT-IRC sec. 6425; Regs. sec. 1.6425-1(b)

4506
Request for Copy of Tax Form
Used by a taxpayer or authorized representative to request a copy of a tax return or Forms W-2 that were filed with the return.
IT-Regs. sec. 601.702

4506-A
Request for Public Inspection or Copy of Exempt Organization Tax Form
Used by a third-party to request a copy of an exempt organization tax form or to inspect the form at an IRS office.
IT-IRC sec. 6104(b)

4562
Depreciation and Amortization
Used by individuals, estates, trusts, partnerships, and corporations to claim depreciation and amortization; to make a section 179 election; and to substantiate depreciation deductions for automobiles and other listed property.
IT-IRC secs. 167, 168, 179 and 280F; Separate instructions

4563
Exclusion of Income for Bona Fide Residents of American Samoa
Used by bona fide residents of American Samoa to exclude income from sources in American Samoa, Guam, and the Commonwealth of the Northern Mariana Islands, to the extent specified in IRC section 931.
IT-IRC sec. 931; Regs. sec. 1.931-1; Pub. 570

4626
Alternative Minimum Tax-Corporations
Used by corporations to figure alternative minimum tax and environmental tax.
IT-IRC secs. 55, 56, 57, 58, 59, and 291; Separate instructions

4684
Casualties and Thefts
Used by all taxpayers to figure gains or losses resulting from casualties and thefts.
IT-IRC sec. 165; Separate instructions

4720
Return of Certain Excise Taxes on Charities and Other Persons Under Chapters 41 and 42 of the Internal Revenue Code
Used by charities and other persons to compute certain excise taxes which may be due under IRC Chapters 41 and 42.
Ex-IRC secs. 4911, 4912, 4941, 4942, 4943, 4944, 4945, and 4955; Separate instructions

4768
Application for Extension of Time To File a Return and/or Pay U.S. Estate (and Generation-Skipping Transfer) Taxes
Used to apply for estate tax extensions in certain cases.
E&G-IRC secs. 6081 and 6161; Regs. sec. 20.6081-1 and 20.6161-1

4782
Employee Moving Expense Information
Used by employers to show the amount of any reimbursement or payment made to an employee, a third party for the employee's benefit, or the value of services furnished in-kind, for moving expenses during the calendar year.
IT-IRC secs. 82 and 217; Regs. sec. 31.6051-1(e)

4789
Currency Transaction Report
Used by financial institutions to report deposit, withdrawal, exchange of currency, or other payment or transfer, by, through, or to such financial institution which involves currency transactions of more than $10,000.
P.L.92-508; Treasury Regs. (31CFR103)

4797
Sales of Business Property
Used to report details of gain (or loss) from sales, exchanges, or involuntary conversions (from other than casualty and theft) of noncapital assets and involuntary conversions (other than casualty and theft) of capital assets, held in connection with a trade or business or a transaction entered into for profit. Also used to compute recapture amounts under sections 179 and 280F when the business use of section 179 or 280F property drops to 50% or less. IT-IRC secs. 1231, 1245, 1250, 1252, 1254, and 1255; IT-IRC secs. 1202, 1211, and 1212; Separate instructions

4835
Farm Rental Income and Expenses
Used by landowner (or sublessor) to report farm rental income based on crops or livestock produced by the tenant where the landowner (or sublessor) does not materially participate in the operation or management of the farm. (Also see Schedule F (Form 1040).)
IT-IRC sec. 61

4868
Extension of Time to File U.S. Individual Income Tax Return
Used to apply for an automatic 4-month extension of time to file Form 1040. IT-IRC sec. 6081; Regs. sec. 1.6081-4; TD 7885

4876-A
Election To Be Treated as an Interest Charge DISC
Used by a qualifying corporation that wishes to be treated as an Interest Charge Domestic International Sales Corporation (Interest Charge DISC).
IT-Regs. sec. 1.921

4952
Investment Interest Expense Deduction
Used by an individual, estate, or trust to figure the limitation on the deduction for interest expense on borrowed funds allocable to property held for investment. IT-IRC sec. 163(d)

4970
Tax on Accumulation Distribution of Trusts
Used by a beneficiary of a domestic or foreign trust to figure the tax attributable to an accumulation distribution.
IT-IRC sec. 667

4972
Tax on Lump-Sum Distributions
Used to determine the income tax on the income portion of lump-sum distributions.
IT-IRC sec. 402(e); Separate instructions

IRS Tax Forms and Publications

5074
Allocation of Individual Income Tax to Guam or the Commonwealth of the Northern Mariana Islands (CNMI)
Used as an attachment to Form 1040 filed by an individual who reports adjusted gross income of $50,000 or more, with gross income of $5,000 or more from Guam or CNMI sources.
IT-IRC sec. 935; Regs. sec. 301.7654-1(d)

5213
Election to Postpone Determination as to Whether the Presumption that an Activity is Engaged in for Profit Applies
Used by individuals, trusts, estates, and S corporations to postpone a determination as to whether an activity is engaged in for profit. IT-IRC sec. 183(e)

5227
Split-Interest Trust Information Return
Used by section 4947(a)(2) trusts to determine whether the trust is treated as a private foundation, and subject to excise taxes under Chapter 42. Ex-IRC sec. 6011; Separate instructions

5300
Application for Determination for Employee Benefit Plan
Used to request a determination letter as to the qualification of a defined benefit or a defined contribution plan, and the exempt status of any related trust. IT-IRC sec. 401(a); Separate instructions

5303
Application for Determination for Collectively Bargained Plan
Used to request a determination letter as to the qualification of a collectively bargained plan. Also used by multi-employer plans covered by PBGC insurance to request a determination letter regarding termination. IT-IRC sec. 401(a); Separate instructions

5304
Savings Incentive Match Plan for Employees of Small Employers
Used by employees to contribute salary deductions to an established Simple IRA.

5305
Individual Retirement Trust Account
Used as an agreement between an individual and the individual's trustee for the establishment of an individual retirement account. IT-IRC sec. 408(a)

5305-SEP
Simplified Employee Pension-Individual Retirement Accounts Contribution Agreement
Used as an agreement between an employer and his or her employees to establish a simplified employee pension.
IT-IRC 408(k)

5305A-SEP
Salary Reduction and Other Elective Simplified Employee Pension - Individual Retirement Accounts Contribution Agreement
Used as an agreement between an employer and his or her employees to establish a simplified employee pension with an elective deferral.
IT-IRC sec. 408(k)(6)

5306
Application for Approval of Prototype or Employer Sponsored Individual Retirement Account
Used by banks, savings and loan associations, federally insured credit unions, and such other persons approved by the Internal Revenue Service to act as trustee or custodian, insurance companies, regulated investment companies and trade or professional societies or associations, to get the approval as to form of a trust or annuity contract which is to be used for individual retirement accounts or annuities. Also to be used by employees, labor unions and other employee associations that want approval of a trust which is to be used for individual retirement accounts.
IT-IRC sec. 408(a), (b), or (c)

5306-SEP
Application for Approval of Prototype Simplified Employee Pension-SEP
Used by program sponsors who want to get IRS approval of their prototype simplified employee pension (SEP) agreements. IT-IRC sec. 408(k)

5307
Application for Determination for Adopters of Master or Prototype, Regional Prototype or Volume Submitter Plans
Used to request a determination letter as to the qualification of a defined benefit or defined contribution plan (the form of which has been previously approved) other than a collectively bargained plan.
IT-IRC sec. 401(a); Separate instructions

5308
Request for Change in Plan/Trust Year
Used by employer or plan administrators to request approval of change in a plan year or a trust year.
IT-IRC sec. 412(c)(5), sec. 442

5309
Application for Determination of Employee Stock Ownership Plan
Used by corporate employers who wish to get a determination letter regarding the qualification of an Employee Stock Ownership Plan under IRC 409 or 4975(e)(7). IT-IRC 409-4975(e)(7)

5310
Application for Determination Upon Termination
Used by an employer who wishes a determination letter as to the effect of termination of a plan on its prior qualification under IRC section 401(a).
IT-IRC secs. 401(a); Separate instructions

5310-A
Notice of Merger, Consolidation or Transfer of Plan Liabilities
Used by every employer or plan administrator for any plan merger, consolidation, or transfer of plan assets or liability required to be reported. IT-IRC sec. 6058(b), 414(l), 401(a)(2); Separate instructions

5329
Return for Additional Taxes Attributable to Qualified Retirement Plans (Including IRAs), Annuities, and Modified Endowment Contracts
Used to report excise taxes or additional income tax owed in connection with individual retirement arrangements, annuities, modified endowment contract, and qualified retirement plans. IT-IRC secs. 72, 4973, 4974, and 4980A; Separate instructions

5330
Return of Excise Taxes Related to Employee Benefit Plans
Used to report and pay the excise tax imposed by IRC section 4971 on a minimum funding deficiency, by Code section 4973(a)(2) on excess contributions to a section 403(b)(7)(A) custodial account, by section 4972 on nondeductible contributions to qualify plans, by section 4975 on prohibited transactions, by section 4976 on disqualified benefits from welfare plans, by 4977 on certain fringe benefits, and by sections 4978, 4978A 4978B, 4979A on certain ESOP transactions, by section 4979 on excess contributions to plans with cash or deferred arrangements, and by section 4980 on reversions of qualified plan assets to employers. Ex-IRC sec. 6011; Separate instructions

5452
Corporate Report of Nondividend Distributions
Used by corporations to report their nontaxable distributions.
IT-CFR 1.301-1, 1.316-1, and 1.6042-2

Free Tax Help

5471
Information Return of U.S. Persons With Respect to Certain Foreign Corporations
Used by U.S. persons to report their activities with related foreign corporations.
IT-IRC secs. 951-972, 6035, 6038 and 6046; Separate instructions

Sch. M (Form 5471)
Transactions Between Controlled Foreign Corporation and Shareholders or Other Related Persons
Used by a U.S. person who controls a foreign corporation to report the activities between the U.S. person and the foreign corporation.
IT-IRC sec. 6038

Sch. N (Form 5471)
Return of Officers, Directors, and 10% or More Shareholders of a Foreign Personal Holding Company
Used by officers, directors, and shareholders of foreign personal holding companies to report information concerning the foreign personal holding company. IT-IRC sec. 6035

Sch. O (Form 5471)
Organization or Reorganization of Foreign Corporation, and Acquisitions and Dispositions of its Stock
Used by U.S. persons to report acquisitions or dispositions of interests in foreign corporations. IT-IRC sec. 6046

5472
Information Return of a 25% Foreign-Owned U.S. Corporation or Foreign Corporation Engaged in a U.S. Trade or Business
Used for reporting the activities between foreign owned corporations and persons related to transactions made by the corporations.
IT-IRC sec. 6038A, 6038C

5498
Individual Retirement Arrangement Information
Used to report contributions to individual retirement arrangements (IRAs) and the value of the account.
IT-IRC sec. 408(i) and (o); Prop. Regs. sec. 1.408-5; See the separate Instructions for Forms 1099, 1098, 5498, and W-2G

5500
Annual Return/Report of Employee Benefit Plan (with 100 or more participants)
Used to report on deferred compensation plans and welfare plans that have at least 100 participants.
IT-IRC sec. 6058(a); ERISA section 103; Separate instructions

Sch. A (Form 5500)
Insurance Information
Used as an attachment to Form 5500 or 5500-C/R to report information about insurance contracts that are part of a qualified deferred compensation plan. ERISA section 103(e)

Sch. B (Form 5500)
Actuarial Information
Used to report actuarial information for a defined benefit plan. (Attached to Form 5500 or 5500-C/R).
IT-IRC sec. 6059; ERISA section 103(a); Separate instructions

Sch. C (Form 5500)
Service Provider and Trustee Information
Used as an attachment to Form 5500 to report information about service providers and trustees of qualified deferred compensation plans.
ERISA section 103.

Sch. E (Form 5500)
ESOP Annual Information
Used to report on employee stock ownership plans which have an outstanding securities acquisition loan or corporation maintaining plan deducted dividends paid on its stock under Code section 404(k).
IT-IRC sec. 6047(e)

Sch. F (Form 5500)
Fringe Benefit Annual Information Return
Used to report the annual information required by Code section 6039D(d) for plans described in section 120, 125, and 127. IT-IRC sec. 6039D(d)

Sch. G (Form 5500)
Financial Schedules
Used to provide certain additional financial information required by Form 5500. ERISA sec. 103

Sch. P (Form 5500)
Annual Return of Fiduciary of Employee Benefit Trust
Used as an annual return for employee benefit trusts which qualify under section 401(a) and are exempt from tax under section 501(a). (Attach to Form 5500 or 5500-C/R.) IT-IRC secs. 6033(a) and 6501(a)

Sch. SSA (Form 5500)
Annual Registration Statement Identifying Separated Participants with Deferred Vested Benefits
Used to list employees who separated from employment and have a deferred vested benefit in the employer's plan of deferred compensation. (Attached to Form 5500 or 5500-C/R.) IT-IRC sec. 6057

5500-C/R
Return/Report of Employee Benefit Plan (with fewer than 100 participants)
Used to report on deferred compensation plans and welfare plans that have fewer than 100 participants.
IT-IRC sec. 6058(a); ERISA section 103; Separate instructions

5500EZ
Annual Return of One-Participant Owners and Their Spouses Pension Benefit Plan
Used to report on pension, profit-sharing, etc. plans that cover only an individual or an individual and the individual's spouse who wholly own a business.
IT-IRC sec. 6058(a); Separate instructions

5558
Application for Extension of Time to File Certain Employee Plan Returns
Used to provide a means by which a person may request an extension of time to file Forms 5500, 5500-C/R, 5500EZ, or 5330.

5578
Annual Certification of Racial Nondiscrimination for a Private School Exempt from Federal Income Tax
Used by certain organizations exempt or claiming to be exempt under IRC section 501(c)(3) and operating, supervising, or controlling a private school (or schools) to certify to a policy of racial nondiscrimination.
IT-IRC sec. 6001; Rev. Proc. 75-50, 1975-2; C.B. 587

5712
Election to be Treated as a Possessions Corporation Under Section 936
Used by a corporation to elect to be treated as a possessions corporation for the tax credit allowed under IRC section 936. IT-IRC sec. 936(e)

5712-A
Cost Sharing or Profit Split Method Under Section 936(h)(5): Election and Verification
Used by a domestic corporation if it elects to compute its taxable income under either the cost sharing method or the profit split method. IT-IRC sec. 936(h)(5)

5713
International Boycott Report
Used by persons with operations in or related to any country associated in carrying out an international boycott. IT-IRC sec. 999; Separate instructions

IRS Tax Forms and Publications

Sch. A (Form 5713)
International Boycott Factor
Used by taxpayers in computing the loss of tax benefits under the international boycott factor method.
IT-IRC sec. 999(c)

Sch. B (Form 5713)
Specifically Attributable Taxes and Income
Used by taxpayers in computing the loss of tax benefits under the specifically attributable taxes and income method.
IT-IRC sec. 999(d)

Sch. C (Form 5713)
Tax Effect of the International Boycott Provisions
Used to summarize the loss of tax benefits resulting from the application of the international boycott provisions.
IT-IRC sec. 999

5735
Possessions Corporation Tax Credit Allowed Under Section 936
Used by qualified possessions corporations to compute credit allowed by IRC section 936. IT-IRC sec. 936

Sch. P (Form 5735)
Allocation of Income and Expenses Under Section 936(h)(5)
Used by corporations that have elected the cost sharing or profit split method of computing taxable income. The form is attached to Form 5735.
IT-IRC sec. 935(h)(5)

5754
Statement By Person(s) Receiving Gambling Winnings
Used to list multiple winners of certain gambling proceeds.
IT-IRC sec. 3402(q); Regs. secs. 31.3402(q)-1(e) and 1.6011-3; See the separate Instructions for Forms 1099, 1098, 5498, and W-2G

5768
Election/Revocation of Election by an Eligible Section 501(c)3 Organization to Make Expenditures to Influence Legislation
Used by certain eligible IRC section 501(c)3 organizations to elect or revoke election to apply the lobbying expenditures provisions of code section 501(h).
IT-IRC secs. 501(h) and 4911

5884
Work Opportunity Credit
Used by individuals, estates, trusts, and corporations claiming a work opportunity credit and any S corporation, partnership, estate or trust which apportion the work opportunity credit among their shareholders, partners, or beneficiaries. See also Form 3800.
IT-IRC secs. 38, 51, and 52

6069
Return of Excise Tax on Excess Contributions to Black Lung Benefit Trust Under Section 4953 and Computation of Section 192 Deduction
Used by exempt Black Lung Benefit Trusts as a worksheet to determine deduction under section 192 and to report tax under section 4953.
IT/Ex-IRC secs. 192 and 4953

6088
Distributable Benefits from Employee Pension Benefit Plans
Used to report the 25 highest paid participants of a deferred compensation plan, which is attached to Form 5310. IT-IRC sec. 401(a)

6118
Claim for Income Tax Return Preparers
Used by income tax return preparers to file for refund of penalties paid. IT-IRC sec. 6696

6177
General Assistance Program Determination
Used by a General Assistance Program of a state or political subdivision of a state in order to be designated as a Qualified General Assistance Program for purposes of certifying individual recipients of the program for the jobs credit.
IT-IRC sec. 51(d)(6)(B)

6197
Gas Guzzler Tax
Used by automobile manufacturers and importers to report the tax on "gas guzzler" types of automobiles. The form is filed as an attachment to Form 720.
Ex-IRC sec. 4064

6198
At-Risk Limitations
Used by individuals, partners, S corporation shareholders, and certain closely-held corporations to figure the overall profit (loss) from an at-risk activity for the tax year, the amount at-risk, and the deductible loss for the tax year.
IT-IRC sec. 465; Separate instructions

6199
Certification of Youth Participating in a Qualified Cooperative Education Program
Used by a qualified school to certify that a student meets the requirements of Sec. 51(d)8 as a member of a targeted group eligible for the jobs credit. IT-IRC sec. 51

6251
Alternative Minimum Tax-Individuals
Used by individuals to figure their alternative minimum tax.
IT-IRC secs. 55, 56, 57, 58, and 59; Separate instructions

6252
Installment Sale Income
Used by taxpayers, other than dealers, to report a sale or other disposition of real or personal property on the installment method.
IT-IRC sec. 453; Pub. 537; Separate instructions

6406
Short Form Application for Determination for Amendment of Employee Benefit Plan
Used for amending a plan on which a favorable determination letter has been issued.
IRC secs. 401(a) and 501(a); Separate instructions

6478
Credit for Alcohol Used as Fuel
Used by taxpayers to figure their credit for alcohol used as fuel. The credit is allowed for the small ethanol producer, alcohol mixed with other fuels and for straight alcohol fuel. See also Form 3800. IT-IRC secs. 38 and 40

6497
Information Return of Nontaxable Energy Grants or Subsidized Energy Financing
Used by every person who administers a government program for a Federal, state, or local governmental entity or agent thereof, that provides grants or subsidized financing under programs a principal purpose of which is energy production or conservation if the grant or financing is not taxable to the recipient.
IT-IRC sec. 6050D; Regs. sec. 1.6050D-1

6627
Environmental Taxes
Used to report environmental taxes on petroleum, certain chemicals, Ozone-depleting chemicals, and certain imported substances. This is an attachment to Form 720.
Ex-IRC secs. 4611, 4661, 4671. and 4681; Separate instructions

6765
Credit for Increasing Research Activities (or for claiming the orphan drug credit)
Used by individuals, estates, trusts, and corporations claiming a research credit for increasing the research activities of a trade or business. Also used to claim the orphan drug credit. See also Form 3800.
IT-IRC secs. 28 and 41; Separate instructions

Free Tax Help

6781
Gains and Losses From Section 1256 Contracts and Straddles
Used by all taxpayers that held section 1256 contracts or straddles during the tax year.
IT-IRC secs. 1092 and 1256

7004
Application for Automatic Extension of Time to File Corporation Income Tax Return
Used by corporations and certain exempt organizations to request an automatic extension of 6 months to file corporate income tax return.
IT-IRC sec. 6081(b); Regs. sec. 1.6081-3

8023
Corporate Qualified Stock Purchase Elections
Used by a purchasing corporation to elect to treat the purchase of a corporation stock as the purchase of a corporation assets. IT-IRC sec. 338; Temp. Regs. sec. 1.338-2T

8027
Employer's Annual Information Return of Tip Income and Allocated Tips
Used by large food or beverage employers to report each establishment's gross receipts, charge receipts and charge tips, and allocated tips of employees.
IT-IRC sec. 6053(c); Regs. sec. 31.6053-3; Separate instructions

8038
Information Return for Tax-Exempt Private Activity Bond Issues
Used by issuers of tax-exempt private activity bonds to provide IRS with information required by section 149(e).
IT-IRC sec. 149(e); Temp. Regs. sec. 1.149(e)-1T; Separate instructions

8038-G
Information Return for Tax-Exempt Governmental Obligations
Used by the issuers of tax-exempt governmental bonds (with issue prices of $100,000 or more) to provide IRS with information required by section 149(e). IT-IRC sec. 149(e); Temp. Regs. sec. 1.149(e)-1T; Separate instructions

8038-GC
Information Return for Small Tax-Exempt Governmental Bond Issues, Leases and Installment Sales
Used by the issuers of tax-exempt governmental bonds (with issue prices of less than $100,000) to provide IRS with information required by section 149(e).
IT-IRC sec. 149(e); Temp. Regs. sec. 1.149(e)-1T;

8038-T
Arbitrage Rebate and Penalty in Lieu of Arbitrage Rebate
Issuers of tax-exempt governmental bonds use Form 8038-T when paying to the United States the arbitrage rebate and the penalty in lieu of the rebate, etc., under section 143(g) and 148(f) and sections 103(c)(6)(D) and 103A(i)(4) of the Internal Revenue Code of 1954. IT-IRC secs. 143(g), 148(f)

8082
Notice of Inconsistent Treatment or Amended Return
Used by partners, S corporation shareholders and residual holders of an interest in a REMIC to report inconsistent treatment of partnership, S corporation or REMIC items or to report amendment of partnership, S corporation or REMIC items. Form 8082 is also used by the TMP (tax matters partner or tax matters person) to make an administrative adjustment request (AAR) on behalf of the partnership, S corporation, or REMIC.
IT-IRC sec. 6222 and 6227(c); Separate instructions

8160
Tax Package Postcard
The IRS sends a postcard to Corporations in lieu of mailing a tax package that they may not need. This is an effort by the IRS to save the cost of printing and mailing.

8233
Exemption From Withholding on Compensation for Independent Personal Services of a Nonresident Alien Individual
Used by nonresident alien individuals to claim exemption from withholding on compensation for independent personal services because of an income tax treaty or the personal exemption amount. Also used by nonresident alien students, teachers, and researchers to claim exemption from withholding under a U.S. tax treaty on compensation for services.
IT-IRC sec. 1441; Reg. sec. 1.1441-4

8264
Application for Registration of a Tax Shelter
Used by tax shelter organizers to register certain tax shelters with the IRS, for purposes of receiving a tax shelter registration number.
IT-IRC sec. 6111; Temp. regs. secs. 301.6111-1T; Separate instructions

8271
Investor Reporting of Tax Shelter Registration Number
Used by persons who have purchased or otherwise acquired an interest in a tax shelter required to be registered to report the tax shelter registration number. Form is attached to any tax return on which a deduction, credit, loss, or other tax benefit is claimed, or any income reported, from a tax shelter required to be registered. IT-IRC sec. 6111; Regs. secs. 301.6111-1T

8274
Certification by Churches and Qualified Church-Controlled Organizations Electing Exemption from Employer Social Security and Medicare Taxes
Used by churches and certain church-controlled organizations to elect exemption from social security and Medicare taxes by certifying the organization is opposed to these taxes for religious purposes.
Emp-IRC sec. 3121(w)

8275
Disclosure Statement
Used by taxpayers to disclose items on a tax return for purposes of avoiding the portions of the accuracy-related penalty due to negligence, disregard of rules or regulations, or a substantial understatement of income tax. It is used by return preparers for disclosures related to preparer penalties for understatements due to an unrealistic position or for willful or reckless conduct. Separate instructions
PA-IRC sec. 6662; Regs. sec. 1.6662-1-1.6662-5; Separate instructions

8275-R
Regulation Disclosure Statement
Used to disclose items to avoid portions of the accuracy-related penalties due to a position taken contrary to the regulations.
PA-IRC sec. 6662; Regs. sec. 1.6662-1-1.6662-5; separate instructions

8279
Election To Be Treated as a FSC or as a Small FSC
Used by qualifying corporations that wish to be treated as a Foreign Sales Corporation (FSC) or Small Foreign Sales Corporation (Small FSC).
IT-IRC sec. 927

8281
Information Return for Publicly Offered Original Issue Discount Instruments
Used by issuers of publicly offered debt instruments having OID to provide the information required by section 1275(c).
IT-IRC sec. 1275(c); Temp. Regs. sec. 1.1275-3T

8282
Donee Information Return (Sale, Exchange or Trade of Donated Property)
Used by exempt organizations who sells, exchanges, transfers, or otherwise disposes of the charitable property within 2 years after the date of the receipt of the contribution. The return is filed with the IRS and a copy is given to the donor.
IT-IRC sec. 6050L

IRS Tax Forms and Publications

8283
Noncash Charitable Contributions
Used by individuals, closely held corporations, personal service corporations, partnerships, and S corporations to report contributions of property other than cash in which the total claimed value of all property exceeds $500. IT-IRC secs. 170; 1.170A-13 and Temp. Regs. sec. 1.170A-13T; Separate instructions

8288
U.S. Withholding Tax Return for Dispositions by Foreign Persons of U.S. Real Property Interests
Used to transmit the withholding on the sale of U.S. real property by foreign persons. IT-IRC sec. 1445; Regs. secs. 1.1445-1 through 1.1445-7; Temp. Regs. secs. 1.1445-9T through 1.1445-11T

8288-A
Statement of Withholding on Dispositions by Foreign Persons of U.S. Real Property Interests
Anyone filing Form 8288 must attach copies A and B of Form 8288-A for each person subject to withholding. IT-IRC sec. 1445; Regs. secs. 1.1445-1 through 1.1445-7, Temp. Regs. secs. 1.1445-9T through 1.1445-11T

8288-B
Application for Withholding Certificate for Dispositions by Foreign Persons of U.S. Real Property Interests
Used to apply for a withholding certificate based on certain criteria to reduce or eliminate withholding under section 1445.
IT-IRC sec. 1445; Regs. secs. 1.1445-3 and 1.1445-6 and Rev. Proc. 88-23

8300
Report of Cash Payments Over $10,000 Received in a Trade or Business
Used by a trade or business to report receipt of more than $10,000 cash in a transaction in the course of such trade or business.
IT-IRC sec. 6050I; Regs. 1.6050I-1

8308
Report of a Sale or Exchange of Certain Partnership Interests
Used by partnerships to report the sale or exchange of a partnership interest where a portion of any money or other property given in exchange for the interest is attributable to unrealized receivables or substantially appreciated inventory items (section 751(a) exchange). IT-IRC sec. 6050K

8328
Carryforward Election of Unused Private Activity Bond Volume Cap
Used by the issuing authority of tax-exempt private activity bonds to elect under section 146(f) to carryforward the unused volume cap for specific projects. IT-IRC sec. 146(f)

8329
Lender's Information Return for Mortgage Credit Certificates (MCCs)
Used by lenders of certified indebtedness amounts to report information regarding the issuance of mortgage credit certificates under section 25.
IT-IRC sec. 25; Regs. sec. 1.25-8T

8330
Issuer's Quarterly Information Return for Mortgage Credit Certificates (MCCs)
Used by issuers of mortgage credit certificates to report information required under section 25.
IT-IRC sec. 25; Regs. secs. 1.25-8T

8332
Release of Claim to Exemption for Child of Divorced or Separated Parents
Used to release claim to a child's exemption by a parent who has custody of his or her child and is given to the parent who will claim the exemption. The parent who claims the child's exemption attaches this form to his or her tax return.
IT-IRC sec. 152(e)(2); Temp. Regs. sec. 1.152-4T; Publication 504

8362
Currency Transaction Reported by Casinos
Used by casinos licensed by a state or local government having annual gaming revenues in excess of $1 million to report each deposit, withdrawal, exchange of currency or gambling tokens or chips or other payment or transfer, by, through, or to such casino, involving currency of more than $10,000. P.L. 91-508; Treasury Regs. secs. 31 CFR 103.22; 31 CFR 103.26; and 31 CFR 103.36

8379
Injured Spouse Claim and Allocation
To process a claim for refund of your share of an overpayment shown on a joint return with your spouse.

8390
Information Return for Determination of Life Insurance Company Earnings Rate Under Section 809
Used by certain life insurance companies to gather information to compute various earnings rates required by section 809.
IT-IRC sec. 809; Separate instructions

8396
Mortgage Interest Credit
Used by qualified mortgage credit certificate holders to figure their mortgage interest credit and any carryover to a subsequent year.
IT-IRC sec. 25

8404
Computation of Interest Charge on DISC-Related Deferred Tax Liability
Used by shareholders of Interest Charge Domestic International Sales Corporations (IC-DISCs) to figure and report their interest on DISC-related deferred tax liability.
ITC 995(f); Regs. sec. 1.995(f)

8453
U.S. Individual Income Tax Declaration for Electronic Filing
Used by qualified filers who file Forms 1040 and certain related schedules, 1040A and 1040EZ via electronic transmission or magnetic media. These filers must file Form 8453 to transmit the individual taxpayer's and return preparer's signature(s) for the return.
IT-IRC secs. 6012 and 6017

8453-E
Employee Benefit Plan Declaration and Signature for Electronic and Magnetic Media Filing
Used by qualified filers who file Forms 5500, 5500-C or 5500-R via electronic transmission or magnetic media.
IT-IRC sec. 6058

8453-F
U.S. Fiduciary Income Tax Declaration and Signature for Electronic and Magnetic Media Filing
Used by qualified filers who file Form 1041 and related schedules via electronic transmission.
IT-IRC sec. 6012

8453-P
U.S. Partnership Declaration and Signature for Electronic/Magnetic Media Filing
Used by qualified filers who file Form 1065 and related schedules via electronic transmission.
IT-IRC secs. 6031

8453-NR
U.S. Nonresident Alien Income Tax Declaration for Magnetic Media Filing
Used by qualified filers who file Forms 1040NR and certain related schedules via electronic transmission. IT-IRC secs. 874 and 6012

Free Tax Help

8582
Passive Activity Loss Limitations
Used by individuals, estates, and trusts to figure the amount of any passive activity loss for the current tax year for all activities and the amount of the passive activity loss allowed on their tax returns.
IT-IRC sec. 469; Separate instructions

8582-CR
Passive Activity Credit Limitations
Used by individuals, estates, and trusts to figure the amount of any passive activity credit for the current year and the amount allowed on their tax returns.
IT-IRC sec. 469; Separate instructions

8586
Low-Income Housing Credit
Used by owners of residential rental projects providing low-income housing to claim the low-income housing credit.
IT-IRC sec. 42; Separate instructions

8594
Asset Acquisition Statement
Used by the buyer and seller of assets used in a trade or business involving goodwill or a going concern value.
IT-IRC 1060, Temp. Regs. sec. 1.1060-1T

8606
Nondeductible IRA Contributions, IRA Basis, and Nontaxable IRA Distributions
Used by individuals to report the amount of IRA contributions they choose to be nondeductible and to figure the nontaxable part of any distributions they received and their basis in their IRA(s) at the end of the calendar year.
IT-IRC sec. 408(o)

8609
Low-Income Housing Credit Allocation Certification
Used by housing credit agencies to allocate a low-income housing credit dollar amount. Also, used by low-income housing building owners to make elections and certify certain necessary information.
IT-IRC sec. 42

Sch. A (Form 8609
Annual Statement
Must be completed by the building owner each year of the 15-year compliance period, whether or not a low-income housing credit is claimed for the year. It is attached to the owner's copy of Form 8609.
IT-IRC sec. 42

8610
Annual Low-Income Housing Credit Agencies Report
Used by housing credit agencies to transmit Forms 8609 and to report the dollar amount of housing credit allocations issued during the calendar year.
IT-IRC sec. 42

8611
Recapture of Low-Income Housing Credit
Used by taxpayers to recapture low-income housing credit taken in a prior year because there is a decrease in the qualified basis of a residential low-income housing building from one year to the next. IT-IRC sec. 42(j)

8612
Return of Excise Tax on Undistributed Income of Real Estate Investment Trusts
Used by real estate investment trusts to report the excise tax on undistributed income.
EX-IRC sec. 4981

8613
Return of Excise Tax on Undistributed Income of Regulated Investment Companies
Used by regulated investment companies to report the excise tax on undistributed income.
EX-IRC sec. 4982

8615
Tax for Children Under Age 14 Who Have Investment Income of More Than $1,400
Used to figure the tax for a child with investment income in excess of $1,400 is taxed at his or her parent's rate and, if so, to figure the child's tax.
IT-IRC sec. 1(g); Temp. Regs. sec. 1.1(i)-1T

8621
Return by a Shareholder of a Passive Foreign Investment Company or Qualified Electing Fund
Used by a U.S. person who owns an interest in a foreign investment company to compute amounts included in gross income. Also used to make elections and terminations of elections. IT-IRC secs. 1291, 1293, and 1294; Separate instructions

8689
Allocation of Individual Income Tax to the Virgin Islands
Used as an attachment to Form 1040 filed by an individual who reports adjusted gross income from Virgin Islands sources. IT-IRC sec. 932

8697
Interest Computation Under the Look-Back Method for Completed Long-Term Contracts
Used by taxpayers to figure the interest due or to be refunded under the look-back method of section 460(b)(2) on certain long-term contracts entered into after February 28, 1986, that are accounted for under either the percentage of completion-capitalized cost method or the percentage of completion method.
IT-IRC sec. 460(b)(1)(B); Separate instructions

8703
Residential Rental Project Certification
Used by operators of residential rental projects to provide annual information the IRS will use to determine whether the projects continue to meet the requirements of section 142(d). Operators indicate on the form the specific test the bond issuer elected for the project period and also indicate the percentage of low-income units in the residential rental project. IT-IRC secs. 142

8709
Exemption From Withholding on Investment Income of Foreign Governments and International Organization
Used by foreign governments or international organizations to claim exemption from withholding under sections 1441 and 1442 on items of income qualifying for tax exemption under section 892. IT-IRC secs. 892

8716
Election To Have a Tax Year Other Than a Required Tax Year
Used by partnerships, S corporations, and personal service corporations to elect to have a tax year other than a required tax year. IT-IRC sec. 444

8717
User Fee for Employee Plan Determination Letter Request
Used by applicants for Employee Plan determination letters to transmit the appropriate user fee. Rev. Proc. 90-17, 1990-1 C.B. 479

8718
User Fee for Exempt Organization Determination Letter Request
Used by applicants for Exempt Organization determination letters to transmit the appropriate user fee. Rev. Proc. 90-17, 1990-1 C.B. 479

8736
Application for Automatic Extension of Time to File U.S. Return for a Partnership, a REMIC, or for Certain Trusts
Used to apply for an automatic three-month extension of time to file Form 1041 (trust), Form 1065, or Form 1066.
IT-IRC sec. 6081; Temp. Regs. secs. 1.6081-2T and 1.6081-3T

IRS Tax Forms and Publications

8752
Required Payment or Refund Under Section 7519
Used by partnerships and S corporations to figure and report the payment required under section 7519 or to obtain a refund of net prior year payments.
IRC secs. 7519 and 444.

8800
Application for Additional Extension of Time to File U.S. Return for a Partnership, REMIC, or for Certain Trusts
Used to apply for an additional extension of up to three months of time to file Form 1041 (trust), Form 1065, or Form 1066. A separate Form 8800 must be filed for each return.
IT-IRC sec. 6081; Temp. Regs. secs. 1.6081-2T and 1.6081-3T

8801
Credit for Prior Year Minimum Tax--Individuals and Fiduciaries
Used by taxpayers to figure the minimum tax credit allowed for tax year and any carryover to a subsequent year.
IT-IRC sec. 53

8804
Annual Return for Partnership Withholding Tax (Section 1446)
Used to report the total liability under section 1446 for the partnership's tax year. Form 8804 is also a transmittal form for Form 8805. IT-IRC sec. 1446; Rev. Proc. 89-31; Separate instructions

8805
Foreign Partner's Information Statement of Section 1446 Withholding Tax
Used to show the amount of effectively connected taxable income and the tax payments allocable to the foreign partner for the partnership's tax year.
IT-IRC sec. 1446; Rev. Proc. 89-31; Separate instructions

8809
Request for Extension of Time To File Information Returns
Used to request an extension of time to file Forms W-2, W-2G, 1098, 1099, or 5498.
PA-IRC sec. 6081; Regs. sec. 1.6081-1

8810
Corporate Passive Activity Loss and Credit Limitations
Used by closely held C corporations and personal service corporations that have passive activity losses and/or credits.
IT-IRC sec. 469; Separate instructions

8811
Information Return for Real Estate Mortgage Investment Conduits (REMICs) and Issuers of Collateralized Debt Obligations
Used by REMICs and Issuers of Collateralized Debt Obligations to report entity information needed to compile Publication 938, *Real Estate Mortgage Investment Conduits (REMIC) Reporting Information*.
IT-IRC secs. 860A-G and 1272(a)(6)(C)(ii)

8812
Additional Child Tax Credit
This credit is in addition to the child and dependent care credit and earned income credit that you may be able to claim. This may give you a refund even if you do not owe any tax.

8813
Partnership Withholding Tax Payment (Section 1446)
Used to make payment to the Internal Revenue Service of withholding tax under section 1446. Each payment of section 1446 taxes made during the partnership's tax year must be accompanied by Form 8813.
IT-IRC sec. 1446; Rev. Proc. 89-31; Separate instructions

8814
Parent's Election to Report Child's Interest and Dividends
Used by parents who elect to report the interest and dividends of their child under age 14 on their own tax return. The form is used to figure the amount of the child's income to report on the parent's return and the amount of additional tax that must be added to the parent's tax.
IT-IRC 1(g)(7)

8815
Exclusion of Interest From Series EE U.S. Savings Bonds Issued After 1989
Used by individuals who paid qualified higher education expenses and cashed series EE U.S. savings bonds during the year to figure the amount of bond interest that is excludable from income.
IT-IRC sec. 135

8816
Special Loss Discount Account and Special Estimated Tax Payments for Insurance Companies
Used by insurance companies that elect to take an additional deduction under section 847.
IT-IRC sec. 847

8817
Allocation of Patronage and Nonpatronage Income and Dividends
Used by certain cooperatives to show income and deductions by patronage and nonpatronage sources.
IT-IRC sec. 1381

8818
Optional Form To Record Redemption of Series EE U.S. Savings Bonds Issued After 1989
Used to keep a record of series EE bonds that were issued after 1989 and cashed in a year higher education expenses were paid.
IRC Sec. 135

8819
Dollar Election Under Section 985
Used to make election to use U.S. dollar by U.S. and foreign business in countries whose currency is hyper-inflationary.
IRC sec. 985

8820
Orphan Drug Credit
An individual, estate, trust or corporation seeking credit for qualified clinical testing expenses paid or incurred during tax year.

8821
Tax Information Authorization
Used as an authorization for an appointee to inspect and/or receive confidential tax information, but not to represent taxpayers. Do not use for alcohol and tobacco taxes and firearms activities. IT-Title 26, CFR, Part 601

8822
Change of Address
Used to notify the Internal Revenue Service of a change of address.

8824
Like-Kind Exchanges
Used by taxpayers to report the exchange of like-kind property. Also used to report section 1043 dispositions.
IRC sec. 1031, 1043; Separate instructions

8825
Rental Real Estate Income and Expenses of a Partnership or an S Corporation
Used by partnerships and S corporations to report income and deductible expenses from rental real estate activities. IRC sec. 61

Free Tax Help

8826
Disabled Access Credit
Used by an eligible business to claim the disabled access credit. The credit is a general business credit under section 38 and is figured under provisions of section 44. IT-IRC section 44

8827
Credit for Prior Year Minimum Tax-Corporation
Used by a corporation to compute the minimum tax credit for alternative minimum tax incurred in prior tax years and any minimum tax credit carryforward that may be used in future years. IT-IRC 53

8828
Recapture of Federal Mortgage Subsidy
Used by individuals to report recapture tax upon early disposition of a federally subsidized residence. IT-IRC sec. 143(m)

8829
Expenses for Business Use of Your Home
Used by Schedule C (Form 1040) filers to figure the allowable expenses for business use of a home and to any carryover of amounts not deductible in the current year. IT-IRC 280A

8830
Enhanced Oil Recovery Credit
Used to claim the enhanced oil recovery credit. The credit is a general business credit under section 38 and is figured under the provisions of section 43. IT-IRC 43

8834
Qualified Electric Vehicle Credit
To figure the credit for qualified electric vehicles placed in service during the year. Credit is 10% of the cost of the qualified vehicle. Maximum credit you may take for each vehicle is $4,000.

8835
Renewable Electricity Production Credit
To claim the renewable electricity production credit. The credit is allowed for the sale of electricity produced in the US or US possessions from qualified energy resources.

8839
Qualified Adoption Expenses
You may be able to take the adoption credit if you paid qualified adoption expenses in 1997 of 1998 and the adoption was final in or before 1998.

8841
Deferral of Additional 1993 Taxes

8842
Election to Use Different Annualization Periods Under the Annualized Income Installment Method for Corporate Estimated Tax

8843
Statement of Exempt Individuals and Individuals with a Medical Condition
If you are an alien individual, file this form to explain the basis of your claim that you can exclude days of presence in the US for purposes of the substantial presence test, i.e., you were unable to leave the US because of a medical condition or medical problem.

8844
Empowerment Zone Employment Credit

8845
Indian Employment Credit

8846
Credit for Employer Social Security Taxes Paid on Certain Employee Cash Tips

8847
Credit for Contributions to Certain Community Development Corporations

8849
Claim for Refund of Excise Tax
The claims may be for amounts you reported on Form 720, 730, or 2290. Also to claim refunds of excise taxes imposed on fuels, chemicals and other articles that are later used for nontaxable purposes.

8850
Prescreening Notice and Certification Request for the Work Opportunity and Welfare to Work Credits
Employers use this form to prescreen and to make a written request to a state employment security agency to certify an individual for the work opportunity credit or work-to-work credit. These are individuals who begin work before July 1, 1999.

8851
Summary of Medical Savings Accounts
This report, submitted by MSA administrators, will be used to furnish information about MSAs to Congress and to determine when the maximum number of MSAs allowed by law is reached.

8853
Medical Savings Accounts and Long Term Care Insurance Contracts
To report newly established MSAs to figure your MSA deduction and to figure your taxable distributions from MSAs.

8857
Request for Innocent Spouse Relief
If you are divorced, separated or no longer living with your spouse, you may now request separation of liability between you and your spouse for an understatement of tax on a joint return.

8859
District of Columbia First Time Home Buyer Credit
To claim the District of Columbia first time home buyer credit. Must file Form 1040 to claim this credit.

8860
Qualified Zone Academy Bond Credit
Eligible holders of qualified zone academy bonds issued after 1997 use this to claim credit offered in lieu of receiving periodic interest payments while the bond is outstanding.

8861
Welfare-To-Work Credit
Used by employers to claim the Welfare-To-Work credit for wages paid or incurred to long term family assistance recipients during the tax year. For those who began working after Dec. 31, 1997 and before July 1, 1999. Credit is 35% of qualified first year wages and 50% of qualified second year wages.

8863
Education Credits
To claim education credits for qualified expenses paid in 1998 for a student enrolled at or attending an eligible education institution. Education credits are the Hope Credit and the Lifetime Learning Credit.

9423
Collection Appeal Request
To file a request for an appeal of a specific collection action

9452
Filing Assistance Program
To figure your gross income and determine your filing requirements under some special situations.

9465
Installment Agreement Request
To request approval to make installment payments for the amount owed to the IRS. If approved, you will be charged $43.

State Tax Assistance

These state taxpayer service departments are the basic starting place for free assistance and guidance pertaining to your state taxes.

Alabama
Taxpayer Assistance
Alabama Income Tax Division
P.O. Box 327465
Montgomery, AL 36132-7465
or
1021 Madison Ave.
Montgomery, AL 36132   334-242-2677
www.ador.state.al.us

Alaska
(No individual income tax; corporation tax only)
Alaska Department of Revenue
Income and Excise Audit Division
P.O. Box 110420
Juneau, AK 99811-0420   907-465-2370
www.revenue.state.ak.us

Arizona
Personal Income Tax
Arizona Department of Revenue
P.O. Box 29002
Phoenix, AZ 85038
www.revenue.state.az.us

Corporation Tax
Arizona Department of Revenue
P.O. Box 29079
Phoenix, AZ 85038-9079
Information and forms: 602-255-3381

Arkansas
Arkansas Department of Finance Administration
Attn: Income Tax
P.O. Box 3628
Little Rock, AR 72203
www.ark.org/dfa/taxs/index.html
General Information Hotline   501-682-1100
Refund Information   501-682-0200

California
Franchise Tax Board
P.O. Box 942840
Sacramento, CA 94240-00400   1-800-852-5711
www.ftb.ca.gov/index.htm
Forms   1-800-338-0505
Hearing Impaired   1-800-822-6268

Colorado
Taxpayer Services
Department of Revenue
1375 Sherman Street
Denver, CO 80261
www.state.co.us/gov_dir/revenue_dir/forms_download.html
Personal and corporate   Fax: 303-534-1209
Forms   303-534-1208

Connecticut
Department of Revenue Services
25 Sigourney St.
Hartford, CT 06106
www.drs.state.ct.us/forms/forms.html
Information and forms (in state)   1-800-382-9463
Information   860-566-8520
Forms   860-297-4753

Delaware
Delaware Division of Revenue
820 North French Street   302-577-3300
Wilmington, DE 19801   1-800-292-7826 (in state only)
www.state.de.us/revenue

Florida
Florida Department of Revenue
5050 W. Tennessee St.
Tallahassee, FL 32399-0100   850-488-6800
http://sun6.dms.state.fl.us/dor
Corporate   850-488-4454

Georgia
Income Tax Division
270 Washington, Room 215
Atlanta, GA 30334
www2.state.ga.us/departments/dor/forms.shtml
Information   404-656-6286
Personal forms   404-656-4293

Hawaii
Taxpayer Services Branch
Hawaii State Tax Collector
P.O. Box 259
Honolulu, HI 96809   808-548-4242
www.state.hi.us/tax/
Information (in-state)   1-800-222-3229
Forms   808-587-7572 or 808-587-7573

Idaho
Idaho Department of Revenue and Taxation
P.O. Box 36
Boise, ID 83722
www.state.id.us/tax/
Taxpayer Assistance   208-334-7660
Forms and refunds   208-334-7789

Illinois
Illinois Department of Revenue
Business Processing Division
P.O. Box 19004
Springfield, IL 62794-9004   1-800-732-8866 (in state)
www.revenue.state.il.us
Information   217-785-6760
Personal and business forms   217-785-7087

Indiana
Indiana Department of Revenue
Government Center North
Room N105
Taxpayer Services Division
Indianapolis, IN 46204   317-232-2240
www.ai.org/dor/
More than 10 forms   317-486-5103
Refunds   317-233-4018

Iowa
Iowa Department of Revenue and Finance
Taxpayer Service
Hoover State Office Building
1305 E. Walnut
Des Moines, IA 50319
www.state.ia.us/government/drf
Information and forms   515-281-3114
Bulk form orders   515-281-5370

Free Tax Help

Kansas
Kansas Department of Revenue
Box 12001
9153 SW Harrison St.
Topeka, KS 66612-2001
www.ink.org/public/kdor/
Personal — 785-296-0222

Kentucky
Kentucky Revenue Cabinet
200 Fairoaks, Building #2
Frankfort, KY 40601
www.state.ky.us/agencies/revenue
Information — 502-564-3658

Louisiana
Louisiana Department of Revenue and Taxation
P.O. Box 201
Baton Rouge, LA 70821-0201
www.rev.state.la.us
Information — 504-925-4611
Forms — 504-925-7532

Maine
Maine Revenue Services
24 State House Station
Augusta, ME 04333-0024
http://janus.state.me.us/revenue/
Information — 207-626-8475
Forms — 1-800-624-7894

Maryland
Comptroller of the Treasury
Income Tax Information
301 W. Preston St.
Baltimore, MD 21201
www.comp.state.md.us
410-974-3918
1-800-MDTAXES (628-2937)

Massachusetts
Massachusetts Dept. of Revenue
Taxpayer Assistance
100 Cambridge Street, 2nd Floor
Boston, MA 02204
www.state.ma.us/dor
617-887-6367
1-800-392-6098 (in state)

Michigan
Department of Treasury
430 West Allegan Street
Lansing, MI 48922
www.treas.state.mi.us
Information — 1-800-487-7000
Forms — 517-373-6598

Minnesota
Minnesota Department of Revenue
600 N. Robert
St. Paul, MN 55145
www.taxes.state.mn.us
Personal — 1-800-652-9094
651-296-3781
Corporate — 1-800-657-3777
651-296-6181

Mississippi
Mississippi State Tax Commission
P.O. Box 1033
Jackson, MS 39215 — 601-923-7800
www.mstc.state.ms.us

Missouri
Taxpayer Services Bureau
Missouri Department of Revenue
P.O. Box 385
Jefferson City, MO 65105-0385
http://dor.state.mo.us
Individual information — 573-751-3505
Corporate information — 573-751-4541
Forms — 1-800-877-6881

Montana
Montana Department of Revenue
Income Tax Division
P.O. Box 5805
Helena, MT 59604
www.state.mt.us/revenue
Personal — 406-444-2837
Corporate — 406-444-3388/6941

Nebraska
Nebraska Dept. of Revenue
Taxpayer Assistance
P.O. Box 94818
Lincoln, NE 68509
www.nol.org/home/NDR
Corporate and Income Tax — 1-800-742-7474
402-471-5729
Forms — 1-800-626-7899 (in state)

Nevada
(No Income Tax)
Department of Taxation
1550 E. College Pkwy., Suite 115
Carson City, NY 89706 — 775-687-4820
www.state.nv.us/taxation

New Hampshire
(No Income Tax)
Department of Revenue
45 Chenell Dr.
Concord, NH 03301 — 603-271-2191
www.state.nh.us/revenue

New Jersey
New Jersey Division of Taxation
50 Barrack Street, CN 269
Trenton, NJ 08646
www.state.nj.us/treasury/
609-292-6400
1-800-323-4400 (in state only)

New Mexico
New Mexico Taxation and Revenue
P.O. Box 630
Santa Fe, NM 87509-0630 — 505-827-0909
www.state.nm.us/tax/

New York
New York State Department of Taxation and Finance
Taxpayer Assistance Bureau
State Campus
Bldg. #8, 9th Floor
Albany, NY 12227
www.tax.state.ny.us
General Information — 1-800-225-5829
Forms — 1-800-462-8100
Refunds — 1-800-443-3200 (in state)

North Carolina
Information:
North Carolina Department of Revenue
P.O. Box 25000
Raleigh, NC 27640 — 919-733-4684
www.dor.state.nc.us

Refund Information:
North Carolina Dept. of Revenue
P.O. Box R
Raleigh, NC 27634 — 919-733-4682

North Dakota
Office of State Tax Commissioner
600 East Boulevard Avenue
Bismarck, ND 58505-0599 — 701-328-2770
1-800-638-2901 (in state)
www.state.nd.us/taxdpt/

State Tax Assistance

Ohio
Taxpayer Services
Ohio Department of Taxation
P.O. Box 2476
Columbus, Ohio 43266-0076
www.state.oh.us/tax/
Forms   1-800-282-1782 (in state)
Information   614-728-9992

Oklahoma
Oklahoma Tax Commission
2501 Lincoln Boulevard
Oklahoma City, OK 73194   1-800-522-8165
www.oktax.state.ok.us
Information   405-521-4321
Forms   405-521-3108

Oregon
Oregon Department of Revenue
Tax Help Section
955 Center Street, NE
Salem, OR 97310   (Automated) 503-378-4988
www.dor.state.or.us

Pennsylvania
Individual:
Pennsylvania Department of Revenue
Taxpayer Services
4th and Walnut Sts.
Harrisburg, PA 17128-0101   717-787-8346
www.revenue.state.pa.us

Corporate:
Pennsylvania Department of Revenue
Business Trust Fund Taxes
Department 280904   717-787-2416
Harrisburg, PA 17128-0904   717-787-1064 (Business)
www.revenue.state.pa.us

Forms:
Pennsylvania Department of Revenue
2850 Turnpike and Middletown Industrial Pike
Harrisburg, PA 17057-5492
Questions   717-787-8201
    1-800-362-2050 (in state)

Rhode Island
Rhode Island Division of Taxation
1 Capitol Hill
Providence, RI 02908
www.tax.state.ri.us
Information   401-222-2905
Forms   401-222-3934
Corporate   401-222-3061

South Carolina
South Carolina Department of Revenue
P.O. Box 125
Columbia, SC 29214
www.dor.state.sc.us
Information   803-898-5709
Services   803-898-5080

South Dakota
(No Income Tax)
445 E. Capitol Ave.
Pierre, SD 57501-3129   605-773-3311
www.state.sd.us/state/executive/revenue/

Tennessee
Tennessee Taxpayer Services
State Office Bldg., 3rd Floor
500 Deaderick St.
Nashville, TN 37242
www.state.tn.us/revenue
Information   615-741-3581
    1-800-829-1040

Texas
(No Income Tax)
State Comptroller of Texas
111 E. 17th St.
Austin, TX 78774   512-463-4600
www.window.state.tx.us/taxinfo/

Utah
Utah State Tax Commission
160 East 3rd South
Salt Lake City, UT 84134
http://txdtm01.tax.ex.state.ut.us
Forms: 801-297-6700

Vermont
Vermont Department of Taxes
Pavillion Office Building
109 State St.
Montpelier, VT 05609-1401
www.state.vt.us/tax/
Taxpayer Assistance   802-828-2865
Business   802-828-2551
Corporate   802-828-5722/5723

Virginia
Virginia Department of Taxation
P.O. Box 1115
Richmond, VA 23218-1115
www.tax.state.vt.us/
Personal   804-367-8031
Corporate   804-367-8036
Forms   804-367-8055

Washington
Department of Revenue
Taxpayer Information
P.O. Box 47478
Olympia, WA 98504   1-800-647-7706
http://dor.wa.gov/

West Virginia
West Virginia Department of Revenue
P.O. Box 3784   304-558-3333
Charleston, WV 25337-3784   1-800-982-8297
www.state.wv.us/taxrev/

Wisconsin
Taxpayer Services
Wisconsin Department of Revenue
P.O. Box 8906
Madison, WI 53708
http://badger.state.wi.us/agencies/dor/
Personal information and forms   608-266-2486
Corporate information and forms   608-266-2772
Bulk form orders   608-267-2025

Wyoming
Department of Revenue
122 W. 25th St.
Cheyenne, WY 82002   307-777-7961
http://revenue.state.wy.us

Free Experts: Free Help in Finding A Free Expert

Not only is the world full of experts who are willing to help resolve your information problems for free, there are organizations whose sole mission is to put you in touch with these specialists. Here is a list of some of these clearinghouses arranged by subject area. Remember that these experts spend their lives studying specific areas and are waiting to help you for free. Just keep in mind that a polite, courteous phone attitude can do wonders.

The websites included with the contacts often have searchable databases where you can find the expert you need with only a couple of clicks of your mouse. For instance, if you go to the Census Bureau websites at www.census.gov, you will find a subject contacts section where you can ask the expert {http://www.census.gov/contacts/www/contacts.html}. If you are looking for commodities information, the National Agricultural Statistics Service at www.nass.usda.gov has a Commodity and Price Specialists Directory on their website at {http://www.usda.gov/nass/nassinfo/speccomm.htm}. There are over 11,000 experts in government offices just waiting to help you.

* Agriculture and Commodities

Agricultural Research Services
U.S. Department of Agriculture
14th and Independence Avenue, SW
Washington, DC 20250   202-720-3656
www.ars.usda.gov
E-mail: arsweb@nal.usda.gov

A staff of research specialists are available to provide specific answers or direct you to an expert in any agricultural-related topic.

National Agricultural Library
10301 Baltimore Boulevard
Beltsville, MD 20702-2351   301-504-5755
www.nal.usda.gov

The National Agricultural Library serves as an information clearinghouse for agricultural-related topics.

National Agricultural Statistics Service
U.S. Department of Agriculture, NAS
14th and Independence Avenue SW
Room 5805 South   800-727-9540
Washington, DC 20250   Fax: 202-690-1311
www.usda.gov/nass
E-mail: nass@nass.usda.gov

The Agricultural Statistics Service (ASS) provides contacts for agricultural production, stocks, prices and other data.

* Arts and Entertainment

Performing Arts Reading Room
Library of Congress
101 Independence Avenue, SE
Room LM-113
Washington, DC 20540   202-707-5507
http://lcweb.loc.gov/rr/perform

This center which works jointly with the Library of Congress offers reference services on any aspect of the performing arts.

* Best and Worst Industries and Companies

Bureau of the Census
U.S. Department of Commerce   301-457-3030
Washington, DC 20230   Fax: 301-457-3670
www.census.gov

Over 100 analysts monitor all the major industries in the United States and the companies within these industries, which range from athletic products to truck trailers.

Office of Industries
U.S. International Trade Commission
500 E Street SW, Room 504   202-205-3296
Washington, DC 20436   Fax: 202-205-3161
www.usitc.gov

Experts analyze impact of world trade on United States industries ranging from audio components to x-ray apparatus.

* Business Advice

Business Assistance Program
Office of Business Liaison
US Department of Commerce
Room H-5898C
Washington, DC 20230   202-482-3176

They can answer questions about business programs and services as well as provide information on a range of business topics.

Library
U.S. Department of Commerce
14th and Constitution Avenue, NW, Room 7046
Washington, DC 20230   202-482-5511
http://lawlibrary.osec.doc.gov

This library also provides reference services on all aspects of business.

* Country Experts

Country Officers
U.S. Department of State
2201 C Street NW
Washington, DC 20520   202-647-4000
www.state.gov

Hundreds of experts are available to provide current political, economic, and other background information on the country they study. Call to ask for the number of a specific country officer.

U.S. Department of Commerce
International Trade Administration   800-USA-TRADE
Washington, DC 20230   202-482-2867
www.ita.doc.gov

Teams of experts from these regions can provide information on marketing and business practices for every country in the world.

International Agriculture
Economic Research Service
U.S. Department of Agriculture
1800 M Street NW
Washington, DC 20005-4788   202-694-5050
www.econ.ag.gov
E-mail: service@econ.ag.gov

This office provides information on agricultural-related aspects of foreign countries.

Foreign Agricultural Service (FAS)
U.S. Department of Agriculture
14th and Independence Avenue, SW
Washington, DC 20250
www.fas.usda.gov

The Foreign Agricultural Service (FAS) provides data on world crops, agricultural policies, and markets.

International Minerals Information
USGS National Center   888-275-8747
12201 Sunrise Valley Drive   703-648-7732
Reston, VA 20192   Fax: 703-648-4888
http://minerals/usgs.gov/minerals

Free Help in Finding A Free Expert

E-mail: dmenzie@usgs.gov
Foreign country experts monitor all aspects of foreign mineral industries.

* Crime

National Criminal Justice Reference Service
National Institute of Justice
Box 6000   301-519-5500
Rockville, MD 20849-6000   800-851-3420
www.ncjrs.org
E-mail: askncjrs@ncjrs.org

Database and reference services provide bibliographies and expertise free or sometimes for a nominal fee.

Uniform Crime Reporting Section
Federal Bureau of Investigation (FBI)
935 Pennsylvania Avenue, NW
Washington, DC 20535-0001   202-234-3000
www.fbi.gov/ucr.htm

Statistics are available from this office on eight major crimes against person and property.

* Demographics, Economic and Industry Statistics

Bureau of the Census
Customer Service   301-457-4100
Washington, DC 20233   Fax: 301-457-4714
www.census.gov

Staff will guide you to the billions of dollars worth of taxpayer supported data.

* Economics:
National, Regional and International

Bureau of Economic Analysis
U.S. Department of Commerce
Washington, DC 20230   202-606-9900
www.bea.doc.gov

This office is the first place to call for economic data.

* Education

Office of Educational Research and Improvement
U.S. Department of Education
555 New Jersey Avenue, NW
Washington, DC 20208-5500   202-219-1556
www.ed.gov/offices/OERI

A network of 16 information clearinghouses that identify literature, experts, audiovisuals, funding, etc.

National Library of Education
U.S. Department of Education   800-424-1616
400 Maryland Avenue, SW   TTY: 202-205-7561
Washington, DC 20202   Fax: 202-401-0552
www.ed.gov/NLE
E-mail: library@ed.gov

This hotline provides referrals to other information sources on any aspect of education.

* Energy

Energy Information Administration
National Energy Information Center
1000 Independence Avenue, SW
Washington, DC 20585   202-586-8800
www.eia.doe.gov
E-mail: Infoctr@eia.doc.gov

This office provides general reference services on U.S. Department of Energy data.

Energy Efficiency and Renewable Energy Network
P.O. Box 3048   800-DOE-EREC
Merrifield, VA 22116   Fax: 703-893-0400
www.eren.doe.gov
E-mail: doe.erec@nciinc.com

Free help on how to save energy as well as information on solar, wind, or any other aspect of renewable energy.

U.S. Department of Energy
Office of Scientific and Technical Information
P.O. Box 62   865-576-1188
Oak Ridge, TN 37831   Fax: 865-576-2865

www.osti.gov
E-mail: OSTIWEBMASTER@apollo.osti.gov

This office provides research and other information services on all energy related topics.

* Health

National Health Information Center   800-336-4797
P.O. Box 1133   301-565-4167
Washington, DC 20013-1133   Fax: 301-984-4256
http://nhic-nt.health.org
E-mail: nhicinfo@health.org

Contact this center for leads to both public and private sector health organizations, research centers and universities.

National Center for Health Statistics
U.S. Department of Health and Human Services
Division of Data Services
6525 Belcrest Road
Hyattsville, MD 20782-2003   301-458-4636
www.cdc.gov/nchs/index.htm

This clearinghouse can provide data on any aspect of health.

* Housing

Library and Information Services Center
U.S. Department of Housing and Urban Development
451 7th Street SW, Room 8141
Washington, DC 20410   202-708-2370

This library provides information on all aspects of housing, and staff will direct you to a program which meets your needs.

* Import and Export Statistics

Foreign Trade Reference Room
U.S. Department of Commerce   202-482-2185
14th and Constitution Avenue, NW, Room 2233   TDD: 202-482-4512
Washington, DC 20230   Fax: 202-482-4614
www.ita.doc.gov

This library can provide data on many aspects of United States trade.

* Metals and Minerals

Mineral Resource Program
913 National Center   703-648-4968
Reston, VA 20192   Fax: 703-648-7757
http://minerals.usgs.gov

Commodity specialists collect, analyze and disseminate information on the occurrence, quality, and quantity, availability of mineral resources.

* Prices, Employment, Productivity And Living Conditions Statistics

Bureau of Labor Statistics
Division of Information Services
2 Madison Avenue, NE, Room 2860   202-691-5200
Washington, DC 20212   TDD: 800-877-8339
www.bls.gov   Fax on demand: 202-606-6325
E-mail: blsdata staff@bls.gov   Question by fax: 202-691-7890

There are subject specialists in such areas as plant closings, labor force projections, producer price indexes, work stoppages.

* World Import and Export Statistics

Office of Trade and Economic Analysis
International Trade Administration
14th and Constitution Avenue, NW   202-482-2185
Washington, DC 20230   Fax: 202-482-5819
www.ita.doc.gov/td/industry/otea/index.html

This is place for numbers concerning trade for most countries.

General Sources

These three offices are the places to get help in locating experts in government as well as the private sector and trade associations.

Free Experts

* Associations
Information Central
American Society of Association Executives 202-626-2723
1575 I Street NW TDD: 202-626-2803
Washington, DC 20005-1168 Fax: 202-371-8825
www.asaenet.org

If you cannot find a relevant association after referring to *Gale's Encyclopedia of Associations* (which is available in most libraries), this organization will help find the right one.

* Government Experts
Federal Information Center
P.O. Box 600 800-688-9889
Cumberland, MD 21501-0600 301-722-9000
www.fic.info.gov TTY: 800-326-2996

Federal Information Centers are located throughout the country and the staff will find you an expert in the government on most any topic.

* Technical Research
Science, Technology, and Business Division
Reference Section
Library of Congress
101 Independence Avenue, SE 202-707-5639
Washington, DC 20540-4751 Fax: 202-207-1925
http://lcweb.loc.gov/rr/scitech

This reference section offers both free and fee-based reference and bibliographic services.

State Starting Places For Finding Experts

If you have trouble locating the exact office you need from the listings elsewhere in the book, this is the section for you. The first place you should start is with State Information Offices listed below. The operators at these offices are normally trained to handle information requests from people who don't know where to go within the state bureaucracy. If you are not successful, try either or both of the other offices listed.

Governor's Office

Because the responsibilities of various state offices often overlap, it may be helpful to begin your data search by contacting the state governor's office. While every state has a central switchboard to field inquiries regarding state business, the number is usually helpful only if you already know which agency is responsible for gathering and interpreting the information you are after. If you are hazy in this regard, the state governor's office will certainly know the appropriate agency department and, if you are lucky, even the name of the special contact person to call.

State Library

A vast amount of research information is available from the state library. After all, it is the official repository of state agency documents and the first place to start if you want to do all of the footwork yourself. In addition, most state libraries also shelve copies of federal government documents and publications.

State libraries are paid for with tax dollars and are open to the public. Collections usually include state legal codes, state historical documents, archival records, genealogy type information, business and economic records, statistical abstracts and annual reports.

In each library these is generally a government information person who can provide telephone and personal assistance to researchers. In addition, there is often a staff specialist to help with statistical questions.

The following is a list of state operators, librarians, and governor's offices.

State Information and Governor's Offices

Alabama
State Information Office: 334-242-8000; {www.state.al.us}

Governor's Office: Office of the Governor, State Capitol Room N-104, 600 Dexter Ave., Montgomery, AL 36130; 334-242-7100, Fax: 334-242-0937; {www.governor.state.al.us}.

State Library: Alabama Public Library Service, 6030 Monticello Drive, Montgomery, AL 36130; 334-213-3900, 800-723-8459 (Montgomery area), Fax: 334-213-3993; {www.apla.state.al.us}.

Alaska
State Information Office: 907-465-2111; {www.state.ak.us}

Governor's Office: Office of the Governor, P.O. Box 110001, Juneau, AK 99811-0001; 907-465-3500, Fax: 907-465-3532; {www.gov.state.ak.us}.

State Library: Alaska State Libraries, P.O. Box 110571, Juneau, AK 99811-0571; 907-465-2921, Fax: 907-465-2665; {www.educ.state.ak.us/lam}, E-mail: {asl@eed.state.ak.us}.

Arizona
State Information Office: 602-542-4900; {www.state.az.us}

Governor's Office: Office of the Governor, 1700 West Washington Street, Phoenix, AZ 85007; 602-542-4331, Fax: 602-542-1381; {www.governor.state.az.us}.

State Library: Department of Library Archives and Public Records, State Capitol, Suite 200, 1700 West Washington Street, Phoenix, AZ 85007; 602-542-4035, 800-255-5841 (Arizona only); {www.lib.az.us}, E-mail: {webedit@dlapr.az.us}.

Arkansas
State Information Office: 501-682-3000; {www.state.ar.us}

Governor's Office: Office of the Governor, State Capitol Building, Room 250, Little Rock, AR 72201; 501-682-2345; {www.state.ar.us/governor}.

State Library: Arkansas State Library, 1 Capitol Mall, Little Rock, AR 72201; 501-682-2053, Fax: 501-682-1529; {www.asl.lib.ar.us}, E-mail: {shawkes@asl.lib.ar.us}.

California
State Information Office: 916-322-9900; {www.state.ca.us}

Governor's Office: Office of the Governor, State Capitol Building, Sacramento, CA 95814; 916-445-2841, Fax: 916-445-4633; {www.ca.gov}.

State Library: California State Library, Library and Courts Building I, 914 Capitol Mall Room 220, Sacramento, CA 95814; 916-654-0174; {www.library.ca.go}.

Colorado
State Information Office: 303-866-5000; {www.state.co.us}

Governor's Office: Office of the Governor, 136 State Capitol Building, Denver, CO 80203-1792; 303-866-2471; {www.state.co.us/gov_dir/governor_office.html}.

State Library: Colorado State Library, 201 East Colfax Avenue, Denver, CO 80203-1704; 303-866-6900, Fax: 303-866-6940; {www.cde.state.co.us/index_library.htm}.

Connecticut
State Information Office: 860-240-0222; {www.state.ct.us}

Governor's Office: Office of the Governor, State Capitol, 210 Capitol Avenue, Hartford, CT 06106; 860-566-4840; {www.state.ct.us/governor}.

State Library: Connecticut State Library, 231 Capitol Avenue, Hartford, CT 06106; 860-566-4777, Fax: 860-566-8940; {www.cslib.org}.

Delaware
State Information Office: 302-739-4000; {www.state.de.us}

Governor's Office: Office of the Governor, Legislative Hall, Dover, DE 19901; 302-739-4104; {www.state.de.us/governor/index.htm}.

Free Experts

State Library: Delaware State Library, 43 South DuPont Highway, Dover, DE 19901; 302-739-4748, Fax: 302-739-6787; {www.lib.de.us}, E-mail: {emcneeley@lib.de.us}.

District of Columbia
Information Office: 202-727-6161; {www.ci.washington.dc.us}

Mayor's Office: Executive Office of the Mayor, 441 4th NW, Room 1100, 1 Judiciary Square, Washington, DC 20001; 202-727-2980.

Central Library: Martin Luther King Jr. Memorial Library, 901 G Street NW, Washington, DC 20001; 202-727-0321, {http://dclibrary.org}.

Florida
State Information Office: 850-488-1234; {www.state.fl.us}

Governor's Office: Office of the Governor, The Capitol, Tallahassee, FL 32399-0001; 850-488-4441; {www.state.fl.us/eog}.

State Library: Florida State Library, 500 Bronough Street, Tallahassee, FL 32399; 850-487-2651; {http://dlls.dos.state.fl.us/stlib}.

Georgia
State Information Office: 404-656-2000; {www.state.ga.us}

Governor's Office: Office of the Governor, State Capitol Building, Constituent Services Room 111, Atlanta, GA 30334; 404-656-1776, Fax: 404-657-7332; {www.gagovernor.org}.

State Library: Office of Public Library Services, 156 Trinity Avenue, Atlanta, GA 30303; 404-657-6220; {www.public.lib.ga.us}.

Hawaii
State Information Office: 808-586-0221; {www.state.hi.us}

Governor's Office: Office of the Governor, Executive Chambers, State Capitol, Honolulu, HI 96813-2901; 808-586-0034, Fax: 808-586-0006; {http://gov/state.hi.us}, E-mail: {gov@gov.state.hi.us}.

State Library: Hawaii State Library, 478 South King St., Honolulu, HI 96813; 808-586-3704; {www.hcc.hawaii.edu/hspls/}.

Idaho
State Information Office: 208-334-2411; {www.state.id.us}

Governor's Office: Office of the Governor, 700 West Jefferson, 2nd Floor, Boise, ID 83702; 208-334-2100, Fax: 208-334-3454; {www.state.id.us/gov/govhmpg.htm}.

State Library: Idaho State Library, 325 West State Street, Boise, ID 83702; 208-334-2150, Fax: 208-334-4016; {www.lili.org/isl}, E-mail: {swhite@state.id.us}

Illinois
State Information Office: 217-782-2000; {www.state.il.us}

Governor's Office: Office of the Governor, 207 Statehouse, Springfield, IL 62706; 217-782-0244 (voice/TDD), Fax: 217-524-4049; {www.state.il.us/gov/}.

State Library: Illinois State Library, 300 South 2nd Street, Springfield, IL 62701; 217-785-5600, 800-665-5576 (within Illinois), TDD: 217-524-1137; {www.sos.state.il.us/depts/library/isl_home.html}.

Indiana
State Information Office: 317-232-1000; {www.state.in.us}

Governor's Office: Office of the Governor, 206 State House, Indianapolis, IN 46204; 317-232-4567, Fax: 317-232-3443; {www.state.in.us/gov}.

State Library: Indiana State Library, 140 North Senate, Indianapolis, IN 46204; 317-232-3675, TDD: 317-232-7763, Fax: 317-232-3728; {www.statelib.lib.in.us}.

Iowa
State Information Office: 515-281-5011; {www.state.ia.us}

Governor's Office: Office of the Governor, State Capitol Building, Des Moines, IA 50319; 515-281-5211; {www.state.ia.us/governor}.

State Library: Iowa State Library, 1112 East Grand Avenue, Des Moines, IA 50319-515-281-4105; {www.silo.lib.ia.us}.

Kansas
State Information Office: 913-296-0111; {www.state.ks.us}

Governor's Office: Office of the Governor, State Capitol 2nd Floor, Topeka, KS 66612; 785-296-3232, TDD: 800-748-4408, Fax: 785-296-7973; {www.ink.org/public/governor}, E-mail: {governor@ink.org}.

State Library: Kansas State Library, 300 SW Tenth Ave., Room 343-N, Topeka, KS 66612; 785-296-3296, 800-432-3919 (Kansas), Fax: 785-296-6650; {http://skyways.lib.ks.us/kansas/KSL}.

Kentucky
State Information Office: 502-564-3130; {www.state.ky.us}

Governor's Office: Office of the Governor, 700 Capitol Avenue, Frankfort, KY 40601; 502-564-2611, Fax: 502-564-2611; {www.state.ky.us/agencies/gov/govmenu6.htm}.

State Library: Kentucky Department for Libraries and Archives, 300 Coffee Tree Road, P.O. Box 537, 40602-0537; 502-564-8300, Fax: 502-564-5773; {www.kdla.state.ky.us}.

Louisiana
State Information Office: 504-342-6600; {www.state.la.us}

Governor's Office: Office of the Governor, P.O. Box 94004, Baton Rouge, LA 70804; 225-342-7015, Fax: 225-342-7099; {www.gov.state.la.us}.

State Libraries: Louisiana State Library, P.O. Box 131, Baton Rouge, LA 70821, 701 N. 4th St., Baton Rouge, LA 70802; 225-342-4923, Fax: 225-219-4804; {http://smt.state.lib.la.us}.

Maine
State Information Office: 207-582-9500; {http://janus.state.me.us}

Governor's Office: Office of the Governor, #1 State House Station, Augusta, ME 04333; 207-287-3531, TTY: 207-287-6548, Fax: 207-287-1034; {www.state.me.us/governor/index.html}.

State Library: Maine State Library, LMA Building, State House, Station 64, Augusta, ME 04333; 207-287-5600, TTY: 207-287-5622, Fax: 207-287-5615; {www.state.me.us/msl/mslhome.htm}.

Maryland
State Information Office: 800-449-4347; {www.state.md.us}

Governor's Office: Office of the Governor, State House, Annapolis, MD 21401; 410-974-3901, 800-811-8336 (Maryland), Fax: 410-974-3275; {www.gov.state.md.us}, E-mail: {governor@gov.state.md.us}.

State Library: Maryland State Archives, 400 Cathedral Street, Baltimore, MD 21201; 410-396-5551, Fax: 410-396-3772; {www.sailor.lib.md.us/index.html}, E-mail: {askus@sailor.lib.md.us}.

Massachusetts
State Information Office: 617-722-2000; {www.state.ma.us}

Governor's Office: Office of the Governor, State House, Room 360, Boston, MA 02133; 617-727-6250, TTY: 617-727-3666, Fax: 617-727-9725; {www.state.ma.us/gov}.

State Starting Places For Finding Experts

State Library: 341 State House, Boston, MA 02133; 617-727-2590; {www.magnet.state.ma.us/lib}.

Michigan

State Information Office: 517-373-1837; {www.state.mi.us}

Governor's Office: Governor, Office of the Governor, P.O. Box 30013, Lansing, MI 48909; 517-335-7858, Fax: 517-335-6863; {www.migov.state.mi.gov}.

State Library: Michigan State Library, 717 West Allegan, P.O. 30007, Lansing, MI 48909; 517-373-1580; {www.libofmich.lib.mi.us}.

Minnesota

State Information Office: 612-296-6013; {www.state.mn.us}

Office of the Governor, 130 State Capitol, 75 Constitution Avenue, St. Paul, MN 55155; 651-296-3391, 800-657-3717, TDD: 651-296-0075 or 800-657-3598; {www.mainserver.state.mn.us/governor}.

State Library: Minnesota Department of Children, Families and Learning, 1500 Highway 3610, Roseville, MN 55113; 651-582-8719, Fax: 651-582-8898; {http://cfl.state.mn.us/library}.

Mississippi

State Information Office: 601-359-1000; {www.state.ms.us}

Governor's Office: Office of the Governor, P.O. Box 139, Jackson, MS 39205; 601-359-3150; {www.govoff.state.ms.us}.

State Library: Department of Archives and History Library, Capers Building, 100 South State Street, P.O. Box 571, Jackson, MS 39205; 601-359-6876, Fax: 601-359-6964; {www.mdah.state.ms.us}.

Missouri

State Information Office: 573-751-2000; {www.state.mo.us}

Governor's Office: Office of the Governor, Capitol Building, Room 216, P.O. Box 720, Jefferson City, MO 65102-0720; 573-751-3222, Fax: 573-751-1495; {www.gov.state.mo.us}.

State Library: Missouri State Library, P.O. Box 387, Jefferson City, MO 65102-0387; 573-751-3615, Fax: 573-751-3612; {http://sos.state.mo.us/lib-ser/libser.html}, E-mail: {SOSmain@mail.sos.state.mo.us}.

Montana

State Information Office: 406-444-2511; {www.state.mt.us}

Governor's Office: Office of the Governor, State Capitol, Helena, MT 59620-0801; 406-444-3111, TDD: 406-444-3607; {www.state.mt.us/governor/governor.htm}.

State Library: Montana State Library, 1515 East 6th Avenue, P.O. Box 201800, Helena, MT 59620; 406-444-3115, Fax: 406-444-5612; {http://msl.state.mt.us}, E-mail: {msl@state.mt.us}.

Nebraska

State Information Office: 402-471-2311

Governor's Office: Office of the Governor, P.O. Box 94848, Lincoln, NE 68509-4848; 402-471-2244; {http://gov.nol.org}.

State Library: Nebraska Library Commission, The Atrium, 1200 North Street, Suite 120,, Lincoln, NE 68508-2023; 402-471-2045, 800-307-2665 (Nebraska), Fax: 402-471-2083; {www.nlc.state.ne.us}.

Nevada

State Information Office: 702-687-5000; {www.state.nv.us}

Governor's Office: Office of the Governor, Capitol Building, Carson City, NV 89701, 775-684-5670; {www.state.nv.us/gov/govhtm}.

State Library: Nevada State Library and Archives, 100 North Stewart Street, Carson City, NV 89701-4282; 775-684-3360; 800-922-2880 (Nevada); {http://dmla.clan.lib.nv.us/docs/nsla}.

New Hampshire

State Information Office: 603-271-1110; {www.state.nh.us}

Governor's Office: Office of the Governor, State House, 107 N. Main St., Room 208, Concord, NH 03301-4990; 603-271-2121; {www.state.nh.us/governor/index.html}.

State Library: New Hampshire State Library, 20 Park Street, Concord, NH 03301; 603-271-2144, Fax: 603-271-6826; {www.state.nh.us/nhsl}.

New Jersey

State Information Office: 609-292-2121; {www.state.nj.us}

Governor's Office: Office of the Governor, P.O. Box 001, Trenton, NH 08625; 609-292-6000; {www.state.nj.us/governor/index.shtml}.

State Library: New Jersey State Library, 185 West State Street, P.O. Box 520, Trenton, NJ 08625-0520; 609-292-6220; Fax: 609-292-2746; {www.nh.state.lib.org}.

New Mexico

State Information Office: 505-827-4011; {www.state.nm.us}

Governor's Office: Office of the Governor, State Capitol Building, Santa Fe, NM 87503; 505-827-3000; {www.governor.state.nm.us}.

State Library: New Mexico State Library, 1209 Camino Carlos Rey, Santa Fe, NM 87505-9860; 505-746-9700; {www.stlib.state.nm.us}, E-mail: {webmaster@stlib.state.nm.us}.

New York

State Information Office: 518-747-2121; {www.state.ny.us}

Governor's Office: Office of the Governor, State Capitol, Albany, NY 12224; 518-474-8390; {www.state.ny.us/governor}.

State Library: New York State Library, Cultural Education Center, Empire State Plaza, Madison Avenue, Albany, NY 12230; 518-474-5355; {www.nysl.nysed.gov}.

North Carolina

State Information Office: 919-733-1110; {www.state.nc.us}

Governor's Office: Office of the Governor, 20301 Mail Service Center, Raleigh, NC 27699; 800-662-7952 (North Carolina), 919-733-5811/4240, Fax: 919-715-3175/2120; {www.governor.state.nc.us}.

State Library: State Library of North Carolina, Archives and History/State Library Building, 109 East Jones Street, Raleigh, NC 27601; 919-733-3270, Fax: 919-733-5679; {http://statelibrary.dcr.state.nc.us}.

North Dakota

State Information Office: 701-224-2000; {www.state.nd.us}

Governor's Office: Office of the Governor, 600 East Boulevard Avenue, Bismarck, ND 58505; 701-328-2200, TDD: 701-328-2887, Fax: 701-328-2205; {www.health.state.nd.us/gov}, E-mail: {governor@state.nd.us}.

State Library: North Dakota State Library, 604 East Boulevard Avenue, Department 250, Bismarck, ND 58505; 701-328-4622, 800-472-2104; {http://ndsl.lib.state.nd.us}.

Ohio

State Information Office: 614-466-2000; {www.state.oh.us}

Governor's Office: Office of the Governor, 77 South High Street, 30th Floor, Columbus, OH 43215; 614-466-3555, 614-644-HELP; {www.state.oh.us/gov}.

Free Experts

State Library: State Library of Ohio, 65 South Front Street, Columbus, OH 43266; 614-644-7061, Fax: 614-466-3584; {http://winslo.state.oh.us}.

Oklahoma
State Information Office: 405-521-2011; {www.state.ok.us}

Governor's Office: Office of the Governor, 212 State Capitol Building, Oklahoma City, OK 73105; 405-521-2342, Fax: 405-521-3353; {www.state.ok.us/~governor}, E-mail: {governor@state.ok.us}.

State Library: Oklahoma State Library, 200 NE 18th St., Oklahoma City, OK 73105; 405-521-2505; {www.odl.state.ok.us}.

Oregon
State Information Office: 503-378-3111; {www.state.or.us}

Governor's Office: Office of the Governor, State Capitol Building, Salem, OR 97310; 503-378-4582 (24 hours), TTY: 503-378-4859, Fax: 503-378-4863; {www.governor.state.or.us}.

State Library: Oregon State Library, 250 Winter Street, NE, Salem, OR 97310; 503-378-4277, 503-588-7119(24hours), TTY/TDD: 503-378-4276; {www.osl.state.or.us/oslhome.html}.

Pennsylvania
State Information Office: 717-787-2121; {www.state.pa.us}

Governor's Office: Office of the Governor, 225 Main Capitol, Harrisburg, PA 17120; 717-787-2500; {www.state.pa.us/PA_Exec/Governor/overview.html}.

State Library: State Library of Pennsylvania, P.O. Box 1601, Harrisburg, PA 17105; 717-787-5986; {www.statelibrary.state,.pa.us/Libstate.htm}.

Rhode Island
State Information Office: 401-222-2000; {www.state.ri.us}

Governor's Office: Office of the Governor, 222 State House, Providence, RI 02903; 401-222-2080, Fax: 401-861-5894; {www.governor.state.ri.us}.

State Library: Rhode Island State Library, 82 Smith Street, State House, Room 208, Providence, RI 02903; 401-222-2473, Fax: 401-331-6430; {www.state.ri.us/library/web.htm}.

South Carolina
State Information Office: 803-734-1000; {www.state.sc.us}

Governor's Office: Office of the Governor, P.O. Box 11829, Columbia, SC 29211; 803-734-9400; {www.state.sc.us/governor}, E-mail: {governor@govoepp.state.sc.us}.

State Library: South Carolina State Library, 1500 Senate Street, P.O. Box 11469, Columbia, SC 29211; 803-734-8666, TDD: 803-734-7298, Fax: 803-734-8676; {www.state.sc.us/scsl}.

South Dakota
State Information Office: 605-773-3011; {www.state.sd.us}

Governor's Office: Office of the Governor, 500 East Capitol, Pierre, SD 57501; 605-773-3212; {www.state.sd.us/governor}, E-mail: {sdgov@state.sd.us}.

State Library: South Dakota State Library, Mercedes MacKay Building, 800 Governors Drive, Pierre, SD 57501; 605-773-3131, 800-423-6665; {www.state.sd.us/state/executive/deca/st_lib/st_lib.htm}.

Tennessee
State Information Office: 615-741-3011; {www.state.tn.us}

Governor's Office: Office of the Governor, State Capitol, Nashville, TN 37243-0001; 615-741-2004; {www.state.tn.us/governor}.

State Library: Tennessee State Library and Archives, 403 7th Avenue, North, Nashville, TN 37243-0312; 615-741-2764; {www.state.tn.us/sos/statelib/tslahome.htm}.

Texas
State Information Office: 512-463-4630; {www.state.tx.us}

Governor's Office: Office of the Governor, P.O. Box 12428, Austin, TX 78711-2428; 512-463-2000, Fax: 512-463-1849; {www.governor.state.tx.us}.

State Library: Texas State Library, 1201 Brazos, P.O. Box 12927, Austin, TX 78711-2927; 512-463-5455; {www.tsl.state.tx.us}, E-mail: {reference.desk@tsl.state.tx.us}.

Utah
State Information Office: 801-538-3000; {www.state.tn.us}

Governor's Office: Office of the Governor, 210 State Capitol, Salt Lake City, UT 84114; 801-538-1000, Fax: 801-538-1528; {www.governor.state.ut.us}, E-mail: {governor@state.ut.us}.

State Library: Utah State Library, 2150 South 300 West, Suite 16, Salt Lake City, UT 84115; 801-715-6789; E-mail: {blind@mail.state.lib.ut.us}.

Vermont
State Information Office: 802-828-1110; {www.state.vt.us}

Governor's Office: Office of the Governor, 109 State Street, Montpelier, VT 05609-0101; 802-828-3333, Fax: 802-828-3339; {www.state.vt.us/governor/index.htm}.

State Library: Vermont Department of Libraries, 109 State Street, Montpelier, VT 05609-0601; 802-828-3265, Fax: 802-828-2199; {http://dol.state.vt.us}, E-mail: {smcshane@dol.state.vt.us}.

Virginia
State Information Office: 804-786-0000; {www.state.va.us}

Governor's Office: Office of the Governor, State Capitol, 3rd Floor, Richmond, VA 23219; 804-786-2211; {www.state.va.us/governor}.

State Library: The Library of Virginia, 800 East Broad Street, Richmond, VA 23219; 804-692-3500; {www.lva.lib.va.us}.

Washington
State Information Office: 360-753-5000; {http://access.wa.us}

Governor's Office: Office of the Governor, P.O. Box 40002, Olympia, WA 98504; 360-902-4111, TTY/TDD: 360-753-6466, Fax: 360-753-4110; {www.governor.wa.gov}.

State Library: Washington State Library, 415 15th Avenue, SW, P.O. Box 42460, Olympia, WA 98504; 360-753-5592; {www.statelib.wa.gov}, E-mail: {webmaster@statelib.was.gov}.

West Virginia
State Information Office: 304-558-3456; {www.state.wv.us}

Governor's Office: Office of the Governor, State Capitol Complex, Charleston, WV 25305; 304-558-2000, 888-435-2731, Fax: 304-342-7025; {www.state.wv.us/governor}, E-mail: {governor@governor.state.wv.us}.

State Library: West Virginia Library Commission, 1900 Kanawha Boulevard East, Charleston, WV 25302; 304-558-204, 800-642-9021 (West Virginia), Fax: 304-558-2044; {http://wvlc.lib.wv.us}.

Wisconsin
State Information Office: 608-266-2211; {www.state.wi.us}

Governor's Office: Office of the Governor, 125 South State Capitol, Madison, WI 53702; 608-266-1212, Fax: 608-267-8983; {www.wisgov.state.wi.us}.

State Starting Places For Finding Experts

State Library, Division for Libraries, Technology and Community Learning, 125 South Webster Street, P.O. Box 7841, Madison, WI 53707-7841; 608-267-9219, Fax: 608-267-1052.

Wyoming

State Information Office: 307-777-7011; {www.state.wy.us}

Governor's Office: Office of the Governor, State Capitol, Cheyenne, WY 82002; 307-777-7434; {www.state.wy.us/governor/governor_home.html}.

State Library: Wyoming State Library, Supreme Court and State Library Building, 2301 Capitol Avenue, Cheyenne, WY 82002; 307-777-7283; {www-wsl.state.wy.us}.

Free Research on Any Topic

Our government is the single largest source of information in the world. Government now represents about 37% of our country's Gross National Product. The commercial publishers in the United States publish about 55,000 books per year. That represents all the books you find each year in bookstores and libraries. However, one little publisher in the government, called the National Technical Information Center, produces over 90,000 titles a year. That's almost twice the amount published by all the commercial publishers combined! And most people have never even heard of this office. There are hundreds of other government publishers that no one knows exist, such as the Office of Health Care Policy Research that will send you a free report showing what works and what doesn't in treating depression, or the U.S. International Trade Commission who will send you a free study on the market for computer games in the United States. Did you know that your Congressman or Senator's office can send you a free report from a list of 10,000 current event topics? These reports are prepared for every member of Congress by the Congressional Research Service. People who make the most important decisions in the world keep up on current events this way, and you can have access to these reports, too.

One Million Of The Best Experts In The World For FREE

Students, researchers, and even average citizens don't have to have a lot of money to get expert opinions and help in finding the answers to their problems. Did you know that some of the most highly respected experts work for the government? Why pay for an office visit to a local doctor to get the latest facts on cholesterol, when you can call an expert at the National Institutes of Health and get your questions answered for free? Why go to your local stockbroker or even to a hot shot Wall Street analyst to get information about the future of biotechnology? You can contact dozens of free experts in the U.S. Government who get paid $60,000 or $70,000 a year just to study biotechnology — and they won't try to sell you any stocks, either.

There are other experts available through the government — like legal experts. Most students and researchers believe that the only way to learn about laws is to spend hours in a stuffy old law library, or to hire a high-priced lawyer. This isn't so. If you want to know about franchising law, don't hire a franchising attorney — call the U.S. Federal Trade Commission. Talk to an attorney that wrote the franchise law, not just studied it in law school! Lawyers, like doctors and other professionals, can't keep up because the laws change every day. They are likely to charge you their hourly fee to go out and learn the current law for you. So why hire an attorney at $200 an hour when you can call a lawyer who wrote the law and pay him absolutely nothing? Want to know more about the laws governing sexual harassment? Call the Equal Employment Opportunity Commission. Want to know about the laws governing dry cleaners who might be polluting your neighborhood? Call the U.S. Environmental Protection Agency and get the most up-to-date information.

I estimate that our government supports approximately one million specialists who spend their careers studying everything from AM radio advertising to zippers. In the past I've found and used government experts on potatoes, underwear, and even urinal screens. The government is the only employer in the world who can afford to pay experts like these. The person studying cholesterol can tell you what will be in the medical journals next year because their office is spending millions of dollars researching the subject today. Your local doctor can't possible keep up on all the changes that are happening in the field of medicine. And he won't know what current research is underway, either.

More Current Than Your Library

The materials available in the library can't possibly keep up with our fast changing society. You want to know about Russia? A librarian is likely to show you the encyclopedia or maybe some books about the country. Chances are they will all be out of date. How can an encyclopedia or a book that takes a year or more to be edited and printed tell you what's going on TODAY in Russia? Instead, you can call the country desk officers at the U.S. Department of State, the U.S. Department of Commerce, or at the U.S. Information Agency and find out what's going on in Russia as of LAST NIGHT. And it will cost you absolutely nothing!

Our world is changing quickly everywhere, not just in the area of world affairs. Where are you going to find the latest rules for governing "900" numbers? At the Federal Communications Commission. Where are you going to find the current guidelines for mammogram screening for women? At the Breast Cancer Information Clearinghouse at the National Institute of Health. Where are you going to find the country's fastest growing cities? At the Bureau of Economic Analysis at the U.S. Department of Commerce. Where are you going to find the best jobs for the year 2000? At the Bureau of Labor Statistics. All of this information is easy to get your hands on, and it's free.

More Complete Than The Superficial Media

Besides the local library, the media seems to be our country's other major source of information. The media is driven by sound bites that are just one or two minutes long. This used to be true of only electronic media, but now it's also becoming true of newspapers and even magazines. More and more print media is beginning to look just like *USA Today*.

A sound bite is a headline. And this headline usually is the result of a reporter reading over a press release and condensing it into a one minute sound bite. They know that's all we'll listen to. But if you're a researcher, a student writing a paper, or if the specific subject affects you, you'll have to find more information. Where are you going to get this detailed information?

Go to the government. On most issues, you can get enough information to make an informed decision or to write an unbiased report. For example, if you see a spot on CNN telling you about the growth of the yogurt industry, don't call CNN. They probably are just reporting from a press release that the National Association Of Yogurt Manufacturers sent to them. Call the yogurt industry expert at the U.S. Department of Commerce. They spend years studying the yogurt industry and can send to you or tell you where to get all the latest unbiased information about the true growth of the yogurt industry. Or, what if you see a report on ABC Nightly News telling you about the problems people are having with silicone breast implants? The reporter is probably excerpting from a press release. Do you call ABC for more detailed information? No. For those who can afford it, a call to your local doctor is a more obvious choice. But most doctors can't keep up on all the latest developments in all aspects of health care, and probably have no idea how that report on ABC will affect you. But if you call the government's Silicone Breast Implant Hotline at the Food and Drug Administration, they can tell you all the latest developments on the topic, and even send you information that will make it possible for you to make an informed decision on further treatment.

We seem to put a lot of value in anything that is in print or even on the broadcast news, particularly if it's on a topic that we don't know much about. If you really want to know about Latvia or even some topic like hemorrhoids, you can talk to someone in the government who has probably spent the last 10 years of their lives studying these subjects. They'll know more than any journalist will ever know, and their expertise is free.

The Key To Living In The Information Age

I believe that learning to use government resources is the key to living in the information age. Computers are just a piece of this complicated puzzle. I have heard it said that in the last 50 years more information has been created than in the entire history of man up to that point. Whether that is true or not, we are all aware that we are living in the midst of an information explosion. When I grew up in the 1950s, if you wrote a book it was as though you walked on water. Now everybody and his brother seems to be writing a book! Look at me — I flunked English in college and I have two New York Times bestsellers. And with this huge growth in information and literature, everyone is creating specialized databases. If you want to know about solar heated swimming pools, you can tap into a solar database and probably get 500 articles that have been written about solar heated swimming pools. Now you have a bigger problem: How do you decide which articles are the best ones? Where can you get these articles?

Instead of going through this time-consuming procedure you can contact the government's solar heated swimming pool expert at the U.S. Department of Energy. This expert probably spent the last 12 years of his life studying this subject and reading all of these articles (and probably writing a good portion of them, too!) More importantly, he can probably tell you what will be in the database next year because he is working on new research today. That's really learning to live in an information society — getting information that is better, faster, and cheaper than you can find from traditional information sources.

So the tool that is the key to the information explosion is not the computer, but the telephone. Unlike the world of computers where 800 numbers are set up to provide you with help in using your computer, there is no one to teach you how to use the telephone effectively. The key to getting the most information by using the telephone lies in how you treat the people who are sitting on the other end of the line waiting to give you the information you need.

Ten Basic Telephone Tips

Here are a few important tips to follow when you attempt to get information of any kind from a government agency over the telephone. Above all, remember that patience is often rewarded even by government bureaucrats!

Introduce Yourself Cheerfully
Starting the conversation with a cordial and upbeat attitude will set the tone for the entire interview. Let the official know that this is not going to be just another mundane telephone call, but a pleasant interlude in an otherwise hectic day.

Be Open and Candid
Be as candid as possible with your source. If you are evasive or deceitful in explaining your needs or motives, your source will be reluctant to provide you with anything but the most basic information.

Be Optimistic
Relay a sense of confidence throughout the conversation. If you call and say "You probably aren't the right person" or "You don't have any information, do you?" it's easy for the person to respond, "You're right, I can't help you." A positive attitude encourages your source to dig deeper for an answer to your question. If they appreciate your attitude, it stand to reason that they will want to do all they can to help you.

Be Courteous
You can be optimistic and still be courteous. Remember the old adage that you can catch more flies with honey than you can with vinegar? Government officials love to tell others what they know, as long as their position of authority is not questioned or threatened.

Be Concise
State your problem simply. Be direct. A long-winded explanation may bore your contact and reduce your chances for getting a thorough response.

Don't Be A "Gimme"
A "gimme" is someone who expects instant answers and displays a "give me that" attitude. Be considerate and sensitive to your contact's time, feelings, and eccentricities. Although, as a taxpayer, you may feel you have the right to put this government worker through the mill, that kind of attitude will only cause the contact to give you minimal assistance.

Be Complimentary
This goes hand in hand with being courteous. A well-placed compliment ("Everyone I spoke to said you are the person I need to ask.") about your source's expertise or insight will serve you well. We all like to feel like an "expert" when it comes to doing our job.

Be Conversational
Briefly mention a few irrelevant topics such as the weather or the latest political campaign. The more conversational you are without being too chatty, the more likely your source will be to open up and want to help you.

Free Research On Any Topic

Return the Favor

You might share with your source information or even gossip you have picked up elsewhere. However, be certain not to betray the trust of either your client or another source. If you do not have any relevant information to share at the moment, call back when you are further along in your research.

Send Thank You Notes

A short note, typed or handwritten, will help ensure that a government official source will be just as cooperative in answering future questions.

How To Use These Clearinghouses

The Information Clearinghouses described in this section are government offices set up to provide taxpayers with free information, reports, articles, and referrals. Some of the clearinghouses may charge a small fee for some of their services, such as the copying of articles. If the office you contacted did not have the specific information you needed, be sure to ask them who might have this information. If they can't answer your questions, ask if there is anyone else in their office who might be able to help you. If this doesn't work, contact the appropriate office listed in the preceding chapter entitled, "Free Experts: Free Help in Finding A Free Expert."

Animals and Agriculture

* Agriculture Exports Clearinghouse

Foreign Agricultural Service
U.S. Department of Agriculture, Room 5074   202-720-7115
Washington, DC 20050   Fax: 202-720-1727
E-mail: fasinfo@fas.usda.gov
www.fas.usda.gov

The Foreign Agricultural Service compiles and disseminates agricultural trade and commodity production information to agribusinesses and the general public. They offer private companies and cooperatives assistance in marketing their products overseas by collecting and publicizing information on foreign buyers and advertising U.S. export availability. They have a monthly magazine, commodity and trade reports, publications, and fact sheets (many of which are free). They can answer such questions as:
1) What are the market prospects for U.S. food and farm products in Japan?
2) What are some overseas markets and buying trends for a particular product?
3) What are some overseas promotional activities?
4) How do I begin an export business?
5) How do I advertise my product directly to buyers overseas?

* Economic Research Service (Agriculture)

U.S. Department of Agriculture
1800 M St., NW, ERS, Room 3100   202-694-5110
Washington, DC 20036-5831   Fax: 202-694-5641
E-mail: service@econ.ag.gov   Fax on Demand: 202-694-5700
www.econ.ag.gov

The Economic Research Service conducts research on the economic and socio-demographic issues of rural America; the marketing, trade, and consumption of farm commodities; U.S. and foreign economic policies and their effects on trade; and more. They produce monographs and journal articles ranging from very technical research reports to easy-to-read leaflets. They offer situation and outlook reports providing a mixture of outlook and in-depth analysis of current commodity, trade, resource, and policy issues. Most of the information is available free of charge. They can answer such questions as:
1) What are the links between development and world trade?
2) What information exists on the U.S. and world markets for agricultural products?
3) How can farmers better conserve water resources?
4) What are the benefits of organic farming?
5) How can farmers adjust their techniques to keep pace with global market trends?

* National Agricultural Statistics Service

NASS-USDA   800-727-9540
Room 5805, South   202-720-3896
Washington, DC 20250   Fax: 202-690-1311
E-mail: nass@nass.usda.gov
www.usda.gov/nass/

The National Agricultural Statistics Service collects data on crops, livestock, poultry, dairy, chemical use, prices, and labor, and publishes the official USDA State and national estimates through its Agricultural Statistics Board. There are nearly 400 reports annually covering domestic agriculture, such as estimates of production, stocks, inventories, prices, disposition, utilization, farm numbers and land, and other factors. They provide national profiles from regular surveys of thousands of farmers, ranchers, and agribusinesses that voluntarily provide data on a confidential basis. Publications are available and range from free to $12. They can answer such questions as:
1) How has the use of a specific chemical for crop growth changed over the past five years?
2) Has the size of farms increased or decreased over the past ten years?
3) What statistics exist on wildlife damage to crops?
4) How has the weekly crop weather effected crop growth?
5) What data is there on livestock slaughter?

* Alternative Farming Systems Information Center

U.S. Department of Agriculture
National Agricultural Library
10301 Baltimore Blvd., Room 304   301-504-6559
Beltsville, MD 20705-2351   Fax: 301-504-6409
E-mail: afsic@nal.usda.gov
www.nal.usda.gov/afsic

The Alternative Farming Systems Information Center encourages research, education, and information delivery about farming systems that preserve the natural resource base while maintaining economic viability. The Center is the focal point for information on all types of alternative farming practices. They can refer you to organizations or experts, identify current research, furnish you with bibliographies, and more. Brief data base searches are free, while exhaustive searches are conducted on a cost recovery basis. They can answer such questions as:
1) How do you establish and maintain an organic garden?
2) What is involved in building a compost pile?
3) What are the effects of herbicide and fertilizer run off?
4) How can I avoid ground water contamination?
5) What are some solar energy alternatives for agriculture?

* Animal Welfare Information Center

National Agricultural Library
U.S. Department of Agriculture
10301 Baltimore Blvd., 5th Floor   301-504-6212
Beltsville, MD 20705-2351   Fax: 301-504-7125
E-mail: awic@nal.usda.gov
www.nal.usda.gov/awic

The Animal Welfare Information Center is the focal point for all aspects of animal welfare. They have information on the care, handling, and management of animals used in research; training guides and manuals for animal care personnel; ethical issues; animal behavior; and pain control. They have a publications list of free fact sheets, bibliographies, and other resources. They can answer such questions as:
1) What information is there on the ethical and moral issues relating to animals and the philosophy of animal rights?
2) What alternatives are there to the use of live animals in research?
3) What videos exist on the care of animals?
4) What are some of the legislation regarding animal welfare?
5) What are some of the resources available regarding the raising of poultry?

* Aquaculture Information Center

National Agricultural Library
U.S. Department of Agriculture
10301 Baltimore Blvd.   301-504-5724
Beltsville, MD 20705-2351   Fax: 301-504-6409
E-mail: afsaqua@nal.usda.gov
www.nal.usda.gov/afsic/aqua/aquasite.htm

The Aquaculture Information Center collects information on the culture of aquatic plants and animals in freshwater, brackish, and marine environments. Examples include: catfish farming, oyster culture, salmon ranching, and trout farming. They have a publications list of free fact sheets, bibliographies, and other resources. They can answer such questions as:
1) How do you start a catfish farm?
2) What are the effects of sodium, cadmium, and lead on aquatic plants?
3) What types of algae are edible?
4) What is involved in raising snails?
5) What can be done to stop the pollution of freshwater environments?

* Food and Nutrition Information Center

Agriculture Research Services
National Agriculture Library, Room 304   301-504-5719
10301 Baltimore Blvd.   Fax: 301-504-6409
Beltsville, MD 20705-2351   TTY: 301-504-6856
E-mail: fnic@nal.usda.gov
www.nal.usda.gov/fnic

The Food and Nutrition Information Center serves many types of users including educators, students, researchers, and consumers. Reference services are provided. Subjects covered include human nutrition research and education, diet and diet-related diseases, food habits, food composition, nutrition education, and more. The Center offers a variety of services which include answers to specific questions, lending books and audiovisuals, and providing computerized literature searches. A publications list is available, many of which are free. They can answer such questions

Free Research On Any Topic

as:
1) What studies exist on the effects of the school breakfast program?
2) What information can you provide to parents concerned about their overweight children?
3) Do you have information on anorexia nervosa?
4) Is it dangerous to consume caffeine while pregnant?
5) Are canned peaches as nutritious as fresh?

* Alternative Farming Systems Information Center (Horticulture)

AFSIC
U.S. Department of Agriculture
10301 Baltimore Blvd., Room 304   301-504-6559
Beltsville, MD 20705-2351   Fax: 301-504-6409
www.nal.usda.gov/afsic

The Alternative Farming Systems Information Center covers technical horticultural or botanical questions, economic botany, wild plants of possible use, herbs, bonsai, and floriculture. They can answer such questions as:
1) How can you grow lavender commercially as a source of essential oils?
2) How do you grow and dry herbs?
3) How much would landscaping improve the worth of a home?
4) Which plants can be used for medicinal purposes?
5) How can I control garden insects without using chemical sprays?

* Meat and Poultry Hotline

Food Safety and Inspection Service
U.S. Department of Agriculture   800-535-4555
Washington, DC 20250-3700   Fax: 202-690-2859
www.fsis.usda.gov

The Meat and Poultry Hotline takes calls from consumers regarding cases of meat or poultry food poisoning or complaints about meat or poultry spoilage, due to improper packaging or processing. They can also provide you with health-oriented information on safe handling and storage of meats and poultry. They can answer such questions as:
1) What should be done during a power outage?
2) What is salmonella and how can people be protected?
3) What are the different type of foodborne illnesses?
4) How long should you cook poultry?
5) What information should be included on meat and poultry labels and what does it mean?

* Organic Gardening

Public Information Center, 3404
U.S. Environmental Protection Agency
401 M St., SW   202-260-7751
Washington, DC 20460-0003   Fax: 202-260-6257
E-mail: public-access@epamail.epa.gov
www.epa.gov

The Public Information Center has free information sheets on organic gardening, composting, and recycling. They can answer such questions as:
1) What plants should be planted near each other to deter pests?
2) What are the dangers of pesticides?
3) Who can I talk to regarding composting and recycling?
4) What are the advantages of organic fertilizers?
5) What is required to maintain a lawn?

* Plant Information Service

U.S. Botanic Garden
245 1st St., SW   202-225-8333
Washington, DC 20024   Fax: 202-225-1561
www.aoc.gov/pages/usbgpage.htm

The U.S. Botanic Garden serves as a center for plant information offering a telephone information service as well as responding to written inquiries, Monday through Friday from 9:00 to 11:30 a.m. They can answer such questions as:
1) What are the benefits of organic gardening?
2) How can I use insects to control garden pests?
3) Which house plants are poisonous?
4) What are the dangers of chemical fertilizers?
5) Which herbs grow best indoors?

* Rural Information Center

National Agricultural Library
U.S. Department of Agriculture (USDA)   301-504-5547
10301 Baltimore Blvd., Room 304   800-633-7701
Beltsville, MD 20705-2351   Fax: 301-504-5181
E-mail: ric@nal.usda.gov
www.nal.usda.gov/ric

The Rural Information Center is designed to provide information and referral services to local government officials, businesses, community organizations, and rural citizens working to maintain the vitality of America's rural areas. The Center provides: customized information products to specific inquiries; refers users to organizations or experts in the field; performs database searches; furnishes bibliographies; identifies current USDA research and Cooperative Extension System programs; and assists users in accessing the National Agricultural Libraries' extensive collection. There is a cost recovery fee for photocopying articles and searches. They can answer such questions as:
1) Which organizations focus on rural health issues?
2) What resources for the historic preservation of farmland are available in rural areas?
3) How can tourism be promoted in small towns?
4) What are examples of the more innovative economic development projects in rural communities?
5) What rural organizations focus specifically on research and development?

* Seafood Hotline

Office of Seafood
Food and Drug Administration
200 C St., SW   800-SAFEFOOD
Washington, DC 20204   Fax: 202-401-3532
E-mail: oco@fdacf.sw.dhhs.gov
http://vm.cfsan.fda.gov/seafood1.html

The Seafood Hotline can provide consumers with information on how to buy and use seafood products, including storing and handling of seafood, and questions on seafood labeling and nutrition. The Hotline has many free publications on a variety of seafood issues. They can answer such questions as:
1) Can fish be kept frozen for a year?
2) How do you know if a seafood vendor is reputable?
3) What are the dangers of eating raw shellfish?
4) What information is available on canned tuna?
5) What are some seafood safety concerns for people with particular medical conditions?

Business and Industry

* Advertising Practices
Federal Trade Commission (FTC)
6th and Pennsylvania Ave., NW 202-326-2222
Washington, DC 20580 Fax: 202-326-3259
E-mail: consumerline@ftc.gov
www.ftc.gov/bcp/menu-ads.htm

This division of the Federal Trade Commission promotes the distribution of truthful information to the public through law enforcement and oversight activities in the following areas: general advertising for deceptive claims; advertising claims for food and over-the-counter drugs, particularly claims relating to safety or effectiveness; tobacco advertising; and performance and energy-savings claims for solar products, furnaces, window coverings, wood burning products, and more. They can answer such questions as:
1) How do you file a complaint with the FTC?
2) When and where is the advertising of tobacco products legal, and what are the reasons behind this?
3) How long are over-the-counter drugs tested before they are released on the market?
4) What penalties are levied against a company that has been charged with deceptive advertising?
5) How effective are over-the-counter diet pills?

* Federal Aviation Administration
Office of Public Affairs
800 Independence Ave., SW
Washington, DC 20591 202-267-3883
E-mail: gramick@postmaster2.dot.gov
www.faa.gov

The Federal Aviation Administration (FAA) is the starting place for any information on airlines, airports, and aircraft. The FAA regulates air commerce, develops civil aeronautics, installs and operates airports, conducts aeronautic research and provides guidance and policy on accident prevention in general aviation. They keep statistics on air travel, accidents, and more. There are free publications on airline careers, aviation, and airplanes, as well as videos and curriculum guides. They can answer such questions as:
1) Which airlines had penalties of $50,000 or more for safety and security issues?
2) What videos are available on aviation?
3) What historical information is available on women in aviation?
4) What are the current statistics on air traffic accidents?
5) What methods are used to reduce the noise level of new aircraft?

* Board of Governors of the Federal Reserve System (Banking)
Publications Services, MS-127
20th and C Sts., NW 202-452-3244
Washington, DC 20551 Fax: 202-728-5886
www.bog.frb.fed.us

The Federal Reserve System, the central bank of the United States, is charged with administering and making policy for the Nation's credit and monetary affairs. The Federal Reserve helps to maintain the banking industry in sound condition, capable of responding to the Nation's domestic and international financial needs and objectives. It has publications and audiovisual materials prepared which are designed to increase public understanding of the functions and operations of the Federal Reserve System, monetary policy, financial markets and institutions, consumer finance, and the economy. They can answer such questions as:
1) How did the Federal Reserve begin and how does it function today?
2) What is the history of the U.S. monetary policy and how is it formulated?
3) Is there a brief overview available on banking regulation?
4) What is the evolution of money?
5) How are checks used, processed, and collected?

* Business Assistance Service
Office of Business Liaison
U.S. Department of Commerce, Room 5062 202-482-1360
Washington, DC 20230 Fax: 202-482-4054
www.doc.gov/obl

The Office of Business Liaison is responsible for keeping the Department of Energy Secretary informed of issues affecting the business community. The Office provides information and guidance on programs throughout the Federal government. Although it cannot provide legal advice or intervene on an inquirer's behalf with a federal agency, it can alleviate the necessity of making numerous attempts to locate or obtain federal information, programs, and services. Most requests are for information having to do with government procurement, exporting, marketing, statistical sources, and regulatory matters. They can answer such questions as:
1) Where can someone get information on what the government is buying and what steps are required to sell to the government?
2) Who can advise a business on unfair trade practices?
3) Where are the statistics on a specific type of business?
4) Where is there information on federal databases?
5) Is there U.S. tariff information available?

* Central and Eastern Europe Business Information Center
U.S. Department of Commerce
International Trade Administration
14th and Constitution Ave., NW, Room 7414 202-482-2645
Washington, DC 20230 Fax: 202-482-4473
www.ita.doc.gov

The Central and Eastern Europe Business Information Center serves as a clearinghouse for information on business conditions in Eastern European countries, and on emerging trade and investment opportunities in those countries. It also serves as a source of information on U.S. government programs supporting private enterprise, trade, and investment in Eastern Europe. The Center also serves as a referral point for voluntary assistance programs. A variety of printed materials are available directly from the Center, as are bibliographies on data available from other sources. Most of the services are free of charge. They can answer such questions as:
1) What are the export procedures for a particular product to Poland?
2) What are the population, economic, commercial, and trade statistics on Romania?
3) Is there a list of contacts for export information in Bulgaria?
4) What political and economic issues should be considered when investing in businesses in Eastern Europe?
5) How can I advertise directly in Eastern European countries?

* Commodity Futures Trading Commission
Office of Public Affairs
Commodity Futures Trading Commission
3 Lafayette Center
1155 21st St., NW 202-418-5080
Washington, DC 20581 Fax: 202-418-5525
www.cftc.gov/

The Commodity Futures Trading Commission (CFTC) promotes economic growth, protects the rights of customers, and ensures fairness of the marketplace through regulation of futures trading. CFTC regulates the activities of numerous commodity exchange members, public brokerage houses, commodity trading advisers, and others, as well as approves the rules under which an exchange operates. They have free publications and can refer you to other offices within CFTC for specific information. They can answer such questions as:
1) What is the purpose of futures trading?
2) How do you read a commodity futures price table?
3) Do brokers have to be registered, and if so, how does one check on a broker?
4) What are some of the important issues that people should be aware of before entering the futures market?
5) What do I do if I suspect my broker of dishonest or unethical behavior?

* Federal Communications Commission
Federal Communications Commission
Public Service Commission 888-225-5322
445 12th St., SW 202-418-0190
Washington, DC 20554 Fax: 202-418-0232
E-mail: psd@fcc.gov TTY: 202-418-2555
www.fcc.gov

Free Research On Any Topic

The Federal Communications Commission regulates interstate and foreign communications by radio, television, wire, satellite, and cable. It is responsible for the development and operation of broadcast services and the provision of rapid, efficient nationwide and worldwide telephone and telegraph services at reasonable rates. They take complaints and have free information on all areas falling within their responsibility. They can answer questions such as:
1) What can be done if someone is having trouble with their cable company?
2) Where do you complain if you find the local D.J.'s show to be offensive?
3) What are the rules regarding pay per call services?
4) Where can you learn more about cellular radio regulations?
5) What happens when radio signals are picked up by consumer electronic products?

* Export Country Experts
U.S. Foreign and Commercial Services
Export Promotion Services
U.S. Department of Commerce
Room 2810   202-482-3809
Washington, DC 20230   Fax: 202-482-5819
www.doc.gov

The Country Desk Officers at the U.S. Department of Commerce can provide businesses with information on a market, company, or most any other aspect of commercial life in a particular country. These specialists can look at the needs of an individual U.S. firm wishing to sell in a particular country in the full context of that country's overall economy, trade policies, and political situation, and also in light of U.S. policies toward that country. Desk officers keep up to date on the economic and commercial conditions in their assigned countries. Each desk officer collects information on the country's regulations, tariffs, business practices, economic and political developments, trade data and trends, market size, and growth. They have free reports and other information available or they can refer callers to other country specialists. They can answer such questions as:
1) How can I expand my business through a foreign franchise?
2) How can I reduce my company's distribution and transportation costs overseas?
3) What type of export opportunities exist for computer manufacturing companies who want to expand to Germany?
4) What are some recent foreign labor trends in Japan?
5) Which markets are growing the fastest overseas?

* Economic Research Service
U.S. Department of Agriculture
1800 M St., NW   202-694-5050
Washington, DC 20036-5831   AutoFax: 202-694-5700
E-mail: service@econ.ag.gov
www.econ.ag.gov

The Economic Research Service conducts research on the economic and socio-demographic issues of rural America; the marketing, trade, and consumption of farm commodities; U.S. and foreign economic policies and their effects on trade; and more. They produce monographs and journal articles ranging from very technical research reports to easy-to-read leaflets. Situation and outlook reports providing a mixture of outlook and in-depth analysis of current commodity, trade, resource, and policy issues are also available. Most of the information is free of charge. They can answer such questions as:
1) What are the links between development and world trade?
2) What information exists on the U.S. and world markets for agricultural products?
3) How can farmers better conserve water resources?
4) What are the benefits of organic farming?
5) How can farmers adjust their techniques to keep pace with global market trends?

* Economics: National, Regional, and International
Bureau of Economic Analysis
U.S. Department of Commerce
1441 L St., NW   202-606-9900
Washington, DC 20230   Fax: 202-606-5310
www.bea.doc.gov

The Bureau of Economic Analysis (BEA) provides information on national and regional economics. BEA collects basic information on such key issues as economic growth, inflation, regional development, and the Nation's role in the world economy. It distributes a number of publications that measure, analyze and forecast economic trends, and are available on recorded messages, online through the Economic Bulletin Board, and in BEA reports. They can answer such questions as:
1) What is the average per capita income in the United States?
2) Will the rate of inflation increase or decrease over the next five years, and by what percent?
3) What percentage of the Gross National Product (GNP) does the government spend on health care?
4) How does the United States' national unemployment rate compare to other industrialized countries?
5) What was the unemployment rate in Pennsylvania from 1989-1993?

* Exporter's Hotline
Trade Information Center
U.S. Department of Commerce   800-USA-TRADE
Washington, DC 20230   Fax: 202-482-4473
www.ita.doc.gov/ita   TDD: 800-TDD-TRADE

The Trade Information Center is a comprehensive one-stop shop for information on U.S. government programs and activities that support exporting efforts. This hotline is staffed by trade specialists who can provide information on seminars and conferences, overseas buyers and representatives, overseas events, export financing, technical assistance, and export counseling. They also have access to the National Trade Data Bank, which provides basic export information, country-specific information, and industry-specific information. They can provide a great deal of free assistance, but there is a fee charged for data bank searches and other technical assistance. They can answer such questions as:
1) What countries are increasing or decreasing imports of a particular product, and at what rates?
2) What 10 countries are the top importers of a specific product?
3) How can a businessman meet prescreened prospects who are interested in a product or service?
4) How can a business assess their export potential?
5) How can a businessman obtain background data on potential foreign partners?

* Fishery Statistics and Economics Division
Office of Research and Environmental Information
National Marine Fisheries Service
National Oceanic and Atmospheric Administration
U.S. Department of Commerce
1315 East-West Highway, SSMC3   301-713-2328
Silver Spring, MD 20910   Fax: 301-713-4137
http://remora.ssp.nips.gov/mrfss

The Fisheries Statistics and Economics Division publishes statistical bulletins on marine recreational fishing and commercial fishing, and on the manufacture and commerce of fishery products. This Division has several annual and biannual reports available. They can answer such questions as:
1) How many fish were imported in a year, and what kind?
2) What is the most popular fish to export?
3) What kinds of fish are frozen?
4) What statistics exist on processed fish?
5) How many fish were caught by weekend fishermen?

* Office of Industries
United States International Trade Commission
500 E St., SW   202-205-3296
Washington, DC 20436   Fax: 202-205-3161
E-mail: cunningham@usitc.gov
www.usitc.gov

The Office of Industries at the U.S. International Trade Commission has experts assigned to every commodity imported into the U.S. These experts are responsible for investigation of the customs laws of the United States and foreign countries; the volume of imports in comparison with domestic production; the effects relating to competition of foreign industries; and all other factors affecting competition between articles of the U.S. and imported articles. They are knowledgeable about the domestic and foreign industry, and have statistical and factual information. They also have information regarding the tariff schedules. There is no charge for this information. They can answer such questions as:
1) What is the rate of duty for a product from a particular country?
2) What is the rate of import-export, the size of the market and the major producers of women's sweaters?
3) How much of a product is exported and what is the size of the potential market?
4) What happens if someone suspects an imported article is being subsidized or sold at less then fair value?
5) What can a company do if they feel they are being unfairly effected by import trade?

Business and Industry

* Technical Data Center (Job Safety)

Technical Data Center
Occupational Safety and Health Administration
U.S. Department of Labor
200 Constitution Ave., NW, Room N2625   202-693-2350
Washington, DC 20210   Fax: 202-219-5046
www.osha.gov

The Technical Data Center compiles technical information on all industries covered by the Occupational Safety and Health Administration (OSHA). The Center maintains a library of 6,000 volumes and 200 journals, as well as an extensive microfilm collection of industry standards and OSHA rule-making records. The Center is also the docket office and holds the hearing records on standards, the comments, and final rules. Literature searches are conducted free of charge. They can answer such questions as:

1) What are some hazard training programs that can be implemented in the workplace to teach employees to work safely in a variety of situations?
2) When was a particular company inspected and what violations were found?
3) What are the health hazards of a particular chemical?
4) What are some dangers of working around chemicals while pregnant?
5) Have there been similar reports of spinal cord injuries in a particular job?

* Federal Mediation and Conciliation Service (Labor-Management)

Federal Mediation and Conciliation Service (FMCS)
2100 K St., NW   202-606-8100
Washington, DC 20427   Fax: 202-606-4216
E-mail: publicinformation@fmcs.gov
www.fmcs.gov

The Federal Mediation and Conciliation Service represents the public interest by promoting the development of sound and stable labor-management relationships; preventing or minimizing work stoppages by assisting labor and management in settling their disputes through mediation; advocating collective bargaining, and much more. They can answer such questions as:

1) What is "alternative dispute resolution", and how can it by used?
2) How can companies work to develop effective labor-management committees?
3) What statistics exist on dispute mediation, preventive medication, work stoppages, and contract mediation?
4) What are some steps that companies can take to improve communication between labor and management?
5) What happens when a Federal agency and employee representative reach a negotiation impasse?

* Federal Labor Relations Authority

Federal Labor Relations Authority
607 14th St., NW   202-482-6550
Washington, DC 20424-0001   Fax: 202-482-6636
Bulletin Board: 202-512-1387
www.flra.gov

The Federal Labor Relations Authority oversees the Federal service labor-management relations program. It administers the law that protects the right of employees of the Federal Government to organize, bargain collectively, and participate through labor organizations of their own choosing. They can answer such questions as:

1) What laws protect Federal employees?
2) What steps can be taken when labor and management have reached an impasse?
3) How does an employee file a union grievance procedure?
4) How do I get a copy of my local union's collective bargaining agreement?
5) Is an agency permitted to negotiate a particular bargaining proposal?

* Labor Statistics Clearinghouse

Division of Information Services
Bureau of Labor Statistics   202-606-5886
U.S. Department of Labor   Fax: 202-606-7890
2 Massachusetts Ave., NE, Room 2860   TDD: 202-606-5897
Washington, DC 20212   Fax on Demand: 202-606-6325
E-mail: blsdatastaff@bls.gov
http://stats.bls.gov/opbinfo.htm

The Bureau of Labor Statistics (BLS) is the principal data-gathering agency of the Federal Government in the field of labor economics. The Bureau collects, processes, analyzes, and disseminates data relating to employment, unemployment, and other characteristics of the labor force; prices and consumer expenditures; wages, other worker compensation, and industrial relations; productivity; economic growth and employment projections; and occupational safety and health. This office can also provide you with a release schedule for BLS major economic indicators and the recorded message number. BLS can refer you to experts within the Bureau who can answer your specific question, provide you with historical information, and refer you to tables and charts for data. The BLS has publications, periodicals, magnetic tapes, diskettes, and more for sale. They can answer questions such as:

1) What are the employment statistics and the outlook for a particular occupation?
2) What is the unemployment rate for a particular state?
3) What is the current wage for a word processor in Seattle, and what are the usual benefits associated with that position?
4) What is the employment projection for a specific job?
5) What is the consumer/producer price index and how has it changed over time?

* Mine Safety Clearinghouse

Office of Information and Public Affairs
Mine Safety and Health Administration
U.S. Department of Labor
4015 Wilson Blvd.   703-235-1452
Arlington, VA 22203   Fax: 703-235-4323
E-mail: ksnyder@msha.gov
http://199.115.12.200

The Mine Safety and Health Administration develops mandatory safety and health standards, ensures compliance with such standards, assesses civil penalties for violations, and investigates accidents. It cooperates with and provides assistance to states in the development of effective state mine safety and health programs and improves and expands training programs. The Clearinghouse can provide general information regarding the Mine Safety and Health Administration, as well as free brochures, manuals, and other publications regarding mine safety and health. They can answer such questions as:

1) How can mine operators train miners effectively to prevent accidents and to avoid unsafe conditions?
2) What are the inspection procedures for a mine?
3) What is the latest information on the treatment and prevention of black lung and other respiratory diseases that are common to miners?
4) What is the latest research on robotics and automation in the mining industry?
5) What mines have been ordered to close because of safety concerns?

* Mineral Commodity Statistics Information

Minerals Information
U.S. Geological Survey   888-ASK-USGS
983 National Center   703-648-6100
Reston, VA 20192   Fax: 703-648-6057
E-mail: minerals@usgs.gov
http://minerals.usgs.gov

The U.S. Geological Survey (USGS) Minerals Resources Program is staffed by mineral experts who distribute a wide variety of mineral-related information and publications to meet and support the needs of the public, as well as government agencies and the scientific and industrial sectors. The staff provides information on the most current as well as past published reports pertaining to minerals, mining, processing, and research. They have statistics on import sources, uses, government stockpile, reserves, world resources, and substitutes. Dozens of commodity specialists are also available to assist you. They can answer such questions as:

1) What will the price of silver be over the next five years?
2) What is the role of gold in the international monetary system?
3) How can industries improve the quality of domestic steel?
4) How many tons of coal did U.S. industries produce last year?
5) What methods are used to recycle scrap metal?

* Minority Energy Information Clearinghouse

Office of Minority Economic Impact
U.S. Department of Energy
Forrestal Building, Room 5B-110
1000 Independence Ave., SW   202-586-5876
Washington, DC 20585   Fax: 202-586-3075
E-mail: ann.young@hq.doe.gov
www.hr.doe.gov/ed/omei/OMEI.HTM

The Minority Energy Information Clearinghouse develops and disseminates information related to energy programs that have an impact upon minorities, minority business enterprises, minority educational institutions, and other minority organizations. They can direct callers to government programs that will assist minority businesses in entering the energy field, as well as giving information about

Free Research On Any Topic

educational programs for minority students who are energy majors. They can answer such questions as:
1) What type of fellowships are available to minority college students attending Historically Black Colleges and Universities who want to pursue energy-related careers?
2) What types of energy-related loans are available to minority businesses?
3) Can I receive a listing of minority energy conferences or workshops?
4) How does the Clearinghouse's electronic bulletin board work?
5) How has recent energy legislation had an impact upon minority businesses?

* Overseas Private Investment Corporation
Investor Information Service
1100 New York Ave., NW
MS 7412
Washington, DC 20527
www.opic.gov
202-336-8663
Fax: 202-408-5155

Investor Information Service assists U.S. firms in gathering information on foreign countries and their business environments, as well as facilitating the flow of information about developing countries to potential U.S. investors. OPIC created the Investor Information Service (IIS). Country-specific information is available in kit form on more than 100 countries, as well as on 16 regions. Kits include materials covering the economies, trade laws, business regulations, political conditions and investment incentives of developing countries and regions. Kit costs range from $10-$420. They can answer such questions as:
1) What information exists for someone who wants to set up a fast food business in Greece?
2) What is the latest information on the foreign economic trends and their implications for the U.S. in Hungary?
3) What issues should be considered in purchasing an overseas venture?
4) Is it possible to meet with local business representatives, and experienced U.S. investors, and to attend briefings by the U.S. Ambassador in a foreign country?
5) What is the current investment climate in France? Is it favorable to new U.S. businesses?

* Pension Benefit Guaranty Corporation
Communications and Public Affairs Department
1200 K St., NW, Suite 240
Washington, DC 20005-4026
www.pbgc.gov
202-326-4040
Fax: 202-326-4042

The Pension Benefit Guaranty Corporation works to ensure the solvency and viability of company-sponsored pension plans. They can provide you with information and publications on pension plans, as well as information pertaining to laws and regulations on pensions. They can answer questions such as:
1) What is the federal pension law?
2) What are pensions plans and how do they operate?
3) What information on plans is a company required to give to members?
4) What are the rights and options of participants?
5) What is the employer's responsibilities regarding pension plans?

* Pension and Welfare Benefits Administration
U.S. Department of Labor
200 Constitution Ave., NW, N5619
Washington, DC 20210
www.dol.gov/dol/pwba/welcome.html
202-219-8776
Fax: 202-219-5362

The Pension and Welfare Benefits Administration (PWBA) helps to protect the economic future and retirement security of working Americans. It requires administrators of private pension and welfare plans to provide plan participants with easily understandable summaries; to file those summaries with the agency; and to report annually on the financial operation of the plans. PWBA has publications and other information available. They can answer questions such as:
1) What is the effect of job mobility on pension plans?
2) What is the Employee Retirement Income Security Act (ERISA)?
3) What studies have been done on the investment performance of ERISA plans?
4) What information are pension plans required to provide to participants?
5) What employee benefit documents are available from the Department of Labor?

* Federal Procurement Data Division
General Services Administration
7th and D St., SW, Room 5652
Washington, DC 20407
202-401-1529
Fax: 202-401-1546

E-mail: linda.hornsby@gsa.gov
www.fpds.gsa.gov

The Federal Procurement Data Center stores information about federal procurement actions, from 1978 to present, that totaled $25,000 or more. The systems contain information on purchasing or contracting office; date of award; dollars obligated; principal product or service; name and address of contractor; and more. Searches and printouts are available on a cost recovery basis. They can answer such questions as:
1) How many contracts did a particular company receive in a given year?
2) Who in the government is buying winter parkas?
3) What types of contracts are being awarded in Franklin county?
4) What has the National Park Service purchased in the last month?
5) Who do I need to talk to in order to sell my particular product?

* Science, Technology and Business Division
Library of Congress
101 Independence Ave., SE
Washington, DC 20540
www.loc.gov
202-707-5639

The Science, Technology and Business Division's collection numbers 3.5 million books, nearly 60,000 journals, and 4.4 million technical reports. The collections include such treasures as first editions of Copernicus and Newton and the personal papers of the Wright Brothers and Alexander Graham Bell. The Division has primary responsibility for providing reference and bibliographic services and for recommending acquisitions in the broad areas of science and technology. Reference services are provided to users in person, by telephone, and by correspondence. Indirect reference service is provided through bibliographic guides (Tracer Bullets) and research reports prepared by Division subject specialists and reference librarians. Copies of reference guides are available at no charge. They can answer such questions as:
1) Where can someone begin looking for information on lasers and their applications?
2) What are good sources of information on volcanoes?
3) What resources exist on extraterrestrial life?
4) Where could someone find sources for information on medicinal plants?
5) How would someone go about creating a hologram?

* U.S. Securities and Exchange Commission
Office of Public Affairs
450 5th St., NW
Washington, DC 20549
www.sec.gov
202-942-0020
Fax: 202-942-9654
TTY: 202-628-9039

The Securities and Exchange Commission (SEC) administers federal securities laws that seek to provide protection for investors; to ensure that securities markets are fair and honest; and to provide the means to enforce securities laws through sanctions. They have free publications, a public reference room, disclosure reports, and information on how individuals can protect themselves. They can answer such questions as:
1) What are pyramid schemes and how do they work?
2) Where can someone find out if there have been complaints about a particular broker or adviser?
3) How does someone choose investments safely?
4) Who needs to register with the SEC and what is required?
5) What is the SEC and how does it operate?

* U.S. Small Business Administration
Answer Desk
409 3rd St., SW
Washington, DC 20416
www.sbaonline.sba.gov/helpdesk
800-827-5722
202-205-6400
Fax: 202-205-7064

The Small Business Administration (SBA) aids, counsels, assists, and protects the interests of small business, and ensures that small business concerns receive a fair portion of government purchases, contracts, and subcontracts. SBA also makes loans and licenses, and regulates small business investment companies. The Small Business Answer Desk helps callers with questions on how to start and manage a business, where to get financing, and other information needed to operate and expand a business. They have a publications catalogue, with most items available for under $5.00. They can answer such questions as:
1) What programs or forms of assistance are available to women entrepreneurs?
2) What help exists for a business interested in developing an export market?
3) Is there a way a business can receive free management consulting?
4) Are there programs designed specifically for businesses in small towns?
5) How does a company enter the federal procurement market?

Business and Industry

* National Center for <u>Standards and Certification</u>

National Institute of Standards and Technology
Building 820, Room 164   301-975-4040
Gaithersburg, MD 20899   Fax: 301-926-1559
E-mail: ncsci@nist.gov
http://ts.nist.gov/ts/htdocs/210/217/bro.htm

The National Center for Standards and Certification Information provides a free service which will identify standards for selling any product to any country in the world. This federal agency will tell you what the standard is for a given product or suggest where you can obtain an official copy of the standard. They can answer such questions as:

1) What U.S. industries standards pertain to certain products?
2) What foreign standards apply to a product?
3) What is the latest GATT information on proposed foreign regulations?
4) Where can I locate the organizations that have standards information?
5) How are military standards different for U.S. standards?

* <u>Transportation</u> Research Information Services

Transportation Research Board
2101 Constitution Ave., NW   202-334-2934
Washington, DC 20418   Fax: 202-334-2003
www.nas.edu/trb

The Transportation Research Information Services (TRIS) is the prime source of transportation research information in the United States. TRIS is an information clearinghouse designed to identify worldwide sources of transportation research information. TRIS contains more than 250,000 abstracts of completed research and summaries of research projects in progress. TRIS is regularly used by transportation administrators, operators, academics, planners, designers, engineers, and managers. TRIS contains information on various modes and aspects of transportation including planning, design, finance, construction, maintenance, traffic operations, management, marketing, and other topics. Publications are available for a fee. They can answer such questions as:

1) What is the latest research on airport capacity?
2) What information exists on the privatization of toll roads?
3) What data should be considered when building a bypass?
4) What studies have been conducted on land traffic getting to and from airports?
5) What technology exists to weigh trucks in motion rather than at weigh stations?

* <u>Women's Bureau</u> Clearinghouse

U.S. Department of Labor
200 Constitution Ave., NW, Room S3306   800-827-5335
Washington, DC 20210   202-219-4486
E-mail: wb-wwc@dol.gov   Fax: 202-219-5529
www.dol.gov/dol/wb/welcome.html

The Women's Bureau Clearinghouse was designed and established to assist employers in identifying the most appropriate policies for responding to the dependent care needs of employees seeking to balance their dual responsibilities. They can also provide information on women's issues, as well as work force issues that affect women. They offer information and guidance in areas such as women-owned businesses, women workers, alternative work schedules, dependent care issues, and much more. They also have publications and other information available, much of which is free. They can answer such questions as:

1) What are some elder care program options?
2) What is the earning difference between men and women?
3) How does flex time work in companies similar to mine?
4) What are some examples of alternate work schedules and how do they work?
5) What literature and other resources are available on employer-supported child care?

* Office of American <u>Workplace</u>

U.S. Department of Labor
200 Constitution Ave., NW   202-219-6098
Washington, DC 20210   Fax: 202-219-8762
www.dol.gov/dol/oaw/

Working together, labor and management in every sector of the American economy are creating joint programs devoted to productivity, organizational efficiency, and a better work environment. The Office of American Workplace seeks to gather information about the various programs, as well as labor and management efforts. They have a free newsletter, as well as other information on this topic. They can answer such questions as:

1) Which firms and organizations in the private sector have labor-management programs?
2) How can a program be instituted to improve labor-management relations?
3) What types of cooperative arrangements have been attempted in companies similar to mine?
4) What involvement have labor unions had in starting these programs in the workplace?

Free Research On Any Topic

Consumer and Housing

* Animal Welfare Information Center
National Agricultural Library
U.S. Department of Agriculture
10301 Baltimore Blvd., 5th Floor   301-504-6212
Beltsville, MD 20705-2351   Fax: 301-504-7125
E-mail: awic@nal.usda.gov
www.nal.usda.gov/awic

The Animal Welfare Information Center is the focal point for all aspects of animal welfare. They have information on the care, handling, and management of animals used in research; training guides and manuals for animal care personnel; ethical issues; animal behavior; and pain control. They have a publications list of free fact sheets, bibliographies, and other resources. They can answer such questions as:

1) What information is there on the ethical and moral issues relating to animals and the philosophy of animal rights?
2) What alternatives are there to the use of live animals in research?
3) What videos exist on the care of animals?
4) What are some of the legislation regarding animal welfare?
5) Are there resources available regarding the raising of poultry?

* Auto Safety Hotline
Office of Defects Investigation (NEF-10)
National Highway Traffic Safety Administration
U.S. Department of Transportation
400 7th St., SW   800-424-9393
Washington, DC 20590   Fax: 202-366-7882
E-mail: hotline@nhtsa.dot.gov
www.nhtsa.dot.gov

The Auto Safety Hotline can provide information on recalls, defects, investigations, child safety seats, tires, drunk driving, crash test results, seat belts, air bags, odometer tampering, and other related topics. They also accept reports of automobile safety problems. The Hotline publishes the New Car Assessment Program, which provides comparable data on the frontal crashworthiness of selected new vehicles. They have free fact sheets and publications on these topics and more. They can answer such questions as:

1) What is the safest new car?
2) Which child car seats have been recalled?
3) What should you do if you suspect an odometer has been tampered with?
4) How many states have seat belt laws, and what are the statistics regarding their use and benefits?
5) What are the statistics for drunk driving, and what information exists for alcohol's involvement in fatalities?
6) What is the fuel efficiency of a particular car?

* Federal Communications Commission
Federal Communications Commission
445 12th St., SW   202-418-0190
Washington, DC 20554   Fax: 202-418-0232
E-mail: fccinfo@fcc.gov
www.fcc.gov

The Federal Communications Commission regulates interstate and foreign communications by radio, television, wire, satellite, and cable. It is responsible for the development and operation of broadcast services and the provision of rapid, efficient nationwide and worldwide telephone and telegraph services at reasonable rates. They take complaints and have free information on all areas falling within their responsibility. They can answer questions such as:

1) What can be done if someone is having trouble with their cable company or does not understand their cable bill?
2) Where do you complain if you find the local D.J.'s show to be offensive?
3) What are the rules regarding pay per call services?
4) Where can you learn more about cellular radio regulations?
5) What happens when radio signals are picked up by consumer electronic products?

* Consumer Product Safety Commission
Office of Information and Public Affairs
U.S. Consumer Product Safety Commission   800-638-2772
Washington, DC 20207   Fax: 301-504-0862
E-mail: info@cpsc.gov
www.cpsc.gov

The Consumer Product Safety Commission (CPSC) protects the public against unreasonable risks of injury from consumer products; assists consumers in evaluating the consumer products and minimizes conflicting state and local regulations; and promotes research and investigation into the causes and prevention of product-related deaths, illnesses, and injuries. The CPSC Hotline can provide you with information on product recalls and will take reports of hazardous products or product-related injuries. You can write to the CPSC for a complete list of publications which describe some of the common hazards associated with the use of consumer products, recommending ways to avoid these hazards. They can answer such questions as:

1) What toys are currently being recalled?
2) What types of consumer products are the most dangerous?
3) What safety information exists for the school playground?
4) Are there special precautions you should take for the elderly?
5) What is some current information regarding poisons?

* Credit Information
Office of Consumer Affairs
Federal Deposit Insurance Corporation
550 17th St., NW, Room F-130   202-942-3100
Washington, DC 20429   800-934-3342
E-mail: consumer@fdic.gov
www.fdic.gov

The Federal Deposit Insurance Corporation (FDIC) was established to promote and preserve public confidence in banks, protecting the money supply through provision of insurance coverage for bank deposits and periodic examinations of insured state-chartered banks that are not members of the Federal Reserve System. The FDIC can provide you with information and an overview of the FDIC, and the major consumer and civil rights laws and regulations that protect bank customers. They can answer questions on such topics as:

1) Equal Credit Opportunity and Age
2) Equal Credit Opportunity and Women
3) Fair Credit Billing
4) Fair Credit Reporting Act
5) Truth in Lending

* National Credit Union Administration
Public Information
1775 Duke St.   703-518-6330
Alexandria, VA 22314-3428   Fax: 703-518-6429
E-mail: pacamail@ncua.gov
www.ncua.gov

The National Credit Union Administration is responsible for chartering, insuring, supervising, and examining federal credit unions and administering the National Credit Union Share Insurance Fund. They have free publications and can refer you to the correct office for more information on credit unions. They can answer such questions as:

1) How are credit unions chartered?
2) What are the rules and regulations regarding the organization of credit unions?
3) Is there a master list of all federally insured credit unions?
4) How are credit unions liquidated?
5) How are credit unions insured?

* Food and Nutrition Information Center
National Agricultural Library
U.S. Department of Agriculture
10301 Baltimore Blvd., Room 304   301-504-5719
Beltsville, MD 20705   Fax: 301-504-6409
E-mail: fnic@nal.usda.gov   TTY: 301-504-6856
www.nal.usda.gov/fnic

The Food and Nutrition Information Center serves many types of users including educators, students, researchers, and consumers. Reference services are provided. Subjects covered include human nutrition research and education, diet and diet-related diseases, food habits, food composition, nutrition education, and more. The Center offers a variety of services which includes answers to specific questions,

Consumer and Housing

lending books and audiovisuals, and providing computerized literature searches. A publications list is available, many of which are free. They can answer such questions as:
1) What studies exist on the effects of the school breakfast program?
2) What information can you provide to parents concerned about their overweight children?
3) Do you have information on anorexia nervosa?
4) Is it dangerous to consume caffeine while pregnant?
5) Are canned peaches as nutritious as fresh?

* Federal Trade Commission (Fraud)

Public Reference Branch, Room 130   877-FTC-HELP
Pennsylvania Ave. at 6th St., NW   202-326-2222
Washington, DC 20580   Fax: 202-326-2050
www.ftc.gov   TTY: 202-326-2502

The Federal Trade Commission (FTC) protects consumers against unfair, deceptive, or fraudulent practices. The FTC enforces a variety of consumer protection laws enacted by Congress, as well as trade regulation rules issued by the Commission. Its actions include individual company and industry-wide investigations, administrative and federal court litigation, rulemaking proceedings, and consumer and business education. The FTC has a wealth of information and free publications on a variety of topics. They can answer such questions as:
1) What are the laws regarding shopping by mail or phone?
2) What are some things people should know before looking for a job with a head hunter?
3) What information exists for people checking out mortgages or refinancing?
4) What should someone do if their lifetime membership in a health club expires?
5) What can be done to protect against credit card fraud?

* Horticulture Clearinghouse

U.S. Department of Agriculture
10301 Baltimore Blvd.   301-504-5204
Beltsville, MD 20705   Fax: 301-504-6927
www.nal.usda.gov

The Horticulture Clearinghouse covers technical horticultural or botanical questions, economic botany, wild plants of possible use, herbs, bonsai, and floriculture. They can answer such questions as:
1) How can you grow lavender commercially as a source of essential oils?
2) How do you grow and dry herbs?
3) How much might landscaping improve the worth of a home?
4) Which plants can be used for medicinal purposes?
5) How can I control garden insects without using chemical sprays?

* HUD USER (Housing)

P.O. Box 6091   800-245-2691
Rockville, MD 20849   Fax: 301-519-5767
E-mail: huduser@aspensys.com   TDD: 800-483-2209
www.huduser.org

HUD USER, a service of the U.S. Department of Housing and Urban Development, is an information source for housing and community development researchers and policymakers that collects, creates, and distributes a wide variety of materials. You can find information on low-income housing, community development strategies, environmental hazards, land development regulations, population shifts, and housing for elderly and disabled people. A free monthly newsletter and a publications catalogue is available. They can answer such questions as:
1) What information is there on housing for people with special needs?
2) How does one remove lead-based paint from their home?
3) What are "enterprise zones" and what are their goals?
4) What are some federal programs and other sources of assistance for homelessness?
5) What video programs are there on housing issues?

* Housing Discrimination

Fair Housing Enforcement Division
Office of Fair Housing and Equal Opportunity
U.S. Department of Housing
   and Urban Development (HUD)
Washington, DC 20410-2000   800-669-9777
www.hud.gov/fhe

The U.S. Department of Housing and Urban Development administers the law that prohibits discrimination in housing on the basis of race, color, religion, sex, and national origin; investigates complaints of housing discrimination; and attempts to resolve them through conciliation. Two common forms of discrimination are redlining and steering. Redlining is the illegal practice of refusing to originate mortgage loans in certain neighborhoods on the basis of race or ethnic origin. Steering is the illegal act of limiting the housing shown by a real estate agent to a certain ethnic group. HUD refers complaints to state and local fair housing agencies. They can answer such questions as:
1) How do I file a discrimination complaint?
2) What are the regulations regarding housing discrimination?
3) Is sexual harassment a violation of the Fair Housing Act?
4) Can someone be denied housing because of a mental disability?
5) Do landlords have to pay for physical changes to your apartment if you need them, such as grab bars in the bathroom or wider doors?

* Public Housing Drug Strategy Clearinghouse

Drug Information and Strategy Clearinghouse
U.S. Department of Housing and
   Urban Development (HUD)
P.O. Box 6424   800-578-3472
Rockville, MD 20850   Fax: 301-251-5767

Sponsored by the Department of Housing and Urban Development, the Drug Information and Strategy Clearinghouse provides housing officials, residents, and community leaders with information and assistance on drug abuse prevention and drug trafficking control techniques. They have created a database containing information on improving resident screening procedures, strengthening eviction policies, increasing cooperation with local law enforcement, implementing drug tip hotlines, forming resident patrols, starting child care centers, and organizing drug education/prevention activities. The clearinghouse also provides information packages, resource lists, HUD regulations, referrals, and a newsletter. There is no charge for most information. They can answer such questions as:
1) How can housing authorities apply for government grants?
2) What are some anti-drug strategies that have been successfully carried out in public housing units?
3) What are the latest drug abuse prevention theories and have there been demonstration projects based on these models?
4) What resident patrols and related programs have been successful in building drug-free neighborhoods?
5) How can there be an increase in cooperation with local law enforcement and other agencies?

* National Injury Information Clearinghouse

U.S. Consumer Product Safety Commission
4330 East-West Highway   301-504-0424
Washington, DC 20207   Fax: 301-504-0025
E-mail: info@cpsc.gov
www.cpsc.gov/about/clrnghse.html

The National Injury Information Clearinghouse maintains thousands of detailed investigative reports of injuries associated with consumer products. It has access to automated databases with several million incidents of injuries that have been reported by a nationwide network of hospital emergency departments. You can find the victim's background, including age, race, injury diagnosis, consumer product involved, and more. The Clearinghouse distributes documents and will fulfill search requests, usually at no charge. They can answer such questions as:
1) How many children under the age of five are injured each year while playing with toys?
2) Are all-terrain vehicles considered dangerous?
3) How many injuries/deaths have been reported within the last five years for all-terrain vehicles?
4) How many fires are caused each year by range/ovens?
5) Which children's clothing manufacturers produce flame retardant materials and how effective are they?

* U.S. Postal Service (Mailing)

Office of Consumer Affairs
475 L'Enfant Plaza, SW
Room 5821   202-268-2281
Washington, DC 20260-2200   Fax: 202-268-2304
www.usps.gov

The Postal Service provides mail processing and delivery services to individuals and businesses and protects the mail from loss or theft. They can answer all your postal service questions and provide you with publications and referrals to other postal service departments. They can answer such questions as:
1) How can a business protect itself against mail fraud?
2) What services does the Postal Service offer?

Free Research On Any Topic

3) How does a business set up a mail room?
4) What international mail services are offered?
5) How can a person stop undesirable material from being delivered to their home?

* Meat and Poultry Hotline

Food Safety and Inspection Service
U.S. Department of Agriculture　　　　　　800-535-4555
Washington, DC 20250-3700　　　　　　　Fax: 202-690-2859
E-mail: fsis.webmaster@usda.gov　　　　　TDD/TTY: 800-256-7072
www.fsis.usda.gov

The Meat and Poultry Hotline takes calls from consumers on cases of meat or poultry food poisoning or complaints about meat or poultry spoilage due to improper packaging or processing. They can also provide you with health-oriented information on safe handling and storage of meats and poultry. They can answer such questions as:

1) What should be done during a power outage?
2) What is salmonella and how can people be protected?
3) What are the different type of foodborne illnesses?
4) How long should you cook poultry?
5) What information should be included on meat and poultry labels and what does it mean?

* Mortgage Information Center

Program Evaluation Division
Assistant Secretary for Housing
U.S. Department of Housing and Urban Development (HUD)
451 7th St., SW
Attn: B133　　　　　　　　　　　　　　202-755-7470, ext. 145
Washington, DC 20410　　　　　　　　　Fax: 202-755-7455
Bulletin Board: 202-708-3563

Monthly reports are compiled by the Program Evaluation Division of HUD in areas relating to the mortgage market, securities, taxation, market trends, interest rates, among others. You can receive a free survey of mortgage lending activity and a survey of FHA and conventional mortgage rates. They can answer such questions as:

1) What are the average mortgage rates for different parts of the country?
2) What is the difference in mortgage rates over the past 10 years?
3) What is the average interest rate on new home loans versus existing home loans?
4) What is the number of unsold new houses in a given month?
5) What is the current FHA rate?

* Organic Gardening

Public Information Center, 3404
U.S. Environmental Protection Agency
401 M St., SW　　　　　　　　　　　　　202-260-7751
Washington, DC 20460　　　　　　　　　Fax: 202-260-6257
E-mail: access@epamail.epa.gov
www.epa.gov

The Public Information Center has free information sheets on organic gardening, composting, and recycling. They can answer such questions as:

1) What plants should be planted near each other to deter pests?
2) What are the dangers of pesticides?
3) Who can I talk to regarding composting and recycling?
4) What are the advantages of organic fertilizers?
5) What is required to maintain a lawn?

* Pension Benefit Guaranty Corporation

Public Affairs
1200 K St., NW　　　　　　　　　　　　202-326-4040
Washington, DC 20005-4026　　　　　　　Fax: 202-326-4042
www.pbgc.org

The Pension Benefit Guaranty Corporation works to ensure the solvency and viability of company-sponsored pension plans. They can provide you with information and publications on pension plans, as well as laws and regulations on pensions. They can answer questions such as:

1) What is the federal pension law?
2) What are pensions plans and how do they operate?
3) What information on plans is a company required to give to members?
4) What are the rights and options of participants?
5) What is the employer's responsibilities regarding pension plans?

* Pension and Welfare Benefits Administration

U.S. Department of Labor
200 Constitution Ave., NW, N5656　　　　202-219-8921
Washington, DC 20210　　　　　　　　　Fax: 202-219-5362
www.dol.gov/dol/pwba

The Pension and Welfare Benefits Administration (PWBA) helps to protect the economic future and retirement security of working Americans. It requires administrators of private pension and welfare plans to provide plan participants with easily understandable summaries; to file those summaries with the agency; and to report annually on the financial operation of the plans. PWBA has publications and other information available. They can answer questions such as:

1) What is the effect of job mobility on pension plans?
2) What is the Employee Retirement Income Security Act (ERISA)?
3) What studies have been done on the investment performance of ERISA plans?
4) What information are pension plans required to provide to participants?
5) What employee benefit documents are available from the Department of Labor?

* Plant Information Service

U.S. Botanic Garden
245 1st St., SW　　　　　　　　　　　　202-225-8333
Washington, DC 20024　　　　　　　　　Fax: 202-225-1561
www.aoc.gov/

The U.S. Botanic Garden serves as a center for plant information offering a telephone information service, as well as responding to written inquiries from Monday through Friday, from 9:00 to 11:30 a.m. They can answer such questions as:

1) What are the benefits of organic gardening?
2) How can I use insects to control garden pests?
3) Which house plants are poisonous?
4) What are the dangers of chemical fertilizers?
5) Which herbs grow best indoors?

* Seafood Hotline

Office of Seafood
Food and Drug Administration
200 C St., SW　　　　　　　　　　　　　800-SAFEFOOD
Washington, DC 20201　　　　　　　　　Fax: 202-401-3532
E-mail: oco@fdacf.sw.dhhs.gov
http://vm.cfsan.fda.gov/seafood1.html

The Seafood Hotline can provide consumers with information on how to buy and use seafood products, including storing and handling of seafood, and questions on seafood labeling and nutrition. The Hotline has many free publications on a variety of seafood issues. They can answer such questions as:

1) Can fish be kept frozen for a year?
2) How do you know if a seafood vendor is reputable?
3) What are the dangers of eating raw shellfish?
4) What information is available on canned tuna?
5) What are some seafood safety concerns for people with particular medical conditions?

* Social Security Administration

Social Security Administration
Office of Public Inquiries
6401 Security Blvd.　　　　　　　　　　800-772-1213
Room 4-C-5 Annex　　　　　　　　　　 410-965-7700
Baltimore, MD 21235-6401　　　　　　　TTY: 800-325-0778
www.ssa.gov

The Social Security Administration administers the Social Security and Medicare programs. They can assist certain beneficiaries in claiming reimbursement and developing and adjudicating claims. They can answer such questions as:

1) If you were to retire today, how much would you receive in benefits?
2) What should be done once you turn 65?
3) What is supplemental security income and how do you apply for it?
4) What disability insurance benefits do you qualify for?
5) What survivor benefits are available to children?

* Internal Revenue Service (Taxes)

U.S. Department of Treasury
1111 Constitution Ave., NW
Washington, DC 20224　　　　　　　　　800-829-1040
Fax on Demand: 703-487-4160
www.irs.ustreas.gov

Consumer and Housing

The Internal Revenue Service is responsible for administering and enforcing the internal revenue laws and related statutes. It's mission is to collect the proper amount of tax revenue at the least cost to the public. They can answer such questions as:
1) How do you get copies of your back tax forms?
2) What is required when you deduct your home office?
3) What are the rules about writing off a vacation/work trip?
4) What happens if you can't pay your taxes?
5) Can you deduct your mother as a dependent if she lives with you?

* Women's Bureau Clearinghouse

U.S. Department of Labor
200 Constitution Ave., NW
Room S3306
Washington, DC 20210

800-827-5335
202-219-4486

E-mail: wb-wwc@dol.gov
www.dol.gov/dol/wb/welcome.html
Fax: 202-219-5529

The Women's Bureau Clearinghouse was established to assist employers in identifying the most appropriate policies for responding to the dependent care needs of employees seeking to balance their dual responsibilities. They can also provide information on women's issues, as well as work force issues that affect women. They can offer information and guidance in areas such as women-owned businesses, women workers, alternative work schedules, dependent care issues, and much more. They also have many free publications and other information available. They can answer such questions as:
1) What are some elder care program options?
2) What is the earning difference between men and women?
3) How does flex time work in companies similar to mine?
4) What are some examples of alternate work schedules and how do they work?
5) What literature and other resources are available on employer-supported child care?

Free Research On Any Topic

Criminal Justice

* Bureau of Alcohol, Tobacco, and Firearms
Distribution Center
U.S. Department of Treasury
P.O. Box 5950
Springfield, VA 22150-5950   703-455-7801
www.atf.treas.gov

The Bureau of Alcohol, Tobacco, and Firearms (ATF) is responsible for enforcing and administering firearms and explosives laws, as well as those laws covering the production, use, and distribution of alcohol and tobacco products. ATF can provide you with a wealth of information, statistics, and publications. They can answer such questions as:
1) What explosive incidents and stolen explosives occurred in a year by state and by type of explosives?
2) What are the different types of firearms available?
3) What are the license requirements for a given state to carry a weapon?
4) How do law enforcement officials trace firearms?

* National Criminal Justice Reference Service
National Institute of Justice/NCJRS
Box 6000
Rockville, MD 20849   800-851-3420
                             301-519-5500
E-mail: askncjrs@aspensys.com   Fax: 301-251-5212
www.ncjrs.org/homepage.htm

The National Criminal Justice Reference Service brings the latest criminal justice research findings to criminal justice policymakers, practitioners, and researchers from around the world. Their database features summaries of books, reports, articles, and audiovisual materials. They have a free bi monthly catalogue which lists new publications (many of which are free), upcoming conferences, and more. They can answer such questions as:
1) What videotapes are there on criminal justice topics?
2) What information exists on community safety issues?
3) How effective is parole and probation?
4) What drug abuse programs are in place for offenders?
5) What is date rape?

* Drug and Crime Data Center and Clearinghouse
1600 Research Boulevard
Rockville, MD 20850   800-666-3332
E-mail: ondc@ncjrs.org
www.ncjrs.org/drgshome.htm

The Data Center and Clearinghouse serves the drugs-and-crime information needs of federal, state, and local policy makers, criminal justice and public health practitioners, researchers and universities, private corporations, the media, and the general public. The most current data is available on illegal drugs, drug law violations, drug-related crime, drug-using offenders in the criminal justice system, and the impact of drugs on criminal justice administration. The Clearinghouse maintains a database of some 1,500 annotated bibliographies of statistical and research reports, books, and journal articles on drugs and crime. All documents are free. They can answer such questions as:
1) What are the economic costs of drug-related crime?
2) What data exists on the quantity and flow of illicit drugs from cultivation to consequences?
3) What percentage of high school seniors used cocaine last year?
4) What tactics have been used to build integrity and reduce drug corruption in police departments?
5) What percentage of rapists report that their victims were well known to them?

* National Clearinghouse on Election Administration
Federal Election Commission   202-694-1100
999 E St., NW   800-424-9530
Washington, DC 20463   Fax: 202-219-8500
www.fec.gov

The National Clearinghouse on Election Administration is an agency of the Federal Election Commission. Its overall objective is to enhance the honesty, integrity, and efficiency of the federal election process by providing information and assistance to state and local election officials, to state legislatures and legislative reference bureaus, and to other interested organizations regarding the conduct of Federal elections. They can answer such questions as:
1) What research reports are available on state campaign finance laws?
2) Where can I obtain advice and assistance in making polling places more accessible to the elderly and handicapped?
3) What statistics exist that could summarize state and national voting age populations, the number of registered voters, turnout, and results in presidential elections for 1960 through 1988?
4) What landmark judicial decisions have been made involving elections over the past twenty years?
5) What are the registration techniques and procedures in a particular state?

* Equal Employment Opportunity Commission (EEOC)
Publications and Information Center
P.O. Box 12549   800-669-EEOC
Cincinnati, OH 45212-0549   Fax: 513-489-8695
www.eeoc.gov

The purpose of the Equal Employment Opportunity Commission is to eliminate discrimination based on race, color, religion, sex, national origin, or age in hiring, promoting, firing, setting wages, testing, training, and all other terms and conditions of employment. The Commission conducts investigations of alleged discrimination, and provides voluntary assistance programs for employers, unions, and others. They have free publications and information available. They can answer such questions as:
1) What questions cannot be asked in an employment interview?
2) What constitutes sexual harassment?
3) What federal law prohibits employers from discriminating between men and women in the payment of wages, and to whom does the law apply?
4) What can be done if you feel you have been unfairly discriminated against?
5) What information exists to train personnel officers on the prevailing laws and regulations?

* Bureau of Justice Assistance Clearinghouse
P.O. Box 6000
U.S. Department of Justice   800-688-4252
Rockville, MD 20849   Fax: 301-251-5212
E-mail: askncjrs@aspensys.com
www.ncjrs.org

The Bureau of Justice Assistance Clearinghouse (BJA) informs state and local criminal justice practitioners about BJA products and programs. They provide federal funding and technical assistance to state and local units of government to improve the criminal justice system. They can answer such questions as:
1) What information is available regarding a variety of anti-drug programs?
2) What programs are in place to improve the efficiency of the criminal justice system?
3) What are the estimated costs of drug testing for a pretrial service program?
4) What training programs exist for narcotics enforcement?
5) What are the treatment alternatives to street crimes?

* Justice Statistics Clearinghouse
Bureau of Justice Statistics
U.S. Department of Justice
Box 6000   800-732-3277
Rockville, MD 20849   301-519-5500
E-mail: askncjrs@aspensys.com
www.ncjrs.org/stathome.htm

The Bureau of Justice Statistics (BJS) supports this clearinghouse for those seeking crime and criminal justice data. In addition to distributing BJS publications, the Clearinghouse responds to statistics requests by offering document database searches, statistics information packages, referrals, and other related products and services. They can answer such questions as:
1) What is the annual national estimate of the amount of crime against persons and households?
2) What are some of the characteristics of victims?
3) How differently are juveniles handled from adults?

Criminal Justice

4) How prevalent is organized crime?
5) What is the recidivism rate, and when criminals are rearrested, with what crimes are they normally charged?

* <u>Juvenile Justice</u> Clearinghouse
National Criminal Justice Reference Service
U.S. Department of Justice, Box 6000
Rockville, MD 20849   800-638-8736
E-mail: askncjrs@aspensys.com
http://ncjrs.aspensys.com:81/ncjrshome.html

The Juvenile Justice Clearinghouse disseminates publications, research findings, and program evaluations supported by the Office of Juvenile Justice and Delinquency Prevention. In addition, the staff can prepare customized responses to information requests. They can answer such questions as:

1) How do juvenile courts vary in handling drug and alcohol cases?
2) What can a community do in response to youth gangs?
3) What methods have been successful in dealing with juvenile reinstitution?
4) How many juveniles were arrested last year for possession of illegal drugs?
5) What methods are effective in reducing violence in the schools?

* National Clearinghouse for Poverty Law (Legal Services)
205 W. Monroe, 2nd Floor   312-263-3830
Chicago, IL 60606   Fax: 312-263-3846

The National Clearinghouse for Poverty Law is the most comprehensive source for information concerning civil poverty law. Also, the Clearinghouse has many publications dealing with issues of vital interest to the non poverty lawyer. Problems with health care, housing, and social security strike people in all economic situations. These are just some of the 20 major areas of law that Clearinghouse publications cover, providing practical information useful to people in all economic and social strata. The Clearinghouse, as a resource center and a legal research system, offers the most complete source of civil poverty law publications that can be found. They have a free publications list. They can answer such questions as:

1) What information exists on the eligibility requirements for Medicare home health care?
2) What models exist on establishing pro bono programs?
3) What are the various issues concerning the tax burden on the poor?
4) What are the litigation issues concerning homeless persons and emergency shelter?
5) Where can information be obtained on child custody cases?

* National Center for <u>Missing and Exploited Children</u>
699 Prince St.   800-843-5678
Alexandria, VA 22314   703-274-3900
www.missingkids.org   Fax: 703-274-2220

The National Center for Missing and Exploited Children serves as a clearinghouse of information on missing and exploited children; provides technical assistance to citizens and law-enforcement agencies; offers training programs to law-enforcement and social service professionals; distributes photos and descriptions of missing children nationwide; coordinates child protection efforts with the private sector; networks with nonprofit service providers and state clearinghouses on missing persons; and provides information on effective state legislation to ensure the protection of children. They can answer such questions as:

1) How can a parent work through the civil and criminal justice systems in order to regain custody of the child her ex-husband stole from her?
2) How can a parent protect children against day care abuse?
3) What are some of the warning signs of child sexual exploitation?
4) What is the profile of a runaway and the patterns of runaway behavior?
5) What information is available to help a child testify in court?

* Office for <u>Victims</u> of Crime Resource Center
U.S. Department of Justice
Box 6000   800-627-6872
Rockville, MD 20849   Fax: 301-251-5212
E-mail: askncjrs@aspensys.com
www.ncjrs.org/victhome.htm

The Office for Victims of Crime Resource Center is sponsored by the Office of Victims of Crime. It can provide access to resources, such as more than 7,000 victim-related books and articles, national victimization statistics, federally sponsored victim-related research studies, and information on state victim compensation programs. From the Clearinghouse, you can get free publications, borrow hard-to-find publications, and buy selected videotapes. Information specialists can also conduct database searches. They can answer such questions as:

1) What is the relationship between child abuse and delinquency?
2) What information is there for police when confronting a domestic violence incident?
3) What are some of the programs which compensate victims of crime?
4) What is the criminal justice response to victim harm?
5) How can one improve the use and effectiveness of the Neighborhood Watch program?

Free Research On Any Topic

Education And The Arts

* ERIC Clearinghouse on Adult, Career, and Vocational Learning

Ohio State University Center on Education and
Training for Employment   800-848-4815
1900 Kenny Rd.   614-292-7069
Columbus, OH 43210   Fax: 614-292-1260
E-mail: ericacve@magnus.acs.ohio_state.edu
http://ericacve.org

The Clearinghouse on Adult, Career, and Vocational Learning provides materials covering all levels of adult and continuing education from: basic literacy training through professional skill upgrading; vocational and technical education covering all service areas for secondary, postsecondary, and adult populations; and career education and career development programs for all ages and populations. A publications list and price sheet are available. They can answer questions such as:

1) What research exists on the effectiveness of flex time and job share programs?
2) What is the job placement rate of graduates from vocational schools?
3) What are the statistics on job satisfaction and wage earnings?
4) What are the benefits of vocational education?
5) What information exists on how people can find a job and make effective career choices?

* ERIC Clearinghouse on Educational Assessment and Evaluation

College of Library and Information Services
1129 Shriver Laboratory   800-464-3742
University of Maryland   301-405-7449
College Park, MD 20742   Fax: 202-319-6692
E-mail: feedback@ericae.net
http://ericae.net

The Clearinghouse on Assessment and Evaluation provides information on the assessment and evaluation of education projects or programs, tests and other measurement devices, methodology of measurement and evaluation, and more. A publications list and price sheet are available. They can answer such questions as:

1) Do statistics show that tests discriminate against certain minority groups?
2) What tests are given to handicapped children and what is the research behind these tests?
3) Is the Scholastic Aptitude Test (SAT) an effective tool of measurement?
4) What is computer-assisted testing?
5) How often are SAT tests updated and who designs the questions?

* Bilingual Education Clearinghouse

National Clearinghouse for Bilingual Education
George Washington University
Center for the Study of Language and Education
2011 Eye St., NW
Suite 2001   202-467-0867
Washington, DC 20006   Fax: 202-467-0867
E-mail: askncbe@ncbe.gwu.edu
www.ncbe.gwu.edu

The Bilingual Education Clearinghouse provides information to practitioners in the field on curriculum materials, program models, methodologies, and research findings on the education of limited English proficient (LEP) individuals. They also offer an electronic information system, free to users, where access is available to a database of curriculum materials and literature related to the education of LEP persons. An electronic bulletin board is also available which contains news from federal, state, and local education agencies, conference announcements, and other current information. Their newsletter and other publications are available, many of which are free of charge. They can answer such questions as:

1) How do you mainstream language minority students?
2) What computer programs exist to assist in teaching limited English proficient students?
3) What are some of the issues and practices involved in meeting the needs of gifted and talented minority language students?
4) How can parents become involved in the education of limited English students?
5) How can teachers integrate multi-cultural materials in instructional programs?

* ERIC Clearinghouse on Counseling and Student Services

School of Education
101 Park Building   800-414-9769
University of North Carolina at Greensboro   910-334-4114
Greensboro, NC 27412-5001   Fax: 910-334-4116
E-mail: ericcass@iris.uncg.edu
www.uncg.edu/~ericcass2

The Clearinghouse on Counseling and Student Services provides documents relating to all levels of counseling and personnel services including preparation, practice, and supervision of counselors at all education levels and in all settings; personnel procedures such as testing and interviewing; group work and case work; career planning; and more. They have free publications, and will conduct searches for a fee. They can answer such questions as:

1) How can counselors enhance a student's self-esteem through counseling?
2) What are the emerging priorities for the counseling field in the 1990's?
3) What dropout prevention programs have been effective?
4) What is the current high school dropout rate?
5) What tests are available to students who are undecided on a choice of career?

* ERIC Clearinghouse on Disabilities and Gifted Education

The Council for Exceptional Children
1920 Association Dr.
Reston, VA 22091   800-328-0272
E-mail: ericec@cec.sped.org
http://ericec.org

The Clearinghouse on Disabilities and Gifted Education provides information on all aspects of education and development of handicapped persons, including prevention of handicaps, identification and assessment of handicaps, and intervention and enrichment programs. All aspects of the education and development of gifted persons are covered as well. A publications list and price sheet are available. They can answer such questions as:

1) What are the issues concerning the mainstreaming of a handicapped student?
2) How do you "home school" a gifted child?
3) What is the research concerning the post-school status of learning disabled students?
4) What preschool services are available for children with handicaps?
5) Under what criteria is a child considered gifted?

* ERIC Clearinghouse on Educational Management

College of Education
5207 University of Oregon   541-346-5043
Eugene, OR 97403-5207   800-438-8841
E-mail: eric@eric.oregon.edu   Fax: 541-346-2334
http://eric.uoregon.edu

The Clearinghouse on Educational Management distributes information on the following subjects: the leadership, management, and structure of public and private educational organizations; practice and theory of administration; preservice and inservice preparation of administrators; and tasks and processes of administration. The Clearinghouse also provides information on sites, buildings, and equipment for education, and planning, financing, construction, renovating, and evaluating educational facilities. They can answer such questions as:

1) What are "mentor teachers" and how do you prepare them to assist new teachers?
2) How do you best confront racism in schools?
3) How do you recruit, select, and retain good teachers?
4) What research has been done on the various methods of school discipline?
5) What elements must be considered in the design of a new school?

* Educational Research

Office of Educational Research and Improvement's
Information Service
U.S. Department of Education
Education Information Branch
Capitol Plaza Building, Suite 300

Education and the Arts

555 New Jersey Ave., NW
Washington, DC 20208-5641   800-424-1616
www.ed.gov/offices/OERI

The Education Information Branch staff specialists can provide information on topics such as early childhood education, elementary and secondary education, higher education, adult and vocational education, education finance, longitudinal statistical studies, and special education. They have publications and reports, many of which are free. They can answer such questions as:

1) What statistics are there on the number of students who receive loans, grants, and work-study assistance from state sources?
2) What are the statistics on private postsecondary education, such as enrollment, earned degrees conferred, full and part-time faculty members and their salaries, and more?
3) What information is available on how to choose a school for a child and what makes a school good?
4) How can parents help their children become better readers?
5) What are the enrollment outcomes for recent master's and bachelor's degree recipients?

* Educational Resources Information Center

ACCESS ERIC
Aspen Systems Corporation
2277 Research Blvd.   800-LET-ERIC
Rockville, MD 20850   Fax: 301-309-2084
E-mail: accesseric@access.eric.org
www.accesseric.org

Educational Resources Information Center (ERIC) is a nationwide information service set up to collect materials about current developments in education and make them available to the public. The system includes 16 clearinghouses, each of which is responsible for acquiring, processing, and disseminating information about a particular aspect of education. The ERIC database contains bibliographic information, including key descriptors and abstracts, on over 950,000 research documents, journal articles, curricular materials, and resource guides. The Clearinghouses offer a wide variety of services and products, and can answer questions about: subject fields, run computer searches, develop short bibliographies, newsletters, and other free or inexpensive materials; publish monographs; publish handbooks; and develop materials to help you use ERIC.

ACCESS ERIC is the main center for the ERIC clearinghouses. It answers all questions on how to use ERIC and helps anyone stay up-to-date on the latest developments in the education field. They can answer such questions as:

1) How can I use ERIC to answer my education question?
2) What is required to have a database search run on a topic?
3) How can I have something that I have written entered into the ERIC system?
4) Where can I find the latest statistics on an education topic?
5) How can school administrators develop new management tools and practices?

* ERIC Clearinghouse on Elementary and Early Childhood Education

University of Illinois at Urbana-Champaign
Children's Resource Center   800-583-4135
51 Gerty Dr.   217-333-1386
Champaign, IL 61820   Fax: 217-333-3767
E-mail: ericeece@uiuc.edu
http://ericeece.org

The Clearinghouse on Elementary and Early Childhood Education provides information covering all aspects of the cognitive, emotional, social and physical development, and education of children from birth through early adolescence, excluding specific elementary school curriculum areas. Among the topics covered are: prenatal and infant development and care; child care programs and community services for children at local, state, and federal levels; parent, child, and family relationships; home and school relationships; foster care and adoption; and more. A publications list and price sheet are available. They can answer such questions as:

1) How do you start a day care center?
2) How do you choose a day care center and how do you assess a preschooler's development?
3) How can parents become involved in the education of their children?
4) How do you meet the needs of homeless children?
5) How do you help children with their social development?

* ERIC Clearinghouse on Higher Education

George Washington University   800-773-ERIC
One Dupont Circle, Suite 630   202-296-2597
Washington, DC 20036-1183   Fax: 202-452-1844
E-mail: mkozi@eric-he.edu
www.eriche.org

The Clearinghouse on Higher Education provides information covering education beyond the secondary level that leads to a four-year, masters, doctoral or professional degree and that includes courses and programs designed to enhance or update skills obtained in these degree programs. Areas include: academic advising, faculty, continuing education, legal issues, curriculum development, and more. They can answer such questions as:

1) What research and assessments are available on the trends and issues in higher education today?
2) What percentage of staff of higher education facilities are minorities and women?
3) What information is available on the issue of student stress?
4) How do we raise academic standards as a country?
5) What techniques are useful in improving a student's organizational skills?

* ERIC Clearinghouse on Information and Technology

Syracuse University School of Education   800-464-9107
621 Skytop Rd., Suite 160   315-443-3640
Syracuse, NY 13244-5290   Fax: 315-443-5448
E-mail: eric@ericir.syr.edu
www.ericir.syr.edu/home

The Clearinghouse on Information and Technology provides information covering educational technology and library and information science at all levels. Instructional design, development, and evaluation with emphasis on educational technology; computers, audio and video recordings, and more. They can answer such questions as:

1) What is the latest research on the value of using computers and applying video technology to enhance learning?
2) What are the various studies comparing the different types of computer based media?
3) Is there an overview of instructional television and its effectiveness for teaching children?
4) At what grade level are computers introduced in the classroom, on average?
5) Are audio recordings an effective tool for teaching foreign languages?

* ERIC Clearinghouse on Community Colleges

University of California at Los Angeles
3051 Moore Hall   800-832-8256
Box 951521   310-825-3931
Los Angeles, CA 90095   Fax: 310-206-8095
www.gseis.ucla.edu/eric/eric.html

The Clearinghouse on Community Colleges provides information covering the development, administration, and evaluation of two-year public and private community and junior colleges, technical institutes, and two-year branch university campuses. They have free publications and will conduct database searches for a fee. They can answer such questions as:

1) What are the main problems involved with transfer students?
2) How many students working on A.A. degrees in nursing are mothers and other women returning to further their education?
3) How do you implement a cultural exchange or study abroad program?
4) How do you recruit and retain minorities and women at junior colleges?
5) What percentage of students attending two-year programs receive financial assistance?

* ERIC Clearinghouse on Languages and Linguistics

Center for Applied Linguistics   800-276-9834
4646 40th St., NW   202-362-0700
Washington, DC 20016-1859   Fax: 202-362-3740
E-mail: eric@cal.org
www.cal.org/ericcll

The Clearinghouse on Languages and Linguistics provides information on languages and language sciences; all areas of foreign language, second language, and linguistics instruction; cultural and intercultural context of languages; international exchanges; teacher training; and more. Mini-bibliographies and fact sheets are available free of charge. Ready-made search printouts are available for a fee, and prices vary for specific searches. They can answer such questions as:

1) How do you institute teaching English as a second language in the workplace?
2) How do you develop a curriculum and training program for volunteer tutors for limited-English proficient adults?

Free Research On Any Topic

3) What are the pros and cons of language immersion programs in schools?
4) What are the issues regarding the foreign language requirement?
5) What are some available opportunities abroad for teaching English as a foreign language?

* National Clearinghouse on Literacy Education

Center for Applied Linguistics
4646 40th St., NW
Washington, DC 20016-1859
E-mail: ncle@cal.org
www.cal.org/ncle
202-362-0700
Fax: 202-362-3740

The National Clearinghouse on Literacy Education produces and disseminates materials summarizing current research and information available on selected topics; develops a directory of effective adult literacy programs and projects; and supports a user services program to respond to information requests. They have a publications list available, and many of the items are free. They can answer such questions as:

1) What organizations offer programs for senior citizens interested in learning to read and write?
2) How can workplaces promote English as a second language?
3) What free resources are available to adult literacy instructors?
4) What percentage of U.S. immigrants are illiterate? What programs exist to help them?
5) What type of educational materials and programs are available to teach English to out-of-school youth?

* Museum Reference Center

Smithsonian Institution
Office of Museum Programs
900 Jefferson Dr., SW
Washington, DC 20560
E-mail: libmail@sil.si.edu
www.sil.si.edu/Branches/mrc-hp.htm
202-786-2271
Fax: 202-357-2311

The Museum Reference Center serves as a clearinghouse for museum programs providing professional development training, advisory assistance, and research services to the national and international museum community and the Smithsonian staff. The Center participates through the sponsorship of workshops, internships, and professional visitor programs, an audiovisual production loan program, publications, and more. They can answer such questions as:

1) Where can information be obtained regarding internship programs for museum careers?
2) What is the latest research on climate control and security for museums?
3) What information exists on how to train docents and volunteers?
4) Where can examples of exhibit designs be found?
5) Where can information be found on collection sharing?

* Performing Arts Library

John F. Kennedy Center for the Performing Arts
2700 F St., NW
Washington, DC 20566
202-416-8780

The Performing Arts Library is a joint project of the Library of Congress and the Kennedy Center, and offers information and reference assistance on dance, theater, opera, music, film, and broadcasting. The Performing Arts Library serves the research and information needs of the public, artists, and staff of the Center. The Library also identifies and locates the creative and resource materials necessary to develop new works and productions in the performing arts. Reference service is available by phone, in person, or by mail. They can answer such questions as:

1) How can an orchestral program of Irish composers be tailored for a young audience?
2) What information exists on different dance companies based in New York?
3) Is there information on what is required to start a record company?
4) Are their recordings of interviews or videotapes of famous actresses discussing their works?
5) Where can recordings be located on poetry readings?

* ERIC Clearinghouse on Reading, English and Communication Skills

Indiana University
Smith Research Center, Suite 150
2805 East Tenth St.
Bloomington, IN 47408-2698
E-mail: ericcs@indiana.edu
www.indiana.edu/~eric_rec
800-855-5847
812-855-5847
Fax: 812-855-4220

The Clearinghouse on Reading, English and Communication Skills provides information on reading, English, communication skills, identification, diagnosis and remediation of reading problems, and more. A catalogue of publications including prices is available. The Clearinghouse will also conduct custom database searches for a fee. They can answer such questions as:

1) How do you teach elementary students listening skills?
2) How can parents help their child to read?
3) How do you help a quiet student communicate in the classroom?
4) Where can teachers obtain written activities for junior high social studies classes?
5) Is there information on sex stereotypes in children's literature?

* ERIC Clearinghouse for Science, Mathematics, and Environmental Education

Ohio State University
1929 Kenny Rd.
Columbus, OH 43210
E-mail: ericse@osu.edu
www.ericse.org
800-276-0462
614-292-6717
Fax: 614-292-0263

The Clearinghouse for Science, Mathematics, and Environmental Education acquires educational literature on the following topics: development of curriculum and instructional materials; teachers and teacher education; learning theory; educational programs; and computer applications. They can answer such questions as:

1) Is there information on how to teach a lesson on environmental education?
2) What can be done to boost students' enthusiasm for math?
3) What are some of the common safety hazards in science classrooms?
4) Where can teachers obtain free science instructional materials?
5) Are there financial aid programs available to teachers interested in continuing education?

* ERIC Clearinghouse for Social Studies/Social Science Education

Social Studies Development Center
Indiana University
2805 East Tenth St., Suite 120
Bloomington, IN 47408
E-mail: ericso@indiana.edu
www.indiana.edu/eric_chess.htm
800-266-3815
812-855-3838
Fax: 812-855-0455

The Clearinghouse for Social Studies/Social Science Education acquires journal articles and documents at all levels of social studies and social science education, including anthropology, economics, geography, sociology, social psychology, civics, and political science, as well as on history and social topics. A publications catalogue is available, including prices. They can answer such questions as:

1) What are some interesting learning activities designed to teach social studies?
2) What resources exist to supplement teachers' lessons on Africa and African Culture?
3) How do you teach geography at home?
4) How can you teach the law incorporating Supreme Court cases?
5) How can teachers stimulate children's interest in anthropology?

* ERIC Clearinghouse on Teaching and Teacher Education

American Association of Colleges for Teacher Education
1307 New York Ave., NW, Suite 300
Washington, DC 20005
E-mail: query@aacte.edu
www.ericsp.org
800-822-9229
202-293-2450
Fax: 202-457-8095

The ERIC Clearinghouse on Teacher Education acquires, publishes, and disseminates documents conveying research, theory, and practice in teacher education and in all aspects of health education, physical education, recreation education, nutrition education, and more. They can answer such questions as:

1) What are the teacher certification requirements?
2) How effective are student teachers in the classroom?
3) What computer games are there to help kids learn math?
4) What techniques can a teacher use to improve classroom productivity?
5) What are "at risk" students and how can they best be served?

* ERIC Clearinghouse on Urban Education

Teachers College
Columbia University Institute for Urban and Minority Education
Main Hall
800-601-4868

Education and the Arts

Room 303, Box 40
New York, NY 10027
E-mail: eric-cue@columbia.edu
http://eric-web:tc.columbia.edu

212-678-3433
Fax: 212-678-4012

The Clearinghouse on Urban Education provides information on the programs and practices in schools in urban areas. In addition, the education of racial/ethnic minority children and youth in various settings is studied: on the local, national, and international level; theory and practice of education equity; and urban and minority experiences. A publications list and price sheet are available. They can answer such questions as:

1) What is the current research on effective programs for reducing the dropout rates among inner city high school students?
2) What research is available on the number of pregnant, minority teenagers who obtain their high school diplomas in inner city schools?
3) What information is there on mentoring programs?
4) What issues are involved in linking schools with human service agencies?
5) Are urban schools financed equitably?

Free Research On Any Topic

Energy and Environment

* EPA Control Technology Center Hotline (Air Pollution)
U.S. Environmental Protection Agency (EPA)
AEERL
Research Triangle Park, NC 27711 919-541-0800

The EPA Control Technology Center Hotline provides technical support to state and local agencies and to EPA regional offices in implementing air pollution control programs. They can answer such questions as:
1) What type of computer software can my company use to assess pollution control problems and evaluate potential solutions?
2) What impacts have control technologies had on air pollution?
3) What type of air pollution permits does my company need to operate in my state?
4) How can my company reduce its air pollution control costs?
5) What are the best cost-effective methods to maintain my company's air pollution control equipment?

* BACT/LAER Clearinghouse (MD-13) (Air Pollution)
U.S. Environmental Protection Agency (EPA)
Clean Air Technology Center 919-541-0800
Research Triangle Park, NC 27711 Fax: 919-541-5742
www.epa.gov/ttn/cact

The BACT/LAER Clearinghouse assists state and local air pollution control agencies in selecting the best available control technology (BACT) and the lowest achievable emission rate (LAER). It controls new or modified sources in a nationally consistent manner. They can answer such questions as:
1) How can my agency get assistance in compiling inventories of air toxic emissions?
2) How does the EPA estimate air toxic emissions?
3) Where can I get a listing of national emissions estimates and factors for air that is made toxic from motor vehicles?
4) Where can I find out about the toxic emissions for a particular consumer product?
5) How can my company achieve the lowest achievable emission rate for our product?

* Asbestos and Small Business Ombudsman Clearinghouse
U.S. Environmental Protection Agency (EPA)
401 M St., SW 800-368-5888
Washington, DC 20460 703-305-5938
www.epa.gov Fax: 703-305-6462

The assigned mission of the Asbestos Ombudsman Clearinghouse is to provide to the public sector, including individual citizens and community services, information on the handling and abatement of asbestos in schools, the workplace, and the home. In addition, interpretation of the asbestos-in-school requirements and publications are provided to explain recent legislation. The EPA Asbestos Ombudsman receives complaints and requests for information and provides assistance with regard to them. They can answer such questions as:
1) What is asbestos, and in what era was it used?
2) How do I know if I have asbestos in my home or at work and how do I find help to contain or eliminate it?
3) What do I do if I have been exposed to asbestos?
4) How can I safe-proof my house from asbestos?
5) Are the schools in my particular neighborhood safe from asbestos?

* Boating Safety Hotline
Office of Boat Safety
U.S. Coast Guard
U.S. Department of Transportation
2100 2nd St., SW 800-368-5647
Washington, DC 20593 202-267-1077
E-mail: BoatWeb@mail.rmit.com Fax: 202-267-4285
www.uscgboating.org/

The Boating Safety Hotline can provide you with information on such topics of interest to boaters as safety recalls, publications, Coast Guard department contacts and addresses, public education courses, and free Coast Guard Services. They have a wealth of free information and publications to share. They can answer such questions as:
1) What statistics exist on boating accidents?
2) How can parents teach children about water safety?
3) What things do people need to consider in evaluating floatation devices?
4) What licenses or regulations should boaters be aware of before they hit the water?
5) Where can people receive information on water charts and other navigational aids?

* National Climatic Data Center
National Oceanic and Atmospheric Administration
U.S. Department of Commerce
Federal Building
151 Patton Ave., Room 120 704-271-4800
Asheville, NC 28801 Fax: 704-271-4876
E-mail: orders@ncdc.noaa.gov
www.ncdc.noaa.gov

The National Climatic Data Center (NCDC) provides an important historical perspective on climate. Through the use of over a hundred years of weather observations, reference databases are generated. NCDC's data and information are available to everyone including the general public, the legal profession, engineering, industry, agriculture, and government policy makers. They can answer such questions as:
1) What were the weather conditions like in a particular part of a state on a specific day, and can this information be used for a court case?
2) In what parts of the country is the climate moderate allowing energy bills to be held to a minimum?
3) What information is available on severe storms, such as the occurrences of storms, data on the paths of individual storms, deaths, injuries, and estimated property damage?
4) Are droughts becoming more widespread?
5) Is the greenhouse theory becoming a reality?

* Energy Efficiency and Renewable Energy Clearinghouse
P.O. Box 3048 800-363-3732
Merrifield, VA 22116 Fax: 703-893-0400
Bulletin Board: 800-273-2955
www.eren.doe.gov

The Energy Efficiency and Renewable Energy Clearinghouse can provide information on how to save energy, as well as information on solar, wind, or any other aspect of renewable energy. They have the latest research on renewable energy technologies and energy conservation, and can refer you to other valuable resources. A list of free publications is available. They can answer questions such as:
1) How can you convert a home to solar heat?
2) How do heat pumps work and are they efficient?
3) What should you look for in a wood-burning appliance?
4) What can be done to improve the energy efficiency of a home?
5) Is the wind a practical source of energy?

* Safe Drinking Water Hotline
U.S. Environmental Protection Agency (EPA)
401 M St., SW
Washington, DC 20460 800-426-4791
E-mail: hotline_sdwa@epamail.epa.gov Fax: 202-260-8072
www.epa.gov/safewater

The Safe Drinking Water Hotline responds to questions concerning the Safe Drinking Water Act, water standards, regulations, and the Underground Injection Program. It will also provide selected free publications. They can answer such questions as:
1) How do I find out if there is lead in my drinking water?
2) What is the Underground Injection Program?
3) What are some of the newer techniques for removing and disposing of water pollutants?
4) What research is being done to develop safer drinking water?
5) What can I do if there is too much fluoride in my drinking water?

Energy and Environment

* **EROS Data Center (Earth Resources)**
  U.S. Geological Survey
  Mundt Federal Bldg.   605-594-6511
  Sioux Falls, SD 57198   Fax: 605-594-6589
  http://edcwww.cr.usgs.gov

The Earth Resources Observation Systems (EROS) Data Center is a national archive, production, and research facility for remotely sensed data and other forms of geographic information. It receives, processes, and distributes data from the U.S.' Landsat satellite sensors and from airborne mapping cameras. The Center houses over 2,000,000 worldwide scenes of Earth acquired by Landsat satellites and nearly 6,000,000 aerial photographs of U.S. sites. Maps and photographs range from $6 to $65 and can be obtained from the Center's customer service department. The staff can answer such questions as:

1) How can I receive a listing of aerial photographs of a particular hurricane that I am studying?
2) How do the Landsat satellite sensors work?
3) How can EROS help my company's geologic exploration projects?
4) How can EROS help my company form a geochemical assessment of a potential land site that we are interested in developing?
5) Can the Center furnish me with a printout of land ownership lists in my particular county?

* **Earth Science Information Centers**
  U.S. Geological Survey
  508 National Center   703-648-6892
  Reston, VA 20192   888-ASK-USGS
  E-mail: esicmail@usgs.gov   Fax: 703-648-4888
  http://mapping.usgs.gov/esic.html

Earth Science Information Centers (ESIC) offer nationwide information and sales service for U.S. Geological Survey map products and earth science publications. This network of ESICs provides information about: geologic, hydrologic, and land use maps, books, and reports; aerial, satellite, and radar images and related products; earth science and map data in digital format and related applications software; and geodetic data. ESICs can fill orders for custom products and provide information about earth science materials from many public and private producers. They can answer such questions as:

1) Where can maps of Indian lands be located?
2) What earth-science teaching aids are available?
3) Where can accurate topographic maps be found which show the location and measurable elevation of natural and man made features?
4) Where can out-of-print maps be located?
5) Where can wetlands be found in the state of Ohio?

* **National Earthquake Information Center**
  U.S. Geological Survey
  Box 25046, DFS, MS967   303-273-8500
  Denver, CO 80225   Fax: 303-273-8450
  E-mail: sedas@gldfs.cr.usgs.gov
  wwwneic.cr.usgs.gov

National Earthquake Information Center compiles, computes, and distributes digital and analog data on earthquakes that have occurred around the world. They have information on seismograms, earthquake magnitudes, intensities, and epicenter locations. They can answer such questions as:

1) What information exists on the most recent earthquake in California?
2) How many fault lines are known in California and where are they located?
3) What should people do in the event of an earthquake?
4) Where has there been seismic activity around the world in a given month?
5) What is the largest earthquake on record?

* **Emergency Planning and Community-Right-To-Know Information Hotline**
  Booz, Allen & Hamilton, Inc.
  401 M St., SW   800-535-0202
  Washington, DC 20466   Fax: 703-412-3333
  www.epa.gov/swercepp/crtk.html

The Emergency Planning and Community-Right-To-Know Information Hotline (EPCRA) provides information on what types of waste may be hazardous to the public's health. All information is open to local agencies, citizens, attorneys, consultants, and communities. EPCRA helps answer questions on the best ways to remove and store hazardous and solid waste. They can answer such questions as:

1) What constitutes a hazardous chemical release?
2) Which releases are especially dangerous?
3) What type of emergency planning is available for those working around or in contact with hazardous waste?
4) How are companies and communities regulated?
5) What documents are available to the average citizen concerned about waste?

* **Emissions Clearinghouse**
  Emission Factor Clearinghouse, MD-14
  U.S. Environmental Protection Agency (EPA)
  Research Triangle Park, NC 27711   919-541-5285
  www.epa.gov/ttnchie1/oindex.html

The Emissions Clearinghouse is a means of exchanging information on air pollution control matters. It addresses the criteria pollutants and toxic substances from stationary and area sources, as well as mobile sources. The *Emission Factor Clearinghouse Newsletter* is issued quarterly, and contains information on recent publications, inquiries about EPA emission inventory policy, newly developed emission factors, and requests for assistance in dealing with general or specific air pollution emissions. The Clearinghouse does have a database for which there is a user fee. They can answer such questions as:

1) How can I get a FAX Chief system?
2) What information exists on the underground storage of fuel tanks?
3) How can I find an engineer to assist me with my emissions questions?
4) What are atmospheric tanks and how are they used?

* **National Energy Information Center**
  U.S. Department of Energy
  1F048 Forrestal Building
  1000 Independence Ave., SW   202-586-8800
  Washington, DC 20585   Fax: 202-586-0727
  E-mail: infoctr@eia.doe.gov
  www.eia.doe.gov

The National Energy Information Center provides general reference services on U.S. Department of Energy data. It can provide statistical and analytical data, information, and referral assistance on a wide variety of energy-related issues. A publications directory, including many free publications, is available. They can answer such questions as:

1) What energy-related educational materials exist for elementary and secondary students?
2) What are some of the issues surrounding the Clean Air Act Amendments?
3) What is the short-term energy outlook?
4) What companies have purchased uranium and how much?
5) What is the petroleum supply statistics for a particular month?

* **National Environmental Data Referral Service**
  NEDRES Office
  National Oceanic and Atmospheric Administration
  U.S. Department of Commerce
  Environmental Information Services
  1305 East-West Highway   301-713-0575
  Silver Spring, MD 20910   Fax: 301-713-1249
  E-mail: barton@esdim.noaa.gov
  www.esdim.noaa.gov/

The National Environmental Data Referral Service (NEDRES) is designed to provide convenient, economical, and efficient access to widely scattered environmental data. NEDRES is a publicly available service which identifies the existence, location, characteristics, and availability conditions of environmental data sets. NEDRES database contains only descriptions, and not the actual data. Major subject categories include climatology and meteorology, oceanography, geophysics and geology, geography, hydrology and limnology, terrestrial resources, toxic and regulated substances, and satellite remotely sensed data. For more information on the NEDRES database, contact the office listed above. They can provide the information and pointers to data on such questions as:

1) What data exists on the air quality in the U.S.?
2) Where can information be found on the Chesapeake Bay?
3) Where can data be located on the estuarine water of California?
4) How has acid rain affected the environment?
5) How has pollution affected the ocean environment?

* **Environmental Financing Information Network**
  Labat-Anderson, Inc.
  401 M St., SW, 2731R
  Washington, DC 20460   202-260-0420
  E-mail: efin@epa.gov

Free Research On Any Topic

www.epa.gov/efinpage

The Environmental Financing Information Network is an online database service. They help state and local officials find different ways to finance and improve the environment in which we live. They assist towns in locating funds to update wastewater treatment plants and other environmental projects all the way down to the sewage system. Information on State Revolving Funds and Public-Private Partnerships is included. They can answer such questions as:

1) How can we get financial funding for a nonprofit organization?
2) What are the pros and cons of forming a public or private partnership?
3) What other cities have revamped their waste management system?
4) How can towns or cities find technical assistance to help with new waste technology?
5) What ways can a state economically enhance their waste treatment systems?

* U.S. Environmental Protection Agency (EPA)
Public Information Center
401 M St., SW   202-260-2080
Washington, DC 20460 Fax: 202-260-6257
E-mail: public_access@epamail.epa.gov
www.epa.gov

The Public Information Center of the Environmental Protection Agency should be the first point of contact for all environmental issues. They have free publications on a variety of environmental topics, and can refer you to other experts within the EPA for more specific responses to your inquiries. They can answer such questions as:

1) What cars have the best gas mileage?
2) What are the current pesticide regulations?
3) What environmental education materials exist for teachers?
4) What can be done to reduce pollution?
5) What is radon, and how can it be removed from a home?

* Center for Environmental Research Information
Technology Transfer
U.S. Environmental Protection Agency (EPA)
26 W. Martin Luther King Dr.
Cincinnati, OH 45268   513-569-7369
To order publications   513-569-7562
E-mail: mailto:ord.ceri@epamail.epa.gov Fax: 513-569-7566
www.epa.gov/docs/ord/

The Office of Research and Development (ORD) has centralized most of its information distribution and technology transfer activities in the Center for Environmental Research Information (CERI). CERI also serves as a central point of distribution for ORD research results and reports. They have statistics, regulations, and publications available at no charge. They can answer such questions as:

1) How can I protect my home from pesticides and pollution?
2) What types of pollution can cause harm to my family?
3) What safety guidelines must a company or lab follow?
4) How can a business get grant money to do research?
5) What certifications must companies meet in regulating their pollution?

* National Marine Fisheries Service
Public Affairs
National Oceanic and Atmospheric Administration
U.S. Department of Commerce
1315 East-West Highway
Room 9272
Silver Spring, MD 20910   301-713-2370
www.nmfs.gov   Fax: 202-501-2953 (constituent services)

The National Marine Fisheries Service (NMFS) manages the country's stocks of saltwater fish and shellfish for both commercial and recreational interests. NMFS enforces the Magnuson Fishery Conservation and Management Act to assure that fishing stays within sound biological limits. Scientists conduct research relating to these management responsibilities in science and research centers and have special knowledge of the fish in their geographical area. They can answer such questions as:

1) What is currently being done to protect whales and what statistics exist regarding these mammals?
2) What are some issues currently under discussion regarding fishing on an international level?
3) What is the Habitat Conservation Program and where can someone find out more information about it?
4) What information exists on seafood inspection?
5) What is currently being done to restore the marine habitat in the Chesapeake Bay?

* Forest Service
U.S. Department of Agriculture
Public Affairs
201 14th and Independence Ave., SW   202-205-1760
Washington, DC 20250   Fax: 202-205-0885
E-mail: mailroom@fs.fed.us
www.fs.fed.us

This country's national forests offer more than 114,300 miles of trails, a Scenic Byway System consisting of nearly 5,000 miles of highways in 32 states, 70 wild and scenic rivers covering nearly 3,500 miles and much more. *A Guide to Your National Forest* lists regional offices, several private and one Forest Service Interpretative Association, and a list of State Boards of Tourism where camping information may be obtained. They can answer such questions as:

1) What state forests in Maryland offer good sailing opportunities?
2) How far in advance must I reserve a campsite?
3) What is the best time of year to plan a camping trip in Tennessee?
4) Which rivers in North Carolina are recommended for canoeing or rafting?
5) How do I receive a listing of national scenic and historic trails?

* Geologic Inquiries Group
U.S. Geological Survey (USGS)
907 National Center   703-648-4383
Reston, VA 22092   Fax: 703-648-4888
http://geology.usgs.gov

The Geologic Inquiries Group is the primary information group of the Geologic Division of the USGS. The Group can provide information and answers to questions concerning all aspects of geology, such as the geology of specific areas, energy and mineral resources, earthquakes, volcanoes, geochemistry, geophysics, and other geoscience disciplines, and geologic map coverage. They have publications available, some of which are free. They can answer such questions as:

1) Where can information be obtained on a particular volcano?
2) Where can geologic maps for a specific area of a state be located?
3) What educational materials exist for teachers who want to teach their students about geology?
4) What geologic information is available on earthquakes?
5) What help is available for someone doing a science project on volcanoes?

* National Geophysical Data Center
National Oceanic and Atmospheric Administration
Mail Code E/GC
325 Broadway, Dept. NGB   303-497-6826
Boulder, CO 80303   Fax: 303-497-6513
E-mail: info@ngdc.noaa.gov
www.noaa.gov

The National Geophysical Data Center (NGDC) combines in a single center all data activities in the fields of solid earth geophysics, marine geology and geophysics, and solar-terrestrial physics. NGDC fills thousands of requests each year for data services and publications. Typical specialized data services may include digitization of analog charts, derivation of geomagnetic indexes, and customized computer graphics. They can answer such questions as:

1) Where can historical earthquake data be obtained?
2) Where can data on solar flare activity be located?
3) What causes avalanches, and what methods are used to ensure the safety of skiers in areas where avalanches typically occur?
4) Where are thermal springs and thermal wells located in Nevada?
5) Where can information on earthquake damage to transportation systems be obtained so that new systems can better withstand the effects of an earthquake?

* National Response Center (Hazardous Chemicals)
U.S. Coast Guard Headquarters
2100 2nd St., SW, Room 2611
Washington, DC 20593   800-424-8802

The National Response Center receives notification and calls reporting oil spills, hazardous chemical releases, biological and radiological releases that have spilled into the environment. They pass the accidents on to a Federal On-Scene Coordinator, who coordinates and begins the clean-up efforts. The Hotline is open to the general public and to companies to call with sightings. Most of the information available from the Center is free. They can answer such questions as:

1) Has there ever been a report of hazardous waste spilled in a specific neighborhood or location?
2) How can I get a report released about a company regarding hazardous waste?
3) What is hazardous waste?
4) How does the Environmental Protection Agency enforce hazardous waste storage?

Energy and Environment

* RCRA Hotline (Hazardous Waste)
U.S. Environmental Protection Agency (EPA)
401 M St., SW 800-424-9346
Washington, DC 20460 703-412-9810
www.epa.gov/epa.oswer Fax on Demand: 202-651-2060

RCRA stands for the Resource Conservation and Recovery Act which has the goals of: protecting human health and the environment from the potential hazards of waste disposal; conserving energy and natural resources; reducing the amount of waste generated, including hazardous waste; and ensuring that wastes are managed in an environmentally sound manner. They can answer questions regarding recycling, hazardous waste, solid waste issues, and much more. They have a catalogue of publications, as well as a publication, *Solving the Hazardous Waste Problem: EPA's RCRA Program*, which provides an overview of RCRA. They can answer such questions as:

1) What are the hazardous waste disposal regulations in my state?
2) Which plant pesticides are considered safe?
3) What are the laws and regulations concerning hazardous waste transportation?
4) How can I begin a recycling program in my community?
5) What are some of the most recent technologies and management strategies for hazardous waste control?

* National Water Information Center
U.S. Geological Survey
501 National Center
Reston, VA 20192 888-ASK-USGS
E-mail: h2info@usgs.gov
http://water.usgs.gov/

The National Water Information Center answers general questions on hydrology, water as a resource, and hydrologic mapping, as well as providing information on the products, projects, and services of the Water Services Division. The Center also provides information and materials for specific needs and is a reference office for Water-Resources Investigation reports released before 1982. The Information Center has maps showing a wide range of water-resources information. The staff can answer such questions as:

1) How can my company improve its waste disposal practices?
2) Where can I receive information on water resource conditions in my state?
3) What can people do to help reduce the problem of acid rain?
4) How can my company prevent ground water contamination?
5) Where can I receive introductory information on ground water hydraulics?

* Indoor Air Quality Information Clearinghouse
P.O. Box 37133 800-438-4318
Washington, DC 20013 Fax: 202-484-1510
E-mail: iaquinfo@aol.com

The Indoor Air Quality Information Clearinghouse of the Environmental Protection Agency can provide information and assistance on indoor air quality problems. It brings together information on more than 17 issues (from asbestos to wood preservatives), for the range of agencies involved in addressing those issues, from health agencies to energy departments. This office also has information on home humidifiers, residential air cleaners, Sick Building Syndrome, indoor air quality, new carpet, and more. They can answer such questions as:

1) What is Sick Building Syndrome, and what agency do I contact if I suspect my building is unsafe?
2) How do I identify and eliminate radon gas from my home?
3) How do I determine if the paint in my home is lead based?
4) What is the most recent legislation concerning asbestos-in-school requirements?
5) What is the Toxic Substance Control Act?

* Bureau of Land Management
Office of Public Affairs
U.S. Department of the Interior
1849 C St., NW, Room 406-CS 202-452-5125
Washington, DC 20240 Fax: 202-452-5124
www.blm.gov

There are close to 270 million acres of public lands located primarily, but not exclusively, in the West and in Alaska comprising one-eighth of our nation's land area. It is the charge of the Bureau of Land Management (BLM) to administer and care for these lands. To accomplish this task, the BLM has a variety of programs and activities, from the very new Heritage Education program aimed at involving and educating young people about America's cultural heritage to finding out about the availability of public lands for sale. They have free publications and can direct you to other resources within the BLM. They can answer such questions as:

1) Where are campgrounds located on BLM lands and what facilities or recreational areas do they have?
2) What videos are available concerning rivers?
3) How can I find out which public lands are for sale in my state?
4) How do I stake a mining claim on federal lands?
5) How can I receive a listing of wildlife habitats on public lands?

* U.S. Nuclear Regulatory Commission
Public Document Room 202-634-3273
Washington, DC 20555 Fax: 202-634-3343
www.nrc.gov

The Nuclear Regulatory Commission (NRC) licenses and regulates civilian use of nuclear energy to protect public health and safety and the environment. The NRC licenses persons and companies to build and operate nuclear reactors and other facilities, and to own and use nuclear materials. The Commission makes rules, sets standards, and carefully inspects companies to ensure that they do not violate existing safety rules. They can answer such questions as:

1) What information exists on abnormal occurrences in nuclear facilities?
2) What is the construction permit process for nuclear facilities?
3) What specific operational information must nuclear facilities submit to the NRC?
4) What statistics are available related to nuclear power?
5) How are radioactive materials packaged for transport?

* National Oceanic and Atmospheric Administration
14th St. and Constitution Ave. 202-482-6090
Washington, DC 20230 Fax: 202-482-3154
www.noaa.gov

The National Oceanic and Atmospheric Administration gathers data, conducts research, and makes predictions about the state of the environment in which we live. NOAA charts the seas and skies, and enriches our understanding of the oceans, atmosphere, space, and sun. They can refer you to other offices and experts for specific questions, and they also offer a variety of publications and films. They can answer such questions as:

1) What research is being conducted on tropical weather and how can we better predict hurricanes?
2) How has the greenhouse effect changed the environment?
3) What are the physical and chemical processes that occur within the Earth's atmosphere?
4) What is being done to protect marine mammals?
5) What research exists on the solar activity in the upper atmosphere?

* Oceanographic Information
National Oceanographic Data Center (NODC)
National Environmental Satellite, Data, and Information Service
National Oceanic and Atmospheric Administration
U.S. Department of Commerce
1315 East West Highway 301-713-3277
Silver Spring, MD 20910 Fax: 301-713-3302
E-mail: services@nodc.noaa.gov
www.nodc.noaa.gov

The National Oceanographic Data Center (NODC) provides global coverage of oceanographic data and services. NODC's databases cover physical and chemical properties of the world's oceans, seas, and estuaries, plus information on selected continental shelf and coastal waters. Simple questions usually can be answered without charge by telephone or mail, but more complicated ones requiring research or computer processing normally carry a fee. They can answer such questions as:

1) How does the Pacific Ocean temperature vary over a year?
2) How has the Atlantic Ocean been effected by pollution and what data exists on this topic?
3) What are the responsibilities of the NODC and what directories of information do they maintain?
4) Is there any bottom current data on the South China Sea?
5) Is the water warmer in Miami Beach or Myrtle Beach?

* National Park Service
Office of Public Inquiries
1849 C St., NW
Washington, DC 20240 202-208-6843
www.nps.gov

Free Research On Any Topic

Along with other responsibilities, the Park Service administers 350 maintained areas in the National Park System, collects the National Register of Historic Places and a registry of natural sites, and manages the Urban Park and Recreation Recovery Program. It provides technical assistance in planning, acquisition and development of recreation resources, conducts surveys of historic buildings and engineering works, has available programs and resources for teachers, and administers a program in interagency archeological services. Information, including brochures, maps, and a publications catalogue can be ordered from the Government Printing Office. The Office of Public Inquiries can refer you to other Park Service offices and can answer such questions as:

1) What archeological digs are currently in progress and where are they located?
2) What statistics are available on Park Service use, such as total visits, visits by region and state, and overnight stays?
3) Where can I locate videos on historic people or national landmarks?
4) How do I find out whether or not my home is eligible for listing on the National Historic Register?
5) How can I receive a listing of the lesser known National Parks?

* National Pesticide Telecommunication Network

Oregon State University
NPTN Ag Chem Extension
333 Weniger   800-858-PEST (7378)
Corvallis, OR 97331-6502   Fax: 541-737-0761

The National Pesticide Telecommunication Network (NPTN) is a toll-free telephone service that provides a wide variety of health information on pesticides. Phones are staffed by pesticide specialists with agricultural, environmental, and public health backgrounds. Inquiries are also answered by graduate students in such fields as biology, anatomy, biochemistry, and entomology. They can answer such questions as:

1) Where can I get information on pesticides that might be found in drinking water wells?
2) What are some guidelines for the safe use of pesticides by farmers?
3) What plants have a natural ability to repel insects?
4) How do I make the transition from pesticide lawn control to natural pest control?
5) What is the toxicity and proper use of the pesticide R-11? How can I dispose of it safely?

* Pollution Prevention Information Clearinghouse

Labat-Anderson, Inc.
401 M St., SW   202-260-1023
Washington, DC 20460   Fax: 202-260-0178
E-mail: ppic@epamail.epa.gov

The Pollution Prevention Information Clearinghouse is designed to help national and international industries reduce pollutants that are released into our environment. They specialize in using education and public awareness to prevent excessive pollution. The Clearinghouse has four information exchange directories that can be ordered. There is no charge for any service. They can answer such questions as:

1) How can pollution prevention benefit businesses?
2) How do you implement a pollution prevention program?
3) Are there training opportunities for pollution control/waste management?
4) How do you get technical assistance for pollution control?
5) What are the differences between large and small waste generators?

* EPA Radon Information Hotline

U.S. Environment Protection Agency (EPA), OAR
401 M St., SW (MS6604J)
Washington, DC 20460   800-767-7236
www.epa.gov/iaq/radon

The EPA Radon Information Hotline can answer all your questions concerning radon. The staff can answer such questions as:

1) What is radon? How does it affect people?
2) How do I determine whether or not my home has a radon problem?
3) How can I obtain a radon detector for my home? How does it work?
4) What are some effective radon prevention methods?
5) What are some control methods for eliminating radon in well water?

* National Sea Grant Depository

Pell Library Building
The University of Rhode Island
Bay Campus   401-874-6114
Narragansett, RI 02882   Fax: 401-874-6160
E-mail: nsgd@gso.uri.edu
http://nsgd.gso.uri.edu

The National Sea Grant Depository provides a wide variety of information on America's oceans, Great Lakes, and coastal zones. It maintains the only complete collection of publications generated by the National Sea Grant College Program. Publications include information on: oceanography, marine education, fisheries, coastal zone management, aquaculture, marine recreation and law. The collection includes journal reprints, technical and advisory reports, handbooks, charts, maps, manuals, directories, books, audiovisual materials, computer programs, annual reports, conference proceedings, and newsletters produced by Sea Grant funded researchers. The staff can answer such questions as:

1) What are some of the most common fish found in Alaska?
2) How do I begin a fish culture enterprise?
3) What is the impact of pollution on the marine environment?
4) What can people do to prevent the pollution of coastal waters?
5) What are some of the potential risks to coastal investment?

* Small Business Ombudsman Clearinghouse

U.S. Environmental Protection Agency (EPA)
Small Business Ombudsman, 1230C   800-368-5888
401 M St., SW   703-305-5938
Washington, DC 20460   Fax: 703-305-6462
www.epa.gov

The Small Business Ombudsman Clearinghouse helps your business comply with all environmental regulations. They provide information on current policies, safety precautions, and general information on keeping the air you breathe healthy. They are available to assist private citizens, small communities, enterprises, trade associations, technical consultants, and laboratories. Listings on all aspects of current EPA regulatory developments are available at no charge. Over 200 EPA publications are maintained for distribution. They can answer such questions as:

1) Am I covered under the new Clear Air Act requirements?
2) How do I get an I.D. number for hazardous waste disposal?
3) What are the requirements for any underground storage waste?
4) How do I know if my community is following proper safety guidelines?
5) What type of waste material could be hazardous to my community?

* National Snow and Ice Data Center

World Data Center-A For Glaciology
CIRES, Box 449
University of Colorado   303-492-5171
Boulder, CO 80309   Fax: 303-492-2468
E-mail: nsidc@kyros.colorado.edu
www-nsidc.colorado.edu

The National Snow and Ice Data Center provides a national and international focus for snow and ice data information services. The Center provides: broad user access to snow and ice data through specialized data reports and inventories in Glaciological Data; through special data sets maintained in the Center; through tailored bibliographies; and through access to the Snow and Ice Library. There is a small fee for some services. They can answer such questions as:

1) How does exhaust from jet aircraft affect cloud cover?
2) Where can data be accessed on glacier fluctuations?
3) How has snow cover varied over time in North America?
4) What current research is being undertaken regarding avalanches?
5) What is the difference between fresh water ice and sea ice?

* Solid Waste Information Clearinghouse

P.O. Box 7219   800-67-SWICH
1100 Wayne Ave., Suite 700   301-585-2898
Silver Spring, MD 20910   Fax: 301-589-7068
E-mail: info@swana.org
www.swana.org

The Solid Waste Information Clearinghouse (SWICH) is concerned with how state and local offices and industries get rid of solid waste. The general public is also welcome to request information. SWICH can show how to economically and ecologically get rid of waste by source reduction, recycling, composting, planning, education, public training, public participation, legislation and regulation, waste combustion, and collection. They can answer such questions as:

1) How can I implement a recycling program in my community?
2) What is the most economical way to dispose of a waste product?
3) How have other communities started and benefitted from recycling?
4) What types of disposal is available to my community or business?

Energy and Environment

* National Space Science Data Center
National Aeronautics and Space Administration
Goddard Space Flight Center 301-286-7354
Greenbelt, MD 20771 Data Request: 301-286-6695
E-mail: request@nssdca.gsfca.nasa.gov Fax: 301-286-1771
http://nssdc.gsfc.nasa.gov/

The National Space Science Data Center (NSSDC) is an organization that provides a variety of valuable services for scientists throughout the world. The Center furthers the use of data obtained from space and earth science investigations, maintains an active data repository, and supports scientific research. The data are contained on more than 120,000 magnetic tapes, tens of thousands of film products, and optical, video, and magnetic disks. NSSDC works with individual users to address their specific requirements. There is a charge for most data, but it is only on a cost recovery basis. They can answer such questions as:

1) What satellites are currently operating in space and which ones are planned for future launch?
2) What data from space can provide estimates of marine phytoplankton in the ocean?
3) Where can photographs taken from APOLLO be located?
4) What data is available to researchers studying the ozone?
5) What information exists on a particular rocket launch?

* Technology Transfer Competitiveness
Administrator
Federal Laboratory Consortium
P.O. Box 545 360-683-1005
Sequim, WA 98382 Fax: 360-683-6654
www.federallabs.org/

The mission of the Federal Laboratory Consortium is to facilitate technology transfer among government, business, and academic entities in order to promote American economic and technological competitiveness. It sponsors conferences and seminars and publishes a free monthly newsletter. For very specific questions from researchers who find themselves at an impasse, the Consortium will conduct a database search to refer the inquirer to an appropriate lab. Write or call for a free general information packet explaining the organization, how to access its services, facilities available for testing, and examples of technology transfers. They can answer such questions as:

1) How can the heat pipes used to cool satellites be converted for use in a business?
2) How can toothpaste used by astronauts benefit those that are used on Earth?
3) What research is being conducted on electric cars?
4) Where can a business locate information on humidity control for a warehouse?

* Technology Transfer Program
NASA Scientific and Technical Information Facility
Technology Transfer Office
NASA-CASI
800 Elkridge Landing Rd. 410-859-5300, ext. 242
Linthicum Heights, MD 21090-2934 Fax: 301-621-0134
www.sti.nasa.gov/

Technology Transfer is an ideal way to apply the National Aeronautics and Space Administration's (NASA) experience and discoveries to your research or business. The transfer of aerospace technology which embraces virtually every scientific and technical discipline is paying off in a broad spectrum of practical applications in industry. The Technology Transfer System is a network of specialized organizations dedicated to helping industry access, apply, and utilize NASA's pool of innovations and technical resources. This allows you to access a wide range of information, products, services and technical expertise. A staff of experts assists you in pinpointing problems, identifying needs, and exchanging ideas. They can answer such questions as:

1) How can ultra-sensitive measuring devices used to measure space dust be put to use measuring environmental pollutants?
2) How can standard doorknobs be replaced with electronic openers?
3) Is it possible to convert spacesuits for use by firefighters or workers in industrial situations?
4) What lunar tool technology can be used in designing cordless power tools?

* Toxic Substance Control Act
U.S. Environmental Protection Agency (EPA)
Environmental Assistance Division
401 M St., SW 202-554-1404
Washington, DC 20460 Fax: 202-554-5603
E-mail: tsca_hotline@epamail.epa.gov

The Toxic Substance Control Act (TSCA) regulates the storage and removal of toxic substances and spills. They are concerned with safely containing toxic substances that may be harmful to our environment. TSCA is open to the general public as well as to industries and environmental groups. They can answer such questions as:

1) What chemicals can a manufacturer produce, and are they on the toxic inventory list?
2) What can I do if a toxic substance was spilled or contained on my property?
3) What are the latest regulations regarding production and handling of toxic substances?
4) How can I get a listing of places where toxic waste is stored?

* Undersea Research
National Undersea Research Program
National Oceanic and Atmospheric Administration (NOAA)
U.S. Department of Commerce
R/OR2, Room 11853
Building SSMC-3
1315 East-West Highway 301-713-2427
Silver Spring, MD 20910 Fax: 301-713-1967
www.oar.noaa.gov/nurp

The National Undersea Research Program (NURP) develops programs and provides support to scientists and engineers to accomplish research underwater for the study of biological, chemical, geological, and physical processes in the world's oceans and lakes. NURP provides investigators with modern undersea facilities including submersibles, habitats, air and mixed gas SCUBA, and remotely operated vehicles. They can answer such questions as:

1) How do I get a grant from NURP?
2) What is the appropriate undersea center for me to contact in my region?
3) How deep in the sea does NURP support scientists work?
4) What kind of research expenses will be covered under a NURP grant?
5) Does NURP support coral reef research?

* EPA National Small Flows Clearinghouse (Wastewater)
West Virginia University
P.O. Box 6064 800-624-8301
Morgantown, WV 26506 Fax: 304-293-3161

The National Small Flows Clearinghouse is the center for small systems wastewater technology transfer. The Clearinghouse provides training resources and expertise in management and maintenance of small wastewater systems. It assists small communities in meeting environmental goals and water quality requirements. The Clearinghouse offers products and services to aid consultants, local officials, and developers in designing, constructing, operating, and managing small wastewater systems. Its products and services include databases, publications, video programs, workshops, and seminars. The staff can answer such questions as:

1) How can I find out more about the use of constructed wetlands that are used to treat domestic wastewater?
2) How can I find out more about sequencing batch reactors? How do they compare with conventional continuous waste treatment systems?
3) What should I look for when hiring qualified wastewater personnel?
4) How can our community get the most out of our existing wastewater resources and facilities?
5) What are some current technologies for cleansing polluted water?

* Watershed Resource Information System
Terrene Institute
U.S. Environmental Protection Agency (EPA)
4 Herbert St.
Alexandria, VA 22305 800-726-LAKE (5253)
www.epa.gov

The Watershed Resource Information System is an information resource on lake restoration, protection, and management. Its Watershed Information Resource Database contains abstracts and citations of technical materials and information and bibliographies. A specialist will conduct a database search for you for a fee of $25, plus $.10 per page per reference. You may purchase the system for $250 or a demo disk for $20. The staff can answer such questions as:

1) What information exists on different methods for restoring polluted lakes?
2) How can I find out about a particular lake's water quality?
3) What are some effective watershed management techniques?
4) What techniques can be used to reduce the incidence of acidification in lakes?
5) What are some effective methods of reducing toxic substances in lakes?

Free Research On Any Topic

* National Weather Service

National Oceanic and Atmospheric Administration
1325 East-West Highway
Silver Spring, MD 20910   301-713-0622
www.nws.noaa.gov

The National Weather Service, through a network of field offices, predicts the nation's weather and issues storm and flood warnings. They also publish a weekly series of daily weather maps which include the highest and lowest temperatures chart and the precipitation areas. They can send anyone interested a sample copy or subscription information on this material. They also have publications on a variety of weather conditions, as well as films, videos, and slides. They can answer such questions as:

1) What should be done in the event of a hurricane?
2) What is a tornado?
3) How are severe storms forecast and where can more information be obtained about them?
4) Is there information available on monthly and seasonal predictions of temperature and precipitation?
5) What is a flash flood?

* Wetlands Protection Hotline

Labat-Anderson, Inc.
401 M St.
MC4502F   800-832-7828
Washington, DC 20460   Fax: 703-525-0201
www.epa.gov/OWAW/wetlands/vital/protection.html

The Wetlands Protection Hotline is a toll-free telephone service that responds to questions about the value and function of wetlands in our world. The staff is interested in protecting our wetlands and showing how wetlands play an important role in our changing environment. They have free publications and fact sheets available. They can answer such questions as:

1) Where can I get the *1987 Corps of Engineers Wetlands Delineation Manual*?
2) Is there any information available on constructed wetlands?
3) Is it legal to dig out a wetlands area?
4) What is the White House's policy on the protection of wetlands?
5) What regulations must farmers comply with when they have wetlands on their property?

Health

* National Institute on Aging
Public Information Office
Building 31, Room 5C27
31 Center Dr., MSC 2292
Bethesda, MD 20892-2292
800-222-2225
Fax: 301-496-1752
www.nih.gov/nia

The National Institute on Aging conducts research related to the aging process and looks at diseases and other special problems related to the needs of the aged. They have a publications list of free items dealing with a variety of consumer issues. They can answer such questions as:
1) What is a good exercise program for an elderly person?
2) What information exists on menopause and how can symptoms be treated?
3) How can the elderly improve their diet?
4) What is osteoporosis and what can be done to minimize its effects?
5) What factors should people be aware of when taking certain medications?

* National AIDS Information Clearinghouse
P.O. Box 6003
Rockville, MD 20849
800-458-5231
Fax: 301-251-5343
E-mail: hivmail@cdc.gov
www.cdc.gov/nchstp/hiv-aids/dhap.htm

The National AIDS Hotline offers 24-hour service seven days a week to respond to any question about HIV infection and AIDS. Information specialists can refer you to groups in your area, and can direct you to local counseling and testing centers. The Clearinghouse can also connect people with the Clinical Trials Information Center, where they can learn what trials are currently taking place and what the requirements are for participants. They have free resources and publications on AIDS and HIV infection. They can answer such questions as:
1) What videos are available on AIDS that are appropriate for kids?
2) What are the signs and symptoms of infection?
3) How can parents most effectively discuss AIDS with their children?
4) What information exists on AIDS clinical trials?
5) Where can someone get information on caring for an AIDS patient at home?

* National Clearinghouse for Alcohol and Drug Information
P.O. Box 2345
11426 Rockville Pike, Suite 200
Rockville, MD 20852
800-729-6686
Fax: 301-468-6433
TDD: 800-487-4889
www.health.org

The National Clearinghouse for Alcohol and Drug Information (NCADI) gathers and disseminates current information on alcohol and drug-related subjects, and can make referrals to other alcohol, tobacco, and drug resource experts. The Clearinghouse is the national resource center for information on the latest research results, popular press and scholarly journal articles, videos, prevention curricula, print materials, and program descriptions. Services include subject searches on an in-house database and response to inquiries for statistics and other information. NCADI can make referrals to self-help organizations, and can provide information on drug and alcohol abuse treatment. They have a publications catalogue listing, booklets, videos, and posters which range in price from free to $25. They can answer such questions as:
1) How do you implement a drug-free workplace program, and what are the laws regarding drug testing at the workplace?
2) How do you teach kids about the dangers of drugs and alcohol, and what are the warning signs parents should know?
3) What are the effects of Fetal Alcohol Syndrome and where can people turn for more information about it?
4) What are some statistics on drug abuse among college students and what prevention programs exist?
5) What research is being done on children of alcoholics and are there support groups in place for them?

* National Institute of Allergy and Infectious Diseases
NIAID Office of Communications and Public Liaison
Building 31, Room 7A50
31 Center Dr., MSC 2520
Bethesda, MD 20892-2520
301-496-5717
Fax: 301-402-0120
www.niaid.nih.gov/

The National Institute of Allergy and Infectious Diseases (NIAID) conducts and supports research to study the causes of allergic, immunologic, and infectious diseases, and to develop better means of preventing, diagnosing, and treating these illnesses. Some studies look at the role of the immune system in chronic diseases, such as arthritis, and at disorders of the immune system, as in asthma. NIAID has become the lead component at the National Institutes of Health for coordinating and conducting AIDS research. They have publications, journal articles, and more. They can answer such questions as:
1) What research is currently being done on allergies to pollen?
2) What is the current research being undertaken on AIDS?
3) How can I help my child handle asthma?
4) What is Chronic Fatigue Syndrome and what are the options for treating it?
5) What research exists on problems associated with the immune system?

* Alzheimer's Disease Education And Referral Center
P.O. Box 8250
Silver Spring, MD 20907-8250
800-438-4380
Fax: 301-495-3334
E-mail: adear@alzheimers.org
www.alzheimers.org/adear

The Alzheimer's Disease Education and Referral Center distributes information about Alzheimer's disease to health professionals, patients and their families, and the general public. The Center provides information about the diagnosis and treatment of Alzheimer's disease, research, and services available to patients and family members. The bibliographic references of the Center are included in a computerized index that includes references to patient and professional education materials, including information about health promotion programs. A list is available of free publications, in addition to a free newsletter. They can answer such questions as:
1) What are the symptoms of Alzheimer's disease and what are the causes?
2) What research has been done to evaluate special long-term care units for Alzheimer patients?
3) Where are research centers located which deal with Alzheimer's?
4) What are some statistics on Alzheimer's?
5) What help is available for families caring for an Alzheimer's patient at home?

* National Arthritis and Musculoskeletal and Skin Diseases Information Clearinghouse
National Institute of Health
1 AMS Circle
Bethesda, MD 20892-3675
301-495-4484
Fax: 301-718-6366
E-mail: NIAMSWEB-L@mail.nih.gov
TTY: 301-565-2966
www.nih.gov/niams

The National Institute of Arthritis and Musculoskeletal and Skin Diseases handles inquiries on arthritis, bone diseases, and skin diseases. They conduct and support basic and clinical research concerning the causes, prevention, diagnosis, and treatment of these diseases. They serve as an information exchange for individuals and organizations involved in public, professional, and patient education. The Clearinghouse has free publications on a variety of topics and can search their database for other information that might be needed. They can answer questions such as:
1) What can be done to prevent osteoporosis and who is most at risk for acquiring this disease?
2) Does chocolate cause acne and how can acne be treated?
3) What information exists on joint replacement for people who suffer from severe arthritis?
4) What are some different types of birth marks, and how can they be removed?
5) What educational materials are there for a continuing education forum on arthritis?

* Asthma Clearinghouse
National Asthma Education Program
P.O. Box 30105
Bethesda, MD 20824-0105
301-592-8573
Fax: 301-592-8563
www.nhlbisupport.com/asthma/index.html

The Asthma Clearinghouse is a new clearinghouse providing publications, reports, resources, and referrals to experts in the field of asthma. One report, *The Executive Summary: Guidelines for the Diagnosis and Management of Asthma*, explains the diagnosis, therapy, and other important considerations for those that suffer from

Free Research On Any Topic

asthma. They can answer such questions as:
1) What materials are available for kids that explain the causes and treatment of asthma?
2) What conditions trigger an asthma attack?
3) Are there different types of asthma?
4) What are some forms of treatment for asthma sufferers?
5) What are the guidelines for treatment of asthma?

* Blood Resources
National Blood Resource Education Program
P.O. Box 30105   301-592-8573
Bethesda, MD 20824-0105   Fax: 301-592-8563
www.nhlbi.nih.gov/

The National Blood Resource Education Program was established to ensure an adequate supply of safe blood and blood components to meet our country's needs, ensuring that blood and blood components are transfused only when therapeutically appropriate. The Program helps health professionals understand the risks and benefits of blood transfusions, and ensures that patients receive appropriate information regarding transfusions. They also work to increase public awareness that donating blood is a safe process. They can answer such questions as:
1) What should people should be aware of when donating blood?
2) Is it still possible to get AIDS from blood transfusions?
3) Can you donate your own blood before you undergo surgery in the event you might require a transfusion?
4) How long can blood be kept before it is no longer usable?
5) What are some of the problems that people encounter when they have unusual blood types?

* The Cancer Information Service
National Cancer Institute
Building 31, Room 10A03   800-4-CANCER
31 Center Dr.   800-435-3848
Bethesda, MD 20892-2580   Fax: 301-402-0894
www.nci.nih.gov/   TTY: 800-332-8615

The toll-free Cancer Information Service can provide accurate, up-to-date information about cancer and cancer-related resources in local areas. A wide variety of free publications on specific types of cancer, treatment methods, coping methods, and other cancer-related subjects are distributed. A database is available, that can access information on clinical trials and treatment options. The Cancer Information Service can help you locate materials and research on a specific type of cancer. They can answer such questions as:
1) Is the new prostate cancer test accurate, and to what degree?
2) How often should you get a mammogram and at what age should you begin?
3) What are the side effects of a particular anti-cancer drug?
4) What are the different stages of breast cancer?
5) What are clinical trials and where can I participate in them?

* National Clearinghouse on Child Abuse and Neglect Information
330 C St., SW   800-FYI-3366
P.O. Box 1182   703-385-7565
Washington, DC 20447   Fax: 703-385-3206
E-mail: nccanch@calib.com
www.calib.com/nccanch

The Clearinghouse on Child Abuse and Neglect Information was established to help professionals and concerned citizens locate information on child abuse and neglect. They collect and disseminate a wide variety of information including publications, audiovisuals, public awareness materials, and more, and can refer you to other resources. Stock publications and many other services are provided at no cost to the user. User fees are required however, for services such as custom database searches and bibliographies. They can answer such questions as:
1) What statistics exist on the incidence of child abuse and neglect?
2) What laws exist that protect children against child abuse?
3) What is the role of the courts in child protection?
4) What funding sources are there for child abuse and neglect programs?
5) What role do teachers play in the prevention and treatment of child abuse?

* National Institute of Child Health and Human Development
P.O. Box 3006   301-496-5133
Rockville, MD 20847   Fax: 301-496-7101
www.nichd.nih.gov

The National Institute of Child Health and Human Development conducts and supports research in maternal and child health and the population sciences. They will respond to individual inquiries on related topics such as studies on reproductive biology and contraception, fertility, mental retardation, and developmental issues. They have free publications and can refer you elsewhere for additional information. They can answer such questions as:
1) Is reversing letters a sign of a reading disability?
2) What are the possible causes of Down Syndrome?
3) What are some important issues to think about when considering a vasectomy?
4) Where is there research being conducted on mental retardation?
5) What are the newest forms of birth control being used?

* National Information Center for Children and Youth with Disabilities
P.O. Box 1492   800-695-0285
Washington, DC 20013-1492   202-884-8200
E-mail: nichcy@aed.org   Fax: 202-884-8441
www.nichcy.org

The National Information Center for Children and Youth with Disabilities operates a national clearinghouse providing free information to assist parents, educators, caregivers, advocates, and others in helping children and youth with disabilities to become active members of the community. The staff provides personal responses to specific questions, as well as information on local, state, or national disability groups for parents, prepared information packets, publications on current issues, and technical assistance to parent and professional groups. They can answer such questions as:
1) How can I help my hyperactive child?
2) At what age do public schools begin mainstreaming students?
3) Can the Center provide a listing of national Down Syndrome support groups?
4) Where can I obtain captioned films for the deaf?
5) How do I make my home more wheelchair accessible? Are there any financial assistance programs available to help me accomplish this?

* Cholesterol Information
National Cholesterol Education Program
Information Center
National Heart, Lung, and Blood Institute
P.O. Box 30105   301-592-8573
Bethesda, MD 20824-0105   Fax: 301-592-8563
www.nhlbi.nih.gov/

Do you know your cholesterol number or has your doctor advised you to change your diet? The National Cholesterol Education Program (NCEP) is for you. NCEP aims to raise awareness and understanding about high blood cholesterol as a risk factor for coronary heart disease and the benefits of lowering cholesterol levels as a means of preventing coronary heart disease. They have specialists on staff to answer questions and they provide printed information on cholesterol, diet, and high blood pressure to the public and health professionals. They can answer such questions as:
1) Is it possible to eat bacon on a low cholesterol diet?
2) Are medications required when trying to lower cholesterol levels?
3) How does exercise affect cholesterol levels?
4) What are the different types of home cholesterol test kits available?
5) What do the cholesterol numbers mean and what is meant by good and bad cholesterol?

* National Institute on Deafness and Other Communication Disorders Clearinghouse
31 Center Dr.
MSC 2320   301-496-7243
Bethesda, MD 20892-3456   Fax: 301-402-0018
E-mail: nidcd@aeric.com   TTY: 301-402-0252

The National Institute on Deafness and Other Communication Disorders disseminates information on normal and disordered processes of human communication. They have information about hearing, balance, smell, taste, voice, speech, and language for health professionals, patients, and the general public. They have fact sheets, bibliographies, information packets, and directories. They can answer such questions as:
1) What are the treatment options for someone who has aphasia?
2) What can be done for children with frequent ear infections?
3) Are all hearing aids created equal?
4) What can be done to help someone who stutters?
5) What are the current statistics on deafness and hearing disorders?

Health

* National Institute of Dental and Craniofacial Research

Information Office
Building 31, Room 2C35
31 Center Dr., MSC-2290   301-496-4261
Bethesda, MD 20892   Fax: 301-496-9988
E-mail: nidrinso@od31.nidr.nih.gov
www.nider.gov

The National Institute of Dental Research conducts research on the causes, prevention, diagnosis, and treatment of diseases and conditions of the mouth and teeth. They have free publications and posters on a variety of topics, and can refer people to experts for further information. They can answer such questions as:
1) What are the oral problems related to AIDS?
2) What information exists on fever blisters and canker sores?
3) What are the causes of periodontal disease and what are some effective treatment options?
4) Are fluoride treatments safe and when should they be started?
5) What are dental sealants and how effective are they in preventing cavities?

* National Diabetes Information Clearinghouse

1 Information Way   301-654-3327
Bethesda, MD 20892   Fax: 301-907-8906
E-mail: ndic@info.niddk.nih.gov
www.niddk.nih.gov/

The National Diabetes Information Clearinghouse was established to increase the knowledge and understanding of diabetes among patients, health professionals, and the general public. The Clearinghouse has a publications list available, with items ranging in price from free to $25, and a free quarterly newsletter featuring news about diabetes. They can also search their database for information on a specific topic. They can answer such questions as:
1) What is the latest research on the ways to manage diabetes, along with nutrition and diet information?
2) What are the issues and reports regarding diabetes and athletics?
3) What is gestational diabetes and the special risks and dangers it presents?
4) What are the types of insulins currently available, along with the time action of the insulin preparations?
5) What are some common foot care problems frequently experienced by diabetics?

* National Digestive Diseases Information Clearinghouse

2 Information Way   301-496-3583
Bethesda, MD 20892-3570   Fax: 301-496-7422
E-mail: nddic@info.niddk.nih.gov
www.niddk.nih.gov/

The Digestive Diseases Information Clearinghouse provides information about digestive diseases to educate the public, patients and their families, as well as physicians and other health care providers. The Clearinghouse provides information products and services such as factsheets, as well as an inquiry and referral service, information about research developments, and organizational and governmental activities related to digestive diseases. The Clearinghouse also maintains a database containing references to literature, products, programs, and services. A list of free publications is available. They can answer such questions as:
1) What are the surgical procedures involved in having a gall bladder removed and are there options to surgery?
2) What are the symptoms, causes, and treatments of ulcers?
3) How do you prevent heartburn?
4) What is a hiatal hernia and does it always require surgery?
5) What is pancreatitis?

* Disabilities Information Clearinghouse

Clearinghouse on Disability Information Programs
U.S. Department of Education
330 C St., SW, Room 3132
Mary Switzer Building   202-205-8241
Washington, DC 20202   Fax: 202-401-2608
www.ed.gov/offices/

The Clearinghouse on Disability Information responds to inquiries on a wide range of topics. Information is especially strong in the areas of Federal funding for programs serving individuals with disabilities, Federal legislation affecting the disability community, and Federal programs benefiting people with disabilities. A publications list is available, many of which are free. The Clearinghouse also maintains a database of sources for equipment to assist disabled people. They can answer such questions as:
1) What information exists about housing disabled people?
2) What handicapped assistance loans are available?
3) What is the law regarding Equal Employment Opportunities for handicapped persons?
4) What are the requirements for public education of students with handicaps?
5) How can businesses best accommodate workers with disabilities?

* Disease Information

Centers for Disease Control
Information Resources Management Office
Mail Stop C-15
1600 Clifton Rd., NE   404-332-4555
Atlanta, GA 30333   Fax on Demand: 404-332-4565

The Centers for Disease Control (CDC) has developed a Voice Information System that allows anyone using a touch tone telephone to obtain prerecorded information on particular health issues. The materials include information about certain diseases or health areas, symptoms and prevention methods, immunization requirements, current statistics, recent disease outbreaks, and other available printed materials. Currently information is available on AIDS, Chronic Fatigue Syndrome, encephalitis, hepatitis, Lyme disease, malaria, and more. They can answer such questions as:
1) What are the current statistics on AIDS?
2) Have there been recent disease outbreaks and where have they occurred?
3) Are vaccines required for travel to Africa?
4) When should children be immunized?
5) What is Chronic Fatigue Syndrome and where can I learn more about this condition?

* Drug Evaluation Clearinghouse

Center for Drug Evaluation and Research
Food and Drug Administration (FDA)
5600 Fishers Lane
Rockville, MD 20857   301-594-1012
www.fda.gov/cder

The Center for Drug Evaluation and Research responds to inquiries covering a wide spectrum of drug issues. They develop policy with regard to the safety, effectiveness, and labeling of all drug products, as well as evaluate new drug applications. The Center conducts research and develops scientific standards on the composition, quality, safety, and effectiveness of drugs. A list of guidelines is available to help manufacturers comply with the requirements of the regulations. The staff will respond to requests for information regarding the laws, regulations, policies, and functions of the FDA as it pertains to drugs. Materials are available on pharmaceuticals, drug labeling, and consumer education. They can answer such questions as:
1) What are the pros and cons of estrogen?
2) What information exists on the different forms of The Pill?
3) Do over-the-counter hair growth products really work?
4) What research has been done on Norplant?
5) What information is required on drug package labels?

* National Eye Institute

Office of Health, Education and Communication
Building 31, Room 6A32
31 Center Dr.   301-496-5248
Bethesda, MD 20892-2510   Fax: 301-402-1065
E-mail: 2020@b31.nei.nih.gov
www.nei.nih.gov/

The National Eye Institute (NEI) conducts and supports research related to the cause, natural history, prevention, diagnosis, and treatment of disorders of the eye and visual system. NEI distributes information on eye disorders, and can refer people to other organizations. They have free publications on a variety of topics. They can answer such questions as:
1) What is the latest information about cataracts and how can they safely be removed?
2) Are disposable contact lenses safe?
3) What are the causes of blindness?
4) How can glaucoma be detected early and are there treatment options to be considered?
5) What is Age-Related Macular Degeneration?

Free Research On Any Topic

* Food and Drug Information
Office of Consumer Affairs, HFE-88
Food and Drug Administration
5600 Fishers Lane
Room 16-85   301-827-4422
Rockville, MD 20857   Fax: 301-443-9767
www.fda.gov/oca/oca.htm

The Food and Drug Administration (FDA) is charged with ensuring that food is safe and wholesome; that drugs, biological products, medical devices are safe and effective; that cosmetics are safe; that the use of radiological products does not result in unnecessary exposure to radiation; and that all of these products are honestly and informatively labeled. The Office of Consumer Affairs of the FDA handles consumer inquiries on issues under the FDA's responsibility, and serves as a clearinghouse for FDA publications (most of which are free). They can also refer callers to the appropriate office for more information. Topics covered include foods, nutrition, federal regulations, cosmetics, drug labeling, medical devices, pharmaceuticals, and more. They can answer such questions as:

1) What nutritional information is available for pregnant women?
2) Are extended wear lenses safe?
3) What information is required on food labels, and what does it mean?
4) What are the different forms of birth control and how effective are they?
5) What is the status of breast implants and where can someone turn for more information on the subject?

* National Health Information Center
Referral Specialist
Office of Disease Prevention and Health Promotion
P.O. Box 1133   301-565-4167
Washington, DC 20013   800-336-4797
E-mail: nhicinfo@health.org   Fax: 301-984-4256
http://nhic_nt.health.org

The National Health Information Center is a health information referral organization that puts people with health questions in touch with those organizations that are best able to answer them. The Center's main objectives are to identify health information resources, channel requests for information to these resources, and develop publications on health-related topics of interest to health professionals, the health media, and the general public. The Center meets these objectives by using a variety of information resource materials, a database of health-related organizations, and an information referral system. There is a publications catalogue available, with prices ranging from free to $5, and the Center covers topics such as community health, school health, worksite health, nutrition, and more. They can answer such questions as:

1) What health education program materials exist for employers and how can they be implemented at the worksite?
2) What organizations and support groups exist for people suffering from cerebral palsy?
3) What toll-free numbers are available for various health information?
4) What is the latest information about a specific rare disease and where can people turn for support?
5) How physically fit are America's six-year-olds and what statistics exist on this topic?

* Health Care Delivery
Bureau of Primary Health Care
Health Resources and Services Administration
5600 Fishers Lane, Room 7-05
Rockville, MD 29857   301-594-4110

The Bureau of Primary Health Care helps assure that health care services are provided to medically underserved populations and to persons with special health care needs. The Bureau serves as a national focus for the development of primary health care delivery capacity, and for placement of health care professionals in Health Professional Shortage Areas to promote sustained sources of health services. Support for primary health care is provided primarily through Community Health Centers, Migrant Health Centers, Services for Special Populations, Services for Residents of Public Housing, and the National Health Service Corps. They can answer such questions as:

1) How can nurses or doctors get their college loans repaid through service?
2) What programs exist for migrant health care?
3) What programs deal with the special health care needs of the homeless?
4) What research is being undertaken on meeting the health care needs of the elderly in this country?
5) What areas of the country are currently designated as health professional shortage areas?

* Health Care Policy Clearinghouse
Agency for Health Care Policy and Research
P.O. Box 8547   800-358-9295
Silver Spring, MD 20907-8547   TDD: 888-586-6340
E-mail: info@ahcpr.gov   Fax on Demand: 301-594-2800
www.ahcpr.gov

The Agency for Health Care Policy and Research (AHCPR) is the primary source of Federal support for research on problems related to the quality and delivery of health services. AHCPR programs evaluate health services, assess technologies, and improve access to new scientific and technical information for research users. Research findings are disseminated through publications, conferences, and workshops. Materials are available on medical treatment effectiveness, health care costs and utilizations, health care expenditures, health information systems, health technology assessment, and funding opportunities for grants and contracts. They can answer such questions as:

1) What are clinical practice guidelines for the treatment of cataracts?
2) What statistics exist on medical expenditures?
3) How effective is a specific treatment strategy for ulcers?
4) What type of person uses a nursing home and what is their average medical condition upon entering such a facility?
5) What are some treatment options for depression and how effective are they?

* Clearinghouse on Health Indexes
National Center for Health Statistics
U.S. Department of Health and Human Services
Public Health Service
6525 Belcrest Rd.
Hyattsville, MD 20782   301-436-8500
www.cdc.gov/nchswww/default.htm

The National Center for Health Statistics provides information assistance in the development of health measures to health researchers, administrators, and planners. The Clearinghouse's definition of a health index is a measure that summarizes data from two or more components and purports to reflect the health status of an individual or defined group. Services provided to users include annotated bibliographies and a reference and referral service. A publications catalogue is available, with items ranging in price from free to $20. They can answer such questions as:

1) What are the typical characteristics of persons with and without health care coverage?
2) What type of health care is provided to adolescents?
3) What method of contraception is used most frequently in the U.S.?
4) What data exists on the current living arrangements of women of childbearing ages in the U.S.?
5) What survey data exists on the firearm mortality among children?

* National Heart, Lung, and Blood Institute Information Center
P.O. Box 30105   301-592-8573
Bethesda, MD 20824-0105   Fax: 301-592-8563
E-mail: NHLBIinfo@rover.nhlbi.nih.gov
www.nhlbi.nih.gov/

The National Heart, Lung, and Blood Institute is responsible for the scientific investigation of heart, blood vessel, lung, and blood diseases. The Information Center can provide the most current information on cholesterol, high blood pressure, asthma, blood products, and more. Subject specialists can provide information in response to inquiries, which may include publications, bibliographies, program descriptions, referrals to other agencies or organizations free of charge. They can answer such questions as:

1) What are the treatment options for someone suffering from emphysema?
2) What should the level of cholesterol be in blood, and how can it be lowered?
3) What information exists on high blood pressure and is medication the only real option to lowering blood pressure?
4) What is the current research on angioplasty?
5) What help is there for children who have asthma?

* High Blood Pressure Information
National High Blood Pressure Education Program
P.O. Box 30105   301-592-8573
Bethesda, MD 20824-0105   Fax: 301-592-8563
www.nhlbi.nih.gov/

The National High Blood Pressure Education Program is a source of information on educational materials for consumers, providers, and planners of high blood pressure control services. The goal of the Center is to reduce death and disability related to

Health

high blood pressure through programs of professional, patient, and public education. Print and audiovisual materials, as well as research reports are available. A free newsletter, *InfoMemo*, covers topics of interest concerning blood pressure. They can answer such questions as:
1) Is there a way to lower your high blood pressure through diet and exercise?
2) What is the effect of alcohol on blood pressure?
3) What research exists on alternative therapies such as biofeedback in reducing blood pressure?
4) How can a blood pressure education program be instituted in the workplace?
5) What resources exist for health educators who work with patients with high blood pressure?

* Homelessness
National Resource Center on Homelessness
 and Mental Illness
Policy Research Associates, Inc.
262 Delaware Ave.   800-444-7415
Delmar, NY 12054   Fax: 518-439-7612
E-mail: nrc@pranic.com
www.prainc.com/nrc

Under contract with the National Institute of Mental Illness, Policy Research Associates develops and disseminates new knowledge about the coordination of housing and services for homeless mentally ill persons. The Center publishes a newsletter, and has free information packets and can conduct database searches. They can refer you to organizations concerned with homelessness and mental illness, as well as Federal programs in the field. They can answer such questions as:
1) What are some of the health issues particularly related to homeless people?
2) What are grant programs currently available to homeless organizations to improve services?
3) What self-help programs exist for homeless people?
4) What are some of the issues organizations need to consider when dealing with homeless children?
5) What housing demonstration programs have succeeded with the homeless population?

* Public Housing Drug Strategy Clearinghouse
Drug Information and Strategy Clearinghouse
U.S. Department of Housing and
 Urban Development (HUD)
P.O. Box 8577   800-955-2232
Silver Spring, MD 20907   Fax: 301-251-5767

Sponsored by the Department of Housing and Urban Development, the Drug Information and Strategy Clearinghouse provides housing officials, residents, and community leaders with information and assistance on drug abuse prevention and drug trafficking control techniques. They have created a database containing information on improving resident screening procedures, strengthening eviction policies, increasing cooperation with local law enforcement, implementing drug tip hotlines, forming resident patrols, starting child care centers, and organizing drug education/prevention activities. The Clearinghouse also provides information packages, resource lists, HUD regulations, referrals, and a newsletter. There is no charge for most of this information. They can answer such questions as:
1) How can housing authorities apply for government grants?
2) What are some anti-drug strategies that have been successfully carried out in public housing units?
3) What are the latest drug abuse prevention theories and have there been demonstration projects conducted that are based on these models?
4) What resident patrols and related programs have been particularly successful in building drug-free neighborhoods?
5) How can there be an increase in cooperation with local law enforcement and other agencies in preventing drug abuse?

* Indian Health Clearinghouse
Indian Health Service
5600 Fishers Lane, Room 635   301-443-3593
Rockville, MD 20857   Fax: 301-443-0507
www.tucson.ihs.gov

The Indian Health Services provides comprehensive health services through IHS facilities, tribally contracted hospitals, health centers, school health centers, and health stations. Reports, directories, brochures, and pamphlets are available. They can answer such questions as:
1) How can doctors get their student loans repaid by working for the Indian Health Service?
2) Where are there health professional shortages within the Indian Health Service?
3) Where are health service facilities currently located?
4) What are some of the health care needs specific to Native Americans?
5) What research is being conducted on substance abuse programs for Native Americans?

* National Kidney and Urologic Diseases Information Clearinghouse
3 Information Way   301-654-4415
Bethesda, MD 20892   Fax: 301-907-8906
E-mail: nkudic@aerie.com
www.niddk.nih.gov/

The National Kidney and Urologic Disease Information Clearinghouse (NKUDIC) is an information resource and referral organization seeking to increase the knowledge and understanding of kidney and urologic diseases. They can provide education and information on kidney and urologic diseases to patients, professionals, and the public, as well as make referrals to other appropriate organizations. The Clearinghouse provides products and services such as publications, a computerized database of educational materials, and annotated bibliographies and topical literature searches on selected topics. A publications sheet is available, with most items being free. They can answer such questions as:
1) What are the symptoms, diagnosis, and treatment of kidney stones?
2) What are the different types of urinary incontinence that some elderly people experience?
3) What information exists about the success rate of kidney transplant operations?
4) What professionals deal with kidney and urologic diseases in my area and what services do they provide?
5) What help is there for men who suffer from impotence?

* National Maternal and Child Health Clearinghouse
8201 Greensboro Dr.
Suite 600
McLean, VA 22102   703-821-8955
www.nmchc.org

The National Maternal and Child Health Clearinghouse provides education and information services in maternal and child health. The Clearinghouse provides current information through the collection and dissemination of publications on maternal and child health topics, and provides technical assistance in educational resource development, program planning, and topical research. They can also refer individuals to other organizations for further information. A publications catalogue is available, with most items free. They can answer such questions as:
1) What are the dangers of lead poisoning, and how can I protect my children?
2) What are the special nutrition needs of pregnant adolescents?
3) What are some of the concerns and issues pregnant women need to know about to ensure a healthy pregnancy?
4) How can parents be sure they are feeding their children nutritious foods?
5) Where can one go for more information on breastfeeding?

* Medical Devices Clearinghouse
Center for Devices and Radiological Health
Food and Drug Administration
Consumer Staff   888-463-6332
1350 Piccard Dr.   301-827-3990
Rockville, MD 20850   Fax: 301-443-9535
E-mail: dsma@cdrh.fda.gov
www.fda.gov/cdrh/index.html

The Center for Devices and Radiological Health is responsible for analyzing factors affecting the safe and effective use of medical devices and radiation-emitting products by lay users and on patients. They answer consumer inquiries by telephone or mail on general issues relating to medical devices or radiation-emitting products. Inquiries can be answered on such products as thermometers, hearing aids, contact lenses, condoms, magnetic resonance imaging devices, hemodialysis equipment, tampons, medical x-rays, pacemakers, and artificial hearts. Publications cover topics such as pregnancy test kits, IUDs, eyeglass lenses, ultraviolet radiation, including general information on medical devices and radiological health products. They can answer such questions as:
1) How effective are condoms and what standards are they required to meet?
2) Are breast implants still considered unsafe?
3) Is it safe to make your own sterile fluids to wash your contacts?
4) What should people be aware of before they undergo an x-ray?
5) Are ultrasounds safe?

Free Research On Any Topic

* National Library of Medicine

8600 Rockville Pike	888-346-3656
Bethesda, MD 20894	301-496-6095
www.nim.nih.gov	Fax: 301-496-2809
Regional Library	800-338-7657

The National Library of Medicine (NLM) is the world's largest research library in a single scientific and professional field. The collection today stands at four million books, journals, technical reports, manuscripts, microfilms, and pictorial materials. The Library's computer-based Medical Literature Analysis and Retrieval System (MEDLARS) has bibliographic access to NLM's vast store of biomedical information. All of the MEDLARS databases are available through NLM's online network of more than 20,000 institutions and individuals. NLM charges a user fee for access to the system. They can answer such questions as:

1) What videos are available on a specific health topic?
2) How can a researcher access NLM's database from home?
3) How can a search be conducted for a specific health topic?
4) What reference guides exist to help researchers locate materials?
5) Where can information on ethics in health care be found?

* Mental Health Clearinghouse

National Institute of Mental Health

6001 Executive Blvd.	301-443-4513
Room 8184, MSC 9663	Fax: 301-443-4279
Bethesda, MD 20892	Fax on Demand: 301-443-5158
E-mail: nimhinfo@nih.gov	
www.nimh.nih.gov/	

The National Institute of Mental Health conducts and supports research to learn more about the causes, prevention, and treatment of mental and emotional illnesses. The Institute collects and distributes scientific and technical information related to mental illness, as well as educational materials for the general public. A publications list is available, with items ranging from free to $25. They can answer such questions as:

1) What are the latest statistics and information on bipolar disorder?
2) What are the various treatment options for someone suffering from depression?
3) What current research is available on the causes and treatment of schizophrenia?
4) What information should you be aware of when looking for a mental health professional?
5) What help exists for people who experience panic attacks?

* Minority Health Clearinghouse

Office of Minority Health Resource Center

P.O. Box 37337	800-444-6472
Washington, DC 20013	Fax: 301-589-0884
www.omhrc.gov	TT: 301-589-0951

The Office of Minority Health Resource Center's mission is to improve the health status of Asians, Pacific Islanders, Blacks, Hispanics, and Native Americans. Major activities include: the dissemination of accurate and timely information regarding health care issues and status through conferences and workshops; the awarding of grants for innovative community health strategies developed by minority coalitions; and research on risk factors affecting minority health. The Resource Center has information on minority health-related data and information resources available at the federal, state, and local levels and provides assistance and information to people interested in minority health and minority health programs. They have a database of minority health-related publications, as well as organizations and programs that concentrate on minority health. They can answer such questions as:

1) How can minority health goals be achieved?
2) What research is being conducted regarding African Americans and their particular risk for high blood pressure?
3) What are health issues particular to Alaskan Natives?
4) What programs are effective in encouraging pregnant Mexican Americans to seek prenatal care?
5) Are there programs specific to Native Americans with substance abuse problems?

* National Institute of Neurological Disorders and Stroke

Office of Communications and Public Liaison

P.O. Box 5801	800-352-9424
Bethesda, MD 20824	Fax: 301-402-2186
www.ninds.nih.gov	

The National Institute of Neurological Disorders and Stroke conducts and supports research on the causes, prevention, diagnosis, and treatment of neurological disorders and stroke. They have free publications on a wide variety of consumer materials and can refer people to other organizations for further information. They can answer such questions as:

1) What is Bell's Palsy and what are the ways in which it is treated?
2) What are the different forms of multiple sclerosis?
3) What current research is being conducted on strokes?
4) What can be done to minimize or reverse the effects of Parkinson's?
5) Is there relief available for chronic pain sufferers?

* Center for Nutrition Policy and Promotion

Center for Nutrition Policy and Promotion
U.S. Department of Agriculture

1120 20th St., NW, Suite 200 North	202-418-2312
Washington, DC 20036	Fax: 202-208-2321
www.usda.gov/cnpp	

The Center for Nutrition Policy and Promotion conducts applied research in food consumption, nutrition knowledge and attitudes, dietary survey methodology, food composition, and dietary guidance and nutrition education techniques. The Center uses the research data to monitor the food and nutrient content of diets of the American population, assess dietary status and trends in food consumption, further understand the factors that influence consumer food choices, maintain the National Nutrient Data Bank of the nutrient content of foods, provide dietary guidance in food selection and preparation and in food money management. The Center reports results of research in both technical and popular publications, and a publications list is available. They can answer such questions as:

1) What are the dietary guidelines for Americans?
2) What is the composition of specific foods?
3) What data exists on what people eat?
4) What factors influence consumer food choices?
5) How aware are people of the relationship between diet and health?

* National Institute for Occupational Safety and Health

Division of Standard Development and Technology Transfer
Technology Information Branch
4676 Columbia Parkway

Mail Stop C-13	800-35-NIOSH
Cincinnati, OH 45226-1998	Fax: 513-533-8573
E-mail: pubstaff@cdc.gov	
www.cdc.gov/niosh	

The National Institute for Occupational Safety and Health provides technical information on programs and issues dealing with occupational safety and health. The Clearinghouse maintains a database through which they can search for journal articles and other materials on a specific topic. They have publications, reports, and bibliographies, many of which are free. They can answer such questions as:

1) Are video display terminals dangerous to the average individual?
2) What is Carpal Tunnel Syndrome and what can be done to treat it?
3) What are some of the dangers of working in a dry cleaning store?
4) How many deaths occurred on a particular job site?
5) What do I do if I suspect a health problem in my workplace?

* National Clearinghouse For Primary Care Information

8201 Greensboro Dr., Suite 600	
McLean, VA 22102	703-821-8955

The National Clearinghouse For Primary Care provides information services to support the planning, development, and delivery of ambulatory health care to urban and rural areas that have shortages of medical personnel and services. They distribute publications focusing on ambulatory care, financial management, primary health care, and health services administration. The Clearinghouse provides information on federal guidances and policies affecting primary care delivery. A list is available of free publications on community health centers, migrant health centers, childhood injury prevention efforts, clinical care, and many other health concerns. They can answer such questions as:

1) What information should be considered when establishing a rural medical practice?
2) What are some of the ways older adults can improve their nutrition and is there information that can be distributed to these clients?
3) What are particular health problems of the migrant population and how can these be addressed?
4) What are some of the characteristics of successful dental programs in community and migrant health centers?
5) What is the status of medical personnel shortages in inner city hospitals and what is being done to alleviate this crisis?

Health

* National Rehabilitation Information Center

    8455 Colesville Rd., Suite 935   800-34-NARIC
    Silver Spring, MD 20910   800-346-2742
    E-mail: naric@capaccess.org   Fax: 301-587-1967
    http://naric.com/naric

The National Rehabilitation Information Center (NARIC) is a library and information center on disability and rehabilitation. The Center is funded by the National Institute for Disability and Rehabilitation Research to collect and disseminate the results of federally-funded research projects. In addition, the Center includes commercially-published books and journal articles in its collection. They also maintain a database of disability and rehabilitation materials which they will search for a small fee. NARIC provides quick reference and referral services, database searches, and photocopies of documents in the collection. They publish a newsletter and other directories and provide information specialists to field the many questions on various topics of concern to people. A list of publications is available, with items ranging in price from free to $25. They can answer such questions as:

1) What resources, support, and information are available for people suffering from traumatic brain injury?
2) Where can you buy a computer keyboard which responds correctly to your patterns of movement if you have cerebral palsy?
3) How effective have supported employment programs been in improving employment opportunities for people with severe disabilities?
4) What are the different education methods available to educate a deaf child, and what are some of the factors to consider when making this choice?
5) What information exists on helping someone who has suffered a spinal cord injury?

* Office on Smoking and Health

    Centers for Disease Control
    4770 Buford Highway, NE
    Mail Stop K-50   770-488-5705
    Atlanta, GA 30341   800-CDC-1311
    www.cdc.gov/tobacco   Fax: 301-986-5001

The Smoking Hotline can answer all your questions regarding cigarettes and stop smoking methods. They can provide fact sheets, pamphlets, posters and other publications, as well as information in response to inquiries. The Center can access information on the Combined Health Information Database, and their library and reading room are open to the public. The Infomemo newsletter contains information on disease prevention, education, and control. They can answer such questions as:

1) What are the pros and cons of various stop smoking methods?
2) What is the current status report on smoking?
3) How does smoking affect a person's health?
4) What are the ways in which a person over 50 might stop smoking?
5) What are the rules or regulations regarding smoking in an office or other public place?

* National Clearinghouse for Professions In Special Education

    The Council for Exceptional Children   800-641-7824
    1920 Association Dr.   703-264-9476
    Reston, VA 22091   Fax: 703-264-1637
    www.cec.sped.org/cl/ncpseabo.htm

The National Clearinghouse for Professions in Special Education provides information that will help people in making a career choice. They have information about the demand for special educators in the U.S., about college and university programs that prepare people for these careers, about financial assistance available, and more. They can answer such questions as:

1) What fellowships are available to work with the deaf?
2) How is music therapy used to work with individuals with disabilities?
3) What different sorts of careers are possible in special education?
4) What type of training is required to work with autistic children?
5) How has mainstreaming affected the special education job market?

* Sudden Infant Death Hotline

    National Sudden Infant Death Syndrome Resource Center
    2070 Chainbridge Rd., Suite 450   703-821-8955
    Vienna, VA 22182   Fax: 703-821-2098
    E-mail: sids@cirsol.com
    http://38.229.82.3/SIDS/index.HTM

The Sudden Infant Death Clearinghouse was established to provide information and educational materials on Sudden Infant Death Syndrome (SIDS), apnea, and other related issues. The staff responds to information requests from professionals, families with SIDS-related deaths, and the general public by sending written materials and making referrals. The Clearinghouse maintains a library of reference materials and mailing lists of state programs, groups, and individuals concerned with SIDS. Their publications include bibliographies on SIDS and self-help support groups, a publications catalogue, and a newsletter. They can answer such questions as:

1) What is crib death?
2) What are the current views on home monitoring to prevent SIDS?
3) How can parents help the grieving process in children after the death of a sibling?
4) How many children died of SIDS in a given state last year?
5) How can SIDS be distinguished from child abuse and neglect?

* Family Violence and Sexual Assault Institute

    1310 Clinic Dr.   903-595-6600
    Tyler, TX 75701   Fax: 903-595-6799

The goal of the Family Violence and Sexual Assault Institute is to provide information services to practitioners and researchers who are working to prevent family violence and provide assistance for victims. A publications list and price sheet are available. They can answer such questions as:

1) What journal articles and bibliographies are there on elder abuse, as well as what statistics, copies of legislation, and organizations concerned with elder abuse issues exist?
2) What are some of the signs of sexual abuse?
3) What are some centers and organizations concerned with child maltreatment?
4) What bibliographies are there on the characteristics of abusive and neglecting parents?
5) What agency should a person contact first if abuse is suspected?

Free Research On Any Topic

National and World Affairs

* Agriculture Exports Clearinghouse
Foreign Agricultural Service
U.S. Department of Agriculture, Room 5074
Washington, DC 20250
E-mail: fasinfo@fas.usda.gov
www.fas.usda.gov
202-720-7115
Fax: 202-720-1727

The Foreign Agricultural Service disseminates agricultural trade and commodity production information to agribusinesses and the general public. They offer private companies and cooperatives assistance in marketing their products overseas by collecting and publicizing information on foreign buyers and advertising U.S. export availability. They have a monthly magazine, commodity and trade reports, publications, and fact sheets (many of which are free). They can answer such questions as:
1) What are the market prospects for U.S. food and farm products in Japan?
2) What are some overseas markets and buying trends for a particular product?
3) What are some overseas promotional activities?
4) How do I begin an export business?
5) How do I advertise my product directly to buyers overseas?

* Arms Control and Disarmament Agency
Office of Public Information
2201 C St., NW
Washington, DC 20451
Bulletin Board
www.acda.gov
800-581-ACDA
202-647-6575
202-736-4436

The Arms Control and Disarmament Agency (ACDA) coordinates the ongoing negotiations between the United States and other nuclear powers to reduce their arsenals. This federal agency also takes the lead in other efforts to reduce the risk of war by, for example, verifying other countries' compliance with the Nuclear Non-Proliferation Treaty and other international agreements. Weapons sales to foreign governments, technology transfer, and treaties are also important elements of arms control. The Agency can answer such questions as:
1) What details exist on certain weapons systems and what analyses have been done on the impact that such systems have on arms control agreements, treaties, and negotiations?
2) What are some of the economic issues related to defense strategies?
3) What is the INF Treaty?
4) What is the current status of arms control and disarmament goals?
5) What is the current arms control policy of the U.S.?

* Central Intelligence Agency
Public Affairs
Washington, DC 20505
www.cia.gov
703-482-0623
Fax: 703-482-1739

The Central Intelligence Agency (CIA) is strictly a foreign intelligence organization and has no domestic or law enforcement duties. The CIA occasionally issues unclassified publications which provide additional research aids to the academic and business communities. The majority of these reports contain foreign or international economic and political information or are directories of foreign officials. They are available for sale. They can answer such questions as:
1) What is the history of the CIA?
2) What are the steps involved in the intelligence cycle?
3) What agencies or departments are involved with the intelligence community?
4) What involvement does the White House have in intelligence activities?
5) Who oversees the CIA?

* Export Country Experts
U.S. Foreign and Commercial Services
Export Promotion Services
U.S. Department of Commerce
Room 2810
Washington, DC 20230
www.ita.doc.gov
800-872-8723
202-482-6220
Fax: 202-482-4473

The Country Desk Officers at the U.S. Department of Commerce can provide businesses with information on a market, company, and any other aspect of commercial life in a particular country. These specialists can look at the needs of an individual U.S. firm wishing to sell in a particular country in the full context of that country's overall economy, trade policies, and political situation, bearing in mind current U.S. policies toward that country. Desk officers keep up-to-date on the economic and commercial conditions in their assigned countries. Each officer collects information on the country's regulations, tariffs, business practices, economic and political developments, trade data and trends, market size, and growth. They have free reports and other information at their fingertips or they can refer callers to other country specialists. They can answer such questions as:
1) How can I expand my business through a foreign franchise?
2) How can I reduce my company's distribution and transportation costs overseas?
3) What type of export opportunities exist for computer manufacturing companies who want to expand to Germany?
4) What are some recent foreign labor trends in Japan?
5) Which markets are growing the fastest overseas?

* Country Officers
U.S. Department of State
2201 C St., NW
Washington, DC 20520
www.state.gov
202-647-4000

Hundreds of country experts at the U.S. Department of State are responsible for following all activities in their assigned countries, from a political, economic, and social perspective. These officers are in constant contact with embassies, deliver and receive documents from those embassies, and write reports on the current activities in the country. They have several publications they can send, plus up-to-date information on each country's population, culture, geography, political condition, and more. Call to ask for the number of a specific country officer. They can answer such questions as:
1) What is the current political situation of a particular country?
2) What is the current population, as well as the health situation of a country?
3) Are there any travel advisories for a particular country?
4) Is there a brief overview of a specific country available?
5) What is the status of human rights in a particular country?

* U.S. Customs Service
Public Information Office
U.S. Department of the Treasury
P.O. Box 7407
Washington, DC 20044
www.customs.ustreas.gov
202-927-6724

The U.S. Customs Service collects the revenue from imports and enforces customs and related laws. It assists in the administration and enforcement of over 400 provisions of law on behalf of more than 40 government agencies. They have many free publications and information on customs rules and travel tips. They can answer such questions as:
1) What are the rules regarding the bringing of pets into the U.S.?
2) Is there a limit to the amount of a particular item one can bring into the country?
3) What are duty-free exemptions, and restricted or prohibited articles?
4) What is required when a traveler declares articles?
5) What is the current duty rate for a particular item?

* Defense Technical Information Center
8725 John J. Kingman Rd.
Suite 0944
Ft. Belvoir, VA 22060-6218
E-mail: help@dtic.mil
www.dtic.mil
800-225-3842
703-767-8274

The Defense Technical Information Center (DTIC) is the clearinghouse within the Department of Defense (DOD) for acquiring, storing, retrieving, and disseminating scientific and technical information to support the management and conduct of DOD research, development, engineering, and studies programs. DTIC services are available to DOD and its contractors and to other U.S. Government organizations and their contractors. Organizations may also become eligible for service under certain programs. DTIC also responds indirectly to the general public's information requests. Most products and services are free, but, there are some fees for technical reports and

National and World Affairs

on-line access. *A DTIC Handbook for Users* is available. They can answer such questions as:
1) What technical reports exist concerning aeronautics?
2) Is there a listing of defense contractors and/or potential contractors?
3) How does a company obtain defense contract work?
4) What type of security clearance procedures are used for defense contractors?

* Defense Clearinghouse
Directorate for Public Communication
U.S. Department of Defense
1400 Defense Pentagon, Room 1E757
Washington, DC 20301-1400   703-697-5737
www.defenselink.mil

The Department of Defense is responsible for providing the military forces needed to deter war and protect the security of our country. The Directorate for Public Communication is a good starting point for Defense Department information. They have publications available, some of which are free, and they can direct you to other sources within the Department. They can answer such questions as:
1) What is the current Department of Defense budget, and how has it changed since the previous year?
2) What is the status of our troops overseas?
3) What is the federal government's security strategies?
4) What Department of Defense bases have closed within the last year?
5) How can I sell my company's products or services to the Army?

* Federal Emergency Management Agency
500 C St., SW   800-480-2520
Washington, DC 20472   202-646-4600
www.fema.gov   Fax: 202-646-4086

Federal Emergency Management Agency (FEMA) is the part of our government which deals with planning for and/or coordinating relief in various national emergencies. FEMA plans for nuclear attacks, security emergencies, disaster recovery aid, and helps to coordinate food, shelter, and financial aid in the event of any natural or man made disasters. FEMA has a publications catalogue which lists free publications on subjects such as civil defense, earthquakes, floods, hurricanes, tornadoes, and more. They can answer such questions as:
1) How can people best prepare for an earthquake?
2) What information exists on emergency medical services needed during a time of crisis?
3) How can homeowners repair their home after a flood?
4) Are there plans available on how to build an effective fallout shelter?
5) What are some safety tips for winter storms?

* American Foreign Policy Information Clearinghouse
Bureau of Public Affairs
U.S. Department of State
2201 C St., NW, Room 6808   202-647-6575
Washington, DC 20520-6810   Fax: 202-647-7120
E-mail: publicaffairs@panet.us-state.gov
www.state.gov

The Department of State receives thousands of reports daily, and produces hundreds of publications, speeches, and conferences on foreign policy issues. The Bureau of Public Affairs informs the American people on foreign policy and advises the Secretary of State on public opinion. If unable to answer an inquiry directly, the staff will direct you to the appropriate source. This bureau issues various publications covering U.S. foreign relations, some of which are free. They can answer such questions as:
1) Where can someone get a copy of the PLO-Israel Peace Treaty and what information does it contain?
2) Are there resource materials available that would allow a business to learn more about the relationship between the U.S. and a foreign country before they invest in that country?
3) What information exists on global terrorism?
4) Where could one find out more information on human rights practices in a particular country?
5) How can one access the U.S.'s or a foreign country's diplomatic records?

* Immigration and Naturalization Service
Central Office
425 Eye St., NW
Washington, DC 20536   202-514-4316
www.usdoj.gov/ins

The Immigration and Naturalization Service (INS) facilitates the entry of persons legally admissible as visitors or as immigrants to the United States, provides assistance to those seeking permanent resident status, and apprehends those who attempt illegal entry into this country. They have established a telephone service system that provides pre-recorded information on immigration and citizenship-related topics. They can answer such questions as:
1) Where is the local INS office located for a particular community?
2) What are the rules regarding the marriage of a foreign citizen to a U.S. citizen?
3) What are the citizenship requirements for children born outside the U.S.?
4) What constitutes political asylum?
5) What are some visa requirements for travel overseas?

* Agency for International Development (AID)
Document Information Services Clearinghouse
1500 Wilson Blvd.
Suite 1010   703-351-4006
Arlington, VA 22209   Fax: 703-351-4039
www.info.usaid.gov

AID's Center for Development Information and Evaluation (CDIE) produces an evaluation publications series which includes a broad range of subjects of interest to those working in international development. The series comprises project impact evaluations, program evaluations, special studies, program design and evaluation methodology reports, and discussion papers. The CDIE Evaluation Publications List is arranged by general subject category and by type of report within each category. Each document is available for $3. They can answer such questions as:
1) What research has been conducted on family planning issues?
2) How do private volunteer organizations assist in the development of a country?
3) How has the emergency food program operated in a particular country?
4) How have health programs been successfully initiated in developing countries and how can they be sustained?
5) What types of agriculture programs have been attempted and what are the results of those programs?

* National Clearinghouse for U.S.-Japan Studies
Indiana University   800-266-3815
2805 East Tenth St., Suite 120   812-855-3838
Bloomington, IN 47408   Fax: 812-855-0455
E-mail: japan@indiana.edu
www.indiana.edu/~japan

The National Clearinghouse for U.S.- Japan Studies is a database system providing timely and comprehensive information about educational resources available to teach about Japan. The Clearinghouse collects, analyzes, abstracts, and creates a database of materials and resources that can assist school systems and individual teachers in developing and implementing curricula and lessons on broad areas of Japanese culture and society, and on U.S.-Japan relationships. The Clearinghouse also includes items such as videos, films, some simulations, artifact kits, and the like, and teacher-developed materials. They can answer such questions as:
1) What information exists on the Japanese educational system?
2) Where can I obtain copies of Japanese War relocation records?
3) What information is available on the Japanese stock market?
4) What are current U.S. trade policies toward Japan?
5) How can I locate programs that offer study abroad opportunities in Japan?

Free Research On Any Topic

Other

* Boating Safety Hotline

Office of Boating Safety
U.S. Coast Guard
U.S. Department of Transportation   800-368-5647
2100 2nd St., SW   202-267-1077
Washington, DC 20593   Fax: 202-267-4285
E-mail: BoatWeb@mail.rmit.com
www.uscgboating.org

The Boating Safety Hotline can provide you with information on such topics of interest to boaters as safety recalls, publications, Coast Guard department contacts and addresses, public education courses, and free Coast Guard Services. They have a wealth of free information and publications to share. They can answer such questions as:

1) What statistics exist on boating accidents?
2) How can parents teach children about water safety?
3) What things do people need to consider regarding floatation devices?
4) What licenses or regulations should boaters be aware of?
5) Where can people receive information on water charts and other navigational aids?

* Children's Literature Center

Library of Congress   202-707-5535
Washington, DC 20540   Fax: 202-707-4632
http://lcweb.loc.gov/rr/child

The Children's Center prepares lists and scholarly bibliographies and provides other reference services for individuals and organizations who study, produce, collect, interpret, and disseminate children's books, films, television programs, or other forms of materials destined for children's information and recreational use, usually outside of the classroom. The Library holds approximately 200,000 children's books and related items, such as boxed and board games, sound recordings, maps, and illustrations. The Center also provides many publisher's catalogues that list titles to be published in the upcoming year, a wide range of periodicals about children's literature, and lists from rare and used book sellers. They can answer such questions as:

1) How can literature be used in the classroom to teach history to 7th graders?
2) What information sources exist for Japanese children's books published after World War II?
3) How can children learn about people with disabilities through literature?
4) Are there books specific to helping children deal with the issues of death and dying?
5) Where could a writer locate materials to help with a book on teaching children to be aware of strangers?

* Congressional Research Service

Library of Congress   202-707-5700
Washington, DC 20540   Fax: 202-707-6745
http://lcweb.loc.gov/rr

The Congressional Research Service (CRS) at the Library of Congress prepares hundreds of non-partisan background reports each year on current issues large and small, domestic and foreign, social and political. CRS also publishes hundreds of major Issue Briefs each year designed to keep members of Congress informed on timely issues. Written in simple and direct language, these briefs provide background information and are updated daily. These studies generated by CRS cover almost any topic imaginable and are a fantastic resource for students, researchers, and anyone else who needs statistics or an analysis of a subject. You must request free copies of these reports through your U.S. Representative or Senator (202-224-3121 Congress Switchboard). The CRS Reports can answer such questions as:

1) What is the history of abortion rights in the U.S. and what legislation is currently before Congress regarding abortion?
2) What information exists on the protection of endangered sea turtles?
3) What is the current status of nuclear missile proliferation in the world?
4) What reports have been done on obscenity on television and radio?
5) What programs are there for working in a foreign country?

* Federal Assistance Programs Retrieval System

Federal Domestic Assistance Catalog Staff
General Services Administration
300 7th St., SW, Suite 101   202-708-5126
Washington, DC 20407   800-669-8331
www.gsa.gov/fdac

The Federal Assistance Programs Retrieval System (FAPRS) is your online link to the Catalog of Federal Domestic Assistance. It contains federal domestic assistance programs, including federal grants, loans, loan guarantees, and technical assistance. Their database contains more than 1,000 assistance programs administered by 51 federal agencies, with summaries of agency functions, descriptions of assistance programs, eligibility criteria, and contact information. Users include state and local governments, small businesses, researchers, and libraries. Fees are on a cost-recovery basis, with no initiation or monthly fees. Contact FAPRS for telephone and data processing charges. They can answer such questions as:

1) What assistance programs would help a rural hospital obtain needed medical equipment?
2) How can a student obtain a doctorate in housing policy at no cost?
3) How can schools obtain science equipment from the government?
4) How can a choreographer receive funds to create a dance?
5) Where can a business turn for assistance in the field of energy?

* American Folklife Center

Library of Congress   202-707-5510
Washington, DC 20540   Fax: 202-707-2076
http://lcweb.loc.gov/folklife

The American Folklife Center at the Library of Congress has been a national advocate for the preservation and presentation of American folklife. The Center serves a varied constituency (state and local organizations, scholars, researchers, students, and the general public), maintains relations and coordinates programs with other federal agencies, and offers a wide range of programs and services. The Folklife Center has conducted or assisted with surveys or major field projects in many states. It conducts research projects based on the documentary collections of the Library of Congress. It sponsors a variety of conferences, workshops, concerts, and other events at the Library and elsewhere. The Archive houses more that 35,000 hours of audio recordings, controls more than 100,000 pages of manuscript materials, and maintains over 4,000 books, directories, and periodicals dealing with folk music and folklore. They can answer such questions as:

1) What information or recordings exist regarding early jazz?
2) Where can someone locate information on Native American architecture?
3) Where are recordings on Australian folk songs?
4) What data is there on the native crafts of Hawaii?
5) Are there videos available to educate students about various cultures?

* Forest Service

U.S. Department of Agriculture
Public Affairs Office
Mailing:
    P.O. Box 96090
    Washington, DC 20090
201 14th and Independence Ave., SW   202-205-1760
Washington, DC 20250   Fax: 202-205-0885
E-mail: mailroom@fs.fed.gov
www.fs.fed.us

The nation's National Forests offer more than 114,300 miles of trails, a Scenic Byway System consisting of nearly 5,000 miles of highways in 32 states, 70 wild and scenic rivers covering nearly 3,500 miles and much more. *A Guide to Your National Forest* lists regional offices, several private and one Forest Service Interpretative Association, and a list of State Boards of Tourism where camping information may be obtained. They can answer such questions as:

1) What state forests in Maryland offer good sailing opportunities?
2) How far in advance must I reserve a campsite?
3) What is the best time of year to plan a camping trip in Tennessee?
4) Which rivers in North Carolina are recommended for canoeing or rafting?
5) How do I receive a listing of national scenic and historic trails?

Other

* Genealogy Research
Reference Services Branch
700 Pennsylvania Ave., NW 202-501-5400
Washington, DC 20408 Fax: 202-501-7154
E-mail: inquire@nara.gov
www.nara.gov/research

The National Archives maintains the historically valuable records of the U.S. Government dating from the Revolutionary War era to the recent past. They preserve records and prepare finding aids to facilitate their use and makes records available for use in research rooms. They can provide assistance and training aids to help you with your research. They can answer such questions as:
1) Where can information be located regarding ship passenger arrival records?
2) What ship plans are available on World War II navy vessels?
3) How can military service and pension records be accessed?
4) How can people most easily trace their family history?
5) Where are prisoner-of-war records of the Civil War maintained?

* Geographic Names Information
Branch of Geographic Names
U.S. Geological Survey (USGS) 888-ASK-USGS
523 National Center 703-648-4544
Reston, VA 20192 Fax: 703-648-5644
http://mapping.usgs.gov

The USGS Branch of Geographic Names maintains a national research, coordinating, and information center to which all problems and inquiries concerning domestic geographic names can be directed. This office compiles name information, manages a names data repository, maintains information files, and publishes materials on domestic geographic names. The Branch works on standardizing names within the Federal government by keeping track of all the names put on maps that the various government agencies publish. They also assist the Board of Geographic Names in resolving name problems, such as if a name is derogatory or the usage is conflicting. The USGS, in cooperation with the Board of Geographic Names, maintains the National Geographic Names Data Base and compiles The National Gazetteer of the United States of American on a state-by-state basis. They can answer such questions as:
1) Where are islands located referred to as "No Man's Island"?
2) Where can a researcher find the location of a town that no longer exists?
3) What background information exists on the name of a town?
4) What is a variant name for the town of Rocky Gap, Colorado?
5) What are the geographic coordinates for a particular location?

* Geography and Map Division
Library of Congress 202-707-6277
Washington, DC 20540 Fax: 202-707-8531
E-mail: maps@loc.gov
http://lcweb.loc.gov/rr/geogmap

The Geography and Map Division of the Library of Congress provides cartographic and geographic information for all parts of the world to the Congress, federal and local governments, the scholarly community, and to the general public. It is the largest and most comprehensive cartographic collection in the world, numbering almost 4.5 million maps, 60,000 atlases, and 6,000 reference works. The Division also has custody of over 350 globes, 2,000 three-dimensional plastic relief models, and a large number of cartographic materials in other formats. They can answer such questions as:
1) What maps are available for genealogists tracing a family history in Virginia?
2) What maps exist on colonial America?
3) Where can aerial photos be located in order to assess erosion and flood damage in a particular area?
4) Are there maps of old railroad lines available?
5) Where can information be located on Revolutionary War battlefields?

* Bureau of Indian Affairs
Office of Public Affairs
U.S. Department of the Interior
1849 C St., NW 202-208-3711
Washington, DC 20240 Fax: 202-501-1516
www.doi.gov/bureau-indian-affairs.html

The Bureau of Indian Affairs principal objectives are to encourage and assist Indian and Alaska Native people to manage their own affairs under the trust relationship with the federal government; to facilitate the full development of their human and natural resource potential; and to mobilize all aids for their advancement. The Bureau can provide you with a wide variety of information on Native Americans, the history of the Bureau and more. They have publications and fact sheets, and can refer you to other resources for more information. They can answer such questions as:
1) What tribes are currently recognized by the U.S.?
2) What are the demographics of American Indians?
3) Which state has the largest percentage of American Indians?
4) What are the labor force estimates by states for Native Americans?
5) How do Indian Tribes govern themselves?

* Library of Congress
101 Independence Ave., SE
Washington, DC 20540 202-707-5000
E-mail: lcweb@loc.gov
www.loc.gov

The Library of Congress is the national library of the United States, offering diverse materials for research including the world's most extensive collections in many areas such as American history, music, and law. They not only have books and periodicals, but also prints, photographs, films, music, and more. This office can direct you to the correct division within the Library. If your question requires extensive research and you cannot come to the Library, they have lists of freelance researchers to assist you for a fee. Many Divisions have their own databases to search citations or bibliographies or literature guides to help readers locate published materials on a particular subject. There may be a charge involved for some services, although many are free. To begin a search, researchers should first contact their local library, and then, proceed to the Library of Congress if they are unable to find adequate information. The Library can answer such questions as:
1) Where can one find information about medicinal plants?
2) What are some good reference sources for children's literature?
3) Where can information be found on medieval law?
4) How can books in braille be accessed?
5) Where can literature guides on a variety of science topics be found?

* Manuscript Division
Library of Congress 202-287-5387
Washington, DC 20540 Fax: 202-707-6336
http://lcweb.loc.gov/rr/mss

The Manuscript Division holds nearly 50 million items, including some of the greatest manuscript treasures of American history and culture. Among these are Jefferson's rough draft of the Declaration of Independence, James Madison's notes on the Federal Convention, George Washington's first inaugural address, the paper tape of the first telegraphic message, Abraham Lincoln's Gettysburg Address and second inaugural address, Alexander Graham Bell's first drawing of the telephone, and many more. The holdings encompass approximately 11,000 separate collections. The Reading Room is open only to qualified researchers. Only under exceptional circumstances are undergraduates permitted to consult manuscripts. The staff at the Division can answer such questions as:
1) Where can copies of George Washington's speeches be located for a biography of Washington?
2) Are records kept of nongovernmental organizations which have significantly affected American life, such as the NAACP?
3) Where is information held on the first Supreme Court justices?
4) How did the Declaration of Independence change from the rough draft version to the final copy?
5) What resources exist for a researcher studying the generals active in World War II?

* Motion Picture Broadcasting and Recorded Sound Division
Library of Congress 202-707-8572
Washington, DC 20540 Fax: 202-707-2371
http://lcweb.loc.gov/rr/mopic

The Motion Picture Broadcasting and Recorded Sound Division has responsibility for the acquisition, cataloging, preservation, and service of the motion picture and television collections, including items on film, videotape, and videodisc. The Division has similar responsibilities for the Library's collections of sound recordings and radio programs. Viewing facilities are provided for those doing research of a specific nature, and must be scheduled well in advance. The reference staff answers written and telephone inquiries about its holdings. They can answer such questions as:
1) What World War II newsreels were produced in Germany?
2) What collections exist for films produced prior to 1915?
3) Where can a researcher look for information on silent films and their music?
4) Where can Afro-American folk music be found?
5) Are their recordings of authors, poets, and other artists reading their own works, such as Robert Frost?

Free Research On Any Topic

* National Park Service
Office of Public Affairs
U.S. Department of the Interior
P.O. Box 37127
Washington, DC 20013-7127
www.nps.gov

202-208-6843
Fax: 202-219-0916

Along with other responsibilities, the Park Service administers 350 maintained areas in the National Park System, collects the National Register of Historic Places and a registry of natural sites, and manages the Urban Park and Recreation Recovery Program. It provides technical assistance in planning, acquisition and development of recreation resources, conducts surveys of historic buildings and engineering works, has available programs and resources for teachers, and administers a program in interagency archeological services. Information including brochures, maps, and a publications catalogue listing items ranging in price from $1 to $30 can be ordered from the Government Printing Office. The Office of Public Inquiries can refer you to other Park Service offices and can answer such questions as:

1) What archeological digs are currently in progress and where are they located?
2) What statistics are available on Park Service use, such as: total visits, visits by region and state, and overnight stays?
3) Where can I locate videos on historic people or national landmarks?
4) How do I find out whether or not my home is eligible for listing on the National Historic Register?
5) How can I receive a listing of the lesser known National Parks?

* Performing Arts Division
Library of Congress
Thomas Jefferson Bldg.
Washington, DC 20540
http://lcweb.loc.gov/rr/perform

202-707-5507

The Performing Arts Library is a joint project of the Library of Congress and the Kennedy Center, and offers information and reference assistance on dance, theater, opera, music, film, and broadcasting. The Performing Arts Library serves the research and information needs of the public, artists, and staff of the Center. The Library also identifies and locates the creative and resource materials necessary to develop new works and productions in the performing arts. Reference service is available by phone, in person, or by mail. They can answer such questions as:

1) How can an orchestral program of Irish composers be tailored for a young audience?
2) What information exists on different dance companies based in New York?
3) Is there information on what is required to start a record company?
4) Are there recordings of interviews or videotapes of famous actresses discussing their works?
5) Where can recordings of poetry readings be located?

* Prints and Photographs Division
Library of Congress
James Madison Memorial Building, Room LM 337
First St. and Independence Ave., SW
Washington, DC 20540
http://lcweb.loc.gov/rr/print/

202-707-6394
Fax: 202-707-6647

The visual collections of the Library of Congress provide a record of people, places, and events in the United States and throughout the world. The Prints and Photographs Division has custody of more than 10 million images in a variety of forms and media: Architecture, Design, and Engineering collections, Documentary Photographs, Fine Prints, Master Photographs, Popular and Applied Graphic Art, and Posters. Researchers may consult the collections in the Prints and Photographs Reading Room. The Reading Room houses the general and special card catalogues, files of photoprint reference copies, and a limited collection of reference books. Reference specialists are available for assistance. The division will accept limited requests by letter, but the staff cannot make lengthy searches. They can answer such questions as:

1) How can someone obtain a print of the Wright Brothers first flight?
2) What photos taken by Brady exist on the Civil War?
3) Where can someone locate photos of various housing projects undertaken by the Work Projects Administration under President Roosevelt?
4) What material is available to study the architecture of Frank Lloyd Wright?
5) What references are there chronicling the history of political cartooning?

* Rare Books and Special Collections
Library of Congress
Thomas Jefferson Building
Washington, DC 20540
http://lcweb.loc.gov/rr/rarebooks

202-707-5434

The Rare Book and Special Collections Division contains more than 650,000 volumes and broadsides, pamphlets, theater playbills, title pages, prints, manuscripts, posters, and photographs acquired with various collections. The materials the Division houses have come into its custody for a variety of reasons: monetary value, importance in the history of printing, binding, association interest, or fragility. Reference assistance is offered by telephone, in person, and by mail. They can answer such questions as:

1) What information exists on the history of ballooning?
2) What books do you have that contain the Confederate States imprint?
3) What references do you have on the history of print making?
4) Do you have information researchers can study regarding Columbus' discovery of America?
5) Do you have 15th century illuminated manuscripts for art history research?

* Rural Information Center
National Agricultural Library
U.S. Department of Agriculture (USDA)
10301 Baltimore Blvd.
Beltsville, MD 20705
E-mail: ric@nal.usda.gov
www.nal.usda.gov/ric

301-504-5547
800-633-7701
Fax: 301-504-5181

The Rural Information Center is designed to provide information and referral services to local government officials, businesses, community organizations, and rural citizens working to maintain the vitality of America's rural areas. The Center provides customized information products to specific inquiries, refers users to organizations or experts in the field, performs database searches, furnishes bibliographies, identifies current USDA research and Cooperative Extension System programs, and assists users in accessing the National Agricultural Libraries' extensive collection. There is a cost recovery fee for photocopying articles and searches. They can answer such questions as:

1) Which organizations focus on rural health issues?
2) What resources for the historic preservation of farmland are available in rural areas?
3) How can tourism be promoted in small towns?
4) What are some examples of the more innovative economic development projects in rural communities?
5) What rural organizations focus specifically on research and development?

* Science and Technology Division
Library of Congress
John Adams Building
Washington, DC 20540
http://lcweb.loc.gov/rr/scitech

202-707-5639

The Science and Technology Division's collection contains 3.5 million books, nearly 60,000 journals, and 3.7 million technical reports. The collections include such treasures as first editions of Copernicus and Newton and the personal papers of the Wright Brothers and Alexander Graham Bell. The Division has primary responsibility for providing reference and bibliographic services and for recommending acquisitions in the broad areas of science and technology. Reference services are provided to users in person, by telephone, and by mail. Indirect reference service is provided through bibliographic guides (Tracer Bullets) and research reports prepared by Division subject specialists and reference librarians. Copies of reference guides are available at no charge. They can answer such questions as:

1) Where can one begin looking for information on lasers and their applications?
2) What are some good sources of information on volcanoes?
3) What resources exist on extraterrestrial life?
4) Where could someone find sources for information on medicinal plants?
5) How would one go about creating a hologram?

* Women's Bureau Clearinghouse
U.S. Department of Labor
200 Constitution Ave., NW, Room S3002
Washington, DC 20210
E-mail: wb_wwc@dol.gov
www.dol.gov/dol/wb/

800-827-5335
202-219-4486
Fax: 202-219-5529

The Women's Bureau Clearinghouse was designed and established to assist employers in identifying the most appropriate policies for responding to the dependent care needs of employees seeking to balance their dual responsibilities. They can also provide information on women's issues, as well as work force issues that affect women. They can offer information and guidance in areas such as women-owned businesses, women workers, alternative work schedules, dependent care issues, and much more. They also have publications and other information available, much of which is free. They can answer such questions as:

Other

1) What are some elder care program options?
2) What is the earning difference between men and women?
3) How does flex time work in companies similar to mine?
4) What are some alternate work schedules and how do they work?
5) What literature and other resources are available on employer-supported child care?

Free Research On Any Topic

Statistics

* National Agricultural Statistics Service
USDA South Bldg., Room 5805
U.S. Department of Agriculture (USDA)
Washington, DC 20250
E-mail: nass@nass.usda.gov
www.usda.gov/nass/
800-727-9540
202-720-3896
Fax: 202-690-1311

The National Agricultural Statistics Service collects data on crops, livestock, poultry, dairy, chemical use, prices, and labor, and publishes the official USDA state and national estimates through its Agricultural Statistics Board. There are nearly 400 reports annually covering domestic agriculture, such as estimates of production, stocks, inventories, prices, disposition, utilization, farm numbers and land, and other factors. They provide national profiles gathered from regular surveys of thousands of farmers, ranchers, and agribusinesses that voluntarily provide data on a confidential basis. Publications are available and range from free to $12. They can answer such questions as:
1) How has the use of a specific chemical for crop growth changed over the past five years?
2) Has the size of farms increased or decreased over the past ten years?
3) What statistics exist on wildlife damage to crops?
4) How has the weekly crop weather affected crop growth?
5) What data is there on livestock slaughter?

* Federal Aviation Administration
Office of Public Affairs
800 Independence Ave., SW
Washington, DC 20591
E-mail: gramick@postmaster2.dot.gov
www.faa.gov
202-366-4000

The Federal Aviation Administration (FAA) is the starting place for any information on airlines, airports, and aircraft. The FAA regulates air commerce, develops civil aeronautics, installs and operates airports, conducts aeronautic research, and provides guidance and policy on accident prevention in general aviation. They keep statistics on air travel, accidents, and more. There are free publications on airline careers, aviation, and airplanes, as well as videos and curriculum guides. They can answer such questions as:
1) Which airlines had the worst on time rate for a given month?
2) What videos are available on aviation?
3) What is some historical information on women in aviation?
4) What are some statistics on air traffic accidents?
5) What methods are used to reduce the noise level of new aircraft?

* National Clearinghouse for Census Data Services
Administrative Customer Service Division
Bureau of the Census
Washington, DC 20233
www.census.gov
301-457-4100
Fax: 301-457-4714

The National Clearinghouse for Census Data Services provides a referral service for persons who need assistance in obtaining Census Bureau data or in using Census Bureau products. This assistance ranges from market research using census data to tape copying or microcomputer services. The Clearinghouse includes organizations that provide services for accessing and using economic data and information from the Census Bureau's 1990 Census TIGER geographic database. They can answer such questions as:
1) How can I update my business's mailing list using 1990 census statistics?
2) How can the census help me trace my genealogical history?
3) What is the TIGER geographic database, and how can I use it?
4) Which products are available on CD-ROM?
5) Does the Bureau have an on-line data service?

* Census Information on Business
Bureau of the Census
U.S. Department of Commerce
Washington, DC 20233
www.census.gov
301-457-4100
Fax: 301-457-4714

The Bureau of the Census is a statistical agency that collects, tabulates, and publishes a wide variety of statistical data about the people and the economy of our nation. The Bureau makes available statistical results of its censuses, surveys, and other programs to the public through printed reports, computer tape, CD-ROMs, microfiche, and more. It also produces statistical compendia, catalogues, guides, and directories that are useful in locating information on specific subjects. A fee is charged for some of the information and searches. They can answer such questions as:
1) What is the percentage of people who have a bachelor's degree in a particular state?
2) What percent of women in the U.S. had a child last year?
3) What is the total amount of water area in a given state?
4) What are some statistics available on city government expenditures?
5) What are the 10 fastest growing occupations?

* Crime Statistics
Law Enforcement Support Section
Federal Bureau of Investigation
J. Edgar Hoover Bldg.
935 Pennsylvania Ave.
Washington, DC 20535
www.fbi.gov
202-324-3000

The Law Enforcement Support Section of the Federal Bureau of Investigation collects statistics for many towns with over 10,000 people, and can provide you with information such as the number of murders, robberies, assaults, burglaries, auto thefts, and more, although they do not rank cities. Many libraries carry their annual report, *Crime In The U.S.*, for which there is a cost. They can run a search on their database for specific information, although there is a fee assessed for this service. They can answer questions such as:
1) When weapons are involved in a crime, which ones are most frequently used?
2) How has the rate of auto theft in the U.S. changed over the past five years?
3) Is Washington, DC still the murder capitol of the U.S.?
4) Have the number of murders committed changed since the death penalty was reinstituted?
5) What is the difference in the rate of burglaries from small towns to major metropolitan areas?

* Economics: National and Regional
Bureau of Economic Analysis
U.S. Department of Commerce
Washington, DC 20230
www.bea.doc.gov
202-606-9900
Fax: 202-606-5310

The Bureau of Economic Analysis (BEA) provides information on national and regional economics. BEA collects basic information on such key issues as economic growth, inflation, regional development, and the nation's role in the world economy. It distributes a number of publications that measure, analyze, and forecast economic trends, which are available on recorded messages, online through the Economic Bulletin Board, and in BEA reports. They can answer such questions as:
1) What is the average per capita income in the United States?
2) Will the rate of inflation increase or decrease over the next five years, and by what percent?
3) What percentage of the Gross National Product (GNP) does the government spend on health care?
4) How does the United States' national unemployment rate compare to that of other industrialized countries?
5) What was the unemployment rate in Pennsylvania from 1989 to 1993?

* Educational Research
U.S. Department of Education, OERI
555 New Jersey Ave., NW
Washington, DC 20208-5641
www.ed.gov/offices/OERI
800-424-1616
202-219-1556
Fax: 202-219-1321

The Education Information Branch staff specialists can provide information on topics such as early childhood education, elementary and secondary education, higher education, adult and vocational education, education finance, longitudinal statistical studies, and special education. They have publications and reports, many of which are free. They can answer such questions as:
1) What statistics are there on the number of students who receive loans, grants, and work/study assistance from state sources?

Statistics

2) What are the statistics on private postsecondary education, such as enrollment, earned degrees conferred, and full and part-time faculty members and their salaries?
3) What information is available on how to choose a school for a child and what factors make a school a good one?
4) How can parents help their children become better readers?
5) What are the enrollment outcomes for recent master's and bachelor's degree recipients?

* Fishery Statistics Division

NOAA Fisheries Headquarters
1335 East-West Highway, SSMC3
Silver Spring, MD 20910
www.nmfs.gov

301-713-2328
Fax: 301-713-4137

The Fisheries Statistics Division publishes statistical bulletins on marine recreational fishing and commercial fishing, and on the manufacture and commerce of fishery products. This Division has several annual and biannual reports available. They can answer such questions as:
1) How many fish were imported in a year, and what kind?
2) What is the most popular fish to export?
3) What kinds of fish are frozen?
4) What statistics exist on processed fish?
5) How many fish were caught by weekend fishermen?

* Clearinghouse on Health Indexes

National Center for Health Statistics
U.S. Department of Health and Human Services
Public Health Service
6525 Belcrest Rd.
Hyattsville, MD 20782
www.cdc.gov/nchswww/default.htm

301-436-8500

The National Center for Health Statistics provides information assistance in the development of health measures to health researchers, administrators, and planners. The Clearinghouse's definition of a health index is a measure that summarizes data from two or more components and purports to reflect the health status of an individual or defined group. Services provided to users include annotated bibliographies and reference and referral service. A publications catalogue is available, with items ranging in price from free to $20. They can answer such questions as:
1) What are the characteristics of persons with and without health care coverage?
2) What type of health care is generally provided to adolescents?
3) What method of contraception is used most frequently in the U.S.?
4) What data exists on the current living arrangements of women of childbearing ages in the U.S.?
5) What survey data exists on the firearm mortality rate among children?

* United States International Trade Commission

Office of Industries
500 E St., SW
Washington, DC 20436
www.usitc.gov/

202-205-3296
Fax: 202-205-3161

The Office of Industries at the U.S. International Trade Commission has experts assigned to every commodity imported into the U.S. These experts are responsible for investigation of the customs laws of the United States and foreign countries, the volume of imports in comparison with domestic production, the effects relating to competition of foreign industries, and all other factors affecting competition between articles of the U.S. and imported articles. They are knowledgeable about the domestic and foreign industry, and have statistical and factual information. They also have information regarding the tariff schedules. There is no charge for this information. They can answer such questions as:
1) What is the rate of duty for a product from a particular country?
2) What is the rate of import-export, the size of the market, and the major producers of women's sweaters?
3) How much of a product is exported and what is the size of the potential market for that product?
4) What happens if someone suspects an imported article is being subsidized or sold at less then fair value?
5) What can a company do if they feel they are being unfairly affected by import trade?

* Justice Statistics Clearinghouse

Bureau of Justice Statistics
U.S. Department of Justice
Box 6000
Rockville, MD 20849
E-mail: askncjrs@aspensys.com
www.ncjrs.org

800-732-3277
Fax: 301-251-5212

The Bureau of Justice Statistics (BJS) supports this Clearinghouse for those seeking crime and criminal justice data. In addition to distributing BJS publications, the Clearinghouse responds to statistics requests by offering document database searches, statistics information packages, referrals, and other related products and services. They can answer such questions as:
1) What is the annual national estimate of crime against persons and households?
2) What are the characteristics of victims?
3) In what ways are juveniles handled differently from adults in the criminal justice system?
4) How prevalent is organized crime?
5) What is the recidivism rate, and when criminals are rearrested, with what crimes are they normally charged?

* Labor Statistics Clearinghouse

Office of Publications
Bureau of Labor Statistics
U.S. Department of Labor
2 Massachusetts Ave., NE, Room 2863
Washington, DC 20212
E-mail: labstat.helpdesk@ bls.gov
http://stats.bls.gov

202-606-7828
Fax: 202-606-7890

The Bureau of Labor Statistics (BLS) is the principal data-gathering agency of the federal government in the field of labor economics. The Bureau collects, processes, analyzes, and disseminates data relating to employment, unemployment, and other characteristics of the labor force; prices and consumer expenditures; wages, other worker compensation, and industrial relations; productivity; economic growth and employment projections; and occupational safety and health. This office can also provide you with a release schedule for BLS major economic indicators and the recorded message number. BLS can refer you to experts within the Bureau who can answer your specific question, provide you with historical information, and refer you to tables and charts for data. The BLS has publications, periodicals, magnetic tapes, diskettes, and more for sale. They can answer questions such as:
1) What are the employment statistics and the outlook for a particular occupation?
2) What is the unemployment rate for a state?
3) What is the current wage for a word processor in Seattle, and what benefits are normally offered with such a position?
4) What is the employment projection for a specific job?
5) What is the consumer/producer price index, and how has it changed over time?

Index

A

Abatement
    asbestos, 524
Academic standards, 521
Accidents
    boating, 524, 540
Accountants, 263, 338
Accounting video, 299
Acid rain, 527
Acne, 531
Acute care facilities, 188
Adopt-a-Horse program, 418
Adoption, 521
Adult education, 520
Advertising, 262
    food, 509
    fraud, 509
    laws, 260
    tobacco, 509
    video, 300
Aerial photographs, 525
Aerospace, 396
    technology, 529
Affirmative action, 262
Affordable housing, 193
Africa
    fax retrieval system, 402
    teaching about, 522
Afro-Americans
    folk music, 541
Agency for Health Care Policy, 534
Agency for International Development, 395, 539
AgExport Action Kit, 399
Aging research, 531
Agricultural Statistics Board, 507, 544
Agriculture
    conservation, 186
    exporting, 399
    exporting magazine, 403
    Farm Loan Filings, 330
    Food and Security Act of 1986, 330
    foreign experts, 394
    foreign trade, 496
    library, 496
    loans to agricultural businesses, 53
    loans, 46
    overseas trade offices, 399
    research, 496
    statistics, 359, 496, 544
    subsidies, 47
    videos, 301
Agriculture, U.S. Department of
    housing, 420
    SBIR grants, 241
AIDS, 533
    hotline, 531
Air bags, 514
Air pollution
    hotline, 524
    indoor, 290
    permits, 524
Air quality
    in buildings, 288
Aircraft, 544
Airlines, 544
    small towns, 49
Airports, 544
    capacity, 513
    grants, 49
    traffic, 513
Alabama
    Better Business Bureau, 348
    bill status information, 414
    business assistance, 55
    business financing, 55
    Center for the Advancement of Developing Industries, 303
    company directories, 344
    corporation information, 325
    data centers, 364
    district courts, 439
    driver information, 387
    EPA office, 295
    exports, 56
    federal procurement assistance, 237
    housing office, 420
    housing programs, 194
    HUD office, 422
    international trade offices, 406
    inventors assistance, 253
    IRS libraries, 450
    IRS problem resolution centers, 460
    labor office, 372
    licensed professionals, 339
    loan programs, 160
    motor vehicle information, 387
    OSHA office, 290
    Patent Depository Library, 246
    productivity specialists, 312
    SBA offices, 56
    securities office, 335
    Small Business Development Centers, 132
    state information, 499
    state planning office, 382
    state procurement office, 242
    state recycling office, 286
    state tax assistance, 493
    statistical abstracts, 377
    surplus property auctions, 429
    tax form distribution center, 468
    tax hotlines, 464
    tax incentives, 55
    technology transfer programs, 308
    technology-oriented assistance, 303
    trade experts, 404
    unclaimed property office, 435
    Uniform Commercial Code Office, 330
    venture capital, 211
    venture capital clubs, 207
    women and minorities, 56
    women business assistance, 277
    women's business ownership representative, 273
    women's commission, 281
Alaska
    Better Business Bureau, 348
    bill status information, 414
    Bureau of Land Management office, 418, 419
    business assistance, 56
    business financing, 56
    company directories, 344
    corporation information, 325
    data centers, 364
    district courts, 439
    EPA office, 295
    exports, 57
    federal procurement assistance, 237
    housing office, 420
    housing programs, 194
    HUD office, 422
    international trade offices, 406

Index

inventors assistance, 253
IRS libraries, 450
IRS problem resolution centers, 460
labor office, 372
licensed professionals, 339
OSHA office, 290
Patent Depository Library, 246
productivity specialists, 312
recycling office, 286
SBA offices, 57
securities office, 335
Small Business Development Centers, 133
state information, 499
state planning office, 382
state procurement office, 242
state tax assistance, 493
statistical abstracts, 377
surplus property auctions, 429
tax form distribution center, 468
tax hotlines, 464
tax incentives, 57
technology transfer programs, 308
technology-oriented assistance, 303
trade experts, 404
unclaimed property office, 435
Uniform Commercial Code Division, 330
venture capital, 211
women business assistance, 277
women's business ownership representatives, 273
women's commission, 281

Alberta
    Better Business Bureaus, 351

Alcohol
    blood pressure, 535
    clearinghouse, 531
    distribution, 518
    in the workplace, 288
    production, 518

Alcohol abuse
    video, 299

Algae
    edible, 507

All-terrain vehicles, 515
Allergies, 531
Alternative Farming Systems Information Center, 507-508
Alzheimer's disease, 531
Ambulatory care, 536
American Folklife Center, 540
American Home-Based Business Association, 260
American Indians
    see Native Americans
American Society of Association Executives, 353
Americans with Disabilities Act, 223
Angioplasty, 534
Animal rights, 507
Animal Welfare Information Center, 507, 514

Animals
    ethical issues, 507
    research, 507

Anorexia nervosa, 508
Anthropology
    teaching, 522
Anti-cancer drugs, 532
Anti-Trust Guide for Association Members, 353

Apartments
    cooperative, 188
    experimental construction, 191
    loans, 189

Aphasia, 532
Apparel, 396
Apprentices, 262
Aquaculture, 528
    farm ownership loans, 46
Aquaculture Information Center, 507
Aquatic plants, 507
Archeology digs, 528
Architects, 338

Architecture
    Native American, 540
    photographs, 542

Arizona
    Better Business Bureau, 348
    bill status information, 414
    Bureau of Land Management office, 418, 419
    business assistance, 57
    business financing, 58
    company directories, 344
    corporation information, 325
    data centers, 364
    district courts, 439
    driver information, 388
    EPA office, 295
    exports, 58
    federal procurement assistance, 237
    housing office, 420
    housing programs, 195
    HUD office, 422
    international trade offices, 406
    inventors assistance, 253
    IRS libraries, 450
    IRS problem resolution centers, 460
    labor office, 372
    licensed professionals, 339
    loan programs, 160
    motor vehicle information, 388
    OSHA office, 290
    Patent Depository Library, 246
    productivity specialists, 312
    recycling office, 286
    SBA offices, 58
    securities office, 335
    Small Business Development Centers, 133
    state information, 499
    state planning office, 382
    state procurement office, 242
    state tax assistance, 493
    statistical abstracts, 377
    surplus property auctions, 429
    tax form distribution center, 468
    tax hotlines, 464
    tax incentives, 58
    technical assistance, 177
    trade experts, 404
    unclaimed property office, 435
    Uniform Commercial Code Department, 330
    venture capital, 211
    women and minorities, 58
    women business assistance, 277
    women's business ownership representatives, 273
    women's commission, 281

Arkansas
    Better Business Bureau, 348
    bill status information, 414
    business assistance, 58
    business financing, 58
    company directories, 344
    corporation information, 325
    data centers, 365
    district courts, 439
    driver information, 388
    EPA office, 295
    exports, 59
    federal procurement assistance, 237
    housing office, 420
    housing programs, 195
    HUD office, 422
    international trade offices, 406
    inventors assistance, 253
    IRS libraries, 450
    IRS problem resolution centers, 460
    labor office, 373
    licensed professionals, 339
    loan programs, 160
    motor vehicle information, 388

Index

Arkansas (continued)
    OSHA office, 291
    Patent Depository Library, 246
    productivity specialists, 312
    recycling office, 286
    SBA offices, 59
    securities office, 335
    Small Business Development Centers, 133
    state information, 499
    state planning office, 382
    state procurement office, 242
    state tax assistance, 493
    statistical abstracts, 377
    surplus property auctions, 429
    tax form distribution center, 468
    tax hotlines, 464
    tax incentives, 59
    technical assistance, 177
    technology transfer programs, 308
    technology-oriented assistance, 303
    trade experts, 404
    unclaimed property office, 435
    Uniform Commercial Code Office, 331
    venture capital, 211
    venture capital clubs, 207
    women business assistance, 277
    women's business ownership representative, 273
    women's commission, 282
Arms Control and Disarmament Agency, 538
Arrests overseas, 408
Art exhibits, 427
Art shows
    Smithsonian Institute, 427
Arthritis, 531
Artificial hearts, 535
Artists
    National Park Service contracts, 260
Arts
    performing, 522
    reference services, 496
Asbestos, 261, 294
    in buildings, 290
    ombudsman, 524
    schools, 524
    screening process, 289
Asia
    environmental technology, 397
    fax retrieval system, 402
Assaults, 544
Association for Commuter Transportation, 285
Association Law Handbook, 353
Association Liability, 353
Associations
    Meat Packers Association, 22
    reference sources, 498
Asthma, 531, 534
Astronauts
    toothpaste, 529
At risk students, 522
Atlantic Ocean, 527
Atmosphere, 527
Atmospheric tanks, 525
Auctions
    books, 427
    Customs Service, 424
    Federal Deposit Insurance Corporation, 419
    federal government, 418
    Forest Service, 419
    General Services Administration, 424
    Internal Revenue Service, 425
    ships, 426
    Small Business Administration, 426
    state government, 429
    U.S. Department of Defense, 424
    U.S. Marshals Service, 425
    U.S. Postal Service, 425

Audio recordings
    folklife, 540
Audits, 448
    free legal help, 269, 443
    how to appeal, 448
    tax publications, 444
Australia
    folk songs, 540
Autism, 537
Auto defects, 514
Auto Safety Hotline, 514
Auto thefts, 544
Automation
    mining, 511
Automobiles
    see also cars
    driver's licenses, 387
    electric, 529
    fatalities, 514
    owner registration, 387
    safety, 514
Automotive goods, 396
Avalanches, 526

B

BACT/LAER Clearinghouse, 524
Ballooning, 542
Banking
    Federal Reserve, 509
    industry, 509
Bankruptcy, 266
Banks
    auctions, 419
    discrimination, 271
    recorded messages, 361, 362
Barbers, 338
Base closures, 539
Battlefields
    Revolutionary War, 541
Bell, Alexander Graham, 542
Bell's palsy, 536
Better Business Bureaus, 348
    company background reports, 348
    international, 351
Bicycles
    commuting, 285
Bid protests, 234
Bilingual education, 520
Biofeedback, 535
Biological products, 534
Bipolar disorder, 536
Birth control, 532, 534
Black lung, 511
Blindness, 533
    tax information, 450
Blood, 532, 534
    donating, 532
Blue Sky laws, 335
    exemptions, 335
Board games, 540
Board of Geographic Names, 541
Boating
    accidents, 540
    safety hotline, 524
Bonding, 50
Bonds
    general obligation, 53
    industrial revenue, 53
Bone diseases, 531
Bonsai, 508
Books
    Library of Congress, 427
    rare, 542

Index

Botanic Garden, 508
Botany, 508
    economic, 515
Brain injury, 537
Bread baking
    video, 300
Breast cancer, 532
Breast implants, 534, 535
Breastfeeding, 535
British Columbia
    Better Business Bureaus, 351
Broadcasting
    regulation, 514
Broadsides, 542
Brokerage houses, 509
Brokers
    complaints, 509
Brooklyn Business Library, 30, 352
BRS, 29
Budget
    defense, 539
Budgetrack, 411
Bureau of Alcohol, Tobacco, and Firearms, 518
Bureau of Economic Analysis, 544
Bureau of Indian Affairs, 541
Bureau of Justice Statistics, 518, 545
Bureau of Labor Statistics, 267, 545
Bureau of Land Management, 418, 419, 527
    local offices, 418
Bureau of the Census, 359
Burglaries, 544
Burros
    federal government sales, 418
Bus companies
    grants, 49
Business
    accounting help, 263
    advertising laws, 260
    Americans with Disabilities Act, 223
    business reply mail, 261
    buying recycled products, 288
    complaints, 261
    computers, 261
    consulting services, 54, 132
    customer relations, 262
    debt collection, 262
    Eastern Europe, 509
    economic outlook, 381
    economically disadvantaged, 234
    employee development, 372
    energy efficiency, 288
    experts, 496
    fuel efficient company cars, 285
    home-based, 260
    incubators, 48
    industrial loss control video, 299
    laws, 264
    legal help, 264
    licensing information, 54
    loans, 266
    low-income entrepreneurs, 177
    mail preparation, 261
    mail services, 261
    minority business development, 48
    money to cut down on pollution, 290
    overseas office space, 269, 399
    pay disputes, 267
    planning, 260, 263
    pricing, 260
    proposals, 363
    raising capital, 260
    raising money, 266
    regulations, 264
    site location, 363, 372
    site selection, 54
    state assistance for women, 277
    stress, 266
    tax credits, 266
    tax deductions, 260
    tax preparation, 261
    taxation, 448
    taxes, 261
    wage reporting, 463
    women business ownership representatives, 273
    women owned, 270
    work-at-home franchises, 263
    workshops, 262
    zoning permits, 267
Business consulting
    women, 271
Business development
    minorities, 48
    Native Americans, 48
Business opportunity
    franchising, 227
Business opportunity disclosure laws
    state listing, 228
Business plan
    assistance, 177
    how to write, 132
    video, 299, 300
BusinessCommunications Co. Inc., 353

C

Cable
    regulation, 514
Caffeine, 508
Cake decorating
    video, 300
California
    Better Business Bureau, 348
    bill status information, 414
    Bureau of Land Management office, 418, 419
    business assistance, 59
    business financing, 59
    company directories, 344
    corporation information, 325
    data centers, 365
    district courts, 440
    driver information, 388
    EPA office, 295
    exports, 60
    federal procurement assistance, 237
    franchises, 228
    franchising information, 322
    housing office, 420
    housing programs, 195
    HUD office, 422
    international trade offices, 406
    inventors assistance, 253
    IRS libraries, 450
    IRS problem resolution centers, 460
    labor office, 373
    licensed professionals, 339
    loan programs, 160
    motor vehicle information, 388
    OSHA office, 291
    Patent Depository Library, 246
    productivity specialists, 312
    recycling office, 286
    SBA offices, 60
    securities office, 335
    Small Business Development Centers, 134
    state information, 499
    state planning office, 382
    state procurement office, 242
    state tax assistance, 493
    statistical abstracts, 377
    surplus property auctions, 429
    tax form distribution center, 468

Index

California (continued)
    tax hotlines, 464
    tax incentives, 60
    technical assistance, 177
    technology-oriented assistance, 303
    trade experts, 404
    unclaimed property office, 436
    Uniform Commercial Code Division, 331
    venture capital, 211
    venture capital clubs, 207
    women and minorities, 60
    women business assistance, 277
    women's business ownership representatives, 273
    women's commission, 282
Campaign finance
    state laws, 518
Campgrounds, 527
Camping
    national forests, 526
Canada
    fax retrieval system, 402
    inventors assistance, 259
    National Headquarters For Canadian Better Business Bureaus, 351
    venture capital clubs, 208
Cancer Information Service, 532
Cancer, 532
Candy companies
    Brock, 20
    Burnell's Fine Candy, 20
    E.J Brach, 20
    Farley Candy, 21
    Ferrara Panned Candy, 21
    Herbert Candies, 20
    Herman Goelitz, 20
    Maillard, 20
    Nabisco Confectionery, 20
    Powell Confectionery, 20
Canker sores, 533
Canoeing, 526
Care labeling rule, 264
Careers
    education, 520
    opportunities, 322
    state labor information, 372
Caribbean Basin
    fax retrieval system, 403
Carpal Tunnel Syndrome, 268, 289, 295, 536
    video, 300
Carpool
    publications, 285
Cars
    see also Automobiles
    business expenses, 260
    driver's licenses, 387
    expenses, 267
    fuel efficient, 285
    leasing, 264
    motor vehicle offices, 387
    owner registration, 387
    safety, 514
Catalog of Federal Domestic Assistance, 46, 540
Cataracts, 533
Catfish farming, 507
Cavities, 533
Census Bureau, 544
Center for Development Information and Evaluation, 539
Center for Devices and Radiological Health, 535
Center for Drug Evaluation and Research, 533
Centers for Disease Control, 533
Central and Eastern Europe Business Information Center, 509
Central Intelligence Agency, 538
Cerebral palsy, 534, 537
Certification
    teachers, 522
Certified development companies, 50, 54
Chain saw safety
    video, 300

Chase Econometrics, 29, 30
Chemical hazards
    worker safety, 300
Chemicals
    release of, 525
    spills, 529
    use stats, 507
Chesapeake Bay, 526
Child abuse, 532
Child care, 262, 517
    see also day care
    facilities loans, 53
    home-based business, 267
    how to select, 271
    starting a business, 271
    videos, 271
Child custody, 519
Child development
    videos, 301
Child health, 532
Child safety seats, 514
Child support
    delinquent payments, 445
Childhood education, 521
Children
    accidents, 515
    books, 540
    child support payments, 445
    disabilities, 532
    exploited, 519
    handicapped, 520
    immunization, 533
    missing, 519
    overweight, 508
Children's Center, 540
Cholesterol, 532
    free help for employees, 288
Christmas trees, 418
Chronic fatigue syndrome, 533
Chronic pain, 536
Citizenship requirements, 539
Civil defense, 539
Civil poverty law, 519
Civil War, 541
Clean Air Act, 285, 525
Climate, 524
Climatology, 525
Clinical care, 536
Clinical trials, 531
Clothing
    children's, 515
Cloud cover, 528
Coal mines, 187
Coal production, 511
Coast Guard
    boating programs, 524
    travel, 428
Coastal zones, 528
Cocaine
    school use, 518
Collective bargaining, 511
Colorado
    Better Business Bureaus, 348
    bill status information, 414
    Bureau of Land Management office, 418, 419
    business assistance, 61
    business financing, 61
    company directories, 344
    corporation information, 325
    data centers, 365
    district courts, 440
    driver information, 388
    EPA office, 295
    exports, 61
    federal procurement assistance, 237
    help for women entrepreneurs, 271
    housing office, 420

Index

housing programs, 195
HUD office, 422
international trade offices, 406
inventors assistance, 253
IRS libraries, 451
IRS problem resolution centers, 460
labor office, 373
licensed professionals, 339
loan programs, 162
motor vehicle information, 388
OSHA office, 291
Patent Depository Library, 246
productivity specialists, 312
recycling office, 286
SBA offices, 61
securities office, 335
Small Business Development Centers, 135
state information, 499
state planning office, 382
state procurement office, 242
state tax assistance, 493
statistical abstracts, 377
surplus property auctions, 429
tax form distribution center, 468
tax hotlines, 464
tax incentives, 61
technical assistance, 178
technology transfer programs, 308
technology-oriented assistance, 303
trade experts, 404
unclaimed property office, 436
Uniform Commercial Code Division, 331
venture capital, 212
venture capital clubs, 207
women and minorities, 61
women business assistance, 277
women's business ownership representatives, 273
women's commission, 282
Commerce Business Daily, 236
Commerce Clearing House, 30, 413
Commerce, U.S. Department of
    foreign industry experts, 396
    franchise information, 230
    hotlines, 361
    technical assistance, 302
Commercial fishing, 526, 545
Commercial News USA, 403
Commissions, women, 281
Commodities
    agricultural, 538
    foreign marketing, 400
    grants, 46
    loans, 46
    production, 507
Commodity Futures Trading Commission, 509
Communication disorders, 532
Communications
    regulations, 514
Communities
    Community Development Block grants, 54
    tax assistance, 445
Community colleges, 521
Community development, 515
Commuting
    bicycles, 285
Companies
    background reports, 348
    case studies, 321
    Dun & Bradstreet reports, 316
    financial information, 316
    information sources, 316
    public documents, 324
    state labor information, 372
    state level information, 317
Complaints
    brokers, 509
    franchising, 228

handling, 261
housing discrimination, 515
pensions, 516
radio, 514
securities, 512
television, 514
Composting, 507, 508, 528
    video, 301
CompuServe, 29
Computers
    assisted testing, 520
    business, 261
    educational, 521
    personal computers, 28
    screens, 261
    site evaluation software, 363
    terminals, 268
    video, 301
Condominiums
    loans, 189
    mortgage insurance, 187
Condoms, 535
Confederate States, 542
Congress, U.S., 410
    Bill Status Office, 269, 355
    caucuses, 356, 411
    Congressional Budget Office, 412
    Congressional committees, 355
    Congressional Information Service, 356
    Congressional Research Service, 412
    Freedom of Information, 35
    Freedom of Information laws, 32
    investigations, 411
    market studies, 354
    reports on the environment, 290
    special reports, 411
Congressional Caucus for Women's Issues, 272
Congressional hearings
    prepared testimony, 355
    published reports, 355
    unedited transcripts, 355
Congressional Quarterly, 30, 356
Congressional Research Service, 540
    archived issue briefs, 357
    current issue briefs, 357
    index, 356
    reports, 356
    studies, 355
    updates, 357
Congressmen, 354
    federal procurement help, 236
Connecticut
    Better Business Bureaus, 348
    bill status information, 414
    business assistance, 62
    business financing, 62
    company directories, 344
    corporation information, 325
    data centers, 365
    district courts, 440
    driver information, 388
    EPA office, 295
    exports, 62
    federal procurement assistance, 237
    housing office, 420, 421
    housing programs, 196
    HUD office, 422
    international trade offices, 406
    inventors assistance, 253
    IRS libraries, 451
    IRS problem resolution centers, 460
    labor office, 373
    licensed professionals, 339
    loan programs, 162
    motor vehicle information, 388
    OSHA office, 291
    Patent Depository Library, 246

Index

Connecticut *(continued)*
    productivity specialists, 312
    recycling office, 286
    SBA offices, 63
    securities office, 335
    Small Business Development Centers, 135
    state information, 499
    state planning office, 382
    state procurement office, 242
    state tax assistance, 493
    statistical abstracts, 377
    surplus property auctions, 429
    tax form distribution center, 468
    tax hotlines, 464
    tax incentives, 62
    technical assistance, 178
    technology transfer programs, 308
    technology-oriented assistance, 303
    trade experts, 404
    unclaimed property office, 436
    Uniform Commercial Code Division, 331
    venture capital, 213
    venture capital clubs, 207
    women and minorities, 62
    women's business ownership representatives, 273
    women's commission, 282
Conservation
    agricultural, 186
    help for businesses, 288
    loans, 186
    soil and water, 186, 187
Construction
    bonding, 234
    international, 396
    nuclear, 527
    recorded messages, 361
    state housing programs, 195
Consumer Information Center, 264
Consumer Price Index
    recorded messages, 361
Consumer Product Safety Commission, 266, 288, 514
Consumers
    complaint handling, 261
    complaints, 262
    fraud, 515
    injuries, 514
    product recalls, 266
Contact lenses, 533, 535
Continuing education, 521
Contraception, 532
Contracting
    bonding, 50
    set-asides, 271
Contractors
    defense, 539
    federal, 512
Control Data Corp., 30
Conway Data, Inc., 30
Cooling-off rule, 264
Cooperative apartments, 188
Cooperative Extension Services, 262
Cooperatives
    financing, 190
    loans, 189
Copernicus, 542
Copyrights, 245
    Copyright Office, 249
    how to obtain, 249
Coral reefs, 529
Cordless power tools, 529
Corporations, 267
    8-K's, 316
    Annual Report to Stockholders, 316
    Better Business Bureau reports, 348
    CEO, 344
    computer systems, 344
    computer tape files, 325
    custom services, 325
    databases, 344
    export market, 344
    financial statements, 316
    industry trends, 344
    key personnel, 344
    mailing labels, 324
    mailing lists, 344
    manufacturing, 344
    marketing information, 344
    microfiche and microfilm, 325
    new companies, 325
    online access, 325
    products, 344
    public, 316
    public documents, 324
    SIC codes, 344
    state directories, 344
    state divisions, 325
    state information, 324
    state offices, 317
    tax statistics, 439
Cosmetics, 534
Cosmetologists, 338
Council of State Governments, 413
Counseling, 520
Countries
    information, 538
Country experts, 392
Country houses
    fix-up loans, 187, 192
County Cooperative Extension Service, 262, 271
Courts
    child testimony, 519
    juvenile, 519
Crash test results, 514
Creative Strategies Research International, 353
Credit
    age discrimination, 514
    business issues, 262
    fair billing, 514
    recorded messages, 361
    repair, 262
    reporting, 514
    state mortgages, 194
    women and credit histories, 270
Credit cards
    fraud, 515
Credit Practices Division, 271
Credit unions, 50
    charters, 514
    federal, 514
Crib death, 537
Crime
    databases, 497
    drug treatment, 518
    drug-related, 518
    insurance, 262
    juvenile, 518
    postal, 264
    statistics, 359, 497, 544
    tax investigations, 445
    victims, 519
Criminal justice
    efficiency, 518
    reference service, 518
Crops, 507
    growth rates, 544
    wildlife damage, 544
Cultural exchange
    foreign experts, 395
Cultural heritage, 527
Curriculum development, 521
Customs Service, 272, 538
    auctions, 424
    public auction line, 424
    regulations, 409

Index

D

Dairy, 507
Dance, 542
Data centers
    state listing, 364
Data Resources, 30
Databases
    bibliographic, 29
    commercial vendors, 28
    computerized, 352
    congressional bills, 411
    corporations, 344
    crime, 497
    driver's license, 387
    export contacts, 398
    federal legislation, 410
    free, 29
    Gale Directory of Databases, 352
    government and commercial, 322
    information brokers, 352
    international energy, 401
    LEGIS, 355
    marketing information, 352
    online, 28
    patents and trademarks, 249
    pros and cons, 28
    state statistical data, 382
    trade leads, 406
    wholesalers, 30
Date rape, 518
Day care
    see also child care
    abuse, 519
    starting a center, 521
Deafness, 532
Death penalty, 544
Deaths
    consumer products, 514
    job-related, 536
    overseas, 409
    weather-related, 524
Debt
    cancellation, 266
    collateral, 330
    collection, 262
    online search access, 330
    personal or corporate, 330
Decision Resources, Inc., 353
Deer management, suburban
    video, 301
Defense contractors, 539
Defense cuts
    and home loans, 190
Defense Logistics Agency, 236
Defense Technical Information Center, 538
Defense, U.S. Department of
    auctions, 424
    property auctions, 424
    SBIR grants, 241
    selling to the military, 234
    surplus furniture, 260
Delaware
    Better Business Bureau, 348
    bill status information, 414
    business assistance, 63
    business financing, 63
    company directories, 344
    corporation information, 325
    data centers, 365
    district courts, 440
    driver information, 388
    EPA office, 295
    exports, 64
    federal procurement assistance, 237
    housing office, 420
    housing programs, 196
    HUD office, 422
    international trade offices, 406
    inventors assistance, 253
    IRS libraries, 451
    IRS problem resolution centers, 460
    labor office, 373
    licensed professionals, 339
    loan programs, 162
    motor vehicle information, 388
    OSHA office, 291
    Patent Depository Library, 246
    productivity specialists, 312
    recycling office, 286
    SBA offices, 64
    securities office, 335
    Small Business Development Centers, 136
    state information, 499
    state planning office, 382
    state procurement office, 242
    state tax assistance, 493
    statistical abstracts, 377
    surplus property auctions, 429
    tax form distribution center, 468
    tax hotlines, 464
    tax incentives, 63
    trade experts, 404
    unclaimed property office, 436
    Uniform Commercial Code Section, 331
    venture capital, 213
    women business assistance, 277
    women's business ownership representatives, 273
    women's commission, 282
Delphi, 29
Demographics, 359
    foreign, 400
    global, 401
    international, 396
    state labor offices, 371
    statistics, 359, 497
Dental disease, 533
Dental sealants, 533
Depreciation, 267
Depression, 534, 536
Design, 542
Diabetes, 533
DIALOG, 29, 30
Dialog Information Services, 352
Diet
    elderly, 531
    pills, 509
Diets, 507
Digestive diseases, 533
Diplomatic records, 539
Direct payments
    federal, 46
    housing, 186
Directories
    contracting, 234
    export/import, 405
    exporting sources, 403
    industry, 381
    state company directories, 344
    state information, 318
Disabilities
    Americans with Disabilities Act, 223
    business grants, 52
    children, 532
    clearinghouse, 533
    housing, 190
    Job Accommodation Network, 223
    publications, 224
    regional technical assistance centers, 223
    veterans, 51
    women, 272
Disability insurance, 516

Index

Disasters
    business loans, 50
    federal help, 539
    housing loans, 188
    loans, 50
    property recovery, 186
Discipline
    school, 520
Disclosure reports, 512
Discrimination
    banking, 271
    employment, 518
    housing, 515
    sexual, 268, 272
Disease
    diet-related, 507
    outbreaks, 533
District of Columbia
    Better Business Bureau, 348
    business assistance, 64
    business financing, 64
    corporation information, 326
    data centers, 365
    district courts, 440
    driver information, 388
    EPA office, 295
    exports, 64
    federal procurement assistance, 237
    housing programs, 196
    HUD office, 422
    information, 500
    international trade offices, 407
    inventors assistance, 254
    IRS libraries, 451
    IRS problem resolution centers, 460
    labor office, 373
    licensed professionals, 339
    loan programs, 162
    motor vehicle information, 388
    OSHA office, 291
    Patent Depository Library, 246
    Recorder of Deeds, 331
    recycling office, 286
    SBA offices, 65
    securities office, 336
    Small Business Development Centers, 136
    state planning office, 382
    state procurement office, 242
    statistical abstracts, 378
    surplus property auctions, 429
    tax form distribution center, 468
    tax hotlines, 464
    tax incentives, 64
    technical assistance, 178
    trade experts, 404
    unclaimed property office, 436
    venture capital, 213
    venture capital clubs, 207
    women and minorities, 64
    women's business ownership representatives, 273
    women's commission, 282
Doctors
    office mortgages, 191
Domestic violence, 519
Doorknobs, 529
Dow Jones, 30
Down Syndrome, 532
Drake University, 251
Drinking water, 524
Dropouts
    rate, 520
    urban, 523
Droughts
    occurrence rate, 524
Drug abuse, 515
    criminals, 518
    employee assistance programs, 299
    testing, 299
    video, 299
Drug Enforcement Agency
    drug dealer property, 425
Drug Information and Strategy Clearinghouse, 515, 535
Drug products, 263, 533
Drug trafficking, 515
Drug-Free Workplace programs
    video, 299
Drugs
    in the workplace, 288
    over-the-counter, 509, 533
Drunk driving, 514
Dry cleaning, 536
Dun & Bradstreet reports, 316
Duty fees, 538

E

E.G.& G. Dynatrend
    property auctions, 424
Ear infections, 532
Early childhood education, 521
Earned income credit, 267
Earnings
    recorded messages, 361
    women, 517
Earth Resources Observation Systems, 525
Earth Science Information Centers, 525
Earthquakes
    California, 525
    clearinghouse, 525
    highways, 526
    preparation, 539
Eastern Europe
    marketing, 397
Eastern States
    Bureau of Land Management offices, 419
EASYNET, 30
Economic growth, 544
Economic Research Service, 507, 510
Economics
    county business patterns, 371
    data, 497
    foreign countries, 496
    foreign experts, 394
    foreign, 394
    international, 400, 401
    recorded messages, 361, 362
    state labor data, 372
    statistics, 359
    tax analysis, 448
    videos, 301
    world trade, 496
Education
    bilingual, 520
    career, 520
    childhood, 521, 544
    clearinghouses, 497
    counseling, 520
    courses on the tax system, 449
    early childhood, 521
    elementary, 544
    expenses, 267
    finance, 544
    foreign languages, 409
    gifted students, 520
    handicapped, 533
    hotline, 497
    international programs, 402
    statistics, 359
    student tax clinics, 448

Index

tax courses, 447
tax practitioners, 447
tax preparation courses, 442
taxpayer services, 459
teacher, 522
urban, 523
Education, U.S. Department of
    SBIR grants, 241
Educational Resources Information Center (ERIC), 521
Educational technology, 521
Eldercare, 517
Elderly
    election access, 518
    federal tax guide, 450
    housing finance assistance, 194
    rental housing, 189
    supportive housing loans, 189
    tax assistance, 449
    taxes, 443
    video on housing options, 300
Elections
    clearinghouse, 518
    handicap access, 518
    presidential, 518
Electric cars, 529
Electricity
    grants, 47
Electronic Legislative Search System, 411
Electronic openers, 529
Emergencies
    national, 539
    planning, 525
Emergency assistance overseas, 408
Emissions
    air toxic, 524
    clearinghouse, 525
    lowest achievable, 524
Emotional illness, 536
Emphysema, 534
Employee Retirement Income Security Act, 516
Employees
    benefit plans, 267
    rights, 262
    training programs, 54
Employers
    taxes, 267
Employment
    corporate statistics, 344
    discrimination, 518
    federal, 511
    outlook, 511
    projections, 511, 545
    recorded messages, 361
    reference sources, 497
    statistics, 360
Employment Standards Administration, 262
Encephalitis, 533
Encyclopedia of Associations, 321, 353
Energy
    audits on-site, 55
    bills, 524
    carpooling, 285
    conservation business, 268
    conservation grants, 51
    conservation hotline, 289
    conservation loans, 53
    efficiency, 288, 524
    energy-related inventions, 255
    foreign specialists, 394
    fossil, 52
    fuel efficient company cars, 285
    government conservation loans, 285
    house weatherization, 194
    information center, 525
    international, 401, 402
    life-cycle costing, 299
    minorities programs, 511
    patent rights, 51
    reference services, 497
    renewable, 402, 497
    research, 497
    solar, 52, 524
    use in buildings, 299
    utility bills, 288
    wind, 524
    women and minority contracts, 51
Energy efficient lighting
    video, 299
Energy, U.S. Department of
    exporting, 402
    invention evaluations, 251
    SBIR grants, 241
Engineering
    photographs, 542
Enterprise zones, 515
Entertainment
    business-related expenses, 260
Entrepreneur quiz, 263
Entrepreneuring, 512
Entrepreneurs
    women, 270
Environment
    coal mining, 49
    Congressional Research Service Reports, 290
    exporting, 397
    help for businesses, 288
    indoor air pollution, 290
    inventions, 252
    loans to buy energy saving equipment, 285
    locating funds, 526
    oceans, 527
    pollution in your business, 294
    protection, 285
    reports from Capitol Hill, 290
    research, 252
    speakers, 288
    technology, 397
    videos, 301
Environmental education, 522
Environmental Protection Agency
    Clean Air Act, 285
    fuel efficient company cars, 285
    Green Lights Program, 288
    invention evaluations, 252
    regional offices, 297
    SBIR grants, 241
    state offices, 295
Epicenters, 525
Equal Employment Opportunity Commission, 372
ERIC, 521
Estrogen, 533
Estuaries, 527
Europe, Eastern
    fax retrieval system, 402
Exercise
    elderly, 531
Exhaust, 528
Exhibitions, 398
Eximbank, 395
Expenses
    business, 260, 267
Experts, 16
    congressional, 411
    country, 392
    getting information, 17
    government, 24, 265, 498
    industry, 23
    locating an expert, 16
    telephone tips, 17
    value of, 16

Index

Explosives
    laws, 518
    stolen, 518
Exporting, 260
    see also international trade; marketing
    agriculture, 399
    Asia, 397
    assistance, 54, 402
    coal technology, 402
    Commercial News USA, 403
    commodities, 400
    company directories, 405
    counseling, 400, 402
    counseling assistance, 397
    counseling services, 400
    databases, 398
    demographic information, 396, 400, 401
    developing nations, 399
    directory of sources, 403
    Eastern Europe, 395, 397
    environmental, 397
    exhibitions, 398
    fax retrieval system, 402
    financial planning, 401
    financing, 395
    foreign buyers, 398, 406
    foreign labor trends, 403
    foreign market studies, 396
    government assistance, 403
    grants and loans, 406
    guide, 403
    guidebook, 403
    hotline, 392
    international business news, 403
    international trade data, 401
    Japan, 397
    Latin America, 397
    legal assistance, 401
    licensing, 399
    loans, 395
    mailing lists, 396
    national security, 399
    overseas office space, 399
    overseas opportunities, 400
    overseas representatives, 396, 398
    planning services, 401
    price indexes, 400
    procurement, 403
    publications, 403
    regulations, 399, 400
    small business conferences, 395
    small business guide, 404
    Soviet Union (former), 397
    state government assistance, 405
    state money programs, 395
    state programs, 406
    statistics, 497
    technology, 398
    television marketing, 397
    trade fairs, 398
    trade leads databases, 406
    trade lists, 396
    trade locator assistance, 398
    trade opportunities, 398
    video, 300
    video catalog, 398
Exports
    agriculture, 47, 507
    counseling, 510
    financing, 510
    loans, 53
    statistics, 360
Extraterrestrial life, 542
Eye injuries and protection, 289
Eyeglass lenses, 535
Eyes, 533

F

FACS Info Service, Inc., 317
Fair Labor Standards Act, 262
Family history, 541
Family Violence and Sexual Assault Institute, 537
Farm workers
    housing loans, 187
Farmers Home Administration
    emergency disaster loans, 54
    farm loan guarantees, 54
    farm operating loans, 54
    farm ownership loans, 54
    soil and water loans, 54
    youth project loans, 54
Farming
    alternative, 507
    size, 544
Farms
    family, 47
    interest assistance, 46
    loans, 46
FARPS, 30
Fatalities, auto, 514
Federal Assistance Programs Retrieval System, 540
Federal Aviation Administration, 544
Federal Bureau of Investigation, 544
    Freedom of Information Act, 38
Federal Communications Commission, 510, 514
Federal Database Finder, 322
Federal Deposit Insurance Corporation, 514
    auctions, 419
Federal Document Retrieval, Inc., 317
Federal Election Commission, 518
Federal Emergency Management Agency, 539
Federal government
    Offices of Legislative Affairs, 411
Federal Highway Administration
    carpooling, 285
Federal Housing Administration, 419
Federal Information Center, 24, 354
Federal information sources
    airlines, 320
    airports, 320
    bank holding companies, 320
    barge and vessel operators, 320
    cable television system operators, 320
    colleges and schools, 320
    commodity trading advisors, 320
    communication companies, 321
    consumer products, 320
    exporting companies, 320
    foreign corporations, 320
    government contractors, 320
    hospitals and nursing homes, 320
    Land Bank associations, 320
    land developers, 320
    mining companies, 320
    national banks, 320
    nonprofit institutions, 321
    nuclear power plants, 321
    Office of Federal Regulators, 320
    pension plans, 321
    pesticide and chemical manufacturers, 321
    pharmaceutical companies, 321
    radio and television stations, 321
    Savings and Loan associations, 321
    utilities, 320
Federal Labor Relations Authority, 511
Federal Laboratory Consortium, 529
Federal Mediation and Conciliation Service, 511
Federal Procurement Data Center, 233, 512
Federal Reserve System, 509
Federal Trade Commission, 227, 260-267, 509, 515
    Equal Credit Opportunity Act, 271

Index

Franchise and Business Opportunities Rule, 228
    industry reports, 358
    online, 228
    women and credit, 270
Fellowships
    deafness specialists, 537
    minorities, 512
Fertility, 532
Fertilizer runoff, 507
Fertilizers
    chemical, 508
Fetal alcohol syndrome, 531
Fever blisters, 533
Film
    childrens, 540
Finance
    Uniform Commercial Code, 330
Financial assistance overseas, 409
Financial managers
    counseling skills, 301
Financial planning
    video, 300
FINDEX, 353
Fire safety
    video, 300
Firearms
    laws, 518
Firefighters, 529
Firewood
    Forest Service auctions, 419
First aid
    video, 300
Fish
    frozen, 508
    saltwater, 526
Fisheries, 528
    foreign experts, 395
    statistics, 545
Fishermen
    grants, 48
    seized vessels, 49
Fishing
    commercial, 545
    international, 526
    recreational, 545
    videos, 301
Flame retardant materials, 515
Flash floods, 530
Flex time, 517, 520
Flood insurance, 192
Floods
    preparation, 539
    warnings, 530
Floriculture, 508
Florida
    Better Business Bureaus, 348
    bill status information, 414
    business assistance, 65
    business financing, 65
    company directories, 344
    corporation information, 326
    data centers, 365
    district courts, 440
    driver information, 388
    EPA office, 295
    exports, 65
    federal procurement assistance, 237
    housing office, 420
    housing programs, 196
    HUD office, 422
    international trade offices, 407
    inventors assistance, 254
    IRS libraries, 451
    IRS problem resolution centers, 460
    labor office, 373
    licensed professionals, 339
    loan programs, 162
    motor vehicle information, 388
    OSHA office, 291
    Patent Depository Library, 246
    productivity specialists, 312
    recycling office, 286
    SBA offices, 66
    securities office, 336
    Small Business Development Centers, 136
    state information, 500
    state planning office, 382
    state procurement office, 242
    state tax assistance, 493
    statistical abstracts, 378
    surplus property auctions, 430
    tax form distribution center, 468
    tax hotlines, 464
    tax incentives, 65
    technology transfer programs, 308
    technology-oriented assistance, 303
    trade experts, 404
    unclaimed property office, 436
    Uniform Commercial Code Division, 331
    venture capital, 213
    venture capital clubs, 207
    women and minorities, 66
    women business assistance, 278
    women's business ownership representatives, 273
    women's commission, 282
Fluoride, 533
Folklife, 540
Food
    advertising, 509
    composition, 507
    statistics, 359
    surplus, 427
Food and Drug Administration, 263, 534
Food and Nutrition Information Center, 507, 514
Food and Security Act of 1986, 330
Food products, 263
Foodborne illness, 508
Foot care, 533
Forecasts
    weather, 530
Foreign Agricultural Service, 399, 507, 538
Foreign exchange rates
    recorded messages, 361
Foreign experts
    agriculture, 394
    cultural exchange, 395
    economics, 394
    energy, 394
    fisheries, 395
    metric programs, 395
    telecommunications, 395
Foreign investment
    guaranties, 51
    insurance, 51
Foreign languages, 521
    institute, 409
Foreign markets, 392
    market studies, 396
    videos, 398
Foreign policy, 539
Foreign trade
    agriculture, 496
    recorded messages, 361
Forest Service
    auctions, 420
    firewood, 419
    regional offices, 420
Forestry
    videos, 301
Forests
    national, 526
Fortune 500 companies, 260
Fossil energy, 52
Foster care, 521

Index

Franchise and Business Opportunities Rule, 228
Franchise disclosure laws
    state listing, 228
Franchise Opportunities Handbook, 227
Franchises, 227
    Federal Trade Commission, 227
    financial statements, 322
    foreign, 510
    International Franchise Association, 229
    legal information, 230
    publications, 229
    purchasing assistance, 230
    rules and regulations, 228
    state checkpoints, 322
    videos, 230
    work-at-home, 263
Franchising
    reference materials, 230
Fraud
    credit card, 515
    inventions, 250
    mail, 264, 515
Freedom of Information
    1986 amendments, 34, 35, 37
    access denied, 35
    accessible records, 33
    administrative appeal procedures, 38
    administrative appeals, 38, 42
    administrative review, 33
    agency requirements, 35, 40
    agency responses, 43
    amending records, 42
    appeals, 35, 38, 43
    applicability, 33
    books, 32
    business transactions, 32
    citizen's guide, 32
    classified documents, 36
    classified information, 41
    commercial information, 36
    commercial users, 34
    confidential business information, 36
    criminal law enforcement, 41
    disclosure, 32, 33, 35, 39, 41, 43
    exclusions, 37
    exemptions, 32, 35-36, 41
    federal civilian employment, 42
    federal contracts, 42
    Federal Information Center, 39
    fee waivers, 34
    fees, 34, 40
    financial information, 36
    financial institutions, 37
    geological information, 37
    informant records, 38
    judicial appeals, 38, 43
    law enforcement, 37
    lawsuits, 36
    limitations, 33
    litigation records, 42
    making requests, 34
    maps, 32
    medical records, 42
    military service, 42
    Office of Federal Register, 39
    personal privacy, 37
    personnel rules, 36
    photographs, 32
    Privacy Act, 32, 37, 39-43
    protected information, 36
    requests, 32-35, 38, 40, 42, 43
    responses, 35
    sample request letters, 45
    scope of, 32
    security classification, 36
    state offices, 33-35, 38
    state open records laws, 32
    tax code, 36
    violations, 33
Freshwater fish, 507
Frost and Sullivan, Inc., 353
Fuel efficiency, 514
Fuels
    tank storage, 525
Fundraising
    tax implications, 441
Furnaces, 509
Futures trading, 509

G

Gale Directory of Databases, Volume 1: Online Databases, 352
Gale's Encyclopedia of Associations, 19
Gall bladders, 533
Games of chance, 264
Gangs
    youth, 519
Gas mileage, 526
Genealogy, 544
General Accounting Office, 234, 412
    reports, 357
General obligation bonds, 53
General Services Administration, 234
    foreign gifts, 427
        Office of Design and Construction, 234
        procurement, 234
        property auctions, 424
        real estate sales, 426
        regional offices, 425
Generators
    waste, 528
Geochemistry, 526
Geographic information, 525
Geographic names, 541
Geography, 525, 541
    teaching, 522
Geological Survey, U.S., 525
Geology, 525
    inquiries group, 526
    maps, 525
    marine, 526
Geophysics, 525, 526
Georgia
    Better Business Bureaus, 349
    bill status information, 414
    business assistance, 66
    business financing, 66
    company directories, 345
    corporation information, 326
    data centers, 365
    district courts, 440
    driver information, 388
    EPA office, 295
    exports, 67
    federal procurement assistance, 237
    housing office, 420
    housing programs, 196
    HUD office, 422
    international trade offices, 407
    inventors assistance, 254
    IRS libraries, 452
    IRS problem resolution centers, 460
    labor office, 373
    licensed professionals, 340
    loan programs, 163
    motor vehicle information, 388
    OSHA office, 291
    Patent Depository Library, 246
    productivity specialists, 312
    recycling office, 286
    SBA offices, 68

Index

securities office, 336
Small Business Development Centers, 137
state information, 500
state planning office, 383
state procurement office, 242
state tax assistance, 493
statistical abstracts, 378
surplus property auctions, 430
tax form distribution center, 468
tax hotlines, 464
tax incentives, 67
technical assistance, 178
technology transfer programs, 308
technology-oriented assistance, 303
trade experts, 404
unclaimed property office, 436
Uniform Commercial Code, 331
venture capital, 213
women and minorities, 67
women business assistance, 278
women's business ownership representatives, 273
women's commission, 282
Gestational diabetes, 533
Gettysburg Address, 541
Gifts
business-related expenses, 260
Glaciers, 528
Glaucoma, 533
Gold, 511
Government
auctions, 418
experts, 265
locating experts, 498
procurement, 233
state information operators, 318
Government Printing Office, 233
publications on procurement, 234
Government procurement
assistance for veterans, 236
bid and contract protests, 234
Commerce Business Daily, 233, 236
congressional help, 236
Federal Procurement Data Center, 233
help for women, 271, 272
minority and labor surplus area assistance, 236
Office of Small and Disadvantaged Business Utilization, 233
selling to the military, 234
Small Business Administration, 234
small business set-asides, 236
state help, 236
state offices, 237
subcontracting opportunities, 233
surety bonding, 234
U.S. Government Purchasing and Sales Directory, 234
women business owners, 234
women-owned business assistance, 236
Grants
airports, 49
Community Development Block grants, 54
country houses, 187
disabled employees, 52
energy conservation, 51-52
environmental research, 252
exporting, 395, 406
federal, 46, 540
fishermen, 48
food sales, 47
housing, 186, 515, 535
Indian Business Development, 277
inventors, 245
land conservation, 191
low income housing, 191
matching, 53
new technology, 48
overseas travel, 408
pesticide contamination, 46
rural development, 47
small business community, 48
Small Business Innovative Research Grants, 54
technology, 241
training, 395
weatherization, 192
woman-owned businesses, 50
women, 270
Graphic arts, 542
Great Lakes, 528
Greenhouse effect, 524
Gross national product, 544
recorded messages, 361
Guam
IRS libraries, 453
venture capital, 213
Gun safety
video, 300
Guns
distribution, 518
laws, 518

H

Habitat Conservation Program, 526
Hair growth products, 533
Handicapped
education, 520
loans, 533
testing, 520
Hawaii
Better Business Bureaus, 349
bill status information, 414
business assistance, 68
business financing, 68
company directories, 345
corporation information, 326
data centers, 365
district courts, 440
driver information, 388
EPA office, 295
exports, 69
federal procurement assistance, 237
franchises, 228
franchising information, 322
HiTech Business Directory, 303
HiTech Journal, 303
housing office, 420
housing programs, 197
HUD office, 422
international trade offices, 407
inventors assistance, 254
IRS libraries, 453
IRS problem resolution centers, 460
labor office, 373
licensed professionals, 340
loan programs, 163
motor vehicle information, 388
OSHA office, 291
Patent Depository Library, 246
productivity specialists, 312
recycling office, 286
SBA offices, 69
securities office, 336
Small Business Development Centers, 137
state information, 500
state planning office, 383
state procurement office, 242
state tax assistance, 493
statistical abstracts, 378
surplus property auctions, 430
tax form distribution center, 468
tax hotlines, 464
tax incentives, 69
technical assistance, 179

Index

Hawaii (continued)
    technology-oriented assistance, 303
    trade experts, 404
    unclaimed property office, 436
    Uniform Commercial Code Office, 331
    venture capital, 213
    venture capital clubs, 207
    women and minorities, 69
    women business assistance, 278
    women's business ownership representatives, 273
    women's commission, 282
Hazardous materials
    disposal, 290
Health
    education programs, 269
    information center, 534
    insurance, 263
    insurance for divorcees, 272
    reference sources, 497
    research, 497
    rural issues, 508
    statistics, 359, 497
    workplace education programs, 294
    workplace inspection, 268
    workplace issues, 263
Health and Human Services, U.S. Department of
    SBIR grants, 241
Health care
    free, 264
    minorities, 536
    policy, 534
    statistics, 534
    workplace inspections, 290
Health clubs, 515
Health professionals
    shortage areas, 534
Health services administration, 536
Hearing aid dealers, 338
Hearing aids, 532, 535
Hearing disorders, 532
Heart, 534
Heartburn, 533
Heat pumps, 524
Hemodialysis equipment, 535
Hepatitis, 533
Herbicides, 507
Herbs, 508
Heritage Education program, 527
Hiatal hernia, 533
High blood pressure, 534
    free help for employees, 288
Higher education, 544
Hill-Burton law, 264
Hiring discrimination, 518
Hispanic
    loans for entrepreneurs with no money, 160
Historic places, 528
Historic preservation, 508
Historically Black Colleges and Universities
    fellowships, 512
HIV infection, 531
Holder-in-due-course rule, 264
Holograms, 542
Home buying
    video, 300
Home equity
    conversion loans, 190
Home improvement
    country houses, 192
    loans, 189
Home loans, 516
Home-based business
    surplus property auctions, 260
    video, 300-301
Homelessness, 515
    children, 521
    health issues, 535
    Interagency Council, 427
    law issues, 519
Homes
    building inspection, 300
HOPE 3 Program, 423
HOPE program, 191
Horses
    federal government sales, 418
Horticulture, 508
Horticulture Clearinghouse, 515
Horticulture safety
    video, 300
Hospitals
    emergency departments, 515
    experimental construction, 191
    mortgages, 188
Hotlines, 53
    AIDS, 531
    air pollution, 524
    alternative fuels, 285
    auto safety, 514
    boating safety, 524
    copyright forms, 249
    drinking water safety, 524
    economic, 361
    education, 497
    emergency planning, 525
    energy conservation, 289
    exporting, 392
    health, 534
    pesticides, 289, 528
    recycling, 268, 285
    safe drinking water, 294
    seafood, 508
    Small Business Administration, 266
    taxes on retirement plans, 443
    telephone tax assistance, 464
    trade, 510
    wetlands, 530
Housing
    cooperative loans, 189
    development, 515
    direct payments, 186
    disabled persons, 190, 533
    elderly, 189, 515
    environmental hazard removal, 194
    equity loans, 190
    experimental housing loans, 191
    farm labor, 187
    financing agencies, 194
    grants, 186, 515
    home improvement loans, 187
    HUD properties, 421
    insurance refunds, 419
    library, 497
    loans, 186
    low income, 190, 191, 423, 515
    low income rental, 193
    low interest loans, 420
    military home loans, 190
    mortgage insurance, 188
    multifamily equity loans, 191
    multifamily mortgage insurance, 189
    multifamily, 189
    Native American, 192
    nonprofits, 187
    options for seniors, 300
    programs for non-profit organizations, 427
    recorded messages, 361
    reference sources, 497
    rehabilitation loans, 187, 188
    rental, 189, 193
    repossessed homes, 418
    Rural Housing and Community Development Service, 420
    rural, 192
    Section 8, 191
    special credit risks, 192

Index

state money, 194
U.S. Department of Agriculture, 420
veterans, 423
videos, 515
Housing and Urban Development, U.S. Department of, 419
HOPE 3 Program, 423
HUD USER, 515
Human rights
foreign countries, 538
Humidifiers, 527
Humidity, 529
Hurricanes
photographs, 525
predicting, 527
preparation, 539
Hydrology, 525
Hyperactivity, 532

I

I.P. Sharp, 30
Ice, 528
Idaho
Better Business Bureaus, 349
bill status information, 415
Bureau of Land Management office, 418, 419
business assistance, 69
business financing, 70
company directories, 345
corporation information, 326
data centers, 366
district courts, 440
driver information, 388
EPA office, 295
exports, 70
federal procurement assistance, 237
housing office, 420
housing programs, 197
HUD office, 422
international trade offices, 407
inventors assistance, 254
IRS libraries, 453
IRS problem resolution centers, 461
labor office, 373
licensed professionals, 340
loan programs, 163
motor vehicle information, 388
OSHA office, 291
Patent Depository Library, 246
productivity specialists, 312
recycling office, 286
SBA offices, 70
securities office, 336
Small Business Development Centers, 137
state information, 500
state planning office, 383
state procurement office, 242
state tax assistance, 493
statistical abstracts, 378
surplus property auctions, 430
tax form distribution center, 468
tax hotlines, 464
tax incentives, 70
technology transfer programs, 308
trade experts, 404
unclaimed property office, 436
Uniform Commercial Code Division, 331
venture capital, 213
venture capital clubs, 207
women's business ownership representatives, 273
women's commission, 282
Illinois
Better Business Bureaus, 349
bill status information, 415

business assistance, 70
business financing, 71
company directories, 345
corporation information, 326
data centers, 366
district courts, 440
driver information, 388
EPA office, 295
exports, 72
federal procurement assistance, 237
franchises, 228
franchising information, 322
housing office, 420
housing programs, 197
HUD office, 422
international trade offices, 407
inventors assistance, 254
IRS libraries, 453
IRS problem resolution centers, 461
labor office, 373
licensed professionals, 340
loan programs, 163
loans for women entrepreneurs, 270
motor vehicle information, 388
OSHA office, 291
Patent Depository Library, 246
productivity specialists, 312
recycling office, 286
SBA offices, 72
securities office, 336
Small Business Development Centers, 138
state information, 500
state planning office, 383
state procurement office, 242
state tax assistance, 493
statistical abstracts, 378
surplus property auctions, 430
tax form distribution center, 468
tax hotlines, 464
tax incentives, 71
technical assistance, 179
technology transfer programs, 308
trade experts, 404
unclaimed property office, 436
Uniform Commercial Code Division, 331
venture capital, 213
venture capital clubs, 207
women and minorities, 72
women business assistance, 278
women's business advocates, 278
women's business ownership representatives, 273
women's commission, 282
Immigration and Naturalization Service, 539
Immunization, 533
Immunologic diseases, 531
Importing
statistics, 360, 497
Impotence, 535
Income
per capita, 544
recorded messages, 361, 362
Incubator programs, 303
Indian Health Services, 535
Indian reservations
housing, 192
Indiana
Better Business Bureaus, 349
bill status information, 415
bonds, 73
business assistance, 72
business financing, 72
company directories, 345
corporation information, 326
data centers, 366
district courts, 440
driver information, 389
EPA office, 296

Index

Indiana (continued)
- exports, 74
- federal procurement assistance, 237
- franchises, 228
- franchising information, 322
- grants, 73
- housing office, 420
- housing programs, 197
- HUD office, 422
- international trade offices, 407
- inventors assistance, 254
- IRS libraries, 453
- IRS problem resolution centers, 461
- labor office, 373
- licensed professionals, 340
- loan programs, 164
- loans, 72
- motor vehicle information, 389
- OSHA office, 291
- Patent Depository Library, 247
- productivity specialists, 313
- recycling office, 286
- resources, 72
- SBA offices, 74
- securities office, 336
- Small Business Development Centers, 139
- state information, 500
- state planning office, 383
- state procurement office, 242
- state tax assistance, 493
- statistical abstracts, 378
- surplus property auctions, 430
- tax form distribution center, 468
- tax hotlines, 464
- tax incentives, 73
- technical assistance, 179
- technology transfer programs, 308
- technology-oriented assistance, 303
- trade experts, 404
- unclaimed property office, 436
- Uniform Commercial Code Division, 331
- venture capital, 214
- women and minorities, 74
- women business assistance, 278
- women's business ownership representatives, 273
- women's commission, 282

Indians, American
- see Native Americans

Indoor Air Quality Information Clearinghouse, 288, 294
Indoor air quality, 527
Industrial relations, 545
Industrial revenue bonds, 53
Industrial waste, 528
Industry, 510
- analysts, 321, 353
- directories, 381
- experts, 321, 396, 496
- observers, 321
- recorded messages, 362
- sources, 321
- suppliers, 321
- trade associations, 321
- trade magazines, 321

Industry Trends and Analysis, 353
Infectious diseases, 531
Inflation rate, 544
InfoNation, 396
Information
- competitors, 25
- government experts, 24
- identifying industry sources, 24
- industry observers, 25
- manufacturers, 25
- research techniques, 19
- suppliers, 25
- techniques, 26

Information brokers, 352

Information for Public Affairs, 413
Information USA, Inc., 22, 24, 316
Injuries
- consumer products, 514

Inner cities
- education, 523

Insects
- organic control, 508
- pest control, 508

Insulin, 533
Insurance, 46
- credit unions, 514
- crime, 262
- disability, 516
- flood, 192
- foreign investment, 51
- health, 263, 272
- health insurance for divorcees, 272
- housing loans, 186
- mortgage, 188

Insurance agents, 338
Intelligence, foreign, 538
Interagency Council on the Homeless, 427
Interest rates, 516
- recorded messages, 362

Interior, U.S. Department of
- Adopt-a-Horse program, 418

Internal Revenue Bulletin, 445
Internal Revenue Service, 260, 266, 517
- Debt Offset Program, 445
- Director's Newsletter, 447
- district offices, 446
- free CD-ROM for small business, 300
- free publications, 468
- international offices, 445
- international telephone numbers, 448
- Learning Vault website, 463
- libraries, 450
- Practitioner Institutes, 447
- Problem Resolution Centers, 460
- Problem Resolution Program, 269
- property auctions, 425
- public opinion surveys, 443
- publications and forms, 469
- research, 446
- Service Centers, 446
- speakers, 446
- Statistics of Income, 439
- tax form distribution centers, 468

International Demographic Center, 30
International Franchise Association, 229
International Resource Development Inc., 353
International trade, 392
- *see also exporting; marketing*
- experts, 404
- International Visitors Program, 403
- investment opportunities, 398
- National Trade Data Bank, 401
- online, 401
- opportunities, 398, 400
- price indexes, 400
- publications, 403
- recorded messages, 362
- state offices, 406
- state specialists, 404
- trade fairs and missions, 398

International Trade Administration, 25
- country desk officers, 392
- industry reports, 357

International Trade Commission, 25, 545
- market studies, 356
- publications, 356

International Venture Capital Institute, 206
Internships
- museums, 522

Inventors
- associations, 54

Index

copyrights, 245
disclosure statements, 245
energy-related inventions, 51, 255
evaluations, 251
free help, 251
groups, 253
loans, 53
organizations, 251
patents, 245-246
pollution abatement, 252
scams, 250
Small Business Innovative Research Grants, 54
state sources for help, 253
trademarks, 245
INVESTEXT, 353
Investments
    Eastern Europe, 509
    international, 401
    overseas opportunities, 398
    securities, 512
    video, 300
Investor Information Service, 512
Iowa
    Better Business Bureaus, 349
    bill status information, 415
    business assistance, 75
    business financing, 75
    company directories, 345
    corporation information, 326
    data centers, 366
    district courts, 440
    driver information, 389
    EPA office, 296
    exports, 76
    federal procurement assistance, 237
    grants for women entrepreneurs, 270
    housing office, 420
    housing programs, 197
    HUD office, 422
    international trade offices, 407
    inventors assistance, 255
    IRS libraries, 453
    IRS problem resolution centers, 461
    labor office, 373
    licensed professionals, 340
    loan programs, 164
    motor vehicle information, 389
    OSHA office, 291
    Patent Depository Library, 247
    productivity specialists, 313
    recycling office, 286
    SBA offices, 77
    securities office, 336
    Small Business Development Centers, 140
    state information, 500
    state planning office, 383
    state procurement office, 242
    state tax assistance, 493
    statistical abstracts, 378
    surplus property auctions, 430
    tax form distribution center, 468
    tax hotlines, 464
    tax incentives, 76
    technical assistance, 179
    technology transfer programs, 309
    technology-oriented assistance, 303
    trade experts, 404
    unclaimed property office, 436
    Uniform Commercial Code Division, 331
    venture capital, 214
    venture capital clubs, 207
    women and minorities, 76
    women business assistance, 278
    women's business ownership representatives, 274
    women's commission, 282
IUDs, 535

J

Japan
    agriculture, 538
    clearinghouse, 539
    exporting to, 397
Jazz, 540
Jet exhaust, 528
Job Accommodation Network, 223
Job interviews, 518
Job placement rate, 520
Job safety, 511
Job satisfaction, 520
Job search video, 301
Job share programs, 520
Job Training Partnership Act, 266
Juvenile crime, 518
Juvenile delinquency, 519
Juvenile justice, 519

K

Kansas
    Better Business Bureaus, 349
    bill status information, 415
    Bureau of Land Management office, 418
    business assistance, 77
    business financing, 77
    company directories, 345
    corporation information, 326
    data centers, 366
    district courts, 440
    driver information, 389
    EPA office, 296
    exports, 78
    housing office, 420
    housing programs, 197
    HUD office, 422
    international trade offices, 407
    inventors assistance, 255
    IRS libraries, 454
    IRS problem resolution centers, 461
    labor office, 373
    licensed professionals, 340
    loan programs, 164
    motor vehicle information, 389
    OSHA office, 291
    Patent Depository Library, 247
    productivity specialists, 313
    publications, 77
    recycling office, 286
    SBA offices, 78
    securities office, 336
    Small Business Development Centers, 141
    state information, 500
    state planning office, 383
    state procurement office, 242
    state tax assistance, 494
    statistical abstracts, 378
    surplus property auctions, 430
    tax form distribution center, 468
    tax hotlines, 464
    tax incentives, 77
    technology transfer programs, 309
    technology-oriented assistance, 303
    trade experts, 404
    unclaimed property office, 436
    Uniform Commercial Code Division, 331
    venture capital, 214
    women and minorities, 78
    women business assistance, 278
    women's business ownership representatives, 274
    women's commission, 282

Index

Kennedy Center, 542
Kentucky
    Better Business Bureaus, 349
    bill status information, 415
    business assistance, 78
    business financing, 78
    company directories, 345
    corporation information, 326
    data centers, 366
    district courts, 440
    driver information, 389
    EPA office, 296
    exports, 79
    federal procurement assistance, 237
    housing office, 420
    housing programs, 198
    HUD office, 422
    international trade offices, 407
    inventors assistance, 255
    IRS libraries, 454
    IRS problem resolution centers, 461
    labor office, 373
    licensed professionals, 340
    loan programs, 164
    motor vehicle information, 389
    OSHA office, 291
    Patent Depository Library, 247
    productivity specialists, 313
    recycling office, 286
    SBA offices, 79
    securities office, 336
    Small Business Development Centers, 141
    state information, 500
    state planning office, 383
    state procurement office, 242
    state tax assistance, 494
    statistical abstracts, 378
    surplus property auctions, 430
    tax form distribution center, 468
    tax hotlines, 464
    tax incentives, 79
    technical assistance, 179
    technology transfer programs, 309
    technology-oriented assistance, 303
    trade experts, 404
    unclaimed property office, 436
    Uniform Commercial Code Division, 331
    venture capital, 214
    venture capital clubs, 207
    women business assistance, 278
    women's business ownership representatives, 274
    women's commission, 282
Keogh plans, 266, 267
Kidnapping
    parental, 519
Kidney stones, 535
Kidneys, 535

L

Labeling, 262
    drug, 533
    Fair Packaging and Labeling Act, 266
    regulations, 263
Labor
    experts, 497
    federal laws, 264
    foreign trends, 403
    negotiations, 372
    recorded messages, 361
    state information centers, 371
    wage laws, 267
Labor force, 545
Labor-management, 511

Lakes
    acid rain, 529
    conservation, 529
Land
    federal, 527
    use maps, 525
Land development, 515
Landlords, 515
Lands
    outdoor recreation, 191
Landsat, 525
Landscaping, 508
Language immersion programs, 522
Languages, 521
Lasers, 542
Latin America
    fax retrieval system, 403
    marketing, 397
Lavender oil, 508
Law
    clearinghouse, 519
    Freedom of Information, 32-35, 38, 40-43
    poverty, 519
    Privacy Act, 32
Law enforcement, 544
Lawn maintenance, 508
Lawyers, 338
Lead paint, 515
Lead poisoning, 535
Leases
    long term, 188
Legal assistance
    exporting, 401
Legal help, 264
Legi-Slate, 30
LEGIS, 269, 410
Legislation
    animal welfare, 507
    bill sponsor, 410
    congressional committees, 410
    database, 410
    federal, 410, 411
    Internal Revenue Service, 444
    internal revenue, 445
    legislative reporting services, 413
    opinion papers, 411
    state, 413
    state bill status information offices, 414
    state reports, 414
    taxes, 443, 448
Lesko's Info-Power III, 354
Libraries
    agriculture, 496
    business, 496
    housing, 497
    Internal Revenue Service, 450
    Scientific Document Library, 245
    tax forms, 443
Library of Congress, 249, 541
    book auctions, 427
    free market studies, 353
    Reference Referral Service, 354
Licensing
    exports, 399
    inventions, 251
    organization of boards, 338
    state boards, 339
    state offices, 338
Limnology, 525
Linguistics, 521
Literacy
    program directory, 522
    training, 520
Livestock, 507
    slaughter, 544
Loan guarantees
    housing, 186

Index

Loans
    agricultural businesses, 53
    agriculture, 46
    apartments, 189
    business and industrial, 47
    child care facilities, 53
    commodities, 46
    condominiums, 189
    conservation, 186
    credit unions, 50
    disaster, 50
    emergency disaster, 54
    energy conservation, 53, 285
    energy saving equipment, 285
    energy-related, 512
    entrepreneurs with no money, 160
    experimental housing, 191
    exporting, 53, 395, 406
    farm labor housing, 187
    farm operating, 46, 54
    farm ownership, 46, 54
    Farmers Home Administration loan guarantees, 54
    farmers, 53
    farms, 46
    federal money, 46
    federal, 540
    guarantees, 46
    handicapped assistance, 533
    high tech, 53
    home improvement, 187, 189
    home, 516
    housing cooperatives, 189
    housing rehabilitation, 187, 188
    housing, 186
    Indian Loans for Economic Development, 277
    interest subsidies, 53
    inventors, 53, 245
    investment companies, 50
    local government, 53
    microloans, 51
    military housing, 190
    minorities, 53
    mobile homes, 187
    Native American veteran housing, 192
    Native Americans, 49
    nursing homes, 188
    proposals, 266
    rural economic development, 47
    rural electrification, 47
    Small Business Administration, 54
    small business, 50, 512
    small town business, 47
    soil and water, 54
    special regional, 53
    supportive elderly housing, 189
    telephone service, 47
    trailer parks, 188
    veterans, 192
    women, 53, 270
    youth project loans, 54
Local information
    Chamber of Commerce, 319
    courts, 319
    Development Authority, 319
    newspapers, 319
    sources, 319
Logos, 267
Louisiana
    Better Business Bureaus, 349
    bill status information, 415
    business assistance, 79
    business financing, 80
    company directories, 345
    corporation information, 326
    data centers, 366
    district courts, 440
    driver information, 389
    EPA office, 296
    exports, 80
    federal procurement assistance, 238
    housing office, 420
    housing programs, 198
    HUD office, 422
    international trade offices, 407
    inventors assistance, 255
    IRS libraries, 454
    IRS problem resolution centers, 461
    labor office, 374
    licensed professionals, 340
    loan programs, 165
    loans for women entrepreneurs, 271
    motor vehicle information, 389
    OSHA office, 291
    Patent Depository Library, 247
    productivity specialists, 313
    recycling office, 286
    SBA offices, 80
    securities office, 336
    Small Business Development Centers, 142
    state information, 500
    state planning office, 383
    state procurement office, 243
    state tax assistance, 494
    statistical abstract, 378
    surplus property auctions, 430
    tax form distribution center, 468
    tax hotlines, 464
    tax incentives, 80
    technology transfer programs, 309
    technology-oriented assistance, 304
    trade experts, 404
    unclaimed property office, 436
    Uniform Commercial Code, 332
    venture capital, 214
    venture capital clubs, 207
    women and minorities, 80
    women's business ownership representatives, 274
    women's commission, 282
Low income housing, 190
Low income
    technical assistance, 177
Lungs, 534
Lyme disease, 533

M

Macular Degeneration, age-related, 533
Magnetic resonance imaging devices, 535
Magnuson-Moss Act, 264
Mail
    bombs, 264
    fraud, 264
    international, 516
    theft, 515
Mail order rule, 264, 265
Mail Recovery Centers
    regional offices, 426
Mailing lists, 544
    brokers, 335
    exporting, 396
    licensing offices, 338
    sorting options, 338
    specialized rosters, 338
Maine
    Better Business Bureau, 349
    bill status information, 415
    business assistance, 80
    business financing, 81
    corporation information, 326
    data centers, 367
    district courts, 440

Index

Maine (continued)
    driver information, 389
    EPA office, 296
    exports, 82
    federal procurement assistance, 238
    housing office, 421
    housing programs, 198
    HUD office, 422
    international trade offices, 407
    inventors assistance, 255
    IRS libraries, 454
    IRS problem resolution centers, 461
    labor office, 374
    licensed professionals, 340
    loan programs, 165
    manufacturing directory, 345
    motor vehicle information, 389
    OSHA office, 291
    Patent Depository Library, 247
    productivity specialists, 313
    recycling office, 286
    SBA offices, 82
    securities office, 336
    Small Business Development Centers, 142
    state information, 500
    state planning office, 383
    state procurement office, 243
    state tax assistance, 494
    statistical abstract, 378
    surplus property auctions, 430
    tax form distribution center, 468
    tax hotlines, 464
    tax incentives, 82
    technical assistance, 180
    technology transfer programs, 309
    technology-oriented assistance, 304
    trade experts, 404
    unclaimed property office, 436
    Uniform Commercial Code Division, 332
    venture capital, 214
    women business assistance, 279
    women's business ownership representatives, 274
    women's commission, 282
Malaria, 533
Mammograms, 532
Management training, 54
Manitoba
    Better Business Bureau, 351
Manufacturing
    recorded messages, 362
Mapping
    airborne, 525
Maps
    demographic, 363
    geologic, 525
    hydrologic, 525
    out-of-print, 525
    topographic, 525
    water, 527
Marijuana
    cultivation, 518
Marine mammals, 527
Marine recreation, 528
Market research
    state data, 364
Market studies
    computerized databases, 352
    Congress, U.S., 354
    existing, 352
    FINDEX, 353
    free, 353
    from associations, 353
    government, 354
    INVESTEXT, 353
    state planning offices, 381
    telephone research services, 352
    traditional published sources, 352

Marketing, 260
    see also international trade; exporting
    agriculture, 507
    Census information, 544
    commodities, 400
    competitive intelligence, 338
    corporations, 344
    data on foreign countries, 396
    demographic information, 338
    developing nations, 399
    Eastern Europe, 397
    export seminars, 406
    exporting assistance, 395
    exporting new products, 396
    forecasting future markets, 363
    foreign buyers, 398
    foreign market studies, 396
    foreign, 392, 399
    franchising trends, 322
    free help, 265
    government information, 264
    international industry, 396
    inventions, 251
    labor information, 371
    labor market data, 371
    Latin America, 397
    market studies, 352
    online, 401
    overseas, 265, 496
    overseas research, 405
    reports on foreign companies, 396
    state company directories, 344
    state data centers, 363
    state motor vehicle offices, 387
    studies, 54, 265
    suppliers, 322
    television overseas, 397
    trade locator assistance, 398
    transportation, 513
    video, 300, 301
Marriage
    foreign citizens, 539
Marshals Service, U.S.
    property auctions, 425
Maryland
    Better Business Bureau, 349
    bill status information, 415
    business assistance, 82
    business financing, 83
    company directories, 345
    corporation information, 327
    data centers, 367
    district courts, 440
    driver information, 389
    EPA office, 296
    exports, 84
    federal procurement assistance, 238
    franchises, 228
    franchising information, 323
    housing office, 420, 421
    housing programs, 198
    HUD office, 422
    international trade offices, 407
    inventors assistance, 255
    IRS libraries, 454
    IRS problem resolution centers, 461
    labor office, 374
    licensed professionals, 340
    loan programs, 166
    motor vehicle information, 389
    OSHA office, 291
    Patent Depository Library, 247
    productivity specialists, 313
    recycling office, 286
    SBA offices, 85
    securities office, 336
    Small Business Development Centers, 143

Index

state information, 500
state planning office, 383
state procurement office, 243
state tax assistance, 494
statistical abstracts, 378
surplus property auctions, 430
tax form distribution center, 468
tax hotlines, 464
tax incentives, 84
technical assistance, 180
Technology Extension Service, 302
technology transfer programs, 309
technology-oriented assistance, 304
trade experts, 404
unclaimed property office, 436
Uniform Commercial Code Division, 332
venture capital, 214
venture capital clubs, 207
women and minorities, 85
women's business ownership representatives, 274
women's commission, 282
Massachusetts
   Better Business Bureaus, 349
   bill status information, 415
   business assistance, 85
   business financing, 86
   company directories, 345
   corporation information, 327
   data centers, 367
   district courts, 440
   driver information, 389
   EPA office, 296
   exports, 86
   federal procurement assistance, 238
   housing office, 421
   housing programs, 199
   HUD office, 422
   international trade offices, 407
   inventors assistance, 255
   IRS libraries, 454
   IRS problem resolution centers, 461
   labor office, 374
   licensed professionals, 341
   loan programs, 166
   motor vehicle information, 389
   OSHA office, 292
   Patent Depository Library, 247
   productivity specialists, 313
   recycling office, 286
   SBA offices, 86
   securities office, 336
   Small Business Development Centers, 143
   state information, 500
   state planning office, 383
   state procurement office, 243
   state tax assistance, 494
   statistical abstracts, 378
   surplus property auctions, 431
   tax form distribution center, 468
   tax hotlines, 464
   tax incentives, 86
   technical assistance, 181
   technology transfer programs, 309
   technology-oriented assistance, 304
   trade experts, 404
   unclaimed property office, 436
   Uniform Commercial Code Division, 332
   venture capital, 214
   venture capital clubs, 207
   women and minorities, 86
   women business assistance, 279
   women's business ownership representatives, 274
   women's commission, 282
Mathematics
   skill development, 522
MCI, 30
McKinney Act, 427

Meals
   business expenses, 260
Measuring devices, 529
Meat and Poultry Hotline, 508
Media
   tax information, 445
Mediation
   labor-management, 511
Medical devices, 534, 535
Medical expenditures, 534
Medical professionals, 338
Medications
   precautions, 531
Medicinal plants, 508
MEDLARS, 536
Menopause, 531
Mental illness, 536
Mental retardation, 532
Mentor programs, 272
Merchandise trade
   recorded messages, 362
Messengers, 262
Metals
   reference sources, 497
Meteorology, 525
Metric programs
   foreign experts, 395
Mexico
   fax retrieval system, 402
Michigan
   Better Business Bureaus, 349
   bill status information, 415
   business assistance, 87
   business financing, 87
   company directories, 345
   corporation information, 327
   data centers, 367
   district courts, 440
   driver information, 389
   EPA office, 296
   exports, 88
   federal procurement assistance, 238
   franchises, 228
   franchising information, 323
   housing office, 421
   housing programs, 199
   HUD office, 422
   international trade offices, 407
   inventors assistance, 255
   IRS libraries, 455
   IRS problem resolution centers, 461
   labor office, 374
   licensed professionals, 341
   loan programs, 167
   motor vehicle information, 389
   OSHA office, 292
   Patent Depository Library, 247
   productivity specialists, 313
   recycling office, 286
   SBA offices, 88
   securities office, 336
   Small Business Development Centers, 143
   state information, 501
   state planning office, 384
   state procurement office, 243
   state tax assistance, 494
   statistical abstracts, 379
   surplus property auctions, 431
   tax form distribution center, 468
   tax hotlines, 464
   tax incentives, 87
   technical assistance, 181
   technology transfer programs, 309
   technology-oriented assistance, 304
   trade experts, 404
   unclaimed property office, 436
   Uniform Commercial Code Section, 332

Index

Michigan *(continued)*
    venture capital, 215
    venture capital clubs, 207
    women and minorities, 88
    women business assistance, 279
    women's business ownership representatives, 274
    women's commission, 282
Microloans, 51
Microwave cooking
    video, 300
Migrant workers
    health care, 534
Mileage rates, 526
Military
    base closings, 48
    home loans, 190
    retired, 51
    service records, 541
    standards, 513
    subcontracting, 234
    tax assistance, 448
Minerals, 526
    foreign country experts, 497
    reference sources, 497
Minerals Resources Program, 511
Mining
    claims, 527
    regulation, 49
    robotics, 511
    safety, 511
Minnesota
    Better Business Bureau, 349
    bill status information, 415
    business assistance, 88
    business financing, 88
    company directories, 345
    corporation information, 327
    data centers, 367
    district courts, 440
    driver information, 389
    EPA office, 296
    exports, 89
    federal procurement assistance, 238
    franchises, 228
    franchising information, 323
    housing office, 421
    housing programs, 199
    HUD office, 422
    international trade offices, 407
    inventors assistance, 255
    IRS libraries, 455
    IRS problem resolution centers, 461
    labor office, 374
    licensed professionals, 341
    loan programs, 167
    loans for women entrepreneurs, 271
    motor vehicle information, 389
    OSHA office, 292
    Patent Depository Library, 247
    productivity specialists, 313
    recycling office, 286
    SBA offices, 89
    securities office, 336
    Small Business Development Centers, 144
    state information, 501
    state planning office, 384
    state procurement office, 243
    state tax assistance, 494
    statistical abstracts, 379
    surplus property auctions, 431
    tax form distribution center, 468
    tax hotlines, 464
    technical assistance, 181
    technology transfer programs, 309
    technology-oriented assistance, 304
    trade experts, 404
    unclaimed property office, 436
    Uniform Commercial Code Division, 332
    venture capital, 215
    venture capital clubs, 207
    women and minorities, 89
    women business assistance, 279
    women's business ownership representatives, 274
    women's commission, 282
Minorities
    8(a) program, 234
    business development, 48
    Business Development Centers, 55
    energy contracts, 51
    energy programs, 511
    government procurement set-asides, 236
    health issues, 536
    junior college, 521
    loans, 53
    standardized tests, 520
    subcontractors tax incentive, 278
    urban education, 523
Minority Business Development Agency, 230
Minority Business Development Centers, 55
Minority Energy Information Clearinghouse, 511
Misinformation
    jargon, 22
Missing children, 519
Mississippi
    Better Business Bureau, 349
    bill status information, 415
    business assistance, 89
    business financing, 90
    company directories, 345
    corporation information, 327
    data centers, 367
    district courts, 440
    driver information, 389
    EPA office, 296
    exports, 90
    federal procurement assistance, 238
    housing office, 421
    housing programs, 200
    HUD office, 422
    international trade offices, 407
    inventors assistance, 256
    IRS libraries, 455
    IRS problem resolution centers, 461
    labor office, 374
    licensed professionals, 341
    loan programs, 168
    motor vehicle information, 389
    OSHA office, 292
    Patent Depository Library, 247
    productivity specialists, 313
    recycling office, 286
    SBA offices, 90
    securities office, 336
    Small Business Development Centers, 145
    state information, 501
    state planning office, 384
    state procurement office, 243
    state tax assistance, 494
    statistical abstracts, 379
    surplus property auctions, 431
    tax form distribution center, 468
    tax hotlines, 464
    tax incentives, 90
    technology transfer programs, 309
    technology-oriented assistance, 304
    trade experts, 404
    unclaimed property office, 437
    Uniform Commercial Code Division, 332
    venture capital, 216
    women and minorities, 90
    women business assistance, 279
    women's business ownership representatives, 274
    women's commission, 282

Index

Missouri
    Better Business Bureaus, 349
    bill status information, 415
    business assistance, 91
    business financing, 91
    company directories, 345
    corporation information, 327
    data centers, 367
    district courts, 440
    driver information, 389
    EPA office, 296
    exports, 93
    federal procurement assistance, 238
    housing office, 421
    housing programs, 200
    HUD office, 422
    international trade offices, 407
    inventors assistance, 256
    IRS libraries, 456
    IRS problem resolution centers, 461
    labor office, 374
    licensed professionals, 341
    loan programs, 168
    motor vehicle information, 389
    OSHA office, 292
    Patent Depository Library, 247
    productivity specialists, 313
    recycling office, 287
    SBA offices, 93
    securities office, 336
    Small Business Development Centers, 146
    state information, 501
    state planning office, 384
    state procurement office, 243
    state tax assistance, 494
    statistical abstracts, 379
    surplus property auctions, 431
    tax form distribution center, 469
    tax hotlines, 465
    tax incentives, 92
    technical assistance, 182
    technology transfer programs, 309
    technology-oriented assistance, 304
    trade experts, 404
    unclaimed property office, 437
    Uniform Commercial Code Division, 332
    venture capital, 216
    venture capital clubs, 207
    women and minorities, 93
    women business assistance, 279
    women's business ownership representatives, 274
    women's commission, 282
Mobile homes
    loans, 187
    state loans, 194
    veterans, 192
Monetary affairs, 509
Money
    evolution, 509
    housing, 186
    real estate, 186
    recorded messages, 362
    unclaimed tax refunds, 447
    unclaimed, 435
Montana
    Better Business Bureaus, 349
    bill status information, 415
    Bureau of Land Management office, 418, 419
    business assistance, 94
    business financing, 94
    company directories, 345
    corporation information, 327
    data centers, 367
    district courts, 440
    driver information, 389
    EPA office, 296
    exports, 95
    federal procurement assistance, 238
    housing office, 421
    housing programs, 200
    HUD office, 422
    international trade offices, 407
    inventors assistance, 256
    IRS libraries, 456
    IRS problem resolution centers, 461
    labor office, 374
    licensed professionals, 341
    loan programs, 168
    motor vehicle information, 389
    OSHA office, 292
    Patent Depository Library, 247
    productivity specialists, 313
    recycling office, 287
    SBA offices, 95
    securities office, 336
    Small Business Development Centers, 147
    state information, 501
    state planning office, 384
    state procurement office, 243
    state tax assistance, 494
    statistical abstracts, 379
    surplus property auctions, 431
    tax form distribution center, 469
    tax hotlines, 465
    tax incentives, 94
    technical assistance, 182
    technology transfer programs, 309
    trade experts, 404
    unclaimed property office, 437
    Uniform Commercial Code Bureau, 332
    venture capital, 216
    venture capital clubs, 207
    women business assistance, 279
    women's business ownership representatives, 274
    women's commission, 283
Mortgages, 515
    adjustable rate, 190
    graduated, 189
    home equity conversion, 190
    insurance, 188
    rates, 516
    recorded messages, 362
    rehabilitation, 187
    state housing help, 194
    unclaimed money, 419
Motion pictures, 541
Mouth diseases, 533
Moving expenses, 267
Multifamily housing, 189
    equity loans, 191
    mortgage insurance, 189, 193
    reinsurance, 193
Multiple sclerosis, 536
Murder, 544
Museum Reference Center, 522
Museums
    training, 522
Music therapy, 537
Music, 542

N

Narcotics
    enforcement training, 518
National Aeronautics and Space Administration
    SBIR grants, 241
National Agricultural Statistics Service, 507
National Archives, 541
National Association for Female Executives, 272
National Association of Investment Companies, 206
National Association of Securities Dealers, 335

Index

National Association of State Small Business Advocates, 53
National Banks, 271
National Center for Health Statistics, 359, 534
National Center for Missing and Exploited Children, 519
National Climatic Data Center, 524
National Conference of State Legislators, 413
National Credit Union Administration, 514
National forests, 47, 526
National Geophysical Data Center, 526
National Health Information Center, 534
National Health Information Clearinghouse, 266, 271
National High Blood Pressure Education Program, 534
National Injury Information Clearinghouse, 515
National Institute of Occupational Safety and Health, 288
National Institute of Standards and Technology, 299
National landmarks, 528
National Library of Medicine, 354, 536
National Marine Fisheries Service, 526
National Oceanic and Atmospheric Administration, 527
National Park Service, 260, 528
National Passport Information Center, 409
National Pesticide Telecommunication Network, 528
National Register of Historic Places, 528
National Response Center, 526
National Science Foundation
    SBIR grants, 241
National Sea Grant Depository, 528
National Trade Data Bank, 401
National Weather Service, 530
Native Americans
    architecture, 540
    business development grants, 277
    business development, 48
    clearinghouse, 541
    economic development loans, 277
    government procurement assistance, 236
    health issues, 535
    housing, 192
    housing loans, 192
    loans for entrepreneurs with no money, 160
    low-income technical assistance, 177
    reservation development loans, 49
    veterans home loans, 192
Navigational aids, 524
Nebraska
    Better Business Bureaus, 349
    bill status information, 415
    Bureau of Land Management office, 418
    business assistance, 95
    business financing, 95
    company directories, 346
    corporation information, 327
    data centers, 368
    district courts, 440
    driver information, 390
    EPA office, 296
    exports, 96
    federal procurement assistance, 238
    housing office, 421
    housing programs, 200
    HUD office, 422
    international trade offices, 407
    inventors assistance, 256
    IRS libraries, 456
    IRS problem resolution centers, 461
    labor office, 374
    licensed professionals, 341
    loan programs, 169
    motor vehicle information, 390
    OSHA office, 292
    Patent Depository Library, 247
    productivity specialists, 313
    recycling office, 287
    SBA offices, 96
    securities office, 336
    Small Business Development Centers, 147
    state information, 501
    state planning office, 384
    state procurement office, 243
    state tax assistance, 494
    statistical abstracts, 379
    surplus property auctions, 431
    tax form distribution center, 469
    tax hotlines, 465
    tax incentives, 96
    technical assistance, 182
    technology transfer programs, 310
    technology-oriented assistance, 304
    trade experts, 404
    unclaimed property office, 437
    Uniform Commercial Code Division, 332
    venture capital, 216
    venture capital clubs, 208
    women business assistance, 279
    women's business ownership representatives, 274
    women's commission, 283
Neighborhood Watch programs, 519
Neurological disorders, 536
Nevada
    Better Business Bureaus, 350
    bill status information, 416
    Bureau of Land Management office, 418, 419
    business assistance, 96
    business financing, 96
    company directories, 346
    corporation information, 327
    data centers, 368
    district courts, 440
    driver information, 390
    EPA office, 296
    exports, 97
    federal procurement assistance, 238
    housing office, 421
    housing programs, 200
    HUD office, 422
    international trade offices, 407
    inventors assistance, 256
    IRS libraries, 456
    IRS problem resolution centers, 461
    labor office, 374
    licensed professionals, 341
    loan programs, 169
    motor vehicle information, 390
    OSHA office, 292
    Patent Depository Library, 247
    productivity specialists, 313
    recycling office, 287
    SBA offices, 97
    securities office, 336
    Small Business Development Centers, 148
    state information, 501
    state planning office, 384
    state procurement office, 243
    state tax assistance, 494
    statistical abstracts, 379
    surplus property auctions, 431
    tax form distribution center, 469
    tax hotlines, 465
    tax incentives, 96
    technology transfer programs, 310
    technology-oriented assistance, 304
    trade experts, 404
    unclaimed property office, 437
    Uniform Commercial Code Division, 332
    venture capital, 216
    women's business ownership representatives, 274
    women's commission, 283
New Car Assessment Program, 514
New Hampshire
    Better Business Bureau, 350
    bill status information, 416
    business assistance, 97
    business financing, 97
    company directories, 346

Index

corporation information, 327
data centers, 368
district courts, 440
driver information, 390
EPA office, 296
exports, 97
federal procurement assistance, 238
housing office, 421
housing programs, 200
HUD office, 422
international trade offices, 407
inventors assistance, 256
IRS libraries, 456
IRS problem resolution centers, 461
labor office, 374
licensed professionals, 341
loan programs, 169
motor vehicle information, 390
OSHA office, 292
Patent Depository Library, 247
productivity specialists, 313
recycling office, 287
SBA offices, 98
securities office, 336
Small Business Development Centers, 148
state information, 501
state planning office, 384
state procurement office, 243
state tax assistance, 494
statistical abstracts, 379
surplus property auctions, 431
tax form distribution center, 469
tax hotlines, 465
tax incentives, 97
technology transfer programs, 310
technology-oriented assistance, 304
trade experts, 404
unclaimed property office, 437
Uniform Commercial Code Division, 332
venture capital, 216
women business assistance, 279
women's business ownership representatives, 274
women's commission, 283

New Jersey
   Better Business Bureau, 350
   bill status information, 416
   business assistance, 98
   business financing, 98
   Commission on Science and Technology, 302
   company directories, 346
   corporation information, 327
   data centers, 368
   district courts, 440
   driver information, 390
   EPA office, 296
   exports, 99
   federal procurement assistance, 238
   housing office, 421
   housing programs, 201
   HUD office, 422
   international trade offices, 407
   inventors assistance, 257
   IRS libraries, 456
   IRS problem resolution centers, 461
   labor office, 374
   licensed professionals, 341
   loan programs, 170
   motor vehicle information, 390
   OSHA office, 292
   Patent Depository Library, 247
   productivity specialists, 313
   recycling office, 287
   SBA offices, 99
   securities office, 336
   Small Business Development Centers, 148
   state information, 501
   state planning office, 384
   state procurement office, 243
   state tax assistance, 494
   statistical abstracts, 379
   surplus property auctions, 431
   tax form distribution center, 469
   tax hotlines, 465
   tax incentives, 99
   technology transfer programs, 310
   technology-oriented assistance, 304
   trade experts, 404
   unclaimed property office, 437
   Uniform Commercial Code Division, 332
   venture capital, 216
   venture capital clubs, 208
   women and minorities, 99
   women's business ownership representatives, 274
   women's commission, 283

New Mexico
   Better Business Bureaus, 350
   bill status information, 416
   Bureau of Land Management office, 418, 419
   business assistance, 99
   business financing, 100
   company directories, 346
   corporation information, 327
   data centers, 368
   district courts, 440
   driver information, 390
   EPA office, 296
   exports, 101
   federal procurement assistance, 238
   housing office, 421
   housing programs, 201
   HUD office, 423
   international trade offices, 407
   inventors assistance, 257
   IRS libraries, 456
   IRS problem resolution centers, 461
   labor office, 374
   licensed professionals, 341
   loan programs, 170
   motor vehicle information, 390
   OSHA office, 292
   Patent Depository Library, 247
   productivity specialists, 313
   recycling office, 287
   SBA offices, 101
   securities office, 336
   Small Business Development Centers, 148
   state information, 501
   state planning office, 384
   state procurement office, 243
   state tax assistance, 494
   statistical abstracts, 379
   surplus property auctions, 432
   tax form distribution center, 469
   tax hotlines, 465
   tax incentives, 100
   technical assistance, 182
   technology transfer programs, 310
   technology-oriented assistance, 304
   trade experts, 405
   unclaimed property office, 437
   Uniform Commercial Code Division, 333
   venture capital, 217
   women and minorities, 101
   women business assistance, 279
   women's business ownership representatives, 274
   women's commission, 283

New York
   Better Business Bureaus, 350
   bill status information, 416
   business assistance, 101
   business financing, 102
   company directories, 346
   corporation information, 327
   data centers, 368

Index

New York (continued)
    district courts, 440
    driver information, 390
    EPA office, 296
    exports, 103
    federal procurement assistance, 238
    franchises, 228
    franchising information, 323
    housing office, 421
    housing programs, 201
    HUD office, 423
    international trade offices, 407
    inventors assistance, 257
    IRS libraries, 456
    IRS problem resolution centers, 461
    labor office, 375
    licensed professionals, 341
    loan programs, 170
    loans for women entrepreneurs, 271
    motor vehicle information, 390
    OSHA office, 292
    Patent Depository Library, 247
    productivity specialists, 313
    recycling office, 287
    SBA offices, 103
    securities office, 336
    Small Business Development Centers, 149
    state information, 501
    state planning office, 384
    state procurement office, 243
    state tax assistance, 494
    statistical abstracts, 379
    surplus property auctions, 432
    tax form distribution center, 469
    tax hotlines, 465
    tax incentives, 103
    technical assistance, 182
    technology transfer programs, 310
    technology-oriented assistance, 304
    trade experts, 405
    unclaimed property office, 437
    Uniform Commercial Code Division, 333
    venture capital, 217
    venture capital clubs, 208
    women and minorities, 103
    women business assistance, 279
    women's business ownership representatives, 274
    women's commission, 283
Newfoundland
    Better Business Bureau, 351
Newsletters
    foreign trade, 406
Newsreels, 541
Newton, Isaac, 542
Nonprofit organizations
    art exhibits, 427
    environmental funding, 526
    foreign gifts, 427
    free books, 427
    housing, 427
    rental housing, 187
    rural housing, 192
    small business help, 47
    surplus food, 427
    surplus property, 427
Norplant, 533
North Carolina
    Better Business Bureaus, 350
    bill status information, 416
    business assistance, 104
    business financing, 104
    company directories, 346
    corporation information, 328
    data centers, 368
    district courts, 440
    driver information, 390
    EPA office, 296
    exports, 105
    federal procurement assistance, 239
    housing office, 421
    housing programs, 201
    HUD office, 423
    international trade offices, 408
    inventors assistance, 257
    IRS libraries, 456
    IRS problem resolution centers, 462
    labor office, 375
    licensed professionals, 341
    loan programs, 171
    motor vehicle information, 390
    OSHA office, 292
    Patent Depository Library, 247
    productivity specialists, 314
    recycling office, 287
    SBA offices, 105
    securities office, 336
    Small Business Development Centers, 150
    state information, 501
    state planning office, 384
    state procurement office, 243
    state tax assistance, 494
    statistical abstracts, 379
    surplus property auctions, 432
    tax form distribution center, 469
    tax hotlines, 465
    tax incentives, 105
    technical assistance, 183
    technology transfer programs, 310
    technology-oriented assistance, 304
    trade experts, 405
    unclaimed property office, 437
    Uniform Commercial Code Division, 333
    venture capital, 219
    women and minorities, 105
    women business assistance, 279
    women's business ownership representatives, 275
    women's commission, 283
North Dakota
    Better Business Bureaus, 350
    bill status information, 416
    Bureau of Land Management office, 418
    business assistance, 106
    business financing, 106
    company directories, 346
    corporation information, 328
    data centers, 368
    district courts, 440
    driver information, 390
    EPA office, 296
    exports, 107
    federal procurement assistance, 239
    franchises, 228
    franchising information, 323
    housing office, 421
    housing programs, 202
    HUD office, 423
    international trade offices, 408
    inventors assistance, 257
    IRS libraries, 456
    IRS problem resolution centers, 462
    labor office, 375
    licensed professionals, 342
    motor vehicle information, 390
    OSHA office, 292
    Patent Depository Library, 247
    productivity specialists, 314
    recycling office, 287
    SBA offices, 107
    securities office, 336
    Small Business Development Centers, 151
    state information, 501
    state planning office, 384
    state procurement office, 243
    state tax assistance, 494

Index

statistical abstracts, 379
surplus property auctions, 432
tax form distribution center, 469
tax hotlines, 465
tax incentives, 106
technical assistance, 183
technology transfer programs, 310
technology-oriented assistance, 305
unclaimed property office, 437
Uniform Commercial Code Division, 333
venture capital, 219
women and minorities, 107
women business assistance, 280
women's business ownership representatives, 275
women's commission, 283

Nova Scotia
    Better Business Bureau, 351
Nuclear Non-Proliferation Treaty, 538
Nuclear power, 527
Nuclear reactors, 527
Nuclear Regulatory Commission, 527
    SBIR grants, 241
Nuclear war, 538
Nurseries
    free plants, 48
Nursing
    A.A. degrees, 521
Nursing homes, 188, 338, 534
Nutrition
    diabetes, 533
    education, 522
    research, 507

O

Obesity, 508
Occupational Safety and Health Administration, 261, 263, 288, 290, 511
Occupational safety, 536
Oceanographic data, 527
Oceanography, 525
Oceans, 527
Odometer tampering, 514
Office of American Workplace, 513
Office of Corporations, 330
Office of Technology Assessment and Forecast, 245
Office of Uniform Commercial Code, 330
Ohio
    Better Business Bureaus, 350
    bill status information, 416
    business assistance, 107
    business financing, 108
    company directories, 346
    corporation information, 328
    data centers, 369
    district courts, 440
    driver information, 390
    EPA office, 296
    exports, 108
    federal procurement assistance, 239
    housing office, 421
    housing programs, 202
    HUD office, 423
    international trade offices, 408
    inventors assistance, 257
    IRS libraries, 457
    IRS problem resolution centers, 462
    labor office, 375
    licensed professionals, 342
    loan programs, 172
    motor vehicle information, 390
    OSHA office, 292
    Patent Depository Library, 247
    productivity specialists, 314
    recycling office, 287
    SBA offices, 109
    securities office, 336
    services for women entrepreneurs, 271
    Small Business Development Centers, 151
    state information, 501
    state planning office, 385
    state procurement office, 243
    state tax assistance, 495
    statistical abstracts, 379
    surplus property auctions, 432
    tax form distribution center, 469
    tax hotlines, 465
    tax incentives, 108
    technical assistance, 183
    technology transfer programs, 310
    technology-oriented assistance, 305
    trade experts, 405
    unclaimed property office, 437
    Uniform Commercial Code Division, 333
    venture capital, 219
    venture capital clubs, 208
    women and minorities, 109
    women business assistance, 280
    women's business ownership representatives, 275
    women's commission, 283

Oil, offshore drilling, 48
Oklahoma
    Better Business Bureaus, 350
    bill status information, 416
    Bureau of Land Management office, 418
    business assistance, 109
    business financing, 109
    company directories, 346
    corporation information, 328
    data centers, 369
    district courts, 440
    driver information, 390
    EPA office, 296
    exports, 110
    federal procurement assistance, 239
    housing office, 421
    housing programs, 202
    HUD office, 423
    international trade offices, 408
    inventors assistance, 257
    IRS libraries, 457
    IRS problem resolution centers, 462
    labor office, 375
    licensed professionals, 342
    motor vehicle information, 390
    OSHA office, 292
    Patent Depository Library, 247
    productivity specialists, 314
    recycling office, 287
    SBA offices, 111
    securities office, 336
    Small Business Development Centers, 152
    state information, 502
    state planning office, 385
    state procurement office, 243
    state tax assistance, 495
    statistical abstracts, 379
    surplus property auctions, 432
    tax form distribution center, 469
    tax hotlines, 465
    tax incentives, 110
    technology transfer programs, 310
    technology-oriented assistance, 305
    trade experts, 405
    unclaimed property office, 437
    Uniform Commercial Code Office, 333
    venture capital, 220
    venture capital clubs, 208
    women and minorities, 110
    women business assistance, 280
    women's business ownership representatives, 275
    women's commission, 283

Index

Online
    federal legislation, 411
    international markets, 401
Ontario
    Better Business Bureau, 351
Opera, 542
Orchestras, 542
Oregon
    Better Business Bureaus, 350
    bill status information, 416
    Bureau of Land Management office, 418, 419
    business assistance, 111
    business financing, 111
    company directories, 346
    corporation information, 328
    data centers, 369
    district courts, 440
    driver information, 390
    EPA office, 296
    exports, 112
    federal procurement assistance, 239
    franchises, 228
    franchising information, 323
    housing office, 421
    housing programs, 202
    HUD office, 423
    international trade offices, 408
    inventors assistance, 257
    IRS libraries, 457
    IRS problem resolution centers, 462
    labor office, 375
    licensed professionals, 342
    loan programs, 173
    motor vehicle information, 390
    OSHA office, 292
    Patent Depository Library, 247
    productivity specialists, 314
    recycling office, 287
    SBA offices, 112
    securities office, 336
    Small Business Development Centers, 153
    state information, 502
    state planning office, 385
    state procurement office, 243
    state tax assistance, 495
    statistical abstracts, 380
    surplus property auctions, 432
    tax form distribution center, 469
    tax hotlines, 465
    tax incentives, 112
    technology transfer programs, 311
    trade experts, 405
    unclaimed property office, 437
    Uniform Commercial Code Division, 333
    venture capital, 220
    venture capital clubs, 208
    women and minorities, 112
    women business assistance, 280
    women's business ownership representatives, 275
    women's commission, 283
Organic gardening, 508
Organic gardens, 507
Organizational skills, 521
Organized crime, 519
Osteoporosis, 531
Overseas assistance
    citizens arrested overseas, 408
    citizens emergency center, 408
    deaths, 409
    financial, 409
    search for United States nationals, 409
Overseas Private Investment Corporation, 512
    fax retrieval system, 403
Oyster culture, 507
Ozone, 529

P

Pacemakers, 535
Pacific Ocean, 527
Packaging, 262
    meat, 508
Paint
    lead, 527
Pancreatitis, 533
Panic attacks, 536
Parental kidnapping, 519
Parkinson's disease, 536
Parks
    national, 528
    urban, 528
Parole, 518
Partnerships, 267
Passports
    National Passport Information Center, 409
Patent and Trademark Office, 245, 267
    disclosure statements, 245
Patent Libraries, 248
Patent searches
    Derwent, 248
    Mead Data Central, 248
Patents, 245
    attorneys, 246
    CD-Rom discs, 248
    Depository Libraries, 246
    energy-related, 51
    Manual and Index to U.S. Patent Classifications, 248
    publications, 245
    Scientific Document Library, 245
    searches, 245, 246
    specifications, 246
    temporary, 245
    United States, 245
Peaches
    canned, 508
Pennsylvania
    Better Business Bureaus, 350
    bill status information, 416
    business assistance, 112
    business financing, 113
    company directories, 346
    corporation information, 328
    data centers, 369
    district courts, 440
    driver information, 390
    EPA office, 297
    exports, 113
    federal procurement assistance, 239
    housing office, 421
    housing programs, 202
    HUD office, 423
    international trade offices, 408
    inventors assistance, 258
    IRS libraries, 457
    IRS problem resolution centers, 462
    labor office, 375
    licensed professionals, 342
    loan programs, 173
    motor vehicle information, 390
    OSHA office, 292
    Patent Depository Library, 247
    productivity specialists, 314
    recycling office, 287
    SBA offices, 114
    securities office, 336
    Small Business Development Centers, 153
    state information, 502
    state planning office, 385
    state procurement office, 243
    state tax assistance, 495
    statistical abstracts, 380

Index

surplus property auctions, 432
tax form distribution center, 469
tax hotlines, 465
tax incentives, 113
technical assistance, 184
technology transfer programs, 311
technology-oriented assistance, 305
trade experts, 405
unclaimed property office, 437
Uniform Commercial Code Division, 333
venture capital, 220
venture capital clubs, 208
women and minorities, 113
women business assistance, 280
women's business ownership representatives, 275
women's commission, 283
Pension and Welfare Benefits Administration, 512, 516
Pension Benefit Guaranty Corporation, 512, 516
Pension laws, 512
Pension plans, 516
Pensions, 265
    job mobility, 512
    tax laws, 441
Performing Arts Library, 542
Periodontal disease, 533
Permanent resident status, 539
Pesticides
    hotline, 289, 528
    milk, 46
    safety practices, 289
    video, 301
Pets, importing, 538
Pharmaceuticals, 534
Photographers
    National Park Service contracts, 260
Photographs
    aerial, 525
    Apollo, 529
    documentary, 542
    Library of Congress, 542
    master, 542
Physical education, 522
Physics
    solar-terrestrial, 526
Phytoplankton, 529
Plants
    free, 48
    information service, 508
    pesticides, 527
    poisonous, 508
    wild, 515
PLO-Israel Peace Treaty, 539
Poetry readings, 542
Poisoning, 514
Police
    domestic violence, 519
    drug corruption, 518
Political asylum, 539
Politics
    foreign, 394
Pollution
    abatement, 186
    Clean Air Act issues, 290
    in your business, 294
    money for businesses, 290
    oceans, 527
    water, 186
Pollution Prevention Information Clearinghouse, 528
Population
    international, 401
Population shifts, 515
Postal Inspection Service, 264
Postal Service, U.S., 261, 515
    Mail Recovery Centers, 425
    mailing rates, 261
    property auctions, 425
    unclaimed merchandise, 418

Posters, 542
Poultry, 507
    cooking, 508
Poverty
    tax burden, 519
Poverty law, 519
Power tools, 529
Precipitation, 530
Pregnancy
    caffeine consumption, 508
    health issues, 535
Pregnancy test kits, 535
Prentice Hall Legal and Financial Services, 317
Preservatives
    wood, 527
Press, foreign, 400
Prices, 545
    international, 400
    reference sources, 497
Pricing strategies, 266
Primark Financial Information Division, 316
Primary care, 536
Primary health care, 534
Print making, 542
Prisoner-of-war records, 541
Pro bono programs, 519
Probation, 518
Processing
    meat, 508
Procurement, 233
    assistance offices, 236
    exporting, 403
    federal, 512
    programs, 54
    state assistance, 242
    state offices, 242
    technical assistance, 49
Producer Price Index
    recorded messages, 362
Product safety, 262, 266
Product standards, 513
Production
    recorded messages, 362
Productivity, 545
    recorded messages, 362
    reference sources, 497
Productivity analysis, 312
Productivity specialists
    national, 315
Prostate cancer, 532
Public brokerage houses, 509
Public housing, 515
Public lands, 527
Publications
    Annual Confectionery Survey, 19
    Gale's Directory of Databases, 30
    Gale's Encyclopedia of Associations, 19
    Journal of Veterinarian Medicine, 29
    Lesko's Info-Power III, 24
    New York Times, 23
    U.S. Government Manual, 24
    U.S. Industrial Outlook, 24
Puerto Rico
    Better Business Bureaus, 350
    district courts, 440
    federal procurement assistance, 239
    housing office, 421
    HUD office, 423
    international trade offices, 408
    IRS libraries, 457
    Patent Depository Library, 247
    tax form distribution center, 469
    tax hotlines, 465
    trade experts, 405
    venture capital, 220
    women's commission, 283
Pyramid schemes, 512

Index

Q

Quebec
    Better Business Bureau, 351

R

Racism
    schools, 520
Radar images, 525
Radio
    archives, 541
    cellular, 514
    foreign, 400
    regulation, 514
Radioactive material, 527
Radiological products, 534
Radon, 261, 290, 294, 526, 528
    state housing agencies, 194
    videos, 295
Rafting, 526
Ranchers
    farm ownership loans, 46
Rape
    date, 518
    statistics, 518
Rare books, 542
Rare diseases, 534
Rattlesnakes
    removing from human dwellings, 300
Reading
    improvement techniques, 521
    skills, 522
Reading programs, 545
Real estate
    agents and brokers, 338
    developer loans, 190
    developers, 190
    General Services Administration, 426
    loans, 186
    Small Business Administration, 426
    state money, 194
Recalls, auto, 514
Recidivism, 519
Record companies, 542
Recorded messages
    economic, 361
Recreation
    marine, 528
Recreation education, 522
Recreation Recovery Program, 528
Recreational areas, 527
Recycling, 508, 527
    composting, 301
    hotline, 268, 285
    info pack, 290
    local help, 286
    scrap metal, 511
    tax breaks, 290
Redlining, 515
Refugees
    loans for entrepreneurs with no money, 160
Regional Disability and Business Technical Assistance Centers, 223
Regulation
    banking, 509
    communications, 514
Rehabilitation, 537
Renewable energy, 524
Rent supplements, 191
Rental housing, 189
Rental vouchers, 193
Research
    assistance for entrepreneurs, 54
    government-funded, 241
    international demographics, 396
    sampling techniques, 22
    solar energy, 52
    strategies, 352
    survey methods, 22
    taxes, 446
    techniques, 19
    university technology projects, 306
Research Information Services, 317
Resource Conservation and Recovery Act, 527
Respiratory diseases, 511
Retirement
    benefits, 516
    plans, 266, 267
    security, 516
    tax aspects, 443
Revolutionary War, 541
Rhode Island
    Better Business Bureau, 350
    bill status information, 416
    business assistance, 114
    business financing, 114
    company directories, 346
    corporation information, 328
    data centers, 369
    district courts, 440
    driver information, 390
    EPA office, 297
    exports, 116
    federal procurement assistance, 239
    franchises, 228
    franchising information, 323
    housing office, 421
    housing programs, 202
    HUD office, 423
    international trade offices, 408
    inventors assistance, 258
    IRS libraries, 457
    IRS problem resolution centers, 462
    labor office, 375
    licensed professionals, 342
    motor vehicle information, 390
    OSHA office, 293
    Patent Depository Library, 247
    productivity specialists, 314
    recycling office, 287
    SBA offices, 116
    securities office, 336
    Small Business Development Centers, 154
    state information, 502
    state procurement office, 243
    state tax assistance, 495
    statistical abstracts, 380
    surplus property auctions, 433
    tax form distribution center, 469
    tax hotlines, 465
    tax incentives, 115
    technical assistance, 184
    technology-oriented assistance, 305
    trade experts, 405
    unclaimed property office, 437
    Uniform Commercial Code Division, 333
    venture capital, 220
    women business assistance, 280
    women's business ownership representatives, 275
    women's commission, 283
Risk management
    video, 300
Rivers
    videos, 527
Robberies, 544
Robotics
    mining industry, 511
Rockets
    launches, 529
Runaways, 519

Index

Rural America, 507
Rural development grants, 47
Rural Housing and Community Development Service, 420
Rural housing, 192
Rural Information Center, 508, 542

S

S corporations, 267
Safe Drinking Water Hotline, 294
Safety
    community, 518
    construction workers, 300
    drugs, 509
    free consultants, 290
    in the workplace, 299
    job, 511
    mining, 511
    nuclear, 527
    occupational, 536
    pesticide, 528
    safety guarding devices, 300
    video display terminals, 295
    water, 524
    workplace issues, 263
Safety, worker
    videos, 300
Sailing, 526
Salaries
    recorded messages, 362
Salmon ranching, 507
Salmonella poisoning, 508
SAMI, 20
Saskatchewan
    Better Business Bureau, 351
Satellites, 529
    cooling, 529
    Landsat, 525
    regulation, 514
Savings and Loans
    recorded messages, 361
Schizophrenia, 536
Scholastic Aptitude Test (SAT), 520
School administrators, 521
Schools
    breakfast programs, 515
    discipline, 520
    racism, 520
    violence, 519
Scrap metal, 511
SCUBA, 529
Seafood
    hotline, 508
    labeling, 508
Seas, 527
Seat belts, 514
Securities, 516
    broker registration, 335
    complaints, 512
    laws, 512
    state offices, 318, 335
Securities and Exchange Commission, 335, 512
    document rooms, 317
    documents, 317
    filings, 316
    Office of Public Affairs, 317
Security
    museums, 522
Security clearances, 539
Seismograms, 525
Self-employment tax, 267
Self-help
    state housing programs, 194
Seminars, business, 262

Service Corps of Retired Executives, 263, 402
Sexual abuse, 537
Sexual harassment, 268, 272, 515, 518
Shellfish, 508
    saltwater, 526
Ship passenger lists, 541
Shipping subsidies, 49
Ships
    auctions, 426
    U.S. Department of Transportation, 426
Sick Building Syndrome, 288, 527
Silicone implants, 535
Silver
    price, 511
Skies, 527
Skiing, 526
Skin diseases, 531
Skunk control
    video, 300
Slogans, 267
Small business
    computers, 261
    export counseling, 402
    export loans, 395
    free CD-ROM, 300
    loans, 50
    microloans, 51
    ombudsman, 528
    start-up guide, 260
    surplus property sales, 426
    tax education, 447
    tax workshops, 459
    videos, 300
Small Business Administration, 260, 512
    auctions, 426
    Business Information Centers, 300
    Directory of Operating Small Business Investment Companies, 206
    energy conservation loans, 285
    federal procurement, 236
    free CD-ROM for small business, 300
    Office of Women's Business Ownership, 272
    Pre-Solicitation Announcement (PSA), 241
    Procurement Automated Source System (PASS), 234
    real estate sales, 426
    Selling to the Federal Government, 236
    Small Business Innovative Research Grants, 54
    Small Business Investment Companies, 206
    women's business ownership representatives, 273
    Women's Network for Entrepreneurial Training (WNET), 272
    Women's Pre-Qualified Loan Program, 270
Small business advocates, 53
    National Association of State Small Business Advocates, 53
Small Business Answer Desk, 512
Small Business Development Centers, 54, 132
    federal procurement, 236
    help for inventors, 251
Small Business Innovative Research Grants, 302
Small Business Innovative Research Programs, 241, 252
Small Business Institutes, 55
Small Business Investment Companies, 54, 210
Small flows, 529
Smithsonian Institute
    Traveling Exhibition Service, 427
Smoking
    free help for employees, 288
    office, 537
Snail farming, 507
Snow, 528
    variances, 528
Social Security
    taxes, 267
Social Security Administration, 516
Social studies, 522
Social workers, 338
Software
    site location, 363
    telecommunications, 31

Index

Soil conservation, 186, 187
Solar activity, 527
Solar energy, 52, 524
Solar flares, 526
Solar products, 509
Sole proprietorships, 267
Solid Waste Information Clearinghouse, 528
Solid waste management, 290
Sound recordings
    archives, 541
South Carolina
    Better Business Bureaus, 350
    bill status information, 416
    business assistance, 116
    business financing, 116
    company directories, 346
    corporation information, 328
    data centers, 369
    district courts, 440
    driver information, 390
    EPA office, 297
    exports, 117
    federal procurement assistance, 239
    housing office, 421
    housing programs, 203
    HUD office, 423
    international trade offices, 408
    inventors assistance, 258
    IRS libraries, 457
    IRS problem resolution centers, 462
    labor office, 375
    licensed professionals, 342
    motor vehicle information, 390
    OSHA office, 293
    Patent Depository Library, 247
    productivity specialists, 314
    recycling office, 287
    SBA offices, 117
    securities office, 336
    Small Business Development Centers, 154
    state information, 502
    state planning office, 385
    state procurement office, 243
    state tax assistance, 495
    statistical abstracts, 380
    surplus property auctions, 433
    tax form distribution center, 469
    tax hotlines, 465
    tax incentives, 116
    technology transfer programs, 311
    trade experts, 405
    unclaimed property office, 437
    Uniform Commercial Code Division, 333
    venture capital, 220
    women's business ownership representatives, 275
    women's commission, 283
South China Sea, 527
South Dakota
    Better Business Bureaus, 350
    bill status information, 416
    Bureau of Land Management office, 418
    business assistance, 117
    business financing, 117
    company directories, 346
    corporation information, 328
    data centers, 369
    district courts, 440
    driver information, 390
    EPA office, 297
    exports, 117
    federal procurement assistance, 239
    franchises, 228
    franchising information, 323
    housing office, 421
    housing programs, 203
    HUD office, 423
    international trade offices, 408
    inventors assistance, 258
    IRS libraries, 457
    IRS problem resolution centers, 462
    labor office, 375
    licensed professionals, 342
    loan programs, 174
    motor vehicle information, 390
    OSHA office, 293
    Patent Depository Library, 247
    productivity specialists, 315
    recycling office, 287
    SBA offices, 117
    securities office, 336
    Small Business Development Centers, 154
    state information, 502
    state planning office, 385
    state procurement office, 243
    state tax assistance, 495
    statistical abstracts, 380
    surplus property auctions, 433
    tax form distribution center, 469
    tax hotlines, 465
    tax incentives, 117
    technical assistance, 184
    technology transfer programs, 311
    trade experts, 405
    unclaimed property office, 437
    Uniform Commercial Code Office, 333
    venture capital, 221
    venture capital clubs, 208
    women's business ownership representatives, 275
    women's commission, 283
Soviet Union (former)
    marketing, 397
Space, 527
    data, 529
Spacesuits, 529
Speakers
    accident prevention, 289
    environment, 289
    environmental concerns, 288
    Internal Revenue Service, 446
    overseas travel, 408
    safety hazards, 289
Special education, 537
Spinal cord injury, 537
Standards, 513
    academic, 521
    drug products, 533
    military, 513
State business listings
    see individual states
State Executive Directory, 318
State information
    approved occupational safety and health programs, 293
    Attorney General's office, 319
    auctions, 429
    Capital Library, 318
    county and local sources, 319
    data centers, 363
    Department of Commerce, 318
    directories, 318
    economic development, 319
    environment regulators, 318
    financial institutions, 318
    food and drug agencies, 319
    forecasting agencies, 381
    government contractors, 319
    government operators, 318
    labor centers, 371
    labor offices, 372
    legislation, 413
    local newspapers, 319
    minority and small business, 319
    motor vehicles, 387
    Office of Corporations, 317
    Office of Uniform Commercial Code, 318

Index

planning offices, 382
recycling offices, 286
regulators, 318
securities offices, 318
statistical abstracts, 377
unclaimed property offices, 435
utility companies, 318
State information offices, 499
State libraries, 499
State, U.S. Department of
    country experts, 394
Statistical Abstract of the United States, 360
Statistics, 544
    agriculture, 496
    agriculture and food, 359
    alcohol, 518
    business, 509
    Census data, 544
    corporate taxes, 439
    crime, 359, 497, 544
    demographic, 359
    economics, 359
    education, 359
    employment, 360
    exporting, 497
    federal statistical agencies, 359
    fisheries, 545
    health, 359
    import and export, 360
    importing, 497
    income, 443
    international trade, 396
    job satisfaction, 520
    law enforcement, 544
    state abstracts, 377
    taxes, 445, 448-449
    tobacco, 518
    world import and export, 360
    world trade, 497
Statistics of Income Bulletin, 448
Steel, domestic, 511
Steering (housing), 515
Storm windows, 192
Storms, 524
    warnings, 530
Stress, 266, 271
    student, 521
Stroke, 536
Stuttering, 532
Subcontracting, 512
    government procurement, 233
Submersibles, 529
Subsidies, shipping, 49
Sudden Infant Death Syndrome, 537
Sun, 527
Superfund sites, 295
Supplemental security income, 516
Supreme Court
    teaching about, 522
Surety bonding, 234
Surgery, blood, 532
Surplus property, 265, 418
    small business, 426
Surveys
    Internal Revenue Service, 443
Survivor benefits, 516

T

Tampons, 535
Tax Court, U.S., 448, 449
Taxes
    accounting methods, 266
    advisory services, 459
    amending your return, 439
    amortization, 267
    assistance, 269, 447
    assistance for military, 448
    assistance programs, 448, 459
    audit manuals, 444
    audits, 443, 448
    bankruptcy, 266
    benefit for using public transportation, 285
    braille tax information, 450
    breaks for recycling, 290
    Bulletin Index - Digest System, 459
    business use of home, 260, 267
    car expenses, 260, 267
    claims court, 439
    collection, 439, 445
    corporation statistics, 439
    corporations, 267
    credits for accommodating the disabled, 223
    credits for employers, 266
    criminal investigations, 445
    deductible expenses, 260, 267
    delinquency notices, 449
    depletion, 267
    depreciation, 267
    determination letters, 446
    direct selling, 267
    District Courts, U.S., 439
    earned income credit, 267, 441
    educational expenses, 267
    elderly, 443, 449, 450
    electronic filing, 441
    employer's guide, 267
    estate and gift, 441
    examinations, 267
    exempt organizations, 441, 449
    Fax by Phone, 464
    federal, 53, 266
    federal help, 439
    federal tax forms, 474
    foreign language assistance, 441
    foreign tax credit, 441
    free assistance, 445
    free CD-ROM, 300
    free courses, 261
    free publications, 468
    gains and losses, 267
    general information letters, 446
    hearing impaired services, 449
    hotlines, 261, 464
    information for practitioners, 443
    insurance, 267
    interest, 267
    international assistance, 445
    international offices, 445
    international, 448
    laws, 447
    legal help, 443
    legislation, 443
    media assistance, 445
    moving expenses, 267
    newsletters for practitioners, 447
    partnerships, 267
    paying in installments, 449
    penalties, 447
    pension plans, 441
    practitioner education, 447
    preparation courses, 442
    prior year returns, 447
    private letter rulings, 446
    problem resolution, 460
    rate structure, 443
    recommendations for change, 463
    recordkeeping, 267
    refund information, 466
    rent, 267
    representation before IRS, 446

Index

Taxes (continued)
    research, 446
    retirement plans, 266, 267, 443
    revenue yields, 443
    self-employment, 267
    small business, 459
    state assistance, 493
    statistics, 443, 448, 449
    student tax clinics, 448
    tax forms, 443
    Taxpayer Assistance Order to Relieve Hardship, 449
    taxpayer education coordinators, 442
    technical advice memorandum, 447
    Tele-Tax, 464, 466
    U.S. Tax Court, 448, 449
    unclaimed refunds, 447
    volunteer income tax assistance, 441
    wage reporting, 463
    walk-in service centers, 447
    website, 464
Taxpayer Education Coordinators, 442
Teachers
    certification, 522
    education, 522
    mentor, 520
    recruitment, 520
    student, 522
Technical assistance, 177
    Centers of Excellence, 307
    incubator programs, 303
    NASA Applications Center, 308
    seed capital, 302
    Small Business Innovative Research Grants, 302
    state Department of Economic Development, 302
    technical expertise referral services, 307
    technology transfer, 302, 306
    U.S. Department of Commerce, 302
    venture capital, 302
Technology
    aerospace, 529
    educational, 521
    enhanced machine controllers, 299
    exporting, 398
    grants, 48, 241
    international, 401
    references, 498
    technical and managerial assistance, 303
    technical expertise referral services, 307
    technology-based businesses, 302
    university projects, 306
    videos, 299
    waste, 526
    wastewater, 529
Technology Assistance Centers, 55
Technology Capital Network at MIT, 206
Technology transfer, 306, 526, 529
    definition, 306
Teenagers, inner city, 523
Teeth, 533
Tele-Tax, 466
Telecommunications
    foreign experts, 395
    international, 396
Telegraph
    regulation, 514
Telephone
    regulation, 514
Television
    children, 540
    regulation, 514
Temperature, 530
Tennessee
    Better Business Bureaus, 350
    bill status information, 416
    business assistance, 118
    business financing, 118
    company directories, 346
    corporation information, 328
    data centers, 369
    district courts, 440
    driver information, 391
    EPA office, 297
    exports, 119
    federal procurement assistance, 239
    housing office, 421
    housing programs, 203
    HUD office, 423
    international trade offices, 408
    inventors assistance, 258
    IRS libraries, 457
    IRS problem resolution centers, 462
    labor office, 375
    licensed professionals, 342
    loan programs, 174
    motor vehicle information, 391
    OSHA office, 293
    Patent Depository Library, 248
    productivity specialists, 315
    recycling office, 287
    SBA offices, 120
    securities office, 336
    Small Business Development Centers, 155
    state information, 502
    state planning office, 385
    state procurement office, 243
    state tax assistance, 495
    statistical abstracts, 380
    surplus property auctions, 433
    tax form distribution center, 469
    tax hotlines, 465
    tax incentives, 119
    technology transfer programs, 311
    technology-oriented assistance, 305
    trade experts, 405
    unclaimed property office, 437
    Uniform Commercial Code Section, 333
    venture capital, 221
    women and minorities, 120
    women business assistance, 280
    women's business ownership representatives, 275
    women's commission, 283
Terrorism
    abroad, 401
    global, 539
Testing, computer assisted, 520
Tests, standardized, 520
Texas
    Better Business Bureaus, 350
    bill status information, 416
    Bureau of Land Management office, 418
    business assistance, 120
    business financing, 120
    company directories, 346
    corporation information, 328
    data centers, 370
    district courts, 441
    driver information, 391
    EPA office, 297
    exports, 121
    federal procurement assistance, 239
    housing office, 421
    housing programs, 203
    HUD office, 423
    international trade offices, 408
    inventors assistance, 258
    IRS libraries, 457
    IRS problem resolution centers, 462
    labor office, 375
    licensed professionals, 342
    loan programs, 174
    motor vehicle information, 391
    OSHA office, 293
    Patent Depository Library, 248
    productivity specialists, 315

Index

recycling office, 287
SBA offices, 121
securities office, 337
Small Business Development Centers, 155
state information, 502
state planning office, 385
state procurement office, 244
state tax assistance, 495
statistical abstracts, 380
surplus property auctions, 433
tax form distribution center, 469
tax hotlines, 465
tax incentives, 121
technology transfer programs, 311
technology-oriented assistance, 305
trade experts, 405
unclaimed property office, 437
Uniform Commercial Code Office, 333
venture capital, 221
venture capital clubs, 208
women's business ownership representatives, 275
women's commission, 283
Textiles, 396
Theater playbills, 542
Theater, 542
Thermal springs, 526
Thermometers, 535
TIGER geographic database, 544
Tires, 514
Tobacco
    advertising, 509
    production, 518
    use, 518, 531
Toll roads, 513
Toothpaste, 529
Topographic maps, 525
Tornadoes, 530
Tourism, 55
    rural areas, 508
    state boards, 526
Toxic emissions, 524
Toys
    injuries, 515
    recalls, 514
Tracer Bullets, 542
Trade
    Eastern Europe, 402, 509
    international, 392
    international business news, 403
    international data, 401
    international statistics, 396
    recorded messages, 362
    seminars, 398
    statistics, 497
Trade associations, 321
    market studies, 353
Trade fairs, 398
Trade Information Center, 510
Trade magazines, 321
Trade missions, 398
Trade practices, 509
Trade publications, 411
Trade remedies, 401
Trademark searches
    Derwent, 249
    Trademark Scan, 249
    Trademark Search Library, 249
Trademarks, 245, 248, 267
    attorneys, 249
    Official Gazette, 249
    registration, 249
    search library, 248
Traffic
    airport, 513
    operations, 513
Trailer parks
    loans, 189
    mortgages, 188

Trails, 526
Training
    discrimination, 518
    employee training programs, 54
    foreign language, 409
    grants, 395
    literacy, 520
    management, 54
    museums, 522
    narcotic enforcement, 518
    retired military, 51
    teachers, 521
    veterans, 50
Transfusions, 532
Transplants
    kidney, 535
Transportation
    public, 285
    research, 513
    women-owned businesses, 49, 50
Transportation Research Information Services, 513
Transportation, U.S. Department of
    assistance to developing countries, 397
    Bicycle-Pedestrian Program, 285
    carpooling, 285
    SBIR grants, 241
    ship operations, 426
Travel
    advisories, 538
    business expenses, 260
    Coast Guard, 428
    country information, 409
    customs information, 409
    financial assistance overseas, 409
    free booklets, 409
    grants, 408
    overseas, 408
    overseas emergency assistance, 408
    passports, 409
    vaccines, 533
    visa requirements, 409
    warnings, 409
Treasury bill
    recorded messages, 362
Treasury notes
    recorded messages, 362
Treasury securities
    recorded messages, 362
Trees
    pruning for profit, 300
Trout farming, 507
Trucks
    weigh stations, 513
Truth in lending, 514
Tuna
    canned, 508

U

U.S. Government Manual, 354
Ulcers, 533
Ultraviolet radiation, 535
Unclaimed money
    mortgage insurance refunds, 419
Unclaimed property, 435
    finders, 435
    state offices, 435
Underground storage tanks, 525
Undersea research, 529
Unemployment
    rates, 544
    recorded messages, 362
Uniform Commercial Code, 318, 330
    request forms, 330
    state offices, 330

Index

Unions
    discrimination, 518
    grievances, 511
Unordered merchandise statute, 264
Urban education, 523
Urban renewal
    home loans, 188
    mortgage insurance, 188
    rental housing, 189
Urinary incontinence, 535
Urologic diseases, 535
Uruguay
    fax retrieval system, 402
Utah
    Better Business Bureau, 351
    bill status information, 416
    Bureau of Land Management office, 418, 419
    business assistance, 121
    business financing, 122
    company directories, 347
    corporation information, 328
    data centers, 370
    district courts, 441
    driver information, 391
    EPA office, 297
    exports, 122
    federal procurement assistance, 240
    housing office, 421
    housing programs, 203
    HUD office, 423
    international trade offices, 408
    inventors assistance, 259
    IRS libraries, 457
    IRS problem resolution centers, 462
    labor office, 375
    licensed professionals, 342
    loan programs, 174
    motor vehicle information, 391
    OSHA office, 293
    Patent Depository Library, 248
    productivity specialists, 315
    recycling office, 287
    SBA offices, 122
    securities office, 337
    Small Business Development Centers, 157
    state information, 502
    state planning office, 385
    state procurement office, 244
    state tax assistance, 495
    statistical abstracts, 380
    surplus property auctions, 433
    tax form distribution center, 469
    tax hotlines, 465
    tax incentives, 122
    technology transfer programs, 311
    technology-oriented assistance, 305
    trade experts, 405
    unclaimed property office, 438
    Uniform Commercial Code Division, 334
    venture capital, 222
    venture capital clubs, 208
    women and minorities, 122
    women business assistance, 280
    women's business ownership representatives, 275
    women's commission, 283
Utility bills, 288

V

Vaccines, 533
Vehicles
    remotely operated, 529
Venture capital, 206
    clubs, 206
    corporate, 209
    directory, 206
    networking, 54
    publications, 209
    Small Business Administration, 206
    Small Business Investment Companies, 210
    state sources, 210
    technology-oriented businesses, 302
    The National Venture Capital Association, 206
Venture capital clubs
    international, 208
Vermont
    Better Business Bureau, 351
    bill status information, 416
    business assistance, 122
    business financing, 123
    company directories, 347
    corporation information, 329
    data centers, 370
    district courts, 441
    driver information, 391
    EPA office, 297
    exports, 124
    federal procurement assistance, 240
    housing office, 421
    housing programs, 204
    HUD office, 423
    international trade offices, 408
    inventors assistance, 259
    IRS libraries, 458
    IRS problem resolution centers, 462
    labor office, 375
    licensed professionals, 342
    loan programs, 174
    motor vehicle information, 391
    OSHA office, 293
    Patent Depository Library, 248
    productivity specialists, 315
    recycling office, 287
    SBA offices, 124
    securities office, 337
    Small Business Development Centers, 157
    state information, 502
    state planning office, 385
    state procurement office, 244
    state tax assistance, 495
    statistical abstracts, 380
    surplus property auctions, 433
    tax form distribution center, 469
    tax hotlines, 465
    tax incentives, 123
    technical assistance, 184
    technology transfer programs, 311
    trade experts, 405
    unclaimed property office, 438
    Uniform Commercial Code Office, 334
    venture capital, 222
    venture capital clubs, 208
    women and minorities, 124
    women's business ownership representatives, 275
    women's commission, 283
Veterans
    business training, 50
    disabled, 51, 192
    government procurement assistance, 236
    home loans, 192
    housing, 423
    mobile home loans, 192
    Native American home loans, 192
Veterans Administration
    hospitals, 42
Veterinarians, 338
Vickers Stock Research Corp., 317
Victims
    compensation, 519
    crime, 518
Video display terminals, 536
    safety, 295

Index

Videos, 299
    AIDS, 531
    animals, 507
    business-related topics, 301
    child care business, 271
    drug and alcohol abuse in the workplace, 288
    environmental concerns, 288
    foreign marketing, 398
    franchising, 230
    health, 536
    home-based business, 301
    housing programs, 515
    occupational safety and health, 289
    radon, 295
    rivers, 527
    tax assistance, 449
    weather, 530
    worker safety topics, 289
    workplace safety, 268
    workplace safety training, 290
Vietnam veterans
    housing, 194
Vinyl chloride
    information, 289
Violence
    school, 519
Virgin Islands
    IRS libraries, 458
    tax form distribution center, 469
    venture capital, 222
Virginia
    Better Business Bureau, 351
    bill status information, 416
    business assistance, 124
    business financing, 124
    Center for Innovative Technology, 302
    company directories, 347
    corporation information, 329
    data centers, 370
    district courts, 441
    driver information, 391
    EPA office, 297
    exports, 125
    federal procurement assistance, 240
    franchises, 228
    franchising information, 323
    housing office, 421
    housing programs, 204
    HUD office, 423
    international trade offices, 408
    inventors assistance, 259
    IRS libraries, 458
    IRS problem resolution centers, 462
    labor office, 376
    licensed professionals, 343
    loan programs, 174
    motor vehicle information, 391
    OSHA office, 293
    Patent Depository Library, 248
    productivity specialists, 315
    recycling office, 287
    SBA offices, 126
    securities office, 337
    Small Business Development Centers, 157
    state information, 502
    state planning office, 385
    state procurement office, 244
    state tax assistance, 495
    statistical abstracts, 380
    surplus property auctions, 433
    tax form distribution center, 469
    tax hotlines, 465
    tax incentives, 125
    technical assistance, 184
    technology transfer programs, 311
    technology-oriented assistance, 305
    trade experts, 405
    unclaimed property office, 438
    Uniform Commercial Code Division, 334
    venture capital, 222
    venture capital clubs, 208
    women and minorities, 125
    women's business ownership representatives, 275
    women's commission, 283
Visas, 539
    requirements, 409
Visiting Scientists Program, 252
Vocational schools
    job placement, 520
Volcanoes, 526
Voluntary Protection Program, 290
Volunteer Income Tax Assistance (VITA), 442, 459
Volunteering
    museums, 522
Volunteers
    tax assistance, 269, 445, 449
    tax preparation courses, 442
Voter registration, 518
Vouchers
    rental, 193

W

Wage discrimination, 518
Wage rates, 267
Wages, 545
    recorded messages, 362
    survey, 511
Wal-Mart Innovation Network, 251
Wall Street Journal, 419
Warranties, 262, 267
Washington
    Better Business Bureaus, 351
    bill status information, 416
    Bureau of Land Management office, 418
    business assistance, 126
    business financing, 126
    company directories, 347
    corporation information, 329
    data centers, 370
    district courts, 441
    driver information, 391
    EPA office, 297
    exports, 126
    federal procurement assistance, 240
    franchises, 228
    franchising information, 323
    housing office, 421
    housing programs, 204
    HUD office, 423
    international trade offices, 408
    inventors assistance, 259
    IRS libraries, 458
    IRS problem resolution centers, 462
    labor office, 376
    licensed professionals, 343
    loan programs, 175
    motor vehicle information, 391
    OSHA office, 293
    Patent Depository Library, 248
    productivity specialists, 315
    recycling office, 287
    SBA offices, 127
    securities office, 337
    Small Business Development Centers, 158
    state information, 502
    state planning office, 385
    state procurement office, 244
    state tax assistance, 495
    statistical abstracts, 380
    surplus property auctions, 434

Index

Washington (continued)
 tax form distribution center, 469
 tax hotlines, 465
 tax incentives, 126
 technical assistance, 185
 technology transfer programs, 311
 technology-oriented assistance, 305
 trade experts, 405
 unclaimed property office, 438
 Uniform Commercial Code Division, 334
 venture capital, 222
 venture capital clubs, 208
 women and minorities, 127
 women business assistance, 280
 women's business ownership representatives, 275
 women's commission, 284
Washington Alert Service, 411
Washington Document Service, 317
Washington Service Bureau, 317
Washington, DC
 see District of Columbia
Waste
 combustion, 528
 disposal, 527
 hazardous, 525
 management, 526
 solid, 525
Wastewater, 529
Water
 conservation, 186, 187, 294
 drinking, 524
 improvement loans, 187
 mapping, 527
 pollution, 186, 524
 safe drinking water hotline, 294, 524
Water safety, 524
Watersheds, 529
Weapons
 crime, 544
 licensing, 518
Weather, 530
 crops, 544
 observations, 524
 predictions, 527
Weatherization grants, 192
Weigh stations, 513
Welding safety
 video, 300
Welfare recipients
 loans for entrepreneurs with no money, 160
 technical assistance, 177
West Virginia
 Better Business Bureaus, 351
 bill status information, 417
 business assistance, 127
 business financing, 127
 company directories, 347
 corporation information, 329
 data centers, 370
 district courts, 441
 driver information, 391
 EPA office, 297
 exports, 128
 federal procurement assistance, 240
 housing office, 421
 housing programs, 204
 HUD office, 423
 international trade offices, 408
 inventors assistance, 259
 IRS libraries, 458
 IRS problem resolution centers, 462
 labor office, 376
 licensed professionals, 343
 loan programs, 176
 motor vehicle information, 391
 OSHA office, 293
 Patent Depository Library, 248
 productivity specialists, 315
 recycling office, 287
 SBA offices, 128
 securities office, 337
 Small Business Development Centers, 159
 state information, 502
 state planning office, 386
 state procurement office, 244
 state tax assistance, 495
 statistical abstracts, 380
 surplus property auctions, 434
 tax form distribution center, 469
 tax hotlines, 465
 tax incentives, 128
 technical assistance, 185
 technology-oriented assistance, 305
 trade experts, 405
 unclaimed property office, 438
 Uniform Commercial Code Division, 334
 venture capital, 222
 venture capital clubs, 208
 women and minorities, 128
 women's business ownership representatives, 275
 women's commission, 284
Western Association of Venture Capitalists, 206
Wetlands, 186
 hotline, 530
 maps, 525
Wheelchairs, 532
White House
 intelligence activities, 538
Wholesale trade
 recorded messages, 362
Wild and Scenic Rivers, 526
Wild plants, 508
Wildlife
 damage to crops, 544
 habitats, 527
Wind energy, 524
Window coverings, 509
Winstar Telebase, 352
Wire
 regulation, 514
Wisconsin
 Better Business Bureau, 351
 bill status information, 417
 business assistance, 129
 business financing, 129
 company directories, 347
 corporation information, 329
 data centers, 370
 district courts, 441
 driver information, 391
 EPA office, 297
 exports, 130
 federal procurement assistance, 240
 franchises, 228
 franchising information, 323
 housing office, 421
 housing programs, 204
 HUD office, 423
 international trade offices, 408
 inventors assistance, 259
 IRS libraries, 459
 IRS problem resolution centers, 463
 labor office, 376
 licensed professionals, 343
 loan programs, 176
 loans for women entrepreneurs, 271
 motor vehicle information, 391
 OSHA office, 293
 Patent Depository Library, 248
 productivity specialists, 315
 recycling office, 287
 SBA offices, 130
 securities office, 337
 Small Business Development Centers, 159

Index

state information, 502
state planning office, 386
state procurement office, 244
state tax assistance, 495
statistical abstracts, 380
surplus property auctions, 434
tax form distribution center, 469
tax hotlines, 465
tax incentives, 130
technical assistance, 185
technology transfer programs, 311
technology-oriented assistance, 305
trade experts, 405
unclaimed property office, 438
Uniform Commercial Code Division, 334
University-Industry Research Program, 302
venture capital, 222
venture capital clubs, 208
women and minorities, 130
women business assistance, 280
women's business ownership representatives, 276
women's commission, 284
Wisconsin Innovation Service Center, 251
Women
    business consulting, 271
    business loans, 50, 270
    business owners, 517
    business ownership representatives, 273
    business publications, 271
    child care business, 271
    Congressional Caucus for Women's Issues, 272
    credit discrimination, 270
    credit histories, 270
    credit, 514
    disabled, 272
    earnings, 517
    energy contracts, 51
    entrepreneur financing, 272
    entrepreneur get-togethers, 272
    entrepreneuring, 512
    entrepreneurs, 270
    Equal Credit Opportunity Act, 271
    federal procurement, 271
    government contracts, 234
    government procurement assistance, 236
    grants for business, 270
    handling stress, 271
    health insurance, 272
    how to select day care, 271
    legislation, 272
    loans, 53
    mentors for entrepreneurs, 272
    minority business owners, 272
    National Association for Female Executives, 272
    networking, 272
    procurement help, 272
    set-asides for business, 271
    small business assistance, 270
    state business assistance, 277
    transportation companies, 49-50
Women owned businesses, 273
Women's Bureau, 517
Women's commissions, 281
Women's Network for Entrepreneurial Training, 272
Wood burning stoves, 509, 524
Wood preservatives, 527
Work stoppages, 511
Worker compensation, 545
Workplace
    Carpal Tunnel Syndrome, 295
    disposing of hazardous materials, 290
    drug and alcohol abuse, 288, 299
    drug-free, 531
    hazards, 268
    health and safety issues, 263
    health education programs, 269, 294
    health inspection, 268
    inspections, 290
    safety and health programs, 268
    safety consultants, 290
    Sick Building Syndrome, 288
    video display terminals, 295
    worker safety, 299
Workshops
    business, 262
    state data centers, 364
World trade statistics, 497
World War II
    records, 541
Wright Brothers, 542
Wyoming
    Better Business Bureau, 351
    bill status information, 417
    Bureau of Land Management office, 418, 419
    business assistance, 130
    business financing, 131
    company directories, 347
    corporation information, 329
    data centers, 370
    district courts, 441
    driver information, 391
    EPA office, 297
    federal procurement assistance, 240
    housing office, 421
    housing programs, 205
    HUD office, 423
    international trade offices, 408
    inventors assistance, 259
    IRS libraries, 459
    IRS problem resolution centers, 463
    labor office, 376
    licensed professionals, 343
    motor vehicle information, 391
    OSHA office, 293
    Patent Depository Library, 248
    productivity specialists, 315
    recycling office, 288
    SBA offices, 131
    securities office, 337
    Small Business Development Centers, 159
    state information, 503
    state planning office, 386
    state procurement office, 244
    state tax assistance, 495
    statistical abstracts, 380
    surplus property auctions, 434
    tax form distribution center, 469
    tax hotlines, 465
    tax incentives, 131
    technology-oriented assistance, 305
    trade experts, 405
    unclaimed property office, 438
    Uniform Commercial Code Office, 334
    venture capital, 222
    women's business ownership representatives, 276
    women's commission, 284

X

X-rays, 535
Xerox, 260

Y

Youth
    business training, 177
    loans for entrepreneurs with no money, 160
    project loans, 54

Index

Z

Zoning
  business permits, 267